The
Good Food
Guide 1999

Mimi's
Book

The
Good Food
Guide 1999

Edited by Jim Ainsworth

CONSUMERS' ASSOCIATION

Which? Books are commissioned and researched by
Consumers' Association and published by
Which? Ltd, 2 Marylebone Road,
London NW1 4DF

Distributed by The Penguin Group:
Penguin Books Ltd, 27 Wrights Lane,
London W8 5TZ

British Library Cataloguing in Publication Data
A catalogue record for this book is
available from the British Library

ISBN 0 85202 717 6

For a full list of Which? books, please write to:
Which? Books, Castlemead, Gascoyne Way,
Hertford X, SG14 1LH
or access our web site at http://www.which.net

Photoset by Tradespools Ltd, Frome, Somerset
Printed in England by Clays Ltd, St Ives plc

Cover design by Kyzen Creative Consultants
Typographic design by Tim Higgins

Contents

The *Good Food Guide* voucher scheme (£5)

For the first time the *Guide* includes three £5 vouchers that readers will be able to redeem against the price of meals taken in participating restaurants. (Look for the (£5) symbol at the very end of entries to locate those participating.) Only one voucher may be used per booked table, for a minimum of two people. Remember that your intention to use the voucher MUST be mentioned at the time of booking. Some restaurants may restrict use of the voucher at some sessions or for some menus (usually 'special offer' or lower-cost set meals); it is best to ask when booking. Actual vouchers (not photocopies) must be presented. The vouchers will be valid from 1 October 1998 to 30 September 1999, and may not be used in conjunction with any other offers.

The *Guide* online

Internet users can find *The Good Food Guide* online at the Which? Online web site http://www.which.net. For a free CD that will give you more details about Which? Online and how to be connected to the Internet, phone 0645 830254 (quoting IJ166).

Update service

Written details of restaurant sales, closures, chef changes and so on since this edition of the *Guide* was published will be available free of charge from 1 December 1998 to 1 May 1999. Readers should write to: FREEPOST, Update, *The Good Food Guide*, 2 Marylebone Road, London NW1 1YN (no stamp is required if you post your request in the UK). Alternatively, you may email *guidereports@which.co.uk*, or phone 0171-830 7551. As always, readers who send in reports on meals will automatically be sent an Update Sheet.

How to use the *Guide*

FINDING A RESTAURANT

If you are seeking a restaurant in a particular area: *first go to the maps* at the centre of the book. Localities where *Good Food Guide* restaurants can be found are indicated on the maps (the London maps give the name of the restaurant). Once you know the locality (or, for London, the restaurant name), go to the relevant section of the book to find the entry for the restaurant. The *Guide*'s main entries are divided into seven sections: London, England, Scotland, Wales, Channel Islands, Northern Ireland, and Republic of Ireland. In the London section, restaurants are listed alphabetically by name; in all other sections, they are listed by locality (usually the name of the town or village).

In addition to the main entries are the Round-ups (a range of restaurants, cafés, bistros and pubs that are worth a visit but do not merit a full entry): those for London can be found just after the London main-entry section, and those for everywhere else are towards the back of the book just after the Republic of Ireland main-entry section.

If you know the name of the restaurant: *go to the index* at the back of the book, which lists both main and Round-up entries.

If you are seeking award-winning restaurants, those offering a particular cuisine, etc.: *make use of the lists* starting on page 11, which feature the top-rated restaurants, restaurants with outstanding wine cellars, restaurants of the year, new entries in the *Guide*, closures (since the last edition), restaurants that charge 15 per cent for service, London restaurants by cuisine, London party bookings, and budget eating. There is also a page giving an eclectic selection of good places to go if you are looking for breakfast/brunch, vegetarian food, a child-friendly atmosphere, a pre-theatre meal, organic or free-range ingredients, a top-notch pub or a waterside setting.

HOW TO READ A GUIDE ENTRY

A sample entry is set out overleaf. At the top of the entry you will find the restaurant's name, map number, address, telephone and fax numbers, its email address if it has one, any symbols that may apply to the establishment, the mark awarded by the Editor for cooking, and the cost range for a three-course meal. (Full explanations of symbols, the cooking mark and the cost range follow the sample entry.) The middle part of the entry describes food, wines, atmosphere and so on, while the final section gives a wealth of additional information (explained in greater detail on pages 9-10).

LOCALITY County   map 4

▲ *Restaurant Name* ♀ ♦◈ ❋ £ | NEW ENTRY |
Address   COOKING 6
TEL: (01234) 111111   FAX: (01234) 222222   COST £15 to £100
EMAIL: restaurant@place.co.uk

This is where you will find information about the restaurant – cuisine, service, décor, wine list, and any other points of interest not covered by the details at the foot of the entry. Each entry in the *Guide* has been re-researched from scratch, and is based on information taken from readers' reports received over the past year, confirmed where necessary by anonymous inspection. In every case, readers and inspectors have been prepared to endorse the quality of the cooking.

Restaurants that receive a wine award (see explanation of 'glass' and 'bottle' symbols below) conclude with a CELLARMAN'S CHOICE. These wines are usually more expensive than the house wines, but are recommended by the restaurant as particularly suitable for the kind of food it serves.

CHEFS: John and Mary Smith   PROPRIETOR: Mary Smith   OPEN: Mon to Fri L 12 to 2, Mon to Sat D 7 to 10   CLOSED: 25 and 26 Dec, Easter, 2 weeks July, bank hols   MEALS: alc (main courses £9 to £15). Set D £16 (2 courses) to £20. Cover £1.50. Light L available. BYO £5   SERVICE: not inc, card slips closed; 10% for parties of 6 or more   CARDS: Amex, Delta, Diners, MasterCard, Switch, Visa   DETAILS: 50 seats. 15 seats outside. Private parties: 25 main room, 15 private room. Car park. Vegetarian meals. Children's helpings. No children under 7. Jacket and tie. No smoking in dining-room. Wheelchair access (also WC). No music. Air-conditioned   ACCOMMODATION: 5 rooms, all with bath/shower. TV. Phone. B&B £35 to £80. Rooms for disabled. Children welcome. Baby facilities. No dogs. Afternoon teas. Swimming-pool. (*The Which? Hotel Guide*) ⊖ £5

● For an explanation of symbols, see inside front cover.

Cooking mark

Marks are given out of 10, and are for cooking only, as perceived by the *Guide* and its readers. They signify the following:

1–2 COMPETENT COOKING Cafés, pubs, bistros and restaurants which offer sound, basic, capable cooking. Those scoring 2 use better ingredients, take fewer short-cuts, please more reporters, and make good neighbourhood restaurants.

3–4 COMPETENT TO GOOD COOKING These restaurants use fine ingredients and cook them appropriately, although some inconsistencies may be noted. They please reporters most of the time. Those scoring 4 show greater skill in handling materials, and are worthy of special note in the locality.

5–6 GOOD TO VERY GOOD COOKING These restaurants use high-quality ingredients, achieve consistently good results, and are enthusiastically reported. Those scoring 6 show a degree of flair, and are among the best in the region.

7–8 VERY GOOD TO EXCELLENT COOKING A high level of ambition and achievement means that the finest ingredients are consistently treated with skill and imagination. Those scoring 8 are worth a special effort to visit.

9–10 THE BEST These are the top restaurants in the country. They are few in number, and can be expensive, but are highly individual and display impressive artistry. Those scoring 10 are the A-team, and can comfortably stand comparison with the stiffest international competition.

Cost

The price range given is based on the cost of a three-course meal (lunch and/or dinner) for one person, including coffee, house wine, service and cover charge where applicable, according to information supplied by the restaurant. The lower figure is the least you are likely to pay, from either à la carte or set-price menus, and may apply only to lunch. The higher figure indicates a probable maximum cost, sometimes based on a set-price meal of more than three courses, if that is what is offered. This figure is inflated by 20 per cent to reflect that some people may order more expensive wine, extra drinks and some higher-priced 'special' dishes, and that price rises may come into effect during the life-time of this edition of the *Guide*.

Meals

At the bottom of entries information on the types of meals offered is given, with any variations for lunch (L) and dinner (D), and details of availability. An à la carte menu is signified by the letters *alc*. This is followed by a range of prices for main courses, rounded up to the nearest 50p. *Set L* denotes a set-price lunch; *Set D* means set-price dinner. Set meals usually consist of three courses, but can include many more. If a set meal has fewer than three courses, this is stated. If there is a cover charge, this is also indicated. *BYO* signifies that you may bring your own bottle of wine, and the corkage charge (if any) is given.

Service

Net prices means that prices of food and wine are inclusive of service charge, and this is indicated clearly on the menu and bill; *not inc*, that service is not included and is left to the discretion of the customer; *10%*, that a fixed service charge of 10 per cent is automatically added to the bill; *10% (optional)*, that 10 per cent is added to the bill along with the word 'optional' or similar qualifier; and *none*, that no service charge is made or expected and that any money offered is refused. *Card slips closed* indicates that the total on the slips of credit cards is closed when handed over for signature.

Other details

Information is also given on *seating, seating outside* and *private parties*. We say *car park* if the restaurant provides free parking facilities for patrons; *vegetarian meals* only if menus list at least one vegetarian option as a starter and one as a main course (if this is not noted, a restaurant may still be able to offer vegetarian options with prior notice – it is worth phoning to check); *children welcome* if there are no particular restrictions on children, and *children's helpings* if smaller portions are available at a reduced price; *jacket and tie* if it is compulsory for men to wear a jacket and tie to the restaurant; *wheelchair access* if the proprietor has confirmed that the entrance is at least 80cm wide and passages at least 120cm wide in accordance with the Royal Association for Disability and Rehabilitation (RADAR) recommendations, and *also WC* if the proprietor has assured us that toilet facilities are suitable for disabled people (*not WC* means these are not available or the proprietor is not sure). *Music* indicates that live or recorded music is usually played in the dining-room; *occasional music* that it sometimes is; *no music* that it never is.

Accommodation

For establishments offering overnight accommodation, the number of rooms, along with facilities provided in the rooms (e.g. bath/shower, TV, phone), is set out. Prices are given usually for bed and breakfast (*B&B*). *D,B&B* indicates that the price also includes dinner. The first figure given is the lowest price for one person in a single room, or single occupancy of a double, the second is the most expensive price for two people in a double room or suite. *Rooms for disabled* means the establishment has stated that its accommodation is suitable for wheelchair-users. Restrictions for children, and facilities for guests with babies, are indicated. *High teas for children* are noted, and *afternoon tea* means the hotel offers teas to non-residents. Any restrictions on dogs in accommodation are noted. *The Which? Hotel Guide* means the establishment is also listed in the 1999 edition of our sister guide to over 1,000 hotels in Britain.

Miscellaneous information

At the end of London entries, the nearest Underground station is given after the symbol ⊖. For restaurants that have elected to participate in the *Good Food Guide* £5 voucher scheme, a (£5) symbol appears at the very end of entries (see page 6 for further details).

The top-rated restaurants

(See pages 8–9 for explanation of marking system.)

Mark **10** for cooking

London
Chez Nico at Ninety Park Lane, W1
Oak Room Marco Pierre White, W1

Scotland
Altnaharrie Inn, Ullapool

Mark **9** for cooking

England
Fat Duck, Bray
Le Manoir aux Quat' Saisons, Great Milton
Waterside Inn, Bray
Winteringham Fields, Winteringham

Mark **8** for cooking

London
Café Royal, Grill Room, W1
The Capital, SW3
The Square, W1

England
Box Tree, Ilkley
Cliveden, Waldo's, Taplow
Croque-en-Bouche, Malvern Wells
Fischer's Baslow Hall, Baslow
Gidleigh Park, Chagford
Grand Hotel, Mirabelle, Eastbourne
Hambleton Hall, Hambleton
Merchant House, Ludlow
Mr Underhill's, Ludlow
L'Ortolan, Shinfield
22 Mill Street, Chagford

Scotland
La Potinière, Gullane

Wales
Walnut Tree Inn, Llandewi Skirrid

Restaurants with outstanding wine cellars
marked in the text with a 🍾

London
Au Jardin des Gourmets, W1
Bibendum, SW3
Brown's Hotel, 1837 Restaurant, W1
Clarke's, W8
Fifth Floor, SW1
Leith's, W11
Odette's, NW1
Le Pont de la Tour, SE1
Ransome's Dock, SW11
RSJ, SE1
Tate Gallery Restaurant, SW1

England
Adlard's, Norwich
Angel Inn, Hetton
Bowlish House, Shepton Mallet
Box Tree, Ilkley
Buckland Manor, Buckland
La Cachette, Elland
Carved Angel, Dartmouth
Cherwell Boathouse, Oxford
Chewton Glen, Marryat Restaurant,
   New Milton
Corse Lawn House, Corse Lawn
Croque-en-Bouche, Malvern Wells
The Crown, Southwold
Epworth Tap, Epworth
Fox & Hounds, Vistro, Crawley
French Partridge, Horton
Gidleigh Park, Chagford
Gravetye Manor, East Grinstead
Hambleton Hall, Hambleton
Harveys, Bristol
Hotel du Vin & Bistro, Tunbridge
   Wells
Hotel du Vin & Bistro, Winchester
Leodi's, Leeds
Le Manoir aux Quat' Saisons, Great
   Milton
Markwicks, Bristol
Michael's Nook, Grasmere
Old Beams, Waterhouses
Old Manor House, Romsey
Pheasant Inn, Keyston
Pheasants, Ross-on-Wye
Porthole Eating House, Bowness-
   on-Windermere
Priory Hotel, Wareham

Read's, Faversham
Röser's, Hastings
Seafood Restaurant, Padstow
Sharrow Bay, Ullswater
Sir Charles Napier, Chinnor
Sous le Nez en Ville, Leeds
Summer Lodge, Evershot
Le Talbooth, Dedham
Three Horseshoes, Madingley
Village Restaurant, Ramsbottom
Vineyard at Stockcross, Stockcross
Waterford House, Middleham
White Hart, Great Yeldham
White Horse Inn, Chilgrove
White House, Williton
White Moss House, Grasmere

Scotland
Airds Hotel, Port Appin
Altnaharrie Inn, Ullapool
Cellar, Anstruther
Champany Inn, Linlithgow
Clifton House, Nairn
The Cross, Kingussie
Inverlochy Castle, Fort William
Kinnaird, Dunkeld
Knipoch Hotel, Oban
Peat Inn, Peat Inn
La Potinière, Gullane
Summer Isles Hotel, Achiltibuie
Ubiquitous Chip, Glasgow
Valvona & Crolla Caffè Bar,
   Edinburgh

Wales
Fairyhill, Reynoldston
Hotel Portmeirion, Portmeirion
Old Rectory, Llansanffraid Glan
   Conwy
Penhelig Arms Hotel, Aberdovey
Plas Bodegroes, Pwllheli
Walnut Tree Inn, Llandewi Skirrid

Republic of Ireland
Arbutus Lodge, Cork
Le Coq Hardi, Dublin
King Sitric, Howth
Park Hotel, Kenmare
Sheen Falls Lodge, La Cascade,
   Kenmare
Newport House, Newport

Restaurants of the year

This award does not necessarily go to the restaurants with the highest mark for cooking, but rather to ones which have shown particular merit or achievement during the year, whether as all-rounders or in some particular field. It may go to an old favourite or to a new entry, but in either case the places listed below are worth visiting in their own right, and have enhanced the eating-out experience in some way.

London
Brown's Hotel, 1837
    Restaurant, W1
Chez Moi, W11
Rhodes in the Square, SW1

England
Ambleside, Rothay Manor
Applethwaite, Underscar
    Manor
Batcombe, Three Horseshoes
Brighton, Terre à Terre
Bristol, River Station
Corscombe, Fox Inn
Dartmouth, Carved Angel
Golcar, Weavers Shed
Great Yeldham, White Hart
Hastings, Röser's
Haworth, Weaver's
Herstmonceux, Sundial
Huddersfield, Bradley's
King's Lynn, Rococo
Langley Marsh, Langley House
    Hotel
Leeds, Pool Court at 42
Middleham, Waterford House

Middlesbrough, Purple Onion
Moulsford, Beetle & Wedge
Nottingham, Hart's
Oxford, Bath Place
Ramsgill, Yorke Arms
Taunton, Brazz
Tunbridge Wells, Hotel du Vin
    & Bistro

Scotland
Achiltibuie, Summer Isles
    Hotel
Anstruther, Cellar
Dumfries, Wisharts
Edinburgh, Balmoral, Number
    One
Eriska, Isle of Eriska
Gullane, La Potinière
Walls, Burrastow House

Wales
Broad Haven, Druidstone
Dollgellau, Dylanwad Da
Hay-on-Wye, Nino's
Llanarmon Dyffryn
    Ceiriog, West Arms

The *Guide's* longest-serving restaurants

The *Guide* has seen many restaurants come and go. Some, however, have stayed the course with tenacity. (Qualification for this list is that the restaurant has been in each edition of the *Guide* subsequent to its first entry.)

Connaught, W1	46 years
Gay Hussar, W1	42 years
Porth Tocyn Hotel, Abersoch	42 years
Gravetye Manor, East Grinstead	38 years
Sharrow Bay, Ullswater	38 years
French Partridge, Horton	34 years
Walnut Tree Inn, Llandewi Skirrid	34 years
Black Bull Inn, Moulton	32 years
Chez Moi, W11	30 years
Rothay Manor, Ambleside	30 years
Sundial, Herstmonceux	30 years
Le Gavroche, W1	29 years
Summer Isles Hotel, Achiltibuie	29 years
The Capital, SW3	28 years
Miller Howe, Windermere	28 years
Cringletie House, Peebles	27 years
Old Fire Engine House, Ely	27 years
Ubiquitous Chip, Glasgow	27 years
Peat Inn, Peat Inn	26 years
Plumber Manor, Sturminster Newton	26 years
Druidstone, Broad Haven	26 years
Waterside Inn, Bray	26 years
White Moss House, Grasmere	26 years
Carved Angel, Dartmouth	25 years
Isle of Eriska, Eriska	25 years
Old Woolhouse, Northleach	24 years
Airds, Port Appin	23 years
La Potinière, Gullane	23 years
Stane Street Hollow, Pulborough	23 years
Blostin's, Shepton Mallet	22 years
Farlam Hall, Brampton	22 years
Langan's Brasserie, W1	22 years

New Entries

These restaurants are new main entries in the *Guide* this year, although some may have appeared in previous years, or in the Round-ups last year.

London

Back to Basics, W1
Birdcage, W1
Blakes, NW1
Brown's Hotel, 1837 Restaurant, W1
Café Royal, Grill Room, W1
Casablanca, W6
Chor Bizarre, W1
Chung's, W1
Circus, W1
County Hall Restaurant, SE1
Dakota, W11
Fina Estampa, SE1
Foundation, SW1
Four Seasons, W2
Globe, NW3
Ibla, W1
Jenny Lo's Teahouse, SW1
Lee Fook, W2
Leith's Soho, W1
Lindsay House, W1
Mash, W1
Mem Saheb, E14
Mesclun, N16
Mirabelle, W1
New Hoo Wah, W1
Oceana, W1
One Lawn Terrace, SE3
Orrery, W1
Pasha, SW7
Pharmacy Bar & Rest., W1
Phoenix, SW15
Poons, W2
Rasa W1, W1
Rhodes in the Square, SW1
R.K. Stanleys, W1
Sarkhel's, SW18
Sartoria, W1
Snows by the Pond, SW13
Spiga, W1
Teatro, W1
10, EC2
Tentazioni, SE1
Vama–The Indian Room, SW10
Veeraswamy, W1
Villandry Dining Room, W1
Woz, W10

England

Batcombe, Three Horseshoes
Beeston, Brasserie 69
Beverley, Wednesdays
Birmingham, Oceanic
Birmingham, Restaurant Gilmore
Brimfield, Roebuck
Bristol, River Station,
Britwell Salome, The Goose
Burton on the Wolds, Langs
Carnkie, Basset Count House
Carterway Heads, Manor House Inn
Chaddesley Corbett, Brockencote Hall
Chagford, 22 Mill Street
Cheltenham, Le Petit Blanc
Chipping Norton, Chavignol
Cranbrook, Kennel Holt Hotel
Crawley, Fox & Hounds, Vistro
Crondall, Chesa
Eynsham, Baker's
Fernhurst, King's Arms
Halifax, Maypole Inn
Haywards Heath, Jeremy's at Borde Hill
Hindon, Grosvenor Arms
Hove, Quentin's
Huddersfield, Thorpe Grange Manor
Langford Budville, Bindon Country House Hotel, Wellesley Restaurant
Lavenham, Angel
Leeds, Marcell's
Lewdown, Lewtrenchard Manor
Liverpool, Becher's Brook
Liverpool, Tai Pan
Liverpool, Taste
Long Crendon, Angel Inn
Ludlow, Courtyard
Ludlow, Mr Underhill's
Ludlow, Oaks
Maidencombe, Orestone Manor
Manchester, Crowne Plaza Midland, French Restaurant
Manchester, Nico Central
Newcastle upon Tyne, Vermont Hotel, Blue Room
Nottingham, Hart's
Ockham, The Chapel at The Hautboy
Portreath, Tabb's
Powerstock, Three Horseshoes
Ramsgill, Yorke Arms
Redmile, Peacock Inn
Rochdale, After Eight

St Mawes, Tresanton Hotel
Sawley, Spread Eagle
Shipham, Daneswood House
Shrewsbury, Sol
Stockcross, Vineyard at Stockcross
Studland, Shell Bay
Sudbury, Brasserie Four Seven
Sunderland, Brasserie 21
Sutton Gault, Anchor Inn
Tadcaster, Hazlewood Castle, Restaurant 1086
Taunton, Brazz
Thame, The Old Trout
Trevenen, Crahan
Tunbridge Wells, Hotel du Vin & Bistro
West Tanfield, Bruce Arms
Wilmslow, Bank Square
Windermere, Holbeck Ghyll
Windermere, Jerichos
Woodbridge, Captain's Table

Scotland

Auldearn, Boath House
Clydebank, Beardmore Hotel, Citrus
Dornoch, Quail Restaurant
Dumfries, Wisharts
Edinburgh, Balmoral, Number One
Edinburgh, Kelly's
Edinburgh, Stockbridge Restaurant
Glasgow, Lux
Glasgow, Nairns
Glasgow, 78 St Vincent
Glasgow, Stravaigin

Wales

Criccieth, Tir-a-Môr
Ganllwyd, Plas Dolmelynllyn
Llanrhidian, Welcome to Town
St George, Kinmel Arms

Northern Ireland

Limavady, Lime Tree

Republic of Ireland

Dublin, L'Ecrivain
Dublin, Peacock Alley

Channel Islands

Gorey, Village Bistro

15

London restaurants by cuisine

Boundaries between some national cuisines – British, French and Italian particularly – are not as marked as they used to be. Therefore, the restaurants listed below are classified by the predominant influence, although there may be some crossover.

American
Bradleys, NW3
Christopher's, WC2
Dakota, W11
Montana, SW6

Belgian
Belgo Noord, NW1

British
Alfred, WC2
Butlers Wharf Chop House, SE1
City Rhodes, EC4
Connaught, W1
Dorchester, Grill Room, W1
French House Dining Room, W1
Greenhouse, W1
Quality Chop House, EC1
Rhodes in the Square, SW1
R.K. Stanleys, W1
Rules, WC2
St John, EC1
Savoy, Grill Room, WC2
Tate Gallery Restaurant, SW1
Wilsons, W14
Wiltons, SW1

Chinese
Cheng-Du, NW1
Chung's, W1
Dorchester, Oriental, W1
Four Seasons, W2
Fung Shing, WC2
Golden Dragon, W1
Jenny Lo's Teahouse, SW1
Lee Fook, W2
Mandarin Kitchen, W2
Mr Kong, WC2
New Hoo Wah, W1
Poons, W2 and WC2
Royal China, W1 and W2
Zen Central, W1

Fish
Back to Basics, W1
Brady's, SW18
Café Fish, W1
Livebait, SE1 and WC2
Lobster Pot, SE11
Lou Pescadou, SW5
Le Suquet, SW3
Two Brothers, N3
Upper Street Fish Shop, N1

French
Alexandra, SW20
Les Associés, N8
Au Jardin des Gourmets, W1
Balzac Bistro, SW3
Brasserie St Quentin, SW3
Brown's Hotel, 1837 Restaurant, W1
Café Royal, Grill Room, W1
Chavot, SW3
Chez Nico at Ninety Park Lane, W1
Criterion Brasserie, W1
La Dordogne, W4
L'Estaminet, WC2
Le Gavroche, W1
Inter-Continental Hotel, Le Soufflé, W1
Interlude, W1
Mirabelle, W1
Mon Plaisir, WC2
Oak Room Marco Pierre White, W1
Le P'tit Normand, SW18
Pied-á-Terre, W1
Les Saveurs, W1
755 Fulham Road, SW6
Village Bistro, N6

Greek
Daphne, NW1

Hungarian
Gay Hussar, W1

Indian/Pakistani
Café Spice Namaste, E1
Chor Bizarre, W1
Chutney Mary, SW10
Lahore Kebab House, E1
Mem Saheb, E14
Mirch Masala, SW16
Sarkhel's, SW18
Salloos, SW1
Tamarind, W1
Vama – The Indian Room, SW10
Veeraswamy, W1
Zujuma's, SW19

Indian Vegetarian
Kastoori, SW17
Rani, N3
Rasa, N16 and Rasa W1
Sabras, NW10
Sree Krishna, SW17

Indonesian/ Straits
Gourmet Garden, NW4
Melati, W1
Singapore Garden, NW6

Italian
Al San Vincenzo, W2
Assaggi, W2
Bertorelli's, WC2
Billboard Café, NW6
Como Lario, SW1
Daphne's, SW3
Del Buongustaio, SW15
Green Olive, W9
Halkin Hotel, SW1
Ibla, W1
L'Incontro, SW1
Neal Street Restaurant, WC2
Olivo, SW11
Orsino, W11
Orso, WC2
Osteria Antica Bologna, SW11
Red Pepper, W9
Riva, SW13
River Café, W6
Sartoria, W1
Spiga, W1
Zafferano, SW1

Japanese
Café Japan, NW11
Inaho, W2
Matsuri, SW1
Misato, W1
Mitsukoshi, SW1
Miyama, W1
Moshi Moshi Sushi, EC2 and EC4
Nobu, W1
Saga, W1
Sushi-Say, NW2
Tatsuso, EC2
Tokyo Diner, WC2
Wagamama, WC1 and W1
Yo! Sushi, W1

Korean
Bu San, N7

Mauritian
Chez Liline, N4

North African/ Middle Eastern
Adams Café, W12
Agadir, W2

Al Bustan, SW1
Al Hamra, W1
Casablanca, W6
Istanbul Iskembecisi, N16
Iznik, N5
Laurent, NW2
Momo, W1
Pasha, SW7

Peruvian
Fina Estampa, SE1

Spanish
Cambio de Tercio, SW5
Moro, EC1

Thai
Blue Elephant, SW6
Mantanah, SE25
Sri Siam Soho, W1
Thai Garden, E2
Thailand, SE14

London party bookings for 25 or more in private rooms

Agadir, W2
Alexandra, SW20
Atlantic Bar and Grill, W1
Au Jardin des Gourmets, W1
Balzac Bistro, W12
Bluebird, SW3
Blue Elephant, SW6
Café du Jardin, WC2
Café Fish, W1
Cambio de Tercio, SW5
Charco's, SW3
Chinon, W14
Chor Bizarre, W1
Christopher's, WC2
Coast, W1
County Hall Restaurant, SE1
Crescent, W1
Dakota, W11
Delfina Studio Café, SE1
L'Escargot, W1
Euphorium, N1

Fina Estampa, SE1
First Floor, W11
Fung Shing, WC2
Ginna, NW3
Golden Dragon, W1
Halkin Hotel, SW1
Hilaire, SW7
L'Incontro, SW1
Justin de Blank, W1
Lanesborough, The
    Conservatory, SW1
Launceston Place, W8
Leith's, W11
Lou Pescadou, SW5
Maison Novelli/Novelli EC1,
    EC1
Melati, W1
Mem Saheb, E14
Mezzo, W1
Mirabelle, W1
Momo, W1

Odette's, NW1
Orsino, W11
Poons (Leicester Street),
    WC2
Quaglino's, SW1
Rasa W1, W1
Red Pepper, W9
Rules, WC2
The Savoy, Grill Room, WC2
Searcy's at the Barbican,
    EC2
755 Fulham Road, SW6
Snows on the Green, W6
Soho Soho, W1
Sree Krishna, SW17
Sri Siam Soho, W1
Stafford, SW1
Tatsuso, EC2
Vama – The Indian Room,
    SW10
Veeraswamy, W1

Budget eating £

At the restaurants below, it is possible to have a three-course meal, including coffee, half a bottle of house wine and service, for £25 or less per person, at any time the restaurant is open, i.e. at dinner as well as lunch. It may be possible to spend considerably more than this, but by choosing carefully you should find £25 or less achievable.

London

Adam's Café, W12
Agadir, W2
Andrew Edmunds, W1
Anglesea Arms, W6
Back to Basics, W1
Belgo Noord, NW1
Billboard Café, NW6
Blakes, NW1
Brackenbury, W6
Drady's, CW18
Bu-San, N7
Café Japan, NW11
Café Spice Namaste, E1
Cheng-Du, NW1
Chiswick, W4
Chung's, W1
Daphne, NW1
Del Buongustaio, SW15
Eagle, EC1
Fire Station, SE1
Four Seasons, W2
Golden Dragon, W1
Gourmet Garden, NW4
Helter Skelter, SW9
Inaho, W2
Istanbul Iskembecisi, N16
Iznik, N5
Jenny Lo's Teahouse, SW1
Justin de Blank, W1
Kastoori, SW17
Lahore Kebab House, E1
Lansdowne, NW1
Laurent, NW2
Mandarin Kitchen, W2
Mantanah, SE25
Melati, W1
Mem Saheb, E14
Mesclun, N16
Mirch Masala, SW16
Misato, W1
Mr Kong, WC2
Moshi Moshi Sushi, EC2 and EC4
Museum Street Café, WC1
New Hoo Wah, W1
Oceana, W1
Osteria Antica Bologna, SW11
Osteria Basilico, W11
Poons (Leicester Street), WC2
Rani, N3
Rasa, N16
Red Pepper, W9
Sabras, NW10
Sarkhel's, SW18

Spiga, W1
Sree Krishna, SW17
Sri Siam Soho, W1
Thai Garden, E2
Tokyo Diner, WC2
Two Brothers, N3
Upper Street Fish Shop, N1
Wagamama, WC1 and W1
Zujuma's, SW19

England

Aldeburgh, Lighthouse
Aldeburgh, Regatta
Alvechurch, The Mill
Barton-upon-Humber, Elio's
Beeston, Brasserie 69
Beverley, Wednesdays
Birmingham, Chung Ying
Birmingham, Maharaja
Birtle, Normandie
Blakeney, White Horse Hotel
Brighton, Terre à Terre
Brimfield, Roebuck
Bristol, River Station
Buckland, Lamb Inn
Burnham Market, Fishes'
Bury St Edmunds, Maison Bleue at Mortimer's
Canterbury, Canterbury Hotel, La Bonne Cuisine
Carterway Heads, Manor House Inn
Cartmel, Aynsome Manor
Castle Cary, Bond's
Caunton, Caunton Beck
Cheltenham, Le Petit Blanc
Cockermouth, Quince & Medlar
Colchester, Warehouse Brasserie
Corscombe, Fox Inn
Crosthwaite, Punch Bowl Inn
Diss, Weaver's Wine Bar & Eating House
Durham, Bistro 21
Elland, La Cachette
Emsworth, Spencers
Epworth, Epworth Tap
Fernhurst, King's Arms
Folkestone, Pauls
Foulsham, The Gamp
Great Yeldham, White Hart
Halifax, Design House
Halifax, Maypole Inn
Harrogate, Drum and Monkey

Haworth, Weavers
Huddersfield, Bradley's
Huddersfield, Café Pacific
Ipswich, Mortimer's on the Quay
Kelsale, Hedgehogs
Keyston, Pheasant Inn
Kirkham, Cromwellian
Knutsford, Belle Epoque Brasserie
Lavenham, Angel
Leeds, Salvo's
Leeds, Sous le Nez en Ville
Leicester, Welford Place
Lincoln, Wig & Mitre
Liverpool, Far East
Liverpool, Tai Pan
Liverpool, Taste
Liversedge, Healds Hall Hotel
Long Melford, Scutchers Bistro
Ludlow, Courtyard
Nayland, White Hart
Newcastle upon Tyne, Metropolitan
Oswestry, Walls
Oxford, Al-Shami
Oxford, White House
Paxford, Churchill Arms
Plumtree, Perkins
Ponteland, Café 21
Portloe, Tregain
Portreath, Tabb's
Powerstock, Three Horseshoes
Ramsgill, Yorke Arms
Richmond, Chez Lindsay
Rye, Landgate Bistro
Sale, Hanni's
Sawley, Spread Eagle
Scarborough, Lanterna
Shelf, Bentley's
Shepton Mallet, Blostin's
Shotley, Old Boot House
Snape, Crown Inn
Southall, Brilliant
Southall, Lahore Karahi & Tandoori
Staithes, Endeavour
Stanton, Leaping Hare Vineyard Restaurant
Sudbury, Brasserie Four Seven
Sudbury, Red Onion Bistro
Tadcaster, Hazlewood Castle, Restaurant 1086

18

Tadcaster, Singers
Taunton, Brazz
Thame, Old Trout
Thornton Cleveleys, Didier's
  Bistro
Wembley, Sakonis
West Bay, Riverside
Whitby, Magpie Café
Winchester, Hunters
Winchester, Wykeham Arms
Windermere, Roger's
Winkleigh, Pophams
Woodbridge, Captain's
  Table

Scotland
Archiestown, Archiestown
  Hotel
Auchmithie, But 'n' Ben
Bowmore, Harbour Inn
Cairndow, Loch Fyne Oyster
  Bar
Canonbie, Riverside Inn
Edinburgh, Fishers Bistro

Edinburgh, Kalpna
Edinburgh, Shore
Edinburgh, Stockbridge
  Restaurant
Edinburgh, Valvona & Crolla
  Caffè Bar
Fort William, Crannog
Glasgow, Café Gandolfi
Glasgow, Mitchells/Mitchells
  West End
Glasgow, La Parmigiana
Glasgow, Splash
Kinlochmoidart, Kinacarra
Milngavie, Gingerhill
Stein, Lochbay
Troon, Highgrove House

Wales
Bassaleg, Junction 28
Broad Haven, Druidstone
Cardiff, Armless Dragon
Cardiff, Le Monde
Clytha, Clytha Arms
Creigiau, Caesar's Arms

Criccieth, Tir-a-Môr
Crickhowell, Nantyffin Cider
  Mill Inn
Dolgellau, Dylanwad Da
Hay-on-Wye, Nino's
Llanarmon Dyffryn Ceiriog,
  West Arms
Llanfihangel nant Melan, Red
  Lion Inn
Llanrhidian, Welcome to
  Town
Llyswen, Griffin Inn
Mathry, Ann FitzGerald's
  Farmhouse Kitchen
Pembroke, Left Bank
St George, Kinmel Arms
Swansea, La Braseria

Northern Ireland
Belfast, La Belle Epoque
Belfast, Nick's Warehouse
Belfast, Strand
Limavady, The Lime Tree

Closures

Whatever happended to that restaurant? Those listed below have closed
since the last edition of the *Guide*, though one or two may still be open under
new owners or have re-opened under a different name.

London
Atelier, W1
Bahn Thai, W1
Bistrot Soho, W1
La Ciboulette, SW3
Fables, SW6
Gabriel, W1
Noughts 'n' Crosses, W5
Shaw's, SW7

England
Billy Budd's, Dartmouth
Crofts, Frome
Grundy's, Harrogate
Fleur de Sel, Haslemere
Les Plantagenêts,
  Leamington Spa
Cobwebs, Leck
Hope End, Ledbury
Bacchus Bistro, Liskeard
Trawlers, Looe

Wickens, Northleach
Riverside Café, Ware

Scotland
Number Thirty Three, Perth

Wales
Edderton Hall, Forden

Channel Islands
Café du Moulin, St Pierre du
  Bois

Service charges

Restaurants still charging 15% for service (sometimes 'optional')

London
Belgo Noord, NW1
Café du Jardin, WC2
The Collection, SW3
Connaught, W1
Daphne's, SW3.
L'Escargot (Picasso Room),
  W1

Lou Pescadou, SW5
Mitsukoshi, SW1
Miyama, W1
Neal Street Restaurant, WC2
Pasha, SW7
Saga (D only), W1
Le Suquet, SW3
Zen Central, W1

England
Bishopstrow House,
  Warminster
Feathers Hotel, Woodstock

Republic of
  Ireland
Adare Manor, Adare

Themed listings

These lists are not comprehensive, but we hope that the few, sometimes quirky, suggestions will guide readers (whether out of necessity or curiosity) towards restaurants that they might not otherwise have considered. Please check entries for further details.

Waterside views

London
Le Pont de la Tour, SE1
Putney Bridge, SW15

England
Bray, Waterside Inn
Emsworth, 36 on the Quay
Fowey, Food for Thought
West Bay, Riverside
Whitstable, Whitstable
   Oyster Fishery Co

Scotland
Cairndow, Loch Fyne Oyster
   Bar
Fort William, Crannog
Port Appin, Pierhouse

Pre-theatre meals

London
Bank, WC2
Bertorelli's, WC2
Café du Jardin, WC2
L'Estaminet, WC2
Ivy, WC2
Livebait, WC2 and SE1
Magno's, WC2
Mezzo, W1
Orso, WC2
Stephen Bull St Martin's
   Lane, WC2

Breakfast/brunch

London
Bank, WC2
Le Caprice, SW1
Mash, W1
Nicole's, W1
Union Café, W1

England
Windermere, Gilpin Lodge
Grasmere, White Moss
   House
Leicester, Welford Place

Scotland
Edinburgh, Valvona & Crolla
   Caffè Bar

Wales
Talsarnau, Maes-y-Neuadd

Vegetarian

London
Kastoori, SW17
Leith's, W11
Museum Street Café, WC1
Rasa, N16 and Rasa W1
Sabras, NW10

England
Long Melford, Scutcher's
   Bistro
Beverley, Wednesdays
Brighton, Terre à Terre

Wales
Broad Haven, Druidstone

Republic of Ireland
Moycullen, Drimcong House

Children welcome

London
Bank, WC2
Spiga, W1
Zafferano, SW1

England
Great Milton, Le Manoir au
   Quat' Saisons
Malmesbury, Old Bell
Oxford, Le Petit Blanc
York, Melton's

Scotland
Oban, Heatherfield House
Spean Bridge, Old Pines

Wales
Llanwddyn, Lake Vyrnwy
   Hotel

Pubs

London
Anglesea Arms, W6
Lansdowne, NW1

England
East Witton, Blue Lion
Halifax, Maypole Inn
Hetton, Angel Inn
Madingley, Three
   Horseshoes
Paxford, Churchill Arms
Rowde, George & Dragon
Sawley, Spread Eagle

Wales
Llanarmon Dyffryn Ceiriog,
   West Arms

Organic/free-range produce

England
Great Gonerby, Harry's
   Place
Kington, Penrhos Court
Ludlow, Oaks
Montacute, Milk House
Ramsbottom, Village
   Restaurant
Virginstow, Percy's at
   Coombeshead

Scotland
Milngavie, Gingerhill
Cupar, Ostlers Close

Wales
Broad Haven, Druidstone
Fishguard, Three Main Street

Introduction

You probably know how the *Guide* works. In case not, it's very simple. You – that is, anybody reading this – write to us about your experiences. We try to sum up a restaurant (and that includes scoring it out of 10) as best we can from your reports, supplemented by anonymous inspections, plus information about opening times, prices and so on supplied by the restaurant. Then we publish it. Then the restaurateur opens the *Guide* and is surprised, even shocked, to discover that he only scores 4, when he thinks he should have at least 6. Or he finds the service described as 'slow' when he scuttles around all day long hardly pausing for breath. How can this be? Some restaurants even send us photocopies of their visitors' book – with things like 'Delicious meal, Brian and Mavis', or 'As good as my mother's cooking, Gerald' – to prove how good they really are. But if restaurateurs could only see themselves as their customers do (Brian, Mavis and Gerald excepted) many would shut their doors out of sheer embarrassment.

Quite a few restaurants understandably ask the *Guide* for feedback. What went wrong? Is there a conspiracy against them? Would we please spell out, dish by dish, exactly what the problem is? We cannot, of course, offer any individual advice: if we did, the *Guide* would find itself in the invidious position of being a 'consultant' to the very restaurants it sets out independently to assess.

One thing we can do is to tell them, in broad terms, what readers have told us. These are honest opinions, from people who don't fill up a visitors' book with gushing praise, but who tell us what really happens. Here are some of their suggestions. Notice how straight-forward they are.

- **Use good ingredients.** Nothing could be simpler, yet it is surprising how often we hear of second-rate, stale, tired, unfresh materials. They don't have to be expensive: vegetables or fruit picked daily from a garden or allotment will by definition be seasonal, and preferable to more exotic ones flown halfway round the world.
- **Taste your food.** Reports are full of 'bland' food that 'tastes of nothing'. Chefs can put an enormous amount of effort into cooking, all of which is to no avail if the end result disappoints. Customers wonder why – when they can cook better at home, or buy a ready meal from the supermarket with more flavour – they are expected to come out and suffer, then pay for it. If you spotted your own

shortcomings before the customers did, you would save a lot of hassle.

- **Time things accurately.** Easily said, and just as easily done. Why buy the best fish you can find, and then overcook it? Even slow-cooked dishes need careful timing, so that they retain shape and texture rather than disintegrating into a stringy mess. Accurate timing is essential for any cook.

- **Make dishes simple.** Don't ask yourself: how can I make this dish more complicated so that customers will think they are getting more for their money? Ask yourself: what can I usefully leave out? Suddenly, all the unnecessary garnishes will disappear and you will be left with what really matters, the essence of a dish.

- **Think about how flavours relate to each other.** If you want to emphasise the sweetness of something, say scallops, don't add something even sweeter: that will only disguise it. Add something with acidity, but don't overdo it. If you have gone to a lot of trouble to get a sauce just right, don't then go and pile a mound of vinegary red cabbage on top, or you'll spoil it. Even flavour marriages need working at.

- **Provide a no-smoking room.** How will this improve your food? People will be able to smell and taste it.

- **Don't charge the earth.** Customers appreciate that restaurants have to make money to stay in business, but if you expect them to spend a week's wage on a meal for two, then it had better be worth it. If you provide a less expensive menu as an option, they will come to visit more often, and still splash out occasionally.

- **Provide some vegetarian dishes.** Meatless food typically offers a challenge to a chef's ingenuity, and materials are not usually very costly, both good points for the restaurant. For the customer they provide a light option, add to variety, and meet a growing demand.

- **Read your own menu.** It is surprising how often dishes fail to correspond to their menu descriptions, leaving customers to conclude that anybody dozy enough to forget the pea purée can't be a good cook. And please write it sensibly in the first place, too: no flowery language, elaborate metaphors, misuse of terms, or generally wild promises that the food cannot keep.

I'll look at it your way if you'll look at it mine

There are lots more points, many about service, that are also aired on a regular basis. For example:

- Would restaurants please welcome customers, instead of just demanding aggressively, 'Have you booked?'

- Would they please remember who has ordered what; given a pencil and paper, this is not difficult.
- Would staff please make it their business to know what is in dishes, rather than running to the chef every time they are asked a question.
- Would they leave the wine bottle within reach, please.
- Only ask, 'Is everything all right?' if you really mean it, and be prepared to do something about whatever isn't all right.
- Do away with service charges.
- If you are a celebrity chef, and absent much of the time, try not to give the impression that you are behind the stoves when you are not.

Most of these things will seem obvious to readers, who simply cannot work out why they are not equally clear to chefs and restaurateurs. Oddly enough, this works the other way round too. I asked a couple of restaurateurs to compile a list of things they wish customers would do, and here, in the interests of balance, are some of their pleas to us.

- **Turn up on time.** 'Sloppy' timing, when tables booked for 7.30 and 8.30 both turn up at 8, can cause gridlock. If there is a problem, give the restaurant as much notice as possible.
- **Turn up with the right number of people.** Numbers, in large parties particularly, can be difficult for the organiser to control, but bookings for six that turn into eight might mean there is no room for the extra guests; if they reduce to four, the restaurant loses income.
- **Cancellations.** These should be 'reasonable', which doesn't mean cancelling at 8.45 if your booking was for 8.30. If there is a problem, give the restaurant as much notice as possible. And please don't claim to have a booking when you haven't, or give a false number when you book.
- **Stick to the menu.** If you want to change the sauce, or some of the ingredients, this can throw a busy kitchen off balance. Bear in mind that a good chef will have gone to the trouble of balancing flavours and textures in a dish, so any departures may be detrimental.
- **Cooking time.** Remember that tuna is now generally cooked rare, salmon can be 'rosy', calf's liver and lamb are generally 'pink'. If you want to depart from these norms, make it obvious when ordering the dish, rather than waiting until it arrives, since a returned dish disturbs your own meal as well as the rhythm of the kitchen.
- **Dietary requirements.** Demands seem to be increasing every year, and restaurants cannot be prepared for all eventualities, especially on set menus with limited choice. Please give notice if you have any special requirements, be they on grounds of religion, health or simply personal preference. And if you eat oysters, don't drink spirits at the same time, or you will probably be ill.

- **Complaints.** Please complain at the time. Give the restaurant a chance to make amends on the spot, allow staff to turn a potentially damaging situation into an enjoyable experience for you. 'It is not a battle, we are on the same side,' said one restaurateur.

I know from your reports that these points could be challenged over and over again. We, the customers, turn up on time, with a booking, in the right numbers, and are greeted by a blank stare as if we had come from Mars. We left a perfectly clear message about dietary requirements, but it was completely ignored. We asked for the lamb rare and it came well done. We did complain at the time, but all we got was a shrug.

It all leads to the fact that seeing something from another's perspective is never easy. It certainly isn't in agriculture, where small-scale organic Davids slug it out with corporate Goliaths desperate to make money from technology.

A dangerous experiment

The argument for genetically modified foods is persuasive. We have the power to fashion our edible world as never before. For a biochemist, there is probably nothing more natural than to inject a fish gene into a tomato, or vice versa, if it will bring 'benefits' to humankind. We cannot simply dismiss this out of hand on moral grounds, or we would forfeit many current and potential medical benefits.

The most commonly aired arguments against genetic modification are largely based on the sound principle that we do not know what the side-effects might be. Bland assurances from governments and agri-business don't wash any more, not after BSE. To introduce 'experimental' herbicide-resistant crops without some soundly based assurance is madness, albeit perfectly legal madness: the government seems powerless to prevent it. But it only takes a strong wind for cross-pollination to begin an irreversible and unstoppable process. And what happens to the pheasant or grouse eating these seeds, the bird that you or I might eat in a restaurant? Probably absolutely nothing at all. But only probably.

If BSE has taught us anything, it is surely to be cautious about 'tampering' with natural processes, however well-intentioned, however plausibly the benefits are packaged.

The more fundamental argument is addressed by Joanna Blythman on page 29: why do we need genetic modification in the first place? If the aim is to use fewer herbicides, fungicides and pesticides – and we are assured by the agrochemical barons that it is – then there is a perfectly viable, much simpler, and considerably more environ-mentally friendly alternative: organic agriculture. It may not make multinational corporations rich, but for the rest of us it seems a perfectly natural solution.

Support the organic movement

The sad thing is that organic agriculture lags behind the public's willingness to support it. Less than 1 per cent of our land is farmed organically (about a quarter of the European average), which means that three-quarters of the organic produce we buy in the UK has to be imported. It costs farmers money to change to organic agriculture, and the subsidy is less than a third of that for set-aside, where they are paid for growing absolutely nothing. Conventional farming has been heavily subsidised since the war. It is surely time to switch priorities and subsidise a sustainable form of agriculture.

Anybody who questions whether farming can support the world's food needs without the aid of chemicals might refer to Lynda Brown's *The Shopper's Guide to Organic Food* (Fourth Estate, 1998). What we really should be asking is: can conventional farming continue to supply the world's needs without poisoning us all? As insecticide use has increased, so, oddly, have crop losses from insects. Anything that contaminates drinking supplies, puts human health at risk through over-use of antibiotics in animals, through organophosphates, and of course through BSE, has to have a question mark over it. And if we counted the cost of cleaning up water supplies and eradicating BSE, and added it to the price we pay for agricultural produce in the shops, then organic farming would begin to look a darn sight better value.

Restaurants are in a strong position. Their collective buying power is immense, and can make a difference, especially when combined with the sum total of all our individual shopping decisions. We have highlighted a few restaurants on page 20 where the organic philosophy has taken hold, along with some other lists that we hope might be of use or interest: pre-theatre eating in London, breakfast and brunch places, and good pubs. Craig Brown's campaign (page 32) to have us all behaving like Italians is not yet sufficiently advanced for us to assume that children are welcome everywhere, so we have produced a short list of child-friendly restaurants. These lists are not comprehensive: they include just a few suggestions, which we hope will be useful.

Getting up to date

The information in the *Guide* is as up to date as we can make it. Every restaurant is phone-checked, and late changes in the kitchen are signalled with a 'New Chef' flash rather than a score. Late developments also help to account for some glaring omissions. London this year, for example, seems to have lost two of its best chefs. As the *Guide* went to press, Pierre Koffmann was moving from Tante Claire to the Berkeley Hotel, Gordon Ramsay from Aubergine into Koffmann's premises, and L'Oranger was temporarily closed. By the time you read this, other chefs may have moved too: to keep track of them, contact our update service (details on page 6).

And who knows what will be in fashion in 1999? Will it still be North African flavours, or will we have moved on to Australian bush tucker, or will Delia Smith have brought some unheard-of ingredient back from a tropical jungle, without which, this time next year, no kitchen will feel itself complete? One of the few certainties is that prices will carry on rising. Two years ago we gave a value symbol to restaurants serving three courses including wine and service for £20. Last year we had to raise the cost limit to £25. Now, even those are becoming few and far between.

This is because it is a seller's market. Restaurants are still booming. That is why many have two sittings, at least in London and some other city centres, which in turns spawns a big postbag of complaints from readers. A few of the more reasonable restaurants recognise that there is a trade-off: order before 7pm, be out before the mid-evening rush, and you can eat more cheaply. That seems fair. Others are simply money-grabbing: you must be out by 9pm, we will harass you to make sure, we will charge full price, our wine list is very expensive, and don't forget that we will charge 12.5 per cent (or in some cases 15 per cent). Note too, incidentally, that since this is the last item to be reckoned up, we are also paying 12.5 or 15 per cent on the VAT component of our bill. Clever that.

To the extent that restaurants are a barometer of the economy, however, we should not expect the boom to last forever. Already pundits are beginning to sound gloomy, trying to interpret the knock-on effects of Far Eastern banking collapses, and poring over signs of a slowdown in UK growth. When things flatten out, and the financial screw tightens, when customers become less willing to fork out large sums in restaurants, what will they do? Having acquired the eating-out habit, they are unlikely to give it up. Perhaps they will trade down and head for one of the many mid-market chains waiting to hoover up business. Or perhaps we may return to a situation that many regard as 'normal': i.e. we shall be able to book just a day or two ahead instead of months, we shall arrive at 8pm and enjoy a leisurely evening, and pay a fair price for the food, not an inflated one with add-ons at every turn. Nobody, least of all *Guide* readers, wants to see good restaurants go out of business, no matter how hard the economic climate, but a restoration of fair play would confirm that every cloud has a silver lining.

Whatever your experiences in the months ahead, please keep the reports coming: because of our schedule they are particularly useful from January to the end of May. The *Guide* is kept up to date by you, the reader. Your experiences, letters, reports and correspondence are what make this publication unique. They are what give it character, individuality, and a genuinely independent voice. Thank you to all who have contributed; and please, Brian, Mavis and Gerald, write to us too. It has not escaped our attention that the next edition will be for 2000. Let's make it a bumper issue.

When 'prime' is not enough

Joanna Blythman, investigative food journalist and author, on how increasing consumer concern for food safety and quality is forcing restaurants to rethink the way they source their ingredients

Back in 1990, when I interviewed the head chef of a prestigious and well-reviewed country-house hotel, I asked him whether or not he used organic ingredients. It became clear he didn't know what I was talking about. 'I use only prime ingredients, if that's what you mean,' he said.

Today, such a response is unthinkable. Where once chefs could rely on comforting descriptions such as 'prime', 'Scotch' and 'traditional', the series of food scares, most notably BSE, that has swept Britain has brought about a sea change in the way chefs think about ingredients. Nowadays, when high-profile chefs appear on TV, a reference to organic producers is almost *de rigueur* – a measure of the growing interest in sourcing the finest and safest ingredients.

Whose side are supermarkets on?

Although top chefs have always based their reputations on the quality of their raw materials as well as their cooking skill, in the best restaurants the former is now becoming as – or even more – important than the latter: a development that has been driven by consumers. Albeit late in the day, the British have begun to grasp just how vital the provenance of food ingredients is. Such awareness is changing the nation's shopping list and creating higher expectations of restaurants.

If, for example, you routinely use extra virgin olive oil at home, as many households now do, you may not be thrilled to be served some undistinguished 'pure' olive oil or vegetable oil in a restaurant. Consumers don't want inferior-quality ingredients when they eat out.

A typical dilemma was expressed to me in a reader's letter. 'When we eat meat at home, I always buy either free-range or organic. But what about meat in restaurants? Should we assume that every Peking duck, chicken tikka or pork escalope is intensively produced?' The answer to that question, for the vast bulk of relatively undistinguished restaurants is, unfortunately, yes. The animal welfare group Compassion in World Farming in 1998 analysed egg sales in the UK. It found that supermarket sales of free-range eggs accounted for as much as 65 per cent of all egg sales in one major supermarket chain, 57 per cent in another and 41 per cent in a third. And yet national figures show that free-range still accounts for only 12 per cent of the nation's total egg production. The clear inference is that intensively produced battery eggs are now being sold in the main for food-processing, and to restaurants and catering outlets where customers are not aware of their pedigree.

As consumers develop greater food awareness, the pressure on chefs to pay greater attention to food selection intensifies. But that's not the only spur to improvement. The frightening power of supermarkets has affected chefs too. Supermarkets now deal direct with growers, bypassing wholesale markets. As a result, the traditional wholesale fruit and vegetable markets – on which chefs previously relied – have contracted into servicing the residual fruit and veg business for which independent shops have been left fighting. The supermarket effect makes it harder for chefs to lay their hands on the fresh, interesting and diverse produce they want and strengthens their interest in dealing direct with small, more specialised and traditional producers which can provide them with items such as organic salad leaves and unusual potato varieties.

The chicken and egg problem

By using suppliers of this kind, not just for fruit and vegetables but for meat, poultry and dairy foods, chefs can be more certain about the safety of their raw materials too. Post-BSE, safety has become synonymous with quality. Intensive agriculture has made many basic ingredients into potentially lethal weapons. Salmonella in eggs and E-coli in beef are now endemic and threaten to change the way chefs are permitted to cook in the future.

In the black humour of the restaurant world, the joke now goes that you no longer ask for steak 'rare' but 'just over the bacterial critical control point'. Serve a dish with raw eggs, such as mayonnaise, Caesar salad or tiramisù, and as a chef you could be leaving yourself open to claims of negligence for falling foul of food safety regulations.

Unless chefs are prepared to give up serving dishes with uncooked eggs or rare meat forever, the only way forward is to make sure that raw materials are not contaminated to start with. That means using carefully produced, non-intensive ingredients.

In California, where stringent new food safety laws have been enacted, the only restaurants brave enough to ignore the new régime are the 'greats' like Chez Panisse, run by Alice Waters, whose cooking has always been predicated on impeccable raw ingredients with a bias towards organic. These are the restaurants that can risk using raw eggs in their mayo because they trust their provenance.

Food worth fighting for

In Europe, too, leading chefs have been manning the barricades to defend both foods and cooking methods. Over 2,500 chefs are now members of Euro-Toques, an organisation founded a decade ago to preserve and enhance European cuisine. They are fighting, for example, to stop the mandatory pasteurisation of milk, cheese and dairy products that has been sought by the US. The reputation of a classic cheese – Roquefort, for instance – rests to a large degree on the properties of the raw milk used in its production. Pasteurise it and you would lose its glorious character, they argue – and do absolutely nothing for the cause of food safety.

But defending artisan products against the industrial hygiene police is relatively straightforward. Chefs are also having to get rapidly up to speed on complex new food technologies such as genetic modification, which looks set to change the face of food as we know it. In a survey of its chefs commissioned by Euro-Toques in late 1996, some 78 per cent said that they were 'concerned about the use of gene technology in farming and agriculture'. Few chefs, it seems, are impressed by the idea of slow-rot tomatoes or extra-long 'super-salmon'. And in the UK, leading chefs such as Nico Ladenis, Rowley Leigh and Sally Clarke have publicly protested against the way that genetically modified food is being forced on to the market unlabelled, without public consent.

Whether it is fighting for endangered artisan foods, or against the rash introduction of untested new technologies, the refreshing wave of militancy among chefs over food issues demonstrates how the agenda of the thinking chef and the informed consumer are coming closer together. Both constituencies seem to be increasingly united in a desire for food produced in a natural way which does not trash the environment, cause unnecessary animal suffering or jeopardise public health. Now that *is* good news for the discerning restaurant diner.

Children every which way, please

Craig Brown, restaurant critic for the *Sunday Telegraph*, on the changing attitudes towards children in restaurants

The small type beneath most of the entries in the 1999 *Good Food Guide* bears a message that is warm and open-armed. 'Children welcome ... ,' it says, time and time again: 'children welcome ... children welcome ... children welcome.'

But are they? In these Estherised days of child worship, when even the Prime Minister feels bound to declare that the contents of the most expensive public monument in our history must pass the 'Euan test' of being acceptable to his 12-year-old son, we are all of us meant to grit our teeth and revere the demands of that group of human beings which the misanthropic writer Patricia Highsmith once characterised as 'drunken dwarves'. Nowadays, even the prissiest restaurateur who boasts the most delicate collection of eighteenth-century china figures on the daintiest of displays is expected to kowtow to the *Zeitgeist*, put on his cheesiest grin and purr, 'Children welcome.'

Suffer the little children

It was not always so. Back in 1975, when a child called Ronald was taking dinner with his parents in Torquay's very own Fawlty Towers (an establishment cruelly overlooked by successive editors of *The Good Food Guide*), the co-proprietor, a Mr B. Fawlty, was perfectly open in his hostility. When Ronald complained that his chips were 'the wrong shape', Fawlty was bullish in his response. 'Oh dear,' he said. 'What shape do you usually have? Mickey Mouse shape? Smarties shape? Amphibious landing craft shape? *Poke-in-the-eye* shape?' Fawlty then terminated the exchange by elbowing young Ronald in the head under the guise of looking at his watch.

Nearly a quarter of a century on, I'd guess that the poke-in-the-eye shape is the only chip still unavailable in some restaurant, somewhere in Britain. Restaurant chains such as Beefeater and Happy Eater have become studiously child-friendly, providing special children's menus decorated with cartoon or TV characters. These menus tend to offer dishes of reconstituted chicken or fish, moulded into star-shapes or fish-shapes, with gobbledegook kiddie-titles. Wimpy, for instance, now presents a choice of a 'benderumptious pork bendy bender meal' or a 'fantabulous fishy nibbles meal'. Youngsters turning their nose up at these might prefer to go instead for the 'jumbolicious chicken chunkies'.

Children are now regularly offered crayons and colouring-books on arrival, leaving their parents, in my experience, feeling oddly left-out and under-occupied, kicking their heels before the arrival of the first course. One or two restaurants even provide conjurors, clowns and face-painters, ready to whisk children away while their parents continue to guzzle and slurp.

Return to childhood. Do not pass 'Go'

Meanwhile, it's possible to detect a strain of infantilism creeping into many of our more avowedly sophisticated new restaurants. Among those I visited in 1998, Oliver Peyton's Mash in London has an electronic board in the hallway greeting diners with babyish jokes, and brightly coloured furniture and décor that could have been plundered from a particularly trendy nursery. Many new restaurants have themes barely more grown-up than, say, Planet Hollywood. One of the most talked-about new restaurants of the year, Pharmacy, attracted the oohs and ahhs of the in-crowd for what was seen as its daringly avant-garde medical interior, but I suspect its success can be more accurately traced to its deft regression to a let's-pretend world of waiters dressed as doctors and nurses, and toytown loos and colourful bottles on the walls. The recent success of so many Moroccan restaurants also has as much to do with their fancy dress and fairytale furnishings as anything gastronomic.

By and large, I approve of this kiddification. Where restaurants are concerned, I prefer the spontaneous to the stuffy, the noisy to the hushed, the joyful to the reverent. To these ends, I see children as my natural allies. When I read the increasingly rare warning 'No children' beneath a description, however glowing, in this guide, I find my eyes speeding on to the next entry. This is because even if I am not planning to bring my children along, I am uneasy about entering anywhere so sniffy as to bar them.

On the other hand, even Father Christmas might concede that Basil Fawlty had a point. We have all been in restaurants while children have been bawling and screeching, throwing toys, food, cutlery and plates hither and thither while their parents sit back either pretending not to notice or, worse, cooing appreciatively. After young Ronald has told Basil Fawlty that his food tastes like 'pig's garbage', his adoring mother simpers protectively, 'He's very clever, rather highly strung.' All in all, it's hard to blame Fawlty for then snapping back, 'Yes, yes, he should be.'

When in Rome . . .

Are children banned from restaurants because they don't know how to behave? Or do children not know how to behave in restaurants because they are banned from them? In *The Good Food Guide*, it is perhaps permissible to fall back on the cliché about the chicken and the egg. In a restaurant guide to Italy, the phrase 'children welcome' would be as superfluous as 'pasta available' or 'knives and forks provided'. Every Italian restaurant is a family restaurant. The proprietors tend to like children, so children tend to like them. Growing up in a restaurant culture that accepts them, children have no need to shriek their defiance from the table-tops. At the same time, Italian adults enter restaurants fully expecting the odd child to be running around, and a few tears from another table will scarcely ruin their meal.

In return for being treated like human beings, Italian children are granted few concessions: no cartoon-character pasta, no benderumptious nibbley chunki-kiddyburgers, no face-paints or clowns. And this is surely the route we in Britain should also take, cutting down on both sniffiness and sycophancy, aiming for a future in which the restaurant is as natural a place for families as it is for businessmen or lovers, a time when the message 'children welcome' is as unnecessary as 'adults welcome'.

Service with a smile?

David Rodwell, a lawyer at Consumers' Association, on service in restaurants – what it covers, how much the consumer pays for it, and what to do if it fails to come up to scratch

We always seem to end up paying for it – whether it is clearly stated on the menu, left up to our discretion, appears without warning on the bill, or even hits us twice when we are faced with an 'open' credit card slip – what is 'service' anyway?

The Supply of Goods and Services Act 1982 might seem like a good place to start looking. Although the act does not provide a specific definition of 'service', it does explain that 'in a contract for the supply of a service ... there is an implied term that the supplier will carry out the service with reasonable care and skill'.

The 'contract' is entered into at the time the table at the restaurant is booked, or, if there has been no booking, at the time the order is taken. The 'service' covers everything that the customer gets from the restaurant up to the time that he or she pays the bill and leaves. The flip side of the restaurant's legal obligations is that it can put what it likes on the menu (as long as the statements are clear and accurate), charge what it likes (as long as the prices are clear and accurate) and bar anyone it wants (as long as it does not do so on grounds of gender, race or disability).

The 'service charge'

Although the food and drink provided by a restaurant are technically part of 'the service', and must be hygienic and of satisfactory quality according to the law, it is *everything else* provided by the restaurant that needs to be looked at to justify a 'service charge'.

Paying for this 'everything else' is not always a straightforward affair. Ideally, the restaurant should deal with service payments in one of two ways:

(1)   make it clear that the prices are all service-inclusive so that – presuming that the food and service are up to standard – the customer can pay the advertised price for the meal without any embarrassment over 'a tip'. This is the method of charging for service that is recommended by the Consumer Protection (Code of Practice for traders on price indications) Approval Order 1988
(2)   add nothing to the prices for service and leave the matter of a tip completely up to the discretion of the customer.

In both cases, if the meal is being paid for by credit card, the card slip should arrive at the table closed unless the customer specifically asks for it to be left open.

In reality, however, consumers are often confronted by a number of other, less-than-ideal ways of paying for service:

- the menu states that an 'automatic' service charge will be added to the bill. Sometimes this can be as high as 15 per cent, though more often 10 or 12.5 per cent. The problem is that, sub-consciously, you still expect to pay the advertised price of the meal and are unpleasantly surprised to see how much 12.5 per cent uplift actually is on the bill. Furthermore, even though you are not legally *required* to pay this part of the bill if the service has not been satisfactory, many customers feel it's more trouble than it's worth to try to have the bill reduced in the event of bad service

- the menu states that there is an 'optional' service charge of 10, 12.5 or 15 per cent. Even though this charge is stated to be 'optional', just as with the automatic service charge, woe betide the customer who dares to exclude it. If it is 'optional', why is it unilaterally added on to the bill? Adding these so-called optional charges on to the bill is also contrary to the recommendations of the 1988 Consumer Protection Approval Order

- service may be added on to the bill without any warning at all; i.e. it is not mentioned on the menu or anywhere else that is in prominent view of the customer. This is a 'misleading price indication' under the Consumer Protection Act 1987 and, therefore, would be illegal. Customers are not obliged to pay for service at all in such a situation and should report the restaurant to the local Trading Standards department

- whatever way service is dealt with by the restaurant, the customer may still be faced with an open credit card slip when the bill arrives. Where a customer asks for the slip to be left open, fair enough. However, the practice of leaving a credit card slip open where service has already been included in the bill is unscrupulous: although the practice of duping customers in this way is not illegal, it should be. In the view of Consumers' Association, *menus should state that credit card slips will always be closed unless the customer specifically requests otherwise.*

Deciding what is reasonable

'Reasonableness' is the key factor when considering whether a service charge is justified. And that is a two-way street. If a customer thinks that just because he will be paying the bill he has *carte blanche* to be rude and excessively demanding, he is not being reasonable, and should not blame the restaurant for problems resulting from his own behaviour. Likewise, the restaurant is responsible for ensuring that staff are properly trained, competent, and do not act in a superior, churlish, inappropriately familiar or off-hand manner (a non-exhaustive list).

Ambience, too, plays a role in the issue of 'service'. Tables crammed too close together (especially in a restaurant that charges high prices), a table next to the toilets or kitchen doors, poor maintenance of furniture and fittings, intrusive music (for example, in one restaurant, a broken tape deck kept playing songs that cut out and restarted every ten seconds) are all elements that can detract from the enjoyment of the overall experience and affect service.

An increasing problem, especially in London, is pressure to finish the meal as quickly as possible and vacate the table. Unless the restaurant has made it clear before the customer enters into the contract that it limits the time customers have at tables, then it is unreasonable to hurry even very slow eaters, as long as the diner plans to go by closing time. The 'hassle factor' may take the form of discouraging customers from ordering a dessert or coffee, hinting that other people are waiting for the table, or even trying to move diners to the bar to finish a meal. Such pressure entirely justifies reducing the service charge.

Very often – though not always of course – problems can be dealt with by a discreet complaint, which will spur the restaurant into remedying the situation. At the end of the day, 'reasonableness' remains the determinant of what customers (and restaurateurs) want.

How to complain

The key to constructive complaining is to stay calm, succinct and polite but firm. If the problem cannot be amicably resolved, then think about reducing the payment for service.

If the charge has been added to the bill or is included in the prices, deduct a reasonable amount and note how much you have deducted, and briefly why you have deducted it, on the bill (generally retained by the restaurant) and receipt (generally retained by you). If the waiter has a problem with this, ask to speak with the head waiter or manager. If you are not getting anywhere or would rather avoid a confrontation, pay the service charge part of the bill 'under protest', being sure to write those words on the bill and your receipt, and take the matter up with the restaurant in writing at a later date (but do not leave it too much later). If the problem is the behaviour of a restaurant employee other than the waiter – the chef or manager, perhaps – you should clarify that in your note on the bill, so that the waiter knows who is to blame for any reduction of the service charge.

Very few cases of bad service will ever end up in court, but it is worth knowing that you have the option (a genuine 'option'). The small claims procedure in the county courts of England and Wales deals with claims up to £3,000 and is designed to help people who are not legally represented. The process is informal and relatively cheap and quick. If the service charge has been paid under protest and the restaurant ignores your claims for compensation, it is worth remembering that the very fact of issuing legal proceedings often leads to an out-of-court settlement. Another avenue to pursue, if the meal cost more than £100 – even if the amount in dispute is less – and was paid for with a credit card (not a debit or charge card), is your credit card company. The Consumer Credit Act 1974 states that they are jointly liable for any breach of contract or misrepresentation by the restaurant.

Going out to a restaurant is supposed to be a pleasurable experience. It is like taking a short holiday. It is not just about eating and drinking, but also about relaxing, socialising and entertainment. While you should remember that complaints are worth pursuing only if you are a 'reasonable' customer, they should always be made and pursued where justified in order that standards are maintained and improved for you and other customers. On the other hand, if you receive excellent service, whether there is a service charge or not, there should be nothing to prevent you leaving a discretionary 'tip'.

London

Adams Café £ map 12

77 Askew Road, W12 9AH	COOKING 3
TEL/FAX: (0181) 743 0572	COST £22–£29

The appearance of this family-run eating-house, with its North African artefacts and simple tables set close together, is unchanged. So, basically, is Abdel Boukraa's food, although it is listed in a new way: a fixed-price menu offers a one-course 'rapide', plus mint tea or coffee, a 'gourmet' (main course plus starter or dessert) and the three-course 'gastronomique'. With all come appetisers that might be meatballs with hot harissa, and a salad of carrots, onions and mixed olives. Two starters can be substituted for the main dish, and the only supplement is £1.50 for couscous royal, with meatball plus skewers of grilled chicken, lamb and merguez. New to the menu are a tagine with chicken, dates, almonds and potatoes, and another of lamb with artichoke, peas and lime. Starters include ojja – Tunisian ratatouille with egg – and brik à l'oeuf, with or without tuna, the best reason for tucking a napkin under your chin. Enticing desserts, apart from classic pastries, are almond or lemon tart, and crêpes berbères: Moroccan-style pancakes with honey sauce. Drink Moroccan or Tunisian wine – rosé is said to be good – and finish with Arabic coffee and, if you dare, fig eau-de-vie or date liqueur. Service, happily led by Frances Boukraa, is devoted to making customers feel comfortably at home.

CHEF: Abdel Boukraa PROPRIETORS: Abdel and Frances Boukraa OPEN: all week D only 7 to 11 CLOSED: 1 week Christmas to New Year, bank hols MEALS: Set D £9.95 (1 course) to £14.95 SERVICE: not inc CARDS: Amex, Diners, MasterCard, Switch, Visa DETAILS: 60 seats. Private parties: 36 main room, 24 private room. Vegetarian meals. Children welcome. Wheelchair access (1 step; not WC). Music ⊖ Shepherd's Bush, Ravenscourt Park (£5)

Agadir £ map 13

84 Westbourne Grove, W2 5RT	COOKING 3
TEL: (0171) 792 2207	COST £20–£33

Good Moroccan food at low prices is reason enough to visit this modest family-run eating-house. The premises have now been extended downstairs, giving twice as many seats as before, and the décor has been re-done in tasteful pale blue. Pleasures include chorba and harira soups and such starters as briouat (stuffed pastry rolls), stuffed sardines, merguez, and maakouda (an egg and potato pancake). Main dishes are couscous with combinations of chicken, meat and vegetables and one unusual variation: Christina couscous with chicken, onion and raisins. More varied tagines come with almonds, prunes, olives and saffron among ingredients. There are also chargilled kebabs, and pastilla – with chicken replacing traditional pigeon. Finish with traditional Moroccan pastries, then mint tea or Moroccan coffee. The short wine list pleases film buffs with no less than seven from Casablanca starting at £8.50.

CHEF/PROPRIETOR: Mustafa Lagnatha   OPEN: all week D only 6 to 12   MEALS: alc (main courses £5.50 to £9)   SERVICE: 10%, card slips closed   CARDS: Amex, Delta, Diners, MasterCard, Switch, Visa   DETAILS: 105 seats. Private parties: 60 main room, 70 downstairs. Vegetarian meals. Children welcome. Wheelchair access (not WC). Music. Air-conditioned   ⊖ Ladbroke Grove

Alastair Little
map 15

49 Frith Street, W1V 5TE   COOKING 5
TEL: (0171) 734 5103   COST £36–£54

The original Alastair Little restaurant once shone like a beacon of innovation in a Soho beset with nouvelle fiddle-faddle. It rode the crest of the first Mediterranean wave to break on central London's shores, and has held fast to that mode even while others have gone overboard for frantic fusion. Plainness and honesty were and are the watchwords of the cooking, and the style rings true because menus are built around such staples as good home-made pasta, the best oils and authentic – rather than merely trendy – domestic recipes such as maiale al latte (pork cooked in milk).

Scarcely a report falls to mention the almost provocative drabness of the surroundings, and indeed this may not be the most cheering room in winter months, but staff are smilingly personable and the food is as bright as a button. Tagliatelle with wild mushrooms and garlic butter started an August dinner with deep, expressive flavours, before mustard-marinated chicken breast with new potatoes, and grilled leg steak of Somerset lamb on ratatouille. The practice of offering two starters at lunch-time is much appreciated, one reporter relishing the chance to go from 'excellent' brandade with truffled French beans to seafood and chickpea pasta. 'This was plenty for our appetites, although we did pig out on their fabulous focaccia as well.' Puddings are more Franco-British than Italian, bringing in rhubarb crumble and pain perdu, but sometimes offering roast figs with honey ice-cream and mascarpone. If disappointments arise, they tend to do so because those unfamiliar with the style find the utter simplicity of it all bemusing. Wines may be a more mainstream selection than expected in the context (there is only a handful from Italy, for example), and prices soon breach the £20 barrier. House French and Italian are £13.

CHEF: Jonathan Ricketts   PROPRIETORS: Alastair Little, Kirsten Pedersen and Mercedes André-Vega   OPEN: Mon to Fri L 12 to 3, Mon to Sat D 6 to 11.30   CLOSED: bank hols   MEALS: Set L £25, Set D £33   SERVICE: not inc; 12.5% for parties of 8 or more   CARDS: Amex, Delta, MasterCard, Switch, Visa   DETAILS: 55 seats. Private parties: 20 private room. Vegetarian meals. Children's helpings. Wheelchair access (1 step; not WC). No music. Air-conditioned   ⊖ Tottenham Court Road

London Round-ups listing additional restaurants that may be worth a visit can be found after the main London section.

Alastair Little Lancaster Road map 12

136A Lancaster Road, W11 1QU	COOKING 4
TEL: (0171) 243 2220	COST £28–£44

Look out for a jaunty white canopy on a rather dreary stretch of road, and Alastair Little's friendly second restaurant is at hand. Those with an eye for interior design might wish for a painting or two to relieve the bright white blankness of the room, but the place is filled with the right sort of buzz. Meals may kick off with scarcely more than 'an assembly job' – beef carpaccio with well-matured Parmesan and 'scrupulously fresh' rocket leaves, say – but that is the Little style, and it satisfies because of the quality of its components. Italian cooking is well understood, as attested by a dish of 'fabulous' pappardelle con lepre, the richly meaty sauce judged so as not to sog the pasta, or there may be roast salt-beef with mash and onion gravy. A classic bourride was flawlessly rendered at an April lunch, and the rhubarb jelly that followed it, served as a great wobbling slab with vanilla ice-cream, was thought 'the best nursery pudding in London'. Roquefort with pears should cater for more savoury preferences at a meal's end. Service is obliging, and price-banding of the lunchtime menu is thought particularly helpful. The same wine list at the same mark-ups is offered here as at the Soho branch (see entry, above).

CHEF: Edwin Lewis PROPRIETORS: Kirsten Pedersen, Alastair Little and Mercedes André-Vega OPEN: Mon to Sat 12.30 to 2.30 (3 Sat), 7 to 11 CLOSED: bank hols MEALS: alc L (main courses £8 to £12). Set D £27.50 SERVICE: not inc; 12.5% for parties of 8 or more CARDS: Amex, Delta, MasterCard, Switch, Visa DETAILS: 45 seats. 10 seats outside. Private parties: 10 main room. Vegetarian meals. Children's helpings. Wheelchair access (not WC). No music. Air-conditioned ⊖ Ladbroke Grove

Al Bustan ⁂

map 14

27 Motcomb Street, SW1X 8JU	COOKING 1
TEL: (0171) 235 8277 FAX: (0171) 235 1668	COST £23–£62

'Charming décor and even more charming service' seems to set this Lebanese venue apart from many comparable establishments. 'Al Bustan' means 'garden' in Arabic, and the theme is followed through tastefully with trellis screens, and green trees painted on one wall. The cover charge would be worth every penny for the two kinds of unleavened bread, although diners are also provided with a harvest festival of raw vegetables, olives and chilli dip. Hot and cold starters feature in abundance, although one reporter found the hummus and stuffed vine leaves rather uninspiring. Main courses could include grilled king prawns in their shells, and chargrilled boneless baby chicken: given a smear of garlic and butter before cooking, and served with 'remarkably good' tartare-like sauce and good-quality rice. Three kinds of baklava feature on the dessert trolley, although a dinky semolina cake with dates and pistachios might be preferred. Service hits the perfect balance between 'quiet gentility' and 'brisk efficiency'. A few Lebanese wines make their presence felt on the short but mainly French list. House wine is £12.

CHEF: Inam Atalla   PROPRIETORS: Mr and Mrs Atalla   OPEN: all week 12 to 11   CLOSED: 2 weeks Christmas   MEALS: alc (main courses £7 to £16). Set L £13. Cover £2   SERVICE: not inc   CARDS: Amex, Diners, MasterCard, Visa   DETAILS: 70 seats. 20 seats outside. Private parties: 75 main room, 8 to 20 private rooms. Children's helpings. No smoking in 1 dining-room. Wheelchair access (2 steps; not WC). Occasional music. Air-conditioned   ✆ Sloane Square, Knightsbridge

Alexandra
map 12

507 Kingston Road, SW20 8SF   COOKING 1
TEL: (0181) 542 4838   FAX: (0181) 947 3805   COST £15–£38

So dedicated is Eric Lecras to the produce of his native country that he eschews the bounty of Raynes Park in favour of a weekly trip to Calais to stock up. Once laden with meat, fish and vegetables, he ferries it back and transforms it into simple, hearty bistro fare at highly attractive prices. Hors d'oeuvre may include crêpe dieppoise stuffed with seafood in a cognac cream sauce, or duck and hazelnut terrine with an onion tartlet. 'Les main courses' (yes, really) seem to be principally meats in classical sauces, from port and thyme for rack of lamb to mustard for fillet of pork. Nostalgic vegetarians may jump at the chance of a cheese omelette. Nougat glacé with mango coulis, and hot apple tart with calvados sauce are traditional ways to finish. Modestly priced wines are by no means all French, but start with rouge and blanc de maison at £8.95.

CHEF/PROPRIETOR: Eric Lecras   OPEN: Tue to Fri and Sun L 12 to 2, Mon to Sat D 7 to 9.30   CLOSED: D 25 Dec, bank hols   MEALS: alc (main courses £11). Set L £6.95   SERVICE: 12.5% (optional)   CARDS: Delta, MasterCard, Visa   DETAILS: 60 seats. 18 seats outside. Private parties: 32 main room, 30 private room. Vegetarian meals. Children welcome. No cigars/pipes in dining-room. Music   ✆ Wimbledon £5

Alfred
map 15

245 Shaftesbury Avenue, WC2H 8EH
TEL: (0171) 240 2566   FAX: (0171) 497 0672   COOKING 4
EMAIL: manager@alfred.co.uk   COST £26–£41

'Alfred doesn't sell its wares boldly,' commented an inspector. The restaurant is split into three dining-areas and there are no 'flash gimmicks' about the décor, which is all duck-egg-blue walls and sulphur-yellow tables. 'It hits a level of unpretension rarely seen,' noted the same correspondent: food and drink are the stars. The kitchen sets its stall out in a classless kind of way, displaying rabbit and haggis alongside oysters and scallops. The tone of the menu inspires confidence through understatement, and also champions the British larder. Here you will find whisky-cured salmon with honey dressing and cress salad, as well as grilled ribeye steak with Stilton butter. High points from recent samplings have included a neatly assembled salad of crab with a 'perfectly rock-fresh flavour', and braised duck on a mound of champ and spinach with an orange-infused sauce. To finish, impeccable cheeses from Neal's Yard come with quince 'cheese', home-made Alfred chutney and impressive home-baked breads; otherwise, opt perhaps for lemon tart with crème fraîche, or gingerbread with lavender custard. The drinks list goes all the way from Hidalgo sherries to

Somerset cider brandy, with beers and ciders in between. Otherwise the wine list takes a thoroughly modern view of things, and naturally includes representatives from English vineyards. House wines start at £11.95.

CHEF: Robert Gutteridge   PROPRIETOR: Fred Taylor   OPEN: Mon to Sat 12 to 3.30, 6 to 11.30
CLOSED: 25 Dec, 1 Jan, bank hols   MEALS: alc (main courses £9 to £15.50). Set L and D (before 7.30 and after 10) £12.95 (2 courses) to £15.90   SERVICE: not inc   CARDS: Amex, Delta, Diners, MasterCard, Switch, Visa   DETAILS: 56 seats. 28 seats outside. Private parties: 16 main room, 16 private room. Vegetarian meals. Children's helpings. No cigars/pipes in dining-room. No music. Air-conditioned   ⊖ Tottenham Court Road

Al Hamra   map 15

31–33 Shepherd Market, W1Y 7HR   COOKING 6
TEL: (0171) 493 1954   FAX: (0171) 493 1044   COST £37–£60

'A thoroughly pleasant place to enjoy fine Lebanese food,' summed up one reporter, noting the general air of affluence in this square, windowed room in Shepherd Market. In its 15 years, Al Hamra has witnessed a blossoming British love affair with the Mediterranean that has moved from Provence and Italy to the spicier flavours of North Africa and the Middle East, but in all this time its own path has remained steadfast. Perhaps its turn for the limelight has come. Ignore, if you will, prawn cocktail and grilled Dover sole in favour of something more regional. Beyond the usual hummus, baba ganoush and falafel lie pickled aubergines with walnuts, fish roe with garlic and olive oil, spinach-filled pastry with pomegranate seeds, and a few Lebanese versions of pizza.

A long menu invites exploration. Lovers of steak tartare will find its lamb equivalent, minced with onion and spices, while lovers of offal can have a field day with lambs' tongue salad, and fried kidney or sweetbreads in lemon juice. The charcoal grill is applied to lamb in various forms – minced with cracked wheat is typical – as well as to whole boneless chicken. Sweets combine pastry, honey and nuts in manifold ways and come on a trolley. Drink yoghurt, or a wine from the largely French and mostly over-£20 list. Ch. Musar is available in three colours, the New World selection visits six countries in eight bottles, and house French is £12.75.

CHEFS: Mahir Abboud and Ahmed Batah   PROPRIETOR: A.H. Fansa   OPEN: all week noon to 11.45   CLOSED: 25 Dec, 1 Jan   MEALS: alc (main courses £12 to £17.50). Set L £25. Cover £2.50   SERVICE: not inc   CARDS: Amex, Diners, MasterCard, Visa   DETAILS: 85 seats. 32 seats outside. Private parties: 85 main room. Vegetarian meals. Children's helpings. Wheelchair access (not WC). Music. Air-conditioned   ⊖ Green Park

Al San Vincenzo   map 13

30 Connaught Street, W2 2AF   COOKING 4
TEL: (0171) 262 9623   COST £34–£59

Set in a row of well-maintained Regency terraced houses just off the bottom end of Edgware Road, this is a 'deeply authentic, Italian, family, country-style restaurant'. Its domestic appeal stems less from the rather distant tenor of service, more from such gestures as a model Ferrari on display, or a magnum of sparkling Italian wine that was used to prop the door open one warm May evening. Vincenzo Borgonzolo's food also has a welcome streak of individuality that follows no London fashion. His menu, which doesn't appear to change very often, is at home with a spicy soup of pork offal, with crisply fried eel, or with 'correctly cooked' fillet of red mullet served with its liver and a blood orange salad.

Celeriac and prawn risotto has been prepared with 'care and attention', and crisp-skinned, 'springy, sweet sea bass', cooked simply with lemon oil, shows that timing is well controlled. An unusual feature is that small appetites (and bills) are discouraged: 'starters taken as a main course, or starters only, will have a £5 supplement added in the evening.' Cooking to order means that meals can be leisurely. You might finish with panettone bread-and-butter pudding, stuffed dates, or cheeses such as Gorgonzola or Taleggio 'in prime condition'. House wines from the south, at £13, head up a remarkably short Italian list.

CHEF: Vincenzo Borgonzolo   PROPRIETORS: Elaine and Vincenzo Borgonzolo   OPEN: Mon to Fri L 12.30 to 1.45, Mon to Sat D 7 to 10   MEALS: alc (main courses £12 to £21)   SERVICE: not inc; 12½% for parties of 5 or more   CARDS: Delta, MasterCard, Visa   DETAILS: 24 seats. Private parties: 6 main room. No children under 12. No cigars/pipes in dining-room. Music   ⊖ Marble Arch

Andrew Edmunds £

map 15

46 Lexington Street, W1R 3LH

TEL: (0171) 437 5708

COOKING 2

COST £21–£33

Run in tandem with an art gallery of the same name, Andrew Edmunds puts on a smart face, with magnolia-painted walls, a pine-clad ceiling and tables packed close together. The mood is lively and jolly, service is laid-back, and the overall impression seems to be 'take it or leave it': thankfully, most reporters fall into the former camp. Similarly, a handwritten menu gets straight to the point, influences are plucked from far and wide, and results are decidedly appetising. Rillettes of pork with onion chutney, dill pickle and walnut bread were reckoned to be an excellent combination; likewise meaty grilled king prawns with chilli and okra. Among the main courses, there has been praise for roast spatchcock poussin served – intriguingly – 'at room temperature' with asparagus, pine-nuts and a 'quite delicate' orange hollandaise. Desserts are competent renditions of classics such as tarte Tatin, and plum and almond tart. The wine list offers a fair selection at prices few would balk at. House wine is £9. The details below are approximate as the restaurant chose not to return the *Guide*'s questionnaire.

CHEF: Paul Croal   PROPRIETOR: Andrew Edmunds   OPEN: all week 12.30 (1 Sat) to 3, 6 to 10.45 (10.30 Sun)   CLOSED: 24 to 31 Dec, 4 days Easter   MEALS: alc (main courses £7 to £9.50)   SERVICE: not inc; 12% for bills over £50   CARDS: Amex, Delta, MasterCard, Switch, Visa   DETAILS: 56 seats. 4 seats outside. Private parties: 28 main room. Vegetarian meals. No music. Air-conditioned   ⊖ Picadilly Circus

The 2000 Guide *will be published before Christmas 1999. Reports on meals are most welcome at any time of the year, but are particularly valuable in the spring (no later than June). Send them to* The Good Food Guide, *FREEPOST, 2 Marylebone Road, London*

Anglesea Arms £

map 12

35 Wingate Road, W6 0UR
TEL: (0181) 749 1291   FAX: (0181) 749 1254

COOKING 4
COST £20–£35

The Anglesea Arms is a traditional pub through and through, and those prepared to put up with the smoke and noisy crowds are rewarded with excellent food. The very basic décor reflects Dan Evans's aim to provide 'some of the joys in life without breaking the bank', and his cooking is based on a zealous enthusiasm for entirely fresh ingredients, especially fish, so the daily-changing blackboard menu is largely dictated by supplies. A catholic style takes in starters of summer shellfish minestrone; pigeon and foie gras terrine; and Catalan-style chorizo, garlic and eel gratin. Equally varied main dishes might include slow-cooked belly pork with crispy noodles and stir-fried vegetables; diver-caught scallops with minted green split peas, bacon and tarragon; or a simple grilled lamb chump with watercress, chips and sauce paloise. A dessert of 'fabulous' lemon tart with 'zinging' orange sauce was the high spot of one reporter's meal; otherwise try white peach Knickerbocker glory, or toasted banana bread and ice-cream. The 'eclectic' wine list includes 14 by the glass. House wines, a Portuguese red and an Italian white, are £8.75.

CHEFS: Dan Evans and Justin Aubrey   PROPRIETORS: Dan and Fiona Evans   OPEN: all week 12.30 to 2.45 (1 to 3.45 Sun), 7.30 to 10.30   CLOSED: 1 week Christmas, 1 week summer   MEALS: alc (main courses £6.50 to £10)   SERVICE: not inc   CARDS: Delta, MasterCard, Switch, Visa   DETAILS: 60 seats. 18 seats outside. Vegetarian meals. Children's helpings. Wheelchair access (not WC). No music   ⊖ Ravenscourt Park   £5

Anonimato

map 13

12 All Saints Road, W11 1HH
TEL: (0171) 243 2808

COOKING 3
COST £29–£46

Nilton Campos says that he named his restaurant 'in a fit of English/Brazilian/ Italian frustration', an uncomfortable-sounding syndrome that apparently reflects his exasperation with the 'new British' tag that has come to replace 'eclectic' as the signifier of choice for Notting Hill eating out. Walls washed in autumnal hues, contrastingly vibrant blue doors, and oil burners on the tables establish the tone. People come for seared duck breast on soy-braised leeks accompanied by fried plantain seasoned with wasabi and mirin, or a risotto of biltong, spring onions and snake beans. It almost seems as if an ingredient has to earn its place on the menu by sheer exoticism, but culinary techniques are sound enough to carry the style. Cep and potato galette on roast pumpkin with pesto suggests that creativity extends to vegetarian dishes too. Desserts plough a more well-worn furrow for sticky toffee pudding or chocolate mousse cake, but for the adventurous there may be champagne-poached figs with Provolone, guava jelly and biscotti. Staff, commended for being 'very obliging', are fully aware that many dishes will need explanation. Brightly flavoured modern wines are well selected, but a little over half come at more than £20. The bidding opens at £10 for a pair of eastern Italians.

CHEF: Nilton Campos   PROPRIETORS: Nilton Campos and Simon Reader   OPEN: Sun brunch 12 to 4, Mon to Sat D 7 to 11   CLOSED: 25 and 26 Dec, 1 Jan   MEALS: alc (main courses £9 to £13). Set D £18 (2 courses) to £22   SERVICE: 12.5% (optional), card slips closed   CARDS: MasterCard, Switch, Visa   DETAILS: 70 seats. Private parties: 20 private room. Vegetarian meals. Children welcome. Music   ⊖ Ladbroke Grove £5

Assaggi
map 13

The Chepstow, 39 Chepstow Place, W2 4TS   COOKING 3
TEL: (0171) 792 5501   COST £26–£53

Large windows, wooden floors, clean lines and striking colours give this Italian restaurant over the Chepstow pub a bright feel, perfectly in keeping with the food. It avoids most of the Italian clichés in favour of simple dishes unlikely to be found elsewhere. While there are centrepieces of calf's liver with polenta, or truffled veal cutlet, the focus is on the dozen starters, or little tastes (assaggi), which typically eschew meat altogether. Larger than meze or its equivalents, they cost around £7 to £8 each. The mix is a good one, including cheese-based dishes such as zuppa di ricotta; fish, from fresh crab to dried grey mullet roe (shaved over fennel); vegetables, simply grilled with olive oil and herbs; and a few pasta options, such as seafood tagliolini, or gnocchi with saffron, butter and sage. Finish with poached figs with mascarpone, or peach tart. Some 20 Italian wines are well chosen for character and value, starting with Sardinian Nuragus (white) and Monica (red) at £9.95.

CHEF: Nino Sassu   PROPRIETORS: Pietro Fraccari and Nino Sassu   OPEN: Tue to Sat L 12.30 (1 Sat) to 2.30, Sun L 1 to 3, Tue to Sat D 7.30 to 11   CLOSED: 2 weeks Christmas   MEALS: alc (main courses £11.50 to £18)   SERVICE: not inc, card slips closed   CARDS: Amex, Delta, Diners, MasterCard, Switch, Visa   DETAILS: 35 seats. Vegetarian meals. Children's helpings. No music ⊖ Notting Hill Gate

Les Associés ⅋✳
map 12

172 Park Road, N8 8JY   COOKING 2
TEL: (0181) 348 8944   COST £21–£42

This is the sort of neighbourhood French restaurant where the rather plain décor doesn't matter much: candles illuminate the close-set tables, and regulars (who might come to celebrate a birthday) know the Spindlers well enough to create a convivial atmosphere. Expect to start with fish soup, marinated scallop salad, or an 'aubergine packet' containing mushrooms and snails, considered original not least for making 'snails taste like something for once'. Marking itself out from its peers, the kitchen might also offer duck breast cooked in foil with turnips, fillet of beef with lobster sauce, and fish of the day cooked in a parcel with duck liver. There may be crème brûlée or a tart to finish, but desserts are not the highlight. Service has been 'accommodating', and three dozen wines are all French, including house red and white at £9.80.

Restaurateurs justifiably resent no-shows. If you quote a credit card number when booking, you may be liable for the restaurant's lost profit margin if you don't turn up. Always phone to cancel.

CHEF: Marc Spindler   PROPRIETORS: Dominique Chèhére and Marc Spindler   OPEN: Tue to Fri
L 12 to 2, Sun L 1 to 3, Tue to Sun D 7.30 to 10   CLOSED: 10 days Sept, 10 days Jan   MEALS: alc
(main courses £10 to £14.50). Set L Tue to Fri £10.50 (2 courses), Set L Sun £12.50   SERVICE:
not inc, card slips closed   CARDS: Diners, MasterCard, Switch, Visa   DETAILS: 40 seats. 15
seats outside. Private parties: 40 main room. Children's helpings. No smoking in 1 dining-room.
Wheelchair access (not WC). Music   ⊖ Highgate   £5

Atlantic Bar and Grill ♥ ⌂   map 15

20 Glasshouse Street, W1R 5RQ   COOKING 2
TEL: (0171) 734 4888   FAX: (0171) 734 3609   COST £26–£75

In this cavernous old hotel ballroom, which has been effectively, if quirkily,
turned into the trendiest of 1990s joints, marble pillars, dark wood and loud
music contribute to a noise level that is high even when the place is half-empty,
though more usually it is a crush. Understatement is not a characteristic of the
menu, which goes in for seared Bulgarian woodland cep risotto with white
truffle oil and wild parsley, and rosette of Welsh lamb with a whipped cep butter
fondue sauce and roasted aubergine and crushed tomato mille-feuille. 'The first
taste of my "oriental swordfish dumplings with a salsa of plum tomatoes,
coriander, seared shiitake, wilted spinach and soy-infused ginger" was
excellent,' noted one reporter, though it came to appear more one-dimensional
with time. Those who share the kitchen's penchant for salty, spicy, sweet, rich
and sour tastes will probably come off best. Finish perhaps with a 'chewy
meringue', or rather a crisp pavlova filled with raspberry purée, whipped vanilla
cream served with blackcurrant compote and cassis sauce. The USA contributes
some appealing if pricey bins to a well-chosen New World section, but the Old
World rules the waves on the Atlantic wine list. House wines open at £12 a
bottle, and 18 wines come by the small or large glass; and then there are always
the cocktails. CELLARMAN'S CHOICE: Pinot Blanc d'Alsace 1997, Mittnach, £18;
Bonny Doon Carignan 1996, Santa Cruz, California, £22.50.

CHEF: Richard Sawyer   PROPRIETOR: Oliver Peyton   OPEN: Mon to Fri L 12 to 3, all week D 6 to
12 (10.30 Sun)   CLOSED: 25 and 26 Dec, 1 Jan, Easter Sun and Mon   MEALS: alc (main courses
£7 to £18). Set L £14.50, Set D 6 to 7 £14.50 (2 courses) to £16.50. Cover £1   SERVICE: 12.5%
(optional), card slips closed   CARDS: Amex, Delta, Diners, MasterCard, Switch, Visa   DETAILS:
180 seats. Private parties: 10 main room, 70 private room. Vegetarian meals. Children welcome.
Music. Air-conditioned   ⊖ Piccadilly Circus

Au Jardin des Gourmets ▮ ⁂   map 15

5 Greek Street, W1V 6NA   COOKING 5
TEL: (0171) 437 1816   FAX: (0171) 437 0043   COST £26–£61

Despite its Russian ownership, this smart first-floor Soho restaurant lays claim
to being the longest-established place serving French food in the capital. The
promised 'garden' only amounts to a rear balcony with potted plants and trailing
ivy, but the cooking, under Vincent Hiss, could scarcely be more copybook
French. Foie gras, for example, is done two ways in the same dish, as a slice of
cold 'ballottine' with onion chutney and as a warm escalope with Puy lentils,
although the excellent mixed vegetarian hors d'oeuvre might once have been
hard to come by in a French restaurant.

Main courses offer an appealingly wide range of meats and fish: turbot is roasted on the bone, its list of garnitures taking in 'curry, tabbouleh and oyster fritters', while rabbit is fashioned into a 'gâteau' with Alsace bacon, Gruyère and mâche. More mainstream preparations might include roast rack of lamb with a herb crust, or Barbary duck with honey. Meals end either with a French cheese selection, or with an inventive dessert such as 'minestrone' of seasonal fruits with basil and lime sorbet.

Wines are predominantly French (a few bottles from elsewhere can be found under the 'Out of France' heading) and feature the Jardin's accurately named 'Very Special Collection' of château-bottled clarets that stretches back to 1949. A dozen French country wines are priced between £9.75 and £13, and the good news is that you will be charged only for what you drink from this selection. CELLARMAN'S CHOICE: Coldstream Hills Chardonnay Reserve 1995, Yarra Valley, Victoria, Australia, £23.50; Haut-Médoc, Ch. Cissac 1989, £40.

CHEF: Vincent Hiss   PROPRIETOR: Novoport Group Ltd   OPEN: Mon to Fri L 12 to 2.30, Mon to Sat D 6 to 11.15   CLOSED: bank hols   MEALS: Set L £10 (Express Menu) to £30, Set D £16.50 to £30   SERVICE: 12.5%, card slips closed   CARDS: Amex, Diners, MasterCard, Switch, Visa   DETAILS: 80 seats. Private parties: 60 main room, 14 to 60 private rooms. Vegetarian meals. Children's helpings. No smoking in 1 dining-room. Music. Air-conditioned   ● Tottenham Court Road   £5

Avenue   map 15

7–9 St James's Street, SW1A 1EE
TEL: (0171) 321 2111   FAX: (0171) 321 2500   COOKING 5
EMAIL: chefs@egami.co.uk   COST £29–£61

The contrast between location and interior is striking. St James's Street is pure establishment, with ancient shops plying old-fashioned trades in premises that have hardly changed in centuries. The Avenue, meanwhile, flaunts its modernity with fashion and pop videos, a spectacular long bar, and bare gleaming white walls that keep the ceiling a long way from the white-tiled floor. As to the food, reporters don't come here for 'great artifice or originality'; they come because it is simply 'an enjoyable place to eat', with a menu that stays light and varied.

A popular Anglo-Mediterranean approach produces goats' cheese and red onion tart, trompette and rocket risotto, and baby gem salad with poached egg and Parmesan. There are meat dishes – rump of lamb with morels and peas, or veal escalope with tapénade – but fish and vegetable items rather outnumber them: iced tomato and red pepper soup with pesto, or three quickly grilled scallops with a salad of apple and Parmesan. It is left to the British element to strike a nursery note, in smoked haddock fish-cake with Welsh rarebit, or Avenue fishfingers ('actually goujons of plaice', according to one visitor) served with matchstick chips.

At dessert the comforting style translates into banoffi pie, chocolate and orange tart, and steamed apple and calvados pudding. Wines are a good blend of old and new, arranged by varietal or style, and feature some forward-thinking growers from both hemispheres. French house wines are £14.50 a bottle, and 27 wines are available by the glass from £3.50 to £23.50 (the last being non-vintage Krug Grande Cuvée).

CHEF: Dean Carr   PROPRIETOR: Christopher Bodker   OPEN: all week 12 to 3 (3.30 Sun), 5.45 (6.30 Sun) to 12 (12.30 Fri and Sat, 10 Sun)   CLOSED: 25 and 26 Dec, L 31 Dec, 1 Jan   MEALS: alc D (main courses £11.50 to £17). Sun brunch (main courses £9 to £13). Set L Mon to Sat £17.50 (2 courses) to £19.50, Set D 5.45 to 7.30 and 10.15 to closing £14.50 (2 courses) to £16.50   SERVICE: 12.5% (optional)   CARDS: Amex, Diners, MasterCard, Switch, Visa   DETAILS: 180 seats. Private parties: 12 main room. Vegetarian meals. Children welcome. Wheelchair access (1 step; also WC). Music. Air-conditioned   ⊖ Green Park

Back to Basics £

NEW ENTRY   map 15

21A Foley Street, W1P 7LA   COOKING 2
TEL: (0171) 436 2181   FAX: (0171) 436 2180   COST £21–£43

On a corner site in Fitzrovia, Back to Basics is not a rallying-point for the moral majority but a useful and accomplished small seafood restaurant. Outside tables take the overspill in fine weather, and the green interior with its checked tablecloths has a pleasing bistro feel. Stefan Pflaumer chalks up the pick of the market on a blackboard, scrubbing off each item as it sells out. A bowl of plentiful tasty, plump mussels in white wine, garlic and cream contains manifestly fresh shellfish and a sauce that needs a spoon to finish it. Sea bass in basil and chilli oil is grilled to crisp the skin but retain moist flesh, and other options have included tuna steak with salade niçoise, brill with green peppercorn butter, and plaice with ginger and soy. Lamb steak and Scotch ribeye are there as an alternative. Puddings go back to basics for bananas baked in foil with rum, or the simplest apple tart, with slices of fruit, cinnamon added, piled on a pastry shell. Service copes well with even the busiest sessions. The short everyday wine list is supplemented by an 'alternative cellar' of French classics. House wines from France and Australia start at £9.95.

CHEF/PROPRIETOR: Stefan Pflaumer   OPEN: Mon to Fri 12 to 3, 6 to 10   CLOSED: 2 weeks Jan, 3 weeks from end Aug, bank hols   MEALS: alc (main courses £7 to £14)   SERVICE: 10% (optional), card slips closed   CARDS: Amex, Delta, Diners, MasterCard, Switch, Visa   DETAILS: 40 seats. 45 seats outside. Private parties: 40 main room. Vegetarian meals. Children's helpings. Wheelchair access (not WC). Occasional music   ⊖ Oxford Circus

Balzac Bistro ⁵⁄✳

map 12

4 Wood Lane, W12 7DT   COOKING 2
TEL: (0181) 743 6787   FAX: (0181) 997 1378   COST £23–£45

For years this dyed-in-the-wool French bistro has been a favourite lunchtime bolt-hole for staff at nearby BBC Television Centre – perhaps it's a better option than the in-house canteen. It may be fixed engagingly in a time warp, with its gingham cloths, photographs of film stars and parasols over some of the tables, yet it still 'seems right for the present'. This is a kitchen that delivers exactly what is needed when food matters more than fashion: classic French onion soup, beef bourguignonne and rack of lamb persillade. Less predictable are grilled scallops, linguini in butter sauce, roast chicken with Parma ham and mozzarella, and medallions of venison with pineapple, honey and soy. The wine list goes Gallic in a big way, with only the occasional incursion into Spain and Italy. House wine is £9.40.

CHEF: F. Vera   PROPRIETOR: P. Tarelli   OPEN: Mon to Fri L 12 to 2.30, Mon to Sat D 7 to 11 CLOSED: 2 weeks Christmas, bank hols   MEALS: Set L and D £13.90, Set D Sat £13.90 to £15.90. Cover £1   SERVICE: 10%   CARDS: Amex, Delta, Diners, MasterCard, Switch, Visa   DETAILS: 60 seats. Private parties: 60 main room, 40 private room. Vegetarian meals. Children welcome. No smoking in 1 dining-room. Wheelchair access (1 step; not WC). Occasional music. Air-conditioned   ⊖ Shepherd's Bush

---

Bank ♥

1 Kingsway, WC2B 6XF

COOKING 5

TEL: (0171) 379 9011   FAX: (0171) 379 9014

COST £27–£74

map 13

Given the amount of glass that features, from heavy revolving doors, past mirrors and the glass-fronted kitchen to the dining-room's ceiling, one could be forgiven for imagining a bottle bank to be the inspiration for this busy, bustling brasserie where tables are a more champagne bucket apart, and things can happen fast. A risotto that arrives within six minutes of the order being punched into the computer is a triumph of sorts, and judging by some reports you may have to hold on to your plate to finish it. On the other hand, fast-paced food before the theatre is seen as 'efficient', and is no bad thing at breakfast either.

The red girders, blue pillars and yellow walls have witnessed a 'collide-o-scope' of flavours from the Far East, Scandinavia, the Mediterranean, France, even Britain. A supermarket could hardly offer more choice, from Baltic herring to Beluga caviare, from roast rabbit with couscous and spiced crab (that's one dish) to fried chicken and shrimp nam rolls, from prosciutto with pumpkin chutney to Cajun blackened chicken. The miracle is that the kitchen delivers the goods with such consistency: fish soup that is 'copious, hot, everything it ought to be', halibut in 'the thinnest, crispest, lightest batter' with chips and mushy peas, or mushroom risotto with 'buckets of flavour'. To finish, fresh fruit comes with a yoghurt sorbet, the crème brûlée varies from passion-fruit to chocolate flavoured, or there may be blackberry and apple pie. Weekend brunch is family time, with toys, colouring books and a children's menu. As for wines, there is no need to raid the piggy bank to drink a decent bottle as there are plenty to be had under £20. Bins are arranged by style from 'light crisp' to 'round smooth' and have a good mix of other countries (including Uruguay) among the French. House Chardonnay and Cabernet/Merlot from France are £11.50. CELLARMAN'S CHOICE: Loire, Chardonnay 'Le Montaillant', 1996, £15.50; Carignan, Mas des Chimères, £14.

CHEF: Christian Delteil   PROPRIETOR: Antony Allan   OPEN: Mon to Fri L 12 to 3, Sat and Sun brunch 11.30 to 3.30, all week D 5.30 to 11.30 (10 Sun). Breakfast menu 7.30 to 10.30 Mon to Fri   CLOSED: 25 Dec, bank hols   MEALS: alc Mon to Fri L, all week D (main courses £10 to £24). Brunch Sat and Sun (main courses £8.95 to £14.95). Set L (Mon to Fri) and D (all week 5.30 to 7pm) £13.90 (2 courses) to £17.50   SERVICE: 12.5% (optional), card slips closed   CARDS: Amex, Delta, Diners, MasterCard, Switch, Visa   DETAILS: 200 seats. Vegetarian meals. Children welcome. Children's helpings Sat and Sun brunch. Wheelchair access (1 step; also WC). No music. Air-conditioned   ⊖ Covent Garden

---

'My main course was roast widgeon, which I told the waiter I had not eaten before. It may not be entirely the chef's fault that I shall not rush to try it again.' (On eating in Edinburgh)

Belair House map 12

Gallery Road, SE21 7AB
TEL: (0181) 299 9788   FAX: (0181) 299 6793

COOKING 4
COST £27–£77

Until only a couple of years ago, Belair was well on its way to becoming a ruin. Its renovation is a minor miracle, and fully worth a look. Set in parkland, it is a gleaming white late-eighteenth-century mansion, almost next door to Dulwich Picture Gallery. Fears that the atmosphere may be stuffed-shirt are allayed by the bold primary colours of the décor and the attire of staff. The 'groovy-looking' manager even sports a ponytail.

Nigel Davies has moved on since last year, and Colin Barnett has stepped into his shoes. His food would be as much at home in Covent Garden as here, its modern European accents expressed in today's clipped menu-speak: 'duck, pie of black pudding & lentils, caramelised apples'. So far, so trendy. But this food has an earthy dimension, that stems as much from materials as anything: perhaps braised pig's trotter with wild mushrooms and mash, or venison with root vegetables and white-bean purée. Seasonings, though, tend to be kept on a tight leash, with a trickle of sweet syrup for a starter of duck breast with pickled pear, or a hint of lavender in the dauphinoise to partner sea bass.

Desserts stretch to a varied and good-value chocolate selection, or poached spiced fruits with Muscat custard. Service is closely attentive, though it doesn't seem to have got the hang of wine yet. The list is replete with enlivening New World flavours, plus a few French classics elbowing their way in. Prices are brisk, with house selections opening at £14.

CHEF: Colin Barnett   PROPRIETOR: Gary Cady   OPEN: all week 12 to 2.30 (3 Sun), 7 to 10.30 (10 Sun)   CLOSED: Sun D in winter   MEALS: alc (main courses L £7.50 to £12.50, D £15 to £22). Set L Mon to Sat £12.50 (2 courses) to £15.50, Set L Sun £24.95, Set D Sun to Thur £24.95   SERVICE: 12.5% (optional), card slips closed   CARDS: Amex, Delta, Diners, MasterCard, Switch, Visa   DETAILS: 110 seats. 50 seats outside. Private parties: 70 main room. Car park. Vegetarian meals. Children's helpings. No cigars in dining-room. Wheelchair access (1 step; also WC). Music

Belgo Noord £ map 13

72 Chalk Farm Road, NW1 8AN
TEL: (0171) 267 0718   FAX: (0171) 284 4842
EMAIL: myriammavros@belgo-restaurants.co.uk

COOKING 3
COST £22–£46

'Moules – Frites – Bières' is the message. The design of this remarkable basement (there's a new extension above called Belgo Rapido for daytime meals) is high-tech monastic with seductive overtones, lovely swooping shapes on the high ceiling and earthy, metallic colours. Seating is on backless wall benches, and noise levels can be deafening: but that's part of the Belgo experience. Mussels – from sources worldwide – are served every which way, in flavoured broths, open-faced with fillings and so on: the classic marinière version impressed at inspection, as did the 'absolutely ace chips and dense mayonnaise'. Alternatives appear in the shape of Belgian specialities such as wild boar sausages with 'stoemp' (mashed potatoes with cabbage and carrots mixed in) and forest fruits, or duck breast with sauté vegetables and a stem ginger and raspberry beer jus. This is casual eating, and it hits the button. Service by waiters in monks' robes is 'absolutely excellent': as one reporter noted, they seem to have 'a universal love for the work' and – judging by other comments – they are also great with kids. There is a decent enough wine list (with house French at £9.75), but people are really here for the bières: the range is arguably the largest outside Belgium, and there are at least a dozen different-shaped glasses from which to quaff them. A sister branch is in Covent Garden at 50 Earlham Street (tel: (0171) 813 2233).

CHEF: Richard Coates PROPRIETOR: Belgo Group plc OPEN: Mon to Fri 12 to 3, 6 to 11.30, Sat 12 to 11.30, Sun 12 to 10.30 CLOSED: 25 Dec MEALS: alc (main courses £8 to £15). Set L £5 (1 course) to £14.95, Set D £12.95 to £14.95 SERVICE: 15% (optional), card slips closed CARDS: Amex, Delta, Diners, MasterCard, Switch, Visa DETAILS: 140 seats. 8 seats outside. Private parties: 140 main room. Vegetarian meals. Children's helpings. Wheelchair access (not WC). No music. Air-conditioned ⊖ Chalk Farm

Bertorelli's map 13

44A Floral Street, WC2E 9DA COOKING 1
TEL: (0171) 836 3969 FAX: (0171) 836 1868 COST £25–£55

It may be corporate-owned, but that doesn't interfere with the 'typically Italian restaurant atmosphere' praised by one reporter. Opposite the Opera House, Bertorelli's is 'warm, friendly, bustling, and full of a sense of fun.' Maddalena Bonino oversees the cooking at both this and the branch at 19–23 Charlotte Street, and the kitchens work to an up-to-date Italian formula that takes in baked smoked mozzarella stuffed with wild mushrooms, roast monkfish on a ragoût of marinated aubergines with cherry tomatoes and butter-beans; and veal milanese, breadcrumbed and Parmesan-coated but served unusually with salsa verde. A range of pastas is also offered, and vegetables and salads – charged extra – include strips of courgette fritter doused in Italian wine vinegar. The all-Italian *lista dei vini* offers a fair choice under £20 while featuring some highly respected growers. A duo of Veronese house wines starts things off at £9.50 a bottle and a quartet of Super-Tuscans draws things to a more pricey yet starry conclusion. CELLARMAN'S CHOICE: Soave Classico Superiore 1996, Pieropan, £19.50; Chianti Rufina Riserva, Castello di Nipozzano 1994, Frescobaldi, £22.

CHEF: Maddalena Bonino PROPRIETOR: Groupe Chez Gérard OPEN: Mon to Sat 12 to 3, 5.30 to 11.30 MEALS: alc (main courses £8 to £14). Set L and D 5.30 to 6.30 £9.95 (2 courses). Cover £1.50 SERVICE: 12.5% (optional), card slips closed CARDS: Amex, Diners, MasterCard, Switch, Visa DETAILS: 135 seats. Private parties: 35 main room. Vegetarian meals. Children welcome. No smoking in 1 dining-room. Wheelchair access (1 step; not WC). No music. Air-conditioned ⊖ Covent Garden

Bibendum map 14

Michelin House, 81 Fulham Road, SW3 6RD
TEL: (0171) 581 5817 FAX: (0171) 823 7925 COOKING 5
EMAIL: manager@bibendum.co.uk COST £38–£71

Bibendum, now over a decade old, remains one of London's most beautiful dining-rooms. Sir Terence Conran's conversion of the 1905 Michelin building produced a first-floor restaurant which seems to be 'hovering over the Fulham Road', the contours of glasses, vases, decanters and ashtrays following those of the tyre man. The mood changes: along with seat covers from season to season, and from daytime, when natural light floods in, to a more theatrical setting at night. 'Cosseting, reassuringly well designed, smooth and contemporary' is how it feels.

The aim, under Simon Hopkinson, was to cook a few dishes perfectly – the best steak au poivre, the crispest fish and chips, the most intense chocolate truffles – and Bibendum has been a showcase for a wide range of dishes, from classic French soupe de poissons, ballottine of foie gras, and poulet de Bresse à l'estragon, to jellied eel terrine, English asparagus with hollandaise, and roast beef 'with Yorkshire pudding as big as a hat'. The kitchen can cook some memorable things, but the tally of errors at an inspection meal indicated a disturbing heavy-handedness. As one reporter put it, the food now 'roughly divides into so-so and exceptional'. Among the latter are rice dishes: amber-coloured smoked haddock and saffron risotto, the 'finest langoustine risotto on the planet', and cold creamed rice with praline and brandied apricots. Other desserts impress too, from chocolate pecan brownies to passion-fruit ice-cream pot with shortbread.

Staff convey the right balance of formality and easy-going friendliness, and the wine list is one of the most enthralling in the capital. Covering both the Old and New Worlds in depth, it boasts long lines of pedigree wines and rarities: Châteaux Climens, Clos Fourtet, Léoville-Las Cases and Palmer from the 1920s, for example, and eight vintages of Ch. Yquem stretching back to 1945. But there is plenty of good drinking to be had at less-exalted levels, beginning with the house Vin de Pays des Côtes du Tarn at £10.95 a bottle, £2.99 a glass. CELLARMAN'S CHOICE: Bourgogne Blanc, Cuvée des Forgets 1995, Dom. Patrick Javillier, £28.50; Bernardus Winery Marinus Cabernet Sauvignon/Merlot 1994, Carmel, California, £46.50. The ground-floor two-roomed Oyster Bar serves mainly seafood, with a short wine list on the reverse of the menu, but now also offers the excellent restaurant list as well.

CHEFS: Matthew Harris, Athene O'Neill and Alex Guillemot   PROPRIETORS: Simon Hopkinson, Lord Hamlyn, Sir Terence Conran and Graham Williams   OPEN: Mon to Sat 12 to 2.30 (12.30 to 3 Sat), 7 to 11.30 , Sun 12.30 to 3, 7 to 10.30   MEALS: alc (main courses £13 to £23.50). Set L £28   SERVICE: 12.5% (optional), card slips closed   CARDS: Amex, Delta, Diners, MasterCard, Switch, Visa   DETAILS: 72 seats. Private parties: 100 main room. Children's helpings. Wheelchair access (2 steps; not WC). No music. Air-conditioned   ⊖ South Kensington   (£5)

Billboard Café £ map 13

280 West End Lane, NW6 1LJ
TEL: (0171) 431 4188 COOKING 1
EMAIL: billboardcafe@demon.co.uk COST £19–£40

'Tasty and authentic' writes an inspector of the Italian food at this airy, parquet-floored café done out in shades of ivory and white, with big mirrors, plants and soft background jazz adding to the relaxed and cheerful atmosphere. The short menu of starters, pasta and grills is augmented by daily specials, including fish served with 'sauce of the day' (perhaps tamarind and tomato, or watercress). Seared tuna steak was 'a star' at one meal, and 'succulent, subtly flavoured' pounded breast of chicken marinated with lime and coriander has been another success; in a nod to English taste both were accompanied by broccoli, carrots, cauliflower, mange-tout and new potatoes. Desserts might include rich chocolate and rum mousse; or opt for well-kept Italian cheeses. Service is 'charming and patient'. New World wines outnumber Italian on a short, interesting list, with ten offered by the glass; house Italian is £8.95.

CHEF/PROPRIETOR: M.T. Nateghi   OPEN: Sat noon to 11.30, Sun noon to 10.30, Mon to Fri D 6.30 to 11.30   CLOSED: 25 and 26 Dec, 1 Jan   MEALS: alc (main courses L £6.50 to £12, D £6.50 to £13.50). Set D £13   SERVICE: 10%, card slips closed   CARDS: Amex, Delta, MasterCard, Switch, Visa   DETAILS: 50 seats. 6 seats outside. Private parties: 60 main room. Vegetarian meals. Children's helpings. No-smoking area. Wheelchair access (1 step; not WC). Music. Air-conditioned   ⊖ West Hampstead   £5

Birdcage ⅝✳   NEW ENTRY   map 15

110 Whitfield Street, W1P 5RU   COOKING 3
TEL: (0171) 383 3346   COST £36–£43

There could hardly be a greater contrast between Michael Von Hruschka's last posting and his new venture. I-Thai exemplified the extreme in terms of both minimalism and price, while Birdcage is relatively inexpensive and stuffed with 'utterly captivating decoration': from a standing Buddha to a perhaps predictable birdcage, by way of a brass wine cooler towering above the table. A personal Lilliputian pestle and mortar is on hand for grinding spices, the cocktail list is written on manuscript paper and inserted into an ostrich egg shell, and the wine list is a piece of origami resting in a net box.

If the dining-room is intriguing – and it is – then wait till you see the menu, pasted incidentally into an old book. There appear to be no holds barred in Von Hruschka's personal interpretation of fusion cooking, which takes in Indian scrambled egg on lime-infused rice, fish and banana risotto topped with first-class salmon, and a flaky filo triangle filled with spicy vegetable couscous and 'skewered on an ivory letter opener'. A tripartite starter, arranged on a slate tile, might include an 'immaculate' coconut and lemon-grass soup, small carrot spring rolls and a mound of salad. To finish there may be tiramisù with ginger wine, various sorbets and ice-creams, or a 'mystery' dessert. Some two dozen wines come from around the world, most of them over £20, although house Chilean white and Portuguese red are £15.

CHEF: Michael Von Hruschka   PROPRIETORS: Caroline Faulkner and Michael Von Hruschka   OPEN: Mon to Fri L 12 to 3, Mon to Sat D 6 to 12   MEALS: Set L and D £19.50 (2 courses) to £25   SERVICE: not inc   CARDS: Amex, MasterCard, Switch, Visa   DETAILS: 24 seats. 6 seats outside. Private parties: 20 main room. Vegetarian meals. Children welcome. No smoking in dining-room. Wheelchair access (not WC). Music   ⊖ Goodge St   £5

Blakes £   NEW ENTRY   map 13

31 Jamestown Road, NW1 7DB   COOKING 3
TEL: (0171) 482 2959   FAX: (0171) 267 2595   COST £22–£47

Don't be put off by the noise from the ground-floor bar of this popular Victorian pub: it isn't audible over the soft, elegant background jazz in the simple first-floor restaurant. Walls and plasterwork are deep petrol blue and purple, and the subtle lighting, supplemented by enormous church candles, makes for a sympathetic ambience. 'The helpful waitress showed that it is as pleasant to work here as it is to visit,' wrote a reporter. The dinner menu is à la carte, with set menus for large parties only. The owners describe the style as eclectic Mediterranean – reflecting the chef's Algerian origin – and it delivers such North African dishes as heart of baby artichoke with Tunisian mahamssa (semolina rolled into tiny balls resembling spätzli), the artichoke resting on a disc of fried potato and vegetable like a spiced bubble and squeak; and 'moist, succulent' deep-fried mixed seafood with an avocado purée and harissa. Pan-fried magret of duck with roasted parsnips, sweet potatoes and grilled peppers is more European, but again spicing hints at the Maghreb. A half-dozen tempting desserts include baked lemon and passion-fruit cheesecake, served hot with a 'dazzling' fruit coulis. The short eclectic wine list starts at £9.50.

CHEF: L. Belaidi   PROPRIETORS: Robert, Carmen and Irvin Blake   OPEN: Mon to Sat 12 to 3, 6.30 to 10.30 (6.30 to 11 Fri and Sat), Sun 1 to 10   CLOSED: 25 Dec, 1 Jan   MEALS: alc (main courses L £5 to £9.50, D £7 to £14.50)   SERVICE: 12.5% (optional), 15% for parties of 8 or more   CARDS: Amex, Delta, MasterCard, Switch, Visa   DETAILS: 50 seats. 40 seats outside. Private parties: 50 to 56 main room. Vegetarian meals. Children's helpings   ⊖ Camden Town

Bluebird ✍   map 14

350 King's Road, SW3 5UU	COOKING 3
TEL: (0171) 559 1000 FAX: (0171) 559 1111	COST £26–£86

'Like Quaglino's with windows,' summed up one visitor, eyeing the serried ranks of tiny tables culminating in a seafood altar. The place has a vitality about it, and the food tries hard to be interesting. John Torode moved here from Mezzo (see entry) in April 1998, but the food continues along much the same lines: a list of simply written dishes grouped into fish and shellfish, pasta and eggs, meat and poultry and so on, with a wood-fired oven turning out tomato tart, rabbit with mushrooms, and squab pigeon with dauphinoise.

Given the large output (for bookings after 8pm, the restaurant tells us, there is no time-limit on tables) it is not surprising that some meals are better than others; hence our bag of mixed reports: brill 'overcooked' for one reporter, 'brilliantly cooked' for another. Indeed, almost any generalisation we might make, whether to do with noise level, cooking times, attractiveness of the menu, or just general enjoyment, is scuppered by reporters with opposing views, except for smooth-running service, which is universally praised. The food may appear mid-priced, but extras can mount up. Wines are up to date, sometimes a bit pricey, but full of interest. House Vin de Pays d'Oc is £11.75.

CHEF: John Torode   PROPRIETOR: Sir Terence Conran   OPEN: all week 12 (11 Sat and Sun) to 3.30, 6 to 11 (10 Sun)   CLOSED: 24 Dec D, 25 and 26 Dec   MEALS: alc (main courses £9 to £27.50). Set L Mon to Sat £12.75 (2 courses) to £15.75, Set L Sun £17.80, Set D 6 to 7 £12.75 (2 courses) to £15.75   SERVICE: 12.5%   CARDS: Amex, Delta, Diners, MasterCard, Switch, Visa   DETAILS: 270 seats. Private parties: 500 main room, 24 to 90 private rooms. Vegetarian meals. Children welcome. Wheelchair access (also WC). Music. Air-conditioned   ⊖ Sloane Square

The text of entries is based on unsolicited reports sent in by readers, backed up by inspections conducted anonymously. The factual details under the text are from questionnaires the Guide *sends to all restaurants that feature in the book.*

Blue Elephant
map 12

4–6 Fulham Broadway, SW6 1AA
TEL: (0171) 385 6595   FAX: (0171) 386 7665
EMAIL: blueelephantlondon@msn.com

COOKING 2
COST £32–£64

This forerunner of 'theme restaurants' – an exuberant jungle with carp pools, cascades and bridges, massed tropical flowers and waiters in national costume – brings welcome colour to Fulham. The long *carte* offers familiar favourites under strange names, but all are clearly described. Salads – some heavily chillied – include sunburst pomelo, jungle, laab (minced chicken), and exotic yam hua pee, consisting of banana flowers and prawns with grated, roasted coconut in a tamarind dressing. One party appreciated 'subtle flavours and nice presentation' in the Royal Thai Banquet of six starters, six main courses, plus pad Thai noodles, vegetables, rice and coupe Blue Elephant. It costs £30, with tom yum soup extra at £5. Vegetarian menus offer stuffed orchids, variations on yod phaeng, and fried home-made bean-curd. Wines are mostly a Thai food-friendly bunch, although some of the mark-ups are less welcoming. House French is £10.50.

CHEF: Rungsan Mulijan   PROPRIETOR: Blue Elephant International plc   OPEN: Sun to Fri L (Sun buffet brunch) 12 to 2.30, all week D 7 to 12.30 (10.30 Sun)   CLOSED: 24 to 27 Dec, 1 Jan. MEALS: alc (main courses £7.50 to £19.50). Set D £29 to £34. Cover £1.50   SERVICE: not inc CARDS: Amex, Delta, Diners, MasterCard, Switch, Visa   DETAILS: 240 seats. Private parties: 50 main room, 30 to 50 private rooms. Vegetarian meals. Children's helpings. Wheelchair access (2 steps; also WC). Music. Air-conditioned   ⊖ Fulham Broadway

Blue Print Café
map 13

Design Museum, Butlers Wharf, SE1 2YE
TEL: (0171) 378 7031   FAX: (0171) 357 8810

COOKING 4
COST £36–£57

The first-floor restaurant at the Design Museum on Shad Thames is, in the opinion of most visitors, a design triumph, which is as it should be. Plainly set tables and hard-edged spaces are thrown into scenic relief by panoramic views over the Thames. A conservatory room has been created by glassing over the balcony, so that, even in sheeting rain, the prospect may be appreciated.

A correspondent who views the place as 'an old favourite' enthused over a lunch that began with an assemblage of crisp pancetta, roast tomatoes, guacamole, spring onions and mayonnaise, proceeded to a vegetarian main course of polenta with ceps, roast onions, mascarpone, rocket and Parmesan, and concluded with a chocolate brownie. The Mediterranean style is embraced here as enthusiastically as at other Conran venues along the wharf, and reaches out to include an appetiser plate of Spanish cured meats; rabbit fricassee with peppers, olives and basil; and an aubergine, tomato, courgette and ricotta pizza. Vegetables are extra, and desserts range from a glass of Isole e Olena vin santo with biscotti, to cherry and almond tart with Jersey cream, or coffee granita. One reporter described the service as 'over-efficient', but most agree on its professionalism. The imaginative wine list is arranged by grape variety, and is by no means limited to the obvious candidates, but mark-ups are a little off-putting. A French rosé opens the batting at £13.50.

CHEF: Jeremy Lee   PROPRIETOR: Conran Restaurants   OPEN: all week L 12 to 3, Mon to Sat D 6 to 11   CLOSED: 25 and 26 Dec, 1 to 3 Jan   MEALS: alc (main courses £11 to £18)   SERVICE: 12.5% (optional), card slips closed   CARDS: Amex, Diners, MasterCard, Switch, Visa   DETAILS: 120 seats. Private parties: 110 main room. Vegetarian meals. Children welcome. Wheelchair access (also WC). No music   ⊖ Tower Hill, London Bridge

Brackenbury £

map 12

129–131 Brackenbury Road, W6 0BQ
TEL: (0181) 748 0107   FAX: (0181) 741 0905

COOKING 4
COST £18–£41

Although the Brackenbury changed hands in 1997, the new regime wisely retained the services of Marcia Chang Hong, who became head chef and ensured a degree of continuity at this enthusiastically supported Shepherd's Bush venue. The deep-green frontage is echoed within by walls and carpet, but where once the décor bore a hard-edged feel, there is now a welcome softness in the air. Robust brasserie cooking is the chosen mode. Scallops are served with guacamole (a variant on the ubiquitous pea purée) and tomato vinaigrette to start, or there may be a 'trusted combination' such as smoked haddock with a poached egg and hollandaise. One reporter heartily approved a lightly cooked pigeon breast bedded on Savoy cabbage with turnips in a red wine reduction, a satiating first course if ever there was. Fish is geared up for mighty appetites too, fried brill arriving with a stew of chorizo and arrocina beans (one of the defining ingredients of 1998) and a dollop of aïoli. Or there is even 'canteen food' for those who prefer: perhaps cheese omelette with chips and salad. Puddings might include prune and almond tart or smooth pink grapefruit sorbet. Staff are friendly and solicitous in just the right measure. The enterprising wine list takes in some sound modern flavours, from Chilean Sauvignon to Oregon Pinot Noir, and kicks off with southern French house wines at £9.50.

CHEF: Marcia Chang Hong   PROPRIETOR: Place Restaurants Ltd   OPEN: Sun to Fri L 12.30 to 2.45 (3 Sun), Mon to Sat D 7 to 10.45   CLOSED: 4 days Christmas, 4 days Easter, some bank hols   MEALS: alc (main courses £6.50 to £12). Set L Mon to Fri £8.50 (2 courses) to £10.50   SERVICE: not inc   CARDS: Amex, MasterCard, Switch, Visa   DETAILS: 60 seats. 24 seats outside. Private parties: 10 main room. Vegetarian meals. Children's helpings. No cigars/pipes in dining-room. Wheelchair access (not WC). No music   ⊖ Goldhawk Road, Hammersmith

Bradleys

map 13

25 Winchester Road, NW3 3NR
TEL: (0171) 722 3457   FAX: (0171) 431 4776

COOKING 5
COST £24–£50

Behind the grind and fumes of Swiss Cottage traffic, Simon Bradley's small neighbourhood restaurant has established a solid customer base. There is no sense of money having been splashed needlessly on décor, just a bit of antiqued paintwork on the partitions and a dose of polish on the bare wooden floor. The colour scheme is pleasantly muted, the better perhaps to point up emphatic tones in the cooking. The style won't surprise these days. It is copybook North London Mediterranean, with chargrilling, herb-crusting and honey-roasting to the fore, but the hand on the tiller is a secure one, and the results provide great satisfaction.

Among successes have been a 'perfectly judged' light gâteau of aubergine, courgette and dolcelatte with tomato and basil sauce, and sesame-seared tuna on glass noodles. 'Highly original and interesting tastes' are part of the draw too, as in duck with sage fritters and smoked apple sauce. Menu choice, especially at dinner, is wider than average, extending from chargrilled squid with watercress and plum and chilli sauce, to a vegetarian main dish of potato rösti with grilled Mediterranean vegetables, halloumi and black olive dressing. Desserts are a strong suit, and rave notices have come in for memorable soft chocolate pudding with marmalade ice-cream, raspberry crème brûlée, and pear soufflé with ginger sauce. Deft and friendly service helps to make this a classy operation. Only the Champagne region is permitted to represent Europe on the wine list. Otherwise it is an enterprising and commendable selection from South Africa, the Americas and the Antipodes, although mark-ups are vigorous. House Chilean is £9.95.

CHEF: Simon Bradley   PROPRIETORS: Simon and Jolanta Bradley   OPEN: Sun to Fri L 12 to 3, all week D 6 to 11   CLOSED: 25 and 26 Dec, 1 Jan   MEALS: alc (main courses £9 to £15). Set L Sun £12 (2 courses) to £15   SERVICE: not inc; 12% for parties of 5 or more   CARDS: Amex, Delta, MasterCard, Switch, Visa   DETAILS: 60 seats. Private parties: 65 main room. Vegetarian meals. Children's helpings. No cigars/pipes in dining-room. Wheelchair access (not WC). Music. Air-conditioned   ⊖ Swiss Cottage   (£5)

Brady's £

map 12

513 Old York Road, SW18 1TF
TEL: (0181) 877 9599

COOKING 2
COST £16–£25

If friends from a far country or another planet wish to sample British cooking, this is the place to take them. It looks like a normal fish-and-chip shop, but is much more. Starters include potted shrimps, cod's roe pâté, anchovies and rollmops, listed on a blackboard together with the day's fish for grilling. These might include tuna, skate, Dover sole, red mullet, halibut, swordfish or bream. Large or small portions of 'dazzlingly fresh, flaky' battered cod, 'sweet-tasting' haddock or plaice are 'enveloped in a wonderful lightweight batter' before 'skilful, exemplary frying'. 'Decent' chips of the old-fashioned thick-cut variety, and even mushy peas if you wish, make queuing worthwhile.

CHEF: Luke Brady   PROPRIETORS: Luke and Amelia Brady   OPEN: Mon to Sat D only 7 to 10.30 (10.45 Thur and Fri)   CLOSED: Christmas, Easter, bank hols   MEALS: alc (main courses £4.50 to £7)   SERVICE: 10% (optional)   CARDS: none   DETAILS: 48 seats. Children's helpings. Music

Brasserie St Quentin ⅝✕

map 14

243 Brompton Road, SW3 2EP
TEL: (0171) 589 8005

COOKING 3
COST £29–£61

This Knightsbridge outpost of the Groupe Chez Gérard empire is decked out in 'sumptuous' red and gold, Paris brasserie style, with chandeliers, huge bronze-coloured wall mirrors, and closely packed tables: as lavish as the small scale allows. Traditional Francophile offerings pepper the menu, from snails (with asparagus and ceps) in puff pastry, via charcuterie and stuffed duck neck to steak béarnaise. The food may be 'uneven', and not always brilliantly conceived, but it has produced some impressive items, not least among seafood: mussels, a well-dressed salad of sweet crab, and just-cooked skate wing in a rich and tangy caper butter. For dessert, crisp prune pithivier comes unusually with a thyme and lemon sorbet. Gallic service ranges from 'glum' to 'attentive'. Ten wines by the glass head a completely French list, which has an eye for thrift as well as a few big names. Vin de Pays des Côtes du Tarn starts the ball rolling at £10.

CHEF: Malcolm John   PROPRIETOR: Groupe Chez Gérard   OPEN: Mon to Sat 12 to 3, 6 to 11.30, Sun 12 to 3.30, 6.30 to 11   MEALS: alc (main courses £10.50 to £24). Set L and D 6 to 7.30 £13.50 (2 courses) to £16.95   SERVICE: 12.5% (optional), card slips closed   CARDS: Amex, Delta, Diners, MasterCard, Switch, Visa   DETAILS: 55 seats. Private parties: 20 private room. Children welcome. No smoking in 1 dining-room. Occasional music. Air-conditioned
⊖ Knightsbridge, South Kensington

▲ Brown's Hotel, 1837 Restaurant 🍷

NEW ENTRY
map 15

Albemarle Street, W1X 4BP
TEL: (0171) 408 1837   FAX: (0171) 493 9381
EMAIL: brownshotel@ukbusiness.com

COOKING 7
COST £40–£100

The date recalls the year Brown's first opened: the one in which Victoria became queen. Now owned by the same group as Raffles Hotel in Singapore, it has been re-launched on a sea of money, which shows in everything from menu to wines to staff to décor. The high-ceilinged oak-panelled dining room is considered 'elegant without being stuffy', and natural daylight at lunch-time is appreciated. 'Classical' seems to apply equally well to both the décor and the very French food: a generous *carte* in the circumstances, working to a fixed repertoire.

Luxuries include foie gras in a sweet Pacherenc jelly, Beluga caviare, and truffles in the chicken consommé, but no attempt is made to shock with outrageous ingredients. If anything, the reverse is true: there is even a spin on an old British favourite, consisting of langoustines and avocado packed in a timbale, with a light cocktail sauce. 'Refined, and technically excellent' is a fair summary of the output: for example, a fillet of 'flawlessly cooked' turbot, together with steamed scallops, mussels, fine noodles and a strewing of vegetables, or strips of pink Aylesbury duck heaped on to a nest of cabbage, itself resting on a potato galette, ringed by an apple and blackcurrant sauce.

Good sense restricts cheeses to a manageable number 'in peak condition', while 'the crowning achievement' of our inspector's meal was a chocolate soufflé with dark chocolate sauce poured in as it was served. Old-fashioned is one thing, but a mid-meal sorbet, and menus without prices for ladies, seems antediluvian; goodness knows what they do when two ladies eat together. Service from a brigade of formally dressed waiters has been 'uninterested' for one, 'impeccable' for another. The wine list is a leather-bound volume that runs to 50 pages, covering the classic areas in depth and doing full justice to the New World. But sommelier John Gilchrist's real triumph is the provision of some 150 exciting wines by the glass (with additional varietal promotions), which he delights in matching to individual dishes if requested. Prices for a glass range from £4 for Bacchus Chiddingstone from England to £30 for Ch. Haut-Brion 1992, and bottles vary from £18 for a regional French to four figures for a first growth claret with plenty of choice at all levels between. Half-bottles are generous too.

CHEF: Gregory Nicholson   PROPRIETOR: Brown's Hotel   OPEN: Mon to Fri L 12.30 to 2, Mon to Sat D 7 to 10.30   CLOSED: 26 Dec   MEALS: alc (main courses £18 to £35). Set L £27 to £55, Set D £55   SERVICE: not inc   CARDS: Amex, Delta, Diners, MasterCard, Switch, Visa   DETAILS: 88 seats. Private parties: 88 main room, 10 private room. Vegetarian meals. Children's helpings. No children under 8. No-smoking areas. Wheelchair access (1 step; also WC). Occasional music. Air-conditioned   ACCOMMODATION: 118 rooms, all with bath/shower. TV. Phone. Room only £235 to £735. Rooms for disabled. Children welcome. Baby facilities. No dogs. Afternoon teas ⊖ Green Park

Bu-San £

map 13

43 Holloway Road, N7 8JP   COOKING 1
TEL: (0171) 607 8264   FAX: (0171) 700 0961   COST £23–£63

Much of the appeal of this likeable little Korean restaurant derives from its owners, Young Hyung and Kim Lee. He cooks, while she runs front-of-house with staff who are 'very charming, very accommodating and very good natured'. The family grow their own vegetables, which Mr Lee sculpts into fantastic carved shapes as ornamentation for some of his dishes; they also grow their own flowers – ' a remarkable feat in Holloway'. Ferocious kim-chee (pickled cabbage with chilli) is a benchmark dish and it does the business here. Otherwise, the kitchen delivers authentic but accessible Korean dishes with a few Japanese specialities tossed in for good measure. Recent reports have singled out sigumchi namul (seasoned spinach with sesame oil) and yuk hoe (Korean-style steak tartare) among the list of appetisers. More substantial successes have included salmon sashimi and ko ke bokum (fried crab in a mild spicy sauce), not to mention hae mul gui ('wonderfully fresh' seafood cooked at the table). Drink Ginseng tea or Hite Korean beer. House wine is £8.95.

CHEF: Young Hyung Lee   PROPRIETORS: Young Hyung and Kim Lee   OPEN: Mon to Fri L 12 to 2.30, all week D 6 to 10   CLOSED: 1 Jan, D before bank hol Mons, bank hol Mons   MEALS: alc (main courses £7 to £20). Set L £4.20 to £6.60 (all 1 course), Set D £14.75 to £19 (all minimum 2)   SERVICE: 10%   CARDS: MasterCard, Switch, Visa   DETAILS: 46 seats. Private parties: 30 main room. Vegetarian meals. Children's helpings. Music. Air-conditioned   ⊖ Highbury & Islington (£5)

Butlers Wharf Chop House ▼

map 13

36E Shad Thames, Butlers Wharf SE1 2YE   COOKING 2
TEL: (0171) 403 3403   FAX: (0171) 403 3414   COST £32–£77

Among sibling Conran restaurants, in what is now a thriving part of town, the Chop House is tilted towards the traditional English end of the food spectrum, with a long menu that takes in shellfish with mayonnaise, fish and chips with mushy peas, and steak and kidney pudding. There are spit-roasts and grills, casseroles and braises, and game such as potted pigeon with shallot pickle, or wild boar and apple sausages. It does not neglect foreign ideas such as baked goats' cheese with chicory and pickled walnuts, or wild mushroom salad with poached egg and tarragon hollandaise, but tends to do more justice to heartier dishes: for example, guinea-fowl with parsley mash at one meal that was 'full of flavour'. Finish perhaps with Cambridge burnt cream or strawberry shortcake. Less-than-knowledgeable wine service has on occasion failed to live up to the standards set by the list, which has some fine clarets and burgundies and some premium New World bins. Mark-ups can be steep but quality is high at all price levels. House Sauvignon from the Languedoc is £11.95, the house claret is £16.50. CELLARMAN'S CHOICE: Mudhouse Sauvignon Blanc 1997, Marlborough, New Zealand, £22.50; Cumaro 1994, Umani Ronchi, Marches, £29.75.

CHEF: Andrew Johns   PROPRIETOR: Sir Terence Conran   OPEN: Sun to Fri L 12 to 3, Mon to Sat D 6 to 11   CLOSED: 1 to 3 Jan, Good Fri   MEALS: alc D (main courses £11.50 to £29.50). Set L £18.75 (2 courses) to £22.75. Bar menu available   SERVICE: 12.5% (optional), card slips closed   CARDS: Amex, Delta, Diners, MasterCard, Switch, Visa   DETAILS: 105 seats. 45 seats outside. Private parties: 50 main room. Vegetarian meals. Children welcome. Wheelchair access (also WC). No music   ➔ Tower Hill, London Bridge

Byron's
map 13

3A Downshire Hill, NW3 1NR   COOKING 3
TEL: (0171) 435 3544   FAX: (0171) 431 3544   COST £25–£55

Leafiest Hampstead may be the location, but there is nothing too refined or twee about Byron's. The décor makes a virtue of bare-boarded spareness, with ochre walls and large-paned windows conferring a fresh, airy feel. Jonathon Coxon once cooked at Walton's in Chelsea, where all was flounce and furbelow, so the change may have come as a relief. Cooking is correspondingly direct and straightforward, delivering deep-fried prawns with rocket and aïoli, and grilled lamb cutlets on creamed leeks and tarragon, with perhaps a blob of lemon sorbet between courses. Sea bass with lemon and vanilla has impressed less than a robust dish of Stilton-topped beef fillet in a port sauce, accompanied by a generous portion of impeccably proper bubble and squeak. Extra charges for vegetables give the final bill a leg-up. Raspberry crème brûlée and 'very light but tasty' caramelised lemon tart have been good puds. The wine list pitches its tent in France and makes minor forays into other territories, but prices are mostly high. Try Chile for relief, or the house Bordeaux at £11.95.

CHEF: Jonathon Coxon   PROPRIETOR: Richard Horwood   OPEN: Sat and Sun L 11 to 5, all week D 7 to 11 (10 Sun)   CLOSED: 25 and 26 Dec   MEALS: alc (main courses L £6.50 to £16.50, D £12.50 to £16.50)   SERVICE: 12.5% (optional), card slips closed   CARDS: Amex, Delta, MasterCard, Switch, Visa   DETAILS: 45 seats. 15 seats outside. Private parties: 40 main room. Vegetarian meals. Children welcome. Wheelchair access (not WC). Music. Air-conditioned ➔ Hampstead

Café dell' Ugo 🍸
map 13

56–58 Tooley Street, SE1 2SZ   COOKING 1
TEL: (0171) 407 6001   FAX: (0171) 357 8806   COST £23–£46

Escapees from the nearby London Dungeon enjoy ascending to the restaurant above the lively ground-floor bar in this cavernous railway arch. Helping to set an eclectic tone are such decorative features as a classical column complete with bust and bicycle, as well wooden chairs, the odd bench and large gilt-plaster mirrors. There is no porridge on this menu, which roams the world for cross-cultural combinations that sometimes work surprisingly well. A reporter, guided by the 'affable, chatty' manager to crab and almond aïoli with guacamole and saffron crostini, was pleased to find the oddly assorted yet restrained flavours 'a balance rather than a clash', and was happy to follow it with potache, a 'satisfying' Spanish cassoulet of guinea-fowl, chorizo, bacon and chickpeas. For dessert, 'moist, sticky, intensely flavoured' chocolate brownie with a light chocolate and caramel sauce has pleased, or opt for home-made ice-creams. Dapper waiters in house T-shirts and black trousers provide 'efficient, obliging' service. Wines are divided into 'bigger' and 'smaller', not by bottle size but in terms of weight and body, and eight are available by the glass.

CHEF: Nick Lang   PROPRIETOR: Simpsons of Cornhill plc   OPEN: Mon to Fri L 12 to 3, Mon to Sat D 6 to 11   CLOSED: bank hols   MEALS: alc (main courses £9.50 to £13.50). Set D £12 (2 courses) to £15   SERVICE: not inc   CARDS: Amex, Delta, Diners, MasterCard, Switch, Visa   DETAILS: 140 seats. Private parties: 90 main room. Vegetarian meals. Children welcome. Music
⊖ London Bridge

Café du Jardin ▼ 🍷

28 Wellington Street, WC2E 7BD
TEL: (0171) 836 8769 and 8760
FAX: (0171) 836 4123

map 15

COOKING 4
COST £21–£55

The Café occupies a corner site in the heart of Covent Garden so, night or day, the joint is jumping. Big picture windows mean you won't miss a trick, and the front-of-house is capable of getting you out in time for the show or attending to you promptly after the encores. Co-owner Tony Howorth made himself head chef in January 1998 and continues to run the wide-ranging menus with flair and sound judgement.

The style is all-embracing, both as to cooking methods and ethnic orientation, and some vibrant, punchy dishes are the result. A large deep-fried crab-cake is alive with strong Thai seasonings (lemon grass especially), counterpointed with cheesy spring onion risotto and high-octane chilli oil. Monkfish, too, makes an impact: fried and crowned with a Parmesan crisp, its underlay of chunky ratatouille bristling appealingly with capers. The intrepid might be tempted by grilled ostrich, which comes with sauté potatoes, red peppers and duxelles. Vegetables are charged extra, but include excellent crisp, thin chips. Desserts are more mainstream than the rest, although caramelised peach tart with crème fraîche and black pepper sorbet has been sighted. Otherwise, white and dark chocolate mousses are the business, and crème brûlée is jollied up with orange. The wine list spreads its favours between France and the New World, offering a variety of flavours at a range of prices. House French is £9.50 a bottle, £3.15 for a 250ml glass.

CHEF: Tony Howorth   PROPRIETORS: Robert Seigler and Tony Howorth   OPEN: all week 12 to 3, 5.30 to 12 (noon to 11 Sun)   CLOSED: 25 Dec   MEALS: alc (main courses £9.50 to £14.50). Set L £9.95 (2 courses) to £13.50, Set D 5.30 to 7.30 and 10 to 12 £9.95 (2 courses) to £13.50   SERVICE: 15% (optional), card slips closed   CARDS: Amex, Delta, Diners, MasterCard, Switch, Visa   DETAILS: 110 seats. 20 seats outside. Private parties: 60 main room, 60 private room. Vegetarian meals. Children's helpings. Wheelchair access (not WC). Music. Air-conditioned
⊖ Covent Garden

All entries in the Guide are re-researched and rewritten every year, not least because restaurant standards fluctuate. Don't rely on an out-of-date Guide.

Café Fish

map 15

36–40 Rupert Street, W1V 7FR
TEL: (0171) 287 8989 FAX: (0171) 287 8400

COOKING 2
COST £29–£55

Like an angler seeking a better beat, Café Fish has moved a short distance upstream. The new larger premises, just off Shaftesbury Avenue, have a bar and canteen on the ground floor with 'bare, industrial' décor, while the main restaurant upstairs has an attractive green and cream colour scheme and has retained the piscine prints and pictures from the old place. Service is attentive and friendly, and the pleasant ambience makes it easy to forgive close, small, plastic-topped tables. 'Well-cooked and very fresh' fish remains the draw: pan-fried halibut with leek dauphinoise, wilted spinach and assorted mushrooms; monkfish with bacon and creamed potato; and the shellfish platter, a must for seafood devotees, which includes oysters, crab, prawns, mussels, langoustines, clams, cockles and whelks. Tarte Tatin with superb caramelised apples on crisp pastry that came with subtle honey and apple ice-cream was the high point of one reporter's meal. Wines are well chosen and decently priced, with many available by the glass; house French is £9.75.

CHEF: Andrew Magson PROPRIETOR: Groupe Chez Gérard OPEN: all week 12 to 3, 5.30 to 11.30 (10.30 Sun) MEALS: alc (main courses £8 to £18) SERVICE: 12.5% (optional), card slips closed CARDS: Amex, Diners, MasterCard, Switch, Visa DETAILS: 110 seats. Private parties: 20 main room, 94 private room. Vegetarian meals. Children welcome. Non-smoking area. Wheelchair access (also WC). Music. Air-conditioned ⊖ Piccadilly Circus

Café Japan £

map 13

626 Finchley Road, NW11 7RR
TEL/FAX: (0181) 455 6854
EMAIL: koichikonnai@msn.com

COOKING 5
COST £19–£47

The words 'Casual Japanese Restaurant' on the front of the menu suggest that it is aimed at people off duty, so Japanese customers are more likely to be family groups than business associates, and suits are rare. The mainly young, all-female staff are friendly, and the place is 'spruce, clean and very relaxed', with white-painted walls, parquet floor, polished wooden table-tops, wooden chairs, and of course hashi (throw-away wooden chopsticks). Lighting is bright, excessively so for some. What most impressed an inspector was the work of chef Koichi Konnai, now also the proprietor. She writes: 'This is an artist. Everything is done just so, sauces are all different, all perfectly matched to the dishes.' Although Japanese cuisine doesn't include the concept of 'original', this cooking is imaginative, even occasionally experimental. Sushi includes 'fantastic, meaty, succulent, delicate and fragrant eel, as good as in Japan'. Starters (or side-dishes) of spinach with sesame dressing, grilled shishamo of sardine-sized capelin, and aubergine and tofu yakitori have also been applauded. Unusual tempura include anago eel and soft-shell crab. Set meals run from grilled fish with miso soup, rice and pickles to dinners based on sushi or yakitori, and sukiyaki or its poached equivalent, shabu-shabu. Green tea ice-cream, and a creamy, sweet version that incorporates candied chestnuts, make impressive desserts.

Drink saké, hot or chilled, beer, house white or red wines, and try plum wine with ice-cream.

CHEF/PROPRIETOR: Koichi Konnai   OPEN: all week D only 5.30 to 10.30   MEALS: alc (main courses £4.50 to £12.50). Set D £5.50 (2 courses) to £17.50. BYO £5   SERVICE: not inc   CARDS: Delta, MasterCard, Switch, Visa   DETAILS: 33 seats. Private parties: 8 main room. Vegetarian meals. Children welcome. Music. Air-conditioned   ⊖ Golders Green

▲ Café Nico 🍴

map 15

Grosvenor House, Park Lane, W1A 3AA   COOKING 4
TEL: (0171) 495 2275   FAX: (0171) 493 3341   COST £49–£55

There's a slight identity crisis at the multi-purpose Café Nico in Park Lane's Grosvenor House Hotel. It's a breakfast room for residents; an informal café offering soup, sandwiches and coffee to all-comers; and a full-blown restaurant, loosely connected to the hotel's flagship Chez Nico, at lunch and dinner. This can add a pleasing sense of informality, or it can mean that staff start laying up for breakfast while diners are still eating their dessert. Still, the well-spaced tables and stylish art deco surroundings make it a comfortable spot from which to enjoy the views over Hyde Park.

While the rich, robust bistro food (risotto with rocket and foie gras, for example) may not have been knocked up by Nico Ladenis himself, there are first-class renditions of deceptively simple, old-fashioned dishes. A croustade of mushrooms is made with 'beautifully thin pastry', surrounded by hollandaise sauce and 'topped with a perfectly poached egg which dripped over everything'. Duck confit, which 'fell off the bone' in the correct fashion, was refreshingly partnered with grapefruit segments and a mild oriental sauce, while 'very fresh' sea bass had a thick, moist tapénade crust. Main courses might be served with a small ramekin of 'the best mash in London'.

Desserts, a mixture of classic French (crème brûlée, chocolate marquise) and nursery English (treacle pudding, bread-and-butter pudding), are in the same rich vein, unless you opt for sorbet. The wine list provides a sobering reminder that the all-day café is in fact part of a Mayfair hotel, with prices starting at £21 (£5 per glass) and rising to £295.

CHEF: Ralph Porciani   PROPRIETOR: Grosvenor House Hotel   OPEN: Tue to Sun 12 to 3, 6 to 10.30   CLOSED: first 2 weeks Jan.   MEALS: Set L and D £25.50 (2 courses) to £29.50. Light menu available during the day   SERVICE: 12.5% (optional)   CARDS: Amex, Delta, Diners, MasterCard, Switch, Visa   DETAILS: 140 seats. Private parties: 250 main room. Children's helpings. No-smoking area. Music. Air-conditioned   ACCOMMODATION: 450 rooms, all with bath/shower. TV. Phone. Room only £258 to £480. Rooms for disabled. Children welcome. High teas for children. Baby facilities. No dogs. Afternoon teas. Swimming-pool   ⊖ Marble Arch, Hyde Park Corner   (£5)

The Guide *is totally independent, accepts no free hospitality, and survives on the number of copies sold each year.*

The Guide *relies on feedback from its readers. Especially welcome are reports on new restaurants appearing in the book for the first time. All letters to the* Guide *are acknowledged.*

Café Royal, Grill Room | **NEW ENTRY** map 15

Regent Street, W1R 6EL COOKING 8
TEL: (0171) 437 1177 FAX: (0171) 439 7672 COST £39–£87

The Grill Room, a monument to 134 years of London's social life, has taken on new vigour under the joint ownership of Marco Pierre White and Granada. Dining-rooms don't come more rococo than this. Simplicity is blithely disregarded in favour of the grandiose, with gilded and garlanded caryatids set against gilt-encrusted mirrors, red plush furnishings and a painted ceiling. The less glamorous entrance and clutch of 'function rooms' are eclipsed and quickly forgotten amid scrolls, drapes, diaphanous robes, padded seats and well-stocked liquor trolleys.

Marco protegé Spencer Patrick shares the master's penchant for foie gras and shellfish starters, and has an unquenchable appetite for luxuries, but despite a smattering of regular MPW items – oysters in champagne jelly, or parfait of foie gras and chicken livers – there is enough novelty to give the cooking an individual stamp. Combinations, never incongruous, can be as simple as delicately smoked salmon wrapped around fresh crabmeat bound with five-star mayonnaise. Indeed a concern for balance is central, as when sweet, firm, pearly-centred scallops 'at the peak of freshness' are arranged on a circular raft of caramelised endive with a first-class orange butter sauce. The style is precise, with a firm classical foundation evident in, for example, a 'superb' version of pigeon 'en vessie' with unstinting use of foie gras and truffles, served with paper-thin wild mushroom ravioli, along with 'foetal' broad beans and carrots, and a cep-infused sauce. Spencer Patrick combines consistency and high technical skill with a dash of flair too: in a vividly coloured dish of perfectly timed red mullet fillets on a puddle of aromatic tomato butter sauce, the whole confidently flavoured yet delicate.

Desserts tend to concentrate on exemplary productions of simple classics: lemon tart, raspberry soufflé into which the waiter pours raspberry purée, and caramelised apple tart with pastry as fine as tissue paper. Portions are well judged, but there is an appetiser and pre-dessert to cope with, so take a doggy bag for the petits fours just in case. Service is formal, well paced, informative, and 'they all wore very nice aftershave'. If you had the money, they had the wine,' said one reporter, and there are indeed many grand old clarets, mature burgundies and classy New World bins on the lengthy list at some very high prices. However, should you consider splashing out £2,800 on the Ch. Latour 1961 (or even £4,800 on the 1921 Yquem), then be warned that all wines over 30 years old are deemed to be your responsibility should the tasting quality be in any way compromised.

CHEF: Spencer Patrick PROPRIETOR: MPW Criterion Ltd OPEN: Mon to Fri L 12 to 2.30, Mon to Sat D 6 to 11 CLOSED: bank hols MEALS: alc (main courses £21.50 to £25). Set L £24.50, Set pre-theatre D £27 SERVICE: 12.5% (optional), card slips closed CARDS: Amex, Delta, MasterCard, Switch, Visa DETAILS: 45 seats. Private parties: 75 main room. Children's helpings. Wheelchair access (also WC). No music. Air-conditioned ⊖ Piccadilly Circus

Dining-rooms where music, either live or recorded, is never played are signalled by No music *in the details at the end of an entry.*

Café Spice Namaste £

map 13

16 Prescot Street, E1 8AZ
TEL: (0171) 488 9242   FAX: (0171) 488 9339

COOKING 4
COST £21–£38

Just east of the Tower of London, this striking Indian restaurant occupies a converted Victorian magistrates' court. Buzzy and noisy, with vivid maroon, purple and turquoise décor, it looked to one visitor 'like that TV programme where someone comes in and decorates your house'. The food is equally arresting. 'Anything goes,' reckoned one reporter, perhaps thinking of ostrich gizzard kebab, alligator tikka, or a variation on Scotch egg, this one using minced bison, moose and blue boar. Even the cow is not sacred, appearing for example as dry fried beef Kerala-style. These come from the weekly speciality menu, which supplements the long list of regional dishes that form the backbone of Cyrus Todiwala's cooking. He has spent a lot of time in Goa, which seems to be the focus. This combination of varied materials – including Indian Ocean fish – with regional cooking styles makes for an innovative approach and diverting eating, from lambs' liver and kidney cooked in the tandoor, to a complex chicken curry called xacutti. While spicing may not always have the expected zest, timing is typically accurate and incidentals include aromatic pilaus, fluffy naan and 'better than average' pickles and chutneys. Finish, perhaps, with hot carrot halva. Colourfully dressed waiters are supervised by Mrs Todiwala, who is 'brimming with enthusiasm'. Around 30 fairly priced wines start with house French at £10.25.

CHEFS: Cyrus Todiwala and Angelo Collaco   PROPRIETORS: Cyrus Todiwala and Michael Gottlieb   OPEN: Mon to Fri L 12 to 3, Mon to Sat D 6.15 to 10.30 (6.30 to 10 Sat)   CLOSED: 1 week Christmas, bank hol Mons   MEALS: alc (main courses £8 to £14)   SERVICE: 10% (optional); 12½% for parties of 8 or more   CARDS: Amex, Delta, Diners, MasterCard, Switch, Visa   DETAILS: 110 seats. Private parties: 80 main room. Vegetarian meals. Children's helpings. Music. Air-conditioned   ⊖ Aldgate, Tower Hill   £5

Cambio de Tercio ▼ 🍽

map 14

163 Old Brompton Road, SW5 0LJ
TEL/FAX: (0171) 244 8970

COOKING 3
COST £29–£51

At a bullfight, an event of three stages, cambio de tercio is the change from one phase to the next, signalled by a fanfare. No fanfares here, but 'noisy modern Spanish music' fits the dramatic saffron and red décor with bullfighting artefacts and pictures. The front opens out in summer, and at the back is a small, bright conservatory. The menu comprises classics from various Spanish regions. Jamon de Jabugo (from a named pig-farm), paella, 'beautifully tender and sweet' Segovian-style suckling pig, and 'very traditional' crema catalana impressed inspectors and a Spanish guest. Gratinated oysters, and stuffed endives with leek sauce, have made enjoyable starters, while a main dish of ostrich, from Cordoba, presently fashionable in Spain, comes in a rich sauce to counterbalance its lean qualities. Desserts vary, but Spanish cheeses with quince marmalade are recommended. Service by youngish Spanish waiters is informal and 'faultless – chatty, friendly, highly professional'. Their skills extend to wine service, making it a pleasure to choose from the peachy, aromatic whites of Galicia and Navarra and mature reds from Rioja and Ribera del Duero (including two Vega

Sicilia Unicos). Prices are fair, with nine house wines offered by the glass and bottle from £2.60/£11.50. CELLARMAN'S CHOICE: Rioja, Cosme Palacio 1996, £16.50; Crianza, Eventum Viña Magaña 1995, Navarra, £17.50.

CHEFS: Manuel Alburquerque and Sergio Laguarda   PROPRIETORS: Abel Lusa and David Rivero   OPEN: all week 12.30 to 2.30, 7 to 11.30   MEALS: alc (main courses £8.50 to £15) SERVICE: not inc; 12.5% for parties of 6 or more   CARDS: Amex, Delta, MasterCard, Switch, Visa   DETAILS: 45 seats. 10 seats outside. Private parties: 100 main room, 18 and 60 private rooms. Children welcome. Wheelchair access (1 step; not WC). Music   ● Gloucester Road

Canteen map 12

Unit G4, Harbour Yard, Chelsea Harbour, SW10 0XD   COOKING 6
TEL: (0171) 351 7330   FAX: (0171) 351 6189   COST £31–£68

The Canteen has done well against the background of a harbour location that no longer seems to bask in the capital's fickle limelight, and despite harlequin and playing-card motifs that are 'the epitome of the 1980s'. True, part of the dining-room overlooks yachts in the marina, and the atmosphere is 'reassuringly buzzy', but success is mostly due to a kitchen that works hard to maintain high standards. The *Guide's* last six editions have listed five different head chefs, among them Stephen Terry, who moved on to the Oliver Peyton empire (see entries Coast and Mash, London), and Tim Powell and Peter Raffell who went to Marco Pierre White's Criterion (see entry, London). What is significant, however, and greatly to be commended, is that hardly anybody notices the changes: there is barely a blip in quality (Ray Brown has worked in the kitchen for five years), which 'makes it such a pleasure to eat here'.

The food remains in contemporary European mould. Fish figures prominently – seared Cajun tuna with a warm salad of couscous, peppers and olives for example – and meat might take in braised shank of lamb, and calf's liver and bacon. The *carte's* price supplements largely cover the luxury of ballottine of foie gras, or a main course of 'moist, juicy' lobster in a ginger broth with pearl vegetables, adjudged 'beautifully balanced' with 'perfect seasoning'. This dish also demonstrates the kitchen's fondness for 'expertly diced' baby vegetables, a theme picked up in peppered duck breast, where pineapple is chopped within a whisker of disintegration; 'simple but spot-on delivery' helped to complete its appeal. Lightness, and familiar but well-judged flavour combinations, are characteristic of desserts: in a pistachio soufflé with chocolate sauce poured in, or crêpes Suzette with a soufflé encased in the pancakes. Service appears to have improved, and is now considered 'professional, friendly and helpful'. Fine petits fours with coffee are charged extra 'but they are worth it', and wines focus on the major regions of France, where there is remarkably little under £20. House wine is £14.

CHEF: Ray Brown   PROPRIETORS: Michael Caine and Claudio Pulze   OPEN: all week L 12 to 3, D 6.30 to 11 (11.45 Sat)   MEALS: alc (main courses £13). Set L £15.50 (2 courses) to £19.50 SERVICE: not inc, card slips closed   CARDS: Amex, Delta, Diners, MasterCard, Switch, Visa DETAILS: 140 seats. Private parties: 140 main room. Children welcome. No cigars/pipes in dining-room. Wheelchair access (also WC). Music. Air-conditioned   ● Fulham Broadway

The nearest underground station is indicated at the end of London entries.

▲ *The Capital* map 14

22/24 Basil Street, SW3 1AT
TEL: 0171-589 5171 FAX: 0171-225 0011 COOKING 8
EMAIL: capitalhotel.co.uk COST £41–£120

The Capital does not make a big splash like some of its peers, which may be what gives it the feel of 'a gem that not everybody has discovered'. The small dining-room's beigey-apricotty-pinkish décor is 'understated' – apart from wooden sculptures attached to mirrors at either end – and although it may be 'unashamedly formal', it is not in the least bit stuffy. All that seems to change are the flowers, and the introduction of a service charge since last year.

Things are done with 'a sense of purpose and style', and it is a place where people are happy to spend their own money. One who had 'an inbuilt aversion to inflated London prices' was won over by a no-choice £55 dinner menu of jellied consommé, salad, foie gras risotto, lobster mousse, red mullet with olive pasta, honey-roast duck and a selection of desserts. Another found the even longer and more expensive option 'outstanding', while the 'glorious' fixed-price lunch, with half a dozen choices at each stage, is considered a great bargain. It might offer vanilla pasta with sweet tomato and fresh white crabmeat, stir-fried lobster with beanshoots and soy, and two smallish but thick slices of impeccably grilled halibut on a bed of Chinese leaves with a small puddle of 'perfect' lemon butter sauce.

Philip Britten's food may not stray too near the experimental edge, but his strength is 'simple, first-class ingredients perfectly cooked'. One summed up the level of skill by advising 'Don't Try This At Home', an injunction prompted in part by six caramelised scallops on a bed of shredded cabbage, with acidulated apple slices and morel sauce; in the centre an orange mound of warm, wobbly coral mousse that was 'slithery, delicate, sensual, magical'. Dishes may miss the classical mark occasionally – a starter of foie gras and chips puzzled one visitor – but they are generally conceived as a whole. 'Utterly fresh, just-warm' pieces of lobster meat, speckled with vanilla seeds and lemon zest made 'a great marriage' at one meal, while 'juicy' pot-roast pigeon, tasty without being gamey, was served with chargrilled artichoke heart whose flavour 'combined wonderfully'. Desserts are no less interesting or accomplished, ranging from iced bitter chocolate nougat with liquorice sauce, via butterscotch soufflé with fromage blanc sorbet, to a passion-fruit and white chocolate pyramid. Staff are knowledgeable and 'extremely attentive', striking the right balance between friendliness and reserve, although wine service has been criticised on more than one occasion. The lengthy list is heavy on grand clarets, burgundies and Rhônes and therefore light on bottles under £20, but house Sauvignon Blanc and Gamay from the Loire are £14.50 each.

CHEF: Philip Britten PROPRIETOR: David Levin OPEN: all week 12.30 to 2.15, 7 to 11.15
MEALS: alc (main courses £25.50 to £26.50). Set L £23.50 (2 courses) to £28, Set D £55 to £80
SERVICE: 12.5% (optional), card slips closed CARDS: Amex, Delta, Diners, MasterCard, Switch, Visa DETAILS: 36 seats. Private parties: 10 to 24 private rooms. Vegerian meals. Children's helpings. Jacket and tie. No cigars/pipes in dining room. No music. Air-conditioned ACCOMMODATION: 48 rooms, all with bath/shower. TV. Phone. Room only £167 to £260 + VAT. Children welcome. Baby facilities. Dogs by arrangement. Afternoon teas ⊖ Knightsbridge

Le Caprice 🍽 map 15

Arlington House, Arlington Street, SW1A 1RT
TEL: (0171) 629 2239   FAX: (0171) 493 9040   COOKING **5**
EMAIL: mailbox@caprice.co.uk   COST £34–£78

This year sees another changing of the guard at the stoves (and possibly a change of ownership as the *Guide* went to press), but the consistent flow has not been interrupted, and Le Caprice keeps packing them in. A couple who had been to an evening sale at nearby Christie's might be typical customers. They didn't expect the moon in terms of culinary flair or value, but came away pleasantly surprised on both counts. The welcome, indeed, is generally warmer than usual for such a streamlined, modern brasserie, and dishes are rendered with deceptively effortless panache. Fish is a strong point, as in seared sea bream on wild garlic mash with deep-fried shallots; or battered lemon sole with a quenelle of minted pea puree standing in for mushy peas, and malt vinegar offered for sprinkling on the chips. Brunch dishes are well-liked, and take in the range from eggs Benedict through plum tomato and basil galette to authentic steak tartare. Desserts might be ricotta tart and honey ice-cream or roasted fruits with mascarpone. Service copes well with the press of business, and the concise list of modern wines takes in the New World, but confines itself to France, Italy and Spain within Europe. There is a good by-the-glass selection from £3.25.

CHEF: Mark Hix   PROPRIETORS: Jeremy King and Christopher Corbin   OPEN: all week 12 to 3 (3.30 Sun), 5.30 (6 Sun) to midnight; Sun L brunch menu   CLOSED: 25 and 26 Dec, 1 Jan, Aug bank hol   MEALS: alc (main courses £10 to £21.50). Cover £1.50   SERVICE: not inc   CARDS: Amex, Delta, Diners, MasterCard, Switch, Visa   DETAILS: 70 seats. Vegetarian meals. Children welcome. Wheelchair access (not WC). Music. Air-conditioned   ⊖ Green Park

Casablanca NEW ENTRY map 12

264 King Street, W6 0SP   COOKING **2**
TEL: (0181) 741 1177   COST £17–£40

Within this discreet, softly lit ground-floor bar with its low wooden tables and colourful sofas, Arabic 'cabaret' music plays most of the time. Eat here or descend to the larger, less atmospheric canteen-style restaurant below. The Lebanese menu offers about 30 meze, hot and cold, which can be a complete meal in themselves, or precede chargrilled main courses of lamb or chicken, or vegetarian options. Praise has come in for conventional meze of moutabal (aubergine paste), makanek (Lebanese sausages), mouhamarah (a paste of nuts with chilli), and kibbeh nayeh (Lebanese lamb tartare, also spiked with chilli). Grills include tasty shawarma (marinated lamb), and shish taouk chicken. 'Special oriental rice' is like home-cooked Indian biryani. Service is charming and helpful. Drink an arak aperitif or Lebanese wine starting at £11.

CHEF: N. Kattabe   PROPRIETOR: Spice Age Ltd   OPEN: Tue to Sun L12 to 2.45, all week D 6 to 11.30   MEALS: alc (main courses £8 to £14). Set L £6 (2 courses), Set D £16   SERVICE: 10% (optional)   CARDS: Amex, Delta, Diners, MasterCard, Switch, Visa   DETAILS: 80 seats. Private parties: 100 main room. Vegetarian meals. Children welcome. Wheelchair access (1 step; not WC). Music. Air-conditioned   ⊖ Ravenscourt Park, Stamford Brook   £5

See inside the front cover for an explanation of the symbols used at the tops of entries.

Charco's

map 14

1 Bray Place, SW3 3LL
TEL: (0171) 584 0765   FAX: (0171) 351 0365

COOKING 3
COST £28–£45

Below the ground-floor wine bar is a cool, modern, mainly white restaurant with well-spaced and well-appointed tables. The Chelsea location and décor suggest high prices, which happily is not the case: a two-course set lunch is good value, and a *carte* lists six or seven choices at each course. Chris Wellington moves freely from traditional English to Italian to oriental ideas, sometimes combining them in arresting ways: squid with chilli salsa and couscous, or ostrich fillet with spinach pasta and red pepper coulis. Reporters have been more than satisfied, though, with English game terrine with cranberry and Cumberland sauce, and roast cod with mushy peas and chips. Vegetables, including sauté greens with chorizo, and potato wedges with Cajun butter, are charged separately but may be unnecessary as portions are generous. Desserts have included coconut mousse with mango, lime and pink grapefruit. Bottle prices open at £8.25 on the good-value wine list, helpfully arranged by grape variety.

CHEF: Chris Wellington   PROPRIETOR: Pillarcrest Ltd   OPEN: Mon to Sat 12 to 2.30 (3 Sat), 6.30 to 10.30   CLOSED: last 2 weeks Aug   MEALS: alc (main courses £10.50 to £14.50). Set L £9.50 (2 courses)   SERVICE: not inc   CARDS: Amex, Delta, MasterCard, Switch, Visa   DETAILS: 35 seats. 8 seats outside. Private parties: 40 main room, 40 private room. Vegetarian meals. Children welcome. Occasional music. Air-conditioned   ⊖ Sloane Square   (£5)

Chavot

map 14

257–259 Fulham Road, SW3 6HY
TEL: (0171) 351 7823   FAX: (0171) 376 4971

COOKING 7
COST £29–£71

Looking a shade more minimalist nowadays, these two rooms with creamy grey and terracotta walls, sepia photographs, and well-spaced tables are 'stylish, comfortable and modern' in one view, 'soothing and restrained' in another. Eric Chavot's food also has a mollifying effect, partly thanks to its prime and sometimes luxurious ingredients: tian of crab with coriander, 'large, juicy' roast scallops with cep risotto, or a particularly rich starter of foie gras served with a buttery tarte Tatin of endives. It is a style, one reporter felt, that 'would have thrilled me ten years ago' and which may now seem to lack a little excitement, yet which is backed up by sound technique.

Dishes are priced in bands on the *carte*, with fair choice at each stage, although descriptions may sometimes fall short of reality. Of a pan-fried sea bass with crab ravioli, one reporter noted that 'the menu gave no hint that this was to be a Far Eastern extravaganza': first-rate, accurately cooked fish rested on stir-fried vegetables, the whole erupting with 'small and varied flavour explosions' yet with a clear design and powerful Thai influence. Likewise a mundane-sounding starter labelled 'peppers, lamb, feta salad' produced slices of briefly seared pink and flavourful lamb, interspersed with cheese-filled pasta shapes, slicked with potent sweet and herb sauces; 'everything on the plate was there for a purpose, and it worked splendidly'.

Enthusiastic support for a range of seafood reflects its generally secure handling: pan-fried langoustines with squid ink tagliatelle, seared red mullet fillets with aubergine 'spiced up Indian-style', and brill with noodles and mustard sauce. 'Fabulous' desserts proved the highlight for one visitor, while another was confronted by an 'amazing display' of a piano made from pistachio mousse with a lid of clear sugar, held up by a piece of white chocolate, the keys alternating pistachio and chocolate. One reporter summed up the whole experience as 'expensive but worth it'. Predominantly French staff are 'not the chatty types', more professional and businesslike, though service has occasionally fallen short of expectation. Wines are classy and mostly French, but with an informed showing elsewhere, though all at prices 'to make you cringe'. House red and white are £15.

CHEF: Eric Crouillère-Chavot PROPRIETORS: Eric Crouillère-Chavot, Robert Seigler and Tony Howorth OPEN: Mon to Fri L 12 to 2.30, Mon to Sat D 7 to 11 MEALS: alc (main courses £18 to £22). Set L £15.50 (2 courses) to £18.50 SERVICE: not inc CARDS: Amex, Delta, Diners, MasterCard, Switch, Visa DETAILS: 60 seats. Private parties: 12 main room, 12 private room. Children welcome. Wheelchair access (1 step; not WC). No music. Air-conditioned ⊖ South Kensington

Cheng-Du £   map 13

| 9 Parkway, NW1 7PG | COOKING 3 |
| TEL: (0171) 485 8058 FAX: (0171) 794 5522 | COST £23–£52 |

A modern, green and white Chinese restaurant neither bare nor garishly decorated, where service is pleasant and helpful, and where background jazz soothes instead of making people jump. It's a far cry from Chinatown, not least in a menu which emphasises Szechuan and Peking cuisines, but also offers Straits and Cantonese dishes. It would be easy to compose a whole meal of intriguing combinations not seen elsewhere. Start with chicken breast dusted with crushed walnuts or 'Cheng-du original seafood salad', followed by sea-spice veal slices with water chestnuts and bamboo shoots, or General Tseng's (Szechuan) chicken. The 'special selections' menu offers scrambled egg fu-yung with fresh salmon and Chinese chives, or steamed chicken with red dates, black fungi and golden lilies. Even the two set menus – yin and yang– are interesting. Standard dishes are listed too, right up to sweet-and-sour pork, which the menu says is the 'all-time favourite'. All this, along with soft lighting and smiling waiters, makes it one of very few Chinese restaurants where the word 'romantic' is not entirely out of place. The short wine list starrts with house Italian at £9.20.

CHEF: Mr Soon PROPRIETORS: Gingerflower Ltd OPEN: all week 12 to 2.30 (3 Sun), 6.30 to 11.30 CLOSED: 24 to 26 Dec MEALS: alc (main courses £4.50 to £18). Set D £19.50 SERVICE: 12.5%, card slips closed CARDS: Amex, Delta, MasterCard, Switch, Visa DETAILS: 72 seats. Private parties: 80 main room. Vegetarian meals. Children welcome. Wheelchair access (not WC). Music ⊖ Camden Town

Chez Bruce ♥   map 12

| 2 Bellevue Road, Wandsworth Common, SW17 7EG | COOKING 5 |
| TEL: (0181) 672 0114 FAX: (0181) 767 6648 | COST £28–£40 |

The complete lack of pretension at this redoubtable Wandsworth address is a great plus. It faces the Common, with enough natural daylight from its front-end conservatory to feel 'tidy, clean and bright', and the crumpled ceiling, 'wild west' woodwork, and close-together tables merely add to the sense of individuality that draws full houses. Fixed-price menus – with a generous choice at dinner – change daily, and embody a broadly European style that ranges from garlic soup, or escabèche of red mullet, to ham and calf tongue terrine, by way of steak and chips, or rather chateaubriand and frites with béarnaise (for two, with a supplement). Along the way it flaunts its southern credentials with truffle oil, herb crostini, lentil salad and olive mash.

Bruce Poole's food is not indebted to fashionable gimmicks, theatrical construction or whimsical decoration. Rather it aims to use good materials, get the timing right, and serve up dishes that people enjoy eating: big chunks of sauté calf's kidney, with artichokes and skinned broad beans, or a fresh piece of cod generously topped with a horseradish-flavoured breadcrumb crust. Dishes conceived as a whole work best: an unexpected match of pickled cucumber topped with smoked haddock in two forms – a thin, flat, griddled square of fish, and a scoop of creamy mousse – proved 'a knockout' at one meal.

Chocolate seems to be a kitchen favourite for dessert, appearing as St Emilion, in a bitter chocolate tart, or as a small square of cake with a hot chocolate sauce and praline parfait. All-male service copes well with numbers. The two-page wine list caters for all palates and pockets, offering good drinking across the board. France sets the ball rolling at £10.95 for a bottle of house wine, and Italy's Angelo Gaja brings things to a stylish halt at £145.

CHEFS: Bruce Poole and Oliver Couillaud   PROPRIETOR: Bruce Poole   OPEN: all week L 12 to 2 (12.30 to 3 Sun), Mon to Sat D 7 to 10.30   CLOSED: 1 week Christmas, bank hol Mons   MEALS: Set L £18, Set D £25. BYO £10 per head   SERVICE: 12.5% (optional), card slips closed   CARDS: Amex, Delta, Diners, MasterCard, Switch, Visa   DETAILS: 70 seats. Private parties: 20 private room. No young children at D. Wheelchair access (not WC). No music. Air-conditioned ⊖ Balham

---

Chez Liline

map 12

101 Stroud Green Road, N4 3PX
TEL: (0171) 263 6550

COOKING 3
COST £20–£45

The décor in this Mauritian fish restaurant is in authentic 'tropical-provincial' French style, and if the service is relaxed it is because, as the menu points out, everything is not only cooked, but also cut, to order. Any lack of speed and efficiency, however, is amply compensated by the charm of the family who run it, and who also own the fish shop next door. From there they have oceans of choice, and their cooking combines the Indian-influenced style with that of France, whose cultural influence is also deep-rooted. Mussels, for example, are marinière or mauricienne (with tomato, herbs and chilli). Half-lobsters appear in the fruits de mer with its lemon-grass bouillon, and in the cold 'assiette de crustaces', while whole ones may be grilled with herbs or cooked with brandy and cream. Fish include Dover sole and parrot-fish, and the daily menu may extend options to sea bass, turbot or crawfish tails. House wines, from France and Italy, are £9.25.

If you have access to the Internet, you can find The Good Food Guide *online at the* Which? *Online web site (http://www.which.net).*

CHEFS: Mario Ho Wing Cheong and Pascal Doudrich   PROPRIETOR: Mario Ho Wing Cheong
OPEN: Mon to Sat 12.30 to 2.30, 6.30 to 10.30   MEALS: alc (main courses £9.50 to £17). Set L
£10 (2 courses) to £18.75, Set D Mon to Thur £10 (2 courses) to £18.75, Set D Fri and Sat
£18.75   SERVICE: not inc   CARDS: Amex, Delta, MasterCard, Switch, Visa   DETAILS: 44 seats.
Private parties: 26 main room. Children's helpings. No cigars/pipes in dining-room. Music
⊖ Finsbury Park (£5)

Chezmax

map 13

168 Ifield Road, SW10 9AF

COOKING 5

TEL: (0171) 835 0874   FAX: (0171) 244 0618

COST £23–£61

This unreconstructed French bistro, down a steep spiral staircase, is blessed
'with no comfort of any kind', but that doesn't stop it drawing the crowds. The
basement is painted an 'unrestful' shade of green; floor, tables and chairs are
made of wood; and although there is a printed menu (in French only), 'the boss'
delivers details of ingredients, cooking and presentation verbally. Proximity of
tables allows him to orate to several at once, pointing out that galette de
Picandou is a pancake covered with tomatoes and goats' cheese, with dollops of
basil sauce around it, and that pig's trotter is stuffed with its own meat, covered
with mustard breadcrumbs, topped with a piece of grilled foie gras, and
surrounded by peas and broad beans in a red wine sauce.

Many staples are here – snails and mussels, oeuf en cocotte, pear tarte Tatin –
but seafood seems to be as successful as anything: just-cooked scallops on a
well-dressed salad, roast cod, and 'brilliantly fresh' sea bass. One or two dishes,
such as beef with bone-marrow, or roast Bresse pigeon, carry a small supplement. Desserts might include almond pithiviers, lemon tart, or 'rich'
chocolate gâteau. The tasting menu consists of seven courses, and early- and
late-evening deals allow significant savings. Service is on the ball, and the
60-strong wine list incorporates a few bottles from outside France. Southern
French house wine is £11.50.

CHEF: Zak El Hamdou   PROPRIETORS: Graham Thomson and Steven Smith   OPEN: Tue to Fri L
12 to 2.30, Tue to Sat D 6.30 to 11   CLOSED: Christmas, Aug, bank hols   MEALS: Set L £10 (2
courses) to £13.50, Set D 6.30 to 7.30 and after 10.30 £10 (2 courses) to £13.50, Set D £21.50 (2
courses) to £39.50. BYO £5   SERVICE: 12.5% (optional), card slips closed   CARDS: Amex,
Delta, MasterCard, Switch, Visa   DETAILS: 60 seats. Private parties: 30 main room, 14 private
room. Children's helpings. No cigars/pipes in dining-room. No music   ⊖ Earls Court, West
Brompton

Chez Moi

30 YEARS
1999
IN THE GUIDE

map 12

1 Addison Avenue, W11 4QS

COOKING 5

TEL: (0171) 603 8267   FAX: (0171) 603 3898

COST £24–£54

With its relaxed feel and 'considerable charm', Chez Moi is 'endearing' partly on
account of its longevity, having notched up an impressive 30 years in the *Guide*.
The dining-room is 'serene' despite jungle-print cushions and a bold red and
black colour scheme, and staff are 'well mannered and attentive'. Richard
Walton has done his best to bring the food up to date, with Thai chicken,
Moroccan lamb tagine, and Japanese-style scallops, although in the process
some of these novelty additions seem to have lost their balance. This is probably

not helped by the stiff competition in London for cracklingly up-to-date fusion food. The strength here is simple, classic, 'seriously good' French food, the kind that Chez Moi has been serving up with assurance throughout its life.

Into this category might come split-pea soup, chicken liver parfait, and grilled zander with herb butter. The kitchen has produced a perfectly executed dish of lightly cooked quail's eggs and smoked salmon in a crisp pastry case with sauce mousseline, and lemon tart ('a great success') with crème anglaise and fresh-tasting raspberry coulis. Ices and sorbets – 'truly fruity' blackberry, or lychee with Muscat – are 'better than one gets almost anywhere'. A la carte prices tend to be on the high side, though the largely French wine list is generally fair in its mark-ups. Prices start at £10.75 for house South African white and Australian red.

CHEF: Richard Walton   PROPRIETORS: Colin Smith and Richard Walton   OPEN: Mon to Fri L 12.30 to 2, Mon to Sat D 7 to 11   CLOSED: bank hols   MEALS: alc (main courses £12 to £17). Set L £16   SERVICE: not inc   CARDS: Amex, Delta, Diners, MasterCard, Switch, Visa   DETAILS: 45 seats. Private parties: 16 main room. Children's helpings. No babies in arms. No cigars/pipes in dining-room. Wheelchair access (not WC). No music. Air-conditioned   ⊖ Holland Park

Chez Nico at Ninety Park Lane   map 15

Grosvenor House, 90 Park Lane, W1A 3AA   COOKING 10
TEL: (0171) 409 1290   FAX: (0171) 355 4877   COST £54–£140

As one of London's more exclusive addresses, Park Lane is a natural for one of the country's greatest chefs. The spacious dining-room in hotel mould, filled with 'serious-looking people from just about every continent', is well lit, comfortable and allows a degree of intimacy. One who has followed Nico from the early days in Battersea through his many incarnations finds the cooking 'as good as ever', and that unwavering excellence is what draws reporters back for more. The food may not have as much in the way of daring, or passion, or excitement, as at some other top restaurants, but is in a class of its own for sheer consistency and reliability, producing neo-classical French dishes, and a few interesting variations, with what most reporters regard as 'perfection'. The earth may not move, but you couldn't get better real estate.

Several options present themselves. Lunch is still considered good value, although incidentals mount up: £5 for coffee and 'world-class' petits fours, for example. If a ten-course menu sounds like a blow-out, bear in mind that portions are 'ideally sized', according to a reporter who 'would highly recommend that people save up for this gastronomic experience'. As for the *carte*, it helps to pick your way through to the more interesting dishes. Smoked salmon with caviare (one of a few items with a price supplement) might keep corporate and multinational fat cats happy, but hardly sets the pulse racing. You'd be much better off with a starter of truffle-oiled haricot beans with a boudin of foie gras 'full of amazing tastes', or 'perfect pink duck in a dazzling oriental sauce, with stunning vegetables to accompany'.

Nico subjects both humble and luxury ingredients to his classical French techniques, and produces dishes that are invariably intense. Foie gras has been served with orange, and equally successfully with spinach; risotto has swapped its ceps for white truffles, bowling over an inspector in the process with its 'outstanding' materials and 'purity of flavour'; 'simply the best risotto I have come across'. There are never too many tastes on the plate, either, judging by the 'elegant simplicity' of baby Dover sole 'dazzling in flavour', served with a chive butter sauce, and 'a mighty chunk of veal chop (on the bone) over diced ceps'.

Glazed lemon tart and chocolate 'negus' are legendary, thin apple tart is made from top-quality apples at the peak of ripeness (served with 'outstanding' vanilla ice-cream and 'wicked' caramel sauce), and the plate of mini desserts – a triumph of faultless and detailed technique – draws nothing but approval and a string of superlatives. Service is formal, professional and precisely drilled. 'You are made to feel like royalty', observed one couple; not hounded by photographers apparently, but simply well looked after. Look to the short selection at the front of the wine list for a few bottles under £30; look elsewhere for a terrific selection of classy wines that are pricey, but by no means the most expensive in the capital.

CHEFS: Nico Ladenis and Paul Rhodes PROPRIETORS: Nico and Dinah Jane Ladenis OPEN: Mon to Fri l 12 to 2, Mon to Sat D 7 to 11 CLOSED. 10 days Ohristmas, 4 days Easter, bank hol Mons MEALS: Set L £34 to £75 (gourmet menu), Set D £52 (2 courses) to £75 (gourmet menu) SERVICE: 12.5% (optional), card slips closed CARDS: Amex, MasterCard, Visa DETAILS: 65 seats. Private parties: 10 main room, 20 private room. No children under 7. No pipes in dining-room. Wheelchair access (2 steps; not WC). No music. Air-conditioned ⊖ Marble Arch

Chinon
map 12

23 Richmond Way, W14 0AS
COOKING 5
TEL: (0171) 602 5968 FAX: (0171) 602 4082
COST £26–£55

Set in a quiet residential street, Chinon looks as if it could be that elusive thing, a great little local restaurant, and indeed the long narrow dining-room with a patio garden at the back has a lot going for it. Two differently priced dinner menus promise sometimes sophisticated food, while an ambitious *carte* weaves provençale and oriental flavours around a French pre-occupation with mousses, butter sauces, galettes and savoury gâteaux. Portions can be enormous – an 'eight-inch long' squid stuffed with a heady mix of basil and tomato, or an 'absurdly tall' stack of some two dozen giant tempura prawns with a pungent yellow curry oil – and that's just for starters.

There is evident technical skill in the labour-intensive cooking, but materials at inspection left something to be desired, and there is a tendency to pile on ingredients: for example, fat nuggets of rosy venison accompanied by a crisp potato galette, resting on a spinach-wrapped portion of mashed potato, on top of red cabbage, surrounded by oyster mushrooms in a creamy sauce, and some Puy lentils. Puddings are less elaborate, typically running to tarts, ice-creams, perhaps a fruit brulée, a bavarois, and chocolate in various forms. Music is loud, and service is not the warmest in London. The wine list is considered 'generally expensive', although we are unable to confirm that, nor any of the details below, since the restaurant has chosen not to furnish the *Guide* with information.

CHEF: Jonathon Hayes PROPRIETORS: Barbara Deane and Jonathon Hayes OPEN: Mon to Sat D 7 to 10.45 CLOSED: 25 Dec MEALS: alc (main courses £10 to £16). Set D £15 to £20 SERVICE: 12.5% (optional) CARDS: Amex, Delta, MasterCard, Switch, Visa DETAILS: 60 seats. 6 seats outside. Private parties: 30 main room, 30 private room. No children under 10. No cigars/pipes in dining-room. Music. Air-conditioned ⊖ Shepherd's Bush

Chiswick ♥ £

map 12

131 Chiswick High Road, W4 2ED
TEL: (0181) 994 6887   FAX: (0181) 994 5504

COOKING 3
COST £25–£45

The dark, unassuming frontage and resolute anonymity of design are very much how London expects its cutting-edge restaurants to look these days. To some, it may all feel a touch leaden; others don't mind whether the walls look pretty, as long as the menus read right. In this respect, Mark Broadbent has his finger very much on the pulse of modern city cooking, and the style is simple but alluring brasserie food. That translates as leeks vinaigrette with marinated anchovies and a soft-boiled egg, roast cod with purple kale and red wine sauce, and grilled Old Spot bacon chop with Jerusalem artichokes. An April luncher enjoyed 'attractive and refreshing' ceviche of scallops with finely chopped spring onions to start, and his companion did well with a main-course rump steak, a satisfyingly thick cut served with horseradish cream and a pile of excellent chips 'stacked like timber'. Lemon polenta cake with mascarpone awaits robust appetites at a meal's end, perry sorbet the more abstemious. Service is cheery and the wine list provides a further boost. Fifty bottles cover a lot of territory from Alsace to Washington State, while prices range from £10.50 for house vin de pays to three figures for a magnum of Ch. Montrose 1982. CELLARMAN'S CHOICE: Waipara West Riesling 1997, Canterbury, New Zealand, £18.95; Ribera del Duero, La Granja de Monasterio 1994, £19.90.

CHEF: Mark Broadbent   PROPRIETORS: Adam and Kate Robinson   OPEN: Sun to Fri L 12.30 to 2.45, Mon to Sat D 7 to 11   CLOSED: Christmas, bank hol Mons   MEALS: alc (main courses £7.50 to £15). Set L £9.50 (2 courses), Set D 7 to 8 £9.50 (2 courses). BYO £7   SERVICE: not inc; 12.5% for parties of 8 or more   CARDS: Amex, Delta, MasterCard, Switch, Visa   DETAILS: 74 seats. 16 seats outside. Private parties: 10 main room. Vegetarian meals. Children's helpings. No music   ⊖ Turnham Green   £5

Chor Bizarre

NEW ENTRY   map 15

16 Albemarle Street, W1X 3HA
TEL: (0171) 629 9802/8542   FAX: (0171) 493 7756
EMAIL: cblondon@aol.com

COOKING 1
COST £35–£60

The name is a pun on chor bazaar, the thieves' market, and this Mayfair branch of the New Delhi restaurant exuberantly celebrates the fantasy in 'kaleidoscopic' furniture: tables inlaid with silver or mother of pearl, topped with limestone or marble, and decorations, some improbably exotic, others genuine antiques. The menu covers the regions of India, offering a wide choice of vegetarian dishes as well as tandoori, curry and 'street foods' such as Bombay bhel poori, and Delhi chaats, hot or cold. A novelty from the Punjab is tak-a-tak, assorted meats or vegetables named after the sound of the knife on the griddle. For two people the best way to explore the cuisine is to order thalis, small portions served in pots on a silver platter. Many of the wines have recommended matching food selections, and the list opens with six house wines starting at £11.95.

Not inc *in the details at the end of an entry indicates that no service charge is made and any tipping is at the discretion of the customer.*

CHEF: Deepinder Singh Sondhi   PROPRIETORS: Mahendra Kaul and Rohit Klattar   OPEN: all week 12 to 3, 6 to 11.30 (10.30 Sun)   CLOSED: 25 and 26 Dec   MEALS: alc (main courses £7.50 to £13.50). Set L Mon to Fri £12.95 (2 courses) to £14.95, Set L Sat and Sun £9.95, Set D £14.95 to £21   SERVICE: 12.5%, card slips closed   CARDS: Amex, Delta, Diners, MasterCard, Switch, Visa   DETAILS: 85 seats. Private parties: 50 main room, 35 private room. Vegetarian meals. Children welcome. No-smoking area. Music. Air-conditioned   ⊖ Green Park   £5

Christopher's

map 15

18 Wellington Street, WC2E 7DD   COOKING 1
TEL: (0171) 240 4222   FAX: (0171) 836 3506   COST £31–£73

Christopher's American food is not fast but de luxe. Classic steaks and grills, using Scottish or American beef, range from eight-ounce hamburger with fries to ten-ounce fillet. Seafood can be as simple as Maine lobster grilled with drawn butter, but 'modern American' dishes are as multicultural as 'new British', taking in jambalaya risotto, blackened salmon with tomato salsa and black-eyed peas, and Pennsylvania red berry strudel with lemon sherbet. The restaurant is now on ground and first floors, the latter reached by a great curving staircase. The basement Speakeasy café-bar offers 'light eats' and a short, lower-priced menu. 'Special food and drink combinations' are dishes for two accompanied by an imaginative choice of four wines. With weekend brunch and pre- and post-theatre menus, choice is as wide as the prairie. Prestigious bottles from America compete with fine burgundies and clarets on a wine list that now features an impressive 50 wines by the glass. Prices start at £12 a bottle (£3 a glass) for the Mexican house white.

CHEF: Adrian Searing   PROPRIETOR: The Hon. Christopher Gilmour   OPEN: all week L 12 to 2.45, Mon to Sat D 6 to 11.45   CLOSED: Christmas   MEALS: alc (main courses £9.50 to £25). Set pre- and post-theatre D £12.50 (2 courses). Café-bar menu. Cover 50p   SERVICE: 12.5% (optional), card slips closed   CARDS: Amex, Delta, Diners, MasterCard, Switch, Visa   DETAILS: 160 seats. Private parties: 120 main room, 50 private room. Children's helpings. Jacket and tie. No music. Air-conditioned   ⊖ Covent Garden

Chung's £ | NEW ENTRY | map 15

22 Wardour Street, W1V 3HD   COOKING 2
TEL: (0171) 287 3886   FAX: (0171) 287 0630   COST £25–£58

'A valuable addition to the really pleasant Chinatown restaurants,' wrote one enthusiast of this self-styled 'Chinese seafood restaurant' with large tables in a well-lit modern room. Waiters are helpful and friendly, their attention to detail including changing chopsticks after one reporter's sticky starter, and impeccable wine service. Basically Cantonese, the menu includes the usual Szechuan and Peking 'intruders', and though there is a whole page of seafood dishes, meat and poultry are also well-represented. An inspector, who reckoned the best bet is to say how much you want to spend and leave it to the chef, was highly impressed by West Lake roasted duckling with beautifully browned skin, the inside thickly coated with chopped prawns, then breadcrumbed and the whole deep-fried. Other successes have included Malaysian-style satay chicken with chilli-hot peanut sauce; griled salmon steaks with black-bean sauce; and stir-fried scallop and squid with asparagus, chopped spring onion, chilli and lettuce. House wine is £8.50.

CHEF: S.W. Chan   PROPRIETOR: Jon Man   OPEN: all week noon to 4am (buffet L noon to 5pm) MEALS: alc (main courses £6 to £14). Set L £4.50, Set L and D £10 to £28   SERVICE: 10% CARDS: Amex, Delta, MasterCard, Switch, Visa   DETAILS: 120 seats. Private parties: 130 main room, 20 private room. Vegetarian meals. Children welcome. Wheelchair access (not WC). Music. Air-conditioned   ⊖ Piccadilly Circus

Chutney Mary ✠✱

map 12

535 King's Road, SW10 0SZ
TEL: (0171) 351 3113   FAX: (0171) 351 7694
EMAIL: 100540.1020@compuserve.com

COOKING 1
COST £29–£56

'I felt like I was back in either India or a posh hotel in the East,' reflected a well-travelled correspondent after sitting in the upstairs bar of this atmospheric restaurant. In a 'fabulous setting' of rotating ceiling fans, comfortable wicker chairs and luxuriant potted plants, efficient staff wait on customers with faultless charm and courteous good humour. 'Chutney Mary' is Raj-speak for an Indian woman aspiring to be westernised, and the food is deliberately Anglo-Indian, although it slips into regional dialect from time to time. Seafood mulligatawny soup, prawn kedgeree and 'Country Captain' chicken with coconut, vinegar, almonds and raisins represent the old colonial guard, while full-bodied lamb Madras served with coriander rice, and Bombay-style duck curry with palm sugar hit a more authentic note. Crab-cakes and stir-fried squid are favoured starters, and it's worth finishing with sweet crispy samosas or a slab of home-made kulfi. The wine list makes a laudable attempt to match mainly New World wines with the food; otherwise drink beer or tea. House wine is £10.95.

CHEF: Hardev Singh Bhatty   PROPRIETORS: Namita Panjabi and Ranjit Mathrani   OPEN: all week 12.30 to 2.30 (3 Sun), 7 to 11.30 (10.30 Sun)   CLOSED: D 25 Dec   MEALS: alc D (main courses £9 to £16.50). Set L £12.50 (2 courses) to £14.50 (£15 Sun), Set D Mon to Thur after 10pm £12.50 (2 courses) to £14.50. Cover £1.50   SERVICE: 12.5% (optional), card slips closed   CARDS: Amex, Delta, Diners, MasterCard, Switch, Visa   DETAILS: 140 seats. Private parties: 50 main room. Vegetarian meals. Children's helpings. No smoking in 1 dining-room. Wheelchair access (not WC). Music. Air-conditioned   ⊖ Fulham Broadway   (£5)

Circus

NEW ENTRY   map 15

1 Upper James Street, W1R 4BP
TEL: (0171) 534 4000   FAX: (0171) 534 4010
EMAIL: chefs@egami.co.uk

COOKING 4
COST £31–£64

Occupying the ground floor and basement of what was the old Granada Television building on the corner of Beak Street and Golden Square, Circus is the latest venture by the outfit that owns Avenue in St James's (see entry). Designed by David Chipperfield in modern ascetic style, it has white walls, novel but comfortable chairs, and night-light candles on the tables. Pre- and post-theatre business ensures that the buzz continues all through the evening, and the site guarantees popularity.

Richard Lee has a canny understanding of how to ensure gastro-satisfaction for today's city clientele. 'Something like an English version of a Paris brasserie' is how one reporter characterised it, which may be why braised faggot with bubble and squeak is among the options; but there is also the odd item from further afield, such as fried squid with pak choi and a chilli and tamarind dressing. Risotto is well rendered – topped with spinach, smoked haddock and a runny poached egg – and skate wing with crushed new potatoes and a thick 'pesto' of rocket and black olives made a favourable impression on an inspector. Ices and sorbets are spot on for both temperature and texture, and incorporate suitably intense flavours such as mango and pink grapefruit; or plump for something more substantial such as Amaretto cheesecake with coffee sauce, or a cheese plate with chillied apple chutney. Everything is delivered with personable charm and great efficiency. Stylistically grouped wines are well chosen, but prices are not gentle, with few bottles below £20. French country wines open the bidding at £13.50.

CHEF: Richard Lee   PROPRIETOR: Mirror Image Restaurants plc   OPEN: all week L 12 to 3, Mon to Sat D 6 to 12; bar menu noon to 1.30am   CLOSED: 25 and 26 Dec, 1 Jan   MEALS: alc (main courses £10.50 to £17.50). Set L and D before 7.30, from 10.15 to 12 and always in bar £14.75 (2 courses) to £16.75   SERVICE: 12.5% (optional), card slips closed   CARDS: Amex, Delta, Diners, MasterCard, Switch, Visa   DETAILS: 130 seats. Private parties: 12 main room, 16 private room. Vegetarian meals. Children's helpings. No music. Air-conditioned   ⊖ Piccadilly Circus

City Rhodes map 13

1 New Street Square, EC4A 3BF COOKING 6
TEL: (0171) 583 1313   FAX: (0171) 353 1662 COST £38–£81

If food is the new rock and roll, does that make Gary Rhodes the culinary Paul McCartney? Both are masters of the populist flourish concealing a hard core of skill, and both could be considered English traditionalists at heart. Gary Rhodes made his name by giving a new spin to old-fashioned classics such as oxtail, liver, and steak and kidney pie, and this restaurant still flies the flag for Britain – rich game faggot with braised turnip, steak and oyster pie, apple and almond bake with thick custard – as well as embracing modern convention with lighter dishes such as pressed tomato cake with peppered goats' cheese. The spacious, modern dining-room on the first floor of a soulless 1960s office block feels surprisingly formal and austere, rather at odds with the star's own persona but well suited to the predominantly business clientele. Prices, too, seem geared to City expense-account customers.

Nevertheless, most diners report a thoroughly sound experience, heightened by the chance of a brush with celebrity perhaps, but due in no small part to the food, which lives up to its elevated reputation. Presentation is striking: one couple, who enjoyed a superb meal, was amused to see that every dish included something fashioned into a pyramid. Lunch, served at a decent pace, might include a 'delightfully balanced' starter of pressed smoked salmon with warm potato salad, followed by expertly cooked venison on potato and spinach gnocchi, or 'sumptuous' sea trout on horseradish mash. For dessert, the famous bread-and-butter pudding 'just gets better and better', while the British Pudding Plate comprises six individual desserts. A short and sensible wine list is divided by style, with Argentinian house white at £12.50 and Australian red at £15.25.

CHEF: Gary Rhodes and Wayne Tapfield   PROPRIETOR: Gardner Merchant   OPEN: Mon to Fri 12 to 2.30, 6 to 8.45   CLOSED: bank hols   MEALS: alc (main courses £13.50 to £24.50)   SERVICE: 12.5% (optional), card slips closed   CARDS: Amex, Delta, Diners, MasterCard, Switch, Visa   DETAILS: 96 seats. Private parties: 14 private room. Vegetarian meals. Children welcome. Wheelchair access (also WC). No music. Air-conditioned   ⊖ Chancery Lane, Blackfriars

---

▲ Claridge's 💱✳   map 15

Brook Street, W1A 2JQ   COOKING 6
TEL: (0171) 629 8860   FAX: (0171) 872 8092   COST £38–£103

Although the décor may be an art-nouveau confection preserved in amber, Claridge's – which celebrated its centenary in 1998 – is determined not to become a time-warp institution. Service may still be French-formal, and much of the slicing, carving and of course flaming goes on in front of you, but then you'd scarcely expect otherwise. This isn't a gastrodrome. And as long as you remember to pack lots of loose change for tipping the lavatory attendants, there is no reason on earth not to have a good time here.

Menus present a contemporary face, in quail salad with soused morellos, fricassee of John Dory with scallops and artichokes in burgundy, and rabbit saltimbocca with pearl barley and rosemary to ponder, and presentation is exquisite. A flattened cylinder of duck galantine contains cubes of meat with apricot pieces in jelly and is accompanied by a tiny scalloped biscuit topped with bitter orange chutney. Faultless tomato risotto is the partner for a roast fillet of turbot, its balsamic salad leaves piled into a little Parmesan crisp basket. Main courses arrive with a plethora of vegetables, separately served. At dessert stage, artistry achieves its apogee in the shape of 'succulently creamy and rich' mango crème chiboust with sharply contrasting strawberry sorbet and lychee syrup, or iced russet apple soufflé sandwiched between deep-fried apple wafers with a calvados caramel sauce. These are preceded by a palate-clearing jelly, of 'sour, sour, sour' pink grapefruit one evening, a much more efficient vehicle for the purpose than a sorbet. Wines are a plutocrat's paradise. For a mere £1,500 you can have Beychevelle '45. Then again, when even the 1993 second wine of Gruaud-Larose is £60, it is clear nobody is going to be done any financial favours. House French is £17.50, or £4.25 a glass.

CHEF: John Williams   PROPRIETOR: Savoy Group   OPEN: all week 12.30 to 3, 7 to 11   MEALS: alc (main courses £15.50 to £39). Set L £29 to £38, Set D Sun to Thur £39 to £58, Set D Fri and Sat £45 to £58   SERVICE: net prices, card slips closed   CARDS: Amex, Diners, MasterCard, Switch, Visa   DETAILS: 120 seats. Private parties: 14 main room, 14 private room. Vegetarian meals. Children's helpings. Jacket and tie. No smoking in 1 dining-room. Wheelchair access (also WC). Music. Air-conditioned   ACCOMMODATION: 198 rooms, all with bath/shower. TV. Phone. Children welcome. Dogs welcome by arrangement. Afternoon teas   ⊖ Bond Street

---

Dining-rooms where music, either live or recorded, is never played are signalled by No music *in the details at the end of an entry.*

London restaurants by cuisine are listed near the front of the book.

Clarke's

map 13

124 Kensington Church St, W8 4BH
TEL: (0171) 221 9225   FAX: (0171) 229 4564

COOKING 6
COST £34–£56

When Sally Clarke opened her elegant Kensington restaurant 15 years ago, offering a no-choice menu was considered an audacious move. Yet the steady stream of superlatives from readers is a tribute to both her good sense and her skill. Any initial reservations about being denied the luxury of choice (at dinner only; lunch is a more casual affair) are dispelled by the consistently excellent food and the refined harmony of her menus.

Two serene rooms (downstairs for non-smokers, with a view of the kitchen) are decorated in cool, muted creams that none the less exude a welcoming warmth. Exuberant use of seasonal greens is one of the leitmotifs of Sally Clarke's cooking. A May dinner got off to a fine start with San Daniele ham served with a salad of grilled asparagus, mustard leaves, black olives and chives, which was dressed with a wonderfully fresh and fruity oil: 'like a Tuscan spring on a plate'. A main course of chargrilled brill fillet came with unusual but inspired accompaniments of spring cabbage and a fennel fritter 'coated in barely a whisper of batter so light that it almost floated off the plate'. British cheeses in prime condition are a regular fixture, served with a palate-cleansing crisp apple, celery or even radishes and crumbly oatmeal biscuits. The prevailing lightness doesn't preclude indulgence in the form of dark chocolate soufflé, or pannacotta with blood oranges.

The no-choice format leaves the kitchen no leeway for error, and it might appear to play it safe with simplistic-seeming dishes. Yet underpinning it are supreme ingredients handled with precision and skill. All this comes without pretension or formality: staff are friendly, with a confidence-building professionalism. At least the wine list provides diners with the opportunity for some mental exercise: selecting a bottle. Although drawn only from France, Italy and California, wines are so attractively priced, exciting, even unusual, that narrowing the choice to one bin is not easy and a generous selection of halves only serves to increase the possibilites. House French is £9. CELLARMAN'S CHOICE: Qupé Marsanne 1996, Santa Barbara, California, £20; Bonny Doon Old Telegram 1995, Santa Cruz, California, £40.

CHEFS: Sally Clarke and Elizabeth Payne   PROPRIETOR: Sally Clarke   OPEN: Mon to Fri 12.30 to 2, 7 to 10   CLOSED: 10 days Christmas, 2 weeks Aug, 4 days Easter   MEALS: alc L (main courses £14), Set D £42. BYO £10   SERVICE: net prices, card slips closed   CARDS: Amex, MasterCard, Switch, Visa   DETAILS: 90 seats. Private parties: 12 main room. Vegetarian meals. Children welcome. No smoking in 1 dining-room. No cigars/pipes in dining room. Wheelchair access (not WC). No music. Air-conditioned   ⊖ Notting Hill Gate

Coast ♥ 〰

map 15

26B Albemarle Street, W1A 4SW
TEL: (0171) 495 5999   FAX: (0171) 495 2999

COOKING 5
COST £35–£75

Coast belongs to Oliver Peyton's group of restaurants, as do Atlantic, and Mash (see entries, London) and Mash and Air (see entry, Manchester), and Bruno Loubet is now being employed to oversee 'culinary development', whatever that may be, thus bringing together two very sharp minds whose owners have been responsible for some of the more siginificant '90s restaurant openings; yet more are planned as the *Guide* goes to press. Noise bounces around the hard-edged, glass-fronted dining-room, contributing to its sense of pace; the bulging eye-socket lights are as weird as ever, and rounded booths for parties of four are 'reminiscent of fairground waltzers'.

In the kitchen, meanwhile, Adam Gray, who worked with Loubet at the Chelsea Hotel, has an energetic 'no holds barred' approach to cooking that takes in seared salmon spring roll in fermented black bean aïoli, and roast halibut with preserved lemon and chickpea pancake. This is 'most assuredly not comfort food', according to one visitor, whose glass-noodle salad with four perky langoustines and a rust-red tamarind bisque was 'gone in two mouthfuls', but fish and vegetable dishes get a good airing: monkfish and pickled vegetable terrine, or a chilled 'juice' of tomato and celery with goats'-cheese quenelle. More substantial dishes come in the form of rabbit ravioli, or peppered Hereford duck with honey and Asian greens.

Desserts take a 'progressive' view of things too, in palm-sugared tamarillo with basil and rosemary ice-ream, or roasted pineapple with dried dates and apricots, served with yoghurt ice-cream. Service from a hierarchy of staff is efficient. An unusual bargain is that children are not charged for when accompanying their parents for Saturday and Sunday brunch. The wine list offers good drinking at all price levels, ranging from sunny New World whites to serious red Bordeaux and burgundies. Spain and Italy are given due consideration too. An appealingly varied house selection begins with a South African Chardonnay at £12.50. CELLARMAN'S CHOICE: Lenswood Sauvignon Blanc 1997, Adelaide Hills, S. Australia, £28.50; Riquewihr, Pinot Noir d'Alsace 'Jubilee' 1995, Hugel, £25.50.

CHEF: Adam Gray   PROPRIETOR: Oliver Peyton   OPEN: all week 12 to 3 (3.30 Sat and Sun), 6 to 11.30 (10.30 Sun)   CLOSED: 25 and 26 Dec, 1 Jan, Easter Sun and Mon   MEALS: alc (main courses £10.50 to £25). Set D Mon to Fri 6 to 7pm £18.50 (2 courses). Sat and Sun brunch menu 12 to 3.30   SERVICE: 12.5% (optional), card slips closed   CARDS: Amex, Delta, Diners, MasterCard, Switch, Visa   DETAILS: 120 seats. Private parties: 8 main room, 30 private room. Vegetarian meals. Children welcome. Wheelchair access (not WC). Occasional music. Air-conditioned   ⊖ Green Park

The Collection   map 14

264 Brompton Road, SW3 2AS	COOKING 1
TEL: (0171) 225 1212 FAX: (0171) 225 1050	COST £27–£60

From the street, it looks unassuming. A narrow gap between neighbouring shops is the start of a long glass catwalk 'tunnel' leading to this loud and lively meeting place for trendy twenty-somethings. Concrete floors, exposed brick and slender metal columns lend it a futuristic industrial chic. In the mezzanine restaurant, black-clad staff are friendly, fast and professional. The menu favours the Orient – steamed foie gras and pork dumplings with chilli honey dip, grilled chicken skewers with tamarind, or yaki soba noodles with shiitake – but also throws in a diverse Mediterranean strand. More adventurous combinations don't always deliver the hoped-for taste sensations, but a straightforward fennel, almond, rocket and goats'-cheese salad is a simple, well-executed dish', and pumpkin ravioli offers generously filled pasta in a rich buttery sauce. For dessert, chocolate and pecan tart with 'an excellent fudgy consistency' competes with more exotic steamed mango and pineapple parcels with chocolate and coconut sauce. The short wine list offers some interesting New World bottles and a fair choice by the glass, including saké; house Argentinian is £11.50.

CHEFS: Cass Titcombe and Chris Benians   PROPRIETORS: Mogens Tholstrup and Belgo plc
OPEN: Mon to Sat L 12 to 3 (4 Sat), Mon to Sat D 6.30 to 11.30   CLOSED: Christmas, bank hols
MEALS: alc (main courses £9.50 to £16.50). Set L £12.95 (2 courses) to £15.95. Bar food
available   SERVICE: 15% (optional), card slips closed   CARDS: Amex, Delta, Diners,
MasterCard, Switch, Visa   DETAILS: 180 seats. Private parties: 180 main room. Vegetarian
meals. Children welcome. Wheelchair access (also WC). Music. Air-conditioned   ⊖ South
Kensington   (£5)

Como Lario   map 14

22 Holbein Place, SW1W 8NL
TEL: (0171) 730 2954   FAX: (0171) 244 8387   COOKING 2
EMAIL: guicat@aol.com   COST £26–£49

Within a 'zealously clean', hard-edged white dining-room in Chelsea, with a sizeable mural of Lake Como filling one wall, a smart clientele gathers for some refined northern Italian cooking. The menu mixes accepted standards such as spaghettini agli scampi with more obviously new-wave items; for example an antipasto dish of grilled radicchio under a blanket of smoked mozzarella that combines the bitterness of the leaves with 'a lovely charred taste' in the cheese. Grilling is a much-mobilised technique, accurately applied to pieces of monkfish and scallops threaded on to a skewer. Among the rest, calves' kidneys and liver are cooked in red wine and served with polenta, and Gorgonzola and ham are crammed into a chicken breast on chestnut sauce. Simplicity scores again at meal's end in a serving of rich pannacotta with raspberry coulis. Staff work hard to look after everybody, while giving 'the impression that they are thoroughly enjoying themselves too'. The Italian wines would all appear to be non-vintage, if the list is any guide, kicking off with house Sicilian at £9.50.

CHEF: Giancarlo Moeri   PROPRIETOR: Guido Campigotto   OPEN: Mon to Sat 12.30 to 2.45, 6.30
to 11.30   MEALS: alc (main courses £8 to £16). Cover £1.25   SERVICE: not inc   CARDS: Amex,
Delta, Diners, MasterCard, Switch, Visa   DETAILS: 90 seats. Private parties: 55 main room.
Vegetarian meals. Children's helpings. No pipes in dining-room. Wheelchair access (not WC).
No music. Air-conditioned   ⊖ Sloane Square

▲ Connaught   map 15

Carlos Place, Mayfair, W1Y 6AL
TEL: (0171)-499 7070   FAX: (0171)-495 3262   COOKING 6
EMAIL: info@the-connaught.co.uk   COST £37–£136

The *Guide's* most senior restaurant is the one that has probably changed least. A 'must' for foreign visitors on the heritage trail, it sells a brand of timeless oak-panelled formality, where waiters dress in tails and juggle chafing dishes, and the menu speaks an impenetrable dialect. Do you have any idea what zephirs de sole 'tout Paris' might be? Or consommé Prince of Wales, or oysters Christian Dior? Would you care to sing a verse of Homard d'Ecosse Grillé 'My Way'? At least mixed grill, lamb cutlets, and kidneys and bacon are not mucked about with, linguistically or otherwise, and anyone who still likes to choose dessert from a trolley, and who appreciates attentive, very polite and plentiful service will find many things done as well here as anywhere.

Whatever else, the kitchen is a busy one, servicing a menu of over 60 dishes (not counting the trolley), and piling on some posh-sounding extras: champagne to braise the salmon, or garnishes of oyster and truffle. It must have the biggest cream bill in London, too. Although the general tenor of the food may be as old-fashioned as avocado cocktail, or prawns in a creamy curried sauce, it does deliver the goods: a huge dish of steak, kidney and mushroom pie for example (the Monday lunchtime special), or 'firm, superbly cooked' brill with a soufflé topping. Likewise, among traditional puds of sherry trifle, treacle tart, or bread and butter, there is first-rate apple tart in a set custard, or 'smooth and creamy' crème brûlée. An oxygen mask may be necessary to scale the heights of the wine list: a vin de pays chardonnay starts things off at £22, and it is uphill from there on.

CHEF: Michel Bourdin   PROPRIETOR: Savoy Group plc   OPEN: all week 12.30 to 2.30, 6.30 to 10.45   MEALS: alc (main courses £12.50 to £40). Set L £27.50, Set L Sun £32.50, Set D £37.50 (Grill Room) to £55   SERVICE: 15%   CARDS: Amex, Delta, Diners, MasterCard, Switch, Visa   DETAILS: 100 seats. Private parties: 22 main room, 12 to 22 private rooms. Vegetarian meals. Children's helpings. Jacket and tie at D. Wheelchair access (also WC). No music. Air-conditioned   ACCOMMODATION: 90 rooms, all with bath/shower. TV. Phone. Room only £225 to £310. Rooms for disabled. Children welcome. No dogs. Afternoon teas (The Which? Hotel Guide)   ⊖ Bond Street, Green Park

Cookhouse

map 12

56 Lower Richmond Road, Putney, SW15 1JT
TEL: (0181) 785 2300

COOKING 3
COST £28–£37

Small is great in this smart but unassuming restaurant with huge windows, blue walls and plain tables. Its small floor space is shared by up to 28 customers, plus waiting staff, and the chef with his one-person support team. Friendly, relaxed service and an appreciative, mainly young clientele make it a convivial place to enjoy Tim Jefferson's cooking. The menu, written on transparent 'blackboards', offers three or four choices at each course. Fashionable ingredients are used, but there is a welcome absence of fuss about such starters as grilled red mullet with a fennel brochette, or carpaccio of lightly smoked venison with fig and chilli chutney. Main dishes in generous portions can be as purely European as sweetbreads with mushroom mash and Madeira jus, or lamb shank, Puy lentils and gratin dauphinoise. Asian influences appear in soy glazed sea bass with Thai vegetable noodles, or lightly curried green shell mussels. But desserts are re-assuringly home based with plum and almond tart, bread-and-butter pudding, and a 'robust-skinned' crème brulée. Both real and decaffeinated coffee are praised. The £2.50 cover charge includes good bread with anchovy butter, a nibble, and corkage on the wine you bring yourself.

The Guide *office can quickly spot when a restaurateur is encouraging customers to write recommending inclusion. Such reports do not further a restaurant's cause. Please tell us if a restaurateur invites you to write to the* Guide.

CHEF: Tim Jefferson PROPRIETORS: Tim Jefferson and Amanda Griffiths OPEN: Tue to Sat D only 7 to 11 CLOSED: 2 weeks Christmas MEALS: alc (main courses £12 to £13.50). Unlicensed but £2.50 cover charge includes corkage SERVICE: not inc CARDS: Delta, MasterCard, Switch, Visa DETAILS: 28 seats. Private parties: 32 main room. Children's helpings. Wheelchair access (1 step; also WC). Occasional music. Air-conditioned ⊖ Putney Bridge

▲ County Hall Restaurant   [NEW ENTRY]   map 13

County Hall, SE1 7PB   COOKING 4
TEL: (0171) 902 8000   FAX: (0171) 928 5300   COST £39–£62

Londoners won't need directing to County Hall, once the headquarters of political administration when the capital had a council. It sits right on the Thames, facing the Houses of Parliament, and is now a large hotel. Crossing Westminster Bridge southwards, take the first small road on the left, and follow signs for the Marriott Hotel. The cavernous brasserie-like dimensions and crustacean bar are stamped out of the same mould as many of London's more popular addresses.

David Ali (ex-Canteen, see entry) cooks, with Richard Corrigan as consultant. An early inspection produced some highly promising dishes, not least a dark green pillow that turned out to be a warm onion tart wrapped in vine leaves surrounded by chopped and tarragon-seasoned green olives. A restrained pan-Asian tendency brings on a fillet of sea bream on sweet potato with a lime pickle sauce and cool raita, an appealing combination with true zing to it, while another successful fish dish was roast sea bass with grilled asparagus, clams and basil-scented tomato sauce. Ideas are arresting, compositions sound: beef fillet comes with a pea flan, horseradish rémoulade and a sauce of Cabernet Sauvignon, while a vegetarian risotto mixes Gorgonzola with peas and pine-nuts. A Tatin variation using bananas is beautifully executed, properly caramelised and served with caramel ice-cream, yet avoiding over-sweetness. Staff are multi-national, familiar with the menu, and there when you need them. The short highly priced wine list is mainly from France, with a few from the New World. House wines start at £14 and there about ten half-bottles and six wines by the glass.

CHEF: David Ali PROPRIETOR: Whitbread Plc OPEN: all week 12 to 5.30, 5.30 to 11 MEALS: alc (main courses £12.50 to £20) SERVICE: not inc, card slips closed CARDS: Amex, Delta, Diners, MasterCard, Switch, Visa DETAILS: 150 seats. 70 seats outside. Private parties: 8 main room, up to 60 private rooms. Vegetarian meals. Children welcome. Occasional music. Air-conditioned ACCOMMODATION: 200 rooms, all with bath/shower. TV. Phone. Room only £250. Children welcome. No dogs ⊖ Waterloo

▲ Crescent 🍸   map 13

Montcalm Hotel, Great Cumberland Place, W1A 2LF   COOKING 4
TEL: (0171) 402 4288   FAX: (0171) 724 9180   COST £31–£35

The Crescent offers all the cachet of dining in a smart hotel without the usual price tag. There is no à la carte menu in the Montcalm's opulent, elegantly draped restaurant; instead you pay for two or three courses, including half a bottle of wine and coffee. 'By London standards this ranks as a best buy,' commented a satisfied reporter. Choice is generous, too, with about a dozen dishes per course. European techniques paired with oriental flavourings is a recurring theme, executed with some flair: a highlight of one meal was very fresh rare tuna served with an intricate pile of delicate seaweed, peppers and noodles and a lemon grass-infused Vietnamese dressing.

The creative streak extends to more classically inspired dishes, such as a well-composed terrine of smoked pork knuckle, foie gras and prunes, beautifully set off by an accompanying fennel and orange salad. Timing has been variable, at its best producing 'melt-in-the-mouth' sweetbreads and 'nicely pink' calf's liver with grilled aubergines and bordelaise sauce. The short wine list has a slightly French bias, although house wine, at £12, is Californian.

CHEF: Peter Robinson   PROPRIETOR: Nikko Hotels (UK) Ltd   OPEN: Mon to Fri L 12.30 to 2.30, Mon to Sat D 6.30 to 10.30   CLOSED: Good Friday, Easter Mon, L bank hols   MEALS: Set L and D £18.50 (2 courses) to £22.50 (inc wine)   SERVICE: not inc   CARDS: Amex, Diners, MasterCard, Switch, Visa   DETAILS. 00 seats. Private parties. 80 main room, 20 to 80 private rooms. Vegetarian meals. Children's helpings. Music. Air-conditioned   ACCOMMODATION: 120 rooms, all with bath/shower. TV. Phone. Room only £195 to £350. Rooms for disabled. Children welcome. Dogs welcome by arrangement. Afternoon teas   ⊖ Marble Arch   £5

Criterion Brasserie
map 15

224 Piccadilly, W1V 9LB   COOKING 6
TEL: (0171) 930 0488   FAX: (0171) 930 8380   COST £29–£54

Gold mosaics, marble walls and a high ceiling, together with orientalist art and hanging tasselled lamps give this, one of London's most evocative dining-rooms, a feel of Byzantium-for-the-masses. It is a 'spacious and exotic' place, although tables are close together and there are no restrictions on smoking. The appeal is a varied *carte*, 'tempting in the modern manner', with vichyssoise of Jerusalem artichoke, salad of preserved lemons and fennel, roast scallops with sauce vierge, and smoked haddock 'kedgeree'. Cooking shows the work of many hands, not all of the same steadiness, but over time it achieves a degree of consistency that is rare among places of similar size.

Risottos – langoustine, saffron or nero – are a strong point, and output ranges from an utterly simple but 'exquisite' Caesar salad to a more involved roast rabbit stuffed with provençale vegetables, served with a dark and intensely perfumed sauce: a dish that smacks of 'hours of patient kitchen craftsmanship' and which would not be out of place at Marco's flagship Oak Room restaurant across the road (see Le Meridien, below). Fish main courses are given as much prominence as meat, producing hot-smoked salmon, cod with chorizo ('a delight') and a ubiquitous MPW dish, skate wing with capers and winkles.

Tarts show well among desserts, not least on account of good pastry: lemon tart is 'very fine', and passion-fruit curd tart's 'rich, warmly unctuous cream' combines well with its 'intense blast of passion-fruit piquancy'. Bread is good, though you may have to ask for it. Most reports suggest that service lacks both interest and organisation, and the two-hour time-limit on tables in the evening can exert pressure on already fragile staff–customer relations. Wines are good but severely marked up for a brasserie, although house Italian white is £12, Australian red £14.

CHEFS: Peter Rafell and Richard Phillips PROPRIETOR: Marco Pierre White OPEN: all week 12 to 2.30, 6 to 12 (10.30 Sun) CLOSED: 25 and 26 Dec, 1 Jan MEALS: alc (main courses £12 to £15). Set L and D 6 to 6.30 £14.95 (2 courses) to £17.95 SERVICE: 12.5% (optional), card slips closed CARDS: Amex, Delta, MasterCard, Switch, Visa DETAILS: 175 seats. Private parties: 250 main room. Children welcome. Wheelchair access (also WC). No music ⊖ Piccadilly Circus

Crowthers

map 12

481 Upper Richmond Road West, SW14 7PU	COOKING 4
TEL/FAX: (0181) 876 6372	COST £28–£40

Philip and Shirley Crowther have built up their pleasing neighbourhood restaurant since 1982 and it is now an enduring fixture of the local restaurant scene. Décor has been given a facelift, but the cooking continues to tread a steady path through the world of French cuisine. Menus are fixed-price for two or three courses and there is plenty to praise.

A ramekin of baby seared scallops with spiced basmasti rice and a light curry dressing is a favourite way to begin, although choice ranges from herbed onion tart to a strudel of salmon with basil and vermouth. Reporters also approve 'meltingly tender' best end of lamb with a herb crust as a main course, along with roast breast of Barbary duck, which might be spiced up with ginger and lime. Among desserts, tarte au citron is reckoned to be a winner, along with chocolate roulade filled with fromage blanc and strawberries, or a large plate of grilled fruits with a Kirsch sabayon. Service has been described as both 'pleasant' and 'thoughtful'. The list of around three-dozen wines seldom strays over the French border, but choice is sound, prices are realistic, and there are over a dozen half-bottles. House wine is £9.50.

CHEF: Philip Crowther PROPRIETORS: Philip and Shirley Crowther OPEN: Tue to Fri L 12 to 1.30, Tue to Sat D 7 to 10.30 CLOSED: 1 week Christmas, Good Fri, 2 weeks summer MEALS: Set L £18.75, Set D £18.75 (2 courses) to £23.50 SERVICE: not inc CARDS: Delta, MasterCard, Switch, Visa DETAILS: 32 seats. Private parties: 45 main room. Children's helpings. Wheelchair access (1 step; not WC). No music. Air-conditioned £5

Cucina

map 13

45A South End Road, NW3 2QB	COOKING 4
TEL: (0171) 435 7814 FAX: (0171) 435 7815	COST £22–£44

'Lively and modern' is how one reporter summed up this thriving venue around the corner from the Royal Free Hospital. The interior is a pleasing and vibrant mix of 'minimalistic chrome yellow' with wooden flooring and eye-catching artwork on the walls. Only the acoustics seem to cause irritation: go there 'happy to shout and be shouted at,' advised one correspondent.

Cooking sets a course for the Pacific Rim by way of the Mediterranean, and it's vibrant, modern stuff. Chargrilled pork fillet with black pudding, bubble and squeak and thyme jus is about as close to home as it gets Otherwise cruise around the world for roast sweet potatoes with grilled asparagus and Taleggio sauce; wok-fried tiger prawns with chilli jam, shiitake mushroom and coriander risotto; or roast poussin with lemon and maple syrup glaze and Cajun slaw.

Ribeye steak and frites for two is a comfortingly familiar fixture on the menu, and desserts also inhabit less exotic territory: passion-fruit crème brûlée, warm pear and frangipane tart, and home-made vanilla ice-cream with chocolate sauce, for example. Set lunches are reckoned to be a bargain, and service is generally fast and attentive. The wine list is as modern as the menu, with much to intrigue the palate. House wine is £10.95.

CHEFS: Andrew Poole and Stephen Baker   PROPRIETORS: Vernon Mascarenhas, Andrew Poole and Stephen Baker   OPEN: all week L 12 to 2.30 (3 Sun), Mon to Sat D 7 to 10.30 (11 Fri and Sat)   CLOSED: 25 and 26 Dec, Easter Sun and Mon   MEALS: alc (main courses £8.50 to £13). Set L Mon to Sat £10 (2 courses) to £13.50, Set L Sun £12.95 (2 courses) to £15.95, Set D £16.95   SERVICE: not inc   CARDS: Amex, Delta, MasterCard, Switch, Visa   DETAILS: 96 seats. Private parties: 80 main room. Vegetarian meals. Children welcome. No cigars/pipes in dining-room. Wheelchair access (1 step; not WC). No music. Air-conditioned   ⊖ Belsize Park

Dakota ▼

	NEW ENTRY map 13
127 Ledbury Road, W11 2AQ	COOKING 4
TEL: (0171) 792 9191 FAX: (0171) 792 9090	COST £28–£56

Dakota is the new sibling of Montana (see entry), opening in late 1997 among antique-shops on the grander side of Notting Hill, and occupying a large ground-floor room with big windows and blue velvet banquettes. Although the menus may be kissing-cousins, the restaurants' names are still bemusingly at the wrong end of the States to define the cooking, which is south-western in inclination, closer to southern California than the prairies.

Blackened corn, marjoram dumplings and chipotle mash are the kinds of ingredients to expect, and there is an emphasis on clean-cut flavours. Expect quinces, apricots, figs and limes among the soft-shell crabs, Yucatan duck broth and wood-smoked halibut. And expect a roll call of chilli varieties that will impress those in the know. Even more impressive is the restraint with which they are used: often no more than 'a fresh, tastebud-sharpening glow' that won't have you reaching for the fire-extinguisher.

'Big blobs of gorgeous-tasting gunge' is one less than technically precise impression of what arrived on one reporter's plate: the rabbit carnita with guarjillo turned out to be a soft pancake stuffed with rabbit meat and chilli flakes topped with sweet fig relish. Round things off with coconut ice-cream and roasted (and lightly chillied) pineapple, or apricot buttermilk bavarois. Service is commended as 'very willing, but not imposing'. Wines are a style-conscious west coast of America selection, supplemented by a few bins from other countries, but quality isn't sacrificed on the altar of fashion. The list changes every quarter so any diners seized by a pioneer spirit will have to move fast to try the Utah Semillon-Sauvignon. Prices start at £10.50.

CHEF: Daniel McDowell   PROPRIETOR: Montana plc   OPEN: all week 12 to 3.30, 7 to 11.30 CLOSED: 25 Dec, 1 Jan, Aug bank hol weekend   MEALS: alc (main courses £8 to £16). Set L £10 (2 courses), Set D £27.50 to £32.50   SERVICE: 12.5% (optional), card slips closed   CARDS: Amex, MasterCard, Switch, Visa   DETAILS: 93 seats. 30 seats outside. Private parties: 16 main room, 30 private room. Vegetarian meals. Children welcome. No cigars before 10. Music. Air-conditioned   ⊖ Ladbroke Grove

Daphne £

map 13

83 Bayham Street, NW1 0AG	COOKING 1
TEL: (0171) 267 7322 FAX: (0171) 482 3964	COST £22–£37

Daphne continues to look 'bright and cheerful', with its green colour schemes and 'old photographs of old Cyprus', which seem to look even more 'sepia-like' by the day. Two-course lunches are reckoned to be 'superb value' for classic dips, followed perhaps by pork sheftalia. Otherwise, attention focuses on daily specials: depending on the market, you might encounter chargrilled sea bass, tuna steak, or fresh artichokes and broad beans stewed in a 'deep, enjoyable sauce'. However, the pick of the bunch, for one correspondent at least, has to be fresh grilled swordfish 'bursting with juices, tangy with lemon and plenty of chopped parsley'. Here and there the kitchen disappoints with more traditional dishes, but there's no denying the personable, friendly atmosphere of the place or the helpfulness of the staff. The upgraded wine list now includes a few more bottles from Greece and Cyprus. House French is £10.75.

CHEFS: Lambros Georgiou and Myltos Tsaroullas   PROPRIETORS: Panikos and Anna Lymbouri   OPEN: Mon to Sat 12 to 2.30, 6 to 11.30   CLOSED: 25 and 26 Dec, 1 Jan   MEALS: alc (main courses £6.50 to £13). Set L £5.75 (2 courses)   SERVICE: not inc   CARDS: MasterCard, Switch, Visa   DETAILS: 85 seats. 30 seats outside. Private parties: 30 main room. Vegetarian meals. Children's helpings. Music   ⊖ Camden Town   (£5)

Daphne's

map 14

112 Draycott Avenue, SW3 3AE	COOKING 4
TEL: (0171) 589 4257 FAX: (0171) 581 2232	COST £26–£76

Mogens Tholstrup went into partnership with Belgo plc in 1998, but no evidence of change is visible to the naked eye. The burnt-earth Tuscan tones of the tiled restaurant, with its garden room to the rear where the roof slides back in summer, remain as airily pleasing as they ever were, the staff as city-cool, the clientele as Chelsea-smart. However, the cooking of Chris Benians – one of the kitchen's longer-serving incumbents – has now appreciably taken off. He is turning out confident Italian dishes as if to the manner born.

Deceptively simple means are very often the key to the best dishes in this style, the point demonstrated by an inspector's first course of three plump sauté scallops bound in crisp pancetta, served on sliced Jerusalem artichokes with fried cherry tomatoes. The marriage of flavours and counterpointing of textures was flawless, as it was in a dish of seared foie gras on braised endive with sliced pears, pine-nuts and vin santo. Importantly, essentials are done well: for example a risotto of girolles and porcini with wood pigeon, given winey depth with Barolo and astringent tang from Parmesan. Fish receives variously apposite treatment too: tuna comes with peppers, olives, and tomato, grilled Dover sole with olive oil, lemon juice and parsley. Pungently alcoholic tiramisù is the star dessert, but there may also be peach and amaretti tart, or pannacotta with red fruits. A contented buzz of satisfaction and the easy banter of the staff tell their own story. House wine is £12.

CHEFS: Chris Benians and Lee Pascell   PROPRIETOR: Mogens Tholstrup and Belgo plc   OPEN: Mon to Sat 12 to 3 (3.30 Sat), 7 to 11, Sun 12.30 to 3.30, 7 to 10.30   CLOSED: Christmas and New Year   MEALS: alc (main courses L £6.50 to £15, D £9.50 to £21.50)   SERVICE: 15% (optional), card slips closed   CARDS: Amex, Delta, Diners, MasterCard, Switch, Visa   DETAILS: 70 seats. 45 seats outside. Vegetarian meals. Children welcome. No music. Air-conditioned
⊖ South Kensington

Del Buongustaio ▼ £ map 12

283 Putney Bridge Road, SW15 2PT   COOKING 2
TEL: (0181) 780 9361   FAX: (0181) 789 9659   COST £23–£44

The traditions of forthright Italian peasant food are alive and well in this unlikely-looking osteria. Aurelio Spagnuolo looks to Piedmont, Puglia and beyond for ideas, and changes his main menu every month. His view of native cuisine challenges many of the clichés: as one reporter noted, 'There was no need for us to have a single dish containing tomato if we didn't want to.' Pasta is a strong suit: spaghetti might appear with cuttlefish, potato, garlic and chillies. Signor Spagnuolo has also taken it on himself to research painstakingly his country's medieval and Renaissance legacy. From sixteenth-century Sicily, for example, might come hand-made ravioli stuffed with chicken, guinea-fowl, ricotta, Swiss chard, nutmeg and rosemary with butter and sage; while Tuscany – *circa* 1400 – yields tonno rinascimentale con le pere (oven-baked tuna with lemon, olives, pear, oregano and breadcrumbs). Cooking such as this stands or falls on the judicious pairing of ingredients rather than on high-flown gastro wizardry. On Sundays, the denizens of Putney and beyond are treated to a daunting 'degustazione' lunch menu that can stretch from three to the full monty of six courses. The wine list has a split personality, covering Italy from top to toe and Australia from West to East, but a glance at the producers and prices reveals a sound mind behind it. House wines start at £8.80 a bottle, £5.95 for a half-litre jug. CELLARMAN'S CHOICE: Cape Mentelle Semillon/Chardonnay 1996, Margaret River, W. Australia, £15.50; Monferrato, Ruché di Castagnole 1994, Bava, £22.50.

CHEFS: Aurelio Spagnuolo and Gianni Saidù   PROPRIETORS: Rochelle Porteous and Aurelio Spagnuolo   OPEN: Sun to Fri 12 to 3 (12.30 to 3.30 Sun), all week D 6.30 to 11.15 (11.30 Fri and Sat, 10.30 Sun)   CLOSED: 2 weeks Christmas, Aug bank hol   MEALS: alc (main courses £7 to £11.50). Set L Mon to Fri £9.50, Set L Sun £15.50 to £25.50, Set D £22.50. Cover 90p   SERVICE: not inc; 10% for parties of 5 or more   CARDS: Amex, MasterCard, Switch, Visa   DETAILS: 60 seats. Private parties: 60 main room. Vegetarian meals. Children's helpings. No cigars/pipes in dining-room. Wheelchair access (1 step; not WC). Music. Air-conditioned   ⊖ East Putney
£5

The 2000 Guide will be published before Christmas 1999. Reports on meals are most welcome at any time of the year, but are particularly valuable in the spring (no later than June). Send them to The Good Food Guide, *FREEPOST, 2 Marylebone Road, London NW1 1YN. Or email your report to guidereports@which.co.uk.*

'Staff are mostly male, and there's more mincing here than in a sausage factory.' (On eating in Nottinghamshire)

Delfina Studio Café

map 13

50 Bermondsey Street, SE1 3UD
TEL: (0171) 357 0244   COOKING **5**
EMAIL: admin@delfina.org.uk   COST £32–£49

One of the perks for resident artists at Delfina is lunch for £1 in the bright, clean-lined restaurant attached to the modern art gallery. The rest of us may not qualify for such bargain rates, but it's still worth negotiating the backstreets of London Bridge to enjoy chef Maria Elia's works of art on a plate. Naturally, presentation is a priority, but the food is more than just easy on the eye. Strong, rich flavours – 'nothing namby-pamby' – ensure that there's plenty to dazzle the palate as well.

The brief menu reads like a synopsis of fusion food, managing to accommodate European, Moroccan, Mexican and Oriental influences on just one page. Typically there might be duck confit and mango salsa tacos, or langoustine 'haystack' to start, followed by chargrilled lamb cutlets with dhal and red chilli oil, or quail with thyme-scented hollandaise. Seafood is a strong point, whether a starter of crab-cake seasoned with chilli, lemon grass and coriander and served with chive hollandaise, or a 'meaty, moist and tender' fillet of sea bass partnered with a salad of fennel, tomato and capers and a tangy lemon and olive oil sauce. The propensity for serving food in a tall stack on the plate exploits the bright colours of the global larder to dramatic effect. Puddings show the same pizazz: chocolate brownie with a scoop of very light, intensely flavoured espresso ice-cream is 'a real killer – exactly as a brownie should be'. Alternatives might include ginger bavarois with star fruit and lychees, or chocolate and banana samosas. A 'friendly, laid-back' atmosphere and pleasant service from black-clad staff make Delfina 'a lovely place for a long, relaxed lunch'. Like the menu, the short wine list packs in plenty of variety, and there are some interesting choices to match the food. House Spanish is £10.95.

CHEF: Maria Elia   PROPRIETORS: Digby Squires, Delfina Entrecanales   OPEN: Mon to Fri L only 12 to 3   CLOSED: 24 Dec to 4 Jan.   MEALS: alc (main courses £10 to £12.50)   SERVICE: 12.5% (optional), card slips closed   CARDS: Amex, Delta, Diners, MasterCard, Switch, Visa   DETAILS: 70 seats. Private parties: 250 main room, 80 to 250 private rooms. Vegetarian meals. Children's helpings. Wheelchair access (also WC). No music   ⊖ London Bridge   (£5)

▲ Dorchester ▼

map 15

Park Lane, W1A 2HJ
TEL: Grill Room (0171) 317 6336; Oriental (0171) 317 6328   COOKING **4**
FAX: Grill Room (0171) 317 6464; Oriental (0171) 409 0114   COST £37–£116

As with most big hotels, it is possible to get anything from a bar snack to a blowout at this Park Lane landmark, but the two restaurants of significance are the Oriental and Grill Room. The former is a simply furnished, low-ceilinged room with silk wall hangings, expansive tables and a 65-dish *carte* with Cantonese leanings that takes in deep-fried soft-shell crab, marinated pork ribs, and pigeon with orange sauce. Abalone and shark's fin feature prominently, but an emphasis on Westernised dishes – stir-fried Dover sole with broccoli rather than, say, duck webs or fish lips – and prices that may cause even more swallowing are points to consider. A list of specials offers greater interest in the shape of steamed chicken dumplings with crab sauce, and multi-course fixed-price menus come with wine recommendations.

The Spanish-style Grill Room, with dark wooden tables and red leather seats, is quite a contrast, offering a fairly traditional version of British food along the lines of potted shrimps, cock-a-leekie soup, shepherd's pie, and deep-fried cod in yeast batter. The grills that give the room its name include veal or lamb cutlets, Scottish lobster, and calf's liver and bacon, while lunch-times ring the changes on old-fashioned favourites: boiled silverside with caraway dumplings on Mondays, roast pork with apple purée on Thursdays and so on. Vegetarians get a separate menu. Crêpes Suzette (dinner only) are flamed at table, while other desserts come round on one of the many trolleys.

The imposing wine list is the same in both restaurants, and while quality is high across the board so are the mark-ups. A handful of bottles under £20 can be found, including house Vins de Pays d'Oc at £18.50, but expect to spend more for a degree of choice within or without the classical regions. Fifteen eclectic wines by the glass start at £5.50. CELLARMAN'S CHOICE: Chablis 'Vau de Vey' 1995, Dom. Jean Durup, £32; Côte de Beaune Villages 1995, Dom. Louis Latour, £37.

CHEFS:Willi Elsener and Kenneth Poon   PROPRIETOR:The Audley Group Ltd   OPEN:Grill Room Mon to Sat 12.30 to 2.30, 6 to 11, Sun and bank hols 12.30 to 2.30, 7 to 10.30; Oriental Mon to Fri L 12 to 2.30, Mon to Sat D 7 to 11   MEALS:Grill Room alc (main courses £18.50 to £49); Set L £29.50, Set D £39.50. Oriental alc (main courses £16 to £38); Set L £27 to £29.50, Set D £37 to £88   SERVICE:net prices, card slips closed   CARDS:Amex, Delta, Diners, MasterCard, Switch, Visa   DETAILS:Grill Room 81 seats, Oriental 41 seats. Private parties: Grill Room 14 main room, Oriental 5 to 16 private rooms. Vegetarian meals. Children welcome (children's helpings Grill room). Wheelchair access (also WC). No music. Air-conditioned   ACCOMMODATION:244 rooms, all with bath/shower. TV. Phone. Room only £255 to £315. Rooms for disabled. Children welcome. High teas for children. Baby facilities. No dogs. Afternoon teas   ● Hyde Park Corner

Dordogne

map 12

5 Devonshire Road, W4 2EU   COOKING 4
TEL: (0181) 747 1836   FAX: (0181) 994 9144   COST £38–£52

Service, like every other aspect of this outpost of Gallic culture, is entirely French, albeit with competent English. The menu is classic French through and through and inspires confidence by its correct translations and brevity. There are a dozen starters and ten main dishes, plus Irish and Breton oysters, and four overwhelming temptations on the lobster menu. Only a few details would surprise French gastronomes, and reporters enthusiastically recommend such dishes as jellied monkfish and avocado terrine, fish soup, turbot fillet in a saffron sauce or pistachio- and herb-stuffed quails. A selection of vegetables might include accurately cooked French beans, carrot, aubergine, tomato and gratin dauphinoise. One reporter tried and enjoyed all the desserts in the 'assiette gourmande'. Another found that passion-fruit soufflé made a fine finish: but it wasn't quite the end, as filter coffee comes with brandy-snaps, strawberry tartlets, 'melt in the mouth truffles' and more. The £1 cover charge includes bread and a glass of Kir. Wines are exclusively French and favourably priced, starting at £9.50 for house Bergerac 'from the heart of the Dordogne'.

CHEF: Jean-Philippe Charrondière   PROPRIETOR: La Dordogne Ltd   OPEN: Mon to Fri L 12 to 2.30, 7 to 11   CLOSED: bank hols   MEALS: alc (main courses £9.50 to £12.50). Cover £1 SERVICE: 10%   CARDS: Amex, Delta, Diners, MasterCard, Switch, Visa   DETAILS: 80 seats. 20 seats outside. Private parties: 32 main room, 20 private rooms. Vegetarian meals. Children's helpings. No-smoking area. Wheelchair access (1 step; also WC). Music   ⊖ Turnham Green £5

Eagle £ 🍴

map 13

| 159 Farringdon Road, EC1R 3AL | COOKING 2 |
| TEL: (0171) 837 1353 | COST £17–£35 |

Outside it is a standard Victorian corner pub, inside a single, noisy, crowded room with a counter along one side. Behind is the charcoal grill and iron range, above a blackboard menu. The bar is where you buy drinks and order and pay for food, which is brought to the tables. These are basic, the seating even rougher, while the modern British-Iberian food is hearty stuff: 'you won't need a starter.' An inspector's rabbit casserole 'looked small compared with other dishes but was more than I could eat': roughly half a rabbit with a kitchen garden of vegetables including new potatoes, courgettes, turnips and asparagus in a light broth, all topped with Swiss chard. The short menu, which contracts through the evening, might also offer marinated rump steak sandwich, grilled sardines on a mountain of salad, and paella Valenciana; afterwards, fine Spanish cheeses with membrillo, or Portuguese pastel de nata, which gives new meaning to 'custard tart'. Decent wines are sold by the glass or bottle, and there's Flowers Original and Weston's ciders. Service is minimal but amiable.

CHEF: Tom Norrington-Davies   PROPRIETOR: Michael Belben   OPEN: all week L 12.30 to 2.30 (3.30 Sat, 4 Sun), Mon to Sat D 6.30 to 10.30   MEALS: alc (main courses £4 to £11)   SERVICE: not inc   CARDS: none   DETAILS: 60 seats. 24 seats outside. Children welcome. Music ⊖ Farringdon

---

L'Escargot

map 15

| 48 Greek Street, W1V 5LQ | COOKING 6 |
| TEL: (0171) 437 6828/2679   FAX: (0171) 437 0790 | COST £30–£72 |

This has been a restaurant since the 1920s, and has gone through a fair few stages of evolution over the years, most of them seemingly in the last decade. Yet another refurbishment has brought new upholstery to the ground-floor restaurant, as well as the sleek, chic upstairs Picasso room, and highlights of the owner's private art collection are now on permanent display. There is surely no other dining establishment in the country adorned by Picasso, Chagall, Miró, Hockney, Warhol, Léger and Matisse.

Billy Reid is producing some highly assured cooking these days, his signature starter a feuilleté of escargots with button onions, bacon lardons and chewy morels. A pair who ate downstairs enjoyed Scottish langoustines with Oscietra caviare, Little Gem lettuce and lemon cream sauce, and a bowl of earthy celeriac soup enriched with truffle oil. Breast of pheasant sauced with tomato and tarragon was a good winter main course, and Goosnargh duck comes in for praise, perhaps served with pommes fondant and mulled shallots. If you haven't started with the eponymous snails, they may well turn up with skate in a sauce diable. Desserts include an object-lesson lemon tart, fresh fruits set in champagne jelly, and iced caramel and apricot crumble. Attentive and efficient service is generally appreciated. Italy and the New World are the main supports for reams of classical French wines that offer a collector's tour of the main regions at in-your-dreams prices. House Vin de Pays d'Oc is £13.

CHEF: Billy Reid PROPRIETOR: Jimmy Lahoud OPEN: Mon to Fri L 12.15 to 2.15, Tue to Sat D 7 to 11 CLOSED: 25 Dec, bank hol L, Aug (Picasso Room) MEALS: alc (main courses ground-floor £13 to £16). Set L and pre-threatre D ground-floor £14.95 (2 courses) to £17.95, Set L Picasso Room £27.50 to £42, Set D Picasso Room £42 SERVICE: ground-floor 12½% (optional); Picasso Room 15% (optional); card slips closed CARDS: Amex, Delta, Diners, MasterCard, Switch, Visa DETAILS: ground-floor 100 seats, Picasso Room 35. Private parties: 20 main room, 24 to 60 private rooms. Vegetarian meals. Children welcome. No cigars/pipes in dining-rooms. Wheelchair access (3 steps; also men's WC). Music. Air-conditioned
⊖ Leicester Square, Tottenham Court Road

L'Estaminet

map 15

14 Garrick Street, WC2E 9BJ
TEL: (0171) 379 1432 FAX: (0171) 379 1530

COOKING 1
COST £31–£58

Candlelit at dinner, relaxed and 'friendly as ever', L'Estaminet deals largely in French bourgeois cooking: coq au vin, snails in puff pastry with garlic butter, Lyonnais sausage with potato salad. One meal began with a mussel-rich, saffron, potato and leek soup, with second and even third helpings possible from the generous tureen, followed by lamb cutlets with green beans and French fries. The pre-theatre set meal is 'probably the best value in theatre-land', and one visitor discovered that you can return for pudding afterwards, adding ruefully 'wish we'd known that'. Pastry dishes are appreciated, from light and fluffy quiche, to chocolate or glazed strawberry tartlet, and the cheese trolley is a big one. Service is 'superb' at the best of times (making the service charge, for once, well-earned) but comes in for special praise before curtain-up, being 'well-timed, without the slightest hint of rush'. House wine is £9.50.

CHEF: Philippe Tamet PROPRIETOR: Christian Bellone OPEN: Mon to Sat 12 to 2.30 (2 Sat), 5.45 to 11 CLOSED: 24 to 26 Dec, Easter, bank hols MEALS: alc (main courses £9 to £18). Pre-theatre D (until 7.30pm) £10.99 SERVICE: 12.5%, card slips closed CARDS: Amex, Delta, MasterCard, Switch, Visa DETAILS: 50 seats. Private parties: 20 private room. Children welcome. No pipes in dining-room. Wheelchair access (1 step; not WC) Music ⊖ Leicester Square

Euphorium

map 13

203 Upper Street, N1 1RQ
TEL: (0171) 704 6909 FAX: (0171) 226 0241

COOKING 2
COST £28–£51

As modern as the next millennium, this stylish, bright place has skylights, and windows overlooking a garden at the back. Zingy orange and pink colours ensure that, despite metallic tables, austerity is avoided. 'Natural and friendly' service is sometimes extremely relaxed, which helps to make it a 'fun place'. Peter Arrowsmith's concisely worded menus include a few old English ideas and the odd Pacific ingredient to vary the Mediterranean diet, although flavours are sometimes muted. Desserts are less exciting than starters and main dishes such as gazpacho, 'meaty terrine', or vegetable moussaka. Tuna is impeccably grilled, though an accompanying salsa hardly justified the prefix 'red hot' on the menu. A two-course lunch, bar menus, 'kids' menu' and Sunday brunch offer a wide choice. Ten of the twenty-five varied wines are under £20; house red French and white Argentinian are £10.50.

CHEF: Peter Arrowsmith   PROPRIETOR: Marwan Badran   OPEN: all week L 12.30 to 2.30 (12 to 3.30 Sun), Mon to Sat D 6 to 10.30   CLOSED: bank hols   MEALS: alc (main courses £10.50 to £17.50). Set L £13.50 (2 courses) to £18.50. Bar menu available   SERVICE: 12.5% (optional), card slips closed   CARDS: Amex, Delta, MasterCard, Switch, Visa   DETAILS: 85 seats. Private parties: 100 main room, 40 private room. Vegetarian meals. Children's helpings. Wheelchair access (also WC). No music. Air-conditioned   ⊖ Highbury & Islington, Angel

---

Fifth Floor 🍾
map 14

Harvey Nichols, 109-125 Knightsbridge, SW1X 7RJ   COOKING 5
TEL: (0171) 235 5250   FAX: (0171) 823 2207   COST £31–£93

On current trends, Harvey Nichols looks set to become a restaurant complex with a department-store attached. As well as the hustle-bustle of the top-floor Café, there is now a basement bar and eatery, the Foundation (see entry). This, however, is the flagship, a long, civilised and plushly upholstered room, screened off from the adjacent food hall and guarded by what, in another milieu, might be called bouncers. It is popular: one pair could only look longingly towards the bar as they were escorted hurriedly through, all thought of enjoying a pre-dinner cocktail banished by the five-deep crush.

First-class olives stir up the appetite for cooking that walks the line between European rustic and classic brasserie style. Baltic herrings with creamed eggs, spring onions, grilled speck and caraway bread might briskly open a meal, or you may opt to wait 20 minutes for a short-crusted cep and Pecorino tart. Steak tartare, a dish that is quietly becoming fashionable again, may be taken as starter or main, and a pair of lamb-lovers might consider a devilled rack (for two) with sauce Choron. Simplicity pays dividends in lunchtime dishes such as grilled plaice with a coriander and lemon sauce, although labour-intensive complexity is also brought off well in a dessert of chocolate teardrop filled with rich chocolate mousse, served with a chocolate cup of orange ice-cream.

Staff have been trained in the cool and efficient school, rather than the warm and familiar, but that – to many – is how it should be in a place like this. The excellent wine list opens with 40 *grand marque* champagnes, perhaps as a nod to 'ladies who lunch', then moves on to some seriously good clarets and burgundies. Italy, Spain and California all make notable contributions, and there is good-value, quality drinking to be found. House French is £12.50. CELLARMAN'S CHOICE: Côtes du Rhône, Coudoulet de Beaucastel 1995, Ch. de Beaucastel, £25; Neil Ellis Pinotage 1996, Stellenbosch, South Africa, £17.50.

CHEF: Henry Harris   PROPRIETOR: Harvey Nichols & Co Ltd   OPEN: all week L 12 to 3 (3.30 Sat and Sun), Mon to Sat D 6.30 to 11.30   MEALS: alc (main courses £13 to £36.50). Set L £19.50 (2 courses) to £23.50   SERVICE: 12.5% (optional), card slips closed   CARDS: Amex, Delta, Diners, MasterCard, Switch, Visa   DETAILS: 120 seats. Private parties: 120 main room. Vegetarian meals. Children welcome. No pipes in dining-room. Wheelchair access (also WC). No music. Air-conditioned   ⊖ Knightsbridge

Fina Estampa

NEW ENTRY   map 13

150–152 Tooley Street, SE1 2TU   COOKING 4
TEL/FAX: (0171) 403 1342   COST £26–£50

This Peruvian restaurant evolved from a basic, chips-with-everything café, which also offered odd dishes reflecting the chef's origin. Bianca Jones cooks as she learned in her family kitchen, while Richard Jones is front-of-house. Colourful blankets, elaborate mirrors and gold and silver ornaments against a cheerful green background lend a more homely and relaxed feel to the interior than its 100-seat capacity might suggest; a small bar, grand piano, and flowers add to the mood.

Potatoes are a favoured Peruvian ingredient, showing up in starters such as causa rellena, composed mainly of mashed, lime-dressed potato salad with chopped tuna and avocado; and papa a la huancaina, resembling Swiss raclette with new potatoes in a subtle sauce of yellow peppers. Sweet potato makes a colourful, soothing garnish for tangy ceviche of white fish, with or without shellfish. Or there might be lamb seco: 'superb mutton' in a rich dark sauce with haricot beans. Desserts include a 'tarte Tatin cheesecake', which one reporter thought better than it sounds. Courteous Peruvian waiters, smart in semi-formal, quasi-Spanish black jackets, enjoy their work and guide you through the unfamiliar menu. The short wine list is mostly South American, with house wines £8.50.

CHEF: Bianca Jones   PROPRIETORS: Richard and Bianca Jones   OPEN: all week 12 to 2.30, 6.30 to 10.30   CLOSED: D 24 Dec to 27 Dec, bank hols   MEALS: alc (main courses £8 to £15) SERVICE: 10% (optional), card slips closed   CARDS: Amex, Delta, Diners, MasterCard, Switch, Visa   DETAILS: 100 seats. Private parties: 60 main room, 50 and 60 private rooms. Children's helpings. Music   ⊖ London Bridge

Fire Station £

map 13

150 Waterloo Road, SE1 8SB   COOKING 1
TEL: (0171) 620 2226   FAX: (0171) 633 9161   COST £24–£37

Arriving at Waterloo station, head for Exit 2, descend the steps, take a sharp right and there's the Fire Station. You can't miss it because it looks like, well, a fire station. The space has been intelligently exploited to provide a bar and snacking area at the front with serious eating to the rear. Daily-changing menus are chalked on a board, but regular items include a Caesar salad that is judged an object-lesson, not least for the 'civilised size of the croûtons'. Grilled sardines with chopped egg, tapénade and beetroot makes a mammoth starter, and main courses may run to veal saltimbocca with risotto milanese, peppered tuna with niçoise garnishes, or grilled smoked haddock with chickpea pancake and spiced yoghurt. Some find the service 'erratic' when the place is full, which it invariably is, but one reader found it so well drilled as to constitute some kind of training model. The shortish wine list is serviceable rather than distinguished, but prices are right, opening at £8.95 for house French.

All entries, including Round-ups, are fully indexed at the back of the Guide.

CHEF: Paul Bloxham   PROPRIETOR: Regent Inns plc   OPEN: all week L 12.30 to 2.30 (3.30 Sun), Mon to Sat D 5.30 to 11   CLOSED: 1 week Christmas, bank hols   MEALS: alc (main courses £9.50 to £12). Set L Mon to Sat and Set D before 8 £9.95 (2 courses)   SERVICE: not inc; 10% for parties of 5 or more   CARDS: Amex, Delta, Diners, MasterCard, Switch, Visa   DETAILS: 100 seats. Private parties: 90 main room. Vegetarian meals. Children welcome. Wheelchair access (not WC). Music. Air-conditioned   ⊖ Waterloo

First Floor

186 Portobello Road, W11 1LA

TEL: (0171) 243 0072   FAX: (0171) 221 9440

map 13

COOKING 5
COST £22–£48

On the first floor of a pub in the fruit and veg part of Portobello, this upstairs dining-room has its 'posh touches' – crisp white linen tablecloths, chiffon at the windows, a chandelier – as well as slapdash paintwork, lino floor and Victorian-style chairs. It is all 'sufficiently unusual to take a little getting used to', though the overall feel is of light and space. Paul Casey, who took over the stoves in March 1998, echoes this eccentricity in the kitchen, where refried mushrooms are paired with truffled hummus, tandoori chicken meets seared foie gras and coriander relish, and ostrich dim-sum comes with beetroot.

Unsurprisingly, some combinations gel more than others: a starter salad of pan-fried pigeon breast and butter-beans, with soy sauce and smoked bacon dressing, for example, has worked better than scallops with tapénade, while kangaroo and horseradish dim-sum was 'a delicious first' for one, and another appreciated 'thick, rich' lobster ravioli. Precision cooking of main-course cod with a light chilli polenta has been commended, and ribeye steak comes with a stack of fat chips and garlic butter. Portions can be large. To finish, white chocolate and yoghurt torte is flavoured with lemon grass and star anise, while warm chocolate mousse on ginger cake is just the right side of too rich'. Bread comes in for unanimous praise. Service is generally friendly. The wine list sports commendable organic inclusions and global choice, with prices from £9.95. Eight wines are sold by the glass from £3.

CHEF: Paul Casey   PROPRIETOR: Chancery Inns Ltd.   OPEN: Mon to Fri 12 to 3.30, 7.30 to 11, Sat 11 to 4, 7.30 to 11, Sun 11 to 4, 7 to 10   CLOSED: 25 and 26 Dec   MEALS: alc (main courses L £7 to £9, D £10 to £15.50). Set L £9.95 (2 courses) to £12.95, Set D £17.95 to £25.95   SERVICE: 12.5% (optional), card slips closed   CARDS: Amex, Delta, Diners, MasterCard, Switch, Visa   DETAILS: 120 seats. Private parties: 75 main room, 30 and 45 private rooms. Vegetarian meals. Children welcome. No cigars/pipes in dining-room. Music   ⊖ Notting Hill Gate, Ladbroke Grove   £5

Foundation

NEW ENTRY   map 14

Lower Ground Floor, Harvey Nichols,
109–125 Knightsbridge, SW1 7RJ

TEL: (0171) 201 8000   FAX: (0171) 201 8080

COOKING 3
COST £26–£46

As the name suggests, this is the basement restaurant of Harvey Nichols, entered from the east side of the building on Seville Street. It's a dramatic, cavernous space with nightclub lighting, enormous mirrors, big jolly abstracts and a wall of cascading water behind the 30-foot bar; the impression of somewhere hot and happening for the Knightsbridge beau monde to congregate is emphasised by music playing at not much below HMV superstore level. Simon Barnett's menu, which appears entombed in a long, narrow Perspex slab, mines the eclectic seam for all it's worth. A bowl of linguine with mussels and clams offers spanking-fresh seafood, vividly flavoured with black olives and plentiful lemon juice. Breast of guinea-fowl with chickpeas, spinach and chorizo is full of appetising pungency, although lacking its advertised romesco sauce at inspection. Vitello tonnato, sea bass with baby fennel, and salt-cod with truffled green beans and rocket keep the Mediterranean ship afloat, while puddings bring us back home with razor-sharp orange and passion-fruit jelly and sweet cream, caramel ripple cheesecake, and treacle tart. Service can seem a little dazed, perhaps by the ambient noise. A very short wine list doesn't begin to do justice to the top-floor wine department. Cocktails may be more to the point, but own-brand house French is £12.50.

CHEF: Simon Barnett   PROPRIETOR: Harvey Nichols   OPEN: all week L 12 to 3.30, Mon to Sat D 6.30 to 11   CLOSED: 25 Dec, bank hol D   MEALS: alc (main courses £9.50 to £14). Set L Mon to Fri and Sun £13.50 (2 courses) to £16.50, Set D £15 (2 courses) to £19.50   SERVICE: 12.5% (optional), card slips closed   CARDS: Amex, Delta, Diners, MasterCard, Switch, Visa   DETAILS: 110 seats. Private parties: 200 main room. Vegetarian meals. Children welcome. No smoking in 1 dining-room. Music. Air-conditioned   ⊖ Knightsbridge

Four Seasons £ |NEW ENTRY| map 13

84 Queensway, W2 3RL   COOKING 2
TEL: (0171) 229 4320   COST £23–£46

It is not the basic décor that draws the crowds, and service is not always the friendliest, but roast duck, crispy roast pork, and char siu pork fillet were 'the best I have eaten in London', according to an experienced inspector. The long main menu offers few surprises, although it has delivered deep-fried softshell crab, moist inside, the flavour 'just right'. The advice is to stick to either roast meats, for those on a budget, or splash out on specials, which offer around 20 items, many not found in other London Chinese restaurants, such as duck's feet with sea cucumber. Less esoteric options might include stir-fried baby octopus with XO sauce, mange-tout and spring onion with 'a lovely crunch in the mouth'. In braised bean curd, king prawns and spicy sauce the 'spicy touch added to the pleasure of lovely textures and flavours', and braised winter melon with dried scallops shows a 'delicate touch'. House wine is £8.50.

CHEF: M.L. Li   PROPRIETOR: Four Seasons Chinese Restaurant   OPEN: all week; 12 to 11.30 (11 Sun and bank hols)   CLOSED: 24 to 26 Dec   MEALS: alc (main courses £5 to £8.50). Set L and D £10.50 to £16 (minimum 2)   SERVICE: 12.5%, card slips closed   CARDS: Amex, Delta, MasterCard, Switch, Visa   DETAILS: 70 seats. Children welcome. Music. Air-conditioned   ⊖ Bayswater

French House Dining Room   map 15

49 Dean Street, W1V 5HL   COOKING 4
TEL: (0171) 437 2477   FAX: (0171) 287 9109   COST £25–£47

The dining-room above the pub of the same name is a compact – some might say cramped – wood-panelled space where, in an atmosphere of cheery informality, some of the least pretentious food in Soho is being served. It is a place where unusual cuts of meat and offal are treated as matter-of-fact, and where menu descriptions are terse, allowing for some element of surprise when the food arrives. An inspection turned up properly served bone marrow with pick and teaspoon, a salad of flat parsley and capers, and toasted ciabatta. Grilled ox tongue was lightly charred and tender, a good portion served on buttery carrot mash. Fish is usually limited to one choice, perhaps grilled mackerel with beetroot, or something as straightforward as baked Dover sole with lemon butter, and there is always a vegetarian option. The odd problem (food arriving at lower-than-expected temperature) doesn't ultimately detract from what is evidently popular and highly capable cooking. Simple but commendable puddings have included sharply flavoured almond cream with cinnamon-stewed dried fruits, and rhubarb and ginger ice-cream. One or two staff at each sitting cope competently with numbers, and an almost entirely French wine list deals quite as efficiently with the food. Prices start at £9.95

CHEF: Margot Henderson   PROPRIETORS: Margot Henderson and Melanie Arnold   OPEN: Mon to Sat 12 to 3, 6 to 11.15   CLOSED: 25 Dec to 1 Jan, bank hols   MEALS: alc (main courses £8.50 to £15.50)   SERVICE: not inc   CARDS: Amex, Delta, Diners, MasterCard, Switch, Visa   DETAILS: 30 seats. Private parties: 30 main room. Vegetarian meals. Children welcome. No music
⊖ Leicester Square

Fung Shing   map 15

15 Lisle Street, WC2H 7BE   COOKING 4
TEL: (0171) 437 1539   FAX: (0171) 734 0284   COST £29–£69

It may strike some people as Westernised in mood and atmosphere, but Fung Shing's culinary heart remains in the authentic world of high-quality Cantonese cuisine. Fine ingredients and assured technique are its strengths. Judging by reports, it pays to focus on the list of chef's specials, which show the kitchen in its best light: a robust dish of tender ostrich with yellow bean sauce, and exemplary crispy eel with chillies were two high points from one seriously exploratory meal that also included shredded chicken with jellyfish, and deep-fried frogs' legs with chilli and garlic. 'We had a laugh as it seemed we had picked our way through an entire zoo,' concluded the recipient.

Elsewhere, in more familiar territory, the kitchen is still capable of satisfying those who know their way around the menu: sizzling spiced prawns have been carefully cooked, a hotpot of roast duck with yams had 'delightfully rich cooking juices', and pak choi greens were 'capably done', according to one correspondent. A few quibbles (cold rice and bowls, for example) colour some reports, but this is still a cut above most of the competition in Soho Chinatown. Service, one regular tells us, is variable 'depending on the mood of the staff' and there is a two-hour time limit on tables. The owners are at pains to point out that they take wine 'very seriously', deploying some reputable bottles on their mainly European list. House French is £12.

CHEF: T.X. Ly   PROPRIETOR: Forum Restaurant Ltd   OPEN: all week 12 to 11.15   CLOSED: 24 to 26 Dec   MEALS: alc (main courses £9.50 to £16). Set L £16 (2 courses), Set D £16 (2 courses) to £30. BYO £5   SERVICE: 10%, card slips closed   CARDS: Amex, Delta, Diners, MasterCard, Switch, Visa   DETAILS: 120 seats. Private parties: 50 main room, 24 and 50 private rooms. Vegetarian meals. Children welcome. Music. Air-conditioned   ⊖ Leicester Square

Le Gavroche ▼

map 15

43 Upper Brook Street, W1Y 1PF
TEL: (0171) 408 0881 and 499 1826
FAX: (0171) 491 4387 and 409 0939

COOKING 7
COST £40–£130

Enter through a discreet door, pause for a drink in the bar, then be escorted downstairs. Nothing disturbs the tranquility, perhaps solemnity, of the dining-room, and clientele tend to be well off, elderly, on business, or all three, which helps to account for the 'private Mayfair club' feel. Beneath the unchanging and stately surface lies cooking that moves gently with the times. Luxuries remain the foundation, and traditional treatments are in the ascendant – lobster mousse with caviare and a champagne butter sauce, oysters and scallops with black truffles, beef with ceps – but there are also departures such as langoustine hotpot with couscous and preserved lemon, a sign that the kitchen is aware of what the rest of the world is up to.

A certain dexterity is typical, as when shelled langoustines and artichoke hearts, in an intensely flavoured creamy tomato soup, are topped with the empty shells filled with langoustine mousse. Given the level of skill, and the reliability of established ideas, a feeling of confidence underlies such harmonious dishes as pink pigeon breasts on a bed of caramelised onion, on top of rosemary risotto, decked about with celeriac crisps. English menu translations are welcome, though à la carte prices are difficult to justify: nearly £20 for a soufflé, famous as the suissesse version is; and £70 for a chicken for two, even though it is from Bresse and served with truffles. No doubt it is gentlemanly concern for the weaker sex that shields ladies from the sight of these prices on their menu. The set lunch, however, which includes nibbles, water, a half-bottle of wine per head, coffee and petit fours, is a good deal. Service is included, by the way, but credit card slips are left open.

Like the cheeseboard, desserts are very French, along the lines of apricot and Cointreau soufflé, fruit-filled biscuity pastries, or a warm sponge with prune and armagnac ice-cream. Largely French staff are formally dressed, and have terms like 'efficient' and 'impeccable' applied to them. 'The sommelier, when he came to take our wine order, had already memorised our food order and had constructive comments on the wine choice.', which may come as a relief to those cowed by the long lines of aristocratic French bottles. Twenty-three vintages of Latour, thirteen of Pétrus, thirty different Domaine de la Romanée-Contis. . . . Prices are not for the faint-hearted either, although a handful of low-born bins can be found under £20. CELLARMAN'S CHOICE: Chablis St-Martin 'Cuvée Albert Roux' 1994, Dom. Laroche, £40; Pomerol, Ch. La Croix 1992, £44.

CHEF: Michel Roux   PROPRIETOR: Le Gavroche Ltd   OPEN: Mon to Fri 12 to 2, 7 to 11   CLOSED: bank hols, 25 Dec, 1 Jan   MEALS: alc (main courses £27 to £36.50). Set L £40 (inc half-bottle wine), Set L and D £80 (menu exceptionel for whole table only)   SERVICE: net prices   CARDS: Amex, Delta, Diners, MasterCard, Switch, Visa   DETAILS: 60 seats. Private parties: 80 main room, 20 private room. Children welcome. Jacket and tie. No cigars/pipes in dining-room. Occasional music. Air-conditioned   ⊖ Marble Arch

CELLARMAN'S CHOICE: *Wines recommended by the restaurateur, normally more expensive than house wine.*

Gay Hussar

map 15

2 Greek Street, W1V 6NB
TEL: (0171) 437 0973   FAX: (0171) 437 4631

COOKING 3
COST £28–£52

'Your entry in the 1992 *Guide* is still accurate,' began one reporter, sadly adrift from London's most happening decade, but making the point that the Hussar rides on impervious and regardless. Laszlo Holecz has been here since 1977, and in all that time hasn't shown much inclination to embrace anything outside the culinary tradition of his native Hungary. And why should he, when it yields pressed boar's head, chilled wild-cherry soup, and cold pike with beetroot sauce and pickled cucumber among the starters? One reporter recommended the place for 'trencherman' portions, another pointed to 'lots of choice' on the menu: fish terrine with cucumber salad, roast duck with red cabbage and apple sauce, chicken paprika with egg dumplings, and calf's liver have all been approved by reporters. Consider sweet cheese pancakes to finish, or raspberry and chocolate gâteau. Service is 'swift and smilingly efficient', and the proferred wine list must be one of the shortest outside a teetotallers' convention. However a 'Connoisseurs' List' containing the full selection can be requested. House Hungarian Cabernet Sauvignon and Traminer are £10.50.

CHEF: Laslo Holecz   PROPRIETOR: Restaurant Partnership Plc   OPEN: Mon to Sat 12.15 to 2.30, 5.30 to 10.45   CLOSED: bank hols   MEALS: alc (main courses £10.50 to £16). Set L £17.50   SERVICE: 12.5% (optional), card slips closed   CARDS: Amex, Delta, Diners, MasterCard, Switch, Visa   DETAILS: 70 seats. Private parties: 12 main room, 12 and 23 private rooms. Vegetarian meals. Children's helpings. Wheelchair access (1 step; not WC). No music. Air-conditioned
⊖ Tottenham Court Road   (£5)

Globe

NEW ENTRY   map 13

100 Avenue Road, NW3 3HF
TEL: (0171) 722 7200   FAX: (0171) 722 7676
EMAIL: globerella@aol.com

COOKING 3
COST £20–£35

Globe opened in late 1997 next to Swiss Cottage tube station in an office-block site that had previously played host only to fast-food eating. It is an L-shaped room with painted glass panes along one side, where vibrant blue and yellow are the colours, the floor is tiled in red, and lighting is bright. Judging by the pictures, soft funk music and the enormous helpings, it is 'aimed at the young at heart'. The name of the place reflects its culinary orientation. Expect anything. A zesty soup of sweet potato and dhal is swirled with basil and red pepper oils and sprinkled with Parmesan and chopped spring onions, a cheerfully chaotic but improbably subtle melange. Chargrilled salmon on a crisply crusty tortilla cake with a zingy salsa of black beans and corn is well executed, while red snapper – also charred – comes with Japanese noodles and bean-shoot stir-fry. Fish is accorded slightly greater prominence than meat, which may be a simple choice between chicken breast or beef fillet. Finish with black cherry and amaretti tart with pear sorbet and appealingly acid blackcurrant sauce, or one of the retro ice-cream concoctions such as golden honeycomb and flaky chocolate vanilla. Service is by friendly young staff. A brisk rummage through the global wine cellar turns up some good bottles, nearly all below £20. Chilean white and French red house wines are £9.50.

CHEF: Terry Williamson   PROPRIETOR: Neil Armishaw   OPEN: Mon to Fri and Sun L 12 (11.30 Sun) to 3, all week D 6 to 11 (7 to 10 Sun)   MEALS: alc D (main courses £9.50 to £11.50). Set L Mon to Fri £11.50 (2 courses) to £13.50 inc wine, Set brunch Sun £12.50   SERVICE: not inc CARDS: Amex, Delta, MasterCard, Switch, Visa   DETAILS: 65 seats. Private parties: 80 main room, 25 private room. Vegetarian meals. Children's helpings. No cigars/pipes in dining-room. Wheelchair access (not WC). Music. Air-conditioned   ⊖ Swiss Cottage

Golden Dragon £

map 15

28–29 Gerrard Street, W1V 7LP   COOKING 3
TEL/FAX: (0171) 734 1073   COST £25–£46

Subtle wall-papers and a 'classic' mural make this bright, always bustling eating-hall feel less frantic than some. The sheer range and variety of dim-sum is what marks this place out from most of the competition: 'meaty, sweet and tender' deep-fried squid, 'heavenly' steamed scallop dumplings, 'seductively slippery' char siu cheung fun, and 'succulent' steamed spare ribs with 'power-fully garlicky juices tinged with red chilli'. The high proportion of Chinese customers in the evening suggests that the cooking of the full Cantonese menu is now up to the same standard. Capital spare ribs with a 'rich, but not over-sweet' honey glaze has been a happy choice, and subtly marinated sliced duck, served warm with a dipping sauce of chopped garlic in white vinegar was considered an improvement on more common ducks. 'Succulent' steamed eel with black-bean sauce is 'less hot and strong than usual', so the eel's fine flavour comes through. One reporter appreciated 'helpful advice from a polite, smiling waiter' though another found service 'cool, surly and uncommunicative'. The wine list is above the local standard, and teas are excellent; po li and 'fragrantly flavoursome' jasmine are recommended. House wine is £8.50.

CHEF: Yuk Cheung Man   PROPRIETORS: Charlie Tsui and Lawrence Cheng   OPEN: all week 12 (11 Sun) to 11.45   CLOSED: 25 Dec   MEALS: alc (main courses £6 to £18). Set L and D £10.50 to £20 (minimum 2)   SERVICE: 10%   CARDS: Amex, Delta, Diners, MasterCard, Switch, Visa DETAILS: 300 seats. Private parties: 380 main room, 30 private room. Vegetarian meals. Children welcome. Music. Air-conditioned   ⊖ Leicester Square

Gourmet Garden £

map 12

59 Watford Way, NW4 3AX   COOKING 1
TEL: (0181) 202 9639   COST £17–£47

Locals, and many from various Asian countries, tend to meet in this Chinese-Malaysian-Singaporean restaurant near Hendon Central Station. The long menu ventures far from the Cantonese repertoire with Singaporean kweh pi tee (crispy pastry cups filled with prawn and vegetable) and laksa, the famous seafood soup. Even more authentic, in its unrefined heartiness, is fried crab Singapore-style with a strong, sweet chilli, garlic and tomato sauce. An inspector was happiest with Hainanese chicken rice from the menu's Malaysian-Singaporean corner, a 'plate-meal' comprising deep-flavoured chicken with rice cooked in its stock, the stock itself accompanying as a soup. A fine Cantonese dish from 'Chef's Recommendations' is braised quail and 'winter pork' (wind-dried pork sausage), served in a clay pot with black mushrooms in rich gravy. Kong poh frogs' legs jump with flavour. Service can be quite friendly when not too pushed. Wines are very basic (house French is £7.50), so drink oolong tea, or tie kuan yim, elegant yet strong enough to match the food.

CHEF: Kia Lian Tan PROPRIETORS: Kia Lian and Annie Tan OPEN: Wed to Mon 12 to 2.15 (2.45 Sun), 6 to 11.15 (10.45 Sun) CLOSED: Christmas MEALS: alc (main courses £5 to £12). Set L and D £10.80 to £14.80 (all minimum 2) SERVICE: not inc CARDS: Amex, Delta, MasterCard, Switch, Visa DETAILS: 70 seats. Private parties: 75 main room. Vegetarian meals. Children's helpings. No-smoking area. Wheelchair access (not WC). Music. Air-conditioned ⊖ Hendon Central

Granita
map 13

127 Upper Street, N1 1QP   COOKING 4
TEL: (0171) 226 3222   FAX: (0171) 226 4833   COST £22–£42

Solid washes of vividly contrasting primary colours provide an effective backdrop for equally colourful dishes in this Islington landmark, still considered 'textbook trendy' after six years. The food is served at wobbly tables with minimal fuss and no fancy napery, by smart, friendly and sometimes antipodean staff. Impeccably '90s ingredients (considered 'first class') embrace chickpeas, tamarind, pomegranates, melted fontina, grilled focaccia, coconut shrimp, butter-beans, pickled plums, split peas, flat bread, roasted tomato and chilli flakes.

Cooking is careful and generally well judged, and although flavours can 'speak in hushed tones' (unlike the customers), they do so in several languages, from lamb kibbeh with yoghurt and tahini, to Thai mackerel salad with chilli, ginger, lemon grass and coriander, or wild mushroom lasagne with truffle oil and Parmesan. Chargrilling works well, whether applied to squid with chickpeas and feta cheese, to crisp, savoury chicken served with spicy lentils, or to the aubergine that goes into 'splendidly smoky' baba ghanoush. Desserts might include manchego with garrotxa and oatcakes, or a cookie plate. A modern list of around 25 wines delivers a good range of flavours at fair prices.

CHEF: Ahmed Kharshoum PROPRIETORS: Ahmed Kharshoum and Vikki Leffman OPEN: Wed to Sun L 12.30 to 2.30, Tue to Sun D 6.30 to 10.30 (10 Sun) CLOSED: 10 days Christmas, 1 week Easter, 2 weeks Aug MEALS: alc D (main courses £10 to £13). Set L £11.50 (2 courses) to £13.50, Set Sun D £12.50 (2 courses) to £14.50 SERVICE: not inc CARDS: MasterCard, Visa DETAILS: 70 seats. Private parties: 65 main room. Vegetarian meals. Children welcome. No cigars/pipes in dining-room. Wheelchair access (not WC). No music. Air-conditioned ⊖ Angel, Highbury & Islington

Greenhouse
map 15

27A Hays Mews, W1X 7RJ   COOKING 6
TEL: (0171) 499 3331/3314   FAX: (0171) 449 5368   COST £31–£65

At the base of a block of flats, the Greenhouse is set back from the road in a 'hidden part' of Mayfair. The cream 'faux-antique' restaurant is a pleasant though sedate room dominated by large ceiling fans, manicured miniature trees and prints of vegetables and flowers. With lots of elbow room and plush furnishings, it is geared to 'mature, affluent customers', who will find a resolutely British slant to the menu, not least among lunchtime specials: Tuesdays bring a choice of Lancashire cheese and onion tart, or boiled ham with butter-beans. But alongside smoked haddock fish-cakes, and lemon sole with brown shrimps, runs a distinctly Mediterranean strand in the form of pea risotto with girolles and summer truffles, or artichoke and goats'-cheese tart. Variations on traditional ideas, meanwhile, might include jellied bacon and parsley with grated mustardy celeriac.

Simply conceived dishes have worked well: a cake of white Dorset crabmeat, for example, topped by avocado mousse and skirted by dressed tomato concassé, proved a 'harmonious combination'. 'Fine ingredients, well matched and perfectly cooked' also spotlight the skilled cooking in main courses such as roast suckling pig with sage crumbs; chargrilled calf's liver with bacon; and wild duck, cooked pink as requested, with chicory, orange and green peppercorns.

With the barest of nods across the Channel to 'wonderfully transparent' champagne jelly with a bright citrus and passion-fruit accompaniment, desserts are generally in the traditional mould of rhubarb crumble, or bread-and-butter pudding. Service has veered from muddled to 'terrific'. A short wine list covers both France and the New World and includes six half-bottles; David Levin's own Loire Sauvignon or Gamay is the house wine at £12.

CHEF: Graham Grafton   PROPRIETORS: David Levin   OPEN: Sun to Fri L12 to 2.30 (3 Sun), 6.30 to 11 (10 Sun)   CLOSED: 25 and 26 Dec, bank hols   MEALS: alc (main courses £11.50 to £19.50). Set L £19.50 (2 courses), Set L Sun £19.50. Cover £1   SERVICE: not inc; 12½% for parties of 8 or more   CARDS: Amex, Delta, Diners, MasterCard, Switch, Visa   DETAILS: 100 seats. Private parties: 100 main room. Vegetarian meals. Children's helpings. No pipes in dining-room. Wheelchair access (1 step; not WC). No music. Air-conditioned   ⊖ Green Park

The Green Olive
map 13

5 Warwick Place, W9 2PX   COOKING 3
TEL: (0171) 289 2469   FAX: (0171) 289 4178   COST £26–£45

'An ideal neighbourhood restaurant where one feels at ease, and eats well at moderate prices,' concluded one visitor to this stylish rustic Italian. Walls are painted cream, except for one left in natural brick, the floor and neatly turned chairs are wood, the tablecloths white, and service is pleasant, calm and competent. Evening menus are set-price for two to four courses with occasional supplements: for once-humble cod, roasted and served with oven-dried tomato, or squid ink polenta in saffron and mushroom sauce. Fine, fresh ingredients, and clean, light flavours are the norm, as in an 'earthy, slightly smoky' lentil soup served with shredded duck, or a dish combining grilled salmon with spinach, Sardinian couscous, and tomato and basil coulis. Portions are huge, and desserts run to 'wonderfully unsweet' coffee ice-cream, and 'exquisitely intense' passion-fruit sorbet. The wine list is predominantly Italian, with a token 'France and New World' section; house selections start at £12.50.

CHEF: Stefano Savio   PROPRIETOR: Bijan Behzadi   OPEN: Sat and Sun L 12.30 to 2.30, all week D 7 to 10.45 (10.30 Sun)   CLOSED: 25 and 26 Dec   MEALS: alc (main courses £5.50 to £11.50). Set D £20.50 (2 courses) to £26   SERVICE: not inc   CARDS: Amex, Delta, MasterCard, Switch, Visa   DETAILS: 58 seats. Private parties: 20 private room. Vegetarian meals. Children's helpings. Wheelchair access (1 step; not WC). Music. Air-conditioned   ⊖ Warwick Avenue

Gresslin's

map 13

13 Heath Street, NW3 6TP

TEL: (0171) 794 8386   FAX: (0171) 433 3282

COOKING 5

COST £21–£50

Gresslin's continues to play a key role in the culinary renaissance of Hampstead village. The long, narrow, wooden-floored restaurant a minute's walk from the tube station attracts a steady stream of loyal locals, who seem to appreciate the lack of pretention as much as Michael Gresslin's vivacious cooking. He brings whole new resonance to the term 'fusion food'; where once innovative chefs were content to combine ingredients in novel juxtapositions, it is now whole regional cuisines that are grafted together.

Results may be seen in a highly approved starter of grilled duck livers on tabbouleh with teriyaki sauce, or in a main course of buckwheat soba noodles with spring greens, beanshoots and coriander pesto. Twice-baked cheese soufflé may not seem cutting-edge, but partner it with a salad of caramelised apples and pecans and it becomes a more exciting proposition. The same degree of precision is evident in simpler dishes: a chilled summer soup of red pepper and tomato that was 'peppery and garlicky but with subtlety', or seared calf's liver with sage leaves on 'ultra-smooth' mash. Finish with stewed prune cheesecake, date and cashew nut vattalapam with cardamom sauce, or a properly brittle-topped and zesty caramelised lemon tart with raspberry coulis. Most are prepared to commend the 'very pleasant' service, though occasional inattention has been noted. The wine list spans the globe from Kent to Coonawarra within a relatively narrow compass, prices skewed a little towards the upper end. House wines, a Chilean white and a French red, are £9.95.

CHEF/PROPRIETOR: Michael Gresslin   OPEN: Tue to Sun L 12.30 to 2.45, Mon to Sat D 7 to 10.45   CLOSED: bank hols, exc 25 Dec   MEALS: alc (main courses £10.50 to £14). Set L Tue to Sat £7.95 (2 courses) to £10.95, Set L Sun £13.95 (2 courses) to £16.95   SERVICE: 12.5% (optional), card slips closed   CARDS: MasterCard, Switch, Visa   DETAILS: 56 seats. Private parties: 18 main room, 16 to 20 private room. Vegetarian meals. Children's helpings. No-smoking area. Music. Air-conditioned   ⊖ Hampstead

▲ Halkin Hotel

map 14

5 Halkin Street, SW1X 7DJ

TEL: 0171-333 1234   FAX: 0171-333 1100

EMAIL: res@halkin.co.uk

COOKING 5

COST £34–£78

'Expensive but excellent' is how one reporter summed up this Belgravian Italian. It is appreciated for its uncluttered but sharp style: marble and granite floors, well-spaced tables, sparse settings, and immaculate, uneffusive service. Stefano Cavallini's food is not meant to fill the belly but to satisfy with its interplay of flavours and textures. Classic Italian dishes are treated with respect – 'every dish sounds inviting, many intriguing' – from saffron risotto, via duck ravioli with cabbage and foie gras, to saddle of venison with polenta and blueberry sauce. Fish has varied from a simple roast fillet of sea bass with tomatoes, olives and capers, to a more challenging dish of mashed cod and roast quail with broccoli sauce.

Unusual combinations crop up elsewhere too – partridge served with pomegranate, turnip confit and celeriac purée, for example – but these are balanced by some variations on old favourites, including roast fillet of veal with Parma ham. The house style is to serve food tepid rather than hot. Desserts tend to have both a fruity and an indulgent component, as in banana gratin with rum sabayon and chocolate sorbet, or pannacotta served with poached pear in red wine. An excellent list boasts one of the largest and most aristocratic selections of Italian wines in London: shame about the prices. Anywhere that can find only five wines at £20 or under is lazy in the extreme; two of these are house wines at £17.50. At least service is included in the prices.

CHEF: Stefano Cavallini PROPRIETOR: Como Holdings OPEN: Mon to Fri L 12.30 to 2.30, all week D 7.30 to 11 (7 to 10 Sun) MEALS: alc (main courses £23 to £27). Set L £25, Set D £55. BYO £10 SERVICE: net prices, card slips closed CARDS: Amex, Delta, Diners, MasterCard, Switch, Visa DETAILS: 50 seats. Private parties: 50 main room, 30 private room. Vegetarian meals. Children welcome. No cigars/pipes in dining-room. Wheelchair access (also WC). Music. Air-conditioned ACCOMMODATION: 41 rooms, all with bath/shower. TV. Phone. Room only £255 to £550. Children welcome. Baby facilities. No dogs. Afternoon teas *(The Which? Hotel Guide)* ⊖ Hyde Park Corner

Helter Skelter £

map 12

50 Atlantic Road, Brixton, SW9 8JN
TEL/FAX: (0171) 274 8600
EMAIL: helter@dircon.co.uk

COOKING 3
COST £24–£43

'It has the beatnik feel of a vegetarian café,' a vegetarian reporter writes, adding, 'but my carnivore companions were equally well fed.' As well as 'creamy' salmon penne they could have chosen starters of mussels with oriental sweet basil and tomato, or teriyaki roast duck. A blackboard of specials supplements the menu in which Thai curries are prominent, but it was a 'rich, beautifully juicy' duck breast and its accompanying leek mash and sweet-sour red cabbage which was especially commended by one visitor. Other options might include escalope of pork with balsamic vinegar, cheese and onion polenta, or gnocchi with roasted red peppers, red onions and red pesto. Desserts run to cheesecake with hot chocolate sauce, and an original orange and pecan torta di polenta. The ambience is as informal and relaxed as one might expect from its location near Brixton market – which closes before the restaurant opens – and service is 'friendly and laid back'. The short wine list is modestly priced, starting with house South African white and French red at £9.50.

CHEFS: John Swerdlow and Patrice Buée PROPRIETORS: John and Natasha Swerdlow OPEN: Mon to Sat D only 7 to 11 (11.30 Fri and Sat) MEALS: alc (main courses £7 to £13) SERVICE: 10% (optional), card slips closed CARDS: Amex, Delta, MasterCard, Switch, Visa DETAILS: 60 seats. Private parties: 12 main room. Vegetarian meals. Wheelchair access (not WC). Music ⊖ Brixton £5

Hilaire ▼

map 14

68 Old Brompton Road, SW7 3LQ
TEL: (0171) 584 8993 FAX: (0171) 581 2949
EMAIL: bryandick@hilaire.co.uk

COOKING 7
COST £35–£60

'A lovely place to revisit,' summed up one reporter on behalf of several. Another finds the small, sunny yellow, tongue-and-groove dining-room 'one of the most reliable restaurants in London', and, although not all correspondents are agreed that we have the rating right, they seem content to return for more. The food opts to stay in familiar territory rather than go adventuring, but that doesn't stop it from being gently enterprising, in asparagus and tarragon soup, a terrine of calf's and duck liver, or pan-fried scallops with a 'sweet-and-sour' onion relish and rocket. A little native Welshness creeps into some dishes, too, perhaps in a laverbread sauce for roast sea bass, or Lady Llanover's salt-duck.

Bryan Webb is 'not of the school that skimps on ingredients', observed one who dined on breast of chicken with morels on a potato pancake, but he does pack in a lot of flavour – in a 'rich deep broth' of mussel and saffron soup that was 'fresh and fishy' – and get his timing right, as in 'perfectly cooked' turbot on pea mash with a dill and mustard sauce. Part of the menu's appeal is its willingness to weave fish, game and offal into the fabric, producing flavourful roast pheasant, John Dory on a risotto of green beans and peas, and lambs' sweetbreads, either as a 'cake' wrapped in caul, or with bacon and Jersey Royal potatoes.

Cheeses are kept in good condition, and reporters rarely seem to have either room or time for dessert; those who have report favourably on caramelised rice-pudding, and chocolate marquise with matching sorbet and caramel sauce. The fixed-price lunch, also available early and late evening, delivers 'smaller portions on smaller plates' but is considered good value. Service is smooth, friendly, attentive and efficient, although one reporter felt the point of eating here was quite lost in view of the fact that smoking is allowed. The wine list is carefully constructed, with a thoughtful balance of modern and traditional styles. Brief tasting notes are both informative and seductive: La Rosa 1992 from Verona is billed as 'a pink dessert wine, made from the Rosenmuskateller grape – ideal for lovers'. Fourteen house wines start at £12.50 and stay under £20.

CHEF: Bryan Webb   PROPRIETORS: Bryan Webb and Dick Pyle   OPEN: Mon to Fri L 12.15 to 2.30, Mon to Sat D 6.30 to 11.30   CLOSED: bank hols   MEALS: Set L and D 6.30 to 7.30 and 10 to 11.30 £18.50 (2 courses) to £23, Set D £30 to £36.50. BYO £12.50   SERVICE: not inc   CARDS: Delta, Diners, MasterCard, Switch, Visa   DETAILS: 70 seats. Private parties: 50 main room, 30 to 50 private rooms. Children welcome. No cigars/pipes in dining-room. No music. Air-conditioned
⊖ South Kensington (£5)

Ibla
	NEW ENTRY map 15

89 Marylebone High Street, W1M 3DE	COOKING 4
TEL: (0171) 224 3799 FAX: (0171) 486 1370	COST £27–£44

Ibla occupies the premises vacated by Villandry (see entry) when it moved to nearby Great Portland Street. The place still doubles as a delicatessen and has a simple, 'refreshingly down-to-earth' feel: the new owners have 'resisted the temptation to throw money at it', instead painting their inherited shell a shade of lime green and khaki at the front, and glossy maroon at the back.

The name refers to an ancient town in Sicily, but the cooking has a broader Mediterranean outlook. Maurizio Morelli, who used to work at the Halkin, brings a well-developed sense of culinary ingenuity to bear on a wide range of materials, evident in thick-cut pieces of raw sea bass 'of terrific freshness', served with sherry vinaigrette, and in interesting soups of artichoke and quail's egg, snail and mint, or kidney beans with mussels. Morelli cooks with a light touch and admirable restraint, serving a 'perfectly balanced' dish of gnocchi with salmon and asparagus; an individual spinach tart with a potato sauce 'like runny mash, but better than that sounds'; and well-timed pork escalopes wrapped around a mixture of radicchio and gorgonzola, which 'worked better than I might have imagined'. Desserts may not be quite in the same league, but they have produced a gratin of fresh fruits made with 'top-drawer' zabaglione. Bread and olive oil are free, but one reporter was charged £1 for tap water. Service is warm, smiling and attentive. Around 60 wines, mostly Italian, offer a stimulating choice, starting at £14.

CHEF: Maurizio Morelli   PROPRIETOR: Luciano Pellicano   OPEN: Mon to Sat 12 to 2.30, 7 to 10.30   CLOSED: bank hols   MEALS: Set L £13 to £16, Set D £21.50 to £24.50   SERVICE: not inc, card slips closed   CARDS: Amex, Delta, MasterCard, Switch, Visa   DETAILS: 45 seats. Private parties: 30 main room. Vegetarian meals. Children's helpings. No music. Air-conditioned
● Bond Street

Inaho £   map 13

| 4 Hereford Road, W2 4AA | COOKING 3 |
| TEL: (0171) 221 8495 | COST £16–£40 |

Those who share an inspector's nostalgia for Tokyo's 'hole-in-the-wall joints' will appreciate this 'tiny shack'. Decorated in bright blue and crowded with yellow pine tables, tight seating and Japanese oddities, it is 'cosy, noisy and good-natured', and even without nostalgia it is easy to enjoy the 'authentic Japanese food, with spanking-fresh ingredients, simply and well cooked'. The menu opens with 'delicious' hors d'oeuvres such as ohitashi (crunchy cooked spinach dressed with soy and sesame) and nasuden (aubergine coated with miso paste and soya and grilled). Specials of 'melt-in-the-mouth' toro sashimi, tuna tataki, and geso (fried octopus) are considered 'excellent' and good value. A short list of hand-rolled sushi includes highly praised anago (eel); ikura (salmon roe); and cuttlefish with natto (strong-tasting fermented soya bean paste), and the range is completed with a selection of tempura, teriyaki and variously garnished hot or cold udon or soba noodles. Set lunches are good value, and set dinner selections of teriyaki or tempura are a sound introduction for those new to Japanese food. Service is 'charming' and 'competent'. Drink saké or wine from the short list (house French is £7.50) and finish with green tea.

CHEF: Mr S. Otsuka   PROPRIETOR: Mr H. Nakamura   OPEN: Mon to Fri L 12.30 to 2.30, Mon to Sat D 7 to 11   CLOSED: 2 weeks Christmas and New Year, 1 week Aug   MEALS: alc (main courses £6.50 to £12). Set L £8 to £10, Set D £20 to £22   SERVICE: 10%   CARDS: Delta, MasterCard, Visa   DETAILS: 20 seats. Private parties: 20 main room. Vegetarian meals. No children under 10. No cigars/pipes in dining-room. Music. Air-conditioned   ● Notting Hill Gate

L'Incontro   map 14

87 Pimlico Road, SW1W 8PH	
TEL: (0171) 730 6327 and 3663	COOKING 2
FAX: (0171) 730 5062	COST £35–£80

Venetian cooking in the heart of Pimlico is what L'Incontro is about. In the watery city, it would be surrounded by kitsch glass ornament shops, whereas here the nearby businesses deal in antiques. The chic minimalism of the dining-room continues to make a striking impression on newcomers, though the cooking does less to startle. It works a classic vein that brings on gnocchetti with pesto, monkfish with artichokes, and quail with wild mushrooms and polenta. Pasta dishes are well rendered – tagliolini with crab sauce, for example – and fish dishes are cleverly handled, so that a sauce made principally from balsamic vinegar does not overpower poached sea bass. Almond tart and coffee bavarois are the kinds of desserts to expect, as well as the usual ices. Prices have provoked a grumble or two, and the list of largely Italian wines won't offer relief either. House Soave and Valpolicella are £15.75.

CHEFS: Danilo Minuzzo and S. Rettore   PROPRIETOR: I. Santin   OPEN: Mon to Fri L 12.30 to 2.30, all week D 7 to 11.30 (10.30 Sun)   CLOSED: 25 and 26 Dec, Easter Sun, L some bank hols   MEALS: alc (main courses £16 to £27.50). Set L £16.50 (2 courses) to £20.50. Cover £1.50   SERVICE: not inc   CARDS: Amex, Delta, Diners, MasterCard, Switch, Visa   DETAILS: 65 seats. Private parties: 65 main room, 35 private room. Vegetarian meals. Children's helpings. No pipes in dining-room. Wheelchair access (not WC). Music. Air-conditioned   ⊖ Sloane Square

---

▲ Inter-Continental, Le Soufflé ♟   map 14

1 Hamilton Place, W1V 0QY
TEL: (0171) 409 3131 and 318 8577
FAX: (0171) 491 0926   COOKING 5
EMAIL: london@interconti.com   COST £41–£92

A concrete block of corporate uniformity overlooking the roar of Hyde Park Corner, the Inter-Continental cannot be accused of extraneous architectural frills. Once through the spangly entrance, it begins to look a little more alluring: do a right wheel, follow the sound of tinkling ivories, and the dining-room – an earthly paradise of subdued lighting and lavish floral adornments – rises before you.

Peter Kromberg is fast approaching his quarter-century at Le Soufflé, and while the cooking has remained firmly rooted in classical principles over the years, it also keeps pace: there is a healthy-eating symbol against many dishes on the menu, as well as a vegetarian one. The wide-ranging *carte* encompasses crab and lobster feuillantine on rösti with a crustacean stock sauce of magisterial intensity, grilled salmon on new potatoes with Parma ham and béarnaise, and an intriguing dish of breast and confit leg of Gressingham duck with leek ravioli, a ragoût of Puy lentils and deep-fried onion rings.

Everything is produced with great assurance, as can be appreciated from a tasting menu that takes you from duck foie gras to the linguistically crumpled 'moëlleux noisette chocolat fudge acidulé' in six dazzling courses. The soufflés are as light, eggy and sensuous as is only fitting in a restaurant named after them, and service is polished to a high shine: 'formal, but nice with it,' thought one. The wine list treats burgundy and clarets seriously, with some exalted bins available at prices to match. More down-to-earth bottles are offered around £20 and under, starting with house French at £16. CELLARMAN'S CHOICE: Madfish Bay Semillon/Chardonnay 1996, Margaret River, W. Australia, £23; Gigondas 1994, Dom. de Santa Duc, £23.80.

CHEF: Peter Kromberg   PROPRIETOR: Inter-Continental Hotels and Resorts   OPEN: Tue to Fri and Sun L 12.30 to 3, Tue to Sat D 7 to 10.30 (11.15 Sat)   CLOSED: 2 weeks after Christmas, L Aug, bank hols   MEALS: alc (main courses £18 to £26). Set L £19.50 (2 courses) to £33.50, Set D £39 to £46   SERVICE: not inc   CARDS: Amex, Delta, Diners, MasterCard, Switch, Visa DETAILS: 80 seats. Vegetarian meals. Children welcome. No pipes in dining-room. No-smoking area. Music. Air-conditioned   ACCOMMODATION: 460 rooms, all with bath/shower. TV. Phone. Room only £311 to £646. Rooms for disabled. Children welcome. Guide dogs only. Afternoon teas   ⊖ Hyde Park Corner (£5)

Interlude 🛋 ¾   map 15

5 Charlotte Street, W1P 1HD   COOKING 4
TEL: (0171) 637 0222   FAX: (0171) 637 0224   COST £35–£55

When Eric Chavot cooked here, a discreet and classical French tone pervaded the dining-room. Now, curtains are pulled right back, lighting in the evening is bright, and the ambience is a lot more relaxed. Paul Merrett, who came from the Terrace restaurant at Le Meridien, takes inspiration from here, there and everywhere, producing a 'compression of duck confit', a dish of sea bass with sag aloo, tomato pickle and an onion bhaji, and banana ravioli with honeycomb ice-cream.

Components are often piled one atop the other in a delicate balancing act, but at their best dishes present clear, fresh flavours: pressed salmon and leek terrine, for example, accompanied by diced tomato with basil and fennel-scented potato salad. Well-executed roasted squab pigeon has been served with celeriac cream and an improvable red wine and beetroot reduction, while lemon tart, made with good pastry and an intense filling, comes with a red berry compote and a basil sorbet. Well-made petits fours arrive with coffee, and service does well on all counts. A brief showing from the New World opens the wine list, before French classics jostle their way forward, many wearing rather stiff mark-ups. The starting-point is £14 for Languedoc varietals.

CHEF: Paul Merrett   PROPRIETOR: Charles Ullmann   OPEN: Mon to Fri L 12 to 3, Mon to Sat D 7 to 11   MEALS: Set L £19.50 to £34.50, Set D £29.50 to £34.50   SERVICE: not inc; 12½% for parties of 6 or more   CARDS: Amex, Delta, Diners, MasterCard, Switch, Visa   DETAILS: 75 seats. Private parties: 20 main room, 10 to 20 private rooms. Vegetarian meals. No children under 12. No smoking in 1 dining-room. Wheelchair access (1 step; not WC). Occasional music. Air-conditioned   ⊖ Tottenham Court Road (£5)

Istanbul Iskembecisi ¾ £   map 12

9 Stoke Newington Road, N16 8BH   COOKING 3
TEL: (0171) 254 7291   FAX: (0181) 881 3741   COST £17–£29

'The tripe soup is a classic, although not all our party would try it!' writes a regular who appreciates that this very popular restaurant is actually named after that dish. Most of the long list of meze are vegetable-based, with hummus, aubergine, spinach, yoghurt, broad beans, courgettes and potatoes among the ingredients. There are also liver, meatballs, and taramasalata, even Atlantic prawns, a rarity in Turkey. Despite 11 vegetarian main dishes, carnivores come into their own with a wide range of kebabs and grills of chicken or lamb, and 'traditional Turkish dishes' which are mostly meat stewed with vegetables.

Desserts should not be missed. As well as baklava there is kadayif – which the menu describes as shredded wheat (but which came first?) with syrup and ground pistachios – alongside puddings based on rice, and either mixed or cooked fruits such as pear or pumpkin in syrup. Service is very helpful and 'sensitive to our desire to have a long meal'. Drink ayran, a yoghurt-based drink like Indian lassi but thinner and sharper. Turkish and a few other wines are available, with house wine £6.50, and of course Turkish coffee to finish.

CHEF: A. Kurultan   PROPRIETORS: Ali Demir and Ahmet Poyraz   OPEN: all week noon to 5am   MEALS: alc (main courses £5 to £8.50)   SERVICE: not inc, card slips closed   CARDS: MasterCard, Switch, Visa   DETAILS: 70 seats. Private parties: 79 main room. Children's helpings. No children under 4. No smoking in dining-room. Wheelchair access (1 step; not WC). Music. Air-conditioned   ⊖ Manor House

Ivy
map 15

1 West Street, WC2N 9NE
TEL: (0171) 836 4751   FAX: (0171) 240 9550
EMAIL: mailbox@caprice.co.uk

COOKING 5
COST £27–£79

Popular as ever, and close to achieving cult status, this 'remains one of the best restaurants of its kind in London' according to a supporter, who lists a friendly welcome, 'excellent food at reasonable prices' and good service among its attributes. Add the 'classical' appeal of wood panelling and stained-glass windows, a dash of comfort, and a sprinkling of glamour from the nearby thespian world, and it is easy to see how it can get booked up ages ahead. Virtually every item on the menu is designed to reassure and comfort, from creamed morel soup to corned beef hash with fried eggs, from sauté foie gras to kedgeree. Dishes may be as simple as potted shrimps, as familiar as salmon fish-cake or shepherd's pie, but everything is underpinned by good-quality fresh ingredients, and choice is generous.

Appropriate cooking ensures that fish emerges 'moist, tender and tasty', as in the case of a 'superbly spiced' sea bass; good judgement produces a balance of flavours in a 'thick and creamy' chicken and coconut soup, for example; and a light hand with pastry has made a success of crisp tomato galette 'thick with chopped basil'. The chips are highly rated, and savouries – maybe herring roes on toast – offer a genuine alternative to baked Alaska or cinnamon fritters. Staff are confident, assured and attentive 'without being fussy or ingratiating', although there are so many of them that you may not see the same one twice. A cover charge pays for bread, and over a dozen wines are available by the glass, from a list that starts at £9.75 but soon hops over the £20 barrier. The same owners were due to open a revamped Sheekey's in autumn 1998, at 28 St Martin's Court, WC2, and were expected to sell Ivy and Le Caprice as the *Guide* went to press.

CHEFS: Des McDonald and Alan Bird   PROPRIETORS: Jeremy King and Christopher Corbin   OPEN: all week 12 to 3 (3.30 Sun), 5.30 to 12   CLOSED: 25 and 26 Dec, 1 Jan, Aug bank hol   MEALS: alc (main courses £8.50 to £22). Set L Sat and Sun £15.50. Cover £1.50   SERVICE: not inc   CARDS: Amex, Delta, Diners, MasterCard, Switch, Visa   DETAILS: 100 seats. Private parties: 6 main room, 6 private room. Children welcome. Wheelchair access (not WC). No music. Air-conditioned   ⊖ Leicester Square

Iznik £

map 13

19 Highbury Park, N5 1QJ
TEL: (0171) 354 5697 and 704 8099   COOKING 3
FAX: (0171) 354 5697   COST £19–£28

First impressions are not so much of a restaurant as of an Aladdin's cave of hanging lamps, oil and electric; of tiles and plates, abstract, calligraphic and figurative; of oil-paintings and fine wood carvings. Some are antique, some antiqued; some Turkish, others 'Turkish'; all against a background of pale green, yellow ochre and turquoise. Equally impressive is the feeling of happy staff and happy customers. Recorded Turkish music soon charms normally unresponsive ears. Reports suggest the best bet is to avoid main courses, the usual variations of grilled or stewed meats, and opt instead for an authentically Turkish-style meal by choosing a selection from the long list of meze. An inspector was particularly impressed by falafel, crisp outside, melting inside, and unusually garnished with a blob of tasty hummus. Fascinating desserts include dried fruit compotes, but the owners strongly recommend bread pudding (with bread imported from Turkey), and quince with rice-pudding, which they say is the origin of English rice-pudding. Drink yoghurt-based ayran with mint or 'gloriously aromatic' oregano, then Turkish wine (the house version is £7.95 a bottle) and finally Turkish coffee with Turkish delight.

CHEF: Saim Berik   PROPRIETORS: Adem and Pirlanta Oner   OPEN: all week 10 to 4, 6.30 to 11
CLOSED: 25 Dec   MEALS: alc (main courses £6.50 to £9.50)   SERVICE: 10%   CARDS: Delta,
MasterCard, Switch, Visa   DETAILS: 75 seats. Vegetarian meals. Children's helpings. Music
⊖ Highbury & Islington (£5)

Jenny Lo's Teahouse £

NEW ENTRY   map 13

14 Eccleston Street, SW1W 9LT   COOKING 3
TEL: (0171) 259 0399   COST £17–£27

Small is beautiful, nowhere more than in this cream, scarlet and purple room, which attracts 'ladies who lunch' in Belgravia, as well as young people happy to find reasonably priced substantial main-course snacks. The décor consists of a few pictures, a fish tank and a display of books by Jenny's father, the late Ken Lo. Black refectory tables are set out with chopsticks and paper napkins, and paper menus for place mats. On offer are some 20 main dishes with rice, or with noodles, stir-fried or in soup. Side dishes – not 'starters' – which come with mains include stuffed Peking dumplings, long and well-covered spare ribs, and spicy prawns garnished with chilli and onion: so crisply fried they can be crunched complete with the shells. A relish to relish is crisp, salted, vinegared, chopped cucumber. Wuntun soup contains the lightest of slithery dumplings, as well as sparklingly fresh leaves. Service by young Chinese staff is performed with charm. House wines start at £9.50, or drink Wulong (also known as Oolong) tea.

CHEF: Jenny Lo   PROPRIETOR: Jenny Lo's Teahouse Ltd.   OPEN: Mon to Sat 11.30 to 3, 6 to
10   CLOSED: bank hols   MEALS: alc (main courses £5 to £6.50)   SERVICE: not inc   CARDS:
none   DETAILS: 30 seats. 6 seats outside. Private parties: 20 private room. Vegetarian meals.
Children welcome. No music ⊖ Victoria

Justin de Blank £

map 15

120–122 Marylebone Lane, W1M 5FZ COOKING 3
TEL: (0171) 486 5250   FAX: (0171) 935 4046 COST £24–£48

With its planked floor, high echoey ceiling and clattery metal tables, this easy-going place can feel a bit 'like a school gym'. Part of the room is a bar, and the food that comes out of an open-to-view kitchen at the back is no more pretentious than the décor. Materials include Martin Pitt eggs, De Gustibus bread, prize-winning sausages and Valrhona chocolate, and the style is unambitious, with freshness typically scoring over finesse. The simple approach takes in soup, a plate of charcuterie, or 'fresh and accurately grilled' mackerel fillet, and perhaps kedgeree, linguine with pesto, or calf's liver with Ayrshire smoked bacon.

Pastry-work demonstrates a light touch: in a pepper and pesto tart, or a wedge of cauliflower and broccoli tart spiked with feta cheese. At the same time, rich and creamy sauces point to a rather old-fashioned approach: perhaps mushroom-flecked for neatly rolled lemon sole fillets, or binding a dish of sweetbreads on spinach with rösti. Finish with English cheeses (or a goats'-cheese soufflé) or maybe hazelnut meringue. Some two dozen wines start at £9.50 and (apart from champagne) stay below £20.

CHEF: Julie Anderson   PROPRIETORS: Jonathan Choat and Justin de Blank   OPEN: Mon to Sat 12 to 3, 5.30 (6 Sat) to 10.30   CLOSED: Christmas, Easter, bank hols   MEALS: alc (main courses £8 to £15)   SERVICE: not inc; 12.5% for parties of 8 or more   CARDS: Amex, Delta, MasterCard, Switch, Visa   DETAILS: 60 seats. 20 seats outside. Private parties: 150 main room, 40 private room. Vegetarian meals. Children welcome. No pipes in dining-room. Wheelchair access (not WC). Occasional music   ⊖ Bond Street

Kastoori £

map 12

188 Upper Tooting Road, Tooting, SW17 7EJ COOKING 1
TEL: (0181) 767 7027 COST £19–£31

Reporters' thanks for the charm of the Thanki family are matched by enthusiasm for the Indian vegetarian food in this simple eating-house. Some dishes will be known to devotees of the cuisine: such starters as bhajias, samosas and crisp little puris, variously filled; a wide range of fresh vegetable curries; and dosa pancakes. More unusual are family specials deriving from a sojourn in Uganda. They include mogo bhajia (fried cassava); green banana curry; chilli banana; kasodi (corn in coconut milk with ground peanut sauce); and kontola curry, a 'crunchy mountain vegetable with an unexpected creamy finish'. House wines are £7.50; note also Indian Anarkali (red) and Chhabri (white), and a decent list of more familiar names.

CHEF: Manoj Thanki   PROPRIETOR: Dinesh Thanki   OPEN: Wed to Sun L 12.30 to 2.30, all week D 6 to 10.30   CLOSED: 25 Dec, 1 week mid-Jan   MEALS: alc (main courses £4.50 to £6) SERVICE: not inc, card slips closed   CARDS: MasterCard, Visa   DETAILS: 84 seats. Private parties: 20 main room. Vegetarian meals. Children welcome. Wheelchair access (not WC). No music. Air-conditioned   ⊖ Tooting Broadway

The Good Food Guide *is a registered trade mark of Which? Ltd.*

Kensington Place ♟

map 13

201 Kensington Church Street, W8 7LX
TEL: (0171) 727 3184   FAX: (0171) 229 2025
EMAIL: kpr@place-restaurants.co.uk

COOKING 6
COST £23–£44

There was a time when Kensington Place, with its hard lines, functional though highly efficient service, and resolutely simple cooking, stood out as a big, brash beacon of innovation. That it is now part of the general scenery is a testament to just how far-reaching the revolution has been that it helped to set in train.

Rowley Leigh's menus have kept abreast of the times while continuing to offer some of the signature dishes that made the Place's reputation. Scallops with pea purée and mint vinaigrette, or griddled foie gras on a sweetcorn pancake, are long stayers, but the handwritten specials should be investigated too. These might offer grilled squid with a powerful dressing of tomato, chilli and ginger, the seasonings turned full on but not drowning the main component. The grill is used again for cod in a meat stock sauce, its cauliflower mash vividly seasoned with cumin, while slow-braised lamb shank is cooked to a satisfying softness, accompanied by a mass of beans with mushrooms and fragments of chorizo. Favourite puddings include bread-and-butter made with panettone, rhubarb fool, and summer trifle replete with red fruits and alcohol. Other places may offer more comfort, but the direct, easily comprehensible, gutsy food is what keeps this one enduringly popular.

Wines are a bright collection assembled partly by grape, partly by country: a skilful blend of modern styles and traditional flavours providing an apt complement to the cuisine. Prices are good considering the postcode, beginning at £10.50 in France, and wines by the glass are plentiful. CELLARMAN'S CHOICE: Mâcon-Vinzelles 1996, Cave des Grands Crus Blancs, £14.50; Stag's Leap Hawk Crest Cabernet Sauvignon 1995, Napa, California, £19.

CHEF: Rowley Leigh   PROPRIETORS: Nick Smallwood and Simon Slater   OPEN: all week 12 to 3 (3.30 Sat and Sun), 6.30 to 11.45 (10.15 Sun)   CLOSED: 25 Dec, 1 Jan   MEALS: alc (main courses £8 to £18). Set L £14.50 to £16.50, Set L £19.50 (for parties of 9 or more), Set D £24.50 (for parties of 9 or more)   SERVICE: not inc   CARDS: Amex, Delta, MasterCard, Switch, Visa   DETAILS: 140 seats. Private parties: 120 main room. Vegetarian meals. Children's helpings. No pipes/cigars. Wheelchair access (1 step; also WC). No music. Air-conditioned
⊖ Notting Hill Gate

Lahore Kebab House £

map 13

2 Umberston Street, E1 1PY
TEL: (0171) 488 2551 and 481 9737

COOKING 1
COST £12–£17

Anyone searching for good Indian food at bargain-basement prices could do a lot worse than pay a visit to this utterly basic eating-house. Food is cooked on a fierce barbecue behind the counter, and on the wall above is a menu, largely ignored by staff and customers. Small parties can indeed choose from chicken, lamb, and kofte in the form of accurately grilled kebabs or as curries, but for four or more it is easier just to say 'please feed us' and the waiter will bring most of the menu. There might also be dhal, biryani, or, on Fridays only, paya (lamb's trotters). There is no licence, so take your own wine or beer.

CHEF: M. Din   PROPRIETOR: M. Siddique   OPEN: all week 12 to 11.30   MEALS: alc (main courses £3.50 to £4.50). BYO (no corkage)   SERVICE: not inc   CARDS: none   DETAILS: 100 seats. Children welcome. Wheelchair access (not WC). Music. Air-conditioned   ⊖ Aldgate East

▲ Landmark London, The Dining Room   map 13

222 Marylebone Road, NW1 6JQ   COOKING 5
TEL: (0171) 631 8000   FAX: (0171) 631 8080   COST £33–£86

'Welcome to the fusion of cuisines in our Dining Room,' states the menu at the Landmark restaurant, which was once the Winter Garden, as the hotel itself was once the Regent. Food styles have changed about as often as the names since the place opened in 1993, and the current kitchen incumbent, Andrew McLeish, has brought a measure of stability to the cooking. As for the restaurant itself, a reporter felt that muted colours, furniture and fittings gave it the air of a drawing-room.

Novel ideas abound. Paper-thin slices of veal carpaccio, for example, are dressed with a pungent herb vinaigrette and accompanied by a sliver of briefly sauté veal liver, the flavour delicate, the texture silky: a nicely weighted lunchtime starter. Dinner might turn up wild mushroom and truffle risotto or grilled lobster with linguine, spring onions and ginger butter, while zander is baked to 'a well-judged opalescence' and then balanced on a timbale of creamed spinach. Angus beef fillet is given the Med treatment with roasted artichokes and pesto sharpened with balsamic, while two might dine on a roast poulet de Bresse with Savoy cabbage and pancetta in a redcurrant sauce.

Desserts range from the tried-and-true, such as strawberry mousse with lemon sorbet, to the take on Austrian Gugelhupf: a parfait-textured iced confection laced with champagne, set on flaky pastry and garnished with iced fruits. Service by an expertly drilled young male team offers 'wall-to-wall solicitude'. The wine list is as wide-ranging as you might expect in five-star surroundings, but basic 1996 Chablis at £31 will give an idea of how much you'll need in order to investigate its wares. House French, a Sauvignon and a Merlot, are £18.50.

CHEF: Andrew McLeish   PROPRIETOR: The Landmark London   OPEN: Mon to Fri L12 to 3, Mon to Sat D 7 to 10.30   MEALS: alc (main courses £17.50 to £30). Set L £24, Set D £34 to £39.50   SERVICE: net prices, card slips closed   CARDS: Amex, Diners, MasterCard, Switch, Visa   DETAILS: 84 seats. Private parties: 30 main room, 360 private room. Vegetarian meals. Children welcome. No-smoking areas. Wheelchair access (also WC). Music. Air-conditioned   ACCOMMODATION: 305 rooms 304 with bath/shower. TV. Phone. Room only £230 to £385. Rooms for disabled. Children welcome. High teas for children. No dogs. Afternoon teas. Swimming-pool   ⊖ Marylebone   £5

▲ Lanesborough, The Conservatory   map 14

1 Lanesborough Place, SW1X 7TA
TEL: (0171) 259 5599   FAX: (0171) 259 5606   COOKING 4
EMAIL: info@lanesborough.co.uk   COST £33–£77

A lot of work went into making the Lanesborough look the part when it was launched a few years ago, and nowhere was the effort more appreciably concentrated than in The Conservatory dining-room. Where other places might have vases of flowers, here jardinières containing small trees are the order of the day, along with lamps under glass parasols, Chinese prints, and a vaulted glass roof.

Paul Gayler has always worked with the grain of Far Eastern techniques, and was one of the first Western chefs to begin using ingredients such as lemon grass and lime leaves. The style shows up in lettuce spring rolls with crab, soy and ginger, or duck crusted with Szechuan peppercorns and sauced with lime and ginger. Other culinary influences are harnessed too, bringing an Indian approach to a curry of aubergine, chayote and sweet potatoes served with naan bread and pineapple chutney, or a North African one for spiced lamb shank with chickpea polenta and cumin-flavoured root vegetables. More mainstream tastes may be relieved to see Lanesborough fish and chips, or grilled beef fillet with béarnaise. Lime chiffon cheesecake, and waffles with marinated strawberries and cinnamon ice-cream, are among the sweet temptations. Wines match the grandeur of the hotel, burgundies in particular a very distinguished bunch, but if £20 is your limit, you will need to forage. House wines start at £17.50.

CHEF: Paul Gayler   PROPRIETOR: Rosewood Hotels   OPEN: all week 12 to 2.30, 6.30 to 12   MEALS: alc (main courses £14 to £29.50). Set L £19.50 (2 courses) to £24.50, Set D Sun to Thur £29.50, Set D Fri and Sat £33   SERVICE: net prices   CARDS: Amex, Diners, MasterCard, Switch, Visa   DETAILS: 106 seats. Private parties: 100 main room, 14 to 100 private rooms. Vegetarian meals. Children's helpings. Wheelchair access (also WC). Music. Air-conditioned   ACCOMMODATION: 95 rooms, all with bath/shower. TV. Phone. Room only £225 to £3,500. Rooms for disabled. Children welcome. High teas for children. Baby facilities. Guide dogs and small dogs welcome. Afternoon teas   ● Hyde Park Corner

Langan's Brasserie

map 15

Stratton Street, W1X 5FD
TEL: (0171) 491 8822   FAX: (0171) 493 8309

COOKING 2
COST £32–£57

The welcome to Langan's begins as soon as you emerge from Green Park tube station, a red neon sign at the end of Stratton Street arrowing you in the right direction. Langan's puts on an all-action show on two floors, the ground-floor room much the more glamorous, and an army of waiters wield big brasserie menus with consummate polish. Begin, perhaps, with field mushrooms and bacon gratinated under a layer of creamy Lancashire cheese, or generous seafood salad dressed with basil oil. Among main courses of grilled calf's liver and bacon, and monkfish kebab with a chili and lime dressing, praise has come in for goose braised in Guinness. Vegetables such as creamed spinach, or boiled Jersey Royals in season, carry an extra tariff, and desserts are as old-fashioned as pineapple in kirsch, poire Belle-Hélène, and 'thin and flimsy' treacle tart with a jug of thin custard. Although the restaurant tells us there is no time limit on tables, our inspector was offered either an 11pm booking or a '7pm, out by 9pm' slot; he chose the latter and felt rushed. Predominantly French wines start at £11.

CHEFS: Ken Whitehead, Dennis Mynott and Roy Smith   PROPRIETORS: Richard Shepherd and Michael Caine   OPEN: Mon to Fri 12.15 to 11.45, Sat D only 7 to 11.45   CLOSED: bank hols   MEALS: alc (main courses £13 to £15). Cover £1   SERVICE: 12.5% (optional)   CARDS: Amex, Delta, Diners, MasterCard, Switch, Visa   DETAILS: 200 seats. Private parties: 12 main room. Vegetarian meals. Children's helpings. Wheelchair access (2 steps; not WC). Music. Air-conditioned   ● Green Park

Lansdowne £

map 13

90 Gloucester Avenue, NW1 8HX
TEL: (0171) 483 0409

COOKING 2
COST £22–£32

This infectiously rowdy Primrose Hill gastro-pub was among the first of its kind in the capital a few years ago, and the successful formula doesn't seem to change. The tone is set by bare floorboards, mismatched furniture, 'rumbustiously cheerful' staff, and a system of ordering at the bar and hoping someone doesn't usurp your seat while you're distracted. 'Hearty but unstructured food' is what to expect, from spiced spinach soup with yoghurt and coriander, through grilled tuna with polenta chips and tomato salsa, to Black Mountain ribeye with baby vegetables and tarragon oil. Grilling is the preferred cooking method for meats, roasting more likely for fish – cod with salsa verde, for example – or vegetables that go into a tart with goats' cheese. Homely puddings have included crunchy meringue with strawberries and cream, gooseberry crumble, and zabaglione with almond semifreddo. A short, invitingly priced wine list is chalked up on the board, and offers robust modern flavours to suit the food. House French is £8.50.

CHEFS: Amanda Pritchett and Mark Watkins   PROPRIETOR: Amanda Pritchett   OPEN: Tue to Sun L 12.30 to 2.30, all week D 7 to 10   CLOSED: 25 and 26 Dec   MEALS: alc (main courses £7.50 to £9.50). Set L Sun £15   SERVICE: not inc, card slips closed   CARDS: Delta, MasterCard, Switch, Visa   DETAILS: 70 seats. 32 seats outside. Private parties: 24 private room. Vegetarian meals. Children welcome. No music   ⊖ Chalk Farm

Launceston Place ▼

map 14

1A Launceston Place, W8 5RL
TEL: (0171) 937 6912   FAX: (0171) 938 2412
EMAIL: lpr@place-restaurants.co.uk

COOKING 2
COST £27–£59

Occupying converted shop premises on a long, gracefully curving corner at the top of an improbably tranquil Kensington street, this is the refined country cousin of more raffish Kensington Place (see entry). A network of interconnecting rooms – all muted colours and soft furnishings – feels pleasantly homely, perhaps suggesting a penchant for English heritage cookery, until pigeon crostini with rocket brings you splashing down in the Mediterranean. Indeed, a willingness to try out new combinations runs through much of the menu, producing a rhubarb dressing for grilled sea bass, a pumpkin and mustard relish for fillet steak, and even deep-fried lychees paired with shrimp mousse and chilli sauce. An inspection meal following a change of kitchen regime yielded mixed results, but coffee and chocolate tart with espresso ice-cream was attractively 'dense in texture, intense in flavour. It is all served with 'quiet efficiency' at an unobtrusive pace. Wines on the compact list are simply arranged in ascending order of cost – starting at £10.75 for house vin de pays Chardonnay – and offer a good choice of grapes and styles at fair prices. CELLARMAN'S CHOICE: Seresin Sauvignon Blanc 1997, Marlborough, New Zealand, £20; St-Emilion, Ch. Vieux Sarpe 1993, £31.

CHEFS: Philip Reed and Terence Eden   PROPRIETORS: Nick Smallwood and Simon Slater
OPEN: Sun to Fri L 12.30 to 2.30 (3 Sun), 7 to 11.30   CLOSED: bank hols   MEALS: alc (main
courses £9.50 to £16.50). Set L and D 7 to 8 £14.50 (2 courses) to £17.50, Set L Sun £19.50
SERVICE: not inc   CARDS: Amex, Delta, MasterCard, Switch, Visa   DETAILS: 85 seats. Private
parties: 85 main room, 12 to 30 private rooms. Vegetarian meals. Children's helpings. No
cigars/pipes in dining-room. Wheelchair access (1 step; not WC). No music. Air-conditioned
⊖ Gloucester Road

Laurent £ map 13

| 428 Finchley Road, NW2 2HY | COOKING 1 |
| TEL: (0171) 794 3603 | COST £19–£30 |

Enter the modest room to find travel posters on white plaster walls, and red and
white check plastic cloths on close-set tables. In the shortest menu competition,
Laurent is a strong contender. Start with brique à l'oeuf, a deep-fried triangle of
filo pastry containing an egg, 'crispy and gooey at the same time, and proceed to
couscous: with vegetables, lamb and merguez sausage, chicken, or fish. The
grains are 'light, dry and as separate as a sand-dune'. When – or if, for portions
are large – it comes to desserts, choose from ice-creams, sorbets, crème caramel or
crêpes Suzette. Of the North African wines, Gris de Boulaouane rosé or powerful
Berkane red match the food best; house wines are £8.50.

CHEF/PROPRIETOR: Laurent Farrugia   OPEN: Mon to Sat 12 to 2, 6 to 11   CLOSED: last 3 weeks
Aug, bank hols   MEALS: alc (main courses £7 to £11). BYO £1.20 per person   SERVICE: not
inc   CARDS: Amex, Delta, MasterCard, Visa   DETAILS: 36 seats. Private parties: 10 main room.
Vegetarian meals. Children's helpings. Wheelchair access (1 step; not WC). No music
⊖ Golders Green

Lee Fook **NEW ENTRY** map 13

| 98 Westbourne Grove, W2 5RU | COOKING 1 |
| TEL: (0171) 727 0099   FAX: (0171) 727 8773 | COST £26–£55 |

Chefs and proprietors of other reputable Chinese restaurants are often to be seen
at this long-running Bayswater venue: a sure sign that Ringo Lo has carved out a
reputation for authenticity. The dining-room has a fresher, lighter feel than
before, thanks to recent renovation: flowers in large vases by the window and a
mural on one wall add to the mood. Excellent roast meats – especially pork –
come highly recommended, and the standard menu also provides decent
versions of crispy duck, deep-fried bean curd with chillies, and stir-fried greens
with ginger and garlic. However, it pays to be adventurous and dip in to the
weekly specials menu, where you might be rewarded with superior braised
seafood in a lotus leaf, deep-fried chicken with fermented red bean paste, or
minced pork with salted fish: 'a fine peasant dish with lots of rustic flavours,'
commented one who knows. Service is 'plentiful', polite and helpful. Drink
jasmine or chrysanthemum tea. House wine is £12.

The Guide *is totally independent, accepts no free hospitality, and survives on the number
of copies sold each year.*

CHEF: Ringo Lo   PROPRIETORS: Mr Low, Mr How and Mr Chan   OPEN: all week 12 to 11.30 CLOSED: 25 Dec   MEALS: alc (main courses £6.50 to £28). Set L and D (minimum 2) £16 to £19.50. Minimum charge £9 at D.   SERVICE: not inc   CARDS: Delta, Diners, MasterCard, Switch, Visa   DETAILS: 80 seats. Private parties: 90 main room. Vegetarian meals. Children welcome. Music. Air-conditioned   ⊖ Bayswater

Leith's

map 13

92 Kensington Park Road, W11 2PN

TEL: (0171) 229 4481   FAX: (0171) 221 1246

COOKING 5

COST £35–£62

Former sous-chef Alastair Ross has taken over from Alex Floyd, who left to cook at Leith s Soho (see entry below). The style remains much the same, however: a classically based menu that incorporates some contemporary touches without slavishly following fashion. It s a grown-up alternative to the hip new restaurants of Notting Hill, probably where the young and hip end up eating 20 years later. The genteel, even sedate dining-room feels like part of somebody s home, albeit an extremely affluent one. There are comfortable armchairs at table, plenty of fine linen, and lots of elbow room.

Lightness, refinement and precision are hallmarks of the cooking, and although some of the more adventurous combinations may not quite deliver all they promise, main courses seem to be soundly rendered. Brill with langoustines for one reporter was 'beautifully cooked, retaining all its fine flavour and texture', and came with a light, well-made basil and shellfish sauce. Another well-judged dish was roast pigeon, accompanied by perfectly timed girolle mushrooms and baby vegetables in a light artichoke broth. An intriguing dessert of gooseberry and candied ginger soufflé turned out to be a 'real gem , served with ginger ice-cream.

Some reporters have found the service efficient and good throughout, others would prefer more warmth and enthusiasm. Co-owner – and occasional sommelier – Nick Tarayan is prepared to put his mouth (and those of his colleagues) behind the impressive list, which features many exciting and unusual wines as well as the expected classics: 'If you don't like a wine which we recommend, we'll change it for something else and have it with our supper.' Styles and prices span a broad spectrum, the house selection starting at £15.50. CELLARMAN'S CHOICE: Mud House Sauvignon Blanc 1997, Blenheim, New Zealand, £26.50; Ribera del Duero, La Granja de Monasterio 1994, £22.50.

CHEF: Alastair Ross   PROPRIETORS: Christopher Bland, Caroline Waldegrave, Nick Tarayan and Alex Floyd   OPEN: Tue to Fri L 12.15 to 2.15, Mon to Sat D 7 to 11.30   CLOSED: 2 weeks Christmas/New Year, bank hols exc Good Fri   MEALS: alc D (main courses £18.50 to £25.50). Set L £16.50 (2 courses) to £19.50, Set D £27.50 (2 courses) to £35   SERVICE: 12.5% (optional), card slips closed   CARDS: Amex, Delta, Diners, MasterCard, Switch, Visa   DETAILS: 70 seats. Private parties: 45 main room, 4 to 36 private rooms. Vegetarian meals. No children under 7. No music   ⊖ Notting Hill Gate

indicates that there has been a change of chef since last year's Guide, *and the Editor has judged that the change is of sufficient interest to merit the reader's attention.*

London Round-ups listing additional restaurants that may be worth a visit can be found after the main London section.

Leith's Soho ♥   NEW ENTRY   map 15

41 Beak Street, W1R 3LE   COOKING 4
TEL: (0171) 287 2057   FAX: (0171) 287 1767   COST £30–£54

Atelier in Beak Street has gone, replaced by this smart and sassy younger sister to the original Leith's (see entry above). Clean, understated lines, muted wood tones and bright lighting provide a sleek, modern environment where the media types of West Soho congregate. 'Good food at reasonable prices in convivial surroundings' should help Leith's stand out from the crowd in an area brimming with restaurants. Alex Floyd has transferred from the main restaurant and cooks a simplified, brasserie-style menu. There is some fashionable '70s retro – prawn cocktail, Angus steak, fresh fruit with ice-cream – plus some sharp versions of modern classics: tuna carpaccio, cod with a niçoise crust and fish in a green Thai curry broth. As at Leith's, vegetarians are imaginatively catered for with, for example, roast cep, salsify and scrambled egg feuilleté.

Skate with capers and tomato concassé was a 'wonderfully good rendition at inspection, and skills in timing and balance are evident in a moist and tender roast guinea-fowl stuffed with a well-flavoured black pudding, given an extra dimension by a well-made sage jus. Desserts might include dense banana tarte Tatin with fine caramel and sultana ice-cream, or apricot bread-and-butter soufflé. The compact wine list skilfully blends the familiar with the less well known – Mexican Chenin Blanc, for one – while keeping prices affordable, starting at £11.50 for the vin de pays Grenache (in both colours). Thirty-three wines are available by the glass. CELLARMAN'S CHOICE: Preludio Viognier/ Chardonnay 1997, Juanico, Uruguay, £16.50; Rocca Rosso 'Cuvée Real' 1995, Angelo Rocca, Apulia, £18.50.

CHEF: Alex Floyd   PROPRIETORS: Christopher Bland, Caroline Waldegrave, Nick Tarayan and Alex Floyd   OPEN: Mon to Sat 12 to 2.30, 6 to 11.15   CLOSED: 2 weeks Christmas/New Year, bank hol Mons   MEALS: alc (main courses £8.50 to £16.50). Set L and D before 7pm £16.50 (2 courses) to £19.50   SERVICE: 12.5% (optional), card slips closed   CARDS: Amex, Delta, Diners, MasterCard, Switch, Visa   DETAILS: 50 seats. Private parties: 20 main room, 22 private room. Vegetarian meals. Children's helpings. No children under 5. No-smoking area. Wheelchair access (not WC). No music. Air-conditioned   ⊖ Piccadilly Circus, Oxford Circus

Lindsay House ♥   NEW ENTRY   map 15

21 Romilly Street, W1V 5TG   COOKING 6
TEL: (0171) 439 0450   FAX: (0171) 437 7349   COST £42–£56

Ring a bell to get in, though nobody seems to know why. This Soho townhouse, with ground- and first-floor dining-rooms, has kept enough of its original features, including uneven wooden floors, to exude 'the slightly raffish air of an Irish country house', which seems an apt place for Richard Corrigan to inhabit. After a spate of large, over-designed, minimalist restaurants, 'how refreshing to discover an intimate, unrushed establishment cooking honest-to-goodness earth-bound food'. The sense of relaxation is helped by not having to vacate the table half-way through the evening, evidently a novelty for some reporters.

The respite from Pacific-fusion cooking is also welcomed. Although a vegetarian option is available, the real pleasures of Corrigan's food are to be found among the offaly bits – sauté veal kidney with girolles, braised veal tongue in a dark sticky sauce with roast garlic, or 'sensational' sweetbreads with spinach and mash – which seem to aim more for refinement than gutsiness. There are five or six dishes per course to choose from, and combinations range from 'imaginative' and 'inspired' to 'bizarre', taking in oysters with sauerkraut, warm chicken ballottine in pesto broth, and a salad of shredded, jellified skate wing with aubergine purée and red pepper.

Fresh and well-sourced materials have contributed to cannelloni 'bursting with lobster', 'juicy' red snapper with a 'profoundly cheesy' ham risotto, and red mullet in several guises: on one occasion 'so crispy it sort of went to dust as one ate it', on another 'perfectly' grilled with 'excellent' flavour, served with a rather contrived cannelloni of salt cod. At its best the food is 'dazzling', and desserts play their part: ripe fig tart with ice-cream and tobacco syrup, or a stack of pineapple slices, dredged in chilli and coriander, served with coconut cream. 'If there's a better lunchtime bargain, I can't think of it.' Service is polite yet amiable and responsive. Overheated wines have been served on more than one occasion, suggesting that there may be a problem with storage. This is a pity because the extensive and innovative list is fairly priced and runs the gamut of varietals from Albariño to Zinfandel, with much that is rare in between. Guides are provided to grapes and styles, and a two-page quick selection simplifies choice for those pushed for time, starting at £12.50. CELLARMAN'S CHOICE: Tokay-Pinot Gris d'Alsace Rotenberg 1988, Zind-Humbrecht, £32; Bandol, Ch. De Pibarnon 1992, £28.

CHEF: Richard Corrigan   PROPRIETOR: Corrigan Restaurants Ltd.   OPEN: Mon to Fri L 12 to 2.30, Mon to Sat D 6 to 10.45   CLOSED: last 2 weeks Aug, bank hols   MEALS: alc L (main courses £15 to £20). Set D £38.   SERVICE: 12.5% (optional), card slips closed   CARDS: Amex, Delta, Diners, MasterCard, Switch, Visa   DETAILS: 60 seats. Private parties: 20 main room, 8 to 20 private rooms. Vegetarian meals. Children's helpings. No pipes/cigars in dining-room. No music. Air-conditioned   ⊖ Leicester Square

Livebait   maps 13, 15

43 The Cut, SE1 8LF
TEL: (0171) 928 7211   FAX: (0171) 928 2279
21 Wellington Street, WC2E 7DN   COOKING 2
TEL: (0171) 836 7161   FAX: (0171) 836 7141   COST £33–£55

'Fresh and funky' are watchwords for the hugely innovative fish cookery going on at both branches of Livebait: a small green-and-white-tiled restaurant opposite the Young Vic theatre, and a new Covent Garden venue with similar décor and an identical menu. What dishes may lack in presentational nicety they more than make up for in recherché allure, so get ready for blue-fin tuna with red chilli blini and Indian fennel relish. Some things work (tempura-battered Cornish squid on mango salsa was 'an interesting assemblage of materials') and some things don't, as is almost inevitable in this high-risk idiom, but in full flow the kitchen is capable of delivering some highly enjoyable dishes. 'Perfectly cooked, faintly translucent' seared Scottish scallops with baked tomatoes and mozzarella pleased one reporter greatly. Side-orders such as mashed potato with Bayonne ham provide further interest, although puddings were described by one reporter as 'unmemorable'. A tempting international wine list is fairly priced, and it is heartening to see Beaujolais – a Brouilly and a Fleurie – served chilled. Prices start at £11.75.

CHEFS: Theo Kyriakou and Manu Feldel PROPRIETOR: Groupe Chez Gérard OPEN: Mon to Sat 12 to 3, 5.30 to 11.30 MEALS: alc (main courses £14 to £29.50). Set D 5.30 to 7 £14.50 (2 courses) SERVICE: 12.5% (optional), card slips closed CARDS: Amex, Delta, Diners, MasterCard, Switch, Visa DETAILS: 100 seats (The Cut), 120 seats (Wellington Street). Private parties: 100 main room. Children welcome. No cigars/pipes in dining-room. Wheelchair access (also WC at Wellington Street only). Music ⊖ Waterloo, Covent Garden

Lobster Pot

map 13

3 Kennington Lane, SE11 4RG
TEL: (0171) 582 5556 FAX: (0171) 582 9751

COOKING 1
COST £22–£65

Look for the lobster pots on the pavement and be ready for piped seagull cries when you ring the doorbell; once inside be prepared for the canned shanties and – on occasion – staff striding about the place in yellow oilskins and waders. In his quirky, small fish restaurant just off the Elephant and Castle roundabout, Hervé Régent delivers bouillabaisse ('a myriad of fishy flavours in one of those thick, gungy, brown liquors that the French manage so well'), alongside punchy red rouille, grated cheese and toasted baguette. Fish is timed with pinpoint accuracy, including the eponymous lobsters, which are prepared to taste. Breton pancakes or ice-creams are the best ways to finish. The set-price three-course lunch is especially good value. Wines are exclusively French, of course, with mark-ups surprisingly on the high side. House wines are £10.50.

CHEF: Hervé Régent PROPRIETORS: Hervé and Nathalie Régent OPEN: Tue to Sat 12 to 2, 7 to 10.45 CLOSED: 24 Dec to 5/6 Jan MEALS: alc (main courses £14.50 to £29.50). Set L £15.50. Set L and D £22.50 (Menu Gastronomique) SERVICE: net prices, card slips closed CARDS: Amex, Delta, Diners, MasterCard, Switch, Visa DETAILS: 38 seats. Private parties: 30 main room, 14 private room. Children's helpings. No cigars/pipes in dining-room. Wheelchair access (not WC). Music. Air-conditioned ⊖ Kennington (£5)

Lola's

map 13

The Mall Building, 359 Upper Street, N1 0PD
TEL: (0171) 359 1932 FAX: (0171) 359 2209

COOKING 5
COST £25–£44

Occupying the first floor of an old tram shed, with enough glass and daylight to produce an airy 'conservatory feel', Lola's rates highly for atmosphere, value, service and simple but inventive cooking. As Morfudd Richards makes clear, theirs is a global approach, as distinct from fusion cooking, a point echoed in the words of a visitor who noted a 'coherence and originality which puts it far above the Pacific Rim jumble'. Ideas come from the Mediterranean (including Morocco), backed by a strong vein of rustic 'European peasant' dishes, but each culinary tradition retains its identity, as in a fattoush salad with halloumi, hummus and flat bread for example, or a 'colourful, thick, aromatic and unbelievably tasty' chicken harira soup.

Vegetables and fish – grilled squid or sea bass – figure as prominently as meat, producing roasted vegetables dressed with good oil on a 'dainty little pizza', or delicate pancakes rolled round a ricotta and spinach filling, then halved and stood on end 'like one of those office pen and pencil holders'. Desserts might include rhubarb and pistachio trifle, or the increasingly popular 'lost bread'. Staff are 'charming and efficient', and wines fit the global description, incorporating variety in both style and price, starting at £9.50.

CHEF: Juliet Peston   PROPRIETORS: Morfudd Richards and Carol George   OPEN: Mon to Sat 12 to 2.30 (3 Sat), 6.30 to 11, Sun 12 to 3, 7 to 10   CLOSED: 24 to 27 Dec, L 1 Jan, L bank hols   MEALS: alc Mon to Fri L, all week D (main courses £10 to £14.50). Set L Mon to Fri £12 (2 courses) to £16.50. Brunch menu Sat and Sun   SERVICE: not inc   CARDS: Amex, Delta, Diners, MasterCard, Switch, Visa   DETAILS: 80 seats. Vegetarian meals. Children welcome. Music. Air-conditioned   ⊖ Angel

Lou Pescadou   map 13

241 Old Brompton Road, SW5 9HP   COOKING 2
TEL: (0171) 370 1057   FAX: (0171) 244 7545   COST £21–£59

A porthole front window, pictures of boats, and nautical-coloured oilcloths on the tables set the piscatorial tone in this long-established seafood restaurant. Some find the place 'deeply old-fashioned' in the way it harks back to eating-places of the 1950s, but staff are young and friendly and the kitchen goes about its work capably. Oysters, clams, mussels and other shellfish dominate starters: a mixed plate of 'bulots, bigorneaux et crevettes grises' is loaded with 'enough shrimps and shellfish for two', and comes with a generous pot of 'fabulous' mayonnaise. Main courses tend towards robust offerings such as monkfish with Meaux mustard, roast fillet of brill with garlic, or 'exceptional' sweet-flavoured scallops set off by a well-judged provençale sauce. Carnivorous alternatives include navarin of lamb, and grilled chicken with lemon. Dessert-lovers have singled out 'exemplary' crème brûlée with peaches, and a trio of intensely flavoured sorbets. The short French wine list is bolstered by a pair of specials each month. House wine is £10.50.

CHEF: Laurent David   PROPRIETORS: Daniel Chobert and Laurent David   OPEN: all week 12 to 3, 7 to 12   CLOSED: Christmas   MEALS: alc (main courses £6.50 to £12.50). Set L Mon to Fri £9.90, Set L and D Sat and Sun £13.50. Cover £1.50   SERVICE: 15% (optional), card slips closed   CARDS: Amex, Delta, Diners, MasterCard, Switch, Visa   DETAILS: 60 seats. 23 seats outside. Private parties: 45 main room, 45 private room. Vegetarian meals. Children welcome. Wheelchair access (not WC). No music. Air-conditioned   ⊖ Earls Court

Magno's 🍽   map 15

65A Long Acre, WC2E 9JH   COOKING 1
TEL: (0171) 836 6077   FAX: (0171) 379 6184   COST £27–£51

'French and reliable' just about sums up this Covent Garden brasserie. Its major use by readers seems to be as a pre-theatre venue, although the two-course meal at £10.95 is also available afterwards. One couple began with spinach and cheese quiche, and avocado with prawns, followed by turkey strips in Chinese spices, and a two-fish dish of salmon and cod. If there's time, finish with white chocolate and raspberry tart, or crème brûlée. The à la carte trips through a standard repertoire of mussels, or beef in red wine, enlivened with an occasional novelty such as ostrich in coconut sauce. A predominantly French wine list has a few hefty mark-ups, but prices start at £10.95 and there is much below £20. Note that a service charge is usually added, although not (the restaurant tells us) to pre- and post-theatre meals; credit card slips are left open.

CHEFS: P. Jauffrineau and D. Bourg PROPRIETORS: S. Caltagirone and F. Falcone OPEN: Mon to Fri L 12 to 2.30, Mon to Sat D 5.30 to 10 MEALS: alc (main courses £10 to £14). Set L and D £13.95 (2 courses) to £16.95, Set D pre-theatre (before 7.15) and post-theatre (10 to 11.30) £10.95 (2 courses) SERVICE: 12.5%; not inc for pre- and post-theatre D CARDS: Amex, Delta, Diners, MasterCard, Switch, Visa DETAILS: 70 seats. Private parties: 70 main room. Vegetarian meals. Children's helpings. No cigars/pipes in dining-room. Wheelchair access (not WC). Occasional music. Air-conditioned ⊖ Covent Garden £5

Maison Novelli/Novelli EC1

map 13

29–30 Clerkenwell Green, EC1R 0DU
TEL: (0171) 251 6606
FAX. (0171) 490 1083

COOKING 6 Maison Novelli
3 Novelli EC1
COST £31–£81

There are two parts to this operation: as you face it from outside, Maison Novelli is on the left, and Novelli EC1 on the right. The former is 'a really good French restaurant', done out in characteristic purple and blue, with bare wooden floors, potted palms and closely packed tables. The menu is 'strong on fish and the humbler parts of animals': perhaps grey mullet with wild mushrooms in a frothy sauce, or chickpea soup with fried cured gizzards and black pudding. Pig's trotter varies by the day, but has incuded an 'admirable' version stuffed with wild mushrooms and black pudding.

The style is wide-ranging, and dishes can seem very busy: marinated mackerel and scallop on a lemon grass kebab with beetroot oil, cardamom and rocket for example, or tuna carpaccio with bean sprouts, oyster beignet, sesame oil and ginger juice. At its best the food is 'thoroughly distinguished', and among successes have been a mound of crab meat surrounded by a herbed gazpacho sauce, a trade mark cassoulet terrine ('low on beans, high on sausage, foie gras, lamb and other meats') and desserts of cold wild berry soufflé, and caramelised citrus tart with a sharp-tasting runny filling.

The first-floor brasserie dining-room at Novelli EC1 shares the purple-blue colour scheme with its neighbour, along with decorative corkscrew spirals and a rather Napoleonic letter N. Sit cheek-by-jowl and expect a generous *carte* of 'vibrant and well-conceived' food with a slightly jauntier air than the restaurant's: a tarte fine of aubergine tapénade with chorizo and mozzarella perhaps, or spiced honey-glazed lamb knuckle with chickpea salsa.

A 'trotter of the day' is available too, but fish and vegetable dishes claim a lot of attention: a pancake gâteau with mushrooms for example, or a piece of cod wrapped in pancetta, with a blob of smoked haddock brandade in the hollow centre. To finish, chocolate tart with a smear of prune is served with a fromage blanc sorbet, and what looks like a large green parcel turns out to be a banana leaf, enclosing poached green figs and banana. It is a toss-up which of the two outlets has the poorest service: both have been dogged by 'interminable waits' which have taken the edge off meals, and one couple who booked at Maison Novelli for Valentine's night were asked to pay two weeks in advance. The wine lists have not been sent to us, but start with house French at £15 in Maison Novelli and £11.50 in Novelli EC1.

CHEFS: Richard Guest (Maison Novelli) and Igor Timchishin (Novelli EC1)   PROPRIETOR: Jean-Christophe Novelli   OPEN: Maison Novelli Mon to Fri L 12 to 3.30, 6.30 to 11.15 (12 Sat); Novelli EC1 Mon to Fri 11 to 11   MEALS: Novelli EC1 alc (main courses £9.50 to £16); Maison Novelli alc (main courses £15 to £24.40)   SERVICE: 12.5% (optional)   CARDS: Amex, Delta, Diners, MasterCard, Switch, Visa   DETAILS: Maison Novelli 80 seats, 10 seats outside; private parties: 50 main room, 35 private room. Novelli EC1 70 seats, 12 seats outside; private parties: 40 main room, 80 private room. Vegetarian meals. Children welcome. No cigars/pipes in dining-rooms. Music   ✈ Farringdon

Mandarin Kitchen £

map 13

14–16 Queensway, W2 3RX   COOKING 4
TEL: (0171) 727 9012   FAX: (0171) 727 9468   COST £19–£60

Rumour has it that this grotto-like Chinese restaurant sells more lobsters than any other eating-place in London. Expertly timed fresh seafood of all kinds is the reason why legions of regulars and newcomers queue up early in the evening. 'I paid my first visit here for over a year and must go more often,' noted one reporter who dined 'sumptuously and reasonably' with a companion on mixed seafood soup, a huge 'pot of crab' with bean noodles and dry shrimps in chilli sauce, followed by toffee bananas. Apart from top-grade Scottish wild lobsters (whole creatures served six ways) and four dishes employing south and west coast crabs, the kitchen works wonders with an exotic haul of live eels, carp, Chinese pomfret, yellow croaker, geoduck (Alaskan king clams, which are served with garlic and soy dip) and more besides. If fish is not your fancy, the menu promises everything from Cantonese roast duck, and chicken with two kinds of mushrooms, to pork with preserved cabbage, and veal chop seasoned with black pepper. Service is 'remarkably swift' even when the place is bursting at the seams. Drink green tea, beer or something from the shortish wine list. House French is £9.90.

CHEF: K.W. Man   PROPRIETOR: Helen Cheung   OPEN: all week 12 to 11.30   MEALS: alc (main courses £5.90 to £26). Set D £9.90 (min 2). BYO £5   SERVICE: not inc   CARDS: Amex, Delta, Diners, MasterCard, Switch, Visa   DETAILS: 110 seats. Private parties: 120 main room. Vegetarian meals. Children welcome. Music. Air-conditioned   ✈ Queensway

Mantanah £

map 12

2 Orton Buildings, Portland Road,
South Norwood, SE25 4UD   COOKING 4
TEL: (0181) 771 1148   FAX: (0181) 771 2341   COST £21–£43

Coloured bright blue, outside and in, and decorated with a wealth of ethnic artefacts, Mantanah has a warmth that is matched by its willing service. The owners say that to ensure authenticity Thai ingredients are flown in weekly. They also mention that they are not afraid of innovation, which is undoubtedly true when it comes to naming dishes. Midnight Curry is chicken with pumpkin, coconut milk and shredded lime leaves, and Crying Dracula is stir-fried pig's liver with green chillies and spring onions. Among starters, Pearl of Mantanah has impressed for its 'vividly spiced' sticky sago dumplings filled with radish and nuts, served with a sweet-sour dipping sauce.

The long menu also lists many regular Thai dishes, and of the 100-plus items some 30 are vegetarian: from Pink Lady (deep-fried aubergine with chilli sauce) to New Adventure, a hot-and-sour curry whose many constituents include 'a famous southern vegetable, sa-taw'. Desserts travel less well than other Thai specialities and meet a mixed reception here. Note iced coffee to cool the palate as a final touch. The short, well-described wine list opens with house French at £7.75.

CHEF: Mrs Tym Srisawatt   PROPRIETOR: Mantanah Ltd   OPEN: Tue to Sun D only 6.30 to 11 CLOSED: 25 and 26 Dec, 1 Jan   MEALS: alc (main courses £5.50 to £7.50). Set D £16 to £20 SERVICE: not inc, card slips closed   CARDS: Amex, Delta, MasterCard, Switch, Visa   DETAILS: 40 seats. Private parties: 40 main room. Vegetarian meals. Children's helpings. No cigars. No music. Air-conditioned (£5)

Mash ♟

	NEW ENTRY map 15
19–21 Great Portland Street, W1M 5DB	COOKING 4
TEL: (0171) 637 5555 FAX: (0171) 637 7333	COST £31–£53

Restaurants are getting more like supermarkets, cramming as many different operations as they can under one roof. Mash functions as a bar, deli and brewery as well as a restaurant, which in turn takes breakfast and weekend brunch as seriously as lunch and dinner. Many design features – orange brewing tanks, 'lizard-eye' light fittings, and clinically curvy 'sci-fi' lines – may be familiar to frequenters of London's Coast or Manchester's Mash (see entries), while others, like the message-flasher, are more of a novelty.

The first-floor dining-room, reached by a 'gravel carpet' staircase, resembles a large cafeteria, divided more by light and shade than anything, with bare floors and tables, a 'fake bakery', and a pair of wood-fired ovens. These are successful with pizzas, producing a first-rate thin, crispy but slightly chewy base that works particularly well with a traditional topping of mozzarella, roast tomato and basil pesto. The kitchen also makes a good job of calf's liver, and comes up trumps with a dish of sea bass and grilled artichoke. Bruno Loubet's involvement may explain some of the more unusual ideas such as expertly baked marinated quail with sweetcorn relish and thin slices of crisp deep-fried taro root.

Desserts tend to come with an ice-cream: 'gooey' chocolate fondant with a wafer of oven-dried pineapple and piña colada ice, or rhubarb compote with crisp polenta shortcake and a custardy basil ice-cream that was 'a revelation' for its reporter. There is no shortage of things to drink, from fruit juices, cocktails and infusions, via four in-house beers, to wines that hop over the £20 barrier quick as a flash, although good drinking can be had for less. As at its Mancunian cousin, the eclectic list arranges wines by varietal, so a South African Sauvignon Blanc rubs shoulders with Pavillon Blanc du Ch. Margaux. House wines from South Australia are £12.50. CELLARMAN'S CHOICE: Vasse Felix Semillon/Chardonnay/Sauvignon Blanc 1996, Margaret River, W. Australia, £23.50; Rioja Alta, Coleccione 2100 1996, Marqués de Murietta £17.

CHEF: Craig Gray   PROPRIETOR: Oliver Peyton   OPEN: all week 12 to 3, 6 to 11.30 (10.30 Sun)
CLOSED: 25 and 26 Dec, 1 Jan, Easter Sun and Mon   MEALS: alc (main courses £6.50 to £13.50).
Set L Sat £16.50. Breakfast menu Mon to Fri 8 to noon; brunch menu Sat and Sun L; bar menu all
week 12 to 11.30   SERVICE: 12.5% (optional)   CARDS: Amex, Delta, Diners, MasterCard,
Switch, Visa   DETAILS: 140 seats. Private parties: 10 main room. Vegetarian meals. Children
welcome. Wheelchair access (not WC). Music. Air-conditioned   ⊖ Oxford Circus

Matsuri   map 15

| 15 Bury Street, SW1Y 6AL | COOKING 4 |
| TEL: (0171) 839 1101   FAX: (0171) 930 7010 | COST £26–£94 |

The word 'Matsuri' means 'festivals', and this swish Japanese restaurant in an
even swisher corner of Mayfair is tastefully bedecked with photographs of
celebrations, lanterns and other decorative artefacts. The kitchen focuses on two
culinary styles, one centuries old, the other modern. On the one hand is the
traditional artistry of sushi, on the other the Westernised flamboyance of
teppanyaki. Go for dinner and you will be able to participate in the full works, as
lobsters, Scotch fillet steak, turbot, duck and saddle of lamb are given the
hot-plate treatment in front of your eyes.

As an appetiser consider sashimi (prepared 'to suit your taste and budget',
says the menu), yakitori, or seaweed salad, and perhaps finish refreshingly with
lemon sorbet or assorted fruits. At lunch-time lacquered bento boxes contain all
sorts of delights, and special meals are built around, say, fried oysters or grilled
eel; you can even call in for a Japanese pizza or some teppan noodles with
seafood and vegetables. Sixteen brands of regional saké top the wine list, which
also includes some reasonably priced bottles from the New World. Chilean
house white is £16 and South African house red is £16.50.

CHEF: Kanehiro Takase   PROPRIETOR: Central Japan Railway Co/Kikkoman   OPEN: Mon to Sat
12 to 2.30, 6 to 10   CLOSED: bank hols   MEALS: alc (main courses L £11 to £22, D £15 to £30).
Set L £11.50 (2 courses) to £40, Set D £40 to £55   SERVICE: 12.5% (optional), card slips
closed   CARDS: Amex, Diners, MasterCard, Visa   DETAILS: 133 seats. Private parties: 30 main
room, 8 to 18 private rooms. Vegetarian meals. Children's helpings (Sat only). Wheelchair
access (also WC). Music. Air-conditioned   ⊖ Green Park, Piccadilly Circus

Melati £   map 15

21 Great Windmill Street, W1V 7PH	
TEL: (0171) 734 6964 and 437 2745	COOKING 1
FAX: (0171) 434 4196	COST £25–£41

As one reporter noted, genuine Malay/Indonesian restaurants are still surprisingly thin on the ground in London, so Margaret Ong's long-established
venue is a gem to be treasured. Since 1981, she and her team have been feeding
legions of diners in this venue in the heart of Soho. The menu is long, flavours are
big and bold, portions are man-sized, and most customers come away feeling
well satisfied. If you are looking for speed, value and satisfaction, go for a bowl
of Singapore laksa, some noodles or one of the composite rice dishes: nasi goreng
istimewa is the pick of the bunch, with its skewers of satay, savoury chicken and
slices of fried egg, not forgetting cooling pickles on the side. Otherwise, there are
classics such as beef rendang, galio sotong (squid cooked in coconut gravy) and a

heathy meatless contingent that encompasses everything from pergedel (potato cake) to pacri nenas (sweet-and-sour pineapple). Desserts are a weird and wonderful bunch: look for es kacang (red beans, mixed fruit, shaved rice and syrup) or the enigmatically titled Sam's Triple. Drink Tiger beer, jasmine tea or house wine at £8.45.

CHEF: Sjamsir Alamsjah   PROPRIETORS: Margaret Ong and Sjamsir Alamsjah   OPEN: all week 12 to 11.30 (12.30 Fri and Sat)   CLOSED: Christmas   MEALS: alc (main courses £5.50 to £7.50). Set L and D £17.50 to £22.50 (inc wine)   SERVICE: not inc, card slips closed   CARDS: Amex, Diners, MasterCard, Visa   DETAILS: 120 seats. Private parties: 35 main room, 35 private room. Vegetarian meals. Children's helpings. Wheelchair access (1 step; not WC). Music. Air-conditioned   ⊖ Piccadilly Circus £5

Mem Saheb £   NEW ENTRY map 15

65 Amsterdam Road, E14 3UU
TEL: (0171) 538 3008   FAX: (0181) 9840655   COOKING 2
EMAIL: memsaheb@demon.co.uk   COST £20–£37

The view from this riverside restaurant takes in the Millenium Dome, and though the modern building may look 'unpromising', inside it is 'really comfortable, almost luxurious', with attractive flowers on widely spaced tables with thick linen cloths. A shortish menu offers some familiar dishes alongside a more unusual range of genuine Bangladeshi options, such as batera (quail) masala stuffed with rice, in a tomato and onion sauce 'free of oil or ghee', and the cooking is distinguished by fresh spicing and good cuts of meat. Fish are also important here: trout and salmon as well as pomfret, ayre, and boal, a freshwater monster imported from Bangladesh, its large, deboned, steaks accurately cooked in 'a thick, spicy gravy with lots of onion'. Five 'combination dishes' offer a half-portion each of such pairings as chicken tikka masala in a 'rich, creamy sauce' and lamb pasanda with cashew-nuts. Occasional Festival celebrations show off the cooking of different Indian regions, maybe Calcutta or Goa. House wine is £6.95, or drink imported Sunny Beaches beer.

CHEF: Anwar Hussain   PROPRIETORS: Mridul Kanti Das, Mr R. Hoque and Mrs I. Kadir   OPEN: Mon to Fri L 12 to 2.30, all week D 6 to 11.30   CLOSED: 25 and 26 Dec   MEALS: alc (main courses £6 to £10). Set L £10.95. Cover £1   SERVICE: not inc   CARDS: Amex, Delta, Diners, MasterCard, Switch, Visa   DETAILS: 70 seats. 20 seats outside. Private parties: 60 main room, 36 private room. Vegetarian meals. Children welcome. No-smoking area. Wheelchair access (not WC). Music. Air-conditioned £5

Mesclun £   NEW ENTRY map 12

24 Stoke Newington, Church Street, N16 0LU   COOKING 3
TEL: (0171) 249 5029   FAX: (0171) 275 8448   COST £20–£39

Behind the unassuming entrance, next door to a more ostentatious Thai restaurant, are the plain white walls, wooden floorboards, bare tables, plants and candles that prompted one visitor to exclaim, 'Ahhhh! Bistro!' True to its name, the food is a (largely European) mix that takes in celery and taleggio tart, calf's liver with smoked bacon and mash, and salads naturally including a mesclun version. Indeed saladings underpin a number of dishes, from a moulded tower of ratatouille sandwiching a disc of mozzarella, to grilled crottin de Chavignol wrapped in Parma ham.

'Uncomplicated' and 'straightforward' sums up how the restaurant sees its food – perhaps exemplified by large crevettes with béarnaise, or roast corn-fed chicken with Mediterranean salsa – a view confirmed by an inspector who noted 'no really fancy techniques' but 'a decent level of accomplishment and a degree of imagination'. Meat is free-range or organic, taking in beef sirloin, roast chump of lamb, and roast duck breast with an attractively 'gamey, liverish' flavour in a well-judged raspberry-infused sauce. Among desserts, the bittersweet chocolate tart stands out for its 'seriously intense' flavour, and light, smooth, creamy texture. Service is notably good, and around 30 wines are carefully chosen to beat the £20 price point, starting with house Italian red and Australian white at £9.95.

CHEF: Dirceu Pozzebon   PROPRIETORS: Salih Cicek and Dirceu Pozzebon   OPEN: Mon to Sat D only 6 to 11, Sun brunch 11 to 11   MEALS: alc (main courses £6 to £12)   SERVICE: 10% (optional), card slips closed   CARDS: Delta, Diners, MasterCard, Switch, Visa   DETAILS: 34 seats. Vegetarian meals. Children's helpings. Wheelchair access (also women's WC). Music (£5)

Mezzo   map 15

100 Wardour Street, W1 3LE	COOKING 3
TEL: (0171) 314 4000 FAX: (0171) 314 4040	COST £26–£69

The largest, loudest and brashest member of the ever-expanding Conran empire, Mezzo inspires both love and hate but little in between. To some, this monumental 700-seater complex (two restaurants, three bars and a café) is the embodiment of Soho style; to others it's 'fairly naff'. For each correspondent who raves about the 'sheer professionalism and the fantastic buzz' there is another to deplore the 'lack of intimacy and warmth' and the 'unbelievable din'.

Mezzonine on the ground floor is the place for quick-fix fusion food (Malay noodles, wok-fried lobster, Chinese roast duck), while down the extravagant spiral staircase Mezzo offers a more traditional menu of grills, rotisserie dishes and crustacea. On a good day, the kitchen – seen through a massive sheet of glass running the depth of two floors – can turn out a 'zingy, healthy, light and cohesive' starter of squid with green mango, tamarind and chilli, followed by 'fabulous' rib of beef 'timed to perfect pinkness on the rotisserie' and 'a winner' of an apple cake with 'heavenly' clotted cream. Even Mezzo's detractors concede that service is on the ball, no mean feat considering the multitudes clamouring to be fed. The reasonably priced wine list starts off with French house wine at £11.75; abstainers can choose Japanese, lemon grass, or fresh mint tea.

CHEF: Tom Meenahan   PROPRIETOR: Sir Terence Conran   OPEN: Mezzo Sun to Fri L 12 to 3 (4 Sun), all week D 6 to 12 (1.30 Fri and Sat, 11.30 Sun); Mezzonine Mon to Sat L 12 to 3 (4 Sat), all week D 5.30 to 1 (3 Fri and Sat, 11.30 Sun)   CLOSED: 25 and 26 Dec   MEALS: Mezzo alc (main courses £10.50 to £17.50). Set L £12.50 (2 courses) to £15.50, Set pre-theatre D £14. Cover £5 (on live music nights). Mezzonine alc (main courses £6.50 to £13.50); Set L £7.95 (2 courses), Set pre-theatre D £7 (2 courses)   SERVICE: 12.5% (optional)   CARDS: Amex, Delta, Diners, MasterCard, Switch, Visa   DETAILS: Mezzo 350 seats, Mezzonine 180 seats. Private parties: 350 main room, 40 private room. Vegetarian meals. Children welcome. Wheelchair access (also WC). Music. Air-conditioned   ⊖ Piccadilly Circus

Mirabelle ☖

| | NEW ENTRY | map 15 |

56 Curzon Street, W1Y 8DL
TEL: 0171-499 4636   FAX: 0171-499 5449

COOKING 6
COST £30–£62

Marco Pierre White seems to be the one man capable of breathing new life into famous old restaurants. His establishments are food-led rather than design-driven, although in the Oak Room, Café Royal and Criterion (see entries, London) he has a fine collection of dining-rooms. Mirabelle's, reached via an 'anonymous mansion block' entrance, a trompe l'oeil lounge and long bar, is more low key, but it rises above the slightly kitsch cartoon-like murals; it shoehorns the tables in, making it feel like a very 'upmarket brasserie', and has a patio for fine-weather eating.

The food confirms the brasserie impression with a long MPW-style *carte*. First courses emphasise seafood and foie gras, and many of the dishes are familiar from his other outlets: squid ink risotto with calamari, foie gras parfait, tomato and crab mille-feuille, or 'wonderfully fresh, beautifully timed' scallops, simply adorned with tomato, oil, salt and basil. The menu has a vitality about it, requiring all manner of techniques for success, and combining last-minute grills of lobster or steak with more drawn-out preparation: boneless oxtail, for example, reassembled into a small cake held together by caul, topped by a filigree potato galette that adds a 'lovely crunchy counterpoint'.

A good line in fish brings smoked haddock with Jersey Royals, sea bass with fennel and béarnaise, and very fresh skate wing with capers, shelled winkles and a superior version of beurre noisette. Clarity of expression is a feature of the cooking, notable in desserts too: a 'delightfully-textured' bitter chocolate tart with milk ice-cream, and a slice of pineapple with peppery caramel sauce and fromage blanc ice cream. Hierarchical service has varied from 'amateurish' to 'well-drilled'. Wines on the lengthy main list concentrate on French classics backed up by some New World plums, and an extensive fine wine list is also available on request. But the real talking point is on the dessert card, where 50 different vintages of Ch. d'Yquem are proudly offered, culminating in a bottle from 1847 at £30,000. Yes, that is four zeros. Otherwise, prices are what you would expect for the West End, with around a dozen bins available under £20. CELLARMAN'S CHOICE: Pacherenc du Vic-Bilh 1995, Dom. Laplace, £18.50; Ata Rangi Pinot Noir 1996, Martinborough, New Zealand, £44.

CHEFS: Charlie Rushton and Lee Bunting   PROPRIETOR: Marco Pierre White   OPEN: all week 12 to 2.30, 6 to 12   MEALS: alc (main courses £12.50 to £25). Set L £14.95 (2 courses) to £17.95 SERVICE: 12.5% (optional), card slips closed   CARDS: Amex, Delta, MasterCard, Switch, Visa DETAILS: 110 seats. 40 seats outside. Private parties: 40 private rooms. Vegetarian meals. Children welcome. No music. Air-conditioned   ⊖ Green Park

Mirch Masala ⁂ £

map 12

1416 London Road, Norbury, SW16 4BZ
TEL: (0181) 679 1828 and 765 1070

COOKING 3
COST £11–£24

Behind the bright fascia, in one of the less prosperous sections of this very long road, is a large, rectangular, canteen-like dining-room with an open kitchen at the back. Decorations are sparse, tables plastic 'marble' topped, and the cooking distinctively Pakistani. Typical is lamb tikka, cooked on a skewer, but freed from it before serving, the meat blackened to a crust and tender inside. Another fine 'warmer' (their name for starters) is butter chicken wings, the meaty upper joints, in a subtle vegetable sauce. Non-vegetarian 'steamers' or main courses are either karahi, served in wide metal dishes, or deigi in round-bottomed metal pots. Staff, some performing cooking and serving duties, could not be more helpful. They ask how hot you like it, confirming the menu's claim that everything is cooked fresh to individual taste. Vegetarians welcome the unusually wide choice. Among commercial desserts, rasgullah (Indian cheese-cake in a milky sauce) is refreshing enough to dispel any lingering spice tastes. Unlicensed, so BYO or drink lassi. Low prices make it great value, which partly explains the lively family parties.

CHEF: Raza Ali   PROPRIETORS: Raza Ali, Mrs Azra Ali, Raiz Ali and Nandi Jutla   OPEN: Tue to Sun (also open bank hol Mons) noon to midnight   MEALS: alc (main courses £2.50 to £9). Unlicensed, but BYO (no corkage)   SERVICE: not inc, card slips closed   CARDS: Delta, Diners, MasterCard, Switch, Visa   DETAILS: 70 seats. Private parties: 100 main room. Vegetarian meals. Children's helpings. No smoking in 1 dining-room. Wheelchair access (also WC). Music. Air-conditioned   (£5)

Misato £   map 15

| 11 Wardour Street, W1V 3HE | COOKING 2 |
| TEL: (0171) 734 0808 | COST £17–£38 |

Real Japanese food is not necessarily expensive. Certainly not here, which attracts hordes of ravenous young people with decent sushi and sashimi, followed by grilled fish with salt or teriyaki sauce, perhaps with side-dishes of fried tofu or ohitashi (chilled spinach in sauce). Bento boxes contain fried chicken, omelette, bean curd, pickles and rice, plus a 'main dish' such as fried pork, prawns, or even a home-made burger. There are plenty of rice and noodle dishes. You may have to queue for a table, where you will be served by pleasant staff. House wines are £10.

CHEF: Shigeki Shidata   PROPRIETOR: T.M. Shokai Ltd   OPEN: all week 12 to 2.45, 5.30 to 10.15   CLOSED: 3 days Christmas, 1 Jan   MEALS: alc (main courses £4.50 to £12). Set L £5 to £6.80   SERVICE: not inc   CARDS: none   DETAILS: 40 seats. Vegetarian meals. Children welcome. No-smoking area. Occasional music   ⊖ Leicester Square, Piccadilly Circus

Mr Kong £   map 15

21 Lisle Street, WC2H 7BA	
TEL: (0171) 437 7341 and 9679	COOKING 4
FAX: (0171) 437 7923	COST £19–£40

Mr Kong's Cantonese cooking is serious, and the long menu delights those who dive deeply into its authentic ingredients. They can explore geoduck, frogs' legs with ginger wine, Mandarin chicken with jellyfish, and much more from the 'chef's special' menu. There are hotpots of stewed lamb with bean-curd sticks, fried chicken and dried salted fish with vegetables, braised belly-pork with yam, and stewed sea-cucumber and fish lips. Other unusual seafoods include top shell, surf clams and razor clams. Less exotic, but pleasing none the less, are 'complex, fiery, stir-fried fillet steak in garlicky sauce' and egg-fried rice. Among other successes, a dish of paper-bag chicken with shiitake mushrooms and bamboo shoots is not on the menu because, they say, 'everyone knows it'. Highly praised vegetables include deep-fried bean curd on greens with oyster sauce. Décor cannot be said to be pristine, although a legion of waiters provides good, friendly service. House French is £7.50.

CHEFS: Mr K. Kong and Mr Y.W. Lai PROPRIETORS: Mr K. Kong, Mr Y.W. Lai, Mr M.T. Lee and K.C. Tang OPEN: all week 12 to 3am CLOSED: 25 Dec MEALS: alc (main courses £6 to £18). Set D £9.30 to £22 (all minimum 2) SERVICE: not inc CARDS: Amex, Delta, Diners, MasterCard, Switch, Visa DETAILS: 120 seats. Private parties: 30 main room, 20 private room. Vegetarian meals. Children welcome. Music. Air-conditioned ⊖ Leicester Square, Piccadilly Circus
(£5)

Mitsukoshi
map 15

Dorland House, 14 20 Regent Street, SW1Y 4PH   COOKING 4
TEL: (0171) 930 0317   FAX: (0171) 839 1167   COST £54–£100

The basement restaurant of the London outpost of Tokyo's leading store is squarely aimed at Japanese residents and visitors. A conventionally austere and elegant mood is set by spectacular vases of flowers in a glass walled enclosure, with white stone chips on the floor, although the décor is beginning to show its age. Despite the all-Japanese orientation, both menu and wine list have English translations: the former taking in a short *carte*, supplemented by a useful choice of set menus, the most curious of which is bento-kaiseki, combining the exquisite small dishes of a formal meal with the convenience of a lacquered, partitioned box.

An inspector recommends the Mitsukoshi dinner of seasonal specialities, which might include sesame tofu, grilled aubergine with minced chicken, and a nimono – a boiled dish – of kabocha squash with a green tea flavoured sauce. His sushi included superb toro, the supreme cut of tuna, and other fine fish, which outshone the accompanying miso soup. A spectacular dessert is kuzukiri, cold arrowroot noodles on a bed of ice served with a hot syrup dip. Drinks include very fine saké in a glass carafe, served chilled on a bed of ice as an aperitif, or as an accompaniment to sushi and many other dishes.

CHEF: Y. Motohashi PROPRIETOR: Mitsukoshi Restaurants Ltd. OPEN: Mon to Sat 12 to 2.30, 6 to 9.30 CLOSED: Christmas, Easter MEALS: alc (main courses £4.50 to £27). Set L £17 to £50, Set D £18 to £50 SERVICE: 15%, card slips closed CARDS: Amex, Diners, MasterCard, Switch, Visa DETAILS: 54 seats. Private parties: 22 main room, 12 to 22 private rooms. Vegetarian meals. Children welcome. Music. Air-conditioned ⊖ Piccadilly Circus

Miyama
map 15

38 Clarges Street, W1Y 7PJ   COOKING 4
TEL: (0171) 499 2443   FAX: (0171) 493 1573   COST £28–£69

This very traditional Japanese restaurant is a handy address for a modestly priced bowl of rice or noodles in soup, garnished with flaked salmon, ume (dried plums), or tempura. These may be accompanied by a side dish of ohitashi (boiled spinach in a subtle sauce with grated bonito) or a grilled yakitori skewer of chicken and onion. An à la carte menu offers the standard range of sushi, sashimi, grilled or fried fish, tempura, and there is a small teppanyaki section. Nabemono dishes prepared at table include sukiyaki or shabu shabu with beef, and udon suki with white noodles, chicken, fish and vegetables in hot broth. Fixed-price meals (or 'suggested set courses') are designed to make choosing easier. The wine-list, a vintage-free zone, covers a wide range from Bereich Bernkastel at £9.50 to Château Talbot at £56.40.

CHEFS/PROPRIETORS: Mr F. Miyama and Mr T. Miura   OPEN: Mon to Fri L 12 to 2.30, all week D 6 to 10.30   MEALS: alc (main courses £8.20 to £26). Set L £12, Set D £34 to £42   SERVICE: 15%   CARDS: Amex, Delta, Diners, MasterCard, Switch, Visa   DETAILS: 64 seats. Private parties: 15 main room. Children welcome. Wheelchair access (not WC). Music. Air-conditioned   ● Green Park

Momo
map 15

25 Heddon Street, W1R 7LG
TEL: (0171) 434 4040   FAX: (0171) 287 0404

COOKING 3
COST £23–£44

Atmosphere figures prominently in the appeal of this Maghrebi restaurant, stoked up by white-stone walls, dark wooden beams, metal lanterns, carpets and Islamic tiles. Tables are close together, there are no restrictions on smoking, and, according to the restaurant, Moroccan music is 'sometimes loud and obtrusive', especially as the night wears on; but 'guests are free to dance on the floor/chairs/tables/bar'. So it is laid-back, then, and suits anybody who enjoys eating while lounging on a sofa.

At the heart of the food are couscous dishes – perhaps with skewered lamb and merguez – and a range of tagines, partnering chicken with olives and preserved lemons, or typically combining meat and fruit: quail with raisins, onions and almonds, for example. Savoury pastries also make an appearance, in the form of briouat (with cheese, mint and potato, for instance) or pastilla of pigeon with almonds and cinnamon. 'Not as spicy as I imagined it would be,' summed up one observer, who was not alone in his view. There are more pastries to finish, as well as sweet couscous, and 'Berber' pancake with honey and almonds. A short, serviceable wine list echoes the French-North African theme, starting with Algerian red at £10.50. As the *Guide* went to press plans were afoot to open on Sundays and Saturday lunch-times.

CHEF: Abdellah El-Rgrachi   PROPRIETOR: Mourad Mazouz   OPEN: Mon to Fri L 12.30 to 2.30, Mon to Sat D 7.30 to 11   MEALS: alc (main courses £10.50 to £16). Set L £12.50 (2 courses) to £15   SERVICE: 12.5% (optional), card slips closed   CARDS: Amex, Delta, Diners, MasterCard, Switch, Visa   DETAILS: 95 seats. 40 seats outside. Private parties: 200 main room, 100 private room. Vegetarian meals. Children welcome. Wheelchair access (also WC). Music. Air-conditioned   ● Piccadilly Circus

Monkeys
map 13

1 Cale Street, Chelsea Green, SW3 3QT
TEL: (0171) 352 4711

COOKING 4
COST £29–£56

The Benhams' restaurant occupies a prime site in a particularly well-heeled part of town, its idiosyncratic name reflected in the plethora of toy primates that fills most of the available shelf space. Athough fairly small, tables are well-spaced, and an obvious attempt to offer value for money is made with fixed-price menus that offer sound, essentially French cooking with an occasional nod to modern British ways. It can be rich, as in a 'decidedly melt-in-the-mouth' warm foie gras salad, but at lunch-time it is possible to eat just a main course, or a combination of any two.

Game is a forte, and 'nicely tender' saddle of venison has been served with a hearty port sauce, red cabbage, Brussels sprouts and mash. Tender mallard and wigeon have also been praised. Sauté scallops with lentils and ratatouille appear among starters, and perhaps grilled sea bass for mains. Sauces come in silver boats in the old-fashioned manner. Puddings have been thought to let down the overall quality, but coffee is suitably strong. As to service, 'Tom Benham himself is excellent, seems to know everybody, and explains the menu well'. A large selection of frequently changing house wines is on offer, all at £15.

CHEF: Tom Benham   PROPRIETORS: Tom and Brigitte Benham   OPEN: Mon to Fri 12.30 to 2.30, 7.30 to 10.30   CLOSED: 1 week Christmas, 3 weeks Aug.   MEALS: Set L £20 to £00, Set D £25 to £35   SERVICE: not inc   CARDS: Delta, MasterCard, Switch, Visa   DETAILS: 32 seats. Private parties: 8 main room. Children welcome. No pipes in dining-room. No music. Air-conditioned ⊖ Sloane Square

Mon Plaisir
map 15

| 21 Monmouth Street, WC2H 9DD | NEW CHEF |
| TEL: (0171) 836 7243   FAX: (0171) 240 4774 | COST £24–£54 |

Finding a nook in the warren of little rooms and passageways adds to the enjoyment of eating at this long-running classic French bistro in the heart of Theatreland. 'Classic' denotes not merely the gastronomic maps on the walls, but also the hearty bourgeois cooking, now overseen by newcomer Patrick Smith, who has worked at Lindsay House, Alfred and L'Escargot. The food can stray into the realms of sea bass seasoned with Szechuan peppercorns and served with polenta, but regulars still expect their poulet rôti chasseur and truffe au chocolat. Service is 'speedy, attentive, young and French'. A handful of wines from Australia and New Zealand prop up the serviceable if unremarkable French selections. House wines are £8.95 for red and £9.20 for white.

CHEF: Patrick Smith   PROPRIETOR: Alain Lhermitte   OPEN: Mon to Fri L 12 to 2.15, Mon to Sat D 5.50 to 11.15   CLOSED: Christmas, 4 days Easter, bank hols   MEALS: alc (main courses £9 to £18.50). Set L £14.95, Set D before 7.15 £10.95 (2 courses) to £13.95, Set D £19.95 (minimum 2). BYO £8   SERVICE: 12.5% (optional), card slips closed   CARDS: Amex, Delta, Diners, MasterCard, Switch, Visa   DETAILS: 96 seats. Private parties: 28 main room. Vegetarian meals. Children welcome. No cigars/pipes in dining-room. Wheelchair access (2 steps; not WC). Music. Air-conditioned   ⊖ Covent Garden

Montana
map 12

| 125–129 Dawes Road, Fulham Broadway, SW6 7EA | COOKING 2 |
| TEL: (0171) 385 9500   FAX: (0171) 386 0337 | COST £24–£52 |

Montana is the elder sister of Dakota (see entry), although the cooking at each is of the south-western USA rather than the northern badlands. The L-shaped corner venue is decorated in American Indian style, so feathers and head-dresses proliferate under the sultry purple ceiling. Soft-shell crab with blackened sweetcorn and a sauce of smoked tomatoes and jalapeños is a typically lively starter, while a main course of 'moist, succulent' duck breast comes with a cake of sweet potatoes seasoned with chilli and cilantro (coriander), and a sweet fig jam. Sweetly dressed salads may be ordered separately, and meals end with perhaps lime tart and strawberry coulis, or cherry and cheese chimichanga served with Rocky Road ice-cream, replete with lumps of marshmallow. Wines are arranged by style and offer as much choice below £20 as above, though the more prized Californian bins fall into the latter category. House French is £11.50.

CHEFS: Daniel McDowell and Allie Sewell PROPRIETORS: Drew Barwick and Kevin Finch
OPEN: Fri to Sun L 12 to 3.30, Mon to Sat D 7 to 11 CLOSED: 25 and 26 Dec MEALS: alc D (main courses £10 to £12.50). Set L Fri £12.50 (2 courses) to £15, Set D £24.95. Brunch menu Sat and Sun SERVICE: 12.5% (optional), card slips closed CARDS: Amex, Delta, MasterCard, Switch, Visa DETAILS: 65 seats. Private parties: 35 main room. Vegetarian meals. Children welcome. Wheelchair access (not WC). Music. Air-conditioned ⊖ Fulham Broadway

Moro

map 13

34–36 Exmouth Market, EC1R 4QE
TEL: (0171) 833 8336 FAX: (0171) 833 9338

COOKING 5
COST £27–£38

The room spills on to the street at the front, the kitchen is open to view at the back (look out for the wood-burning oven and charcoal grill), and in between a long zinc bar dispenses blackboard snacks (tapas, raciones, meze, call them what you will) to casual callers. Plain wooden tables and chairs confirm the informality. When it opened in the spring of 1997, Moro tapped into a Maghreb-inspired vein of cooking that has come to permeate many other kitchens. Paradoxically, its freshness of appeal derives from its ancient roots: the meeting of Arabic and European cultures, whose high point was during the Moorish occupation of Spain from the eighth to the fifteenth centuries. If we think fusion food is a modern idea, we should think again. Despite preserved lemons, pomegranates, dates, chickpeas, harissa and membrillo, this is not doctrinaire or purist food, simply an appealing blend of the familiar and exotic.

Although it sounds as if a menu decoder might help with some items – mojama, cecina, fatayer, gozleme – staff are happy to explain, and the food itself is easily understood: from bold-flavoured white bean soup to quail on flatbread. Good materials have produced fresh-tasting crab brik, and chargrilled squid with harissa, perfectly timed and with 'simple but exact flavours'. The chargrill has also worked to good effect on veal chop (with chorizo and cabbage), and leg of lamb (with okra and coriander). Desserts stick to a smaller repertoire that takes in rosewater and cardamom ice-cream, and almond tart with quince and oloroso. Valdespino sherries head the fairly priced, Spanish-led wine list, and house French is £9.50.

CHEFS: Mr and Mrs Sam Clark, and Jake Hodges PROPRIETORS: Mr and Mrs Sam Clark, Jake Hodges and Mark Sainsbury OPEN: Mon to Fri 12.30 to 2.30, 7 to 10.30 CLOSED: Christmas, Easter, bank hols MEALS: alc (main courses £11 to £13). Tapas menu available 12.30 to 10.30
SERVICE: not inc CARDS: MasterCard, Switch, Visa DETAILS: 80 seats. 20 seats outside. Vegetarian meals. Children welcome. Wheelchair access (also WC). No music ⊖ Farringdon

The Guide *always appreciates hearing about changes of chef or owner.*

Moshi Moshi Sushi 🍴✳ £ map 13

Unit 24, Liverpool Street Station, EC2M 7QH
TEL/FAX: (0171) 247 3227
7–8 Limeburner Lane, EC4M 7HY   COOKING 1
TEL: (0171) 329 1160   FAX: (0171) 248 1807   COST £13–£30

Music tapes come round almost as often as the plates on the conveyor belt at this pioneer of kaiten (conveyor-belt gastronomy), which still offers sushi from one pound a plate. There are tables where you can sit and order from the menu, but most of the fun is to be had perching on a stool watching the chefs at work, and grabbing colour-coded plates as they rattle past. Ask the chefs for specials such as salmon roe, uni (sea urchin) and toro (tuna belly), which are reckoned to be a better bet than the basic nori rolls. Sashimi and vegetarian sushi are always available and there are also geta – literally 'wooden slippers', actually platters of assorted sushi or sashimi – which are great value. Drink free green tea or order wine, beer or saké from cheerful relaxed staff.

CHEFS: Enrico Venzon, Sui Hong Lee and Ravi Raveendran   PROPRIETOR: Caroline Bennet
OPEN: Mon to Fri 11.30 to 9   CLOSED: 24 Dec to 3 Jan, bank hols   MEALS: alc (plate prices £1 to £2.50). Geta (1-plate meals) £4.50 to £11.50. Cover 50p   SERVICE: net prices, card slips closed   CARDS: Delta, Diners, MasterCard, Switch, Visa   DETAILS: 75 seats. Vegetarian meals. Children welcome. No smoking in dining-room. Music   ⊖ Liverpool Street   (£5)

MPW map 12

Second Floor, Cabot Place East,
Canary Wharf, E14 4QT | NEW CHEF |
TEL: (0171) 513 0513   COST £33–£58

Cabot Place is the main shopping mall at Canary Wharf. Alight from the Docklands Light Railway, and head on up to the celestial glass-domed heights, where Canada Tower looms above, and where, at the very top, is a restaurant of slightly awkward semi-circular layout. Robert McQuattie Arnott arrived, just as the *Guide* was going to press, to interpret the Marco mode, which had of late taken in pig's trotter and frisée in a sherry vinaigrette, a risotto of baby squid with roast lobster and grilled scallops, and a brioche version of bread-and-butter pudding. Service tends towards the ice-cool norm of such places. Wines are well-chosen, but don't exert themselves to provide much choice below £20. The cheapest, however, a Piedmont Cortese and a red Vin de Pays d'Oc, are £10.

CHEF: Robert McQuattie Arnott   PROPRIETORS: Jimmy Lahoud and Marco Pierre White   OPEN: Mon to Fri 12 to 2.30, 5.30 to 9   CLOSED: 25 Dec, bank hols   MEALS: alc (main courses £10 to £19.50)   SERVICE: 12.5% (optional), card slips closed   CARDS: Amex, Delta, MasterCard, Switch, Visa   DETAILS: 150 seats. Private parties: 200 main room, 15 private room. Vegetarian meals. Children welcome. Wheelchair access (not WC). No music. Air-conditioned

The 2000 Guide will be published before Christmas 1999. Reports on meals are most welcome at any time of the year, but are particularly valuable in the spring (no later than June). Send them to The Good Food Guide, FREEPOST, 2 Marylebone Road, London NW1 1YN. Or email your report to guidereports@which.co.uk.

Museum Street Café ✦ £ map 15

47 Museum Street, WC1A 1LY
TEL/FAX: (0171) 405 3211 COOKING 5
EMAIL: koerbernathan@museumstreetcafe COST £22–£35

At Easter 1998, the Café reassessed its modus operandi, and introduced a few changes. It no longer opens in the evenings, but has returned to its spiritual identity as an all-day café, doing early breakfasts and afternoon teas during the week and brunches on Sundays. The menu, which was always evolving in this direction, is now almost exclusively vegetarian, although you can have scrambled eggs with smoked salmon for brunch without fear of being lynched.

Hard by the British Museum, it is a long narrow room that benefits from a skylight and some colourful modern daubs and Chinese prints on the walls. The food is impeccably sourced: Valrhona chocolate goes into an unforgettable cake, Appledore organic vegetables and saladings are used, and cheeses come from Neal's Yard. An inspector was struck by the authoritative use of herbs and spices that give lift to even the simplest dishes. A swirl of chipotle cream ignited a bowl of roasted sweet potato soup, on which six coriander leaves floated. A mass of torn basil gave bite to a pasta dish in which roasted red peppers, sweated onions and the scent of saffron joined penne quills cooked al dente. Other lunchtime dishes have been white bean and roasted vegetable chilli with Montgomery Cheddar, and frittata with Roseval potatoes, spinach and Taleggio. Non-chocoholics might settle at the end for apricot and almond tart, or banana with Greek yoghurt, honey and almonds. Aromatic espresso, from Illy, should not be missed. A dozen wines are intelligently chosen, every bottle having earned its place, and prices are keen as mustard. Languedoc varietals, a Marsanne and a Merlot, open the proceedings at £9.50.

CHEFS/PROPRIETORS: Mark Nathan and Gail Koerber OPEN: all week L only 12 to 3 (Sun brunch 11.30 to 3.30) CLOSED: 2 weeks Christmas, Easter, bank hols MEALS: alc (main courses £6.50 to £8.0). Breakfast and afternoon tea menus Mon to Fri 8 (9 Sat, 11.30 Sun) to 6. BYO £5 SERVICE: not inc CARDS: Amex, Delta, MasterCard, Switch, Visa DETAILS: 36 seats. 5 seats outside. Private parties: 18 main room. Vegetarian meals. Children welcome. No smoking in dining-room. Wheelchair access (2 steps; also men's WC). No music ⊖ Holborn, Tottenham Court Road

Neal Street Restaurant map 15

26 Neal Street, WC2H 9PS [NEW CHEF]
TEL: (0171) 836 2740 FAX: (0171) 240 3964 COST £35–£78

Antonio Carluccio's shrine to fungus is located on a cobbled thoroughfare in the heart of old Covent Garden. Most readers will be familiar with his jovial TV appearances, and his passion for wild mushrooms and truffles is such that one or the other is built into nearly every savoury dish on the menu in the winter months. Kirk Vincent, who arrived too late for us to receive any feedback, has worked in Italy, and inherits a rich vein of cooking that might take in veal kidneys in vin santo, or guinea-fowl with chanterelles, and tiramisù to finish. Wines, though not exclusively Italian, afford little in the way of financial relief beyond house Sardinian white or Montepulciano d'Abruzzo at £11.

CHEF: Kirk Vincent   PROPRIETOR: Antonio Carluccio   OPEN: Mon to Sat 12.30 to 2.30, 6 to 11
CLOSED: 24 Dec to 1 Jan, bank hols   MEALS: alc (main courses £12 to £21). Set L £25   SERVICE:
15% (optional), card slips closed   CARDS: Amex, Delta, Diners, MasterCard, Switch, Visa
DETAILS: 65 seats. Private parties: 12 main room, 24 private room. Vegetarian meals. Children
welcome. No pipes in dining-room. Wheelchair access (1 step; not WC). No music.
Air-conditioned   ⊖ Covent Garden

New Hoo Wah £ | **NEW ENTRY** map 15

| 37 Gerrard Street, W1V 7LJ | COOKING 1 |
| TEL: (0171) 434 0540   FAX: (0171) 434 0521 | COST £16–£43 |

New Hoo Wah may look like a typical large Chinatown restaurant, simply
decorated with magnolia walls bearing Chinese prints, but the cooking sets it
apart. Although the long *carte* covers Szechuan and Peking cooking, this is
principally a Cantonese place as the 'lunch special menu' makes clear. Lovers of
'the slithery and slippery' are happy to catch eel, snakefish and, for the
adventurous, a number of snake dishes. An inspector enjoyed soft-shell crab,
bean curd with crabmeat, abalone with sea cucumber; and a whole deep-fried
lacquered pigeon, with moist meat, crisp skin and lots of flavour. Dim-sum,
prepared in full view on a stall, are also highly rated: har kau (steamed prawn
dumplings), and 'wonderfully gelatinous' stewed pork knuckle with egg in
honey black vinegar sauce, have been praised. Various set menus are available;
one reporter enjoyed a 'monk jump over wall' banquet, based on the
long-cooked, wonderfully garnished soup of that name. Service is commended
for politeness, efficiency and command of English but can be impersonal. House
wine is £7.50.

OPEN:all week 12 to 11.30 (11.45 Fri and Sat)   MEALS:alc (main courses £4 to £12). Set L and D
£9.50 to £20   SERVICE:10%   CARDS:Amex, Delta, Diners, MasterCard, Switch, Visa
DETAILS:Children welcome. No-smoking area. Music. Air-conditioned   ⊖ Leicester Square

Nico Central ✑ | map 15

| 35 Great Portland Street, W1N 5DD | COOKING 4 |
| TEL: (0171) 436 8846   FAX: (0171) 436 3455 | COST £34–£43 |

One of Nico's Park Lane-trained chefs has taken up the reins at his old
stamping-ground north of Oxford Street. The L-shaped room with art deco
fittings and mirrored dado rail hasn't changed much over the years. Waiters still
run athletically up and down stairs, and there is, as ever, a slight feeling of a
quart being poured into a pint pot when the tiny tables are filled up with
paraphernalia. The menu is formula-Nico, as it has been developed during the
empire's diversification of the last few years, mostly classical French brasserie
cooking using good materials.

Meals might begin robustly with goats' cheese and red pepper terrine dressed
with olive oil and thyme, or a risotto of baby artichokes. Main courses tend to
impress the most, as in herb-crusted roast monkfish in a restrained red wine
sauce, although braised shin of veal has been less successful. Vegetable
selections (charged extra) have seemed rather perfunctory. Desserts appear more
inventive than at other Nico branches, and have included chocolate blinis wih
caramelised apple and nougat glacé, as well as an appreciably alcoholic Grand

Marnier bavarois with powerful lemon sauce. Both service and wines are largely French, the former commended as 'speedy and efficient', the latter rather more pedestrian and pricey. The starting-point is £12.50.

CHEF: Jean-Philippe Patruno   PROPRIETOR: Restaurant Partnership plc   OPEN: Mon to Fri L 12 to 2, Mon to Sat D 7 to 11   CLOSED: Christmas, Easter, bank hols   MEALS: Set L £22 (2 courses) to £25, Set D £27   SERVICE: net prices   CARDS: Amex, Delta, Diners, MasterCard, Switch, Visa   DETAILS: 50 seats. Private parties: 12 private room. Vegetarian meals. No children under 8. No cigars/pipes in dining-room. Wheelchair access (not WC). No music. Air-conditioned ⊖ Oxford Circus

Nicole's   map 15

158 New Bond Street, W1Y 9PA   COOKING 4
TEL: (0171) 499 8408   FAX: (0171) 409 0381   COST £42–£71

The clothes shop's 'cool stylishness' is echoed in the light, clean looking dining-room, which makes 'a smart impression' on those who head downstairs to it. Cooking is in Italian-Californian mould, and lunch seems to cause the biggest frisson. The aim is not necessarily to send customers back into the world with Kate Moss figures, though: 'the food was surprisingly robust and the portions generous.' Taken together, bar and restaurant menus cover everything from roast pepper risotto or steak sandwich (ciabatta, of course), to pan-fried cod with mash and parsley sauce, or 'mixed grill' of lamb cutlet, calf's liver, pancetta and black pudding. Any gaps in the shopping day can be filled by breakfast or afternoon tea.

The kitchen takes its supplies seriously, from organic leaves and Italian-grown vegetables to grilled Glenbervie beef fillet, served with foie-gras crostini and roast parsnips. Presentation is uncluttered, and the kitchen opts for a preponderance of chargrilling because it is 'simple, healthy and tasty'. But that has not stopped reporters from enjoying 'notably sweet' deep-fried scallops with thick-cut chips and zingy tartare sauce, and a 'huge gooey pile of hazelnut and chocolate meringue'. Good choice of wines by the glass adds to the appeal of the short, well-chosen list, which opens with house French at £11.75.

CHEF: Annie Wayte   PROPRIETOR: Stephen Marks   OPEN: restaurant Mon to Sat L 12.30 to 3.30 (4 Sat), Mon to Fri D 6.30 to 10.45; breakfast menu 10.30; bar menu Mon to Sat 11.30 to 5.30 CLOSED: 25 and 26 Dec, bank hols   MEALS: alc (main courses £14 to £24). Cover £1   SERVICE: 12.5% (optional), card slips closed   CARDS: Amex, Delta, Diners, MasterCard, Switch, Visa DETAILS: 90 seats. Private parties: 100 main room. Vegetarian meals. Children welcome. No-smoking area. Music. Air-conditioned   ⊖ Green Park, Bond Street

▲ Nobu   map 15

Metropolitan Hotel, 19 Old Park Lane, W1Y 4LB   COOKING 5
TEL: (0171) 447 4747   FAX: (0171) 447 4749   COST £31–£90

A Japanese restaurant with South American input might not sound like the first requirement of the discerning squillionaire, but that is what this hotel on the fringe of Mayfair has to offer. Staff flit about the long, narrow room in Issey Miyake and Donna Karan, more labels fill the close-packed tables, and a babble from customers bounces off the low ceiling. Superstar chef Nobuyuki Matsuhisa opened here in 1997, adding it to his portfolio of restaurants in New York,

Beverly Hills and Aspen, Colorado, appointing New Zealander Mark Edwards as his representative in the kitchen.

The dual geographical orientation of the cooking results in an appetiser of yellowtail sashimi with jalapeño, or Peruvian spicy salmon skewer, but the more obvious Japanese creations impress most. Freshly prepared sushi, especially tuna, is particularly fine. Soft-shell crab in a roll with sashimi and grilled eel also comes in for praise, and udon noodle dishes and tempura-battered vegetables add to the range of choice. The menu requires advanced proficiency with Japanese gastronomy to decode, so some opt for the £60 multi-course omakase that finishes with a generous platter of sushi. Otherwise, end with an ice-cream, tropical fruit, or coco manger blanco (you've guessed it, Peruvian blanc mange) with chill-roasted pineapple. A broad range of sakés, including one from Napa Valley, supplements a stylistically catalogued, state-of-the-art wine list. Prices are on the high side, though house Côtes de Duras Sémillon and Merlot are £14.50.

CHEFS: Nobuyuki Matsuhisa and Mark Edwards PROPRIETORS: Nobuyuki Matsuhisa, Robert De Niro and Como Holdings OPEN: Mon to Fri L 12 to 2.15, all week D 6 to 10.15 (9.45 Sun) MEALS: alc (main courses £6.50 to £27.50). Set L £22.50 to £40, Set D £60 SERVICE: 12.5% (optional), card slips closed CARDS: Amex, Delta, Diners, MasterCard, Switch, Visa DETAILS: 150 seats. Private parties: 40 main room. Vegetarian meals. Children welcome. Wheelchair access (also WC). No-smoking area No music. Air-conditioned ACCOMMODATION: 155 rooms, all with bath/shower. TV. Phone. Room only £195 to £1,300 (not inc VAT). Rooms for disabled. Children welcome. Baby facilities. Afternoon teas ⊖ Hyde Park Corner

Novelli W8

map 13

122 Palace Gardens, W8 4RT
TEL: (0171) 229 4024 FAX: (0171) 243 1826

COOKING 5
COST £34–£62

It helps to be young to eat here. At least, that's what the older generation concludes after sitting in 'uncomfortable' chairs, sampling the noise level, and coping with the lack of space. Lunch-times in the blue and purple dining-room may be quieter, and indeed the fixed-price lunch is considered 'amazing' value when compared with the *carte*. The Novelli style puts an individual spin on some classic ideas, producing pressed cassoulet terrine for example, and takes an interest in offal such as tongue salad with beetroot marmalade and lentils, or pig's trotter of the day, perhaps stuffed with chicken mousse, saucisson and shiitake, served with a smooth celeriac mash.

The food is colourful – judging by a capuccino pea soup with foie gras and cep powder, or a 'sweet tasting and flavourful' chilled gazpacho with crab and cucumber – and fish is given as much prominence as meat, turning up roast mullet with vanilla risotto, alongside a 'well-balanced' dish of poached rabbit leg stuffed with piperade risotto, served with a fine red pepper sauce. A few 'meagre helpings' have spoiled it for some, but chips are 'perfection' and desserts are considered a strong point: steamed chocolate pudding with vanilla ice is 'good to look at, good to eat'. Service may be more willing than attentive, but the bill comes with a 'suggested gratuity' anyway. A short, pricey wine list starts with house French at £13.50.

CHEF: Mike Bird   PROPRIETOR: Jean-Christophe Novelli   OPEN: Tue to Sat L 12 to 3, all week D 6 to 11   CLOSED: 2 weekds from 23 Dec   MEALS: alc (main courses £11.50 to £14)   SERVICE: 12.5% (optional)   CARDS: Amex, Delta, Diners, MasterCard, Switch, Visa   DETAILS: 65 seats. 14 seats outside. Children welcome. No cigars/pipes in dining-room. Music   ⊖ Notting Hill Gate

Oak Room Marco Pierre White

map 15

Le Meridien Hotel, 21 Piccadilly, W1V 0BH   COOKING 10
TEL: (0171) 437 0202   FAX: (0171) 437 3574   COST £49–£186

The restaurant is 'in the Meridien but not of it', according to one visitor. Indeed, a note on the menu disclaims any connection between the two. Powerful Edwardian design takes in vast panels of limed oak, and six enormous chandeliers 'hanging from the highest ceiling of any restaurant I can recall', set off by 'awe-inspiring' flower arrangements. Fine art on the walls chimes well with the rococo splendour, making this an impressive room, though not necessarily one to cheer the spirit. The menu mixes refined and complex starters with rich and often involved main courses, and 'wonderfully excessive' desserts; it is 'world-class' cooking.

A la carte meals begin with a taster, typically a single sweet-tasting seared scallop with a puddle of squid ink and a pile of chewy deep-fried squid tentacles, and first courses consist mostly of shellfish and foie gras, many of which will be familiar to Marco fans: indeed, some are on offer at other MPW restaurants, including Criterion Brasserie and Mirabelle (see entries).This may not make for great excitement, but it doesn't diminish their impact when they are produced with such definitive skill, as in a sensuous-looking escalope of foie gras with a fanned, lightly glazed mango and a carrot and ginger sauce, or 'exquisitely made' vinaigrette of leeks and langoustine with caviare en gelée (jellied dishes are something of a trade mark).

There is no shortage of luxury ingredients, but one sign of a good kitchen is what it can do with ordinary-sounding materials. This kitchen's answer is a mille-feuille of crab layered with tomato and avocado, served with a tomato vinaigrette: 'widely copied', submitted one reporter, 'but I have yet to eat one which comes even close to this'. Game dishes are handled as well as any: for example, a dish of roast greyleg partridge with choucroute, 'transformed into haute cuisine' by virtue of excellent ingredients and perfect delivery that includes a truffled stock-based sauce. This may not be particularly original, but in the view of one of our most widely travelled inspectors, 'I can safely say that it is not possible to make this dish any better.'

'There is only one dessert for me here,' confided a reporter, who was understandably smitten with the iced nougat-centred pyramide, while another found the pan-fried soufflé Rothschild as good as ever. Even a simple-looking feuillantine of raspberries, with three thin layers of biscuity pastry, hides great technical skill and requires balanced judgement to get it as right as this. 'First-rate workmanship in the service of sensual delight' was how one observer summed up a chocolate 'cadeau', a sort of layered cake with a tall hat, with 'wizard' chocolate flavour and good textural variety. Plentiful petits fours are 'of the highest order'.

Service is smooth, providing nothing disturbs the routine, but has also been considered 'arrogant' and 'going through the motions'. Sooner or later the question of price arises. 'If I was going to spend this sort of money on a restaurant, this is the sort of food I would want to eat,' declared one, but the 'stonkingly expensive' package is not helped by hefty supplements: £15 for a lobster starter, and £20 for a piece of sea bass with a caviare topping and a deep-fried oyster, even though it could not be bettered. On a *carte* that already costs £80 these additions seem merely greedy. Anybody of a nervous financial disposition might consider the fixed-price three-course lunch (with two choices per course), although smelling-salts may be necessary for wine prices that 'bring tears to your eyes'. The list is uncompromisingly aristocratic and set out frustratingly in old-fashioned style with barely legible prices, starting at £30.

CHEF/PROPRIETOR: Marco Pierre White   OPEN: Mon to Fri L 12 to 2.30, Mon to Sat D 7 to 11.15   CLOSED: 2 weeks Christmas, 2 weeks Aug   MEALS: Set L £29.50, Set D £75 to £85   SERVICE: not inc   CARDS: Amex, Delta, MasterCard, Switch, Visa   DETAILS: 80 seats. Vegetarian meals Children welcome. Wheelchair access (also WC). No music. Air-conditioned   ⊖ Piccadilly Circus

Oceana 🍴✳ £

NEW ENTRY   map 15

Jason Court, 76 Wigmore Street, W1H 9DQ   COOKING 2
TEL: (0171) 224 2992   FAX: (0171) 486 1216   COST £26–£54

Comfortable high-backed chairs, and strong rich colours on columns and wall panels, combine to give this basement room a warm feeling, reinforced by casually dressed owner Tony Kitous and his only slightly more formally dressed staff. Co-owner Pierre Khodja adds subtle North African spices and flavours to his brand of modern European cooking, which may not be readily apparent from the menu, although lamb (marinated neck, as a starter) comes on tabouleh, and rump (as a main) with merguez. Recommended dishes have included Mediterranean cheeses with vegetables, and mushrooms with aubergine caviare and garlic bread, while carnivores might opt for boudin blanc with spinach, or breast of duck with aubergine marmalade. Fishy selections run to dressed crab, and roast sea bass with fennel salad, while lemon tart and seductive ice-creams might be among the rich and creamy desserts. A varied, 40-strong wine list has eight house wines by the glass or bottle (£9.70).

CHEF: Pierre Khodja   PROPRIETORS: Tony Kitous and Pierre Khodja   OPEN: Mon to Fri L 12 to 3, Mon to Sat D 6 to 11.15   CLOSED: 25 Dec, bank hols   MEALS: alc (main courses £10.50 to £16.50). Set L and D (before 7.15pm) £12.50   SERVICE: 12.5% (optional), card slips closed CARDS: Amex, Delta, Diners, MasterCard, Switch, Visa   DETAILS: 90 seats. Private parties: 120 main room, 8 to 18 private rooms. Vegetarian meals. Children welcome. No smoking in 1 dining-room. Wheelchair access (2 steps; also WC). Music. Air-conditioned   ⊖ Bond Street
(£5)

'After the veteran maitre d' soothingly explained how the worldwide demand for sea bass made it impossible for us to have any, we felt much better. For £100 a head we had previously expected to get any damn fish we fancied from the menu. We now thought of more-deserving rich businessmen in far-flung lands, and felt more than a little contrite at our own greed.' (On eating in Oxfordshire)

L'Odéon ♥ map 15

65 Regent Street, W1R 7HH
TEL: (0171) 287 1400   FAX: (0171) 287 1300 | NEW CHEF |
EMAIL: lodeon@cara.co.uk   COST £31–£77

A table beside the long window frontage of this large first-floor dining-room secures a good view on to Regent Street below, and curtained bays prevent the space from feeling cavernous. As the *Guide* went to press, the kitchen was about to come under the control of Breton chef Erwan Louaisil. It may be difficult to anticipate the style he will adopt, but he has worked at Daniel's in New York, and is a protégé of Pierre Garnier in Paris, so things look promising. Reports, please. An eclectic wine list, sourced from Bibendum wine merchants, is grouped by grape and style, some 80 bins offer plenty of choice at reasonable prices, while a dozen fine burgundies and clarets are provided for those in search of more traditional fare. The house selection starts at £13.50. CELLARMAN'S CHOICE: Bourgogne 'Cuvée Icarus' 1994, Paul Boutinot, £15.50; Bordeaux, Ch. de Fontenille 1995, £19.50.

CHEFS: Erwan Louaisil   PROPRIETORS: Pierre and Kathleen Condou   OPEN: all week 12 to 2.30, 5.30 to 11.30 (7 to 10.30 Sun.)   CLOSED: 25 and 26 Dec, 1 Jan, bank hols   MEALS: alc (main courses L £14.50 to £22.50, D £15 to £26). Set L and D 5.30 to 7pm £14.50 (2 courses) to £18. Bar meals available all week L and D. Afternoon tea. Cover £1.50   SERVICE: not inc; 12.5% for parties of 6 or more   CARDS: Amex, Delta, Diners, MasterCard, Switch, Visa   DETAILS: 220 seats. Private parties: 200 main room, 20 private room. Vegetarian meals. Children welcome. No-smoking area L only. Wheelchair access (also WC). Music. Air-conditioned   ⊖ Piccadilly Circus

Odette's ♦ map 13

130 Regents Park Road, NW1 8XL
TEL: (0171) 586 5486 and 8766   COOKING 6
FAX: (0171) 586 2575   COST £20–£57

Odette's is that rare combination, a restaurant that serves its neighbourhood well but is also worth travelling across town for: 'a real find', one visitor called it. There is a wine bar below stairs, a bright, exuberant garden room at the back, and a more sedate room at the front, with mahogany bar, gilt mirrors of all shapes and sizes, and crisp linen all contributing to a feel of 'comfortable opulence'. The food is 'worth every penny', but the no-choice £10 lunch has to be one of the capital's best permanent offers: one appreciative couple negotiated a first-course exchange – from ox-cheek to a creamy chicken and almond soup – followed it with 'perfectly cooked' fillets of John Dory on shredded fennel, and finished with thin slices of glazed banana on fresh berries with pistachio ice-cream: 'excellent value,' they concluded.

'Simple and distinct' flavours are the style, a legacy of David Kennedy's well-spent time with Terence Laybourne at 21 Queen Street (see entry, Newcastle upon Tyne). Despite some perky flavours – harissa with lemon sole, or a mix of coriander, chilli, garlic and ginger to spice up fresh crab – ideas are generally restrained: tartlet of asparagus with Jersey royals and chives, or sauté black-leg chicken with peas and broad beans. For one reporter, monkfish with risotto and saffron sauce, and a 'tarte Tatin' of caramelised onions and goats' cheese were main courses 'of the highest order', while a winter dish of duck wrapped in Savoy cabbage with lentils has elicited several superlatives.

Desserts are approached with similar vigour. There may be a jellied rhubarb and blood orange terrine, chocolate espresso tart with crème fraîche, or a warm winter fruit salad that is 'like eating fruit in Glühwein'. Wines on the wide-ranging yet quality-focused list are arranged by style and succinctly annotated; combined with a healthy choice of bottles under £20, two pages of halves and 30 wines by the glass, this is a good way to encourage experimentation. House wines from Argentina are £10.95. CELLARMAN'S CHOICE: Palliser Estate Sauvignon Blanc 1997, Martinborough, New Zealand, £20.50; Coteaux Varois, Ch. Routas 'Infernet' 1995, £16.70.

CHEF: David Kennedy   PROPRIETOR: Simone Green   OPEN: all week L 12.30 to 2.30 (Sat and Sun wine bar only), Mon to Sat D 7 to 11   CLOSED: 1 week Christmas, bank hols   MEALS: alc (main courses £9 to £16.50). Set L £10   SERVICE: not inc   CARDS: Amex, Delta, Diners, MasterCard, Switch, Visa   DETAILS: 00 seats. 10 seats outside. Private parties: 30 main room, 9 and 30 private rooms. Vegetarian meals. Children's helpings. No cigars/pipes in dining-room. No music   ⊖ Chalk Farm

Olivo
map 13

21 Eccleston Street, SW1W 9LX   COOKING 2
TEL: (0171) 730 2505   FAX: (0171) 824 8190   COST £27–£53

Efficient air-conditioning, designer lights, bright blue and yellow décor, and clean lines add up to cool Sardinia. That there is no such thing as Italian cooking in Italy, only regional cooking, is amply proved by Olivo's menu, which on a single day can include wild boar salami with fennel, skate salad with balsamic vinegar and pine-nuts, chargrilled grey mullet, and sebada (a cheese-filled, deep-fried pastry shell with honey). Dinner follows the Italian format of antipasti, minestra (pasta, soup or risotto) and secondi piatti of fish or meat. The charcoal grill produces many of the main dishes, and a set-lunch menu offers a smaller choice with perhaps only four main courses. The decently priced all-Italian wine list features several from Sardinia. House wines are £10.

CHEF: Marco Melis   PROPRIETORS: Jean-Louis Journade and Mauro Sanna   OPEN: Mon to Fri L 12 to 2.30, all week D 7 to 11   CLOSED: Christmas, bank hols   MEALS: alc D (main courses £8 to £15). Set L £15 (2 courses) to £17. Cover £1.50   SERVICE: not inc   CARDS: Amex, Delta, MasterCard, Switch, Visa   DETAILS: 55 seats. Children's helpings. No children under 5. No cigars/pipes in dining-room. No music. Air-conditioned   ⊖ Victoria

One Lawn Terrace
NEW ENTRY   map 12

1 Lawn Terrace, SE3 9LJ
TEL: (0181) 355 1110   FAX: (0181) 255 0111   COOKING 4
EMAIL: enquiries@one-lawn-terrace.co.uk   COST £27–£57

Nick Hall, a lifelong resident of SE3, has at last realised his burning ambition to bring quality eating to the area by opening this bright, expansive brasserie in premises that were formerly a printing works. The large yellow upstairs room is wooden-floored and wide, and broken by a mezzanine on steel struts where more tables are crowded in. Although functionality is the first principle, it extends, unusually, to side-plates for bread and real napkins.

Sanjay Dwivedi has absorbed the modern European culinary idiom, and his lengthy menus seem to offer something for everyone, including kids. Escabèche of grilled sardines with tapénade, rabbit confit with mustard macaroni, and chocolate and pistachio mille-feuille with lemon and lime coulis indicate the vibrancy of the approach. An inspection meal was somewhat uneven in quality, but offered lightly cooked calf's liver with rissoles of polenta and a red wine sauce, and a stunning dessert of blood orange and strawberry trifle with burnt orange ice-cream. An alternative pudding, in every sense of the word, might be fruit neapolitan layered with pepper tuiles and thyme ice-cream. Presentation may not be the first priority, but the willingness to experiment has definitely caught Blackheath's mood. Designer-clad staff are young, enthusiastic and chatty. Wines on the intelligently put together list offer a broad range of styles and varietals from some of the world's more exciting small growers. Eight house wines start at £11.95 a bottle.

CHEF: Sanjay Dwivedi   PROPRIETOR: Nick Hall   OPEN: Wed to Fri and Sun L12 to 2.30 (3 Sun), all week D 6 to 10.30 (11 Fri and Sat)   CLOSED: 25 and 26 Dec, 1 Jan   MEALS: alc (main courses £11 to £15). Set L £12.95 (2 courses) to £16.50, Set D Mon to Thur before 7.45pm £13.95 (2 courses) to £17.50. Sun brunch menu also available 12 to 3   SERVICE: 12.5% (optional), card slips closed   CARDS: Amex, Delta, MasterCard, Switch, Visa   DETAILS: 150 seats. Private parties: 150 main room, 24 private room. Vegetarian meals. Children's menu. No pipes/cigars in dining-room. Wheelchair access (also WC).Music. Air-conditioned   £5

192 ♥ 🍺   map 13

192 Kensington Park Road, W11 2ES   COOKING 1
TEL: (0171) 229 0482   FAX: (0171) 229 3300   COST £22–£48

No thoroughfare in 'seriously hip' Portobello is more trendy than Kensington Park Road, with its colourful street crowd and mixture of shops. 192, which has spawned a generation of British chefs, including Adam Robinson, Rowley Leigh, Dan Evans and 'the godfather himself, Alastair Little', has switched focus under the Groucho Club's direction. It doesn't look much different – still in need of 'urgent attention' to its fabric, and still drawing a mixed media crowd – but the wine list has been strengthened and now provides a major draw.

Salads are much in evidence – Caesar, usually, plus maybe one of crab, bacon and avocado – alongside steamed mussels with coriander and chilli, or a tempura combining 'dazzlingly fresh' prawns with 'uninspiring' vegetables. Stuffed rabbit leg, or Moroccan lamb shank are likely main courses, followed perhaps by chocolate torte. Service may be 'a bit unco-ordinated', but staff are 'friendly and helpful'. Wines appeal both to the palate and pocket – many are under £20 – with a good number offered by the glass. Early-birds can quaff Beaumont des Crayères champagne for a mere £22 (between 5.30pm and 7.30pm). CELLARMAN'S CHOICE: Poggio all Gazze Sauvignon 1996, Tenuta dell'Ornellaia, Bolgheri, £20; Deakin Estate Shiraz 1996, Victoria, Australia, £13.90.

See inside the front cover for an explanation of the symbols used at the tops of entries.

CHEF: Michael Knowlson PROPRIETOR: The Groucho Club plc OPEN: all week 12.30 to 3 (3.30 Sat and Sun), 7 to 11.30 (11 Sun) CLOSED: 25 and 26 Dec, 1 Jan, Aug bank hol MEALS: alc (main courses £7 to £13.50). Set L Mon to Fri £10.50 (2 courses), Set L Sat and Sun £12 (2 courses) SERVICE: not inc; 12½% for parties of 7 or more CARDS: Amex, Delta, Diners, MasterCard, Switch, Visa DETAILS: 105 seats. 10 seats outside. Private parties: 22 private room. Vegetarian meals. Children welcome. No-smoking area. Wheelchair access (not WC). Occasional music ⊖ Ladbroke Grove, Notting Hill Gate

Orrery ♀

NEW ENTRY   map 15

55 Marylebone High Street, W1M 3AE   COOKING 6
TEL: (0171) 616 8000   FAX: (0171) 616 8080   COST £36–£78

An orrery is a mechanical model of the solar system, one of which sits at the entrance to the dining-room. That answers the first question most people ask. The second – why? – may have something to do with a similarly named restaurant of Sir Terence's back in the 1950s. As at Bluebird (see entry) we have the whole works: shop, food-store and first-floor restaurant, although this is a 'small Conran' by industry standards. The long, narrow, simply adorned but handsome dining-room looks out through large semi-circular windows over Marylebone churchyard. It is airy, relaxing and attractively lit, with blond wood, banquette seating, and 'confessional' wooden baffles separating groups of tables, making it all 'unquestionably classy' to look at. And it is equally stylish, day or night.

Brothers Chris and Jeff Galvin make the running with trademark Conran material, particularly shellfish, which might turn up as jellied lobster, crayfish salad, potted crab, or an 'expertly made and presented' langoustine raviolo to begin. Foie gras is there too, in a terrine. Cooking has varied, from 'underdone' duck to 'overcooked' lobster, but at its best has produced 'perfectly cooked' cod with champ and caper sauce, and 'superb' pink roast squab pigeon. 'When the kitchen gets it right, there is little you can fault'.

Pastry work is praised, from a crumbly shallot tart served with duck livers, via Granny Smith apple tart with simultaneously crispy and buttery pastry, to highly commended petits fours, and the apricot tart bourdaloue with vanilla sauce is reckoned a good one. Service is well directed (there appear to be so many sommeliers they are in need of a collective noun) but disgruntlements have included waiting time, loud neighbours and passive smoking. The lengthy wine list circles the planet to field a host of celestial bins at fairly astronomical prices. France is given the full treatment and Italy, California and Australia make some starry contributions. House wines from France are £12 for white, £13 for red. CELLARMAN'S CHOICE: Hess Chardonnay 1995, Napa, California, £31; St-Hallett Old Block Shiraz 1994, Barossa Valley, S. Australia, £30.75.

CHEF: Chris Galvin PROPRIETOR: Conran Restaurants OPEN: all week 12 to 3, 7 to 11 (10.30 Sun) MEALS: alc D (main courses £14.50 to £22). Set L Mon to Fri £26.50, Set L Sat and Sun £19.50 (2 courses) to £23.50. Set D Sun £28.50 (inc glass of champagne). Bar meals available SERVICE: 12.5% (optional), card slips closed CARDS: Amex, Delta, Diners, MasterCard, Switch, Visa DETAILS: 76 seats. Private parties: 9 main room. Vegetarian meals. Children welcome. No pipes in dining-room. Wheelchair access (also WC). Occasional music ⊖ Regents Park

▌ denotes an outstanding wine cellar; ♀ denotes a good wine list, worth travelling for.

Orsino 🍷 map 12

119 Portland Road, W11 4LN
TEL: (0171) 221 3299 FAX: (0171) 229 9414 COOKING 2
EMAIL: joeallenldn@btinternet.com COST £23–£52

The sister branch of Covent Garden's Orso (see entry below) is situated on a wedge-shaped site reminiscent of the bow of a boat. A revolving frosted-glass door, concealed lighting, giant flowers in a tall steel bucket and highly decorated plates enhance the stylishness. Short, daily-changing menus are inventive, while remaining faithful to modern Italian cooking. Deep-fried calamari with tomato and hot pepper sauce offers lightly battered squid rings and a dip with 'a powerful, lingering kick' to it, while roast sea bass with white beans, tomato and herbs is built around a pair of basil-and-parsley-coated fillets 'bursting with flavour'. A certain robustness permeates meat dishes too, so that venison steaks come with roast celeriac and a sauce of green peppercorns and red wine. Fruity, if not scrupulously seasonal, puddings may take in raspberry and pear torta with tropical fruit compote, or peach and strawberry tart with marinated strawberries, the latter impressing not least for the quality of its short pastry. Service has on occasion been 'lackadaisical', but clearly a lot of effort has gone into compiling the wine list. Around 50 Italians of interest and note are offered at reasonable prices. Umbrian house wines are £11.50 a litre.

CHEF: Anne Kettle PROPRIETOR: Orsino Restaurants Ltd OPEN: all week 12 to 11.30 CLOSED: 24 and 25 Dec MEALS: alc (main courses £12.50 to £15.50). Set L £11.50 (2 courses) to £15.50 SERVICE: not inc CARDS: Amex, MasterCard, Switch, Visa DETAILS: 100 seats. Private parties: 8 main room, 36 private room. Vegetarian meals. Children welcome. No-smoking area. No music. Air-conditioned ⊖ Holland Park

Orso 🍷 map 15

27 Wellington Street, WC2E 7DA
TEL: (0171) 240 5269 FAX: (0171) 497 2148 COOKING 2
EMAIL: joeallenldn@btinternet.com COST £26–£50

'Gutsy and well-flavoured' Italian regional cooking has been Orso's stock-in-trade since opening in 1985 and it continues with a virtually unchanged formula. The menu calls into play pizzas, pastas and risottos, and the kitchen keeps its larder generously stocked with ingredients of the moment. Green cauliflower salad with roasted peppers, capers, black olives and oregano shows up among the starters, while main courses could range from grilled scallops with bitter broccoli to veal and porcini stew with Parmesan mash. The restaurant's location, deep in Covent Garden's theatreland, means that 'brilliant-value' pre-theatre menus are a great draw and staff respond impressively to time constraints (a limit of two and a half hours is set on tables). One couple who cruised comfortably through three courses and coffee in an hour enthused over a rich bean soup and a 'great' dish of chargrilled Mediterranean vegetables, which served as an overture to mixed fish salad with a peppery dressing on new potatoes, green beans and onions, while a decent Amaretto tart brought the curtain down satisfactorily. The all-Italian wine list (champagne excepted) is similar to Orsino's (see above), with Antinori being just one of the star producers featured. A reasonable choice of bottles under £20 starts with house white and red at £11.50 a litre.

CHEF: Martin Wilson   PROPRIETOR: Orso Restaurants Ltd   OPEN: all week 12 to 11.45 CLOSED: 24 and 25 Dec   MEALS: alc (main courses £11.50 to £13.50). Set L Sat and Sun £14 (2 courses) to £16. Set pre-theatre D 5 to 6.45pm £13 (2 courses) to £15   SERVICE: not inc CARDS: Amex, MasterCard, Switch, Visa   DETAILS: 110 seats. Vegetarian meals. Children welcome. No-smoking area. No music. Air-conditioned   ⊖ Covent Garden

Osteria Antica Bologna ₹ £　　　　　　　　map 12

| 23 Northcote Road, SW11 1NG | COOKING 3 |
| TEL: (0171) 978 4771 | COST £21–£38 |

Aurelio Spagnuolo brings the cooking of Ancient Rome to a fascinated Wandsworth and Battersea. This culinary archaeology takes place in a compact little restaurant on a busy high road, the décor of barrel-ends and timber tables refreshingly unstuffy, and the contented babble of the clientele telling its own story. To explore the Roman legacy, try leporem madidum: rabbit stewed in honey, wine, fennel, ginger and rosemary served with barley and leek 'risotto'.

The cooking is never less than earthy and filling, although in typically inventive Italian style it deals enthusiastically in fish and vegetables: stuffed squid, the 'smooth and silky' white flesh contrasting in colour and texture to the filling of Pecorino, garlic, olives, capers and chubby mussels; or a lively Sicilian dish of ribbon pasta (tuppeddoni) with spring onions, rocket and broad beans, enhanced by two mild cheeses, goats' and ricotta. Sformatino, a mascarpone and ricotta pudding with hot chocolate sauce, is a substantial way to finish, melon sorbet with fresh melon and pineapple a lighter one. Service by 'switched-on Italians' keeps things moving smartly, and is both helpful and knowledgeable where wine is concerned. The list covers the length and breadth of Italy and features some good modern producers. Pugliese house wines are £7.90 for a 75cl jug. CELLARMAN'S CHOICE: Soave Classico Superiore 1995, Pra, £15.50; Chianti Classico Poggio Paiano 1995, £18.50.

CHEF: Aurelio Spagnuolo   PROPRIETORS: Aurelio Spagnuolo and Rochelle Porteous   OPEN: Mon to Fri 12 to 3, 6 to 11 (11.30 Fri), Sat 12 to 11.30, Sun 12 to 10.30   CLOSED: 10 days Christmas and New Year   MEALS: alc (main courses £6 to £11). Set L Mon to Sat £7.50 (2 courses). Cover 70p   SERVICE: not inc; 10% for parties of 5 or more   CARDS: Amex, Delta, MasterCard, Switch, Visa   DETAILS: 75 seats. 15 seats outside. Private parties: 40 main room. Vegetarian meals. Children's helpings. No cigars/pipes in dining-room. Wheelchair access (not WC). Music. Air-conditioned   (£5)

Osteria Basilico £　　　　　　　　　　map 13

29 Kensington Park Road, W11 2EU
| TEL: (0171) 727 9957 and 9372 | COOKING 1 |
| FAX: (0171) 229 7980 | COST £20–£39 |

This cheerful trattoria attracts the Portobello crowds and can sometimes feel cramped and smoky. But the atmosphere is also buzzy and fun, and the kitchen delivers a long list of pizze ('all made with mozzarella,' the menu points out) classic pasta dishes, plus some items with a more up-to-date ring: a starter of pan-fried sausage and spinach with balsamic vinegar, or rocket and Parmesan as a side salad, for example. Specials of the day might include baked shank of lamb, grilled sea bream and, for vegetarians, a dish of baby spinach with goats' cheese, asparagus and roasted peppers. The decently priced Italian wine list is a bonus, and Prosecco makes an excellent aperitif; house wine is £7.90.

CHEF: Alex Palano   PROPRIETOR: A. Tirabuschi   OPEN: all week 12.30 to 3 (4 Sat, 3.15 Sun), 6.30 to 11 (10.30 Sun)   CLOSED: D 24 Dec, all day 25 and 26 Dec and 1 Jan   MEALS: alc (main courses £6 to £12). BYO £5   SERVICE: 12.5% (optional)   CARDS: Amex, Delta, MasterCard, Switch, Visa   DETAILS: 80 seats. 20 seats outside. Private parties: 10 main room. Vegetarian meals. Children welcome. Occasional music. Air-conditioned   ⊖ Ladbroke Grove

Oxo Tower ♥ ⁵⁄✳   map 13

| Oxo Tower Wharf, Barge House Street, SE1 9PH | COOKING 5 |
| TEL/FAX: (0171) 803 3888 | COST £37–£75 |

The eighth floor of Oxo Tower (there's a lift) is a prime spot for a view across the Thames to some landmark sights, sweeping round from the City and St Paul's Cathedral to the Houses of Parliament. A window table helps to make the most of it, but is not essential, and the 'wow response' is elicited day or night, on clear days and cloudy ones. The restaurant's focus is on contemporary European food, and a generous *carte* ranges wide, taking in starters of creamed leek and smoked haddock tart with poached egg, ceviche of queen scallops, and baby artichokes barigoule.

Richness and a degree of luxury are the norm, evident in a whole sea bass for two, veal kidneys with mustard sauce, and cannon of lamb with creamed garlic, ceps and Madeira sauce. Among reported successes have been a huge wild mushroom ravioli 'packed with flavour', and a dish of John Dory and scallops on risotto with a champagne sauce: fish is as prominent as meat on both the *carte* and fixed-price lunch menu. Passion-fruit soufflé, lemon tart, and raspberry sablé continue the classically driven approach, while the brasserie next door serves slightly less expensive food with more Pacific Rim flavours. Although not quite as imposing as at Harvey Nichols' Fifth Floor restaurant (see entry, London), the wine list is still a grand affair conducted mostly in France, but with several flirtations outside. Prices can reflect the high quality, yet a number of good bottles come in under £20, even £15, beginning with the house French at £12.50.

CHEF: Simon Arkless   PROPRIETOR: Harvey Nichols & Co Ltd   OPEN: restaurant Sun to Fri L 12 to 3, 6 to 11 (10.30 Sun); brasserie all week 12 to 3 (3.3.0 Sun), 5.30 to 11 (10.30 Sun)   MEALS: alc (main courses brasserie £10.50 to £15.50, restaurant £13.50 to £22.50). Set L restaurant £24.50, Set D brasserie before 6.45 £18.50 (2 courses) to £21.50   SERVICE: 12.5% (optional)   CARDS: Amex, Delta, Diners, MasterCard, Switch, Visa   DETAILS: 140 seats. Brasserie 100 seats outside, restaurant 75 seats outside. Vegetarian meals. Children welcome. No smoking in 1 dining-room. Wheelchair access (also WC). Music (brasserie only). Air-conditioned   ⊖ Waterloo, Blackfriars

Le Palais du Jardin   map 15

| 136 Long Acre, WC2E 9AD | COOKING 2 |
| TEL: (0171) 379 5353   FAX: (0171) 379 1846 | COST £30–£52 |

The Palais has grown since it opened in 1992, acquiring a mezzanine level, but still serving French brasserie food. Monochrome décor contributes to the early-'90s hard-edged feel, and at busy sessions the decibel level may seem off the scale. Simple dishes have pleased – seared tuna salad, and well-timed grilled salmon with a tapénade crust were the highlights of a Saturday lunch for one party – or there might be more complex offerings such as sauté foie gras with mango tarte Tatin on ginger sauce. Fish-cakes, or rather 'gâteaux de poisson', come with chips and tomato sauce, while meat dishes tend to be more elaborately garnished. Desserts aim for rich territory in lemon tart with mascarpone cream, and chocolate tart with a red berry compote has been highly recommended. 'Waiters swoop around in sharp suits and groovy haircuts' and generally get the job done well. The principally French wine list also has a few from the New World, starting with house wines from £9.50.

CHEFS: Winston and Miles Matthews   PROPRIETOR: Le Palais Du Jardin Ltd   OPEN: Mon to Sat 12 to 3.30, 5.30 to 12, Sun 12 to 11   CLOSED: 25 and 26 Dec   MEALS: alc (main courses £9.50 to £15.50)   SERVICE: 12.5% (optional), card slips closed   CARDS: Amex, Delta, Diners, MasterCard, Switch, Visa   DETAILS: 350 seats. 20 seats outside. Private parties: 150 main room. Vegetarian meals. Children's helpings. Wheelchair access (2 steps; also WC). Music. Air-conditioned   ⊖ Covent Garden, Leicester Square

Pasha

NEW ENTRY   map 14

1 Gloucester Road, SW7 4PP   COOKING 3
TEL: (0171) 589 7969   FAX: (0171) 581 9996   COST £24–£39

Mosaic floors, exotic lanterns, a petal-strewn fountain, low, silk-cushioned chairs and loud North African music make this fashionably Moroccan-themed restaurant feel like 'a set from *Casablanca*'. The cooking makes up in quality what it lacks in authenticity: bean dishes, such as Merguez sausage with fava bean kofte, and yellow lentil soup, are 'hearty and nutritious-feeling', while a layered pastry pastilla of almond, pigeon and cinnamon is generously sized and not too sweet. Sesame crusted tuna with coriander, olives, tomatoes and rocket has also proved a well-balanced combination, and a side order of aubergine chips with lemon and mint has been singled out for praise. Finish with an unusual Turkish Delight crème brûlée. Service is costumed and theatrical, adding to the sense of occasion, though more patchily efficient than it should be for a 15 per cent 'optional' levy. France and Iberia account for the lion's share of a 40-strong wine list that pivots around the £20 to £25 mark. House vine de pays is £10.50.

CHEFS: Chris Benians, James Mc Murrough and Jason Sant   PROPRIETORS: Mogens Tholstrup and Belgo Group plc   OPEN: Mon to Sat 12 to 3, 7 to 11.30 (10.30 Sun)   CLOSED: Christmas, bank hols   MEALS: alc (main courses £10 to £15). Set L £11.95 (2 courses) to £13.95   SERVICE: 15% (optional), card slips closed   CARDS: Amex, Delta, Diners, MasterCard, Switch, Visa   DETAILS: 85 seats. Private parties: 45 main room. Vegetarian meals. Children welcome. No pipes in dining-room. Music. Air-conditioned   ⊖ Gloucester Road

Le P'tit Normand

map 12

185 Merton Road, SW18 5EF   COOKING 3
TEL: (0181) 871 0233 and 877 0996   COST £17–£43

Check tablecloths and Edith Piaf provide an appropriately traditional background for simple French country cooking, much of it in domestic mould, the sort of thing we might expect a French grandmother to knock up: onion soup, crêpes Dieppoises, carré d'agneau provençale. Blackboard specials set the pulse racing faster than the printed menu, and might take in wild mushroom feuilleté, cheese soufflé, or veal kidney with Meaux mustard sauce. The set lunch in particular is considered 'excellent value', and that goes for Sunday too. One weekday reporter enjoyed fillet of herring on warm slices of potato, and sauté of pork in a mushroomy sauce 'served in a dish left on the table', with accompanying vegetables included in the price. Desserts might take in tarte Tatin or crème brûlée. Choose from a dozen and a half wines, keep an eye on blackboard additions, and ask to see the range of calvados. House French is £8.95.

CHEF: Jean-Pierre Iung   PROPRIETOR: Philippe Herrard   OPEN: Mon to Fri and Sun L 12 to 2, all week D 7 to 10 (10.30 Fri and Sat)   MEALS: alc (main courses £9 to £12.50). Set L Mon to Fri £5 (2 courses), Set L Sun £11.95   SERVICE: 12.5% (optional), card slips closed   CARDS: Amex, Delta, Diners, MasterCard, Switch, Visa   DETAILS: 40 seats. Private parties: 26 main room. Children's helpings. No pipes in dining-room. Wheelchair access (1 step; not WC). Music. Air-conditioned   ⊖ Southfields

Pharmacy Bar & Restaurant   NEW ENTRY   map 13

150 Notting Hill Gate, W11 3QG   COOKING 4
TEL: (0171) 221 2442   FAX: (0171) 243 2345   COST £26–£70

'I don't think there can be much chance of this being confused with a real pharmacy,' observed one visitor, noting the 'security officer' on the door and coat-check girls inside, although the Royal Pharmaceutical Society apparently thinks otherwise, so 'Bar & Restaurant' has been added to help avoid confusion. Whatever else, the name has been a boon to headline writers, the place has 'taken Notting Hill by storm', and is 'a lot of fun'. Walk through the ground-floor bar where white plastic seats are made to look like aspirin – 'ideal for a pain in the backside?' – and upstairs to the calmer dining-room. This being a Damien Hirst place, there is 'still life' in the form of butterflies glued on to large canvases, which hang on expensive-looking wallpaper covered in minute pharmaceutical icons.

'The reality is a lot less exciting than the hype,' reflected one reporter, but there is much of interest from a young chef who has trained with the best in France. Dishes are pleasingly straightforward, sometimes as simple as an 'impeccably done' tian of 'utterly fresh' Dorset crab with Poilâne toast, or scrambled eggs with black truffle, or a root vegetable salad with goats' cheese. There is much chargrilling – of crisp-skinned fleshy sea bass 'brilliantly timed' and strewn with a few vegetables – as well as a bit of spit-roasting: of Landes duck, or suckling pig for example. Desserts alternate between a very English apple crumble and a rather French pain perdu with a fruit gratin. Service can be 'somewhat distracted'. Wines, helpfully divided into £20 price bands, score for interest and quality. House Italian red and French white are £10.50.

CHEF: Sonja Lee   PROPRIETORS: Damien Hirst, Matthew Freud and Jonathan Kennedy   OPEN: Mon to Sat L and Sun brunch 12.30 to 2.45, all week D 7 to 10.45 (10 Sun)   CLOSED: L bank hol Mons   MEALS: alc (main courses £10 to £25). Set L £13.50 (2 courses) to £15.50. Bar menu available   SERVICE: 12.5% (optional), card slips closed   CARDS: Amex, Delta, Diners, MasterCard, Switch, Visa   DETAILS: 105 seats. Vegetarian meals. Children's helpings. Wheelchair access (also WC). No music. Air-conditioned   ⊖ Notting Hill Gate

Phoenix

NEW ENTRY map 12

162–164 Lower Richmond Road, SW15 1LY   COOKING 4
TEL: (0181) 780 3131   FAX: (0181) 780 1114   COST £24–£47

The partnership that runs Sonny's (see entries, London and Nottingham) opened this dramatic new Fulham venue in 1996. Although the entrance is on Pentlow Road, the restaurant puts its best face – a terrace awash with great white parasols – forward on to Lower Richmond Road. Inside is similarly bright, white and cavernous, while tables are close enough for a neighbourly chat.

Peter Goffe Wood juxtaposes culinary cultures on the menu, though not generally on the same plate, in a repertoire that runs from asparagus nori rolls with soy dipping sauce, through lamb chops with baked aubergine and provençale dressing, to biscotti and vin santo. A first-course plate of charcuterie – excellent home-cured duck, pork loin and chorizo with appropriately sharp pickles and relishes – was followed at inspection by a piece of lightly cooked halibut on the bone, served with tapénade and resting on leeks dressed in a saffron vinaigrette: a stimulating assemblage of flavours. Vegetables are charged extra, and mash is recommended. Stateside puddings, such as toasted banana bread with maple ripple ice-cream and caramel sauce, improbably manage to avoid both 'stodge and sickliness', or there is generally a tangy sorbet such as passion-fruit or mango for lighter appetites. Staff are praised for being both 'polite and good-looking', proving you can have it all. The wine list offers an inspired round-up of modern, international drinking, and doesn't just stick to Chardonnay and Cabernet. House French, a Colombard and a Merlot, are £9.50.

CHEF: Peter Goffe Wood   PROPRIETORS: Rebecca Mascarenhas and James Harris   OPEN: all week 12.30 to 2.30 (3.30 Sun), 7 to 10.30 (11.30 Fri and Sat, 10 Sun)   CLOSED: bank hols   MEALS: alc (main courses £7.50 to £13.50). Set L £12 (2 courses), Set L Sun £17.50   SERVICE: not inc   CARDS: Amex, Delta, Diners, MasterCard, Switch, Visa   DETAILS: 90 seats. 45 seats outside. Private parties: 90 main room, 24 private rooms. Vegetarian meals. Children's helpings. Wheelchair access (also WC). No music. Air-conditioned   ⊖ Putney Bridge   £5

Pied-à-Terre

map 15

34 Charlotte Street, W1P 1HJ
TEL: (0171) 636 1178   FAX: (0171) 916 1171   COOKING 7
EMAIL: p-a-t@dircon.co.uk   COST £39–£107

The exterior is 'oh-so-discreet', the monochromatic interior equally understated, relieved (if that is the word) by '60s pop art icons Lyndon B. Johnson and Chairman Mao: it certainly avoids the solemnity of some of London's classier dining venues. If the world outside is moving in the direction of simplicity, there is precious little sign of it in this kitchen. Tom Aikens's dishes tend to be complex constructions that rely on labour-intensive techniques. They put a contemporary spin on classical French cooking, and seem designed to test just how far an idea will go, as if aiming to be the ultimate expression of something.

In this quest, some dishes consist of variations on a theme, among them a quail consommé with confit quail, wild mushroom ravioli, quail breast and poached quail egg: a 'superb mix of textures and tastes' using top-drawer materials. One member of a party ate braised pig's head and tongue with steamed trotter, deep-fried brains and ears. 'We all thought he was incredibly brave and the maître d' said he was proud of him!' Outside service hours the kitchen is busy making crab ravioli to place beside John Dory fillets, and boudin of veal shin to accompany braised sweetbreads. Does it all work? Flavours can be bold, although due to the involved nature of some dishes they can vie for attention.

Desserts follow the same route, producing a plate of caramelised apples between sheets of wafer-thin crunchy pastry, surrounded by dollops of apple sorbet in pastry cups: 'yes, it was fancy,' admitted the reporter, 'but the fuss was worth making.' To add to the kitchen's labours, meals begin with first-rate amuse-gueules, then a coffee cup of some sophisticated soup (cauliflower with an oyster perhaps, or celery with scallop), and finish with a 'sensational choice' of classy petits fours with coffee. These can sometimes steal the show. Bruno Asselin, mentioned in despatches for being 'one of the warmest and most knowledgeable sommeliers in the trade', has an uphill job trying to sell very fine but expensive wines to customers who can buy some of them at a fraction of the price elsewhere. House vin de pays is £15.

CHEF: Tom Aikens   PROPRIETORS: David Moore and Tom Aikens   OPEN: Mon to Fri L 12.15 to 2.15, Mon to Sat D 7.15 to 10.45   CLOSED: 1 week Christmas, 1 week New Year, 2 weeks end Aug   MEALS: Set L £23 (2 courses) to £35.50, Set D £32.50 to £60   SERVICE: 12.5% (optional), card slips closed   CARDS: Amex, Delta, MasterCard, Switch, Visa   DETAILS: 36 seats. Private parties: 7 main room, 16 private room. Wheelchair access (2 steps; not WC). No music. Air-conditioned   ● Goodge Street

---

Le Pont de la Tour ▮

map 13

| 36D Shad Thames, Butlers Wharf, SE1 2YE | COOKING 5 |
| TEL: (0171) 403 8403   FAX: (0171) 403 0267 | COST £41–£83 |

The view of the City skyline, Docklands developments, Tower Bridge, and – who knows? – maybe one day the Millennium Dome as well certainly makes Shad Thames a prime site. It represents an alternative, and equally glamorous, side of London to the West End. Most of the restaurants along the wharf have something or other to do with Sir Terence Conran, who could give lessons in Parisian-style brasserie catering to the French.

Menus toe the Mediterranean line more tenaciously than most, but that doesn't stop them incorporating English asparagus with hollandaise, or calf's liver and mash with grilled Suffolk bacon. Chargrilling and roasting are much in evidence, producing grilled vegetables in a salad with goats' cheese and marinated tomatoes, and roast pigeon with lentils and foie gras sauce. The kitchen generally shows a light touch, too, in items such as spiced crab salad with avocado and coriander, or a main course of sauté scallops provençale. The crêpe parmentier starter with soured cream, smoked salmon and caviare, praised again this year, is becoming something of a signature dish. Inconsistencies and inaccuracies have also surfaced during the year, disappointing some reporters. Puddings, however, have their staunch supporters. Caramel fondant has been 'stunning', and simpler options – lemon tart, or vanilla petit pot topped with blackcurrants – are highly commended too.

The final tally is almost unavoidably high, not least because of extra charges for vegetables, although the massive wine list often has something to do with it too. Temptation looms in long lines of vintage champagnes, grand burgundies, top-class clarets and eminent New World productions. Although prices quickly tower skywards, the helpful sommelier will steer you towards cheaper bottles. House Vins de Pays d'Oc is £11.95. CELLARMAN'S CHOICE: Mas de Daumas Gassac 1996, Aimé Guibert, £34.75; Penley Estate Cabernet/Shiraz 1993, Coonawarra, S. Australia, £30.

CHEFS: David Burke and Andrew Sargent   PROPRIETORS: Sir Terence Conran and David Burke   OPEN: Sun to Fri L 12 to 3, all week D 6 to 11.30 (11 Sun)   CLOSED: 25 and 26 Dec, Good Fri   MEALS: Set L Mon to Fri £28.50. alc Sun brunch (main courses £12 to £14.50), all week D (main courses £16.50 to £23.50). Pre- and post-theatre D Mon to Sat before 6.45 and after 10.30 £19.50. Bar food available   SERVICE: 12.5% (optional), card slips closed   CARDS: Amex, Delta, Diners, MasterCard, Switch, Visa   DETAILS: 125 seats. 70 seats outside. Private parties: 20 private room. Vegetarian meals. Children welcome. Wheelchair access (not WC). No music ⊖ Tower Hill, London Bridge

Poons £

map 15

| 4 Leicester Street, WC2H 7BL | COOKING 1 |
| TEL/FAX: (0171) 437 1528 | COST £13–£38 |

This central London branch of Poons continues to steam along, pleasing a mixed Chinatown clientele with its quality and delighting them with its prices. It goes in for rapid turnover, basic casseroles, wind-dried meats, rice hotpots and noodle dishes, and specialities such as roast duck with pickled plums, and quail's eggs with exotic mixed vegetables including fungi and bean curd. For the adventurous there might be Dover sole subtly flavoured with tangerine peel, artfully served off the bone, but with head, tail and lower skin intact. House French wine is £7.30.

CHEF: Yuan Jin He   PROPRIETOR: W.N. Poon   OPEN: all week 12 to 11.30   CLOSED: Christmas   MEALS: alc (main courses £4 to £10). Set L and D (minimum 2) £7 to £17   SERVICE: not inc   CARDS: Amex, MasterCard, Switch, Visa   DETAILS: 138 seats. Private parties: 65 main room, 32 private rooms. Vegetarian meals. Children welcome. Wheelchair access (not WC). No music. Air-conditioned   ⊖ Leicester Square   £5

Poons

NEW ENTRY map 13

| Unit 205, Whiteleys, 151 Queensway, W2 4YJ | COOKING 2 |
| TEL: (0171) 792 2884   FAX: (0181) 458 0968 | COST £21–£62 |

This outpost of the Poon empire is on the first-floor gallery above Whiteleys shopping mall. Tables outside are for light meals and snacks, while inside is an unusually stylish dining-room with large mirrors, and spotlights embedded in the black ceiling. Four set menus are a cut above the norm, and the *carte* covers most of the standard Cantonese repertoire with a few excursions further afield: shredded beef soup with Szechuan pickled vegetables has been favourably received. Fresh materals and accurate timing have made a success of mussels in black-bean sauce, and stir-fried scallops with asparagus, and the kitchen has produced a 'remarkably delicate' haute cuisine version of Singapore vermicelli noodles. From a serious list of more than 50 dim-sum, reporters have singled out light char siu buns, shark fin and coriander dumplings, and 'red-hot', ultra-light yam croquettes. Service throughout has been described as 'exceptional' and 'impeccable', both for food and drinks. The wine list was being updated as the *Guide* went to press, but house wine is £11.

CHEF: Chiu Sai Wing   PROPRIETOR: Mr Poon   OPEN: all week 12 to 11 (10.45 Sun); dim-sum L 12 to 4 Mon to Fri, 12 to 4.45 Sat and Sun   CLOSED: Christmas   MEALS: alc (main courses £2 to £9 L, £5 to £25 D). Set L and D £15 to £25 (all minimum 2)   SERVICE: not inc   CARDS: Amex, Delta, Diners, MasterCard, Switch, Visa   DETAILS: 100 seats. 48 seats outside. Private parties: 120 main room. Vegetarian meals. No children under 5. Wheelchair access (not WC). Music. Air-conditioned   ⊖ Queensway

Putney Bridge

map 12

The Embankment, SW15 1LB
TEL: (0181) 780 1811   FAX: (0181) 780 1211

COOKING 4
COST £28–£55

Blond and dark wood, steel piping, lots of glass and the Thames lapping at the door combine to give this stylish modern building a 'nautical' or 'Parisian' feel, according to taste; it has impressed the architectural trade enough to pick up a few design awards too. A large downstairs bar for drinking and casual eating spills on to the towpath, while the restaurant sits above, ringing the 'modern British' bell with commendable enthusiasm.

Seafood, vegetables and pasta all figure at least as prominently as meat (which majors on chicken and lamb), producing a range of dishes from grilled swordfish to chilli and Cheddar tart, from spinach gnocchi with smoked haddock to saffron broth with cod and chickpeas. Ingredients do not always seem to have given of their best though, prices are considered high, and standards vary: consistency matters, and Putney Bridge could do with more of it. A savoury Welsh rarebit complements desserts of passion-fruit gratin or chocolate pyramid.

Bread is 'excellent', service 'friendly', and wines are considerately arranged by grape or style. The Old World's upper hand is offset by judicious offerings from the New, and while some of the mark-ups are a bit high, prices start at a useful £10.90 for a bottle, £3 a glass. Digestifs are worth a look too.

CHEF: Paul Hughes   PROPRIETOR: Trevor Gulliver   OPEN: Mon to Sat 12 to 3, 6 to 11, Sun 12.30 to 3, 7 to 10.30   MEALS: alc (main courses £9.50 to £16). Set L Mon to Sat £13.50 (2 courses) to £17.50, Set L Sun £19.50. Bar meals available.   SERVICE: not inc; 12.5% (optional) for parties of 5 or more   CARDS: Amex, Delta, Diners, MasterCard, Switch, Visa   DETAILS: 152 seats. Private parties: 170 main room. Vegetarian meals. Children's helpings. Wheelchair access (also WC). Occasional music. Air-conditioned   ⊖ Putney Bridge   £5

Quaglino's 🍞

map 15

16 Bury Street, SW1Y 6AL
TEL: (0171) 930 6767   FAX: (0171) 839 2866

COOKING 5
COST £30–£83

It is still only six years since the Conran relaunch of Quaglino's, and yet it seems to have been with us half a lifetime. The theatrical sweep of the interior, where just about everybody loves the feeling of descending the marble staircase in ready-when-you-are-Mr-de-Mille mode into a space 'like the hull of a luxury liner', still impresses, as do the furiously darting waiters and dreamily drifting cigarette girls. Star-spotting remains one of the attractions for some: one reporter wandered out in front of the seafood altar in search of celebrity but could see only the Arsenal football team.

Henrik Iversen has been shuffled across town within the Conran structure (he was at the Butlers Wharf Chop House; see entry). Menus remain firmly entrenched in modern brasserie mould, and the cooking seems to have its fair share of hits. Crab and leek tart uses 'sparklingly fresh crabmeat' in delicate, crumbly pastry, and fish cookery generally is wondrously accurate, given the number of covers clamouring to be fed. 'Good clean flavour and first-class texture' marked out one reporter's swordfish, there is always shoulder of pork with crackling and apple sauce, and vegetarian dishes exert some imagination: perhaps in pea, herb and Parmesan risotto fritter with grilled asparagus. Vegetable side-orders range from crisp-cooked French beans to heavily salted frites. Puddings include all today's favourites as well as one or two more unusual offerings, such as orange parfait with poached figs. A well-compiled wine list is supplemented by classic cocktails, including a slate of Martini variations. House Vins de Pays d'Oc are £11.75.

CHEF: Henrik Iversen   PROPRIETOR: Sir Terence Conran   OPEN: all week 12 to 2.30, 5.30 to 11.30 (12 Fri and Sat, 11 Sun)   CLOSED: D 24 Dec, 25 Dec, L 26 Dec, L 31 Dec, L 1 Jan   MEALS: alc (main courses £10.50 to £29). Set L and D 5.30 to 6.30 £15.50 (2 courses) to £19   SERVICE: 12.5% (optional), card slips closed   CARDS: Amex, Delta, Diners, MasterCard, Switch, Visa   DETAILS: 267 seats. Private parties: 300 main room, 40 private room. Vegetarian meals. Children welcome exc in bar. Wheelchair access (also WC). Music. Air-conditioned   ⊖ Green Park, Piccadilly Circus

Quality Chop House ✯✶

map 13

94 Farringdon Road, EC1R 3EA   COOKING 3
TEL: (0171) 837 5093   COST £23–£50

Charles Fontaine has expanded, or rather his restaurant has, into the premises next door. The extension is unobtrusive, sharing the same etched glass and offering equally uncomfortable sit-up-and-beg seats. Although the self-styled 'no-nonsense' approach still covers egg, bacon and chips, Toulouse sausage and mash, corned beef hash, and lamb chops, there is now more emphasis on fish: jellied eels, potted shrimps, smoked herring and potato salad, lobster mayonnaise, steamed mussels with coriander. First courses tend to be 'compositions rather than cooking', but mains have turned up grilled marlin with hollandaise, a well-judged salmon fish-cake, and decent braised lemon sole surrounded by 'good black olives and falling-apart tomatoes'. Desserts are as straightforward as ever: 'crisp' strawberry tart, a 'refreshing' dish of poached summer fruits, and 'excellent' crème brûlée. Service is helpful and 'comfortably matter of fact', and some two dozen wines start at £10.

CHEF/PROPRIETOR: Charles Fontaine   OPEN: Sun to Fri L 12 to 3 (4 Sun), all week D 6.30 (7 Sun) to 11.30   CLOSED: Christmas and New Year   MEALS: alc (main courses £7 to £15)   SERVICE: not inc   CARDS: Delta, MasterCard, Switch, Visa   DETAILS: 60 seats. Private parties: 10 main room. Vegetarian meals. Children's helpings. Wheelchair access (1 step; not WC). No smoking in 1 dining-room. No music. Air-conditioned   ⊖ Farringdon

Quincy's ♥

map 13

675 Finchley Road, NW2 2JP   COOKING 3
TEL: (0171) 794 8499   COST £33–£39

This modestly proportioned restaurant on one of the narrower stretches of Finchley Road remains abidingly popular. Regulars are enticed by fixed-price menus on which the once identifiably French accent grows more muted as the seasons pass. Now there is roast rabbit with green olives, cannellini beans and gremolata, as well as duck breast in hoisin with Chinese vegetables, but David Philpott is sufficiently accomplished to bring lustre to these other styles of cooking too. A reporter who started with pumpkin gnocchi on saffron and orange sauce, went on to roast pheasant with cider apples and parsnip purée, and finished with lemon parfait and a cranberry compote commented that 'execution and presentation are still good, portions are wholesome and flavours nicely balanced'. It may feel a tight fit when the place is full, but service is attentive, and most reporters come away happy. The wine list isn't very long, but every bottle is an intelligent choice, with a sprinkling of New World wines adding to the palette of flavours from France. Prices are scrupulously fair, rising from £9 for the house Duboeuf to £35 for vintage champagne.

CHEF: David Philpott   PROPRIETOR: David Wardle   OPEN: all week D only 7 to 11   CLOSED: Christmas   MEALS: Set L £25   SERVICE: not inc   CARDS: Amex, Delta, Mastercard, Switch, Visa   DETAILS: 30 seats. Private parties: 8 main room. Vegetarian meals. Children's helpings. No cigars/pipes in dining-room. Wheelchair access (1 step; not WC). Music. Air-conditioned ⊖ Golders Green

Quo Vadis
map 15

26–29 Dean Street, W1A 6LL
TEL: (0171) 437 9585   FAX: (0171) 434 9972

COOKING 6
COST £29–£77

Damien Hirst's décor is nothing if not stimulating. The upstairs bar is the place to gawp at intestinal art, and while the ground-floor dining-room may feel rather more Charles Rennie Macintosh it does have its share of visual diversions, including a large golden hand coming out of the wall, and 'a pair of resin elk antlers with a malfunctioning neon tube between them'. A degree of formal restraint from some staff does not prevent this from being a 'user-friendly' restaurant, and while the £250 caviare starter seems to have disappeared, choice is very generous. Quite a few dishes will be familiar to Marco Pierre White fans, and fish and seafood account for about half the diet, from scallops with sauce vierge, or terrine of red mullet and langoustines to start, to skate wing with clams, and seared tuna with a soft green olive tapénade.

Well reported risottos include one of langoustine, made special by a 'russet-brown trickle of reduced peppery langoustine esssence', and a creamy and buttery version with plump mussels and saffron strands, described as 'one for purists'. A livery, earthy dimension is explored too, in the form of 'rich, dense and gamey' Bresse pigeon with baby turnips and shredded cabbage – 'what more perfect a triumvirate could you wish for?' – that came in in a light, smoky, and 'very lickable' cassis jus. Equally impressive at one meal was a 'seriously big' piece of seared calf's liver, with Alsace bacon, pungent fried sage leaves and braised fennel, accompanied by first-rate olive-oil mash.

A high level of skill keeps the kitchen motoring, not least in desserts of almond ice with a jug of bitter chocolate sauce poured over at table, and 'unctuous' lemon tart with a 'heady mix of many egg yolks, tart lemon and sugar'. A whole page of vintages of Penfolds Grange – among many delectable offerings from Australia and elsewhere – indicates the scope and depth of the phenomenal wine list, although the policy of holding customers responsible for

157

a wine's condition if it is 30 years old or more (as at Café Royal's Grill Room; see entry) is not very user-friendly. On the other hand, the sommelier's selection suggests several attractive bins under £30, starting at £13 for a French Merlot.

CHEFS: Tim Payne and Phil Coope PROPRIETORS: Marco Pierre White, Jimmy Lahoud, Jonathan Kennedy and Matthew Freud OPEN: Mon to Fri L 12 to 3, all week D 6 to 12 (10.30 Sun) MEALS: alc (main courses £13 to £25). Set L and pre-theatre D £14.95 (2 courses) to £17.95 SERVICE: 12.5% (optional), card slips closed CARDS: Amex, Delta, MasterCard, Switch, Visa DETAILS: 120 seats. Private parties: 40 main room, 16 private room. Vegetarian meals. Children welcome. No music. Air-conditioned ⊖ Tottenham Court Road, Leicester Square

Rani ✱ £
map 12

7 Long Lane, N3 2PR
TEL/FAX: (0181) 349 4386
EMAIL: nomeatrani@AOL.com

COOKING 1
COST £22–£33

Since 1984 the Pattnis have sought to offer a distinctive version of South Indian and Gujarati cooking in their converted shop close to Finchley Central tube station. The menu canters through bhel pooris, kachoris, aloo papri chat and other starters before parading 'slow-cooked' vegetables and pulses such as akhaa bhindi bateta (okra with baby potatoes and onions) or akhaa ringal (Kenyan aubergines pressed with spices and ground peanuts). Home-made pickles and chutneys are one of the star turns, although we have had no reports yet on their new-style 'fusion' cooking: over a dozen pizzas ranging from margherita to pineapple and chilli, not to mention cappuccino and Italian-style ice-creams. Lassi, falooda and spiced tea are alternatives to Cobra beer and a handful of wines. House wine is £9.70.

CHEF: Sheila Pattni PROPRIETOR: Jyotindra Pattni OPEN: Sun 12.15 to 10.30, Mon to Sat D only 6 to 10.30 CLOSED: 25 Dec, 1 Jan MEALS: alc (main courses £4 to £7). Set L and D £6.80 to £11.45 (minimum 2; all 2 courses) SERVICE: 10% (optional), card slips closed CARDS: Amex, Delta, MasterCard, Switch, Visa DETAILS: 70 seats. Private parties: 50 main room, 12 private room. Vegetarian meals. Children's helpings. No smoking in 1 dining-room. Wheelchair access (1 step; not WC). Music ⊖ Finchley Central (£5)

Ransome's Dock 🍾
map 12

35-37 Parkgate Road, SW11 4NP
TEL: (0171) 223 1611 and 924 2462
FAX: (0171) 924 2614

COOKING 5
COST £24–£59

Readers' reports indicated a dip in standards last year at Martin Lam's bright and buzzy waterside restaurant, but now it's back on form and generating plenty of praise. 'Excellent in every way,' commented one reporter; 'an impressive performance,' agreed another. 'Here is a chef who shops wisely and cooks intelligently, serving up real food with big flavours.' Quality British produce is a strong theme – Craster kippers, Morecambe Bay shrimps, Cumbrian ham – treated simply but with enough Mediterranean flourishes to signal that modern British is the intention. English asparagus is grilled and served with pecorino cheese, while Norfolk smoked eel might garnish a warm buckwheat pancake or be served on bruschetta with horseradish.

The star turn at inspection was a dish of 'juicy and opaque' scallops that had been chargrilled to caramelised perfection, their sweetness offset by spicy chorizo sausage and 'light and fluffy' celeriac and parsley purée. 'Perfectly timed' Trelough duck breast was very tender with good crisp skin; sirloin steak, cooked with the same precision, was accompanied by 'giant chips'. Rocombe Farm organic ice-creams are a fixture, and desserts might also include lemon curd mousse with blueberries, tarts such as cherry and almond, and prune and armagnac soufflé 'risen in textbook fashion'. Service is brisk and pleasant, by informed and considerate staff who cope well under pressure. The catholic wine list is full of appealing and unusual bins from some of the world's top growers, at prices that don't require a king's ransom. They are helpfully grouped by grape or style, ranging from 'aromatic and dry whites' to 'very big reds'. The house selection starts at £12.50. CELLARMAN'S CHOICE: Cloudy Bay Sauvignon Blanc 1998, Marlborough, New Zealand, £19.75; Crozes-Hermitage 1996, Alain Graillot, £23.

CHEF: Martin Lam   PROPRIETORS: Martin and Vanessa Lam   OPEN: all week L (brunch Sat and Sun) 11.30 to 5 (3.30 Sun), Mon to Sat D 6 to 11   CLOSED: Christmas, Aug bank hol   MEALS: alc (main courses £9 to £17). Set L £11.50 (2 courses). Brunch menu Sat and Sun. BYO £6   SERVICE: 12.5% (optional), card slips closed   CARDS: Amex, Delta, Diners, MasterCard, Switch   DETAILS: 55 seats. 20 seats outside. Private parties: 14 main room. Car park D and weekends only. Vegetarian meals. Children's helpings. No pipes in dining-room. Wheelchair access (1 step; also WC). Music. Air-conditioned

Rasa ⁵✳ £   map 12

55 Stoke Newington Church Street, N16 0AR   COOKING 3
TEL: (0171) 249 0344   FAX: (0171) 249 8748   COST £21–£28

Both this and the new branch (see entry below) are brightly decorated, mainly in pinks, each with an octagonal skylight, neither compromising on quality. Strictly vegetarian Keralan food is the draw, and for those who find difficulty in choosing from the long menu, waiters – casually dressed, friendly and competent – will suggest a set meal, but it is more fun to forage. Among 'pre-meal snacks' is an 'unmissable' poppadum selection; they come plain and spiced, together with chinnappam, a little cake of rice-flour and shallots with cumin and black sesame seeds, and achappam, a crisp coconut-flavoured rice-flour waffle. From 'Rasa's own starters' reporters have enjoyed the 'fresh, well-balanced, spicing' of Mysore bonda: crisp-fried vegetable balls in chickpea-flour batter with a creamy coconut chutney. Other outstanding dishes include spinach and curd cheese curry, tarka dhal, and crisp, spicy, potato-filled masala dosa, while among staples are 'fluffy and tangy' lemon rice, and 'crispy, spongy, yeasty' appam. Mango sorbet, and home-made kulfi with excellent creamy texture' are probably the best ways to finish. The modest wine list, although a vintage-free zone, is very respectable. House wines are £7.95.

CHEF: Sivadas Sreedharan   PROPRIETOR: Rasa Ltd   OPEN: Tue to Sun L 12 to 2, all week D 6 to 11.30   CLOSED: 25 and 26 Dec   MEALS: alc (main courses £4.50 to £5.50). Set L and D £15 (2 courses)   SERVICE: not inc, card slips closed   CARDS: Amex, Delta, Diners, MasterCard, Switch, Visa   DETAILS: 45 seats. Private parties: 20 main room. Vegetarian meals. Children welcome. No smoking in dining-room. Wheelchair access (1 step; also WC). Music. Air-conditioned

Rasa W1 🌶🗙   NEW ENTRY   map 15

6 Dering Street, W1R 9AB	COOKING 3
TEL: (0171) 6291346	COST £31–£44

'A successful cloning exercise' was one visitor's view after eating at the new branch of Rasa in Dering Street. It is less cramped than the Stoke Newington original (see entry above), the décor is more lavish, and prices are higher, but Keralan vegetarian food takes in the same range of poppadums, lentil patties, stuffed pastries, dosas, curries and kulfi. There are exciting breads too, such as uzhunappam, made from rice-flour, cumin seeds, shallots and coconut, while rice might be flavoured with lemon, coconut or tamarind. House wine is £9.50.

CHEFS: Anil Narayan and Sivadas Sreedharan PROPRIETOR: Rasa W1 Ltd. OPEN: all week 12 to 3, 6 to 11 CLOSED: 24 Dec to 8 Jan MEALS: alc (main courses £5.50 to £9). Set L and D £22.50 SERVICE: 12.5% (optional), card slips closed CARDS: Amex, Delta, MasterCard, Switch, Visa DETAILS: 85 seats. Private parties: 50 main room, 50 private room. Vegetarian meals. Children welcome. No smoking in dining-room. Wheelchair access (not WC). Music. Air-conditioned ⊖ Oxford Circus, Bond Street

Redmond's   map 12

170 Upper Richmond Road West, SW14 8AW	COOKING 5
TEL: (0181) 878 1922	COST £29–£40

The low-key plain glass frontage to the Haywards' small suburban restaurant offers little clue to the bright and startling things going on within. Judy Bibby's Kandinsky-like abstracts mounted on primrose walls add lustre to the room, and Redmond Hayward's lively fusion cooking makes a good stab at stimulating most palates. An inventory of modish ingredients will tick off lime leaves, truffle oil, bulgar and polenta (not to mention beetroot and rhubarb), which appear in dishes that have been carefully composed rather than slung together in hope. 'A vibrant heap of chicken, vegetables and herbs had all the keynote flavours of Thai cooking,' according to an autumn Sunday luncher, who went on to roast mallard with 'outstandingly good' pommes Anna and a powerful, concentrated sauce.

Fish dishes are similarly confident – well-timed skate wing with an improbably subtle sauce of anchovies and rosemary delighted another reporter – and vegetarian options are bold and adventurous. Calvados ice-cream is a favourite dessert accompaniment, while an oozy, juicy summer pudding that poured forth seasonal berries was 'one of the very best I have eaten'. One of the benefits of not being in central London is that prices can be kept on a tighter leash, and reporters commend the sound value it all represents, an agreeable impression that extends to the intelligently chosen wine list too. Prices start at £11.50 for Languedoc Sauvignon and £12.50 for red Côtes du Ventoux, and there is a generous range of half-bottles.

All entries, including Round-ups, are fully indexed at the back of the Guide.

Net prices *in the details at the end of an entry indicates that the prices given on a menu and on a bill are inclusive of VAT and service charge, and that this practice is clearly stated on menu and bill.*

CHEF: Redmond Hayward   PROPRIETORS: Redmond and Pippa Hayward   OPEN: Sun to Fri L
12 to 2.30 (3 Sun), Mon to Sat D 7 to 10.30   CLOSED: bank hols exc Good Friday   MEALS: Set L
Mon to Fri £16.50 (2 courses) to £21.50, Set L Sun £14.50 (2 courses) to £17.50, Set D Mon to Fri
£18.50 (2 courses) to £22.50, Set D Sat £22.50   SERVICE: not inc; 10% for parties of 6 or more
CARDS: Delta, MasterCard, Switch, Visa   DETAILS: 50 seats. Private parties: 10 main room.
Vegetarian meals. Children's helpings. No cigars/pipes in dining-room. Wheelchair access (not
WC). No music. Air-conditioned

Red Pepper £

map 13

8 Formosa Street, W9 1EE
TEL: (0171) 266 2708   FAX: (0171) 289 4178

| NEW CHEF |
COST £22–£44

Even the owners describe this Italian restaurant as cramped and say that the lack
of wall decorations means that the food provides all the colour. Its stock-in-trade
includes a range of pasta dishes, and more than a dozen pizzas from the
wood-burning oven, although we learnt of the appointment of two new chefs
too late for feedback on their performance. Reports please. Prices on the
all-Italian wine list start at £9.

CHEFS: Carlo Salodini and Manni Pasquale   PROPRIETORS: B. and N. Behzadi   OPEN: Sat L
12.30 to 2.30, Sun L 12.30 to 3.30, all week D 6.30 to 10.45 (10.30 Sun)   CLOSED: 25 and 26 Dec,
1 Jan   MEALS: alc (main courses £6 to £13)   SERVICE: not inc; 12.5% for parties of 5 or more
CARDS: Delta, MasterCard, Switch, Visa   DETAILS: 50 seats. 20 seats outside. Private parties:
25 main room, 25 private room. Vegetarian meals. Children's helpings. Wheelchair access (not
WC). Music. Air-conditioned   ⊖ Warwick Avenue

Rhodes in the Square | NEW ENTRY |

map 13

Dolphin Square, SW1
TEL: (0171) 798 6767   FAX: (0171) 798 5685

COOKING 7
COST £33–£84

Gary Rhodes's latest incarnation arises on the north side of Dolphin Square, the
Pimlico apartment-block-cum-hotel that is home to squads of glitterati and
Honourable Members alike. An expansive, high-ceilinged room done in
simmering midnight blue is set off by sparkling chrome railings and portholes,
with constellations of little ceiling spots. 'It is like dining in the grand ballroom
of an ocean liner.'

This is currently the best example of the Gary Rhodes style, whereby British
and other classics are re-invented, often humorously, sometimes arrestingly:
ham consommé with featherlight pea pancakes, for example, or 'an impeccably
made omelette' topped with lobster thermidor. Pigeon faggot the size of a
billiard ball comes on potato cake with mustard cabbage, and fish has included a
whole red mullet, stuffed with peppers, aubergine, anchovies and garlic, sauced
with fennel and cream. Even better is a crisp pastry shell containing a layer of
spinach, a soft-poached egg and creamy risotto, all in a beurre blanc sauce; this,
to one who'd had her fair share of meals out, was 'one of the best dishes I've
eaten all year'.

Ideas keep coming, not least among desserts. Pineapple is sliced to carpaccio
thinness and served on a giant square plate with a brandy-snap basket filled
with its sorbet. Star of desserts, though, is a British pudding plate that
incorporates lemon meringue tart of incredible sweet/sharp balance, a bourbon

biscuit straight out of the Fabulous Food cookbook, and a cylinder of apple crumble ice-cream with cold vanilla-specked custard. Excellent coffee, good breads and 'faultless service that never missed a beat', all contribute to success. The food deserves more enterprising wines than it gets (although there are some good producers) and customers deserve more sympathetic pricing. The cheapest white is an Argentinian blend at £15.50, the red a basic claret at £19.

CHEFS: Gary Rhodes and Roger Gorman PROPRIETOR: Gardner Merchant/Dolphin Square Trust OPEN: Sun to Fri L 12 to 2.30, all week D 7 to 10 (9 Sun) MEALS: alc (main courses £14.50 to £22.50). Set L £19.50, Set L Sun £21.50 SERVICE: 12.5% (optional), card slips closed CARDS: Amex, Delta, Diners, MasterCard, Switch, Visa DETAILS: 90 seats. Private parties: 8 main room. Vegetarian meals. Children's helpings. Wheelchair access (also WC). Music. Air-conditioned ⊖ Pimlico

Riva   map 12

169 Church Road, SW13 9HR	COOKING 5
TEL/FAX: (0181) 748 0434	COST £26–£48

'Riva comes closer to the experience of eating out in Italy than any other restaurant I've visited in the UK,' summed up one visitor. In an undistinguished parade of shops on the outskirts of Barnes, it doesn't go out of its way to attract attention, a stance that reflects the ordinary quotidian nature of the operation. Décor is subdued, and the mirrored dining-room feels restful: a tasteful but uneventful backdrop to seasonal northern Italian food. Despite the enormous televisual exposure of Italian food in Britain, Riva still manages to avoid the clichés and come up with some unusual dishes.

First courses include a few antipasto-style assemblies – a plate consisting of a tiny artichoke heart filled with a dab of rich cheese fonduta, a few slender asparagus spears topped with a poached egg and Pecorino shavings, and a spoonful of tender young broad beans on an oniony dressing – but these are done with care and have a sense of unity. Well-balanced flavours point to an experienced hand in the kitchen, producing linguine with clams, rocket and fine shavings of pungent bottarga, and seared calf's liver 'as soft as butter', served with loose-textured polenta, 'masses of fresh porcini mushrooms' and a rich gravy.

There may be rum-flavoured panettone to finish, or blueberry and prune pancake with a dash of grappa, and although presentation may be old-fashioned – a piped border of cream rosettes for a silky-smooth chocolate pudding – it is the 'rich and intense' flavour that counts. Service is well paced, and wines combine interest and variety with tolerable prices, starting with house Tocai and Merlot at £9.95.

CHEF: Francesco Zanchetta PROPRIETOR: Andrea Riva OPEN: Sun to Fri L 12 to 2.30, all week D 7 to 11.30 (9.30 Sun) MEALS: alc (main courses £8.50 to £13.50) SERVICE: 10%, card slips closed CARDS: Amex, Diners, MasterCard, Switch, Visa DETAILS: 45 seats. 8 seats outside. Private parties: 40 main room. Vegetarian meals. Children's helpings. No cigars/pipes in dining-room. Wheelchair access (not WC). Music. Air-conditioned

Card slips closed *in the details at the end of an entry indicates that the total on the slips of credit cards is closed when handed over for signature.*

River Café ♟ map 12

Thames Wharf Studios, Rainville Road, W6 9HA	COOKING 6
TEL: (0171) 381 8824 FAX: (0171) 381 6217	COST £42–£65

Clean lines, self-assured design, and a smattering of famous faces help to make this a 'seriously chic' place to eat at. It embodies a simple, open style of Italian cooking, at the same time glamorising the fertile repertoire of peasant food in which fish and vegetables play a significant role. The wood-fired oven is a boon, although it can also roast nearby customers. This ancient yet fashionable cooking method (which needs skilful handling) is applied to anything from turbot to guinea-fowl, the latter stuffed with prosciutto, mascarpone and thyme, and served with lentils, herbs and rocket.

Despite translations, dishes are awash in apparently baffling ingredients – pagnotti, salmoriglio, granchio, rombo – that seem to demand A-level menu-Italian to decode. But waiters 'delight in the opportunity this gives them for instruction', and reporters don't mind too much in view of the often exemplary results that appear. This is confident food, producing bruschetta with a mound of Cornish crab and an unfussy herb salad, or an impressive dish of polenta (how often does that happen?) with a mix of girolles, trompettes and pied de mouton, enlivened with a hefty dose of garlic. Bollito misto may be more homely than fashionable but is still carefully cooked, and served with mostarda di Cremona.

Textbook chocolate nemesis is as smooth and rich as can be, and caramel ice-cream has been 'stunning'. Tables have time limits, prices are high, and not all reporters are equally happy with their food, citing disappointments with risotto, the texture of meat (lamb in particular), and 'elusive' tastes, but all that is par for the course here: it simply doesn't speak to everybody. At its best service is friendly and well informed, though it can be 'detached', and there are many grumbles about unsympathetic treatment. The all-Italian wine list (champagne excepted) has been expanded by four pages of 'reserve wines', some from older vintages. Puiatti's elegant Collio Chardonnays, Aldo Conterno's grand Barolos and Selvapiana's renowned 'Bucerchiale' Chianti Rufinas are just a few of the welcome arrivals. House wines are £9.50. CELLARMAN'S CHOICE: Pinot Grigio 1996, Franz Haas, Alto Adige, £19; Chianti Rufina 1995, Selvapiana, £16.50.

CHEFS: Rose Gray, Ruth Rogers and Theo Randall   PROPRIETORS: Richard and Ruth Rogers, and Rose Gray   OPEN: all week L 12.30 to 3, Mon to Sat D 7 to 9.30   CLOSED: 1 week Christmas, bank hols   MEALS: alc (main courses £17 to £24)   SERVICE: 12.5% (optional), card slips closed   CARDS: Amex, Delta, Diners, MasterCard, Switch, Visa   DETAILS: 95 seats. 40 seats outside. Car park. Children's helpings. No cigars/pipes in dining-room. No music
⊖ Hammersmith

R.K. Stanleys [NEW ENTRY] map 15

6 Little Portland Street, W1N 5AG	
TEL: (0171) 462 0099 FAX: (0171) 462 0088	COOKING 3
EMAIL: manager@rkstanleys.co.uk	COST £26–£43

Fred Taylor, owner of Alfred (see entry, London), has a new venture. The problem he has addressed is how to package beer and sausages in a non-laddish way, and without sounding Bavarian about it. He has come up with a self-consciously '50s feel – red banquette seating, plastic table tops – in a large, square box of a room that begins to look like a canteen when office lunchers congregate in party booths and along the benches.

The 'Magnificent Seven' bangers, around which the enterprise revolves, are made in-house and range from a Simple Stanley ('I would like to be able to buy sausages like that') served with mash, onions and deep-fried kale, via Glamorgan (leeks and Caerphilly cheese) and Thai sausage, to a game version 'full of flavour' that came with mustard mash, honey-glazed parsnips and red cabbage. Meat loaf with greens and mushroom ketchup, and a dish of scallops with black pudding and mushy peas, provide diversion, as do shellfishy starters of crab bisque or steamed mussels. The 'heartily filling and satisfying' effect is completed by rhubarb crumble, and treacle tart with custard. Service is young and obliging, and drinks include a short range of wines by the glass (among them three English whites), Dunkerton's organic cider, and beers from Bombardier to Belgian Kriek, from Spitfire to German smoked beer. House wine is £10.50.

CHEF: Robert Gutteridge   PROPRIETOR: Fred Taylor   OPEN: Mon to Sat 12 to 3.30, 6 to 11.30   CLOSED: Christmas, bank hols   MEALS: alc (main courses £7 to £12)   SERVICE: 12.5% (optional)   CARDS: Delta, MasterCard, Switch, Visa   DETAILS: Children's helpings. Non-smoking area. Wheelchair access (2 steps; also WC). No music. Air-conditioned   ⊖ Oxford Circus

Royal China maps 13, 15

13 Queensway, W2 4QJ	
TEL/FAX: (0171) 221 2535	
40 Baker Street, W1M 1DH	COOKING 4
TEL/FAX: (0171) 487 4688	COST £30–£77

There has never been any doubt about the quality of dim-sum at both these branches – har gau prawn dumplings, turnip paste, spring rolls, chicken and duck feet for one party – but over the past year cooking on the rest of the *carte* has picked up a gear. Both share the spectacular décor of black and gold lacquer panels and service from 'slim, elegant waitresses in glistening, sequinned gold costumes'. Menus include such luxuries as abalone (and superior abalone), shark's fin and lobster; various whole ducks and chickens, and sauté fillet of Dover sole with spicy salt. Although set menus (for a minimum of two) are not particularly liberal in terms of number of dishes, the *carte* is correspondingly generous in scope. Among dishes that have been endorsed at the Queensway branch are seafood golden cups (stir-fried scallops, prawns, mushrooms and water chestnuts on crispy pastry), stewed pork belly with assorted vegetables, and stewed aubergine with minced pork in spicy sauce. Baker Street, meanwhile, has turned up impressive cold hors d'oeuvres (jellyfish with sesame oil, for example), crispy aromatic duck, sauté steak with lemon grass, and crisply fried golden batter chicken. Some 50 wines include very choice bottles at generally fair prices, starting with house French red and white at £9.50.

'A vegetarian selection is offered on the menu, but the proprietor boomed when asked what there was: "You don't come here to eat vegetarian – have the fish!"' (On eating in Dorset)

CHEFS: Simon Man, Wai-Hung Law and David Pang PROPRIETOR: Pearl Investments Ltd
OPEN: Queensway Mon to Sat 12 to 11, Sun 11 to 10; dim-sum all week 12 to 5; Baker Street all
week 12 to 11 (11.30 Fri and Sat); dim-sum all week 12 to 5   MEALS: alc (main courses £5.50 to
£40). Set D £23 to £29   SERVICE: 12.5%   CARDS: Amex, Delta, Diners, MasterCard, Switch,
Visa   DETAILS: 200 seats (Queensway), 100 seats (Baker Street). Private parties: 200 main
room, 20 private rooms (Queensway), 40 main room, 12 private room (Baker Street). Vegetarian
meals. Children welcome. Music. Air-conditioned   ⊖ Queensway, Baker Street

RSJ 🍾

13A Coin Street, SE1 8YQ
TEL: (0171) 928 4554   FAX: (0171) 401 2455

map 13

COOKING 4
COST £26–£52

Nigel Wilkinson set up shop on this corner site at the end of a well-converted
Victorian terrace 20 years ago, and must have witnessed quite a few changes to
the neighbourhood. While the area's fortunes have lifted, RSJ's strengths have
kept it well on top. 'Remarkably consistent, remarkably good value,' summed
up one visitor, and 'an invaluable South Bank restaurant' for after the theatre.
Aim for the first-floor dining-room, where a generous and well-balanced *carte*
offers modern dishes of sweetcorn and crab soup with coriander cream, pot-roast
sea bass with aubergine caviare and tapénade, and saddle of rabbit with (daring,
this) risotto of lobster. Indeed, risotto is something of a house speciality.

The good-value fixed-price lunch is singled out for its 'imaginative and
enjoyable' dishes, among which might be a starter of terrine of pork knuckle,
followed by smoked haddock and spinach lasagne with poached egg and
hollandaise, finishing with orange mousse flan. Service is 'smiling and willing'.
Lovers of Cabernet Franc, Chenin Blanc or Sauvignon Blanc will appreciate
Nigel Wilkinson's unique and much-lauded wine list, which concentrates
(almost) entirely on the Loire and demonstrates just how good these grapes can
be when handled by great winemakers. An attractive quartet from Australia's
Adam Wynn is provided for those able to resist the lure of the Loire, plus a few
burgundies and a solitary Bordeaux. House Saumur is £10.75. CELLARMAN'S
CHOICE: Savennières, Clos de Coulaine 1996, Claude Papin, £17.95; Anjou
Villages, Croix de Mission 1996, J.Y. Lebreton, £16.95.

CHEF: Peter Lloyd PROPRIETOR: Nigel Wilkinson OPEN: Mon to Fri L 12 to 2, Mon to Sat D 5.30
to 11   MEALS: alc (main courses £10 to £15.50). Set L and D £14.95 (2 courses) to £16.95
SERVICE: 12.5% (optional), card slips closed CARDS: Amex, Diners, MasterCard, Switch, Visa
DETAILS: 90 seats. 12 seats outside. Private parties: 10 main room, 20 private room. Vegetarian
meals. Children's helpings. No cigars/pipes in dining-room. Music. Air-conditioned
⊖ Waterloo (£5)

Rules

35 Maiden Lane, WC2E 7LB
TEL: (0171) 836 5314   FAX: (0171) 497 1081

map 15

COOKING 4
COST £37–£56

In an era when new restaurants in the capital may be here and gone in a matter of
months, it is rare to see one of this longevity. Rules celebrated its bicentennial in
1998. With tables crammed cheek by jowl, the atmosphere is one of convivial
hubbub, which seems only right in theatreland. Rules famously trades in
seasonal game, much of it sourced from the owner's estate in the Pennines.

Here be grouse, hare, teal and woodcock, simply and carefully roasted to order in the British manner. Outside autumn and winter, specialities include rump of lamb with butter-beans in Madeira, venison shank in gin sauce, and grilled Dover sole.

Like previous incumbents, David Chambers has managed to inveigle a few more newfangled items on to the menus, offering wild mushroom and goats'-cheese soufflé with truffle dressing, and roast cod on fennel confit with sweet peppers and tomato. Similarly, there may be summer berries in a champagne jelly with raspberry and elderflower sorbet for pud, but what most customers are probably here for are pear and blackberry pie or treacle sponge and custard. The overwhelming majority of readers' letters speak of service that is 'unhurried but attentive and professional'. A brisk, brief list of wines is headed up by a selection 'from the former colonies', which turns out to mean exotic places like California. House French is £11.75.

CHEF: David Chambers PROPRIETOR: John Mayhew OPEN: all week noon to 11.30 CLOSED: 5 days Christmas MEALS: alc (main courses £14 to £18). Set L Sat and Sun £17.95 (2 courses), Set D 3 to 6 £15.95 (2 courses) SERVICE: not inc CARDS: Amex, Delta, Diners, MasterCard, Switch, Visa DETAILS: 135 seats. Private parties: 65 main room, 16 to 32 private rooms. Vegetarian meals. Children's helpings. No music. Air-conditioned ⊖ Covent Garden, Charing Cross (£5)

Sabras £

map 12

263 Willesden High Road, NW10 2RX   COOKING 4
TEL: (0181) 459 0340   COST £19–£33

Refurbishment has toned down the décor, but not the food, which is 'as good as ever'. The Desais continue to serve up 'sensational' Gujerati home-cooking, plus other vegetarian delicacies from all over India. Farsan (home-made spicy savouries) include samosas, red onion bhajia and perhaps less familiar kachori (peas in pastry). Bombay specialities take in a range of puris, including a deluxe sev puri 'bursting with flavour', according to a reporter who continued with a North Indian chevati dal ('a complex blend of four types of lentil'), 'fine' mutter paneer and, from the list of 'South Indian specialities', a 'remarkable' Hyderabad masala dosa. Shak-bhaji (Gujerati seasonal vegetables) range from sweet potatoes to Bombay potatoes, from lilla beans to ravaiya; this last, the menu explains, is 'baby aubergines and bananas stuffed with gram flour, coconut, garlic and special aromatic herbs and spices, slow cooked'. There are a few Indian desserts and Mövenpick ices to finish, and a remarkable list of drinks, from simple wines to good premium beers, by way of fruit juices 'zapped with own secret ingredients', and lassi: salt or sweet, including one with acacia honey, another with sugar and ground pistachio. House wine is £9.95.

CHEFS/PROPRIETORS: Hemant and Nalinee Desai OPEN: Tue to Sun D only 6.30 to 10.30 CLOSED: 25 Dec MEALS: alc (main courses £4 to £7). Set D £6.95 to £14.95 SERVICE: 10%, card slips closed CARDS: Amex, Delta, Diners, MasterCard, Switch, Visa DETAILS: 32 seats. Private parties: 32 main room. Vegetarian meals. Children welcome. Wheelchair access (not WC). Music ⊖ Dollis Hill (£5)

See inside the front cover for an explanation of the symbols used at the tops of entries.

Saga

map 15

43–44 South Molton Street, W1V 1HB

TEL: (0171) 408 2236   FAX: (0171) 628 7507

COOKING 1
COST £30–£77

Amid the fashion shops of South Molton Street is 'an anachronistic little "rustic" Japanese fence'. This is the entrance to Saga, with its karaoke bar upstairs and white-walled basement restaurant. A standard menu cruises extensively through appetisers, sashimi, tempura, noodles and so forth: high points from reports have included nasu dengaku (rich, sweet grilled aubergine flavoured with miso), and agedashi dofu (a bowl of deep-fried tofu in dashi broth), not to mention a western flight of fancy in the shape of deep-fried crab and avocado rolls. Best bets, however, are likely to be the seasonal specialities and dishes of the day: these are written in untranslated Japanese, although it might be worth taking pot luck and trying something without knowing what it is. Saga also has a notable list of sakés arranged by class and region, which come in tokkuri (carafes) presented in wooden boxes to keep them warm. House wine is £13.50.

CHEF: Mr Shimada   PROPRIETOR: Mr K. Hashimoto   OPEN: Mon to Sat 12.30 to 2.30, 6.30 to 10, Sun D only 6 to 9.30   MEALS: alc (main courses £6.50 to £22). Set L £7 to £25, Set D £35 to £42. Cover £1 D   SERVICE: not inc L, 15% D   CARDS: Amex, Delta, Diners, MasterCard, Switch, Visa   DETAILS: 100 seats. Private parties: 20 main room, 6 to 12 private rooms. Vegetarian meals. No children under 4. No cigars/pipes in dining-room. Music. Air-conditioned   ⊖ Bond Street   £5

St John

map 13

26 St John Street, EC1M 4AY

TEL: (0171) 251 0848 and 4998

FAX: (0171) 251 4090

COOKING 5
COST £31–£55

Let's make no bones about it: this bar/restaurant is 'the place to consume dead animals and drink'. Vegetarians do get a look-in but only if they don't object to sitting next to someone eating a duck's neck. The spartan atmosphere of this former smokehouse, all white stone and concrete with grey floorboards, is striking ('like eating out in rural Hungary'), while staff uniforms bear a passing resemblance to butchers' kit. 'Nose to tail eating' is the promise on the pig-emblazoned menu, which makes a serious attempt to prove that you can indeed eat everything except the squeal. The whole thing adds up to a 'lively, fun experience', thought one reporter.

Rolled pig's spleen and bacon, or bloodcake with fried eggs, are more than just a challenge to carnivores, and it is good to see the celebrated roast bone marrow and parsley salad still defiantly on the menu. Game and fish put in more than a token appearance and are prepared with the same high level of skill. One reporter enjoyed 'a good, earthy dish' of lightly smoked eel, samphire and potato salad, the meaty-textured fish set off by the crunch and fresh, clean taste of the samphire. The Shropshire lamb that followed was served off the bone with chicory and a thin gravy. Well-made puddings such as apple dumpling, Eccles cake with Lancashire cheese, and gooseberry fool have an old-fashioned wholesomeness. An exclusively French wine list also offers draught beers and a comprehensive range of Cognacs. House wine is £11.

CHEF: Fergus Henderson   PROPRIETORS: Trevor Gulliver, Fergus Henderson and Jon Spiteri
OPEN: Mon to Fri L 12 to 3, Mon to Sat D 6 to 11.30   CLOSED: Christmas and New Year   MEALS:
alc (main courses £4 to £15)   SERVICE: not inc   CARDS: Amex, Delta, Diners, MasterCard,
Switch, Visa   DETAILS: 100 seats. Private parties: 150 main room, 20 private room. Vegetarian
meals. Children welcome. No music   ✆ Farringdon   £5

Salloos

map 14

| 62–64 Kinnerton Street, SW1X 8ER | COOKING 4 |
| TEL: (0171) 235 4444   FAX: (0171) 259 5703 | COST £27–£63 |

Reporters appreciate the 'soothing experience' of dining among the fretted
screens, colourful curtains and pleasing paintings of this elegant Knightsbridge
Indian restaurant. Prices, geared to the neighbourhood, pay for consistently
good cooking of what owner Mr Salahuddin (Salloo) used to enjoy in his Lahore
home. Tandoori dishes are recommended as shared starters for two, and the
menu suggests that they should be enjoyed independently of other dishes. A
reporter's memorable chicken kebab had 'a delicacy and freshness of spicing
rarely found in London'.

Beyond curries, the rest of the shortish menu offers more varied cooking
methods than usual. There is baked chicken in a cheese soufflé mixture,
deep-fried chicken thighs, and Salloos' 'unique speciality', haleem akbari,
shredded lamb cooked in wheat germ and lentils. Halva gajar, warm carrot halva
topped with silver leaf, is an enticing way to finish. Mrs Salahuddin and three
daughters provide friendly service. Opt for a classic French wine, or one of
Corney & Barrow's 20-strong special selection, including Australian Semillon
Chardonnay and a Shiraz Merlot, which should match the finely spiced food.
House wines are £12.50.

CHEFS: Abdul Aziz and Humayun Khan   PROPRIETORS: Mr and Mrs M. Salahuddin   OPEN: Mon
to Sat 12 to 2.30, 7 to 11.15   CLOSED: 25 and 26 Dec   MEALS: alc (main courses £10 to £15). Set
L £16, Set D £25. Cover £1.50   SERVICE: 12.5% (optional), card slips closed   CARDS: Amex,
Delta, Diners, MasterCard, Switch, Visa   DETAILS: 65 seats. Private parties: 65 main room.
Vegetarian meals. Children welcome. No children under 6 after 8pm. No cigars/pipes in
dining-room. No music. Air-conditioned   ✆ Hyde Park Corner, Knightsbridge

Sarkhel's £

NEW ENTRY   map 12

| 199 Replingham Road, SW18 5LY | COOKING 2 |
| TEL: (0181) 870 1483 | COST £23–£36 |

Chef Udit Sarkhel spent nearly ten years at the Bombay Brasserie (see London
Round-ups), before moving to this parade of shops in Southfields. The warm
décor, friendly ambience and 'totally charming' service make it 'a pleasure to eat
here', and the wide-ranging menu looks to many regions of the Subcontinent for
ideas. An inspector who admired excellent chicken chettinad, and baigan bhurta
(chargrilled, mashed aubergines) found them surpassed by dahl masala, and
palak gosht with large, tasty chunks of lamb, still pink inside, garnished with
fresh, dry, shredded spinach leaves. Daily specials might take in South Indian
crab, the mixed white and brown meat served in a scallop shell and spiced, so the
flavour of the crab shone through', and desserts include 'ultra-light' gulab

jamun. The short wine list is unexciting, but one reporter enjoyed jal jeera (listed among starters), a gently sparkling 'palate awakening' aperitif flavoured with cumin and mint. House wine is £9.90.

CHEF: Udit Sarkhel   PROPRIETORS: Udit and Veronica Sarkhel   OPEN: Sun L 12 to 2.30, Tue to Sun D 6 to 10.30 (11 Fri and Sat)   CLOSED: 25 and 26 Dec   MEALS: alc D (main courses £4 to £9). Set L £9.95   SERVICE: not inc   CARDS: Delta, MasterCard, Switch, Visa   DETAILS: 38 seats. Private parties: 40 main room. Vegetarian meals. Children welcome. Music. Air-conditioned   ⊖ Southfields £5

Sartoria ▼   NEW ENTRY   map 15

20 Savile Row, W1X 1AE   COOKING 5
TEL: (0171) 534 7000   FAX: (0171) 534 7070   COST £41–£71

Never one to let a design opportunity pass him by, Sir Terence Conran has made the most of the tailoring link in this Italian addition to his ever expanding restaurant collection. Taking its cue from Italian rationalism of the 1930s, the squarish dining-room is a clean-lined space with grey upholstery against a white background, sharp lighting and, on warm days, a side that opens up to the New Burlington Street air. Glass cases contain half-finished suits (bastes in the trade), and graphics reinforce the bespoke connection with a needle and thread on seat covers, a pin cushion for the bill, and a button motif on everything: one even hoves into view as you drain the coffee cup.

Darren Simpson's time at the River Café shows in, for example, a salad of artichokes with boiled lemons and artichokes, and chocolate nemesis, and although he may be slightly handicapped in not having a wood-burning oven, he still produces an appealing range of sometimes dramatic-looking dishes. A note on the menu advises that risotto is prepared to order (20 minutes), and the risotto nero served to an inspector confirmed what a good idea this was. Antipasti (the longest section on the menu) might include carpaccio, bruschetta with broad beans, and a dish of deep-fried veal sweetbreads and baby artichokes, partnered with lightly battered chard and a first-rate tarragon-flavoured gribiche-like sauce called dragoncella.

Main-course fish and meat get equal billing with three dishes each – quail with zucchini and grapes, perhaps, or prime turbot so perfectly cooked 'it quivered and wobbled when set down', served with beetroot and more chard – and desserts include poached cherries with ricotta, and a sweet puff pastry tart of green tomatoes with 'wonderful' zabaglione. Service is well paced. The wine list will excite Italian enthusiasts with its string of super-Tuscans – Ornellaia, Sassicaia and Solaia – as well as bottles from Gaja, Conterno and Jermann among many modish producers. Prices are more suited to a super-model's pocket, but wines under £20 can be found, starting with the Arcadian house wines at £14. CELLARMAN'S CHOICE: Pomino Bianco 1996, Frescobaldi, £20; Valpolicella Classico 1996, Allegrini, £19.

CHEF: Darren Simpson   PROPRIETOR: Conran Restaurants   OPEN: all week L 12 to 3, Mon to Sat D 6.30 to 11.15   CLOSED: 25 and 26 Dec, 1 Jan.   MEALS: alc (main courses £15 to £19.50) SERVICE: 12.5% (optional), card slips closed   CARDS: Amex, Delta, Diners, MasterCard, Switch, Visa   DETAILS: 120 seats. Private parties: 8 main room, 24 private rooms. Vegetarian meals. Children welcome. Wheelchair access (also WC). No music. Air-conditioned   ⊖ Oxford Circus, Piccadilly Circus

Les Saveurs de Jean-Christophe Novelli   map 15

37A Curzon Street, W1Y 7AF
TEL: (0171) 491 8919 FAX: (0171) 491 3658

COOKING 3
COST £37–£112

Since the last edition of the *Guide* Jean-Christophe Novelli has added this prestigious address to his portfolio, although it is a source of regret to some that he no longer cooks, since that has always been the root of his appeal. The windowless basement dining-room looks smart rather than characterful, with light walnut panelling and green upholstery, but tables are expansively spread and a sense of moneyed well-being pervades. Set-price lunch includes a glass of champagne and coffee, dinner offers a generous eight or more choices per course (a few of which attract a supplement) and, unusually for this kind of cooking, vegetables and salad are ordered separately and charged extra.

The food aims high: poached oysters with caviare fondue, wild mushrooms steamed in a pancake, and seared scallops in a broad-bean ragoût with a reduction of orange, vanilla and cardamom. Although materials are varied and of high quality, they did not translate into particularly successful dishes at inspection, the highlight of which was a first-rate combination of boneless rabbit cutlets with confit leg on a pea risotto. Desserts include fig tart with pistachio ice-cream, an apple and cinnamon 'Bavarian', and a chocolate plate that mixes hot with cold, dark with white. The wine list is 'thicker than *Hugh Johnson's World Atlas of Wine*', but many prices are 'hideous'. House vin de pays is £15.50.

CHEF: Nick Wilson PROPRIETOR: Jean-Christophe Novelli OPEN: Tue to Fri L 12.30 to 2.30, Mon to Sat D 6.30 to 10.30 (11.30 Fri and Sat) MEALS: Set L £19.50 (2 courses) to £25, Set D £25 (2 courses) to £75 SERVICE: 12.5% (optional) CARDS: Amex, Delta, Diners, MasterCard, Switch, Visa DETAILS: 65 seats. Private parties: 14 private room. Children welcome. No cigars/pipes in dining-room. Music. Air-conditioned ⊖ Green Park

▲ *The Savoy, Grill Room* map 15

The Strand, WC2R 0EU
TEL: (0171) 836 4343 FAX: (0171) 240 8749
EMAIL: info@the-savoy.co.uk.

COOKING 5
COST £43–£110

The Savoy, for those who don't know, is around a courtyard off the Strand: the only thoroughfare in Britain where it is mandatory to drive on the right. To call the Grill Room 'clubby' may be to under-egg the pudding; on one midweek evening in April, the clientele was fully 90 per cent male. That may or may not matter, but it confirms this as one of London's most traditional eating-spaces, with food to match.

Familiar strains resound in omelette Arnold Bennett, roast pigeon with peas and bacon, or the various grills, although there are more contemporary noises in the shape of a large spinach raviolo containing a hulking piece of salmon, topped with deep-fried leek threads and surrounded by a moat of champagne cream sauce. The full Savoy experience, though, comes with the trolley. Its cargo changes daily – Wednesday brings a pot-roasted guinea-hen with horseradish crust and celeriac cream – and is attended by a white-coated surgeon who carves your share before you.

Another trolley passes back and forth with desserts, its variety enough to induce 'an ecstasy of indecision' in one who settled for a 'technically perfect' hunk of clafoutis and a wobbly raspberry mousse. Imaginative petits fours come with coffee for those who can't decide at all. Wine service is as correct as everything else, clean muslins on hand for sieving elderly clarets that constitute the main business of the cellar. House wines start at £18.50, or opt for one of the varied range of 'aerated waters'.

CHEF: Simon Scott   PROPRIETOR: Savoy Group plc   OPEN: Mon to Fri L 12.30 to 2.30, Mon to Sat D 6 to 11.15   CLOSED: Aug, bank hols (exc 25 Dec)   MEALS: alc (main courses L £13.50 to £24, D £19 to £47.50). Set pre-theatre D £27.95 (2 courses) to £29.75   SERVICE: not inc   CARDS: Amex, Diners, MasterCard, Switch, Visa   DETAILS: 85 seats. Private parties: 20 main room, 20 to 500 private rooms. Vegetarian meals. Children welcome. Jacket and tie. Wheelchair access (also WC). No music. Air-conditioned   ACCOMMODATION: 207 rooms, all with bath/shower. TV. Phone. Room only £225 to £895. Rooms for disabled. Children welcome. Baby facilities. Afternoon teas. Swimming-pool *(The Which? Hotel Guide)*   ⊖ Embankment

▲ Savoy, River Restaurant

map 15

The Strand, WC2R 0ET
TEL: (0171) 836 4343   FAX: (0171) 240 8749   COOKING 4
EMAIL: info@the-savoy.co.uk.   COST £46–£105

The setting is 'luxurious, as befits a grand hotel', and is one of the very few on the north bank of the Thames to afford a river view worth the name. It is also one of the few left with a dance band and a 'carver's trolley' (as in the Grill Room, see above) offering a daily special: if it's Tuesday it must be roast saddle and best end of lamb. The lunchtime trolley is the more varied of the two, offering poached turbot most days, and steak and kidney pie with oysters on Friday. As for the rest, it aims to appeal to as many tastes as possible: grilled brill in wasabi butter for the modernists, roast cod on parsley sauce with a poached egg for old schoolboys, and Irish cobbler potato tart for those who have had enough of luxury.

For those who haven't, the 'Gourmet' menu might include a caviare taster, goose liver terrine, ceps, langoustines and truffles, as well as a glass of wine with each course. Another trolley delivers desserts, although the *pièce de résistance* consists of dark and light chocolate ices sitting on a tray containing carbon dioxide which, when triggered with a splash of water, 'produces a theatrical mist which stops all diners in their tracks'. Portions are considered generous. Service from smartly attired staff is 'impeccable but also friendly', and house wine is £18.50.

CHEF: Anton Edelmann   PROPRIETOR: Savoy Group plc   OPEN: all week 12.30 to 2.30, 6 to 11.30   MEALS: alc (main courses £25 to £42). Set L £28.50, Set D Sun to Thu £39.50, Set D Fri and Sat £43.50, pre-theatre D all week 6 to 7.30pm £28.50   SERVICE: net prices, card slips closed   CARDS: Amex, Delta, Diners, MasterCard, Switch, Visa   DETAILS: 180 seats. Private parties: 50 main room. Car park. Vegetarian meals. Children welcome. Jacket and tie. No pipes in dining-room. Wheelchair access (3 steps; also WC). Music. Air-conditioned   ACCOMMODATION: See entry above for details   ⊖ Embankment

▲ *means accommodation is available.*

Searcy's at the Barbican map 13

Level 2, Barbican Centre, Silk Street, EC2Y 8DS	COOKING 4
TEL: (0171) 588 3008 FAX: (0171) 382 7247	COST £32–£57

To see the Barbican complex at its best, advises one visitor, go at night, when the lake becomes 'a shimmering gloss under the lights, the fountains play and the water moves'. Searcy's aluminium-framed windows provide a sweeping vantage point, for all that its plain table settings and unbroken expanses of white plaster give it the feel of an 'industrial cafeteria'. The advantage of such anonymity is that 'anybody could fit in here', and Tom Ilic reflects that inclusiveness in his menus, which move without missing a beat from skate and citrus salad with lemon-grass vinaigrette, through baked cod with black olive crust and salsa verde, to apple and pear crumble with orange yoghurt ice-cream.

Confidence with the kinds of muscular flavours favoured by his now-departed mentor, Richard Corrigan, is evinced in a first course of fried sweetbreads and agreeably sticky black pudding, arranged around a heap of shredded carrot dressed with cardamom vinaigrette. Kid has been something of a star, carved in cutlets like lamb, and 'boasting a succulence and tenderness I had not thought possible'. Desserts may let the side down, although one party unanimously commended a blackberry and apple mille-feuille with Granny Smith sorbet. Predominantly French service tries hard, and around 50 wines offer a reasonable array of styles from the Old World supported by an occasional rewarding foray into the New. Prices start in France at £10.95.

CHEF: Tom Ilic   PROPRIETOR: Searcy Tansley & Co.   OPEN: Sun to Fri L 12 to 2.30, all week D 5 to 11 (6.30 Sun)   CLOSED: 24 and 25 Dec   MEALS: alc (main courses £14.50 to £18). Set L and D £18.50 (2 courses) to £21.50   SERVICE: not inc   CARDS: Amex, Delta, Diners, MasterCard, Switch, Visa   DETAILS: 130 seats. Private parties: 30 main room, 10 to 280 private rooms. Vegetarian meals. Children's helpings. No-smoking area. Wheelchair access (also WC). Occasional music. Air-conditioned   ⊖ Barbican, Moorgate (£5)

755 Fulham Road map 12

755 Fulham Road, SW6 5UU	COOKING 6
TEL: (0171) 371 0755 FAX: (0171) 371 0695	COST £25–£57

This may be only a short drive from the style-conscious Kensington and Chelsea end of Fulham Road, but number 755 feels distinctly suburban. The dining-room is a low-ceilinged box decorated in jazzily patterned pastel yellow and greyish blue, and the cooking is modern French using some pretty upmarket ingredients, including lobster – steamed with potato salad and baby spinach – and truffles, perhaps in a frothy cannellini bean soup. Techniques are sound too, as one might expect of a chef who has spent time cooking at Turner's, Pied-à-Terre and Kensington Place.

Alan Thompson doesn't rely on standard chargrilling or wok cooking, but undertakes some involved constructions: a robust dish of snails encased in breadcrumbed balls of chicken mousse, served with 'excellent mushrooms' and Puy lentils, for example, or seared scallops with aubergine crisps and 'dashings' of salt cod vichyssoise, a dish distinguished by its 'classy delivery'. Even an appetiser prawn comes in a fine, light, golden tempura batter, with expertly made aïoli and mango chutney dips. As one diner observed, after eating a simple but well-executed rare roast grouse, with a smooth bread sauce and fondant potato, this is 'grown-up food'.

A keen understanding of flavours results in well-balanced dishes, not least in desserts such as pear Tatin with good pastry and 'just the right sweetness'. Prices are considered 'good value for this standard of cooking', and service from Georgina Thompson, though slow-paced, is polite and helpful. Wines are split between Old and New Worlds, and while prices seem to have crept up generally, house French is only £12.50.

CHEF: Alan Thompson   PROPRIETORS: Alan and Georgina Thompson   OPEN: Tue to Sun L 12.30 to 2.30, Tue to Sat D 7 to 11 (12 to 4 Sun)   CLOSED: 2 weeks Christmas, Aug, bank hols   MEALS: alc (main courses £14.50 to £19.50). Set L £10 (2 courses) to £14, Set D £18 (2 courses) to £22   SERVICE: not inc   CARDS: Amex, Delta, MasterCard, Switch, Visa   DETAILS: 60 seats. Private parties: 40 main room, 35 private room. Vegetarian meals. Children's helpings. Wheelchair access (not WC). Music. Air-conditioned   ⊖ Parsons Green   £5

Simply Nico   map 13

48A Rochester Row, SW1P 1JU   COOKING 4
TEL: (0171) 630 8061   FAX: (0171) 828 8541   COST £33–£55

Light wood, framed drawings, mirrors and white cloths combine to produce a 'smart and well-cared-for feel' in this narrow ochre-yellow room in West-minster. There is 'no chi-chi and dome-lifting here, thank goodness', concluded one reporter, 'just reliable cooking with no culinary fireworks'. Whatever the food may lack in pyrotechnics it makes up for in its ability to comfort, with cep risotto, smoked haddock fish-cake with poached egg and hollandaise, or plump seared foie gras on a caramelised apple galette. It follows a tried-and-tested European route, serving up fish soup with rouille and croûtons, for example, and with rare exceptions it delivers satisfaction: skate wing with anchovies and capers on a cake of fried linguine that was 'crisp outside and soft inside', or roast breast of guinea-fowl with stuffed cabbage and a 'concentrated essence-of-fowl sauce'.

Desserts of lemon tart, cherry clafoutis or chocolate mousse with pistachio ice-cream adopt the same steady-as-she-goes philosophy. The inclusive pricing policy (as long as you don't choose side veg or dishes with supplements attached) is much appreciated, 'so the fixed price three-course meal for £27 cost us exactly that', and it is one of very few restaurants to have a menu in braille. Service is 'attentive without being intrusive', and capable of adapting itself to customer requirements. An international collection of 50-plus wines offers a fair spread of styles and flavours. House French is £11.50. Simply Nico is now also a brand name, owned by The Restaurant Partnership, with outlets in the City and Chelsea (see London Round-ups).

CHEF: Richard Hugill   PROPRIETOR: The Restaurant Partnership   OPEN: Mon to Fri L 12 to 2, Mon to Sat D 7 to 11   CLOSED: Christmas, Easter, bank hols   MEALS: Set L £22 to £25, Set D £27   SERVICE: net prices, card siips closed   CARDS: Amex, Delta, Diners, MasterCard, Switch, Visa   DETAILS: 42 seats. Private parties: 12 main room. Vegetarian meals. No children under 10. No pipes/cigars in dining-room. No music. Air-conditioned   ⊖ Victoria

Use the lists towards the front of the book to find suitable restaurants for special occasions.

Singapore Garden

map 13

83–83A Fairfax Road, NW6 4DY
TEL: (0171) 328 5314   FAX: (0171) 624 0656
EMAIL: SGR@aol.com

COOKING 2
COST £19–£62

Garden by name and décor, with assorted pictures and colourfully dressed waitresses, this restaurant reminded one visitor of the home country, not least because dishes arrive at the serving hatch with electronic bleeps sounding like those that warn Singapore taxi drivers when they are speeding. The long menu includes a page of Singaporean-Malaysian specialities plus around 15 seasonal dishes. Blachan in the name of a dish denotes fiery, chilli-spiced, fermented shrimps, and might be applied to squid or okra, while chiew yim indicates Cantonese-style chopped garlic and chillies, perhaps used for soft-shell crab. Praise has come in for steamed sea bass with ginger and spring onion, and spring greens stir-fried with garlic. The wine list, with exemplary detailed descriptions, mingles the familiar and the lesser known, and has a strong New World bias. House wines are £10.95 and £11.95.

CHEF: Mrs S.K. Lim   PROPRIETORS: the Lim family   OPEN: all week 12 to 2.45, 6 to 10.45 (11.15 Fri and Sat)   CLOSED: 25 to 28 Dec   MEALS: alc (main courses £5.50 to £36). Set L £6.25 (2 courses) to £8, Set D £17.50 to £22.50   SERVICE: 12.5% (optional), card slips closed   CARDS: Amex, Delta, Diners, MasterCard, Switch, Visa   DETAILS: 100 seats. 12 seats outside. Private parties: 100 main room. Vegetarian meals. Children welcome. No cigars in dining-room. Music. Air-conditioned   ⊖ Swiss Cottage

Snows by the Pond

NEW ENTRY   map 12

14–15 Barnes High Street, SW13 9LW
TEL: (0181) 876 1471   FAX: (0181) 876 1090

COOKING 2
COST £22–£45

Sebastian Snow divides his time between here and the Green (see entry, below) as best he can, cooking lunch at one, dinner at the other; so you may catch him, or you may not. The new venture occupies a large square room in a terraced house in genteel, affluent Barnes, helped towards a sunny Mediterranean disposition by vivid lines on pastel walls. It is a convivial place, with fair prices for both food and wine, and Snow devotees will be familiar with the mix of French, Italian and British dishes, from foie gras with fried egg to squid ink risotto. Chargrilling and roasting between them account for such successes as a 'beautifully blistered slab of feta' served on a chickpea and black olive salad, and moist flakes of roast cod and slices of red pepper served on a salt-cod cake.

Flavours can be robust and assertive, as in a starter of linguine with chicken livers and spicy chorizo, or 'light and refined', as in a dish of seared red mullet with artichoke ravioli in a fish stock bouillon. Desserts such as polenta cornmeal cake with mascarpone pick up on the European theme, and they 'can outshine everything else', as they did at inspection with a light but 'wicked' sticky toffee pudding served with clotted cream. Young, enthusiastic and friendly staff are dressed in casual black and, even when the pressure is on, a manageress of 'considerable charm' holds everything together. A short, sensibly chosen wine list starts at around £10.

CHEF/PROPRIETOR: Sebastian Snow   OPEN: Tue to Sun L 12 (11 Sat and Sun) to 3, Tue to Sat D 6 to 11   CLOSED: bank hols   MEALS: alc (main courses £9 to £12). Set L £10 (2 courses) to £13 SERVICE: not inc; 12.5% for parties of 6 or more   CARDS: Amex, Delta, MasterCard, Switch, Visa   DETAILS: 75 seats. Private parties: 75 main room. Vegetarian meals. Children's helpings. No pipes in dining-room. Wheelchair access (not WC). Music. Air-conditioned

Snows on the Green

map 12

| 166 Shepherd's Bush Road, W6 7PB | COOKING 2 |
| TEL: (0171) 603 2142   FAX: (0171) 602 7553 | COST £25–£50 |

Brook Green is the village appellation given to this bit of Shepherd's Bush, and Sebastian Snow's now-expanded original restaurant overlooks that patch of verdure. Fruity shades of orange and peach, bare wooden tables and inlaid tiles point to a Mediterranean orientation, confirmed in antipasti and simple shellfish and pasta dishes. The range extends, as at the Pond, to more robust daube of beef, or spiced haunch of venison with red cabbage and a truffly sauce, perhaps followed by flaky-pastry apple tart with caramel sauce and vanilla ice-cream, or a 'spot-on' steamed pear and ginger pudding. Vegetables and salads are charged extra, as is bruschetta, which all helps to push up the bill, but 'courteous, friendly and helpful' staff add to the appeal. Wines are a cheering, cosmopolitan collection, with whites offering greater price relief than reds. The bottom line is £10.75.

CHEF/PROPRIETOR: Sebastian Snow   OPEN: Sun to Fri L 12 to 3, Mon to Sat D 6 to 11   CLOSED: bank hols and Sun in summer   MEALS: alc (main courses £6.50 to £12). Set L £13 (2 courses) to £16.50   SERVICE: not inc; 12.5% for parties of 6 or more   CARDS: Amex, Delta, Diners, MasterCard, Switch, Visa   DETAILS: 100 seats. Private parties: 75 main room, 40 private room. Vegetarian meals. Children's helpings. No cigars/pipes in dining-room. Wheelchair access (not WC). Music. Air-conditioned   ⊖ Hammersmith

Soho Soho

map 15

| 11–13 Frith Street, W1V 5TS | COOKING 2 |
| TEL: (0171) 494 3491   FAX: (0171) 437 3091 | COST £28–£58 |

So smack in the middle of Soho that they named it twice, this venue was established by Groupe Chez Gérard as an oasis of provençale cooking over a decade ago. The mood, in the first-floor room particularly, is of a modern brasserie, and the cooking reflects that: marseillaise fish soup is the real deal, full of 'deep shellfish nuances' and accompanied by saffron mayonnaise, grated Gruyère and croûtons. Deep-fried squid with aïoli, or foie gras terrine in Sauternes aspic are other classic ways to start, and the house speciality is wild boar, stewed in red wine and served with chestnuts and linguine, although it might be further improved by a ladleful of liquor. Elsewhere, thick, rich sauces are quite the thing, even for basil-crusted cannon of lamb with potato gratin. An agreeably light assiette of desserts brings forth lemon tart with good bite, 'perfectly velvety' crème brûlée, and brandy-snaps filled with lavender cream. Service is well schooled in the professional niceties. An entirely French wine list opens with house Vins de Pays d'Oc at £9.95.

CHEF: Stephane Bailhe   PROPRIETOR: Groupe Chez Gérard   OPEN: Mon to Fri L 12 to 2.30, Mon to Sat D 6 to 11.30   CLOSED: 25 Dec, 1 Jan, Good Fri, Easter Sun   MEALS: alc (main courses £9 to £17). Cover £1.50   SERVICE: 12.5% (optional)   CARDS: Amex, Diners, MasterCard, Switch, Visa   DETAILS: 60 seats. Private parties: 30 main room, 60 private room. Car park. Vegetarian meals. Children welcome. Music. Air-conditioned   ⊖ Leicester Square

Sonny's   map 12

94 Church Road, SW13 0DQ	COOKING 5
TEL: (0181) 748 0393 FAX: (0181) 748 2698	COST £24–£48

After 12 years here, Rebecca Mascarenhas has decided it is time the restaurant had a major refit. This was due to take place as the *Guide* went to press, so we have no details, but reopening is scheduled after a few weeks with Leigh Diggins continuing as head chef. He takes a contemporary approach to European ideas, sometimes directly – red mullet with grilled vegetables and a tomato and basil dressing – and sometimes with an individual slant, as in scallops with vanilla risotto, or both kinds of artichoke in a salad with roasted red pepper and black olives.

Materials range from home-smoked chicken, via foie gras with celeriac and apple salad, to brill with samphire, or salmon with caramelised endive. A few niggles have surfaced during the year, but the food is generally confident without showing off, indicating a chef who is comfortable with his materials and with the traditions he draws on. Desserts generally contain a fruity element, such as rhubarb Bakewell tart, or black cherry and chocolate yoghurt mousse. Forty-plus wines from all over the place are arranged in price order, starting at £9.95; half are under £20 and nearly as many are available by the glass.

CHEF: Leigh Diggins   PROPRIETOR: Rebecca Mascarenhas   OPEN: all week L 12.30 to 2.30 (3 Sun), Mon to Sat D 7.30 to 11   CLOSED: most bank hols   MEALS: alc (main courses £9.50 to £13.50). Set L Mon to Sat £12 (2 courses), Set L Sun £17.50   SERVICE: not inc   CARDS: Amex, Delta, Diners, MasterCard, Switch, Visa   DETAILS: 100 seats. Private parties: 24 private room. Vegetarian meals. Children's helpings. No music. Air-conditioned   ⊖ Hammersmith (£5)

Sotheby's Café ⬩✳   map 15

34–35 New Bond Street, W1A 2AA	COOKING 3
TEL: (0171) 293 5077	COST £25–£38

Though you may see no external evidence, the Café at Sotheby's is to the left of the lobby. Its manager writes that patrons are more than welcome to browse around the premises after lunch, sizing up the merchandise and perhaps ending up with a rather lovely Victorian jardinière or a case of antique claret into the bargain. Appetites will have been whetted beforehand by such things as leek and morel tartlet lubricated with truffle oil, or fillet of haddock with grilled pepper relish and spinach. Choice is kept sensibly to a minimum, and the lobster club sandwich – a crustacean, bacon and mayo stack on soft brioche – seems a stayer. Finish with British cheeses such as Cotherstone and Oxford Blue with oatcakes, or more lightly with blood-orange sorbet. Cheesecakes of one sort or another seem a constant. In addition to lunches, you can breakfast on scrambled eggs with smoked salmon, or pop in for cream teas after the midday rush subsides. Wines are a predominantly French but well-chosen bunch, with most bins available by the glass, starting at £3.75.

CHEF: Caroline Crumbly   PROPRIETOR: Sotheby's   OPEN: Mon to Fri and Sun L only 12 to 3 CLOSED: last 2 weeks Aug, 23 Dec to 5 Jan   MEALS: alc (main courses £10 to £14)   SERVICE: net prices, card slips closed   CARDS: Amex, Delta, Diners, MasterCard, Switch, Visa   DETAILS: 45 seats. Vegetarian meals. No smoking in dining-room. Wheelchair access (not WC). No music. Air-conditioned   ⊖ Green Park

Spiga £   NEW ENTRY   map 15

84–86 Wardour Street, W1V 3LF   COOKING 3
TEL: (0171) 734 3444   FAX: (0171) 734 3332   COST £23–£40

Under the same ownership as Zafferano (see entry), and with a sister restaurant, Spighetta (see London Round-ups), Spiga sports this year's hottest kitchen accessory, a wood-fired oven. The place is stark, modern, brightly lit, with a bar along one side and a kitchen in the far corner. Bustling, full, noisy and 'unacceptably smoky' with loud Muzak, it is not going to be everyone's cup of tea, but the food majors on fresh ingredients. Plain and simple dishes are cooked confidently, where they are cooked at all, since there is much marinating, assembling and serving raw: salads of tomato with basil and mozzarella, or of tuna with pickled aubergine, and beef carpaccio or thinly sliced smoked swordfish.

Pizzas are huge – about a foot across – but there is 'no problem eating one each'. The bases are thin, and worth crossing town for in one reporter's estimation. Choose from rich fried aubergine, standard margherita, Napoli with anchovies, or caprino with goats' cheese, tomato and rocket. In addition, there are pasta dishes, fish and meat options – sweet leg of lamb with aubergine purée and grilled red pepper – and desserts that include a coffee-cup with layers of chocolate mousse and coffee cream: 'I'd like to single this out for special praise.' Service is from an army of well-regimented but unsmiling staff. A couple of dozen decent Italian wines start at £10.50.

CHEF: Michele Franzolin   PROPRIETOR: A–Z Restaurants   OPEN: Mon to Sat 12 to 3, 6 to 11 (12 Thur to Sat), Sun noon to 10.30   CLOSED: Christmas, bank hols   MEALS: alc (main courses £6 to £13.50)   SERVICE: 12.5% (optional), card slips closed   CARDS: Amex, Delta, MasterCard, Switch, Visa   DETAILS: 100 seats. Vegetarian meals. Children's helpings. Wheelchair access (also WC). Music. Air-conditioned   ⊖ Piccadilly Circus, Tottenham Court Road

The Square ♥   map 15

6–10 Bruton Street, W1X 7AG   COOKING 8
TEL: (0171) 495 7100   FAX: (0171) 495 7150   COST £47–£79

The Square is 'everything you want from a great restaurant', according to a reporter who appears easily satisfied by 'sublime cooking, fine service, brilliant wines, and a good atmosphere in swish surroundings'. Given a parquet floor, large abstract paintings, and plenty of space between smartly set tables, the room conveys a feeling of light and space. It is elegant, relaxing and, for this part of London, 'surprisingly unsnooty'. Fish features as prominently as meat among main courses, while starters typically combine shellfish – pistou soup with lobster, or 'brilliantly seared' scallops with girolles and a tomato butter sauce – with a little offal: foie gras with caramelised endive, or a skilfully handled lobe of foie gras with a sparse honey and pan-juice sauce.

Although dishes may sound ordinary, they often leave reporters searching for superlatives. Bresse pigeon comes in several forms, usually (though not invariably) pink and successful: perhaps served with a tarragon and foie gras mousseline stuffed inside a Savoy cabbage leaf, or with wild mushrooms and red wine sauce. Seasonality is something the kitchen seems to delight in flouting occasionally, serving up turbot with asparagus in October, and an apple and mincemeat tart in July, but fine ingredients, a high level of technical command, and clarity of flavour are what count. This is not hearty, gutsy food, nor is it showy. It is the marriage of ingredients and balance in dishes that so often impress, all done with a lightness of touch, as in a velouté of truffles with top-drawer tortellini of girolles and parmesan, or in chunks of steamed turbot in a creamy curry sauce, with an 'excellent' coriander risotto.

Desserts are no less appealing for having a conventional air about them: a large black fig sliced into a clear red juice, with light, puffy beignets and mascarpone; or a 'classic mille-feuille' (i.e. made with pastry for once) of pears with cream of Williams pear. Cheeses are French and in good condition. Service is courteous, 'never seems to be any hurry', and generally manages to balance efficiency and friendliness. The only downside is the cost, with prices rising somewhat faster than inflation. Wines can be expensive too, although this is a reflection of their pedigree and rarity. The classical list is big on burgundy (proprietor Nigel Platts-Martin's particular passion) and first-class clarets and Rhônes, while Australia and California are also accorded the respect they deserve. For particularly good-value whites look to the Mâconnais; otherwise the sommelier's selection of ten wines opens at £18.50. CELLARMAN'S CHOICE: Bourgogne Blanc 1995, Jean-Philippe Fichet, £29.50; Bourgueil Cuvée Beauvais 1990, Pierre-Jacques Drouet, £29.50.

CHEF: Philip Howard PROPRIETORS: Nigel Platts-Martin and Philip Howard OPEN: Mon to Fri L 12 to 3, all week D 6.30 to 10.45 (10 Sun) CLOSED: 25 and 26 Dec, 1 Jan. MEALS: alc (main courses £15 to £17). Set D £45 SERVICE: 12.5% (optional), card slips closed CARDS: Amex, Delta, Diners, MasterCard, Switch, Visa DETAILS: 70 seats. Private parties: 70 main room, 18 private room. Vegetarian meals. No children under 9. No cigars in dining-room. Wheelchair access (also WC). No music. Air-conditioned ⊖ Green Park

---

Sree Krishna £

map 12

192–194 Tooting High Street, SW17 0SF   COOKING 1
TEL: (0181) 672 4250   COST £19–£30

Although the menu includes common curry-house korma, dopiaza, dansak, vindaloo and the rest, the point of this South Indian restaurant is its regional vegetarian cuisine, which even takes in a 'tasty and aromatic' north–south 'fusion' bread, coconut paratha. Other approved dishes include appams (rice pancakes), iddly (rice and urad dahl-steamed savoury sponge cakes), kalan (a hottish mango curry), carrot poriyal (a dryish stir-fry), and sambhar, a wet vegetable curry that was a 'good mix of piquant and spicy'. The paratha and carrot dishes are additions to the menu, along with stir-fried vegetable thorans, kappa (cassava) and more. Those who think of India as unchanging will appreciate this restaurant's familiar brown and brass décor and its 'fairly efficient' service. Italian house wines are £7.50.

CHEF: Terab Ali   PROPRIETORS: T. Haridas, J. Dharmasggan, Ms Pillai   OPEN: all week 12 to 3, 6 to 11 (12 Fri and Sat)   CLOSED: 25 and 26 Dec   MEALS: alc (main courses £4 to £6.50). BYO £2   SERVICE: 10%, card slips closed   CARDS: Amex, Diners, MasterCard, Visa   DETAILS: 60 seats. Private parties: 60 main room, 70 private room. Vegetarian meals. Children's helpings. Wheelchair access (also WC). Music. Air-conditioned   ⊖ Tooting Broadway   £5

Sri Siam Soho £ {map 15}

16 Old Compton Street, W1V 5PE   COOKING 2
TEL: (0171) 434 3544   FAX: (0171) 287 1311   COST £22–£47

For some devotees of Thai food, Sri Siam is 'an old Soho standby' that continues to serve commendable food in a setting that combines 'London chic with ethnic'. Two dining-areas with parquet floors, beige walls and subtly stencilled bamboo leaves and birds create a pleasing effect. The 60-dish menu covers all the staples, and there's also a full selection for vegetarians. An assortment of decoratively arranged meatless hors d'oeuvre proved to be the high point of one meal: in particular, the recipients singled out deep-fried sweetcorn cakes and 'golden bags' (filo pastry filled with vegetables and tied with a thread of green kelp seaweed). Main dishes are competently handled, although some have commented that seasoning could have more zing and distinctiveness here and there. Pla neaung (steamed salmon with preserved plum and ginger) and kaeng pak (green vegetable curry) have been well received; likewise 'stingingly spicy' hot-and-sour papaya salad. Coconut ice-cream is a refreshing dessert, or finish with exotic fruit. Fairly priced New World wines stand out on the shortish list. House wine is £9.50. A second branch is at 85 City Wall, EC2; tel: (0171) 628 5772.

CHEF: W. Rodpradith   PROPRIETOR: Oriental Restaurant Group plc   OPEN: Mon to Sat L 12 to 3, all week D 6 to 11.15 (10.30 Sun)   CLOSED: 25 Dec, 1 Jan   MEALS: alc (main courses £6.50 to £10). Set L and D £12.95 to £19.95 (some min 2)   SERVICE: 12.5% (optional), card slips closed   CARDS: Amex, Delta, Diners, MasterCard, Switch, Visa   DETAILS: 145 seats. Private parties: 80 main room, 20 and 30 private rooms. Vegetarian meals. Children welcome. Wheelchair access (not WC). Music. Air-conditioned   ⊖ Tottenham Court Road, Leicester Square   £5

▲ Stafford {map 15}

St James's Place, SW1A 1NJ
TEL: (0171) 493 0111   FAX: (0171) 493 7121   COOKING 3
EMAIL: info@thestaffordhotel.co.uk.   COST £32–£81

Down a little-known cul-de-sac in the inner recesses of St James's, the Stafford is a grand hotel on a domestic scale and with a transatlantic tone. You may start Stateside for a cocktail in the bar, where baseball caps and American football helmets are suspended above, before arriving on the shores of unreconstructed Old Blighty for Chris Oakes's Classics menu, where steak and kidney pudding and poached salmon in lemon and parsley butter present the defiantly uncool side of culinary Britannia. Other menus, however, bring more enterprising contemporary dishes to light: smoked duck breast with mango and lime chutney, perhaps, or red mullet on a potato galette with champagne sauce and mange-tout. Earthiness and homeliness are also appealing aspects of Chris Oakes's cooking, apparent in venison with cabbage and bacon, and Devonshire apple cake with vanilla ice-cream, though there is always room for something unusual such as tea and honey parfait with plum compote. The wine list is encyclopedic, and comes at five-star prices. Basic négociant Chablis at just under £30 gives a flavour of it. House French is £17.50.

CHEF: Chris Oakes PROPRIETOR: Shire Inns OPEN: Sun to Fri L 12.30 to 2.30, all week D 6 to 10.30 (6.30 to 9.30 Sun) MEALS: alc (main courses £19 to £28). Set L £20 (2 courses) to £23.50, Set D £23.50 (2 courses) to £27 SERVICE: net prices, card slips closed CARDS: Amex, Delta, Diners, MasterCard, Switch, Visa DETAILS: 40 seats. Private parties: 55 main room, 2 to 44 private rooms. Vegetarian meals. Children welcome. Jacket and tie. Wheelchair access (not WC). No music. Air-conditioned ACCOMMODATION: 80 rooms, all with bath/shower. TV. Phone. Room only £199 to £450. Rooms for disabled. Children welcome. Afternoon teas *(The Which? Hotel Guide)* ⊖ Green Park

---

Stephen Bull ♥ 🍴

map 15

5–7 Blandford Street, W1H 3AA
TEL: (0171) 486 9696 FAX: (0171) 490 3128
EMAIL: sbull2@compuserve.com

COOKING 6
COST £37–£51

In 1999 Stephen Bull clocks up a decade at this small and trim dining-room off Marylebone High Street. Décor is light and uncluttered, tables necessarily close, the mood professional but not formal. Despite other ventures (see entries below), Stephen Bull has never spread himself too thinly, always keeping a manageable hold on each enterprise, and generally maintaining a consistent standard. New chef Robert Jones is no exception, producing dishes very much in Bullish mode. Contemporary ingredients fit neatly into the style of cooking, which makes a virtue of handling humble materials and less-fashionable cuts with understanding. This is not flamboyant food – indeed ideas are often straightforward – but they tend to be imbued with enough novelty not to be clichés.

A sense of restraint is typical – small slivers of chorizo not overpowering the crisp-skinned, well-timed pink sea bream they accompany – and a sure hand has made a success of 'light as a feather' gnocchi with leeks and girolles in a well-judged cheese sauce, one of four vegetarian options. Dishes typically get their kicks from an accompanying relish, maybe a scoop of stunning foie gras parfait in a wood-pigeon salad, or a dab of horseradish cream on top of calf's liver: two thickish pink slices, with a lump of kidney and a sweet, earthy beetroot sauce. 'A decent, thoughtful, well-constructed dish' was the judgement on this, a sentiment that could apply almost across the board.

Dessert combinations may be as standard as rhubarb crumble tart with ginger ice-cream, but good workmanship turns out a sound result, including an iced coffee parfait with a fanned poached pear and a puddle of dark chocolate sauce that finished one first-rate meal. Around 100 wines drawn mostly from France and the New World are helpfully arranged by style and clearly annotated. Prices are fair, starting at £11.50 for house red, £14 for white, with plenty of attractive bins offered below £20, as well as 16 half-bottles. CELLARMAN'S CHOICE: Bergerac, Ch. Tour des Gendres, Cuvée des Conti 1997, £14.95; Fitou Vieilles Vignes 1995, Dom. de Roudène, £13.95.

CHEF: Robert Jones PROPRIETOR: Stephen Bull OPEN: Mon to Fri L 12.15 to 2.30, Mon to Sat D 6.30 to 10.30 CLOSED: 1 week Christmas, bank hols MEALS: alc (main courses £14 to £15). BYO £5 SERVICE: 12.5% (optional), card slips closed CARDS: Amex, Diners, MasterCard, Switch, Visa DETAILS: 55 seats. Private parties: 55 main room. Vegetarian meals. Children's helpings. No cigars/pipes in dining room. Wheelchair access (1 step; not WC). No music. Air-conditioned ● Bond Street

---

Stephen Bull St Martin's Lane ▼   map 15

12 Upper St Martin's Lane, WC2H 9DL   COOKING 5
TEL: (0171) 379 7811 FAX: (0171) 836 3855   COST £36–£51

Stark. Windowless. Pictureless. Adorned with nothing. The dining-area at SBSML is all of those and more, the more being a handy location for theatreland, with obliging early- and late-evening menus, an escape from the mediocrity of much in Covent Garden and Leicester Square, and an inventive and individual approach to modern food. On the surface, things look quiet enough, but there is a lot going on in this kitchen: a vegetable platter, for instance, might consist of carrot and coriander bavarois, mushroom vol-au-vent, black olive couscous and falafel, while 'warm salad' has included a rabbit, bacon and snail version. Given that the results are 'consistently good' and 'reasonably priced', no wonder it draws enthusiastic reports.

Part of the appeal lies in an intelligent use of unshowy ingredients, from shin of beef or ox tongue to variously flavoured gnocchi: perhaps made with saffron and served with finely diced olive, artichoke heart and a rocket salad. There is enough on the plate to arouse interest but distractions are avoided, so heightening the pleasure, as in an escalope of salmon sitting on a mound of dauphinoise-like celeriac, surrounded by a deep red wine sauce and roasted garlic cloves, 'the kind where you squeeze out the pulp and indulge yourself'. Desserts have spanned the gamut from old-fashioned junket – 'creamy and light' – to a jazzier coconut rice-pudding brûlée with tropical fruit salsa, while service has an efficient and businesslike air about it. Wines are introduced with a 'Quick' list of 26 bottles (most available by the glass) and 16 half-bottles to help speed the theatre crowd on their way. The main list is usefully grouped by style with accompanying food-matching suggestions, and each wine has a lively tasting note to aid selection. Given the location, prices are reasonable too: house vins de pays are £10.75 the white, £11.95 the red. CELLARMAN'S CHOICE: Costières de Nîmes Blanc 1996, Ch. de St-Cyrgues, £14.50; Ribera del Duero 1995, Pago de Carraovejas, £26.

CHEF: John Bentham PROPRIETOR: Stephen Bull OPEN: Mon to Fri L 12 to 2.30, Mon to Sat D 5.45 to 11.30 CLOSED: 1 week Christmas, bank hols MEALS: alc (main courses £11 to £14.50). Set pre- and post-theatre D 5.45 to 7, 11 to 11.30 £10 to £13.50 (all 2 courses) SERVICE: 12.5% (optional), card slips closed CARDS: Amex, Diners, MasterCard, Switch, Visa DETAILS: 66 seats. Private parties: 75 main room. Vegetarian meals. Children's helpings. No cigars/pipes in dining-room. Wheelchair access (1 step; not WC). No music. Air-conditioned ● Leicester Square

Stephen Bull Smithfield ♥ ✳

map 13

71 St John Street, EC1M 4AN
TEL: (0171) 490 1750   FAX: (0171) 490 3128   COOKING 3
EMAIL: sbull2@compuserve.com   COST £31–£50

A bustlingly popular branch of Stephen Bull's little London empire on fashionable St John Street offers metropolitan cooking in tune with the times. The plate of Spanish delicacies remains a fixture, either as a starter or main course, and seafood specialities – scallop ceviche with honey and lime, or Irish rock oysters at 90p apiece – are always bright and fresh. A reporter who ate here twice in three evenings praised a bowl of fine mussel soup, roasted skate au poivre with baby leeks, and juniper-cured salmon with horseradish crème fraîche. Meat dishes are usually simpler than fish, but successfully pair such things as Scotch ribeye with roast chicory and celeriac, or neck end of lamb with sauté potatoes and olives. Piquancy is achieved in desserts such as kirsch parfait with blackberry compote, and farmhouse cheeses come with pear chutney.

An up-to-the-minute wine list features popular grape varieties from trendy producers, but more traditional options are also provided. Wines are grouped and annotated in the same fashion as at other Stephen Bull establishments (see entries above) and prices are equally fair, starting at £11.50 for a Spanish Tempranillo. CELLARMAN'S CHOICE: Falerno del Massico Bianco 1996, Fattoria Matilde, Campania £19.00; Pago de Carrovejas 1995, Ribera del Duero £23.

CHEF: Danny Lewis   PROPRIETOR: Stephen Bull   OPEN: Mon to Fri L 12 to 2.30, Mon to Sat D 6.30 to 10.30   CLOSED: 1 week Christmas, bank hols   MEALS: alc (main courses £10 to £12) SERVICE: not inc, card slips closed   CARDS: Amex, Diners, MasterCard, Switch, Visa   DETAILS: 110 seats. Private parties: 100 main room. Vegetarian meals. Children's helpings. No smoking in 1 dining-room. Wheelchair access (1 step; not WC). Occasional music. Air-conditioned
⊖ Farringdon

Stepping Stone ✳

map 12

123 Queenstown Road, SW8 3RH   COOKING 3
TEL: (0171) 622 0555   FAX: (0171) 622 4230   COST £25–£46

This popular, bright neighbourhood restaurant does a good job of 'discouraging us south-of-the-river residents from driving any further into London in search of an excellent dinner'. The frequently changing *carte* offers a fashionable blend of modern and traditional in the shape of onion soup, goats'-cheese and chicory pizza, or smoked haddock gratin, while main courses have taken in skate with lentils and lemon basil butter, and calves' kidneys with parsnip purée and mustard sauce. The good-value set-price menu offers two choices at each course: perhaps white-bean crostini or marinated red peppers, followed by roast plaice with stir-fried vegetables, or cheese and onion tart with a salad of wild mushrooms and jerusalem artichokes. Desserts range from pear and almond tart to steamed marmalade pudding with whisky custard, and cheeses are from Neal's Yard. The wine list offers a wide choice, many from the New World, as well as the entreaty to 'be adventurous . . . we will gladly change the bottle if it is not to your liking'. House wines change frequently and are priced around £10.

CHEF: Peter Harrison PROPRIETOR: Bestgroom Ltd OPEN: Sun to Fri L 12 to 2.30, Mon to Sat D
7 to 11 (10.30 Mon) CLOSED: 5 days Christmas, bank hols MEALS: alc (main courses £9 to
£16). Set L £10.75 (2 courses), Set L Sun D £15 SERVICE: not inc CARDS: Amex, Delta, Diners,
MasterCard, Switch, Visa DETAILS: 56 seats. Private parties: 56 main room. Vegetarian meals.
Children's helpings. No smoking in 1 dining-room. Wheelchair access (not WC). No music.
Air-conditioned ⊖ Clapham Common

Sugar Club   map 13

21 Warwick Street, W1R RSB   COOKING 5
TEL: (0171) 437 7776 FAX: (0171) 437 7772   COST £36–£54

In the summer of 1998 Sugar Club finally outgrew its Notting Hill premises, and
moved to Soho, the old site being reborn as Bali Sugar. Stainless steel fixings,
reddish timber floors, and muted sand colours lend the place an agreeably cool
metropolitan air, while one wall is dominated by a shimmeringly intense giant
daub. The first sign of quality comes with hugely improved breads: a
crisp-crusted caraway and thyme roll makes a properly appetising opener to
Peter Gordon's almost exclusively Pacific Rim cooking. Despite a flourish of
something Hispanic – a starter of chorizo with piquillo peppers, chillies,
garrotxa (goats' cheese), almonds and capers on sour-dough bread – the most
vivid cooking influences are drawn from Asia. Sashimi of Iki Jimi yellowtail
with black-bean and ginger salsa, for example, offers slices of 'superbly fresh'
fish in a texturally contrasted dressing.

Flavours tend to go off like fireworks, though not entirely at random, as in the
case of fried halibut coated with chopped shiso leaves, accompanied by a salad of
new potatoes, baby spinach, red cabbage, galangal and truffle. Grilled kangaroo
loin is the signature, a thick piece sitting on mustard mash. To finish, chocolate
mousse cake with crème fraîche and raspberries finds a good bittersweet
balance, the dish topped with a velvety thick layer of chocolate frosting. A
generous offering of wines by the glass opens a list that has much to commend it
in terms of discriminating selection, although mark-ups may deter many from
real exploration. Italian house wines start at £10.50.

CHEF: Peter Gordon PROPRIETORS: Ashley Sumner and Vivienne Hayman OPEN: all week 12
to 3, 6 to 11 MEALS: alc (main courses £11.50 to £17.80) SERVICE: 12.5% (optional), card slips
closed CARDS: Amex, Diners, MasterCard, Switch, Visa DETAILS: 130 seats. 25 seats
outside. Private parties: 50 main room. Vegetarian meals. No children under 14. Wheelchair
access (not WC). No music. Air-conditioned ⊖ Oxford Street

Le Suquet   map 14

104 Draycott Avenue, SW3 3AE   COOKING 3
TEL: (0171) 581 1785 FAX: (0171) 225 0838   COST £22–£73

Pierre Martin's bustly seafood restaurant is sited plumb in the middle of the
smartest part of Chelsea. People cram the tiny dining-room to overflowing and,
when the weather obliges, sit outside to eat fish and shellfish of exemplary
freshness, simply presented in salads and feuilletés or with textbook Madras or
meunière sauces. Oysters, mussels, scallops and sea-urchins are the order of the
day, while white fish such as sole comes with hollandaise full of keen vinegary

bite. High-rollers may opt for turbot in champagne sauce or a lobster salad, but prices for more luxurious items rise steeply. Meats include sirloin steak with peppercorns or shallots, or perhaps navarin of lamb, but that is really to miss the point. Desserts may not inspire, but espresso is excellent. Plastic menus lay it all out in formula fashion, and service moves at breakneck pace. Surprisingly for a French-owned restaurant, the wines are bereft of vintages and producers on the list. Vins de maison are £10.50.

CHEF: Philippe Moron   PROPRIETOR: Pierre Martin   OPEN: all week 12 to 2.30, 7 to 11.30 (all day Sat and Sun)   MEALS: alc (main courses £11.50 to £30). Set L £13. Cover £1   SERVICE: 15% (optional), card slips closed   CARDS: Amex, Delta, Diners, MasterCard, Switch, Visa   DETAILS: 50 seats. 8 seats outside. Private parties: 18 main room, 18 private room. Children welcome. Music   ⊖ South Kensington

Sushi-Say
map 12

33B Walm Lane, NW2 5SH   COOKING 3
TEL: (0181) 459 7512   FAX: (0181) 459 2971   COST £27–£47

The curious long, narrow dining-room, decorated in basic rustic fashion with various Japanese artefacts, has a warm ambience. Sit at one of half a dozen tables, or at the small bar where chef-patron Katsuharu Shimizu prepares traditional sushi and sashimi. The repertoire extends way beyond raw fish, though menu translations from Japanese are approximate and sometimes don't do justice to a dish: a reporter was impressed by 'sweet and delightful' edamame (green soya beans), described as Japanese peas; and 'sticky soya beans' understates the strong fermented flavour of natto. Also approved have been buta kakuni (diced belly pork); satoimo nitsuke (yams in a special sauce); and tendon (deep-fried prawn and vegetables on rice). A range of set dinners offers a good way to enjoy the cuisine: the Sushi-Say version, for example, includes appetiser, vegetable nimono, yakitori, fried tofu, chicken teriyaki, tempura and sushi. Service is charmingly led by Mrs Shimizu. The list of sakés, complete with tasting notes, repays investigation. Alternatively, French house wine is £9.

CHEF: Mr K. Shimizu   PROPRIETORS: Mr and Mrs K. Shimizu   OPEN: Tue to Sun D only 6 to 10.30   CLOSED: 25 and 26 Dec, 1 Jan, 1 week Easter, 1 week Aug   MEALS: alc (main courses £7 to £18). Set D £16 to £26   SERVICE: not inc   CARDS: Amex, Delta, MasterCard, Switch, Visa   DETAILS: 36 seats. Private parties: 20 main room, 6 private room. Vegetarian meals. Children welcome. No-smoking area. Wheelchair access (not WC). No music. Air-conditioned ⊖ Willesden Green

Tamarind
map 15

20 Queen Street, W1X 7PJ   COOKING 2
TEL: (0171) 629 3561   FAX: (0171) 499 5034   COST £28–£65

The smart Mayfair setting is a clear indication that this is Indian food for people 'who are not short of a bob or two'. One wall of the pine-floored, green and gold, low-ceilinged basement dining-room is a window on to the kitchen, which turns out a range of standard dishes – shami kebab, traditional chicken curry, rogan josh – alongside less usual wild mushrooms in pickled mango dressing, or John Dory with crispy spinach. 'My lamb kebab ground with mint and coriander sounded better than it tasted,' reckoned one reporter, while 'chickpea, spinach, lentil and potato kebab tasted better than it sounded'. The tandoor is applied to nan bread, monkfish with saffron and yoghurt, game in season, and first-rate marinated king prawns with an appealing 'smoky' dimension. To finish, creamy-textured kulfi is generously saffroned, and halva is served with 'perfectly decent' carrot fudge. An up-to-date wine list covers a variety of styles, but there is not much under £20. Six house wines start at £13.50.

CHEF: Atul Kochhar   PROPRIETOR: Halcyon Hotel   OPEN: Sun to Fri L 12 to 3 (2.30 Sun), all week D 6 to 11.30 (10.30 Sun)   CLOSED: 25 Dec, 1 Jan   MEALS: alc (main courses £10.50 to £18). Set L and post-theatre D £16.50   SERVICE: not inc L, 12.5% D   CARDS: Amex, Delta, Diners, MasterCard, Switch, Visa   DETAILS: 100 seats. Private parties: 100 main room. Vegetarian meals. Children welcome. Music. Air-conditioned   ⊖ Green Park

Tate Gallery Restaurant 🍾

map 13

Millbank, SW1P 4RG
TEL: (0171) 887 8877   FAX: (0171) 887 8902

| NEW CHEF |

COST £30–£57

Richard Zuber, who has come all the way from Sydney, arrived too late for us to discover whether a change of direction was planned for the hitherto Anglo-French cooking at this 'cluttered, bustling room' with its famous Whistler mural. It has, in any case, always been better known for its legendary cellar of French classics and modern New World masterpieces. Novices who require a guided tour should ask for help from sommelier Hamish Anderson, otherwise ten house wines (from £12.50 to £19.50) provide a quick character sketch, and the Lloyd Grossman selection paints a pretty picture for his chosen five. CELLARMAN'S CHOICE: Monthélie 1995, Dom. Denis Roussey, £21.50; Bordeaux, Ch. Talbot 1989, £27.95.

CHEF: Richard Zuber   PROPRIETOR: Trustees of the Tate Gallery   OPEN: all week L only 12 to 3 (4 Sun)   CLOSED: Christmas   MEALS: alc (main courses £9.50 to £15.50). Set L £15.75 (2 courses) to £18.50. Minimum £15.75   SERVICE: not inc, card slips closed   CARDS: Amex, Diners, MasterCard, Switch, Visa   DETAILS: 100 seats. Vegetarian meals. Children's helpings. No-smoking area. Wheelchair access (also WC). No music

Tatsuso

map 13

32 Broadgate Circle, EC2M 2QS
TEL: (0171) 638 5863   FAX: (0171) 638 5864

COOKING 4
COST £31–£101

Beyond the plain glass frontage, enter a tiny lobby dominated by a ferocious-looking suit of samurai armour. On the ground floor is a teppanyaki bar, where chefs grill meat and fish at stainless steel tables, while downstairs a tranquil wood-panelled dining-room deals in fine Japanese cuisine. On the set menus some items appear simply as 'assorted appetisers', or 'special hot dish of the day', for the basis of this type of meal is that every dish is cooked by a different method. Oriental subtleties include the 'grilled dish' toban yaki (sliced Scotch beef poached in a tiny earthenware pot over an open flame), and braised mackerel with radish sauce. There is a full range of sushi, sashimi, tempura, and sunomono as well as sukiyaki and its variations. Connoisseurs of fried fish may enjoy grey mullet with leek, or turbot deep-fried without coating. As an alternative to fine, but expensive, wines drink Tatsuso's own superb saké: dry, rich and mellow as fine old silk. Finish with glowing gold 'green' tea.

CHEFS: Nobuyuki Yamanaka   PROPRIETOR: Terutoshi Fujii   OPEN: Mon to Fri 11.30 to 2.30, 6 to 9.45   CLOSED: 25 Dec, bank hols   MEALS: alc (main courses £10.50 to £26.50). Set L £28 to £75, Set D before 9pm £29 to £66   SERVICE: 13%, card slips closed   CARDS: Amex, Delta, Diners, MasterCard, Switch, Visa   DETAILS: 120 seats. Private parties: 50 main room, 6 to 50 private rooms. Vegetarian meals. Children welcome. Wheelchair access (also WC).No music. Air-conditioned

Teatro   NEW ENTRY   map 15

93–107 Shaftesbury Avenue, W1V 7AE   COOKING 5
TEL: (0171) 494 3040   FAX: (0171) 494 3050   COST £27–£53

Footballer Lee Chapman and his wife, actress Leslie Ash, have scored highly in this new venture, perhaps because they have signed Stuart Gillies whose cooking, according to one visitor, is distinguished by 'clarity, precision and a grasp of culinary logic'. The setting is not auspicious: in a former NCP car park on the corner of Shaftsbury Avenue and Dean Street, reached by a bleak staircase and a narrow corridor devoted to merchandising. A great deal of money has been poured into making the low-ceilinged interior as fashionably bare as possible, the result either 'clinical' or exuding 'clean comfort' according to taste.

Happily, minimalist chic doesn't extend to the food, which goes in for the richness of lobster risotto, crab bisque and 'foie gras du jour', plus a refined take on Mediterranean/Middle Eastern flavours: salmon with lemon couscous, or rack of lamb with a pine-nut crust and aubergine confit. There is no doubting either flair or technique. Beetroot soup with a swirl of minted crème fraîche shows a good balance of sweetness and acidity, while sweetcorn ravioli with truffle oil and wild mushrooms converted a sweetcorn agnostic with its 'staggeringly intense' flavour. Grilled halibut, 'cooked to pearly opalescence', has been 'superbly judged', served with a punchy horseradish butter. Rich puddings – banana sticky toffee, treacle tart, or crème brûlée – rather lack the inventive edge of the rest of the food. Courteous, designer-clad staff are commendably well-informed. The wine list has a French bias and a New World selection that looks more towards America than Australia, starting with house wine at £11.

CHEF: Stuart Gillies   PROPRIETORS: Lee Chapman and Leslie Ash   OPEN: Mon to Fri L 12 to 3, Mon to Sat D 6 to 11.45   CLOSED: 25 to 31 Dec.   MEALS: alc (main courses £14.50 to £18.50). Set L and D £15 (2 courses) to £18. Cover £1.50   SERVICE: not inc   CARDS: Amex, Delta, Diners, MasterCard, Switch, Visa   DETAILS: 100 seats. Private parties: 100 main room. Vegetarian meals. Children's helpings. No pipes in dining-room. Wheelchair access (also WC). No music. Air-conditioned   ⊖ Piccadilly Circus

10   NEW ENTRY   map 13

Cutlers Gardens Arcade, Devonshire
Square, EC2M 4YA   COOKING 4
TEL: (0171) 283 7888   FAX: (0171) 626 4859   COST £27–£56

Behind black iron gates close by Liverpool Street station, in a recently constructed arcade, 10' is a basement restaurant and bar. Designed by Julyan

Wickham, whose previous successes include Bank (see entry), the room is made cheerily un-subterranean by means of large murals depicting kitchen still-lifes in pastel colours, and inventive use of mirrors. Judging by the animated buzz at lunch-times, it seems enthusiastically supported by City trade.

Richard Ross offers a lively-sounding brasserie menu, strong on oriental influences, but bringing in such indelibly British standards as breakfast salad of fried egg, bacon, black pudding and hash browns, or roast chicken with bubble and squeak, and baked rice pudding with prunes. An inspection lunch turned up fine crab risotto sprinkled with shaved horseradish, a piece of properly timed roast cod with spinach and garlic mash in a meat stock sauce, and Chinese-spiced duck hotpot, the meat braised in honey, garlic, ginger and soy, and accompanied by soft egg noodles. Finish with plum and rhubarb trifle, or spotted dick and custard with currants spilling out all over the plate. Service, anonymous in the contemporary manner, is well-drilled and highly efficient. The restaurant has not supplied us with a wine list, but house French is £11.50 a bottle.

CHEF: Richard Ross   PROPRIETOR: City Bars & Restaurants plc   OPEN: Mon to Fri 11.30 to 2.30, 5.30 to 9.30   CLOSED: bank hols   MEALS: alc (main courses £13 to £22.50). Set D £15.95 SERVICE: 12.5% (optional), card slips closed   CARDS: Amex, Delta, Diners, MasterCard, Switch, Visa   DETAILS: 130 seats. Private parties: 140 main room. Vegetarian meals. Children welcome. Wheelchair access (also WC). Music. Air-conditioned   ⊖ Liverpool Street

Tentazioni ⚑✶

	NEW ENTRY	map 13

2 Mill Street, Lloyd's Wharf, SE1 2BD	COOKING 5
TEL/FAX: (0171) 237 1100	COST £34–£44

Unlike other warehouse conversions within shouting distance, this one has not had millions of pounds thrown at it. It doesn't look the part of a fine restaurant: the ground floor is a wine bar with rag-rolled yellow walls, while the dining-room is up a short flight of 'ship's stairs' to a mezzanine-cum-balcony. Nor does it have much in the way of slick service, which is more 'homely' than anything. But it does have an honesty and integrity about it, in marked contrast to many of the more cynical operations to which London is prey. The food is Italian, and, while it goes in for pesto, rocket and truffle oil, manages to avoid most of the clichés.

The menu changes every couple of weeks to accommodate regulars, relying on a sense of ingenuity to convert often humble materials into dishes of character. Fish, vegetables and fowl account for the bulk of the output, which might run to ricotta gnocchi, aubergine terrine, or steamed hake fillet with basil purée. One meal began with a first-class lentil soup 'of substance and body' accompanied by two pink quail breasts, followed by a 'revelatory' dish of rabbit: a conical 'jambonette' of just-cooked meat enclosing a bare stuffing of herbs, part-sliced and laid on a splodge of polenta. To finish, yoghurt mousse with strawberries comes on a black pepper syrup, and Gorgonzola is served with pears. A four-course dinner option includes a glass of wine at each, or there is a short, sharp Italian list starting at £10.50.

CHEF: Alessio Brusadin   PROPRIETORS: Alessio Brusadin and Mauro Santoliquido   OPEN: Mon to Fri L 12 to 2.30, Mon to Sat D 7 to 10.45 (10.15 Sun)   CLOSED: 25 Dec, Easter, bank hols   MEALS: alc (main courses £12.50 to £15). Set D £38 (incl wine)   SERVICE: not inc   CARDS: Amex, Delta, Diners, MasterCard, Switch, Visa   DETAILS: 35 seats. Private parties: 35 main room. Children welcome. No smoking in 1 dining-room. Music   ⊖ London Bridge   (£5)

Thai Garden 🎇 £   map 12

249 Globe Road, E2 0JD   COOKING 3
TEL: (0181) 981 5748   COST £24–£34

This small café in an East End 'enclave of slightly upmarket old hippie shops' is popular with young locals. Its green and white walls carry 'arty photos of seashells' and the closeness of smallish tables 'just adds to the cosiness'. A long menu is divided into vegetarian and seafood sections, and makes for interesting reading and eating. An inspector enjoyed a combination of mixed starters, including 'tasty and spicy' mushroom and prawn satay; and yam woon sen: a hot and sour vermicelli salad with mushrooms, nuts and raisins. Of main dishes, 'authentic' Pad Thai goong (noodles, deep-fried prawns, eggs, peanuts, dried parsnips, onion and coriander) has been 'subtle and sophisticated', while crisply deep-fried pomfret is served on a 'truly wonderful rich, hot and sweet sauce'. Gaeng pad, a curry of aubergines, red pepper, mushroom and onion, comes in a 'tasty, caramelly' sauce of soy, chilli and coconut cream. Fixed-price menus – a basic lunch, and a range of dinners – are well-balanced, and service is pleasant if not always fast. All 20 wines, including champagne, are below £20; house French is £7.50.

CHEF: Naphathorn Duff   PROPRIETORS: Suthinee and Jack Hufton   OPEN: Mon to Fri L 12 to 2.45, all week D 6 to 10.45   CLOSED: bank hols   MEALS: alc (main courses £4.50 to £6.50). Set L £7.50, Set D £16 to £21   SERVICE: 10%, card slips closed   CARDS: MasterCard, Visa   DETAILS: 32 seats. Private parties: 20 main room, 12 private rooms. Vegetarian meals. Children welcome. No smoking in 1 dining-room. Wheelchair access (1 step; not WC). Music   ⊖ Bethnal Green   (£5)

Thailand 🎇   map 12

15 Lewisham Way, SE14 6PP   COOKING 5
TEL: (0181) 691 4040   COST £28–£48

The illuminated map of South-east Asia forming most of this restaurant's ceiling is as bright and colourful as the cooking of chef-patron Mrs Herman. She is a Laotian from north-east Thailand, and her fiery inheritance is reflected in the menu (entirely in English, clearly described) by Laotian dishes meant to be eaten with the fingers along with sticky rice. A speciality – minced pork with fried rice balls – comes with pungent spices and a touch of sweetness balanced by the sharpness of lime. Papaya salad is authentically spicy, and seafood has included hot-and-sour prawn soup flavoured unusually with bergamot, as well as mussels in their shells (listed as 'fresh – in season') sauced with 'a rich blend of exotic spices which did not overwhelm them'.

Starters include satay, spring rolls, spicy sausages, fish-cakes, and chicken wings, as well as spiced crabmeat with chicken steamed in cabbage leaves. Main dishes offer a full range of red and green curries and stir-fries, plus grilled prawns and steamed stuffed squid. Bean curd is a main ingredient of vegetarian dishes, and 'fish of the royal Lao recipe' could prove worth exploring. One way to cool the palate is with sweet sticky rice at the heart of several desserts, or try the short, mainly Italian wine list. Alternatively there are Tiger and Singha beers, and 50 malt whiskies.

CHEF/PROPRIETOR: Gong Herman   OPEN: Tue to Sat D only 6 to 10   CLOSED: 25 Dec   MEALS: alc (main courses £6 to £11). Set D £20   SERVICE: not inc, card slips closed   CARDS: MasterCard, Visa   DETAILS: 25 seats. Private parties: 25 main room. Vegetarian meals. No smoking in dining-room. Music. Air-conditioned   ⊖ New Cross, New Cross Gate

33 St James's
map 15

33 St James's Street, SW1A 1HD   COOKING 4
TEL: (0171) 930 1272   FAX: (0171) 930 7618   COST £41–£77

Although not big by London standards, the restaurant makes a simple, bold statement with its palatial glass frontage and larger-than-life Dutch and Spanish pastiches by Paul Karslake that cover lavish expanses of mustard-yellow walls. A degree of invention produces an appealing menu, although dishes tend to revisit territory familiar to regulars: smoked haddock risotto with poached egg, seared scallops glazed under a curry Sauternes sauce, or pan-fried foie gras layered between slices of crisp potato, with a Bramley apple sauce.

First courses generally concentrate on vegetable and farinaceous items – wild mushroom pappardelle, mussel ravioli, or salad of chargrilled vegetables with chorizo – while mains bring on a varied range of materials from ostrich fillet to peppered pink calf's liver with dauphinoise and mustard sauce, by way of braised pig's cheek with potato pie and spinach purée. The set-price menu is confusingly called an à la carte, which description more properly applies to the 'Gourmet' menu, which may offer grilled skate with capers and caviare to start, followed by Dover sole with lemon and sea salt, or pot-roast saddle of rabbit stuffed with sundried tomatoes, pancetta and herbs. A fruity element is common among desserts: summer pudding, rhubarb and strawberry tartlet, or warm griddled pineapple with coconut ice-cream, for example. Service is 'cheerful and attentive'. Wines are resourceful, with a sure eye for interest and quality, but prices are on the high side. House Muscadet is £17, Côtes du Rhône £18.

CHEF: Kristian Smith-Wallace   PROPRIETOR: Vincenzo De Feo   OPEN: Mon to Fri L 12 to 2.30, Mon to Sat D 6 to 11.30 (midnight Fri and Sat)   MEALS: alc (main courses £12 to £23.50). Set L £18.95 (2 courses), Set D £24.95 (2 courses). Cover £1   SERVICE: 12.5% (optional), card slips closed   CARDS: Amex, Delta, Diners, MasterCard, Switch, Visa   DETAILS: 75 seats. Private parties: 90 main room, 35 private room. Vegetarian meals. Children's helpings. No-smoking area. Wheelchair access (not WC). Occasional music. Air-conditioned   ⊖ Green Park   (£5)

Tokyo Diner £
map 15

2 Newport Place, WC2H 7JJ   COOKING 2
TEL: (0171) 287 8777   FAX: (0171) 434 1415   COST £15–£22

Although no longer unique, this pioneer of affordable Japanese food still holds its own in terms of quality and value. Choices include soba and udon soup noodles; very mild Japanese curries with rice and pickle; and donburi (boxes of rice with toppings that range from egg and onion to chicken or pork). Bento boxes contain dressed noodle salad, sashimi (usually salmon), salad, rice and a meat or fish 'main course' in their four compartments. Sushi include 'sea chicken', a curiosity explained on the menu (along with useful hints on eating Japanese style) as 'the most popular cooked tuna in Japan'. The restaurant is light, bright and cheerfully decorated, although the tables and seats are tiny. Drink Japanese beer or saké, and remember that tips are not accepted.

CHEF: Miyuki Handa   PROPRIETOR: Richard Hills   OPEN: all week 12 to 12   MEALS: alc (main courses £5.90 to £7.50). Bento box meals £9.50 to £12.50.   SERVICE: none, card slips closed   CARDS: Delta, MasterCard, Switch, Visa   DETAILS: 75 seats. Private parties: 35 main room. Vegetarian meals. Children welcome. No-smoking area. Wheelchair access (not WC). Music. Air-conditioned   ⊖ Leicester Square/Piccadilly Circus

Turner's
map 14

| 87–89 Walton Street, SW3 2HP | COOKING 7 |
| TEL: (0171) 584 6711   FAX: (0171) 584 4441 | COST £27–£68 |

'One of the best and most pleasant restaurants we have visited,' summed up one reporter. Turner's appeals for its unpretentious, calm and professional approach: 'we felt genuinely welcome, and I reckon so did everyone else.' It has to rank among London's best-value lunches. One couple was 'bowled over' by theirs: one had smoked duck salad with walnuts, then pink lamb and kidney on a tower of risotto in a rich red wine sauce, and 'feather-light' strawberry cheesecake; the other ate warm salad of monkfish, chunky pieces of chicken with courgettes and garlic jus, and a 'light and refreshing' raspberry-based trio of sorbet, ice-cream and meringue. At £15 a head, that's good going.

Turner's food is founded on classical ideas but is not hidebound. Crab sausage with peas in a cream sauce is 'a nice variation on a theme'; silky-textured, full-flavoured foie gras pâté comes with a crisp salad; and saddle of rabbit (as a first course) has been stuffed with white beans and spicy sausage. Prime materials include roast pigeon, rack of English lamb in a herb crust, and beef with a bone-marrow and garlic sauce, while a well-tended stockpot provides the necessary depth: an intense port and thyme reduction to accompany pink breast and confit leg of duck, for example.

Although it keeps abreast of the times, the food never seems to fall for the clichés that sustain others, preferring to maintain steady interest, for example with a dessert of iced lemon chiboust with blueberry compote and madeleines. Or there may be a savoury of baked goats' cheese with bacon and potato. Service is generally good, with only a couple of grumbles from reporters over the past year. Charles Curran has left the kitchen and Brian Turner himself was cooking as the *Guide* went to press. William Fèvre Chablis is a feature of the well-bred, predominantly French and rather pricey list, but there are a few sporting chances for those with a £20 budget. House red and white Bordeaux are £13.50.

'The starter plates were cleared the moment we had finished and, at the same time, the main courses were presented with the comment from the restaurant manager, "Sorry to rush you, but the chef wants to go home."' (On eating in Cumbria)

CHEF/PROPRIETOR: Brian Turner   OPEN: Sun to Fri L 12.30 to 2.30, all week D 7.30 to 11 (6.30 to 8.30 Sun)   CLOSED: 1 week Christmas, bank hols   MEALS: Set L Mon to Fri £12.50 (2 courses) to £15, Set L Sun £21.50, Set D £26.50 (2 courses) to £38.95   SERVICE: not inc   CARDS: Amex, Delta, Diners, MasterCard, Switch, Visa   DETAILS: 54 seats. Private parties: 54 main room, 6 private room. Children's helpings. Wheelchair access (1 step; not WC). Music. Air-conditioned ⊖ South Kensington

Two Brothers £

map 12

297–303 Regents Park Road, N3 1DP

COOKING 2

TEL: (0181) 346 0469   FAX: (0181) 343 1978

COST £18–£38

The Manzi brothers' Finchley fish restaurant continues to delight for the impeccable freshness of what it serves, the range of choice (which alone elevates it out of the chip-shop category) and the 'stimulating and entertaining' buzz of the atmosphere. Behind the broad dark-blue frontage it has 'a slight 1950s feel', with mirrored pillars and mood-setting pictures of whales and sharks. Blackboard specials supplement the printed menu, which deals in battered cod's roe, sardines fried with herbs and garlic, and Arbroath smokies with tomato in a cheese cream sauce. Main courses include Mediterranean prawns in 'pungent, copious' garlic butter, halibut steak, rock eel, or salmon fried in soy sauce and ginger timed to 'sweet succulence'. Portions are large, but if you've room puddings are good too, be they 'creamy, custardy, but light' bread-and-butter, or perhaps orange segments in caramel sauce with lemon sorbet. Service is 'endearingly friendly and down to earth'. The predominantly white wine list is serviceable and modestly priced, and kicks off with house Côtes de Duras from the proprietors' own vineyard at £9.30.

CHEFS/PROPRIETORS: Leon and Tony Manzi   OPEN: Tue to Sat 12 to 2.30, 5.30 to 10.15   CLOSED: Christmas, last 2 weeks Aug, bank hols (exc Good Fri) and day following   MEALS: alc (main courses £8 to £14.50)   SERVICE: not inc, card slips closed   CARDS: Amex, Delta, MasterCard, Switch, Visa   DETAILS: 90 seats. Children's helpings. No-smoking area. Music. Air-conditioned   ⊖ Finchley Central

Union Café

map 15

96 Marylebone Lane, W1M 5FP

COOKING 3

TEL: (0171) 486 4860

COST £28–£53

A handy bolt-hole for the Oxford Street crowd, Union Café, now five years old, is a single large space with wooden floors, large windows and an open-to-view kitchen behind a long stainless steel counter. The short menu looks modish, and has an element of 'cuisine assemblée' about it, with plates of Parma ham, charcuterie and smoked salmon, and salads with marinated squid or mozzarella. Alternatively, soup – maybe chilled coriander vichyssoise – makes a good start. Bacon and pork come from Heal Farm, free-range eggs from Martin Pitt, and cheese from Neal's Yard, although there is no mention of the source of rocket, which they must buy 'by the hundredweight'.

Among successes have been seafood dishes of sweet chargrilled scallops with crispy pancetta, and deep-fried lemon sole with chips and properly made tartare sauce. Fruit and ices feature prominently in desserts, including a light mascarpone custard tart with mango, peach and raspberry, and Baghdad marmalade ice-cream that was 'not exactly The Mother of All Ice-Creams' but did have a potent bittersweet tang. Service is perfectly good for the most part, though it has also been 'cool' and 'disdainful'. Drinks include fruit smoothies, a few beers, and around 20 interesting wines starting at £10.50 for South African white and Portuguese red.

CHEFS: Caroline Brett and Sarah Conway   PROPRIETORS: Caroline Brett and Sam Russell
OPEN: Mon to Sat 12.30 to 3, 6.30 to 10.30 (Sat brunch 11 to 4.30, Mon to Fri breakfast 9.30 to
12)   CLOSED: 2 weeks Christmas, bank hols   MEALS: alc (main courses £9 to £13.50)
SERVICE: 12.5% (optional), card slips closed   CARDS: Delta, MasterCard, Switch, Visa
DETAILS: 80 seats. Private parties: 75 main room. Vegetarian meals. Children welcome.
No-smoking area. Wheelchair access (not WC). No music   ⊖ Bond Street

Upper Street Fish Shop £

map 13

324 Upper Street, N1 2XQ
TEL/FAX: (0171) 359 1401

COOKING 1
COST £14–£27

To some it is just old-fashioned, to others 'an honest restaurant amid the pretentious clutter of Upper Street'. On the blue and white tablecloths are ketchup, HP sauce, vinegar and tartare sauce. Fish is notable for its freshness, and basic cod and luscious halibut have been recommended; also home-made fish soup, which is white, in traditional English style. Although there are chips with (nearly) everything, the world beyond creeps in with moules marinière, and a plate of deep-fried shellfish comprising mussels, oysters, butterflied prawns, scampi and tiger prawn tails in filo pastry. Home-made desserts include comfortingly stodgy ginger pudding with custard. Service is by 'bustling, genial ladies' who will bring a pot of tea – or you can drink your own wine.

CHEF: Stuart Gamble   PROPRIETORS: Alan and Olga Conway   OPEN: Tue to Sat L 12 to 2.15,
Mon to Sat D 6 (5.30 Fri and Sat) to 10.15   MEALS: alc (main courses £6 to £10). Unlicensed;
BYO (no corkage)   SERVICE: not inc   CARDS: none   DETAILS: 50 seats. Private parties: 10 main
room. Children's helpings. Wheelchair access (1 step; not WC). No music. Air-conditioned
⊖ Angel

Vama – The Indian Room

| NEW ENTRY | map 12

438 King's Road, SW10 0LJ
TEL: (0171) 351 4118   FAX: (0171) 565 8501
EMAIL: andyv@aol.com

COOKING 2
COST £20–£71

Vama makes a bit of a splash near the World's End stretch of the King's Road, its glass frontage open to the street in fine weather, its stone floors and tan walls creating a calming effect. There is a plant-filled conservatory at the back for those in more romantic mood, the whole looked after by smartly dressed staff and 'a charming motherly Indian lady'. The shortish menu divides itself into vegetarian and the rest, with traditional chicken tikka, sag gosht and palag paneer balanced by a few slightly more adventurous dishes: tandoori crab, lobster or quail, for example, or a mix of spiced mushrooms including morels. Among highlights so far have been large, marinated, grilled prawns and scallops, along with dhal, nan, roti, a 'light, fresh, tasty' rasmalai, and cumin-flavoured lassi. Prices are high by Indian standards, and some 30 wines start at £9.75.

CHEF: Brinder Narula   PROPRIETORS: Andy Varma, Arjun Varma and Ritu Dalmia   OPEN: all week 12 to 3, 6 to 11.30   CLOSED: 25 and 26 Dec   MEALS: alc (main courses £5 to £20). Set L £5.95 to £9.95. Cover £1   SERVICE: 12.5% (optional), card slips closed   CARDS: Amex, Delta, MasterCard, Switch, Visa   DETAILS: 84 seats. 10 seats outside. Private parties: 100 main room, 40 private room. Car park. Vegetarian meals. Children welcome. Wheelchair access (not WC). Music. Air-conditioned   ⊖ Sloane Square   £5

Veeraswamy   **NEW ENTRY** map 15

99 Regent Street, W1R 8RS   COOKING 1
TEL: (0171) 734 1401   FAX: (0171) 439 8434   COST £25–£49

The owners of Chutney Mary (see entry) have given this old colonial restaurant just off Regent Street a complete makeover, with blond wood, bright lighting, vivid blocks of colour, and a frosted-glass centrepiece between tables down the middle; a little nostalgia is indulged in black and white photographs of Piccadilly Circus in the 1920s, when the restaurant first opened. Symbols on the shortish menu indicate relative chilli heat, but a degree of anglicisation ensures that none is very hot. Variety and contrast are achieved by including grills and roasts, vegetarian dishes, and a few from the Subcontinent's northern and southern extremities. Others have even less specific origins: cod and salmon fish-cakes with ginger and herbs, Britain's very own chicken tikka masala, and kulfi with dark chocolate sauce. Among other interesting offerings are half a dozen oysters stir-fried with coconut and spices, and kingfish with turmeric and mango. Nan is light and soft, service is smart and attentive, and wines are cannily arranged for compatibility with spice heat, starting with house vin de pays at £10.95.

CHEF: Gowtham Kumar   PROPRIETORS: Ranjit Mathrani and Namita Panjabi   OPEN: Mon to Fri 12 to 2.30, 5.30 to 11.30, Sat 12.30 to 3, 5.30 to 11.30, Sun 12.30 to 3, 6 to 10   CLOSED: D 25 Dec   MEALS: alc (main courses £9 to £13.50). Set L Mon to Sat £11 (2 courses) to £14, Set L Sun £11 (1 course) to £13.75, Set D 5.30 to 6.30 and 10 to 11.30 £11 (2 courses) to £14. Cover £1 (not on set meals)   SERVICE: 12.5% (optional), card slips closed   CARDS: Amex, Delta, Diners, MasterCard, Switch, Visa   DETAILS: 160 seats. Private parties: 70 main room, 40 private room. Vegetarian meals. Children welcome. No pipes in dining-room. Wheelchair access (not WC). Music. Air-conditioned   ⊖ Piccadilly Circus   £5

Village Bistro   map 12

38 Highgate High Street, N6 5JG
TEL: (0181) 340 5165 and 0257   COOKING 1
FAX: (0181) 347 5584   COST £27–£42

The place may feel a little more 'twee Sussex tea-shop' than French bistro, according to one reporter, but the atmosphere of 'easy, unpretentious' intimacy and the 'pleasingly personal' service are greatly appreciated. A party of four who tested the menu's range enjoyed tomato, aubergine and scallop soup, monkfish terrine with sweet peppers and olives, and sauté guinea-fowl with bacon, shallots and herbs. Culinary accents are not uniformly French, and merguez sausages with couscous, or coriandered salmon with king prawns and curry oil, are quite as likely to crop up. Show-stopping desserts may include chocolate meringue with coffee sauce, as well as baked bananas with banana fritters and ice-cream described as 'a schoolboy's outsize treat'. Classic French wines at manageable mark-ups are the main focus of the wine list, with prices opening at £10.50.

CHEF: Nicholas Rochford and Christopher Durnin PROPRIETOR: Darela Ltd OPEN: all week 12 to 3, 6 to 11 MEALS: alc (main courses £10 to £13). Set L Mon to Sat £13.50 (2 courses) SERVICE: not inc CARDS: Amex, Delta, MasterCard, Switch, Visa DETAILS: 56 seats. Private parties: 34 main room, 20 private room. Vegetarian meals. Children's helpings. No cigars/pipes in dining-room. Music. Air-conditioned (£5)

Villandry Dining Room ⅙✳ | NEW ENTRY | map 15

170 Great Portland Street, W1N 5JB   COOKING 3
TEL: (0171) 631 3131   FAX: (0171) 631 3030   COST £26–£49

The principle may remain the same – a food shop and restaurant on one site – but Villandry's move from cramped make-do premises to this large customised emporium is a dramatic one. It now appears 'vibrant and self-confident'. The main entrance is in Bolsover Street, but to miss browsing round the deli on the Great Portland Street side would be a great pity; allow half an hour. Much of the well-chosen, often organic produce makes its way on to the menu in the refectory-like dining-room, with its hard, noise-reflecting surfaces, stark white walls, bare floors, and plain wooden tables with paper cloths. There is no strict division into courses, just a free-ranging *carte* that takes in a plate of charcuterie, braised lamb shank with roasted vegetables, and maybe sauté squid with chickpeas, chorizo and red peppers.

Soups, whether humble cabbage or more exotic coconut and coriander, tend to be 'warm, thick and comforting', and risotto is well done, perhaps underneath grilled John Dory and scallops, or an artichoke version with grilled chicken breast. A mixed salad with flat bread might sound mundane but for one May diner it delivered 'plenty of interest' with broad beans, pea shoots, leeks, 'lashings of dill', tabbouleh and 'all sorts of crunchy bits'. Timing has been variably successful, even with slow-cooked beef brisket. Among desserts, tarts of lemon and walnut, and poached nectarine and almond are well reported. Service is friendly, even 'matey', but can be unco-ordinated. Wines are mostly French, some rather highly priced for the circumstances; five house wines range from £11.50 to £19. A juice/coffee/wine bar is due to open shortly after the *Guide* is published.

CHEFS: Roz Carrarini and Steve Evernett-Watts PROPRIETORS: J.C. and Roz Carrarini OPEN: Mon to Sat 12.30 to 3, 7 to 10 CLOSED: 5 days Christmas, bank hols MEALS: alc (main courses £7.50 to £15) SERVICE: 12.5%, card slips closed CARDS: Amex, Delta, MasterCard, Switch, Visa DETAILS: 80 seats. 16 seats outside. Private parties: 40 main room, 10 and 20 private rooms. Vegetarian meals. Children welcome. No smoking in dining-room. Wheelchair access (not WC). No music. Air-conditioned ⊖ Great Portland Street

'Service still leaves something to be desired. There seems little point in taking orders for aperitifs and subsequently presenting the customer with a list of cocktails.' (On eating in Kent)

Vong ✦

map 14

Berkeley Hotel, Wilton Place, SW1X 7RL
TEL: (0171) 235 1010   FAX: (0171) 235 1011   COOKING 5
EMAIL: vong-savoygroup@btinternet.com   COST £35–£74

It is not difficult to make a 'Hollywood entrance' down the staircase into this elegant basement dining-room, where smartly clad, attentive and know-ledgeable staff add a touch of glamour to the enterprise. The kitchen produces carefully crafted food, with 'lots of attention to visuals'. Gold glazed earthen-ware, pure white or black china, and neat little Japanese trays provide the background to Jean-Georges Vongerichten's vision of Thai-French fusion food, where foie gras comes in a peanut and ginger sauce with mango, and Dover sole is given a spiced almond sauce.

Spicing is not chilli-hot, but characteristically 'fresh' and 'subtle', sometimes yielding 'wonderful combinations', from a fresh, clean flavoured' crab spring roll with tamarind dipping sauce, to quail rubbed with Thai spices: 'a brilliant blend of flavours'. A 'black plate' starter (£30 for two) samples several items, including perhaps 'very crisp' breadcrumbed king prawn with a sweet-and-sour dip, or 'an exquisite blend' of raw tuna rolled with a spicy chilli Thai dip.

Occasionally dishes pile on extra flavours with diminishing returns, but it is hard to resist the sense of excitement generated by experiment, which extends to desserts such as Valrhona chocolate cake with lemon-grass ice-cream and a treacle biscuit. Rice crackers come in place of bread, and petits fours have made an impression. Lunch is considered good value, dinner only if you're on expenses, and wines only if you make a bottle go a long way. The complete absence of Thai wines is not a problem, given the very high quality from Europe and the New World. Most bottles are over £20, but prices start at £14.50.

CHEFS: Jean-Georges Vongerichten and Daniel del Vecchio   PROPRIETOR: Savoy Group plc
OPEN: Mon to Sat L 12 to 2.30, all week D 6 to 11.30   CLOSED: 25 and 26 Dec   MEALS: alc (main courses £13 to £26). Set L £15 (2 courses) to £20, Set pre-theatre D (6 to 7pm) £17.50, Set D £45   SERVICE: 12.5% (optional), card slips closed   CARDS: Amex, Delta, Diners, MasterCard, Switch, Visa   DETAILS: 130 seats. Private parties: 145 main room. Vegetarian meals. Children welcome. No smoking in 1 dining-room. Music. Air-conditioned   ⊖ Hyde Park Corner

Wagamama ✦ £

map 15

4 Streatham Street, WC1A 1JB
TEL: (0171) 580 9365   FAX: (0171) 323 9224
10A Lexington Street, W1R 3HS   COOKING 1
TEL: (0171) 292 0990   FAX: (0171) 734 1815   COST £14–£25

Queues are now shorter, even non-existent at off-peak hours, not because Wagamama is any less popular, but because there are two branches at present, and more on the way. Accept the noise (at least there is no music), mixed hi-tech and low-tech ordering, the refectory tables, and the system – ideal for the kitchen, less so for customers – by which dishes arrive when ready; thus you and your companions may not eat at the same time. Yes, accept all this, and the jargon-ridden 'healthy' menu, and enjoy very generous portions of freshly prepared noodles stir-fried, pan-fried or in soup. The variety of meat, seafood and vegetable content suits most tastes, although some reporters talk of blandness. There are rice-based dishes too, while side dishes (known elsewhere as starters) include ever-popular gyoza (Chinese dumplings), which one regular visitor finds 'sometimes immaculate'. The mostly New World wine list is sensibly short, bolstered by a range of soft drinks, some claiming to be even healthier than wine: can this be possible? As we went to press a new branch was about to open at 101a Wigmore Street (tel: (0171) 409 0111).

CHEF: David Chia (Streatham Street), Jo Allen (Lexington Street) PROPRIETOR: Wagamama Ltd OPEN: Mon to Sat 12 to 11, Sun 12.30 to 10.30 CLOSED: 25 and 26 Dec. MEALS: alc (main courses £4.50 to £7). Set L and D £7 to £8 (all 2 courses) SERVICE: not inc CARDS: Amex, Delta, MasterCard, Switch, Visa DETAILS: 175 seats (Streatham Street), 104 seats (Lexington Street). Vegetarian meals. Children welcome. No smoking in dining-room. No music. Air-conditioned ⊖ Tottenham Court Road (Streatham Street), Piccadilly Circus (Lexington Street)

White Onion   map 13

297 Upper Street, Islington, N1 2TU	COOKING 4
TEL/FAX: (0171) 359 3533	COST £23–£45

Upper Street may have more than its fair share of good restaurants, but White Onion has no trouble holding its own among the competition. Busy and self-assured, it is the smartest of Bijan Behzadi's plot of vegetables, which includes Green Olive and Red Pepper (see entries, both London), as well as the newly opened Purple Sage. The Onion hides a tasteful and 'elegantly chic' split level dining-room behind an inconspicuous plain glass front, with simple black lacquered wooden furniture, black and white walls, discreet lighting and well-spaced tables. It is also handy for Islington's Almeida Theatre, and theatre-goers appreciate the late opening hours.

The modern European food might include cod with butter-beans, or calf's liver with garlic confit, and is high on aesthetic appeal, as well as 'taste, texture, freshness of ingredients, quality and quantity' in one couple's estimation. Dishes are simply expressed and fulfil the promise of the menu, which might list pan-fried sea bass with crispy sweet potatoes and beurre blanc, or pastilla of guinea-fowl with caramelised shallots and port sauce. Pan-fried foie gras served on a warm mozzarella and rocket salad (unlikely as it may sound) is still proving a winner.

A 'good and interesting selection' of desserts might include coconut soufflé, or a dark and light chocolate 'ravioli'. Confident and efficient service plays its part, as does the 50-strong wine list, dominated by France (try Alsace for a white) but more fun elsewhere. Prices start at £9.50 for Sicilian house wine.

CHEF: Eric Guignard PROPRIETOR: Bijan Behzadi OPEN: Tue to Sun L 12 to 2.30 (3 Sun), all week D 6.30 to 11 (7.30 to 10 Sun) CLOSED: 1 week Jan MEALS: alc D (main courses £8 to £13.20). Set L Tue to Sat £10 (2 courses) to £14.50, Set L Sun £15 (2 courses) to £19.50 SERVICE: not inc CARDS: Amex, Delta, MasterCard, Switch, Visa DETAILS: 63 seats. Private parties: 30 main room. Vegetarian meals. Children's helpings. Wheelchair access (1 step; also WC). Music. Air-conditioned ⊖ Angel, Highbury & Islington

Report forms are at the back of the book; write a letter if you prefer; or email us at guidereports@which.co.uk.

Wilsons

map 12

236 Blythe Road, W14 0HJ	COOKING 1
TEL: (0171) 603 7267 FAX: (0171) 602 9018	COST £30–£47

Caledonian cuisine in the glens of Shepherd's Bush is on offer at Bob Wilson's non-dressy and cheerily welcoming little restaurant. The sense of tradition admirably extends to the inclusion of a dram in the price of the haggis starter with bashed spuds and swede. Salmon of course features, either fashioned into fish-cakes served on parsley sauce or as a peppered escalope baked with leeks in white wine. The wail of the pipes grows fainter once lamb cutlets are sauced with mustard and redcurrants, and may have been drowned out altogether as pheasant is fried with sauerkraut and chorizo in a red wine jus. Whatever the accent, it is presented in enjoyably domestic fashion in an atmosphere of genuine conviviality. Vegetables are charged extra, but cash customers are granted a five per cent discount for helping to save on bank charges. A short but serviceable wine list opens with vins de pays at £10.50.

CHEF: R. Hilton   PROPRIETORS: R. Wilson and R. Hilton   OPEN: Sun to Fri L 12.30 to 2 (2.30 Sun), Mon to Sat D 7.30 to 10   MEALS: alc (main courses £9 to £15). Set L Sun £13.50 (2 courses)   SERVICE: 12.5% (optional), card slips closed   CARDS: Delta, Diners, MasterCard, Switch, Visa   DETAILS: 44 seats. Private parties: 44 main room. Vegetarian meals. Children's helpings. No pipes in dining-room. Wheelchair access (1 step; not WC). Music. Air-conditioned   ⊖ Hammersmith Broadway, Shepherd's Bush

Wiltons

map 15

55 Jermyn Street, SW1Y 6LX	COOKING 4
TEL: (0171) 629 9955 FAX: (0171) 495 6233	COST £37–£106

Tourists who visit London to see Beefeaters, Buckingham Palace and Madame Tussaud's ought to visit Wilton's as well: it is an enduring Establishment restaurant that maintains an Edwardian style of eating, just about as far removed from contemporary brasserie fusion food as you could imagine. Although it has only been at its present address since 1984, it has a venerable 250-year history of moving around St James's, supplying oysters to royalty along the way, and now offers mostly fish, a few grills, and game in season.

Simplicity is a strength, yielding dressed crab, lobster cocktail, smoked salmon and scrambled eggs, potted shrimps, omelettes (including Arnold Bennett), and plainly grilled or poached fish such as Dover sole, plaice or halibut. There is little more to it than that, apart from grilled lambs' kidneys, fillet steak, and desserts of sherry trifle, crème brûlée, or pear Belle Hélène, although in traditional fashion it also offers a choice of savouries to finish. Service is predictably on the formal side, although it typically melts as the meal progresses. Outside a few token offerings, wines are French and pricey. A page of champagnes doubtless helps the oysters down. House white is £16.50, red £17.

CHEF: Ross Hayden   PROPRIETORS: the Hambro family   OPEN: restaurant Sun to Fri 12.30 to 2.30, 6.30 to 10.30; oyster bar Sun to Fri 12.30 to 6.30   MEALS: alc (main courses £8 to £29). Set L Sun £21.95. Cover £1.50   SERVICE: not inc   CARDS: Amex, Diners, MasterCard, Switch, Visa   DETAILS: 80 seats. Private parties: 18 main room, 18 private room. Vegetarian meals. Jacket and tie. Wheelchair access (1 step; not WC). No music. Air-conditioned   ⊖ Green Park

Woz

NEW ENTRY   map 12

46 Golborne Road, W10 5PR

COOKING 2

TEL: (0181) 968 2200   FAX: (0181) 968 0550

COST £23–£43

The gentrification of west London continues apace, and may soon reach the top end of Golborne Road, where it will find Antony Worrall Thompson's latest concept ready and waiting. It is on two levels: a brightly lit ground-floor with modern portraits on the walls, and a dimly lit and homelier basement with rustic décor and chairs 'like French farmhouse furniture'. The formula is café-type lunches and a no-choice five-course dinner party in the evenings. A selection of antipasti, perhaps including superb mozzarella with chillied pesto, or strips of tender calf's liver in onion dressing, is followed by salad – on one night a complex assemblage of smoked chicken, king prawns and chicory with walnut dressing – before a casserole-style main course of pork with courgettes cooked in milk, or perhaps rack of lamb with rosemary, salsa verde and three 'vicious' red-hot chillies. One perfect cheese is served – Cashel Blue or 'divinely running' Brie with chutney – before a pudding such as bitter chocolate and prune torte with raspberry compote. Friendly service adds to the charm. Wines, drawn mostly from Italy, are full of character, the majority staying helpfully under £20. Chilean house wines are £12.95 a bottle.

CHEFS: Antony Worrall Thompson and David Massey   PROPRIETORS: Antony and Jacinta Worrall Thompson   OPEN: Tue to Sun L 12 to 4, Mon to Sat D 7 to 11   CLOSED: 24 to 30 Dec   MEALS: alc L (main courses £6 to £11). Set L £9.95 (2 courses), Set D £22.95 to £25.95   SERVICE: not inc; 12.5% for parties of 8 or more   CARDS: Amex, Delta, MasterCard, Switch, Visa   DETAILS: 65 seats. Private parties: 35 main room. Vegetarian meals. Children's helpings. No cigars/pipes in dining-room. Music. Air-conditioned   ⊖ Westbourne Park

Yo Sushi 🍶✳

map 15

52/53 Poland Street, W1V 3DF

TEL: (0171) 287 0443   FAX: (0171) 287 2324

COOKING 1

EMAIL: info@yosushi.co.uk

COST £12–£25

Yo! Sushi turns traditional ideas of sushi bars upside-down. Behind the glowing neon frontage it is big and bare, filled with noisy music and giant video screens. Chefs – some human, some mechanical – turn out large quantities of sushi on various coloured plates to indicate prices. Grab them as they come round on the kaiten (conveyor belt), claimed to be the world's longest, or order specials of the day, listed on boards. A chart helps to identify tuna, cuttlefish, eel, sweet shrimp, octopus, scallop and salmon roe. Of vegetarian sushi the best are traditional cucumber or shinko (pickled turnip). Unlimited still and sparkling water is available on tap at each counter place, and robot drinks trolleys deliver flasks of hot or iced saké, Sapporo beer and Japanese tea.

CHEF: Nacer Arab   PROPRIETOR: Simon Woodroffe   OPEN: all week 12 to 12   CLOSED: 25 and 26 Dec   MEALS: alc (plate prices £1 to £4.50)   SERVICE: not inc, card slips closed   CARDS: Amex, Delta, Diners, MasterCard, Switch, Visa   DETAILS: 120 seats. Vegetarian meals. Children's helpings. No smoking in dining-room. Music. Air-conditioned   ⊖ Oxford Circus

All entries, including Round-ups, are fully indexed at the back of the Guide.

Zafferano

map 14

15 Lowndes Street, SW1X 9EY	COOKING 7
TEL: (0171) 235 5800 FAX: (0171) 235 1971	COST £30–£61

'Modern rustic' décor mirrors the food perfectly. This is a restaurant (now in its fifth year) with a sense of purpose, showing how prime ingredients can, with care and a degree of ingenuity, be made to sing. Cream wash walls, terracotta floors and upholstered chairs make it an 'informal, relaxed, yet smart' place to eat, and a generous menu deals in food that is light and satisfying at the same time. Don't worry that some of it may sound ordinary: spaghetti with clams, and a spring vegetable soup with prawns and basil pesto, are among dishes that have impressed. Often the very simplicity appeals: pheasant ravioli with rosemary, fillet of plaice in a basil crust, or flaky cod with creamy lentils and parsley sauce.

The 'rustic' appeal shows in the kitchen's dexterity with often humble materials – calves' feet and artichoke salad, or borlotti bean and spelt soup – and it seems to work its most successful turns with fish and pasta, turning out linguine with spicy crab, or steamed hake with garlic, parsley and vinegar. Desserts are on a par for impact, from moist and crunchy nougat parfait with intense and bitter chocolate sauce, to cannelloni siciliani: crisp, golden pastry filled with tangy-sweet candied fruit. Service has, on the whole, been efficient and friendly. Italian wines are full of interest, and despite long runs of aristocratic bottles from Tuscany and Piedmont, more affordable drinking is not neglected. House Sette Soli and Montepulciano d'Abruzzo are £10.70.

CHEF: Giorgio Locatelli   PROPRIETOR: Zafferano Restaurants Ltd   OPEN: Mon to Sat 12 to 2.30, 7 to 11   CLOSED: 2 weeks Christmas, Easter, 2 weeks Aug, bank hols.   MEALS: Set L £17.50 (2 courses) to £20.50, Set D £25.50 (2 courses) to £33.50   SERVICE: not inc   CARDS: Amex, Delta, MasterCard, Switch, Visa   DETAILS: 63 seats. Vegetarian meals. Children's helpings. Wheelchair access (not WC). Music. Air-conditioned   ❷ Knightsbridge

Zen Central

map 15

20 Queen Street, W1X 7PJ	
TEL: (0171) 629 8089 and 8103	COOKING 4
FAX: (0171) 493 6181	COST £41–£79

Zen earned its place in history, over a decade ago, by making it smart to eat in Chinese restaurants. Its bold green and white décor may smack of the eighties, but the black leather armchairs are now 'nicely crinkled and worn in', while soft lighting, large well-spaced tables and efficient air-conditioning contribute to a relaxed atmosphere.

There is no doubting the quality of ingredients, including such luxuries as whole fresh abalone, suckling pig, shark's fin and lobster, and everything is cooked with care, if not always with abundant flair. Workaday dishes have included soft-shell crab with peppercorn salt, Peking ravioli in chilli sauce, and plump frog's legs in butter and garlic, while others come more highly recommended: tender veal cutlets in black pepper sauce, or braised bean curd with mushrooms and broccoli. A rustic Cantonese dish of fried rice Fook Chow style – made with finely chopped prawns, scallops, duck meat, spring onion and egg – evoked childhood memories for one visitor, while another enthused about red bean paste pancake, 'among the best in London'. The conventional wine list has a few choice bottles and starts with house red Merlot at £16.

CHEF: Chris Kwan   PROPRIETOR: Tealeaf Ltd   OPEN: all week 12.15 to 2.30, 6.30 to 11.15 (11 Sun)   CLOSED: 24 and 25 Dec   MEALS: alc (main courses £10.50 to £25). Set L £28, Set D £38 to £45.   SERVICE: 15% (optional)   CARDS: Delta, Diners, MasterCard, Switch, Visa   DETAILS: 90 seats. Private parties: 80 main room, 22 private room. Vegetarian meals. Children welcome. Wheelchair access (not WC). Music. Air-conditioned   ⊖ Green Park (£5)

Zujuma's £   map 12

58A Wimbledon Hill Road, SW19 7PA	COOKING 2
TEL: (0181) 879 0916 FAX: (0181) 944 0861	COST £20–£44

The tie with Whitbreads has been cut and Zuju Shareef is now involved full-time as chef/patronne. Glass jars and vibrant south Indian colours remain, although there have been minor changes to the exotic ethnic décor. Notwithstanding smartly dressed staff, the sense of visiting Zuju at home is, if anything, stronger than before; she may even emerge from the kitchen to discuss your order. Her 'modern Hyderabadi' cooking uses olive oil instead of ghee, and many dishes are steamed, a style that is consistent sometimes to a fault. To avoid duplicating starters and side dishes, choose either the non-Indian formula of starter followed by a main dish, or forgo starters and order a mushqaab, a sort of mini-thali with three accompaniments for the selected main dish. Choice is wide: three ways each with lamb, chicken, fish and vegetarian bases. Biryani is a pot of layered lamb, rice and aubergines in a coconut, tamarind and sesame sauce, with yoghurt raita and kiwi salad. Despite a profusion of flame symbols, the use of chilli and pepper is restrained but can be increased on request. Drink Kingfisher beer or choose from the short wine list, which kicks off with Chilean house red at £10.25.

CHEF: Zuju Shareef   PROPRIETOR: Zujuma's Restaurants Ltd   OPEN: all week 11.30 to 2.30, 6.30 to 11 (10.30 Sun)   MEALS: alc (main courses £8 to £14.50). Set L £7.95 (2 courses) to £11.95   SERVICE: not inc, card slips closed   CARDS: Amex, Delta, MasterCard, Switch, Visa   DETAILS: 60 seats. Children welcome. No-smoking area. Music. Air-conditioned ⊖ Wimbledon (£5)

London Round-ups

Eating out in London is largely a question of picking the location that offers the right kind of food for the occasion. To assist *Guide* readers, the Round-up section provides details of a range of restaurants, bistros and cafés that are well worth a visit, but do not merit a full entry. Each is included for a specific reason: you may find lunchtime bolt-holes for shoppers, good hotel dining-rooms, chippies, Cantonese soup kitchens, up-and-coming brasseries, even a new star or two in the making. Entries are based on readers' recommendations, often backed up by inspectors' reports. In some cases we have put an establishment in the Round-ups rather than in the main-entry section because there are changes in the air or because there has been a dearth of votes in its favour. Reports on these places are especially welcome, as they enable us to extend our overall coverage of good food in the capital. Weekend closures and unusual opening times are given in the entries.

Apprentice　　　　　　　　　　SE1
Butlers Wharf　　　　　　　　　　map 13
(0171) 234 0254
Training ground for chefs, so food is prepared and served by students: perhaps gnocchi with tomato and basil sauce or a cured salmon parcel with citrus dressing to start, then lamb-en-croûte or chargrilled sea bass with saffron couscous. Finish with warm chocolate tart or passion-fruit bavarois. Closed Sat and Sun.

L'Arte　　　　　　　　　　　　W1
126 Cleveland Street　　　　　　map 15
(0171) 813 1011
Unpretentious Fitzrovia restaurant decorated in black and white. A successful formula of rustic Italian cooking, with a daily-changing menu that might take in grilled goats' cheese, deep fried prawns with mixed vegetables, fish stew and pizzas. For dessert try hot apple and raisin tart or zabaglione with vin santo. Short, mainly Italian wine list starts at £8.50. Closed Sat L and Sun.

Belgo Centraal　　　　　　　　WC2
50 Earlham Street　　　　　　　map 15
(0171) 813 2233
Peer into the relentlessly busy kitchen beneath your feet and take the service lift to an underground world of waiters attired in monkish habits, and choose from mussels served a dozen ways: try them with chips and mayonnaise. The menu also stretches to chargrilled sea bass and spit-roasted chicken. Don't forget to explore the excellent range of Belgian beers.

La Belle Epoque　　　　　　　SW3
151 Draycott Avenue　　　　　　map 14
(0171) 460 5005
Vast open-fronted brasserie in a complex also containing L'Oriental and La Salle restaurants, and selling food and take-away items. A shellfish menu offers half a lobster with Marie-Rose sauce, dressed crab or scallops with lentils, while meat dishes might be rosette of veal with sweetbread, sausage and kidneys. Typical desserts have included bread-and-butter pudding and pecan pie with maple syrup. Fair selection of wines at reasonable prices.

Beotys　　　　　　　　　　　　WC2
79 St Martin's Lane　　　　　　map 15
(0171) 836 8768/8548
Young pretenders have their brief moments of glory in the West End, but Beoty's continues to run as enduringly as 'The Mousetrap'. The Frangos family set up this Greek-Cypriot restaurant in 1945 and are still in residence; so, too, is their head waiter, who joined in 1956. Stuffed

vine leaves, kleftiko and arnaki melitzanes (lamb cooked with aubergines in red wine sauce) flesh out a menu that studiously avoids current trends. This is also the world of 'les escargots de Bourgogne', 'le filet de boeuf grillé, sauce béarnaise' and 'le suprême de volaille à la Kiev'. Closed Sun.

Bombay Brasserie   SW7
Courtfield Close   map 14
(0171) 370 4040/373 0971
One of the most opulent Indian restaurants in the capital celebrated its sixteenth birthday in 1998. The décor is all polished wood floors, ethnic artefacts, chandeliers and potted plants, and the menu charts a course right across the Sub-continent. Here you will find tandoori specialities from the North-West Frontier, intensely flavoured seafood dishes from Goa, roadside and beach snacks from Bombay and much more besides. Lunch is an extravagant buffet.

Books for Cooks   W11
4 Blenheim Crescent   map 13
(0171) 221 1992
Compact bookshop off Ladbroke Grove which is a foodie bibliophile's heaven, packed to the rafters with a vast selection of cookbooks, new and old. Dedication to the cause runs to a tiny kitchen at the back of the shop, where recipes are put to the test. After building up a hunger browsing the shelves, customers can enjoy the results, but note that booking is essential. Regular cookery workshops pass on the skills to recreate those favourite dishes at home. Open Mon to Sat from 9.30 to 6.30.

Le Braconnier   SW14
467 Upper Richmond Road   map 12
(0181) 878 2853
This popular French 'poacher' offers good-value set meals in comfortable surroundings. Start with lobster and crab timbale, followed by braised shank of lamb, and finish with an excellent prune and armagnac terrine. Short wine list.

Friendly, if somewhat unknowledgeable service. Closed Sat L and Sun.

Cactus Blue   SW3
86 Fulham Road   map 14
(0171) 730 5550
' Funky' place, with décor dominated by wrought iron and a glass-boxed staircase, which attracts a mixed crowd of 'lounge lizards' and 'glamorous babes'. Cocktails and 'Mexican food with Californian spins' place it a cut above the average Tex-Mex joint. Try tamarillo or spiky cactus soups; tequila-cured salmon with tortilla, crème fraîche and black caviare; or oregano ancho-rubbed chicken with roast garlic and blue-cheese cornbread. Closed L Mon to Fri. More reports, please.

Le Cadre   N8
10 Priory Road   map 12
(0181) 348 0606
Popular north London French restaurant where David Misselbrook has built up a regular clientele. Start with a crottin of goats' cheese en croûte, followed by sea bream on a bed of spinach, calf's liver with pancetta, or monkfish in a crab sauce. Desserts might include chocolate truffle with green Chartreuse sauce, or caramelised apple tart. Excellent service. Closed Sat L and Sun.

Café du Marché   EC1
22 Charterhouse Square   map 13
(0171) 608 1609
'I feel as though I am not in the City, but somewhere in France,' writes a reporter who considers this 'one of the jewels of London'. The location is tantalisingly remote (look for the alleyway off Charterhouse Square) and the interior is pure rusticity. Handwritten menus promise such things as salad of lambs' tongue with boudin noir, grilled red mullet with tomato risotto, and lemon treacle tart with vanilla custard. Closed Sat L and Sun.

Café Portugal SW8
6A Victoria House, map13
South Lambeth Road
(0171) 587 1962
Authentic Portuguese restaurant run by
the friendly Brancos. Home-made food,
sandwiches and great patisserie. Choose
from the long selection of tapas, or start
with hot soup in the winter and gazpacho
in the summer. Main courses might be
stuffed squid or rabbit casserole. Finish
with hot apple pie or Portuguese rice-
pudding.

Cantina del Ponte SE1
36C Shad Thames map 13
(0171) 403 5403
Conran's Italian job which shares the
wonderful view with its illustrious
neighbour Le Pont de la Tour (see Main
entry, London). Sit outside or by the
window and make the most of it. The
menu devotes sections to pastas, risottos
and pizzas, but does extend further to
include swordfish, or lamb with
peperonata. Service can buckle under
pressure.

Chapel NW1
48 Chapel Street map 13
(0171) 402 9220
Close to Edgware Road tube station, this
foodie pub has pleasant staff and relaxed
surroundings. A frequently changing
menu offers generous helpings of moist
breast of chicken with pesto, venison
stew, or rosace of monkfish and scallops.
Finish with apricot and almond tart or
banoffi pie. Eclectic wine list at
reasonable prices.

Chez Gérard W1
8 Charlotte Street map 15
(0171) 636 4975
Attractive restaurant (part of a chain)
famous for its steak and frites, and
predominantly French cooking. Prix-fixe
dinner menu might offer soupe du jour or
pâté followed by steak or chicken. From
the *carte* choose oysters or mussels to start
followed by lamb cutlets, escalope of veal,
or grilled salmon with lemon and

watercress. Desserts might include tarte
Tatin or nougat glacé. Good-value wines.
Welcoming service when not too full.
Closed Sat L. Other branches are at 31
Dover Street, W1, tel. (0171) 499 8171,
119–120 Chancery Lane, WC2, tel.
(0171) 405 0290, and 64 Bishopsgate,
EC2, tel. (0171) 588 1200.

Chuen Cheng Ku W1
17 Wardour Street map 15
(0171) 734 3281/3509
One of the old stagers in Soho
Chinatown, famous for its totem pole
outside the door and for its dim-sum.
Dining areas on many levels are packed
with Chinese and occidentals sampling
delicacies throughout the day: not
surprising, since the whole experience is
reckoned to be 'the most extraordinary
value'. Heated trolleys 'doing the rounds'
between tables encourage
experimentation: 'the variety of textures
is a delight,' commented one fan who
singled out scallop cheung fun, and
turnip paste, among others. The full
menu holds fast to its Cantonese origins.

Clerkenwell Restaurant & Bar EC1
73 Clerkenwell Road map 13
(0171) 831 7595
Cheerful Italian restaurant offering a
weekly-changing *carte* for lunch on
Monday to Friday only. Open the same
evenings in December only. Choose from
chargilled cuttlefish with black olives, or
grilled goats'-cheese salad with Puy lentils
and peppers, followed by pan-fried fillets
of red sea bream with ratatouille, or
roasted rump of new-season's lamb.
Desserts might include warm pecan pie
with ice-cream, or fried sweet ravioli of
mascarpone with poached pear. Excellent
selection of Italian wines.

Diwana Bhel Poori NW1
121 Drummond Street map 13
(0171) 387 5556
This is *the* Indian vegetarian café in
Drummond Street. Fresh ingredients,
well-balanced spicing and hefty portions
– not to mention outstanding value for

money – are the keys to its enduring success. Samosas 'bursting' with mashed vegetables, sev poori and dahi vada continue to draw enthusiastic reports. Also in the running are the dosas (look for the triangular version containing chunks of paneer), sag bhaji and the splendidly generous thalis. Drink incomparable lassi and enjoy the laid-back, down-to-earth atmosphere.

Ebury Wine Bar SW1
139 Ebury Street map 13
(0171) 730 5447
Friendly, busy bistro with mainly Spanish staff and food, although the menu goes global with crab and chicken spring rolls with noodle salad, lamb and pancetta meatloaf with pesto minted potatoes, and seared duck breast with mango and coriander. Similarly, desserts range from figs poached in Shiraz to Greek yoghurt with honey and toasted almonds. Reporters have enjoyed 'juicy' olives, 'tasty' canapés, brandade of salt cod on chargrilled leeks, fried squid with aoili, and crisp bruschetta of peppers. Bar snacks are available every day until 10.30pm.

Efes Kebab House W1
80 Great Titchfield Street map 15
(0171) 636 1953
Fitzrovia may be an 'up-and-coming' area, but Efes has been up there for almost 25 years. This Turkish stalwart is still chargrilling lamb and chicken with skill and offering a range of some 20 hot and cold mezes. Attentive service by staff who look as though they have been there for the duration. The take-away section has proved a revelation for one kebab-loving local worker. Closed Sun.

English Garden SW3
10 Lincoln Street map 14
(0171) 584 7272
Chelsea town house converted into a 'light and bright' conservatory-style restaurant with horticultural overtones. Menus attempt to follow the seasons, and offer grilled scallops with slow-roasted shallots, roast rump of lamb with honey-glazed vegetables, or grilled sea bass with vanilla, lemon and potato crust. Service is, for the most part, charming and helpful. The wine list is dominated by France, with a few token detours further afield.

Enoteca Turi SW15
28 Putney High Street map 12
(0181) 785 4449
One of many small restaurants at the river end of the high street, Enoteca offers good-value Italian cooking and a reasonably priced Italian wine list with 17 by the glass. Among recommendations have been mussels with pesto, calf's liver with cabbage, and baked rabbit. Puddings might be home-made lemon tart with raspberry coulis or Italian chocolate terrine with amaretti biscuit. Closed Sat L and Sun.

Formula Veneta SW10
14 Hollywood Road map 14
(0171) 352 7612
Rather glitzy venue dealing in fashionable Italian cooking at fair prices. Fish might include monkfish with aubergine and pancetta, or even chargrilled sturgeon with a coulis of rucola, parsley, basil and lemon. Otherwise, pastas and risottos share the billing with, say, pan-cooked beef with anchovy and caper sauce, or veal escalope in artichoke and Emmental cheese sauce. A garden at the rear of the restaurant is open during the summer. Closed Sun.

Four Regions SE1
County Hall map 13
(0171) 928 0988
Expensive Chinese with magnificent river views in what was once the GLC staff canteen. Set menus (minimum two) are around the £20 to £30 mark, or choose from soups, king prawns or satay chicken, followed by fresh lobster or 'succulent' crispy tropical duck with orange. Efficient and friendly service.

Frederick's N1
Camden Passage map 13
(0171) 359 2888
If wedding bells are in the air, you might consider tying the knot in the Clarence Room on the first floor of this celebrity-friendly Islington venue. Downstairs are three distinct dining areas – one overlooks the garden – where Andrew Jeffs's contemporary cooking incorporates both luxurious and peasant touches: sesame-roasted lobster comes with spring onion and crème fraîche risotto, or roast rump of lamb is served with Madeira jus, champ and minted peas. Desserts might feature raspberry brioche pizza with vanilla ice-cream. Closed Sun, exc for large parties.

Gate W6
51 Queen Caroline Street map 12
(0181) 748 6932
Vegetarian cooking with an up-beat international flavour is the order of the day in Adrian and Michael Daniel's high-ceilinged Hammersmith restaurant. The menu globetrots for tostadas, grilled halloumi cheese on Moroccan chickpea salad with Yemenite chilli sauce, and green Thai curry. Finish with raspberry compote and crème fraîche, or poached peaches with butterscotch sauce. There are seats outside for fine-weather meals. Closed Sat L and Sun.

Geales W8
2 Farmer Street map 13
(0171) 727 7969
Family-owned since 1919, this fish restaurant just behind the Gate cinema offers main-course fish priced by weight, from halibut to skate, lemon sole to salmon, served with chips and peas. Start with soup or prawn cocktail and finish with apple crumble or chocolate eclairs. Closed Sun and Mon.

Gecko NW1
7–9 Pratt Street map 13
(0171) 424 0203
DJs pump out music throughout the week in this contemporary, style-conscious Camden venue. The food gets its kicks from around the world: the West contributes nachos, chargrilled burgers and salade niçoise; the East has its say with satays, samosas, chicken curry with stir-fried vegetables, and Malaysian mee goreng. Closed Sat L and Sun.

Gilbey's W5
77 The Grove, Ealing map 12
(0181) 840 7568
Converted former corner shop, with back room opening on to pleasant garden. Sister branch to those in Amersham (see entry, England round-ups) and Eton. Brilliant wine list at shop prices, starting with house wines at only £6. Modern British cooking with oriental overtones offering dishes such as pan-fried calf's liver and bacon with olive mash, or marinated seafood. Good-value set meals, but extras mount up on the *carte*.

Goolies W8
21 Abingdon Road map 13
(0171) 938 1122
Narrow restaurant on two levels: bar and casual eating area on the lower, and a more formal dining-room on the upper. Friendly atmosphere. Daily-changing set lunch menu with a *carte* at dinner. Start with a consommé of lobster or a marbre of rabbit, followed by chargrilled tuna served rare or 'tender' lamb cutlets. Mainly New World wines. Closed Sat L and Sun D.

Le Gothique SW18
Royal Victoria Patriotic Building map 12
(0181) 870 6567
On the first floor of an extraordinary Gothic building whose foundation stone was laid by Queen Victoria. There are tables outside for summer eating, and wedding receptions can be held here. A la carte menus offer Mediterranean fish soup with rouille, or terrine of partridge with apple and raisin chutney, followed by venison steak cooked in red wine or fresh filleted monkfish with leeks. Note that the car park and gardens close at midnight. Closed Sat L, and Sun.

Great Nepalese

NW1
48 Eversholt Street   map 13
(0171) 388 6737

Something of an institution, the Great Nepalese has two dining areas with generously sized tables. Good popadoms, pickles and dips have been commended, or try freshly cooked onion bhajia, masco bara (a Nepalese pancake with a simple lentil filling), chilli chicken or king prawn masala. Drink Indian Cobra beer or the Spanish house wine. Friendly, if slightly slow service from smartly dressed waiters.

Greek Valley

NW8
130 Boundary Road   map 13
(0171) 624 3217

The Bosnics' north London taverna offers abundant hot and cold starters ranging from assorted home-made dips, and whole red pepper with garlic and feta cheese, to loutza (grilled smoked ham) and spanakopittes (feta cheese and spinach pastries). Following on, there might be chicken breast in hot paprika sauce or various different kebabs, while sweets could include Greek figs in syrup, or pancakes. Friday night is 'party night' with live music. Dinner only, and closed Sun.

La Grignote

NW3
77 Heath Street   map 13
(0171) 433 3455

Popular with Hampstead locals. Excellent value Sunday lunch menu offers fish soup with croûtons, perhaps followed by wild boar sausage and celeriac mash, finishing with lime soufflé for dessert. More expensive à la carte menu and wine list. Extremely friendly service. Closed Sun.

Jindivick

N1
201 Liverpool Road   map 13
(0171) 607 7710

Roomy corner restaurant offering a 'seductive' blend of cooking difficult to typecast. Emperor bream with asparagus and vierge sauce, treacle-roasted duck breast with shallots and pak choi, and fig and plum puff-pastry pizza with vanilla ice-cream have all figured on the daily-changing menu. Excellent for weekend brunch and families.

Lavender

SW11
171 Lavender Hill   map 12
(0171) 978 5242

'Admirable little place' that provides creditable food in easy-going surroundings. Menus change daily and the kitchen comes up with some good ideas: as homespun as boiled bacon with mash and spinach, or as cosmopolitan as pan-fried salmon fillet with marinated puy lentils, roast fennel salad and coriander sweetcorn dressing. Begin with salad of chicken livers and finish with 'zesty' orange cake with sour cream and caramel syrup. Friendly service. Other branches are at 24 Clapham Road, SW9, 112 Vauxhall Walk, SE11 and 61 The Cut, SE1.

Lemonia

NW1
89 Regents Park Road   map 13
(0171) 586 7454

Long-running north London establishment offering hearty helpings of authentic Greek food. Meze (for a minimum of two people) is the speciality of the house, but the menu also promises avgolemono soup, pork souvlaki, ordikia (chargrilled marinated quails), kleftiko, and baby squid simmered in wine with herbs. Three-course weekday lunches and special deals are great value. Closed Sat L and Sun D.

London Hilton, Windows Rooftop Restaurant

W1
22 Park Lane   map 15
(0171) 493 8000

Spectacular setting and wonderful views over London on a clear day. Superb simple and flavourful food, but service has not impressed. Adequate wine list. From the *carte* try a warm salad of red mullet with anchovy vinaigrette, or poached foie gras with white beans, followed by fillet of lamb with crispy pancakes, or pot-roasted monkfish. Closed Sun D.

Mandalay W2
444 Edgware Road map 13
(0171) 258 3696
Cheerful Burmese café run by the
friendly Ally brothers. Only 28 seats so
booking is recommended. One special
lunch offer might consist of curry
(chicken, meatball, vegetable, or shrimp
and potato), served with rice and salad;
another of a crispy spring vegetable roll
followed by banana fritters, and tea or
coffee. Closed Sun.

Mandola W11
139 Westbourne Grove map 13
(0171) 229 4734
Enterprising but 'cramped' little café
serving a mixed-bag of authentic African
dishes in a setting of plain wooden tables
and ethnic artefacts. Starters are mostly
dips and salads (aubergine with grated
vegetables is a winner), main courses
tend to revolve around stews and curries.
Otherwise look for kustaletta (lamb
cutlets marinated in Sudanese spices fried
with spring onions and tomatoes).
Desserts are likely to be Afro variations on
Middle Eastern staples such as baklava.
'Smiley', feel-good service. Unlicensed,
but BYO (£1 corkage).

Manzi's WC2
1–2 Leicester Street map 15
(0171) 734 0224
In 1998, the Manzi family celebrated
their 70th anniversary at one of London's
most redoubtable seafood restaurants. Eat
bistro-style on the ground floor or more
formally in the upstairs Cabin Room.
Simple fried and grilled fish are probably
the best bets from a menu that deals
heavily in the likes of scallops Mornay,
sole meunière and lobster thermidor. If
you fancy staying in town, it's worth
noting that Manzi's is also a hotel. Closed
Sun L.

Marquis W1
121A Mount Street map 15
(0171) 499 1256
The Fiori family have been at this glitzy
address since 1959, although things have

changed dramatically in recent years. The
menu now beats to the '90s
Mediterranean pulse, with a tweak here
and there from other quarters. Gnocchi of
rocket and ricotta receives a langoustine
sauce, breast of chicken wrapped in
pancetta and filled with a mozzarella and
porcini stuffing is served on butternut
squash purée, while seared tuna steak
and grilled vegetables are enlivened with
avocado and lime butter. Closed Sat L and
Sun.

Mezzanine SE1
National Theatre, Upper Ground map 13
(0171) 452 3600
Restaurant in the National Theatre
building with views over the river.
'Lovely atmosphere and exceptional
service.' Recommended dishes have
included salmon fish-cakes on wilted
greens, deep-fried cod with pesto butter,
marinated Mandarin duck, and calf's liver
cooked 'just right'. Finish with capuccino
crème or strawberry and ginger charlotte.
Closed Sun.

New World W1
1 Gerrard Place map 15
(0171) 434 2508
One of the top locations in Soho
Chinatown for 'trolley' dim-sum wheeled
around by legions of tireless staff. Crowds
pack the three floors of this huge place for
a massive selection taking in all kinds of
steamed dumplings, deep-fried nibbles,
roast meats, soups and cooked-to-order
items such as aubergines stuffed with
prawns. The full menu has a strong
Cantonese bias and includes everything
from familiar beef with oyster sauce to
more esoteric offerings such as steamed
minced pork with salted duck egg.

Patisserie Valerie W1
R.I.B.A., 66 Portland Place map 15
(0171) 580 5533
On the first floor of the R.I.B.A. building.
Large, airy room with a terrace for
summer eating, and tables in niches in
the entrance gallery. Choose from
pastries, toasted sandwiches, soups or

pasta. More substantial dishes might include croque monsieur/madame, omelettes or risotto con porcini. Generous portions, all well garnished. Excellent coffee. Charming service. Closed Sun.

Pizzeria Castello   SE1
20 Walworth Road   map 13
(0171) 703 2556

Lively pizzeria close to the Elephant & Castle and one of the top names among the independents. Pizzas and pastas are naturally the mainstays of the menu, although the kitchen does branch out with specials such as rocket and Parmesan salad, gazpacho and sauté king prawns. There are also some quaffable Italian wines to go with the food. Great value. Closed Sat L and Sun.

Poons   WC2
27 Lisle Street   map 15
(0171) 437 4549

White-fronted building with red fascia and bistro-style red and white check tablecloths. Try fried aubergine, Cantonese dim-sum, crispy belly pork or lamb and tofu hotpot. Charming service from Shirley Poon assisted by smart waitresses.

Porte des Indes   W1
32 Bryanston Street   map 13
(0171) 224 0055

Spectacular dining-room in this sister restaurant to the Blue Elephant – able to accommodate up to 300 people on two floors – with regional cuisine from across India, plus French/Creole cuisine of Pondicherry. Seasonal menus, food festivals and special vegetarian menus are on offer too. From the house menu try parsee fish (fillets of sole in a mint and coriander chutney) or beignets of aubergine. Main courses could be adrak ke panje (lamb chops marinated in spices and chargrilled), or poulet rouge. The house pudding is Coupe Pondicherry. Closed Sat L.

Randall & Aubin   W1
16 Brewer Street   map 15
(0171) 287 4447

Converted Soho butcher's and grocery shop, now specialising in 'fruits de mer' and the output of a rotisserie. Have a bowl of whelks with lemon and vinegar, Cumberland sausages with mustard, or a hot chicken baguette with frites if you want to eat cheaply. Alternatively, splash out on roast stuffed blackleg chicken with peas, beans and mascarpone sauce, whole lobster with potato salad, or go for broke with 50 grams of caviare plus chopped egg, parsley, creme fraîche and blinis.

Roussillon   SW1
39 Ranelagh Grove   map 14
(0171) 730 5550

As the *Guide* went to press, the restaurant formerly known as Marabel closed for a thorough refurbishment and name change. Provençale chef Alexis Gauthier has pleased reporters with sound, well-balanced French cooking with modern touches. Assuming the cooking continues in the same vein after the refit, expect 'correct' risotto with morels, 'tasty' grilled turbot with figs and artichokes, 'tender' pigeon with seared foie gras and wild berries, and traditional clafoutis to finish. Reports, please.

Salt House   NW8
63 Abbey Road   map 13
(0171) 625 4178

Converted corner pub with an informal atmosphere and constantly changing paintings for sale on the walls. Good-value modern rustic cooking offers generous portions. Recommended dishes have included chicken and lentil salad, goats' cheese tart, chicken breast with strawberry and Chablis sauce, and lemon bavarois. Blackboard wine list. Closed Mon L.

Simply Nico – Barbican   EC1
7 Goswell Road   map 13
(0171) 336 7677

Simply Nico – Chelsea   SW10
7 Park Walk   map 14
(0171) 349 8866

New branches of the original (see main entry, London) opened by the Restaurant Partnership. Similar three-course menus throughout. Among recommended dishes have been chicken liver parfait with port jelly and brioche, ballottine of quail with sage mousse, roast saddle of lamb with provencale vegetables, and breast of Duck sarladaise. Finish with rice-pudding croquettes with apricot coulis or hot chocolate fondant.

62 Restaurant & Theatre Bar   SE1
62 Southwark Bridge Road   map 13
(0171) 633 0831

Small restaurant adjacent to Southwark Playhouse decorated in strong colours. Lunchtime bar menu (also available before and after the theatre) offers soup, pasta, fish-cakes or a cheese platter. Main menu choices might be chargrilled squid or gravadlax followed by roasted cod with tapénade. Lemon and raspberry tart and poached peaches with mango sorbet have been recommended. Combined theatre and dinner tickets available. Closed Sat L and Sun.

Sofra   WC2
36 Tavistock Street   map 115
(0171) 240 3773

One of a chain of Turkish eating-houses with restaurants, cafés and delicatessens dotted around central London. All-day opening, great value for money and the prospect of live guitar music are part of the package, and each outlet follows the same ground rules. 'Divine' meze 'all fresh and spicy' could be followed by grills, casseroles such as incik (knuckle of lamb on the bone cooked in its own juices) and a healthy contingent of seafood (fillets of swordfish steamed in foil with black pepper, coriander, bay leaves and tomatoes, for example). The 'introductory' set menu is an unbeatable deal.

Soho Spice   W1
124/126 Wardour Street   map 15
(0171) 434 0808

Light, airy, strikingly decorated Indian restaurant packed with young people. A short Hyderabadi menu has some unusual offerings. Start with chilli aubergines or try a main dish of dum ka murg (tender chicken with sauted onions, chillogi and cashew-nuts flavoured with saffron). Or try a main course of chicken with lentil and vegetable curries in separate bowls, with a pot of yoghurt and naan all included in the price. Very fast service.

La Spighetta   W1
43 Blandford Street   map 15
(0171) 486 7340

Smart, up-to-the-minute pizzeria in a downstairs room complete with wall sculptures and a wood-fired oven. Pizzas come in 12 versions with excellent thin bases and all kinds of toppings from margherita to spada (with watercress and marinated swordfish). Otherwise there are pastas and daily specials such as pan-fried cod with saute fennel and tomato. Finish with tiramisù. Friendly service from a willing young crew, and carefully chosen, affordable wines.

Spread Eagle   SE10
2 Stockwell Street   map 12
(0181) 853 2333

This ancient coaching-inn has acquired a new chef, Michael Smith, who was in the 1998 *Guide* at First Floor (see main entry, London). The repertoire is now in a more traditional French style, supported by a new kitchen and welcoming front-of-house staff. Typical dishes might be celery and Stilton soup or scampi to start, followed by herb-crusted monkfish or pot-roasted guinea-fowl with couscous, finishing with chocolate praline parfait. Reports, please.

Star of India   SW5
154 Old Brompton Road   map 14
(0171) 373 2901

Long-established restaurant where high

prices are fully justified by the location, unique ambience, friendliness of the Mahammad brothers and the wealth of choice on the wide-ranging menu. Starters might include murg chaat (diced chicken in a tamarind dressing) or samundri rattan (gratinated baby scallops steeped in garlic). Main courses offer medallions of duck breast with papaya and ginger, or salmon marinated in dill, mustard, lemon and honey and cooked in the tandoor. A selection of ice-creams and sorbets is supplemented by fresh pinapple, or steamed milk pudding. House French wine is £9.50. Closed bank holidays.

Thai Bistro   W4
99 Chiswick High Road   map 12
(0181) 995 5774
Small, informal Thai restaurant with communal tables and bench seating. Regional and vegetarian menus in addition to the main one, which offers dishes such as kanom bang na moo (minced pork with peanut sauce) or laab issan (chopped beef with hot chilli). Desserts might run to banana in coconut milk, ice-creams or sorbets. Friendly service even when busy. Drink Thai beer or choose from the short wine list.

Toffs   NW10
38 Muswell Hill Broadway   map 12
(0181) 883 8656
Toffs is suitable for both eating in the tiny dining-room, or take-aways. Try a bowl of fish soup, or choose from haddock, cod etc. in crispy batter, with non-greasy chips, home-made tartare sauce and excellent gherkins. Closed Sun and Mon.

T'su   SW3
118 Draycott Avenue   map 14
(0171) 584 5522
Smart modern Japanese outlet, particularly useful at lunch-time. Conveyor-belt format, with comfortable bar stools (with backs). Well-prepared sushi with bright, refreshing flavours circulate, and pricing is based around plates of different colours. Other

alternatives, ordered from keen and informative young staff, appear in the shape of sashimi, miso soup and chicken soba noodles. Drink saké or choose from the short, reasonably priced wine list.

Vasco & Piero's Pavilion   W1
15 Poland Street   map 15
(0171) 437 8774
This old stager among London's Italian restaurants has recently had a facelift, but the food remains much as before. Fixed-price dinners continue to offer the best value, and you can eat affordably from menus that might promise salad of octopus with borlotti beans and chickpeas, grilled sea bass with fennel, and calf's liver with fresh sage. Lunchtime visitors have also endorsed featherlight carpaccio of lamb and grilled salmon with French beans. Closed Sat and Sun.

Vegetarian Cottage   NW3
91 Haverstock Hill   map 13
(0171) 586 1257
No good for carnivores, but the rest of us can look forward to a comprehensive range of Chinese vegetarian dishes. Mushrooms are braised and served with black moss, and bean curd comes Szechuan style or in a curry sauce. Seafood features and scallops are stir-fried with vegetables or steamed with garlic in a spicy sauce. Friendly and helpful service.

Wigmore Restaurant   W1
36 Wigmore Street   map 15
(0171) 487 4874
Basement restaurant decorated in art nouveau style. Lunch might offer chilled gazpacho or chicken and ham terrine, followed by chargrilled salmon escalope or glazed duck breast with rösti potatoes, finishing with chocolate terrine or summer pudding. A good-value £10 two-course dinner menu deals in similar dishes. Short wine list starts with house French at £9.50. Closed for dinner mid-July to September, and Sat L and Sun D.

Willie Gunn's　　　　　　　SW18
422 Garratt Lane　　　　　　　map 12
(0181) 946 7773
On a corner site, with huge picture
windows, this wine bar and restaurant
offers good, modern British cooking.
Recommended dishes have included
fish-cakes with parsley sauce and chips,
summer pudding, and grilled peaches
with mascarpone lemon cream.
Fortnightly-changing menus might also
offer mussels with gremolata, or
sweetbreads, followed by Lincolnshire
sausages with mash, or pork loin with
caramelised apples.

Wodka　　　　　　　　　　W8
12 St Albans Grove　　　　　　map 14
(0171) 937 6513
Long-standing Polish restaurant with

wonderful selection of vodkas.The menu
du jour might offer chilled beetroot soup
or seared tuna with couscous followed by
roast pork shank or kulebiak (salmon in
pastry) with mushroom and spinach.
Finish with caramelised pear tart or
crème brûlée. Closed Sat L and Sun L.

Yoshino　　　　　　　　　　W1
3 Piccadilly Place　　　　　　map 15
(0171) 287 6622
In an alleyway just off Piccadilly this
small thoroughly Japanese restaurant is
best visited with an expert as there is no
English menu. Excellent sushi, or try the
sashimi which comes in a large basket
(swordfish, tuna, shrimps, squid etc.)
with eel rice or salmon egg rice. Drink
saké or Japanese beer. Charming staff.
Closed Sun and bank hols.

England

ALDEBURGH Suffolk map 6

Lighthouse £

77 High Street, Aldeburgh IP15 5AU	COOKING 1
TEL/FAX: (01728) 453377	COST £17–£33

First off, 'it's nothing like a lighthouse'. If anything, the main dining-room downstairs recalls its former life as a shop, now decked out as a bistro with tiled tables and rustic décor, while a smaller no-smoking area upstairs opens on to the kitchen. It is informal, friendly, often busy, and well served by enthusiastic staff. Fresh fish is the strength – 'just as it ought to be' in a coastal town like Aldeburgh – coming from the beach fishermen, from Colchester or, in the case of oysters, from Loch Fyne. The menu changes in some way each day, but might offer Norfolk potted shrimps on toast, Cromer crab salad, or cod fillet in beer batter with chips. Most of the cooking is done to order – chargrilled tuna with rice and salsa, or skate wing with herb butter and capers – and the food generally succeeds because it combines simplicity with a dash of flair. There are meat dishes of duck confit, calf's liver, or sausage and mash for variety, and puddings such as bread-and-butter, lemon tart or banana pancakes. Some 60 well-chosen, briefly annotated wines are sympathetically priced, starting with nine house recommendations around £10 each.

CHEFS: Sara Fox, Guy Welsh and Gavin Battle   PROPRIETORS: Peter Hill and Sara Fox   OPEN: all week 12 to 2.30, 7 to 10   CLOSED: Sun D and Mon L in winter   MEALS: alc (main courses £5.50 to £10). Set D £13.50 (2 courses) to £15.75   SERVICE: not inc, card slips closed   CARDS: Delta, MasterCard, Switch, Visa   DETAILS: 90 seats. 20 seats outside (summer only). Private parties: 50 main room, 25 private room. Vegetarian meals. Children's helpings. No-smoking area. Wheelchair access (1 step; not WC). No music £5

Regatta ⅝✳ £

171 High Street, Aldeburgh IP15 5AN	COOKING 3
TEL/FAX: (01728) 452011	COST £22–£40

Speculation about Robert Mabey's departure to Norwich has seemingly come to nothing, and the man himself is still in residence at this nautically inclined seaside restaurant (although his outlets in Ipswich and Sudbury have been sold). Locals and visitors alike are thankful that he has not gone away. East Coast fish shows up strongly – especially among the blackboard specials – whether it be cod, sprats, skate or sea bass. Reporters have also strongly endorsed meat and game in all manner of guises: rillettes of pork is served with grilled bruschetta and pickled samphire, a warm salad of duck comes with 'thin, perfectly crisped' lardons and a Thai dressing, while pheasant pudding with a suet crust has been copiously and 'superbly' sauced. Puddings also receive plenty of glowing praise – especially ice-creams such as Grand Marnier and chocolate chip, although the range also includes old favourites like jam roly-poly and steamed spicy pear pudding with caramel sauce. The wine list, from Lay & Wheeler, runs to 40 reasonably priced bins with a leaning towards the New World. House French is £8.95.

CHEFS: Robert Mabey and Nigel Ramsbottom   PROPRIETORS: Robert and Johanna Mabey
OPEN: all week 12 to 2, 6 to 10 (booking essential in winter)   MEALS: alc (main courses £8 to £14)   SERVICE: not inc   CARDS: Amex, Delta, MasterCard, Switch, Visa   DETAILS: 100 seats. 6 seats outside. Private parties: 40 main room. Vegetarian meals. Children's helpings (not Sat D). No smoking in 1 dining-room. Wheelchair access (3 steps; also WC). Occasional music   £5

ALTRINCHAM   Greater Manchester   map 8

Juniper

21 The Downs, Altrincham WA14 2QD   COOKING 7
TEL: (0161) 929 4008   FAX: (0161) 929 4009   COST £34–£62

Juniper sits in a parade of shops in a prosperous-looking Manchester suburb, sporting traces of Tuscany and Charles Rennie Mackintosh in its huge Ucello-style mural, art deco wall lights, and buckets of greenery. The food is sustained by a high degree of technical accomplishment in which contributing flavours don't fuse into an anonymous whole, but stay interesting. A short *carte* works within a fairly narrow spectrum of frothy soups, finely wrought terrines, prime fillets of meat or fish arranged in heaps, sparse vegetable garnishes, and slicks of different oil-based emulsions that appear in various guises throughout a meal.

Typical of the style are a light, creamy, frothy white truffle soup with noodles and anchovy, and a 'wonderfully gutsy and refreshing' parfait of finely ground aubergine with garlic and herbs, surrounded by fruity olive oil and chopped leek. Meat and fish are well sourced, producing a chunk of well-hung beef fillet that is cooked rare, properly seared and rested, and fillets of brill arranged on a mound of spätzli noodles, surrounded by puddles of pesto scattered with diced tomato: 'very fresh fish, well timed, with good, powerful flavours.' Quantities are not large, but dishes are carefully crafted – there always seem to be several things going on at once, as if Paul Kitching thinks in three dimensions – and always keep the main component centre stage.

Don't be surprised to find an old-fashioned dish such as coq au vin on the menu either. As Paul Kitching notes, if you wait long enough, almost any dish will come back under the spotlight again. In fact, his repertoire changes slowly, leaving one regular pleading for more variety. In a city centre, with other restaurants to choose from, this might not be such a problem, but Juniper is the best restaurant for a considerable distance, and so carries an extra burden. Freshly made bread rolls – white, wholemeal or fruit – are praised, and 'classy desserts' add greatly to the appeal, from glazed lemon tart to the soufflés: a Christmas pudding one full of 'traditional flavour', or a mixed berry version with honey ice-cream. Service is well-drilled, informative and friendly. Wines are rooted in France, but now include a handful of southern hemisphere bottles. House vin de pays is £15.

CHEF: Paul Kitching   PROPRIETORS: Nora and Peter Miles   OPEN: Tue to Fri L 12 to 2, Mon to Sat D 7 to 10   CLOSED: bank hols   MEALS: alc (main courses L £12 to £16, D £16 to £19) SERVICE: not inc, card slips closed   CARDS: Amex, Delta, MasterCard, Switch, Visa   DETAILS: 50 seats. Private parties: 40 main room, 14 private room. Children welcome. Music. Air-conditioned

---

ALVECHURCH Worcestershire   map 5

The Mill ♥ ✸ £

Radford Road, Alvechurch B48 7LD
TEL: (0121) 447 7005   FAX: (0121) 447 8001   COOKING 4
5 mins from junction 2 of M42   COST £24–£36

Although there is no stream – the three-storeyed red-brick mill is now consigned to a suburban setting – old beams and an iron cogwheel hint at its former industrial life. The light dining-room conveys a 'garden-room impression', and shiny cutlery and glasses confirm the place is well cared for. It is family-run and 'very comme il faut', with courteous, precise service from the McKernons touched with 'simple sincerity'. Carl Timms combines good raw materials with technical skill in his French-oriented dishes of duck confit, smoked haddock and asparagus tart, or turbot with orange and basil sauce. His mid-week set-price dinner is composed from dishes on the *carte*, which itself changes half a dozen times a year.

Geoff McKernon writes that they have tried to introduce a few more luxuries in the shape of lobster ravioli, and terrine of foie gras, but these have not gone down as well as the cyclical favourites: salmon wrapped around a poached egg, fillet of beef with caramelised onions and red wine sauce. 'Nicely balanced' flavour combinations are a feature of desserts, which might include chocolate and raspberry truffle cake, or iced mandarin parfait with rhubarb syrup. Wines are set out on a main list offering a good spread of styles and flavours at favourable prices (including nine vintages of Lebanon's Château Musar), backed up by a fine-wine list – available on request – featuring mature burgundies, venerable Riojas and a plethora of vintage clarets. House French is £9.25. CELLARMAN'S CHOICE: Chablis Fourchaume 'Dom. des Valery' 1996, Jean Durup; £18.50; Bonny Doon Ca' del Solo Big House Red 1995, Santa Cruz, California, £15.50.

CHEF: Carl Timms   PROPRIETORS: Stefan, Geoffrey and Vivienne McKernon   OPEN: Tue to Sat D only 7 to 8.30 (9 Fri and Sat). Sun L by arrangement only   CLOSED: 2 to 3 days after Christmas, first week Jan, first two weeks Aug   MEALS: alc (main courses £11.50 to £16). Set D Tue to Thur £15 (2 courses) to £17.50   SERVICE: not inc   CARDS: Amex, MasterCard, Visa   DETAILS: 30 seats. Private parties: 30 main room. Car park. Vegetarian meals. Children welcome (very young children at early D only). No smoking in dining-room. Music   (£5)

The Good Food Guide *is a registered trade mark of Which? Ltd.*

AMBERLEY West Sussex　　　　　　　　　　　　　　　　　　　map 3

▲ *Amberley Castle, Queen's Room* 🍴✳

Amberley BN18 9ND
TEL: (01798) 831992　FAX: (01798) 831998　　　　　COOKING 3
on B2139, between Storrington and Bury Hill　　　　　COST £31–£55

There can be few more evocative settings for a meal than this ancient castle near the south coast. The oldest part dates from the twelfth century, the bulk of it from the fourteenth, and anybody with an I-Spy book can tick off portcullis, drawbridge, dried-up moat and crenellated towers, not to mention suits of armour, swords and pikes. The top half of the Great Hall serves as the dining-room, where dinner, at well-spaced, immaculately set tables, is the main business: the à la carte has gone, and one-price meals are five courses, the basic three course format extended by the addition of soup or sorbet after the starter, and cheese before dessert.

Given the price, a few luxuries are not surprising – peppered foie gras pâté with spiced fig chutney, or a seaweed-wrapped terrine of lobster and potato – and the general thrust is towards food that satisfies: meaty fish such as brill, served with wild mushroom risotto, or roast chump of lamb with grilled polenta. Puddings, which serve a similar purpose, stay closer to home and may well be the highlight: warm rhubarb and apple crumble with vanilla custard, or bitter chocolate soufflé. Aristocratic French wines occupy most of the list, and although the New World gets a look-in, prices generally are very high. Seven house wines start at £13.95 (£4.50 a glass).

CHEF: Sam Mahoney　PROPRIETORS: Martin and Joy Cummings　OPEN: all week 12 to 2, 7 to 9.30　MEALS: Set L Mon to Sat £12.50, Set L Sun £21.50, Set D £35　SERVICE: not inc, card slips closed　CARDS: Amex, Delta, Diners, MasterCard, Switch, Visa　DETAILS: 38 seats. 20 seats outside. Private parties: 48 main room, 12 private room. Car park. Vegetarian meals. No children under 10. Jacket and tie. No smoking in dining-room. Occasional music ACCOMMODATION: 15 rooms, all with bath/shower. TV. Phone. B&B £145 to £300. No children under 10. No dogs. Afternoon teas

---

AMBLESIDE Cumbria　　　　　　　　　　　　　　　　　　　map 8

Glass House 🍴✳

Rydal Road, Ambleside LA22 9AN　　　　　　　　　　　COOKING 3
TEL: (01539) 432137　FAX: (01539) 431139　　　　　　COST £18–£48

Attached to a glass-blowing studio, and dating from the early 1500s, this converted water mill near the Bridge House is made of glass and metal held together by large quantities of polished wood. 'It feels congruent,' according to a reporter in the interior design business. 'Casual' service tends to lack streamlined organisation, but on the other hand it contributes to the relaxed atmosphere thrown up by walkers and families. All-day opening is a plus too, and children have their own menu.

Throughout, meat takes second place to fish and vegetables. At their best, good ingredients, clear flavours and accurate cooking times combine to impress, in a range of dishes from mackerel escabèche, or coarse pork terrine with aubergine chutney, to salmon with pesto mash and saffron vegetables. 'I think they are offering something honest and a cut above the norm,' ventured one reporter. At the 'simple but tasty' end of the spectrum might be blue cheese crostini with tomato and pesto, or a leek and Stilton tart made with light pastry, while dinner brings out Roquefort and olive pizza, and saddle of rabbit with tagliatelle. Desserts draw less enthusiasm than breads, which are variously flavoured with dates, walnuts, apricots, caraway, or curry and raisin. Apart from beers and soft drinks, there are 20 lively wines (mostly under £20), plus a selection by the glass. House wines begin around £12.

CHEF: Stuart Birkett   PROPRIETOR: Adrian Sankey   OPEN: all week 12 to 10 (all-day menu 12 to 5.30, D menu 6.30 to 10)   CLOSED: 25 to 27 Dec   MEALS: alc (main courses all-day menu £4 to £8, D £9.50 to £14.50)   SERVICE: not inc, card slips closed   CARDS: Delta, MasterCard, Switch, Visa   DETAILS: 80 seats. 30 seats outside. Private parties: 80 main room. Car park. Vegetarian meals. Children's helpings. No smoking in dining-room. Occasional music   £5

▲ Rothay Manor ▼ ✱

Rothay Bridge, Ambleside LA22 0EH
TEL: (01539) 433605   FAX: (01539) 433607
EMAIL: hotel@rothaym.demon.co.uk
off A593 to Coniston, ¼m W of Ambleside

COOKING 2
COST £22–£48

This is a distinctive-looking and comfortably furnished house in pleasant gardens beside the River Rothay, just a few hundred yards from the centre of Ambleside. It has been in the Nixon family, and on the gastronomic tourist map, for over 30 years, and many reporters have been eating here since they were in short trousers or mini-skirts. 'Returning to old haunts can be a disappointment,' observed one, 'but not in this case.' Another returnee was less fortunate, but the feel of a 'civilised place to enjoy a quiet and fairly traditional lunch' or dinner captures it well.

Lunch is a cold buffet, augmented by a few hot dishes such as poached salmon or beef bourguignon, and dinner typically offers a choice of three items per course. Prawns in marie-rose sauce (remember that?) might be stuffed into a smoked salmon parcel, pork fillet comes with a mild curry and apricot sauce, and 'nicely pink' grouse has been served with spicy red cabbage. Finish with cheesecake, profiteroles or apple strudel. Wines are a globe-trotting collection, with some good producers making their presence felt in the Australian and German sections, as well as the more traditional reaches of the Rhône, Loire and Burgundy. Four house wines are £12 each. CELLARMAN'S CHOICE: Stoneleigh Vineyards Sauvignon Blanc 1996, Marlborough, New Zealand, £17.50; Lirac 'Les Queyrades' 1992, Dom. Méjan, £19.50.

'At a restaurant which will definitely never appear in The Good Food Guide, the following exchange took place last weekend:
Customer: "Tell me, how is the plaice Dieppe prepared?"
Waitress: "Well, first we defrost it, then we put it in the microwave, then we smother it in sauce." (On eating in Essex)

CHEFS: Jane Binns and Colette Nixon PROPRIETORS: Nigel and Stephen Nixon OPEN: all week 12.30 to 2 (12.45 to 1.30 Sun), 7.45 to 9 CLOSED: 3 Jan to 5 Feb MEALS: alc (main courses £6.50 to £8.50). Set L £13.50, Set D £24 (2 courses) to £30. BYO £5 SERVICE: not inc, card slips closed CARDS: Amex, Delta, Diners, MasterCard, Switch, Visa DETAILS: 75 seats. Private parties: 10 main room, 28 private room. Car park. Children's helpings. No children under 6 at D. No smoking in dining-room. Wheelchair access (1 step; also WC). No music. Air-conditioned ACCOMMODATION: 18 rooms, all with bath/shower. TV. Phone. B&B £78 to £140. Rooms for disabled. Children welcome. High teas for children. Baby facilities. Guide dogs only. Afternoon teas (*The Which? Hotel Guide*) (£5)

AMERSHAM Buckinghamshire   map 3

Kings Arms

30 High Street, Old Amersham, HP7 0DJ   COOKING 3
TEL: (01494) 726333 FAX: (01494) 433480   COST £22–£46

'A pub which seems to operate as a restaurant, and takes its food very seriously' is a fair summing-up of this old coaching-inn. It represents a 'bit of old England', with a comfortable, timbered interior, and offers food that is 'carefully produced and served competently'. A basket of fresh bread arrives, perhaps followed by pink, well-flavoured chicken liver pâté with toast, or a warm salad of smoked haddock with a creamy chive sauce and a softly poached egg. The food aims to be satisfying rather than mould-breaking, offering liver and bacon with mash and onion gravy, a fish of the day – perhaps grilled cod, sitting on a small mound of 'crisp and crunchy' cabbage, in a creamy sauce 'saved from over-richness by the addition of capers' – and homely puddings of sticky date and toffee, or chocolate tart. Wines are helpfully arranged by style, fairly priced, and include a couple of local whites. House Chilean red and South African white are £9.75.

CHEF: Gary Munday PROPRIETOR: John Jennison OPEN: Tue to Sun L 12 to 2, Tue to Sat D 7 to 9.30 CLOSED: 26 to 31 Dec MEALS: alc Tue to Sat L, Tue to Fri D (main courses £14.50 to £16.50). Set L Tue to Fri £10.50 (2 courses) to £13.50, Set L Sun £15, Set D Tue to Fri £17, Set D Sat £25. BYO £5 SERVICE: not inc CARDS: Amex, Delta, Diners, MasterCard, Switch, Visa DETAILS: 35 seats. Private parties: 12 main room, 12 to 50 private rooms. Car park. Vegetarian meals. Children's helpings. No cigars/pipes in dining-room. Wheelchair access (not WC). No music (£5)

APPLETHWAITE Cumbria   map 10

▲ Underscar Manor 🔆

Applethwaite CA12 4PH
TEL: (01768) 775000 FAX: (01768) 774904   COOKING 6
off A66, ½m N of Keswick   COST £36–£66

The views from this Italianate villa are diverting, whatever the weather. Skiddaw's bulk looms behind, and windows face south to Derwentwater and Cat Bells. Squirrels scurry about the lawn, and guinea-fowl dig it up, all drawing the eye away from ruched curtains, drapes of wispy material that make it feel 'as if it were always Christmas', and the 'souvenir shop' décor of toy bears and pot squirrels. The kitchen's strength is a vein of 'impressive classical cooking' that deals in seared foie gras on a caramelised apple tart, roast saddle of venison with a cabbage parcel, and rice pudding with a crispy topping. Dishes may sound fussy on the menu with all ingredients listed, but what arrives on the plate is thoughtfully constructed food which first and foremost tastes good.

The high level of skill that characterises the cooking is put to good use in, for example, a twice-baked cheese soufflé 'crisp outside, moist inside', and a 'smooth, creamy' chicken liver parfait with a greengage compote in a potato basket. 'An awful lot of work has gone into this,' reckoned one appreciative observer of his wedge of 'light as a feather' Bakewell tart. Sound judgement is deployed throughout, keeping the sometimes spicy flavours in check: in a salsa to accompany the cheese soufflé, or in a peppered and grilled duck breast, served with 'Thai' cabbage and a glossy, expertly made sauce.

There are flounces – good-quality butter is sculpted into roses, and domes are lifted – but what counts is that for materials, cooking and service, the place delivers. A generous selection of cheeses arrives in good condition, together with an array of celery batons, grapes, sliced apples, biscuits and more freshly made bread. The fixed-price lunch is judged 'utterly reasonable', with a choice of four items per course, and the largely French wine list is considerate to drinkers wanting change from £20.

CHEF: Robert Thornton   PROPRIETORS: Pauline and Derek Harrison, and Gordon Evans   OPEN: all week 12 to 1, 7 to 8.30 (9 Sat)   MEALS: alc (main courses £19 to £20). Set L £25, Set D £30   SERVICE: not inc, card slips closed   CARDS: Amex, Delta, MasterCard, Switch, Visa   DETAILS: 55 seats. 12 seats outside. Private parties: 30 main room. Car park. Vegetarian meals. No children under 12. Jacket and tie. No smoking in dining-room. Occasional music   ACCOMMODATION: 11 rooms, all with bath/shower. TV. Phone. DB&B £95 to £250. No children under 12. Afternoon teas (*The Which? Hotel Guide*)

ARNCLIFFE   North Yorkshire   map 8

▲ *Amerdale House* ✽

| Arncliffe, Littondale BD23 5QE | COOKING 4 |
| TEL: (01756) 770250 | COST £36–£43 |

Arncliffe shelters beneath limestone hills in a particularly remote part of the Yorkshire Dales, where narrow country lanes, a gently flowing river and craggy outcrops set the scene. Ornithologists may be enthralled by dippers and curlews flitting about the meadows, those who come to eat by the serious cooking going on at Amerdale House.

The scope of the dinner menus is small – just a pair of alternatives at main course and pudding, with three at the first course, and a no-choice filler between starter and main – but attention to detail is precise. Imagination extends to remaking avocado prawns by adding banana and a curried mayonnaise, and intermediate offerings by no means stick to soup or sorbet, but might take in tomato and basil tart, Thai fish-cakes, or asparagus hollandaise. Then it's fish or meat for main, perhaps grilled halibut with wild mushrooms, or a nearly-cassoulet dish of duck confit with haricots and Toulouse sausage. Pedigree northern cheeses with home-made oatcakes are the alternative to puddings such as apple tart with cinnamon ice-cream, or chocolate marquise with mint cream.

Wines are French or New World with a smattering of Spanish red, the majority under £20. Prices open at £9.85 for white and £10.50 for red.

CHEF: Nigel Crapper   PROPRIETORS: Paula and Nigel Crapper   OPEN: all week D only 7.30 to 8.30   CLOSED: mid-Nov to mid-Mar   MEALS: Set D £28. BYO (corkage negotiable)   SERVICE: not inc, card slips closed   CARDS: Delta, MasterCard, Switch, Visa   DETAILS: 24 seats. Car park. Children welcome. No smoking in dining-room. No music   ACCOMMODATION: 11 rooms, all with bath/shower. TV. D,B&B £62.50 to £131. Children welcome. High teas for children. Baby facilities. No dogs (*The Which? Hotel Guide*)

ASENBY   North Yorkshire   map 9

▲ Crab & Lobster 🕴✳

Dishforth Road, Asenby YO7 3QL
TEL: (01845) 577206   FAX. (01845) 577109   COOKING 2
off A168, between A19 and A1   COST £23–£60

Little changes at this tackle-strewn thatched pub off the A1, except that Crab Manor, a Georgian house set in seven surrounding acres, is due for completion as the *Guide* goes to press, offering accommodation plus a few sporting options in the grounds. The food, meanwhile, includes most known ways of cooking fish, and a few more besides: seafood bruschetta, tandoori tiger prawns, garlic and chilli crab, Thai fish soup, smoked haddock risotto, lobster thermidor, fish Wellington, and good old fish, chips and peas. There are Loch Fyne oysters on ice for those who prefer more straightforward options, and a few meat dishes too: spicy beef tortilla, or roast lamb fillet with dauphinoise potatoes. Finish with cherry Bakewell tart, raspberry brûlée, or steamed orange pudding with custard, and drink from a short list of wines, many below £20, starting with house Duboeuf at £10.50.

CHEF: Michael Pickard   PROPRIETORS: David and Jackie Barnard   OPEN: all week 12 to 2.30, 6.30 to 10 (noon to 10 Sun in spring and summer)   MEALS: alc (main courses £8 to £22). Set L £11.50 (2 courses) to £14.50   SERVICE: not inc, card slips closed   CARDS: Amex, Delta, MasterCard, Switch, Visa   DETAILS: 150 seats. 100 seats outside. Private parties: 100 main room, 10 to 40 private rooms. Car park. Vegetarian meals. Children welcome. No smoking in dining-room. Occasional music   ACCOMMODATION: 9 rooms, all with bath/shower. TV. Phone. B&B £45 to £90. Rooms for disabled. Children welcome. Afternoon teas   (£5)

ASHBOURNE   Derbyshire   map 8

▲ Callow Hall 🍴 🕴✳

Mappleton Road, Ashbourne DE6 2AA
TEL: (01335) 343403   FAX: (01335) 343624
¾m NW of Ashbourne, turn left off A515 at crossroads
with Bowling Green pub on left; Mappleton Rd first   COOKING 4
on right   COST £26–£58

The Spencers of Ashbourne have been caterers to quality since the 1720s, with the result that this country-house hotel may seem more like a cottage industry on a grand scale. The industriousness extends not just to in-house baking but to smoking and curing as well, while a sense of grandeur is re-inforced by the antlered heads that line the hallway, and in the ruched curtains at the tall windows of the lounge. Crimson tones dominate the main dining-room, where the country-house culinary style is accorded full honours. Among starters, scallops and prawns are stuffed into a pastry 'cushion' and given a prawn sauce, before a second-course refresher of either sorbet or maybe a simply grilled fillet of white fish. Main courses revolve around prime cuts such as mozzarella-glazed beef fillet with duxelles, or chicken breast with white wine and tarragon sauce.

An up-to-date vegetarian option is always offered, perhaps goats' cheese and roasted tomato tart dressed with chilli oil. Strawberry and white chocolate bavarois with fruit coulis, or homely plum tart with custard round things off. Despite the sense of ceremony, service is friendly as well as efficient. 'Drink wine and live longer!' urges the cover of the wine list, and the range of bottles contained therein provides sufficient encouragement to do just that. Fine French fare is followed by a worldly collection of varietals and styles drawn from England, Switzerland and Canada, as well as the more expected countries. House French is £10.25. CELLARMAN'S CHOICE: Premières Côtes de Blaye, Ch. Haut Grelot 1996, £13.25; Te Awa Farm Cabernet/Merlot 1996, Hawkes Bay, New Zealand, £17.75.

CHEFS: David and Anthony Spencer   PROPRIETORS: David, Dorothy and Anthony Spencer OPEN: Sun L 12 to 1.30, Mon to Sat D 7.15 to 9 (Sun D residents only)   CLOSED: 25 and 26 Dec, 1 Jan   MEALS: alc D (main courses £18 to £19.50). Set L Sun £18.25, Set D £37   SERVICE: not inc   CARDS: Amex, Diners, MasterCard, Switch, Visa   DETAILS: 60 seats. Private parties: 35 main room, 20 to 25 private rooms. Car park. Vegetarian meals. Children's helpings. No smoking in dining-room. No music   ACCOMMODATION: 16 rooms, all with bath/shower. TV. Phone. B&B £75 to £140. Rooms for disabled. Children welcome. High teas for children. Baby facilities. Dogs by arrangement and not in public rooms. Fishing (*The Which? Hotel Guide*) £5

ASHBURTON Devon   map 1

▲ *Holne Chase* ▮ ⌂ ✳

Ashburton TQ13 7NS
TEL: (01364) 631471   FAX: (01364) 631453
EMAIL: info@holne-chase.co.uk   COOKING 4
2m N of Ashburton on road to Two Bridges   COST £28–£47

The 'chase' – a theme apparent in the sporting prints decorating this white-painted Victorian house overlooking the Dart Valley – can be joined by anybody wanting to fish, ride or shoot, and the 'country-house party' feel is never far away. With the departure of Wayne Pearson, Ross Duncan moved up to take control of the kitchen, continuing to use vegetables, fruits, herbs and saladings from the walled garden, baking bread in-house, and taking advantage of such local materials as fish, game and West Country cheeses.

A country-house strand is evident in the cooking too: in quail galantine stuffed with oyster mushrooms, and in slices of tender venison arranged in a pyramid over a base of crisp bubble and squeak. Fish has impressed, from tagliatelle with mussels, prawns and just-seared scallops, to accurately timed red mullet fillets spread with herbs, built into a tower and topped with 'a splendidly mad-looking thatch of crisp onion shreds'. Vegetables are integral –

glazed onions and lightly vinegared beetroot cubes with venison, for example – and within its own parameters the food can be both gently 'innovative and interesting'.

Among desserts, iced nougat with mango and caramel has provided a pleasing contrast between astringency and sweetness. Service is 'polished without being pompous' and the Hugheses oversee a friendly operation. Wines are largely supplied by St James's merchants Berry Bros & Rudd, so it is no surprise to see high-quality bins from the traditional French regions in the majority. A quartet of Vega Sicilia Unicos and a small selection from the New World broaden the appeal. House wines are priced between £11.25 and £12.90 a bottle (£3/£3.50 a glass). CELLARMAN'S CHOICE: Berrys' Puligny-Montrachet NV, Gérard Chave, £29.80; Margaux, Ch. Siran 1982, £47.15.

CHEFS: Ross Duncan and Philippa Hughes   PROPRIETORS: Sebastian and Philippa Hughes   OPEN: all week 12.15 to 2, 7.15 to 8.45   MEALS: Set L £20 to £29.50, Set D £25 to £29.50. Light lunches available   SERVICE: not inc, card slips closed   CARDS: Amex, Delta, Diners, MasterCard, Switch, Visa   DETAILS: 45 seats. 30 seats outside. Private parties: 80 main room, 10 private room. Car park. No children under 10 at D. No smoking in dining-room. Wheelchair access (1 step; also WC). Occasional music   ACCOMMODATION: 17 rooms, all with bath/shower. TV. Phone. B&B £75 to £155. Rooms for disabled. Children welcome. High teas for children. Baby facilities. Dogs welcome in bedrooms only. Afternoon teas. Fishing (*The Which? Hotel Guide*)   £5

AYLESBURY Buckinghamshire   map 3

▲ *Hartwell House* ♥ ⚡✳

Oxford Road, Aylesbury HP17 8NL
TEL: (01296) 747444   FAX: (01296) 747450
EMAIL: info@hartwell-house.com   COOKING 4
on A418, 2m from Aylesbury towards Oxford   COST £34–£68

As the glossy brochure points out, Hartwell has a venerable history. The site was mentioned in the Domesday Book, Louis XIV stayed here, and it was home to the forebears of American General Robert E. Lee. The brochure is not the only glossy thing about it either. Historic House Hotels have done a smart restoration job, and behind the Jacobean and Georgian façade are some opulently decorated rooms. It has been 'corporatised', with conference facilities, swimming-pool and gym, and there is a degree of formality about the arrangements, which is not to everybody's taste, and of course the food is not cheap, but it is worth turning up for.

Roger Barstow's haute-cuisine ambitions match the surroundings, as he serves up some modern interpretations of classic dishes on a long evening *carte*: an assortment of Japanese-style tuna with horseradish and chilli dressing; pork rillette made from Gloucester Old Spot; or tapénade-glazed red mullet with aubergine and roast garlic. He goes to the trouble of making morel raviolis to float in Jerusalem artichoke soup, and piles on the luxury of ceps and truffles with roast Aylesbury duckling, but keeps an eye out for sharp flavours too, as in a coconut brulée and sorbet with lime syrup, or passion-fruit parfait encased in dark chocolate. Wines aren't cheap either, but there's no doubting their quality. Grand names from the Old World mingle with star producers from the New (imbibers on a budget should look to South America) while the sweet-of-tooth (and flush-of-wallet) may well be tempted by one of four rare Vouvrays from Gaston Huet. House wines from southern France are £12.90. CELLARMAN'S CHOICE: Coteaux de l'Ardèche, Cépage Viognier 1995, £21; Lirac, La Fermade, 1994, Dom. Maby £24.50.

CHEF: Roger Barstow   PROPRIETOR: Historic House Hotels Ltd   OPEN: all week 12.30 to 1.45, 7.30 to 9.30 (9.45 Fri and Sat)   CLOSED: closed to non-residents 24 to 26 Dec   MEALS: Set L £20.50 (2 courses) to £27.50, Set D £42   SERVICE: net prices, card slips closed   CARDS: Delta, MasterCard, Switch, Visa   DETAILS: 60 seats. 20 seats outside. Private parties: 60 main room, 18 to 30 private rooms. Car park. Vegetarian meals. No children under 8. Jacket and tie at D. No smoking in dining-room. Wheelchair access (also WC). Occasional music   ACCOMMODATION: 46 rooms, all with bath/shower. TV. Phone. Room only £125 to £280. Rooms for disabled. No children under 8. Afternoon teas. Swimming-pool. Fishing (*The Which? Hotel Guide*)

BAKEWELL Derbyshire   map 8

Renaissance ⅚✳

| Bath Street, Bakewell DE45 1BX | COOKING 4 |
| TEL: (01629) 812687 | COST £28–£46 |

Hidden in a quiet street away from the town centre, this heavily beamed old house has done time as a restaurant under several owners. Attractively decorated, it offers a comfortable welcome in the form of a red and green bar area, and a dining-room reached through two latticed arches. In these days of mixing and matching, the proudly French menus may almost count as a branch of ethnic cooking. Luxury ingredients such as truffles and foie gras are conscientiously imported from Eric Piedaniel's homeland, the former perhaps topping poached scallops on leek purée, the latter cooked with apple in puff pastry and sauced with cider. There is no shyness, though, about offering such relatively simple bistro-style dishes as veal tournedos wrapped in bacon with 'a rustic mustard sauce'. A memorable market dish one night was a fish casserole that mixed salmon and tuna among other items in a powerful lobster broth. Crêpes Suzette done by the book crop up among desserts, as does an impressive fig tart that boasts 'a creamy base and crisp pastry' and comes with prune and armagnac sauce. The wine list trips lightly through classic French regions but also finds space for a small New World showing. House Chardonnay and Merlot are £9.80.

CHEF: Eric Piedaniel   PROPRIETORS: Eric and C. Piedaniel, and D. Beraud   OPEN: Tue to Sun L 12 to 2 (reservations only), Tue to Sat D 7 to 9.30   CLOSED: 31 Dec, first 2 weeks Jan, first 2 weeks Aug   MEALS: Set L and D £18.95 plus supplements   SERVICE: not inc   CARDS: Delta, MasterCard, Switch, Visa   DETAILS: 70 seats. Private parties: 50 main room, 25 private room. Vegetarian meals. Children's helpings. No smoking in dining-room. Wheelchair access (2 steps; not WC). Music

---

Prices quoted in the Guide *are based on information supplied by restaurateurs. The prices quoted at the top of each entry represent a range, from the lowest meal price to the highest; the latter is inflated by 20 per cent to take account of likely price rises during the year of the* Guide.

BARNET Hertfordshire	map 3

Mims

63 East Barnet Road, Barnet EN4 8RN	COOKING 6
TEL/FAX: (0181) 449 2974	COST £24–£37

Reports continue to flood in for this unassuming neighbourhood restaurant, with its dark tables and hand-scrawled, daily-changing menu. Those schooled by experience in what Ali Al-Sersy can do are satisfied to report that the message is 'steady as he goes'. When a chef genuinely impresses, it is often with the most disarmingly simple means, as attested by a pair of Sunday lunchers who began with caramelised onion tart made with soft, friable pastry, and roast mackerel with a poached egg and potato salad, both delivering powerful flavours without the need for excess garnish. Skate with a caper crust on a bed of spinach and rösti potatoes emphasises the confidence with which fish is handled. Menu descriptions have a way of underselling a dish, but that often adds to the pleasure when what turns up is so good.

Then again, there is a deceptive richness about much of the cooking, even when all the menu may have announced is 'roast rump of lamb, roast vegetables'. Foie gras is used to memorable effect in a sauce with sauté young guinea-fowl, for instance, and nothing quite prepared one diner for the presentation of cinnamon ice-cream: a chocolate cylinder garnished with a huge fright-wig of spun sugar ('I didn't know whether to eat it or comb it'). Otherwise, tiramisù has been reckoned one of the best for miles, though cafetière coffee could do with pepping up. Service comes in for criticism as to pace, and can be a touch prickly under pressure. French house wines are £9.50 (£2.75 a glass).

CHEF: A. Al-Sersy PROPRIETORS: P. Azarfar and A. Al-Sersy OPEN: Tue to Fri L 12 to 3, Tue to Sat D 6.30 to 11, Sun 12 to 10.30 CLOSED: 25 and 26 Dec MEALS: Set L £10.50 (2 courses) to £15, Set D £16 (2 courses) to £20.50 SERVICE: not inc CARDS: Delta, MasterCard, Visa DETAILS: 45 seats. Private parties: 60 main room. No children under 7. No cigars/pipes in dining-room. Wheelchair access (also WC). Music (£5)

BARNSLEY South Yorkshire	map 9

Armstrongs ♟

102 Dodworth Road, Barnsley S70 6HL	COOKING 4
TEL: (01226) 240113	COST £24–£51

'An absolute triumph in Barnsley,' was how one correspondent described this pleasantly furnished Victorian town house. Nick Pound continues to offer plenty of good deals, from special two-course lunches to mid-week fixed-price dinners. His culinary imagination is allowed full rein in the evening, when he embarks on a world tour, picking up roast breast of duck with kumquats and fennel, and fillet of beef nivernaise along the way. Fish is strongly represented in the shape of pan-fried squid with Peruvian black potatoes, and Cornish sea bass with pak choi greens and fresh water chestnuts.

In simpler vein, thick slices of smoked salmon come with a potato pancake, while 'moist' chicken breast receives a 'confidently robust' rosemary and garlic sauce. Crème brûlée has been described as 'technically perfect and thickly glazed', or you might finish with iced butterscotch meringue cake, or a sultana tartlet with jasmine tea sorbet. Deborah Swift runs front-of-house with an assured touch. Wines on the appealingly varied list are accompanied by snippets of useful information. The northern hemisphere has the edge over the southern on quantity, but quality is high wherever you look. Prices are fair, with the house selection beginning at £10.95.

CHEF: Nick Pound   PROPRIETORS: Nick Pound and Deborah Swift   OPEN: Tue to Fri L 12 to 1.30, Tue to Sat D 7 to 9.30   MEALS: alc (main courses £13 to £17.50). Set L Tue to Fri £7.50 (2 courses) to £14.50, Set D Tue to Fri £16.95   SERVICE: not inc   CARDS: Amex, Delta, MasterCard, Switch, Visa   DETAILS: 50 seats. Private parties: 40 main room. Car park. Vegetarian meals. Children's helpings. No pipes/cigars in dining-room. Wheelchair access (1 step; not WC). Music

---

BARNSTAPLE Devon   map 1

▲ *Lynwood House* ⁵⭑

Bishop's Tawton Road, Barnstaple EX32 9EF
TEL: (01271) 343695   FAX: (01271) 379340   COOKING 3
1m S of town centre, before A377 roundabout   COST £33–£53

A 'Victorian gentleman's residence' on the southern outskirts of town is the setting for this family-run restaurant-with-rooms, where round mahogany tables, potted plants and candles emphasise the era. It 'feels like a home', with a welcome to match. Fish is a mainstay of both the 'lighter meal' menu – goujons of lemon sole, prawn omelette – and the à la carte, which might include brill in crab sauce, scallops wrapped in bacon, or a pot of mixed seafood in a 'thermidor' sauce. Chunky fish soup has long been a successful way to begin, and wing of skate with black butter has had the thumbs-up, but there may also be venison medallions, or crisp-skinned duck, plus a couple of vegetarian options. A 'savoury of the day' makes a welcome alternative to calorific puddings of bread-and-butter, or meringue with a hot toffee sauce. A generally sound and varied list of wines begins with house French at £9.90.

CHEFS: Ruth and Matthew Roberts   PROPRIETORS: the Roberts family   OPEN: Mon to Fri L 12 to 1.45, Mon to Sat D 7 to 9.30   MEALS: alc (main courses £14.50 to £29)   SERVICE: not inc   CARDS: Amex, Delta, Diners, MasterCard, Switch, Visa   DETAILS: 40 seats. Private parties: 60 main room, 20 private room. Car park. Vegetarian meals. Children's helpings. No smoking in dining-room. Wheelchair access (1 step; also WC). No music   ACCOMMODATION: 5 rooms, all with bath/shower. TV. Phone. B&B £47.50 to £67.50. Children welcome. No dogs in public rooms   (£5)

BARTON-UPON-HUMBER North Lincolnshire   map 9

▲ *Elio's* £

11 Market Place, Barton-upon-Humber DN18 5DA   COOKING 1
TEL/FAX: (01652) 635147   COST £19–£55

A courtyard extension offers the tempting prospect of al fresco dining outside Elio-Mario Grossi's long-serving 'ristorante' in Barton's marketplace. Sound local supplies of game, vegetables and particularly fish are deployed for a repertoire of dishes that moves beyond 'Pavarotti trattoria' into something more modern. Daily specials are the pick of the bunch: here you might find carpaccio, chargrilled tuna steak with roasted peppers, or calf's liver alla veneziana with polenta. Otherwise choose from a clutch of pizzas, pasta dishes and old favourites along the lines of chicken cacciatore, fillet steak topped with Gorgonzola on a port and cream sauce, or saltimbocca alla Romana. Italian ice-creams, zabaglione, and oranges in Grand Marnier are typical sweets. House wine is £8.95

CHEFS: Elio-Mario Grossi, Nicolas Lyon and Louise Kuyath   PROPRIETOR: Elio-Mario Grossi
OPEN: Tue to Fri L 12 to 2, Mon to Sat D 6.30 to 10.30   CLOSED: 25 and 26 Dec, bank hols, last two weeks Aug   MEALS: alc (main courses £6.50 to £19.50). Set L £7.95 (2 courses)   SERVICE: not inc, 10% for parties of 6 or more   CARDS: Amex, Delta, Diners, MasterCard, Switch, Visa
DETAILS: 65 seats. 16 seats outside. Private parties: 75 main room, 8 private room. Car park. Vegetarian meals. Children's helpings. Wheelchair access (1 step, not WC). Music
ACCOMMODATION: 2 rooms, both with bath/shower. TV. Room only £35 to £45. No dogs (£5)

BARWICK Somerset   map 2

▲ *Little Barwick House* ♥ ⁵⁄✳

Barwick BA22 9TD
TEL: (01935) 423902   FAX: (01935) 420908   COOKING 5
off A37, take second left opposite Red House pub   COST £28–£33

In a quiet village just outside Yeovil, set amid folly-strewn rolling countryside, this comfortable and welcoming Georgian house is 'totally relaxing'. 'There are no pretensions of grandeur,' since it is an easy-going family enterprise. Meals might begin with a drink outside in fine weather, and there are two waves of pre-meal nibbles, so anybody aiming to take advantage of all four subsequent courses should bring a good appetite. The bright red dining-room's flexible menu also offers a two- or three-course option, centred around a 'wide, appealing choice' of dishes with a couple of daily extras.

Veronica Colley does a good job managing the conflicting demands of traditionalists and modernists, serving up pots of creamy, cheese-topped smoked haddock, alongside duck breast marinated in garlic, chilli, ginger and soy sauce. It is all underpinned by the 'wholesome feeling' of good ingredients. Among main courses to draw praise is a version of fish and chips that included five or six different species, 'all clearly fresh and lightly fried', and Sussex pie made with beef and mushroom. Cheese has been recommended, and crème brûlée is popular, or there may be chocolate brownie with warm butterscotch sauce. The wine list meanders round the vinous globe, taking a rather mysterious route, but the range of varietals is good and very affordable prices make the journey worthwhile. Nine house wines from France, Germany and South Africa are all £10.90 a bottle.

'You must leave the car in the drive and walk in via the outhouse and kitchens, passing a notice saying, "Do not feed the chefs." ' (On eating in Scotland)

CHEF: Veronica Colley   PROPRIETORS: Christopher and Veronica Colley   OPEN: Mon to Sat D only 7 to 9 (9.30 Sat); Sun D for residents only   CLOSED: 25 Dec to 1 Jan   MEALS: Set D £20.90 (2 courses) to £25.90   SERVICE: net prices, card slips closed   CARDS: Amex, MasterCard, Switch, Visa   DETAILS: 40 seats. Private parties: 40 main room. Car park. Vegetarian meals. Children's helpings. No smoking in dining-room. No music. Air-conditioned   ACCOMMODATION: 6 rooms, all with bath/shower. TV. Phone. D,B&B £73.50 to £127. Children welcome. High teas for children (*The Which? Hotel Guide*) (£5)

BASLOW Derbyshire   map 9

▲ *Fischer's Baslow Hall* ♥ ⁵✳

Calver Road, Baslow DE45 1RR   COOKING 8
TEL: (01246) 583259   FAX: (01246) 583818   COST £35–£70

Not far from Chatsworth House, this stone-built Edwardian mansion, up a short, curved, tree-lined drive, is surrounded by garden. Drinks are taken on cushion-strewn sofas round an immense fireplace in the lounge, and walls are hung with a variety of paintings and prints. The dining-room is small considering the size of the house, its understated Chinese theme emphasising a turn-of-the-century bourgeois feel. A fine display of appetisers sets the tone, indicating the detail and workmanship that characterises Max Fischer's approach, and the coffee-cup of soup served at table reaps high praise, be it parsley with a poached quail's egg, or shellfish bisque with the flavour of roasted shells.

Lunch offers a choice of four items per course, dinner six or more, and Max Fischer follows the seasons as closely as anybody. In classic fashion he offers shellfish, foie gras and vegetable dishes to start: lobster salad with peas and asparagus, or disarmingly simple fat roast scallops, 'zingily fresh and beautifully seasoned', with a dark slick of intense sherry and ethereal truffle oil. Dishes generally have a strong focus, and timing makes the most of prime materials: fresh, sweet, firm-fleshed bream on a bed of mashed potato, or squab pigeon and foie gras wrapped in Savoy cabbage. As for industry, pig's trotter takes the biscuit, its sticky skin filled with a refined eggy meaty mix, its sauce reduced to just the right consistency.

Contrasts of sweetness and tartness show to good effect in desserts, some of which play on an integrated idea – raspberry soufflé well partnered with chocolate sauce – while others take a more segmented approach: a plate of elaborately worked exotic fruit desserts, for example, or variations on a theme of rhubarb. The kitchen runs the show and sets the pace, and service is smooth, relaxed, courteous. Café Max provides a less expensive alternative, offering maybe duck spring roll, monkfish with pease pudding, and lemon and mascarpone meringues. The wine list features quality drinking from both hemispheres, and, while there are few bargains, mark-ups are far from outrageous. House wines from France and Italy are £13. CELLARMAN'S CHOICE: Morton Estate Sauvignon Blanc 1996, Hawkes Bay, New Zealand, £18; Cumaro Rosso Conero 1994, Umani Ronchi, Italy, £24.

The Guide*'s top-rated restaurants are listed near the front of the book.*

CHEF: Max Fischer   PROPRIETORS: Max and Susan Fischer   OPEN: Sun to Fri L 12 to 1.30, Mon to Sat D 7 to 9.30 (Sun D residents only)   CLOSED: 25 and 26 Dec   MEALS: Set L Mon to Fri £20 (2 courses) to £24, Set L Sun £24, Set D £45   SERVICE: not inc   CARDS: Amex, Delta, Diners, MasterCard, Switch, Visa   DETAILS: 76 seats. Private parties: 40 main room, 12 and 24 private rooms. Car park. Children's helpings. No children under 12 after 7pm. No smoking in dining-room. Wheelchair access (3 steps; also WC). No music   ACCOMMODATION: 6 rooms, all with bath/shower. TV. Phone. B&B £80 to £130. Children welcome. High teas for children. Baby facilities. No dogs (*The Which? Hotel Guide*)

BATCOMBE Somerset

map 2

Three Horseshoes ♥ ⁵⫶✳

NEW ENTRY

Batcombe BA4 6HE

TEL: (01749) 850359   FAX: (01749) 850615

3½m S of A361 Shepton Mallet to Frome road, at the east of the village

COOKING 5
COST £20–£39

Although slightly off the beaten track, this grey-stone hostelry is easy to locate behind the gargoyled and majestically spired village church. It is prettily decorated in uncluttered fashion and has a 'child-friendly' garden. Carole Evans used to be at Poppies (at the Roebuck; see entry, Brimfield), where she worked very much in the vanguard of the country-pub renaissance. Menus may embrace potted crab with toast fingers, cauliflower and Stilton soup, and roast leg of lamb with mint sauce (in which context the serving of passion-fruit coulis with Denhay ham might cause surprise), but the plaudits Carole Evans gains are for the industrious attention to detail she brings to the transformation of impeccable materials.

Grey mullet is fried enough to crisp the skin, its sauce an expressive tomato potion full of deep-fried capers, the olive oil mash 'bashed' in the approved manner rather than liquidised. A bright green moat of garden-pea sauce deepens the appeal of a thick piece of good tournedos. When it comes to afters, the kitchen is unashamedly happy to give people what they want: 'icky sticky' toffee pudding, or glazed lemon tart with a spoonful of top-gear raspberry coulis poured over it. With fine home-made breads and service that, on early reports, seemed inexperienced but was learning fast, this place will certainly add lustre to the Somerset scene. Wines are an attractively priced bunch, drawn mostly from France with a few New World bins helping to broaden the appeal. Half-bottles are generous, and half a dozen house wines from France, South Africa and Australia are all £9.95 a bottle. CELLARMAN'S CHOICE: Bourgogne Blanc 'Les Setilles' 1995, Olivier Leflaive, £14.50; Los Vascos Cabernet Sauvignon 1995, Chile, £14.

CHEF: Carole Evans   PROPRIETOR: West Country Village Inns   OPEN: all week 12 to 1.45, 7 to 9 (9.30 Sat)   MEALS: alc (main courses L £5.50 to £8, D £5.50 to £13.50). Set L Sun £7.95 (1 course) to £15.95   SERVICE: not inc   CARDS: Delta, MasterCard, Switch, Visa   DETAILS: 78 seats. 40 seats outside. Private parties: 30 main room. Car park. Vegetarian meals. Children's helpings. No smoking in dining-room. No music

---

New main entries and restaurant closures are listed near the front of the book.

Clos du Roy 🍳

1 Seven Dials, Saw Close, Bath BA1 1EN	COOKING 3
TEL: (01225) 444450 FAX: (01225) 404044	COST £22–£51

The restaurant inhabits a horseshoe-shaped first-floor room overlooking a pedestrian precinct by the Theatre Royal, perhaps not Bath's comeliest environ, but comfortable enough. A musical theme predominates, not just courtesy of the pianist but in the décor, too, which boasts wall-mounted lutes among its diversions. François Gardilloux arrived from the South of France towards the end of 1997, to continue the straightforward, contemporary French style established by the owner: a neatly presented and disarmingly simple first course of sauté scallops with tomato vinaigrette, or a more elaborate caramelised onion tart topped with foie gras in a honeyed red wine sauce. Rack of lamb with a mustard and herb crust is an old friend, or there may be diverting fish specials such as sea bass with braised fennel and a veal jus. The menu-writing is French-florid, so farandoles and carnivals are all over the place, Galia melon is 'rehoused' with Parmesan cheese wafers, and you may finish with the suggestively Dali-esque 'Infamous Chocolate Fantasy Plate'. French service is generally well paced and observant, but has been known to affect the famous shrug when things go wrong. The stylistically organised wine list is by no means confined to France, and the sound choices are keenly priced. House wines are £9.95.

CHEF: François Gardilloux   PROPRIETORS: Philippe and Emma Roy   OPEN: all week 12 to 2.30, 6 to 10.30   MEALS: alc (main courses £11 to £17.50). Set L £9.95 (2 courses) to £12.95, Set D £16.50 (2 courses) to £19.50   SERVICE: not inc; 10% (optional) for parties of 6 or more; card slips closed   CARDS: Amex, Delta, Diners, MasterCard, Switch, Visa   DETAILS: 95 seats. 20 seats outside. Vegetarian meals. Children's helpings. No children under 8. No cigars/pipes in dining-room. Wheelchair access (not WC). Music   £5

Hole in the Wall 🍷 ✽

16 George Street, Bath BA1 2EN	COOKING 4
TEL/FAX: (01225) 425242	COST £21–£49

The entrance is high on a raised pavement, but steps inside lead back down to what can feel like a basement until you look out of the back window and see daylight. The old fireplace, carriage lamps, tartan banquette seating, hard-wearing carpet and bare wooden tables might recall a pub, but the menus tell a different story. A contemporary mix of mostly European ideas runs from foie gras on toasted brioche, to more intricate terrine of skate and whole scallops held together by 'a sort of brown smoky mousse', wrapped in a cabbage leaf, and served with a warm vinaigrette containing caper berries.

A degree of novelty keeps interest high, as in clear vegetable soup with truffle and lamb tortellini, but dishes rarely stray too far from such classical combinations as duck with orange, or a variation on jambon persillé that pleased one reporter: made with chunks of pig's tongue and wild rabbit in a 'lovely slithery' gelatinous medium, served with piccalilli. Both kitchen and front-of-house have put on an uneven performance during the past year, disappointing some, captivating others. The latest we have is encouraging, indicating that the kitchen is powered by 'real cooking'. Test that with an individual, light chocolate tart in chocolate-coloured pastry, served with a cherry sauce. Wines are sourced mainly from the Old World, although some choice bins from the New make a valuable contribution to the range of styles. Prices start in France at £11.50, and 26 wines by the glass begin at £2.75 and end at £6 for champagne. CELLARMAN'S CHOICE: Graves, Ch. Beauregard-Ducasse 1995, £22; Ch. Musar 1991, Gaston Hochar, Lebanon, £17.

CHEF: Eric Lepine   PROPRIETORS: Christopher and Gunna Chown   OPEN: Mon to Sat 12 to 2, 6 to 11   MEALS: alc (main courses L all £5.50, D £15 to £18). Set L £11.50, Set D Mon to Fri £19.50   SERVICE: not inc   CARDS: Amex, Delta, MasterCard, Switch, Visa   DETAILS: 80 seats. Private parties: 24 main room, 20 to 30 private room. Vegetarian meals. Children's helpings. No smoking in 1 dining-room. No music. Air-conditioned   £5

▲ Lettonie ♀ ⅘✳

| 35 Kelston Road, Bath BA1 3QH | COOKING 7 |
| TEL: (01225) 446676   FAX: (01225) 447541 | COST £41–£75 |

They've moved at last, from a suburban shopping parade in Bristol to these swish new premises: a Georgian house of mellow Bath stone with a large reception hall and a dark, comfortable lounge bar with swagged curtains. The dining-room, decorated with 'institutional' paintings, overlooks a terraced garden that slopes away towards the Avon Valley. It seems the most natural thing in the world for a brilliant owner-chef to move from cramped premises that don't do justice to his talent to spacious ones that do, although in the process a one-man band tends to become a small brigade, or a small brigade a large one, and the cooking changes. So it has to some extent here.

The style retains much that is familiar from the old Lettonie. This is high French cooking with distinctive Latvian flourishes, including the magnificent flaming duck egg and caviare starter, as well as bortsch terrine with beef pirogi and soured cream. Clever devices and time-consuming workmanship also remain a characteristic, for example a whole scallop shell sealed with puff pastry, enclosing half a dozen slices of scallop and roe; or a boudin blanc, cut into small pieces, heavily seared, and arranged alongside blobs of dark mushroom essence around a mix of salad leaves and trompette mushrooms. Pig's trotter is another labour-intensive and successful dish, perhaps stuffed with sweet breads, chicken and mushrooms, in a parsley cream sauce.

Among the stars of 'acclaimed' desserts have been pear mousse with toffee ice-cream, a 'light, puffed up' caramel sponge tart reminiscent of Bakewell, and dark chocolate ice and banana sorbet in a pastry basket, surrounded by caramel-coated banana slices. Reports over the year have been mixed, one correspondent, for example, finding that 'Martin Blunos has not lost his touch', another wondering if some dishes have lacked a sense of purpose and direction; and prices have risen, though that was perhaps to be expected. Service has had its ups and downs in terms of both warmth and competence, but 'unobtrusive' and 'totally professional' seem to sum it up well, and the wine waitress has been commended for her knowledge. Wines are predominantly French, with some particularly good burgundies, and a few choice bins from other countries add depth. Five house wines from France, Portugal and New Zealand start at £15.80. CELLARMAN'S CHOICE: St-Aubin premier cru 'Les Frionnes' 1996, Sylvain Langoureau, £40; Givry 1994, 'Clos Jus' 1994, Mouton, £31.

CHEF: Martin Blunos   PROPRIETORS: Siân and Martin Blunos   OPEN: Tue to Sat 12 to 2, 7 to 9.30   MEALS: Set L £25, Set D £44.50   SERVICE: not inc   CARDS: Amex, Delta, Diners, MasterCard, Switch, Visa   DETAILS: 34 seats. Private parties: 16 main room, 16 private room. Car park. Children's helpings. No smoking in dining-room. Music   ACCOMMODATION: 5 rooms, all with bath/shower. TV. Phone. B&B £95 to £165. Children welcome

Moody Goose ✸

7A Kingsmead Square, Bath BA1 2AB	COOKING 4
TEL/FAX: (01225) 466688	COST £23–£50

Just in case you were wondering, there is indeed a moody (or at least blue) goose standing in the middle of the dining-room at this smart basement restaurant. Whatever its temperament, it makes its presence felt; one luncher was tempted to give it a pat on the head, but a pat on the back for Stephen Shore's inventive cooking sufficed instead. There is a sense of restless experimentation about the menus that might deliver galantine of partridge stuffed with mushrooms and apricot, or roast cod with aubergine fritters, followed by top-drawer chocolate tart with vanilla sauce, though one reporter was less convinced by the matching of lime and walnuts with lamb's liver. This is the modern British idiom in full flow, cheerfully borrowing the popular bits from French haute cuisine – as in a highly successful foie gras parfait with diamonds of Sauternes jelly and toasted brioche – but offering rice-pudding with apple and cinnamon for afters as well. Seasonality remains the guiding principle throughout. 'A warm welcome and thoroughly professional service' help to send people away happy. The competently compiled wine list majors in France, and opens with an international delegation of house wines from £10.50.

CHEFS: Stephen Shore and Andy Blackburn   PROPRIETORS: Stephen and Victoria Shore   OPEN: Mon to Sat 12 to 2, 6 to 9.30 (10 Sat)   CLOSED: 2 weeks Feb, bank hols (open 25 Dec)   MEALS: alc (main courses L £9.50 to £12.50, D £15 to £17.50). Set L £10 (2 courses) to £13.50, Set pre-theatre D (until 7pm) £10 (2 courses) to £13.50   SERVICE: not inc   CARDS: Amex, Delta, Diners, MasterCard, Switch, Visa   DETAILS: 30 seats. Private parties: 25 main room, 8 private room. Children's helpings. No children under 7. No smoking in dining-room. No music

No. 5 Bistro £ ✸

5 Argyle Street, Bath BA2 4BA	
TEL: (01225) 444499 FAX: (01225) 318668	COOKING 3
EMAIL: chome@globalnet.co.uk	COST £20–£44

'As bistro-ish a bistro as I have ever come across' is one reporter's summing up of No. 5, with its bare pine floor and poster-crowded walls, candles in bottles and lazily turning ceiling fan. The printed menu is supplemented by blackboard specials, and while there's fish soup with saffron aïoli, and pork medallions in brandy cream, a strain of gentle creativity is also allowed in, in the form of roasted quails on wild rice with apricots, chilli and lemon. Kick off perhaps with 'superlatively juicy' salmon and cod fish-cakes wrapped in rösti with lemon and caper sauce, and follow that with rich and colourful charred tuna steak with a tomato and chilli salsa. Grilling fruits with a sabayon is a favoured dessert technique, or there may be 'rib-stickingly good' rice-pudding with a generously brandied sauce of dried apricots. Delays can occur when things get busy, and the background pop is relentless. Wines are a slightly perfunctory selection, but note that you can take your own on Mondays and Tuesdays. House offerings start at £8.95.

CHEFS: Stephen Smith, Paul Hearne and Sarah Grantins PROPRIETORS: Stephen Smith and Charles Home OPEN: Tue to Sat L 12 to 2.30, Mon to Sat D 6.30 to 10 (10.30 Fri, 11 Sat) CLOSED: 1 week Christmas MEALS: alc (main courses L £5.50 to £8, D £10 to £12.50). BYO Mon and Tue (no corkage) SERVICE: not inc CARDS: Amex, Delta, Diners, MasterCard, Switch, Visa DETAILS: 35 seats. Private parties: 16 main room. Vegetarian meals. Children's helpings. No smoking in dining-room. Wheelchair access (2 steps; not WC). Music

▲ Queensberry Hotel, Olive Tree ♥ ✸

Russel Street, Bath BA1 2QF
TEL: (01225) 447928 FAX: (01225) 446065
EMAIL: queensbury@dial.pipex.com

COOKING 5
COST £23–£49

The Queensberry is just far enough away from the hustle and bustle of Bath to provide a refuge even at the height of the tourist season, although the journey is easily walkable. The atmosphere in the basement dining-room is 'lively and jolly, the décor bright and breezy', a term that arguably applies to the food too: for example, prawns, salmon and monkfish set in well-flavoured aspic and decorated with parsley leaves; fine and generous grilled lobster with herb butter; or breast of Gressingham duck with well-wrought red wine sauce. The guiding principles of lightness and freshness are not forgotten even when it comes to a steamed chocolate sponge pudding with matching sauce and ice-cream. Wines are a food-friendly collection, chosen with one eye on quality and the other on value for money, with some serious French bins rounding things off well. House wines from Gascony and the Côte de Tarn are £11.50; six wines by the glass cost £2.50. CELLARMAN'S CHOICE: Alamos Ridge Chardonnay 1995, Mendoza, Argentina, £13.50; Qupé Syrah 1994, Santa Maria Valley, California, £28.

CHEF: Mathew Prowse PROPRIETORS: Stephen and Penny Ross OPEN: Mon to Sat L 12 to 2, all week D 7 to 10 (9 Sun) CLOSED: 5 days Christmas MEALS: alc (main courses £11.50 to £16.50). Set L £11.50 (2 courses) to £13.50, Set D Sun to Fri £21 SERVICE: not inc, card slips closed CARDS: Delta, MasterCard, Switch, Visa DETAILS: 60 seats. Private parties: 40 main room, 40 private room. Vegetarian meals. Children's helpings. No smoking in dining-room. Wheelchair access (4 steps; also WC). Occasional music. Air-conditioned ACCOMMODATION: 29 rooms, all with bath/shower. TV. Phone. B&B £89 to £195. Rooms for disabled. Children welcome. High teas for children. Baby facilities. Guide dogs only. Afternoon teas (The Which? Hotel Guide)

Occasional music in the details at the end of an entry means live or recorded music is played in the dining-room only rarely or for special events. No music means it is never played.

▲ *Royal Crescent, Brasserie/Pimpernel's* ✠

16 Royal Crescent, Bath BA1 2LS	COOKING 5 Brasserie, 4 Pimpernel's
TEL: (01225) 823333 FAX: (01225) 339401	COST £36–£73

Under the same ownership as Cliveden (see entry, Taplow), the Royal Crescent now has two restaurants. Refurbishment has left an understated entrance (don't walk past it), and the Brasserie is where the restaurant always used to be. Despite the changes, this still presents a slightly formal face, with beige walls and starched white tablecloths, but offers a lively enough menu of seared tuna with tomato salsa, roast codling with chorizo, and smooth textured rabbit boudin with black pudding mash and a dark sticky sauce. Generous portions seem to be the norm, with a huge scallop wrapped in crispy pancetta, served on a spicy samosa with a pungent curry oil to start, and a 'gargantuan' braised shin of veal in a gelatinous sauce, 'a classic of its kind', served with a strewing of sculpted vegetables and a creamy lick of celeriac purée. Finish with warm chocolate fondant, or raspberry crumble with ginger ice-cream. The wine list is short, trendy and to the point, but with house wine over £20 a bottle it might make sense to drink one of the 17 wines by the glass from £3 upwards.

Pimpernel's, which puts a Far Eastern spin on European food, is in a 'starkly Georgian' dining-room (nothing Asian about it) down a staircase, underneath the pavement. Its three-course menu goes in for tiger prawns with a dribble of lemon grass cream, baked foie gras with fresh mango chutney, and squab pigeon with lime sauce and ginger dressing, although flavours of citrus, chilli, garlic, soy and fish sauce tend to be 'rounded down rather than up', leaving sweetness a dominant characteristic. Presentation is a forte, from the black and turquoise cartwheel plates on which dramatically arranged main courses arrive, to the large mesh of spun sugar that decorated an inspector's ripe mango and papaya with mint sorbet. Our information suggests that the cheese extravaganza is not the dessert of choice. While the menu remains the same for much of the time, the short selection of wines changes monthly. Prices start around £20.

CHEF: Steven Blake   PROPRIETOR: Cliveden Plc   OPEN: Brasserie all week 12.30 to 2, 7 to 9.30 (10 Sat); Pimpernel's Tue to Sat D only 7 to 10   CLOSED: Jan (Pimpernel's only)   MEALS: Brasserie alc (main courses £14.50 to £20), Set L £15.50 (2 courses) to £19.50, Set D £23 (2 courses) to £31; Pimpernel's Set D £42   SERVICE: not inc   CARDS: Delta, Diners, MasterCard, Switch, Visa   DETAILS: 45 seats (Brasserie), 24 seats (Pimpernel's). Private parties: 65 main room (Brasserie), 24 main room (Pimpernel's), 40 and 80 private rooms. Car park. Vegetarian meals. No children under 16 (Pimpernel's). No smoking in 1 dining-room. Air-conditioned. Occasional music   ACCOMMODATION: 45 rooms, all with bath/shower. TV. Phone. Room only £170 to £675. Children welcome. High teas for children. Baby facilities. Well-behaved dogs welcome. Afternoon teas. Swimming-pool (*The Which? Hotel Guide*)

Woods

9–13 Alfred Street, Bath BA1 2QX	COOKING 2
TEL: (01225) 314812 FAX: (01225) 443146	COST £18–£45

The Prices have occupied this L-shaped ground-floor dining-room, in a lofty Georgian terrace opposite the Assembly Rooms, for 20 years. William Morris curtains, steel and cane chairs and horsy prints combine to produce the feel of a 'local let's-eat-out' place, and there is no shortage of dishes to keep regulars happy: spiced leg of lamb with mint and fruit couscous, or poached fillet of cod with a crust of herbs and Parmesan, for example. In the event that main courses fail to set the blood racing, there are plenty of 'irresistible' starters, including chicken terrine with a 'much-needed' tomato chutney, and, the highlight of one meal, a mound of fresh crab lightly seasoned with coriander, lemon and black pepper, with a herby sauce around it. 'Cholesterol Corner' might offer crème caramel with orange, or sticky praline pudding with butterscotch sauce and clotted cream. Service is 'shirt-sleeved, very attentive, constantly on the prowl', and, given the two-course lunch deal, the place is understandably popular. Unless you are a big spender, aim for the dozen wines under £15, all available by the glass, including house French at £10.

CHEF: David Price   PROPRIETORS: Mr and Mrs D.G. Price   OPEN: all week L 12 to 2.30, Mon to Sat D 6 to 11   CLOSED: 26 Dec and 1 Jan   MEALS: alc (main courses £7.50 to £15.50). Set L £7 (2 courses), Set L Sun £14, Set D Mon to Thur £8 (2 courses) to £15, Set D Fri £11.25 to £15, Set D Sat £19.95   SERVICE: not inc   CARDS: MasterCard, Visa   DETAILS: 140 seats. 12 seats outside. Private parties: 100 main room, 40 private room. Vegetarian meals. Children's helpings. No cigars/pipes in dining-room. Wheelchair access (1 step; also WC). Music £5

BEAMINSTER Dorset   map 2

▲ *Bridge House* 🍴 ⚡✖

3 Prout Bridge, Beaminster DT8 3AY   COOKING 2
TEL: (01308) 862200   FAX: (01308) 863700   COST £19–£37

This thirteenth-century stone house with thick walls and mullioned windows is a 'civilised and restful' place to be. A log fire burns in the lounge, the conservatory looks on to a well-tended high-walled garden, and the dining-room is a wash of pink-painted wood. Simon Clewlow cooks along similar lines to his predecessor, and while the food might not have been out of place a decade ago – slices of Barbary duck breast with a raspberry vinegar sauce, for example – it still makes 'a fresh impression', and uses good raw materials, many of them local. There is a welcome lack of pretence about both food and setting, but dishes are neatly presented. Flans and tarts tend to be wedges cut from a large one, as in a spring version made with crumbly pastry, air-dried ham from nearby Denhay Farm, and sun-dried tomatoes. Vegetables, served separately, include a good version of gratin dauphinois. 'Professionally made' ice-creams figure among desserts, and there is a locally sourced help-yourself cheeseboard. Value is considered good, especially at lunch-time, and the abolition of supplements to the fixed-price menu is a welcome development. Fair pricing is a feature of the wine list: 12 house wines under £10.50 a bottle is particularly good going, among them an English white.

CHEF: Simon Clewlow   PROPRIETOR: Peter Pinkster   OPEN: all week 12 to 2, 7 to 9   MEALS: Set L £11.50, Set D £20.50. BYO £8   SERVICE: not inc, card slips closed   CARDS: Amex, Delta, Diners, MasterCard, Switch, Visa   DETAILS: 36 seats. 12 seats outside. Private parties: 40 main room, 16 private room. Car park. Vegetarian meals. Children's helpings. No smoking in dining-room. No music   ACCOMMODATION: 13 rooms, all with bath/shower. TV. Phone. B&B £64 to £112. Rooms for disabled. No children under 12. Dogs welcome in bedrooms only and not left unattended. Afternoon teas (*The Which? Hotel Guide*)

BEESTON Nottinghamshire   map 5

Brasserie 69 £   NEW ENTRY

69 Chilwell Road, Beeston NG9 1EQ   COOKING 2
TEL: (0115) 925 9994   COST £23–£46

Stephen Cook took over this small terraced property in 1997, and his apposite
surname has not been lost on local headline writers. It is a low-budget operation
– brick walls, tiled floors and painted woodwork are the main decorative
features – but the upstairs 'smokers' retreat' has been refurbished, and
renovation is on the cards for the dining-room as the *Guide* goes to press. Cook
cooks a monthly-changing menu of brasserie-style food, from asparagus with
hollandaise to lamb brochette, from honey-glazed duck to baked aubergine with
melted goats' cheese ('fresh, soft, oozing') in a tomato sauce with good French
bread to dip in. Fish dishes – firm, fresh sea bass, or simply grilled Dover sole on
a bed of spinach – are displayed on a blackboard, as are desserts. Service is
friendly, and 20 or so affordable wines start with house French at £8.50.

CHEF/PROPRIETOR: Stephen Cook   OPEN: Tue to Sat D only 7 to 10.30; L and Sun D by
arrangement for parties of 10 or more   MEALS: alc (main courses £8.50 to £19)   SERVICE: not
inc, card slips closed   CARDS: Delta, MasterCard, Switch, Visa   DETAILS: 30 seats. Private
parties: 30 main room. Vegetarian meals. No children under 10. No smoking while others eat.
Music (£5)

BEVERLEY East Riding of Yorkshire   map 9

Wednesdays ▼ £   NEW ENTRY

8 Wednesday Market, Beverley HU17 0DG   COOKING 2
TEL/FAX: (01482) 869727   COST £23–£44

Open not just on Wednesdays but all week, this plainly but cheerfully decorated
restaurant takes its name from its address in the covered market near the minster.
Wendy Rowley is playing an enthusiastic part in bringing modern oriental and
Mediterranean ways to the East Riding, and has a particular mission to look after
vegetarians: that fashionable contemporary dish, the 'stack', appears here
constructed of goats' cheese and spiced aubergine with a relish of sweet peppers.
Crisply fried duck and bacon in a warm salad with plum vinaigrette is a
signature starter, much enjoyed at inspection, while fish preparations – steamed
halibut with tomato sauce and roasted red peppers dressed in good olive oil –
show sound understanding. Accompanying vegetables could do with sprucing
up a bit, but yoghurt and cardamom cream served with sun-dried fruits and lime
syrup is a diverting dessert. There may be delays when the place is busy, but staff
are willing enough. Around 60 wines put together from some cleverly chosen
producers offer quality at manageable prices. The worldly collection is grouped
by style, beginning with 'light, fresh, unoaked' whites and ending with
'particularly fine' reds. CELLARMAN'S CHOICE: Stag's Leap Wine Cellars
Chardonnay 1995, Napa Valley, £27; Pierro Pinot Noir 1996, Margaret River, W.
Australia, £23.

CHEFS: Wendy Rowley and Tim Durrance   PROPRIETORS: Matthew and Wendy Rowley, and Bob Griffin   OPEN: all week 12 to 2, 7 to 9.30 (10 Fri and Sat)   MEALS: alc (main courses £7.50 to £15)   SERVICE: not inc, card slips closed; 5% for parties of 8 or more   CARDS: Delta, MasterCard, Switch, Visa   DETAILS: 65 seats. 16 seats outside. Private parties: 32 main room. Vegetarian meals. Children's helpings. Wheelchair access (not WC). Music

---

BIRCH VALE Derbyshire

map 8

▲ Waltzing Weasel

New Mills Road, Birch Vale SK22 1BT
TEL/FAX: (01663) 743402
on A6015, ½m W of Hayfield

COOKING 3
COST £21–£40

Above Stockport, on the way to the Derbyshire peaks, the Weasel is a stone-built pub still recognisable as such, with 'more of a pubby feel' than such conversions usually achieve when they turn to food. Mike Atkinson greets and serves behind the bar, where light lunches and snacks typically embrace hot buttered shrimps on toast, ham and eggs, lasagne, or poached salmon. Dinner is a more serious (and more expensive) affair of protein-rich main courses, served on polished oak tables in the dining-room; a casserole of the day plugs into the 'European peasant' tradition. The food benefits greatly from good sourcing, evident in seafood pâté tasting 'satisfyingly of the sea', and moist duck of a 'really excellent flavour'. Roasts are well handled – pink slices of leg of lamb, for instance, moistened by a sparse rosemary and garlic jus – and accompanied by a generous quantity of self-service vegetables. Desserts, unfortunately, have let the side down. Unaffected service from friendly young staff is a plus, as is the moderately priced wine list.

CHEF: George Benham   PROPRIETOR: Michael Atkinson   OPEN: all week 12 to 2, 7 to 9   MEALS: alc L (main courses £7 to £12.50). Set D £21.50 (2 courses) to £25.50   SERVICE: not inc, card slips closed   CARDS: Amex, Delta, MasterCard, Switch, Visa   DETAILS: 40 seats. Private parties: 40 main room. Car park. Vegetarian meals. Children's helpings. No children under 6. Wheelchair access (1 step; not WC). Occasional music. Air-conditioned   ACCOMMODATION: 8 rooms, all with bath/shower. TV. Phone. B&B £38 to £95. Children welcome

---

BIRDLIP Gloucestershire

map 2

▲ Kingshead House ▼

Birdlip GL4 8JH
TEL: (01452) 862299
on B4070 towards Stroud
¼m off A417 between Gloucester and Cirencester

COOKING 2
COST £25–£48

Uneven Cotswold flagstone floors and inglenooks set the scene in this 'country cottage style' restaurant. Prints 'like something out of Mrs Beeton' decorate the walls, a fitting backdrop for Judy Knock's 'homespun' dishes. Her food is carefully made, generally well timed, and founded on good raw materials: roast rack of lamb, or 'nicely pink' duck. A simple first-course of crab and lobster en gelée has impressed, although the enthusiasm for adding components to a dish is not always shared by reporters, and saucing and cool temperatures have let some dishes down. Dinner is now three courses for a set price (determined by the main course), and might finish with Il Diplomatico (an Italian sponge with chocolate, rum and coffee), or Lord John Russell's iced pudding – a bombe of orange and lemon ices with a Cointreau sauce – which dates from 1860, when Cointreau was as great a novelty as alcopops are now. Wines, on the other hand, date mostly from the 1990s, but encompass a good range of styles and varietals, including a Bacchus-Seyval from local vineyard Crickley-Windward. Prices are fair, with house wines starting at £10.50, and half-bottles are generous. CELLARMAN'S CHOICE: Menetou-Salon, Clos du Blanchais 1996, Pellé, £16.50; Hautes Côtes de Nuits, Clos du Vignon 1993, Le Brun, £18.50.

CHEF: Judy Knock   PROPRIETORS: Judy and Warren Knock   OPEN: Tue to Fri and Sun L 12.30 to 1.45, Tue to Sat D 7.30 to 9.45   CLOSED: 25 to 27 Dec, 1 Jan.   MEALS: alc (main courses £8 to £13). Set L Sun £16.50, Set D £25 to £27.50   SERVICE: not inc; 10% for parties of 6 or more   CARDS: Amex, MasterCard, Visa   DETAILS: 34 seats. 10 seats outside. Private parties: 32 main room. Car park. Vegetarian meals. Children's helpings. Wheelchair access (1 step; not WC.) Music   ACCOMMODATION: 1 room, with bath/shower. B&B £40 to £70. TV. Children welcome. Small dogs welcome in bedroom by prior arrangement (£5)

BIRKENHEAD Merseyside   map 8
Beadles

15 Rosemount, Oxton, Birkenhead L43 5SG   COOKING 2
TEL: (0151) 653 9010   COST £27–£37

Although the Gotts have been serving customers for over 20 years in their 'simple but elegant' dining-room, they still move with the times. The short menu might start with a salad of good black pudding and ham hock, field mushroom soup, or strips of raw salmon marinated in yoghurt and mint, perhaps closer to gravlax than the advertised 'sushi' style. Good-quality fillet steak has been served with Chinese mushrooms and red wine sauce, while Italian cotechino sausage 'in a wonderful natural skin' has come with an earthy-tasting mixed-bean casserole. Roy Gott's advice is always helpful, desserts don't appear to be a highlight, but most wines on the short and varied list stay helpfully below £15, including house French at £8.

CHEF: Bea Gott   PROPRIETORS: Roy and Bea Gott   OPEN: Wed to Sat D only 7.30 to 9.30   CLOSED: 2 weeks Aug   MEALS: alc (main courses £11 to £12.50)   SERVICE: not inc; 10% for parties of 6 or more   CARDS: Delta, MasterCard, Switch, Visa   DETAILS: 36 seats. Private parties: 32 main room. No children under 7. No smoking in dining-room before coffee. Wheelchair access (1 step; not WC). Music

---

BIRMINGHAM West Midlands   map 5
Chung Ying £

16–18 Wrottesley Street, Birmingham B5 4RT   COOKING 1
TEL: (0121) 622 5669 FAX: (0121) 666 7051   COST £21–£49

The gastronomic fortunes of Birmingham's Chinese restaurants are forever changing, but Chung Ying continues as one of the most reliable places of its kind in the city. Dining-areas are spread over two floors, and the kitchen is capable of

237

feeding up to 250 people from a gargantuan menu running to more than 300 dishes. What it delivers are big platefuls of robust Cantonese cooking of the old school, which means an emphasis on hotpots, casseroles, one-plate meals built around rice, soup and noodles, plus a strong showing in the seafood department. The familiar side of things is represented by the likes of steamed scallops, sliced beef with oyster sauce, and chicken with ginger and spring onion. Less familiar – and more challenging – are specialities such as steamed fish-head in black-bean sauce, braised ox tripe with spices, and sizzling eel balls. A separate list of 50 dim-sum, featuring such delicacies as Shanghai dumplings, yam croquettes, and pan-fried turnip paste, is aimed at daytime snacking. House wine is £10.

CHEF: T.C. Tsang   PROPRIETOR: Sui Chung Wong   OPEN: all week noon to 11.30 (10.30 Sun)   CLOSED: 25 Dec   MEALS: alc (main courses £5 to £11). Set D £12.50 to £19 (all minimum 2)   SERVICE: 10% (optional)   CARDS: Amex, Delta, Diners, MasterCard, Switch, Visa   DETAILS: 250 seats. Private parties: 120 main room, 120 private room. Vegetarian meals. Children welcome. Wheelchair access (2 steps, not WC). Music. Air-conditioned £5

Leftbank

79 Broad Street, Birmingham B15 1AH   COOKING 1
TEL: (0121) 643 4464   FAX: (0121) 643 5793   COST £23–£54

The high-ceilinged hundred-year-old branch of Barclays near the city centre retains a few grilles and a vault door for old time's sake, and is decorated with oils, gilt and rattan, and lit by candles. Modern European food is the preoccupation, evident from the roll call of rocket, truffle butter sauce, grilled goats' cheese on bruschetta, onion marmalade, saffron risotto, smoked garlic mash, black pudding, sun-dried tomatoes and tapénade dressing. The kitchen has turned out 'thick and concentrated' mushroom and Stilton soup, salmon and cod fish-cakes, and lambs' kidneys with parsnip mash but, for a couple of reporters at least, the food has not met expectations in terms of either taste or texture. House wine is £9.95.

CHEF: William Marmion   PROPRIETOR: Caroline Benbrook   OPEN: Mon to Fri L 12 to 2, Mon to Sat D 7 to 10   CLOSED: 25 Dec to 1 Jan, bank hols   MEALS: alc (main courses £11.50 to £18.50). Set L £12 (2 courses) to £14.50   SERVICE: not inc; 10% for parties of 10 or more   CARDS: Amex, Delta, Diners, MasterCard, Switch, Visa   DETAILS: 70 seats. Private parties: 55 main room, 16 private room. Vegetarian meals. Children's helpings. No cigars in dining-room. Wheelchair access (1 step; also WC). Music. Air-conditioned

Maharaja £

23–25 Hurst Street, B5 4AS   COOKING 2
TEL: (0121) 622 2641   FAX: (0121) 622 4021   COST £20–£30

Although it stands on a street corner a few doors from the Birmingham Hippodrome, the unassuming Maharaja makes no great show of things. Blink and you might almost miss the black and gold canopied frontage, but inside there's a feel of cultured intimacy that is immediately pleasing: the artefacts on the walls are genuine Indian and so is the background music. The kitchen continues to deliver a confident version of Punjabi and Mughlai cooking that relies on top-notch ingredients and freshly ground spices. Specials of the day add variety to the menu, which seems to have changed little over the years. Starters such as aloo tikkian and panir pakora precede a clutch of tandooris, tikkas and familiar-sounding curries such as chicken bhuna masala, lamb pasanda and king prawn biryani. Breads and rice show up well, and the list of vegetable dishes is a touch above the norm. Drink lassi, Kingfisher lager or dip into the promising list of two dozen affordable wines. House wine is £7.30.

CHEFS: Gurmaj Kumar and Jaskarn Dhillon PROPRIETOR: Mr N.S. Batt OPEN: Mon to Sat 12 to 2, 6 to 11 CLOSED: Christmas, bank hols, last week July, first week Aug. MEALS: alc (main courses £6 to £8). Set L and D £12.15 SERVICE: 10%, card slips closed CARDS: Amex, Delta, Diners, MasterCard, Switch, Visa DETAILS: 62 seats. Private parties: 30 main room. Vegetarian meals. Children welcome. Wheelchair access (1 step; also WC). Music. Air-conditioned

Oceanic   NEW ENTRY

89-91 Livery Street, B3 1RJ	COOKING 1
TEL: (0121) 236 7500 FAX: (0121) 236 7550	COST £26–£56

This Birmingham newcomer, which opened in the autumn of 1997, occupies the basement of an old factory on the edge of the Jewellery Quarter, in a part of town that is more gritty than pretty. Down the steps is a bar, and a 'very designerish' mirrored restaurant with 'spiky, bold colours', whose main feature is dark blue, glossy, reflective acetate suspended from the ceiling. The result is a 'confident, brash look' that suits the set-up fine. The kitchen has not pitched its aims too high, and succeeds admirably. Fish predominates and is cooked with care – chargrilled salmon with rocket, or seabass fillet with Mediterranean vegetables –and lively, fresh, well-balanced flavours are the norm: smoked halibut and blueberry terrine, or tiger prawns with chilli sauce. Desserts are as simple as crème brûlée, or fried bananas with hot fudge sauce. Though the fixed-price lunch (with five mains to choose from) is fair value, à la carte prices might give cause for concern. Around 20 well-spread wines start with house Spanish at £10.50 (£2.80 a glass).

CHEF: Mr J. Santos PROPRIETOR: Various Marketing Ltd OPEN: Mon to Fri L 12 to 2.30, Tue to Sat D 7 to 10 (10.30 Sat) MEALS: alc (main courses £9.95 to £18.95). Set L £12.50 (2 courses) SERVICE: not inc CARDS: Amex, Delta, Diners, MasterCard, Switch, Visa DETAILS: 55 seats. Private parties: 60 main room, 10 to100 private rooms. Vegetarian meals. No children under 12. Music (£5)

Restaurant Gilmore   NEW ENTRY

27 Warstone Lane, Birmingham B18 6JQ	COOKING 2
TEL: (0121) 233 3655 FAX: (01543) 415511	COST £21–£49

Paul Gilmore established his small, unpretentious restaurant, in a converted Victorian rolling mill in the Jewellery Quarter, in the spring of 1997. Bare brick walls and red velvet drapes at small stained-glass windows lend warmth, tables are close, and old cookery books provide a hint of the enthusiasm which is 'one of the place's endearing qualities'. There are 'no themes or gimmicks', just simple ingredients and down-to-earth cuts of meat – the city's market provides fish, beef comes from Scotland – given an interesting twist with combinations and accompaniments: apple and chilli soup, breast of chicken with cumin and pickled ginger, or grilled loin of tuna on a saffron and chive risotto. A preference for oily dressings was a feature of an inspection meal, whose highlight was a simply presented roast rack of English lamb in a well-reduced wine jus with basil and garlic mash. Cheeses are unpasteurised farmhouse, and appealing desserts have included rich bitter chocolate crème brûlée with warm brandied cherries, and rhubarb and port syllabub with pistachio nut brittle. Wines are a short, interesting mix of Old and New Worlds with a few pricier French bottles. House Vin de Pays d'Oc is £9.50.

CHEF: Paul Gilmore   PROPRIETORS: Paul and Denise Gilmore   OPEN: Tue to Fri L 12 to 2, Tue to Sat D 7 to 9.30   CLOSED: 25 to 31 Dec, 2 weeks Jan, 2 weeks Aug, bank hol Tue   MEALS: Set L £14.50, Set D £19.50   SERVICE: not inc   CARDS: Amex, Delta, Diners, MasterCard, Switch, Visa   DETAILS: 36 seats. Private parties: 36 main room. Vegetarian meals. Children's helpings. No-smoking area. Music. Air-conditioned   (£5)

BIRTLE Greater Manchester   map 8

▲ *Normandie* ♏ £

Elbut Lane, Birtle BL9 6UT
TEL: (0161) 764 3869 and 1170
FAX: (0161) 764 4866   COOKING 4
off B6222, 3m NE of Bury   COST £19–£41

A winding road leads off the Bolton to Rochdale road, climbing towards the moors and this long-established family-run restaurant. Stone-built 'like an old pub', it incorporates a modern annexe and boasts a view over most of Manchester. The bar is less colourful than the dining-room, whose egg-yellow walls, sky-blue paint and rust-pink tablecloths are the scene for Paul Bellingham's largely Anglo-French cooking. This might vary from simple coq au vin to a warm salad of vegetables on a chickpea galette, and a degree of innovation is often evident: in a first course of salty smoked cod mousse with beetroot terrine, perhaps, or fillet of beef topped with a snail ravioli.

Some partnerships work well – steamed brill with a good lobster sausage, for instance, or roast and braised pheasant with mushroom dumplings – although flavours, singly or in combination, have failed to excite. Nevertheless, there is much to enjoy, including pink calf's liver with 'a dense and creamy texture', served with a strongly flavoured onion and Madeira sauce. For one party, 'moist and light' blueberry and polenta cake was the hit among desserts, but hot toffee pudding and chocolate mousse have also drawn applause. Wines are mostly from France, with eight country wines offering good-value drinking (the house Vin de Pays des Côtes du Tarn is £9.95), while a few choice selections from the New World broaden the appeal. CELLARMAN'S CHOICE: Stormy Cape Chenin Blanc 1997, South Africa, £13.50; Saumur Champigny 1996, Ch. de Villeneuve, £19.50.

CHEF: Paul Bellingham   PROPRIETORS: Mr and Mrs M. Moussa   OPEN: Mon to Fri L 12 to 2, Mon to Sat D 7 to 9.30   CLOSED: 2 weeks from 26 Dec, 1 week Easter, bank hols exc 25 Dec   MEALS: alc (main courses £10 to £16.50). Set L £12.50, Set D £15   SERVICE: none, card slips closed   CARDS: Amex, Delta, Diners, MasterCard, Switch, Visa   DETAILS: 50 seats. Car park. Vegetarian meals. Children welcome. No cigars/pipes in dining-room. Wheelchair access (1 step; also WC). Music   ACCOMMODATION: 23 rooms, all with bath/shower. TV. Phone. B&B £49 to £79. Rooms for disabled. Children welcome. Baby facilities. No dogs. Afternoon teas   £5

BISHOP'S TACHBROOK Warwickshire   map 5

▲ Mallory Court ⁵✷

Harbury Lane, Bishop's Tachbrook CV33 9QB
TEL: (01926) 330214   FAX: (01926) 451714
EMAIL: reception@mallory.co.uk   COOKING 5
off B4087, 2m S of Leamington Spa   COST £43–£80

Although just off the M40, this attractive old house with leaded windows and creeper-covered walls feels quite serene amid manicured lawns, flowerbeds, a swimming-pool and croquet pitch. The lounge is bright and floral, the dining-room 'serious', with yellow fabric, wood panelling and widely set tables; high-quality fixtures and fittings point towards the luxury end of the market. So does Allan Holland's Anglo-French food, which goes in for foie gras terrine, oyster tagliatelle with champagne and caviare, and artichoke salad with truffle dressing, although it seems equally happy with earthier dishes of warm black-pudding tart, or roast squab pigeon with pea purée, bacon and beans.

Ingredients are first-rate, and flavour combinations tend to be classically inclined, from red mullet tapénade with sauce vierge to pistachio crème brûlée and vanilla ice-cream, or pavé of chocolate with mandarins and crème anglaise. Whatever you think of the prices, note that they include service, which is some consolation when it comes to the heavily marked-up wine list, lovely as some of the bottles undoubtedly are. Three of the seven house wines are under £20.

CHEF: Allan Holland   PROPRIETORS: Allan Holland and Jeremy Mort   OPEN: all week 12.30 to 2, 7 to 9.45   MEALS: alc (main courses £18 to £30). Set D £35. BYO £12   SERVICE: net prices, card slips closed   CARDS: Amex, Delta, Diners, MasterCard, Switch, Visa   DETAILS: 50 seats. 25 seats outside. Private parties: 27 main room, 18 to 20 private room. Car park. Vegetarian meals. No children under 9. No smoking in dining-room. Wheelchair access (2 steps; also WC). Occasional music   ACCOMMODATION: 18 rooms, all with bath/shower. TV. Phone. B&B £150 to £275. Rooms for disabled. No children under 9. No dogs. Afternoon teas. Swimming-pool

---

BLACKPOOL Lancashire   map 8

September Brasserie

15–17 Queen Street, Blackpool FY1 1PU   COOKING 3
TEL: (01253) 623282   FAX: (01253) 244355   COST £20–£42

This 'classic' first-floor brasserie has no lounge, just an open-plan kitchen, bare tables, plain china and simple cutlery and glassware. If the décor looks 'a trifle frayed', staff certainly don't: they are organised enough to cope with set-price meals, a *carte* and blackboard specials. This is 'solid food', with a few local ingredients adding interest: Lytham shrimps accompany Irish trout, and there is a tart of Lancashire cheese and Bury black pudding.

Down-to-earth dishes – braised lamb shank 'falling off the bone' and 'full of flavour', served with mashed carrots – work as well as more novel ideas, such as duck confit wrapped in a capsicum pancake. One who began with a scallop shell filled with scallops, prosciutto and ceps, and finished with pear mousse with 'nicely caramelised' poached pears and eau-de-vie, declared the whole meal 'professionally cooked and attractively served'. Service in the evening can be 'leisurely'. There is no house wine, but prices start around £11. Note the specialist promotions, an organic selection, and the option to bring your own for £5 corkage.

CHEF: Michael Golowicz   PROPRIETORS: Michael Golowicz and Pat Wood   OPEN: Tue to Sat 12 to 2, 7 to 10   CLOSED: 1 week winter, 1 week summer   MEALS: alc (main courses £6 to £14.50). Set L £12.50 (2 courses) to £15.50, Set D £14.50 (2 courses) to £17.80. BYO £5   SERVICE: not inc, card slips closed   CARDS: Amex, Diners, MasterCard, Visa   DETAILS: 45 seats. Private parties: 35 main room. Vegetarian meals. Children's helpings. Music   (£5)

BLAKENEY Norfolk   map 6

▲ White Horse Hotel £

4 High Street, Blakeney NR25 7AL
TEL: (01263) 740574   FAX: (01263) 741303   COOKING 2
off A149 between Cley and Morston   COST £22–£40

'An encouraging place of cheerful eccentricity,' concluded one reporter after eating and staying at this exceptionally friendly hotel. Standing just up the hill from Blakeney quay, it started life as a village watering-hole: a 'lively' bar (with its own menu) runs all day long. Serious dining takes place in the restaurant, a split-level room in what was originally the stables. Christopher Hyde cooks with a light touch, and his menus, bolstered by blackboard specials, are a mix of the 'straight-up, old-fashioned and up-to-date'. Starters of 'nourishing' king prawn risotto, bruschetta with chickpea and chilli purée, and an 'excellent' warm salad of Toulouse sausage and bacon with lentil dressing have pleased reporters enormously. Mains are equally assured: loin of lamb on grilled aubergine with tomato and cinnamon sauce, and grilled fillet of brill on potato bhaji. A 'beautifully presented' tiramisù parfait with coffee cream hit the button for one diner, while another praised rich chocolate mousse. Three dozen wines are drawn from the Adnams list. House vins de pays is £7.95.

CHEF: Christopher Hyde   PROPRIETORS: Daniel Rees and Sue Catt   OPEN: Tue to Sat D only 7 to 9   MEALS: alc (main courses £8 to £15). Bar food available   SERVICE: not inc, card slips closed   CARDS: Amex, Delta, MasterCard, Switch, Visa   DETAILS: 32 seats. Private parties: 30 main room. Car park. Vegetarian meals. Children's helpings. No children under 8. No-smoking area. Wheelchair access (1 step; not WC). Occasional music   ACCOMMODATION: 10 rooms, all with bath/shower. TV. Phone. B&B £25 to £85. Children welcome. High teas for children. Baby facilities. No dogs (The Which? Hotel Guide)

▲ means accommodation is available.

▲ *Devonshire Arms, Burlington Restaurant* ⁵✖

Bolton Abbey BD23 6AJ
TEL: (01756) 710441 FAX: (01756) 710564
EMAIL: dev.arms@legend.co.uk
at junction of A59 and B6160, 5m NW of Ilkley

COOKING 5
COST £29–£76

Built as a coaching-inn in the seventeenth century, the Devonshire Arms is part
of an estate that stretches along the River Wharfe, past the ruins of twelfth-
century Bolton Priory, and on to the moors. It has been modified over the years to
keep pace with developments, with a health and leisure centre round the back
and, most recently, an informal modern brasserie serving 15 dishes that can be
taken as either a starter or main course (at £8.75), plus a few more expensive
grills and roasts, and a children's menu. Dinner in the swankier Burlington
Restaurant is three courses, but there is now also a six-course look-what-
I-can-do menu called 'chef's choice' that deals in velouté of celeriac with truffles,
langoustine and scallop risotto, and loin of venison with polenta cake and more
truffles.

The 'ordinary' menu, if we may call it that, is not short of luxuries either, but it
also has an earthier side, as in a terrine of black pudding, pig's cheek and
vegetables, which impressed an autumn visitor with its differing textures and
'great depth of flavour'. Meaty main courses of squab pigeon with wild
mushrooms, or beef fillet with truffled lentils are balanced by red mullet with
confit tomatoes, or chunky-flaky cod with a crab and asparagus risotto. Puddings
tend to put fruit in a rich context: pineapple tarte Tatin with coconut ice-cream,
or mascarpone and amaretti cheesecake with poached plums. Service could be
better organised. Spanish house wines are £14.50 a bottle, and 40 wines are
offered by the glass.

CHEF: Andrew Nicholson PROPRIETORS: The Duke and Duchess of Devonshire OPEN: Sun L
12 to 2.30, all week D 7 to 10 MEALS: Set L Sun £18.95, Set D £30 to £50 SERVICE: not inc,
card slips closed CARDS: Amex, Delta, Diners, MasterCard, Switch, Visa DETAILS: 70 seats.
10 seats outside. Private parties: 90 main room, 12 to 90 private rooms. Car park. Vegetarian
meals. Children's helpings. No smoking in dining-room. Wheelchair access (also WC). No
music ACCOMMODATION: 41 rooms, all with bath/shower. TV. Phone. B&B £110 to £275.
Rooms for disabled. Children welcome. Baby facilities. Afternoon teas. Swimming-pool. Fishing
(*The Which? Hotel Guide*) £5

▲ *Eastwell Manor* ⁵✖

Eastwell Park, Boughton Lees TN25 4HR
TEL: (01233) 219955 FAX: (01233) 635530
on A251, 3m N of Ashford

COOKING 6
COST £29–£69

The manor is a gloriously Gothic and extravagantly chimneyed pile in the Kent
countryside. An atmospheric courtyard, darkened oak panels, and the smell of
woodsmoke drifting from open fires all do their bit to make the place feel
ancient. Set lunches look good value in the context, but the *carte*'s generosity
(nine choices per course) is impressive considering how labour-intensive some

of the dishes are: saddle and braised leg of rabbit are served with Pommery pasta and tarragon jus, and a crépinette of guinea-fowl appears with pancetta, broad beans and morel sauce.

Materials are first-rate: organic pork, game from the estate, Appledore salad leaves, and pristine dived scallops 'as good as you'll get', although serving the last with sweet ginger purée and beetroot jus obscures rather than enhances the scallops' own sweetness. More-classical partnerships tend to work better, as in a confident and professional rendition of partridge with shredded Savoy cabbage and 'a gem' of well-reduced but not sticky sauce. Seafood has drawn praise too: for example, immaculately roast cod served with a watercress risotto, with earthy-tasting beetroot and a discreet dash of horseradish making 'a most interesting combination'.

Desserts demonstrate an inventive turn of mind, ranging from warm Cox's apple soup served with an apricot and raisin samosa and a cider sorbet, to strawberry spring rolls that come with crème fraîche ice-cream and thyme syrup. Good home-made bread adds to the appeal, and service is on the ball: thankfully the white gloves have gone, and domes are now used with more discretion. Wines are mostly French and of high quality but – apart from a short house selection under £15 – not very kind to those of modest means.

CHEF: Ian Mansfield   PROPRIETOR: Turrloo Parrett   OPEN: all week 12 to 2.30, 7 to 9.30 (10 Fri and Sat)   MEALS: alc (main courses £17.50 to £24). Set L Mon to Sat £12.50 (2 courses) to £16.50, Set L Sun £24.50   SERVICE: not inc   CARDS: Amex, Delta, Diners, MasterCard, Switch, Visa   DETAILS: 80 seats. Private parties: 110 main room, 12 to 70 private rooms. Car park. Vegetarian meals. Children's helpings. No smoking in dining room. Music   ACCOMMODATION: 23 rooms, all with bath/shower. TV. Phone. B&B £140 to £330. Rooms for disabled. Children welcome. Baby facilities. Afternoon teas. (*The Which? Hotel Guide*)

BOWNESS-ON-WINDERMERE Cumbria   map 8

▲ *Linthwaite House* ♟ ⅝✕

Crook Road, Bowness-on-Windermere LA23 3JA
TEL: (01539) 488600   FAX: (01539) 488601   COOKING 4
EMAIL: admin@linthwaite.com   COST £21–£52

Linthwaite House offers arresting views down wooded hillside from its 14-acre eyrie high above Lake Windermere. The elegant and comfortable dining-room has deep-piled red carpet and matching curtains, and the tone of service from well-trained staff is dignified and formal. Ian Bravey's cooking fits the country-house style like a glove: fixed-price dinner menus in particular are classics of the genre. A chef's bonne-bouche (always 'hot and vegetarian', we are assured) sets the ball rolling. First courses range from potato rösti topped with morels and girolles to terrine of foie gras with poached (yes, poached) brioche. At inspection, a starter of pigeon-breast salad with shallots and pine-nuts on raspberry-dressed leaves offered tender meat and good accompaniments. Main courses have included fine chargrilled pork tenderloin with a suggestion of five-spice seasoning, glazed with balsamic and honey, although 'meagre' saucing may not always be a match for the top-notch ingredients. Real tarte Tatin with vanilla custard is 'wonderfully caramelised, sweet and delicious', while sticky toffee pudding and superb British and Irish cheeses also come in for praise.

Wines, supplied in the main by Cumbria merchant Frank Stainton and Bibendum in London, are a globe-trotting collection organised by grape/style. Claret buffs are catered for, and moderate drinkers are offered a considerate number of half-bottles or half-carafes. House white from New Zealand is £14.75 and Chilean house red is £19.50.

CHEF: Ian Bravey   PROPRIETOR: Handmade Hotels   OPEN: Sun L 12.30 to 1.45, all week D 7.15 to 9, light lunch menu Mon to Sat L   CLOSED: 2 to 6 Jan.   MEALS: alc (main courses £8 to £10). Set L Sun £14.95, Set D £33.50. BYO £7   SERVICE: net prices, card slips closed   CARDS: Amex, Delta, MasterCard, Switch, Visa   DETAILS: 40 seats. 30 seats outside. Private parties: 50 main room. Car park. Vegetarian meals. No children under 7 at D. No smoking in dining-room. Wheelchair access (1 step; also WC). Music   ACCOMMODATION: 18 rooms, all with bath/shower. TV. Phone. B&B £70 to £180. Rooms for disabled. Children welcome. High teas for children. Baby facilities. No dogs. Afternoon teas. Fishing (*The Which? Hotel Guide*) (£5)

Porthole Eating House ▮

3 Ash Street, Bowness-on-Windermere LA23 3EB	COOKING 4
TEL: (015394) 42793 FAX: (015394) 88675	COST £18–£52

Halfway along Bowness's only pedestrianised street, the Porthole looks the part of a whitewashed Cornish cottage, suggesting that fish and shellfish might be the main attraction. But this is no fisherman's hideout. It is a set of small interconnected rooms with glossy red ceilings, wooden tables, shelves full of bric-à-brac, a warm fire, and a distinctly convivial air. Lunch is the more casual meal, perhaps offering lasagne, lamb casserole, blackened salmon fillet, or 'rustic' steak and kidney pudding with proper suet pastry. With the exception of a few interlopers such as fish-cakes or Thai-style gambas, and steak five ways, the *carte* remains largely in traditional Italian mould, featuring Parma ham with melon, spaghetti bolognese, or chicken saltimbocca with sage. English-style vegetables accompany. A 'garnish' of some sort seems to be a trade mark, even with rich and creamy tiramisù, which comes with pomegranate seeds and a strawberry. Service is friendly, relaxed and capable, from staff who are 'courteous and welcoming'. It would be easy to run out of superlatives when trying to do justice to Judith Burton's superb wine list which is full of the great, the rare and the downright unusual. It's good to see Italy and Germany being paid the attention they merit; France, of course, is accorded due respect, and the New World selections are spot-on. There is plenty of choice under £20, beginning with Italian house wines at £11.

CHEF: Andrew Fairchild   PROPRIETORS: Gianni and Judy Berton   OPEN: Mon, Wed, Thur, Fri and Sun L 12 to 2.30, Wed to Mon D 6.30 to 10.30   CLOSED: 18 Dec to end Feb   MEALS: alc (main courses L £7 to £8, D £9 to £15). Set L Sun £10   SERVICE: not inc, card slips closed CARDS: Amex, Diners, MasterCard, Switch, Visa   DETAILS: 40 seats. 40 seats outside. Private parties: 40 main room. Vegetarian meals. Children's helpings. Music

▮ *denotes an outstanding wine cellar;* ▾ *denotes a good wine list, worth travelling for.*

BRAITHWAITE Cumbria map 10

▲ *Ivy House* ♟ ✂

Braithwaite CA12 5SY
TEL: (017687) 78338 FAX: (017687) 78113 COOKING 3
just off B5292 Keswick to Braithwaite road COST £27–£35

The seventeenth-century house is in a quiet village a couple of miles from Keswick, between Bassenthwaite and Derwentwater, and the form is an early dinner of four courses. Start in the warm and welcoming lounge, climb the stairs to a dark green dining-room with mirrors, candles and chandeliers, and prepare for some 'old-fashioned country cooking' of the sort that 'fills people up and makes them happy'. A sorbet or soup – broccoli and sweet potato, or creamy cauliflower 'with "home-made" written all over it' – is preceded by Thai pork satay, black pudding with wholegrain mustard, or perhaps tomato tart, from a choice of half a dozen items, and main courses have included sirloin steak with garlic butter, and Parmesan-crusted salmon in a mussel chowder. Different cultures might meet – coconut curry sauce and couscous for one chicken dish – and a reporter whose corn-fed chicken came with red wine sauce and bacon declared it 'cooked with skill'. Puddings are in the mould of sticky toffee, tiramisù, or raspberry torte. Service is on the formal side, and also 'pretty swift', so meals finish early. All but four of the 48 wines come in under £20; indeed, some cost less than £10, but this hasn't been at the expense of interest or quality. Exciting producers have been selected from both hemispheres and given enthusiastic tasting notes. Argentinian house wines are £9.50 a bottle, £2 a glass. CELLARMAN'S CHOICE: Chardonnay 'La Fagge' 1995, Castello d'Alba, Tuscany, £18.95; Caballo Loco No 1 NV, Jorge Cordech, Chile, £17.95.

CHEFS: Wendy Shill, Peter Holten, Ryan Stanger PROPRIETORS: Nick and Wendy Shill OPEN: all week D only 7.30 (1 sitting) CLOSED: Jan MEALS: Set D £19.95 SERVICE: not inc CARDS: Amex, Delta, Diners, MasterCard, Switch, Visa DETAILS: 32 seats. Private parties: 10 main room. Car park. No children under 6. No smoking in dining-room. Music ACCOMMODATION: 12 rooms, all with bath/shower. TV. Phone. D,B&B £49.95 to £112.90. Rooms for disabled. Children welcome. High teas for children. Baby facilities. Dogs by arrangement

---

BRAMPTON Cumbria map 10

▲ *Farlam Hall*

Brampton CA8 2NG
TEL: (01697) 746234 FAX: (01697) 746683
EMAIL: farlamhall@dial.pipex.com COOKING 3
on A689, 2½m SE of Brampton (not at Farlam village) COST £39–£48

'The families that run Farlam Hall put on long dresses and smart suits and treat you like house guests,' noted a couple from London who revelled in the sumptuous décor and 'endless sofas' that set the tone in this amiable Victorian country house. Gastronomically speaking, 'not a trimming is missed', from canapés to petits fours. In between, guests are offered a short four-course dinner menu that changes every evening. One typical meal kicked off with home-baked apricot and sesame bread before light tartlets of goats' cheese and anchovy with apple sauce. Following this came a dish of boned quail stuffed with chicken and pistachio served with a potent mushroom gravy and a 'robust plateful' of decent vegetables. The cheeseboard is generous and patriotic, and there are smiles all round for comforting desserts of 'succulent' raspberry Linzertorte, or home-made banana ice-cream in a biscuit case with cherry and nectarine compote. Coffee is served in the lounge, where devotees of Scrabble can try out their prowess. France holds pride of place on the affordable wine list, although other countries have their say. House wines are £13.50.

CHEF: Barry Quinion   PROPRIETORS: the Quinion and Stevenson families   OPEN: all week D only 8 to 8.30   CLOSED: 25 to 30 Dec   MEALS: Set D Sun to Fri £30, Set D Sat £31 SERVICE: not inc, card slips closed   CARDS: Amex, MasterCard, Switch, Visa   DETAILS: 45 seats. Private parties: 24 main room. Car park. No children under 5. No cigars/pipes in dining-room. Wheelchair access (2 steps; not WC). No music   ACCOMMODATION: 12 rooms, all with bath/shower. TV. Phone. D,B&B £115 to £240. No children under 5. Afternoon teas (*The Which? Hotel Guide*)

BRAY Berkshire
map 3

Fat Duck ♥

| 1 High Street, Bray SL6 2AQ | COOKING 9 |
| TEL: (01628) 580333   FAX: (01628) 776188 | COST £40–£86 |

This may not have the slickness and superficial veneer that some may expect from highly rated restaurants, but the food does tend to stop people in their tracks. The dining-room's interplay between natural and metallic takes in low-beamed white-painted ceilings, a copper-clad bar, dull gold tabletops, black wrought-iron chairs, huge platinum-grey mirrors, candle sconces dripping 'heavy Edgar Allan Poe wax', and a rusting metal urn spilling out 'giant fungi and interesting-shaped bits of wood'. For one visitor the sensual food is 'like early Picasso', in that 'it breaks moulds, and crosses boundaries' while tasting 'utterly delectable'. It is not trendy, rather an expression of 'one man's strange and fevered brain and its translation on to the plate'.

An understanding of the science of cooking underlies the operation – it is as much laboratory as restaurant – and most dishes seem to involve about three days' intricate planning and manufacture, but results are not in the least bit clinical, just 'very natural, with nothing tortured or forced'. Cod, for example, has been rubbed with vanilla, liquorice, coriander, cardamom, mint, lemon and lime zest, and served with cockscombs that 'sat on the plate like exaggerated Dennis Healey eyebrows'; it came with a runner-bean purée, and Puy lentils 'boiled in Badoit, which – apparently – acts like bicarbonate of soda and renders them soft without exploding'. This partnering of seafood with offal or cheap cuts of meat – veal sweetbreads ('easily the best I have ever had', from an inspector) with smoky clams, or four langoustines and shards of pig's trotter under a sheet of silky pasta – gives dishes more impact in the mouth, more power. In the hands of a lesser chef this might appear merely overworked; here it is simply 'magic'.

Vegetable accompaniments are no less involved – cauliflower is braised with beurre noisette to a 'brown goo' that tasted both 'mellow and intense', pommes purée are as good as any – as are desserts. Chocolate coulant is made by folding powdered cocoa-flavoured pastry into a meringue mix, then using it to surround a nugget of ganache to produce a lava flow of liquid filling that 'volcanoes out at the touch of a spoon'. A wobbly lemon tart set between a pastry base and blow-torched top has proved 'a triumph of art over gravity', slowly detumescing as the surface tension is broken. Well-sourced cheeses have included first-rate Berthault Epoisses, at its best 'pure farmyard, dung and straw to sniff, but tasting like nectar'; the reporter ended by licking the box.

This is not a place for vegetarians. Given the quality, prices are very reasonable, and 'there is nothing stiff or ma'amish' about the service: Nigel the maitre d' is knowledgeable, charming, witty and friendly. Improvements during the past year have included bread, now sour dough baked in a wood-fired oven, and the introduction of wines by the glass, taken from a new house selection of 15 whites and 15 reds, to assist mixing and matching with each course. Prices are not cheap but producers throughout the impressive list are top-drawer, and there is much here to titillate a wine buff's palate. CELLARMAN'S CHOICE: Vin de Pays de l'Hérault, Dom. de L'Hortus 1996, £29, Châteauneuf-du-Pape 'Les Caillots' 1995, A Brunel, £38.50.

CHEF: Heston Blumenthal   PROPRIETORS: Heston and Susanna Blumenthal   OPEN: Tue to Sun L 12 to 2 (2.30 Sun), Tue to Sat D 7 to 9.30 (10 Fri and Sat)   CLOSED: 2 weeks Christmas   MEALS: alc (main courses £15.50 to £27). Set L Tue to Sat £17.50 (2 courses). BYO £15   SERVICE: not inc   CARDS: Amex, Diners, MasterCard, Switch, Visa   DETAILS: 50 seats. 25 seats outside. Private parties: 55 main room. Vegetarian meals. Children's helpings. Wheelchair access (1 step; not WC). Occasional music

---

▲ Waterside Inn ❦

Ferry Road, Bray SL6 2AT
TEL: (01628) 620691   FAX: (01628) 784710   COOKING 9
EMAIL: 100552.1641@compuserve.com   COST £50–£163

One of the country's Frenchest of French restaurants occupies a stretch of the Thames in one of the home counties' most English villages. It started life as a pub and hasn't changed much outside, but inside, rather like an embassy, it suddenly becomes French territory, 'as though one has entered a benign kingdom'. Framed culinary awards, menus, cookery books and portraits remind everyone just who the empire belongs to. A square dining-room, dark and intimate, opens out into an extension bathed in sunlight on the right day, which in turn overlooks a colourful pagoda, an enormous weeping willow, and a small jetty where the launch (available for hire) ties up. The scene is altogether more theatrical at night when the dining-room, decorated in 'slightly over the top Chinoise style', lights up like a stage set.

The appeal here is not excitement, certainly not novelty, rather it is classical French food which aims for a kind of perfection: 'technically, the dinner was a tour de force,' observed our inspector. Some dishes appear disarmingly simple – two poached eggs in a pastry case with asparagus tips and a mousseline sauce, for example – but are definitive versions. The *carte* offers fair choice and good balance among starters, fish and shellfish dishes, along with main courses of grilled pigeon or rabbit, or loin of lamb with sweetbreads in puff pastry; the *menu exceptionnel* samples the range in five courses. Prices, previously fully inclusive, have come down slightly in order to accommodate a 12.5% 'discretionary' service charge, and the *Guide* is pleased to note that credit card slips are now closed. Even at these prices, however, it is striking how each dish manages to justify its cost: 'if we had this type of money to spend, we would not hesitate to spend it here.'

Luxuries appear in abundance and the cooking is confident, though not without an occasional blemish, as if to show it is still human. But for 'brilliant fine-tuning of flavours' it is difficult to beat a 'dazzlingly fresh' and sweet giant scallop, fiercely seared and caramelised, served with chunky ceps, bitter rocket leaves and finely julienned, slightly sour apples. One outstanding dish is Challandais duck (for two), accompanied by olive and anchovy sauce with spinach purée on one occasion, by lemon and thyme jus on another. The bird itself is cooked a uniform pink, carved at table in grand-hotel style, with a texture 'almost like a refined version of rare roast beef', unfatty yet moist, its gently gamey flavour etched into the memory of its reporter.

The kitchen's light hand is particularly evident at dessert stage, in soufflés of mirabelles or peach, and in a crumbly sablé biscuit sandwiching finely sliced pears, served with a punchy raspberry coulis. Service is a 'well-oiled machine' and the wine list is a magnum opus, resolutely and classically French (ports and madeiras are the only *étrangers*) and catholic in its repertoire. Prices are as high as the roll-call of *grands crus* and first growths are long, climbing quickly to three figures and often reaching four without seeming to pause for breath. House white is £19, the red £29.50. CELLARMAN'S CHOICE: Bourgogne Blanc 1987, François Jobard, £41; Margaux, Ch. Palmer 1991, £68.

CHEFS: Michel Roux and Mark Dodson   PROPRIETOR: Michel Roux   OPEN: Wed to Sun L 12 to 2 (2.30 Sat and Sun), Tue to Sun D 7 to 10   CLOSED: 26 Dec to 28 Jan, 5 to 8 Apr; also Sun D 1 Oct to 30 Apr   MEALS: alc (main courses £30 to £40). Set L £29.50 to £67.50, Set D £67.50 SERVICE: 12.5% (optional), card slips closed   CARDS: Amex, Diners, MasterCard, Switch, Visa DETAILS: 75 seats. Private parties: 80 main room, 8 private room. Car park. Vegetarian meals. No children under 12. No cigars/pipes in dining-room. Wheelchair access (1 step; not WC). Music ACCOMMODATION: 9 rooms, all with bath/shower. TV. Phone. B&B £135 to £245. No children under 12. No dogs

---

BRIGHTON East Sussex   map 3

Black Chapati

12 Circus Parade, New England Road,
Brighton BN1 4GW   COOKING 4
TEL: (01273) 699011   COST £18–£37

Greater comfort is one of this year's innovations at the Chapati. More space among tables and softer lighting now reward the many devotees of Stephen Funnell's and Lauren Alker's Eastern cooking. Although the name may suggest a predominantly Indian bias, the cooking is in fact more broadly based, and is predicated on a diligent and conscientious understanding of various national cuisines, each of which is accorded its due integrity. Thus, tuna is grilled rare and served on buckwheat noodles and spinach, dressed with Japanese shoyu sauce. Lamb patties use a coconut-milk pastry made to a Sri Lankan formula, while hot-and-sour soup with pieces of poached sea bass and rice noodles is Vietnamese in inspiration.

The balance of seasonings in a dish, which can resemble precision engineering in Eastern cookery, is carefully attended to, so that flavours ring out clear and true, and central ingredients are not swamped. Organic produce is used where available, and fish and seafood are all native species to ensure freshness. Only at dessert stage, when you may be anticipating new takes on gulab jamun or kulfi, does the spotlight swing recognisably back to Europe, although coconut ice-cream with poached kumquats certainly throws lemon tart and crème brûlée into relief. The proprietors feel that their food 'is not usually wine-compatible', which is why there are only around half a dozen wines. Breton cider is a favoured alternative, at £5.50 the litre.

CHEFS/PROPRIETORS: Stephen Funnell and Lauren Alker   OPEN: Tue to Sat D only 7 (6.30 Sat) to 10.30   CLOSED: 2 weeks Christmas, 2 weeks July   MEALS: alc (main courses £10 to £12.50). Set D Tue to Fri before 9.30 (7 Fri) £7.50 (2 courses) to £10 (set D must be pre-booked) SERVICE: 10%, card slips closed   CARDS: Amex, Delta, MasterCard, Switch, Visa   DETAILS: 32 seats. Private parties. 16 main room. Vegetarian meals. Children welcome. Wheelchair access (not WC). Music (£5)

One Paston Place

1 Paston Place, Brighton BN2 1HA	COOKING 6
TEL: (01273) 606933 FAX: (01273) 675686	COST £25–£51

In their three or four years of ownership the Emmersons have put an individual stamp on this one-roomed restaurant with their confident style of cooking and management. Forget any thoughts of a hidebound repertoire that centres on beef, lamb, chicken and pork, and be prepared for one in which fish and game can play a starring role: saddle of rabbit comes with a potato and artichoke galette, and red mullet and sea bream with sea urchin sauce. 'Inventive and colourful' first courses are the norm: a light crab soup with Thai spices, marbled rabbit terrine with walnut dressing, or scallop and potato salad, for instance.

In the view of one reporter, although main courses 'do not usually surprise, they are always deeply satisfying', and might include stuffed squab pigeon with boudin blanc and wild mushrooms, or stuffed quail with cep pancake and foie gras jus. And if the food has an element of comfort, it is not at the expense of interest; consider roast scallops with grilled cauliflower, and pavé of ostrich with Szechuan pepper and celeriac mash. Banana tarte Tatin, or an orange, Grand Marnier and bitter chocolate soufflé might be among desserts. Service is highly commended. 'It is one of the easiest places I know in which to attract staff attention; but it is also one in which you will be left to pour your own wine if that is what you wish.' The predominantly French list is not quite in the same class, although the interesting house selection looks good value, starting at £9.90 for Syrah and Chardonnay.

CHEF: Mark Emmerson   PROPRIETORS: Mark and Nicole Emmerson   OPEN: Tue to Sat 12.30 to 2, 7.30 to 10   CLOSED: first 2 weeks Jan, first two weeks Aug   MEALS: alc (main courses £15 to £17.50). Set L £14.50 (2 courses) to £16.50   SERVICE: 10%, card slips closed   CARDS: Amex, Delta, Diners, MasterCard, Switch, Visa   DETAILS: 48 seats. Private parties: 10 main room. No children under 5 at D. No cigars/pipes in dining-room. Wheelchair access (not WC). Music. Air-conditioned

Terre à Terre ⅍ £

71 East Street, Brighton BN1 1HQ
TEL: (01273) 729051 FAX: (01273) 327561

COOKING 4
COST £23–£37

After disappearing from the main listings last year because of an awkwardly timed move, Terre à Terre makes a welcome return. It is the same as before, only bigger and better and, in a town where quirky integrity is not exactly a new idea, stands out 'as a truly one-off place'. The three large rooms are painted various intensities of orange and divided by columns and short walls – tables near the front are quieter – and the brasserie feel is evident in polished wooden floors, bare tables, comfortable chairs, simple cutlery, paper napkins and basic glassware.

This is a restaurant with a mission. The food is strictly vegetarian (with several marked as vegan), but any preconceptions have to be left aside. Choice is generous, the cooking style 'totally eclectic', drawing from all over the Mediterranean, Central Europe, the Far East and America. 'If anything can be turned to good use to provide flavour, texture and colour, it is,' reckoned one visitor. Culinary boundaries are thus breached in many dishes: in a plate of varied 'tapas' that includes sushi, couscous and pizza, for example, or a tower that combines Italian, German and English components in a fettucine and sauerkraut base, a smoked Cheddar and mustard centre, and a top surmounted by thick slices of buttered apple.

Intelligent adaptation coupled with soundly based techniques enable the kitchen to produce a starter of light pastry puffs filled with lovage-flavoured celeriac purée, surrounded by a moat of bortsch, and a smoothly textured Catalan baked custard with a crisp caramelised topping, served with half a well-ripened passion-fruit. Good Italian-style breads are an extra, staff are 'efficient and friendly', and organic French house wine is £9.50.

CHEFS: Paul Morgan, Lawrence Glass and Rickie Hodgson PROPRIETORS: Amanda Powley and Philip Taylor OPEN: Tue to Sun 12 to 10.30 CLOSED: 3 days Christmas MEALS: alc (main courses £8 to £9) SERVICE: not inc CARDS: Delta, Diners, MasterCard, Switch, Visa DETAILS: 70 seats. Private parties: 70 main room. Vegetarian meals. Children's helpings. No smoking in 1 dining-room. Wheelchair access (1 step; also WC). No music

Whytes

33 Western Street, Brighton BN1 2PG
TEL: (01273) 776618

COOKING 3
COST £29–£37

The Whytes' small but expansively welcoming restaurant just off the seafront feels like the sort of place where you might expect to find cream teas rather than confident Anglo-French cooking. Reports praise the down-to-earth humanity of the approach, and guests applaud many incidental felicities, such as parsnip crisps with crudités. A starter salad that pairs plaice fillets and Parma ham was judged 'an unusual and successful combination' by one reader, while another enjoyed a soup of celery, Stilton and apple. The odd Far Eastern note creeps in to main courses such as roast best end of lamb on wilted pak choi with 'Asian pesto', and crisp-roasted duckling sauced with ginger and lime. Desserts, recited at table, might take in lemon meringue ice-cream in a brandy-snap basket.

Wines are currently an eclectic bunch with prices opening at £9.40. As we went to press a new list containing more information to aid selection was being prepared.

CHEF: Ian Whyte   PROPRIETORS: Ian and Jane Whyte   OPEN: Tue to Sat D only 7 to 9.30 CLOSED: 26 to 30 Dec, last week Feb and first week Mar, bank hols   MEALS: Set D £16.45 (2 courses) to £20.50. BYO £5   SERVICE: not inc   CARDS: Amex, MasterCard, Visa   DETAILS: 36 seats. Private parties: 12 private room. Vegetarian meals. Music

---

BRIMFIELD Herefordshire   map 5

▲ *Roebuck* ✸✱ £   NEW ENTRY

Brimfield SY8 4NE
TEL: (01584) 711230   FAX: (01584) 711654
just off A49 Leominster to Ludlow road, 4m W of   COOKING 3
Tenbury Wells   COST £20–£49

Regular readers will remember this as a beacon in the area under its previous chef, Carole Evans, who has moved to the Three Horseshoes in Batcombe (see entry). The Willson-Lloyds, who bought the Roebuck in 1997, have maintained both the feel of a village pub and the basic layout: a bar with beams and dark wooden panelling, and a modern dining-room with bamboo chairs and pastel prints. Good raw materials – many of them local and thus seasonal – underpin an ambitiously long menu for the circumstances, supplemented by a daily selection of blackboard extras.

The varied repertoire straddles the traditional/modern divide, taking in anything from pigeon breast on saffron risotto, via half a dozen 'properly baked' filo pouches filled with a spicy crab mix, to a neat mound of overlapping slices of 'crisscross-seared' pink calf's liver, surrounded by a translucent bacon-flavoured sauce. Vegetables are 'old-fashioned' in quantity and presentation, the plainer ones making the running, and desserts have included rhubarb and apple crumble, and individual steamed autumn pudding with apricots, pecans and pear. Incidentals have not quite caught up with the rest of the operation, but service is well suited, and wines are broadly arranged by style on the short, carefully chosen and good-value list, starting with house French at £9.95.

CHEFS: Jonathan Waters and David Willson-Lloyd   PROPRIETORS: David and Susan Willson-Lloyd   OPEN: all week 12 to 2.30, 7 to 9.30   CLOSED: D 25 Dec   MEALS: alc (main courses £7.50 to £18.50). Set L £13.50, Set D £19.50 (set meals by arrangement only). BYO (corkage negotiable)   SERVICE: not inc, card slips closed   CARDS: Delta, MasterCard, Switch, Visa DETAILS: 90 seats. 20 seats outside. Private parties: 38 main room. Car park. Vegetarian meals. Children's helpings. No smoking in dining-room. Wheelchair access (not WC). No music ACCOMMODATION: 3 rooms, all with bath/shower. TV. Phone. B&B £45 to £60. Children welcome. High teas for children. Baby facilities. Afternoon teas (*The Which? Hotel Guide*)   £5

Card slips closed *in the details at the end of an entry indicates that the total on the slips of credit cards is closed when handed over for signature.*

▲ *means accommodation is available.*

Bell's Diner ⚡✖

1 York Road, Montpelier, Bristol BS6 5QB
TEL: (0117) 924 0357   FAX: (0117) 924 4280
take Picton Street off Cheltenham Road (A38) – runs   COOKING 5
into York Road   COST £23–£36

When the owners of Bell's Diner moved to River Station (see entry, below), Chris Wicks took over the running of this corner site, and is more than holding his own among the modern Bristol newcomers. A series of well-maintained interconnecting rooms, with dark petrol-blue woodwork, floors of grey slate and solid wood, and properly spaced tables now set with linen cloths, give it a gloss that makes it one of Bristol's 'nicest restaurants'. Mediterranean flavours – and that includes Moroccan spiced meatballs with preserved lemons and couscous – constitute the focus, but there is more besides, from duck egg and asparagus frittata, via nettle and wild garlic soup, to New England cod chowder. One couple dining in September was pleased to see the menu 'littered with autumnal fungi'. Set-price meals are good value, though there are enough supplements (as many as five out of eight choices) to suggest the format might be reviewed.

A good showing of fish and vegetable dishes keeps the tone light, and cooking is done 'with competence, understanding and no gimmicks', as in a 'big slab' of seared sea trout with pea and mint purée, broad beans, and a sorrel butter sauce. Even unassuming dishes are thoughtfully put together, for example a chunky barbecued duck breast with young leeks, asparagus and balsamic dressing. If the 'rich, accomplished' liquorice parfait with a fresh, tangy apple compote is on the menu, take it; otherwise expect lemon tart, chocolate brownie, or pannacotta with stewed rhubarb 'like the best old-fashioned home-cooking'. Efficient, unpretentious and informal service is 'as good as ever' – note there are two sittings on Friday and Saturday evenings – and the short list of intelligently chosen wines is well priced, starting with house Breganze at £8.95.

CHEF/PROPRIETOR: Christopher Wicks   OPEN: Tue to Fri and Sun L 12 (10.30 Sun) to 3, Mon to Sat D 7 to 10.30   CLOSED: 22 Aug to 1 Sept   MEALS: alc L (main courses £8 to £12.50). Set D £12.50 (2 courses) to £15.50   SERVICE: not inc, card slips closed; 10% for parties of 8 or more   CARDS: Delta, MasterCard, Switch, Visa   DETAILS: 60 seats. Private parties: 30 main room. Vegetarian meals. Children's helpings. No smoking in dining-room. Music   £5

Glass Boat

Welsh Back, Bristol BS1 4YB   COOKING 4
TEL: (0117) 929 0704   FAX: (0117) 929 7338   COST £25–£48

The setting is a renovated barge moored by Bristol Bridge in the heart of the city. It makes a novel venue for Michel Lemoine's assured modern cooking, which is based on a bedrock of Anglo-French cuisine spiced up with themes from elsewhere. Smoked cod is baked with lemon, thyme and garlic and served on a bed of Jerusalem artichoke purée, while duck is cooked long and slow and given a sauce of caramelised kumquats and orange segments. Lively invention runs to braised lamb in bread dough, fillet of salmon with a coconut crust, and peppered pineapple plus a sweet-and-sour sauce. Vegetarians are treated to dishes such as sweet butternut squash and mushrooms on a sage and lemon sauce. Desserts continue the eclectic mood, in almond and pine kernel pithiviers with star anise sauce, or chocolate pudding with vanilla whipped cream. The wine list casts its net wide for quality and value, those from Burgundy and Bordeaux standing out. House wines start at £9.95.

Under the same ownership, and with the same chef, Byzantium (at 2 Portwell Lane, Bristol) aims to bring an equally innovatory, and perhaps even more exotic, approach to the redeveloped dockside. It serves curried mushrooms with dry banana and popped rice, alongside more conventional hake with citrus and mustard butter, against a background of 'entertainment' in the form of jazz and belly dancing. Early reports indicate that it has not quite hit the nail on the head.

CHEF: Michel Lemoine   PROPRIETOR: Arne Ringner   OPEN: Mon to Fri L 12 to 2.30, Mon to Sat D 6.30 to 10.45   CLOSED: 24 Dec to 4 Jan, L bank hol Mons   MEALS: alc (main courses £13 to £19.50). Set L £10.95 (2 courses), Set D £17.50. BYO £5   SERVICE: not inc, card slips closed   CARDS: Amex, Delta, MasterCard, Switch, Visa   DETAILS: 100 seats. Private parties: 100 main room, 40 private room. Vegetarian meals. Children welcome. Wheelchair access (not WC). Music. Air-conditioned £5

Harveys 🍾

12 Denmark Street, Bristol BS1 5DQ	COOKING 5
TEL: (0117) 927 5034 FAX: (0117) 927 5001	COST £27–£69

A glass of sherry is probably the best way to get in the mood here. Harveys has been making and shipping it for centuries, and not just Bristol Cream either. The medieval wine cellars where they used to bottle it now look bright and modern with antique Bristol-blue bottles, colourful paintings, and large tables set with spotless glassware. Contemporary French cooking is the kitchen's preoccupation, as in a starter of duck and foie gras terrine with Chinese spices and candied onions, or pan-fried fillet of salmon with squid beignets, olive oil, tomato and basil. Menus change roughly six times a year, with luxuries such as langoustines and truffles, or scallops and caviare, attracting a supplement, or there is a six-course 'Discovery' menu with the option of six matching wines.

Soups are well reported – pumpkin with crab, or asparagus with a heap of brown shrimps in the centre – while roasting and pan-frying are the principal main-course treatments, as in roast pigeon with salted, herbed new potatoes and a sherry vinegar jus. Desserts make interesting use of fruit, producing a raspberry sablé with fig purée and rhubarb coulis, or a honey and pear cake to accompany spiced crème brûlée. If you indulge in that sherry, it had better be a large one if it's going to last while you peruse the long lines of first-growth clarets and fine burgundies that make up the bulk of Harveys' impressive wine list. Despite the plethora of grand names, it is possible to keep your feet on the ground with a good choice of bottles under £20. House wines are mostly £13. CELLARMAN'S CHOICE: Harveys Bicentenary *premier cru* Chablis 'Vaillons' 1994, J Moreau et Fils, £24; Montagne St-Emilion, Ch. Jura Plaisance 1990, £23.

CHEF: Daniel Galmiche PROPRIETOR: John Harvey & Sons OPEN: Mon to Fri L 12 to 2, Mon to Sat D 7 to 10.30 CLOSED: third week Feb, first 2 weeks Aug, bank hols MEALS: Set L £14.95 (2 courses) to £17.95, Set D £33.95 (2 courses) to £47. BYO £6.95 SERVICE: net prices CARDS: Amex, Delta, Diners, MasterCard, Switch, Visa DETAILS: 65 seats. Private parties: 100 main room, 40 private room. Vegetarian meals. No children under 10. No smoking while others eat. Music. Air-conditioned

Hunt's

26 Broad Street, Bristol BS1 2HG COOKING 5
TEL/FAX: (0117) 926 5580 COST £34–£48

The Hunts' restaurant is very much part of old mercantile Bristol, for it once dealt in tea and coffee when such commodities had shops to themselves. It now purveys Andrew Hunt's classical and confident cooking, which still seems to exert a powerful pull on a local clientele not short of good places to eat. New this year are one-plate lunches, which may take in salmon with orange and fennel salad, or pork noisette sauced with grain mustard and Gruyère, both served with new potatoes. Star turns from the main *carte* have included seared scallops with tomato, basil and coriander 'embellished with immaculate greenery', and 'beautifully timed, slightly pink' partridge with a rich Madeira sauce. Cornwall provides the monkfish, which is fricasseed with saffron, while sights are trained north of the border for Drambuie parfait with raspberry coulis. Nougat glacé left one reporter speechless with admiration. 'Friendly but discreet' service is the balance most people look for. Helpfully descriptive tasting notes fill out the ambitious wine list, which hauls in many good producers at sensible prices. French house selections open with Côtes de Duras Sauvignon Blanc at £9.95.

CHEF: Andrew Hunt PROPRIETORS: Andrew and Anne Hunt OPEN: Tue to Fri 12 to 2, Tue to Sat 7 to 10 CLOSED: 10 days Christmas, 1 week Easter, 2 weeks Aug MEALS: alc (main courses £14.50 to £16). Light L available SERVICE: not inc, card slips closed CARDS: Amex, Delta, MasterCard, Switch, Visa DETAILS: 40 seats. Private parties: 26 main room. Children's helpings. Wheelchair access (1 step; not WC). Music £5

Markwicks

43 Corn Street, Bristol BS1 1HT COOKING 6
TEL/FAX: (0117) 926 2658 COST £26–£54

A quietish shopping street by day, Corn Street turns into a lively thoroughfare at night, full of clubs and discos. Descend the spiral staircase, though, and all is calm within the cocooned basement that used to be a bank vault. Oak panels convey an Edwardian feel, 'bunch of grapes' lamps suggest art deco, and embossed walls 'in beige (but I mean that nicely)' hint at something Regency. Astute front-of-house staff miss nothing, yet this still contrives to be a 'happy and relaxed place' with an atmosphere of 'great confidence'. Elegant glassware, plain white plates and starched napery indicate the serious focus.

Stephen Markwick's unshowy food adopts a classical European approach: in provençale fish soup with rouille, guinea-fowl with morel mushroom sauce, and a plate of lamb's offal with mustard sauce and onion marmalade. His cooking is founded on sound principles. 'We are incorporating more organic foods,' he writes, and the materials are nothing if not prime, as one couple discovered with their 'juicy' rack of lamb with leeks, and grilled fillet of turbot – 'palpably fresh and properly cooked, bouncy and firm' – that came with a superior version of ratatouille and herby sauce vierge. Timing is accurate, flavouring is well judged, and textures are part of the appeal, evident for example in a mushroom risotto draped with pink pigeon breasts.

Daily fish specials and generous main courses come complete, with potatoes and a salad on the side, so there hardly seems any point in ordering extra vegetables. Desserts vary from a fruity banana and pineapple compote with mango sauce, via Paris-Brest, to a thin pastry tart filled with a rich chocolate confection and strawberries. Some fine-tuning to the wine list has resulted in a harmonious range of varieties, styles and flavours at extremely favourable prices – the house selection of 20 bins priced between £10 and £20 striking just the right note and introductions from the New World and Italy are particularly sound. CELLARMAN'S CHOICE: Albariño Lagar de Cervera 1997, Rias Baixas, Galicia, £13.50; Cornas la Geynale 1994, Robert Michel, £25.

CHEF: Stephen Markwick PROPRIETORS: Stephen and Judy Markwick OPEN: Tue to Fri L 12 to 2, Tue to Sat D 7 to 10 CLOSED: 1 week Christmas, 1 week Easter, 2 weeks Aug MEALS: alc (main courses £15 to £17). Set L £13.50 (2 courses) to £17, Set D £23.50 SERVICE: not inc, card slips closed CARDS: Amex, Delta, Diners, MasterCard, Switch, Visa DETAILS: 40 seats. Private parties: 10 main room, 6 to 20 private rooms. Vegetarian meals. Children's helpings. No music

River Station £

NEW ENTRY

The Grove, Bristol BS1 4RB
TEL: (0117) 914 4434 FAX: (0117) 934 9990

COOKING 5
COST £21–£50

Dockside crime presumably having been wiped out, the old river-police station near the city centre has been given a new lease of life. Run by the team that brought us Bell's Diner (now leased and run separately, see entry above), it is an uncompromisingly modern building, whose black walnut tables, elm floor, marble, glass, zinc and stainless steel could not be a bolder display of cosmopolitan ambition. The ground floor is a non-bookable deli and espresso bar serving snacks and cold foods, while the main dining-room is a floor above, with a balcony over the water for fine weather. This is a purposeful place, with a mission to serve simple good food. It takes away the fuss from eating out, and relies on its skill with matter-of-fact dishes for effect.

In place of elaborate descriptions, the menu simply lists ingredients in a dish: 'deep-fried crab-cakes, sweet chilli sauce + pickled papaya', or 'salad of smoked eel + mustard leaves, lardons + poached egg'. Despite well-hung chargrilled Scottish sirloin with chips and béarnaise, the repertoire leans towards the fish, vegetable and farinaceous end of the spectrum with asparagus and hollandaise, pumpkin ravioli with roasted walnut salsa, or 'beautifully underdone' seared scallops, served with coriander-flecked noodles and black beans in a chilli-hot sauce.

What is more, the cooking is accurate, producing a rich thick artichoke broth – 'just the sort of home-made thing that impresses for being tasty and not contrived' – and hearty duck breast 'cooked pinkish', properly rested and thickly sliced, as well as a 'splendid' tarte fine with a topping of quince compote and a neat pattern of apple slices, served with a dollop of crème fraîche. A sharp modern list of 60-plus wines, divided broadly by style, stays mostly under £20, and all 12 house wines, plus a few others, are available by the glass. Prices start at £9 a bottle.

CHEF: Peter Taylor   PROPRIETORS: Shirley-Anne Bell, Mark Hall, John Payne and Peter Taylor   OPEN: Sun to Fri L 12 to 2.30, all week D 6 to 10.30 (11 Fri and Sat)   MEALS: alc (main courses £8 to £16.50). Set L £10.50 (2 courses) to £15, Set D Sun to Thur £12.95 (2 courses) to £16. Weekend brunch menu 11.30 to 2.30. Cold food available all week in downstairs coffee bar   SERVICE: not inc   CARDS: Amex, Delta, Diners, MasterCard, Switch, Visa   DETAILS: 120 seats. 30 seats outside. Private parties: 120 main room. Vegetarian meals. Children's helpings. No-smoking area. No music

Rocinantes ▼

85 Whiteladies Road, Bristol BS8 2NT   COOKING 4
TEL: (0117) 973 4482   FAX: (0117) 974 3913   COST £24–£44

Regulars at this tapas bar and restaurant in genteel Clifton are seemingly so determined to enter into the Spanish spirit of things that they are happily prepared to sit at outside tables on a chilly April evening. The structure of the place – loud, busy bar at the front, quieter dining-area at the back and upstairs – seems authentic too, and while this 'is not a place for posh frocks', the atmosphere is convivial enough. Fine tapas in the bar include freshly sliced Serrano ham, patatas bravas, proper brandade and spiced olives. Eating from the main menu, a reporter was impressed by genuine earthiness in a terrine of pigeon and pork wrapped in Serrano and cabbage leaf, served with creamily rich celeriac rémoulade. Organic meats are accorded star billing, perhaps grilled lamb steak with a butter sauce containing anchovy, garlic and rosemary, or duck confit with green lentils and roast vegetables.

Not everything on the bill of fare is Spanish; a modern Italian influence makes itself felt, and there has been Moroccan lamb tagine with preserved lemons and couscous. Spanish cheeses such as Picos blue or ewes' milk Manchego are the savoury alternatives to mainstream puddings of blueberry cheesecake or lemon tart. Friendliness without intrusiveness distinguishes the service. Twenty-one wines (including five organics) are offered by the glass between £2.10 and £2.75 on the predominantly Old World wine list, or there is always the trendy range of beers for those who like to drink straight from the bottle. Palacio Leon house wines are £9.50.

CHEF: Barny Haughton and Brian Dougherty   PROPRIETORS: Barny Haughton and Matthew Pruen   OPEN: all week 12 (10 Sun) to 3, 6 to 11 (10.30 Sun)   CLOSED: 25 and 26 Dec, 1 Jan   MEALS: alc (main courses £8.50 to £15). Set L Mon to Fri £9.50 (2 courses). Tapas menu in bar area   SERVICE: not inc; 10% for parties of 5 or more   CARDS: Amex, Delta, Diners, MasterCard, Switch, Visa   DETAILS: 90 seats. 40 seats outside. Private parties: 30 main room. Vegetarian meals. Children welcome. Wheelchair access (1 step; not WC). Music

Dining-rooms where music, either live or recorded, is never played are signalled by No music *in the details at the end of an entry.*

BRITWELL SALOME Oxfordshire
map 2

The Goose ⁵⁄✗
| NEW ENTRY |

Britwell Salome OX9 5LG   COOKING 5
TEL: (01491) 612304   FAX: (01491) 614822   COST £30–£46

A simple country pub is the setting for one of the bigger splashes made in rural Oxfordshire this year. Chris and Kate Barber opened in January on the outskirts of this rather racily named village, he having previously cooked at Buckingham and St James's Palaces, a pair of grandish stately homes in London. The bar area may be quite plain, but the two dining-rooms are done in a handsome deep bluey-green that looks most enticing after dark. Relaxed confidence and an absence of formality characterise the service, and the cooking is firmly in the vein of modern simplicity, with attention focused on a few well-chosen ingredients.

Choice at both lunch and dinner is restricted to three options at each course, with variable prices during the day, a fixed price in the evening. One of the first courses is always a soup, perhaps creamy, smooth asparagus or earthy wild mushroom, and scallops have turned up too, sliced around a mound of soft couscous. Rack of lamb with beetroot is something of an essay in pink, the meat very rare and the root juices bleeding into the sauce, while a leg of crisp-skinned roast chicken may come on a plateful of turnip and parsnip purée, surrounded by admirably intense cep gravy. Fish alternatives might be baked halibut on mussel ragoût, or tuna, briefly grilled and served on green beans with two dressings, one containing sun-dried tomato, the other a pesto-laced truffle oil. A plated cheese selection brings together a mixture of impressive British and French examples, 'all in good nick', while puddings include rhubarb ice-cream with raspberries, flavoured crème brûlée, and satisfying banana bavarois. 'We came away feeling the Goose has filled a niche,' wrote one party. The modestly proportioned wine list is priced almost entirely below £20. Choices are pretty inspired, although whites are fairly deeply rooted in Sauvignon and Chardonnay territory. Prices are from £9.95.

CHEF: Chris Barber   PROPRIETORS: Chris and Kate Barber   OPEN: Tue to Sun L 12 to 2.30 (3.30 Sun), Tue to Sat D 7 to 10   MEALS: alc L Tue to Sat (main courses £10 to £15). Set L Sun £20 (2 courses) to £25, Set D £20 (2 courses) to £25   SERVICE: not inc   CARDS: Delta, MasterCard, Switch, Visa   DETAILS: 60 seats. 25 seats outside. Private parties: 32 main room. Car park. Children's helpings. No smoking in dining-room. Wheelchair access (1 step; not WC). Occasional music

BROADHEMBURY Devon
map 2

Drewe Arms

Broadhembury EX14 0NF
TEL/FAX: (01404) 841267   COOKING 3
off A373, between Cullompton and Honiton   COST £31–£37

Broadhembury – little more than a collection of thatched cottages with a church and an inn – enchants visitors: 'a quintessential English village,' one called it. 'We are very much a pub with a dining-room, with everything that entails,' writes Nigel Burge; that means a convivial atmosphere, bar snacks and a couple of blackboard menus. Fish is very much the main business, sometimes with a Scandinavian twist – gravad lax, or marinated herring with a tot of aquavit – and sometimes not. The freshness of scallops and Dover sole has impressed, and simple treatments are a plus: steamed sea bass with pesto, turbot with hollandaise, crab salad. Alternatively, there might be rare beef sandwiches, or tenderloin of venison with wild mushroom sauce. 'Not cheap, but value for money' was a brief summing-up by one reporter who finished with a 'gorgeous' tarte Tatin. Wines focus on Chardonnay and Sauvignon blanc, but there is interest elsewhere, most bottles are under £20, and half-bottle and by-the-glass offerings are fair.

CHEFS/PROPRIETORS: Kerstin and Nigel Burge   OPEN: all week L 12 to 2, Mon to Sat D 7 to 10   CLOSED: 25 Dec   MEALS: Set L and D £21. BYO minimum £5   SERVICE: not inc   CARDS: none   DETAILS: 30 seats. 40 seats outside. Private parties: 20 main room. Vegetarian meals. Children's helpings. Wheelchair access (1 step; also women's WC). No music   £5

BROADWAY Worcestershire   map 5

▲ *Dormy House* ♈ ⁑✶

Willersey Hill, Broadway WR12 7LF
TEL: (01386) 852711   FAX: (01386) 858636
EMAIL: reservations@dormyhouse.co.uk   COOKING 4
just off A44, 1m NW of Broadway   COST £28–£62

On a steep wooded escarpment above Broadway, looking out towards the Vale of Evesham, Dormy House bills itself as 'a seventeenth-century farmhouse with twentieth-century comforts'. The 'quite plush' Tapestries dining-room inhabits a conservatory with attractively set tables, comfortable chairs and lots of space. Menus embrace both à la carte and set-price meals, as well as a six-course 'gourmet' option, while the vegetarian *carte* might offer vegetable fritters in light tempura batter, alongside a more adventurous dish of beetroot and sweetcorn fritters with an onion and orange marmalade on tzatziki sauce.

Many ideas derive from the country-house tradition, but given Cornish cod in a real ale batter, and steamed jam roly-poly, Alan Cutler clearly is not a slave to them. He is a busy man, judging by the number and intricacy of dishes, but a sound assessment of workable flavour combinations keeps the whole thing on track, from grilled tuna on salad niçoise with a smoked gazpacho sauce, to crêpes suzette. Finding a wine to drink may take some time: introductions to each region and individual notes accompanying the numerous bins make such fascinating reading that it's hard to concentrate on the matter in hand. Classicists will delight in the French collection, but modernists won't be disappointed either. Ten French house wines start at £10.50 a bottle, £2.05 a glass. CELLARMAN'S CHOICE: Petit Chablis 1996, Dom. Thierry Hamelin, £19.34; Lussac-St Emilion, Ch. Lyonnat 1994, £21.95.

'The summer menu had chicken as the main course, and I was told curtly when I ordered it, "The chicken will be beef." When I asked how it would be done, he replied, "The same."'
(On eating in Buckinghamshire)

CHEFS: Alan Cutler and Colin Seymour   PROPRIETOR: Jorgen Philip-Sorensen   OPEN: Sun to Fri
L 12.30 to 2, all week D 7 to 9.30 (9 Sun)   MEALS: alc Mon to Fri L, all week D (main courses L
£8.50 to £9, D £15.50 to £20). Set L Sun £19.50, Set D £30.50 to £35. BYO £8.50   SERVICE: not
inc   CARDS: Amex, Delta, Diners, MasterCard, Switch, Visa   DETAILS: 80 seats. Private parties:
40 main room, 8 and 14 private rooms. Car park. Vegetarian meals. Children welcome before
7.30pm. Children's helpings. No smoking in 1 dining-room. Occasional music
ACCOMMODATION: 49 rooms, all with bath/shower. TV. Phone. B&B £71 to £142. Rooms for
disabled. Children welcome. High teas for children. Baby facilities. Dogs welcome in bedrooms
only (£5 charge for dogs). Afternoon teas (*The Which? Hotel Guide*)

▲ *Lygon Arms*

High Street, Broadway WR12 7DU
TEL: (01386) 852255   FAX: (01386) 858611   COOKING 6
EMAIL: info@the-lygon-arms.co.uk   COST £38 £72

The departure of Roger Narbett and arrival of Graham Nesbitt in the kitchen
seems to have made little difference at this landmark Cotswold inn. Except, that
is, for the barrel-vaulted dining-room, which seems to get a new coat of paint
every time the head chef changes: one wall features the dark wooden balustrades
of the famous minstrels' gallery, another is taken up with mullioned windows,
and all around are stags' heads, coats of arms and suits of armour. The reason for
the seamless transition might lie in Graham Nesbitt's country-house experience,
and in the fact that some of his predecessor's dishes continue on the menu.

His own skill has a lot to do with it too. An inspection meal combined
outstanding raw materials with impeccable timing: 'every dish I ate was clever',
including a starter of 'brilliant' nuttily seared scallops, surrounding a squat
tower of filo pastry filled with Cornish crab that was spiced with chilli and
coriander. There are plain chargrills for the traditionally minded, but that seems
a waste given the originality of a mushroom and rabbit broth with apple and
tarragon ravioli, and the accomplishment of roast loin of 'terrifically tasty'
Cotswold lamb served with a mound of correctly made risotto.

Technical proficiency, a feature of the cooking throughout, helps to make a
resounding success of chocolate and hazelnut soufflé, served with nougatine
ice-cream and a jug of chocolate sauce that the waiter pours in. Pre-meal nibbles
and petits fours with coffee are not up to the same standard, and teamwork and
organisation among waiting staff could be improved. Wines are predominantly
French, of high quality and priced accordingly, but house red and white are £14.

CHEF: Graham Nesbitt   PROPRIETOR: The Savoy Group   OPEN: all week 12.30 to 2, 7.30 to
9.15   MEALS: alc (main courses £20 to £24). Set L £24.50, Set D £38   SERVICE: not inc, card
slips closed   CARDS: Amex, Delta, Diners, MasterCard, Switch, Visa   DETAILS: 120 seats. 40
seats outside. Private parties: 95 main room, 12 to 95 private rooms. Vegetarian meals.
Children's helpings. No children under 8 at D. No smoking in dining-room. Wheelchair access
(also WC). Music   ACCOMMODATION: 65 rooms, all with bath/shower. TV. Phone. B&B £105 to
£165. Rooms for disabled. Children welcome. High teas for children. Baby facilities. Afternoon
teas. Swimming-pool (*The Which? Hotel Guide*)

---

 indicates that there has been a change of chef since last year's Guide, and the Editor
has judged that the change is of sufficient interest to merit the reader's attention.

Le Poussin ♥ ⅝✳

The Courtyard, Brookley Road,	
Brockenhurst SO42 7RB	COOKING 7
TEL: (01590) 623063 FAX: (01590) 622912	COST £27–£52

The restaurant, between a hairdresser's and a bookshop, is small – no more than half a dozen tables – and the décor stylish, with deep forest-green chairs, and tartan covers under white tablecloths. Beyond tiny posy-holders, salt sprinklers, and coloured prints of 'what look like rare-breed chickens', the poussin theme is not taken to extremes. Good lighting ensures that 'for once one can see what one is eating', which is a blessing because the food is worth looking at. A 'beautifully made' dish of chicken ballotine, for example, is arrayed in four constituent parts: slices of 'seriously pink' chargrilled chicken liver, a small salad of interesting leaves, asparagus tips, and the sliced ballottine itself in a little grain mustard dressing.

Meals can be two, three or four courses long, typically with a choice beween two items, and are put together using 'formidable technical skills'. Alex Aitken collects mushrooms, perhaps partnering morels with breast of guinea-fowl, or oyster mushrooms with a piece of brill, bone still in, with a 'quite simply perfect' sauce that incorporates champagne vinegar and truffle: 'posh ingredients used with a point'. Sheer excitement may be elusive, but the food is certainly 'interesting', and 'fabulous' raw materials (of which the brill was an example) show to good effect in the regularly appearing trio of meats – fillets of venison, beef and pork – all pink, served with little cones of shredded cabbage.

Soufflés are a forte, typically accompanied by a sauce and a sorbet, and all the elements were rated 'perfect' in themselves at one meal, even if they did all involve just the one flavour, passion-fruit. Freshly made bread and creamy butter add to the appeal, although nibbles and petits fours are not quite up to the same standard as the rest. Service is 'professional but frosty'. Alex Aitken has taken over the buying and selling of the wines, and 'a special edition' of Le Poussin's list with notes handwritten by him is now available. The classic regions of France are given thorough treatment, mature vintages abound, and there is a fair choice at all price levels. Twelve wines from Worlds Old and New are available by the glass from £3. CELLARMAN'S CHOICE: St-Aubin 1993, Roland Dagneau, £17.50; Weinert Cavas de Weinert 1992, Mendoza, Argentina, £19.50.

CHEFS: Alex Aitken and Angus Hyne   PROPRIETORS: Alex and Caroline Aitken   OPEN: Wed to Sun 12 to 1.30, 7 to 9.30   MEALS: Set L £10 (2 courses) to £15, Set D £22.50 (2 courses) to £27.50   SERVICE: not inc   CARDS: MasterCard, Switch, Visa   DETAILS: 24 seats. 8 seats outside. Private parties: 24 main room. Car park. Vegetarian meals. Children welcome. No smoking in dining-room. Wheelchair access (also WC). Music

---

The 2000 Guide *will be published before Christmas 1999. Reports on meals are most welcome at any time of the year, but are particularly valuable in the spring (no later than June). Send them to* The Good Food Guide, *FREEPOST, 2 Marylebone Road, London NW1 1YN. Or email your report to guidereports@which.co.uk.*

BROMSGROVE Worcestershire   map 5

▲ Grafton Manor ⁵✱

Grafton Lane, Bromsgrove B61 7HA
TEL: (01527) 579007 FAX: (01527) 575221
EMAIL: steven@grafton.unet.uk   COOKING 4
off B4091, 1½m SW of Bromsgrove   COST £32–£55

The red-brick, mullion-windowed manor devotes some of its spare acres to growing herbs, vegetables and fruit (including quince and medlar), and the scale inside is impressive too, from a first-floor lounge with a big log fire, to a non-smoking dining-room with crisp napery, simple white china and fresh flowers. Simon Morris's well-known love of Indian food reaches a climax every January when he runs a two-week Indian festival; it is worth checking dates when booking. The rest of the time, the style reverts to its southern European calling: chickpea, snail and chorizo broth with aïoli, for example, or goats' cheese in a couscous crust with a dollop of pesto, 'a hefty portion with hefty tastes'.

Bold flavours – sea bass served with roughly textured potatoes dotted with bitter olives and sweet tomatoes – sit comfortably beside more indulgent ones, for example 'rich, creamy and subtly balanced' ravioli filled with chicken and smoked bacon, served with truffle-infused Parmesan cream. The four-course dinner offers greatest choice, invention and variety, and high standards are reached with apparent ease, not least in desserts such as chilled coconut rice-pudding with a 'fruity kick' from its accompanying lime sorbet. Good bread includes cumin-flavoured 'Goan rolls', and although mark-ups can be high there is enough on the French-dominated wine list to suit most pockets, starting with eight house wines around £12 to £13. Wedding parties may close the dining-room on Saturday evenings.

CHEF: Simon Morris PROPRIETORS: the Morris family OPEN: Sun to Fri L 12.30 to 1.30, all week D 7 to 9.30 MEALS: Set L £20.50, Set D £27.85 to £32.75 SERVICE: not inc, card slips closed CARDS: Amex, Delta, Diners, MasterCard, Switch, Visa DETAILS: 70 seats. Private parties: 60 main room, 50 private room. Car park. Vegetarian meals. Children's helpings. No smoking in dining-room. Wheelchair access (2 steps; not WC). No music ACCOMMODATION: 9 rooms, all with bath/shower. TV. Phone. B&B £85 to £150. Rooms for disabled. Children welcome. Dogs welcome in kennels only. Afternoon teas. Fishing (The Which? Hotel Guide)

BROXTON Cheshire   map 7

▲ Frogg Manor ⁵✱

Nantwich Road, Broxton CH3 9JH   COOKING 3
TEL: (01829) 782629 FAX: (01829) 782459   COST £24–£63

Here be frogs indeed, though only imitation ones. They lounge on the sundial and huddle among the reeds, reflecting the proprietor's passion for the genus Ranidae. The setting is a well-kept Georgian country mansion, where John Sykes seems to do most things himself. A certain nostalgia pervades the menu, from the announcement of its fixed price in guineas to many of the dishes themselves, which take in sausage and mash (as a starter), prawns marie-rose with melon, and fillet steak in wine and brandy. That said, Paraguayan chicken pancake marks a departure from the common round.Grilled chèvre accompanied by a sauté of peppers, spring onions and celery has been 'good, rustic and simply presented', or there might be halibut fillet rolled in mixed grains and served with mustard sauce; portions tend to be generous Those whom the Frogg Manor mood takes certainly fall under its spell: 'the food and surroundings were lovely,' says one letter, 'and we could have stayed a lot longer.' Wines are stylistically grouped, and include a handful of good producers, but prices are not giveaway. Monthly-changing house wines are £10.

CHEFS: John E. Sykes and Stuart Brown   PROPRIETOR: John E. Sykes   OPEN: all week D only 7.15 to 10.30 (L by appointment only)   MEALS: Set L £16.80, Set D £27.30   SERVICE: not inc, card slips closed   CARDS: Amex, Delta, Diners, MasterCard, Switch, Visa   DETAILS: 55 seats. Private parties: 55 main room. Car park. Vegetarian meals. Children's helpings. No smoking in 1 dining-room. Music   ACCOMMODATION: 6 rooms, all with bath/shower. TV. Phone. Room only £50 to £125 Children welcome. Dogs welcome in 1 room only Afternoon teas (*The Which? Hotel Guide*) (£5)

BRUTON Somerset   map 2

Truffles

95 The High Street, Bruton BA10 0AR   COOKING 4
TEL/FAX: (01749) 812255   COST £21–£36

Very little seems to change in the diminutive front room of this old weaver's cottage, which for more than a decade has served as the setting for the Bottrills' smartly provincial restaurant. Martin Bottrill continues to cook what might be called 'strenuously inventive' food, pulling together worldwide influences and themes for his monthly fixed-price menus. In March, for example, you might kick off with Jerusalem artichoke mousse, which is served with smoked prawns, gravad lax and a mustard dressing. Follow perhaps with stuffed fillets of whiting wrapped in nori seaweed, deep-fried in tempura batter and served with oriental sauce, or with a tranche of calf's liver on a bed of polenta mash with a lime and sage jus. To finish, there is Truffles' layered gâteau, although a brighter finale might be iced fig parfait 'teardrop' served with a bitter chocolate shell and a lemon cream sauce. Cut-price mid-week suppers are also worth knowing about, although these need to be pre-booked. Two dozen half-bottles provide a commendable back-up to the ever-changing list of around 40 bins, most of which are supplied by Christopher Piper Wines. House wines start at £9.95.

CHEF: Martin Bottrill   PROPRIETORS: Denise and Martin Bottrill   OPEN: Sun L 12 to 1.30, Mon to Sat D 7 to 9   CLOSED: 2 weeks end Feb   MEALS: Set L Sun £13.95, Set D Tue to Thurs £12.95 (2 courses), Set D Mon to Sat £22.50   SERVICE: not inc, card slips closed   CARDS: MasterCard, Visa   DETAILS: 22 seats. Private parties: 22 main room. Vegetarian meals. Children's helpings. No children under 5. No smoking while others eat. Wheelchair access (2 steps; not WC). No music   (£5)

'The waiter told me that duck sometimes comes like that: that is, impossible to cut.' (On eating in London)

BUCKLAND Gloucestershire   map 5

▲ Buckland Manor 🍷 🥪 ⁑

Buckland WR12 7LY
TEL: (01386) 852626 FAX: (01386) 853557
EMAIL: buckland-manor-uk@msn.com   COOKING 4
off B4632, 2m SW of Broadway   COST £39–£72

The thirteenth-century manor-house in the Severn Valley sits next to the church amid acres of pristine grounds, its flowerbeds ablaze with colour in summer. In the dining-room, oak panelling has been rendered creamy white to lighten the tone, the better to set off the oil paintings and royal-blue curtains and carpet. Kenneth Wilson took up the cudgels in spring 1998, maintaining the essentially English cooking (with gentle French inflections) that is the familiar country-house style. Lunch is fixed price, dinner à la carte, the latter encompassing cold ballottine of quail stuffed luxuriously with duck confit, pistachios and truffles, and main courses such as Dover sole fricassée with wild mushrooms, broad beans and tarragon.

An early inspection yielded a fine tart of mature goats' cheese resting on a sweetly jammy tomato base surrounded by good rocket pesto, and a complicated main dish in which a fillet of pot-roasted salmon arrived on a risotto of lemon and thyme in a pink shellfish bisque, topped with a pasta case of langoustine. Soufflés baked to order are the defining dessert of this style, and a 'fine, wobbling' strawberry one, served with a pastry case of chocolate sorbet, is fittingly feather-light. Alternatives might include poached pear sablé, or a version of crêpes suzette. It is all despatched in a 'courteous, but stiffly formal' manner, the bread silver-served and the brioche for smoked salmon elegantly swathed in linen. The wine 'book' now runs to 570 bins, each with its own tasting note, plus an impressive 141 half-bottles. France is given the full treatment, Burgundy in particular standing out with its collection of top producers, including several Domaine de la Romanée-Contis, while California just has the edge in a strong New World showing. House wines and French country wines offer good drinking up to £24, with around 25 by the glass. CELLARMAN'S CHOICE: Pouilly-Fuissé, Tête de Cuvée 1996, Jean-Marie Guffens, £36; Pessac-Léognan, Ch. Le Pape 1993, £26.

CHEF: Kenneth Wilson PROPRIETORS: Roy and Daphne Vaughan OPEN: all week 12.30 to 1.45, 7.30 to 9 MEALS: alc (main courses £18.50 to £22). Set L £29.50. BYO £10. Bar menu L SERVICE: not inc CARDS: Amex, Delta, Diners, MasterCard, Switch, Visa DETAILS: 38 seats. 20 seats outside. Private parties: 38 main room. Car park. No children under 12. Jacket and tie. No smoking in dining-room. Wheelchair access (2 steps; not WC). No music ACCOMMODATION: 13 rooms, all with bath/shower. TV. Phone. B&B £178 to £325. Rooms for disabled. No children under 12. No dogs. Afternoon teas. Swimming-pool (*The Which? Hotel Guide*)

Report forms are at the back of the book; write a letter if you prefer; or email us at guidereports@which.co.uk.

See inside the front cover for an explanation of the symbols used at the tops of entries.

BUCKLAND Oxfordshire

map 2

▲ *Lamb Inn* ▼ ✸ £

| Lamb Lane, Buckland SN7 8QN | COOKING 2 |
| TEL: (01367) 870484   FAX: (01367) 870675 | COST £20–£49 |

Under the stewardship of Peta and Paul Barnard, the eighteenth-century Lamb has become a 'popular and worthwhile' eating venue, serving the needs of its neighbourhood and beyond. A dining-room, done out in shades of blue and yellow, has been tacked on to the original building, adding a touch of sophistication to what is essentially a rustic country pub. An atmosphere of 'well-being and enjoyment' pervades the place. One menu serves both the bar and restaurant, and the repertoire is constantly changing. Here you might find home-cured fillet of beef, or roast widgeon with plum, cinnamon and apple sauce, alongside a warm salad of Cajun spiced monkfish, or whole sea bass baked on a bed of sea salt with Pernod sauce. An inspector who visited for Sunday lunch was impressed by the green pea and ham soup, and a succulent fillet of salmon in filo pastry with a creamy sauce of prawns and avocado. Brûlées, fruity tarts and flans make up the majority of desserts. A cleverly chosen wine list reflects the lively interest in the subject taken by the Barnards; indeed, wine tastings are a regular event. Some 70 bins ensure that most palates are catered for, and prices are such that most pockets will be happy, too. House wines start at £8.95 a bottle (£1.75 a glass).

CHEF: Paul Barnard   PROPRIETORS: Paul and Peta Barnard   OPEN: all week 12 to 2 (2.30 Sun), 6.30 to 9.30   CLOSED: 25 and 26 Dec.   MEALS: alc (main courses £6 to £17). Set L Mon to Sat £8.50 (2 courses), Set L Sun £19.25   SERVICE: not inc, card slips closed   CARDS: Amex, Delta, MasterCard, Switch, Visa   DETAILS: 60 seats. 40 seats outside. Private parties: 75 main room, 16 private room. Car park. Vegetarian meals. Children's helpings. No smoking in dining-room.Music   ACCOMMODATION: 4 rooms, all with bath/shower. TV. Phone. B&B £35 to £55. Children welcome. Afternoon teas. Garden   (£5)

BURNHAM MARKET Norfolk

map 6

Fishes' £

| Market Place, Burnham Market PE31 8HE | COOKING 3 |
| TEL: (01328) 738588   FAX: (01328) 730534 | COST £19–£43 |

'Nothing changes' volunteered one reporter who returned after an interval. This all-female enterprise still has a 'homely sitting-room' with newspapers, an informal atmosphere, and a menu offering 'seafood for thought'. Brancaster oysters come either fresh, or perhaps baked with Stilton, gravlax is made in-house, and soups are highly rated, whether vegetable or 'real' crab soup with chunky pieces. Other crustacean dishes typically include scallops au gratin, and (for a supplement to the set-price lunch) a plate of lobster, crab, crevette, prawns and shrimps.

One correspondent considers it 'everything you would expect from a fish restaurant', which means fresh fish 'perfectly cooked' and simply sauced: herb butter for plaice, sorrel for salmon, or black butter and capers for skate wing. A dish combining ham, smoked chicken and duck is usually on hand as an alternative. As with many fish restaurants, sweets are not given a high priority, but that hasn't stopped one reporter enjoying a 'world-beating' treacle tart with sour cream. Bread is good, more is offered, and wines are cannily chosen with an eye for value, including a handful from the excellent Chabisienne Co-operative. Prices start at £8.50.

CHEFS: Gillian Cape and Paula Ayres   PROPRIETOR: Gillian Cape   OPEN: Tue to Sun L 12 to 2 (2.15 Sun), Tue to Sat D 6.45 to 9.30 (9 Mon to Fri in winter, and bank hol Sun), and L and D bank hol Mon   CLOSED: 24 to 27 Dec, 3 weeks Jan   MEALS: alc (main courses £6.50 to £13.50). Set L Tue to Sat £12.25, Set L Sun £14.25. BYO £5   SERVICE: not inc, card slips closed   CARDS: Amex, Delta, Diners, MasterCard, Switch, Visa   DETAILS: 42 seats. Private parties: 12 main room. Children's helpings. No children under 5 at D after 8.30. Wheelchair access (1 step; not WC). No music   (£5)

BURPHAM West Sussex   map 3

George and Dragon

Burpham BN18 9RR
TEL: (01903) 883131
2½m up single-track, no-through road signposted   COOKING 3
Warningcamp off A27, 1m E of Arundel   COST £23–£33

'Please remove muddy boots before entering,' says a sign on the door – a reminder that this country pub is in prime walking country, with stunning views all around. It also has high aspirations and caters for a prosperous, gentrified crowd. Bar meals and a serious dedication to real ale are two of its pubby attributes, although the kitchen also woos customers with its upmarket restaurant menu. Dinner is fixed-price for two or three courses, and there is clearly some imagination at work in the kitchen. King scallops served on a sweet potato and lentil mash with creamy green pepper sauce, or smoked quail salad with quail's eggs set the mood, before main courses ranging from rack of Southdown lamb with rosemary crust on an apricot and brandy sauce, to steamed fillet of brill with Noilly Prat and lime sauce. Desserts tend to be substantial, as in pavlova, chocolate brandy mousse, and passion-fruit cheese-cake. Around four dozen wines trip affordably around the globe. House wines are £10.

CHEFS: Kate Holle and Gary Scutt   PROPRIETORS: Kate Holle and James Rose   OPEN: Sun L 12.15 to 2, Mon to Sat D 7.15 to 9.30   CLOSED: 25 Dec, restaurant closed bank hols   MEALS: Set L £16, Set D £16.75 (2 courses) to £19.75. Bar meals available all week   SERVICE: 10%, card slips closed   CARDS: Amex, Delta, MasterCard, Switch, Visa   DETAILS: 36 seats. Private parties: 36 main room. Car park. Vegetarian meals. No children under 8. No pipes in dining-room. Wheelchair access (not WC). Music   (£5)

'Air-dried Cumbrian ham ... came swimming in a damson sauce (not mentioned on the menu).... For the main course we had both ordered venison with (you're ahead of me!) a damson sauce.... It was at [dessert] stage that I asked if I could have a damson dessert, as I have never had a meal with damsons at every course. A laugh and an apology meant that I was able to fulfil this unique experience.' (On eating in Cumbria)

BURTON ON THE WOLDS Leicestershire	map 5

Langs | NEW ENTRY |

147 Melton Road, Burton on the Wolds LE12 5TQ	COOKING 5
TEL/FAX: (01509) 880980	COST £20–£42

This barn conversion, next door to a garden centre, opened for business in December 1997. Stone-flagged floors and a beamed ceiling survive as reminders of its origins, but refurbishment has brought swish red and gold striped wallpaper, deep-pile carpets, rattan chairs, and crisp white damask tablecloths. In the words of one early visitor, it is 'a restaurant of integrity and ambition', which cooks in the contemporary mode of Moroccan-style sea bream, and duck confit with glazed plums and damson essence. A confident chef, Gordon Lang has an enterprising penchant for trotters and oxtail, hotpots and navarins, although he may not indulge this much beyond grilled lambs' liver, or pot-roast beef with sage dumplings, preferring instead to major on chargrilled chicken with Caesar salad, or beef tournedos.

Good timing and a predilection for direct flavours give the cooking its direction, producing at one meal a generous piece of moist salmon 'salted and seared to a caramel-coloured crispness', served with dauphinoise potatoes 'browned to a turn', and a buttery saffron-flecked emulsion. Desserts tend to be simple classics: Eton mess, peach melba, or queen of puddings on 'fresh and frothy home-made custard'. Service is 'swift and unobtrusive', and the wine list combines affordable bottles with special ones, starting with Côtes du Rhône red and Jurançon white at £10.75 (£2.75 a glass).

CHEF: Gordon Lang   PROPRIETORS: Gordon Lang and Paul Simms   OPEN: Tue to Fri and Sun L 12.15 to 2 (Sun), Tue to Sat D 7 to 9.45   MEALS: alc (main courses £11.50 to £15). Set L Tue to Fri £9.95 to £11.95 (2 courses), Set L Sun £12.95   SERVICE: not inc, card slips closed   CARDS: Delta, MasterCard, Switch, Visa   DETAILS: 40 seats. 8 seats outside. Private parties: 50 main room. Car park. Vegetarian meals. Children's helpings. Wheelchair access (also WC). Music

BURY ST EDMUNDS Suffolk	map 6

Maison Bleue at Mortimer's ✳ £

30/31 Churchgate Street, Bury St Edmunds IP33 1RG	COOKING 3
TEL: (01284) 760623	COST £21–£52

What was once plain Mortimer's has now been expanded and relaunched under the ownership of the indefatigable Régis Crépy of Suffolk repute (see Great House, Lavenham). 'Relaunched' is a particularly apposite way to put it, since the theme of the place is firmly nautical. A lifebuoy hangs on the wall, and in the room at the back a large mural depicts a beach with lighthouse and a bunch of ferocious-looking seagulls. Not surprisingly, the menu deals mostly in the bounty of the sea: fried sardines with asparagus on tomato salsa, for example, or 'wonderfully oaky' home-smoked salmon with a potato and onion cake and thyme vinaigrette. Care in presentation shows in the sectioning of lobster in a Cantonese-style ginger and spring onion broth, and in the filleting of skate, which appears à la grenobloise: with butter, croûtons, capers and lemon. For those not interested in what the sea can deliver, there might be shank of lamb in red wine, or grilled sirloin steak. Strawberry mille-feuille with crème anglaise makes a good finisher, or there may be chocolate terrine with orange sauce, but the commercial ice-creams and sorbets don't inspire. Crab-shaped chocolates come with coffee. Staff are as keen as mustard. The French, Italian and New World wines are intelligently chosen and offer reasonable value. House French is £10.

CHEF: Pascal Canevet   PROPRIETOR: Régis Crépy   OPEN: Mon to Sat 12 to 2.30, 6.30 to 9.30 (10 Sat)   CLOSED: 3 weeks Jan   MEALS: alc (main courses £6.50 to £17). Set L £9.95 (2 courses) to £12.95, Set D Mon to Fri £17.95   SERVICE: not inc   CARDS: Amex, Delta, MasterCard, Switch, Visa   DETAILS: 80 seats. Private parties: 40 main room, 40 private room. Children's helpings. No smoking in 1 dining-room. Occasional music

---

CAMBRIDGE   Cambridgeshire   map 6

Midsummer House

Midsummer Common, Cambridge CB4 1HA	COOKING 6
TEL: (01223) 369299 FAX: (01223) 302672	COST £36–£74

This Victorian villa occupies a prime spot facing the common, with a conservatory dining-room overlooking a colourful garden. Reporters during the year have experienced a 'warm, friendly atmosphere', and the restaurant's strong sense of colour and design – in both décor and food – has been a feature of Anton Escalera's ownership. Despite his Spanish links, the cooking is firmly in contemporary French mould. A seasonally changing three-course menu (supplemented by a five-course no-choice weekday dinner option) makes good use of prime materials, and aims for direct, clean, identifiable flavours.

The repertoire revolves around a finite number of ideas, thus a Tatin of sea bass might appear in spring, one of lamb fillet in summer. Likewise roast halibut or sea bass will be served with saffron risotto on one menu, fillet of beef with a 'creamy, buttery and cheesy' wild mushroom risotto on another, a dish that, topped with foie gras, also displays the food in one of its richer moods. The end result, typically piled in a tower, is essentially simple, but skills include accurate timing – producing 'perfectly pink' saddle of lamb with a rosemary and shallot cream sauce – a good sense of the balance of flavours, and proper regard for textures. Lemon tart has been appreciated for its soft filling and crisp pastry case, or there may be hot chocolate fondant with vanilla bonbon, or pear crumble with iced caramel. A large selection of petits fours, including tarts, chocolates and biscuits 'deserve a mention of their own'. Wines are mostly French, and mostly over £20, but with a few good bottles from the New World. Ten house wines start at £11.95.

CHEF: Anton Escalera   PROPRIETORS: Russell Morgan and Anton Escalera   OPEN: Tue to Fri and Sun L 12 to 2.15, Tue to Sat D 7 to 10.15   MEALS: Set L Mon to Fri £23, Set L Sun £24.50, Set D Tue to Fri £39.50 to £50, Set D Sat £39.50 (glass of champagne included on Sun L and £50 menus). BYO £8.50 SERVICE: not inc   CARDS: Amex, Delta, MasterCard, Switch, Visa   DETAILS: 35 seats. Private parties: 30 main room, 10 to 15 private rooms. Vegetarian meals. Children's helpings. No smoking while others eat. Wheelchair access (1 step; not WC). No music   £5

22 Chesterton Road ♥

| 22 Chesterton Road, Cambridge CB4 3AX | COOKING 3 |
| TEL: (01223) 351880   FAX: (01223) 323814 | COST £33–£49 |

This pretty, candlelit 'Victorian shoebox of a room', in a terrace near the Cam, is decorated in peaches and blues and feels like a private house. It is the setting for four-courses, one of them a leaf salad, with the option of an extra fish dish for a supplement of £6: perhaps haddock kedgeree with green curry sauce, or pan-fried skate with chilli and basil cream. The food aligns along an East–West axis, offering pork and mushroom galantine with hoisin sauce, and salmon fish-cakes with chilli and coconut sauce. It looks good too – an artist's palette of sorbets with a slick of raspberry paint and a pastry 'paintbrush' – although greater attention to prime ingredients and clarity of flavours would have impressed our inspector more. Among dishes that have worked well are a thick pea and mint soup, braised lamb shank and pearl barley 'with bags of flavour', and rich chocolate bread-and-butter pudding. A few misnomers can creep into the menu (sauce gribiche without eggs, capers or gherkins, for instance), and service is 'stringently by the book', but wines have been selected with intelligence, enthusiasm and a keen eye for quality at a good price. Don't forget to take a look at the seasonally changing selection of interesting bins at the back of the list. Four house wines at £9.25 or £11.25 are sourced from Bordeaux, Hungary, Chile and Australia. CELLARMAN'S CHOICE: Chardonnay del Salento Barrique Kym Milne 1994, Italy, £14.75; Weinert Malbec 1992, Mendoza, Argentina, £16.50. The owners have opened a second restaurant, called Brasserie 22, at 160 High Street, Newmarket, Suffolk.

CHEF: Ian Reinhardt   PROPRIETORS: David Carter and Louise Crompton   OPEN: Tue to Sat D only 7 to 9.45; L by arrangement for parties of 10 or more   CLOSED: 1 week Christmas   MEALS: Set D £23.50   SERVICE: not inc   CARDS: Amex, Delta, MasterCard, Switch, Visa   DETAILS: 38 seats. Private parties: 26 main room, 12 private room. Vegetarian meals. No children under 12. No smoking while others eat. Occasional music. Air-conditioned

---

CANTERBURY Kent   map 3

▲ Canterbury Hotel, La Bonne Cuisine ⁵⅍ £

71 New Dover Road, Canterbury CT1 3DZ	
TEL: (01227) 450551 FAX: (01227) 780145	COOKING 5
EMAIL: labonne.cuisine@btinternet.com	COST £22–£40

'One of those bourgeois Victorian mansions that are so big they are destined to become either small hotels or flats,' writes an architecturally minded correspondent of this handsome red-brick edifice that is just a short jog from the cathedral. The interiors have been lavishly appointed – the dining-room a vision in shimmering primrose – and the kitchen boasts the talents of Jean-Luc Jouvente, a chef steeped in classical French technique who has cooked for the 'beau monde' of Monte Carlo.

A Mediterranean influence is evident in the preference for olive oil over cream and butter, which helps to lighten that classicism, but in any case 'flair and flavour' are the hallmarks of the menus. Smoked duck breast is served in fanned slices, dressed with walnut oil, and accompanied by a mille-feuille filled with avocado mousse, while fish treatments are innovative but carefully thought through, bringing a sea-urchin sauce to John Dory roasted with ginger and samphire. Meat alternatives might include guinea-fowl breast stuffed with morels, or rack of lamb with a sauce of acacia honey. Not all desserts have pleased, but true tarte Tatin with caramel ice-cream or Montélimar nougat glacé with a coulis of fruits of the forest should inspire confidence. French service may be tenderly youthful, but does a capable job with charm. The cooking deserves much better than the present short, basic wine list, but at least prices are restrained. House wines from southern France are £8.90.

CHEF: Jean-Luc Jouvente   PROPRIETORS: Mr and Mrs Bevan   OPEN: all week 12 to 2, 7 to 10 (9 Sun)   MEALS: alc (main courses £8.50 to £12.50). Set L Mon to Sat £12.50 to £15.95, Set D £15.95   SERVICE: not inc, card slips closed   CARDS: Amex, Delta, Diners, MasterCard, Switch, Visa   DETAILS: 55 seats. Private parties: 55 main room, 25 private rooms. Car park. Vegetarian meals. Children's helpings. Jacket and tie. No smoking in 1 dining-room. Occasional music. Air conditioned   ACCOMMODATION: £5 rooms, all with bath/shower. TV. Phone. B&B £48 to £75. Children welcome. Baby facilities. No dogs in public areas. Afternoon teas (*The Which? Hotel Guide*)

CARLTON North Yorkshire   map 9

▲ *Foresters Arms* ⁵✳

Carlton in Coverdale, Carlton DL8 4BB
TEL/FAX: (01969) 640272   COOKING 4
off A684, 5m SW of Leyburn   COST £26–£55

Horses can outnumber cars along Coverdale's narrow, meandering lanes, and the absence of casual trippers may help to explain why the seventeenth-century inn has managed to avoid being tarted up or themed. Flag floors, beams and an open fireplace convey the air of a real pub, with all the informality that implies. 'Light' lunches in the bar – boar's liver and bacon with onion, or grilled Yorkshire ham and eggs – give way at dinner to weightier ham knuckle with pease pudding, or saddle of lamb with apricots. But there is no mistaking Barrie Higginbotham's mission to make his blackboard of fish dishes the talk of North Yorkshire, from spiced fish-cakes, or fillet of salmon with potato rösti, to whole roast haddock with capers and lemon butter sauce.

Baked crab gâteau deserves its regular billing thanks to a light, soufflé-like texture, generous helping of 'wonderfully fresh' white crabmeat, and al dente asparagus spears. First-rate supplies and cooking are also evident in, for example, a thick, chunky piece of hake served alongside Toulouse sausage with a delicate bisque-like shellfish sauce. Vegetarians get a fair deal, and desserts might include an 'old favourite' such as apple and ginger crumble or baked treacle tart. Fifty-plus wines are split between Old and New Worlds, with a few posher bottles over £20. House Chilean Merlot and Hungarian Chardonnay are £9.60.

'There were very few obvious pieces of pig's ear in evidence. So few, in fact, that we re-christened the dish "côtes de porc Van Gogh".' (On eating in Berkshire)

CHEF/PROPRIETOR: B.K. Higginbotham   OPEN: Tue to Sun L 12 to 2, Tue to Sat D 7 to 9.30
CLOSED: 25 Dec, 3 to 4 weeks Jan   MEALS: alc (main courses £9 to £19). Light L available Tue to
Sat   SERVICE: not inc, card slips closed   CARDS: Delta, MasterCard, Switch, Visa   DETAILS: 60
seats. 24 seats outside. Private parties: 40 main room, 15 private room. Car park. Vegetarian
meals. Children's helpings. No smoking in 1 dining-room. Wheelchair access (not WC). Music
ACCOMMODATION: 3 rooms, all with bath/shower. TV. B&B £35 to £60. Children welcome. High
teas for children. Baby facilities. Dogs welcome by arrangement. Afternoon teas (*The Which?*
Hotel Guide)

CARNKIE Cornwall   map 1

Basset Count House ✶✶ | NEW ENTRY |

Lower Carnkie TR16 6SP
TEL: (01209) 215181   COOKING 5
just outside Redruth on B3297 to Helston   COST £18–£36

This 'absolutely stupendous' converted Georgian count house opened as the last
edition of the *Guide* was going to press. A listed building just outside Redruth on
the site of an old tin mine, it feels like a 'restrained modern country house' with
lots of gleaming dark wood, muted sponged walls, deep low sofas, table-lamps
with richly coloured shades, swathes of fabric and old oil-paintings. John
Milan, a pub owner of note in the area, has had the good sense to bring in Ann
Long, who last appeared in the 1993 *Guide* at Long's in Blackwater. Her
handwritten menus combine regular dishes, such as fillet steak in sherry and
cream, with more interesting smoked salmon with nan bread and basil cream, in
what might be seen as an updated version of country cooking.

Dishes reflect the ingenuity of a real cook who enjoys the endless variations
that familiar ingredients can be coaxed to produce: a starter of warm Stilton
rarebit with pear tartlet, or an intriguing spin on kedgeree, the smoked fish and
rice formed into a flattish cake and fried. 'Creamy yet firm', this opens to reveal a
soft-boiled quail's egg, and comes with a puddle of glossy sauce. Good gratin
dauphinoise features among the vegetables served with main courses of duck
breast with honey and Chinese spices, or sweet and 'perfectly roasted' best end
of lamb.

From a list that included treacle tart and mango bavarois, one visitor picked
out an old favourite of Ann Long's repertoire, meringue with a chewy centre and
crisp outside, tasting of toasted hazelnuts and served with black and white
grapes. Warm, newly baked bread adds to the appeal. Some 50 wines, mostly
under £20, are culled from Western Europe and the New World, starting with
house French at £9.50.

CHEF: Ann Long   PROPRIETOR: R.J. Milan   OPEN: Sun L 12 to 2, Wed to Sat D 7 to 9   MEALS:
Set L Sun £12.50, Set D £19.50 (2 courses) to £23   SERVICE: not inc, card slips closed   CARDS:
Delta, MasterCard, Switch, Visa   DETAILS: 36 seats. Private parties: 25 main room, 12 private
room. Car park. Vegetarian meals. No children under 10. No smoking in dining-room. No music

---

The Guide *is totally independent, accepts no free hospitality, and survives on the number
of copies sold each year.*

CARTERWAY HEADS Northumberland   map 10

▲ *Manor House Inn* 💺✕ £   NEW ENTRY

Carterway Heads, Shotley Bridge DH8 9LX
TEL: (01207) 255268   COOKING 3
on A68, 3m W of Consett   COST £15–£33

The stone-built inn looks out over fine unravaged countryside. Two bars and a
dining-room are trim and well kept without trowelling on the old-world charm,
and the Browns' developing jug collection is proudly hung from beams above
diners. A surprisingly wide range of choice is offered, chalked up on a
blackboard, the cooking neither overly trendy nor lapsing into pub-grub
stalwarts. Intensely smoky bacon goes into a warm salad with mange-tout and
tiny prawns in a well-made gentle vinaigrette. Other starter options (many of
which may be taken as main courses) have included garlic-crusted green-lip
mussels, pasta in a creamy sauce of mushrooms and garlic, and locally cured
kippers. One or two novelties such as chicken breast stuffed with smoked
salmon crop up among favourites like Cumberland sausage with mash and
mustard sauce, while guinea-fowl cooked in its skin delivers forcefully
flavoured meat with a sauce of brandy and apricot. Main courses are served with
a great heap of vegetables, but you may want to leave room for indulgent English
puddings such as ginger grundy: a 'rich but addictive' mixture of pineapple,
cream and crystal ginger on a crunchy chocolate and ginger base. The owners
bring a definite sense of jollity to the proceedings. France and the southern
hemisphere supply most of the wines on a sanely priced list that opens with
house French at £7.75.

CHEF: Peter Tiplady   PROPRIETORS: Chris and Moira Brown   OPEN: all week 12 to 2.30, 7 to
9.30 (9 Sun)   CLOSED: D 25 Dec   MEALS: alc (main courses £4.50 to £12). Set L and D £12.50 (2
courses) to £14.75   SERVICE: not inc, card slips closed   CARDS: Amex, MasterCard, Switch,
Visa   DETAILS: 58 seats. 16 seats outside. Private parties: 45 main room. Car park. Vegetarian
meals. Children's helpings until 8 in lounge. No smoking in dining-room. No music
ACCOMMODATION: 4 rooms. TV. B&B £24.50 to £43. Children welcome. Dogs by arrangement
£5

CARTMEL Cumbria   map 8

▲ *Aynsome Manor* 💺✕ £

Cartmel LA11 6HH
TEL: (01539) 536653   FAX: (01539) 536016   COOKING 2
off A590, ½m N of village   COST £19–£35

'Excellent service' from the Varley family and their local staff is one reason why
people set a course for this 400-year-old manor house on the Cartmel peninsula.
Visitors also approve of the food. The evening menu runs to five courses,
although diners are welcome to have fewer if they wish; a note on the menu now
promises that 'a vegetarian option is available on request'. What the kitchen
offers is dyed-in-the-Lakeland-wool country-house cooking with an occasional
nod to the local larder: rolls of air-dried Cumberland ham stuffed with cheese
and herb pâté have pleased, along with deep-fried bananas stuffed with Stilton

and served with curry mayonnaise, which one regular reckoned were 'exceptional'. Main courses that have found favour have included steak with red wine and shallot sauce, and duck with peach and brandy sauce; fish has also been given the seal of approval. Desserts are from a trolley of these-you-have-loved favourites: 'rather large' pies and gâteaux, fruit salad and the like. The wine list is forever evolving, but prices are fair and the choice catholic. At the time of going to press, house wines were £10.50 a litre.

CHEFS: Victor Sharratt and Christopher Miller   PROPRIETORS: the Varley family   OPEN: Sun L 1pm, Mon to Sat D 7 to 8.30 (residents only Sun D)   CLOSED: 2 to 28 Jan   MEALS: Set L £11.95, Set D £15.50 to £19.50   SERVICE: not inc, card slips closed   CARDS: Amex, Delta, MasterCard, Switch, Visa   DETAILS: 28 seats. Private parties: 30 main room. Car park. Vegetarian meals. Children's helpings. No children under 5 at D. Jacket and tie. No smoking in dining-room. No music   ACCOMMODATION: 12 rooms, all with bath/shower. TV. Phone. D,B&B £53.50 to £109. Children welcome. High teas for children. Baby facilities. Dogs welcome in bedrooms only. Afternoon teas (The Which? Hotel Guide) £5

▲ *Uplands* ⚞

Haggs Lane, Cartmel LA11 6HD
TEL: (015395) 36248   FAX: (015395) 36848
EMAIL: uplands@kencomp.net
2½m SW of A590, 1m up road opposite Pig   COOKING 5
and Whistle   COST £23–£42

As with Miller Howe (see entry, Windermere), John Tovey has sold his interest in Uplands, which now belongs solely to Tom and Diana Peter, 'and the Nat West!' The change has been marked by a face-lift – colours are now pale yellow, ivory and green – and menus have lost their blue border, so reminiscent of Miller Howe, although the style of cooking remains as before. Indeed, the unchanging nature of Uplands constitutes its appeal for some: 'nothing spectacular', summed up one, but 'of all the places we visit time and again Uplands is the one that consistently never lets us down'. Add good value and friendly but unobtrusive service, and it is easy to see why 'every other guest seemed to be a regular. I would be if I lived in the area.'

The pattern is three courses at lunch, four at dinner, perhaps starting with wild mushrooms in hot garlic and cheese sauce on saffron tagliatelle, or a 'smooth, light' hot salmon soufflé with 'bags of flavour', wrapped in smoked salmon and served with an impressive watercress sauce. Soup is a well-loved institution – it comes in a generous tureen, accompanied by a whole small loaf of warm brown bread – as is the selection of four vegetables which arrives with the main course, be it baked fillet of sea bass with a chive sauce, or 'lamb at its best': loin cooked pink and served with a sharp redcurrant and caper sauce. Desserts offer the biggest choice of any course, perhaps incorporating a 'splendid, rich' chocolate Grand Marnier mousse, passion-fruit ice-cream, or sticky toffee date pudding. New World wines take up nearly half the list, and prices are fair, starting with house French at £9.90.

The Guide *always appreciates hearing about changes of chef or owner.*

CHEF: Tom Peter   PROPRIETORS: Tom and Diana Peter   OPEN: Thur to Sun L 12.30 for 1 (1 sitting), Tue to Sun D 7.30 for 8 (1 sitting)   MEALS: Set L £15, Set D £27   SERVICE: not inc, card slips closed   CARDS: Amex, Delta, MasterCard, Visa   DETAILS: 28 seats. Private parties: 20 main room. Car park. Children welcome. No smoking in dining-room. Wheelchair access (2 steps; also men's WC). No music   ACCOMMODATION: 5 rooms, all with bath/shower. TV. D,B&B £140 (double room). No children under 8. Dogs welcome in bedrooms only (*The Which? Hotel Guide*)   (£5)

CASTLE CARY Somerset   map 2

▲ *Bond's* ⁵⁺✕ £

Ansford Hill, Castle Cary BA7 7JP
TEL/FAX: (01963) 350464   COOKING 2
on A371, 400yds past station towards Wincanton   COST £24–£58

The Bonds' ivy-clad house was once a coaching-inn for travellers *en route* through the West Country. The fare on offer these days might well have baffled those early patrons, but Yvonne Bond is determined to show that globetrotting cuisine is not the exclusive preserve of the cities. Quail is wok-fried with parsnips and bacon and served on an orange-dressed salad, crab soup is thickened with rice and comes with 'fiery rouille', while poussin may arrive in Spanish attire, stuffed with chorizo and sauced with sherry. One pair who stayed in summer found nothing to fault in anything they ate; the first night's dessert of ginger ice-cream with kiwi and grapes was 'such a good balance of tastes' that it was ordered again on the second. Great care is taken over the serving of cheeses, which come as a selection of not fewer than five. Keith Bond is a militant for wine-pricing fairness, and the list opens with six well-chosen house wines that are charged proportionately if you don't manage the whole bottle. The remainder is a concise, imaginative selection of up-to-the-minute drinking.

CHEF: Yvonne Bond   PROPRIETORS: Yvonne and Kevin Bond   OPEN: all week D only 7 to 9 (7 to 7.30 Sun and Mon)   CLOSED: 1 week Christmas   MEALS: Set D £14.50 to £23.50. Light L available all week 12 to 2   SERVICE: not inc, card slips closed   CARDS: MasterCard, Visa   DETAILS: 20 seats. 6 seats outside. Private parties: 20 main room. Car park. Vegetarian meals. Children's helpings. No children under 8. No smoking in dining-room. No music   ACCOMMODATION: 7 rooms, all with bath/shower. TV. Phone. B&B £41 to £85. No children under 8 exc babies. Baby facilities. No dogs. Afternoon teas   (£5)

CASTLE COMBE Wiltshire   map 2

▲ *Manor House Hotel* ⁵⁺✕

Castle Combe SN14 7HR
TEL: (01249) 782206   FAX: (01249) 782159
EMAIL: enquiries@manor-house.co.uk   COOKING 4
on B4039, 3m NW of junction with A420   COST £31–£86

'Even the taxi driver thought it was the loveliest place to which he had ever delivered a punter,' reckoned one visitor who enthused about the village, the setting, and the originally fourteenth-century house on the edge of the Cotswolds. Inside are lots of small interlinking lounges and studies,

Jacobean-style furniture, and a 'large, sweeping and ballroomish' dining-room with well-spaced tables. Thanks to the staff, 'we felt very comfortable in what could have been a stuffy atmosphere'. A *carte* and set-price options might offer well-flavoured and -textured tuna carpaccio, or a soufflé of calf's sweetbreads. Alternatively, a 'classical section', mostly for two people, reverts to grilled Dover sole and old-style crêpe Suzette 'flamed at your table'.

The kitchen takes its country-house duties seriously, piling on plentiful appetisers, a pre-meal soup, writing menus in curly script, prices in words, tossing in a mid-meal sorbet, and generally using a lot of ingredients in a dish: one visitor's 'good, livery' duck came with sweet apple juice, vanilla oil, baked apple segments, spinach, braised fennel, leeks, green beans wrapped in a bundle, and dauphinoise potatoes. 'I still don't know what confit means when applied to turbot' confessed one reporter, who nevertheless enjoyed a 'firm, nutty' piece of it. Some accompaniments are first-rate, as in a buttery hollandaise that had been mixed with smoky aubergine and garlic, to accompany beef fillet, while others are less successful. As for the bill, with coffee and sweetmeats at £6.50, 'it would be more cost-effective to try and get yourself sent on a conference here'. That way you might be able to enjoy some of the classier wines on the extensive list. House Chilean Merlot is £18.95, French Sauvignon £23.50.

CHEF: Mark Taylor PROPRIETOR: Manor House Hotel (Castle Combe) Ltd OPEN: all week 12 to 2, 7 to 10 MEALS: alc (main courses £22.50 to £27). Set L Mon to Sat £16.95 (2 courses) to £18.95, Set L Sun £20, Set D £35 SERVICE: not inc, card slips closed CARDS: Amex, Delta, Diners, MasterCard, Switch, Visa DETAILS: 105 seats. 20 seats outside. Private parties: 105 main room, 12 to 30 private rooms. Car park. Vegetarian meals. Children welcome. Jacket and tie. No smoking in dining-room. Wheelchair access (also WC). No music ACCOMMODATION: 45 rooms, all with bath/shower. TV. Phone. Room only £115 to £350. Rooms for disabled. Children welcome. No dogs. Afternoon teas. Swimming-pool. Fishing (*The Which? Hotel Guide*)

CAUNTON Nottinghamshire   map 5

Caunton Beck £

Caunton NG23 6AB   COOKING 2
TEL: (01636) 636793   FAX: (01636) 636828   COST £20–£46

The format that Michael and Valerie Hope have devised, already in operation at the Wig & Mitre (see entry, Lincoln), is very much of the 1990s. Mercifully free of the restrictive opening times and practices that can sometimes bedevil country eating, this beamed inn flings open its doors at 8am and doesn't close them until 11pm, seven days a week. During that time it offers a wide variety of dishes strewn across no fewer than five menus: seasonal, daily, sandwich, breakfast, and a three-course '£25 for two people' deal (including a half-bottle of wine), which one couple enjoyed not least for its 'ample portions'. The place is roomy, light and airy inside, with tables in nooks and crannies, and french windows open on to an al fresco eating-area outside. The same food is served throughout, ingredients are good, and ideas vary from a modern salad of chorizo sausage with smoked quail's eggs, via steak and kidney pie with dumplings, to treacle sponge. Wines, arranged broadly by style, begin with house French at £10.25.

CHEFS: Paul Vidic, Jamie Matts and Adrian Graves PROPRIETORS: Michael and Valerie Hope, and Paul Vidic OPEN: all week 8am to 11pm MEALS: alc (main courses £5.50 to £16.50). Set L and D (exc Sat D) £25 for 2 people, inc wine. BYO by prior arrangement SERVICE: not inc CARDS: Amex, Delta, Diners, MasterCard, Switch, Visa DETAILS: 120 seats. 40 seats outside. Private parties: 30 main room, 30 private room. Car park. Vegetarian meals. Children's helpings. Wheelchair access (also WC). No music (£5)

CHADDESLEY CORBETT Worcestershire   map 5

▲ *Brockencote Hall* ⁵✕ | NEW ENTRY |

Chaddesley Corbett DY10 4PY
TEL: (01562) 777876 FAX: (01562) 777872
on A448, Kidderminster to Bromsgrove road,   COOKING 3
just outside village   COST £28–£65

This classical house in 70 acres of parkland includes a conservatory lounge with tented roof, as well as three adjoining dining-rooms, among its creature comforts. The view across grassland is enlivened by the scurryings of rabbits, while equally dashing staff convey an impression of eager concern within. Didier Philipot has come and gone in the kitchens here, but seems firmly re-installed now, and offers well-wrought modern French food in the form of a bilingual menu. Sauté duck foie gras on a buckwheat pancake with mango chutney sends out a mixture of messages, as might 'bayildi' of spring lamb with peppermint and provençale vegetables.

Complexity looms, in a dish of saffroned red mullet escabèche served with expertly timed sliced scallops, tapénade and basil oil, while roasted Aberdeen Angus fillet on smoked bacon and potato rösti offers a more mainstream choice. Desserts might include warm orange salad in honey butter with gingerbread ice-cream, or rich, hot toffee soufflé with nougat glacé and chocolate sauce. The wine list is old-style French, dividing Bordeaux into its various regions and encompassing some highly illustrious bottles, but not offering a great deal in the way of everyday wines. Seven French house wines open at £11.40.

CHEF: Didier Philipot PROPRIETORS: Alison and Joseph Petitjean OPEN: Sun to Fri L 12 to 1.30, all week D 7 to 9 (9.30 Sat) MEALS: alc (main courses £22.50). Set L £19.50, Set D £24.50 SERVICE: net prices, card slips closed CARDS: Amex, Diners, MasterCard, Switch, Visa DETAILS: 75 seats. Private parties: 50 main room, 12 to 32 private rooms. Car park. Children's helpings. No smoking in dining-room. Wheelchair access (1 step; not WC). No music ACCOMMODATION: 17 rooms, all with bath/shower. TV. Phone. B&B £92 to £145. Rooms for disabled. Children welcome. High teas for children. Baby facilities. No dogs. Afternoon teas (£5)

If you have access to the Internet, you can find The Good Food Guide *online at the* Which? *Online web site (http://www.which.net).*

'Service before dinner was a British farce. There was more service from various servers in various rooms to announce that the service we needed was coming than the actual service we eventually obtained.' (On eating in Oxfordshire)

▲ *Gidleigh Park* ▮ ⅍

Chagford TQ13 8HH
TEL: (01647) 432367   FAX: (01647) 432574
EMAIL: gidleighpark@gidleigh.co.uk
from Chagford Square turn right at Lloyds Bank into
Mill Street, take right fork after 150 yards, follow lane   COOKING 8
for 1½m   COST £42–£87

On the edge of Dartmoor, this 'imitation half-timbered' house is one of the most
relaxing places to spend a few days. 'If ever we win the lottery we are going to
come and stay here for a month while we decide what to do.' Expect wood fires,
comfortable chairs, oak panelling and a charming welcome: staff put everybody
at ease, nobody feels like a poor relation, and the sense of teamwork is strong,
both out front and in the kitchen. The food is 'generally excellent, occasionally
brilliant', as well as being 'therapy for the stomach', and Michael Caines cooks
with a mix of power, skill, finesse and evident generosity.

Luxuries are never far away, and truffles appear frequently: with pasta, in an
'outstanding' risotto with wild mushrooms, or sliced on to a 'just cooked' piece
of braised turbot with a chive butter sauce. 'Wobbly' fresh foie gras, with
buttered apple and tiny glazed turnips served on a thin slice of black pudding,
was one reporter's idea of 'the dish I would want for my last supper'. Salads
impress too: warm quail salad with poached quail's eggs and crispy bacon for
example, or small towers of mixed leaves balanced on Parmesan tuiles,
interspersed with tiny mounds of ratatouille.

The kitchen's adaptability allows it to deal equally well with light summery
dishes –'simple but oh so good' red mullet drizzled with olive oil – and earthier
winter fare, from 'gamey and sweet' roast partridge to pithivier of pigeon with
wild mushroom and truffle mousse. The highlight of one meal was half a dozen
seared scallops, set around a tian of stacked slices of marinated aubergine,
grilled red and yellow pepper, and tomato; underneath were slicks of four
colourful and intense sauces: anchovy, mayonnaise, herbs and tomato. It was
judged 'a brilliant idea, beautifully and perfectly executed', in which all items
worked well individually and with each other. What held the cooking back at
inspection were a few 'technical imperfections' and a sense that not all dishes
were equally well considered.

Cheeses tend to include some British or local, some Irish and some French,
while desserts have been 'stunning': pistachio parfait with hot chocolate
mousse, 'paper-thin' hot apple tart with vanilla ice-cream, or a 'superbly crafted'
dish combining a crisp almond tuile biscuit filled with roughly chopped cherries
'seriously marinated in kirsch', with a scoop of intense cherry ice-cream: 'very
good, very simple, totally professional'. Paul Henderson's legendary wine list
continues to delight with its exciting range of Californian and Italian reds,
which are in good company with the fine vintage clarets and burgundies. Alsace
and Germany are afforded the respect they deserve too. Mark-ups reduce in
relative terms as the bottles become more expensive, and there is plenty of good
drinking to be had between £20 and £30. Eight wines by the glass are available
from £4 (a Cuvinet machine keeps open bottles fresh). CELLARMAN'S CHOICE:
Puligny-Montrachet 1995, J. Chavy, £32; Madiran, Ch. Montus 1990, £25.

CHEF: Michael Caines   PROPRIETORS: Paul and Kay Henderson   OPEN: all week 12.30 to 2, 7 to 9   MEALS: Set L Mon to Thurs £20.50 (2 courses) to £57.50, Set L Fri to Sun and bank hols £25.50 (2 courses) to £57.50, Set D £57.50 to £62.50. BYO £10. Light L available   SERVICE: net prices, card slips closed   CARDS: Amex, Delta, Diners, MasterCard, Switch, Visa   DETAILS: 35 seats. Private parties: 25 main room. Car park. Children's helpings. No smoking in dining-room. No music   ACCOMMODATION: 14 rooms, all with bath/shower. TV. Phone. DB&B £225 to £425. Children welcome. Baby facilities. Afternoon teas. Fishing

---

▲ 22 Mill Street ⅝✳ | NEW ENTRY |

22 Mill Street, Chagford TQ13 8AW   COOKING 8
TEL: (01647) 432244   COST £21–£35

From a Round-up entry in the last edition of the *Guide* to a score of 8 is a bit of a jump for Duncan Walker and his partner Amanda Leaman, who runs front-of-house, but an inspector enjoyed one of her 'best meals ever' at this small terraced property with a glass shop-front and green-painted woodwork. The colour turns to gold in the uncluttered, modern dining-room, which feels smart without having had money thrown at it. Duncan Walker has worked with Shaun Hill, who used to cook at Gidleigh Park (see entry, above) before moving to the Merchant House (see entry, Ludlow), and the debt to his mentor is notable in format, style of dishes and in some of the detail, not least the extremely fine bread: 'I would have recognised that buttermilk roll anywhere.'

The blend of country informality on the one hand and 'revolutionary talent' and enthusiasm from the kitchen on the other makes this a rare gem. Just one dish gives an idea: layers of saffron-coloured pasta flecked with red, stacked like a pile of poppadums, spilling out chunks of fresh crabmeat – this is 'big-hearted and generous' food – surrounded by a thickish brick-red crustacean stock sauce with a warm roasted flavour, and topped with deep-fried lemon zest and parsley. Technically perfect, the dish was 'completely unfussy'; all the components, including colourful grilled red pepper and sticks of green spring onion, contributed to the success of the whole.

Lunch might offer such apparently simple things as cream of asparagus soup, or wild mushroom risotto, or such classics as bourride, or smoked haddock with spinach, poached egg and hollandaise, but the menu is a master of under-statement. It did not prepare one evening visitor for a 'gamey, tender' squab pigeon, roasted whole, perfectly timed, separated into its constituent parts, placed on an 'intense' green pea purée, and topped with briefly seared livers. 'Glorious vegetables' included small dice of crusty, caramelised beetroot, roast shallots, and blobs of buttery silky spinach, all combining as well with each other as with the pigeon.

'Brilliance' and 'excitement' are obvious all the way through. A mundane-sounding dessert of warm poached peaches with caramel ice-cream, for example, turned out to be much more: a central squat round tower of caramel ice-cream sandwiched between crisp, lacy biscuits, surrounded by a blistered, lightly cinnamon- and peach-flavoured sabayon containing the poached peach halves. Menu choice is sensibly limited, appetisers and petits fours are top-drawer, and value for money is hard to beat, helped by some three dozen wines, starting with house Australian at £9.30.

CHEF: Duncan Walker PROPRIETORS: Amanda Leaman and Duncan Walker OPEN: Tue to Sat L 12 to 2, Mon to Sat D 7.30 to 9 (also open bank hol Suns) CLOSED: 25 and 26 Dec, bank hol Mons MEALS: alc L (main courses £6 to £9). Set L £12.95 (2 courses) to £14.95, Set D £20.50 (2 courses) to £24.50 SERVICE: net prices, card slips closed CARDS: MasterCard, Switch, Visa DETAILS: 30 seats. Private parties: 12 main room, 12 private room. Children welcome. No smoking in dining-room. Wheelchair access (not WC). Music ACCOMMODATION: 2 rooms, both with bath/shower. TV. B&B £31 to £43. Children welcome

---

CHEESDEN Greater Manchester   map 8

Nutters ⁑✗

Edenfield Road, Cheesden, nr Rochdale OL12 7TY	COOKING 6
TEL/FAX: (01706) 650167	COST £26–£46

This may be a barren spot of bleak, windswept moorland near Rochdale, but the restaurant is heralded by signs attached to 'anything vertical to which a sign can be attached', and can be full by 7pm on a weekend: TV appearances and a book 'seem to have worked miracles on turnover'. Inside the dog-leg door is a collection of kitchen pans set into a board: 'It must be art,' concluded one visitor. Andrew Nutter has 'correctly prioritised: food then décor', and certainly food is the more contemporary of the two, although you might not guess it from the 'melody' of mixed fish or 'symphony' of miniature desserts. A single menu lays out the slightly overlapping lunch and dinner options and stresses that there is no obligation to eat three courses.

Starters have a particularly imaginative streak, evident from black pudding wuntuns, mushrooms in filo on a disc of chorizo paste, or a salad of melting raclette cheese and cured ham with 'lovely earthy' potatoes and a pickled onion dressing. The kitchen has also produced asparagus soup good enough to impress a visiting Parisienne, and caramelised duck breast to rival anything its reporter had eaten in south-west France. Timing is accurate, producing a seared salmon fillet, crisp outside, moist inside, on a bed of chicory and mâche, with a tomato and basil dressing. Cod and skate also feature among the fish, chicken and beef among the rest, and even that northern favourite, beef with Stilton, is prepared with sensitivity, using 'superbly tasty' fillet, cut thin and cooked rare, with 'just the right amount of a hint' of cheese.

Tarts (hot apple and frangipane, or caramelised lemon), timbales (chilled chocolate), mousses (white chocolate and raspberry), parfaits (banana and rum) and cheesecakes (Black and White Minstrel) keep up the variety in desserts. Mr Nutter senior is a gracious and unpretentious maître d', dispensing unhurried, friendly service, and wines are from an overwhelmingly French list, although house red and white at £10.50 are Australian.

CHEF: Andrew Nutter PROPRIETORS: Rodney, Jean and Andrew Nutter OPEN: Wed to Mon 12 to 2, 6.45 to 9.30 (12 to 9 Sun) CLOSED: first 2 weeks Aug MEALS: alc (main courses £9.50 to £16). Set L Sun £19.95, Set Gourmet Menu D £29.50 SERVICE: not inc CARDS: Amex, Delta, MasterCard, Switch, Visa DETAILS: 52 seats. Private parties: 52 main room. Car park. Vegetarian meals. Children's helpings. No smoking in dining-room. Wheelchair access (also WC). Music

CHELTENHAM Gloucestershire   map 5

Le Champignon Sauvage ▼

24–26 Suffolk Road, Cheltenham GL50 2AQ   COOKING 7
TEL/FAX: (01242) 573449   COST £28–£61

Despite its unremarkable location on a busy inner-city street, 'this is no ordinary restaurant', an inspector insists. David Everitt-Matthias's cooking unites faultless technique with clear and original flavour combinations, while his wife Helen manages front-of-house with panache, creating an atmosphere of relaxed well-being in the stylish dark-blue and yellow dining-room. Although some readers have found the pricing a little steep, there is a generosity in both the abundant use of top-quality ingredients and the succession of extras that punctuate the meal: at dinner there might be a complimentary rich and aromatic blanquette of butter-beans with truffle oil ('a superb way to begin'), first-rate breads warm from the oven, and a pre-dessert lemon-scented geranium cream with a brittle brûlée topping and contrasting passion-fruit sorbet. Surprises aplenty, then, but never novelty for its own sake. It is a measure of the kitchen's finesse that while the cooking has unexpected twists it always retains a sense of proportion and balance.

Meat dishes are characterised by uncompromisingly bold flavourings that complement rather than compete with each other: a lamb chump, for example, with robust Mediterranean-inspired accompaniments of pungent goats' cheese and potato purée, sun-dried tomatoes, aubergines and tapénade, considered 'a first-class dish, much more than the sum of its parts'. A spice-marinated duck leg on a split-pea purée is 'full of beguiling flavours', served with two intense sauces, a scattering of petits pois, pak choi and sweet cicely. Fish dishes are in lighter vein. Crab ravioli features fine, elastic pasta and a frothy crab sauce infused with tarragon and truffle oil that is 'light, yet strong and intense in taste', while oysters and scallops are poached and served in a light velouté sauce with leeks.

An impressive selection of cheeses is 'an experience not to be missed', although the dazzlingly inventive desserts are hard to pass up. Exotic spicing is a feature of these: iced gingerbread parfait with orange and liquorice sorbet, pineapple tarte Tatin and coconut sorbet, and a 'rich, creamy, yet not cloying' Thai-spiced cream layered with thin flaky pastry and served with mango and a rich mulled red wine syrup. Wines are mostly from classical French regions with a sprinkling from the New World. Quality is the priority, although prices are mostly reasonable, and there is no shortage of choice under £20, starting with house French at £9.95. CELLARMAN'S CHOICE: Azay le Rideau 1995, Pascal Pibaleau, £12.50; Savigny-lès-Beaune, 'Les Lavières' 1995, Charles Vienot, £24.50.

CHEF: David Everitt-Matthias PROPRIETORS: David and Helen Everitt-Matthias OPEN: Mon to Fri L 12.30 to 1.30, Mon to Sat D 7.30 to 9.15 CLOSED: 10 days Christmas, 2 weeks summer, 4 days Easter, bank hols MEALS: Set L £14.50 (2 courses) to £18.50, Set D Mon to Fri £15.50 (2 courses) to £38, Set D Sat £28 (2 courses) to £38. Menu rapide L £14.50 (2 courses) inc wine SERVICE: not inc CARDS: Amex, Diners, MasterCard, Switch, Visa DETAILS: 28 seats. Private parties: 22 main room. Children welcome. No smoking before 10 at D. Wheelchair access (1 step; not WC). No music £5

Mayflower

32–34 Clarence Street, Cheltenham GL50 3NX	COOKING 1
TEL: (01242) 522426 FAX: (01242) 251667	COST £12–£55

The redoubtable Kong family tell us that their mailing list of loyal and devoted customers has topped the 1,000 mark – a sure sign that they are doing the right things. After 16 years in business, their distinctive Regency blue and gold restaurant is something of a landmark in a town bristling with eating-places. Their menu is a lengthy stroll through the more accessible regions of Cantonese, Peking and Szechuan cuisine. Expect anything from king prawns sauté with celery in satay sauce, to sliced roast duck with pickled ginger and onions, to deep-fried 'nest of chicken' with prawn rolls. Vegetarian offerings include sizzling 'mock duck' with black beans and chilli, and a version of Singapore fried rice noodles. Cut-price business lunches, banquets and monthly theme evenings complete the picture. The Mayflower also promotes wine seriously, and the list of around 100 bins has a broad international spread with fair prices to match. House wine is £9.25.

CHEFS: Mr C.F. Kong and Mrs M.M. Kong   PROPRIETORS: the Kong family   OPEN: Mon to Sat L 12 to 1.45, all week D 6 to 10.30   CLOSED: 24 to 26 Dec   MEALS: alc (main courses £5 to £10.50). Set L £6.75, Set D £17 to £19.50   SERVICE: not inc   CARDS: Amex, Delta, Diners, MasterCard, Switch, Visa   DETAILS: 80 seats. Private parties: 80 main room, 40 private room. Vegetarian meals. Children welcome. Music. Air-conditioned   £5

Le Petit Blanc £

NEW ENTRY

Queen's Hotel, The Promenade,	
Cheltenham GL50 1NN	COOKING 5
TEL: (01242) 266800 FAX: (01242) 266801	COST £22–£48

The Promenade ('Cheltenham's best street') is wide, tree-lined, and 'very spa' with a number of grand buildings, including the Queen's Hotel, whose ground floor this easy-going modern brasserie occupies. It is a high-ceilinged, sparsely furnished, mirrored room (tables for two are 'tiny') with arched windows and newly painted murals, and, like its counterpart in Oxford, is open all day for a wide variety of dishes and eating-options.

The food combines a classical French provincial feel – a 'rough, generous, enormously appetising' starter of salmon niçoise with mustard and pesto dressings – with more homespun items such as Oxford sausages ('tasting of meat, what a change!') with onion gravy and chips. Despite the brasserie tag, the food is pretty serious, judging by a deep-fried, crisp-crusted, salsa-topped crab-cake sitting on a creamy chive-flecked risotto. Raw materials are good, 'utter freshness' is the norm, and careful timing extends to slow-cooked dishes such as a 'top-class' braised rabbit cassoulet combining flageolets, haricots blanc, lentils and chorizo.

Desserts are no less appealing, whether a pineapple and kirsch parfait on a thin layer of meringue, served with mango coulis, or a wedge of 'intense, totally decadent' chocolate tart, combining crisp pastry with a mousse-like filling, served with mascarpone ice-cream. An extra charge is made for bread and vegetables, both of which are good, and service is well informed, friendly and helpful; 'the head waiter was at Oxford', meaning the other branch. Wines match the style, with some well-chosen varietals under £20, and eight wines by the glass including house vin de pays at £9.95 a bottle.

CHEF: Stephen Nash   PROPRIETOR: Blanc Restaurants Ltd   OPEN: all week 12 to 3, 6 to 11 (10.30 Sun)   CLOSED: 25 Dec   MEALS: alc (main courses £7.50 to £14.50). Set L £12 (2 courses) to £14, Set D 6 to 7.30 £12 (2 courses) to £14. Bar food available all day   SERVICE: not inc, card slips closed; 10% for parties of 8 or more   CARDS: Amex, Delta, Diners, MasterCard, Switch, Visa   DETAILS: 152 seats. 12 seats outside. Vegetarian meals. Children's helpings. No smoking in dining-room. Music. Air-conditioned   (£5)

CHESTER Cheshire   map 7

▲ Chester Grosvenor Hotel, Arkle ♥ 🍷 ⁙✸

Eastgate Street, Chester CH1 1LT   COOKING 6
TEL: (01244) 324024   FAX: (01244) 313246   COST £34–£88

As Paul Reed moved to the Crowne Plaza Midland (see entry, Manchester) after a dozen years here, Simon Radley arrived from Nunsmere Hall (see entry, Sandiway) to take charge of the prestigious kitchen. The setting is unexciting. Walking through the mock library, its shelves stocked with yards of books, into a windowless, mahoganied dining-room with equine pictures 'of no particular merit' and less than bright lighting, the overall feel is 'dim, subdued and a little dated'. But serious wine glasses, leather-bound menus, and black-uniformed staff make it obvious they mean business. The sensibly sized menu format remains much as before: seven or eight options per course of imaginative and stylish, rather than cutting-edge, food. Luxury ingredients are conspicuous by their presence, but the balance is good.

A broadly classical style turns up stuffed pig's trotter with Puy lentils, neatly presented fillet of veal 'en croute' with a Dijon mustard sauce, and a cleanly flavoured 'noisy' terrine of pencil leeks with nuggets of lobster that 'just squeaked as you ate it'. Some components – the vanilla potatoes served with gamey-tasting pot-roast Bresse pigeon for instance – don't have the impact they might, while others work extremely well: an intensely flavoured fig marmalade with confit of duck leg at one meal. To finish, poached peaches are given a champagne sabayon, while a rich, creamy, tangy lemon brûlée is served with a quenelle of raspberry sherbet. The standard three-course format is supplemented by appetisers to start, a sorbet before the main course, a bread trolley, and petits fours with coffee.

The hefty wine list impresses with its roll-call of famous names and renowned vintages, and not just from France. Such venerable wines don't come cheap (you can spend £4,000 on one bottle if you feel so inclined), but there are over 60 bottles under £20 and house French is £12. CELLARMAN'S CHOICE: Vichon Winery Chevrignon 1994, Napa Valley, California, £28; St-Chinian 'Cuvée Signée' 1993, Dom. des Jougla, £19.50.

▲ *means accommodation is available.*

CHEF: Simon Radley PROPRIETOR: Grosvenor Estate Holdings Ltd OPEN: Tue to Sun L 12 to 2.30, Mon to Sat D 7 to 9.30 (10 Sat) CLOSED: 24 Dec D to 31 Dec, bank hols MEALS: Set L £25 to £48, Set D £40 (2 courses) to £48, Gourmet Menu £40. Brasserie and bar meals available. BYO £5 SERVICE: not inc CARDS: Amex, Diners, MasterCard, Switch, Visa DETAILS: 40 seats. Private parties: 22 main room. Vegetarian meals. Children's helpings. No smoking in dining-room. Wheelchair access (also WC). Music. Air-conditioned ACCOMMODATION: 85 rooms, all with bath/shower. TV. Phone. Room only £125 to £210. Rooms for disabled. Children welcome. High teas for children. Baby facilities. Guide dogs only. Afternoon teas

---

CHILGROVE West Sussex   map 3

▲ *White Horse Inn* 🍾

Chilgrove PO18 9HX
TEL: (01243) 535219 FAX: (01243) 535301   COOKING 2
on B2141, between Chichester and Petersfield   COST £30–£42

During 1999 Barry Phillips and Neil Rusbridger will clock up 30 years at this Sussex landmark famed for its wines, and their 'casual and unfussy' approach is appealing. The bar (for smokers) has its own menu – bits of paper stuck to a board – while the dining-room's fixed-price offerings might turn up a starter salad of warm potato and Toulouse sausage, or a 'pleasantly accomplished' filo pastry basket with sliced courgettes. Fish varies by the day, liver and sweetbreads make a welcome appearance, and game has included local pigeon breast, and a pheasant and partridge pancake with mushroom sauce. Vegetables and desserts, in an inspector's view, do not live up to the rest of the food. The wine list, on the other hand, cannot fail to please, and its 90 pages set out famous wines by the multitude: 21 vintages of Mouton-Rothschild, 16 of Pétrus and 16 of Domaine de la Romanée-Conti, and that's without considering the half-bottles, magnums and even Jeroboams. Germany, for once, is given the attention it deserves, while dessert wines are drawn from the Crimea, Italy and South Africa, as well as the expected regions. The house selection of the week combines good value with simplicity of choice for those not up to the full list, and starts at £11.50. CELLARMAN'S CHOICE: Ockfener Bockstein Riesling Spätlese 1990, Dr Fischer, £15; Bourgogne Rouge 1995, Bertrand Ambroise, £18.

CHEF: Neil Rusbridger PROPRIETORS: Barry Phillips and Neil Rusbridger OPEN: Tue to Sat 12 to 2, 7 to 9.30 CLOSED: last week Oct, Feb MEALS: Set L £16.50 (2 courses) to £19.50, Set D £23. Bar meals Tue to Sun L SERVICE: 10% (12½% Sat D), card slips closed CARDS: Delta, Diners, MasterCard, Switch, Visa DETAILS: 65 seats. 50 seats outside. Private parties: 30 main room, 12 private rooms. Car park. Vegetarian meals. Wheelchair access (not WC). No music. Air-conditioned ACCOMMODATION: Cottage with 5 rooms, all with bath/shower. TV. Phone. B&B £30 to £100. Rooms for disabled. Dogs welcome by arrangement.

All entries in the Guide *are re-researched and rewritten every year, not least because restaurant standards fluctuate. Don't rely on an out-of-date* Guide.

Not inc *in the details at the end of an entry indicates that no service charge is made and any tipping is at the discretion of the customer.*

CHINNOR Oxfordshire map 2

Sir Charles Napier 🍾

Sprigg's Alley, nr Chinnor OX9 4BX
TEL: (01494) 483011 FAX: (01494) 485311
exit 6 from M40, at Chinnor roundabout turn right,
continue straight up hill; Sprigg's Alley signposted COOKING 4
after 1m COST £30–£52

Despite surreal statues and sculptures, outside and in, this feels like a well-worn, comfortable pub with a dining-room. One of Heath Robinson's old frying-pans acts as a weight to close the door behind you, while brick fireplaces, wooden beams and assorted chairs and sofas emphasise the informality. 'Idiosyncratic, and delightfully so,' reckoned one visitor, adding praise for the personal stamp of Julie Griffiths. Reporters generally consider the food 'interesting', perhaps because there is less reliance on the usual cuts of meat, and a more enterprising enthusiasm for seafood, fowl and vegetable dishes, or perhaps because of the kitchen's passion for a range of contemporary ingredients and bright flavours: spiced chickpeas with deep-fried squid, minted pea risotto with griddled scallops, or gingery papaya salsa served with crispy Gressingham duck. Desserts – hot date cake with toffee sauce, meringue with berries and cream – show a strong traditional bias. One reporter noted a surcharge of £1 when a second starter was taken in place of a main course.

The wine list is priced to suit all pockets, with bottles ranging from £11.75 to £180, and thanks to some judicious selection offers value for money at every level. The sheer variety of the offerings provides ample reason for experimentation. Informed notes introduce unusual grapes and nudge the curious towards favourite producers. CELLARMAN'S CHOICE: Polish Hill Riesling 1996, Clare Valley, S. Australia, £16.50; Frankland Estate Olmo's Reward Cabernet 1992, Great Southern, W. Australia, £18.50.

CHEF: David Jones PROPRIETOR: Julie Griffiths OPEN: Tue to Sun L 12.30 to 2 (3.30 Sun), Tue to Sat D 7.30 to 9.30 CLOSED: 26 and 27 Dec MEALS: alc (main courses £9.50 to £16.50). Set L Tue to Sat and D Tue to Fri £15.50 (2 courses). BYO £6 SERVICE: 12.5% (optional), card slips closed CARDS: Amex, Delta, MasterCard, Switch, Visa DETAILS: 80 seats. 80 seats outside. Private parties: 40 main room, 40 private room. Car park. Vegetarian meals. Children's helpings. No children under 7 at D. No-smoking area. Wheelchair access (not WC). Music

CHIPPING NORTON Oxfordshire map 2

Chavignol 🍷 ⅝✖ [NEW ENTRY]

7 Horsefair, Chipping Norton OX7 5AL COOKING 6
TEL/FAX: (01608) 644 490 COST £36–£67

Lovells at Windrush Farm, in the *Guide* last year at Minster Lovell, has moved. Or rather, the Maguires bought out the company, and set up a new venture on the site of La Madonette in this old Cotswold wool town, with Marcus Ashenford as chef; so it is in effect the same team. Mark Maguire, in more casual mode than previously, dresses to match the dark blue and pale yellow décor, and 'seems like a good man who cares'. All is relaxation, smiles and easy co-operation in the small dining-room with its plain, pictureless walls and black wrought-iron candle-holders.

The food takes an individual stance, and can appear complex, but 'transmits a sense of artistry and pleasure'. Red mullet, for example, is poached and served chilled with a salt cod beignet, and deep-fried wild mushrooms come on a soft ball-of-wool pasta base, surrounded by an earthy aubergine purée and truffle oil. Saucing is no less impressive, and local game – pigeon or venison – has come with potato gratin and a deep-flavoured meat gravy, while Trelough duck (confit leg and pink breast) is served with a light duck mousse and a first-rate cassis sauce. 'You have to like protein here,' reckoned one couple, who evidently did.

Presentation is arresting, but workmanship is always subordinate to the overall effect, as in a couple of 'stunning' desserts: a light caramel mousse with a fanned William pear and puffy sabayon, or lemon parfait hidden in a brandy-snap box, topped with a scoop of rich chocolate ice-cream and a 'TV aerial' of spun sugar. Quality has a high priority on the wine list, and classical France is given the full treatment. Small selections from around the globe add variety, and there is plenty of choice in the region of £20, although it is easy to spend more if you wish.

CHEF: Marcus Ashenford   PROPRIETORS: Mark and Donna Maguire   OPEN: Tue to Sat 12.30 to 1.45, 7 to 9.30   CLOSED: 3 weeks Jan.   MEALS: Set L £18.50 (2 courses) to £25, Set D £25 (2 courses) to £42.50   SERVICE: not inc   CARDS: Amex, Delta, Diners, MasterCard, Switch, Visa   DETAILS: 28 seats. Private parties: 22 main room, 10 private room. Vegetarian meals. Children welcome. No smoking in dining-room. No music

---

CHOBHAM Surrey   map 3

Quails

1 Bagshot Road, Chobham GU24 8BP   COOKING 3
TEL/FAX: (01276) 858491   COST £23–£48

New seats promised last year have duly arrived to brighten up the dining-room with their turquoise and yellow upholstery. The short menu with six or seven choices in each course is 'French and modern British', says chef Christopher Wale, but the latter now prevails, although a modest fixed-price-menu presents the cooking of a different French region each month. Sauté prawns with oriental sauce, fillet of cod rubbed with Thai spices on stir-fried beanshoots, and rack of lamb studded with garlic on a bed of couscous with a mint jus have been commended. Desserts, perhaps chocolate crème brûlée or poached tamarillos, are generally approved. Smartly dressed young waitresses are cheerful and efficient. A reporter did not mind giving his credit card number when booking ahead for a party of six but resented being charged £15 per head at the time of booking. A worldly collection of wines helpfully arranged by style offers good drinking at reasonable prices. House French is £9.75.

CHEF: Christopher Wale   PROPRIETORS: the Wale family   OPEN: Tue to Fri L 12.30 to 1.30, Tue to Sat D 7 to 9.30   CLOSED: 26 Dec, 1 Jan   MEALS: alc (main courses £13 to £15.50). Set L Tue to Fri £11.95 (2 courses) to £14.95, Set D Tue to Fri £15.95 (2 courses) to £18.95   SERVICE: not inc   CARDS: Amex, Delta, Diners, MasterCard, Switch, Visa   DETAILS: 50 seats. Private parties: 50 main room. Car park. Vegetarian meals. Children welcome. Wheelchair access (not WC). Music. Air-conditioned   £5

CHRISTCHURCH Dorset   map 2

Splinters

11/12 Church Street, Christchurch BH23 1BW	COOKING **3**
TEL/FAX: (01202) 483454	COST £26–£51

Splinters is a row of knocked-through terraced houses with shop-front windows in a cul-de-sac that has the glorious Christchurch priory at its end. Within, it is such a warren of little rooms that 'finding one's way out again is quite a task'. Highly polished pew seating and tightly packed tables re-inforce the mood, and may not prepare you for the daring culinary escapades that the kitchen prides itself on. Set-price menus are supplemented by daily specials, which include a fillet steak dish du jour, perhaps tricked out with hot Jamaican curry sauce and deep-fried onion rings. Salmon fillet on black olive and basil butter sauce with baby leeks uses good fish, 'cooked to a thorough, consistent opacity', or there may be sauté foie gras with sweetbreads, pommes Anna and a white truffle sauce for a £3 supplement. Starters run to calf's liver on salad leaves surrounded by a wreath of raspberries, onions and pancetta, further garnished with tapénade on croûtons. Showboating desserts may include a green study that matches mint choc-chip ice-cream with vivid green crème de menthe sorbet, moated with green sugar syrup, and with the word 'green' inscribed in chocolate on the rim of the plate. Staff are welcoming and know what they're serving. Wines offer a reasonable international spread, starting at £11.90.

CHEF: Jason Davenport   PROPRIETORS: Timothy Lloyd and Robert Wilson   OPEN: Tue to Sun L 12 to 2.30, Tue to Sat D 7 to 10 (10.30 Sat)   CLOSED: 28 to 30 Dec   MEALS: Set L £13.95 (2 courses) to £15.95, Set D £23.95 (2 courses) to £27.95   SERVICE: not inc   CARDS: Amex, Delta, Diners, MasterCard, Switch, Visa   DETAILS: 42 seats. Private parties: 12 main room, 8 to 22 private rooms. Children's helpings. No smoking in dining-room. Music   £5

CLAYGATE Surrey   map 3

Le Petit Pierrot

4 The Parade, Claygate KT10 0NU	COOKING **2**
TEL: (01372) 465105 FAX: (01372) 467642	COST £26–£35

Apart from the native ingredients, such as Gressingham duck, and a menu in both French and English, this small restaurant would not seem out of place across the Channel. Green, cream and gold wallpaper, a tented ceiling, French pictures and a large mirror add to the provincial feel. A typically bilingual potage of smoked haddock, beans and bacon, using good fish stock, was enjoyed by an inspector, and simpler dishes from the two-course lunch menu might include spinach and prawn omelette, and plaice with mushrooms. Passion-fruit dessert, served warm with marmalade cheesecake cream and passion-fruit coulis, amounted to a 'very good, light marmalade sponge'. The 90-strong wine list ranges widely over the French regions and includes 20 half-bottles. Even burgundies are not greedily priced; house wine is £9.95.

CHEF: Jean-Pierre Brichot   PROPRIETORS: Jean-Pierre and Annie Brichot   OPEN: Mon to Fri L 12.15 to 2, Mon to Sat D 7.15 to 9.30   CLOSED: 1 week Christmas, 2 weeks end Aug, bank hols   MEALS: Set L £10.75 (2 courses) to £18.75, Set D £21.75   SERVICE: not inc   CARDS: Amex, Diners, MasterCard, Visa   DETAILS: 32 seats. Private parties: 32 main room. Vegetarian meals. Children welcome. No children under 9. No pipes in dining-room. Wheelchair access (1 step; not WC). Music   £5

CLITHEROE Lancashire   map 8

Auctioneer 🍴✻

New Market Street, Clitheroe BB7 2JW   COOKING 4
TEL: (01200) 427153   FAX: (01200) 444518   COST £18–£45

The Auctioneer attracts passers-by in summer with a 'splendid' display of colourful window-boxes and hanging baskets. Henk Van Heumen's ethnically themed menus have been a feature of Clitheroe life for a decade now, and his urge to explore is undimmed. Renditions of any given cuisine are cheerfully approximate rather than strictly purist (hence the generous use of cream sauces in some Sicilian and Sardinian dishes), but the quality of materials is not in doubt. Brochettes of tiger prawns and scallops wrapped in bacon are 'fine, juicy seafood', while mustard and herb-coated lamb cutlets are timed to make the most of the flavour of mature meat, and Catalan-style pork medallions with beans and chorizo are 'full-flavoured, properly rustic and salty'. Desserts from the main *carte* include chocolate marquise with saffron sauce and a highly commended raspberry crème brûlée. Ten imaginative house wines, all at £11, are the inviting preamble to a fairly priced and broadly based wine list.

CHEF: Henk Van Heumen   PROPRIETORS: Henk and Frances Van Heumen   OPEN: Tue to Sun 12 to 1.30, 7 to 9 (9.30 Sat)   MEALS: alc (main courses £12.50 to £17.50). Set L £6.95 (2 courses) to £8.95, Set D £19.75   SERVICE: not inc   CARDS: Amex, Delta, MasterCard, Switch, Visa   DETAILS: 48 seats. Private parties: 24 main room, 24 private rooms. Vegetarian meals. Children's helpings. No babies. No smoking in dining-room. Music   £5

COCKERMOUTH Cumbria   map 10

Quince & Medlar 🍴✻ £

13 Castlegate, Cockermouth CA13 9EU   COOKING 2
TEL: (01900) 823579   COST £23–£27

The Quince & Medlar has evolved from a café into a rather more formal but still very relaxed restaurant. Parsnip and potato pancakes are topped with beetroot, horseradish and creme fraîche, and served with 'fresh as a daisy' salad, while a pie of Cumberland farmhouse cheeses and ricotta on a bed of noodles is 'delicate, subtle and light as a feather'. Other offerings might include warm asparagus and quail's egg salad, or roasted root vegetables with cheesy polenta, while desserts range from iced lemon parfait to Cointreau soufflé. Some reporters have felt it unnecessary for the vegetable-based dishes to be accompanied by piles of additional vegetables, but the kitchen's heart is in the right place. Service endears with its charm and friendliness. A handful of organic wines stand out on the affordable list, and house wine is £7.

CHEFS/PROPRIETORS: Colin and Louisa Le Voi   OPEN: Tue to Sat D only 7 to 9.30   CLOSED: 1 week mid-Nov, 24 to 26 Dec, 2 weeks mid-Jan   MEALS: alc (main courses £8.50). BYO £5   SERVICE: not inc, card slips closed   CARDS: MasterCard   DETAILS: 26 seats. Private parties: 14 main room. Vegetarian meals. No children under 5. No smoking in dining-room. Wheelchair access (2 steps; not WC). Music

---

COLCHESTER Essex   map 3

Warehouse Brasserie ✻ £

12 Chapel Street North, Colchester CO2 7AT	COOKING 3
TEL/FAX: (01206) 765656	COST £15–£36

A bumper postbag testifies to the enduring popularity of Messrs Brooks' and Burley's splendid brasserie. The location may be less than promising, but 'if every town in Britain   had a restaurant of this quality', few would have reason to quibble. Brisk, unshowy but infectiously enthusiastic service helps to keep the atmosphere buzzing: 'young, vibrant, noisy and very happy' is how one reporter summed up the mood of the place. The kitchen now draws heavily on supplies of organic produce, including meat, vegetables, herbs and salad stuff, and lunch-time is a crowd-puller, largely because of the 'fantastic-value' fixed-price menu. Warm pigeon breast salad followed by roast cod on celeriac and potato mash generated an effusive response from one visitor; another put pen to paper after sampling 'great' confit of duck with bubble and squeak, and then navarin of lamb, and chocolate pudding. Dinner brings its own delights in the shape of home-cured gravlax with dill sauce, smoked haddock and prawn fish-cakes with chive sauce, and roast loin of lamb stuffed with rosemary and thyme. Creamy 'French-style' ice-creams are a favourite way to finish. The wine list looks worldwide for value and quality, starting at £8.95.

CHEFS: Anthony Brooks, Mark Burley, Paul James and Cheryl Hilham   PROPRIETORS: Anthony Brooks and Mel Burley   OPEN: all week L 12 to 2, Mon to Sat D 7 to 10   MEALS: alc (main courses £7.50 to £12). Set L Mon to Sat £5.95 (2 courses) to £7.95, Set D Mon to Thur £9.95 (2 courses) to £12.95   SERVICE: not inc, card slips closed   CARDS: Amex, Delta, Diners, MasterCard, Switch, Visa   DETAILS: 100 seats. Private parties: 110 main room. Vegetarian meals. Children's helpings. No smoking in 1 dining-room. Wheelchair access (1 step; also WC). No music. Air-conditioned   £5

COLERNE Wiltshire   map 2

▲ Lucknam Park ❦ ✻

Colerne SN14 8AZ	
TEL: (01225) 742777 FAX: (01225) 743536	
EMAIL: lucknampark@compuserve.com	COOKING 5
off A420 at Ford, 6m W of Chippenham	COST £57–£94

The mile-long avenue that leads to the door of Lucknam is flanked by a double row of beeches, so that 'bathed in liquid green light' on a summer's evening, it may have a beguiling other-worldly feel to it. Five hundred acres of parkland surround an immaculately preserved Palladian mansion that has been run as a hotel for a little over a decade, and which makes a strikingly professional impression as soon as you step through the portico.

A choice of menus is offered at dinner, including a £40 version with only a brace of options per course, although dishes from the 'Classical' menu may be selected (at a supplement) by those who want potted shrimps, fish and chips, or steak with bèarnaise sauce. Finally, there is the maximum-impact *carte*, which is where Paul Collins really flexes his muscles. The expected luxuries are well rendered, as in a generous slab of foie gras terrine adorned with Muscat jelly in 'amber cubes like superior fruit gums'. Cannelloni of lobster, tomato and basil might be another way to start, before fillets of John Dory with crab risotto and tarragon sauce. Meat is served in hearty quantities, and has included good spring lamb with garlic cream and broad beans. Soothing desserts, such as apricot soufflé with five-spice sabayon, or chocolate and Amaretto gâteau, come with wine suggestions appended. Service is generally charming, and the 'jolly and cheerful' sommelier has been particularly praised. He presides over a lengthy and predominantly French list, with claret and burgundy vintages going back a long way. Prices are high – lottery winners will have a field day – but those on a limited budget might look to the intriguing regional French section, or to England or South America. CELLARMAN'S CHOICE: Collard Chenin Blanc 1995, Hawkes Bay, New Zealand, £23; Cornas 1991, J- L. Colombo, £45.

CHEF: Paul Collins   PROPRIETOR: Lucknam Park Hotels Ltd   OPEN: Sun L 12.30 to 2.30, all week D 7.30 to 9 (Fri and Sat 7 to 10)   MEALS: alc (main courses £26 to £29). Set D £40. Light snacks available in Pavilion restaurant   SERVICE: not inc, card slips closed   CARDS: Amex, Delta, Diners, MasterCard, Switch, Visa   DETAILS: 80 seats. Private parties: 80 main room, 36 in private rooms. Car park. Vegetarian meals. Children's helpings. No children under 12 at D. Jacket and tie. No smoking in dining-room. Wheelchair access (1 step; also WC). Music ACCOMMODATION: 41 rooms, all with bath/shower. TV. Phone. Room only £130 to £625. Rooms for disabled. Children welcome. High teas for children under 12. Baby facilities. No dogs. Afternoon teas. Swimming-pool (*The Which? Hotel Guide*)

COOKHAM Berkshire   map 3

Alfonso's

19–21 Station Hill Parade, Cookham SL6 9BR   COOKING 3
TEL: (01628) 525775   COST £30–£45

A genuine and personable family atmosphere is one reason why the Baenas' long-serving restaurant in a parade of shops has such a loyal following. Light green walls and fresh linen cloths help to make the interior hospitable, and the feel is of 'a veritable small oasis'. There are a few echoes of the owners' native Spain in dishes such as warm piquillo pepper flan 'perfumed' with Don Zolio Xeres, and a terrine of Alicante nougat on chocolate cream with Cointreau-soaked cherries, but elsewhere the kitchen globetrots for inspiration. Mille-feuille of Torbay crab and chervil served on a crab bisque and olive oil emulsion was 'to die for', according to one correspondent; others have enjoyed pasta with spinach, oven-dried tomatoes and ham as a starter. Further afield, main courses have come up with loin of Berkshire pork marinated Argentine-style and cooked on wood embers, Mongolian beef platter drizzled with olive oil and a Japanese beer reduction, and roast rack of lamb served with a

289

timbale of Algerian couscous. Ten Spanish wines are supplemented by a short selection from around the world; house French is £9.25.

CHEF: Richard Manzano   PROPRIETORS: Mr and Mrs Alfonso Baena   OPEN: Mon to Fri L 12.30 to 2, Mon to Sat D 7 to 10   CLOSED: 25 Dec, 1 Jan, bank hols   MEALS: Set L £7.50 (2 courses), Set L and D £18 (2 courses) to £21.50   SERVICE: not inc   CARDS: Amex, Delta, Diners, MasterCard, Visa   DETAILS: 34 seats. Private parties: 34 main room. Car park. Vegetarian meals. Children's helpings. No pipes in dining-room. No smoking while others eat. Wheelchair access (not WC). Occasional music. Air-conditioned

---

COPPULL MOOR   Lancashire   map 8

Coppull Moor ✦

311 Preston Road, Coppull Moor PR7 5DU   COOKING 1
TEL: (01257) 792222   FAX. (01257) 793666   COST £25–£47

Anyone for a six-course dinner? That's the offer at this refurbished small pub on the A49, heavily decorated with ink drawings and assorted *objets d'art*. It retains an 'old-fashioned' feel, not least because everybody sits down at 8 o'clock, having chosen from a wordy menu that might offer 'goose and vegetable terrine served with a classical Cumberland sauce and a tomato and mixed leaf salad with a warm dressing', or 'prime fillet steak chargrilled and served with an onion sauce and garnished with savoury tomatoes and topped with a large field mushroom cooked with shallots and herbs'. Apart from beef, a typical menu might centre around saddle of lamb, wild duck, or baked sea bream – after soup, fish-cake, or smoked haddock with risotto – and finish with steamed chocolate pud or blueberry and cassis ice-cream. Coffee is included, water is free and, even more refreshingly, gratuities are not accepted. Sixty-plus well-spread wines start with house Australian at £14.50.

CHEF/PROPRIETOR: Barry Rea   OPEN: Sun L 12.30 (1 sitting), Tue to Sun D 8 (1 sitting)   MEALS: Set L £15.50, Set D Tue to Thur £26.50, Set D Fri to Sun £28.50   SERVICE: net prices   CARDS: none   DETAILS: 33 seats. Private parties: 18 main room, 6 to 15 private rooms. Car park. Vegetarian meals. No children under 14. No smoking in dining-room. Wheelchair access (not WC). Music

---

CORSCOMBE   Dorset   map 2

▲ Fox Inn £

Corscombe DT2 0NS
TEL/FAX: (01935) 891330
off A356, 6m SE of Crewkerne   COOKING 2
                                                           COST £19–£40

(DORSET 1999 PUB)

'Can you find a more beautiful pub in England?' challenges Martyn Lee, staking his claim to priority with a sixteenth-century building that is thatched, stone-built, flag-floored, inglenooked, with climbing roses over the front and a big welcome inside. For a village pub to be both off the beaten track and yet as busy as this seems a contradiction in terms, but there is no doubting the reason for its popularity: 'unusually good-quality pub food'. Fish from West Bay is a strong suit, delivering roast cod, grilled lemon sole, salmon fish-cakes and a 'Kerala-style' fish curry, and Will Longman's approach is a combination of cosmopolitan and 'rock-solid English', making use of free-range eggs, garden herbs and local game such as griddled venison, or rabbit braised in the Aga in cider, mustard and cream. Puddings aim to comfort – treacle tart, sticky toffee, rich chocolate pot – and the whole thing is backed up by 'very friendly' and 'highly efficient' service. Drink real ale, something home-made such as elderflower cordial or sloe sherry, or a wine under £20 from the short list. House wines are £9.50.

CHEFS: Will Longman and George Marsh PROPRIETOR: Martyn Lee OPEN: all week 12 to 2, 7 to 9 (9.30 Fri and Sat) CLOSED: 25 Dec (exc for drinks at L) MEALS: alc (main courses £5 to £15). BYO £6 SERVICE: not inc, card slips closed CARDS: Amex, Delta, MasterCard, Switch, Visa DETAILS: 65 seats. 35 seats outside. Private parties: 20 main room, 20 private room. Car park. Vegetarian meals. Children welcome. Wheelchair access (1 step; not WC). No music ACCOMMODATION: 3 rooms, all with bath/shower. TV. B&B £45 to £70. No children. No dogs

---

CORSE LAWN Gloucestershire   map 2

▲ *Corse Lawn House* 🍷 ✳

Corse Lawn GL19 4LZ
TEL: (01452) 780771 FAX: (01452) 780840   COOKING 3
on B4211, 5m SW of Tewkesbury   COST £27–£59

A group of tall red-brick Georgian buildings stands proud in the flatlands of the Vale of Gloucester, reflected in the great pond (that was once a drive-through coach wash) in front of them. The Hines have notched up two decades here, and run things to a tried-and-true formula that doesn't strive after modishness for its own sake, but puts its trust in the value of established practice. Top-class breads made from unbleached flour start things off in fine style, before smoked chicken and avocado salad or warm crab terrine with herb butter sauce, and then perhaps chargrilled salmon with capers and cucumber. Oriental embellishments are brought to bear in Chinese-spiced pork with lime leaves, ginger and honey, and meals might end with a study in rhubarb (fool, sorbet and compote), or lemon tart. A couple of reports this year have spoken of a kitchen ticking over rather than noticeably exerting itself, which seems a shame given the level of experience. The lengthy wine list takes a leisurely stroll through classical French regions (travelling as far back in time as the 1940s in the case of Bordeaux), then journeys through Europe on its way to a quick tour of the New World. Quality is consistently high and half-bottles are numerous. House French is £9.95. CELLARMAN'S CHOICE: Reuilly 1996, Dom. Henri Beurdin, £16.20; Chénas, Dom. de Mongrin 1994, Gaec des Duc, £18.80.

CHEFS: Baba Hine and Andrew Poole PROPRIETOR: the Hine family OPEN: all week 12 to 2, 7 (7.30 Sun) to 9.30 CLOSED: 25 and 26 Dec. MEALS: alc (main courses £16 to £20). Set L £14.95 (2 courses) to £17.95, Set D £25 SERVICE: not inc, card slips closed CARDS: Amex, Diners, MasterCard, Visa DETAILS: 80 seats. 30 seats outside. Private parties: 80 main room, 20 to 35 private rooms. Car park. Vegetarian meals. Children's helpings. No smoking in dining-room. Wheelchair access (also WC). No music ACCOMMODATION: 19 rooms, all with bath/shower. TV. Phone. DB&B £70 to £140. Rooms for disabled. Children welcome. High teas for children. Baby facilities. Dogs welcome exc in restaurant. Afternoon teas. Swimming-pool (*The Which? Hotel Guide*)

CRANBROOK Kent	map 3

▲ *Kennel Holt Hotel* 🍴✕ `NEW ENTRY`

Goudhurst Road, Cranbrook TN17 2PT	COOKING 5
TEL: (01580) 712032 FAX: (01580) 715495	COST £37–£44

The ambition of this tall-chimneyed manor-house (Elizabethan originally) is signalled by five carefully nurtured acres of scenery, including a pond surrounded by perfectly white-painted stakes, and formally clipped hedges. Go through a yew archway to an oak front door and into an entrance hall full of antiques and garden games. Old books, furniture, beams and rugs abound, log fires smoke gently, visitors help themselves to a drink from the well-stocked bar and eat in a 'stylishly understated' dining-room. The owners, with backgrounds in advertising and food styling, and a love of the Dordogne in particular, arrived in 1992, Valentine Rodriguez five years later. A clear sense of purpose is evident from the sourcing of materials – local Biddenham asparagus, Frances Smith saladings, Rye scallops – to a balanced menu with well-defined ideas. Guinea-fowl is paired with foie gras, for example, in both a terrine, and in a rich, earthy main course of stuffed breast served with wilted spinach, waxy potatoes and a julienne of root vegetables: 'complex flavours, a lot of ingredients and a successful outcome' was the judgement.

Ouput varies from tuna spring rolls to stuffed leg of rabbit with cabbage and Marsala sauce, and a degree of comfort is evident in some of the dishes: pea, ham and mint soup with a poached egg, or a tower built of rice and lobster permeated with a fragrant mixture of saffron, cumin and cardamom. Desserts – a high point – have included roundels of 'wickedly rich and short biscuit' filled with creamy lemon curd and served with a lime custard, and 'the best bread-and-butter pudding ever eaten in 53 years'. Service is 'attentive, discreet and personable', and wines are predominantly French, from the classic regions, with a centre of gravity somewhat over £20, though house red and white are £12.50.

CHEF: Valentine Rodriguez PROPRIETORS: Neil and Sally Chalmers OPEN: Tue to Fri and Sun L 12.30 to 1.45, Tue to Sat D 7.30 to 8.45 CLOSED: 2 weeks Jan, Sun L May to Sept MEALS: Set L and D £25 to £30. BYO £10 SERVICE: 10% (optional), card slips closed CARDS: Amex, Delta, MasterCard, Switch, Visa DETAILS: 25 seats. Private parties: 10 main room, 16 private room. Car park. Vegetarian meals. No infants. Children's helpings. No smoking in dining-room. Occasional music ACCOMMODATION: 10 rooms, all with bath/shower. TV. Phone. B&B £85 to £125. Rooms for disabled. Children welcome. Baby facilities (*The Which? Hotel Guide*)

CRAWLEY Hampshire	map 2

Fox & Hounds, Vistro   `NEW ENTRY`

Crawley SO21 2PR	
1½m off A272 Winchester to Stockbridge road	COOKING 2
TEL: (01962) 776285 FAX: (01962) 776005	COST £22–£58

A vistro is a cross between a wine bar and a bistro. The idea has succeeded admirably in, for example, Winchester and Tunbridge Wells. Now here is a French version, in an ancient pub – each storey juts out above the one below – which has been modernised and divided into different eating-areas decorated in pastel blues and yellows. The emphasis is on sampling a range of wines by the glass throughout a meal. Three suggestions are normally made for each dish, for example Banyuls, Coteaux du Layon or champagne to accompany foie gras terrine, but the wine list itself offers a vast number by the glass, and owner Jerome Debris is only too pleased to chip in with advice. The food is as French as andouillette with cider sauce, or garlic sausage with lentils, and goes in for salads of confit goose gizzard, or pig's trotter and warm potatoes. Only opened in 1997, it has already divided the opinion of reporters, but has scored well for such traditional items as chicken with a mustard cream sauce, and veal Marengo.

In all, some 150 wines are offered by the (small/large) glass or bottle, ranging in price from £1.80/£2.20 (£10.50 a bottle) for a vins de pays to £10/£15 (£55) for a prestige cuvée champagne, with plenty of enjoyable drinking to be had at all levels in between. This is just the place to come to experiment with wine and food matching, or to try wines you couldn't normally afford, even though some of the finer wines listed are available only by the bottle. CELLARMAN'S CHOICE: Vin de Pays des Côtes de Gascogne 1996, Dom. Lalanne, £11.70; Bourgeuil Vieilles Vignes 1985, Pierre Caslot, £26.50.

CHEF: Pierre-Olivier Michel   PROPRIETOR: Vistro Ltd   OPEN: Tue to Sun L 12.15 to 2.15, Tue to Sat D 7.15 to 9.30   MEALS: alc (main courses £9.50 to £15.50). Set L Tue to Sat £9.50 (2 courses) to £12.50, Set Sun L and D £14.50 (2 courses) to £17.50   SERVICE: not inc   CARDS: Delta, MasterCard, Switch, Visa   DETAILS: 60 seats. Private parties: 30 main room, 14 to 25 private rooms. Car park. Vegetarian meals. Children's helpings. No children under 7. Wheelchair access (not WC). Music   £5

CRONDALL Hampshire   map 3

Chesa   NEW ENTRY

Bowling Alley, Crondall GU10 5RJ   COOKING 5
TEL/FAX: (01252) 850328   COST £39–£52

Looking every inch the suburban villa, Chesa is built in the grounds of a larger restaurant (now a private house) that Peter Hughes and his partner ran for a number of years. There is no getting round the 'unmemorable décor' and 'conservative atmosphere', in a dining-room that is 'only the same size as yours or mine', but this is the sort of place that, in one visitor's view, reflects priorities across the Channel, 'where they don't care what the décor's like so long as the grub is good'. At heart the style is Anglo-French, with provençale fish soup and rouille, cheese quiche with Cumberland sauce, and salad of duck leg confit, and there is a strong emphasis on native materials: 'as far as is possible, all produce used is British'.

The industrious kitchen turns out purées, terrines, ice-creams, parfaits, pastry and 'wonderfully crumbly' cheese straws and 'imaginative and skilfully executed' amuse-gueules that get meals off to a fine start. From then on it is accomplished cooking all the way. For an inspector, salmon and sea bass fish-cake was 'everything a fish-cake should be', with a dash of chilli, more fish than potato, coated in egg and breadcrumbs, deep-fried, and surrounded by a velouté sauce. Alcohol is used judiciously: Madeira in the rich and gamey sauce that accompanies boned quail stuffed with dark, nutty rice and dried apricot, or calvados and orange in the sauce for a large duck breast. Rösti potatoes arrive with meat, boiled with fish; otherwise everybody shares the same selection of vegetables. Waterloo, St Andrew and Golden Cross are among the weekly-changing crop of British cheeses, and desserts have ranged from glacé ginger crème brûlée with Earl Grey syrup, to a dark, intense chocolate mousse served with nougat ice-cream. All this doesn't come cheap, but wines on the short list begin at around £12 for house red and white.

CHEF: P.H.O. Hughes   PROPRIETORS: P.H.O. Hughes and E.J. Clark   OPEN: Wed to Fri and Sun L 12.30 to 1 (booking essential), Wed to Sat D 7.30 to 8.30   CLOSED: first 3 weeks Jan   MEALS: Set L £23 (2 courses), Set D £26 to £33. BYO £7.50   SERVICE: 10% (optional), card slips closed   CARDS: Amex, MasterCard, Switch, Visa   DETAILS: 20 seats. Private parties: 14 main room. Car park. Children welcome. No pipes/cigars in dining-room. Wheelchair access (also WC). No music

---

CROSTHWAITE Cumbria   map 8

▲ *Punch Bowl Inn* £

Crosthwaite LA8 8HR	COOKING 4
TEL: (015395) 68237 FAX: (015395) 68875	COST £20–£36

The Punch Bowl comfortably straddles the divide between pub and restaurant, looking more like the former, serving food more like the latter, and the in-betweenness has gathered many devotees. Steven Doherty now divides his time between the open-plan, split-level, low-beamed Crosthwaite original and his new venture Spread Eagle (see entry, Sawley), but despite an early wobble the consensus view is that things have settled down and 'standards of cooking and service are admirable', even if prices seem to have crept up a bit. Given chicken schnitzel, and gravlax with blinis, this is not aiming to be cutting-edge food, but it is well-sourced, properly cooked and attractively presented, as reporters have found with a thick and 'very satisfying' slice of coarse rabbit terrine, and a generous fillet of flaky fresh-tasting cod with cheesy sauce. Bacon and sausage come from Woodall's at Waberthwaite, and one visitor was pleased with his grilled bacon in ciabatta that came with salad leaves and mustard mayonnaise: 'a posh bacon buttie', he called it.

Those who visit in spring can enjoy the Lyth Valley's famous damson blossom, those who return in autumn benefit from the fruit, perhaps stewed and wrapped in a pancake. Alternatively, there might be banana tarte Tatin with toffee cream, or crisp-topped chocolate 'nemesis' made from good-quality chocolate and served with a creamy ice-cream. Service is 'cheerful', and 'no nonsense' when it comes to wine: house wine is £12 a litre, £6 for a half-litre.

CHEFS: Steven Doherty and Duncan Collinge   PROPRIETORS: Steven and Marjorie Doherty, Alan Bell and Lionel Yates   OPEN: all week 12 to 2, 6 to 9   CLOSED: 25 Dec   MEALS: alc (main courses £7 to £10.50). Set L Sun £9.25 (2 courses) to £11.25. Light snacks available   SERVICE: not inc, card slips closed   CARDS: MasterCard, Switch, Visa   DETAILS: 60 seats. 20 seats outside. Car park. Vegetarian meals. Children's helpings. No-smoking area. No music ACCOMMODATION: 3 rooms, all with bath/shower. TV. DB&B £35 to £50. Children welcome. No dogs

CRUDWELL Wiltshire   map 2

▲ *Crudwell Court* ▾ ✳

Crudwell, Nr Malmesbury, Crudwell SN16 9EP
TEL: (01666) 577194   FAX: (01666) 577853
EMAIL: crudwellcrt@compuserve.com   COOKING 2
on A429, 3m N of Malmesbury   COST £18–£46

'Very English, very charming,' summed up one visitor: the hotel and restaurant
next to the church has a delightful walled garden, but isn't a grand place, rather
simply decorated with stripped wood, potted plants and comfortable furniture.
The repertoire covers much familiar territory, some dishes going back a few
years – soft herring roes in a tarragon cream sauce, or a stiff cone-shaped sole
'mousseline' with a tomatoey lobster sauce – but well-balanced meals might also
take in grilled goats' cheese and artichoke salad, or pork medallions in a
mushroom and leek sauce. Duck has appeared in a couple of citrussy guises:
pink breast in a pool of lime and ginger sauce, and fanned slices in a tangy orange
and kumquat sauce. Vegetables are served on a side plate, desserts may let the
side down, and wine service may not be very knowledgeable, but the wines
themselves impress with a range of vintages and styles at fair prices, particularly
in the French regions. House French is £9.75, and there is a good choice of
half-bottles. CELLARMAN'S CHOICE: Sancerre 1996, André Dezat et Fils £18;
David Wynn Shiraz 1996, Eden Valley, S. Australia, £17.50.

CHEF: Chris Amor   PROPRIETOR: Nick Bristow   OPEN: all week 12 to 2, 7 to 9.30   MEALS: Set L
Mon to Sat £7.50 (2 courses) , Set L Sun £11.50, Set D £19.50 to £25.95   SERVICE: not inc, card
slips closed   CARDS: Amex, Delta, Diners, MasterCard, Switch, Visa   DETAILS: 90 seats.
Private parties: 55 main room, 35 to 55 private rooms. Car park. Vegetarian meals. Children's
helpings. No smoking in dining-room. Occasional music   ACCOMMODATION: 15 rooms, all with
bath/shower. TV. Phone. DB&B £45 to £114. Children welcome. Baby facilities. Dogs welcome
in bedrooms only. Afternoon teas. Swimming-pool (*The Which? Hotel Guide*)   £5

CUMNOR Oxfordshire   map 2

Bear & Ragged Staff ✳

Appleton Road, Cumnor OX2 9QH
TEL: (01865) 862329   FAX: (01865) 865366   COOKING 2
EMAIL: bruce@cumnorbear.ash9.co.uk   COST £23–£52

'Splendid place,' writes a regular reporter of this fourteenth-century stone-built
house in a village four miles from Oxford city centre. Fish from Newlyn is the
main business: seared scallops with pesto potatoes, sea bass with asparagus, or
fillet of cod with tomato confit and foie gras. A printed menu and a blackboard
operate in tandem, and meat is by no means neglected. Poached egg salad with
Toulouse sausage and bacon offers a very Franco-British way to begin, and there
may be shank of lamb, or venison with poached pears and black pudding to
follow. Desserts deserve 'special mention', according to a reporter whose party
enjoyed white chocolate mousse with dark chocolate sauce, and steamed date
and walnut pudding with toffee sauce. Prices cause some head-scratching,
varying from 'too expensive', to 'outstanding value for money' from one who ate

a fixed-price three-course lunch. A round-the-world wine list starts with a changing selection of house wines at £9.75.

CHEF: Bruce Buchan   PROPRIETORS: Bruce and Kay Buchan   OPEN: Sun to Fri L 12 to 2, Mon to Sat D 7 to 10   CLOSED: 3 or 4 days Christmas   MEALS: alc (main courses £13 to £16). Set L Mon to Fri £12.50 (2 courses) to £14.50. Bar snacks all week. BYO £5   SERVICE: not inc, card slips closed   CARDS: Amex, Diners, MasterCard, Switch, Visa   DETAILS: 80 seats. Private parties: 50 main room. Car park. Children's helpings. No smoking in 1 dining-room. Wheelchair access (also WC). Music   £5

DARTMOUTH Devon   map 1

Aragua ▼

St Saviours Square, Dartmouth TQ6 9DH   COOKING 3
TEL/FAX: (01003) 832224   COST £23–£47

In a quiet corner of Dartmouth, flanked by St Saviour's Church and the British Legion, this family-run restaurant makes a good stab at looking South American, helped by potted palms and a huge wooden armadillo. But despite huevos rancheros (fried eggs with black beans and tomato-chilli-coriander sauce) and Caracas-style roast pork with lentils, the thrust is not entirely Latin American: the menu also makes room for duck liver terrine, and pannacotta with plum compote. Choice may not be particularly wide, but Aragua does provide Dartmouth with 'exciting new combinations of flavours', including lobster and papaya salad, and grilled sweetcorn soup with coriander and red pepper salsas.

Presentation and careful cooking are appreciated, producing black pasta with 'light and non-greasy' mussel fritters, and fish soup accompanied by a 'home-made breadstick the size of a knife handle' containing rouille at one end and aïoli at the other. Desserts are no less interesting, judging by churros fritters with chocolate ice and coffee crystals, and mango ice-cream with pecan-ginger brownie. Wines from Chile, Argentina and Mexico form the backbone of a short but resourceful list, with contributions from six other countries adding a bit of weight at some very slim prices. Four wines of the week are also available by the glass, as are half-a-dozen almacenista sherries. CELLARMAN'S CHOICE: St-Véran 1996, Dom. des Deux Roches, £16.50; Antiguas Reservas Cabernet Sauvignon 1994, Cousiño Macul, Maipo, Chile, £16.50.

CHEFS: Franz and Elizabeth Conde   PROPRIETORS: Franz and Elizabeth Conde, and Patricia Thomas   OPEN: Fri to Sun L 12 to 2, Wed to Sat D 7 to 9 (9.30 Sat and summer)   CLOSED: first 3 weeks Dec, last 2 weeks Mar, last week June   MEALS: alc D (main courses £12 to £18). Set L £15 (2 courses)   SERVICE: net prices, card slips closed   CARDS: Amex, Delta, MasterCard, Switch, Visa   DETAILS: 40 seats. Private parties: 40 main room. Car park. Children's helpings. No smoking while others eat. Music   £5

Several sharp operators have tried to extort money from restaurateurs on the promise of an entry in a guidebook that has never appeared. The Good Food Guide *makes no charge for inclusion.*

▲ *denotes an outstanding wine cellar;* ▼ *denotes a good wine list, worth travelling for.*

Carved Angel

2 South Embankment, Dartmouth TQ6 9BH
TEL: (01803) 832465   FAX: (01803) 835141

COOKING 7
COST £38–£67

'It took us 12 years to organise ourselves to have lunch at this splendid restaurant,' confided a couple who came all the way from Taunton, and were glad they made the effort. The 'airy, elegant' dining-room has a splendid view over the Dart estuary (or you can 'watch passers-by licking their ice-creams'), while the open-plan design makes it easy to see goings-on in the kitchen. The principles here are well established, and take their inspiration from the 'European/Elizabeth David tradition'. First, develop good supply lines, using local raw materials as far as possible: seafood is the most obvious resource to land on the doorstep. Then present the food simply, 'with no garnishing for garnishing's sake'; everything on the plate should be there for a good reason.

It is this approach that has kept the Angel's halo in place for over a quarter of a century. The food has always maintained a proudly British dimension – in roast partridge with bread sauce and medlar jelly, for example – although the kitchen is not slow to pick up on other bright ideas and flavours: prawn soup made with coconut, chilli and lime, and served with a fish wuntun, perhaps, or best end of lamb with spiced couscous and aubergine. For dessert, expect hot chocolate soufflé with vanilla ice-cream, or rhubarb and kumquat compote, from half a dozen alternatives on the *carte*.

Not all reporters find such simplicity of style to their taste, although it is worth noting the absence of hidden extras. The overwhelming majority view, however, is of consistently good food. Service has been both 'speedy, friendly and efficient', and slow enough to allow 'a long, relaxing lunch'. Other details, from bread and olives to pickles, coffee and petit fours, are notably good, and menu options start with a set one-course dinner. The owners have now opened the Carved Angel Café at 7 Foss Street, serving teas and light lunches.

In sympathy with the food, every wine on the list has earned its place: there are no fillers or makeweights here. Fine wines from France are ably supported by judicious selections from the New World, while a quartet from England keeps the British flag flying. Numerous aperitifs and digestifs are listed, and half a dozen house wines from France and New Zealand are £15. CELLARMAN'S CHOICE: Jackson Estate Sauvignon Blanc 1997, Marlborough, New Zealand, £22; Monthélie 1992, Eric de Suremain, £29.

CHEFS: Joyce Molyneux and Nick Coiley   PROPRIETORS: Joyce Molyneux, Nick Coiley, Meriel Matthews and Zoë Wynne   OPEN: Tue to Sun L 12.30 to 2.30, Tue to Sat D 7 to 9.30   CLOSED: 1 week Christmas, 6 weeks from 1 Jan   MEALS: alc L (main courses £18 to £25). Set L Tue to Sat £15 and £25 (both 2 courses) to £30, Set L Sun £38, Set D £28 (1 course) to £48. BYO £5 per person   SERVICE: net prices, card slips closed   CARDS: Delta, MasterCard, Switch, Visa DETAILS: 48 seats. Private parties: 40 main room, 18 private rooms. Vegetarian meals. Children welcome. No smoking in dining-room. Smoking lounge. No music (£5)

The text of entries is based on unsolicited reports sent in by readers, backed up by inspections conducted anonymously. The factual details under the text are from questionnaires the Guide *sends to all restaurants that feature in the book.*

Cutter's Bunch

33 Lower Street, Dartmouth TQ6 9AN	COOKING 2
TEL: (01803) 832882	COST £28–£44

A stone's throw from Lower Ferry behind Dartmouth Yacht Club, Cutter's Bunch is a lively bistro with bags of fun and atmosphere. People really seem to enjoy themselves here. Nick Crosley is keen on local produce, but his menus are also peppered with ideas from around the globe. Alsace onion tart and Mediterranean fish soup share the billing with crab-stuffed chicken wings with chilli and ginger dip, borek (filo parcels filled with feta cheese, spinach and lamb) and Moroccan-style poussin with saffron and olive rice. Nearer to home you might also find local lobster with calvados cream sauce, or Dartmoor venison with a red wine and cassis sauce. Bringing up the rear is a blackboard of desserts, perhaps including iced chocolate terrine and strawberry crème brûlée. The wine list offers excellent value and a catholic selection drawn from most major producing countries. House wine is £10.50.

CHEF: Nick Crosley   PROPRIETORS: Nick and Jo Crosley   OPEN: Thur to Mon (and Tue July and Aug) D only 7 to 9.45   CLOSED: Sun and Mon Nov to May (exc bank hols and Easter)   MEALS: alc (main courses £12 to £17.50). BYO by arrangement   SERVICE: not inc, card slips closed   CARDS: Delta, MasterCard, Switch, Visa   DETAILS: 28 seats. Private parties: 32 main room. Children's helpings. No pipes. Music   £5

DEDDINGTON Oxfordshire   map 5

Dexter's

Market Place, Deddington OX15 0SE	
TEL/FAX: (01869) 338813	
from A4260 Oxford to Banbury road turn right into	COOKING 4
Market Square in Deddington	COST £21–£55

Drawing in its horns only slightly since last year – by closing on Sunday evening and all day Monday – Dexter's still adopts a bright approach to world cooking, and is all the more welcome for doing it 'in the desert surrounding Banbury'. Seating may not be generous, but the plates are, and ingredients are sound. Salmon and coriander fish-cakes come with a pot of garlic mayonnaise and a salad of crisp variegated leaves with a mustard dressing, and loin of lamb has been served with slices of black pudding ('a good filler'), along with potato rösti and 'a rich sauce of excellent flavour'. Dishes are perked up with varied seasonings: chilli and tomato salsa for swordfish; ginger, soy and honey for sea bass; or mustard mash for a duck leg wrapped in Parma ham; 'this kitchen is very good at varying the intensity of mustard to suit what it is presented with.' Desserts aim for the comfort zone with tiramisù, St Emilion au chocolat, and bread-and-butter pudding. A one-page global wine list starts in Argentina and finishes in Burgundy and Bordeaux. House Vin de Pays d'Oc is £10.50.

£5 *indicates that the restaurant has elected to participate in the* Good Food Guide *voucher scheme. For full details see page 6.*

CHEF: Jamie Dexter Harrison, Bradley Morris and Stuart Cox   PROPRIETORS: Jamie Dexter Harrison and Roger Blackburn   OPEN: Tue to Sun L 12 to 2.15, Tue to Sat D 7 to 9.30 (10 Sat) CLOSED: Christmas and New Year   MEALS: alc (main courses £10 to £16.50). Set L £8.50 (2 courses) to £11, Set D Tue to Fri £16.95 (2 courses) to £19.95. BYO £10   SERVICE: not inc, card slips closed   CARDS: Delta, MasterCard, Switch, Visa   DETAILS: 36 seats. Private parties: 42 main room. Vegetarian meals. Children's helpings. No children under 5. No cigars/pipes in dining-room. Wheelchair access (not WC). Occasional music

---

DEDHAM Essex   map 6

▲ *Fountain House* ▼ ⁵⟪✳

| Dedham Hall, Brook Street, Dedham CO7 6AD | COOKING 1 |
| TEL: (01206) 323027   FAX: (01206) 323293 | COST £26–£34 |

Watercolour landscapes on the wall are a reminder that this is Constable country. The River Stour runs nearby, and Fountain House is up a gravel drive near the centre of the village. Wendy Sarton's weekly-changing menu is generous in its offerings, packing in almost 30 dishes over three courses. Her style is admirably straightforward, mixing old favourites of carrot and orange soup, smoked haddock Florentine, or Normandy pork fillet, with feta cheese and roast pepper salad, or chicken liver Stroganoff. A dozen or so desserts generally combine fruit and cream in equal measure, from mango cheesecake or strawberry vacherin to a dried fruit compote with vanilla ice-cream. Wines are grouped by varietal/style, prices are extremely fair (with some real bargains to be had among the fine wine bin-ends) and half-bottles are exemplary. French house wines plus one Italian in all three colours range between £9 and £12. CELLARMAN'S CHOICE: Allan Scott Sauvignon Blanc 1997, Marlborough, New Zealand, £17; Côte de Brouilly, Dom. de la Voûte des Crozes 1996, Nicole Chanrion, £15.

CHEF: Wendy Sarton   PROPRIETORS: Wendy and James Sarton   OPEN: Sun L 12 to 2.30, Tue to Sat D 7 to 9.30   MEALS: Set L £18.50, Set D £19.95   SERVICE: not inc, card slips closed CARDS: Delta, MasterCard, Switch, Visa   DETAILS: 50 seats. Private parties: 50 main room. Car park. Vegetarian meals. Children's helpings. No smoking in dining-room. Wheelchair access (not WC). Occasional music   ACCOMMODATION: 6 rooms, all with bath/shower. TV. B&B £40 to £90. Children welcome. High teas for children. Baby facilities. No dogs (£5)

▲ *Le Talbooth* ▮

| Gun Hill, Dedham CO7 6HP | COOKING 4 |
| TEL: (01206) 323150   FAX: (01206) 322309 | COST £29–£72 |

'Le Talbooth,' according to one regular visitor, 'is how everybody thinks of England – thatched roof, beams, the river running past at the back.' In the evening, when it is floodlit, the impression created is more dramatic, while the interior may seem rather lifestyle-magazine for some, with its illuminated repro paintings, carriage lamps and white piano. Reporters over the past year have varied in their assessments of the cooking, one praising 'very well-cooked' Dover sole meunière, as well as mini-steaks of veal loin with mushrooms and a green peppercorn sauce. At inspection, things were patchier: a crisply sauté gingered crab-cake on a bed of spinach impressed greatly, while a pairing of salmon and sea bass was not well timed. Steamed sultana pudding with 'perfect' custard has been one of the more successful desserts.

The wine list is good on burgundy (revealing the hand of local wine merchants Lay & Wheeler), is quite long on claret, and features some fine selections from the New World, where South Africa, in particular, contributes a greatly increased number of bins. Eight house wines, in all three colours, start at £11.50. CELLARMAN'S CHOICE: Stellenzicht Chardonnay 1997, Stellenbosch, South Africa, £18.95; Warwick Trilogy 1995, Stellenbosch, South Africa, £17.95.

CHEF: Terry Barber   PROPRIETORS: Gerald, Diana and Paul Milsom   OPEN: all week 12 to 2 (4 Sun in winter), 7 to 9.30   CLOSED: Sun D in winter   MEALS: alc (main courses £14.50 to £26). Set L £16.50 (2 courses) to £19, Set D £20.50 to £24   SERVICE: 10%, card slips closed   CARDS: Amex, Delta, Diners, MasterCard, Switch, Visa   DETAILS: 75 seats. 60 seats outside. Private parties: 80 main room, 34 private room. Car park. Vegetarian meals. Children's helpings. No smoking while others eat. Occasional music   ACCOMMODATION: 10 rooms, all with bath/shower. TV. Phone. B&B £85 to £175. Rooms for disabled. Children welcome. No dogs *(The Which? Hotel Guide)* £5

DENMEAD Hampshire   map 2

Barnards ⅝✸

Hambledon Road, Denmead PO7 6NU
TEL/FAX: (01705) 257788   COOKING 2
on B2150, 2m NW of Waterlooville   COST £19–£54

David and Sandie Barnard's popular restaurant runs to a well-tried formula: they understand their customers and offer sound cooking that pleases the palate. All tastes are catered for (including a full menu for vegetarians, cut-price midweek deals and so forth), and the value for money is undeniable. David's cooking is steeped in Anglo-French classics: sauté chicken livers are served in a puff pastry case with a Madeira sauce, while smoked salmon mousse is wrapped in slices of smoked salmon and presented on a cucumber salad. Mains could range from pan-fried noisettes of lamb with creamy pepper sauce to grilled salmon fillet with stir-fried vegetables, while desserts might feature anything from dark and white chocolate mousse with coffee-bean sauce to lemon tart coupled with a lemon sorbet. The short wine list is dotted with respectable names from around the globe. House French from Pierre Perrin is £10.

CHEF: David Barnard   PROPRIETORS: David and Sandie Barnard   OPEN: Tue to Fri L 12 to 1.30, Tue to Sat D 7 to 9.30   CLOSED: 1 week Christmas, 1 week Easter and 1 week Aug   MEALS: alc (main courses £13.50 to £22). Set L £8.50 (2 courses) to £10, Set D Mon to Thur £10 (2 courses) to £12.50, Set D Fri and Sat £15 (2 courses) to £17.50. BYO £3.95   SERVICE: not inc, card slips closed   CARDS: Amex, Delta, MasterCard, Switch, Visa   DETAILS: 38 seats. 12 seats outside. Private parties: 34 main room, 20 and 34 private rooms. Car park. Vegetarian meals. Children's helpings. No smoking in dining-room. Music   £5

The Guide relies on feedback from its readers. Especially welcome are reports on new restaurants appearing in the book for the first time. All letters to the Guide are acknowledged.

DERBY Derbyshire map 5

Darleys

Darley Abbey Mill, Darley Abbey, Derby DE22 1DZ
TEL: (01332) 364987 FAX: (01332) 541356 COOKING 4
just off A6, 2m N of Derby city centre COST £20–£53

Occupying part of an old mill beside a weir on the River Derwent, Darleys was refurbished towards the end of 1997. Now bright and modern, with high-backed blue chairs standing out against pastel colours, it combines the smartness of linen tablecloths and polished glasses with a relaxed feel, helped by uniformed but not starchy staff who are attentive, knowledgeable and polite. Monthly-changing menus tend to put a contemporary spin on classic ideas, producing for example a Thai version of duck confit, the leg honey-basted and crisp-skinned, served with stir-fried vegetables.

First-course terrines are attractively varied: pressed pork and foie gras, or tomato and basil with roast artichokes and tapénade, or a chunky one combining ham hock with quail eggs and apricot, served with gribiche sauce and a delicately spiced grape chutney. Ingredients are fresh, there is a light hand in the kitchen, and dishes are decorative but not fussily presented. The food also has a strongly seasonal feel to it, one June visitor enjoying a succession of summery Sunday lunch dishes from warm peppered salmon on a niçoise salad with 'splashings of pesto', to a 'medley' of fruits served with a 'subtle and spicy' mousse of soured cream and ginger. Alternatively, there may be white chocolate and raspberry trifle, or warm rice-pudding dumplings served 'fritter-style'. The well-chosen wines are, unusually these days, totally European, and very fairly priced, starting with house French at £10.

CHEF: Philip Leech PROPRIETOR: David Pinchbeck OPEN: all week 12 to 2.30 (3 Sun), 7 to 10 (6.30 to 10.30 Fri and Sat) CLOSED: 1 Jan MEALS: alc (main courses £11 to £17). Set L £13.50. BYO £5 SERVICE: not inc CARDS: Amex, Delta, Diners, MasterCard, Switch, Visa DETAILS: 70 seats. Private parties: 70 main room. Car park. Vegetarian meals. Children's helpings. No smoking in dining-room. Music. Air-conditioned (£5)

DINTON Buckinghamshire map 3

La Chouette

Westlington Green, Dinton HP17 8UW
TEL/FAX: (01296) 747422 COOKING 5
off A418, 4m SW of Aylesbury COST £19–£60

Frédéric Desmette cooks his native Belgian food in the archetypal English setting of a former village pub, complete with beams and wooden floors. His own bird photography – owls a speciality – covers the walls. It is a one-man-and-a-helper style of operation, and the limitations occasionally show through when M. Desmette is trying to cook and cover front-of-house at the same time. He is naturally good at both, and is considered 'a host of such character' that he 'dispels all doubts about the Belgians' capacity for humour'. But the food deserves his full attention, for when it is good, it is very good.

Alongside familiar fillet of salmon or ribeye of beef '(sans os!)' are to be found goose rillettes, char, and veal sweetbreads in mustard sauce. M. Desmette also likes to come up with a few 'surprises' on his menu, but obviously we can't tell you about those. Except to say that on one occasion the surprise pudding was a sorbet; it surprised the reporter too. Apart from Cloudy Bay and a couple of Italians, the wines are all French, and of extremely high quality. This is reflected in the prices, but bottles under £20 can be found, particularly if you resist the clarets. If powerful reds appeal, then why not give one of Alain Brumont's darkly brooding Madirans a try? House wine is £10.50, but don't overlook the Belgian beers. CELLARMAN'S CHOICE: Côtes de Gascogne, Dom. du Tariquet 1995, £14.50; Coteaux d'Aix en Provence, Dom. de Trévallon 1992, £38.

CHEF/PROPRIETOR: Frédéric Desmette   OPEN: Mon to Fri L 12 to 2, Mon to Sat D 7 to 9   MEALS: alc (main courses £10 to £16). Set L £10, Set D £26.50 to £36. BYO by arrangement   SERVICE: 12.5% (optional), card slips closed   CARDS: Amex, Delta, MasterCard, Visa   DETAILS: 40 seats. 12 seats outside. Private parties: 45 main room. Car park. Children's helpings. No cigars/pipes in dining-room. Music

---

DISS Norfolk   map 6

▲ *Salisbury House* £✳

84 Victoria Road, Diss IP22 3JG   COOKING 2
TEL/FAX: (01379) 644738   COST £21–£49

This sixteenth-century timber-framed building on the outskirts of Diss, originally a grain store, then the miller's house, hides behind a neat Victorian frontage. There are two eating options. The formal dining-room, with chandelier and oriental carpet, offers three, four or five courses at a set price, and includes canapés, coffee and petits fours. The lemon-yellow bistro next to the kitchen has a *carte* and operates, as Barry Davies puts it, 'without as much service'. Dishes cover similar 'country-house' territory in both: from soups, salads and terrines to start, via meat balls, or 'slightly grainy' salmon mousse with strong-tasting lime leaf sauce, to roast birds including quail, served with walnut mashed potatoes and a thin herb-flecked jus. It is a busy kitchen, more taken with elaborate processing (into mousse, bavarois, soufflé, roulade and parfait) than is currently fashionable. Finish, perhaps, with meringue nests filled with fudge ice-cream, or a frozen terrine of gingerbread with 'chewy' white chocolate. The bistro wine list is a short selection from the restaurant one, which aims for variety and generally fair pricing. House vin de pays is under £10.

CHEF: Barry Davies   PROPRIETORS: Barry and Sue Davies   OPEN: Tue to Fri L 12.15 to 1.45, Tue to Sat D 7.15 to 9.15   CLOSED: 2 weeks summer   MEALS: restaurant Set L £24.95 to £32.50, Set D £24.95 to £32.50; bistro alc (main courses £6 to £8.50). BYO £7   SERVICE: not inc   CARDS: MasterCard, Visa   DETAILS: 36 seats. 10 seats outside. Private parties: 20 main room, 14 to 22 private rooms. Car park. Vegetarian meals. Children's helpings. No smoking in dining-room. Wheelchair access (not WC). Music   ACCOMMODATION: 3 rooms, all with bath/shower. TV. B&B £45 to £82. Rooms for disabled. Children welcome. No dogs (*The Which? Hotel Guide*) £5

Weaver's Wine Bar & Eating House £

Market Hill, Diss IP22 3JZ COOKING 2
TEL: (01379) 642411 COST £19–£38

The original building that is now the Bavins' likeable 'eating house' was constructed centuries ago by a breakaway section of the Guild of Weavers. Today, exposed beams and brickwork are still to be seen, although the dining-rooms have been embellished with greenery and flowers and a truly pleasant atmosphere prevails. The *carte* shows a fair degree of imagination, although it doesn't shun traditional steak and kidney pudding. Among starters you might find local asparagus with a soft poached egg and a brilliant dressing of nut brown butter and balsamic vinegar. Main courses have called into play medallions of beef fillet, served over a fusilli and paprika goulash with a 'refreshing' chive creme fraîche, as well as herb-crusted salmon on roasted Mediterranean vegetables with beurre blanc. A separate fixed-price menu (not available Saturday evening) is undeniably good value, delivering perhaps breaded mushrooms on fondue cheese and wine sauce, 'extremely tender' loin of pork with apple and brandy sauce, and toffee and apple cheesecake. The well-annotated, 80-strong wine list has noticeable leanings towards the Antipodes. House wine is £9.75.

CHEF: William Bavin PROPRIETORS: William and Wilma Bavin OPEN: Tue to Fri L 12 to 1.30, Mon to Sat D 7 to 9.30 CLOSED: 1 week Christmas, 1 week end Aug. MEALS: alc (main courses £10 to £13.50). Set L £7.95 (2 courses) to £10.75, Set D Mon to Fri £13.50 SERVICE: not inc, card slips closed CARDS: Amex, Delta, Diners, MasterCard, Switch, Visa DETAILS: 80 seats. Private parties: 50 main room, 50 private room. Vegetarian meals. Children's helpings. No smoking before 2 L, 9.30 D; no cigars. Music

---

DORRINGTON Shropshire map 5

▲ Country Friends ¾✳

Dorrington SY5 7JD
TEL: (01743) 718707 COOKING 6
on A49, 5m S of Shrewsbury COST £37–£49

The black and white half-timbered house beside the main road is owner-run with minimal help. It is a 'dark and comfortable' place with a 'provincial' feel and a relaxed atmosphere. Fixed-price menus at lunch and dinner, with six or seven choices per course, are where the effort is concentrated. Ideas are not usually controversial, encompassing perhaps twice-baked soufflé of Llanboidy cheese and celeriac, or rabbit terrine with a cranberry and red pepper chutney, and supplies tend to be local: Ludlow venison, for example, served as a steak on a bean purée with juniper sauce.

Although the food may not go in for brio and daring, it does pick up some modern flavours, in crispy salmon with Thai red curry sauce for example, or spicy fish-cakes with peanut dressing, and is always well made, indeed 'technically very expert', leaving one visitor with the 'strong impression that a great deal of care and thought had gone into everything'. Charles Whittaker is equally at home making tarragon dumplings to accompany Trelough duck breast, or filling a chicken breast with smoked chicken mousse and encasing it in puff pastry.

Textures tend to be smooth, and flavours are subtle but never dull, as in pistachio parfait with caramelised banana, or queen of puddings with gin and lime ice-cream. 'Old-fashioned' service tops up all liquids regularly, whether smart burgundy or Washington State Chardonnay, whether from New Zealand or as close as Hereford. House wines (three French, one Australian) are £11.95.

CHEF: Charles Whittaker   PROPRIETORS: Charles and Pauline Whittaker   OPEN: Tue to Sat; 12 to 2, 7 to 9 (9.30 Sat)   CLOSED: 2 weeks mid-July   MEALS: alc (main courses £6.75 to £9). Set L and D £24 (2 courses) to £30. Light L available   SERVICE: not inc   CARDS: Delta, MasterCard, Switch, Visa   DETAILS: 40 seats. Private parties: 40 main room. Car park. Vegetarian meals. Children welcome. No smoking in dining-room. Wheelchair access (1 step; not WC). No music   ACCOMMODATION: 3 rooms 1 with bath/shower. DB&B £65 to £102. Children welcome. No dogs
(£5)

DREWSTEIGNTON Devon   map 1

▲ *Hunts Tor* 🏃✳

Drewsteignton EX6 6QW   COOKING 3
TEL/FAX: (01647) 281228   COST £30–£40

The scale of this peaceful village with its thatched cottages, tiny roads, two pubs, post office and a church, is reflected in the restaurant, which seats only 8 people. It is 'the English equivalent of a French chambre d'hôte', where guests find themselves in conversation with each other, although the cooking adopts a more 'aspirational' approach than its typical French counterpart, turning to pesto dressing, avocado salsa and chargrilled vegetables to accompany its Dorset air-dried ham, salmon fillet, or pigeon breast. A three-course dinner might take in galette of aubergine and duck liver, pork fillet with sweet soy and ginger shiitake mushrooms, and cold caramelised rice-pudding accompanied by clotted cream and mango salad. The format is clear, and the rules brook no deviation: dinner needs to be booked 24 hours in advance, and everybody eats at 7.30. There is no choice on the menu, but 'we had the chance to say in advance if there was something that we did not like'. This gives Sue Harrison the opportunity to shine, and she takes it. 'The food was brilliant,' summed up one reporter. House French starts at £10.80.

CHEF: Sue Harrison   PROPRIETORS: Sue and Chris Harrison   OPEN: all week D only 7.30 (1 sitting; 24 hours' notice required)   CLOSED: end Oct to beginning Mar   MEALS: Set D £20 to £23   SERVICE: not inc   CARDS: none   DETAILS: 8 seats. Private parties: 8 main room. Car park. Vegetarian meals. No children under 10. No smoking in dining-room. Music   ACCOMMODATION: 3 rooms, all with bath/shower. TV. B&B £40 to £75. Children over 10 and babies welcome. Dogs welcome in bedrooms only (*The Which? Hotel Guide*)

All details are as accurate as possible at the time of going to press, but chefs and owners often change, and it is wise to check by telephone before making a special journey. Many readers have been disappointed when set-price bargain meals are no longer available. Ask when booking.

DRYBROOK Gloucestershire   map 5

Cider Press ✦✶

The Cross, Drybrook GL17 9EB   COOKING 4
TEL: (01594) 544472   COST £28–£42

A modest former shop, on the road through the unassuming little hamlet of
Drybrook in the Forest of Dean, makes an appealing venue for a country
restaurant. Fish is the speciality of Christopher Challener's repertoire, so much
so that diners are invited to call again on the day of their booking to find out what
has been bought that morning, and stake a claim to a fancied item before anyone
else gets there. The treatments range far and wide for inspiration: gilt-head
bream, for example, is buried in sea salt and baked in the Spanish manner,
before being filleted at table and served with salpicon. Red mullet is 'larded'
with anchovies, rubbed with olive oil and salt and then grilled, and comes with a
bhaji of guva (a type of mange-tout), tomato and spices. Starters take in scallops
with spring onions and ginger and an oriental dip, as well as kipper and apple
pâté with a warm bagel. Meat eaters will not be disappointed either: reporters
have praised 'tender' Cotswold lamb, and mustard-glazed local duck in plum
and honey sauce. Puddings have made less of an impression: the ad-lib
international cheese selection may be a better bet. Staff are 'friendly and helpful',
although service is occasionally a little 'quirky'. The wine list skims the surface
of some familiar regions, and keeps most of its findings below £20. House vin de
pays is £7.95 for red and £8.75 for white.

CHEF: Christopher Stephen Challener   PROPRIETOR: Bernadette Elizabeth Fitzpatrick   OPEN:
Wed to Sat D only 7 to 11 (L Wed to Mon by arrangement)   CLOSED: early Jan   MEALS: alc (main
courses £13.50 to £15)   SERVICE: not inc   CARDS: Delta, MasterCard, Visa   DETAILS: 22 seats.
Private parties: 28 main room. Children welcome. No smoking in dining-room. Wheelchair
access (also WC). No music

DURHAM Co Durham   map 10

Bistro 21 ▾ 🍞 ✦✶ £

Aykley Heads House, Aykley Heads,
Durham DH1 5PS   COOKING 4
TEL: (0191) 384 4354   FAX: (0191) 384 1149   COST £22–£48

Near Durham Police HQ and hospital to the north of the city, this former
farmhouse has been 'beautifully restored'. The entrance isn't obvious, but so far
all reporters have been hungry enough to find it. Walk down a glass-lined
corridor to a cream-painted dining room with greeny-blue trimmings, wooden
floor, and paper napkins confirming its relaxed bistro attitude. Craig Edmund
arrived at the beginning of 1998, but the style established by Terence Laybourne
(see entry, 21 Queen Street, Newcastle) continues with a generous *carte* of dishes
ranging from Thai coconut soup via eggs Benedict to shepherds pie.
   The variety is appealing (extra dishes are chalked on a blackboard) without
any sense of barrels being scraped to produce it, offering roast lobster with garlic
butter and chips, alongside thin tomato tart with basil oil, or marinated pork
steak with rosemary. Vegetables are served and charged separately. Desserts

typically combine a fruity element – rhubarb and strawberry trifle – with a more indulgent one: warm chocolate tart with coconut ice, or sticky toffee. An up-to-the-minute wine list offers 50 bins of varying styles and grape varieties, ranging in price from £9.50 for House Duboeuf to £35 for a bottle of Bolly. CELLARMAN'S CHOICE: Sancerre 'Les Boffants' 1996, Charles Dupuy, £19.90; Bonny Doon 'Le Cigare Volant' 1995, Santa Cruz, California, £29.80.

CHEF: Craig Edmund   PROPRIETORS: Terence and Susan Laybourne   OPEN: Mon to Sat 12 to 2.30, 6 to 10.30   CLOSED: Christmas, bank hols   MEALS: alc (main courses L £8.50 to £13.50, D £8.50 to £18.50). Set L £12 (2 courses) to £14.50   SERVICE: not inc   CARDS: Amex, Delta, Diners, MasterCard, Switch, Visa   DETAILS: 95 seats. 24 seats outside. Private parties: 55 main room, 10 to 20 private rooms. Car park. Vegetarian meals. Children's helpings. No smoking in dining-room. Wheelchair access (also WC). Music

---

EAST BOLDON Tyne & Wear   map 10

Forsters ⅝✳

2 St Bedes, Station Road, East Boldon NE36 0LE
TEL: (0191) 519 0929
just off A184 Newcastle to Sunderland road,   COOKING 3
3m NW of Sutherland   COST £24–£43

One reporter considers a meal in this light, modern, square suburban dining-room 'an essential part of any visit to the Sunderland area'. Barry Forster serves the same sort of 'not messed about' food he always has, offering reliable cooking at a realistic cost, chosen from a *carte* or a weekday fixed-price menu. Anglo-French is his style, ranging from spicy lamb sausages with Yorkshire pudding and red wine gravy, via grilled salmon with chive beurre blanc, to guinea-fowl breast with Savoy cabbage and creamy mustard sauce. Vegetarians need to order their food 48 hours in advance, but might choose chive and Parmesan risotto or Cheddar soufflé. Soup, salad and pasta starters are balanced by weightier grilled haddock topped with Welsh rarebit, and similar options are offered by puddings of vanilla crème brûlée, bitter chocolate and orange parfait, or sticky toffee. Evenings are backed up by 'gentle, unobtrusive service' from Sue Forster, and by a short list of modestly priced wines mostly from France. House Duboeuf is £8.50.

CHEF: Barry Forster   PROPRIETORS: Barry and Sue Forster   OPEN: Tue to Sat D only 7 to 9.30 CLOSED: Christmas, New Year, 2 weeks May, 1 week Aug, bank hols   MEALS: alc (main courses £12 to £15). Set D Tue to Fri £17.50. BYO £5   SERVICE: not inc   CARDS: Amex, Diners, MasterCard, Visa   DETAILS: 28 seats. Private parties: 30 main room. Car park. Children's helpings. No children under 7. No smoking in dining-room. Music   £5

EASTBOURNE East Sussex   map 3

▲ Grand Hotel, Mirabelle

Jevington Gardens, Eastbourne BN21 4EQ   COOKING 8
TEL: (01323) 410771   FAX: (01323) 412233   COST £27–£67

The Grand is a huge Victorian hotel, set back from the seafront behind trees that are mature enough to provide privacy. Inside is a 'never-ending' run of corridors and meeting-rooms, culminating in the rather 'institutional' restaurant housed in the east wing; to save time, it has its own entrance. Pre-meal drinks are taken in the soft grey and appropriately plum-yellow lounge, while the dining-room's high ceiling and well-spaced tables give it an expansive feel, helped by 'smooth, unhurried and stylish' service. It was 'a rare find' for one visitor and, after going through a rocky patch before changing ownership, now seems set on a purposeful course.

The kitchen deals in contemporary haute cuisine, exemplified by crab cannelloni, fillet of beef with morel cream and foie gras butter, or a 'perfectly composed' escabèche made unusually with lemon sole. Menus tend to play down complexity, enabling dishes to deliver more than anticipated: for example a tumbling pile of seared sea bass, tuna, red mullet, salmon, scallops and mussels, each species precisely cooked and 'showing its different character-istics', sitting on a single sheet of black pasta, with a saffron sauce for dramatic contrast, the whole thing crowned with a wuntun of lobster.

Many dishes have a 'multi-dimensional ring' to them, requiring skill and precision to make them work. One 'worthy of the highest commendation' at inspection combined seared foie gras with ravioli that 'sang of ceps', topped with feathery crispy noodles, surrounded by a sherry vinegar jus for even greater depth of flavour. For dessert, one couple, overcome with curiosity, sampled the novelty of a deep-fried blueberry ice-cream perched on a biscuit, surrounded by a soup of melon and lemon-grass; doubts only surfaced about whether they'd made the right choice when they watched a six-inch-tall tian of chocolate being delivered to another table. Skill is impressive across all departments, and is applied equally to appetisers and delicate pastries and petits fours. House French wines are £12.50.

CHEFS: Keith Mitchell and Simon Hulstone PROPRIETOR: Elite Hotels OPEN: Tue to Sat 12.30 to 2, 7 to 10 CLOSED: 2 weeks Jan, 2 weeks Aug, bank hols exc L 25 Dec MEALS: alc (main courses £16.50 to £22.50). Set L £15.50 (2 courses) to £18.50, Set D £26.50 to £32.50 SERVICE: 10%, card slips closed CARDS: Amex, Diners, MasterCard, Switch, Visa DETAILS: 50 seats. Private parties: 50 main room. Car park. Vegetarian meals. Children's helpings. No cigars/pipes in dining-room. Wheelchair access (also WC). Music. Air-conditioned ACCOMMODATION: 164 rooms, all with bath/shower. TV. Phone. Rooms for disabled. Children welcome. Afternoon teas. Swimming-pool (£5)

EAST GRINSTEAD West Sussex   map 3

▲ *Gravetye Manor* ▮ ⁵✴

Vowels Lane, East Grinstead RH19 4LJ
TEL: (01342) 810567 FAX: (01342) 810080
EMAIL: gravetye@relaischateaux.fr   COOKING 7
off B2110, 2m SW of East Grinstead   COST £43–£110

A long drive leads through a wooded 1,000-acre estate to this Elizabethan house and its tranquil 'natural garden'. The last is a Victorian addition, the work of William Robinson, and although the house itself looks an impressive four centuries old, the north wing was added as recently as 1992. The interior is distinguished by dark oak panelling, mullioned stone windows, and a solid sense of comfort and 'old English style'. 'If I am as well looked after as this house,' mused one visitor, 'then I shall be all right.' And he was.

Mark Raffan's food embraces British, French and Italian ideas, and makes sure the result is pretty comforting, as in roast Hebridean scallops in a puff pastry tartlet, terrine of duck confit and foie gras, or creamy vegetable risotto. When in distinctly 'new British' mood, he might turn out a variant on an old favourite, such as cod tempura with pea purée, or pink calf's kidney served with a steak suet pudding topped with a couple of shelled oysters. The *carte*'s balance is maintained with a good showing of fish – seared red mullet and roast squid salad, perhaps – and non-meat options such as a warm, flavourful, moulded artichoke mousse surrounded by vegetables deep-fried in batter. The appearance of offal and game among the meats is also welcome: perhaps roast pigeon on a potato and foie gras galette, or noisette of local venison served with a horseradish mousseline. Sauces have the depth of flavour expected of a good stock base, and demand to be spooned until there is nothing but 'a dark stain left on the plate'.

Savouries provide a realistic alternative to dessert, set-price lunch and dinner menus typically offer a choice of three items per course, and although food and service (described as 'polite perfection') are universally appreciated. Classic wines from classic vintages are the hallmark of a lengthy wine list, where France gets full treatment and there is much worth examining from Germany. Prices are not low but quality is assured. French house white is £18, red £19.50. CELLARMAN'S CHOICE: Meursault-Blagny 1995, Louis Latour, £54; Bourgogne Pinot Noir 1994, Joseph Faiveley, £19.50.

CHEF: Mark Raffan   PROPRIETORS: Peter Herbert and family   OPEN: all week 12.30 to 1.45, 7.30 to 9.30 (9.45 Sat, 8.45 Sun)   CLOSED: D 25 Dec exc for residents   MEALS: alc (main courses £21 to £34). Set L £30, Set D £38.   SERVICE: net prices, card slips closed   CARDS: MasterCard, Switch, Visa   DETAILS: 55 seats. Private parties: 8 main room, 16 private room. Car park. Vegetarian meals. No children under 7. Jacket and tie. No smoking in dining-room. Wheelchair access (not WC). No music   ACCOMMODATION: 18 rooms, all with bath/shower. TV. Phone. Room only £130 to £260. No children under 7 except babies. Baby facilities. Fishing (*The Which? Hotel Guide*)

EAST WITTON North Yorkshire   map 8

▲ *Blue Lion*

East Witton DL8 4SN
TEL: (01969) 624273   FAX: (01969) 624189
on A6108 Ripon to Leyburn road, 2m SE of   COOKING 3
Middleham   COST £21–£46

As John Dalby returned to the kitchen in February 1998, the food took a turn for the better in this traditional Wensleydale pub. Its is 'a place to sit, relax and unwind', either in the old, dark, wood-panelled bar, or in the evening at one of the well-spaced tables in the dining-room. Dinner is a *carte* that might start with terrine of ham knuckle and chicken livers with split pea purée, followed by roast venison or peppered duck breast, while the bar's blackboard menu lists a generous choice of dishes, including a wedge of bacon and leek tart, served with garlicky aioli, and a meaty, moist fillet of sea bass with a crispy skin, served with chargrilled peppers, aubergine and fennel.

Chargrilled steaks are also an option, a vegetarian menu might offer tomato and tapénade tart, portions are generous, sauces tend to be creamy, and vegetables 'really taste of what they should'. A savoury is offered as an alternative to desserts of rich dark chocolate tart, good vanilla and banana ice-creams, and 'nicely caramelised' pear Tatin. Although France dominates the wine list, bottles from elsewhere are full of interest, prices are fair, and a short and useful selection under £16 sets the ball rolling with house red and white at £9.50.

CHEF: John Dalby   PROPRIETORS: Paul and Helen Klein   OPEN: Sun L 12 to 2.15, Tue to Sat D 7 to 9.30   MEALS: alc D (main courses £11.75 to £16.45), Sun L £14.70. Bar meals available L and D all week   SERVICE: not inc   CARDS: Delta, MasterCard, Switch, Visa   DETAILS: 60 seats. 20 seats outside. Private parties: 30 main room, 14 private room. Car park. Vegetarian meals. Children's helpings. Wheelchair access (also WC). No music   ACCOMMODATION: 12 rooms 9 with bath/shower. TV. Phone. B&B £47.50 to £85. Children welcome. Baby facilities. Afternoon teas (*The Which? Hotel Guide*)

EDENBRIDGE Kent   map 3

Honours Mill

87 High Street, Edenbridge TN8 5AU   COOKING 5
TEL: (01732) 866757   COST £23–£50

The old water-mill has been 'interestingly converted' into a well-appointed restaurant. There are beams everywhere, a stream still runs underneath, and the balcony overlooking the mill pond is scheduled to come into operation before this edition of the *Guide* appears. The whole place has a 'cool' air about it, and crisp white damask tablecloths and napkins 'assure you that a treat is in store' according to one visitor, who added, 'This is what a serious restaurant should look like.' Menus are serious too: the less expensive dinner option (similar to lunch) includes a half-bottle of house wine, the more expensive yields greater choice and more indulgent dishes: terrine of foie gras with Sauternes jelly, crab risotto with roast tomatoes and Parmesan shavings, and pork fillet with ceps.

Traditional ideas such as roast lamb in puff pastry, or a rich cassoulet Toulousain with chunks of pork, duck and sausage, are balanced by a few livelier items. Warm sausage of smoked haddock comes with a mild curry sauce, and a casserole of snails with wild mushrooms, although there is a suggestion that, by pulling out an extra stop, the kitchen might deliver even more in the way of excitement. The high point for one couple was the finish: pecan pie flavoured with cinnamon, and Sussex Pond pudding, chosen from a list that might also include passion-fruit crème caramel, or blackcurrant and almond tart. Service is 'warm and friendly', and any drinker wanting change from £20 is advised to explore the short vins de pays section on the overwhelmingly French wine list; half-bottles are plentiful and prices start around the £10 mark.

CHEF: Martin Radmall   PROPRIETORS: Neville, Duncan and Giles Goodhew   OPEN: Tue to Fri and Sun L 12.15 to 2, Tue to Sat D 7.15 to 10   CLOSED: 2 weeks Christmas, Good Friday   MEALS: Set L Tue to Fri £15.50 to £32.75, Set L Sun £23.50, Set D Tue to Fri £26 (inc wine), Set D Tue to Sat £32.75   SERVICE: not inc   CARDS: Delta, MasterCard, Switch, Visa   DETAILS: 42 seats. 18 seats outside. Private parties: 42 main room. Children's helpings. No music   £5

ELLAND   West Yorkshire   map 8

La Cachette   £

7–10 Town Hall Buildings, Elland HX5 0EU   COOKING 2
TEL: (01422) 378833   FAX: (01422) 377899   COST £17–£42

This light and airy Victorian building – with three separate dining-areas plus a wine bar – offers largely modern British food alongside more traditional items. Opt for grilled lemon sole, or steak with a brandy and green peppercorn sauce, or try more adventurous chargrilled squid with chilli and coriander, or wild boar steak with a port and honey sauce. Deep-fried Brie might be as old as the hills, but as 'comfort food' it works well, served here successfully with Cumberland sauce. Modernised bread-and-butter pudding comes as a crimp-edged tart, with strawberry slices, custard and sorbet. Service is relaxed, and three-course 'menu du soir' with half a bottle of wine is extremely good value. The wine list is price-conscious across the board too – there is plenty of good drinking under £15 – and takes an interest in fine producers wherever they may be. Ten house wines start at £7.95 a bottle, £1.40 a glass. CELLARMAN'S CHOICE: Isabel Winery Sauvignon Blanc 1997, Marlborough, New Zealand, £16.95; Faugères Rouge 1994, Dom. Léon Barral, £14.95.

CHEF: Sean Walker   PROPRIETOR: C&O Partnership   OPEN: Mon to Sat 12 to 2.30, 6 to 10 (11 Fri and Sat)   CLOSED: 26 Dec   MEALS: alc (main courses £7 to £14). Set D £10.95 to £13.95 (inc wine); set D not available after 7pm Sat. Bar menu L and D   SERVICE: not inc, card slips closed   CARDS: Amex, Delta, MasterCard, Switch, Visa   DETAILS: 140 seats. Private parties: 60 main room, 14 to 50 private rooms. Vegetarian meals. Children welcome. Wheelchair access (2 steps; not WC). Music. Air-conditioned   £5

ELY   Cambridgeshire   map 6

Old Fire Engine House ▼ ⚶

25 St Mary's Street, Ely CB7 4ER   COOKING 2
TEL: (01353) 662582   FAX: (01353) 666282   COST £26–£42

A photograph of the fire brigade with their engine, taken in 1912, graces the small bar of this stalwart just a few yards from the cathedral. It has bare stone floors, a large walled garden, and devotes more of its rooms to artwork than to eating. The food does not aim to be fashionable, ambitious or exciting. Indeed, Michael Jarman writes that 'we are pleased when customers tell us that we are exactly the same as they remember 25 years ago'. They pickle their own herrings, make an old-fashioned coarse-textured pork terrine called mitoon, conjure up simple seasonal soups – lovage in May, for example – and use good materials: impressively fresh plaice, or noisettes of lamb in flaky pastry. Vegetables are improvable, and desserts, like everything else, have 'home-made' written all over them: light lemon syllabub, or plum crumble with custard. Don't expect polished, professional service; staff are friendly, welcoming, informal, and offer second helpings. Vintage clarets, mature burgundies and Rhônes come at very reasonable prices on the Francophile wine list, particularly in the closing fine-wine section. Fans of the New World will be disappointed with severely limited choices, but house red and white from Concha y Toro are good value at £8. CELLARMAN'S CHOICE: Concha y Toro Chardonnay 1995, Marqués de Casa, Maipo, Chile, £11.50; Côtes du Rhône 1994, Guigal, £13.50.

CHEF: Terri Kindred   PROPRIETORS: Ann Ford and Michael Jarman   OPEN: all week L 12.30 to 2, Mon to Sat D 7.30 to 9   CLOSED: 2 weeks from 24 Dec, bank hols   MEALS: alc (main courses £11 to £14.50). BYO (£3.50)   SERVICE: not inc   CARDS: Delta, MasterCard, Switch, Visa DETAILS: 36 seats. 20 seats outside. Private parties: 36 main room, 12 and 22 private rooms. Car park. Vegetarian meals. Children's helpings. No smoking in 1 dining-room. No music

---

EMSWORTH Hampshire   map 2

Spencers ¦✳ £

36 North Street, Emsworth PO10 7DG   COOKING 3
TEL/FAX: (01243) 372744   COST £20–£35

Green shutters make this restaurant and brasserie look 'rather French' from outside. The main dining-room, up a short steep flight of stairs, has bare wooden tables, bench seating, and a penchant for fish. A dozen or so main-course dishes – billed as 'Catch of the Day', and subject to a clutch of round-the-world treatments – might include scallops glazed with mustard and cheese sauce, chargrilled tuna with sun-dried tomato and olive pesto, or sea bass with spring onion, ginger and soy. The fish itself impresses for freshness, flavour and texture, as in a 'springy' lemon sole served with a 'rather greasy' pepper sauce and copious vegetables. Meaty alternatives (on a menu shared with the brasserie) are in plentiful supply – grilled ribeye steak, calf's liver, and breast of duck or guinea-fowl – while first courses have included a fine-textured goose terrine, and smoked pigeon and mango salad with 'interesting leaves and a lovely dressing'. Desserts run to passion-fruit tart with mascarpone, fresh fruit pavlova, and a white-chocolate and chestnut mousse. Around 30 fairly priced wines begin with a six-strong house selection from £8.95, also available by the glass from £1.80.

CHEF: Denis Spencer   PROPRIETORS: Denis and Lesley Spencer   OPEN: Tue to Sat D only 7.30 to 10.30   CLOSED: 25 and 26 Dec   MEALS: alc (main courses £7 to £11)   SERVICE: not inc CARDS: Amex, Delta, Diners, MasterCard, Switch, Visa   DETAILS: 34 seats. Private parties: 24 main room, 10 private room. Vegetarian meals. Children's helpings. No smoking in dining-room. Music. Air-conditioned (£5)

CELLARMAN'S CHOICE: *Wines recommended by the restaurateur, normally more expensive than house wine.*

Dining-rooms where music, either live or recorded, is never played are signalled by No music *in the details at the end of an entry.*

---

36 on the Quay ♥ ❊

47 South Street, Emsworth PO10 7EG	COOKING 6
TEL: (01243) 375592 FAX: (01243) 375593	COST £31–£62

This small, smartly attired eighteenth-century smugglers' inn down by the quayside combines a sense of space and intimacy, thanks to well-spread tables, a fresh primrose-yellow colour scheme, and a window looking out to yachts and the sea. Karen Farthing ably oversees front of house, while Ramon puts a skilled and contemporary spin on some time-honoured ideas. Emsworth is lucky to have them. While lunch typically offers a choice of two items – a main course fillet of brill, for example, or boned, roast baby chicken with a casserole of lentils and root vegetables – dinner moves up a gear into the realms of skate wrapped around scallops, served with a light cream of basil and scallop coral. Locally caught fish and shellfish figure prominently.

'Really inventive food within a classical framework' is what keeps the kitchen motoring. Imagination and workmanship transform a rabbit and mustard partnership into a triumphant first course in which pastry rectangles enclose two pink 'eyes' of rare loin embedded in a two-tone layer of light celeriac and dark confit; tightly curled stacks of pasta unravel to pick up a light, well-judged creamy mustard sauce. Sheer professionalism keeps the sometimes complex treatments well under control, as in a refined take on liver and onions, for example, which sandwiches creamy chopped leeks and discs of pasta between thin slices of liver, the tower surrounded by a well-reduced stock sauce. Follow up with warm chocolate tart, or a plate of four miniature apple desserts.

Classic bins from France are in the majority on the impressive wine list, but the New World makes the most of its minor contribution. While the pedigree of producers is beyond dispute, it would be helpful to see a few more bottles under £20, although French house red and white afford some relief at £13.50 each. CELLARMAN'S CHOICE: Torreon de Parades Chardonnay 1995, Rapel, Chile, £21.50; Bourgueil 'Grand Mont' 1993, P.J. Druet, £27.75.

CHEF: Ramon Farthing PROPRIETORS: Ramon and Karen Farthing OPEN: Tue to Fri L 12 to 2, Mon to Sat D 7 to 10 CLOSED: 4 days after Christmas, bank hols exc Good Fri MEALS: Set L £16 (2 courses) to £19, Set D £31.95 to £37.50 SERVICE: not inc CARDS: Amex, Delta, Diners, MasterCard, Switch, Visa DETAILS: 40 seats. Private parties: 30 main room, 10 private room. Car park. Children's helpings. No smoking in 1 dining-room. Music

---

EPWORTH North Lincolnshire　　　　　　　　　　　　　　　　　　　map 9

Epworth Tap ▮ ❊ £

9 – 11 Market Place, Epworth DN9 1EU	
TEL: (01427) 873333 FAX: (01427) 875020	COOKING 4
3m S of M180 junction 2	COST £24–£40

'The wine's the thing' in Helen Wynne's likeable and lively venue housed in a converted village pub. The place has bags of atmosphere, and the cooking is based resolutely on carefully sourced raw materials: vegetables from local farms, fish from Brixham and Loch Fyne, meat from a butcher in Grimsby. 'A meal at the Epworth Tap should leave you neither bloated nor broke,' remarked one reporter who was mightily impressed by the value for money. Food may play a supporting role to wine, but there is plenty to enjoy: start with a timbale of smoked salmon and cucumber or grilled goats'-cheese salad and finish off with sticky toffee pudding or ginger sorbet. In between, the choice ranges from casserole of venison with star anise to pan-fried brill with saffron and lime cream sauce.

John Wynne will happily advise on the wines, which are taken seriously but served without fuss or pretension. Venerable burgundies, *cru classé* clarets and fine Rhônes are offered at eminently reasonable prices, as are some prestige bins from the New World. House wines are £10.50. CELLARMAN'S CHOICE: Montagny 1996, Jean-Marc Boillot, £20; Madfish Bay Shiraz 1996, Margaret River, W. Australia, £17.50.

CHEF/PROPRIETOR: Helen Wynne   OPEN: Wed to Sat D only 7.30 to 9.15   CLOSED: 2 weeks after Christmas, bank hols   MEALS: alc (main courses £9.50 to £12.50). Set D Sat £20. BYO £5 SERVICE: not inc, card slips closed   CARDS: Delta, MasterCard, Switch, Visa   DETAILS: 50 seats. Private parties: 24 main room, 24 private room. No children under 6. No smoking in 1 dining-room. Music (£5)

ERPINGHAM Norfolk   map 6

▲ *Ark* ♟ ⅚✳

The Street, Erpingham NR11 7QB
TEL: (01263) 761535   COOKING 4
3m off A140 Cromer road, 4m N of Aylsham   COST £22–£43

Anybody who cooks appreciates the importance of a well-stocked garden. Here at this flint house with its stone-flagged hall, the garden is visible from the dining-room, and plays a significant part in the kitchen's output. French provincial cooking is Sheila Kidd's inspiration, although not in the narrow sense of a standard unvarying repertoire. Some dishes emerge more or less direct from this tradition, such as 'weeping lamb' with potato and mushroom gratin, or Roquefort soufflé with pears and walnuts, but the thrust is a self-taught cook's natural response to materials, producing saddle of hare with cream, poached egg on toasted brioche with wild mushrooms, or leg of mutton with creamed turnip and caper sauce.

Garden vegetables may be turned into a salad to accompany skate and sea-trout with mayonnaise, or be pickled to provide a relish for poached cod. Sheila Kidd also cures gravlax in-house, and spices damsons to serve with chicken liver parfait or with 'old-fashioned' pork terrine. This country brand of high-quality home-cooking extends to desserts of summer pudding, old English ratafia trifle, and raspberry syllabub. Eleven house wines, priced around £10, open a list which travels the major regions in search of good value and concludes stylishly with two pages of fine wines. The adventurous might like to try English Gooseberry Fizz. CELLARMAN'S CHOICE: Bourgogne Blanc 1994, Serafin Père et Fils, £17.50; Lalande de Pomerol, Ch. Canon Chaigneau 1989, £27.50.

Report forms are at the back of the book; write a letter if you prefer; or email us at guidereports@which.co.uk.

CHEF: Sheila Kidd   PROPRIETORS: Mike and Sheila Kidd   OPEN: Sun L 12.30 to 2, Tue to Sat D 7 to 9.30   CLOSED: 25 and 26 Dec, 2 weeks early Oct, Tue in winter, bank hols   MEALS: Set L £14.50, Set D £19.75 (2 courses) to £26   SERVICE: not inc   CARDS: none   DETAILS: 30 seats. 8 seats outside. Private parties: 30 main room, 8 private rooms. Car park. Vegetarian meals. Children's helpings. No smoking in dining-room. No music   ACCOMMODATION: 3 rooms, 2 with bath/shower. TV. DB&B £65 to £125. Rooms for disabled. Children welcome. Baby facilities

---

EVERSHOT Dorset   map 2

▲ *Summer Lodge* 🍾

Summer Lane, Evershot DT2 0JR
TEL: (01935) 83424   FAX: (01935) 83005   COOKING 6
EMAIL: sumlodge@sumlodge.demon.co.uk   COST £26–£74

The Corbetts' tranquil country-house hotel has an unusually high number of regulars among its guests, and a fair number write to the *Guide* in its praise. There is a strong feeling of generosity about the whole establishment,' noted a satisfied customer of 15 years' standing, who found the food this year to be even better than on his previous visit. Tim Ford still practises the comfortable, cosseting style of country-house cooking that he learned at Sharrow Bay (see entry, Ullswater). He goes to some lengths to source ingredients locally, and the menu pays generous tribute to his suppliers, who provide naturally reared Dorset lamb, free-range pork and chicken, venison from nearby Melbury Park, fish from Lyme Bay, and West Country cheeses, including Montgomery's Cheddar and Dorset Blue Vinney. Dinner might consist of seared red mullet with creamed celeriac and basil oil, an intermediate course of soup or sorbet, then skate with a caper sauce, or perhaps local lamb with fresh asparagus. However, many dishes carry supplements in the evening, which can push up the total. Set lunches generate most enthusiasm, providing extraordinary value for money and interesting choices: pot-roast chicken with morel stuffing has benefited from a well-flavoured sauce, while a beautifully presented asparagus mousse in langoustine sauce was 'a brilliant combination of delicate flavours'.

Desserts are suitably indulgent for a spoiling weekend stay. Choose from dark chocolate tart, bread-and-butter pudding, or milk chocolate cheesecake with coffee sauce. Service is usually 'tiptop', although some have found it slow under pressure. Quality is the key in a huge wine list which opens its doors to most of the world's wine-producing countries. Particular highlights are fine German Rieslings, pedigree Italian producers and some highly prized bins from North America. Prices open at £11.75 for a Minervois or a Vin de Pays d'Oc Sauvignon Blanc, and there is an excellent choice of half-bottles.

CHEF: Timothy Ford   PROPRIETORS: Nigel and Margaret Corbett   OPEN: all week 12.30 to 2, 7.30 to 9 (9.30 Fri and Sat)   MEALS: alc (main courses L £9.50 to £12, D £20 to £26.50). Set L £12.75 to £17.50, Set D £36. BYO £7.50, champagne £15   SERVICE: not inc, card slips closed   CARDS: Amex, Delta, Diners, MasterCard, Switch, Visa   DETAILS: 40 seats. 16 seats outside. Private parties: 20 main room, 24 private room. Car park. Vegetarian meals. Children's helpings. No children under 7 at D. No smoking while others eat. Wheelchair access (also WC). Occasional music   ACCOMMODATION: 17 rooms, all with bath/shower. TV. Phone. B&B £125 to £275. Rooms for disabled. Children welcome. Baby facilities. Dogs welcome in bedrooms only. Afternoon teas. Swimming-pool (*The Which? Hotel Guide*) £5

EXETER Devon   map 1

Lamb's ✦✗

15 Lower North Street, Exeter EX4 3ET
TEL: (01392) 254269   FAX: (01392) 431145   COOKING 2
EMAIL: lambsexeter@aol.com   COST £28–£46

Contrary to the impression given in last year's *Guide* entry, Lamb's is closer to the famous Iron Bridge than the cathedral: in fact, it's right underneath it. Dark green is the defining colour within, and the place feels spruce and modestly elegant. Alison Aldridge cooks imaginatively but stays within defined culinary parameters, and much of what she produces is of a high order. 'Crisp and rich' crab-cakes aromatised with lemon grass and served with coriander salsa were a thoroughly pleasing opener at inspection, followed by soundly executed best end of Devon lamb with minted ratatouille and potatoes seasoned with a touch of balsamic. West Country produce is justly celebrated, whether it be local duck with orange and ginger, or the Somerset cider brandy that is used to flame tenderloin of pork. Regionality even extends to desserts, the star being Exeter pudding, a 'substantial but light' suet creation striped with raspberry jam, and served with raspberry sauce, fresh vanilla custard and clotted cream: 'we are still talking about it'. Coffee could do with stiffening up a bit, but home-made petits fours are good. Wines are carefully chosen with an eye to value, and there are squads of halves. House selections from France, Argentina and Devon are £10.

CHEF: Alison Aldridge   PROPRIETORS: Alison and Ian Aldridge   OPEN: Tue to Fri L 12 to 2, Tue to Sat D 7 to 10   CLOSED: Christmas and New Year   MEALS: alc (main courses £11 to £16.50). Set L £15 (2 courses) to £19, Set D Tue to Thur £15 (2 courses) to £19, Set D Fri and Sat £20. BYO negotiable   SERVICE: not inc   CARDS: Amex, Delta, MasterCard, Switch, Visa   DETAILS: 46 seats. 10 seats outside. Private parties: 26 main room, 26 private room. Vegetarian meals. Children's helpings. No smoking in 1 dining-room. Wheelchair access (1 step; not WC). Music
£5

EYNSHAM Oxfordshire   map 2

▲ Baker's ✦✗ | NEW ENTRY |

4 Lombard Street, Eynsham OX8 1HT   COOKING 5
TEL: (01865) 881888   FAX: (01865) 883537   COST £19–£58

Eynsham, an unassuming village five miles out of Oxford, was once a coaching-stop on the London to Bristol route. Travellers then were none too keen to linger, given the attentions of marauding highwaymen, but the scene is more hospitable now, thanks in no small part to Baker's. The restaurant-with-rooms has been stylishly renovated in contemporary taste, the dining-room a relaxed, wood-floored space with large mirrors and panelled fireplace.

Refinement with robustness might sum up Philip Baker's cooking style, and this balance shines through in duck confit, ham and foie gras with a beetroot dressing, and in sauté scallops with spring onion mash and salsa verde. Firm, well-timed sea bass derives power from a sauce of lobster juices, while beef has been treated to creamed shallots and a smoked bacon and potato pancake.

Opponents of the al dente school should note that accompanying vegetables have been described as 'aggressively undercooked'. Rice-pudding comes topped with a raspberry gratin that lifts the dish, and approving words are also spoken of steamed orange sponge with crème brûlée ice-cream. Service is generally well led by Amanda Hill but can go a little awry when she is absent. Wines are a commendably broad-minded selection, though whites plough the Sauvignon and Chardonnay furrow fairly deeply, and prices show heartening restraint. House wines are from £10.95.

CHEF: Philip Baker   PROPRIETORS: Philip Baker, Amanda Hill and Donald Baker   OPEN: all week L 12 (12.30 Sun) to 2.30, Tue to Sat D 7 to 10.30   CLOSED: bank hols exc 25 Dec   MEALS: alc D (main courses £14.50 to £19). Set L Mon to Sat £8.50 (2 courses) to £10.50, Set L Sun £11 (2 courses) to £13.50, Set D £16 (2 courses) to £20   SERVICE: not inc   CARDS: Delta, MasterCard, Switch, Visa   DETAILS: 50 seats. Private parties: 60 main room, 15 private room. Car park. Vegetarian meals. Children's helpings. No smoking in 1 dining-room. No pipes/cigars in dining-room. Wheelchair access (not WC). Music   ACCOMMODATION: 2 rooms, both with bath/shower. TV. Phone. B&B £60. Children welcome. No dogs

---

FARNBOROUGH Kent   map 3

Chapter One

Farnborough Common, Locksbottom,
Farnborough BR6 8NF   COOKING 3
TEL: (01689) 854848   FAX: (01689) 858439   COST £29–£54

Chapter One implies there's more to follow, and indeed the owners have now embarked on Chapter Two in Blackheath. Within the long, low, white building that is neon-lit in blue, the kitchen, under John Wood, offers menus that are infused with fashionably novel ideas while also satisfying more traditional tastes; lunchtime bar snacks follow similar lines. Home-smoked salmon is served with onions and capers, and fillet steak comes with both salsa verde and béarnaise. Descriptions make free with culinary terminology, so that fish soup is paired with 'rouille tortellini', while 'spinach brandade' accompanies baked cod. Meals end with the likes of hot banana soufflé, or lime and vanilla cheesecake with cherry tea sorbet. Wines are divided between 'French' and 'Rest of the World', the latter offering best value for money. House wines, flagged only by their nationalities, start at £10 for 'Italian'.

CHEF: John Wood   PROPRIETOR: Selective Restaurants Group   OPEN: all week 12 to 2.30 (3.30 Sun), 6.30 to 10.30 (11.30 Fri and Sat)   MEALS: alc D (main courses £13.50 to £17.50). Set L Mon to Sat £16 (2 courses) to £19.50, Set L Sun £16. Bar L available Mon to Sat   SERVICE: 10% (optional), card slips closed   CARDS: Amex, Delta, Diners, MasterCard, Switch, Visa   DETAILS: 120 seats. Private parties: 120 main room, 60 private room. Car park. Vegetarian meals. Children's helpings. No cigars/pipes in dining-room. Occasional music. Air-conditioned   (£5)

Prices quoted in the Guide are based on information supplied by restaurateurs. The prices quoted at the top of each entry represent a range, from the lowest meal price to the highest; the latter is inflated by 20 per cent to take account of likely price rises during the year of the Guide.

FAVERSHAM Kent   map 3

Read's 🍾

Painter's Forstal, Faversham ME13 0EE
TEL: (01795) 535344   FAX: (01795) 591200   COOKING 7
on Eastling road, 2m S of Faversham   COST £29–£61

Painter's Forstal consists of a few timbered houses sheltering among Kent copses, and Read's, which, as reporters have attested over two decades, occupies an 'unprepossessing' building. Ignore that, for the interior is more than pleasant, the approach is highly professional and David Pitchford's cooking is one of the jewels in the Home Counties crown. Diligently sourcing the pick of local produce, he favours an essentially English culinary idiom, adding Mediterranean elements where appropriate.

The menu offers plenty of choice, its detailed descriptions interspersed with well-chosen literary quotations that span the intellectual range from Dr Johnson to Miss Piggy. Seasonality is all. A spring menu turned up new Jersey Royals with Whitstable scallops, dressed with white truffle oil. Main courses include four cuts of Romney Marsh lamb – from the saddle, fillet, best end and kidney – as well as fillets of salmon trout on buttered hop shoots with a lemon and chive butter sauce. Real understanding of textures and flavours, which underpins the technique and elevates Read's into the upper echelons, is shown to good effect on the six-course tasting menu. It concludes with a selection of three desserts, on one occasion tangy lemon meringue tartlet, raspberry sorbet and caramel soufflé. From the main menu, 'Chocoholics Anonymous' – a quintet of chocolate delicacies – is a perennial favourite. Home-made breads and good coffee served with fudge point up attention to detail, although service varies 'between discreetly attentive and rather aggressive hurrying up'.

Reporters lacking time to come to grips with the extensive wine list have welcomed a condensed version: some 60 bins under £20 offering a refreshing range of styles and varietals. The finer fare includes Penfolds Grange, Vega Sicilia Unico, and first-growth and 'super-second' clarets. Ten wines by the glass begin at £3.50. CELLARMAN'S CHOICE: Gewurztraminer d'Alsace 1990, Trimbach, £22; Cape Mentelle Cabernet/Sauvignon 1993, Margaret River, W. Australia, £21.

CHEF: David Pitchford   PROPRIETORS: David and Rona Pitchford   OPEN: Tue to Sat 12 to 2, 7 to 9.30   CLOSED: 26 Dec, 1 Jan   MEALS: Set L £17.50, Set D Tue to Fri £21 to £38, Set D Sat £38 SERVICE: not inc, card slips closed   CARDS: Amex, Delta, Diners, MasterCard, Switch, Visa DETAILS: 40 seats. 15 seats outside. Private parties: 60 main room, 20 private room. Car park. Vegetarian meals. Children's helpings. No pipes/cigars in dining-room. Wheelchair access (1 step; not WC). No music   (£5)

Card slips closed *in the details at the end of an entry indicates that the total on the slips of credit cards is closed when handed over for signature.*

'We were met and greeted by the obsequious owner, who asked if everything was all right when we hadn't had anything'. (On eating in Lincolnshire)

FERNHURST Surrey	map 3

King's Arms ✳✳ £ | NEW ENTRY |

Midhurst Road, Fernhurst GU27 3HA   COOKING 3
TEL: (01428) 652005   COST £21–£42

On the face of it there is little to distinguish this Bargate stone pub from any other seventeenth-century inn hereabouts: a few hanging baskets and flowering tubs outside, low beams, oak tables and an inglenook fireplace inside. It still functions as a pub too, but the Hirsts earned their stripes in London – Michael cooking at Green's in Duke Street – and then, according to one grateful visitor, 'they realised that Surrey had far more need of their talents'. The style is contemporary, with dishes chalked on a board: roast tomato tart, corned beef hash and fried egg, sweetcorn fritter, half a lobster, pork and leek sausage.

A typical May meal began with a pile of assorted wild mushrooms on brioche, lubricated with a balsamic dressing of garlic and herbs, followed by 'juicy' pink rack of lamb with 'indifferent' bubble and squeak and a 'fine' wild mushroom sauce. Puddings are mostly traditional English, including plum and blackberry crumble, raspberry mousse, and steamed lemon sponge, while service is from 'intelligent, highly motivated and hard-working' staff. Wines are helpfully arranged by style, backed up with a fine wine section and a page of house offerings starting at £9, and prices are fair.

CHEF: Michael Hirst PROPRIETORS: Michael and Annabel Hirst OPEN: all week 12 to 2.30, 7 to 10 CLOSED: some days Christmas, bank hol Mons, and Sun D Dec to Feb MEALS: alc (main courses £5.50 to £14) SERVICE: not inc CARDS: Delta, MasterCard, Switch, Visa DETAILS: 45 seats. 40 seats outside. Private parties: 28 main room, 12 private room. Car park. Vegetarian meals. Children's helpings. No children under 14 at D. No smoking in 1 dining-room. No music

FERRENSBY North Yorkshire	map 9

▲ General Tarleton ✳✳

Boroughbridge Road, Ferrensby HG5 0PZ   COOKING 5
TEL: (01423) 340284 FAX: (01423) 340288   COST £25–£42

Sir Banastre Tarleton, baronet, distinguished himself on the losing side in the American War of Independence, became MP for Liverpool, and then returned to the colours under Wellington. It is thought one of his men opened this roadside inn in the early nineteenth century, and named it after him. It is now owned by the partnership that gave us the long-running Angel Inn at Hetton (see entry); indeed, John Topham lists himself as chef at both. The team here has been much preoccupied over the past year, refurbishing and upgrading, and the results are plain to see.

The kitchen's remit is to mix unpretentious but up-to-date bar/brasserie food with more ambitious impulses in a fixed-price dinner menu of four courses plus coffee. The new-wave Italian mode is celebrated in a crisp pesto-splashed tomato tart adorned with Parmesan shavings, and in a pasta dish that brings together mussels, spicy sausage, peppers and garlic. One reporter thought his terrine of Tuscan vegetables and goats' cheese 'an absolute dream', and was scarcely less impressed by a slow-cooked shoulder of English lamb sitting majestically on olive oil mash and rosemary sauce. Desserts are crowd-pleasers such as sticky toffee pudding, and an intriguing chocolate Jaffa slice, which 'had a layer that was exactly the same as the orangey bit in the middle of a Jaffa cake'. Reports have spoken of long waits for the food, but most seem to find patience rewarded. Wines are listed in no particular order other than by colour, and are a generally enlivening bunch. House wines start at £9.95.

CHEF: John Topham   PROPRIETOR: The Angel Inn at Hetton Partnership   OPEN: Sun L 12 to 2.30, Mon to Sat D 6.30 to 9.30   MEALS: alc D (main courses £10 to £15). Set L £17.50, Set 'early bird' D until 7.45 £10 (2 courses) to £12.45, Set D £26.50. Bar food available all week L and D   SERVICE: not inc, card slips closed   CARDS: Amex, MasterCard, Switch, Visa   DETAILS: 60 seats. 100 seats outside. Private parties: 36 main room, 36 private room. Car park. Vegetarian meals. Children welcome. No smoking in 1 dining-room. Wheelchair access (1 step; also WC). No music   ACCOMMODATION: 14 rooms, all with bath/shower. TV. Phone. Room only £49.50. Rooms for disabled. Children welcome. Baby facilities. Dogs welcome by arrangement. Afternoon teas. Garden   £5

FOLKESTONE Kent   map 3

Pauls £

2A Bouverie Road West, Folkestone CT20 2RX	COOKING 1
TEL: (01303) 259697 FAX: (01303) 226647	COST £17–£31

After 24 years, Paul Hagger has his customers pretty well sussed. They are mostly locals who crowd into the appealingly informal dining-room with its cheerfully coloured cloths and racks of wine bottles, tempted perhaps by the 'lunch club' deal of a main course from the buffet and coffee for £4.95, or the £9.95 three-course 'supper club' offer. There is no need to join either of these clubs, just turn up in the normal way for seafood and pepper bake at lunch (there's a Carvery on Sunday), or black pudding with apple, followed by salmon steak with cream and mussels at dinner. Otherwise, the *carte* might offer skate wing with beurre noir, or pink rack of lamb with honey glaze. Vegetarians get a fair deal. Alcohol and cream in the cooking, and the presence of snails in garlic butter, plus a dessert trolley filled with spongey creamy things, all indicate that the aim is to be no more cutting-edge than the market can withstand. The bulk of the global wine list is under £20, and classic clarets from good vintages (many under £40) are a steal.

CHEF: Darren Byer   PROPRIETORS: Penny and Paul Hagger   OPEN: all week 12 to 2.30, 7 to 9.30   CLOSED: 1 week after Christmas   MEALS: alc Mon to Sat L, all week D (main courses £10 to £11). Carvery Sun L £10.95, Buffet Mon to Sat L £4.95 (1 course), Set D Sun to Fri £9.95. BYO £6 (must be pre-arranged)   SERVICE: not inc   CARDS: Delta, MasterCard, Switch, Visa   DETAILS: 120 seats. 40 seats outside. Private parties: 100 main room, 20 and 40 private rooms. Vegetarian meals. Children welcome. Wheelchair access (2 steps; not WC). No music   £5

'The best way to describe my main course is that it did not contain any horseradish. Most other ingredients you might care to imagine were present.' (On eating in Cambridgeshire)

FOULSHAM Norfolk   map 6

The Gamp £ 🍴✳

| Claypit Lane, Foulsham NR20 5RW | COOKING 2 |
| TEL: (01362) 684114 | COST £18–£32 |

This relatively sizeable Norfolk village is famed throughout the county for the splendour of its Christmas decorations. It ought by now to be pretty well known for this rambling cottage restaurant too, drolly named after the umbrella that was once used to patch a hole in the roof. The simple, modestly proportioned menus showcase a hearteningly domestic style of cooking that avoids ostentation. Start with potted local crab tricked out with prawns and lemon, and move on perhaps to lamb cobbler cooked with onions and baby veg. One December luncher was glad of a generous bowl of potato and watercress soup with hot bread, skewered rump steak on wild rice served with plentiful accompaniments, and chocolate-flavoured cherry Bakewell tart, not to mention the 'real winter welcome' that preceded it all. Other 'sweet endings', as the menu has it, may be strawberry and passion-fruit sorbet or rhubarb crème brûlée. The concise international wine list has some pedigree names on it, but still, alas, no vintages. Best to ask. House French is £7.95.

CHEFS: Andy Bush and Simon Nobbs   PROPRIETORS: Daphne and Andy Bush   OPEN: Wed to Sat (and 1st and 3rd Sun of month) L 12 to 1.30, Tue to Sat D 7 to 9.30   CLOSED: first 2 weeks Jan   MEALS: alc Wed to Sat L, Tue to Sat D (main courses £9 to £13). Set L first and third Sun of month £11.95, Set D Tue to Fri £11.95. BYO £5   SERVICE: not prices, card slips closed   CARDS: Delta, MasterCard, Switch, Visa   DETAILS: 40 seats. Private parties: 40 main room. Car park. Vegetarian meals. Children's helpings. No smoking in dining-room. Wheelchair access (also WC). No music

---

FOWEY Cornwall   map 1

Food for Thought

| The Quay, Fowey PL23 1AT | COOKING 4 |
| TEL: (01726) 832221   FAX: (01726) 832077 | COST £30–£49 |

The erstwhile Customs House enjoys views over Fowey harbour to the wooded hills beyond. It is charmingly decorated with much indoor foliage and walls of exposed shale, the main room a long, elegant space with a bar in the middle. The Billingsleys are practised hosts, and offer a menu that majors in local fish and seafood. Devotees will be delighted to find lobster and crab in a risotto with a langoustine bisque sauce among starters, and scallops given right royal treatment in a main course that sees them bedded on leeks, and sauced with Sauternes and cream. Moules marinière are a stalwart, while the more meatily inclined might begin with sliced beef fillet dressed in chilli, ginger and Szechuan peppercorns, and go on to Barbary duck breast with red onion marmalade and a cassis sauce. Confidence is inspired by the fact that the kitchen appears equally at home with something as simple as asparagus with 'brilliant' beurre blanc, as with salmon escalope in a sauce of black treacle, juniper and sherry. On the pudding menu, sharply flavoured fruit sorbets compete with dark chocolate mousse in coffee-bean sauce. Service works hard to make everybody feel at home, and French house wine is £8.95.

CHEF: Martin Billingsley   PROPRIETORS: Martin and Caroline Billingsley   OPEN: Mon to Sat D only 7 to 9.30   CLOSED: Christmas, Jan and Feb   MEALS: alc (main courses £10.90 to £15.90). Set D £19.95   SERVICE: not inc, card slips closed   CARDS: MasterCard, Switch, Visa   DETAILS: 40 seats. Private parties: 30 main room. Children's helpings. No children under 12. Wheelchair access (not WC). No music

---

FRESSINGFIELD Suffolk   map 6

Fox and Goose ♥

Fressingfield IP21 5PB
TEL: (01379) 586247   FAX: (01379) 586688
EMAIL: paoleary@compulsive.com   COOKING 3
on B1116, 3½m S of Harleston   COST £25–£55

The building, still owned by the adjacent church, dates from 1509, and while it may feel Old World – log fires burn in the grate, and money is not lavished on décor – the cooking sets its face very much towards the new. Options are many, from bar snacks to set meals to a *carte*, plus menus for vegetarians and children, and they cover a lot of ground between them. Grilled halloumi cheese comes with pitta bread and black olives; tiger prawns and salmon are served in coconut milk with lime leaves, lemon grass and chilli; or there may be a warm salad of smoked haddock with bacon and poached egg. Kids can choose between crispy Peking duck pancakes, and fried egg with beans, sausage and chips, while the Sunday roast – Orkney beef with Yorkshire pudding – needs ordering in advance. Finish with British and Irish cheeses, or a rich pudding such as treacle tart or chocolate pot. The wine list is strongest in Bordeaux and Burgundy, with additional variety and style provided in short selections from other regions/countries. A page of house recommendations from around the world starts at £13.50.

CHEF: Maxwell Dougal   PROPRIETORS: Tim and Pauline O'Leary   OPEN: all week 12 to 2, 7 to 9 CLOSED: 25 and 26 Dec   MEALS: alc (main courses £10 to £15). Set L Mon to Fri £9.50 (2 courses) to £12.50, Set L Sun £13.50, Set D Wed to Fri and Sun £17.50. BYO £10   SERVICE: not inc   CARDS: Delta, MasterCard, Switch, Visa   DETAILS: 46 seats. 16 seats outside. Private parties: 30 main room, 20 private room. Car park. Vegetarian meals. Children's helpings. No music £5

GATESHEAD Tyne & Wear   map 10

▲ Eslington Villa Hotel ⁵⅊

8 Station Road, Low Fell, Gateshead NE9 6DR
TEL: (0191) 487 6017   FAX: (0191) 420 0667
leave A1 (M) at Team Valley Trading Estate, approach
Gateshead along Team Valley; at top of Eastern   COOKING 3
Avenue, turn left into Station Road   COST £23–£50

This quiet hotel on the outskirts of Gateshead offers a pleasant antidote to bustling city life, with a conservatory overlooking a sloping garden at the back, and a suburban dining-room with polished wooden tables. Fixed-price menus may be centred around poached salmon or braised beef, with soup or a spicy sausage salad to begin, while the *carte* goes in for calf's liver on herb risotto, or roast rack of lamb with rosemary and garlic. A few more enterprising dishes appear among starters on the *carte*: wild boar sausage with olive oil mash, for example, or king prawn tempura with a chilli ginger sauce. Despite the hearty, meaty element, vegetarians get a fair deal with main courses of tomato tart or wild mushroom risotto, and seafood might include Dover sole, oysters, grilled scallops, or mussels wth pasta and pesto. Finish with steamed chocolate sponge, blueberry tart served with matching ice-cream and maple syrup, or peppered pineapple with coconut ice-cream. Service is a strength, and three dozen wines cover a lot of ground in terms of geography, price and grape variety, starting with house French at £10.50.

CHEF: Ian Lowery   PROPRIETORS: Nick and Melanie Tulip   OPEN: Sun to Fri L 1£ to 1.45, Mon to Oal D 7 to 9.30   MEALS: alc Mon to Fri L, Mon to Sat D (main courses £17 to £18). Set L Sun £9.95 (2 courses), Set D Mon to Fri £18.45 (2 courses) to £22.45. BYO £3   SERVICE: not inc   CARDS: Amex, Delta, Diners, MasterCard, Switch, Visa   DETAILS: 55 seats. 12 seats outside. Private parties: 42 main room, 18 private room. Car park. Vegetarian meals. Children's helpings. No smoking in dining-room. Wheelchair access (also WC). Music   ACCOMMODATION: 12 rooms, all with bath/shower. TV. Phone. B&B £44.50 to £69.50. Children welcome. Baby facilities (*The Which? Hotel Guide*)   (£5)

GILLINGHAM Dorset   map 2

▲ *Stock Hill House* £✕

Stock Hill, Gillingham SP8 5NR
TEL: (01747) 823626   FAX: (01747) 825628
EMAIL: reception@stockhill.net   COOKING 5
off B3081, 1m W of Gillingham   COST £32–£52

The year 1999 looks like being one of transition for the Hausers. Since arriving here in 1985 they have planted 1,500 trees in the surrounding parkland, and geared the kitchen garden up to supply all the herbs and half the vegetables they need. The Victorian house is richly furnished and immaculately maintained, with a lofty, elegant dining-room where 'glasses glisten, and cutlery glints'. Peter Hauser's food is built along an Anglo-French axis, with occasional forays into his native Austria, although enlargement of the kitchen and additions to the team as the *Guide* goes to press will doubtless bring a measure of change.

Dinner has been described as 'a self-indulgent experience', from canapés and an appetiser soup through to home-made chocolates with coffee. In between might come anything from an old favourite such as snails in garlic and parsley butter, to pan-fried sea bream with risotto. Local materials feature, and the food's comfort rating is helped along by foie gras and truffle pâté, and steamed Dorset game pudding with Guinness gravy. Given the Austrian background, *fürst puckler törte mit beeren saft* should come as no surprise, and there cannot be many people still fashioning swans out of meringue. Service, one observer noted, varies from relatively inexperienced but in training, via one or more 'superbly competent' waitresses from Germany or Austria, to Nita herself, 'briefly chatty, smiling and watchful'. Italy and California are new to the wine list this year, and the Austrian bins now number a patriotic ten, but France remains the focal point. Five house wines from France and Austria start at £13.50.

CHEF: Peter Hauser PROPRIETORS: Peter and Nita Hauser OPEN: all week 12.30 to 1.45 (1.30 Sun), 7.30 to 8.45 (8.30 Sun). Booking essential MEALS: Set L £20 to £22, Set D £30 to £32 SERVICE: not inc, card slips closed CARDS: MasterCard, Switch, Visa DETAILS: 36 seats. Private parties: 24 main room, 12 private room. Car park. Vegetarian meals. Children's helpings. No children under 7. No smoking in dining-room. No music ACCOMMODATION: 10 rooms, all with bath/shower. TV. Phone. D,B&B £120 to £280. No children under 7. High teas for children over 7. No dogs (The Which? Hotel Guide)

GOLCAR West Yorkshire map 8

▲ Weavers Shed

Knowl Road, Golcar HD7 4AN
TEL: (01484) 654284 FAX: (01484) 650980 COOKING 5
on B6111, 2m W of Huddersfield from A62 COST £20–£50

Stephen Jackson has realised his dream of running a 'restaurant-with-rooms' by converting the neighbouring mill-owner's house into five bedrooms. It is 'probably the friendliest restaurant we have visited' in the eyes of one family, who also appreciated the classy blend of old (the 'shed' itself is eighteenth-century) and new. Clever lighting makes the best of everything, and menus from grand restaurants decorate the walls; some of their gestures are faithfully copied, too, from large plate-settings (removed unused), via an opening coffee cup of soup, to petits fours and 'traditional posset' (milk with a shot of eau-de-vie) to finish. The kitchen is dedicated to '90s dishes of red mullet with roast tomato couscous, and calf's liver with crispy bacon polenta, not to mention 'really sensuous' foie gras with a squiggle of sticky-sweet balsamic vinegar reduced to 'the consistency of thick black treacle'.

Clinically precise presentation makes a dramatic impact, and timing is spot on, from fat, juicy scallops sprinkled with coral powder, via rare beef, to thick slices of Lunesdale duckling, served at one meal with chilli noodles, butternut squash sauce, and curry-flavoured butter. The kitchen's own nearby garden supplies the vegetables. Desserts exhibit as much workmanship as everything else: for example, a buttery banana tarte Tatin with a blob of pecan ice-cream and a dash of maple syrup. Well-chosen wines from around the world are tailored to suit all pockets, starting with four house wines at £10.95.

CHEFS: Ian McGunnigle, Stephen Jackson and Robert Jones PROPRIETOR: Stephen Jackson OPEN: Tue to Fri L 12 to 2, Tue to Sat D 7 to 10 CLOSED: 25 and 31 Dec, 1 Jan, bank hols MEALS: alc (main courses £11.50 to £16). Set L £9.95 (2 courses with wine) to £13.95. BYO £5 SERVICE: not inc CARDS: Amex, MasterCard, Switch, Visa DETAILS: 55 seats. Private parties: 40 main room, 30 private room. Car park. Vegetarian meals. Children welcome. No cigars/pipes in dining-room. Wheelchair access (2 steps; also WC). Music ACCOMMODATION: 5 rooms, all with bath/shower. TV. Phone. Rooms for disabled. Children welcome. Baby facilities. No dogs (The Which? Hotel Guide) £5

The Guide *is totally independent, accepts no free hospitality, and survives on the number of copies sold each year.*

GORING Oxfordshire map 2

Leatherne Bottel

Goring RG8 0HS
TEL: (01491) 872667   FAX: (01491) 875308
on B4009 out of Goring, 5m S of Wallingford

COOKING 4
COST £36–£63

Overlooking the upper reaches of the Thames, and with the Berkshire Downs in sight, the Bottel makes the most of its bucolic setting with seating outside when the seasons oblige. The dining-room has been extended into the area once occupied by the bar, and is stylishly done up with attractive sculptures, apricot rag-rolled walls and huge vases of flowers and wild grasses. Keith Read mobilises herbs and spices in novel ways to breathe life into some classic dishes: horseradish is made into a savoury ice-cream, for example, to accompany quickly grilled local goats' cheese on a tarragon croûton, a stunning idea that stops short of making the eyes water. Salt played a prominent role in a spring salad of smoked halibut, Parmesan, salmon caviare, rocket and quail's eggs, but the ensemble worked well. Lemon-balm leaves and stalks of lemon-grass may be the seasonings for a crisp-skinned grilled fillet of sea bass, but thick slices of spicy chorizo have been described as 'mugging' the delicate flavour of roasted John Dory. Well-made ice-creams with properly emphasised flavours (rum and banana, or boozy prune and armagnac) compete with creamy, piquant lemon tart with raspberry coulis at dessert stage. Service at busy times can become stretched and shambolic. Wines offer a range of impressive growers, especially in France, but prices are not gentle. Bypass the list's preface – a red rag to politically correct sentiment – to find house selections at £14.50.

CHEFS: Keith Read and Julia Storey   PROPRIETOR: Keith Read   OPEN: all week L 12.15 to 2 (2.30 Sat, 3.30 Sun), Mon to Sat D 7.15 to 9.15   CLOSED: 25 Dec   MEALS: alc (main courses L £6.50 to £9.50, L and D £16.50 to £19.50). Set D Mon to Thur £19.50   SERVICE: 12.5%, card slips closed   CARDS: Amex, MasterCard, Visa   DETAILS: 50 seats. 75 seats outside. Private parties: 20 main room, 12 private room. Car park. No pipes in dining-room. Wheelchair access (not WC). No music. Air-conditioned   £5

GRANGE IN BORROWDALE Cumbria map 10

▲ *Borrowdale Gates Hotel*

Grange in Borrowdale CA12 5UQ
TEL: (017687) 77204   FAX: (017687) 77254
off B5289, about 3m S of Keswick, ¼m N of Grange

COOKING 5
COST £25–£42

Borrowdale is considered by some to be unsurpassed for grandeur among Cumbria's valleys, and this comfortably appointed Victorian house boasts fine views of green mountains with their heads in the clouds. The dining-room is a bright, spacious place done in pale peach, with smart napery and a requirement for equally trim attire on the part of patrons. Former chef Michael Heathcote was replaced in summer '98 by Wendy Lindars, who retains the fixed-price menu format (four courses plus coffee in the evenings), but the cooking itself seems to have moved up a gear from an already pretty impressive pace.

Creamed courgette and mint soup at a Sunday lunch was both rich and full of flavour, as was smoked salmon bavarois with a salad of pickled cucumber. A grilled tranche of cod catches the mood of the moment, here served with wilted spinach and warm pesto, and locally reared meats are given a fair shout too, perhaps in the form of thinly carved roast loin of Lakeland pork garnished with caramelised apple slices. The cheese platter again comes in for commendation for variety and ripeness, while summer pudding arrives 'oozing with purple juices and stuffed with berries'. Chocoholics might gravitate towards a dark truffle torte on brandy-soaked sponge with coffee-bean sauce. Staff are watchful without being overbearing, reinforcing the professionalism of the whole operation. The wine list is strong in France and gains extra vigour from some astute New World selections. Plenty of good drinking is to be had under £20, beginning with house wines from the Parkinsons' favourite producer, Georges Blanc, at £12 a bottle, £2.50 a glass. CELLARMAN'S CHOICE: Mâcon-Azé 'Dom. d'Azenay' 1995, Georges Blanc, £17.50; Bourgogne Pinot Noir 1995, Dom. Pierre Berthau, £18.75.

CHEF: Wendy Lindars   PROPRIETORS: Terence and Christine Parkinson   OPEN: all week 12.15 to 1.30, 7 to 8.45   CLOSED: Jan   MEALS: Set L Sun £14.50, Set D £26.50. Light L menu available Mon to Sat   SERVICE: not inc   CARDS: Amex, Delta, MasterCard, Switch, Visa   DETAILS: 60 seats. Private parties: 12 main room. Car park. No children under 5. Jacket and tie preferred. No smoking in dining-room. Wheelchair access (also WC). No music   ACCOMMODATION: 28 rooms, all with bath/shower. TV. Phone. D,B&B £53.50 to £160. Rooms for disabled. Children welcome. High teas for children. Baby facilities. No dogs. Afternoon teas (*The Which? Hotel Guide*)   £5

GRASMERE Cumbria   map 8

▲ *Michael's Nook* 🍾

Grasmere LA22 9RP   COOKING 6
TEL: (015394) 35496   FAX: (015394) 35645   COST £38–£66

This is a far cry from the humble poetic shepherd's nook after which it is named: rather a well-established hotel 'run in a most civilised manner'. During their 30 years at this creeper-covered Victorian house overlooking Grasmere, the Giffords have filled it with English period furniture, pictures and porcelain, reflecting their background in the antiques business, and achieve an easy mix of formality and comfort. Reg Gifford's other hobbies include breeding Great Danes and exotic cats (evidence of which are also to be found) and picking good chefs: despite their comings and goings over the years he has maintained an impressive record. Mark Treasure left for the Feathers (see entry, Woodstock), and William Drabble arrived from London, having learned his trade at The Capital, Chez Nico and latterly Pied-à-Terre (see entries, all London).

The food is in modern French mould, and luxuries are never far away: foie gras might be combined with ham hock in a terrine, with pigeon in a boudin, or simply roasted, and there is lobster and truffle oil to play with, and ceps and morels. Presentation is a strength, as when tuna niçoise ingredients are piled into a turret and topped with a yolky mix of oil and cream. Dexterity is much in evidence, producing crisp-skinned sea bass fillets looking 'like a granite tor' sitting on thin slices of deep-fried courgette, surrounded by a fragrant bouillon; a light dish but one with 'plenty of character'.

Technical accomplishment does not always achieve the desired result – pink best end of lamb 'neither tender nor tasty' at one meal – but finesse shows to good effect in a trio of apple desserts, and in a tarte Tatin of pineapple served with a rich, creamy coconut ice-cream. The hefty wine list spans the globe in its search for quality, interest and variety, and while it reaches the heights of first- and second-growth clarets, and burgundies from Domaine de la Romanée-Conti, it also offers plenty of good drinking at less-exalted levels (a few bins cost under £10). House wines from France and Australia are priced between £10.50 and £14.50 a bottle. CELLARMAN'S CHOICE: Gewurztraminer d'Alsace 'Fleur de Guebwiller' 1994, Schlumberger, £20.50; Lawson's Padthaway Shiraz 1990, Padthaway, S. Australia, £26.50.

CHEF: William Drabble PROPRIETORS: Mr and Mrs R.S.E Gifford OPEN: all week 12.30 to 1, 7.30 to 8.30. Booking essential MEALS: Set L £34.50, Set D £45 SERVICE: not inc CARDS: Amex, Delta, Diners, MasterCard, Switch, Visa DETAILS: 50 seats. Private parties: 40 main room, 40 private room. Car park. No children under 7. Jacket and tie. No smoking in dining-room. Wheelchair access (1 step; also WC). No music ACCOMMODATION: 14 rooms, all with bath/shower. TV. Phone. D,B&B £135 to £270. Children welcome by arrangement. No dogs. Afternoon teas (The Which? Hotel Guide) £5

▲ White Moss House ▮ ✳

Rydal Water, Grasmere LA22 9SE
TEL: (015394) 35295 FAX: (015394) 35516
on A591, at N end of Rydal Water

COOKING 6
COST £35–£43

This traditional Lakeland restaurant – once the property of William Wordsworth, and in the *Guide* now for over a quarter of a century – is a small, unassuming place, well placed for walkers. Start with an aperitif in the lounge, done in duck-egg blue with floral upholstery, and eat in the plainer dining-room, where wooden tables are set with candles and jugs of iced water. One sitting and a no-choice five-course menu is a familiar format in these parts. It works in the kitchen's favour, allowing it to reduce wastage and control timing: orders are taken by Sue Dixon, and dinner then flows at a well-judged pace.

The food is not cutting-edge; rather it embraces an old-fashioned way of doing things, but they are done well. Thick vegetable soups typify the 'home-made, domestic' approach, while the hot savoury soufflé is an innovation for the Dixons, according to one observer, who was impressed by the fact that some 16 'can arrive at table without any of them collapsing'.

Local produce stretches from Cumbrian sika venison, via rack of Westmorland organic lamb, to free-range maize-fed guinea-fowl, the breast perhaps thickly sliced, the leg distinguished by a light, crispy skin, served in a creamy sauce with apple. Vegetables 'done to a turn' arrive on a separate plate. 'Rich and fruity' huntsman's pudding is a regular, or there may be apple and blackberry Grasmere with a ginger topping, described as 'an up-market crumble'. To finish, cheeses are chosen 'blind' from a long list. Bread is dark, malty slices, 'and if you want more you ask', and breakfast 'deserves a special mention'. The stunning array of wines is sensibly arranged by region within France, followed by comparable varietals from elsewhere, so New World Sauvignons follow the Loire, for example. While each section carries its own introduction, Sue Dixon will provide intelligent advice if further guidance is required. Prices range from fair to impressively low, with the opening personal selection beginning at £9.50 a bottle, £1.90 a glass. CELLARMAN'S CHOICE: Mâcon Chardonnay 1996, Dom.Talmard, £13.95; Médoc, Ch. Des Tourelles 1990, £14.75.

CHEFS: Peter Dixon and Colin Percival   PROPRIETORS: Sue and Peter Dixon   OPEN: Mon to Sat D only 8 (1 sitting)   CLOSED: Dec to Feb   MEALS: Set D £27.50   SERVICE: not inc, card slips closed   CARDS: MasterCard, Switch, Visa   DETAILS: 18 seats. Car park. Children's helpings. No smoking in dining-room. Wheelchair access (not WC). No music   ACCOMMODATION: 8 rooms, all with bath/shower. TV. Phone. D,B&B £83 to £190. Children welcome. No dogs. Fishing (*The Which? Hotel Guide*)   £5

GREAT GONERBY Lincolnshire   map 6

Harry's Place 🍴✳

17 High Street, Great Gonerby NG31 8JS
TEL: (01476) 561780   COOKING 7
on B1174, 2m NW of Grantham   COST £50–£78

'We revisited Harry's Place after a gap of three years and were delighted to find it unchanged and the cooking as superb as ever.' So began one tribute to this small and dedicated family enterprise. The scale is domestic: the front parlour is the dining-room, walls are painted 'gypsy pink', furniture is a mix of stripped pine and antiques, and candles burn on the tables. Caroline Hallam is a skilled hostess, 'bustling round and loading food on to the table', and a tiny *carte* of three courses, with the day's date, offers a choice of two items at each stage.

'Right from the word go you notice the herbs,' reported one visitor, picking up basil, dill, mint and chives in puff pastry pizza-style appetisers. These are hallmarks of the style: not exotic flavours, but familiar ones, yet fresh and vibrant, that give the food its edge and power. Other materials bolster strength: Orkney king scallops; 'immaculately fresh' lobster from Filey in a salad with mango, avocado and truffle oil; and loin of Cornish lamb, seared pink, sliced and served in a simple stock and alcohol reduction. There are no fireworks here, just honest and skilful cooking.

Circumstances allow Harry Hallam the opportunity to balance flavours and to time things accurately, and he takes it, producing a creamy soup based on gamey guinea-fowl stock, 'perfectly in tune with' its other component, celeriac. Chicken is free-range and corn-fed, grouse might be from Yorkshire, and the centrepiece of one meal was a thickish slice of River Dee salmon ('we never use farmed fish'), lightly sauté to be rare in the middle, with a translucent, gently acidic sauce of cooking juices, shallots and red wine. More herbs gave each mouthful an unpredictability that kept interest buoyant, helped by three piles of well-judged and 'characterful' vegetables. Among desserts – of Bramley apple and calvados soufflé, or chocolate mousse with Grand Marnier custard – the light, soft, eggy caramel-infused mousse brûlée stands out, perhaps accompanied by a small pile of fresh raspberries. A short, unbalanced wine list that starts around £16.50 and soon escalates in price is the only letdown.

CHEF: Harry Hallam   PROPRIETORS: Harry and Caroline Hallam   OPEN: Tue to Sat 12.30 to 2, 7 to 9.30   CLOSED: bank hols   MEALS: alc (main courses £22.50 to £27.50)   SERVICE: not inc   CARDS: Delta, MasterCard, Visa   DETAILS: 10 seats. Private parties: 10 main room. Car park. Children's helpings. No children under 5. No smoking in dining-room. Wheelchair access (1 step; not WC). No music   £5

GREAT MILTON Oxfordshire   map 2

▲ *Le Manoir aux Quat' Saisons* 🍾 ⅝✳

Church Road, Great Milton OX44 7PD
TEL: (01844) 278881 FAX: (01844) 278847
EMAIL: lemanoir@oxfordserve.co.uk   COOKING 9
off A329, 1m from M40 junction 7   COST £50–£140

Raymond Blanc's ambition over the past 15 years here has been to offer the best in food and hospitality. He is 'a genuinely nice man', his talent makes him one of Europe's outstanding chefs, and the Manoir has provided a fitting stage on which to perform. The set incorporates a quiet and contemplative Japanese garden, vegetable and herb gardens, a lawn and numerous life-size bronzes. Inside, Blanc family snaps personalise the drawing-rooms' mix of soothingly expensive wallpaper and objets d'art. Colourful modern paintings decorate the yellow dining-room, and the conservatory, candlelit at dinner, is attractively spacious and light.

The backbone is a seasonally changing *carte* with a mix of old Blanc favourites, new dishes and 'specialities'; a 'gourmand' option offers a good cross-section. Starters of offal (mostly liver) and shellfish – macaroni with langoustines in truffle butter – point to French cuisine at its 'hautest', a theme taken up by main courses of roast Agen pigeon with foie gras ravioli, or Landes chicken with morels and Jura wine sauce. But the Japanese theme is well established too, producing a first course of marinated eel, octopus and baby mackerel with black beans and thin slithery noodles on a bed of dark seaweed.

At its best the food can excite. Indeed that is one of Raymond Blanc's strengths: the risks he takes give his food an edge that more classical exponents lack. When this works it can be thrilling, as for example in a deceptively simple chilled essence of clear tomato ladled over a tower of tomato flesh, considered 'sublime'. The design of some dishes can be less convincing, for example when they appear as a plate of separate components rather than an integrated whole, although the parts themselves are invariably exquisite.

Although timing of some items – fish and pasta for example – has disappointed, desserts have shown the kitchen on top form, with caramelised pear baked in brioche, and a mille-feuille of ganache and chocolate wafers, accompanied by a 'sensational' caramel sauce with nuts and a dash of lime, typifying the skills that made Blanc's name. Good bread and first-rate appetisers add to the pleasure. 'Some staff are charming and knowledgeable, others are not', and one or two gaffes in service have been unworthy of the Manoir's aspirations. Commendably, Raymond Blanc welcomes children of all ages, and takes vegetarians seriously.

Wine buffs with money to spend – and they will need plenty – will have their pulses raised by page upon page of excellent clarets and burgundies in the hefty list. Although it is strongly Francophile, other regions are paid the attention they deserve; indeed, the only surprise is that there is no saké to complement the Japanese theme found in the cuisine and gardens. South-west France makes a good starting point for the few affordable bottles. Wine service can suffer from 'youthful inexperience' but is otherwise very correct. CELLARMAN'S CHOICE: Chardonnay Trocken 1995, Weingut Wieninger, Austria, £45; Chorey-lès-Beaune 1995, Mailland Père et Fils, £36.

CHEFS: Raymond Blanc and Jonathan Wright   PROPRIETOR: Raymond Blanc   OPEN: all week 12.15 to 2.15, 7 to 9.15   MEALS: alc (main courses £29 to £42). Set L £32 to £72, Set D £72. BYO £20   SERVICE: not inc   CARDS: Amex, Delta, Diners, MasterCard, Switch, Visa   DETAILS: 124 seats. Private parties: 8 main room, 55 private room. Car park. Vegetarian meals. Children's helpings. No smoking in dining-room. Wheelchair access (also WC). No music. Air-conditioned   ACCOMMODATION: 28 rooms 19 with bath/shower. TV. Phone. Room only £210 to £435. Rooms for disabled. Children welcome. Baby facilities. Dogs welcome in outdoor kennels only. Afternoon teas (*The Which? Hotel Guide*)

GREAT MISSENDEN Buckinghamshire   map 3

La Petite Auberge

107 High Street, Great Missenden HP16 0BB	COOKING 4
TEL: (01494) 865370	COST £36–£50

Entering the Martel's cottage restaurant in the high street is like stepping into someone's front room. It may seem sparsely decorated, with only a few pictures of French scenes to brighten up the white walls, but Mrs Martel's chatty presence out front certainly lends life to the place. The short *carte* is written in French with English translations, and it majors in the classics. What impresses is the sheer quality of the raw materials and the skill with which they are handled. Superbly fresh scallops are transformed into a 'wobbly' mousse which appears surrounded by pools of lemon dressing, while free-range guinea-fowl is served with a fine 'rustic' rösti and a flavoursome jus dotted with girolles.

There's also a deceptive simplicity about dishes such as grilled king prawns, splayed open and served on a creamy sauce flecked with strips of soft leek, or tender veal sweetbreads on a brown gravy jus, discreetly laced with calvados. Vegetables taste as if they have just been plucked from the garden, while desserts include a 'fabulous' caramelised lemon tart, and hot apple with cinnamon ice cream. The short, carefully chosen wine list is exclusively French, and prices are fair across the range. Muscadet de Sèvre et Maine is £10.50.

CHEF: Hubert Martel   PROPRIETORS: Mr and Mrs Hubert Martel   OPEN: Mon to Sat D only 7.30 to 10   CLOSED: two weeks Christmas   MEALS: alc (main courses £14 to £16)   SERVICE: not inc   CARDS: MasterCard, Visa   DETAILS: 30 seats. Private parties: 30 main room. Children welcome. Wheelchair access (also WC). Music

---

The 2000 Guide will be published before Christmas 1999. Reports on meals are most welcome at any time of the year, but are particularly valuable in the spring (no later than June). Send them to The Good Food Guide, FREEPOST, 2 Marylebone Road, London NW1 1YN. Or email your report to guidereports@which.co.uk.

GREAT YELDHAM Essex

map 3

White Hart  £

Poole Street, Great Yeldham CO9 4HJ
TEL: (01787) 237250 FAX: (01787) 238044

COOKING 4
COST £19–£42

'Think of beams, beams and beams, exposed inside and out, and you'll get some idea of this beautiful old building,' claims one visitor. The Huntsbridge formula (see also Three Horseshoes, Madingley, and Pheasant Inn, Keyston) is an appealing one; indeed, it provides a model for informal eating that traditional pubs have conspicuously failed to match. All the food, from 'snacks' of ploughman's or pasta, to two-course weekday lunches, plus a generous *carte*, is available throughout: in the large bar, in both non-smoking dining-rooms, and on the stone-flagged terrace in fine weather. The style is a sympathetic combination of traditional and contemporary, turning up chorizo risotto with roasted red peppers, and loin of venison with Swiss chard.

There is plenty for non-meat eaters, including a Mediterranean vegetable and mozzarella tart, and Dover sole with new potatoes and parsley butter. Despite some uneven delivery, there is much to praise in dressings (which use good-quality olive oil), and in saucing, fish and vegetables. Finish, perhaps, with warm rice-pudding, tiramisù, or first-rate raspberry crème brûlée, and if black olive and onion bread is on offer, take it. Service from young staff is 'friendly and efficient'. The wine list, by confining itself to around 100 bottles, manages to offer plenty of interest without becoming unwieldy. Good-quality drinking is to be had at all price levels, with mark-ups decreasing the higher you get. House wines start at £ 9.45. CELLARMAN'S CHOICE: Viognier 'Cold Heaven' 1996, Santa Maria, California, £29; Rosso di Montalcino 1995, Costanti, £22.

CHEF: Roger Jones PROPRIETOR: Huntsbridge Ltd OPEN: all week 12 to 2, 7 to 10 (9.30 Sun) CLOSED: D 25 and 26 Dec, D 1 Jan MEALS: alc (main courses £7.50 to £15). Set L Mon to Sat £7.50 (2 courses) to £10.50. Snack menu available. BYO £5.50 SERVICE: not inc, card slips closed CARDS: Amex, Delta, Diners, MasterCard, Switch, Visa DETAILS: 100 seats. 36 seats outside. Private parties: 80 main room, 28 private room. Car park. Vegetarian meals. Children's helpings. No smoking in dining-room. Wheelchair access (not WC). Music

GRIMSTON Norfolk

map 6

▲ *Congham Hall* ✳

Lynn Road, Grimston PE32 1AH
TEL: (01485) 600250 FAX: (01485) 601191
off A148 or B1153, 7m E of King's Lynn

COOKING 3
COST £24–£51

Congham is a Georgian country-house hotel awash with modern amenities. It even boasts a cricket pitch, should there be eleven of you. Nearby are bird sanctuaries, the tranquil Norfolk coastline, and Royal Sandringham, and it is worth wandering around the sumptuous grounds of the Hall itself. Meals are taken in the Orangery, an elegant glass-ceilinged room where Stephanie Moon's assured cooking keeps abreast of the times.

Rabbit loin with smoked bacon, pulses and wild mushrooms as a starter suggests a gutsier approach than is often the way in country houses, and first courses are followed by an intermediate offering that may be as simple as sorbet or as refined as seared foie gras with apple sauce and caramelised chestnuts, depending on appetite. Sea bass, lobster and sole come together in a saffron and dill sauce for the fishily inclined, while meat-eaters might plump for beef fillet topped with horseradish and thyme mousse, served with cocotte potatoes and a Madeira jus. Vegetarians have their own ample menu, and then everyone is reunited for puddings of pear and almond tart with lavender ice-cream, or flambé bananas with meringue and banana and tamarind wafers. Despite its map of Europe, the wine list is not thus confined, but high prices will prove a straitjacket for many. Try Spain. Half-bottles are plentiful, and house wines are £12.75.

CHEF: Stephanie Moon   PROPRIETORS: Christine and Trevor Forecast   OPEN: all week 12.30 to 2, 7.30 to 9.30   MEALS: Set L Mon to Sat £9.50 (2 courses) to £13.50, Set L Sun £18.50, Set D £25 to £32. BYO £10   SERVICE: not inc, card slips closed   CARDS: Amex, Delta, Diners, MasterCard, Switch, Visa   DETAILS: 50 seats. 40 seats outside. Private parties: 50 main room, 18 private room. Car park. Vegetarian meals. No children under 12. Jacket and tie at D. No smoking in dining-room. Wheelchair access (2 steps; not WC). No music   ACCOMMODATION: 14 rooms, all with bath/shower. TV. Phone. B&B £80 to £210. No children under 12. Dogs in kennels. Afternoon teas. Swimming-pool (*The Which? Hotel Guide*)

HALIFAX West Yorkshire   map 9

Design House ▼ £

Dean Clough Mills, Halifax HX3 5AX   COOKING 3
TEL: (01422) 383242   FAX: (01422) 322732   COST £22–£46

Dean Clough is a success story that could bear repeating all over West Yorkshire. The site was a carpet mill, testament to Halifax's role in the woollen industry, that has been preserved and converted into suites of offices and, in one small corner, a restaurant. A modern interior mixes glass, chrome and wood with a blue and orange colour scheme, while a short modern menu offers simple but appealing dishes of baked organic eggs with creamed mushrooms, or chargrilled calf 's liver. Occasionally something bolder swims into view: two pieces of lightly battered plaice, served on couscous flavoured with garlic and coriander, on a puddle of chillied mango purée.

Other fish has worked well too, including firm, fresh, oven-baked cod with 'exceptional' scallops, full of flavour and 'undercooked to perfection', in a bowl of aniseedy fish stock. Breast of corn-fed chicken has come with a similar clear stock containing mushrooms and leeks. David Watson's direct approach continues into desserts of lemon-curd rice-pudding, plum mousse, and baked vanilla cream. Value is good overall and staff are friendly and knowledgeable. Wines from around the world are intelligently chosen, arranged simply by style, and sport refreshingly low mark-ups. Italian house wines are £9.50 and 20 half-bottles are on offer.

The Guide *always appreciates hearing about changes of chef or owner.*

CHEF: David Watson   PROPRIETOR: John Leach   OPEN: Mon to Fri L 12 to 2, Mon to Sat D 6.30 to 10   CLOSED: 25 to 27 Dec, 1 and 2 Jan   MEALS: alc (main courses £8 to £16). Set L and D Mon to Fri £10.95 (2 courses) to £13.95   SERVICE: not inc   CARDS: Amex, Delta, MasterCard, Switch, Visa   DETAILS: 70 seats. 12 seats outside. Private parties: 70 main room. Car park (D only). Vegetarian meals. Children's helpings. No smoking while others eat. Music. Air-conditioned

Maypole Inn £   [NEW ENTRY]

32 Warley Town, Halifax HX2 7RZ   COOKING 4
TEL: (01422) 831106   COST £17–£39

'I liked the fact that the [Maypole] inn has not been spoilt,' observed a regular visitor to this slightly out-of-the-way village pub on the outskirts of Halifax. An open-plan log fire dominates the 'rustic' bar, where drinkers crowd in for pints of hand pulled beer and snacks. Upstairs is the restaurant, a comfortable room with lilac-coloured walls, dried flowers and thick candles on the tables, where neatly turned-out staff work smoothly and attentively.

Chef Ian Kendell moved back to Yorkshire after spells in several high-profile London kitchens (including Canteen and Kensington Place; see entries, London): not surprisingly his cooking is '90s brasserie style, fashionable and defined by the contents of the global larder. Two starters typify his range: on the one hand a chunky lobster, crab and spring onion terrine surrounded by a trickle of olive oil and balsamic vinegar; on the other, a brunch-like warm salad of superlative black pudding, crisp bacon, croûtons and a poached egg. Mains are equally convincing: honey-roast duck breast on braised cabbage with lemon grass and soy, or perfectly timed roast rack of lamb with mint crust and a side helping of buttery mash, for example. Generous desserts range from fruit crumble topped with a portion of cold fruit compote to chocolate and rum pavé. The wine list is a well-chosen, cosmopolitan slate of around 50 bins. House wine is £8.75.

CHEF: Ian Kendell   PROPRIETOR: Sue Hardy   OPEN: Sun L 12.30 to 2.30, Tue to Sat D 6.30 to 9.30 (10 Sat)   CLOSED: 25 and 26 Dec   MEALS: alc (main courses £6.50 to £13.50). Set L Sun £9.75 (2 courses) to £12.50, Set D Tue to Sat 6.30 to 8 (7.30 Fri, 7 Sat) £9.75 (2 courses) to £12.50. Bar menu available Sun L and Tue to Fri D.   SERVICE: not inc, card slips closed   CARDS: Delta, MasterCard, Switch, Visa   DETAILS: 50 seats. 60 seats outside. Private parties: 50 main room. Car park. Vegetarian meals. Children's helpings. Music   (£5)

HAMBLETON Rutland   map 6

▲ *Hambleton Hall* ▮ ✻

Hambleton LE15 8TH
TEL: (01572) 756991   FAX: (01572) 724721
EMAIL: hotel@hambletonhall.com   COOKING 8
off A606, 3m SE of Oakham   COST £31–£95

Overlooking Rutland Water, with venerable yew trees and a beautiful garden, this is a fine place to come on a summer evening, and equally appealing in winter when log fires make 'warmth' and 'homely' the watchwords. Visitors feel pampered by the comfortable lounges, plentiful cushions and sense of calm. In their 20 years here, Tim and Stefa Hart have produced a very classy establishment that is neither overbearing nor stuffy; it is 'surprisingly unpretentious', straddling the formal–casual dimension with ease, even in the more traditionally furnished Regency-striped dining-room.

Choice is more than generous – some 30 dishes for a dining-room that seats 40 people at most – with game, offal, daily-delivered fish and shellfish, a wealth of cooking methods, and a bright Anglo-Mediterranean tilt to it all. Between them, menus take in classic winter dishes of braised leg of hare with mashed potatoes and root vegetables in a red wine sauce, summery ones of morels with asparagus and chicken mousse, and rich ones of Bresse pigeon with a mille-feuille of foie gras, turnips and baby onions. The food has flashes of excellence – 'some of our food was brilliant', noted an inspector – and among successes have been 'massive, succulent' roast scallops 'cooked (almost not cooked) to perfection', in a sauce vierge with 'lashings of olive oil', and a fillet of Aberdeen Angus beef, served on 'the most intense of red wine sauces' with a blotter of fondant potatoes and a strewing of vegetables.

Labour-intensive treatments and luxury ingredients can make it tricky to sustain standards, as well as adding to the cost: prices are 'a serious drawback' (extravagantly truffled risotto comes in at £30), inhibiting return custom, detracting from enjoyment, and conveying a sense of elitism that Hambleton otherwise makes such a successful effort to counter. But set-price options, even without choice, can be attractive; the 'tasting menu' at £60 offers six courses. The assiette of desserts was the highlight of a meal for one reporter, while others have enjoyed individual ones from passion-fruit soufflé and ice-cream, via an intensely flavoured lemon tart with a compote of raspberries, to caramelised apple tart with a scoop of vanilla ice-cream and a compote of blackberries.

The dining-room, we are pleased to note, is now non-smoking. Service is young, friendly, well briefed and professional, and the informative sommelier comes in for special praise for his 'helpful hints' and selections of wines by the glass. The encyclopedic list has vintage ports stretching back to the 1950s and fine clarets and grand burgundies to the 1960s, while California stands out in an excellent New World section. Modest wines for those on a budget can also be found, and lovers of sweet wine have plenty to look forward to. CELLARMAN'S CHOICE: Lavaux, Epesses 'La Braise d'Enfer' 1996, Les Frères Dubois, Switzerland, £31; Ribera del Duero Reserva 1994, Viña Pedrosa, £34.

CHEF: Aaron Patterson   PROPRIETORS: Tim and Stefa Hart   OPEN: all week 12 to 1.30, 7 to 9.30   MEALS: alc (main courses £20 to £30). Set L Mon to Fri £19.50, Set D £35 to £60   SERVICE: net prices, card slips closed   CARDS: Amex, Delta, MasterCard, Switch, Visa   DETAILS: 40 seats. Private parties: 40 main room, 14 and 20 private rooms. Car park. Vegetarian meals. Children's helpings. No babies. No smoking in dining-room. Wheelchair access (2 steps; also WC). No music   ACCOMMODATION: 15 rooms, all with bath/shower. TV. Phone. B&B £145 to £295. Rooms for disabled. Children welcome. Baby facilities. Dogs welcome by arrangement. Afternoon teas. Swimming-pool (*The Which? Hotel Guide*)

The Guide office can quickly spot when a restaurateur is encouraging customers to write recommending inclusion. Such reports do not further a restaurant's cause. Please tell us if a restaurateur invites you to write to the Guide.

HAMPTON HILL   Greater London   map 3

Monsieur Max

133 High Street, Hampton Hill TW12 1NJ   COOKING 5
TEL: (0181) 979 5546   FAX: (0181) 979 3747   COST £23–£50

Last year's *Guide* commented that Max Renzland was not one for excess frill or furbelow in the design of his restaurants. To prove us wrong he has this year installed a new floor, re-made the entrance lobby and upgraded the air-conditioning. Not only that, but readers also tell us the cooking is on an upward swing too. More or less opposite an Esso station in the heart of suburbia, the restaurant offers what has become the trademark Renzland style of French country cuisine given a gloss of sophistication by tip-top raw materials and artful presentation.

A ballottine of foie gras accompanied by green beans and leaves could have graced a much loftier establishment, its 'silky texture and generous flavour' lending it true distinction. Marinated herring with a warm potato and spring onion salad is a robust stalwart from the proprietor's time in Chelsea, while a serving of Cantabrian anchovies is left to speak for itself, garnished with little more than shallots and grilled pain Poilâne. One man's roast chump of lamb was 'pretty bloody' (a compliment, this) and very tender, given lift by a raviolo of sweetbreads and parsley and a rich wild mushroom ragoût. To finish, there may be an exemplary tarte fine aux pommes constructed of wafer-thin buttery pastry and the sweetest apples – 'it slipped down like a dream' – or chocolate fondant with crème anglaise and wild cherries. Service is obliging. The wine list, printed in the left margin of the menu, is more cosmopolitan for reds than for whites, which are mostly French. Choices are sound, but mark-ups are high. House wines are £12.50.

CHEFS: Max Renzland, Alex Bentley and Morgan Meunier   PROPRIETOR: Max Renzland   OPEN: Sun to Fri L 12 to 2.30 (3 Sun), all week D 7 to 10.30 (11 Fri and Sat)   CLOSED: 25 and 26 Dec   MEALS: Set L Mon to Fri £11 (2 courses) to £14, Set L Sun £19.50, Set D £19.50   SERVICE: 12.5% (optional), card slips closed   CARDS: Delta, MasterCard, Switch, Visa   DETAILS: 90 seats. Private parties: 16 main room, 16 to 20 private rooms. Children welcome. No cigars/pipes in dining-room. Wheelchair access (not WC). No music. Air-conditioned   £5

HAROME   North Yorkshire   map 9

Star Inn ⅝✸

Harome YO6 5JE
TEL: (01439) 770397   FAX: (01439) 771833   COOKING 3
off A170, 3m SE of Helmsley   COST £21–£50

It is rumoured that J.B. Priestley used to sit in the bar of this ancient Yorkshire pub, and at first glance it still looks the part: six centuries young, complete with thatch on the roof, beams and furniture crafted by 'Mouseman' Thompson. But since the arrival of Andrew and Jacquie Pern in 1996, it has undergone a near miraculous transformation: 'a Star reborn!' quipped one correspondent. Andrew cooks, Jacquie dashes around elegantly out front. The food has oodles of North Country generosity and classical creamy richness, but it is also stylish, deft and based around prime local ingredients: game is from the moors, herbs are harvested from the garden, fish arrives fresh from Whitby or Hartlepool. Go for lunch (sit in the garden in fine weather) and you might be offered re-invented pub staples ranging from sandwiches filled with steak and blue cheese shavings to light dishes like grilled black pudding with parsley mash and home-baked beans. Reporters have found even more to enjoy from the daily blackboard: duck breast braised with Toulouse sausage, 'gorgeous' partridge breasts crowned with foie gras, and baked monkfish with champ and herb butter have been singled out, while gooseberry and gin fool, fruit roly-poly, and lemon tart have drawn plenty of applause. Gospel Green Sussex Cyder is an English interloper on the keenly priced wine list, which features some classic burgundies and a sprinkling from the New World. House wine is £9.50.

CHEF: Andrew Pern   PROPRIETORS: Andrew and Jacquie Pern   OPEN: Tue to Sun L 11.45 to 2 (Sun 12 to 6), Tue to Sat D 6.45 to 9.30.   CLOSED: 2 weeks Jan   MEALS: alc (main courses £6 to £15). Light L available. BYO £5   SERVICE: not inc, card slips closed   CARDS: MasterCard, Switch, Visa   DETAILS: 65 seats. 30 seats outside. Private parties: 35 main room, 10 private room. Car park. Vegetarian meals. Children's helpings. No smoking in dining-room. Wheelchair access (not WC). No music

---

HARROGATE North Yorkshire   map 8

The Bistro

1 Montpellier Mews, Harrogate HG1 2TG   COOKING 2
TEL: (01423) 530708   FAX: (01423) 567000   COST £28–£44

Tables are set close in this courtyard bistro, which maintains a 'pleasant relaxed atmosphere' even when bursting with conference visitors. The cooking takes a breezy approach to Mediterranean and other ideas, generating gnocchi with walnut pesto, tartlet of smoked haddock with spinach and poached egg, and roast cod with an olive crust, basil purée and risotto of sun-dried tomatoes. Marc Papon has produced good fish soup, 'excellent' tagliatelle with scallops, and meat dishes of lamb shank, honey- and soy-roasted duck, and calf's liver with polenta cake. For pudding, try lemon tart. Some two dozen largely French wines stay mostly below £20. House Vin de Pays d'Oc is £10.50.

CHEF: Marc Papon   PROPRIETOR: Maurizio Capurro   OPEN: Tue to Sat 12 to 2, 7 to 10 CLOSED: 10 days Christmas   MEALS: alc (main courses £10 to £14.50)   SERVICE: not inc CARDS: Delta, MasterCard, Switch, Visa   DETAILS: 36 seats. 12 seats outside. Private parties: 36 main room. Vegetarian meals. Children's helpings. Music   £5

Drum and Monkey £

5 Montpellier Gardens, Harrogate HG1 2TF   COOKING 4
TEL: (01423) 502650   FAX: (01423) 522469   COST £16–£41

'Still as good as ever' reckoned one visitor to this busy Harrogate landmark, where William Fuller will clock up 20 years in 1999. The advice is to arrive early for lunch, and book ahead for weekends. Eat in the darkly wooded bar downstairs, or in the long maroon-coloured upstairs dining-room, and be prepared for a menu that offers nothing but fish and shellfish, garnered from Whitby, Brixham, Fleetwood and Loch Fyne. It comes hot or cold, on its own or with a sauce, from simple to complicated, in traditional or modern guise, and large or small: the shellfish platter incudes half a lobster, and grilled Dover soles weigh up to 1.5 lbs. Soups, salads, smoked fish pâté and prawn cocktail start things off, garlic butter turns up on the hot shellfish platter, scallops come with lime, coriander and ginger, and seafood pie is topped with cheese and potato. Finish with chocolate mousse, sherry trifle or frozen blueberry yoghurt, and drink from a short, fairly priced wine list that starts at £7.85.

CHEFS: Keith Penny and Tina Nuttall   PROPRIETOR: William Fuller   OPEN: Mon to Sat 12 to 2.30, 6.30 to 10.15   CLOSED: 24 Dec to 2 Jan   MEALS: alc (main courses £4 to £14). BYO £3.50 SERVICE: not inc   CARDS: Delta, MasterCard, Switch, Visa   DETAILS: 50 seats. Private parties: 8 main room. Children's helpings. No music

---

HARWICH Essex   map 6

▲ The Pier at Harwich ▼

The Quay, Harwich CO12 3HH   COOKING 2
TEL: (01255) 241212   FAX: (01255) 551922   COST £28–£54

Ferries and huge container lorries come and go around the pier and the Orwell estuary and you can watch their progress from the windows of the upstairs dining-room. The theme of the place is predictably nautical – all 'ship's wheels, knotted ropes, bells, lights' – and it should come as no surprise that fish is the prime contender on the menu. A number of dishes are now priced as starters or main courses, which encourages flexibility, although the core repertoire remains intact. Pan-fried sardines, Dover sole meunière, and plainly grilled fillet of sea bass have all been enjoyed of late, although the choice extends to rock oysters, lobster (from the restaurant's own tanks), non-piscine alternatives in the shape of toasted goats'-cheese salad, and chargrilled sirloin steak. Accompaniments include 'masses and masses' of vegetables, and desserts might feature sorbets or a gâteau of fresh raspberries and strawberries. Downstairs is the Ha'penny Pier, a boon for families with children hungry for fish and chips and knickerbocker glory. Service is amiable.

The fish-friendly wine list offers a broad selection of good-value drinking from France and the New World, as one would expect when local merchants Lay & Wheeler are the suppliers. House wines are an unusual duo: the red is a Moldavian Merlot, the white a Trebbiano from the Italian Marches, both £9.95 a bottle.

CHEF: Chris Oakley   PROPRIETOR: The Pier at Harwich Ltd   OPEN: all week 12 to 2, 6.30 to 9.30   CLOSED: D 25 and 26 Dec   MEALS: alc (main courses £8.50 to £19). Set L Sun £14.50 (2 courses) to £17.50. Bistro menu available all week L and D   SERVICE: 10%, card slips closed CARDS: Amex, Delta, Diners, MasterCard, Switch, Visa   DETAILS: 70 seats. Private parties: 70 main room. Car park. Children's helpings. Music   ACCOMMODATION: 6 rooms, all with bath/shower. TV. Phone. B&B £52.50 to £85. Children welcome. Baby facilities (The Which? Hotel Guide)

HASTINGS East Sussex   map 3

Röser's

64 Eversfield Place, St Leonards on Sea,
Hastings TN37 6DB   COOKING 7
TEL/FAX: (01424) 712218   COST £27–£70

A marked absence of hype attends this Victorian house on the front, just along from the pier, where the restaurant and its proprietors are the acme of modesty. The dining-room – whose bow-fronted window and booths of banquette seating might be taken as a statement against modernity – may have something to be modest about, but the cooking certainly doesn't. This is one of the top half-dozen restaurants on the south coast and, judging by our postbag, seems to be an as-yet-undiscovered gem for many readers. The appeal of Gerald Röser's food is that it remains uncomplicated by flourish and gesture, and he invariably manages to produce 'a bit of magic' that transforms the materials into something exciting, without for a moment detracting from their essential nature. At one meal, for example, home-made pasta came with a ragoût of chanterelles, trompettes and ceps, in a 'beautifully judged' sauce flecked with black truffle: 'essentially a simple dish that was brought to life by virtually every single component'.

Menus consist of a *carte*, a very attractive three-course set-price deal, plus a few daily extras, and although the style has a broadly European thrust, its individuality defies simple pigeon-holing. Each dish has its own focus: perhaps pike soufflé with a smoked salmon and dill sauce to begin, then medallions of sika venison with a butter-bean and winter savory purée. It is a world in which guinea-fowl, pigeon, duck and goose are as likely to appear as chicken, where oysters might be fried, wild boar made into a sausage, and local brill served up with kohlrabi and truffle. Herbs and spices are used judiciously – sage leaves and coriander seeds mixed with diced tomato flesh to accompany red mullet, for instance – and desserts are a high point, particularly the caramelised lime cream: a light, free-standing mousse with a crisply blow-torched icing sugar top, surrounded by blobs of bitter orange sauce. The wine list is a weighty tome with page after page of fine burgundies and mature classed-growth clarets. Selections from outside France are just as appealing, with eight bins from England making a particularly pleasing appearance. House wines include Louis Latour Chardonnay at £14.95. CELLARMAN'S CHOICE: Chablis 1996, Moreau et Fils, £16.50; Gigondas, Dom. du Grand Montmirail 1990, Pascal Frères, £22.50.

CHEF: Gerald Röser   PROPRIETORS: Gerald and Jenny Röser   OPEN: Tue to Fri L 12 to 2, Tue to Sat D 7 to 10 (booking essential)   CLOSED: first 2 weeks Jan, last 2 weeks Jun   MEALS: alc (main courses £14.50 to £27). Set L £18.95, Set D Tue to Fri £21.95   SERVICE: net prices, card slips closed   CARDS: Amex, Delta, Diners, MasterCard, Switch, Visa   DETAILS: 26 seats. Private parties: 16 main room, 30 private room. Vegetarian meals. Children welcome. No cigars/pipes in dining-room (£5)

Net prices *in the details at the end of an entry indicates that the prices given on a menu and on a bill are inclusive of VAT and service charge, and that this practice is clearly stated on menu and bill.*

HAWORTH West Yorkshire

map 8

▲ *Weavers*  £

15 West Lane, Haworth BD22 8DU
TEL: (01535) 643822   FAX: (01535) 644832

COOKING 2
COST £22–£42

At the top of a cobbled street, backing on to the Parsonage Museum and a handy car park, Weavers wears its tackle proudly. Bobbins and shuttles dangle from the bar ceiling, commemorative plates and old photographs decorate the dining-room, and thick millstone grit walls enclose the lot. After 20 years the Rushworths know their market well, and serve 'hearty portions (i.e. normal for Yorkshire)' of simple, honest and traditional British food, such as lamb shank with root mash, or Pennine meat and potato pie made with local beef and served with 'lashings of gravy', helped along by a few trendier items such as an 'upside down' tart of Mediterranean vegetables. They deserve credit for not trying to make their food fussy or ambitious, and for taking care with essentials: producing a well-judged, boned and rolled shoulder of lamb that was 'homely, straightforward and tasty'. To start, deep-fried potato skins come with chive mayonnaise, and herb-flecked cheese sausages with an apple and raisin chutney, while puddings might include bread-and-butter, or crème brûlée with Yorkshire rhubarb. For value, note the early-evening Sampler Menu, and the 20-strong 'best-seller' selection of wines under £17.25 on a carefully chosen list.

CHEF/PROPRIETOR: Colin and Jane Rushworth   OPEN: Tue to Sat D only 6.45 to 9.15   CLOSED: 2 weeks Christmas, 2 weeks June   MEALS: alc (main courses £7.50 to £15). Set D Tue to Fri (before 7.45) £10.95 (2 courses) to £13.50. BYO £3.50   SERVICE: not inc, card slips closed   CARDS: Amex, Delta, Diners, MasterCard, Switch, Visa   DETAILS: 65 seats. Private parties: 16 main room, 16 private room. Vegetarian meals. Children's helpings. No smoking in dining-room. Music. Air-conditioned   ACCOMMODATION: 4 rooms, all with bath/shower. TV. Phone. B&B £50 to £75. Children welcome. No dogs (*The Which? Hotel Guide*) £5

HAYDON BRIDGE Northumberland

map 10

General Havelock Inn

Ratcliffe Road, Haydon Bridge NE47 6ER
TEL: (01434) 684376
on A69, 100yds W of junction with B6319

COOKING 1
COST £19–£35

Aim through the bar of this roadside pub, past some nostalgic advertising signs, to a stone-clad dining-room at the back overlooking the river. It is a peaceful spot, handy for visitors to Hadrian's Wall five or six miles away, with a handwritten menu of old favourites ranging from Stilton and celery soup to chicken with tarragon. What the food may lack in surprise it makes up for in reassuringly simple cooking: perhaps a lemon butter sauce for North Sea haddock, or fillet of pork with rosemary in a wine and cream sauce. Fruity or chocolatey puddings follow – apple tart, or dark chocolate mousse – and some two dozen wines stay comfortably under £20.

CHEF: Angela Clyde   PROPRIETORS: Ian and Angela Clyde   OPEN: Wed to Sun L 12 to 1.15, Wed to Sat D 7.30 to 8.45   CLOSED: first week Jan, first 2 weeks Sept   MEALS: alc Wed to Sat L (main courses £6 to £6.50). Set L Sun £12.25, Set D £20. Bar L available   SERVICE: not inc   CARDS: none   DETAILS: 28 seats. 8 seats outside. Private parties: 32 main room. Vegetarian meals. Children's helpings. Wheelchair access (1 step; also WC). Occasional music

---

HAYWARDS HEATH   West Sussex   map 3

Jeremy's at Borde Hill ⅚✶ | NEW ENTRY |

Balcombe Road, Haywards Heath RH16 1XP   COOKING 5
TEL: (01444) 441102   COST £27–£52

Entrepreneurial Jeremy Ashpool has added this new venture to his existing restaurant at the Crabtree (see entry, Lower Beeding). Set in the privately owned gardens of Borde Hill, just north of Haywards Heath, the restaurant is reached through landscaped parkland: those just coming to eat don't have to pay the admission charge. Occupying part of the old stable courtyard, the dining-room opens on to a terrace overlooking a sumptuous walled garden with vine-entwined arches and herbaceous borders.

As at the Crabtree, Jeremy Ashpool intends to lead from the rear, in this case following the lead of his co-chef Kate Neal. It is a conscientious approach, in which the kitchen bakes its own excellent breads, makes ice-creams and sorbets, and seeks to refine versions of classic European cooking, rather than striving for the whole-world-on-a-plate philosophy. Expect Mediterranean fish soup with all the accoutrements, rack of lamb on puréed flageolet beans with roasted garlic, or a 'superbly executed' dish of flaked smoked haddock on a bed of spinach, surmounted by a soft-poached egg with a creamy mustard sauce. Top-drawer ingredients have included a deeply flavoured fillet of brill served with new potatoes and a chive butter sauce. Here is a kitchen aiming for restraint rather than stridency, and managing an impressive level of consistency, not least among desserts such as a 'richly flavoured', transparent, berry-filled rose-petal jelly, or a cube of chocolate torte topped with clementine sorbet. Staff display 'a lot of charm and efficiency at the same time'. A compact list of around 50 wines packs in lots of interest and flavour and features some good growers. Prices start in Italy at £10 and end in Burgundy at £42, with plenty worth drinking in between.

CHEFS: Jeremy Ashpool and Kate Neal   PROPRIETOR: Jeremy's Restaurants Ltd.   OPEN: Tue to Sun L 12.30 to 2, Tue to Sat D 7.30 to 10   CLOSED: 25 Dec.   MEALS: alc (main courses £11.50 to £18). Set L £13.50 (2 courses) to £17.50, Set D £15 (2 courses) to £19   SERVICE: 10%, card slips closed   CARDS: Amex, MasterCard, Switch, Visa   DETAILS: 45 seats. 20 seats outside. Private parties: 40 main room. Vegetarian meals. Children's helpings on request. No smoking in dining-room. Wheelchair access (1 step; not WC). Occasional music   (£5)

£ *means that it is possible to have a three-course meal, including coffee, half a bottle of house wine and service for £25 or less per person, at any time the restaurant is open, i.e. at dinner as well as lunch. It may be possible to spend considerably more than this, but by choosing carefully you should find £25 or less achievable.*

HERSTMONCEUX East Sussex

map 3

Sundial ✸

Gardner Street, Herstmonceux BN27 4LA
TEL: (01323) 832217

COOKING **5**
COST £32–£77

Now into their fourth decade at this seventeenth-century country-style auberge, the Bertolis are practised restaurateurs. An old-world feel pervades the place; even the menu is written in French with parenthetical English subtitles. Carpaccio of smoked goose marinated in olive oil with Parmesan is one of the more attention-grabbing starters, but seafood is the first love, whether it be a simple dish of tagliatelle with white crabmeat, or a mixture of lobster, prawns and crab served in a salad or baked in a feuilleté case. All fish is punctiliously selected, with the result that some dishes are available for a minimum of two or more customers. Early claimants may bag themselves a fillet of sea bass served with olive oil, lemon vinegar and carrot purée, or a simply fried Dover sole with beurre noisette and tartare sauce. Roasts for two indicate a certain sense of occasion on the part of the kitchen, and here include not just authoritative chateaubriand, but milk-fed lamb with thyme and rosemary too.

Desserts seem to bring things back to the trattoria mode with a bump: squishy gâteaux, a potpourri of sorbets, or chocolate profiteroles are the order of the day. The Sundial enjoys tenacious support, not least because, as one reporter observes, the Bertolis imbue the place with real personality. The wine list is cursory in all regions (including Italy, oddly) save classic France, where mature clarets and burgundies tumble forth in profusion. House wines start at £12.95 for Soave and Valpolicella.

CHEF: Giuseppe Bertoli PROPRIETORS: Giuseppe and Laure Bertoli OPEN: Tue to Sun L 12 to 2 (2.30 Sun), Tue to Sat D 7 to 9.30 (10 Sat) CLOSED: 25 Dec to 20 Jan, 15 Aug to first week Sept MEALS: alc (main courses £17.50 to £27.50). Set L Tue to Sat £19.50, Set L Sun £22.50, Set D £27.50 SERVICE: 10%, card slips closed CARDS: Amex, Delta, Diners, MasterCard, Switch, Visa DETAILS: 50 seats. 25 seats outside. Private parties: 60 main room, 22 private room. Car park. Vegetarian meals. Children's helpings. No smoking in dining-room. Wheelchair access (1 step; not WC). Music £5

HETTON North Yorkshire

map 8

Angel Inn 🍾

Hetton BD23 6LT
TEL: (01756) 730263 FAX: (01756) 730363
off B6265, 5m N of Skipton

COOKING **6**
COST £27–£45

'A jewel in the crown of the Yorkshire Dales' sums up the way most visitors come to feel about the Angel, which appears to go from strength to strength, perhaps because, as the owners declare, the kitchen is more interested in cooking to please customers than to entertain itself. It is a 400-year-old grey-stone former farm building not far from Skipton, with colourful window-boxes, beamed ceilings, and log fires burning in winter. John Topham's menus are a world away from heritage pub cooking, as may be seen from the moment the appetiser arrives: a strongly flavoured chunk of jellied lamb pâté with fruity chutney one chilly night in June. Crisp tomato tart dressed with pesto, Parmesan and basil delivers bright flavours and good textural punch, not least from the frying of the basil leaves. Black pudding with a glaze of Lancashire cheese underneath a fillet of smoked haddock is equally cosmopolitan.

Attention to detail is in evidence throughout, as in roast loin of lamb with decent fat and plenty of earthy savour, combined with sweet dried tomatoes, roast garlic and top-notch dauphinoise. A pair who took the fish route enjoyed charred squid salad, followed by 'a beautiful piece of halibut in a red wine sauce.' Pastrywork is clearly a source of pride, to the extent that three out of five puddings may be tarts of one sort or another, the lemon version given a raspberry coulis, while the heavy-duty Yorkshire curd tart comes with cinnamon ice-cream. Well-trained staff lend the place an air of professionalism. The proprietors also own the General Tarleton at Ferrensby (see entry). The wine list goes in search of the best, and finds it primarily in Bordeaux, Burgundy and Italy. Prices are fair too, with ten house wines from France, Chile and Australia starting at £9.95 a bottle, £1.85 a glass. A long list of half-bottles rounds things off nicely. CELLARMAN'S CHOICE: Pouilly-Fumé, Dom. de Berthier 1996, Jean-Claude Dagueneau, £16.95; Volnay 'Les Angles' 1993, Lucien Boillot, £22.50.

CHEFS: John Topham and Richard Smith   PROPRIETORS: Denis and Juliet Watkins, and John Topham   OPEN: restaurant Sun L 12 to 2, Mon to Sat D 6 to 9.30; bar brasserie open all week 12 to 2.30, 6 to 10   CLOSED: 25 Dec, 1 Jan, 1 week Jan   MEALS: Set L Sun £19.50, Set D £28.95   SERVICE: not inc, card slips closed   CARDS: Amex, MasterCard, Switch, Visa   DETAILS: restaurant 54 seats; bar brasserie 60 seats. 45 seats outside. Private parties: 40 main room. Car park. Vegetarian meals. Children welcome. No-smoking area. Wheelchair access (1 step; also WC). No music. Air-conditioned   £5

HINDON Wiltshire   map 2

▲ *Grosvenor Arms* ⁵⁺ | **NEW ENTRY** |

High Street, Hindon SP3 6DJ   COOKING 4
TEL: (01747) 820696   FAX: (01747) 820869   COST £22–£43

Head for the crossroads in the centre of the village to find this L-shaped Georgian inn, the original roughcast walls rendered in plaster and painted white. A courtyard with trestle tables makes an appealing spot for benign-weather dining, and inside is sparely but stylishly decorated, the main feature a Venetian-blinded picture window into the kitchen, so you can watch them at it. Ownership is the same as at the Three Horseshoes (see entry, Batcombe), which brings its own kind of reassurance.

Paul Suter has been a chef since he was fresh out of school, and worked at various *Guide*-listed establishments in the south-west. Here he brings fresh, modern cooking to the country-pub ambience and makes a pretty impressive fist of it. Truffle oil goes into a dish of linguine with leeks, mushrooms, mustard and Pecorino, while salmon and prawns are presented rillettes-fashion and dressed with lemon and herbs. Fish is 'incredibly fresh and moist' – seared snapper fillet on stewed baby leeks with cherry tomatoes in a fish stock and cream sauce, for example – or there may be 'unbelievably tasty' stuffed roast saddle of local rabbit, parcelled up in Parma ham and cushioned on chive-speckled mash.

Desserts include passion-fruit délice on mango coulis, or poached pear with caramel sauce and cinnamon ice-cream. Service is 'amiable and forthcoming'. Wines are the same as those at Three Horseshoes, although there are far fewer half-bottles. France dominates the gently priced list, which opens with six house wines all at £9.95 a bottle, £2.50 a glass.

CHEF: Paul Suter   PROPRIETORS: Martin Tarr and Paul Toogood   OPEN: all week 12.30 to 2, 7 to 9.30 (10 Fri and Sat)   MEALS: alc (main courses £7 to £13)   SERVICE: not inc   CARDS: Delta, MasterCard, Switch, Visa   DETAILS: 60 seats. 30 seats outside. Private parties: 20 main room. Car park. Vegetarian meals. No children under 5. No smoking in dining-room. No music ACCOMMODATION: 7 rooms, all with bath/shower. TV. Phone. B&B £45 to £75. No children under 5. Dogs welcome. Afternoon teas   (£5)

HINTLESHAM Suffolk   map 6

▲ Hintlesham Hall 🍷 🍴

Hintlesham IP8 3NS
TEL: (01473) 652268   FAX: (01473) 652463   COOKING 4
on A1071, 4½m W of Ipswich   COST £32–£77

Return visitors find themselves impressed anew by this beautiful house. It divides into a number of comfortable drawing- and dining-rooms, decorated with traditional country-house paintings, Chinese carpets, huge mirrors and long curtains. 'Everything matches something else.' The food echoes some of the luxurious notes, too, in a caramelised escalope of foie gras with roasted figs, and a partnership of morels, asparagus and truffles with breast of guinea-fowl, for example. A range of menu options and prices reflects the choice of ingredients as much as workmanship: perhaps roast loin of lamb with grilled vegetables on the *carte*, and chump of lamb with pesto mash on the set-price lunch menu.

Contemporary techniques and ingredients abound, from confit of tuna to spicy fish-cakes, while warm chorizo finds its way variously into a monkfish starter and a dish of duck confit. There is usually one vegetarian dish per course – perhaps a deep-fried goats'-cheese pasta parcel, or a double-baked cheese soufflé made with Shropshire blue – and a savoury alternative to desserts of chocolate rice-pudding, mango tart or pineapple beignets. Staff are plentiful and mostly attentive, but service has had its ups and downs, and communication between kitchen and dining-room has gone awry. France forms the backbone of a carefully chosen list, although Spain is singled out for special attention and Italy deserves a mention too. Good drinking is to be had at all price levels, with a nicely varied bunch of house recommendations beginning at £12.90. CELLARMAN'S CHOICE: Verdicchio Casal di Serra 1996, Umani Ronchi, £15.05; Malbec 1992, Luigi Bosca, Argentina, £15.25.

CHEF: Alan Ford   PROPRIETOR: David Allan   OPEN: Sun to Fri L 12 to 1.45, all week D 7 to 9.30 MEALS: alc (main courses £17 to £24). Set L £19.50, Set D Sun to Thur £26. BYO £11, sparkling £15   SERVICE: not inc, card slips closed   CARDS: Amex, Diners, MasterCard, Switch, Visa DETAILS: 120 seats. Private parties: 81 main room, 16 to 81 private rooms. Car park. Vegetarian meals. Children welcome. No children under 10 at D. Jacket and tie. No smoking in dining-room. Wheelchair access (1 step; also WC). No music   ACCOMMODATION: 33 rooms, all with bath/shower. TV. Phone. B&B £89 to £300. Rooms for disabled. Children welcome. High teas for children. Swimming-pool (*The Which? Hotel Guide*)   (£5)

HINTON CHARTERHOUSE Bath & N.E. Somerset   map 2

▲ Homewood Park ⁵✗

Hinton Charterhouse BA3 6BB
TEL: (01225) 723731   FAX: (01225) 723820 | NEW CHEF |
off A36, 6m SE of Bath   COST £22–£80

Since the last edition of the *Guide*, Gary Jones has stepped on to the chefs'
merry-go-round and been whisked off to Waldo's at Cliveden (see entry,
Taplow). Andrew Hamer worked with him at this ivy-clad Georgian house for a
couple of years, after spells cooking on a yacht off America's east coast, and in the
British Virgin Islands for Richard Branson. Before that he worked his way up the
ladder at the Manoir (see entry, Great Milton), so we can safely assume he knows
his way round a kitchen, although his appointment came too late for us to receive
any feedback.

He oversees an ambitious *carte* that seems well supplied with truffles, caviare,
sweetbreads and a few seasonal materials, perhaps taking in raviolis of
langoustine with asparagus and samphire, followed by breast of Trelough
duckling with lentil mousse and caramelised apples, before warm poached pear
with vanilla blinis. The tasting menu is six courses plus the usual country-house
add-ons. House wines are £14.50. Reports please.

CHEF: Andrew Hamer   PROPRIETOR: Homewood Park   OPEN: all week 12 to 2, 7 to 9.30
MEALS: alc (main courses £23 to £26). Set L Mon to Sat £19.50, Set L Sun £22.50. Set D (Tasting
Menu) £52   SERVICE: not inc   CARDS: Amex, Delta, Diners, MasterCard, Switch, Visa
DETAILS: 60 seats. Private parties: 40 main room, 16 to 30 private rooms. Car park. Vegetarian
meals. Children's helpings. No smoking in dining-room. Wheelchair access (also WC). No
music   ACCOMMODATION: 19 rooms, all with bath/shower. TV. Phone. B&B £105 to £315.
Children welcome. Baby facilities. Guide dogs only. Afternoon teas. Garden. Swimming-pool
(*The Which? Hotel Guide*)

HOLT Norfolk   map 6

Yetman's ▾ ⁵✗

37 Norwich Road, Holt NR25 6SA   COOKING 4
TEL: (01263) 713320   COST £41–£52

Alison Yetman is 'a dedicated and original cook' who works in established
country mould from her low-ceilinged cottage. She concentrates on dinner, plus
Sunday lunch, and, although he 'doesn't waste words', Peter Yetman is an
'excellent' friendly host who ensures that everything runs smoothly. With brash
professional chefs ruling the cities, this more traditionally based cooking can
appear less flamboyant, but it is no less skilled. Many dishes are recognisably
from the British and French provincial repertoire – Jerusalem artichoke soup,
asparagus and Gruyère tart, steak and kidney pudding – and well-sourced
materials include grain-fed beef, free-range eggs (perhaps served on toasted
brioche with hollandaise), and local organic pork.

Grilling and roasting are favoured techniques for main courses, applied
equally to fish – maybe salmon, served with samphire – and interspersed with
perhaps poached turbot fillet with potted shrimp sauce. Cheeses are from Neal's
yard, and desserts are in the style of rhubarb crème brûlée, or muscat-poached

pears. Portions may be 'copious'. The well-designed wine list circumnavigates the globe in search of enjoyable, good-value bins to complement the food, and succeeds admirably. Sauvignon remains the most popular varietal, though Seresin has snatched the Kiwi crown from Cloudy Bay, while an English trio makes a welcome debut. An ever-changing group of wines by the glass starts at £3.50. CELLARMAN'S CHOICE: Seresin Sauvignon Blanc 1997, Marlborough, New Zealand, £16.75; Margaux, Ch. Labégorce 1992, £32.50.

CHEF: Alison Yetman   PROPRIETORS: Alison and Peter Yetman   OPEN: Sun L 12.30 to 1.30, Wed to Sat D (Mon in summer) 7.30 to 9 (9.30 Sat)   MEALS: Set L and D £22.75 (2 courses) to £31   SERVICE: not inc, card slips closed   CARDS: Amex, Delta, MasterCard, Switch, Visa DETAILS: 32 seats. Private parties: 20 main room, 10 private room. Vegetarian meals. Children's helpings. No smoking in dining-room. Wheelchair access (1 step; not WC). No music

---

HONLEY West Yorkshire   map 8

Mustard & Punch

6 Westgate, Honley HD7 2AA   COOKING 4
TEL: (01484) 662066   COST £25–£41

Mustard jars and *Punch* cartoons continue to set the tone in this quirkily decorated bistro-style restaurant with its wooden floors, checked cloths and hats on the ceiling. Despite a few quibbles about the service, all are in agreement about the quality of the food. The two-course fixed-price lunch menu is remarkable value, and promises distinctive flavours with plenty of texture and colour. 'Soldiers' of prawn and sesame toasts stationed neatly around a pile of sweet-and-sour vegetables were deemed 'a great success', while baked pike quenelles with shellfish bisque and rich, dark rabbit stew with fluffy herb dumplings suggest a kitchen that is equally at home with refinement and big, earthy gestures.

Evening meals have also convinced reporters, particularly those with a penchant for multi-ethnic themes. Marinated roast duck breast with a spring roll and Chinese flavourings was a bold attempt at fusion food, while a brochette of king prawns and monkfish spiced with cumin and coriander, served with soured lime cream and 'nutty' Basmati rice took one reporter back to his 'first visits to curry houses in the early sixties'. Rounding things off are decent desserts such prune and armagnac tart, or gin and tonic sorbet. On Friday evenings the restaurant is given over to a fish menu and every few months there are special jazz dinners with live music. The wine list runs to three dozen bins with a global outlook, including plenty of modern New World stuff at keen prices. Chilean house wine is £9.50.

CHEFS: Christopher Dunn and Andrew Wood   PROPRIETORS: Anna Young and Dorota Pencak OPEN: Tue to Fri L 12 to 2, Tue to Sat D 7 to 10   CLOSED: 25 Dec   MEALS: alc (main courses £9.50 to £15). Set L £5.95 (2 courses), Set D Tue to Thur £13.50 (2 courses)   SERVICE: not inc CARDS: MasterCard, Switch, Visa   DETAILS: 54 seats. Vegetarian meals. Children's helpings. No cigars/pipes in dining-room. Music

---

▲ *means accommodation is available.*

HORNCASTLE Lincolnshire   map 9

Magpies ▉ ⅍

| 71–75 East Street, Horncastle LN9 6AA | COOKING 4 |
| TEL: (01507) 527004   FAX: (01507) 524064 | COST £21–£42 |

Magpies is in one of the town's older buildings, a low-ceilinged, cottagey place on the coast road. The Lees have nearly a decade under their belts here, and have created a relaxed atmosphere dedicated to enjoyment: 'certainly not the sort of place where you feel obliged to talk in whispers,' as one noted with relief. Matthew and Simon Lee draw influences from today's best-loved cooking styles, but adhere firmly to established principles, rather than going for the experimental approach. Thus, roast scallops come with chive velouté, chicken liver parfait with red onion marmalade, and brandy and cream are stirred into crab bisque. 'Pink and tasty' rack of lamb with flageolet beans, garlic confit and rosemary and Madeira jus was ideal for a November diner, as was his light, but enjoyable bread-and-butter pudding with calvados ice-cream. Duck may well be sourced from Normandy, and come with Puy lentils and port sauce, although the beef is Lincolnshire through and through, and classically sauced with shallots, mushrooms and red wine.

To finish, there may be nougat glacé fashioned into a pyramid and garnished with orange and passion-fruit, or 'excellent' chocolate marquise. Service is 'friendly and prompt'. Quality walks hand in hand with interest and variety in a global wine list that features enough gems to attract the eye (and beak) of any passing magpie. Non-feathered collectors will be equally attracted by the fair prices. French house wines are £10. CELLARMAN'S CHOICE: Montagny *premier cru* 1996, Jean-Marc Boillot, £24; Châteauneuf-du-Pape 1994, Dom. du Vieux Télégraphe, £26.

CHEFS: Matthew and Simon Lee   PROPRIETORS: the Lee family   OPEN: Tue to Fri L 12.30 to 2, Tue to Sat D 7.15 to 10.30   CLOSED: Restricted opening Jan, 2 weeks Aug   MEALS: alc (main courses £8 to £14). Set D £22 (2 courses) to £25   SERVICE: not inc   CARDS: Delta, MasterCard, Visa   DETAILS: 40 seats. Private parties: 40 main room. Vegetarian meals. Children's helpings. No smoking in dining-room. Music (£5)

HORNDON ON THE HILL Essex   map 3

▲ *Bell Inn* ⅍

High Road, Horndon on the Hill SS17 8LD	
TEL: (01375) 642463 FAX: (01375) 361611	
off M25 at junction 30/31, signposted Thurrock,	COOKING 2
Lakeside; take A13, then B1007 to Horndon	COST £26–£41

The five-centuries-old Bell wears its history like a glove: stories are told of a heretic burned at the stake in the courtyard during Mary Tudor's reign, while the interior is all exposed beams and panelling. Tables are laid out in the busy bar, or you can book a place in the vaulted dining-room. One menu applies throughout and is peppered with dishes that speak emphatically of the present. Colourful ideas abound. Scallops are served with black pasta and orange butter sauce, fillets of red mullet are bedded on pak choi greens with an oriental sauce. Away from fish, the kitchen also delivers calf's-liver mousse with black pudding salad, stuffed pig's trotter, and spiced confit of duck with honey, soy and roast parsnips. Desserts could take in orange steamed pudding or chocolate parfait drizzled with Earl Grey. The Bell is noted for its range of real ales; otherwise the well-chosen list of around 100 wines features 13 by the glass. Australian house wines are £9.50 a bottle.

CHEF: Sean Kelly   PROPRIETORS: John and Christine Vereker   OPEN: Sun to Fri L 12 to 1.45, all week D 7 to 9.45   CLOSED: 25 and 26 Dec   MEALS: alc (main courses £10 to £13.50)   SERVICE: not inc, card slips closed   CARDS: Amex, Delta, MasterCard, Switch, Visa   DETAILS: 80 seats. 36 seats outside. Private parties: 10 main room, 26 and 36 private rooms. Car park. Vegetarian meals. Children's helpings. No smoking in dining-room. No music   ACCOMMODATION: 14 rooms, all with bath/shower. TV. Phone. Room only £50 to £75. Rooms for disabled. Children welcome. Baby facilities. Dogs welcome (*The Which? Hotel Guide*)

HORTON Northamptonshire   map 5

French Partridge 🍷 ⁵✻

Horton NN7 2AP
TEL: (01604) 870033   FAX: (01604) 870032   COOKING 6
on B526, 6m SE of Northampton   COST £33–£40

The Partridges have been going for so long at this white-fronted house with 'burnished copper' nameplate – they started in 1963 – that they don't so much follow trends as wait patiently for them to come round again. Thus there is no jazzy décor, just green walls, brown curtains and black banquette seating, there are no nibbles in the bar, and no appetisers or presents from the chef at table. The intermediate course is not the boring old soup-or-sorbet routine either, but real food: typically a fish option such as grilled tuna with oriental spicing, or a first-rate puff pastry tart, perhaps with tomatoes, feta cheese and herbs. This is one of four courses (portions are well judged) that make dinners such extremely good value.

Despite occasional forays into exotica, the cooking has the strong stamp of regional France about it: not just in individual dishes, although there is no shortage of them – braised lamb shank with garlicky flageolet beans, or pigeon breasts with Puy lentils and bacon – but also in spirit. This is a family affair, with two generations in the kitchen, distaff side out front, and an air of simple honesty pervading the workmanship: pounding and sieving to make potted tongue, turning pheasant into sausages, or stuffing a chicken breast with cream cheese, butter and garlic to rescue a classic Kiev from its awful pre-packed reputation.

Pastrywork is impressive, not least among desserts such as apple tart, and the kitchen is not above an occasional piece of whimsy: a tongue-in-cheek Bertie Bassett's liquorice ice-cream, surrounded by tiny liquorice all-sorts in a crème anglaise. 'I really enjoy drinking wine here because I know I'm not being ripped off,' wrote one reporter, and prices on the Partridges' estimable list are indeed fair. The wines themselves are a great source of contentment: a canny selection from France and Germany (with a sole contribution from England), backed-up by some fine New World bins; 'stickies' are particularly appealing. House wines start at £10. CELLARMAN'S CHOICE: St-Véran 1995, Jean Manciat, £15; Marsannay 'Les Ouzeloy' 1992, Joseph Roty, £16.

CHEFS: David and Justin Partridge PROPRIETORS: David and Mary Partridge OPEN: Tue to Sat D 7.30 to 9 CLOSED: 2 weeks Christmas, 2 weeks Easter, 3 weeks mid-July to Aug MEALS: Set D £26 to £27 SERVICE: net prices CARDS: none DETAILS: 50 seats. Private parties: 10 main room. Car park. Children welcome. No smoking in dining-room. Wheelchair access (not WC). No music (£5)

HOVE East Sussex   map 3

Quentin's   NEW ENTRY

42 Western Road, Hove BN3 1JD   COOKING 1
TEL: (01273) 822734   COST £28–£34

'Hove, actually,' is the in-joke cry of local residents when asked if they live in Brighton, lumped in unitary splendour as one entity since last year. Quentin's is at the very-definitely-Hove end of the Western Road, which starts in central Brighton. That said, there are certainly no frills in the décor, which is dominated by jumbled heavy furniture, bare floorboards and sepulchral lighting. Quentin Fitch cooks in the modern idiom, marinating chargrilled chicken breast in lime juice, star anise and honey, or keeping things simple with an asparagus-topped red onion tart served with salads. Fish varies according to the day's catch (the seafront is only a block away), while duck breast with a parsnip rösti at inspection was a well-conceived dish, deriving richness from a burgundy sauce. Chocolate and orange bombe delivers explosive flavour, or there may be a version of crème brûlée. Service is friendly and efficient. The brief wine list lingers largely in France and, should you have £185 spare, offers '83 Latour. House French is £9.95.

CHEF: Quentin Fitch PROPRIETORS: Quentin and Candy Fitch OPEN: Tue to Fri L 12 to 2, Tue to Sat D 7 to 9.30 (10 Sat) CLOSED: last week Aug, first week Sept, bank hols MEALS: alc L (main courses £13). Set L £6.95 (1 course) to £18.95, Set D £16.95 (2 courses) to £18.95 SERVICE: not inc CARDS: Amex, Delta, Diners, MasterCard, Switch, Visa DETAILS: 28 seats. Private parties: 8 main room, 20 private room. Vegetarian meals. No infants at D. No cigars/pipes in dining-room. Wheelchair access (not WC). Music. Air-conditioned

---

HOVINGHAM North Yorkshire   map 9

▲ Worsley Arms ⁵⃨

Hovingham YO6 4LA   COOKING 2
TEL: (01653) 628234 FAX: (01653) 628130   COST £24–£46

Built by Sir William Worsley in 1841 as the centrepiece for a spa that never materialised, this broad-fronted inn has recently found a new lease of life. The place now wears two hats. Those looking for casual, bistro-style meals in a setting redolent of willow and leather should head for the Cricketers Bistro: here you will find anything from sandwiches and creative salads (sauté chorizo sausage, potatoes, sun-dried tomatoes, olives and deep-fried capers) to braised ham shank with pease pudding, or confit of salmon with buttered pasta. Grander gestures appear in the main dining-room, where chef Andrew Jones steers a course between fillets of Yorkshire beef with wild mushrooms, and seared sea bass with braised baby fennel and mussels. Desserts are 'well-presented' offerings along the lines of glazed lemon tart with clotted cream, or chocolate marquise. Sunday lunch is clearly popular with the Yorkshire set, although reports have been mixed. Around 60 well-spread wines are augmented by a cluster of half-bottles. Own-label house wines are £11.50.

CHEF: Andrew Jones   PROPRIETOR: Euan Rodger   OPEN: bistro all week 12 to 2, 7 to 9.30 (9 Sun); restaurant Sun L 12 to 2 (also Mon to Sat by arrangement), all week D 7 to 9.30   MEALS: bistro alc (main courses £8 to £15); restaurant Set L £16, Set D £25. BYO £6.50   SERVICE: not inc, card slips closed   CARDS: Amex, Delta, Diners, MasterCard, Switch, Visa   DETAILS: 40 seats. 20 seats outside. Private parties: 60 main room, 10 and 40 private rooms. Car park. Vegetarian meals. Children's helpings. No smoking in dining-room. Wheelchair access (not WC). Occasional music   ACCOMMODATION: 18 rooms, all with bath/shower. TV. Phone. B&B £60 to £90. Rooms for disabled. Children welcome. High teas for children. Baby facilities. Dogs in bedrooms only. Afternoon teas (*The Which? Hotel Guide*)   (£5)

HUDDERSFIELD West Yorkshire   map 9

Bradley's £

84 Fitzwilliam Street, Huddersfield HD1 5BB   COOKING 2
TEL: (01484) 516773   FAX: (01484) 538386   COST £13–£41

Stained-glass windows and ornately carved wood contrast with metal ceiling slats and recessed lights in Andrew Bradley's split-level bistro just out of Huddersfield town centre. Friendliness, a buzzy atmosphere and, above all, 'superb' value for money are keys to its success. The early-bird menu remains an outstanding bargain – especially as the price includes half a bottle of wine. Even more financially enticing is the set lunch: the blackboard promises generous, well-tried bistro-style dishes such as Mexican burritos, or cream of vegetable soup, before sauté chicken drumsticks (three of them) in a skilfully crafted mushroom and tarragon sauce, or Cumberland sausage with orange and thyme. Desserts also show up favourably: nuttily textured walnut and poppy-seed sponge, or cherry cheesecake with raspberry coulis, for example. Those wishing to delve into the *carte* will find plenty to please in the shape of aubergine caviar, rump of lamb with rosemary-scented ratatouille, and fillet of salmon with basil tagliatelle. The wine list is a serviceable selection at realistic prices. House wine is £9.25.

CHEFS: Jonathan Nichols and Glen Varley   PROPRIETORS: Andrew Bradley and Jonathan Nichols   OPEN: Mon to Fr L 12 to 2, Mon to Sat D 6 to 10 (10.30 Fri and Sat)   CLOSED: bank hols   MEALS: alc (main courses £8.50 to £15). Set L £5.90, Set D 6 to 7.30 (7 Sat) £13.50 (inc wine). BYO £5   SERVICE: not inc   CARDS: Delta, MasterCard, Switch, Visa   DETAILS: 65 seats. Private parties: 65 main room. Car park (D only). Vegetarian meals. Children's helpings. Wheelchair access (not WC). Music. Air-conditioned

---

Café Pacific £

3 Viaduct Street, Huddersfield HD1 5DL   COOKING 3
TEL: (01484) 559055   COST £19–£32

Underneath the arches in Viaduct Street is this vibrant open-plan café where food is definitely the main attraction. The kitchen looks worldwide for ideas and inspiration, with much attention focused on the Mediterranean and Far East.

Diverse cultures sit happily together in the shape of roast stuffed peppers in herbed filo pastry with aloo gobi, or loin of lamb with vegetable tempura and bang-bang dressing. Elsewhere, you might find tabbouleh salad with merguez sausage, harissa and lemon, or burrito of re-fried beans, salsa and Monterey Jack cheeses, or even confit of duck with stir-fried slaw, ginger and soy. Then it's back home for black pudding, caramelised shallots and toffee apples, fish-cakes with parsley sauce, and ribeye steak and chips. Desserts are equally eclectic, ranging from Belgian chocolate bread-and-butter pudding to vin santo, raisin and meringue bombe. The helpfulness and caring attitude of staff has come in for high praise. A 30-strong wine list goes for the New World in a big way, and prices are kind on the wallet. House wine is £8.95.

CHEF/PROPRIETOR: Scott Hessel   OPEN: Tue to Fri 12 to 2.30, Tue to Sat 6 to 10 (10.30 Fri and Sat)   MEALS: alc (main courses £7 to £11). Set D Tue to Thur and 6 to 7.30 Fri and Sat £11.50 SERVICE: not inc   CARDS: Delta, MasterCard, Switch, Visa   DETAILS: 55 seats. Private parties: 70 main room. Vegetarian meals. Children's helpings. Wheelchair access (not WC). Music. Air-conditioned

▲ *Lodge Hotel* ♈ ✻

48 Birkby Lodge Road, Birkby,
Huddersfield HD2 2BG   COOKING 3
TEL: (01484) 431001   FAX: (01484) 421590   COST £23–£48

The Lodge is a substantial stone-built house in the prosperous suburb of Birkby, with an oak-panelled lounge, real fire and some interesting art nouveau features, including a 'remarkable' chandelier, in the dining-room. It benefits from being family-run – Mr Birley is a 'cheerful, knowledgeable' front-of-house man – and is considered good value for money. Dinner is four courses and, apart from a mid-meal soup or sorbet, offers half a dozen choices at each stage, perhaps starting with ravioli of lobster and crab in a clear seafood broth, or a twice-baked blue-cheese soufflé on a 'fruitily dressed' salad garnished with a fan of poached pear.

Seasoning and timing are well handled, and good materials show through, as in a roast squab pigeon ('one of the larger, more tender French-style birds') served with wild mushrooms and shallots, or saddle of lamb – 'full of spring lamb flavour' – that came with a rather 'jammy' sauce of stock, blackcurrants and honey. The cheeseboard is 'well above average', and there is a generous choice of dessert wines by the glass to accompany caramel-glazed rice-pudding, chilled pineapple soufflé, or warm bitter chocolate tart. The all-embracing, helpfully annotated wine list offers good-value drinking at all price levels, with the odd gem here and there raising excitement levels. House wines are £10.95 or £11.25. CELLARMAN'S CHOICE: Cloudy Bay Chardonnay 1996, Marlborough, New Zealand, £24.95; Pinot Noir 1996, Michel Laroche, Corsica £11.95.

'One of the new dishes was the most outlandish thing I have seen on a British menu for many years, unless you count ham, pineapple and sweetcorn pizza. How anyone could come up with a combination like that, unless on drugs or strong blue cheese late at night, beats me.' (On eating in Berkshire)

CHEFS: Garry and Kevin Birley, and Richard Hanson   PROPRIETORS: Garry and Kevin Birley
OPEN: Mon to Fri and Sun L 12 to 2, Mon to Sat D 7.30 to 9.30   MEALS: Set L £10.95 (2 courses)
to £13.95, Set D £23.95 to £26   SERVICE: not inc, card slips closed   CARDS: Amex, Delta,
Diners, MasterCard, Visa   DETAILS: 82 seats. 20 seats outside. Private parties: 62 main room,
10 to 24 private rooms. Car park. Vegetarian meals. Children's helpings. No smoking in
dining-room. Wheelchair access (also WC). Music   ACCOMMODATION: 13 rooms, all with
bath/shower. TV. Phone. B&B £60 to £80. Children welcome. Baby facilities. Afternoon teas
(*The Which? Hotel Guide*)   £5

Thorpe Grange Manor   NEW ENTRY

Thorpe Lane, Almondbury, Huddersfield HD5 8TA
TEL/FAX: (01484) 425115   COOKING 5
off A629, 2m E of Huddersfield   COST £22–£47

After three years at Raymond Blanc's Manoir aux Quat' Saisons (see entry, Great
Milton), 24-year-old Jason Neilson has opened his own manor, a couple of miles
outside Huddersfield. A spacious and secluded eighteenth-century house
surrounded by rolling lawns, it is an imposing showcase for the talents of so
young a chef, but by all accounts his abilities match his ambition. 'One of the
most exciting ventures to hit Huddersfield,' commented one reporter, after
visiting it three times in as many weeks.

Menus are light, modern and restrained, yet the classical training is evident in
refined, well-flavoured sauces that accompany most dishes: honey and lime jus
with slow-roasted guinea-fowl, light beetroot dressing with terrine of Cornish
crab, or, on a richer note, Madeira sauce with a mille-feuille of wild mushrooms.
A first-class assiette of Yorkshire lamb incorporates tender loin chops, slim slices
of liver and kidney and a 'nice thick chunk of saddle, just flavour through and
through', set off by a potato and black olive purée and a 'brilliant' sauce made
from the reduced meat juices. The light touch continues with desserts: a 'not
over-rich' truffle of chocolate on a delicately orange-scented crème anglaise, or
poached mango and rice-pudding, its intense flavours balanced by passion-fruit
coulis. Extras, too, are well up to scratch, from squidgy home-made foccacia
bread laden with sun-dried tomatoes to good coffee and petits fours. Service is
friendly and attentive without being obtrusive. The wine list features plenty of
mid-range offerings, plus a choice of six house wines at £9.95.

CHEF: Jason Neilson   PROPRIETORS: Ronald, Gillian and Jason Neilson, and Ruth Woods
OPEN: Tue to Fri and Sun L 12 to 2, Tue to Sat D 7 (6 Tue to Thur) to 10   CLOSED: bank hols
MEALS: alc (main courses £14 to £16). Set L £12.50 (2 courses) to £14.95, Set D £19.95
SERVICE: not inc   CARDS: Delta, MasterCard, Switch, Visa   DETAILS: 65 seats. 20 seats outside.
Private parties: 80 main room. Car park. Vegetarian meals. Children's helpings. No cigars/pipes
in dining-room. Wheelchair access (also WC). Music   £5

✑ *indicates that there has been a change of chef since last year's* Guide, *and the Editor
has judged that the change is of sufficient interest to merit the reader's attention.*

If a restaurant is new to the Guide *this year (did not appear as a main entry in the last
edition),* NEW ENTRY *appears opposite its name.*

HUNSTRETE Bath & N.E. Somerset   map 2

▲ *Hunstrete House* 🥪 ✳

Hunstrete, Chelwood BS39 4NS
TEL: (01761) 490490   FAX: (01761) 490732   COOKING 5
off A368, 4m S of Keynsham   COST £34–£83

The house is a low, pale-stone building just off the main road, with a courtyard
for al fresco eating. Three or four comfortable lounges, with log fires and old
pictures, look out on to parkland and grazing deer, though mock Greek pillars
make the dining-room seem more classically inclined. Stewart Eddy took over
the stoves shortly after the last edition of the *Guide* appeared, but the kitchen's
focus remains a generous *carte*, supplemented by a seven-course tasting menu
and simpler lunches.

The food is modern, some of it highly wrought, much of it refined, and nearly
all of it looking good: a 'stunning' terrine of just-seared salmon, for example,
sitting on a vegetable 'escabeche' of broad beans, tomato flesh and carrot, all
infused with the taste of orange, fennel and dill. Dishes are technically
impressive, and sometimes very busy, as in a starter of roast langoustines with
wafer-thin slices of dried tomato, deep-fried courgettes, parsley and basil, plus a
host of other accoutrements; or in a main course of trimmed best end of lamb,
with small mounds of garlicky kidney and sweetbread. Cheeses are a feature,
with their own 'menu', and desserts have included espresso ice-cream with
mocha sauce, and vanilla crème brûlée.

Meals begin with olives, nibbles and perhaps a coffee cup of frothy soup, and
end with petits fours, though some materials could be improved, and our
inspector left wondering exactly who, at these prices, the food was intended for.
Wines reflect the ambition of the restaurant rather than everyday needs, with
relatively few bottles under £20, although house Bordeaux is £14.95.

CHEF: Stewart Eddy   PROPRIETORS: Mr and Mrs M.H. Fentum   OPEN: all week 12 to 2, 7 to
9.30   MEALS: alc (main courses £24.50 to £25.50). Set L £19.95, menu Dégustation £55
SERVICE: not inc   CARDS: Amex, Delta, Diners, MasterCard, Switch, Visa   DETAILS: 70 seats. 16
seats outside. Private parties: 50 main room, 14 and 30 private rooms. Car park. Vegetarian
meals. Children's helpings. No smoking in dining-room. Wheelchair access (not WC). No music.
Air-conditioned   ACCOMMODATION: 23 rooms, all with bath/shower. TV. Phone. D,B&B £98 to
£250. Children welcome. High teas for children. No dogs. Afternoon teas. Swimming-pool (*The
Which? Hotel Guide*)

HURSTBOURNE TARRANT Hampshire   map 2

▲ *Esseborne Manor* 🍸 🥪

Hurstbourne Tarrant SP11 0ER
TEL: (01264) 736444   FAX: (01264) 736725   COOKING 5
on A343, 1½m N of Hurstbourne Tarrant   COST £29–£53

The manor is a small but beautiful rural house set in an immaculate garden, high
on the Wessex Downs. Chintzy chairs in the drawing-room, a 'bright and airy'
dining-room stretching the length of the house, and fresh flowers everywhere
add up to the feel of 'elegance'. Ben Tunnicliffe has taken over the stoves since
the last edition of the *Guide* and, despite one or two disappointments in the

meantime, the latest we have is that he is acquitting himself well, serving a short set-price menu (not available Fridays and Saturdays) and a *carte*.

Contemporary ideas abound, from a starter of oven-dried tomatoes with lime leaves and grilled halloumi cheese, to barbecued duck with mango salsa. Among fish and vegetable dishes that have won applause are a layered lobster and lasagne starter with 'intensely flavoured' lobster stock, sea bass with niçoise sauce, and a light saffron and leek bavarois on a base of lentils and red pepper. Vegetables are the same for all, apart from boiled potatoes with fish, and gratin dauphinois with meat. Desserts have included a plate of four chocolate puddings, one of them an 'out of this world' soufflé in an egg cup. 'Pleasant, charming' waitresses do a good job, and wines are offered without any pressure. France takes pride of place on a list which continues to combine quality with mostly fair prices, while judicious selections from the New World supplement the range of flavours. Half a dozen house wines start at £13.50 a bottle, £3 a glass.

CHEF: Ben Tunnicliffe PROPRIETOR: Ian Hamilton OPEN: all week 12 to 2, 7 to 9.30 MEALS: alc (main courses £12 to £19). Set L and D Sun to Thur £17 SERVICE: not inc, card slips closed CARDS: Amex, Delta, Diners, MasterCard, Switch, Visa DETAILS: 35 seats. 30 seats outside. Private parties: 45 main room, 12 private room. Car park. Vegetarian meals. Children's helpings.Wheelchair access (also women's WC). Occasional music ACCOMMODATION: 15 rooms, all with bath/shower. TV. Phone. B&B £88 to £135. Rooms for disabled. Children welcome. High teas for children. No dogs in public rooms. Afternoon teas (*The Which? Hotel Guide*) (£5)

HUXHAM Devon   map 1

▲ *Barton Cross* 🍴✳

Huxham, Stoke Canon EX5 4EJ
TEL: (01392) 841245   FAX: (01392) 841942   COOKING 2
on A396 to Tiverton, 4m N of Exeter   COST £35–£41

'Seventeenth-century charm with twentieth-century luxury,' promises the brochure promoting the Hamiltons' personally run hotel. The setting consists of three renovated and modernised thatched cottages built around a courtyard garden. Inside is a galleried dining-room where guests can enjoy Paul George Bending's creditable cooking. His fixed-price dinner menus (two or three courses) are defined by the seasons, and the kitchen takes its work seriously. In spring you might begin with ravioli of Cornish crab in mussel, leek and white wine sauce, while in autumn you might choose wild-mushroom tart topped with foie gras. A home-made sorbet or soup precedes main courses, which could range from roasted noisettes of spring lamb and kidneys wrapped in Parma ham and served on rosemary mash, to fillets of sea bass and salmon with Chinese spices. To finish, there are home-made ices, cappuccino crème brûlée or blackberry crêpe soufflé. Around 100 well-annotated wines provide plenty of sound drinking at fair prices. House wines start at £9.25.

NEW CHEF   *is shown instead of a cooking mark where a change of chef occurred too late for a new assessment of the cooking.*

CHEF: Paul George Bending   PROPRIETORS: Brian and Gina Hamilton   OPEN: Mon to Sat D only 6.30 to 9.30 (10.30 Sat)   MEALS: alc (main courses £14.50). Set D £20.50 (2 courses) to £25 SERVICE: not inc, card slips closed   CARDS: Amex, Delta, MasterCard, Switch, Visa   DETAILS: 50 seats. 12 seats outside. Private parties: 50 main room, 10 to 12 private rooms. Car park. Vegetarian meals. Children's helpings. No smoking in dining-room. Wheelchair access (also WC). Occasional music   ACCOMMODATION: 8 rooms, all with bath/shower. TV. Phone. B&B £55 to £95. Rooms for disabled. Children welcome. Baby facilities   (£5)

HYTHE Hampshire   map 2

Boathouse

29 Shamrock Way, Hythe Marina Village,
Hythe SO45 6DY | NEW CHEF |
TEL: (01703) 845594   FAX: (01703) 846017   COST £23–£49

This marina brasserie overlooking the Solent is hearteningly free of pretence. It consists of an open-plan dining-room and bar with a relaxed atmosphere and casually dressed staff. There is 'not a tie in sight' and, given the boating backdrop, customers might appear in anything from shorts to sou'westers. Cathal Leonard, who has worked with previous chef Ian McAndrew, took over the stoves just as the *Guide* was going to press, too late for us to receive any feedback. But we would be surprised if fish does not continue to feature on the contemporary British menu, with its brasserie fare of smoked haddock with champ and poached egg, grilled red mullet with couscous and vierge dressing, and apple and raisin crumble. A short list of young wines offers some interesting bottles under £20, particularly from Italy. Prices start at £9.75.

CHEF: Cathal Leonard   PROPRIETOR: Leisure Great Britain (Oakley) Ltd   OPEN: Tue to Sun L 12 to 2.30, Tue to Sat D 7 to 10   CLOSED: bank hols   MEALS: alc (main courses L £8 to £10, D £10 to £16). Set L Tue to Sat (2 courses) £10.50. BYO £5   SERVICE: not inc   CARDS: Delta, MasterCard, Switch, Visa   DETAILS: 50 seats. 25 seats outside. Private parties: 70 main room, 12 private room. Children welcome. Wheelchair access (also WC). Music   (£5)

ILKLEY West Yorkshire   map 8

Box Tree ▮ ✸

37 Church Street, Ilkley LS29 9DR   COOKING 8
TEL: (01943) 608484   FAX: (01943) 607186   COST £37–£66

Considered 'quaint, tiny, ornate and dated', this eighteenth-century farmhouse is also 'elegant and sumptuous', with display cabinets of Wedgwood china, elaborately framed pictures of the Yorkshire Dales, and close-set tables in the narrow dining-room. Set-price menus have gone, and all meals are now à la carte, but the food remains simply conceived with a clear focus: cream of carrot soup with goats'-cheese ravioli, sauté snails with garlic purée and parsley sauce, or roast rump of veal with mushrooms and grain mustard sauce. Vegetarian options might include tagliatelle with poached egg and truffle sauce, or feuilleté of wild mushrooms with pesto.

'Spasmodic signs of brilliance' emanate from the kitchen, not least among first courses of poached oysters with an 'intense and superb' oyster mousseline, or expertly sauté scallops 'full of flavour', served with a gingery, peppery, lemon-grassy chutney of apples, pears and pineapple. There is a feeling that main courses have been 'almost a lecture in what food should be rather than a simple meal that one should enjoy', with reports commonly referring to the small portion size, even though the principal materials generally find favour: extremely young spring lamb, or 'beautifully cooked' turbot, for example.

Puddings appear to be uniformly 'brilliant', from a 'perfectly cooked' raspberry soufflé served with a jug of purée, to a 'simple, fresh, tangy' dish of poached strawberries in a caramelised orange sauce. 'The rhubarb mousse-cum-brûlée was so good we ordered another one between us.' Service has let the side down seriously on occasion, but wines would go a long way towards reinstating the *entente cordiale*. The vast list features great Australians and Italians as well as the more expected first-class French bottles. Prices can reach four figures, but there are around 70 bins under £20 and a good number by the glass from £3. CELLARMAN'S CHOICE Bourgogne Blanc 1996, Jean Yves Devevey, £15; Bourgogne Rouge 'Les Bons Batons' 1996, Dom. Michele et Patrice Rion, £14.

CHEF: Thierry LePrêtre-Granet PROPRIETOR: The Box Tree Restaurant (Ilkley) Ltd OPEN: Tue to Sun L 12 to 2.30, Tue to Sat D 7 to 10 MEALS: alc (main courses £12.50 to £20) SERVICE: not inc CARDS: Amex, MasterCard, Switch, Visa DETAILS: 50 seats. Private parties: 16 main room. Vegetarian meals. Children welcome. No smoking in dining-room. Wheelchair access (not WC). Occasional music

---

IPSWICH Suffolk   map 6

Mortimer's on the Quay ✣ £

Wherry Quay, Ipswich IP4 1AS   COOKING 2
TEL/FAX: (01473) 230225   COST £17–£42

On a sunny day views out to the marina are exceedingly 'picturesque', noted one reporter who found his way to this likeable restaurant on Wherry Quay. Fresh fish – mostly from suppliers in Grimsby – is the reason for coming here: the kitchen makes no concessions towards meat eaters, although vegetarians are not excluded. The printed menu is supplemented by a list of blackboard specials and choice is determined by the market. Some dishes are fixtures: potted shrimps, marinated herrings with assorted flavourings, crab pâté, and smoked salmon with scrambled eggs continue to find favour as starters. The rest is classic fish cookery of the old school: a combination of fresh flavours and abundant sauces. Chargrilled turbot with béarnaise, fillet of salmon florentine, and monkfish with tomato, onion and fennel are typically well-received offerings. Puddings are creamy and alcoholic, ranging from chocolate pot laced with rum to blackcurrant bavarois with cassis. There are some very respectable names on the 60-strong wine list, especially among whites. House wine is £8.50.

Report forms are at the back of the book; write a letter if you prefer; or email us at guidereports@which.co.uk.

CHEFS: Kenneth Ambler and Eric Kerta PROPRIETOR: Kenneth Ambler OPEN: Mon to Fri L 12 to 2, Mon to Sat D 6.30 to 9 (8.30 Mon) CLOSED: 23 Dec to 5 Jan MEALS: alc (main courses £7 to £18). BYO £3 SERVICE: not inc CARDS: Amex, Delta, Diners, MasterCard, Switch, Visa DETAILS: 85 seats. Private parties: 15 main room, 25 private room. Vegetarian meals. Children's helpings. No smoking in 1 dining-room. Wheelchair access (1 step; not WC). No music (£5)

Scott's Brasserie

4A Orwell Place, Ipswich IP4 1BB   COOKING 3
TEL: (01473) 230254   FAX: (01473) 218851   COST £28–£34

Enter the smallish bar, where snacks and light bites can be taken during the week (Caesar salad, say, a club sandwich, or steak and chips), walk to the back and ascend the stairs to an attractive first-floor brasserie bedecked with watercolours, copper pan lids and abundant greenery. Scott Davidson offers good-value set menus providing plenty to tease the palate along the way. Dishes such as baked snails with smoked garlic and coriander butter, or a cassoulet of venison, Scotch beef and wild mushrooms are supplemented by specials along the lines of langoustine bisque, grilled skate wing with lime and honey dressing, and wild boar sausages with braised red cabbage, caraway, red onion and wine sauce. Desserts tend towards richness, as in bread-and-butter pudding, coffee cream profiteroles, and blackberry and mascarpone crème brûlée. The majority of the 30 wines on the list derive from France, although there is a sprinkling from elsewhere. House wine is £9.95.

CHEF: Scott Davidson PROPRIETORS: Charles Lewis and Scott Davidson OPEN: Mon to Fri L 12 to 2.45, Mon to Sat D 6.30 to 10 CLOSED: bank hols MEALS: Set L and D £14.95 (2 courses) to £18.95. BYO £5. Bar food available SERVICE: not inc; 10% for parties of 8 or more CARDS: Amex, Delta, MasterCard, Switch, Visa DETAILS: 70 seats. Private parties: 36 main room, 28 to 36 private rooms. Vegetarian meals. No children under 14. No cigars/pipes in dining-room. Music (£5)

IXWORTH Suffolk   map 6

Theobalds ❢ ⅝✳

68 High Street, Ixworth IP31 2HJ   COOKING 4
TEL/FAX: (01359) 231707   COST £29–£52

Exposed timbers, beams and an inglenook fireplace point to the house's venerable age. Built in 1650, on the village's main street, it is substantial enough in its present incarnation to accommodate generously sized and well-spaced tables. Menus roll gently from one season to the next, and make an impression for their variety, which typically takes in shellfish starters of poached mussels or grilled scallops, perhaps grilled goats' cheese with aubergine and pesto, and usually a twice-baked cheese soufflé; even the fixed-price lunch offers around half a dozen items per course.

Despite an occasional foray into spicy Szechuan prawns and scallops, or braised peppers with couscous and coriander sauce, Simon Theobald's English country approach deals largely in traditional ideas such as breast of duck with cinnamon apples and calvados sauce, or 'tender and rich' roast partridge with bacon and wild mushrooms. Alcohol courses through the sauces – Madeira for venison, Beaujolais for calf's liver – and also turns up in chocolate truffle cake with Cointreau sauce, and Grand Marnier mousse, though not in crème caramel. Home-baked bread and fine petits fours add to the appeal, service is 'knowledgeable, unobtrusive, attentive', and wines are a worldly bunch, arranged simply by colour and price. The specially recommended bottles (about half the total) are succinctly annotated, and half-bottles remain a strong point. Prices start at £13.25. CELLARMAN'S CHOICE: St-Romain sous le Château 1995, Dom. Guillemard, £29.95; Saumur-Champigny, Ch. du Hureau 1995, P. et G. Vatan £22.30.

CHEFS/PROPRIETORS: Simon and Geraldine Theobald   OPEN: Tue to Fri and Sun L 12.15 to 1.30, Tue to Sat D 7.15 to 9.15   CLOSED: 2 weeks Aug   MEALS: alc D (main courses £10.50 to £17). Set L Tue to Fri £13.50 (2 courses), Set L Sun £18.50. BYO £6   SERVICE: not inc   CARDS: Delta, MasterCard, Switch, Visa   DETAILS: 38 seats. 10 seats outside. Private parties: 36 main room. Vegetarian meals. Children's helpings. No children under 8 at D. No smoking in dining-room. No music   (£5)

JEVINGTON East Sussex   map 3

Hungry Monk ⅝✱

Jevington BN26 5QF
TEL/FAX: (01323) 482178   COOKING 3
off A22 between Polegate and Friston   COST £36–£55

The Monk celebrated 30 years of trading this year, and marked the occasion by publishing a recipe-book to let amateur practitioners in on some of the secrets of its current repertoire. In the centre of a tiny village off the London to Eastbourne road, the Mackenzies continue to please a loyal Sussex following with their old-fashioned approach. Ornately framed paintings, napkin rings and discreet classical music may seem to many to belong in another era, but menus have evolved cautiously with the times. Salmon wrapped in prosciutto, and sauced with red wine and shallots, indicates a willingness to continue trying out new ideas, as does a rack of lamb accompanied by a carrot and coriander rissole in a redcurrant, rosemary and garlic sauce.

One idea that is bound to run and run is banoffi pie, for the Monk was its originator. Alternative puddings might include mocha-bocker glory or chestnut mille-feuille with kirsch-soaked cherries. Service is watchful and capable. The extensive wine list exhibits a fondness for French classics, mature clarets in particular looking very good, and has a better-than-usual choice of German wines as well as a few English bottles. House selections embrace France and New Zealand, and start at £11.

CHEFS: Sharon Poulton and Claire Burgess   PROPRIETORS: Nigel and Susan Mackenzie   OPEN: Sun L 12 to 2, all week D 7 to 10   CLOSED: 24 to 26 Dec, bank hols exc Good Fri   MEALS: Set L and D £24.95. BYO £6   SERVICE: not inc, card slips closed, 12.5% for parties of 8 or more   CARDS: Amex   DETAILS: 40 seats. Private parties: 40 main room, 6 to 16 private rooms. Car park. Vegetarian meals. Children's helpings. No children under 4. No smoking in dining-room. Occasional music. Air-conditioned   (£5)

KELSALE Suffolk   map 6

Hedgehogs ✠ £

Kelsale IP17 2RF
TEL: (01728) 604444   FAX: (01728) 604499   COOKING 2
on A12, 1m N of Saxmundham   COST £17–£28

Hedgehog signs announce the approach to this sixteenth-century thatched, oak-beamed, brick-floored building, where candles provide illumination at dinner. Stephen Yare deals in traditional Anglo-French-Italian dishes from deep-fried whitebait to duckling with cherries to cannelloni of smoked haddock. He may throw in an occasional Thai dip for a starter of crispy strips of beef, or a tomato salsa to accompany grilled salmon and polenta 'chips' (real chips come with rump steak), but mostly he stays with the simple country style of lentil soup, pork and duck paté served with smoked duck salad, or navarin of lamb. 'Satisfactory' desserts might include apple and frangipane tart, iced Amaretto and panettone parfait, or roasted pineapple with vanilla ice. Some 30 wines go out of their way to be affordable, starting with house Vin de Pays du Gers at £7.75.

CHEF/PROPRIETOR: Stephen Yare   OPEN: Tue to Fri and Sun L 12 to 2, Tue to Sun D 7 to 9.30 CLOSED: second week Jan , last week Oct   MEALS: alc (main courses £7.50 to £10.50). Set L £7.50 (2 courses), Set D £9.95   SERVICE: not inc, card slips closed   CARDS: Delta, MasterCard, Switch, Visa   DETAILS: 60 seats. 20 seats outside. Private parties: 30 main room, 24 private rooms. Car park. Vegetarian meals. Children's helpings. No smoking in dining-room. Wheelchair access (1 step; also WC). Music   £5

KENILWORTH Warwickshire   map 5

Restaurant Bosquet ♟

97A Warwick Road, Kenilworth CV8 1HP   COOKING 5
TEL: (01926) 852463   COST £34–£51

The Ligniers' friendly and informal restaurant feels so much like a private house that you wonder if you ought to ring the doorbell on arrival. Bernard Lignier can be glimpsed down the hall in the kitchen while his wife acts as hostess in the small dining-room. The setting may be domestic but the cooking is an accomplished and single-minded rendition of the cuisine of south-west France, with sophisticated saucing, a dash of imagination and generous use of luxuries such as foie gras, truffles and lobster.

If the same ingredients crop up more than once on the same menu, it is because Bernard Lignier picks the choice produce of the day, working it into different dishes and creating some surprising yet successful combinations in the process. Asparagus, for example, might be slipped into a mille-feuille of sweetbreads and truffle, making an effective counterpoint to an intense Madeira sauce, yet is equally pleasing when presented more simply with a truffle dressing. One reporter enjoyed 'soft and yielding' saddle of venison with a well-balanced juniper and mandarin sauce, while mandarin zest has been flecked into a dark chocolate ice-cream, part of a 'plate of various killer chocolate manifestations' that also included a light and frothy tart and an airy mousse. A sharp yet creamy lemon tart was handled with the same flair and served with an excellent orange sorbet. Wines are as exclusively French as the cuisine and range from Ch. Mouton-Rothschild 1985 to less grand, but none the less appealing, bins from the south-west. House wines start at £11.50. CELLARMAN'S CHOICE: Jurançon Sec 'Cuvée Marie' 1996, Charles Hours, £20; Gamay de Touraine 1996, £12.50.

CHEF: Bernard Lignier   PROPRIETORS: Bernard and Jane Lignier   OPEN: Tue to Sat L (by arrangement only) 12 to 1.15, Tue to Sat D 7 to 9.15   MEALS: alc (main courses £15 to £16). Set L £23, Set D Tue to Fri £23   SERVICE: not inc   CARDS: none   DETAILS: 26 seats. Private parties: 30 main room. Children's helpings. Wheelchair access (2 steps; not WC). No music

Simpson's

101–103 Warwick Road, Kenilworth CV8 1HP   COOKING 4
TEL: (01926) 864567   FAX: (01926) 864510   COST £26–£43

Judging by the 'trophy motors' outside, Simpson's appears to cater for 'affluent Middle England at play'. It is a 'clean, bright and airy' place with foody cartoons on bare brick walls, green wickerwork chairs, and close-together tables. This may be the heart of England, but the kitchen manages to get its hands on some 'superb fish', as one couple found who began with precisely grilled tuna, served with couscous, herb salad and gazpacho, followed by a dish of cod on a bed of piquant cabbage with a red-wine sauce.

Greek-born Andreas Antona brings a dash of native seasoning to the Anglo-French melting pot. Alongside black pudding with glazed apples and cider sauce, or breast of chicken with leeks, morels and foie gras sauce, we find tarragon-flavoured lamb kleftico sufficiently powerful to remind one visitor of the real thing back in Cyprus. Accompanying vegetables – in this case shiitakes, artichokes and green beans – are particular to each dish, and presentation is attractive, judging by a yellow saffron risotto that came with pink Parmesan and deep-fried green rocket leaves. To finish, brochette of exotic fruits comes with chilled rice-pudding and Malibu sauce, while pavé of chocolate with raspberries and vanilla sauce is 'melt in the mouth-fantastic'. Service is 'attentive, quiet and expert'. Traditional and 'hippy' teas are offered in what looks like a fine wooden cigar box. House French is £10.95.

CHEFS: Andreas Antona, Luke Tipping and Andrew Waters   PROPRIETOR: Andreas Antona   OPEN: Mon to Fri L 12.30 to 2, Tue to Sat D 7 to 10   CLOSED: 25 Dec, 1 Jan, bank hols   MEALS: alc L (main courses £5). Set D £19.95 (2 courses) to £24.95   SERVICE: not inc   CARDS: Amex, Delta, Diners, MasterCard, Switch, Visa   DETAILS: 80 seats. Private parties: 8 main room, 80 private room. Car park. Vegetarian meals. Children welcome. No-smoking area. Music. Air-conditioned

---

'One petit four was a semi-molten opaque ochre blob, apparently attempting to escape from its frilly paper casing. I was not sure whether to eat it or say, "Take me to your leader."'
(On eating in Norfolk)

The Guide always appreciates hearing about changes of chef or owner.

KESWICK Cumbria   map 10

▲ *Swinside Lodge* ⅋✳

Grange Road, Newlands, Keswick CA12 5UE
TEL/FAX: (017687) 72948
off A66 Penrith to Cockermouth road; turn left at   COOKING 4
Portinscale and follow Grange road for 2m   COST £28–£37

This quiet Cumbrian retreat by Derwent Water works to a formula of such
striking simplicity that no city restaurateur would dare essay it. A menu with no
choice (except for dessert), a hotel with no wine-cellar (because it is unlicensed,
so bring your own), no lunches, no credit cards, and dinner at a single sitting is
the framework, and yet Graham Taylor keeps them coming back. It helps to have
mountainous Lakeland tranquillity all about and Chris Astley in the kitchen, of
course, but none the less the Lodge is a testament to a special way of doing things
that doesn't change because it doesn't need to.

Dinner might begin, after the prescribed tot of free sherry, with goats'-cheese
soufflé before going on to a soup such as onion and coriander or white bean and
bacon. Borrowdale trout might feature for main course, but meat is more the
norm, as in guinea-fowl breast with deep-fried shredded parsnip and wild
mushrooms in a red wine sauce. Four vegetables accompany. Puddings offer the
likes of caramelised apples with cinnamon ice-cream in a tuile basket, or
rhubarb crème brûlée with rhubarb sorbet. Local cheeses may be taken as an
extra course, before you repair to the lounge for cafetières with chocolates and
fudge. One firm regular noted that Graham Taylor has kept the same staff for a
number of years, suggesting contentment behind the scenes as well as among the
clientele.

CHEFS: Chris Astley   PROPRIETOR: Graham Taylor   OPEN: all week, D only 7.30 to 8 (1 sitting)
MEALS: Set D £25 to £28. Unlicensed: BYO (no corkage)   SERVICE: not inc, card slips closed
CARDS: none   DETAILS: 18 seats. Private parties: 18 main room. Car park. No children under 10.
No smoking in dining-room. No music   ACCOMMODATION: 7 rooms, all with bath/shower. TV.
D,B&B £72 to £160. No children under 10. No dogs. Afternoon teas (*The Which? Hotel Guide*)

KEYSTON Cambridgeshire   map 6

Pheasant Inn ▮ ⅋✳ £

Keyston PE18 0RE
TEL: (01832) 710241   FAX: (01832) 710340   COOKING 4
on B663, 1m S of junction with A14   COST £20–£47

The olives in the bar, marinated with cumin and coriander, are 'more what you'd
expect from a back street café in Marrakesh', and despite reassuringly traditional
warm terracotta walls, dark polished tables, a big fireplace stacked with logs,
and 'a comfortable squishy sofa in the corner', the Pheasant is 'no ordinary
country pub'. It has none of the hearty male beery atmosphere, but nor is it at all
formal. The menu is imaginative without being over-ambitious, and ranges in
style from a French bourgeois sausage of chicken, wild mushroom and basil
with braised lentils, to a 'featherlight, moussey-textured' double-baked

goats'-cheese soufflé, with crisp apple and crunchy walnut salad to balance its rich, smooth texture. Ingredients are fresh and handled with skill and care, as in 'perfectly cooked' scallops with shredded vegetables 'that had barely touched the frying pan' and a generous dash of coriander.

Main courses have produced a classic partnership of 'tender, well-roasted' pigeon breasts with wild mushroom risotto, and 'immaculately fresh' sea bass with linguine and courgettes. To finish, consider thinly sliced caramelised apples on buttery flaky pastry with a scoop of caramel ice-cream, or an 'ace' pistachio soufflé with chocolate ice-cream. Staff are young, helpful, polite and efficient. Adnams beer is well-kept, and around 100 wines are helpfully presented by style, ranging from 'crisp, fresh appetising whites' to 'top-class Bordeaux and Bordeaux-style' reds. House wines start at £9.45, 14 of which are also available by the glass. CELLARMAN'S CHOICE: Pinot d'Alsace Vieilles Vignes 1996, Meyer Fonné, £12.95; Côtes du Roussillon 1996, Dom. du Mas Crémat, £13.50

CHEF: Martin Lee   PROPRIETOR: John Hoskins   OPEN: all week 12 to 2, 6 (7 Sun) to 10   CLOSED: D 25 and 28 Dec   MEALS: alc (main courses L £4.50 to £9, D £7.50 to £15). BYO £5   SERVICE: not inc   CARDS: Amex, Delta, Diners, MasterCard, Switch, Visa   DETAILS: 120 seats. 30 seats outside. Private parties: 30 main room. Car park. Vegetarian meals. Children's helpings. No smoking in 1 dining-room. No music

---

KING'S CLIFFE Northamptonshire   map 6

King's Cliffe House ▼ ⁵✶

31 West Street, King's Cliffe PE8 6XB   COOKING 4
TEL/FAX: (01780) 470172   COST £24–£43

The stone in this part of the village has been around long enough to acquire a dark patina, lending character to the whole not-quite-straight street. The entrance is round the back, through the garden, to a door opened by ultra-polite Andrew Wilshaw, who is full of 'thank-yous' whenever he renders even the smallest service, and remembers who is having what without writing anything down. A bowl of glistening olives and cheese pastries accompanies the menu, which adopts a 'sensible country approach'.

If four nights a week seems like a part-time operation, the owners are quick to disabuse us. Their time is taken up with hot-smoking turbot roe, venison fillet, goose breast and eels from the River Nene, making their own salt cod, baking bread from stone-ground organic flour, and sourcing materials: even local ones such as quince, mulberries, medlars, a host of mushrooms, and game according to season, take some winkling out. It all indicates an honesty of intent, exemplified in a 'simply conceived and presented' main course tart of wild mushrooms with a deep-flavoured Madeira sauce. Cooking is accurately timed, seasoning is spot-on, and flavours are true: as in a starter of seared scallops with mashed lentils and bright coriander pesto, or griddled 'super-fresh' Norfolk asparagus with grated Parmesan.

Four or five interesting British cheeses offer an alternative to desserts such as hot chocolate soufflé, or lemon brulée with 'textbook custard and a lemon-curdy taste'. Considerable time and thought must have gone into compiling the wine list, too, for it's a particularly exciting collection drawn from both hemispheres and offered at very fair prices. Half a dozen house wines are priced between £9.95 and £12.50. CELLARMAN'S CHOICE: Dry River Sauvignon Blanc 1997, Martinborough, New Zealand, £21; Ribera del Duero 1994, Viña Pedrosa, £19.75.

CHEFS/PROPRIETORS: Emma Jessop and Andrew Wilshaw   OPEN: Wed to Sat D only 7 to 9.15   CLOSED: 25 and 26 Dec, 1 Jan, bank hols   MEALS: alc (main courses £10 to £15)   SERVICE: net prices   CARDS: none   DETAILS: 20 seats. Private parties: 20 main room. Car park. Vegetarian meals. Children's helpings. No smoking in dining-room. No music

---

KING'S LYNN Norfolk   map 6

Rococo ▼

11 Saturday Market Place, King's Lynn PE30 5DQ

TEL/FAX: (01553) 771483   COOKING 6
EMAIL: rococorest@aol.com   COST £22–£50

If the relentlessly monochrome style of modern city restaurants has wearied the soul, Rococo, as its name suggests, is not about understatement in any way. The décor in the sitting-area offers not so much a riot of colour as a full-scale armed insurrection. Green and yellow checks on the tables, a dresser done up in shimmering fuschia, not to mention the glow of the paintings, administer a kick-start to the senses. All this is perhaps a better harbinger of the professionalism to come than the modest handwritten menu might suggest.

Boudin noir on a crisp potato cake with apples and grapes is a triumph of earthy textural contrasts, and yet the overall effect is one of lightness. Fish cookery is especially effective, never more so than when several types are brought together: perhaps sea-trout, Dover sole, freshwater prawns and tiny Norfolk shrimps of impeccable flavour, united with a well-wrought chervil butter sauce. Thick cutlets from a rack of lamb are classically partnered with quenelles of rosemary stuffing and a minted pea purée. Even the serving of an interim sorbet of apple and calvados won over a sorbet sceptic. At dessert stage, the artistry continues when a stack of short buttery biscuits is layered with nectarine and pineapple in the upper storeys and crème brûlée in the lower, and is accompanied by a scoop of smoothly rich coconut ice-cream.

When the canapés, freshly baked bread and petits fours are all included in the roll of honour, it becomes clear that this is a kitchen on a red-hot streak, which is well served by a 'relaxed and friendly' front-of-house team. Wines are chosen with knowledge and a sense of adventure, offering a good range of styles and flavours from around the world. The list opens with a 'personal choice' of 16 wines priced between £11.95 and £32.75, any of which would prove rewarding drinking. CELLARMAN'S CHOICE: Mâcon-Viré 1994, Jean Thévenet, £29.95; Rhône, Les Collines de Laure 1996, Jean-Luc Colombo, £21.50.

CHEFS: Nick Anderson and Timothy Sandford   PROPRIETORS: Nick and Anne Anderson   OPEN: Tue to Sat L12 to 2 (1.30 Sat), Mon to Sat D 7 to 10   MEALS: Set L £9.95 (2 courses) to £13.50, Set D £22.50 (2 courses) to £32.50. BYO £4   SERVICE: not inc, card slips closed   CARDS: Amex, Delta, Diners, MasterCard, Switch, Visa   DETAILS: 40 seats. Private parties: 40 main room. Vegetarian meals. Children's helpings. No smoking while others eat. Wheelchair access (also WC). Music (£5)

KINGTON Herefordshire   map 5

▲ Penrhos Court ⁂

Kington HR5 3LH
TEL: (01544) 230720   FAX: (01544) 230754
EMAIL: martin@penrhos.kc3.co.uk   COOKING 2
on A44, 1m E of Kington   COST £39–£47

Nowhere in the *Guide* is more committed to organic food than Penrhos Court, the first restaurant in Britain to be given the Soil Association's stamp of approval. Daphne Lambert and Martin Griffiths, who have carefully restored this 700-year-old property, recognised long before most that food and health are inextricably intertwined; they even run courses on it. This is not a hairshirt operation, though, merely an embodiment of the principles of good eating, woven into a short, daily-changing, four-course menu. The first two courses are fixed: a soup such as spiced lentil with coconut cream, or nettle and potato, or beetroot with chive blossom, followed by Greek salad, or vegetable sushi, or twice-baked mushroom soufflé. Main courses typically offer a meat, a fish and a vegetable dish: for example, chicken with polenta and red pepper sauce, fillet of turbot with crab sauce, or rocket ravioli with tomato sauce. Desserts of summer-fruit trifle, or brandied apricot fool may not have quite the same impact, but the bread is a prizewinner. Some two dozen organic wines on the wide-ranging list stay mostly below £20, and ten house wines, starting at £11.50, are available by the glass.

CHEF: Daphne Lambert   PROPRIETORS: Martin Griffiths and Daphne Lambert   OPEN: all week D only 7.30 to 9.30   CLOSED: Jan   MEALS: Set D £29.50. BYO £3 to £5   SERVICE: not inc, card slips closed   CARDS: Amex, Delta, MasterCard, Visa   DETAILS: 70 seats. 200 seats outside. Private parties: 75 main room, 20 to 120 private rooms. Car park. Vegetarian meals. Children's helpings. No smoking in dining-room. Occasional music   ACCOMMODATION: 19 rooms, all with bath/shower. TV. Phone. B&B £55 to £105.50. Rooms for disabled. Children welcome. High teas for children. No dogs. Baby facilities   (£5)

KIRKHAM Lancashire   map 8

Cromwellian £

16 Poulton Street, Kirkham PR4 2AB   COOKING 4
TEL/FAX: (01772) 685680   COST £25–£33

The Fawcetts offer an attractive combination of unpretentious setting and serious cooking. Evenings begin amid the beams and chintz curtains with a warm welcome from the 'avuncular' Peter Fawcett, a plate of canapés and a look at the short menu that changes eight times a year. Choice may be limited to three or four items per course, but that seems fair given the domestic scale and price tag: 'exceptional value,' concludes one reporter. Josie Fawcett has no culinary axe to grind, and seems just as happy offering a warm potato and black pudding salad as a goats'-cheese crostini with tapénade and pesto dressing.

Chicken and salmon make regular appearances among main courses (fillet steak and the cheeseboard attract a supplement) and their treatments are equally varied: from sweet chilli sauce for salmon, to tabbouleh with lemon and mint sauce for chicken. Soups are 'tasteful and appetising', presentation is 'distinctive', and the oven-baked potatoes in cream are a big draw. Of the strands that go to make up the kitchen's output, the 'traditional' is best represented by comfort-food puddings: crumbles, turnovers, or sponges such as the apple upside down one with caramel calvados sauce and toffee fudge ice-cream. Good-value wines from the New World, and a choice of half-bottles, add to the appeal. House vin de pays is £9.50.

CHEF: Josie Fawcett   PROPRIETORS: Peter and Josie Fawcett   OPEN: Tue to Sat D only 7 to 9   MEALS: Set D £16   SERVICE: not inc, card slips closed   CARDS: Amex, Delta, Diners, MasterCard, Switch, Visa   DETAILS: 28 seats. Private parties: 10 main room, 10 private room. Vegetarian meals. Children welcome. Occasional music   (£5)

KNUTSFORD Cheshire   map 8

▲ Belle Epoque Brasserie 🗱 £

60 King Street, Knutsford WA16 6DT   COOKING 2
TEL: (01565) 633060   FAX: (01565) 634150   COST £19–£43

Immaculately kept interiors, marble-pillared alcoves and a floor of Venetian glass recall the high style of a long-gone, tastefully decadent era, quite a contrast to David Mooney's modern metropolitan brasserie cooking. Chorizo sausage goes into risotto, along with orange, sage and onion; samosas of crab come with red pepper coulis; and local venison steak has a warm cranberry salsa. One reporter was impressed by the vivacity of a dish of buckwheat pancakes, the batter filled with chopped spring onion, encasing a mixture of provençale vegetables and fine olive oil. Fish and chips uses a generous fillet of creamy haddock, and comes with mushy peas, home-made tartare sauce packed with gherkins and capers and (whisper it) 'a flask of malt vinegar'. An original way to finish might be with cherry scones served with cherry liqueur jam and white chocolate cream. A wide selection of wines by the glass heads up a thoughtful list that is replete with exemplary value. Bottle prices open at £9.95.

CHEF: David Mooney   PROPRIETORS: Keith and Nerys Mooney   OPEN: Mon to Fri L 12 to 2, Mon to Sat D 7 to 10   CLOSED: 24 to 26 Dec, bank hols   MEALS: alc (main courses £8 to £14.50). Rapid lunch £5.50 (2 courses)   SERVICE: not inc, card slips closed   CARDS: Amex, Delta, Diners, MasterCard, Switch, Visa   DETAILS: 100 seats. 20 seats outside. Private parties: 60 main room, 18 to 80 private rooms. Children's helpings. No smoking in 1 dining-room. Wheelchair access (2 steps; not WC). Music   ACCOMMODATION: 7 rooms, all with bath/shower. TV. Phone. B&B £45 to £55. No children under 14. No dogs (The Which? Hotel Guide)

LANGAR Nottinghamshire   map 5

▲ Langar Hall 🗱

Langar NG13 9HG
TEL: (01949) 860559   FAX: (01949) 861045
EMAIL: langarhall_hotel@n.direct.co.uk   COOKING 4
between A46 and A52, 4m S of Bingham   COST £21–£75

The house sits at the edge of the village, in 30 acres of parkland in the Vale of Belvoir. In fine weather drinks and food can be served outside; otherwise meals are eaten in the open-plan pillared dining-room amid a display of old hunting and architectural prints. Dishes are simply expressed on menus, allowing Imogen Skirving the opportunity to fill in any details personally, or give 'a recitation of the menu with a few asides and elaborations along the way', as it struck one visitor. First-course soups, terrines and salads might be joined by twice-baked cheese soufflé, fresh-tasting chicken liver parfait, or an impressive wild mushroom risotto.

Good-quality materials are served with 'natural' sauces: fish swims into view more in summer, while game takes priority in autumn and winter, lamb in spring (braised shank with mash, cabbage and green beans, perhaps), and there is 'always beef from a reputable herd', typically chargrilled and served with a red wine and shallot sauce. The cooking does its best to cut down on butter and cream, using the latter only in desserts, among which might be bitter chocolate tart with vanilla ice, lemon tart, or poached rhubarb with ginger ice. Service has not always been entirely clued up. Wines are wide-ranging, varied in style, picked with an eye for quality, and start with a 30-strong house selection between £10 and £20.

CHEF: Toby Garratt   PROPRIETOR: Imogen Skirving   OPEN: all week 12 to 1.45, 7 to 9.30 (10 Fri and Sat)   MEALS: alc (main courses £9.50 to £25). Set L Mon to Sat £10 (2 courses) to £12.50, Set L Sun £17.50, Set D Mon to Fri £15, Set D Sat and Sun £20 to £25   SERVICE: not inc   CARDS: Amex, Diners, MasterCard, Visa   DETAILS: 50 seats. Private parties: 42 main room, 8 to 22 private rooms. Car park. Vegetarian meals. Children welcome. No smoking in 1 dining-room. Wheelchair access (also women's WC). Occasional music   ACCOMMODATION: 10 rooms, all with bath/shower. TV. Phone. B&B £65 to £150. Children welcome. Baby facilities. Dogs welcome by arrangement. Afternoon teas. Fishing (*The Which? Hotel Guide*)   £5

LANGFORD BUDVILLE Somerset   map 2

▲ *Bindon Country House Hotel,*
Wellesley Restaurant 🗲✳

NEW ENTRY

Langford Budville TA21 0RU
TEL: (01823) 400070   FAX: (01823) 400071
EMAIL: bindonhouse@msn.co.uk
off B3187 Wellington to Milverton road,   COOKING 2
7m W of Taunton   COST £26–£66

This small-scale, peaceful and 'superbly beautiful' seventeenth-century house opened in summer 1997 after extensive renovation. Two rounded gabled towers make a striking façade, while the dusky pink and sea-green dining-room goes in for busy carpets, friezes and wallpaper, its prints forging a link with Arthur Wellesley, Duke of Wellington (after whom the dining-room is named). Good materials include loin of locally farmed venison, cooked pink with a scattering of young vegetables, and the simplest techniques such as grilling and roasting turn out to be the most successful: at one meal 'nicely timed' scallops on a bed of fried noodles and fine ratatouille. Be prepared for a copious array of garnishes and extras – two lots of appetisers and pre-dessert cheese – and expect to see dishes built into elaborate towers. It is with the sweet course that the chef really gets into his decorative stride, adding biscuits and spun sugar when, judging by an inspection meal, more attention might have been paid to the dessert itself. Herb flavours are used more than generously throughout, and solicitous staff offer to grind pepper over everything savoury. Nearly 100 wines balance quality and value, starting with eight house wines under £16.50.

CHEF: Patrick Robert   PROPRIETORS: Mark and Lynn Jaffa   OPEN: all week 12 to 2, 7.30 to 9.30   MEALS: alc (main courses L £12 to £15.50, D £14 to £23), Set L £13.95 (2 courses) to £16.95, Set D £27.50   SERVICE: not inc, card slips closed   CARDS: Amex, Delta, Diners, MasterCard, Switch, Visa   DETAILS: 35 seats. 45 seats outside. Private parties: 55 main room, 10 and 45 private rooms. Car park. No children under 14. No smoking in dining-room. Wheelchair access (not WC). Music   ACCOMMODATION: 12 rooms, all with bath/shower. TV. Phone. B&B £75 to £155. Children welcome. High teas for children. Dogs welcome in 1 bedroom only. Afternoon teas. Swimming-pool £5

LANGHO Lancashire   map 8

▲ *Northcote Manor* ♟ ✻

Northcote Road, Langho BB6 8BE
TEL: (01254) 240555   FAX: (01254) 246568   COOKING 6
on A59, 8½m E of M6 exit 31   COST £26–£65

The extended manor-house looks out over the Ribble Valley, on the edge of the Trough of Bowland, a short broom ride from Pendle Hill. It sports a couple of lounges and a large, quiet, airy dining-room with beige walls, assorted pictures and well-spaced tables. Nigel Haworth's avowed aim is to produce food that expresses something of a 'refined rustic' character, and the use of regional materials gives it, as one reporter put it, 'a sense of local identity and overall purpose'. Among these might be black pudding (partnered by pink trout, with a mustard and nettle sauce), cornfed Goosnargh duckling (given a Chinese treatment with spring rolls and plum chutney), and Pendle lamb (with winter vegetables and coriander oil).

There is much else besides, including Colchester oysters, Orkney scallops, and risotto of New Forest mushrooms, but whatever the provenance, presentation is 'top-drawer', materials are first-rate, timing is accurate, and there is an appealing sense of 'innovation without wild experiment' running through the food, from 'moist fresh' haddock on a bed of Jerusalem artichokes, to pink lamb's liver with thyme mash, crispy bacon and roast shallots. Desserts have included 'rich and tangy' mulled pear tarte Tatin and, perhaps most innovative of all, a 'refreshing' Lancashire cheese crème brûlée. Service is 'prompt, friendly and courteous', with intervals between courses 'perfectly timed'. 'A bit pricey' is a typical, though not unanimous, summing up, and a princely collection of wines drawn from some of the world's top producers contributes to this conclusion. Still, there is fair choice under £20, and even a few under £15 if you keep your eyes peeled. CELLARMAN'S CHOICE: Albariño Lagar de Cervera 1997, Rias Baixas, Galicia, £20.65; Quinta do Crasto Reserva 1995, Douro, £20.50.

Report forms are at the back of the book; write a letter if you prefer; or email us at guidereports@which.co.uk.

CHEF: Nigel Haworth   PROPRIETORS: Craig Bancroft and Nigel Haworth   OPEN: all week 12 to 1.30 (2 Sun), 7 to 9.30 (10 Sat)   CLOSED: 25 Dec, 1 Jan   MEALS: alc D (main courses £16.50 to £23.50). Set L £16, Set D £37, Set D £37   SERVICE: 10% (optional)   CARDS: Amex, Delta, Diners, MasterCard, Switch, Visa   DETAILS: 60 seats. Private parties: 30 private room. Car park. Vegetarian meals. Children's helpings. Jacket and tie. No smoking in dining-room. Wheelchair access (2 steps; also WC). Music   ACCOMMODATION: 14 rooms, all with bath/shower. TV. Phone. B&B £80 to £130. Rooms for disabled. Children welcome. Afternoon teas (*The Which? Hotel Guide*)

LANGLEY MARSH   Somerset

map 2

▲ *Langley House Hotel* 🍷 ⅙✳

Langley Marsh, Wiveliscombe TA4 2UF
TEL: (01984) 623318   FAX: (01984) 624573
½m N of Wiveliscombe

COOKING 5
COST £39–£55

Small and personally run, Langley House dates in part from the sixteenth century, and is 'a haven of comfort and tranquillity'. The white-painted house is well cared for, and 'very un-hotelly', which was the highest accolade one reporter could bestow on a hotel. Dinner is three or four courses with no choice before pudding, the menu changes daily, and it is worth noting that Peter Wilson is 'a brilliant fish cook' who has produced 'out of this world' sea bass, and roast cod with a pine-nut crust and a 'rich but exquisite' sauce based on barley and lemon.

Meat dishes have sent correspondents away happy too – 'tender, tasty' Somerset lamb, served with a tartlet of onion and cassis purée – and the enterprise is sharpened by a kitchen garden that yields herbs and vegetables. The 'marvellous selection' of local Somerset and Devon cheeses is 'not to be missed'. Chief among puddings is probably the icky sticky one with toffee sauce, but for one visitor elderberry and elderflower syllabub was 'everything a syllabub should be'. Anne Wilson 'does all the waitressing and running around' with occasional help. Bordeaux and Burgundy remain the twin focal points of the wine list, with quite a few wines available by the magnum or half-bottle. A discerning eye is also cast over other main regions, picking out some sound producers from the New World. House French is £12.50. CELLARMAN'S CHOICE: Montagny 'Les Joncs' 1995, Faiveley, £22.50; Pomerol, Ch. Plince 1989, £26.45.

CHEF: Peter Wilson   PROPRIETORS: Peter and Anne Wilson   OPEN: all week D only 7.30 to 8.30   MEALS: Set D £26.50 to £31.50. BYO £8.50   SERVICE: not inc, card slips closed   CARDS: Amex, MasterCard, Visa   DETAILS: 20 seats. 10 seats outside. Private parties: 18 main room, 20 private room. Car park. Vegetarian meals. Children's helpings. No children under 7. No smoking in dining-room. Wheelchair access (1 step; not WC). No music   ACCOMMODATION: 8 rooms, all with bath/shower. TV. Phone. B&B £72.50 to £127.50. Children welcome. High teas for children. Baby facilities. Dogs welcome in bedrooms only. Afternoon teas (*The Which? Hotel Guide*)
(£5)

Restaurateurs justifiably resent no-shows. If you quote a credit card number when booking, you may be liable for the restaurant's lost profit margin if you don't turn up. Always phone to cancel.

LAVENHAM Suffolk   map 6

▲ *Angel* ✿ £ | NEW ENTRY |

Market Place, Lavenham CO10 9QZ
TEL: (01787) 247388 FAX: (01787) 248344
EMAIL: angellav@aol.com   COOKING 2
on A1141, 6m NE of Sudbury   COST £20–£31

The Angel – just opposite the Great House (see entry below) in Lavenham's
medieval market square – has been a licensed hostelry since 1420. Try to bag a
spot in the original heavily beamed part of the pub, with its massive inglenook
fireplace and coveted 'piano table' in the bay window. Some of the kitchen's
productions may be recognisable pub food: home-made pork pie with chutney,
sausages and mash with onion gravy, or sirloin steaks from locally reared beef.
In the evenings, though, a more adventurous seam produces items such as an
inspector's 'amazingly good' red snapper with ginger, spring onions and lime, or
roast loin of mature lamb with redcurrants and rosemary. Before that, 'simple
and satisfying' cream of celery soup, and fresh seafood tagliatelle that brought
together crab, scallops and prawns in a thin cream sauce, were also impressive.
Puddings include the inevitable sticky toffee, but also a fine, lightly set brûlée
stuffed with raspberries. Themed evenings with regional menus occur regularly.
The international wine list is very reasonably priced, and house wines, which
start at £7.95, are also available by the part-bottle (charged pro rata).

CHEFS: Mike Pursell and Chris Boyle   PROPRIETORS: Roy and Anne Whitworth, John and Val
Barry   OPEN: all week 12 to 2.15, 6.45 to 9.15   CLOSED: 25 and 26 Dec   MEALS: alc (main
courses £7 to £10.50)   SERVICE: not inc, card slips closed   CARDS: Amex, Delta, MasterCard,
Switch, Visa   DETAILS: 100 seats. 60 seats outside. Private parties: 50 main room, 10 to 16
private rooms. Car park. Vegetarian meals. Children's helpings. No smoking in 1 dining-room.
Wheelchair access (not WC). Occasional music   ACCOMMODATION: 8 rooms, all with
bath/shower. TV. Phone. B&B £39.50 to £65. Rooms for disabled. Children welcome. Baby
facilities. Dogs by arrangement. Afternoon teas (*The Which? Hotel Guide*) （£5）

▲ *Great House*

Market Place, Lavenham CO10 9QZ
TEL: (01787) 247431 FAX: (01787) 248007   COOKING 2
EMAIL: greathouse@surflink.co.uk   COST £24–£57

In a village that has managed to retain its medieval heart, the Great House
occupies a prime site on a corner of the market square, its white-painted façade
bedecked with hanging baskets. You don't have to hunt far for wooden beams
and floorboards, nor peruse the menu for long before working out where the
food is coming from. 'Our style of cooking is French, as we all are,' confirms
Martine Crépy. She oversees a rather formal dining-room of closely packed
tables, which may come under pressure on busy Saturday evenings, while
husband Régis stakes out the French claim with 'superb' foie gras, Pernod-
flavoured mussel soup, and crisp-skinned duck magret with a gamey-tasting
sauce. When dishes change, they tend to be variations on a theme, smoked
chicken replacing pigeon breast in a warm salad with poached egg, for example.

Finish perhaps with a block of 'rich, dark, smooth' chocolate terrine with orange sauce, or a 'nicely caramelised' upside-down apple tart with cinnamon sauce. It is refreshing to see as many white wines from Languedoc-Roussillon as from Burgundy on a list that also looks to the New World, and finds room for a brace from Suffolk. The Crépys now also own Mortimer's in Bury St Edmunds (see entry).

CHEF: Régis Crépy   PROPRIETORS: Régis and Martine Crépy   OPEN: Tue to Sun 12 to 2.30, 7 to 9.30 (10 Sat); open bank hols and occasional Mon D   CLOSED: 3 weeks Jan   MEALS: alc (main courses L £6.50 to £10, D £13 to £18). Set L £9.95 (2 courses) to £14.95, Set D £17.95   SERVICE: not inc   CARDS: Amex, Delta, MasterCard, Switch, Visa   DETAILS: 45 seats. 30 seats outside. Private parties: 60 main room. Children's helpings. Music   ACCOMMODATION: 5 rooms, all with bath/shower. TV. Phone. B&B £55 to £110. Children welcome. High teas for children. Baby facilities (The Which? Hotel Guide)

LEEDS   West Yorkshire   map 8

Brasserie Forty Four

44 The Calls, Leeds LS2 7EW   COOKING 5
TEL: (0113) 234 3232   FAX: (0113) 234 3332   COST £21–£45

Head for the tall tower of St Peter's church. The brasserie is round the back in a cobbled street near the river, still very much a part of the city's revitalised centre, and still impressing reporters with its consistency. Top-quality fresh produce is a good foundation, resulting in flavours that 'sing loudly', even in a simple leafy, herby salad of tomatoes, mozzarella and anchovies. A thoroughly modern menu picks its way through the world larder, turning up good olive oil, aged balsamic vinegar, Japanese noodles, Whitby fish and shellfish, and serving up Moroccan lamb meatballs, Indonesian chickpea and cauliflower curry, and 'exciting' Turkish spiced aubergines.

The food is 'beautifully presented' but 'nothing is there just for show'; everything on the plate counts towards the end result, whether a humble sprig of dill on a smoked salmon starter that was 'tastier than we grow in our own garden', or a zingily flavoured Cantonese sweet-and-sour chicken 'straight off the grill' served with water chestnuts, shiitakes and root ginger. Fixed-price menu deals are presumably designed for fast turnover at lunch (one course, bread and coffee for a fiver) and to clear enough room in the restaurant by 8.15pm to let the big spenders rip. In fact, the value for money is genuine, even though vegetables and service add a bit to the cost: with a 'posh pasty' of duck confit, foie gras and truffle on offer as a main course, you can't grumble.

Service may at times be geared to processing diners through the time constraints, but with no sense of pressure, and it has been described variously as crisp, efficient, pleasant, friendly, charming and professional. Over 60 wines, ten of them by the half-bottle, are sharply chosen from all points of the compass, starting at £9.90.

'As a dish, it was a collection of different sorts of effects . . . ultimately not having a lot to do with each other. Instead of saying, "Eat me," the dish said, "Look how clever I am."' (On eating in London)

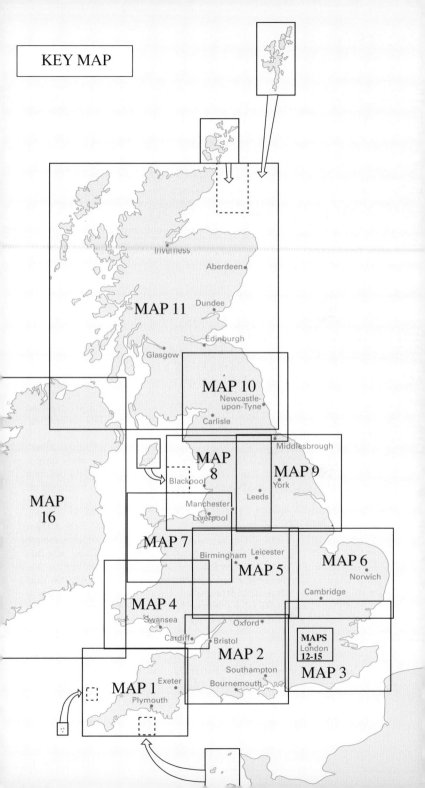

KEY MAP

MAP 11

MAP 10

MAP 8

MAP 9

MAP 16

MAP 7

MAP 5

MAP 6

MAP 4

MAP 2

MAPS
London
12-15

MAP 3

MAP 1

Inverness

Aberdeen

Dundee

Edinburgh

Glasgow

Newcastle-
upon-Tyne

Carlisle

Middlesbrough

Blackpool

York

Leeds

Manchester

Liverpool

Birmingham

Leicester

Norwich

Cambridge

Swansea

Oxford

Cardiff

Bristol

Southampton

Bournemouth

Exeter

Plymouth

MAP 1

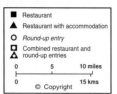

■ Restaurant
▲ Restaurant with accommodation
○ *Round-up entry*
□ Combined restaurant and
△ round-up entries

0	5	10 miles
0		15 kms

© Copyright

Lundy Island

Isles of Scilly
28 miles WSW of Land's End

New
Grimsby • ▲ **St Martin's**
○ *Tresco*

Hugh Town

*Bude
Bay*

*Port Isaac
Bay*

B o d m i

▲ **New Polzeath**
△ **Padstow** •Wadebridge

Watergate Bay •Bodmin

*Collifor
Res.*

•Newquay C O R N W A L L

Ligger Bay

St Austell

○ *Grampound* **Fowey** ■

St Austell Bay

Portreath ■

*St Ives
Bay* ○ *Truro*

St Ives ■ ▲ **Portloe** *Veryan
Bay*

▲ **St Mawes**

St Just **Carnkie** ■

Penzance ■ **Trevenen** ■ *Constantine* **Maenporth**

Falmouth •Falmouth

Porthleven ■ **Mawnan Smith** ▲ *Falmouth
Bay*

*Lands
End* *M o u n t ' s
B a y* **Mawgan** ■ ○ *Gillan*

Lizard Point

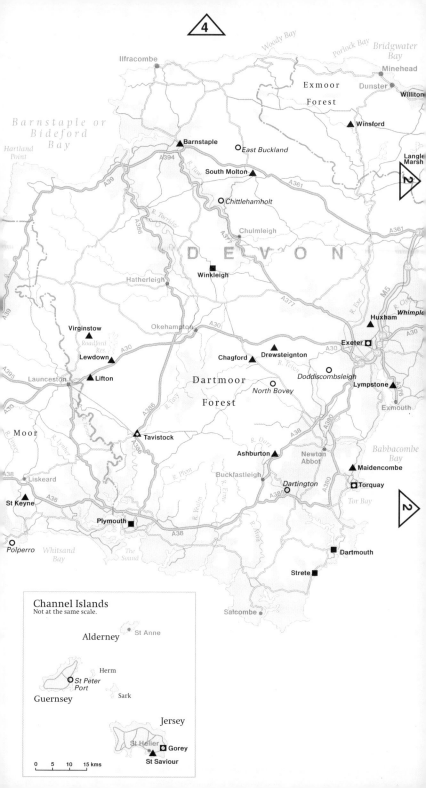

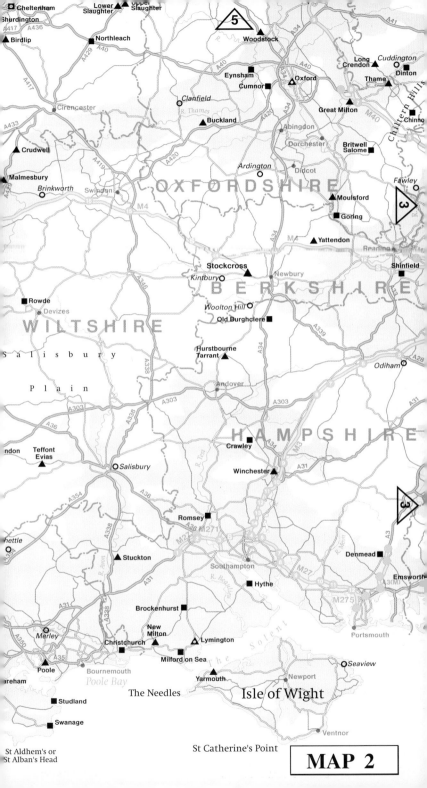

MAP 2

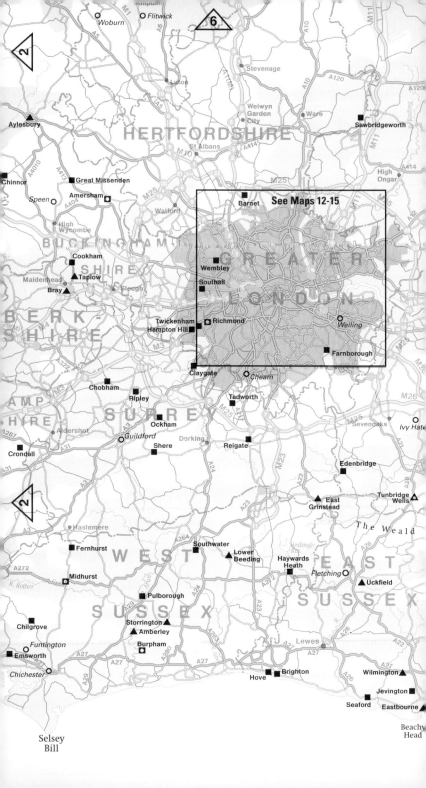

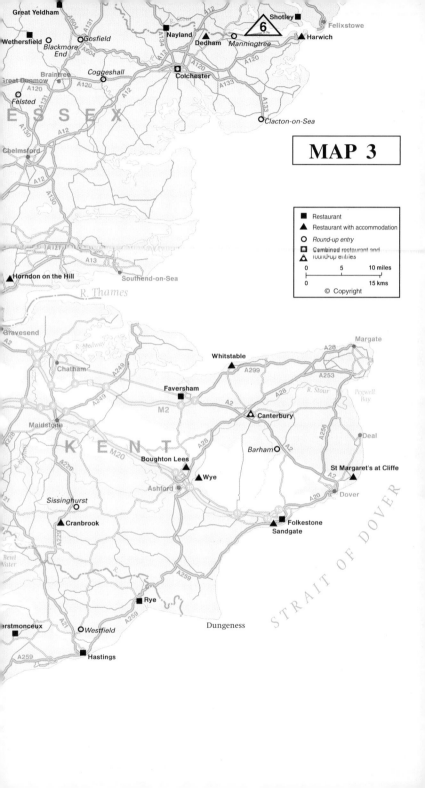

MAP 4

- ■ Restaurant
- ▲ Restaurant with accommodation
- ○ Round-up entry
- ◻ Combined restaurant and
  △ round-up entries

```
0        5      10 miles
0              15 kms
```
© Copyright

CARDIGAN

BAY

Newquay

A487

Cardigan

Fishguard Bay

Newport Bay

▲ Newport

A487

▲ Fishguard

Porthgain   Mathry

St. David's
Head

▲ Pontfaen

Rosebush ■

Ramsey
Island

Welsh Hook ▲

PEMBROKESHIRE

CARMAR

St David's   ○

Solva

Carmarthen

A40

St. Brides
Bay

Broad
Haven ▲

A40   Haverfordwest

Skomer Island

A477

○ Laugharne

Broad Sound

Skokholm Island

Milford
Haven

A478

Pembroke ■

A477

Carmarthen
Bay

Caldey
Island

Reynoldston

BRISTOL

MAP 5

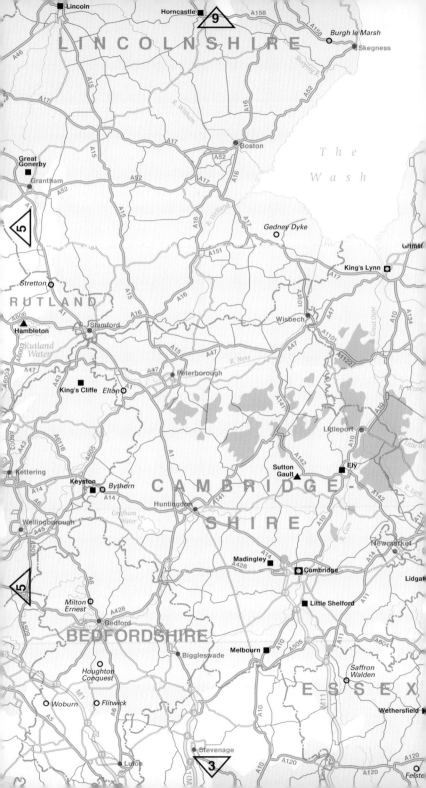

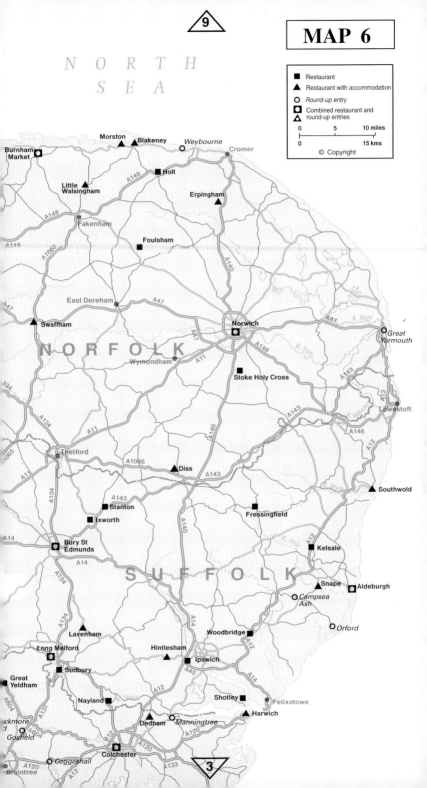

MAP 6

9

NORTH
SEA

Restaurant
Restaurant with accommodation
Round-up entry
Combined restaurant and round-up entries

0   5   10 miles
0   15 kms
© Copyright

Morston
Blakeney
Weybourne
Cromer
Burnham Market
Holt
A148
Little Walsingham
Erpingham
Fakenham
A148
Foulsham
A1065
A140
East Dereham
A47
A47
Swaffham
R. Bure
NORFOLK
Norwich
Great Yarmouth
A143
Wymondham
A146
R. Yare
A11
Stoke Holy Cross
R. Waveney
Lowestoft
A143
A12
A146
Thetford
A1066
Diss
A143
Blyth
A134
A11
A140
Southwold
A134
Stanton
A143
Fressingfield
Ixworth
A14
Bury St Edmunds
Kelsale
R. Alde
A134
SUFFOLK
Snape
Aldeburgh
Campsea Ash
A14
Orford
Lavenham
Woodbridge
A12
Long Melford
Hintlesham
Ipswich
A14
Sudbury
A45
Great Yeldham
Nayland
Stour
Shotley
Felixstowe
A604
Harwich
ckmore
Gosfield
Dedham
Manningtree
A120
Coggeshall
Colchester
A120
A120
Braintree
A133
3

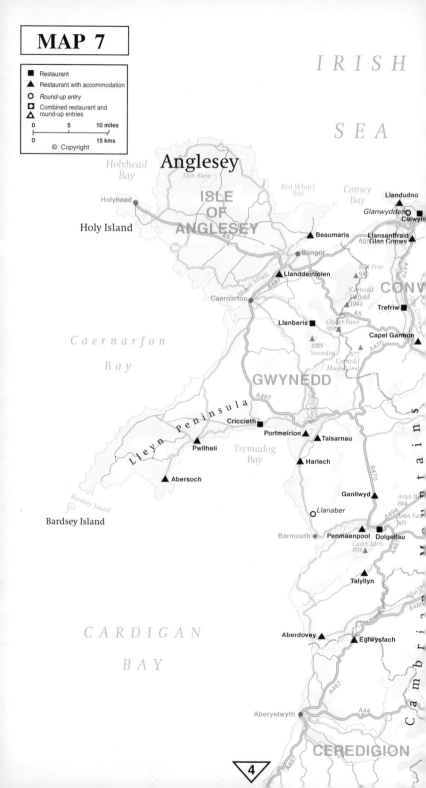

MAP 7

- ■ Restaurant
- ▲ Restaurant with accommodation
- ○ Round-up entry
- ▣ Combined restaurant and
- △ round-up entries

0   5   10 miles
0   15 kms
© Copyright

IRISH

SEA

Holyhead Bay

Anglesey

Llyn Alaw

Holyhead

ISLE
OF
ANGLESEY

Holy Island

Red Wharf Bay

Conwy Bay

Llandudno

Glanwydden

Colwyn

■ Beaumaris

Llansantffraid
Glan Conwy

Bangor

Llanddeiniolen ▲

Foel Fras 941

CONW

Caernarfon

Carnedd Dafydd 1044

Trefriw

A5

Llanberis ■

Glyder Fawr 997

Capel Garmon ▲

1085 Snowdon

872

Carnedd Moel-siabod

Caernarfon Bay

GWYNEDD

A487

Criccieth ■

Portmeirion ▲

Talsarnau ▲

Lleyn Peninsula

Pwllheli ▲

Tremadog Bay

Harlech ▲

▲ Abersoch

Ganllwyd ▲

Bardsey Sound

○ Llanaber

Aran Ben 884

Aran Faw 905

Bardsey Island

Barmouth ●

Penmaenpool ▲

Dolgellau ■

Cader Idris 893

Talyllyn ▲

CARDIGAN

Aberdovey ▲

Eglwysfach ▲

BAY

Cambrian Mountains

Aberystwyth

A44

CEREDIGION

4

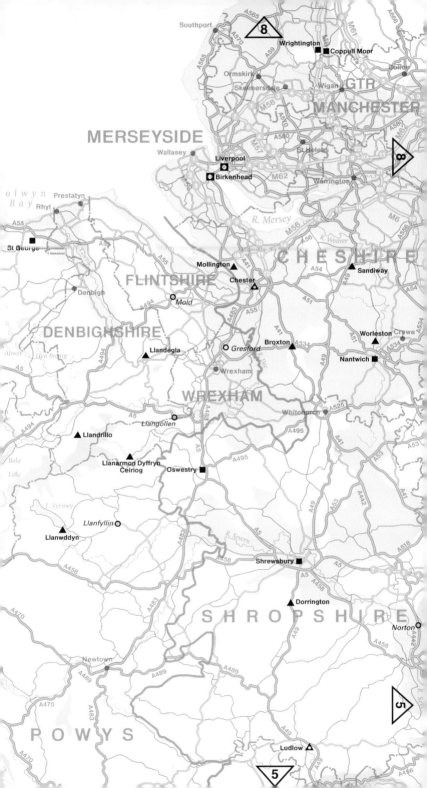

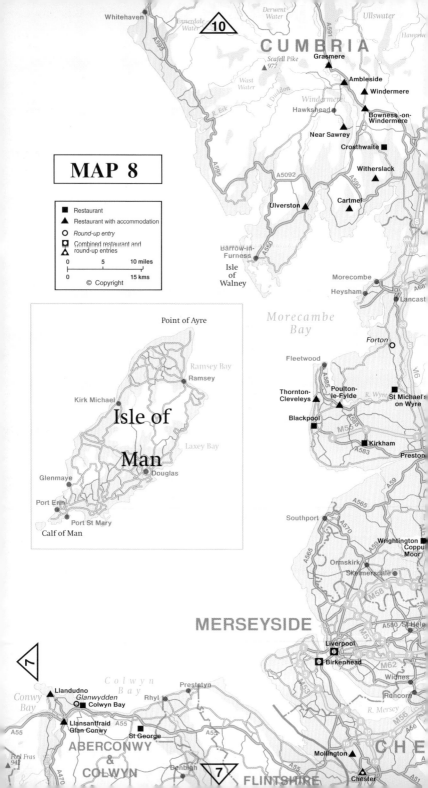

MAP 8

■	Restaurant
▲	Restaurant with accommodation
○	Round-up entry
▣	Combined restaurant and round-up entries
△	

0   5   10 miles
0   5   15 kms
© Copyright

CUMBRIA

Whitehaven
△10
Derwent Water
Ullswater
Ennerdale Water
Scafell Pike 977
Grasmere
Hawswe
Wast Water
R. Duddon
Ambleside
Windermere
Windermere
Hawkshead
Bowness-on-Windermere
R. Esk
A5092
Near Sawrey
Crosthwaite ■
Witherslack ▲
A595
Ulverston ▲
Cartmel ▲
Barrow-in-Furness
Isle of Walney
A590
Morecombe
Heysham
Lancast
A68

Point of Ayre

Morecambe Bay

Ramsey Bay
Ramsey
Forton ○
Fleetwood
Kirk Michael
Thornton-Cleveleys ▲
Poulton-le-Fylde ▲
St Michael's on Wyre ■
R. Wyre

Isle of

Laxey Bay

Man

Blackpool ■
Douglas
M55
Kirkham ■
Glenmaye
Preston
Port Erin
Port St Mary
Calf of Man
A583
A59

Southport
A565
A570
Wrightington ■
Coppu Moor
Ormskirk
Skelmersdale
A565
M58

MERSEYSIDE
A580 /St Hele

Liverpool ◙
Birkenhead ◙
M57
M62
Widnes
Runcorn
R. Mersey
M56

△7
Conwy Bay
Colwyn Bay
Llandudno ▲
Glanwyddno
Colwyn Bay ◙
Prestatyn
Rhyl
Llansantfraid Glan Conwy ▲
A55
St George ■
A55
Mollington ▲
CHE
Port Fras
942
ABERCONWY & COLWYN
Denbigh
△7
Chester
FLINTSHIRE

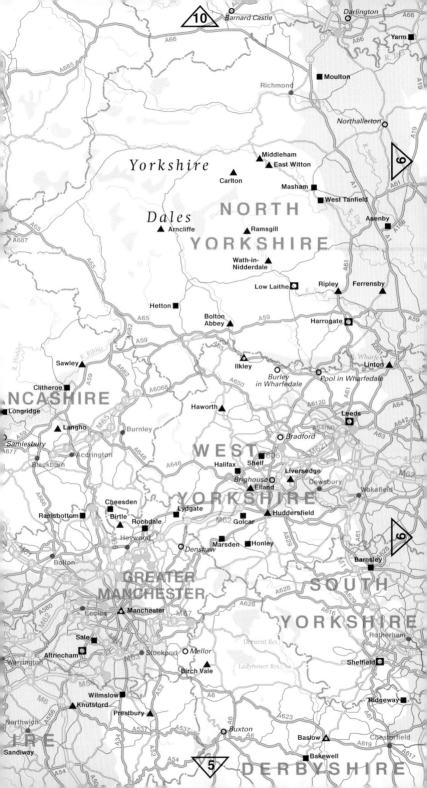

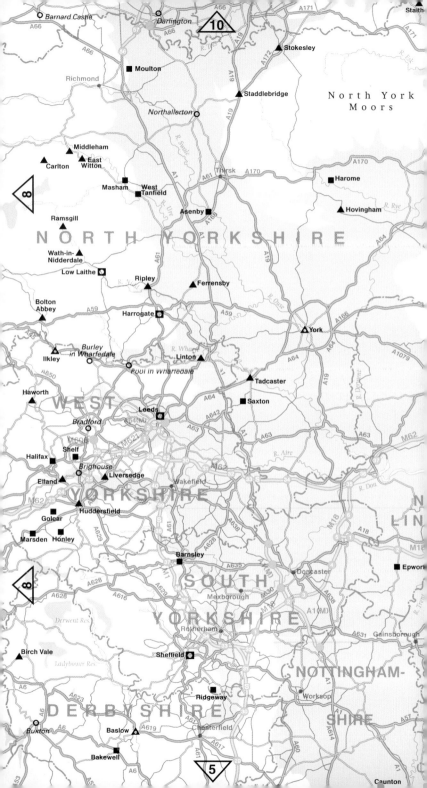

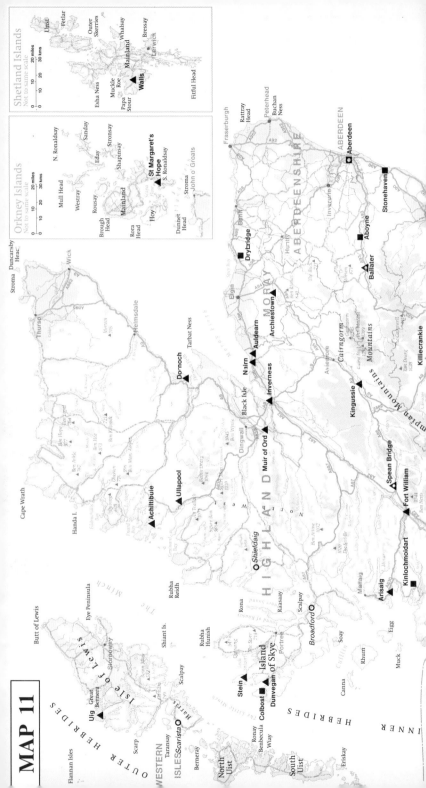

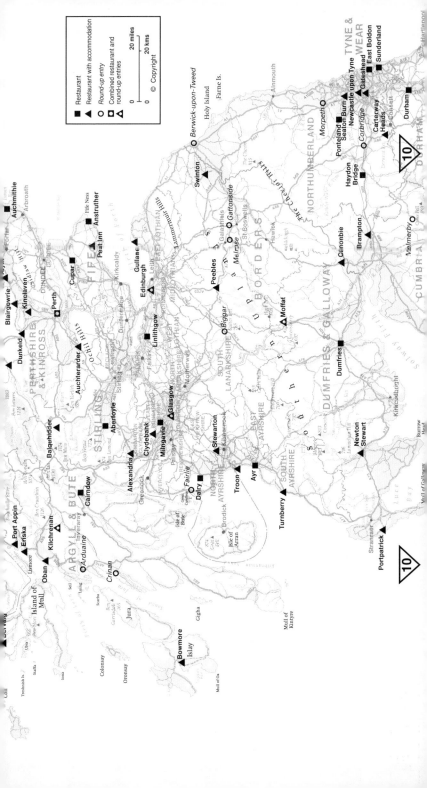

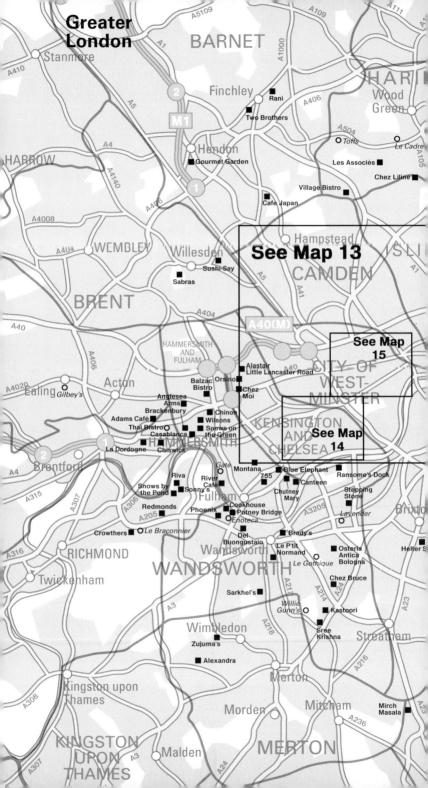

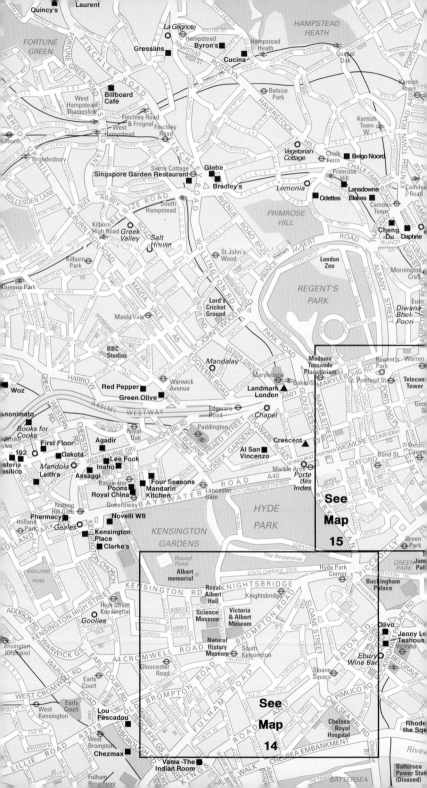

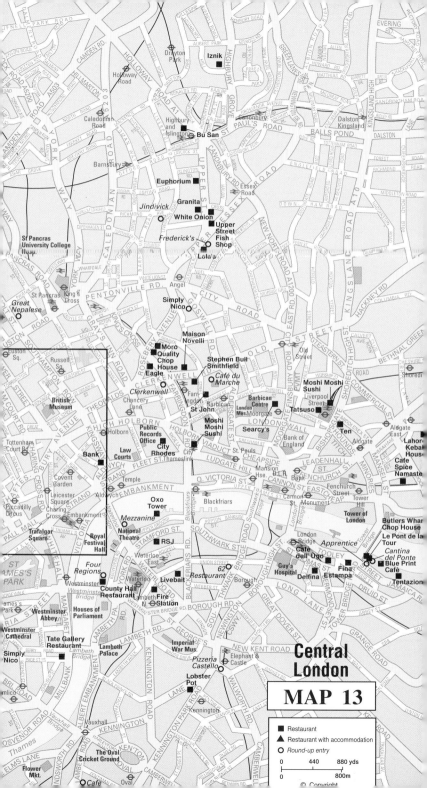

Iznik

Holloway
Road

Drayton
Park

EVERING
RD.

Caledonian
Road

Highbury
and
Islington   Bu San

Dalston
Kingsland

DALSTON

BALLS POND

Barnsbury

Euphorium

Granita
Jindivick   White Onion
Frederick's   Upper
Street
Fish
Shop
Lola's

St Pancras
University College
Hosp.

St Pancras
King's
Cross

Angel

Simply
Nico

Great
Nepalese

Maison
Novelli
Moro
Quality
Chop
House
Eagle   Stephen Bull
Smithfield   Old
Street

Euston
Sq.

Russell
Sq.

Clerkenwell   Café du
Marche
St John   Moshi
Moshi
Sushi
Liverpool
Street
Moshi Moshi
Sushi   Barbican
Centre   Tatsuso
London
Mus. Moorgate

British
Museum

Chancery
Lane

Farring-
don

Barbican
Mansion
House

Searcy's   Ten

Bank
of
England

Lahore
Kebab
House
Cafe
Spice
Namaste

Tottenham
Court Rd.

Holborn

Public
Records
Office
City
Rhodes   St Pauls
Ludgate Hill

CHEAPSIDE   Aldgate
East
Aldgate

Bank   Fenchurch
Street

Covent
Garden   Law
Courts   Temple   City
Thameslink
Blackfriars   Bank   Monument

Tower
Hill

Leicester
Square

Piccadilly
Circus

Charing
Cross   Aldwych
EMBANKMENT   Q. VICTORIA

Oxo
Tower   Blackfriars

Tower of
London   Butlers Wharf
Chop House
Le Pont de la
Tour
Cantina
del Ponte
Blue Print
Café
Tentazioni

Trafalgar
Square

Mezzanine
National
Theatre   RSJ

Royal
Festival
Hall

London
Bridge   Apprentice
Cafe
dell'Ugo
62
Restaurant   Guy's
Hospital   Fina
Estampa
Delfina

Four
Regions
Westminster   County Hall
Restaurant   Livebait
Fire
Station   Borough

Waterloo
East

Houses of
Parliament

Westminster
Abbey

Lambeth
Palace

Imperial
War Mus.

NEW KENT ROAD
Elephant &
Castle   Central
London

Westminster
Cathedral

Simply
Nico

Tate Gallery
Restaurant

Pizzeria
Castello

MAP 13

Lobster
Pot

Kennington

ST
AMES'S
PARK

ames's
Park

The Oval
Cricket Ground

Oval

Flower
Mkt.

Cafe

■ Restaurant
▲ Restaurant with accommodation
○ Round-up entry

0   440   880 yds
0   800m

© Copyright

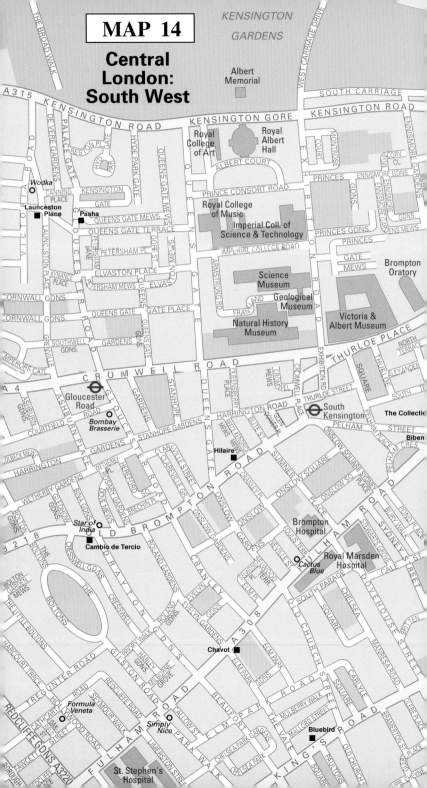

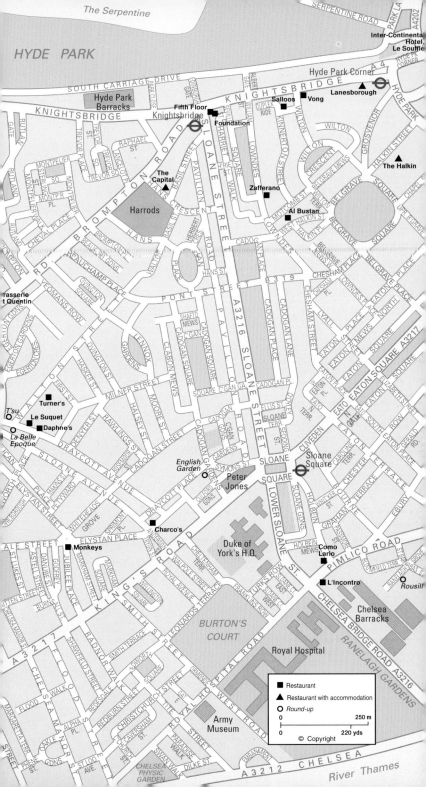

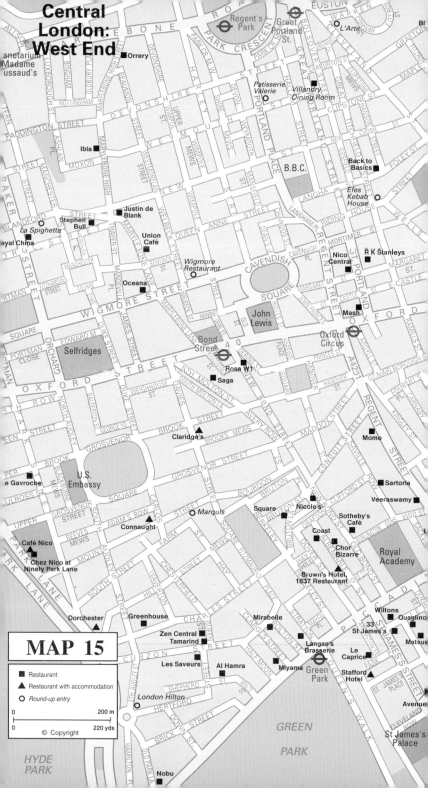

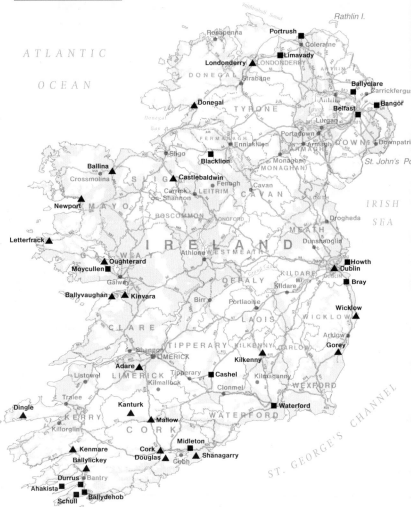

ATLANTIC

OCEAN

Rathlin I.

Rosapenna

Portrush

Coleraine

Londonderry   LONDONDERRY   Limavady

Strabane

Ballyclare

Carrickfergus

Donegal   TYRONE   Bangor

Belfast

Portadown

Donegal Bay

FERMANAGH

Enniskillen

Armagh   Downpatrick

Sligo   DOWN

St. John's Po

Blacklion

MONAGHAN

Castlebaldwin   CAVAN

Ballina

Crossmolina

SLIGO

Fenagh

Cavan

Carrick-on-Shannon   LEITRIM

Newport   MAYO

ROSCOMMON   LONGFORD

IRISH

SEA

Letterfrack   IRELAND

Drogheda

MEATH

Dunshaughlin

Athlone   WESTMEATH

Oughterard   GALWAY

Moycullen

Galway

Howth

Dublin

KILDARE

OFFALY   Kildare

Bray

Ballyvaughan   Kinvara

Birr

Portlaoise

CLARE   Wicklow

WICKLOW

Shannon   TIPPERARY   KILKENNY   CARLOW

LIMERICK   Arklow

Gorey

Adare   Tipperary   Kilkenny

Listowel   LIMERICK   Kilmallock   Cashel   Kilmaganny

Clonmel   WEXFORD

Tralee   Dingle

KERRY   Kanturk   Mallow

Waterford

WATERFORD

Killorglin

CORK

Midleton

Kenmare   Cork   Shanagarry

Douglas

Ballylickey   Cobh

ST. GEORGE'S CHANNEL

Durrus   Bantry

Ahakista

Schull   Ballydehob

ATLANTIC OCEAN

CHEF: Jeff Baker   PROPRIETOR: Michael Gill   OPEN: Mon to Fri L 12 to 2, Mon to Sat D 6.30 to 10 (11 Fri and Sat)   CLOSED: bank hols   MEALS: alc D (main courses £8 to £13.50). Set L £5 (1 course) to £12.95, Set D before 7.15pm £9.75 (2 courses) to £12.95   SERVICE: 10% (optional), card slips closed   CARDS: Amex, Delta, Diners, MasterCard, Switch, Visa   DETAILS: 110 seats. Private parties: 52 main room, 52 private room. Vegetarian meals. Children's helpings. No cigars/pipes in dining room. Wheelchair access (5 steps; also WC). Music. Air-conditioned

Fourth Floor

Harvey Nichols, 107–111 Briggate, Leeds LS1 6AZ	COOKING 3
TEL: (0113) 204 8000 FAX: (0113) 204 8080	COST £26–£53

When Harvey Nichols opened in Leeds in 1996, it seemed to confirm the economic renaissance that the city is currently enjoying. Modern British cooking is how the food on offer in the fourth-floor restaurant is described, which of course means that – bangers and mash with onions and mustard notwithstanding – there is scarcely a recognisably British preparation on the menu, at least until the pudding list is produced. Instead, the food is as trend-conscious as the hard-edged décor of white walls and steel-legged tables. Marinated monkfish on sun-dried tomato couscous might start you off, and be followed by duck breast with parsnip purée and pancetta. 'Clear flavours and a good consistency' characterised one diner's bowl of sweet potato and chilli soup, and bold tastes similarly distinguished a main course of roasted cod on lyonnaise potatoes with parsley hollandaise. Side-orders include chips with aïoli. A woman was heard to gasp, 'This is sheer heaven' of her chocolate marquise. Otherwise, creamed rice-pudding with Yorkshire parkin is a dish designed to woo not just the locals, and espresso and cappuccino have been pronounced 'the best in Leeds'. Efficient service keeps things motoring. Oregon Pinot Gris and California Grenache indicate the catholicity of the wine list. Own-label house wines are £11.95.

CHEF: Simon Shaw   PROPRIETOR: Harvey Nichols plc   OPEN: Mon to Sat L 12 to 3, Thur to Sat D 6 (7 Sat) to 10.30   CLOSED: 25 and 26 Dec   MEALS: alc (main courses £9 to £16). Set L £11.95 (2 courses), Set D £13.50 (2 courses) to £15.95   SERVICE: 10% (optional), card slips closed CARDS: Amex, Delta, Diners, MasterCard, Switch, Visa   DETAILS: 90 seats. 10 seats outside. Private parties: 120 main room. Vegetarian meals. Children's helpings. No-smoking area. Wheelchair access (also WC). Music. Air-conditioned

Leodis 🍸

Victoria Mill, Sovereign Street, Leeds LS1 4BJ	COOKING 4
TEL: (0113) 242 1010 FAX: (0113) 243 1411	COST £22–£48

'Leeds is obviously a boom city,' mused one visitor to this canal-side redevelopment. Lunchtime crowds were hovering outside the door before opening time, as if at the first day of Harrods' sale. What they were waiting for was Steven Kendell's vibrant, modern brasserie cooking that, in January, furnished one reporter with 'outstandingly good' scallops on tomato salad and a Madeira-sauced fillet steak. Portions are on the generous side, but the choice is wide enough to cater for all constitutions. Fish and seafood aficionados are well served with oysters dressed in red wine and shallots, and monkfish with apples in cider. Finish with melon and ginger granita, toffee and banana ice-cream, or more-filling marsala cheesecake. Pastrywork has come in for criticism, as has a slight tendency to 'gild the lily' in presentation, but the overall standard seems consistent enough to justify the enthusiasm of those early arrivers. Caring service extended to handing a copy of the day's *Yorkshire Post* to one solo luncher who was trying not to stare into space.

Phil Richardson has put together a very user-friendly list of wines, dividing them into red, white or sparkling and bracketing those above £20 as 'expensive'. Guest wines, Phil's personal selection page and 'extra fine wines from our cellars at Paris' are welcome features, as are the helpful notes. Overall the prices are reasonable with a good, international range of styles and flavours at the lower end, but it has to be said that some of the classed-growth clarets are very expensive. CELLARMAN'S CHOICE: Coteaux de l'Ardèche, Grand Ardèche Chardonnay 1995, Louis Latour, £18.15; Mamre Brook Cabernet-Shiraz 1994, Barossa Valley, S Australia, £14.95.

CHEF: Steven Kendell   PROPRIETORS: Martin Spalding, Steven Kendell and Phil Richardson
OPEN: Mon to Fri L 12 to 2, Mon to Sat D 6 to 10   CLOSED: 25 and 26 Dec, L bank hols   MEALS:
alc (main courses £9 to £14). Set L and D £13.95 (not available after 7.15 Sat)   SERVICE: not inc
CARDS: Amex, Delta, Diners, MasterCard, Switch, Visa   DETAILS: 180 seats. 60 seats outside.
Private parties: 180 main room. Vegetarian meals. Children's helpings. Wheelchair access (also
WC). Music

Marcell's ⅝✳

NEW ENTRY

300 Harrogate Road, Leeds LS17 6LY
TEL: (0113) 236 9991   FAX: (0113) 236 9940   COOKING 4
EMAIL: s1hawkins@aol.com.   COST £19–£38

Wayne Newsome has cooked his way around some of Yorkshire's big-name establishments, while baking bread by night for a Leeds market stall. Now he's channelled this prodigious energy into running his own restaurant, in a mock-Tudor parade of shops on the outskirts of the city. The breads are as good as ever and the rest is accomplished enough to cause a few ripples in Leeds – a city not short of good restaurants.

The funky bar and lime-green dining-room provide a slightly bizarre setting for some cutting-edge cuisine. Written in unfussy, abbreviated style, the two-course set menu (with vegetables charged extra) might kick off with salad of roast chicken livers, followed by confit of oxtail with red wine jus or breast of duck with roast apricots. Good timing, a sense of proportion and a light hand are evident in dishes such as a hot olive and red onion tart made with 'melt-in-the-mouth' pastry, topped with a scoop of chilled fromage frais and served with a well-flavoured orange emulsion. The modern approach doesn't preclude some polished renditions of traditional dishes: 'tasty, tender' roast leg of lamb came with Yorkshire pudding that 'tasted like Yorkshire pudding should taste' and a good, deep-brown gravy. Desserts might not always match their menu descriptions but are so good that no one seems to mind – apple charlotte was a dark, rich chocolate cake topped with caramelised apple, while banana and toffee crunch was an excellent variation on crème brûlée. 'A good neighbourhood restaurant that's well worth travelling to,' wrote a reporter drawn by a bargain Sunday lunch at £11.95. The imaginative, engagingly written wine list offers plenty of choice under £20, with house wine at £9.75.

CHEF: Wayne Newsome   PROPRIETORS: Wayne Newsome, Errol Gilbert and Stephen Hawkins   OPEN: Sun L 12 to 2, Tue to Sun D 7 to 10 (10.30 Sat)   CLOSED: 1 to15 Jan.   MEALS: Set L Sun £11.95, Set D £12.95 (2 courses)   SERVICE: 10% (optional), card slips closed   CARDS: Amex, Delta, Diners, MasterCard, Switch, Visa   DETAILS: 56 seats. Private parties: 55 main room. Car park. Vegetarian meals. Children's helpings. No children under 9 at weekends after 8pm. No smoking in dining-room. Music   £5

Pool Court at 42

42 The Calls, Leeds LS2 7EW
TEL: (0113) 244 4242   FAX: (0113) 234 3332

COOKING 7
COST £29–£61

'This establishment offers a top-flight chef, superb sourcing, good management, good service and – we believe – good value for money. What a great combination.' So rang one endorsement. The sleek, ovoid, nautically themed dining-room overlooking the water is 'intimate' rather than large, decorated in cool shades of grey and dark blue, with chrome and blond wood, and attractively lit. In today's culinary climate, dishes may not sound exciting – whole grilled Dover sole, roast Lincolnshire duckling – but in fact they are, and the lack of cutting edge, Pacific rim, fusion, crossover and experiment is considered 'a welcome change'. But neither is the food plain. Flavours are positive and well balanced, which makes for 'hugely enjoyable eating'. The ability to make simple food taste extraordinary is a rare skill, and Jeff Baker has it.

Top-notch ingredients, apparent at every turn, help enormously. Fish, for example, has yielded 'juicy' roast Whitby cod with glossy flakes and a salty, crispy crust and, on a lunchtime menu, deep-fried, golden-brown salmon fish-cakes, dry and crispy, with a 'semi-soft mousseline' texture inside, served with herbs and salad leaves. Indeed the lunchtime value is considered 'amazing'. One couple with a four-year-old child ate some of the best food they had tasted in the north of England – including creamed eggs with caviare, and linguine with truffles – and went away with 'change from forty quid'.

Elsewhere, luxuries abound, from chicken consommé with truffled dumplings imparting 'immense depth of flavour', to strips of pink, tender pigeon breast on buttered Savoy cabbage, surrounded by a stock and wine-based sauce with girolles and truffle; 'no lack of flavour here'. Among desserts, consider the crème brûlée, red fruit sablé, chocolate fondant, and baked lemon tart, any of which might appear in the 'assiette' of three desserts. Cheeses are served in good condition with a piece of fruitcake, producing 'a particularly happy pairing' for one reporter's Explorateur. A Classics menu offers the option of a 'multi-course sprint through the à la carte', which is reasonably priced, providing you have the appetite.

Olives and almonds start proceedings, breads are especially good, and service is 'helpful, correct, but not over-formal'. In place of a house wine 'Michael Gill's selection' of a dozen or more bottles heads up the varied list, and although mark-ups can be on the high side there is enough temptation under £20 to satisfy. Prices start around £13.

ENGLAND

CHEF: Jeff Baker   PROPRIETORS: Michael and Hanni Gill   OPEN: Mon to Fri L 12 to 2, Mon to Sat
D 7 to 10 (10.30 Fri and Sat)   CLOSED: bank hols   MEALS: Set L £12.50 (2 courses) to £17, Set D
£24.50 (2 courses) to £39.50   SERVICE: 10%, card slips closed   CARDS: Amex, Delta, Diners,
MasterCard, Switch, Visa   DETAILS: 38 seats. 20 seats outside. Private parties: 38 main room.
Vegetarian meals. Children's helpings. No cigars/pipes in dining-room. Wheelchair access (also
WC). Music. Air-conditioned

Rascasse ⅋

Canal Wharf, Water Lane, Leeds LS11 5BB   COOKING 6
TEL: (0113) 244 6611   FAX: (0113) 244 0736   COST £25–£61

The once run-down Yorkshire end of the Leeds-Liverpool Canal is now a
thriving zone of culture, commerce and good eating, and this former grain store –
overlooking a convoy of colourful barges – is a vibrant, capacious, brightly lit,
'hustly bustly' mecca for modern brasserie cooking. France is the inspiration for
much of it, from foie gras terrine with Poilâne toast, to seared tuna with
ratatouille and beurre noisette, and the evident skill delights, producing 'firm
and tasty' roast scallops with a sharp celeriac purée and truffle-flavoured
dressing, and lobster ravioli in a clear bouillon with shiitake and Chinese
vegetables.

Sauces are properly reduced and glossy without being syrupy, adding to the
pleasure of, for example, pink calf's liver, and 'succulent' guinea-fowl; during
the game season, birds from the Yorkshire Moors join their imported French
poultry cousins. Extras include pomme purée ('we call this mashed potato in
Yorkshire,' explained a reporter) and tapénade. Puddings typically play one
component off against another, as in rice-pudding with spiced poached fruit and
a 'tangy' syrup, or lemon tart with raspberry sorbet that was a 'zingy' mix of
flavours.

The 'Fastrack' menu available at lunch and early evening is a useful resource,
offering perhaps tuna with lime butter, duck confit with roast root vegetables,
and chocolate tart with vanilla ice-cream. 'Most of the staff are French,' observed
a reporter, 'which, even today, still adds a hint of something' (*je ne sais quoi*,
presumably), and although service has been praised, the reception procedure
has been a bit confused on occasion. Well over half the wines on the intelligently
chosen list hail from France. It is particularly good on Burgundy but not afraid to
explore lesser-known regions, like China's Shandong Province or deepest,
darkest West Sussex, in its search for quality and interest at a fair price. House
French is £11. CELLARMAN'S CHOICE: De Gyffarde Sauvignon Blanc 1997,
Marlborough, New Zealand, £19.50; Côtes du Rhône Villages 1995, Paul
Jaboulet Aîné, £13.50.

CHEF: Simon Gueller   PROPRIETORS: Simon Gueller and Nigel Jolliffe   OPEN: Mon to Fri L 12 to
2, Mon to Sat D 6.30 to 10 (10.30 Fri and Sat).   CLOSED: 1 week after Christmas, bank hol
Mons   MEALS: alc (main courses £12.50 to £17.50). Set L and D Mon to Fri until 7.30 £13.50 (2
courses) to £17. Bar L available   SERVICE: not inc   CARDS: Amex, Delta, Diners, MasterCard,
Switch, Visa   DETAILS: 100 seats. 30 seats outside. Private parties: 60 main room. Car park.
Vegetarian meals. Children welcome. No cigars/pipes in dining-room. Wheelchair access (also
WC). Music. Air-conditioned

Salvo's £

115 Otley Road, Headingley, Leeds LS6 3PX
TEL: (0113) 275 5017   FAX: (0113) 278 9452   COOKING 2
EMAIL: 100530.274@compuserve.com   COST £19–£37

Set back from the main road through Headingley, with a discreet, dark blue frontage, and a bar to bring the queues inside, Salvo's is smartly turned out, with pale wood, deep ochre walls, and some 'Jackson Pollock by numbers' on the walls. The long menu, with daily specials on top, offers food that is 'fresh and not too expensive'. Pizza and pasta count for much of the output, and supplies of marinated anchovies and roasted artichokes come from southern Italy, although given a starter of tandoori-style chicken this is not food for purists. Quite a bit of cheese finds its way into dishes: deep-fried Brie, though not exactly cutting-edge, is a good example of its kind, molten Stilton is poured over warm avocado, and a cheese sauce might accompany queen scallops in the shell. Among the ten pizza options is a calzone-style Kiev, the dough formed into something resembling a bowler hat, stuffed with profuse quantities of chicken and garlic, so massive it 'could probably only happen in Yorkshire'; enough to knock any idea of dessert on the head anyway. Italy and the New World dominate the 35-strong good-value wine list, which opens around £10.

CHEFS: Michael Leggiero and Pam Nelson   PROPRIETORS: the Dammone family   OPEN: Mon to Sat 12 to 2, 6 to 10.45   MEALS: alc (main courses £5.50 to £13)   SERVICE: not inc   CARDS: Amex, Delta, MasterCard, Switch, Visa   DETAILS: 65 seats. Private parties: 25 main room. Vegetarian meals. Children's helpings. Wheelchair access (not WC). Music. Air-conditioned

Sous le Nez en Ville ▮ £

The Basement, Quebec House, Quebec Street,
Leeds LS1 2HA   COOKING 4
TEL: (0113) 244 0108   FAX: (0113) 245 0240   COST £20–£46

It would be unfair, reckons one reporter, to characterise this basement restaurant as the tortoise to some of the hares running elsewhere in Leeds, but if its development has been more measured, then results are, at best, scarcely less impressive. The setting is bare board floors, bentwood chairs, modern pictures, plain white napkins and crockery. Fish is one strong suit, offal another. Plaice comes with 'real chips', crisp and dry, cooked in beef dripping, while a pyramid of chicken livers – 'crusty on the outside, melting within, and beautifully sweet' – has been constructed over caramelised shallots. Chargrilling is also applied to venison, ribeye steak, and crisp-skinned, moist-fleshed chicken served with chive-flecked yoghurt and Thai spices.

The kitchen is not afraid to tackle strong flavours, expensive ingredients, inexpensive ingredients, exotic ingredients, classic combinations, or unusual combinations: expect to find deep-fried Brie alongside terrine of foie gras with a clear thyme-infused jelly. The 'early-bird' menu offers simpler fare, but there is still good choice, and dishes are enticing. Willing staff trot off to find out what they don't know, but sometimes seem to lack organisation. It may help first-timers to know that drinks must be ordered at the bar. Wines are strongest within France, even though Spanish, Italian and New World wines are all of good pedigree. Prices are kept well reined in, with plenty of choice below £15. A dozen house wines (including two Hidalgo sherries) start at £8.50 a bottle, £1.55 a glass. CELLARMAN'S CHOICE: Rully 'Les St-Jacques' 1996, François d'Allaines, £16.95; Rioja Reserva, Viña Ardanza 1989, La Rioja Alta, £22.50.

CHEF: Andrew Carter   PROPRIETOR: C.R.C.R. Partnership   OPEN: Mon to Sat 12 to 2.30, 6 to 10 (11 Fri and Sat)   CLOSED: bank hols   MEALS: alc (main courses £7.50 to £14.50). Set D before 7.30 £14.95 (inc wine)   SERVICE: not inc, card slips closed   CARDS: Amex, Delta, MasterCard, Switch, Visa   DETAILS: 86 seats. Private parties: 20 main room. Vegetarian meals. Children welcome. Occasional music   £5

LEICESTER Leicestershire   map 5

Welford Place £

9 Welford Place, Leicester LE1 6ZH	COOKING 3
TEL: (0116) 247 0758 FAX: (0116) 247 1843	COST £21–£44

Occupying a commanding corner spot near the Magistrates' Courts and Registry Office, Welford Place makes a welcome return as a main entry after a year in the Round-up section. The Victorian brick and stone building has not been prettied up, nor had its original 'gentlemens' club' character modernised away, and although this might tend to induce a rather 'sombre' feel in the dining-room, all-day opening and multiple eating-options soon bring a smile to reporters' faces. Breakfast is available until noon, sandwiches and snacks can be eaten any time, and a daily-changing fixed-price menu supplements the seasonally changing *carte*.

Ambition is pitched so as not to over-stretch the kitchen, which focuses on a manageable repertoire and careful buying: for example, generous fillets of bass, salmon, cod and brill, all accurately timed, served with a glossy hollandaise. Cooking relies on sound technique and lightness of touch – pieces of chicken breast in a clean-flavoured lemon and basil sauce – and a sense of immediacy pervades even a simple dish of chunkily sliced, decently herby sausage sauté with small new potatoes. Finish, perhaps, in Italian style with zuppa inglese or a 'wonderfully thick but light' version of tiramisù. Service is young, efficient and 'unpushy', and wines are a sensible middle-ground selection of more or less familiar names arranged stylistically; most are below £20, including house French at £10.25.

CHEF: Lino Poli   PROPRIETORS: Michael and Valerie Hope, and Paul Vidic   OPEN: all week 8 to 11 (9 to 6 Sun)   MEALS: alc (main courses £7.50 to £15.50). Set L and D £12.50. Breakfast and snack menus available   SERVICE: not inc   CARDS: Amex, Delta, Diners, MasterCard, Switch, Visa   DETAILS: 216 seats. Private parties: 80 main room, 20 to 70 private rooms. Vegetarian meals. Children's helpings. No music   £5

All entries, including Round-ups, are fully indexed at the back of the Guide.

indicates that smoking is either banned altogether or that a dining-room is maintained for non-smokers. The symbol does not apply to restaurants that simply have no-smoking areas.

LEWDOWN Devon   map 1

▲ *Lewtrenchard Manor* 🐟✻   **NEW ENTRY**

Lewdown EX20 4PN
from Exeter take A30 to A386, left at T-junction then
right on to old A38 for 6m; left where signposted   COOKING 5
'Lewtrenchard'   COST £27–£46

A grey-stone Elizabethan manor-house with an imposingly solid, even sombre, façade, Lewtrenchard is set in well-manicured gardens complete with fountain and dovecote. The Reverend Sabine Baring-Gould, novelist and author of 'Onward, Christian Soldiers' among other hymns, once lived here, but the Murrays took up residence in 1988. Despite the period weightiness of the interiors, where much dark panelling and carved oak is in evidence, the place is run with an appreciable lightness of tone, and staff treat guests with a sense of humanity often lacking in such country piles.

David Jones, previously sous-chef to Chris Colmer at Ynyshir Hall in Eglwysfach (see entry, Wales), arrived in spring 1998, bringing a lift to the operation. 'The menu eats less exotic than it sounds,' commented a reporter, who for all that was happy to commend most of what she did eat. Seared Cornish scallops have come with parsley mousseline and roasted leeks, while risotto primavera is given a new spin by acquiring chorizo and a Meaux mustard sabayon, making an ecumenical harmony of Italian, Spanish and French components. Robustness characterises main courses such as baked cod with asparagus, broad beans and morel cream sauce, while chump of local lamb with black olive blini, fennel tortellini and basil gravy offers flavour-filled meat, a pancake of properly proved dough, expertly timed pasta and a perfectly judged stock-based sauce. Desserts are full of thought-provoking flavours, too, as in pistachio parfait with a sauce of coconut and lemon grass, or hot blackcurrant soufflé served with a glass of aniseed ice-cream of diverting intensity. The wine list scoops up decent bottles from most of the major countries but focuses particularly on South Africa, where the owners hie from. House selections, of which there are no fewer than 14, start at £10.

CHEF: David Jones   PROPRIETORS: James and Sue Murray   OPEN: Sun L 12.15 to 1.30, all week D 7 to 9   MEALS: Set L Sun £19.50, Set D £30. Bar L available   SERVICE: not inc, card slips closed   CARDS: Amex, Delta, Diners, MasterCard, Switch, Visa   DETAILS: 45 seats. 10 seats outside. Private parties: 8 main room, 20 private room. Car park. Children welcome; under-8s by arrangement. No smoking in dining-room. Wheelchair access (also WC). Music ACCOMMODATION: 9 rooms, all with bath/shower. TV. Phone. B&B £80 to £150. Children welcome; under-8s by arrangement. No dogs in public rooms or left in bedrooms unattended. Afternoon teas. Fishing (*The Which? Hotel Guide*) £5

£5 *indicates that the restaurant has elected to participate in the* Good Food Guide *voucher scheme. For full details see page 6.*

'My waitress thought the question of whether the mousseline of chicken was hot or cold was "a very interesting point".' (On eating in Norfolk)

LIDGATE Suffolk   map 6

Star Inn

The Street, Lidgate CB8 9PP
TEL: (01638) 500275   COOKING 1
on B1063, 6m SE of Newmarket   COST £26–£38

Maria Teresa Axon has brought a touch of Catalan earthiness to this part of
landlocked Suffolk, and her five-centuries old village pub provides a bustling –
if unlikely – setting for food with plenty of Mediterranean gutsiness. Native
dishes, including Catalan salad, paella, and salmon 'a la Gallega' are mainstays
of her short menu, but the kitchen also looks further afield for 'very good'
scallops in bacon, venison in port, and sirloin steak in Stilton sauce. 'Melting'
carpaccio of salmon is a favourite way to begin, and reporters have also enthused
about monkfish marinière: a piscine extravaganza served in a large earthenware
bowl. Service is personable, especially when Maria Teresa is on the premises.
Greene King real ales are alternatives to the modest, affordable wine list. House
wines are £10.

CHEF/PROPRIETOR: Maria Teresa Axon   OPEN: all week L 12 to 2, Mon to Sat D 7 to 10   CLOSED:
24 and 25 Dec, 1 Jan   MEALS: alc (main courses £9.50 to £12.50). Set L Mon to Fri £4.50 (1
course) to £8.50 (2 courses), Set L Sun £12.50. Bar L available Mon to Sat. BYO £2.50   SERVICE:
not inc, card slips closed; 10% for parties of 8 or more   CARDS: Amex, Delta, Diners,
MasterCard, Switch, Visa   DETAILS: 50 seats. 20 seats outside. Private parties: 25 main room,
25 private room. Car park. Vegetarian meals. Children's helpings. Occasional music   £5

LIFTON Devon   map 1

▲ *Arundell Arms* ✸✳

Lifton PL16 0AA
TEL: (01566) 784666   FAX: (01566) 784494   COOKING 4
just off A30, 3m E of Launceston   COST £25–£52

The Arundell is an erstwhile coaching-inn not far from the Cornish border and
the ruins of Tintagel Castle. Its proprietor is nearing the completion of her fourth
decade here, and the whole operation runs with consummate ease. Despite the
heavily creeper-clad pubby exterior, inside is grander than you might expect, the
dining-room a vision in cool pastel peach with a massively dangling chandelier
the centrepiece. This is a kitchen that thrives on sourcing wholesomely reared
and naturally produced local fare, including Devon beef and lamb, fish from
Looe, and ewes' milk cheese from Launceston. Restrained classicism is the
keynote, manifested in asparagus soup with tarragon cream, chicken liver pâté
with apricot chutney, or lambs' kidneys fried and served with pesto and a
garlic-dressed salad, a dish that impressed an inspector for its clear flavours and
textures. To follow, there may be a casserole of mixed fish – sole, monkfish, red
mullet and scallops in a parsleyed cream sauce – or straightforward meat
preparations such as Trelough duckling with red wine and thyme risotto. A trio
of citrus desserts brings top-notch lemon sorbet, lemon tart and orange terrine,
while cheeses are of impeccable pedigree. Relaxed, chatty service is pleasingly
informal. Wines are stronger in the major French regions than in the rest of the

world, but prices are at least fair and there's a good showing of halves. Australian and French house wines start at £9.75.

CHEFS: Philip Burgess and Nick Shopland   PROPRIETOR: Anne Voss-Bark   OPEN: all week 12.30 to 2.30, 7.30 to 9.30   CLOSED: D 24 to 26 Dec   MEALS: Set L £15 (2 courses) to £18, Set D £27.50 to £34.50. Bar food available   SERVICE: not inc   CARDS: Amex, Diners, MasterCard, Switch, Visa   DETAILS: 70 seats. Private parties: 80 main room, 30 private room. Car park. Vegetarian meals. Children's helpings. No young children at D. No smoking in dining-room. Wheelchair access (2 steps; not WC). Music   ACCOMMODATION: 28 rooms, all with bath/shower. TV. Phone. B&B £68 to £107. Children welcome. High teas for children. Baby facilities. Afternoon teas. Fishing (*The Which? Hotel Guide*) £5

LINCOLN Lincolnshire   map 9

Jew's House ✦

15 The Strait, Lincoln LN2 1JD	COOKING 3
TEL: (01522) 524851	COST £24–£50

The Jew's House wears its antiquity well. Built around 1190, it is 'one of the oldest inhabited houses in Britain', according to the brochure. There are no fancy decorations, simply beams and whitewashed stone walls hung with a few art nouveau prints and reproductions of wine labels. Over the years, chef Richard Gibbs has gradually refined his version of Anglo-French cooking. There isn't much in the way of modernistic frippery or wild experimentation, but results on the plate are professional and excite the palate. The classic approach shows in a 'faultless', smooth yet textured cream of celery soup with Stilton, and medallions of top-notch beef in a 'gentle' bordelaise sauce.

From time to time there are forays further afield, as in roast aubergine with sun-dried tomatoes and sage-scented polenta, or grilled salmon with oyster mushrooms, spinach and balsamic vinegar, but it's back to France for desserts. Both lemon tart with crème fraîche and almond tart were deemed 'first-class' by an inspector, but choice extends to chocolate marquise, tarte Tatin with calvados cream sauce, and Grand Marnier soufflé. Cheeses are emphatically Gallic too, although there may be a representative or two from nearer home as well. Service is generally on the ball, discreet and efficient. As you might expect, France looms large on the list of around 40 wines, although there is plenty of sound drinking from elsewhere. House wines start at £9.50.

CHEF: Richard Gibbs   PROPRIETORS: Richard and Sally Gibbs   OPEN: Tue to Sat 12 to 1.30, 7 to 9   MEALS: alc (main courses £12.50 to £15). Set L £12.50 (2 courses) to £15, Set D £25   SERVICE: not inc   CARDS: Amex, Delta, Diners, MasterCard, Switch, Visa   DETAILS: 26 seats. Private parties: 26 main room, 10 private room. Vegetarian meals. Children's helpings. No smoking in dining-room. Music

---

Wig & Mitre £

30 Steep Hill, Lincoln LN2 1TL	COOKING 4
TEL: (01522) 535190 FAX: (01522) 532402	COST £20–£46

What makes Lincoln's compact centre different from dozens of other English market towns and cities is its ancient 'top-of-the-hill' site, crowned with castle and cathedral. Amid buildings dating back to Elizabethan times and before, Wig

& Mitre's narrow frontage opens into a set of rooms where 'everything runs into each other', although the ground floor is more of a bar and upstairs more of a dining-room. But the point here, as the well-established and enlightened policy makes clear, is that the same food is available throughout. This, together with the seven-day-a-week all-day opening hours, puts the customer centre-stage: eat what you like, when, and where.

The food, as at their more recently opened Caunton Beck (see entry, Caunton), consists of 'pub favourites with modern English additions' and covers a multitude of dishes from sardine, lemon and garlic pâté, via Malaysian prawn and noodle soup, to beef braised in real ale and mustard. Dishes are spread over four menus – daily, seasonal, sandwich and breakfast – so the combinations and permutations are virtually endless. There is 'no pretension, no theatre' about the service, but there is sincerity behind the usual 'is everything all right?' enquiry. Around 60 wines, the majority under £20, start with house French at £10.25.

CHEFS: Paul Vidic, Peter Dodd and Mark Cheseldine   PROPRIETORS: Michael and Valerie Hope, and Paul Vidic   OPEN: all week 8am to 11pm   MEALS: alc (main courses £5.50 to £16.50). BYO (corkage negotiable)   SERVICE: not inc   CARDS: Amex, Delta, Diners, MasterCard, Switch, Visa   DETAILS: 120 seats. 24 seats outside. Private parties: 60 main room. Vegetarian meals. Children's helpings. Wheelchair access (4 steps; not WC). No music   (£5)

LINTON West Yorkshire   map 8

▲ *Wood Hall* ⚡

Trip Lane, Linton LS22 4JA
TEL: (01937) 587271   FAX: (01937) 584353
from Wetherby take A661 N for ½m, turn left to
Sicklinghall and Linton, then left to Linton and Wood   COOKING 3
Hall, and turn right in Linton opposite Windmill pub   COST £21–£47

Wood Hall once stood on the banks of the river that now runs through its grounds, its slight transposition occasioned when a detachment of Cromwell's army smashed the original building in a fit of the vapours and threw it in the water. It rose again in 1750, and now boasts a pillared entrance, neatly rollered lawns, and gym equipment that is the last word in fitness technology. It also boasts Phillip Pomfret's weekly-changing menus that offer three courses plus coffee at a fixed price with no supplements. The food is in gently rich and unalarming country-style, embracing salad of smoked chicken, walnuts and snow peas dressed with lemon and honey; pesto-crusted scallops cooked in garlic, vermouth and cream; and Gressingham duck breast with buttered spinach, an orange pancake and a sauce of port and shallots. It is all served with willingness and civility, though very formal. Wines are an entertainingly wide-ranging collection, and there are many classy producers, but prices are high. House selections from France, Argentina and Australia open at £11.95.

The text of entries is based on unsolicited reports sent in by readers, backed up by inspections conducted anonymously. The factual details under the text are from questionnaires the Guide *sends to all restaurants that feature in the book.*

CHEF: Phillip Pomfret   PROPRIETOR: Arcadian International Ltd   OPEN: Sun to Fri L 12 to 2.30 (3 Sun), all week D 7 to 10   MEALS: Set L Mon to Fri £15.95, Set L Sun £13.50, Set D £18 (1 course) to £29.95   SERVICE: not inc   CARDS: Amex, Delta, Diners, MasterCard, Switch, Visa   DETAILS: 80 seats. 20 seats outside. Private parties: 100 main room, 10 to 100 private rooms. Car park. Vegetarian meals. Children's helpings. No smoking in dining-room. Wheelchair access (also WC). Music   ACCOMMODATION: 43 rooms, all with bath/shower. TV. Phone. Room only £99 to £155. Rooms for disabled. Children welcome. High teas for children. Afternoon teas. Swimming-pool. Fishing   £5

LITTLE SHELFORD   Cambridgeshire   map 6

Sycamore House ♥ £✻

1 Church Street, Little Shelford CB2 5HG	COOKING 4
TEL: (01223) 843396	COST £31–£38

Michael Sharpe in the kitchen and his wife Susan out front make a capable and assured team in this admirable little local restaurant, serving up simple, precise cooking in a comfortable cream-painted dining-room. Their short but varied fixed-price menu finds room for homely offerings such as tomato and red pepper soup, or roast partridge on parsnip mash as well as for more jazzy combinations: spaghetti with roasted peppers, beef, soy sauce and spring onions, for example, whose strong flavours complement rather than compete with each other. Ideas are bold – confit duck with black olives, for example – though in practice, our inspector noted, flavourings can be reticent, their potential not always exploited to the full. Puddings might include decent home-made ice-cream, a nicely textured panettone bread-and-butter pudding, or chocolate tart. Some 60 wines of good provenance are offered at remarkably low prices, and that includes vintage champagne. House French is £9.95, but this is the sort of list that presents the perfect excuse to treat yourself to finer fare. CELLARMAN'S CHOICE: Côte de Beaune, Ladoix 1996, Verget, £22; Rosso di Montalcino 1995, Argiano, £15.75.

CHEF: Michael Sharpe   PROPRIETORS: Michael and Susan Sharpe   OPEN: Tue to Sat D only 7.30 to 9   CLOSED: 24 Dec to 1 Jan   MEALS: Set D £22.50. BYO £6   SERVICE: not inc, card slips closed   CARDS: Delta, MasterCard, Switch, Visa   DETAILS: 24 seats. Private parties: 24 main room. Car park. Vegetarian meals. No children under 12. No smoking in dining-room. No music £5

LITTLE WALSINGHAM   Norfolk   map 6

▲ Old Bakehouse £✻

33 High Street, Little Walsingham NR22 6BZ	
TEL/FAX: (01328) 820454	
EMAIL: chrispadley@compuserve.com	COOKING 1
on the B1105, 4½m N of Fakenham	COST £31–£43

Part Georgian, with sixteenth-century ovens – in a much older village with medieval houses still standing – the Old Bakehouse aims for plain but satisfying cooking along Anglo-French lines. Thus lamb kidneys are given a cream and mustard sauce, pork is cooked with prunes, and a coarse-textured terrine baked in a chicken is served with a chicory and orange salad. Among the more interesting dishes, local crab is baked in filo, and there is an old-fashioned pie of steak, kidney and smoked oyster in a red wine gravy. The vegetarian menu has offered warm goats'-cheese tartlet, and that old standby, curried nut roast. Finish with banoffi pie, or blackberry and apple crème brûlée, and drink a reasonably priced wine from the predominantly French list. House vin de table is £10.25.

CHEF: Chris Padley   PROPRIETORS: Chris and Helen Padley   OPEN: Sun L once a month 12.15 to 1.30, Wed to Sat D 7 to 8.30 (9 Sat)   CLOSED: 1 week Nov, 25 and 26 Dec, 2 weeks Jan to Feb, 1 week June   MEALS: alc (main courses £14.50 to £16.50). Set L Sun £13.25   SERVICE: not inc, card slips closed   CARDS: Delta, MasterCard, Switch, Visa   DETAILS: 48 seats. Private parties: 40 main room, 10 private room. Vegetarian meals. No young children. No smoking in dining-room. Music   ACCOMMODATION: 3 rooms, all with bath/shower. TV. B&B £27.50 to £45. No young children. Dogs by arrangement (*The Which? Hotel Guide*) (£5)

LIVERPOOL Merseyside   map 8

Becher's Brook ¾✳   [NEW ENTRY]

29A Hope Street, L1 9BQ   COOKING 5
TEL: (0151) 707 0005   FAX: (0151) 708 7011   COST £25–£73

Liverpool has languished far too long without a major non-ethnic restaurant to do it credit, but hope may now be at hand – on Hope Street. Situated in an end-terrace property between the two cathedrals, opposite the historic Philharmonic pub, it is named after the infamous jump at Aintree racecourse. If the décor screams 'Canadian Native' at you, that is because much of it has been culled from the proprietor's mother's collection of Inuit, Cree and Haida artefacts. Should the mood prove infectious, you can start with a bowl of Nova Scotia clam chowder, and finish with a piece of matured Canadian Cheddar.

David Cooke's wide-ranging culinary net also hauls in grilled foie gras on morel polenta in a plum wine reduction with pickled vegetables; and saffron and red pepper risotto under a puff-pastry lid. He has an affinity with Japanese techniques, and tempura-battered items feature prominently, from canapés all the way to banana with honey and lime ice-cream. An inspection dinner included a fricassee of lambs' kidneys and sweetbreads that demonstrated sensitive timing, the richness of the offals offset by the tang of rosemary and mustard in the accompanying mash; and a superior reworking of the surf 'n' turf theme, in which a veal steak shared the plate with a meaty piece of lobster tail, with button mushrooms and shallots in attendance. Star of the desserts has been rhubarb mousse with honey and chestnut ice-cream and passion-fruit sauce, but there is also pineapple and praline bombe, or the grand plate selection. With discreet, yet knowledgeable service, Becher's Brook looks set to make Liverpool once more a place of gastronomic pilgrimage, although prices in the evening can mount up. France leads the wine list, with passing nods to New World countries fleshing it out. The 'Proprietor's Selection' begins with Touraine Chenin at £10.95.

CHEFS: David Cooke and Gerard Hogan   PROPRIETORS: David and Donna Cooke   OPEN: Mon to Fri L 12 to 2.30, Mon to Sat D 5 to 10 (Fri and Sat later by arrangement)   CLOSED: 25 and 26 Dec, 1 Jan, bank hols   MEALS: alc (main courses £13 to £20). Set L £13.95 (2 courses) to £17.50   SERVICE: not inc, 10% for parties of 8 or more   CARDS: Amex, Delta, Diners, MasterCard, Switch, Visa   DETAILS: 38 seats. Private parties: 38 main room. Vegetarian meals. Children's helpings. No children under 7. No smoking in dining-room. Wheelchair access (not WC). Music (£5)

Far East 🍸✳ £

27–35 Berry Street, Liverpool L1 9DF   COOKING 2
TEL: (0151) 709 3141/6072   FAX: (0151) 708 9798   COST £11–£47

'The Grande Dame' of Liverpool's Chinese restaurants has responded positively to competition from new young-blood venues around the city. Outside has received a facelift and, according to one who knows the place well, 'there has been a notable improvement in the food'. The range of dim-sum (served noon to 6pm) now includes steamed crab-meat balls, mixed meat wrapped in a bean-curd sheet, and sweet lotus cream buns from a list of more than 20 offerings. Authentic Cantonese flavours dominate the full menu of around 200 dishes, which boasts a heavyweight contingent of roast meats, casseroles and noodles, alongside more esoteric offerings. 'Fragrant Bones of a Dragon's Tongue' is a complex rendition of Dover sole (including crunchy deep-fried skeleton) served with asparagus tips and straw mushrooms: it is 'spectacular to look at and absolutely heaven to eat'. Elsewhere, reporters have endorsed intensely flavoured king prawns in chilli and salt, and an 'eight treasure' hotpot with all the correct ingredients assembled with care. A fixed-price buffet is served Monday, Wednesday and Friday evenings, and gourmet dinners are an attraction on Tuesday and Thursday. House wine is £8.50.

CHEF: C.K. Cheung   PROPRIETOR: Sue Yao Leung   OPEN: all week 12 to 11.30 (1am Fri and Sat, 11.15 Sun)   CLOSED: 25 and 26 Dec, Good Fri   MEALS: alc (main courses £7 to £10.50). Set L £6 to £10.50, Set D £14.50 to £19.30. Minimum 2 to 6 for set meals. Dim-sum to 6pm daily   CARDS: Amex, Diners, MasterCard, Switch, Visa   DETAILS: 250 seats. Private parties: 200 main room. Car park. Vegetarian meals. Children's helpings. No smoking in 1 dining-room. Wheelchair access (also WC). Music. Air-conditioned

Tai Pan £   [NEW ENTRY]

W.H. Lung Building, Great Howard Street,
Liverpool L5 9TZ   COOKING 1
TEL: (0151) 207 3888   FAX: (0151) 207 0100   COST £15–£45

Tai Pan resembles its Manchester parent (see entry), in its location above an oriental supermarket, its large size, and its auspicious mural dragon on restful green walls. While the main menu adds some Westernised items to the Cantonese repertoire, a Chinese reporter found the best dishes and dim-sum only on the Chinese and set menus. But never mind: the manager or waiter will translate, so Westerners too can enjoy stir-fried crab with bamboo fungus and broccoli, or perhaps stewed pig's trotters with duck webs. An inspector's recommendations include fried yam cake, deep-fried prawn parcel appetisers, and fried sliced duck and char siu in oyster sauce. Best of all was 'subtle and delicate' fish fillet with sliced pork in mushroom sauce. Sundays see a better range of dim-sum wheeled around on trolleys. House wine starts at £8.50, or go for Tsing Tao or Ginseng beer.

CHEF: Mr Au   PROPRIETOR: Tai Pan Restaurants   OPEN: all week noon to 11.30 (9.30 Sun and bank hols)   MEALS: alc (main courses £6.50 to £10.50). Set L £5.45 (2 courses) to £8.45, Set D £14 to £25. Minimum 2 people for set meals   SERVICE: not inc, card slips closed   CARDS: Amex, Delta, Diners, MasterCard, Switch, Visa   DETAILS: 300 seats. Private parties: 280 main room, 70 private room. Car park. Vegetarian meals. Children welcome. Wheelchair access (also WC). Music. Air-conditioned

Taste £ | NEW ENTRY |

Albert Dock, L3 4AA
TEL: (0151) 709 7097 (ext 310)   FAX: (0151) 708   COOKING 2
8751   COST £18–£29

By writing S in blue and the rest in black, the designers have made it obvious that this Albert Dock-side bistro/café-bar is part of the Tate, in an area now surrounded by 'soon-to-be-trendy shops' and boats at anchor. Its clean lines include a ship-shaped bar of perforated aluminium, a stone-floored main dining-room and a blue-walled equivalent upstairs. Don't come here for originality, but do expect 'very acceptable' food in a 'pleasant environment'. The daytime café bar has a range of options from salads and sandwiches, as well as Scouse (a lamb and vegetable dish described as a 'local speciality'), and more cosmopolitan dishes, such as Nachos platter or Cajun burgers. The evening bistro menu offers sausage and mash with onions, seared tuna, and slightly more sophisticated artichoke and asparagus mixed with egg and Parmesan in mayonnaise. Finish perhaps with baked bananas, or a version of apple and blackberry crumble served 'with a mound of cream and a pool of custard'. Service is from 'young hip staff in orange tee-shirts'. A selection of speciality coffees is on offer, and the short wine list has two dozen uncomplicated wines starting at £8.50, with most under £20.

CHEF: Antony Pressance   PROPRIETORS: Robert and Michael Gutmann   OPEN: all week café-bar all day 10 to 6, bistro D only 7 to 10   CLOSED: 25 Dec   MEALS: alc (main courses café-bar £4 to £5, bistro £6 to £11)   SERVICE: not inc   CARDS: Amex, Delta, MasterCard, Switch, Visa   DETAILS: 120 seats. Private parties: 250 main room. Car park. Vegetarian meals. Children's helpings. No smoking after 5pm. Wheelchair access (also WC). Music. Air-conditioned

▲ Healds Hall Hotel £⊁ £

Leeds Road, Liversedge WF15 6JA
TEL: (01924) 409112   FAX: (01924) 401895   COOKING 2
on A62 between Leeds and Heckmondwike   COST £17–£41

Thanks to the business and conference trade, this eighteenth-century building
has a 'corporate air' about it, but what makes it different from hundreds of other
superficially similar establishments is that it is owner-managed: 'and it shows'.
Staff are relaxed, but fully in control of proceedings, the owners eat in the
dining-room, and the chef wanders in for a chat later in the evening. The style is a
combination of classics – asparagus with hollandaise, roast partridge with
cabbage and lentils – and some contemporary dishes such as crab-cakes with
chilli, ginger and coriander, or crisply deep-fried salt cod brandade arranged on
a generous pool of garlic laden aïoli. Fixed-price menus offer good value and
plenty of interest, perhaps pork pudding made with leg and root vegetables in an
apple suet pastry, while desserts might include a tart of rhubarb or raspberries.
British cheeses are a strength, and nearly all the 50 or so wines come in under
£20, including house French at £8.50.

CHEF: Philip McVeagh   PROPRIETORS: Thomas and Nora Harrington   OPEN: Sun to Fri L 12 to 2,
Mon to Sat D 6.30 to 9.30   CLOSED: 26 Dec, 1 Jan   MEALS: alc D (main courses £11 to £15.50).
Set L Mon to Fri £10.75, Set L Sun £11.50, Set D £18.50. Bar L available Mon to Fri   SERVICE:
not inc, card slips closed   CARDS: Amex, Delta, Diners, MasterCard, Switch, Visa   DETAILS: 50
seats. Private parties: 35 main room, 12 to 130 private rooms. Car park. Vegetarian meals.
Children's helpings. No smoking in dining-room. Wheelchair access (also WC). Music
ACCOMMODATION: 25 rooms, all with bath/shower. TV. Phone. B&B £40 to £75. Rooms for
disabled. Children welcome. High teas for children. Baby facilities. Dogs welcome in bedrooms
only. Afternoon teas

Rockingham Arms

52 Front Street, Lockington YO25 9SH   COOKING 2
TEL: (01430) 810607   FAX: (01430) 810734   COST £31–£45

The Arms is a converted East Riding pub that now functions happily as a country
restaurant without frills. Adam Richardson and Sue Barker hold sway in the
kitchen and work to a regularly changing dinner menu that allows the option of
eating two or three courses. Influences come from near and far, and there is
plenty to intrigue the palate in the shape of smoked haddock topped with
poached egg on spiced potatoes, confit of belly-pork on red pepper and onion
relish, or seared chicken breast with sun-dried tomato, black olive and tarragon
sauce. A fondness for flavours oriental also surfaces in, say, caramelised salmon
with Thai noodles, or magret of duckling braised in coconut milk and served
with coconut rice and pickled plums. Desserts steer a safe and steady course with
ginger sponge and custard, chocolate and hazelnut meringue, and bread-
and-butter pudding with apricot coulis and crème fraîche. Around 60
well-spread, affordable wines are supplemented by a blackboard of bin-ends.
House Vin de Pays d'Oc is £11.95.

CHEFS: Adam Richardson and Sue Barker PROPRIETORS: David and Sue Barker OPEN: Tue to Sat D only 7 to 10 CLOSED: Christmas, 2 weeks in summer, bank hols MEALS: Set D £21.95 (2 courses) to £25.95 SERVICE: not inc CARDS: Delta, MasterCard, Switch, Visa DETAILS: 60 seats. Private parties: 14 main room. Car park. Vegetarian meals. Music (£5)

LONG CRENDON Buckinghamshire map 2

▲ *Angel Inn* 🍷 NEW ENTRY

Bicester Road, Long Crendon HP18 9EE
TEL: (01844) 208268 FAX: (01844) 202497 COOKING 2
on B4011, 2m NW of Thame COST £26–£49

New owners Steve and Angie Good are now firmly ensconced in this upgraded sixteenth-century listed building. The place reveals its antiquity and pedigree in the exposed panel of wattle and daub in what is now the breakfast room. There is a homely bar, complete with settees and armchairs, although the main focus for diners is the large conservatory at the back, with its terrace for summertime drinks. As before, fish remains the star turn, and it pays to consider the list of blackboard specials. Reporters have been particularly satisfied with smoked haddock on mustard and leek mash with cheese sabayon, seared tuna niçoise, and monkfish in saffron butter sauce; even a simple grilled lemon sole has impressed by virtue of its freshness. You might begin with crab salad, or chicken liver parfait with red onion confit, and finish with nougat glacé with caramelised banana and rum sauce, or hot pecan pie dribbled with maple syrup and served with a dollop of 'top-quality' clotted cream. An appealing collection of wines grouped by style and mostly priced between £15 and £20 is backed up by five pages of 'reserve wines' from quality growers in France, Germany and the New World. House wines start at £11.95.

CHEFS: Trevor Bosch and Donald Joyce PROPRIETORS: Steve and Angie Good OPEN: all week L 12 to 2.30, Mon to Sat D 7 to 9.30 (10 Sat) MEALS: alc (main courses £8.50 to £19.50). Set L Sun £12.95 (2 courses) to £14.95 SERVICE: not inc CARDS: Delta, MasterCard, Switch, Visa DETAILS: 75 seats. 30 seats outside. Private parties: 35 main room, 16 to 35 private rooms. Car park. Vegetarian meals. Children's helpings. No smoking in 1 dining-room. Music. Air-conditioned ACCOMMODATION: 3 rooms 4 with bath/shower. TV. Phone. B&B £55 to £65. Children welcome. High teas for children. Baby facilities. Guide dogs only. Afternoon teas (*The Which? Hotel Guide*) (£5)

LONG MELFORD Suffolk map 6

Scutchers Bistro £

Westgate Street, Long Melford CO10 9DP COOKING 3
TEL: (01787) 310200 FAX: (01787) 310620 COST £23–£37

A 'tranquillising choice of pastel shades' helps to create a suitably soothing mood in the Barretts' conversion of 'two Victorian villas'. However, the countrified décor of pine furniture and floral patterned cushions ensures that all is light and airy, rather than soporific. Nicholas Barrett's menus brim over with lively ideas drawn from the global melting-pot: crispy duck with spring onions, cucumber, hoisin sauce and pancakes (a favourite starter) rubs shoulders with carpaccio of beef and Mediterranean vegetables, balsamic vinegar and olive oil. Regulars have also approved smoked haddock and brown shrimp kedgeree, seared scallops on a tomato and shallot salsa, and roast fillet of lamb on courgettes, baby tomatoes, olives and garlic. In addition, there's clear endorsement for vegetarian options such as 'riso' (rice, asparagus and wild mushrooms topped with a poached egg). Vegetables include splendid potato and spring onion mash, while the star among the desserts is a hot vanilla and raspberry soufflé, although this is often reserved for special occasions. Diane Barrett's presence out front ensures that proceedings run along at just the right pace. The wine list continues to offer a fine range of styles and varietals from both hemispheres at some very fair prices, but for some reason has ceased to give the vintage for most of the bins. Ten house wines cost between £9.20 and £12.50 a bottle (£1.80/£2.50 per glass).

CHEF: Nicholas Barrett   PROPRIETORS: Nicholas and Diane Barrett   OPEN: Tue to Sat 12 to 2.30, 7 to 9.30 (open Mothering Sun and Easter Sun)   CLOSED: 24 to 26 Dec, 1st week Jan   MEALS: alc (main courses £7.50 to £14.50)   SERVICE: not inc   CARDS: Amex, Delta, MasterCard, Switch, Visa   DETAILS: 75 seats. 60 seats outside. Private parties: 75 main room. Car park. Vegetarian meals. Children's helpings. No cigars/pipes in dining-room. Wheelchair access (not WC). No music

---

LONGRIDGE Lancashire   map 8

Paul Heathcote's ✤

104–106 Higher Road, Longridge PR3 3SY
TEL: (01772) 784969   FAX: (01772) 785713
from Preston, follow Town Centre signs, drive uphill
though centre of Longridge, then turn left, following   COOKING 7
signs for Jeffery Hill   COST £32–£81

Paul Heathcote becomes ever busier – he has restaurants in Preston and Manchester (see entries), cooks for Preston North End home matches, does outside catering, and runs a 'School of Excellence' in Manchester – but Longridge's kitchen is where he cooks when he's at home. The style is more luxurious than the series of small cottagey rooms might suggest, but it has its feet on the ground too. Beside artichoke and foie gras soup, or poached lobster, are his modern interpretations of humble icons: black pudding with crushed potatoes and baked beans, or ploughman's terrine with pickle dressing.

These slightly mocking dishes do more than just poke fun, of course. They make the point that food has roots, not just in terms of local materials, of which corn-fed Goosnargh duckling is perhaps the prime example, but in its traditions too. Take an idea, deconstruct it, put it back together, and you get such simple but appealing dishes as soft-boiled duck egg with asparagus soldiers, or a thick piece of the 'juiciest' spiced knuckle of ham, combined in a terrine with white beans, served with a mustard dressing. One Good Friday visitor finished with hot cross buns and ricotta fritters: three egg-shaped yeasty buns, 'very hot, very spicy', served with a warm honey custard.

Not all dishes carry a message, though, and many simply stand for themselves: four 'tender and tasty' scallops, for example, perfectly timed, sitting on a smooth creamy cauliflower purée, surrounded by a sweet, sticky sherry caramel sauce.

Soups, such as honey-roast parsnip, or wild mushroom 'sieved and sieved' so that it was 'clear but creamy, with an intense taste of mushrooms', are ideal for dunking with onion- or black pudding-flavoured breads. Meals might finish with pink strawberry soufflé standing proud in a copper pan, or 'majestic' bread-and-butter pudding.

Service is 'crisp' and 'impeccable', if sometimes a little aloof, and the service charge has a ceiling of £15. 'This was the best-value lunch I have ever had,' confessed one reporter, bemused that the dining-room was not full; another noted that from May to September 'four can eat for the price of three' at Friday lunch-time, making it an even more 'tremendous bargain'. Sadly the wine list, of undeniably high quality, cannot be considered a bargain, and those with only £20 to spend will find little beyond token excitement. House French is £13.

CHEFS: Paul Heathcote and Andrew Barnes   PROPRIETOR: Paul Heathcote   OPEN: Fri and Sun L 12 to 2, Tue to Sun D 7 to 9.30   MEALS: alc D Tue to Sat (main courses £18 to £23). Set L £22.50, Set D Tue to Sat £08 to £66, Set D Sun £38. BYO £51, £10 D   SERVICE: 10% (optional, maximum £15), card slips closed   CARDS: Amex, Delta, Diners, MasterCard, Switch, Visa DETAILS: 60 seats. Private parties: 60 main room, 16 private room. Car park. Vegetarian meals. No children under 7. No smoking in dining-room. Wheelchair access (not WC). Music

---

LOWER BEEDING   West Sussex   map 3

Jeremy's at the Crabtree ▲✷

Brighton Road, Lower Beeding RH13 6PT
TEL: (01403) 891257   FAX: (01403) 891606
EMAIL: jeremys.crabtree@btinternet.com   COOKING 4
on A281, just S of village   COST £22–£41

This is not the pub it may look like from outside, but people still perch in what was the bar to eat, or sit in the simply decorated dining-room where crisp white linen brings a degree of formality. Jeremy Ashpool is more of a 'restaurateur' than a chef these days, dividing his time between the Crabtree and his new venture (see entry, Borde Hill) and leaving Fredi Djuric, whom he descibes as a half-Yugoslavian from Paris, in charge of the kitchens. The wide-ranging style continues as before, offering an attractive mix of dishes from deep-fried squid in garlic and coriander batter to chargrilled veal kidney in mustard sauce, from risotto cake to pigeon breast with lentils and bacon.

Soups – of pumpkin, or mushroom and spinach – are well reported, and fish is a strong suit, producing a 'satisfying starter' of simple grilled salmon, and a main course fish-cake with leeks, spinach and grilled tomato. The kitchen sensibly doesn't set itself ambitious targets it can't meet, enabling it to draw applause for braised rabbit, 'moist, perfectly cooked' lamb chops, and desserts of warm toffee sponge pudding, or baked apple stuffed with sultanas and hazelnuts. One reporter was pleased to see the friendly, informal service much improved, although felt it still had some way to go. Wines embrace a good variety of styles at a range of generally fair prices, starting with seven house wines at £10.

▲ *means accommodation is available.*

CHEFS: Fredi Djuric and Jeremy Ashpool   PROPRIETOR: Jeremy's Restaurant Ltd   OPEN: all
week L 12.30 to 2, Mon to Sat D 7.30 to 9.45   MEALS: alc (main courses £8 to £10). Set L Mon to
Sat £10.50 (2 courses), Set L Sun £16.50, Set D £25   SERVICE: not inc L, 10% D, card slips
closed in restaurant only   CARDS: Amex, Delta, MasterCard, Switch, Visa   DETAILS: 45 seats.
15 seats outside. Private parties: 25 main room. Car park. Vegetarian meals. Children welcome.
No smoking in 1 dining-room. Wheelchair access (not WC). No music   £5

LOWER SLAUGHTER Gloucestershire   map 5

▲ *Lower Slaughter Manor* 🍷 ✷

Lower Slaughter GL54 2HP
TEL: (01451) 820456   FAX: (01451) 822150
EMAIL: lowsmanor@aol.com   COOKING 6
off A429, at sign 'The Slaughters'   COST £36–£93

Despite its vaguely alarming name, Lower Slaughter is one of the more serenely
beautiful villages in the Cotswolds. There has been a manor-house in these parts
since before the Norman Conquest, but the present edifice – a mere stripling –
dates from 1658. Ornate plasterwork ceilings and fireplaces lend the public
rooms an air of well-preserved splendour, and the Vaughans work hard to
ensure that arriving guests feel as if they are being wrapped in a warm embrace.

Martin White cooks in unabashedly country-house mode: prime cuts and
fillets of fish are the main commodities, given a luxury touch with veloutés,
purées and mousses, and the only offal in evidence may be foie gras.
Notwithstanding that, reporters confirm the high standard of technique with
which the cooking is executed. Lightly sauté Cornish scallops sitting on a cake of
crab and potato are well matched with a butter sauce containing chervil and dill,
the timing and balancing impressively accurate, while two warm slices of terrine
of duck confit, foie gras and new potato are accompanied by a chunky preserve of
Bramley apples, ginger and cinnamon. Lamb cutlets plumped up with wild
mushroom mousse offer good Welsh meat and come with an apposite sauce
incorporating ratatouille vegetables. Salt levels can be high. To finish, choose
from hot fruit soufflés with a kaleidoscope of vari-coloured coulis, or perhaps
chocolate tart with coffee parfait and vanilla sauce. Little extras are crammed in
all over the place at dinner, starting with smoked salmon sandwiches, then
canapés, then an amuse-gueule at table, a surprise bowl of soup after the first
course, a pre-dessert after the main, and shock-troops of petits fours with coffee
('we took some with us to eat later,' gasped an overloaded reporter). Wines are
strong in the French regions, California, Australia and New Zealand particularly, but don't expect to be pleasantly surprised by the prices. Sancerre at £29.50
is typical. House wines start at £15 for Louis Latour burgundies.

CHEF: Martin White   PROPRIETORS: Roy and Daphne Vaughan   OPEN: all week 12 to 1.30 (2
Sun), 7 to 9.30   MEALS: Set L £15.95 (2 courses) to £19.95, Set D £42. BYO from £10   SERVICE:
not inc   CARDS: Amex, Delta, Diners, MasterCard, Switch, Visa   DETAILS: 40 seats. Private
parties: 30 main room, 20 private room. Car park. Vegetarian meals. No children under 12.
Jacket and tie. No smoking in dining-room. No music   ACCOMMODATION: 15 rooms, all with
bath/shower. TV. Phone. B&B £135 to £350. No children under 12. No dogs. Afternoon teas.
Swimming-pool (*The Which? Hotel Guide*)   £5

LOW LAITHE North Yorkshire   map 9

Dusty Miller

Low Laithe, Summerbridge HG3 4BU
TEL: (01423) 780837   COOKING 6
on B6165, 2m SE of Pateley Bridge   COST £34–£55

Brian and Elizabeth Dennison's old stone house just off the main tourist drag in deepest Nidderdale is not a place for showy gestures, but it scores heavily with its pleasingly relaxed atmosphere. Full credit to Elizabeth's presence out front: she exudes calmness and confidence effortlessly, knows her stuff and manages to put everyone at ease. Brian's cooking has what might be described as 'a wonderful simplicity and yet a brilliance of care and attention'. There is sure technique and dedication in every dish. The handwritten dinner menu is a world away from the faddish gestures of the Pacific Rim: instead it deals in classic Anglo-French specialities based on impeccable raw materials. Main courses of, say, rack of Nidderdale lamb with rosemary jus, and coq au vin, are bolstered by a 'fishmonger's fish of the day'. Before that, you might opt for 'a good soup' (says the menu) or monkfish with lime and bacon, while a handful of comforting desserts features de luxe bread-and-butter pudding, raspberry crème brûlée, peach and almond crumble and so forth. There's also the alternative of a short fixed-price menu based around a single main course such as supreme of chicken André (with tomato, basil and pasta). French house wines are £12.90.

CHEF: Brian Dennison PROPRIETORS: Brian and Elizabeth Dennison OPEN: Tue to Sat D only 7 to 11 CLOSED: 25 and 26 Dec, 2 weeks Aug or Sept, most bank hols MEALS: alc (main courses £17 to £18). Set D £24 SERVICE: not inc CARDS: Amex, MasterCard, Visa DETAILS: 45 seats. Private parties: 30 main room, 15 private room. Car park. No children under 9. Wheelchair access (1 step; not WC). Occasional music

---

LUDLOW Shropshire   map 5

Courtyard £ | NEW ENTRY |

---

2 Quality Square, Ludlow SY8 1AR
TEL: (01584) 878080   COOKING 2
                                                        COST £18–£35

The impetus provided by Shaun Hill, when he opened Merchant House in 1994, seems to have spurred on the local competition, not least in the cobbled courtyard just off the main square, where sage- and terracotta-coloured walls and a few prints give the Courtyard a rather sedate 'tearoom' atmosphere. Jane Malcolm, who worked with Carole Evans (formerly at Poppies, Brimfield, now at the Three Horseshoes in Batcombe – see entry), gives value for money, and uses good raw materials, including hazelnut-crusted rack of lamb – 'good meat, lots of flavour' – served with creamed leeks and a sauce of port and pan juices, and fillet of beef with well-made rösti and a fresh pesto-like salsa verde. Presentation is appealingly simple, as in a Thai chicken salad, and flavours well judged, as in a starter of crab in filo pastry with a lightly chilli-spiced tomato sauce, or 'enjoyable' passion-fruit caramel. Service is bright and friendly, and the wine list of 22 bottles could hardly be shorter or cheaper. House Australian is £8.25.

CHEF/PROPRIETOR: Jane Malcolm   OPEN: Mon to Sat L 12 to 2, Thur to Sat D 7 to 9 (open for D Mon to Sat during Festival)   CLOSED: 25 and 26 Dec, 1 Jan, 2 weeks Jan, early May bank hol   MEALS: alc (main courses £6.50 to £12.50). Snack menu L   SERVICE: not inc   CARDS: Visa   DETAILS: 30 seats. 8 seats outside. Private parties: 14 main room, 14 private room. Vegetarian meals. Children's helpings. No smoking in 1 dining-room. Music. Air-conditioned

Merchant House ⅝✹

| Lower Corve Street, Ludlow SY8 1DU | COOKING 8 |
| TEL: (01584) 875438   FAX: (01584) 876927 | COST £36–£44 |

Shaun and Anja Hill's tiny restaurant pursues a personal vision of hospitality which bucks the current trend. Located in a venerable terrace, it consists of six wooden tables in two interconnecting rooms, with gleaming glassware and a collection of desirable paintings 'that signal a place of discernment and good taste'. It does not always extend a fulsome welcome – make yourself at home if the two owners and their one helper are busy in the kitchen – and makes no attempt to take on the trappings of luxury: the approach is simple but civilised, with 'a total lack of pomp'. It is worth setting the scene because this approach is not to everybody's taste, and one or two disappointments have been registered during the year. In the *Guide*'s opinion, however, Merchant House gets its priorities right. Food comes first.

The draw is Hill's considerable skill, confident cooking, and his 'knack of deploying first-rate ingredients to their ultimate advantage', making a meal here 'one of the great British bargains'. Three courses offer a choice of four items at each stage, and incorporate some old Hill favourites alongside 'newish ideas'. Thus the underlying principle of his much-imitated scallop dish – sliced discs of white muscle, arranged around a purée of brown lentils and coriander, with 'an underlying heat which evoked India' – finds new expression in a 'stunning, earthy' plate of sweet, firm steamed lobster with its 'hot hummus' combination of chickpeas, shallots, garlic, cumin, olive oil and coriander.

While technique can be taken for granted – in the timing of a saffron and artichoke risotto, for example – it is the fact that flavours and textures are intelligently considered that proves ultimately satisfying: in a steamed fillet of John Dory under an acidulated sabayon with juniper-flavoured sauerkraut, or a jointed squab pigeon 'more tender and less gamey' than the norm for our inspector, served on a glossy reduction with morel mushrooms and a turret of garlicky gratin dauphinois potatoes. Dishes are not 'picture perfect', though they are generally attractively presented. Puddings, though good, rarely elicit superlatives. A wedge of apricot tart comes with good pastry, tart fuit and an eggy crème anglaise, or there may be crème brûlée or pannettone bread-and-butter pudding.

Anja Hill and her waitress may be a little diffident, but they are friendly, informal, natural and obliging. There may be a 'longer than comfortable wait' before the main course, but this reflects the domestic nature of the operation. Canapés are first-rate, bread is even better, especially the white milk rolls that 'look like collapsing Yorkshire puddings', and the 50-strong wine selection is as personal as everything else: varied, interesting and fairly priced, starting with house Italian white and French red at £12.50.

CHEF: Shaun Hill   PROPRIETORS: Shaun and Anja Hill   OPEN: Fri and Sat L 12.30 to 2, Tue to Sat D 7 to 9   CLOSED: 1 week Christmas, 2 weeks spring   MEALS: Set L and D £27.50   SERVICE: net prices, card slips closed   CARDS: Delta, MasterCard, Switch, Visa   DETAILS: 24 seats. Private parties: 8 main room. No smoking in dining-room. Wheelchair access (not WC). No music

---

▲ Mr Underhill's ♀ ✸   NEW ENTRY

Dinham Weir, Ludlow SY8 1EH   COOKING 8
TEL: (01584) 874431   COST £33–£46

After spending sixteen years at Stonham in Suffolk – Mr Underhill last appeared in the 1997 edition of the *Guide* – the Bradleys wanted to expand and offer accommodation. 'We thought we would be moving less than two miles, re-opening within a month and not even changing our phone number,' they write. 'Ten months, 18,000 miles and several disappointments later we found ourselves in Ludlow', a town now richly endowed with good eating. They opened in November 1997, in a location that renders the name appropriate: a steep slope runs down from the castle towards a weir on a broad bend along the wooded banks of the River Teme. The custard-coloured house has a secluded garden for drinks, a splendid view through the dining-room's patio doors, its 'light, airy' impression helped by bright modern paintings.

As before, there is no choice until dessert, but the menu is discussed when booking. Typically it makes a fishy start: for example, a mound of small dice of salmon marinated in lemon juice, mixed with minutely chopped red peppers, onion, chilli and herbs, sitting on a good-sized pool of clean-tasting, oil-streaked 'gazpacho to get excited about'. 'Everything is so simple, so classy,' wrote one visitor. A simple-sounding 'Barbary duck with flat leaf parsley', for example, turns out to be an 'unforgettable' dish of pink sliced breast and properly confit leg, arranged beside flat ribbons of briefly steamed courgette and carrot, that was an object lesson in fresh raw material, taste, texture and technical accomplishment.

Dishes are conceived as a whole, with sweet baby carrots making 'a meaningful contribution' to thick, overlapping slices of 'tender, beautifully textured' beef fillet. Other vegetables may be served separately, but are adapted to the dish: fine beans in lemon oil, and gratin dauphinoise for the beef, 'deeply impressive' roast potatoes for the Barbary duck. The kitchen has also turned out a chocolate tart with a soufflé-like texture, and a taste that was was '110 per cent cocoa'. The pattern is three courses and coffee, with cheese as a possible extra: half a dozen English, French and Irish 'in perfect condition', which come with a basket of more 'wonderful' bread. Service from Judy Bradley and well-trained helpers is 'impeccably professional', and value is 'outstandingly good'. Judy is extremely knowledgeable about wine, and this is amply demonstrated by her list, where quality and value are given equal consideration. Arizona is championed in a New World section designed to appeal to enthusiasts, while traditionalists will be satisfied by what France has to offer. The selection of half-bottles was due to be expanded as the *Guide* went to press; four French house wines are priced between £11 and £12.50. CELLARMAN'S CHOICE: Chablis *premier cru* Montmains 1996, Dom. Chevalier, £22; Wirra Wirra Church Block 1996, McLaren Vale, S. Australia, £16.50.

CHEF: Christopher Bradley   PROPRIETORS: Christopher and Judy Bradley   OPEN: all week D only 7.15 to 8.45 (L by arrangement)   MEALS: Set L and D £25   SERVICE: not inc   CARDS: MasterCard, Visa   DETAILS: 30 seats. 40 seats outside. Private parties: 30 main room. Car park. Vegetarian meals. Children welcome. No smoking in dining-room. No music ACCOMMODATION: 6 rooms, all with bath/shower. TV. Phone. D,B&B £70 to £128. Children welcome. No dogs. Afternoon teas. Fishing (£5)

Oaks ♥ ⅝✳   NEW ENTRY

17 Corve Street, Ludlow SY8 1DA
TEL: (01584) 872325   FAX: (01584) 874024   COOKING 4
EMAIL: koak@globalnet.co.uk   COST £33–£46

Ludlow is suddenly a gastronomic El Dorado, and this neighbourhood restaurant – set in an Elizabethan terrace at the foot of a hill leading down from the town centre – is keen to play an integral part in the proceedings. Oak panelling and exposed stone walls within form the backdrop for a comfortable bar, and a pair of elegant dining-rooms boast generously spaced and well-set tables. The two- to four-course menu reads well, and is priced inclusively with no supplements. Ken Adams grows his own herbs and vegetables, smokes his own fish and shellfish, and has established a carefully nurtured network of supply lines for everything from organic flour to saffron. It all goes into cutting-edge cooking that demonstrates a knowing facility with contemporary modes. Guinea-fowl, grilled foie gras, wild mushrooms and bacon congregate in a substantial-sounding first-course salad, a soup brings together crayfish and morels under a puff-pastry cover, while smoked salmon arrives with a tian of smoked scallops, vegetables and seaweed with Japanese seasonings.

Main courses are painstakingly composed: a loin of lamb crusted with red pepper and crumbs (a change from mustard and herbs) is accompanied by a tart of minced lamb and courgettes and a stripe of dark tomato and garlic sauce. The culinary philosophy restricts salt to a minimum, but quite a few items – vegetables in particular – seem to be liberally anointed with lemon juice. Good British and French cheeses are well-kept and come with molasses and walnut bread. Sweeter palates are satisfied by elderflower sorbet and strawberries in a brandy-snap basket, or pecan and maple-syrup tart with lemon-balm ice-cream. Welcoming and knowledgeable staff ensure things run smoothly. Wines have been cleverly chosen to keep both traditionalists and experimentalists happy while focusing on quality. House wines from Portugal, France and Germany are £9.95 or £12.90, and there is a good choice of half-bottles. CELLARMAN'S CHOICE: Hunters Chardonnay 1995, Marlborough, New Zealand, £20; Ch. Musar 1991, Gaston Hochar, Lebanon, £20.50.

CHEF/PROPRIETOR: K.H. Adams   OPEN: Tue to Sat D only 7 to 9.30   MEALS: Set D Tue to Fri £18.50 (2 courses) to £27.50, Set D Sat £22.50 to £28.50   SERVICE: not inc, card slips closed CARDS: Delta, MasterCard, Switch, Visa   DETAILS: 30 seats. Private parties: 20 main room, 15 and 30 private rooms. Car park. Vegetarian menu. Children's helpings. No children under 10. No smoking in dining-room. Occasional music

The Guide's *top-rated restaurants are listed near the front of the book.*

LYDGATE Greater Manchester map 8

▲ *White Hart*

51 Stockport Road, Lydgate OL4 4JJ
TEL: (01457) 872566 FAX: (01457) 875190 COOKING 4
on A6050, 3m E of Oldham COST £24–£44

The stone-built pub in a little Pennine village to the east of Oldham was rescued from virtual dereliction by its present owners in 1994. It has been converted to make a dual catering operation, with informal eating in a ground-floor brasserie (and the name is not entirely Gallic wishful thinking – the place actually was a brewery in the late eighteenth century), while a full-fig restaurant menu is offered upstairs.

John Rudden is having an enterprising go at bringing classy modern cooking to the area and has the technical ability to back it up. Magnificent home-baked breads set the tone in the restaurant. A slice of thoughtfully conceived terrine builds full-flavoured ham hock around a centre of pâté de foie gras, the whole set in a light aspic and served with melba toast. Another first course offers a stimulating assemblage of three nut-brown scallops on smoked salmon, itself on a base of celeriac purée, in a restrained creamy nage. If criticism there be, it is that dishes – particularly main courses – can show a tendency to gild the lily. Notwithstanding that, ingredients seem well sourced, and may turn up as saddle of rabbit stuffed with sweetbreads (a favourite offal here) and wild mushrooms, served with rosemary butter tagliatelle, or hake fillet with roasted leeks, caramelised onions and a sweet-and-sour fish stock sauce. Fine northern cheeses such as Appleby Cheshire and real Lancashire may offer simple contrast to labour-intensive desserts such as poached plums in a cinnamon toast sandwich, or chocolate and orange roulade with mint ice-cream. It is all served with genuine enthusiasm against a background of potted classics and Irish jigs. Wines are a cosmopolitan collection, although the list has been considerably reduced since last year. However, it still offers a reasonable choice of styles and flavours at a fair price. House Chilean Chardonnay and Spanish Tempranillo are £9.75 a bottle.

CHEF: John Rudden PROPRIETORS: Charles Brierley and John Rudden OPEN: restaurant Sun L 12 to 2.30, Tue to Sat D 6 to 9.30; brasserie all week 12 to 2.30, 6 to 9.30 MEALS: restaurant Set L Sun £17.50, Set D £27; brasserie alc (main courses £8 to £15). BYO £10 SERVICE: not inc, card slips closed CARDS: Amex, Delta, MasterCard, Switch, Visa DETAILS: 100 seats. 20 seats outside. Private parties: 70 main room, 24 private room. Car park. Vegetarian meals. Children's helpings. No smoking in 1 dining-room. Wheelchair access (also WC). Music ACCOMMODATION: 5 rooms, all with bath/shower. TV. Phone. B&B £55 to £80. Children welcome. No dogs. Afternoon teas (£5)

LYMINGTON Hampshire map 2

▲ *Gordleton Mill Hotel, Provence*

Silver Street, Hordle, Lymington SO41 6DJ COOKING 6
TEL: (01590) 682219 FAX: (01590) 683073 COST £28–£64

This is one of the more romantic settings along the south coast. A stream with bullrushes, reeds, willow and oak runs through the garden, there are white-painted wooden bridges everywhere, and the sound of running water induces a tranquil feel. The dining-room – 'almost a conservatory' – is nothing if not cheerful, done in sunny and spring-like colours. Toby Hill left to open a restaurant in London (no sign of it as the *Guide* went to press), leaving sous-chef Steven Smith to take control and oversee a *carte* on which fish takes prominence, accounting almost exclusively for starters and for more than half the main courses. Two set-lunch menus are available, the cheaper one having less choice.

The result is a light style in which roasting and pan-frying predominate, producing 'close to perfect' roast scallops with crisp celeriac chips, fillet of turbot with a quenelle of pea purée, and properly seared veal sweetbreads 'in an ultra-light pastry case'. Sauces tend to be vinaigrettes and, in the case of meat, 'essences': of morels for beef, of ceps for pink loin of lamb with artichokes. Dishes are intelligently composed, and if they sometimes lack edge and sparkle, then at least they are well balanced, accurately timed and attractively presented, as in pink roast squab pigeon with a distinctive thyme jus, or sticky risotto with a 'deep shellfish savour', surrounded by a rich bisque-style sauce and a few seared langoustine tails that 'oozed freshness'.

Desserts have included 'text-book' raspberry sablé, three biscuits high, accompanied by a vanilla bavarois and deep scarlet coulis, and a pyramid of crunchy caramel triangles enclosing iced nougatine, served with apricot sorbet and sauce. Service aims to be correct, but seems on occasion to be in need of direction and pace. As the *Guide* went to press, a new wine list was being prepared.

CHEF: Steven Smith PROPRIETOR: William Stone OPEN: Tue to Sun L 12 to 2, Tue to Sat D 7 to 9.45 CLOSED: 2 weeks Nov MEALS: alc (main courses £14 to £18). Set L £16.50 to £20 SERVICE: not inc CARDS: Amex, Delta, Diners, MasterCard, Switch, Visa DETAILS: 55 seats. 14 seats outside. Private parties: 55 main room. Car park. Children welcome. No smoking in dining-room. No smoking in 1 dining-room. Wheelchair access (also WC). Music. Air-conditioned ACCOMMODATION: 7 rooms, 6 with bath/shower. TV. Phone. B&B £97 to £149. No children under 7. Lap dogs only. Afternoon teas. Fishing (*The Which? Hotel Guide*)

LYMPSTONE Devon	map 1

▲ *River House* ⅋✕

The Strand, Lympstone EX8 5EY	COOKING 1
TEL: (01395) 265147	COST £46–£60

Predictably, the River House sits right on the water's edge, with views (on a good day) across the estuary to the Haldon Hills and Powderham Castle. Shirley Wilkes seems to have a soft spot for the Mediterranean – judging by provençale fish soup, and monkfish 'Spanish style' with orange, tomato, garlic, herbs and sherry – while at the same time turning her hand to traditional English standards of smoked fish mousse, Dartmoor beef with baby Yorkshire puddings, and roast lamb with herbs. An array of country-style desserts takes in gooseberry mousse with rhubarb, lemon and almond roulade, and more exotic banana pancakes flavoured with orange and cardamom and flamed in both brandy and Grand Marnier. Wines are well spread in geography and price, and around ten are available by the glass from £3, from £9.95 a bottle.

CHEF: Shirley Wilkes: PROPRIETOR: Michael Wilkes   OPEN: Tue to Sat 12 to 1.30, 7 to 9.30 (10.30 Sat)   CLOSED: 25 to 27 Dec, bank hols   MEALS: Set L and D £31 (2 courses) to £35.50. Light L available   SERVICE: not inc   CARDS: Amex, Delta, MasterCard, Visa   DETAILS: 34 seats. Private parties: 85 main room, 14 private room. Car park. Vegetarian meals. Children's helpings. No children under 6. No smoking in dining-room. Wheelchair access (not WC). No music ACCOMMODATION: 3 rooms, all with bath/shower. TV. B&B £62 to £108. No children under 6. Dogs welcome by arrangement (£5)

MADINGLEY Cambridgeshire   map 6

Three Horseshoes

High Street, Madingley CB3 8AB   COOKING 3
TEL: (01954) 210221   FAX: (01954) 212043   COST £25–£48

Utilitarian tables and old *Vanity Fair* prints decorate this thatched pub in a quiet village just outside Cambridge. A conservatory with pot plants and a trellis overlooks the garden and, in common with other Huntsbridge pub-restaurants (see entries Pheasant Inn, Keyston, and White Hart, Great Yeldham), the same free-ranging food can be eaten in the non-bookable bar, or in the hardly more formal dining-room. It is a best-bits-from-everywhere style of cooking, and although the menu looks simple enough, anybody who walked into the kitchen and opened the cupboard door would find buffalo mozzarella, wasabi, mooli, mirin, ruby chard, black pudding, shiitakes, harissa, tamari, black beans, Asian pesto, pak choi, tabbouleh, rocket, soba noodles, mustard oil, sticky black Thai rice, white chocolate and much more.

Quite a few dishes involve a fair number of these ingredients – terrine of chicken with foie gras, garlic confit, roast red onions, trompette mushrooms and sauce gribiche – and our inspector was ready to award Richard Stokes a prize 'for the chef who can put together the most complicated dishes and just about get away with it'. Chargrilling is the cooking method of choice, applied sensitively to scallops, and to spiced chicken served with potato and garlic cake, grilled okra, sweetcorn salsa, and yoghurt dressing with mint oil. Desserts might include caramelised lemon tart, or panettone bread-and-butter pudding. Service can be on the cool side. The wine list (compiled by Master of Wine John Hoskins for the Huntsbridge group) is a highly attractive collection of bottles, grouped by style and containing as much that appeals from outside France as within. House wines start at £9.45, with 14 of them being offered by the glass at very reasonable prices (£1.80 to £3.95).

CHEF: Richard Stokes   PROPRIETOR: Huntsbridge Ltd   OPEN: all week L 12 to 2, Mon to Sat D 6.30 to 9.30 (10 Sat)   MEALS: alc (main courses £7.50 to £16)   SERVICE: not inc   CARDS: Amex, Delta, Diners, MasterCard, Switch, Visa   DETAILS: 100 seats. 40 seats outside. Private parties: 70 main room. Car park. Vegetarian meals. Children's helpings. Wheelchair access (not WC). No music

---

Use the lists towards the front of the book to find suitable restaurants for special occasions.

To find a restaurant in a particular area use the maps at the back of the book.

MAENPORTH Cornwall

map 1

Pennypots

Maenporth Beach TR11 5HN
TEL: (01326) 250251 FAX: (01326) 251040

COOKING 6
COST £39–£47

Even by Cornish standards the view across Falmouth Bay is arresting. The restaurant occupies the first floor of a new building next to 'an upmarket holiday residences development': drinks are served on the terrace in fine weather, and at other times the dining-room is protected from the elements by a sliding-glass wall. Large, well-spaced tables help to make it feel 'restful and pleasing', and while the ceramic teddy bears and framed certificates and diplomas may not be to everyone's taste, the cooking certainly seems to be.

Fish and shellfish, in plentiful supply locally, might appear as a starter of scallops with Parma ham and balsamic dressing, or a main course fillet of sea bass served in a warm coriander dressing. Given its freshness and quality, a simple 'medley' of assorted seafood, perhaps baked in filo pastry with saffron sauce, makes a lot of sense. Meat does not just play second fiddle however, having produced highlights of 'light and creamy' chicken-liver mousse, and 'wonderful' fillet of beef in rich madeira sauce. Technical ability is not in doubt, and Kevin Viner aims for simplicity without 'lots of needless garnishing', although he could probably make it simpler still if he left out a few nests of deep-fried leeks.

Two courses are an option, but most reporters wisely choose a dessert: perhaps a cold soup of summer fruits; lemon tart with a scoop of 'seriously intense' blackcurrant sorbet; or creamy bread and butter pudding that is 'light years from the usual heavy filler', served with clotted cream. Service from Jane Viner and her assistants is notably good. As the *Guide* goes to press, a beach bar and grill – called Oceans – is due to open on the lower floor; it will have its own open-plan kitchen and is aimed at families on holiday. Wines are widely sourced, carefully chosen to offer good choice under £20, and are graded on the list by sweetness for whites, and body for reds. The seven-strong house selection starts at £9.50.

CHEFS: Kevin Viner, Peter McGregor and Gavin Young PROPRIETORS: Kevin and Jane Viner
OPEN: Tue to Sat D only 7 to 10 CLOSED: Christmas, 1 Jan, 4 weeks in winter MEALS: Set D £24
(2 courses) to £28.50. BYO £4 SERVICE: not inc, card slips closed CARDS: Amex, Delta,
Diners, MasterCard, Switch, Visa DETAILS: 40 seats. Private parties: 40 main room. Car park.
Vegetarian meals. Children's helpings. No smoking before 10pm. Wheelchair access (1 step;
also WC). Music. Air-conditioned

MAIDENCOMBE Devon

▲ Orestone Manor ⚹

NEW ENTRY

Rockhouse Lane, Maidencombe TQ1 4SX
TEL: (01803) 328098 FAX: (01803) 328336
on A379 (formerly B3199) between Torquay and
Teignmouth

COOKING 4
COST £37–£59

Orestone basks in a certain amount of reflected glory. It was once home to Isambard Kingdom Brunel's brother-in-law, and Rudyard Kipling used to live next door, but those not easily dazzled by celebrity will appreciate the trim Georgian country lodge – with its sub-tropical gardens – for itself. The dining-room is done in shades of red and hung with sporting prints, and the ambience is pleasantly informal.

Wayne Pearson has cooked his way around Devon and Cornwall – at Holne Chase, Ashburton last year and before that at Well House, St Keyne (see entries) – gathering plaudits wherever he has been. His style is essentially British country-house, with fashionable ingredients incorporated subtly rather than clumsily sprayed on, although strong accompaniments can occasionally compete with main components. Chicken liver parfait may seem as old as the hills, but is a superb version, dense and creamy, textured with green peppercorns and served with a ringingly intense kumquat chutney. A fish trio that brings together squid pickled in star-anise, sweet-cured mackerel, and smoked salmon with pools of bright red pepper sauce, offers a visually dramatic composition, as well as keen flavour contrasts. At inspection 'proper' egg custard tart was more successful than chocolate marquise with pistachio sauce. Service is 'slick and polished', and a commendable effort to source interesting flavours at level-headed prices is evident on the wine list, house selections opening with red and white Australian blends at £9.95.

CHEF: Wayne Pearson   PROPRIETORS: Mr and Mrs W.J. Dagworthy   OPEN: all week D only 7 to 9 (lunch by arrangement)   CLOSED: first two weeks of Jan   MEALS: Set D £23.50 (2 courses) to £32.50. Snack menu available on request   SERVICE: not inc, card slips closed   CARDS: Amex (3.5% surcharge), Delta, MasterCard, Switch, Visa   DETAILS: 40 seats. Private parties: 80 main room, 12 private room. Car park. No children under 8. No smoking in dining-room. Wheelchair access (2 steps; not WC). Music   ACCOMMODATION: 18 rooms, all with bath/shower. TV. Phone. B&B £55 to £160. Children by arrangement. Baby facilities. Dogs welcome in bedrooms only. Afternoon teas. Swimming-pool (£5)

MAIDEN NEWTON Dorset   map 2

Le Petit Canard ♀ ⁵⋇

Dorchester Road, Maiden Newton DT2 0BE
TEL: (01300) 320536   FAX: (01300) 320536
EMAIL: duckie@globalnet.co.uk   COOKING 5
off A37, 7m N of Dorchester   COST £38–£46

The Chapmans came here from Canada a decade ago, only intending to stay two years, and have been unable to tear themselves away. Home is now this terraced house in the centre of a tiny Dorset village – a small but uncramped restaurant decorated with fairy lights strung across beams, net curtains at the windows, plenty of flowers and spiralling candle-holders on each table. Geoff Chapman's cooking has evolved continuously within the Pacific Rim style, with obvious touches of California amid the Eastern references.

There is a lot going on in dishes to judge by the menu descriptions, but they make clear culinary sense. Thus a first course of sauté scallops with fine green beans, scattered with crisp bacon pieces and a spiked-up dollop of crème fraîche was 'dead simple, dead right'. A meatier starter might be grilled pigeon breast with cured ham sausage, crisp celeriac and tarragon lentils. Kangaroo is a constant on the menu, perhaps chargrilled and served with fragrant, silky mustard mash and a less than powerful red wine sauce. Otherwise, there might be chicken or lamb main courses, with a 'fish of the day' offering. Granny Smith sorbet with vanilla ice-cream makes a colourful dish, and pistachio biscotti can be had as a finale (at a supplement) with a glass of muscat. Vocal jazz is played to drown out the sound of mine host crooning over a hot stove.

The wine list may be compact, but packs in plenty of interest and flavour, particularly from the New World: take Penfolds Trial Bin 'White Grange', for example, or the nostalgic but fully merited sparkler from Canada. Traditionalists should check out the fine-wine bin ends section at the back. Prices are fair, starting around £11 for the frequently changing house selection. CELLARMAN'S CHOICE: Gewurztraminer Bollenberg 1994, Fuchs, £16.95; Elsa's Vineyard Cabernet Sauvignon 1993, Valentin Bianchi, Argentina, £18.95.

CHEF: Geoff Chapman   PROPRIETORS: Geoff and Lin Chapman   OPEN: Tue to Sat D 7 to 8.45   CLOSED: 2 weeks early Jan   MEALS: Set D £24.50. BYO £8   SERVICE: not inc   CARDS: MasterCard, Visa   DETAILS: 30 seats. Private parties: 38 main room. No children under 7. No smoking in dining-room. Music

---

MALMESBURY Wiltshire   map 2

▲ *Old Bell* ⚑✴

Abbey Row, Malmesbury SN16 0AG	NEW CHEF
TEL: (01666) 822344 FAX: (01666) 825145	COST £23–£43

Simon Holling moved up from sous-chef to take charge of the kitchen at this ancient hostelry – one of the oldest hotels in England – as the *Guide* went to press. On offer is a range of bar snacks, and set-price menus that might take in pressed terrine of ham hock with chilli-spiced mango chutney, poached salmon, and mousse of iced dark chocolate and banana with a warm fudge sauce. Staff are young and friendly, and children are made especially welcome: given a supervised den to play in during the daytime, nannies by arrangement, and their own menus. Wines can be a bit pricey, though quality is good and choice varied. House South African is £12.50.

CHEF: Simon Holling   PROPRIETORS: Nigel Chapman and Nicholas Dickinson   OPEN: all week 12.30 to 2.30 (2 Sun), 7.30 to 9.30   MEALS: Set L £15, Set D £19.75 to £26. Light L and D available   SERVICE: not inc, card slips closed   CARDS: Amex, Delta, Diners, MasterCard, Switch, Visa   DETAILS: 60 seats. 50 seats outside. Private parties: 80 main room, 12 to 24 private rooms. Car park. Vegetarian meals. Children's helpings. No smoking in dining-room. Wheelchair access (not WC). Occasional music   ACCOMMODATION: 31 rooms, all with bath/shower. TV. Phone. B&B £65 to £170. Children welcome. High teas for children. Baby facilities. Dogs welcome exc in public areas. Afternoon teas (*The Which? Hotel Guide*)

See inside the front cover for an explanation of the symbols used at the tops of entries.

'While seated at the bar, a party of French visitors were making their selection from the menu. On being asked whether the salmon in the gravad lax was smoked, I commented (on detecting the pungent smell of too many Gitanes cigarettes) that if she simply exhaled on the fish it would have the desired effect!' (On eating in Scotland)

MALVERN WELLS Worcestershire   map 5

Croque-en-Bouche ▮ ⁵⨯

---

221 Wells Road, Malvern Wells WR14 4HF
TEL: (01684) 565612
EMAIL: croque@globalnet.co.uk   COOKING 8
on A449, 2m S of Great Malvern   COST £31–£60

Partly screened by tall trees, with only the name on the window to identify it,
Croque-en-Bouche, now 21 years in the *Guide*, feels as much a private house as a
restaurant. Polished wooden tables are neatly set with plain glassware, and
bottle-stocked shelves indicate the importance of drink to the enterprise, as
much a wine business as anything. The format bears repeating. Dinner, served
three evenings a week, varies from three to five courses for a set price. Marion
Jones cooks, Robin Jones serves, each single-handedly, and there is no
fol-de-rol about either. Because there are just the two of them, arrivals are
carefully timed at intervals, a practice that can cause tension when it goes awry,
though most recognise this as merely being 'organised' and 'efficient'.

The pattern of a full meal is typically soup, a choice of three fish, then three
meat dishes, salad, cheese, and any of six desserts. Marion Jones concentrates on
items she knows well: grilled Bobbington wild boar, smoked Orkney lamb, or
the Japanese fish selection combining chargrilled squid, king prawns and crab
with shiitakes, asparagus, seaweed and pickled cucumber. She rings the
changes by serving Cornish skate now with sea kale shoots from the garden (a
short season), now with mango salsa and herbs. Colourful soups, such as vivid
green split pea with wild garlic and sorrel, come in a large help-yourself tureen.
Creamy dauphinoise potatoes accompany meat dishes such as aubergine-stuffed
leg of Cotswold spring lamb, marinated and roasted pink, served with a
mint-flecked béarnaise sauce.

The dressed salad that follows is a knockout, whether a chargrilled Mediterranean version, or one made with herbs and flowers from the garden. The
cheese trolley is stocked with a good variety, mostly British, served at 'perfect
ripeness'. Desserts can be taken as a sampler plate of the entire selection, or
individually: perhaps a wedge of 'Jaffa' cake combining dark chocolate and
orange, or a pineapple tart layered with crème patissière, topped with toasted
coconut shavings, and served with an 'out of this world' banana and coconut
ice-cream. Petits fours with coffee provide a 'wonderful finish', and value for
money is a regular theme in reports. With well over a thousand attractively
priced wines to choose from, customers might like to have the abbreviated – yet,
still lengthy – list sent to them in advance for leisurely perusal. If not, a short list
which includes the house selection (starting at £10) is available on the night, or
Robin Jones will 'be pleased to offer any advice'. The coverage is so broad that it
is difficult to single out any region for particular praise, but old and rare Rhônes
are a speciality. Bottles are left on the table for diners to serve themselves.
CELLARMAN'S CHOICE: Bonny Doon Ca' del Solo Malvasia Bianca 1996, Santa
Cruz, California, £15.50; Nuits-St-Georges 1993, Dom. de l'Arlot, £25.

▮ *denotes an outstanding wine cellar;* ▼ *denotes a good wine list, worth travelling for.*

CHEF: Marion Jones   PROPRIETORS: Robin and Marion Jones   OPEN: Thur to Sat D only 7 to 9.30   CLOSED: Christmas to New Year, 1 week May, 1 week July, 1 week Sept   MEALS: Set D Thur and Fri £23 to £36, Set D Sat £25 to £38   SERVICE: net prices, card slips closed   CARDS: Delta, MasterCard, Switch, Visa   DETAILS: 22 seats. Private parties: 6 main room, 6 private room. Children welcome. No smoking in dining-room. Wheelchair access (1 step; not WC). No music

Planters

191–193 Wells Road, Malvern Wells WR14 4HE
TEL: (01684) 575065   COOKING 3
on A449, 3m S of Great Malvern   COST £26–£42

Sandra and Chandra continue to jazz up Worcestershire palates in their unlikely little restaurant by Malvern village post office. Unlikely, because what they offer is a genuine version of South-east Asian food. Influences come mainly from Thailand, Indonesia and Sri Lanka, and value for money undeniable. The main menu, which changes every few months, promises tom yum kai (hot and sour chicken soup), vaday (lentil rissoles) and various satays as starters, while mains take in everything from salmon steak in batter with Thai lemon sauce, to stir-fried chicken breast with lemon grass and cashew-nuts, by way of pork cooked in mustard and coconut milk sauce. A new and successful revelation for one devotee was 'excellent' Muslim lamb cooked with yoghurt and spices. Among side-dishes and accompaniments, it's worth noting roti canai (unleavened Malaysian bread) and achar (pickled vegetables). Gourmet feasts, or a fixed-price rijsttafel ('rice table') are alternatives, but the star deal is the reduced-price menu (Tuesday to Friday): have a main course with trimmings for around £10, then, if you choose a starter, dessert comes free. Service is unerringly pleasant and efficient. The wine list is pitched perfectly to suit the food on offer. House French is £8.40.

CHEF: Chandra de Alwis   PROPRIETOR: Sandra Pegg   OPEN: Tue to Sat D only 7 to 9 (9.30 Fri and Sat)   CLOSED: Tue Jan to Easter   MEALS: alc (main courses £8 to £9). Set D Tue to Fri (1 course) £10, Set D Tue to Sat £16.25 to £27.50   SERVICE: not inc, card slips closed   CARDS: MasterCard, Switch, Visa   DETAILS: 40 seats. Private parties: 40 main room. Vegetarian meals. Children welcome. Wheelchair access (1 step; not WC). No music   £5

MANCHESTER   Greater Manchester   map 8

Chiang Rai £

16 Princess Street, Manchester M1 4NB   COOKING 3
TEL: (0161) 237 9511   COST £23–£38

This white basement dining-room, attractively decorated with pots and other artefacts, makes a pleasant setting for 'technically proficient' Thai food distinguished by 'clear, sharp spicing'. Starters are divided into 'Classic' (satay, fried beef balls), 'Seafood' (pastry-wrapped fried prawns, fish-cakes studded with green chilli) and 'Northern Thai' (skewers of grilled marinated pork with hot sauce, and curried noodles with rich coconut cream, turmeric and pickled cabbage). 'Succulent and pungent' hot and sour trout is spatchcocked, filleted, marinaded, baked, and garnished with red and green chillies and pineapple; stir-fried pork is enlivened with garlic and peppers; and green prawn curry is a 'fine, coconutty version'. A separate vegetarian menu offers the likes of aubergine with chilli and basil in yellow-bean sauce. Various set menus offer better-than-average choice, and there are good-value three-course lunches. Staff, mainly Thai, are courteous and knowledgeable, and wines are few but interesting: Tyrell's Long Flat Red makes a good match for strong Thai flavours. A branch of Chiang Rai is at 762–766 Wilmslow Road, Didsbury M20 2DR (tel: (0161) 448 2277).

CHEF: Tussana Panyuak   PROPRIETOR: Andy Parkhouse   OPEN: Mon to Fri L 12 to 2.30, all week D 6 to 11   CLOSED: bank hols   MEALS: alc (main courses £6.50 to £9.50). Set L £5 to £9   SERVICE: not inc (10% on set meals), card slips closed   CARDS: Amex, Diners, MasterCard, Switch, Visa   DETAILS: 90 seats. Private parties: 90 main room. Vegetarian meals. Children welcome. Music

▲ Crowne Plaza Midland, French Restaurant

NEW ENTRY

Peter Street, Manchester M60 2DS
TEL: (0161) 236 3333   FAX: (0161) 932 4100

COOKING 5
COST £43–£65

The Midland, as it was always known, used to be Manchester's main railway hotel. Central Station next door has become the G-Mex centre, and the re-named hotel's French Restaurant has taken on a new chef. Paul Reed arrived in May 1998 from the Arkle restaurant at the Chester Grosvenor Hotel (see entry, Chester) to work his magic on a largely classical menu, deeply entrenched in dairy produce, alcohol and luxury ingredients. It looks as though his first priority may have been to concentrate on quality control of the existing repertoire, before introducing his own more complex and innovative dishes. If so, it is working well, although prices are 'seriously high', if you call £21.50 for a plate of duck breast with ceps and barley risotto serious.

The oval dining-room, still just recognisable from the old days, is high-ceilinged, with dark wood and mirrored panels. Service is 'remarkably attentive', with silver domes being lifted to reveal, perhaps, a casserole of lobster with vegetables in a 'commendably sparse' Sauternes and cream sauce. Among 'healthy options' signalled on the menu are grilled lamb cutlets and sauté fillet of beef.

Prime cuts predominate, and fish tends to be given the dairy treatment: a vegetable-strewn creamy buttery sauce for fillets of Dover sole, arranged on slices of Jerusalem artichoke mixed with chopped truffles. Desserts go in for mousses, parfaits and feuillantines, alongside maybe an iced apricot soufflé with a sharp compote of apricots and a frothy sabayon. 'Excellent' cheeses are served at room temperature, and a vast selection of interesting loaves – including a 'remarkable baked potato and rosemary roll' – is borne around on a trolley: try a blue cheese with the chocolate bread. A heavily bound wine list concentrates on France; prices start at £12.95 for house red and white, and zoom upwards rapidly.

CHEF: Paul Reed   PROPRIETOR: Crowne Plaza Manchester   OPEN: Mon to Sat D only 7 to 11
CLOSED: Christmas, bank hols   MEALS: alc (main courses £16.50 to £24). Set D £35 (5-course
Menu Gastronomique)   SERVICE: not inc   CARDS: Amex, Delta, Diners, MasterCard, Switch,
Visa   DETAILS: 55 seats. Private parties: 500 main room, 25 to 100 private rooms. Vegetarian
meals. Children welcome. Jacket and tie. No cigars. Wheelchair access (also WC). Occasional
music. Air-conditioned   ACCOMMODATION: 303 rooms, all with bath/shower. TV. Phone. Room
only £150 to £170. Rooms for disabled. Children welcome. Baby facilities. Afternoon teas.
Swimming-pool (*The Which? Hotel Guide*)   £5

Koreana £

Kings House, 40A King Street West,
Manchester M3 2WY
TEL: (0161) 832 4330   FAX: (0161) 832 2293   COOKING 2
EMAIL: 113036.1764@compuserve.com   COST £13–£33

Opened in 1985 and still going strong, Koreana has earned its stripes among
central Manchester's contingent of Far Eastern restaurants. 'Unprepossessing'
décor and subdued classical music define the mood in the basement
dining-room, and service is as pleasant as can be. The kitchen delivers capable
renditions of the classic Korean repertoire and the food is reckoned to be
outstanding value for money. The procedure is to build your own three-course
meal for a fixed price, based on dishes listed on the menu; alternatively, there are
five-course banquets for up to four people. Reporters have spoken highly of yook
hwae (oriental 'steak tartare' with a sesame oil dressing and 'a raw egg mixed in
at the table'). Also worth noting are mandoo (a soup containing beef dumplings
and vegetables), gu jul pan (mixed appetisers served in a traditional partitioned
box) and several sorts of bulgogi and galbi (marinated beef or chicken cooked on
a special grill). Drink green tea or the ginseng version; otherwise there is Korean
beer to quench the thirst. House wine is £7.95.

CHEFS: Mrs H. Kim and Mr H.S. Shin   PROPRIETOR: Koreana Ltd   OPEN: Mon to Fri 12 to 2, Mon
to Sat 6.30 (5.30 Sat) to 10.30 (11 Fri and Sat)   CLOSED: 25 to 30 Dec, 1 Jan, L bank hols
MEALS: alc (main courses £7.50 to £9). Set L £6.50 (1 course) to £13.50, Set D £13.50 to £19.50
(min 2)   SERVICE: not inc, card slips closed; 10% for parties of 8 or more   CARDS: Amex, Delta,
Diners, MasterCard, Switch, Visa   DETAILS: 60 seats. Private parties: 80 main room. Vegetarian
meals. Children's helpings. Music   £5

Kosmos Taverna £

248 Wilmslow Road, Manchester M14 6LD   COOKING 2
TEL: (0161) 225 9106   FAX: (0161) 256 4442   COST £18–£38

About as authentic as you can get this far from Greece, Loulla Astin's
long-established taverna serves up just about every dish that travellers are likely
to encounter, and then some. Chicken kebabs, spicy minced lamb, and jumbo
prawns are grilled over charcoal, while slow cooking produces traditional lamb
kleftiko and pork afelia. Chips are on offer, but it is better to go for the cracked
wheat pilaff. Among seasonal items that might show up is a dish of artichokes
with spring lamb in egg and lemon sauce. Meze include the usual array of dips
and salads, along with grilled halloumi or stuffed vine leaves, and white bean

soup is here not as a modish appetiser, but because it is 'the national dish of Greece'. Retsina is £2 a glass, Robola at £12.50 is a more serious white, and house wine is £10.

CHEF: Loulla Astin PROPRIETORS: Stewart and Loulla Astin OPEN: Sun 1 to 11, all week D 6 to 11 (12 Fri and Sat) CLOSED: 25 and 26 Dec, 1 Jan MEALS: alc (main courses £6 to £12.50). Set L Sun £5, Set D (before 7.30) £7.95 SERVICE: not inc CARDS: Amex, Delta, MasterCard, Switch, Visa DETAILS: 90 seats. Private parties: 50 main room. Vegetarian meals. Children's helpings. Music. Air-conditioned (£5)

Lime Tree ⁵✱

8 Lapwing Lane, West Didsbury,
Manchester M20 2WS   COOKING 2
TEL: (0161) 445 1217   COST £20–£45

'A very good night out' was one correspondent's verdict on this amiable neighbourhood restaurant on the fringes of Didsbury. The décor struck one reporter as 'very potted planty', and even though tables are packed quite closely together, the overall impression is 'roominess and privacy'. Ideas are gleaned from the global cauldron, and short menus leap happily between grilled black pudding with apple and mint jelly, and crisp-skinned Chinese-style duckling with wok-fried vegetables and transparent noodles. In between there is space for grilled asparagus with roasted peppers, goats' cheese and tomato vinaigrette, or roast loin of lamb with an individual moussaka, spiced couscous and rosemary jus. The kitchen also seems to have a special liking for salmon: three cured versions are served as a starter with smoked trout mousse, while fresh fillets might be roasted and served with sauté spinach, smoked salmon and a tarragon and lemon butter sauce. Among desserts, lime sorbet with raspberry coulis, and a round block of dark and white chocolate ice-cream have both been favourably received. The wine list has been thoughtfully and knowledgeably assembled. House wine is £9.95.

CHEFS: Jem O'Sullivan and Jason Dickinson PROPRIETOR: Patrick Hannity OPEN: Tue to Fri and Sun L 12 to 2.30, all week D 6 to 10.30 CLOSED: bank hols MEALS: alc (main courses L £4.50 to £9, D £10 to £14). Set L Tue to Fri £9.95 (2 courses), Set L Sun £11.95, Set D 6 to 7 £9.95 (2 courses). SERVICE: not inc CARDS: Amex, Delta, MasterCard, Switch, Visa DETAILS: 85 seats. 20 seats outside. Private parties: 40 main room. Vegetarian meals. Children welcome. No smoking in 1 dining-room. Wheelchair access (1 step; not WC). Music

Little Yang Sing

17 George Street, Manchester M1 4HE   COOKING 2
TEL: (0161) 228 7722 FAX: (0161) 237 9257   COST £23–£44

'The new décor/layout is a big improvement,' writes a regular supporter of this Chinatown stalwart hard by the Metrolink and major city-centre amenities. Mirrors create the illusion of space, the stairs and entrance have been repositioned and the bar no longer dominates. The menu may lack the more esoteric ingredients and specialities offered by nearby competition and some reporters feel that there is an emphasis on so-called 'crossover dishes' to assuage Western palates. Having said that, the kitchen knows what it's about and any adaptation is of the best sort. Dim-sum (served until 5.30pm) are 'well conceived and well executed': fun kuo (fried prawn balls), scallop dumplings and char siu buns have all passed muster. Elsewhere the thrust of the menu is old-school Cantonese without tears: sublime steamed scallops with spring onion and sesame oil, huge slices of perfectly cooked duck 'straight from the wok' with miscellaneous vegetables, seafood chow mein and other one-plate dishes. Little Yang Sing also makes a laudable attempt to please vegetarians and offers a daytime 'kiddies menu'. Service is 'admirable and friendly'. One reporter observed that most of the clientele tend to quaff pints of beer in true Mancunian style, rather than picking their way through the fair list of three dozen wines. House vin de pays is £9.95.

CHEF: Mr Choi   PROPRIETOR: L.Y.S. Ltd   OPEN: all week noon to 11.30   CLOSED: 25 Dec
MEALS: alc (main courses £7 to £10). Set L £8.95, Set D £15 (minimum 2). Dim-sum menu available. BYO £5   SERVICE: 10%   CARDS: Amex, Delta, MasterCard, Switch, Visa   DETAILS: 90 seats. Private parties. 100 main room. Vegetarian meals. Children's menu daytime. Music. Air-conditioned

Mash and Air ♥ 🍺

40 Chorlton Street, Manchester M1 3HW
TEL: (0161) 661 1111 (Air), (0161) 661 6161 (Mash)   COOKING 5
FAX: (0161) 661 1112 (Air), (0161) 661 6060 (Mash)   COST £22–£57

There are precious few brasseries in France, let alone Britain, that actually brew their own beer. The process here takes up four floors, and brewer Paul Home conducts tours around the brightly coloured tanks every Saturday lunch-time. Air (dinner only) occupies the top floor, Mash (open all day) is below, and there is a bar on the ground floor. The hard-surfaced minimalism, and shiny paint in primary colours, may smack of industrial architecture, but floral displays in Mash help to soften things, and Air compensates with smartly set tables, rich blue upholstery and a cityscape seen through large uncurtained windows.

Jason Whitelock deals in bright flavours and modern ideas, using Mash's wood-fired oven to turn out a variety of pizzas, fish of the day served three ways, and first-rate calf's liver with onion gravy. A starter of garlic bread with Lancashire cheese was considered 'a poor description of the puffed-up object which arrived', and which impressed the socks off its reporter. Salads, grilled ciabatta sandwiches and fair prices add to the appeal.

Air goes a step further in its invention, in a dish of roasted, spiced, corn-fed chicken served with a salad of walnuts, dried apricots and figs bound in creamy yoghurt. It notches up an extra degree of excitement, too, in a memorable Moroccan-inspired dish consisting of a light, thin pasta envelope filled with slow-cooked shank of lamb which had been pounded, scented with garlic and other Middle Eastern spices and set on a heap of chopped lemon pickle, around which was a rich glossy reduction scattered with chickpeas, the whole dish 'full of sharp, clear flavours'.

Service throughout is friendly, enthusiastic, 'refreshingly informal' and, in the case of Air at least – to which the 'Glass' symbol refers – well versed in wines, with the sommelier not only able to recommend a choice to match a specific dish but also willing to provide tasting samples to aid selection. Wines are an appealingly varied bunch, arranged by varietal/regional blends with some good-quality bins to be had at a price (the list at Mash is less diverse). An eclectic house selection is priced from £11.50 a bottle/£4 for a large glass, while a pint of Mash beer is £2.40. CELLARMAN'S CHOICE: Allan Scott Sauvignon Blanc 1996, Marlborough, New Zealand, £26; De Loach 'Platinum' 1995, Sonoma County, California, £25.50.

CHEF: Jason Whitelock   PROPRIETOR: Oliver Peyton   OPEN: Air: Mon to Sat D only 7 (6 Thur to Sat) to 11 (11.30 Thur to Sat); Mash: all week noon to midnight (1am Thur and Fri, 2am Sat, 10.30pm)   CLOSED: 25 and 26 Dec, 1 Jan   MEALS: Air: alc (main courses £13 to £16.50); Mash: alc (main courses £5.50 to £12)   SERVICE: 10% (optional)   CARDS: Amex, Delta, MasterCard, Switch, Visa   DETAILS: Air: 150 seats. Private parties: 200 main room, 12 private room. Mash: 120 seats. Private parties: 10 private room. Air: valet parking. Vegetarian meals. Children welcome. Wheelchair access (also WC). Music. Air-conditioned

▲ Moss Nook

Ringway Road, Manchester M22 5WD
TEL: (0161) 437 4778   FAX: (0161) 498 8089   COOKING 6
on B5166, 1m from Manchester Airport   COST £26–£70

Moss Nook has notched up 25 years as a star in the Manchester firmament, and its proximity to the airport has resulted in a fair amount of corporate business, something which is reflected in the tone of the Harrisons' operation. Deep reds lend an air of gravitas to the scene, and service, which is choreographed down to the last dribble of mineral water ('each act performed as if it were part of a religious service') keeps proceedings slightly more serious than they need be.

However, it is worth all the ceremony for Kevin Lofthouse's accomplished cooking, which may be taken à la carte or as a surprise menu (four courses at lunch and six at dinner, available only when booked by the whole table). A spring version delivered a small chicken tart in a finely judged curry sauce with saffron rice, an old-fashioned but well-crafted dish of salmon wrapped in a fillet of lemon sole on watercress sauce, and then generously served fillet of beef on peppercorn sauce. Presentation may recall the days of '80s nouvelle cuisine, with little bundles of French beans tied in a strand of leek, and mashed potato formed into lightly browned cubes like marshmallows. That meal ended with a plethora of unseasonal fruits sandwiched into a feuilleté with a strawberry coulis. Choices from the *carte* have included duck breast with a spiced duck sausage, and venison with wild mushroom timbale. While to some this style may seem a throwback to another era, to others it may come as a relief that there are still corners of England like it. Coffee comes in a silver pot with a woollen handle-cover and a shower of petits fours. A commendable wine list is strong on France and Australasia, but bottles under £20 are fairly thin on the ground. House French is £9.50.

CHEF: Kevin Lofthouse   PROPRIETORS: Pauline and Derek Harrison   OPEN: Tue to Fri L 12 to 1.30, Tue to Sat D 7 to 9.30   CLOSED: 2 weeks Christmas   MEALS: alc (main courses £18.50 to £25). Set L £18.50 (for whole table only), Set D £29.95 (for whole table only)   SERVICE: not inc, card slips closed   CARDS: Amex, MasterCard, Visa   DETAILS: 65 seats. 20 seats outside. Private parties: 55 main room. Car park. No children under 12. Jacket and tie. No music   ACCOMMODATION: 1 room in cottage, with bath/shower. TV. Phone. D,B&B £140

Nico Central　　　　　　　　　　　　　　　　　NEW ENTRY

Mount Street, Manchester M60 2DS　　　　　　　　　　　　　COOKING 5
TEL: (0161) 236 6488　FAX: (0161) 236 8897　　　　　　　COST £19–£52

Rather like a Russian novel, it seems appropriate to introduce the dramatis personae at the outset. Clive Fretwell used to cook at Le Manoir aux Quat' Saisons (see entry, Great Milton), and Nico Ladenis of Chez Nico at 90 Park Lane (see entry, London) is a consultant to Roy Ackerman's Restaurant Partnership. Advertising handouts feature the three of them looking as if they were about to sing in a Three Tenors concert. This is one of two new restaurants occupying the Crowne Plaza Midland, a Manchester landmark known as the Midland Hotel for longer than anybody can remember. A couple of cavernous, airy rooms have been completely revamped. The bar has become a busy meeting place, with tub-shaped armchairs, art-deco-style, and Gothic fireplace; wine racks are reached by stepladders, and the back of the bar forms one wall of the dining-room, another huge space with white-clothed tables, mirrored pillars and potted plants.

'Well-handled modern brasserie food' is Fretwell's new style, his weekly-changing dishes appealing equally to trenchermen and vegetarians: two 'immense' skinless pheasant sausages with a gamey flavour, or tomato and raclette tart with pesto. Starters typically go in for 'gâteaux' – incorporating beetroot and goats' cheese, or a mix of walnuts, ground chickpeas, onions and tomato – and layered terrines, perhaps of woodcock, foie gras and artichoke with a sparse olive oil dressing. Although broadly European, the food also embraces a few Far Eastern flavourings, as in roast guinea-fowl with a sweet and sticky ginger and lime leaf sauce, or braised lamb shank with a creamy coconut sauce and Chinese greens.

Finish with 'very large' crème brûlée, 'dense' chocolate cake with mint and cream sauce, or 'raspberry conversation', an impressively thin short pastry tart of crème anglaise and raspberries topped with a lemon-zesty meringue. Bread and appetisers are good, but French service has brought a trail of woes, largely for its exasperating lack of understanding, although it has also been 'sharp and friendly', and the kitchen's control over timing is not in question. Some of the 60 or so varied wines are ambitiously priced; five are available by the small glass from £3 to £5.50.

CHEF: Clive Fretwell　PROPRIETOR: The Restaurant Partnership　OPEN: all week 12 to 2.30, 5.30 to 11 (10 Sun)　CLOSED: 25 and 26 Dec　MEALS: Set L £12.50, Set D £19 (2 courses) to £24 SERVICE: net prices, card slips closed　CARDS: Amex, Delta, Diners, MasterCard, Switch, Visa DETAILS: 110 seats. Vegetarian meals. Children's helpings. No cigars/pipes in dining-room. No music. Air-conditioned　£5

Pearl City　£

33 George Street, Manchester M1 4PH　　　　　　　　　　　COOKING 1
TEL: (0161) 228 7683　FAX: (0161) 237 9173　　　　　　　COST £23–£43

Very much an old-stager among the burgeoning ranks of restaurants in Manchester's Chinatown, Pearl City attracts a largely Western clientele with its 'old-style Cantonese' cooking. Cut-price lunches and a big choice of set menus are aimed at those wanting the likes of pork with green pepper and black-bean sauce, or beef with ginger and spring onion. More promising is the list of dim-sum, which one seasoned reporter reckoned were probably as good as any in the country. He was particularly impressed with steamed Chinese mushroom with pork and prawn ball, prawns in rice paper, and steamed whelks in satay sauce. From the main menu, roast duck has crispy, glazed skin, sumptuous meat and an unctuous degree of authentic fattiness; other commendable dishes have included green peppers and aubergine stuffed with prawn meat, 'sweetish' Szechuan chilli beef, and 'hefty platefuls' of vermicelli noodles. Service is generally 'good and helpful'. George Duboeuf house wine is £8.50.

CHEF: Tony Cheung   PROPRIETORS: Tony Cheung, P. Lee and P. Keung   OPEN: all week noon to 2am (4am Fri and Sat, midnight Sun)   MEALS: alc (main courses £6.50 to £10). Set L £4.90 to £9.50, Set D £15.50 to £19.50 (minimum 2). Dim-Sum menu until 2am   SERVICE: 10%   CARDS: Amex, Delta, MasterCard, Switch, Visa   DETAILS: 400 seats. Private parties: 160 main room, 240 private room. Vegetarian meals. Children's helpings. Music. Air-conditioned

Simply Heathcotes

Jackson Row, 151 Deansgate, Manchester M2 5WD   COOKING 4
TEL: (0161) 835 3536   FAX: (0161) 835 3534   COST £21–£57

As if completing a tie-breaker, one reporter writes: 'I like Heathcotes because it's trendy without being pretentious and seems to attract everyone, from pop stars to business folk to working-class Mancunian families.' The spacious first-floor dining-room – with coloured walls and 'bright splodgy paintings' – plays to an appreciative crowd. One distinctive contribution of Paul Heathcote (or is it Max Gnoyke, we are never sure) is to turn traditional 'Lancashire domestic' ideas into modern comfort food. This 'ee bah gum factor' doubtless accounts for such dishes as a corned beef terrine, served with slicks of a strangely familiar brown sauce condiment. But there is plenty more besides, from baked cod with black olive mash and pesto, via ceviche of mackerel with celeriac rémoulade, to a 'cassoulet' of chargrilled scallops with chorizo.

Poultry – perhaps chicken on a bed of pease pudding with stout sauce, or confit of duck leg with a pearl barley and red wine 'risotto' – is worth considering, since the pedigree birds come from Goosnargh. Bread-and-butter pudding, and ginger cream with lime leaf sorbet and biscotti, indicate the extreme ends of the dessert menu, which has also produced a 'very big, very sweet' creamy, crisp-topped orange and chocolate brûlée. A welcome development since last year is that the three-course set-price option has come down to £12.50 at both lunch and dinner, and large parties may wish to note that the 'optional' service charge has a ceiling of £20. Staff are young, well-intentioned and learning as fast as they can. A well-constructed list of around 40 wines includes more than a dozen by the glass. House French is £11 a bottle.

CHEFS: Max Gnoyke and James Gingell   PROPRIETOR: Paul Heathcote   OPEN: Mon to Sat 11.45 to 2.30, 5.30 to 11, Sun 12 to 4, 6 to 9   CLOSED: 25 and 26 Dec, 1 Jan, bank hols   MEALS: alc (main courses £11.50 to £20). Set L and D £10.50 (2 courses) to £12.50. BYO £10   SERVICE: 10% (optional), card slips closed   CARDS: Amex, Delta, MasterCard, Switch, Visa   DETAILS: 160 seats. Private parties: 200 main room, 50 private room. Vegetarian meals. Children welcome. No cigars/pipes in dining-room. Wheelchair access (also WC). Music. Air-conditioned

Tai Pan £

Brunswick House, 81–97 Upper Brook Street,
Manchester M13 9TX   COOKING 2
TEL: (0161) 273 2798   FAX: (0161) 273 1578   COST £22–£48

Its location – some distance from the heartland of Manchester's Chinatown and with virtually no pedestrian passing trade – may explain why this 'Hong Kong-style eating-house' is not content to rest on its laurels. 'I have a distinct impression of consolidation,' noted one devotee of the place. The kitchen deals mainly in genuine Cantonese food, although there are occasional detours into the cuisines of Peking and Szechuan. Dim-sum are of a consistently high standard: deep-fried cuttlefish cakes, prawns in rice-paper, spare-ribs with black-bean sauce, and beef dumplings are a few examples of recent successes. The remainder of the 200-dish menu is a broad sweep through the full repertoire, with an impressive helping of vegetarian options to boot. 'Really fine' stir-fried Dover sole with ginger and spring onion is perhaps the pick of the fish dishes, or you might choose sauté fresh and dried squid, crabmeat with straw mushrooms, or fried prawn cake with mange-tout. Elsewhere, crispy Cantonese chicken, 'first-rate' char siu pork and Amoy-style vermicelli noodles have been heartily endorsed. House wine is £8.20.

CHEF: Garry Wan   PROPRIETOR: Mr K.K. Chan   OPEN: all week 12 to 11.30   MEALS: alc (main courses £6.50 to £11.50). Set L £5.45 (2 courses) to £9.45, Set D £14 to £28 (minimum 2) SERVICE: 10% (not on drinks)   CARDS: Amex, Delta, Diners, MasterCard, Switch, Visa   DETAILS: 320 seats. Private parties: 320 main room, 100 private room. Car park. Vegetarian meals. Children welcome. Wheelchair access (also WC). Music. Air-conditioned

---

MARSDEN West Yorkshire   map 8

▲ Olive Branch

Manchester Road, Marsden HD7 6LU
TEL: (01484) 844487   FAX: (01484) 842877   COOKING 2
on A62, between Slaithwaite and Marsden   COST £22–£46

'We enjoyed ourselves,' admitted one couple who ventured out on to the moors one chilly December evening. Since 1993 the Listers have revitalised what was once a Pennine watering-hole on the packhorse route. These days, visitors come by car to sample pub/brasserie food in a 'warm and welcoming' setting of scrubbed pine tables, wine racks and Gerald Scarfe cartoons. There's no fixed menu, but the day's dishes are written on cards and blackboards dotted around the bar. John Lister is forever dreaming up new ideas and he scours the globe with magpie-like curiosity. The results read well on the page and taste good on the plate: scallops 'of particularly fine quality' are served with salad leaves, truffle oil and Parmesan shavings; breast of chicken might be braised in Amaretto liqueur with toasted almonds; while sea bass receives the full oriental treatment with noodles, lime-dressed leaves and red pepper sauce. Pasta has also received the thumbs-up. Brisk, friendly service helps maintain the upbeat mood, and the thoughtfully assembled wine list does its job remarkably well. House French is £9.90.

CHEF: John Lister   PROPRIETORS: John and Ann Lister   OPEN: Wed to Fri and Sun L 12 to 1.45, all week D 6.30 to 9.30 (4 to 8.30 Sun)   CLOSED: 26 Dec, first week Jan   MEALS: alc (main courses £9 to £16). Set L and D £13.50 (not available after 7.30pm Fri and Sat). BYO £7 SERVICE: not inc, card slips closed   CARDS: Amex, Delta, MasterCard, Switch, Visa   DETAILS: 68 seats. Private parties: 68 main room, 35 private room. Car park. Vegetarian meals. Children welcome. Music   ACCOMMODATION: 3 rooms, all with bath/shower. TV. Room only £49.50. Children welcome. No dogs. Afternoon teas (£5)

MASHAM North Yorkshire   map 9

Floodlite £✷

7 Silver Street, Masham HG4 4DX
TEL: (01765) 689000   COOKING 5
off A6108, 9m NW of Ripon   COST £17–£43

Don't expect lavish or pristine surroundings. Décor is not the priority at Charles and Christine Flood's restaurant near the square. But as one of Masham's three main attractions (the other two: beer and fudge), Floodlite can be 'unreservedly recommended' for its food and value. If the place is modest, so are the prices: lunch in particular is considered 'amazing value', while the *carte* is distinguished by its generosity for such a small operation.

One visitor surmised that Charles Flood likes 'pottering about in the kitchen', producing pâtés and terrines (foie gras with celeriac salad, or salmon and pike with dill sauce), and turning out 'varied, rich and intense sauces': hollandaise with fillet steak, beurre blanc with scallops and leeks, and red wine and peppercorns for tenderloin of wild boar. He works with 'first-class' ingredients, including wild roe deer and hare all year round, other game in season, simply grilled Dover sole or salmon with sorrel, and loin of English spring lamb with a herb crust. Trimmed vegetables are 'plainly prepared, but each just right', and the pervading sense of culinary expertise extends to desserts: banana mousse with butterscotch sauce, or a blackberry and apple version of bread-and-butter pudding. Service is 'quiet but attentive', and wines are varied, interesting and fairly priced, starting with around half a dozen by the glass. House Australian is £8.50.

CHEF: Charles Flood   PROPRIETORS: Charles and Christine Flood   OPEN: Fri to Sun L 12 to 2, Tue to Sat D 7 to 9 (Sun D by arrangement)   MEALS: alc (main courses £9 to £16.50). Set L £11.50, Set D £15.   SERVICE: not inc, card slips closed   CARDS: Amex, MasterCard, Visa DETAILS: 36 seats. Private parties: 28 main room, 10 private room. Vegetarian meals. Children's helpings. No smoking in 1 dining-room. Wheelchair access (3 steps; not WC). Occasional music (£5)

' "Just how medium and just how rare is medium rare?" [the chef/proprietor] asked my wife. [He then said] "I'll bring you a blowtorch if you like." ' (On eating in Lincolnshire)

Several sharp operators have tried to extort money from restaurateurs on the promise of an entry in a guidebook that has never appeared. The Good Food Guide *makes no charge for inclusion.*

MAWGAN Cornwall   map 1

Yard Bistro

Trelowarren, Mawgan TR12 6AF
TEL: (01326) 221595   COOKING 1
off B3293, 3m SE of Helston   COST £15–£35

The setting is a delight on a fine summer's evening, especially if you are sipping wine in the courtyard. Inside, in the converted stable block, jazz music plays, and cheerful gingham and red chairs define the mood of the place. The Yard is 'bistro' through and through. Generous helpings of bread and vegetables are greatly appreciated, and the kitchen makes plentiful use of locally caught fish in the shape of, say, fried hake dumplings with saffron pancakes, or grilled John Dory in red Thai spices with black noodles. Elsewhere reporters have praised 'tender and substantial' duck with cranberries, and the regime also gets to grips with roast loin of Cornish lamb in warm basil and goats'-cheese dressing. Puddings might be as simple as local strawberries with clotted cream, but they are judged to be 'first-class'. Prices on the modest wine list are eminently affordable. House wines kick off at £7.50.

CHEF/PROPRIETOR: Trevor Bayfield   OPEN: Tue to Sun L 12 to 2, Wed to Sat D 7 to 9 (open Mon in summer)   CLOSED: 25 Dec   MEALS: alc (main courses L £4.50 to £5.50, D £12 to £13). BYO £3.50   SERVICE: not inc, card slips closed   CARDS: Delta, Diners, MasterCard, Switch, Visa DETAILS: 50 seats. 12 seats outside. Private parties: 60 main room. Car park. Vegetarian meals. Children's helpings. Wheelchair access (also WC). Music   £5

MAWNAN SMITH Cornwall   map 1

▲ Nansidwell

Mawnan Smith TR11 5HU
TEL: (01326) 250340   FAX: (01326) 250440
EMAIL: bomberob@aol.com
off A494 Helston road, take left fork at   COOKING 3
Red Lion in village   COST £31–£67

The kitchen at this comfortable Edwardian house makes good use of its location to acquire fish and shellfish – oysters come from the nearby Helford estuary – and the West Country supplies lamb, beef and cheeses. It is an industrious kitchen too: fish and meats are smoked in-house, and dishes typically include a number of intricate elements, as in poached breast of chicken with goose liver and chestnuts on a rosemary and port butter sauce, or chargrilled calf's liver on a shallot and smoked bacon confit, with a sherry and wild mushroom dressing. Some dishes carrry a hefty supplement (from £6.50 to £7.50), but the range and balance of menus is impressive, taking in veal sweetbreads, steamed bream and scallops, roast loin of Exmoor venison, and a baked herb and cheese soufflé. Al dente steamed vegetables – produced by a local grower – are served in a 'Chinese basket', and desserts might run to honey and praline savarin, or hot plum and chocolate pudding with Cornish clotted ice-cream. A short, well-spread wine list opens with house white Navarra and red Valdepeñas at £12.

CHEF: Anthony Allcott PROPRIETORS: Jamie and Felicity Robertson OPEN: all week 12.30 to 1.30, 7 to 9 CLOSED: Jan MEALS: Set L £15.75, Set D £27.50 SERVICE: not inc CARDS: Delta, MasterCard, Switch, Visa DETAILS: 40 seats. 20 seats outside. Private parties: 40 main room. Car park. Vegetarian meals. Children's helpings. No children under 7 at D. No cigars/pipes in dining-room. Wheelchair access (1 step; not WC). No music ACCOMMODATION: 12 rooms, all with bath/shower. TV. Phone. B&B £95 to £180. Rooms for disabled. Children welcome. High teas for children under 7. Baby facilities. Dogs welcome in bedrooms only.

MELBOURN Cambridgeshire

map 6

Pink Geranium ⅚✳

25 Station Road, Melbourn SG8 6DX
TEL: (01763) 260215 FAX: (01763) 262110
just off A10, 2m N of Royston

COOKING 6
COST £26–£72

Steven Saunders certainly has plenty to occupy him. As well as running this place, his interests extend to appearances on BBC's *Ready Steady Cook*, writing magazine articles and cookery books, and overseeing the recently acquired seventeenth-century Sheene Mill nearby, a seven-day-a-week brasserie serving anything from goat's-cheese soufflé to Thai duck breast hotpot. Pink Geranium, a thatched cottage built around 1500, easily lives up to its name, the exterior washed in pale blush-pink, the intimate interior a riot of floral upholstery. Mark Jordan now heads up the kitchen, producing copybook country-house style meals that may begin with a terrine of braised artichoke and poached lobster with tomato confit and herb oil, or perhaps seared fillet of grey mullet on Mediterranean vegetable ragoût. Mention of the M-word may suggest contemporary clichés, but the cooking has always been more thoughtful than that, and even a twice-baked soufflé that incorporates ricotta, Parmesan and basil is made more interesting with a salsa of apricots, grapes and prunes.

Cooking methods are gentle: rabbit loin bound in Bayonne ham and steamed, or pink chump of lamb accompanied by fondant potato and a niçoise sauce. Menu descriptions accumulate ingredients to a degree that may sound daunting, but there is enough confidence and flair in the performance to pull it all off. Desserts are simpler than the rest, taking in peach melba on raspberry sauce, or pear and vanilla tart on honey crème anglaise. Service, headed by Sally Saunders, is generally slick and professional. The wine list encouragingly leads off with a good selection of bottles under £15 before stretching into the lusher pastures of Puligny-Montrachet and top Pauillac. The bottom line is £10.

CHEFS: Mark Jordan and Steven Saunders PROPRIETORS: Sally and Steven Saunders OPEN: Tue to Sat 12 to 2, 7 to 10 CLOSED: 25 and 26 Dec, 1 Jan MEALS: alc (main courses £15 to £28). Set L Tue to Fri £12 (2 courses) to £16, Set L Sat £18.50 SERVICE: not inc CARDS: Amex, Delta, MasterCard, Switch, Visa DETAILS: 65 seats. Private parties: 18 main room, 18 private room. Car park. Vegetarian meals. Children's helpings. No smoking in dining-room. No music
£5

'There's not much point in having good raw materials if you're going to end up making Our Home-Reared Beef taste like Our Home-Reared Carpet.' (On eating in Shropshire)

MELKSHAM Wiltshire — map 2

▲ *Toxique*

187 Woodrow Road, Melksham SN12 7AY
TEL: (01225) 702129   FAX: (01225) 742773
take Calne road at Melksham centre mini-roundabout;   COOKING 2
turn left into Forest road and Toxique is on the left   COST £31–£49

After a brief excursion to Bath last year, where a sister restaurant, Toxique Fish, came to nought, Helen Bartlett is now back running the kitchen single-handedly at this colourful Wiltshire original. Redecoration with 'new paintings by Peter' was in hand as as we went to press, but the contemporary style of food continues unabated, taking in herb consommé with dumplings, goats'-cheese tart, and crisp-skinned oriental-style duck. Seafood plays a significant role, often a striking one – deep-fried fish cakes with lemon-grass salsa, Scottish salmon served with glazed red onions and mustard mash – but marinated lamb brochette with black olives and sauté polenta shows that meat is not left out in the cold. Finish with rhubarb bread-and-butter pudding, prune and almond tart, or lemon mascarpone mousse. France is the mainstay of the well-chosen wine list, which starts with house red at £11, white at £12.50.

CHEF: Helen Bartlett   PROPRIETORS: Peter Jewkes and Helen Bartlett   OPEN: Sun L 12.30 to 2, Wed to Sat D 7.30 to 10   MEALS: Set Sun L £18.50 (2 courses) to £22, Set D £31   SERVICE: not inc, card slips closed   CARDS: Amex, Delta, MasterCard, Switch, Visa   DETAILS: 40 seats. Private parties: 26 main room, 16, 26 private rooms. Car park. Vegetarian meals. No smoking in dining-room. Music   ACCOMMODATION: 5 rooms, all with bath/shower. D,B&B £95 to £160. Children welcome. High teas for children. No dogs (*The Which? Hotel Guide*) £5

MIDDLEHAM North Yorkshire — map 8

WINE 1999 BY THE GLASS

▲ *Waterford House*

Kirkgate, Middleham DL8 4PG   COOKING 3
TEL: (01969) 622090   FAX: (01969) 624020   COST £28–£50

A roughcast stone-built inn near Middleham's village square, Waterford House celebrated its first decade under the Madells' ownership this year. Although profusely decorated with antiques and paintings, and with a treasure-trove of a wine cellar, it is run without airs and graces as a comforting home-from-home. Everyl Madell cooks in a French-influenced manner that befits that ethos, the menus specialising in crab, avocado and pink grapefruit with mayonnaise, bouillabaisse with aïoli, and roast duck for two with a sauce of spiced apricots, plums and figs fired up with Cointreau. Those are supplemented by spoken daily specials that regularly involve a partnering of two fish, such as marlin and swordfish in tomato and garlic sauce, or salmon and halibut with beurre blanc. Chocolate and pear tart, and lemon crème brûlée, are among the crowd-pleasing puddings on display.

Brian Madell is a past master at putting everyone at their ease, and is constantly at hand to advise on the menu and choice of wines, which may well come as a relief to those daunted by the mighty tome that constitutes the wine list. Around 900 bins are offered, many of the highest quality and at very reasonable prices. Spanish reds are a particular speciality, although all the classics are well represented. An impressive 70 house wines are offered by the glass, but even more remarkable is the fact that, if requested, Brian will open a bottle from the main list and serve a 'glass' (the equivalent of a quarter-bottle) for a quarter of the full price. CELLARMAN'S CHOICE: Sancerre Vieilles Vignes 1994, Dom. Hubert Brochard, £22.75; Pauillac, Ch. Batailley 1982, £34.50.

CHEF: Everyl Madell PROPRIETORS: Brian and Everyl Madell OPEN: all week L (by arrangement only) 12 to 2.30, D 7 to 9.30 MEALS: alc (main courses £13.75 to £17.50). Set L £17.50, Set D £19.50 SERVICE: not inc, card slips closed CARDS: Delta, MasterCard, Switch, Visa DETAILS: 20 seats. Private parties: 26 main room. Car park. Children's helpings. No smoking in dining-room. Occasional music ACCOMMODATION: 5 rooms. TV. Phone. B&B £45 to £90. Children welcome. Baby facilities. Afternoon teas £5

MIDDLESBROUGH Middlesbrough   map 10

Purple Onion

1999

80 Corporation Road, Middlesbrough TS1 2RF   COOKING 3
TEL: (01642) 222250   FAX: (01642) 248088   COST £21–£56

The owners are real McCoys (see also entry, Staddlebridge), from a family who have long rejoiced, and caused others to rejoice, in their hospitality and the fun of good eating. The décor goes one better, described as 'funk' by an inspector amused by Victorian bric-à-brac and art nouveau pictures, ornate mirrors and large plants; and the low note supplied by tubas filled with candles. Music too is aimed at a young clientele, with alternative blues, rock and yes, funk again.

The cuisines celebrated in this remarkable setting are those of San Francisco, Rome, Bangkok – and north-east England. The inspection lunch included 'unusual but successful' fish-cakes: a blend of 'earthily spiced' salmon and white fish, plus fennel salad dressed with black-bean sauce, and 'great' chips. But all was exceeded by a dessert from the blackboard: 'chocolate and chilli sponge filled with marmalade ice-cream drizzled with chocolate sauce and sweet chilli syrup'. Some blackboard! Some dessert! Some praise! A shame it's too long to quote in full. Other eye-catching choices are the house speciality cioppino di mare, a San Francisco fish stew; hand-rolled buffalo mozzarella and tomato salad (hand-rolled buffalo make better-tempered mozzarella than machine-churned); and to boot, a singular home-made vegetable and bean Wellington for vegetarians. But tradition is firmly upheld by Yorkshire pudding with onion gravy, offered as a Sunday lunch starter. A new downstairs cellar bar has special musical evenings, a supper special on Sunday with a live band, and is sometimes used as an overflow to the main restaurant.Wines come from Playford Ros in Thirsk, which regularly updates the cosmopolitan list. House French is £10.95.

CHEFS: Graeme Benn and Tony Chapman PROPRIETORS: John and Bruno McCoy OPEN: all week 12 to 2.30 (3 Sun), 5 to 10.30 (6 to 9.30 Sun) CLOSED: 25 Dec, 1 Jan MEALS: alc (main courses £7.50 to £18). Set L Sun £9.95 (2 courses) to £12.50 SERVICE: not inc CARDS: MasterCard, Switch, Visa DETAILS: 110 seats. Private parties: 30 main room, 30 private room. Vegetarian meals. Children's helpings. Wheelchair access (also WC). Music. Air-conditioned £5

MIDHURST   West Sussex   map 3

Maxine's ⚡✷

Elizabeth House, Red Lion Street,
Midhurst GU29 9PB   COOKING 3
TEL: (01730) 816271   COST £25–£36

A local pair who have been eating here more or less since the de Jagers opened 17
years ago are devoted fans of the fixed-price menu, offered at the same price
lunch and dinner at virtually every session. At Easter, they enjoyed carrot and
coriander soup with rye bread, roast pork with apple sauce, crisp crackling and
herb-scented gravy, and 'deliciously sharp' lemon tart with 'crisply caramelised
top – the best we have ever had'. Robert de Jager's style is homely classicism, all
of a piece with the beamed dining-room reminiscent of an old-fashioned
tearoom. A la carte eating brings on such options as prawn and mango salad with
a Thai dressing, poached salmon in sorrel sauce, or rack of lamb with a sauce of
port, orange and mint. Opinions of the pace of service differ between 'efficient
and unflappable' and tediously slow. House French wine is £9.95.

CHEF: Robert de Jager   PROPRIETORS: Robert and Marti de Jager   OPEN: Wed to Sun L 12 to
1.30, Wed to Sat D 7 to 9.30   MEALS: alc (main courses £9 to £15). Set L and D (exc Sat D)
£15.95   SERVICE: net prices, card slips closed   CARDS: Amex, Delta, MasterCard, Switch,
Visa   DETAILS: 24 seats. Private parties: 30 main room. Children's helpings. No smoking in
dining-room. No music

MILFORD ON SEA   Hampshire   map 2

Rocher's £

69–71 High Street, Milford on Sea SO41 0QG
TEL: (01590) 642340   COOKING 3
on B3058, 3m SW of Lymington   COST £22–£41

Old-fashioned touches, such as napkins arranged as fans and garnishes of
tomato 'roses', help to define the mood in the Rochers' welcoming restaurant.
This is no place for wild experimentation. Alain Rocher's cooking is 'very
straightforward in the best sense of the word', noted one correspondent who
enjoyed a Sunday lunch of gazpacho, halibut with a 'beautifully balanced'
beurre blanc, and a raspberry sorbet of 'great depth'. There is plenty of
comforting Gallic familiarity in dishes such as fanned avocado with bacon or
ribeye steak with grain-mustard sauce, although the 'dinner gastronomique'
menu occasionally branches out into confit of duck salad with balsamic dressing,
or pan-fried guinea-fowl with garlic sauce. Desserts stay firmly in the classic
mould of crème brûlée, tarte au citron and hot chocolate gâteau. Service is 'very
pleasant and relaxed'. A notable selection of Loire wines is the highlight of the
well-balanced, international list; house wine is £10.50.

CHEF: Alain Rocher   PROPRIETORS: Alain and Rebecca Rocher   OPEN: Sun L 12.15 to 1.45,
Wed to Sat D 7 to 9.45   CLOSED: 25 and 26 Dec, 1 Jan.   MEALS: Set Sun L £14.50, Set D £13.95
(2 courses) to £23.50   SERVICE: not inc   CARDS: Amex, Delta, Diners, MasterCard, Switch,
Visa   DETAILS: 26 seats. Private parties: 34 main room. No children under 7. No smoking while
others eat. Wheelchair access (not WC). Music (£5)

MOLLINGTON Cheshire   map 7

▲ *Crabwall Manor* ❢ ⁵⋇

Parkgate Road, Mollington CH1 6NE
TEL: (01244) 851666   FAX: (01244) 851400
EMAIL: sales@crabwall.com | NEW CHEF |
off A540, 3m N of Chester   COST £24–£64

The Manor, which partly dates back to Norman times, is a sprawling red-brick complex that goes in for banqueting and conference catering: 'but not so as you'd notice,' a reporter kindly observed. Former sous-chef Katie Cook took over the kitchens as the *Guide* went to press, but the country-house style of cooking is expected to continue, producing pehaps tagliatelle of oysters, foie gras terrine, best end of lamb with vegetable risotto, and roast pear tartlet. The huge wine list covers most points of the compass but is strongest in France: country wines and Alsace stand out alongside the more expected burgundies and clarets. Prices climb quite quickly, but there is plenty of choice under £20 and lots of half-bottles. House wines from Georges Duboeuf are £13.50. CELLARMAN'S CHOICE: Gewurztraminer d'Alsace, Dom. du Ch. de Riquewihr 1994, Dopff & Irion, £23; Haut-Médoc, Ch. Cissac *cru bourgeois exceptionnel* 1992, £29.50.

CHEF: Katie Cook   PROPRIETOR: Carl Lewis   OPEN: all week 12 to 2, 7 to 9.30   MEALS: alc (main courses £18.50 to £24). Set L £16, Set D £26   SERVICE: not inc, card slips closed   CARDS: Delta, Diners, MasterCard, Switch, Visa   DETAILS: 250 seats. Private parties: 90 main room, 30 to 90 private rooms. Car park. Vegetarian meals. Children's helpings. No smoking in dining-room. Wheelchair access (3 steps; also WC). Music. Air-conditioned   ACCOMMODATION: 48 rooms, all with bath/shower. TV. Phone. Room only £110 to £175. Rooms for disabled. Children welcome. Baby facilities. No dogs. Afternoon teas (*The Which? Hotel Guide*)

MONTACUTE Somerset   map 2

▲ *Milk House* ⁵⋇

The Borough, Montacute TA15 6XB   COOKING 2
TEL: (01935) 823823   COST £29–£38

'A rather eccentric restaurant' summed up one reporter, dishing out the compliments. It doesn't seat many, and opening times are limited, but the Duftons take their mission seriously. In the village square, opposite the entrance to the National Trust's Montacute House, Milk House is clean and well kept, with lace mats on well-spaced tables, an open fire, and a commitment to organic, often local, produce. This yields a haul of meat, fish and dairy products, and many vegetables and fruits are home-grown. Fish, vegetables and game are given a high priority, producing a ramekin of creamy smoked haddock to start, and main courses of braised guinea-fowl, or spiced onion tart. Lee Dufton keeps the cooking manageably simple, turning out lamb leg steaks in a minted garlic and cream sauce, and anything from a hot pistachio sponge pudding to brown sugar meringues with fresh fruit and cream. She is happy to offer vegan dishes, plus the alternative of rice crackers with unhydrogenated vegetable oil instead of bread and butter. Ten organic wines head up the short but good-value list, with house wines at around £10.

CHEF: Lee Dufton   PROPRIETORS: Bill and Lee Dufton   OPEN: Wed to Sat D only 7.30 to 9; L by arrangement   CLOSED: Nov to Apr   MEALS: alc (main courses £12 to £14). Set D £22.50. BYO £5   SERVICE: not inc, card slips closed   CARDS: none   DETAILS: 8 seats. 8 seats outside. Private parties: 24 main room. Vegetarian meals. Children's helpings. No smoking in dining-room. Wheelchair access (not WC). No music   ACCOMMODATION: 3 rooms, all with bath/shower. B&B £48 to £58. Children welcome (*The Which? Hotel Guide*)   £5

MORETON-IN-MARSH Gloucestershire   map 5

Annie's

3 Oxford Street, Moreton-in-Marsh GL56 0LA	COOKING 2
TEL/FAX: (01608) 651981	COST £32–£49

Just off the main street, Annie's is a 'well-presented small restaurant' whose cottagey feel is a welcome contrast to some of the grandiose and expensive piles that seem to dominate the Cotswolds. David Ellis's strand of unpretentious country cooking doesn't rely on either experiment or cliché for effect, rather it persuades with relatively simple dishes done well: grilled Stilton cheese on a crumpet, lambs' kidneys with bacon and mushrooms, and fruit meringue or chocolate biscuit cake. First courses might make use of smoked chicken, duck leg or pigeon breast, while meaty main courses have run to pork tenderloin with Madeira sauce, and rack of lamb with a spiced herb crust. Fresh fish varies by the day, and Anne Ellis writes that 'vegetarians, vegans, and anyone on a special diet can be catered for with prior notice'. Fifty or so wines are mostly French, including house Merlot and Chardonnay at £12.50.

CHEF: David Ellis   PROPRIETORS: David and Anne Ellis   OPEN: Mon to Sat D only 7 to 9.30 (10 Sat), L by arrangement   CLOSED: end Jan, early Feb   MEALS: alc (main courses £15.50 to £20)   SERVICE: net prices, card slips closed   CARDS: Amex, Diners, MasterCard, Visa DETAILS: 30 seats. Private parties: 30 main room. Children's helpings. No smoking while others eat. Music   £5

Marsh Goose 🍷 ⅝✳

High Street, Moreton-in-Marsh GL56 0AX	COOKING 6
TEL: (01608) 653500 FAX: (01608) 653510	COST £23–£42

One who comes antique-hunting in the Cotswolds is philosophical: 'If you can't find the piece you want, you can always be sure of a good lunch at the Marsh Goose.' A newcomer considered it 'an incredible surprise'. A number of small interconnecting rooms, tastefully decorated in soft colours, keep the place feeling intimate. The atmosphere is 'calm and relaxing', and those in the front room can look out through 'old wavy glass' on to the marketplace. The Goose appeals on all fronts: ambience, food and service. 'Everything about our meal was just right.' The consistency is all the more remarkable given that Sonya Kidney and Leo Brooke-Little divide their time between here and the Churchill Arms (see entry, Paxford). Matthew Laughton's arrival has hardly caused a ripple.

'We are now paying more attention to the source of our meat,' writes Mr Brooke-Little, looking for greater peace of mind in the face of 'never-ending food scares'. Gloucester Old Spot pork is a natural-enough choice, perhaps served with apple compote and a sage jus. The menu is a canny mixture of familiar ideas – breast of chicken with leek and tarragon sauce – alongside more unusual items such as a Burgundian snail and smoked goose liver terrine with a garlic and herb sauce, or beetroot-marinated salmon with a lime dressing. The kitchen's sense of judgement keeps these ideas firmly in touch with what customers will swallow, allowing it to serve fillet of red mullet with chorizo sausage and tapénade, or thin slices of rare roast beef salad with a Chantilly cream flavoured with horseradish, capers and spring onion.

Desserts can be filling, but nobody seems to mind. Hot choux soufflé is served with a mango and passion-fruit parfait, and warm plum and frangipane tart comes with clotted cream. The set lunch (with three choices for each of the three courses Tuesday to Saturday, six on Sunday) is good value and very popular with reporters. Service makes for a relaxed time of things, and wines are helpfully grouped by style in a list which has seen the introduction of some more favourably priced wines and the odd 'golden egg', although there are still a few high mark-ups. House wines from Spain, France and Australia start at £9.75. CELLARMAN'S CHOICE: Bourgogne Blanc 1995, Dom. Henri-Clerc, £14.50; Stag's Leap Hawk's Crest Cabernet Sauvignon 1995, Napa Valley, California £18.30.

CHEFS: Sonya Kidney and Matthew Laughton PROPRIETORS: Sonya Kidney, Leo Brooke-Little and Gordon Campbell-Gray OPEN: Tue to Sat L 12.30 to 2.30, Tue to Sat D 7.30 to 9.30 CLOSED: 26 and 27 Dec, 1 and 2 Jan MEALS: alc L Tue to Sat (main courses £11 to £14). Set L Tue to Sat £14, Set L Sun £18, Set D £26.50. DYO £7 SERVICE: not inc CARDS: Amex, Delta, Diners, MasterCard, Switch, Visa DETAILS: 60 seats. Private parties: 22 main room. Children's helpings. No smoking in dining-room. Wheelchair access (also WC). No music

---

MORSTON Norfolk   map 6

▲ Morston Hall ▼ ⅝⋇

Morston NR25 7AA
TEL: (01263) 741041   FAX: (01263) 740419
EMAIL: reception@morstonhall.demon.co.uk   COOKING 5
on A149, 2m W of Blakeney   COST £25–£45

This old flint house, set in three acres of well-tended gardens looking out to open fields and big skies – the area is a 'paradise' for ornithologists – is comfortable, relaxing, and 'a lovely hotel for a quiet break'. Tables are large and well-spaced, staff are 'warm, welcoming, friendly, and willing to talk about the food', which offers no choice apart from cheese or dessert. The format means that everyone sits down more or less together, and puts the responsibility for balance firmly in the kitchen's hands, which generally works well: at one meal for example, confit leg of guinea-fowl, curried cod on steamed spinach, pork with mustard sauce, and cold passion-fruit soufflé with mango ice-cream. While individual dishes may appear small, the overall effect is 'just right'.

Local materials play a part in the food's success, from vegetables via wild fungi to shellfish; menus change by the day, and the cooking displays a high degree of skill and judgement. While main courses may rely on traditional combinations such as roast breast of duck with orange, other dishes explore some less usual territory: wild mushrooms with black pudding, a 'brilliant' mousse of chicken and Roquefort, or 'stunningly good' grilled smoked salmon with a 'perfect' sauce mousseline and guacamole. Vegetables are carefully prepared, and desserts have included a light orange soufflé served in a crisp crêpe with a sharp orange and lime syrup. Like the cuisine, the wine list combines traditional fare with less familiar offerings that reward the adventurous. Perhaps to reassure others, the bins are divided into grape varieties, sub-divided into country of origin and concisely annotated. Prices are fair, beginning at £9.90 for the house vins de pays. CELLARMAN'S CHOICE: Mitchelton Reserve Marsanne 1993, Victoria, Australia, £17; Rioja, Dragon Tempranillo 1995, £11.50.

CHEF: Galton Blackiston and Daniel Smith   PROPRIETORS: Tracy and Galton Blackiston, and Justin Fraser   OPEN: Sun L 12.30 to 1 (1 sitting), all week D 7.30 to 8 (1 sitting)   CLOSED: 1 to 22 Jan   MEALS: Set L £18, Set D £30. BYO £9.50   SERVICE: not inc, card slips closed   CARDS: Amex, Delta, MasterCard, Switch, Visa   DETAILS: 40 seats. Private parties: 40 main room. Car park. Children's helpings. No smoking in dining-room. Wheelchair access (1 step; also WC). No music   ACCOMMODATION: 6 rooms, all with bath/shower. TV. Phone. D,B&B £90 to £180. Children welcome. Dogs welcome (free in kennels, £5 and with own bedding otherwise). Afternoon teas (The Which? Hotel Guide)

MOULSFORD Oxfordshire   map 2

▲ Beetle & Wedge ♥ ✳

Ferry Lane, Moulsford OX10 9JF
TEL: (01491) 651381   FAX: (01491) 651376   COOKING 5
off A329, down Ferry Lane to river   COST £30–£55

A gentle lunch overlooking the Thames from the comfort of the conservatory was one reporter's idea of a 'perfect lazy day', helped in his case by only having to drive an hour out of London. In effect, this is a restaurant of two halves. Richard Smith mans the chargrill in the Boat House, turning out rump steak, salmon with hollandaise, and calves' kidneys with black pudding and mustard sauce. This is the more casual of the two venues, with a feel of the brasserie about its warm goats'-cheese salad, or spicy squid with spring onions and beansprouts. There is no hard and fast division into separate courses on its generous *carte*.

Dishes in the Dining Room are perhaps more crafted, but not a million miles away in style. Here Olivier Bouet has produced sauté foie gras with lyonnaise onions and Sauternes sauce, and grilled fillets of Dover sole ('beautiful fish') with 'fat, juicy' seared scallops and béarnaise sauce. 'It's nice to see a menu not packed with eclectic flavours,' observed one visitor, who judged the cooking to be 'essentially classical with modern British touches'. Puddings bear that out with apple and blackcurrant crumble, and hot rice-pudding with plum compote; one reporter enjoyed 'huge nuggets' of beignet soufflés with lemon-curd sauce, another praised the lemon tart. Overall, timing has been 'spot on', the balance of flavours is well judged, and the cooking's consistency is noteworthy. Service on the whole is both 'friendly' and 'professional'. Kate Smith's Dining Room wine list departs from the norm by placing Italy ahead of France – she believes Italian wines 'represent superb quality at very reasonable prices' – but France wins out in terms of numbers, and the bin-end clarets from 1961 are hard to overlook. Mark-ups can be high, but there is good drinking to be had under £20, beginning with house wines from France and Italy at £12.95 a bottle, £3.50 per glass. CELLARMAN'S CHOICE: Bourgogne Blanc 1994, Dom. Leflaive, £42.50; St-Joseph 1995, Gaillard, £24.50.

CHEFS: Richard Smith and Olivier Bouet   PROPRIETORS: Richard and Kate Smith   OPEN: Boat House all week 12.30 to 2, 7.30 to 10; Dining Room Tue to Sun L 12.30 to 2, Tue to Sat D 7.30 to 10   CLOSED: 25 Dec   MEALS: Boat House alc (main courses £10 to £17.50); Dining Room Set L £27.50, Set D £35   SERVICE: not inc   CARDS: Amex, Delta, Diners, MasterCard, Switch, Visa   DETAILS: 65 seats (Boat House), 30 seats (Dining Room). 75 seats outside. Private parties: 64 private room. Car park. Vegetarian meals. Children's helpings. No smoking in dining-room. Wheelchair access (also WC). Occasional music   ACCOMMODATION: 10 rooms, all with bath/shower. TV. Phone. B&B £95 to £150. Rooms for disabled. Children welcome. High teas for children. Baby facilities. Dogs welcome by arrangement (*The Which? Hotel Guide*)

MOULTON North Yorkshire   map 9

Black Bull Inn ▼

Moulton DL10 6QJ
TEL: (01325) 377289   FAX: (01325) 377422
EMAIL: sarahblackbullinn.demon.co.uk   COOKING 4
1m SE of Scotch Corner, 1m from A1   COST £23–£52

Only the odd low-flying aircraft from nearby Leeming airbase momentarily disturbs the tranquillity of tiny Moulton. An earlier mode of transport is installed to the rear of the Black Bull, in the shape of a carefully maintained '30s Pullman railway carriage forming the centrepiece of the restaurant. Lit in muted tones of an evening, it makes for a thoroughly charming setting. Paul Grundy's culinary style is gently classical, a cut above the domestic in keeping with the context, so that fillets of sole are stuffed with crab and sauced with chive mousseline. Indeed, fish is a strong point, as attested by the reader who enjoyed butterflied Dublin Bay prawns with garlic butter, and then a generous section of monkfish wrapped in filo on a fresh tomato sauce. Meat-eaters are supplied with Aberdeen Angus in various cuts, or perhaps rack of lamb with leek and potato crumble and Madeira sauce. Novel presentation characterised a dessert of baked rice pudding, which came as three quenelles with a scoop of nutmeg ice-cream and a pear marmalade glaze. Service is competent and friendly. Value for money is a major attraction of the predominantly French wine list and, with vintage champagnes at shop prices, the Black Bull would be a particularly good place to head for a celebratory meal. For those less in a mood to splash out, house French is £8.50 a bottle. CELLARMAN'S CHOICE: Muscadet 'Cuvée LM' 1996, Louis Métaireau, £11.50; Chénas 'Manoir des Journets' 1995, £12.50.

CHEF: Paul Grundy   PROPRIETORS: G.H., A.M.C. and S.C. Pagendam   OPEN: Mon to Fri L 12 to 2, Mon to Sat D 6.45 to 10.15.   MEALS: alc (main courses £15 to £20). Set L £14.95. Bar meals available Mon to Sat L. BYO £5   SERVICE: not inc   CARDS: Amex, Delta, Diners, MasterCard, Switch, Visa   DETAILS: 120 seats. 16 seats outside. Private parties: 12 main room, 10 and 30 private rooms. Car park. Vegetarian meals. No children under 7. No music

---

Report forms are at the back of the book; write a letter if you prefer; or email us at guidereports@which.co.uk.

NAILSWORTH Gloucestershire   map 2

William's Bistro

3 Fountain Street, Nailsworth GL6 0BL	COOKING 5
TEL: (01453) 835507 FAX: (01453) 835950	COST £26–£51

William Beeston runs a dual enterprise. A delicatessen fronts on to Fountain Street, where a fresh fish counter is the pride and joy, and – entered from the street to the right, hidden discreetly behind trees – is the Bistro, where fish play a starring role too. A long, low dining-room is done in terracotta pink, the wall adornments including cheese-box lids and a large mirror festooned with dried hops.

Seafood specialities are concentrated in main courses, although you can begin with half a crab, a few oysters, or a spiced lobster salad dressed with chilli and soy. Otherwise, duck confit on sweet potato cakes might start you off. An inspection dish of fresh figs, stuffed with spinach and almonds and gratinated with Gorgonzola, offered 'an inspired assembly of tastes and textures', followed by grilled fillet of sea bass served on crab risotto: the fish superbly timed, the risotto chunky with good crabmeat, the whole dish 'executed accurately and confidently'. One of the vegetable accompaniments was a moulded serving of mash, crumbed and baked, and shaped to look like a pear with a clove for stalk; in case the oblique joke doesn't register, this is, of course, William's pear. Alternatively, there might be sea bream with scallops and spring onions, or tuna on red onion and tomato salsa with tapénade, while a wide choice of puddings may take in caramelised rice-pudding with blueberry compote, and warm chocolate tart with 'thin, crisp, sweet pastry', served with beautifully concentrated vanilla ice-cream. Home-made breads are especially recommended, and youthful, straight-talking service contributes to the atmosphere of happy informality. The somewhat jumbled-up wine list is predominantly French, but everything comes in at well under £20, with £8.50 as the starting-point.

CHEFS: Craig Schofield and Katie Beeston   PROPRIETORS: William and Rae Beeston   OPEN: Tue to Sat D 7 to 9.30   CLOSED: 2 weeks Christmas/New Year, Tue after bank hols   MEALS: alc (main courses £10.50 to £17)   SERVICE: not inc, card slips closed   CARDS: MasterCard, Visa   DETAILS: 50 seats. Private parties: 50 main room. Children welcome. No music

NANTWICH Cheshire   map 5

Churche's Mansion ♥ ⁵⨉

150 Hospital Street, Nantwich CW5 5RY	COOKING 3
TEL: (01270) 625933 FAX: (01270) 627831	COST £31–£64

Practically everything in this sixteenth-century town-centre house is made from wood: bare board floors, wall panelling, carved fireplace surrounds, ceilings and beams. Michael Lea, who took over the kitchen in August 1997, has worked here since 1992, so there has understandably been little change in the cooking's direction. The food still involves a degree of 'dolling up', which contributes to the sense of 'industry' that unfolds over the course of a meal: from nibbles through to petits fours.

In this vein, an inspector felt that a starter of smoked salmon and scallops 'would have gained if a number of components had simply been left out': the celeriac stewed in cream perhaps, or the strips of deep-fried leek, the aubergine, or maybe the red peppers and courgettes. Nevertheless, reporters have enjoyed a range of dishes from monkfish and lobster salad, and Thai-style prawns, to Gressingham duck served with the liver. The most original, straightforward (and thus successful) dish at inspection was a puff pastry banana tart, with rum and raisin ice-cream and a rum and caramel sauce. A special Sunday dinner menu is offered with three choices at each course (instead of the usual eight) and two people eating for the price of one. The wine list will please both classicists and modernists with its blend of old favourites from France (Beaujolais is paid particular attention) and rising stars from Australia, Argentina and California. Half-bottles are generous and house wines start at £11.50. CELLARMAN'S CHOICE: Welmoed Chardonnay 1996, Stellenbosch, South Africa, £14.95; Bagedow Bush Vine Grenache, Barossa Valley, S. Australia, £16.95.

CHEF: Michael Lea   PROPRIETORS: Robin Latham and Amanda Simpson   OPEN: Wed to Sun 12 to 2.30, 7 to 9.30   CLOSED: 2 weeks Jan   MEALS: Set L £15.25 (2 courses) to £18.95, Set D £28.50. Set D Sun £28.50 for 2 people. BYO £8   SERVICE: not inc, card slips closed   CARDS: Delta, Diners, MasterCard, Switch, Visa   DETAILS: 60 seats. 20 seats outside. Private parties: 48 main room, 24 and 48 private rooms. Car park. Vegetarian meals. Children's helpings. No children under 10 at D. No smoking in dining-room. Occasional music   £5

NAYLAND Suffolk   map 6

White Hart £

11 High Street, Nayland CO6 4JF   COOKING 3
TEL: (01206) 263382   FAX: (01206) 263638   COST £21–£45

Holding centre-stage in a 'delightful' Elizabethan village, the White Hart looks as if it has always been there. Inside, a feeling of simple rusticity pervades the heavy beams and bare brick walls that make up the main dining-area. Grafted on to this is chef/proprietor Mark Prescott's classic training at both the Waterside Inn, Bray, and Le Gavroche, London (see entries). Perhaps because the place clings to its pub roots, the cooking is a canny mix of robust English with a dollop of Gallic richness, and a few spicy forays further afield; it is even possible to get up-market sandwiches at lunch-time. Regulars who pack the place for Sunday lunch are treated to exemplary roast beef and gargantuan helpings of slow-roast pork belly (complete with crackling), as well as perfectly wrought game terrine with fig conserve, and juicy steamed cod with herb and cheese crust. Dinner heralds a few more ambitious items in the shape of Irish oysters with red wine vinegar, whole roast Dover sole, and grilled confit of rabbit leg with herb risotto. To finish, praline glacé has been spot-on and the toffee ice-cream is to die for. Local staff are polite, unflustered and friendly. Real ales provide an alternative to the imaginative modern wine list, which is big on juicy flavours. House wines start at £9.25. Plans to provide guest accommodation were in the pipeline as the *Guide* went to press.

CHEF/PROPRIETOR: Mark Prescott   OPEN: all week 12 to 2.30, 6.30 to 9 (9.30 Fri and Sat, 8.30 Sun)   CLOSED: 26 Dec, 1 Jan   MEALS: alc D (main courses £6.50 to £15). Set L £9 (1 course) to £16. Bar food available   SERVICE: not inc   CARDS: Amex, Delta, Diners, MasterCard, Switch, Visa   DETAILS: 80 seats. 50 seats outside. Private parties: 60 main room, 40 private room. Car park. Vegetarian meals. Children's helpings. Wheelchair access (not WC). Music   (£5)

NEAR SAWREY Cumbria	map 8

▲ *Ees Wyke* 🌟

Near Sawrey LA22 0JZ	
TEL/FAX: (015394) 36393	COOKING 2
on B5286 from Hawkshead	COST £28–£34

John and Margaret Williams have run their guesthouse and restaurant, in Beatrix Potter's former holiday home overlooking Esthwaite, for a decade. Visitors are made to feel at home and residents get a good deal on the five-course dinner, eaten amid splendid hilly views at the back. The country style of cooking might take in Flookburgh shrimps in hot spiced butter, pork fillet with wholegrain mustard sauce, and chocolate fudge cake. An intermediate course – soufflé Suissesse perhaps – and the inclusion of both cheese and dessert, help to make an evening of it. Some three-dozen wines are well chosen and fairly priced, starting with Vin de Pays d'Oc at £9.50.

CHEF: John Williams   PROPRIETORS: Margaret and John Williams   OPEN: all week D only 7.30 (1 sitting)   CLOSED: Jan and Feb   MEALS: Set D £21   SERVICE: not inc, card slips closed   CARDS: Amex   DETAILS: 24 seats. Private parties: 35 main room. Car park. No children under 8. No smoking in dining-room. Wheelchair access (1 step; not WC). No music   ACCOMMODATION: 8 rooms, all with bath/shower. TV. D,B&B £54 to £108. No children under 8. Dogs welcome in bedrooms only (*The Which? Hotel Guide*)

NEWCASTLE UPON TYNE Tyne & Wear	map 10

21 Queen Street 🍷

19–21 Queen Street, Princes Wharf, Quayside,	
Newcastle upon Tyne NE1 3UG	COOKING 7
TEL: (0191) 222 0755 FAX: (0191) 221 0761	COST £28–£64

Queen Street may be having a face-lift as part of the quayside regeneration, but number 21's interior is way ahead of it, with blond-wood floors, mint and sea-green blocks of colour, and bright abstract paintings. 'The place has elegance, warmth and simplicity,' reckoned one visitor who came for 'a taste of well-being' and went away happy. Despite smart décor and sophisticated food, the atmosphere is 'totally unpretentious and good-natured', making this 'by far the best establishment in the north-east'.

The frequently changing *carte* offers around eight dishes per course (some with a supplement), and the kitchen's gently evolving ideas are welcomed: sauté Kielder venison with 'unbelievable' blue cheese polenta, or roasted chicken wings arranged around a mound of mustardy celeriac rémoulade, topped by a lobe of griddled foie gras. Luxury ingredients abound – including a 'wonderful' crispy roll containing chunks of lobster meat, corn kernels and wild mushrooms, served with a rich shellfish stock – and foie gras even replaces the garlic stuffing in a variation on chicken Kiev. But the cooking does not rely on riches to impress; it does this perfectly well on the good-value lunch menu with such things as pumpkin and parsley soup, or blue cheese soufflé with poached pears and walnuts. Even though some of the cooking seems a little involved – duck cooked five ways including a glazed and marinated leg, and a garlicky sausage on lentils – raw materials are 'consistently sound', and 'clear and strong' flavours result. Well-flavoured, pink roast chump of lamb, for example, was 'simplicity itself' at inspection, carved into thick slices, served with an evocative provençale 'gâteau' of tomato and aubergine cooked in olive oil, and a light lamb stock.

Well-kept British and French cheeses are served at room temperature, and desserts have included a warm, liquid-centred chocolate cake with coconut sorbet, and 'an inspired combination' of zesty lemon and almond polenta cake with strawberries. Service is generally highly rated: 'all folk are treated with respect and courtesy' by smart staff whose efficiency, knowledge and large numbers add to the 'classy' feel. 'Many wines seem older than the sommelier!' exclaimed one reporter who was subsequently reassured when the Frenchman proved he knew his business. France dominates a list that concentrates on quality rather than providing blanket coverage. House French is £12. CELLARMAN'S CHOICE: Morton Estate Chardonnay 1995, Hawkes Bay, New Zealand, £20; Saintsbury Pinot Noir 1994, Carneros, California, £29.20.

CHEF: Terence Laybourne   PROPRIETORS: Terence and Susan Laybourne   OPEN: Mon to Fri L 12 to 2, Mon to Sat D 7 to 10.45   CLOSED: Christmas, bank hols   MEALS: alc (main courses £18.50 to £22.50). Set L £14 (2 courses) to £17.50   SERVICE: not inc   CARDS: Amex, Delta, Diners, MasterCard, Switch, Visa   DETAILS: 70 seats. Private parties: 60 main room. Children's helpings. No pipes in dining-room. Wheelchair access (not WC). Music

Fisherman's Lodge ✵✖

Jesmond Dene, Newcastle upon Tyne NE7 7BQ	COOKING 6
TEL: (0191) 281 3281 FAX: (0191) 281 6410	COST £26–£70

Down a leafy lane, beside a babbling brook – yet still in Newcastle – this nineteenth-century stone-built lodge makes a good fist of juggling business parties, private functions and ordinary customers. Light wood, mirrors and subdued lighting in the bar give way to a bright dining-room where a generous menu majors in fish and shellfish. Much is traditional, along the lines of lemon sole Walewska, plain grilled Dover sole, or salmon with mushrooms in a white wine sauce ('old fashioned', one called it), but the kitchen is equally at ease turning out queen scallops with a Thai dressing, or seafood tempura with soy sauce. Lobster comes three ways, garlic butter puts in more than one appearance, and there are 'selections' of fish and shellfish: on spinach with a trio of sauces perhaps, or deep-fried with a lemon butter sauce.

There is plenty more besides, though, as the Lodge stakes its claim to a wide audience – rack of Northumbrian lamb with garlic mash, or a dish of duck confit, breast and sausage with a cassis sauce – while vegetarians are typically offered three options per course. Impressive desserts have included pear tarte Tatin with caramel sauce and vanilla ice-cream, and variations on an apple or chocolate theme. Choice also extends to six different kinds of bread and three butters. Despite the emphasis on fish, red and white wines receive equal billing on a varied list that offers twice as many under £20 as over, and starts at £12 for Vin de Pays d'Oc.

CHEFS: Steven Jobson and Paul Amer   PROPRIETORS: Franco and Pamela Cetoloni   OPEN: Mon to Fri L 12 to 2, Mon to Sat D 7 to 11   CLOSED: bank hols   MEALS: alc (main courses £18 to £28). Set L £17.80, Set D Mon to Fri £29.50   SERVICE: not inc   CARDS: Amex, Delta, Diners, MasterCard, Switch, Visa   DETAILS: 65 seats. 35 seats outside. Private parties: 14 main room, 14 and 45 private rooms. Car park. Vegetarian meals. Children's helpings. No children under 9 at D. No smoking in dining-room. Wheelchair access (1 step; also WC). No music

Leela's ✹✸

20 Dean Street, Newcastle upon Tyne NE1 1PG	COOKING 3
TEL: (0191) 230 1261 FAX: (01661) 823916	COST £24–£47

'The first and the only South Indian restaurant in the North East' claims the brochure. Eponymous Leela Paul and her husband have been in residence at this genteel city-centre address since 1990, and their enthusiasm and dedication to the business remain undiminished. Their food is healthy without seeming piously virtuous, they care, and their dishes rely on the fine balancing of distinct flavours. Specialities are drawn from Leela's native Kerala and the adjacent region of Tamil Nadu, with vegetarian and carnivorous ones sitting side by side. Starters move beyond paper dosas, uthappam and dahi vadai into the realms of olli kunu (stir-fried mushrooms with garlic and herbs on a bed of sauté onions), baked peppers stuffed with home-made paneer cheese, and irachi thoran (strips of lamb soaked in almond sauce, then stir-fried). Main dishes are equally diverse, ranging from king prawns marinated in tamarind sauce then slowly cooked with a touch of cream, to marinated pork baked in foil and accompanied by spiced apple salad and pilau rice. An impressive back-up of vegetables and side-dishes features such things as chera veralan (spinach and potatoes with sesame seeds). The wine list was being updated as we went to press, but it remains the product of thoughtfulness and knowledge. House wine is £10.95.

CHEF: Kuriakose Paul   PROPRIETORS: Kuriakose and Leela Paul   OPEN: Mon to Sat 12 to 2.30, 6 to 11.30   CLOSED: first 2 weeks Jan, bank hols   MEALS: alc (main courses £8 to £13). Set L £9.95, Set D £16.95 (2 courses) to £18.95   SERVICE: not inc   CARDS: Amex, Delta, Diners, MasterCard, Visa   DETAILS: 60 seats. Private parties: 40 main room. Vegetarian meals. Children's helpings. No smoking in dining-room. Music   (£5)

Metropolitan £

35 Grey Street, Newcastle upon Tyne NE1 6EE	
TEL: (0191) 230 2306 FAX: (0191) 230 2307	COOKING 3
EMAIL: sean@metropolitanbrasseries.co.uk	COST £19–£38

The Metropolitan strives to play the part of a modern big-city brasserie, and succeeds admirably. The building itself was once the old Bank of England premises on 'glorious Georgian' Grey Street; now it oozes life and energy, with brightly painted walls, intricately moulded high ceilings, glass and mirrors. The piped music is 'groovy', service is informal and the kitchen works to a menu that hits just the right 'metropolitan' note. Samples from a typically enjoyable lunch tell it all: 'excellent' cassoulet soup loaded with duck, garlicky sausage and beans, roast cod with spiced chickpeas, and freshly prepared salt beef and horseradish mash did the business, before North Country cheeses and 'light as a feather' chocolate and Newcastle Brown Ale cake.

Much of the repertoire is served throughout the day, although dinner ushers in a few more ambitious ideas in the shape of tuna carpaccio with wasabi-dressed spring onion and sesame salad, and roast breast and confit of corn-fed chicken with celeriac mash. The wine list, from award-winning merchants Lay & Wheeler, is youthful and up-to-date, as befits the philosphy of the place. A dozen wines are served by the glass, while bottle prices start at £8.95.

CHEF: Nick Gardiner   PROPRIETORS: Sean Parkinson and Nick Gardiner   OPEN: Mon to Sat 12 to 3, 6 to 10.45   CLOSED: 25 and 26 Dec   MEALS: alc (main courses £4 to £13). Set L £8.95 (2 courses) to £11.95. Brasserie menu available 10 to 7   SERVICE: 10% (optional), card slips closed   CARDS: Amex, Delta, Diners, MasterCard, Switch, Visa   DETAILS: 170 seats. Private parties: 32 private room. Vegetarian meals. Children's helpings. No-smoking area. Wheelchair access (also WC). Music. Air-conditioned   £5

▲ *Vermont Hotel, Blue Room* | NEW ENTRY

Castle Garth, Newcastle upon Tyne NE1 1RQ   COOKING 5
TEL: (0191) 233 1010   FAX: (0191) 233 1234   COST £36–£63

County Hall was turned into a luxury hotel some time back, but John Connell's arrival – he used to cook at 21 Queen Street (see entry above) – is more recent. The entrance on bridge level leads to Vermont's sixth floor, and the Blue Room is on the third. It is a 'strictly formal' dining-room – although service is 'friendly and attentive' – sporting a dais with a shining baby grand piano and windows overlooking the Side: an old street leading down to the Quayside. Connell's food is broadly European in style, high French in technique, and quite modern in terms of its penchant for oriental flavours. Thus he might turn out a 'pressing' of foie gras and quail with vegetables to start, or a shellfish risotto, or tiger prawn beignets with lemon grass and coriander gazpacho.

Meat and fish tend to be prime cuts and fillets, in preference to game or offal, and a degree of ingenuity gives them interest: spiced salmon fillet with crushed chickpeas, turmeric oil, parsley jus and tomato crisps, for example. The kitchen is concerned for its food to look stylish, and it usually does: a bright orange-red bisque-like provençale fish soup with aïoli, croûtons and grated Gruyère, or a 'succulent' ball of salmon wrapped in a spinach leaf, served with pieces of lobster and dressed leaves, surrounded by chive-flecked crème fraîche.

Dishes tend to consist of several components, but the overall design seems clear enough, even if goats'-cheese ravioli does seem a rather powerful accompaniment to pink roast rack of Northumberland lamb and its rich-tasting jus. Desserts exhibit as much workmanship as everything else, producing a crunchy-topped crème brûlée with summer fruits and almond pastries, or a cup of frothy, liquid chocolate cappuccino, served with gingerbread ice-cream. House French wines are £11.80. The Brasserie, open all week, serves slightly less-expensive meals from a wide-ranging *carte*.

CHEF: John Connell   PROPRIETOR: Taz Group Ltd   OPEN: Mon to Sat D only 6.30 (7 Sat) to 10 CLOSED: Aug   MEALS: alc (main courses £14.50 to £21). Set D £42. Brasserie menu all week L and D   SERVICE: not inc   CARDS: Amex, Delta, Diners, MasterCard, Switch, Visa   DETAILS: 80 seats. Private parties: 250 main room, 75 to 250 private rooms. Car park. Vegetarian meals. No-smoking area. Wheelchair access (also WC). Music   ACCOMMODATION: 101 rooms, all with bath/shower. TV. Phone. B&B £75 to £155. Rooms for disabled. Children welcome. High teas for children. Baby facilities. Dogs by arrangement. Afternoon teas

---

NEW MILTON Hampshire   map 2

▲ *Chewton Glen, Marryat Restaurant* ▮ ⅝✶

Christchurch Road, New Milton BH25 6QS
TEL: (01425) 275341   FAX: (01425) 272310
EMAIL: reservations@chewtonglen.com
from A35 follow signs to Walkford and Highcliffe,
take second turning on left after Walkford down   COOKING 6
Chewton Farm road   COST £33–£87

An early-eighteenth-century house remodelled with Palladian touches in the late-Victorian era presents a façade of green-shuttered grandeur to the world. Play croquet on the front lawn if you will, or book in for the full-on corporate experience within, where keep-fit facilities or the expansive pool are options. The Chewton Bunny (a pathway, not a local breed of rabbit) will lead you in 20 minutes to the sea.

Pierre Chevillard cooks extensive fixed-price menus at lunch and dinner, with supplements for foie gras, caviare, truffles, even smoked salmon. The style is mostly identikit modern French, with a red pepper sauce vividly accompanying fillet of turbot, or Barbary duck served with blood-orange sauce and garnished with vegetable julienne. At its most extreme, it may encompass a pairing of braised pork cheeks and lobster with Thai seasonings. A pre-Christmas group enjoyed themselves immensely, with a lunch that took in rémoulade of tiger prawns dressed in lobster oil, expertly timed fillet of brill with saffron sauce, textbook steak and kidney pudding with Guinness, and chocolate tart with bitter orange sauce: 'a chocoholic's dream'. Suggested sweet wines are indicated on the menu against the desserts: Jurançon for meringue-encased pineapple filled with exotic sorbets, or a £10 glass of Sauternes for first-class crème brûlée. Service has veered from sluggish to prompt, but does its best to remain attentive throughout.

The varied, 500-strong wine list is perhaps best suited to those with a corporate expense account, as high prices are scattered liberally throughout, not just restricted to the first-class clarets, burgundies and vintage champagnes. That said, the standard is high, wines under £20 can be found – the Languedoc-Roussillon is a good place to start – and house claret is £16.25, New Zealand Chardonnay £17.25. CELLARMAN'S CHOICE: Savennières, Clos du Papillon 1995, Baumard, £25; Cabernet Sauvignon Reserva 1982, Jean Leon, Penedès, £30.85.

CHEF: Pierre Chevillard   PROPRIETOR: Martin Skan   OPEN: all week 12.30 to 1.45, 7.30 to 9.30
MEALS: Set L £13.50 (2 courses) to £18.50, Set D £47   SERVICE: not inc, card slips closed
CARDS: Amex, Delta, Diners, MasterCard, Switch, Visa   DETAILS: 120 seats. Private parties: 120
main room, 10 to 120 private rooms. Car park. Vegetarian meals. Children's helpings. No
children under 7. Jacket and tie. No smoking in dining-room. Wheelchair access (also WC).
Occasional music. Air-conditioned   ACCOMMODATION: 54 rooms, all with bath/shower. TV.
Phone. Room only £220 to £475. Rooms for disabled. No children under 7. Afternoon teas.
Swimming-pool (*The Which? Hotel Guide*)

NEW POLZEATH Cornwall   map 1

▲ *Cornish Cottage Hotel* 🏶✳

New Polzeath PL27 6UF
TEL: (01208) 862213   FAX: (01208) 862259
signposted off B3314 between Wadebridge   COOKING 6
and Port Isaac   COST £23–£54

In a 'genteel' resort, with handy walks along the nearby beach and clifftop, this
doesn't feel much like a cottage, apart perhaps from the false beams and leaded
lights in the dining-room. Reporters have mixed feelings about the rest:
illuminated fountain, 'swirly' carpets, wild wallpaper and 'the most ornate
grandfather clock you'll ever see'. New owners (also hoteliers in Newquay) took
over in November 1997, but Martin Walker remains at the stoves, producing a
range of interchangeable dishes for his *carte* and set-price menus. Main courses
tend to be protein-rich – perhaps beef fillet, or honey-baked pork tenderloin –
and portions can be on the generous side: a big piece of baked haddock on olive
oil mash, surrounded by pesto sauce, or 'loads of duck' breast in thick chunks
with a livery sausage, served on rösti potatoes.

Lobster is available with 24 hours' notice, subject to availability, but first
courses might offer something shellfishy, perhaps a risotto surrounded by a ring
of 'perfectly cooked' scallops, corals included, with a puddle of tapénade.
Desserts take a fairly classical stand, ranging from a soufflé, or bread-and-butter
pudding with dried apricots, to glazed lemon and orange tart, served with
matching and 'zingingly refreshing' sorbets. Throughout, good raw materials
provide a solid foundation, and meals are well paced. Over half the three dozen
varied wines are below £20, and there's an interesting selection by the glass to
accompany cheese or dessert. House wine, at £10.50, is French.

CHEF: Martin Walker   PROPRIETORS: Mr and Mrs D Faulkner   OPEN: all week D only 7 to 9, and
occasional Sun L   MEALS: alc (main courses £12.50 to £18.50). Set D £29.50. BYO £5
SERVICE: not inc, card slips closed   CARDS: Delta, MasterCard, Switch, Visa   DETAILS: 36
seats. 16 seats outside. Private parties: 50 main room. Car park. Vegetarian meals. No children
under 12. No smoking in dining-room. Music   ACCOMMODATION: 15 rooms, all with
bath/shower. TV. Phone. B&B £48 to £111. No children under 12. Afternoon teas.
Swimming-pool (£5)

---

*'This place seems to be popular and I write to counter any recommendations you may
receive. . . . There is a short wine list of mediocre bottles which would go well with the food.'*
(On eating in Staffordshire)

NORTHLEACH Gloucestershire   map 2

Old Woolhouse

Market Place, Northleach GL54 3EE   COOKING 5
TEL: (01451) 860366   COST £57–£69

By keeping to itself, the Old Woolhouse maintains an air of secrecy. It puts up net curtains, doesn't advertise its presence as a restaurant (just hangs a cream and brown sign outside with the name on), and doesn't have a written menu. It is certainly 'a place of great discretion' and can feel like a private dining-club. It is solid, stone-built, with log fires on the go, and its polished bare wooden tables are set with 'exquisite' Hungarian hand-painted crockery. The Astics – 'a charming couple' – do everything themselves. Jenny Astic recites the menu – two starters and three mains – and then comes round later to talk about cheese and dessert.

The food is all the better for being straightforward. Seafood starters have included 'wonderfully fresh' skinless sea bass, scattered with crispy bacon bits and a sprinkle of ground black pepper in a red wine sauce, and a dish of large scallops with their coral, surrounded by mussels in a lightly spicy sauce with garlic and saffron. Main courses are typically meaty, perhaps three thick slices of 'tasty' rib of beef with a tangy, mustard-flavoured brown gravy, or a chicken jointed into 'rustic' pieces, skin still on, tasting 'like chickens used to taste', with a vinegar sauce. Gratin dauphinois potatoes, crispy on top, creamy underneath, are served on a side-plate.

Main courses are followed by a green salad, then cheese, then initially one dessert, but eventually all three are offered for trial: tarts of apple, or prune and marzipan, and maybe strawberry shortcake. Coffee is good. There is no house wine, nothing by the glass, and just one copy of the handwritten parchment list, with 40 or so fancy French wines. Prices are fair – Ch. Beychevelle 1978 at £50, for example – but the selection starts around £25.

CHEF: Jacques Astic PROPRIETORS: Jacques and Jenny Astic OPEN: Tue to Sat D only from 8; other times by arrangement CLOSED: 1 week Christmas MEALS: Set D £40 CARDS: none
DETAILS: 18 seats. Private parties: 18 main room. Children welcome. No music

---

NORWICH Norfolk   map 6

Adlard's 🍾

---

79 Upper St Giles Street, Norwich NR2 1AB   COOKING 6
TEL: (01603) 633522 FAX: (01603) 617733   COST £30–£68

'Charm and character' is the first impression on entering this small, dark, emerald-green dining-room, its 'cave-like feel' offest by colourful prints and paintings. Considering the scale, options are generous: a 'perfectly composed' seven-course 'gourmet' dinner, a no-choice table d'hôte, and a *carte* of variable length, but more extensive in the evening. Fine ingredients underpin the cooking, which gives a lot of mainstream ideas a miss in favour of braised snails with morel sauce, or stuffed pig's trotter. Roast scallops in a fennel bouillon made 'an excellent beginning' for one reporter, while frothed-up white bean soup with 'plentiful bits' of chanterelles and ceps did the job for another.

At its best the food is colourful and intensely flavoured, as in a 'cake' of roasted red pepper and fennel enclosed in courgette and augerbine skin, topped with a mozzarella and tomato beignet, surrounded by a whizzed-up sauce of herbs in oil. But there seems more of an emphasis these days on 'food as art' at the expense of eating pleasure: more substance would be welcome. Slow service and 'modestly sized portions' at relatively high prices have disappointed some reporters, although others find the prices – which may pay for scallops, foie gras with ceps, truffle risotto, calves' sweetbreads and so on – perfectly reasonable, and service pleasant, friendly and helpful.

Extras include freshly baked bread, good purple olives, and first-rate appetisers and pre-desserts, while desserts themselves have ranged from 'disappointing' mango rice-pudding with matching ice-cream, to better prune and armagnac soufflé, and chocolate cake with vanilla ice-cream. New Zealand, Australian and California wines hold their heads high on a list that is long on Old World classics and refreshingly short on hefty mark-ups. Brief but apposite annotations aid selection, while two pages of 'bin beginnings' simplify matters even further. House wines are £11.75, and half-bottles abound. CELLARMAN'S CHOICE: Viña Casablanca Sauvignon Blanc 1997, Lontué Valley, Chile, £15; Salice Salentino Rosso 1994, Agricole Vallone, £15.

CHEFS: Aiden Byrne and Roger Hickman PROPRIETOR: David Adlard OPEN: Tue to Sat L 12.30 to 1.45, Mon to Sat D 7.30 to 10.30 CLOSED: 25 to 31 Dec MEALS: alc (main courses L £11, D £19). Set D £27.50 to £46. BYO £5 SERVICE: not inc CARDS: Amex, Delta, Diners, MasterCard, Switch, Visa DETAILS: 42 seats. Private parties: 45 main room. Vegetarian meals. Children's helpings. No smoking until after main course; no cigars/pipes in dining-room. No music

Marco's ✦

| 17 Pottergate, Norwich NR2 1DS | COOKING 2 |
| TEL: (01603) 624044 | COST £24–£48 |

At what stage a restaurant becomes a local institution may make for much debate, but Marco Vessalio's small-scale Italian which opened in the centre of Norwich in 1970 must be well on its way. The dining-room is brightly decorated, the few tables snugly packed in, and the bilingual menu offers a broader range of choice than the average trattoria. King prawns wrapped in Parma ham with peppers, garlic and parsley are the star attractions in one of the pasta starters, or there may be gnocchi of potato, ricotta and basil with Parmesan cream. A squeeze of lime and a dash of chilli oil used to flavour a partnering of grilled monkfish and halibut suggest a willingness to break new culinary ground. On the other hand, Genoese-style buridda is a highly praised stalwart of the kitchen. Meat-eaters might opt for a fillet of barley-fed beef in a horseradish cream sauce. Desserts extend from great ices and sorbets to Marco's Italianised bread-and-butter pudding: budino di pane. Service, in the view of one reporter, could be sharpened up, while another thought it just fine. The all-Italian wine list (champagne excepted) offers some interesting bins from around the country, helpfully annotated for those less familiar with the nation's grapes and producers. House Sicilian in all three colours is £11.

CHEF/PROPRIETOR: Marco Vessalio   OPEN: Tue to Sat 12.30 to 2, 7.30 to 10   CLOSED: Christmas, bank hols   MEALS: alc (main courses £8.50 to £17). Set L £14.70   SERVICE: not inc, card slips closed; 10% for parties of 8 or more   CARDS: Amex, Diners, MasterCard, Visa   DETAILS: 22 seats. Private parties: 12 main room. Vegetarian meals. Children's helpings. No smoking in dining-room. Wheelchair access (not WC). No music

---

NOTTINGHAM Nottinghamshire ⟨MIDLANDS 1999 NEWCOMER⟩ map 5

Hart's   **NEW ENTRY**

Standard Court, Park Row, Nottingham NG1 6GN   COOKING 6
TEL: (0115) 911 0666   FAX: (0115) 911 0611   COST £21£50

If this is the future, we want more of it, please. Nothing rejuvenates a city centre better than good restaurants, and Tim Hart of Hambleton Hall (see entry) has applied his considerable entrepreneurial nous to finding a site near the castle that works better than some might have predicted (it used to be the General Hospital), decorating it colourfully and tastefully, and filling the kitchen with chefs who mostly know what they are doing. The bright and cheerful space, with vivid geometric paintings, a city view and comfortable chairs, makes a 'smart, enjoyable' venue that is run with serious professionalism: the greeter is communicative and efficient, staff remember who is eating what, and 'the whole place seems well organised'.

Mark Gough has, naturally enough, worked at Hambleton, and his brigade has notched up experience in both Britain and France; hence the thrust of the menu: grilled tuna niçoise, roast scallops with saffron risotto, calf's liver with sage and spinach. These are carefully considered dishes, simple in intent, clear in design, for the most part skilful in execution, and tasty into the bargain: 'light, beautifully judged' fricassee of asparagus with morels and lambs' sweetbreads in spring that was 'all you could ask it to be', or artichoke heart topped with a mound of moist crabmeat with an intriguing chilli edge. Main-course meats have disappointed, but fish has worked well, including a pan-fried fillet of brill draped over spinach and rösti, with shiitake and oyster mushrooms in a creamy sauce.

Desserts are an unquestioned high point, among them a 'small, elegant square' of tiramisù; a soft chocolate sponge pudding with a fondant interior; and a richly textured chocolate tart with pistachio ice-cream. The set lunch looks good value, and a short, graduated, well-focused wine list, supplemented by a few finer bottles, is sympathetically priced, starting at £9.50.

CHEF: Mark Gough   PROPRIETOR: Tim Hart   OPEN: all week 12 to 2, 7 to 10.30   MEALS: alc (main courses £7.50 to £14). Set L Mon to Sat £9.50 (2 courses) to £15, Set L Sun £18. BYO min £5   SERVICE: 10%, card slips closed   CARDS: Delta, MasterCard, Switch, Visa   DETAILS: 85 seats. 20 seats outside. Private parties: 90 main room, 12 private room. Car park at D. Vegetarian meals. Children's helpings. Wheelchair access (also WC). No music

---

Prices quoted in the Guide *are based on information supplied by restaurateurs. The prices quoted at the top of each entry represent a range, from the lowest meal price to the highest; the latter is inflated by 20 per cent to take account of likely price rises during the year of the* Guide.

Sonny's

3 Carlton Street, Hockley, Nottingham NG1 1NL	COOKING 3
TEL: (0115) 947 3041 FAX: (0115) 950 7776	COST £21–£44

Everyone, from teenagers to grannies, seems to have a thoroughly good time at this 'airy, friendly, professional' Midlands sibling of Sonny's in London (see entry). There may be echoes of the 1980s in some ideas on the wide-ranging *carte* – witness an excellent rendition of Mediterranean fish soup, warm crab tart with fennel mayonnaise, or rump steak with sauce Choron – but there's also an up-to-the-minute tendency to draw on themes from around the globe. Seared foie gras comes with sweet potato rösti and ginger, Vietnamese pork salad is perked up with pickled vegetables, while the Middle East yields braised lamb shank with Moroccan spices and couscous. Kick off with a dish of olives and finish with, perhaps, sticky toffee pudding in the classic English tradition. Set Sunday lunch has been a thoroughly enjoyable experience, no doubt helped along by 'affable' service. Ten wines by the glass head the thoughtfully assembled list, which promises sound drinking, especially from France, Italy and Australia. House wines start at £8.95.

CHEFS: Graeme Watson and Pete Smith   PROPRIETOR: Rebecca Mascarenhas   OPEN: all week 12 to 3 (4 Sat), 7 to 10.30 (11 Fri and Sat)   CLOSED: 25 and 26 Dec, bank hols   MEALS: alc (main courses £9 to £13.50). Set L Mon to Fri £8.95 (2 courses) to £11.50, Set L Sun £13.95   SERVICE: not inc   CARDS: Amex, Delta, MasterCard, Switch, Visa   DETAILS: 75 seats. 20 seats outside. Private parties: 70 main room. Vegetarian meals. Children welcome. No cigars/pipes in dining-room. Wheelchair access (not WC). Occasional music. Air-conditioned

---

OCKHAM Surrey   map 3

▲ The Chapel at The Hautboy | NEW ENTRY |

Ockham GU23 6NP	
TEL: (01483) 225355 FAX: (01483) 211176	COOKING 5
EMAIL: richardwatney@btinternet.com	COST £38–£79

The Watneys opened their three-tiered operation in 1997, with a cellar bar, ground-floor brasserie (called The Oboe), and a striking first-floor Chapel restaurant. A minstrels' gallery runs along one end of the mid-nineteenth-century mock-Gothic room, an enormous black chandelier hangs from the 60-foot vaulted ceiling, and walls are oak-panelled, then plastered, then decorated with hand-drawn Tuscan frescoes. Quite an effect. Darren Tidd, meanwhile, who used to cook at the Angel Hotel (see Round-up entry, Midhurst), oversees a generous, set-price, seasonally changing dinner menu, plus an eight-course 'gourmet' version.

Drawing largely on European ideas, with a contemporary style, a few luxuries, and a fair bit of organisation and workmanship, he turns out a very appealing menu: creamed soup of smoked bacon and lentils with cep oil, chilled tuna escabèche, and 'perfectly cooked' pan-fried scallops laid around a 'compote' of tomato, olive and basil, with chanterelle mushrooms and sauce vierge. Anybody who considers life too short to stuff a morel should allow Darren Tidd to do it for them: he distributes them, along with broad beans and salsify, around pot-roasted veal sweetbread sitting on a base of chard. With this comes a plate of creamy mashed potatoes, and a few 'exceptionally light' crisply battered vegetables. Among desserts – banana soufflé with Amarula ice-cream, or Earl Grey parfait with saffron syrup – the assortment of layered chocolate mousses with kirsch-soaked cherries has stood out for being 'rich', yet 'light as a feather'. Forty-plus wines combine variety with fair value. House Bordeaux is £13.95.

CHEF: Darren Tidd   PROPRIETORS: Richard and Mags Watney   OPEN: Chapel restaurant Tue to Sat 12 to 2, 7 to 10; Oboe brasserie all week 12 to 2, 7 to 10   CLOSED: 25 and 26 Dec.   MEALS: Set L £20 (2 courses) to £25, Set D £35 to £50 (gourmet menu)   SERVICE: not inc   CARDS: Amex, Delta, MasterCard, Switch, Visa   DETAILS: 45 seats. Private parties: 55 main room, 120 private room. Car park. Vegetarian meals. Children welcome. No smoking while others eat. Music. Air-conditioned   ACCOMMODATION: 5 bedrooms, all with bath/shower. TV. Phone. B&B £98 to £125. Children welcome. Baby facilities. No dogs. Afternoon teas   £5

OLD BURGHCLERE Hampshire   map 2

Dew Pond ▼ ✳

Old Burghclere RG20 9LH
TEL/FAX: (01635) 278408   COOKING 6
off old A34, 3m W of Kingsclere   COST £37–£52

In March 1999 Keith and Julie Marshall notch up an impressive decade here. The two sixteenth-century knocked-together drovers' cottages retain a domestic feel – it is like 'dining in a private house' – and the setting is a bonus, with rural views across two counties to a twelfth-century church and 'Watership Down'. Indeed, the combination of surroundings and quality of cooking makes the place 'hard to beat' for some distance.

Choice – seven items per course – seems generous in the circumstances, and the food keeps abreast of developments, introducing chorizo into wild mushroom risotto, delivering mussels spiced with chilli, ginger and coconut, and adding charred limes to fillets of sole and brill cooked with vermouth and crème fraîche. Yet dishes have the distinctly common-sense feel of sound underlying principles, as when chargrilled asparagus is served with quail's eggs and lemon butter sauce, or when noisettes of lamb come with provençale vegetables and rosemary-scented juices. Game pops up, too, as roasted pigeon, perhaps, or saddle of roe-deer.

Lemon tart, white chocolate mousse, crème brûlée, sorbet, and strawberry vacherin have all appeared together as a 'memorable' assortment of miniature desserts, and meals are overseen by 'charming, efficient, yet totally unobtrusive' service. Wines on the attractively priced list are sourced from around the world and helpfully grouped by style, while two pages of fine wines and two more of half-bottles add to its appeal. Four house wines from France and Australia are £11.95. CELLARMAN'S CHOICE: Shottesbrooke Sauvignon Blanc 1995, McLaren Vale, S. Australia, £15.25; Côtes du Rhône, Coudoulet de Beaucastel Rouge 1993, £15.90.

🍾 denotes an outstanding wine cellar; ▼ denotes a good wine list, worth travelling for.

CHEF: Keith Marshall   PROPRIETORS: Keith and Julie Marshall   OPEN: Tue to Sat D only 7 to 10
CLOSED: 2 weeks Jan, 2 weeks Aug   MEALS: Set D £25   SERVICE: not inc   CARDS: Amex, Delta,
MasterCard, Switch, Visa   DETAILS: 45 seats. Private parties: 45 main room, 25 and 30 private
rooms. Car park. Vegetarian meals. Children's helpings. No children under 5. No smoking in
dining-room. Wheelchair access (not WC). No music   (£5)

OSWESTRY Shropshire   map 7

▲ *Sebastian* ⅚✳

45 Willow Street, Oswestry SY11 1AQ   COOKING 3
TEL/FAX: (01691) 655444   COST £28–£58

This sixteenth-century house with oak beams and panelling is home to a French
bistro, as the Renoir reproductions and posters of wine chateaux attest. The
cooking is determinedly French provincial, and one could hardly ask for a better
illustration of the way British and French styles have diverged over the years,
than to compare a typical global brasserie menu with Mark Sebastian Fisher's
steadier output of frogs' legs in batter, warm salad of guinea-fowl with boudin
blanc, and loin of lamb with a herb crust and ratatouille. His style is a busy one.
Breast of duck comes with prune quiche, and a mousse topping is a favourite
way of garnishing main courses: fillet of beef with one of veal and truffle,
monkfish with one of salmon and mushrooms. A three-course monthly-
changing menu is sensibly priced (about the same as a main course on the *carte*)
and comes with an appetiser and mid-meal sorbet. Apple-filled pancakes or
strawberry vacherin might be among desserts, and, while the cheeses are all
French, a few foreign wines sneak on to the reasonably priced list, which opens
at £10.95.

CHEF: Mark Sebastian Fisher   PROPRIETORS: Michelle and Mark Sebastian Fisher   OPEN: Tue
to Sat D only 6.30 to 10   CLOSED: 25 and 26 Dec, 1 Jan   MEALS: alc (main courses £16 to £24).
Set D £19.95   SERVICE: not inc, card slips closed   CARDS: Amex, Delta, MasterCard, Switch,
Visa   DETAILS: 40 seats. Private parties: 60 main room. Vegetarian meals. Children welcome.
No smoking in dining-room. Wheelchair access (1 step; not WC). Music   ACCOMMODATION: 3
rooms, all with bath/shower. TV. Phone. Room only £32 to £40. Children welcome. Baby
facilities. Garden   (£5)

Walls ♼ £

Welsh Walls, Oswestry SY11 1AW   COOKING 2
TEL: (01691) 670970   FAX: (01691) 655306   COST £18–£51

Conversion of this Victorian school building never went far enough, thankfully,
to remove the nostalgic feel of its wooden floor, brick walls, tall windows and
solid-looking beams. Geoffrey Hughes has turned it into a venue with broad
appeal, including art exhibitions and jazz evenings. The wine bar serves fishy
starters, pasta, steaks, salads, and a slate of 'specials' such as roast duck with pear
and cinnamon sauce, while the restaurant aims for a degree of innovation. Goose
rillettes are served with onion marmalade, grilled vegetable terrine comes with
caper dressing, and roast salmon is given a gremolata crust and salsa verde. 'We
have introduced some more-fashionable ingredients,' the restaurant writes,

perhaps thinking of roast loin of lamb with chermoula and grilled polenta, rather than sherry trifle or treacle sponge and custard. Wines have also seen a few introductions, and the expanded list is now arranged by varietal and offers a good spread of styles and flavours, with as much attention being paid to quality below £20 as above. House wines are £9. CELLARMAN'S CHOICE: Uva Mira Sauvignon Blanc 1997, Stellenbosch, South Africa, £17.50; Simon Hackett Anthony's Reserve Shiraz 1996, McLaren Vale, S. Australia, £22.50.

CHEFS: Geoffrey Hughes and Simon Newbery   PROPRIETORS: Geoffrey Hughes, Katherine Bottoms and Ruth Williams   OPEN: all week 12 to 2.30, Mon to Sat 6.30 to 10   CLOSED: 26 Dec, 1 Jan   MEALS: alc (main courses L £5 to £14, D £6.50 to £20)   SERVICE: not inc, card slips closed   CARDS: Amex, Delta, Diners, MasterCard, Switch, Visa   DETAILS: 220 seats. 32 seats outside. Private parties: 220 main room, 40 to 60 private rooms. Car park. Vegetarian meals. Children's helpings. Wheelchair access (also WC). Music   £5

OXFORD   Oxfordshire map 2

▲ *Al-Shami* £

25 Walton Crescent, Oxford OX1 2JG	COOKING 2
TEL: (01865) 310066 FAX: (01865) 311241	COST £19–£39

This typical Lebanese restaurant, open all day, offers simple comfort in a light airy dining-room with pleasant and efficient but not rushed service. A selection of Lebanese hors d'oeuvres can make a vegetarian feast, but there is lamb and offal too, and grilled chicken wings with garlic sauce. A reporter enjoyed baked cod fillet with 'tangy and flavoursome' sesame sauce, and suyahdiyah (spiced rice topped with fish). Most main dishes are lamb or chicken grilled on skewers, while shish taouq (chicken marinated in garlic, lemon juice and olive oil) has been excellent. Desserts are Lebanese pastries or ice-cream (or more-expensive Arabic ice-cream), and mint tea is refreshing. A short wine list offers several vintages of Ch. Musar; house wine is £9.99.

CHEF: Mimo Mahfouz   PROPRIETOR: Al-Shami Cuisine & Accommodation Ltd   OPEN: all week noon to midnight   MEALS: alc (main courses £5.50 to £12). Set L £12 (2 courses), Set D £15 (2 courses). Cover £1   SERVICE: not inc   CARDS: MasterCard, Switch, Visa   DETAILS: 90 seats. Private parties: 50 main room, 40 private room. Vegetarian meals. Children welcome. Wheelchair access (also WC). Music   ACCOMMODATION: 12 rooms, all with bath/shower. TV. Phone. B&B £35 to £45. Children welcome. No dogs   £5

▲ *Bath Place* ▾ 🍷 ⚡

OXFORD
1999
SIZZLER

4–5 Bath Place, Holywell Street, Oxford OX1 3SU	COOKING 5
TEL: (01865) 791812 FAX: (01865) 791834	COST £30–£73

Bath Place is an agglomeration of seventeenth-century cottages behind a tiny gated courtyard. The interior is all narrow stairways and creakily uneven floors, and the low-ceilinged dining-room – actually a pair of interconnecting rooms – is lent character by exposed stone walls that once enclosed the city. Strategically angled lighting and floating candles add a crepuscular feel to it in the evening, but if you're expecting gentle country-house cooking, prepare to be startled.

Guillaume Foussier took up the cleavers in the kitchen at the beginning of 1998 and has breathed novelty and vividness into the cooking. Bordelais by birth, he has worked in the USA and on Mayotte in the Indian Ocean, and brings some of the fusion style of California and spice-island ingredients to bear on essentially French technique. Fillets of roast mackerel, 'demonstrably fresh and timed to perfection', are served on chilli-dressed melon dice with a creamy masala sauce, an artfully conceived first course of vibrant flavours. Panaché of fish at inspection offered five types, each on its own sauce, one of fish stock and parsley, another of mango, and so forth, all skilfully composed. Goose breast makes a rarely seen main course, here cooked in cardamom oil, then thinly sliced on prune and liver mousse and given a truffle sauce.

Amid all the innovation, it comes as something of a comfort to find archetypal coq au vin – chicken legs stewed as of old in red wine with whole small onions and bacon – rendered with effortless ease. Flavours keep coming on strong at dessert stage, where aniseed bavarois with liquorice sorbet may compete with tarte Tatin of pineapple, mango and papaya in a cardamom cream sauce. Service does its best, but could be more co-ordinated. Some 60 wines from around the world are grouped by style, and tasting notes tell all that's needed in around a dozen words. Prices are reasonable, starting at £11.95 for house wines. CELLARMAN'S CHOICE: Isonzo Malvasia 1996, Sergio & Marius Druis, £15.75; Nebbiolo d'Alba Santa Rosalia 1996, Giacomo Brezza, £19.50.

CHEF: Guillaume Foussier PROPRIETORS: Kathleen and Yolanda Fawsitt OPEN: Wed to Sun L 12 to 2 (2.30 Sun), Tue to Sat D 7 to 10 (10.30 Sat) CLOSED: last week Dec, first week Jan, last 2 weeks Aug MEALS: alc (main courses £14 to £19). Set L Wed to Sat £14.50 (2 courses) to £19.50, Set L Sun £23.50 SERVICE: not inc; 10% for parties of 5 or more CARDS: Amex, Delta, MasterCard, Switch, Visa DETAILS: 32 seats. 10 seats outside. Private parties: 40 main room. Vegetarian meals. Children's helpings. No smoking in dining-room. Wheelchair access (2 steps; not WC). Music. Air-conditioned ACCOMMODATION: 13 rooms, all with bath/shower. TV. Phone. B&B £80 to £150. Children welcome. Baby facilities. Dogs welcome by arrangement

Cherwell Boathouse 🍾

50 Barwell Road, Oxford OX2 6ST	COOKING 3
TEL/FAX: (01865) 552746	COST £23–£35

'Please make it plain that the place is as simple as its name suggests,' pleaded one correspondent, while another was surprised how basic the surroundings were; even the paper napkins are 'thin and small'. Expect an old boathouse with a steep slipway, bare wood, an oar and a few paintings for decoration, and 'homely' cooking. The fortnightly-changing set menu (the same at lunch and dinner) is short, offering perhaps asparagus salad, crab-cakes, hummus, and maybe chicken and chickpea soup to start. A vegetarian option, such as stuffed artichokes with lentil purée, is usually available alongside maybe pigeon with beans, or a trio of fish – a small fillet each of salmon, whiting and red snapper – served with green tagliatelle. Puddings don't vary much beyond trifle, chocolate nemesis or ice-cream.

With Anthony Verdin as owner it is no surprise that wines are supplied by London merchants Morris & Verdin and that quality is well to the fore. André Jacquart champagnes, Alsace from André Ostertag and mature burgundies from Comtes Lafon are ongoing specialities, bolstered by short but sound selections from the New World. The white and red house selections open at a cheerful £7.50, although mark-ups at all levels are gratifyingly low. CELLARMAN'S CHOICE: Meursault Clos de la Barre 1991, Dom. des Comtes Lafon, £38; Au Bon Climat Pinot Noir 1996, Santa Barbara, California, £20.

CHEFS: Gerard Crowley and Wayne Cullen PROPRIETOR: Anthony Verdin OPEN: Tue to Sun L 12 to 2, Tue to Sat D 6 to 10 CLOSED: 24 to 30 Dec MEALS: alc (main courses £8 to £12). Set L £17.50, Set D £19.50 SERVICE: 10% (optional), not inc CARDS: Amex, Delta, Diners, MasterCard, Switch, Visa DETAILS: 60 seats. 24 seats outside. Private parties: 50 main room, 100 private room. Car park. Vegetarian meals. Children's helpings. No smoking before 2.15 L and 10.30 D. Wheelchair access (1 step; also WC). No music £5

Lemon Tree

268 Woodstock Road, Oxford OX2 7NW   COOKING 4
TEL/FAX: (01865) 311938   COST £25–£49

This trendy 'Californian wannabee' restaurant, designed and owned by Clinton Pugh, occupies a large, detached, double-fronted house about a mile up the Woodstock Road. Progress from a large airy bar at the front, through a glassed-over dining-room, to a garden that opens up for al fresco meals in summer. The modern, fashionable food takes Italian and Mediterranean ideas as a starting-point and doesn't miss an opportunity to present its up-to-date credentials: parsnip chips with grilled mackerel fillet, wasabi dressing for seared tuna, polenta with lambs' liver, smoked chillies with chargrilled pork cutlets, and so on.

Some items are free-range (the pork, for instance), others organic, including chicken: the livers in a salad with mango dressing, the leg stuffed with lemon confit and served with tagliatelle. The food is delivered with panache: chicken and mushroom terrine, for example, attractively presented on a large white plate with red onion marmalade and plenty of the leaves that seem to decorate so many dishes. Desserts gravitate northwards, towards Normandy apple tart, or hot treacle sponge, and cheeses are English. Service from staff in cream denim skirts and jeans is 'more than willing'. Note that there are two sittings on Friday and Saturday evenings, and that bread and olives are charged extra. The short wine list aims for safe modern drinking, starting at £8.75 for Chilean Merlot and white Bordeaux, with half a dozen by the glass.

CHEF: Paul Keeble PROPRIETOR: Clinton Pugh OPEN: all week 12 to 11 CLOSED: 25 to 27 Dec MEALS: alc (main courses £8 to £15) SERVICE: not inc, card slips closed; 10% for parties of 5 or more CARDS: MasterCard, Switch, Visa DETAILS: 100 seats. 50 seats outside. Private parties: 120 main room, 20 private room. Car park. Vegetarian meals. Children's helpings. Wheelchair access (also WC). Music £5

▲ Old Parsonage Hotel, Parsonage Bar

1 Banbury Road, Oxford OX2 6NN
TEL: (01865) 310210   FAX: (01865) 311262   COOKING 1
EMAIL: oldparsonage@dial.pipex.com   COST £28–£48

Although close to the centre of Oxford, the Parsonage is considered 'a haven of peace', and 'a pleasantly relaxing place to meet friends for lunch'. It does not pretend to be a fully fledged restaurant, but serves food of a quality that puts many pubs to shame. The menu has been trimmed a bit and brought up to date, sporting ingredients such as red mullet, coconut, black olive sauce, chillies and couscous. Fish, fowl and vegetables predominate over red meat, producing tuna steak on celeriac with garlic purée, and breast of guinea-fowl on a potato pancake with wild mushroom sauce. A salad of avocado, tomato and mozzarella, and another of chicken and asparagus, proved 'just right for a warm summer night' for one couple. Desserts run to baked Alaska and passion-fruit tart, portions are generous, service is attentive, and a short but varied list of wines includes good choice by the glass and half-bottle. Prices start at £11.50.

CHEF: Alison Watkins PROPRIETOR: Jeremy Mogford OPEN: all week 12 to 3, 6 to 11 CLOSED: 25 to 26 Dec MEALS: alc (main courses £9 to £12.50) SERVICE: not inc, card slips closed CARDS: Amex, Diners, MasterCard, Switch, Visa DETAILS: 37 seats. 30 seats outside. Car park. Vegetarian meals. Children welcome. No pipes in dining-room. Wheelchair access (2 steps; not WC) Music Air-conditioned ACCOMMODATION. 30 rooms, all with bath/shower. TV. Phone. B&B £125 to £170. Rooms for disabled. Children welcome. Afternoon teas. Fishing

Le Petit Blanc 🍴✳

71–72 Walton Street, Oxford OX2 6AG	COOKING 5
TEL: (01865) 510999 FAX: (01865) 510700	COST £24–£45

In the competitive world of the modern brasserie, style and appearance count for a lot, and Le Petit Blanc's light, airy and welcoming feel propels it into the first division. Close-together tables contribute to the 'buzz', an 'informal but civilised' air pervades, and the room at the back has a grandstand view of the kitchen with 'masses of chefs' and a busy spit roast. After disappearing into the Round-up section last year, when Stuart Lyall arrived just as the *Guide* was going to press, Le Petit Blanc returns to the main listings with a flourish.

Day-long opening brings breakfasts and afternoon teas, as well as set-price meals and a freewheeling *carte* that runs from breads to pasta to fish to rotisserie dishes of roast pheasant with juniper, or poussin with pak choi. Along the way reporters have enjoyed crostini of goats' cheese with tomato chutney, 'moist, firm-textured' red mullet with a 'brilliant' tomato, olive and pesto dressing, and (in their droves, it would seem) pink and tender calf's liver. Dishes that are 'well seasoned and full of character' include rich coq au vin with home-made tagliatelle. Apple crumble and Maman Blanc's floating islands reduced one grown man to write of 'mouth boggling flavours'. As at all M. Blanc's establishments children are positively welcomed, able to choose pasta with tomato sauce, or chicken with fries from their own menu. The 'professional cheerfulness and confidence' of staff, who are knowledgeable and attentive, produces a contented response, and electronic order pads help to keep things moving along at a good pace. Around ten wines, from a list of three dozen, are available by the glass, including house vin de pays at £9.95.

CHEFS: Stuart Lyall PROPRIETOR: Raymond Blanc OPEN: all week 12 to 3.30, 6.30 to 11 CLOSED: 25 Dec MEALS: alc (main courses £8 to £13.50). Set L £12.50 (2 courses) to £15, Set D 6.30 to 7 £12.50 (2 courses) to £15. BYO £10 SERVICE: not inc, 10% optional for parties of 8 or more CARDS: Amex, Delta, Diners, MasterCard, Switch, Visa DETAILS: 120 seats. Private parties: 12 main room, 16 private room. Vegetarian meals. Children's helpings. No smoking in 1 dining-room. Wheelchair access (also WC). Music. Air-conditioned (£5)

White House £

2 Botley Road, Oxford OX2 0AB	COOKING 2
TEL: (01865) 242823 FAX: (01865) 793331	COST £24–£41

In a former incarnation, the White House was a tollgate where motorists paid to cross the river into the city; later it became a pub, and now it is 'lounge, bar and restaurant' looking out on to a terrace and walled garden. The inside is done out in shades of yellow and blue and the menu is pure brasserie. Affordable bar meals call into play everything from vegetable tempura with spicy dip to Cumberland sausage with boulangère potatoes, while the full *carte* extends to warm salad of duck, pear and Gorgonzola, and seared tuna with Szechuan peppercorns and oven-dried tomatoes. One successful lunch commenced with 'top-notch' carrot, cardamom and ginger soup, and crisp deep-fried prawn wuntuns with spring onions and a leafy salad potently dressed with soy and chilli. The owners are also wine merchants, and the list of around 30 bins is a well-assembled slate. House vin de pays is £8.95.

CHEF: Christopher Bland   PROPRIETOR: Whites Restaurant Ltd   OPEN: all week 12.30 to 2.30 (3 Sun), 6 to 9.30 (7 to 9 Sun)   CLOSED: D 25 and 26 Dec   MEALS: alc Mon to Sat L, all week D (main courses £7 to £10). Set L Sun £11.95 (2 courses) to £14.95. Bar meals available   SERVICE: not inc   CARDS: Amex, Delta, Diners, MasterCard, Switch, Visa   DETAILS: 60 seats. 40 seats outside. Private parties: 40 main room. Car park. Vegetarian meals. Children's helpings. Wheelchair access (also WC). Music £5

PADSTOW Cornwall   map 1

Margot's ✱

11 Duke Street, Padstow PL28 8AB	COOKING 1
TEL: (01841) 533441	COST £16–£38

Steering a steady course when Padstow's tourist and gastronomic circus is in full swing may have its problems, but this admirable little bistro – which used to be called Bistro Margot Thomas – continues to hold its own. As a crowd-pleasing gesture, the place now opens at lunch-time for light meals of grilled mackerel with salsa and rocket, stir-fried beef fillet with black beans and so on, all at knockdown prices. Evening brings a three-course, fixed-price menu, which is chalked daily on a blackboard. Simplicity and honest freshness are the hallmarks: reporters have singled out marinated aubergine and red pepper with feta and olives, skate wing baked with anchovy, rosemary and garlic accompanied by herb-grilled potatoes, and calf's liver with sherry and balsamic vinegar. Abundant vegetables are served in Chinese-style bamboo steaming baskets, while bread-and-butter pudding laced with calvados retains its supremacy as the signature dessert. The wine list aims for modesty and good value, and succeeds. House Trebbiano and Sangiovese are £9.50.

CHEFS: Adrian Oliver, Kwashie Amalgo and Vicky Woosnam-Mills   PROPRIETOR: Mike Meredith   OPEN: all week 12 to 2, 7 to 9.30 (reduced opening in winter)   CLOSED: Nov to Jan MEALS: alc L (main courses £2.50 to £5). Set D £18.95 (2 courses) to £22.95   SERVICE: not inc, card slips closed   CARDS: Delta, MasterCard, Switch, Visa   DETAILS: 30 seats. Private parties: 30 main room. Vegetarian meals. Children's helpings. No smoking in dining-room. Music £5

▲ *Seafood Restaurant* 🍾

Riverside, Padstow PL28 8BY   COOKING 6
TEL: (01841) 532700   FAX: (01841) 532942   COST £38–£94

My, my, what a postbag; it's amazing what television will do for a restaurant. Even though refurbishment has brought more seats to the monochromatic dining-room with its 'brazen technicolour artwork', two sittings at dinner are still required to satisfy demand. A lively atmosphere generally prevails, and 'the food is simple, the fish fresh' much of the time. But those reporters are sharply divided. Rick Stein has done an enormous amount to educate and encourage public appetite for fish, and his own personal cooking can undoubtedly be taken as benchmark, but he now finds himself putting his name to something that often falls a bit short.

Variety extends from a large platter of fruits de mer to roast cod with saffron mashed potatoes and tapenade, and among successes have been 'exquisite' softshell crabs, a rich-tasting fish soup, and appealing meurette of plaice and lemon sole made with Beaujolais. The spicier dishes work well too, from flavourful chargrilled squid with a chilli and black pepper dressing, to plump, meaty mackerel 'straight from the sea' with spices rubbed into the flesh. But reporters have also found under-par saucing, some poor timing and seasoning, and rather high prices, even for haddock and lemon sole. Like the solitary grilled steak, desserts of lemon tart, Eton mess, or orange and almond cake with vanilla sabayon tend not to cause much of a splash.

Service has had its ups and downs, seeming disorganised and inflexible to some, and polite, well informed and accommodating to others. Highly drinkable wines of humble origin swim alongside some aristocratic ones on a list that is as seafood-friendly as you would expect, and features a fair number of bottles under £20. Whites predominate, of course, but red wine lovers are far from neglected. The house selection of current favourites opens at £12.95. CELLARMAN'S CHOICE: Montagny *premier cru* 'Les Bonneveaux' 1995, Leflaive, £22.50; Mulderbosch Faithful Hound 1994, Stellenbosch, South Africa, £18.50.

CHEF: Rick Stein   PROPRIETORS: Mr and Mrs Rick Stein   OPEN: Mon to Sat 12 to 1.30, 7 to 10 (9 midweek Nov to Mar)   CLOSED: Christmas/New Year   MEALS: alc (main courses £21.50 to £36). Set L £28, Set D £34   SERVICE: not inc   CARDS: Delta, MasterCard, Switch, Visa DETAILS: 100 seats. Private parties: 16 main room. Children's helpings. No children under 5. Wheelchair access (3 steps; not WC). Occasional music. Air-conditioned   ACCOMMODATION: 27 rooms, all with bath/shower. TV. Phone. B&B £35 to £130. Children welcome. Baby facilities (*The Which? Hotel Guide*)

PAINSWICK Gloucestershire   map 2

Country Elephant 🍷✳

New Street, Painswick GL6 6XH
TEL/FAX: (01452) 813564
on A46 Cheltenham to Stroud road   COOKING 4
                             COST £22–£49

The Elephant has shrunk slightly, the Rees brothers now represented only by chef/patron Robert. The *carte* has also diminished, with only three or four choices at each course, though set lunches and dinners change daily according to the market and are well balanced and good value. Fish plays an important part here, as evidenced by baked skate wing, lemon sole en papillotte or, from the set dinner menu, very fresh salmon steak with Cornish crab risotto and carrot butter. Other main dishes might be poulet noir with a scallop and ginger mousse and baby spinach, or fillet of beef with red onion and tarragon jus. Among both starters and desserts are tarts, such as onion confit with Parma ham and braised endive, and mango tarte Tatin. Service is 'observant and helpful' if sometimes uninformed. Forty wines feature on the list, of which ten (plus three dessert wines) are offered by the glass at very friendly prices; house Chenin and Shiraz are £9.80 a bottle.

CHEF/PROPRIETOR: Robert Rees   OPEN: Tue to Sat 12 to 2, 7 to 10   CLOSED: 24 Dec to 3 Jan
MEALS: alc (main courses £14 to £16). Set L £10 (2 courses) to £13, Set D £13 (2 courses) to £18
SERVICE: not inc   CARDS: Amex, Delta, Diners, MasterCard, Switch, Visa   DETAILS: 30 seats. 20
seats outside. Private parties: 30 main room. Vegetarian meals. Children welcome. No smoking
in dining room. Wheelchair access (1 step; not WC). Music (£5)

PAULERSPURY Northamptonshire   map 5

▲ *Vine House* £✳

100 High Street, Paulerspury NN12 7NA
TEL: (01327) 811267   FAX: (01327) 811309   COOKING 4
off A5, 2m SE of Towcester   COST £26–£45

This 300-year-old house of local limestone, just off the A5, feels as if it might once have been a pub. The scale is small, the dining-room modern and comfortable, and Julie Springett runs front-of-house with the air of 'a jovial farmer's wife'. Marcus Springett's short menu changes daily, and his country cooking embraces terrines and pâtés – jellied smoked haddock and prawns, or rabbit confit with smoked bacon – and sausages: from rabbit with black pudding to venison with chestnut. Traditional items such as fillet steak with chips and mushrooms, or garlic-studded chicken breast, sit easily alongside an oriental starter of tuna with sesame and soy, and roast cod with tapénade and provençal vegetables. One or two items might carry a small supplement, but value is fair, and desserts have included hot honey-roasted pineapple, and apple and blackberry crumble. Start with a glass of home-made lemonade or ginger beer, and choose a wine from the predominantly French list; house wines are £9.95.

CHEF: Marcus Springett   PROPRIETORS: Marcus and Julie Springett   OPEN: Thu and Fri L 12.15
to 1.30, Mon to Sat D 7.30 to 9.30   CLOSED: 23 Dec to 4 Jan   MEALS: Set L £16.95, Set D
£24.95   SERVICE: not inc   CARDS: MasterCard, Visa   DETAILS: 45 seats. Private parties: 30
main room, 10 private room. Car park. Children's helpings. No smoking in dining-room.
Wheelchair access (2 steps; not WC). No music   ACCOMMODATION: 6 rooms, all with
bath/shower. TV. Phone. B&B £43 to £66. Children welcome. No dogs

---

£ *means that it is possible to have a three-course meal, including coffee, half a bottle of house wine and service for £25 or less per person, at any time the restaurant is open, i.e. at dinner as well as lunch. It may be possible to spend considerably more than this, but by choosing carefully you should find £25 or less achievable.*

PAXFORD Gloucestershire   map 5

▲ *Churchill Arms* £

Paxford GL55 6XH	COOKING 5
TEL: (01386) 594000 FAX: (01386) 594005	COST £20–£36

The Churchill's pitch – a pub with food, not a restaurant with beer – means that it stays open seven days a week. There are few refinements, no candles or tablecloths, and no bookings, although it can get busy; two people found themselves 'eating in the back of their Range Rover' one evening. A relaxed approach sets the right tone, and generally high-quality food brings most reporters back for more. The menu is chalked up daily, offering around half a dozen each first and main courses, and orders are taken at the bar.

Owners Leo Brooke-Little and Sonya Kidney (who is executive chef both here and at Marsh Goose, see entry Moreton-in-Marsh), adopt the same approach to sourcing materials in both places, using properly reared meat and seasonal vegetables. Dishes range from the ordinary – parsnip soup, or ham, egg and chips – to more unusual: scallops with curried potatoes and pancetta. The kitchen follows no particular style, and seems equally at home with tuna steak and black olive pesto as with an 'unctuous' braised belly of Old Spot pork with deep-flavoured gravy and garlic mash, considered good enough to be 'a lesson for every English pub'. Finish in traditional English way with rice pudding or sticky toffee, and drink Hook Norton beer or one of around 20 wines that start at £8.50.

CHEFS: Sonya Kidney and David Toon   PROPRIETOR: Boardcreate Ltd   OPEN: all week 12 to 2, 7 to 9   CLOSED: D 25 Dec   MEALS: alc (main courses £7 to £12)   SERVICE: not inc   CARDS: Delta, MasterCard, Switch, Visa   DETAILS: 60 seats. 40 seats outside. Private parties: 14 main room. Children's helpings. Wheelchair access (not WC). Occasional music   ACCOMMODATION: 4 rooms, all with bath/shower. TV. Phone. B&B £30 to £60. Children welcome (*The Which? Hotel Guide*)

PENZANCE Cornwall   map 1

Harris's £✴

46 New Street, Penzance TR18 2LZ	COOKING 2
TEL: (01736) 364408 FAX: (01736) 333273	COST £20–£56

'One could be going back in time as one enters this small restaurant' in a narrow side street just off the main shopping thoroughfare. Not to the days of smugglers or tin mining, but to the 1970s (perhaps 1972, when Roger and Anne Harris started here) judging by the atmosphere, pink décor, service and menu with its bonne-femme and meunière sauces, prawns in garlic butter, crab with cheese sauce, and mushrooms cooked with red wine and bacon. Locally sourced supplies include fish and shellfish from Newlyn – poached John Dory or steamed lobster perhaps – and Cornish lamb, as well as 'tender, moist' Scottish venison with beetroot, apple and caraway. Economy of style extends to using a base of leeks and red pepper sauce to support a starter of either red mullet or Cornish goats' cheese, while desserts have included chocolate pot and 'decent, gooey' treacle tart. Service is 'efficient', prices are considered a bit high for the area, and wines focus on France, starting with house wine at £11.50.

CHEF: Roger Harris   PROPRIETORS: Anne and Roger Harris   OPEN: Tue to Sat L 12 to 2, Tue to Sun D 7 to 9.30   CLOSED: 25 and 26 Dec, 3 weeks winter   MEALS: alc (main courses L £6.50 to £9.50, D £15 to £20)   SERVICE: 10%, card slips closed   CARDS: Amex, Delta, MasterCard, Switch, Visa   DETAILS: 40 seats. Private parties: 20 main room. Vegetarian meals. Children welcome. No smoking in 1 dining-room. Music

---

PLUMTREE Nottinghamshire   map 5

Perkins ❊ 🍴 £

Old Railway Station, Plumtree NG12 5NA
TEL: (0115) 937 3695   FAX: (0115) 937 6405   COOKING 2
off A606, 2m S of Nottingham   COST £22–£41

Halfway between a bistro and a restaurant, this bright and airy station conversion adopts an easy-going approach. French prints cover the walls of the bar (where orders are taken) and a couple of small dining-rooms, and a conservatory overlooks the old line. Hugh Cocker (formerly at Penmaenuchaf Hall, see entry Penmaenpool) has joined Marco Smeeth in the kitchen, but with little change to the cooking as we went to press. The strength is 'simple food well executed', and ideas are none the worse for using sound combinations such as moist fillet of salmon with dill sauce, or tender calf's liver with bacon.

Menus combine a good range of materials, with no shortage of fish and vegetables: layers of tomato and aubergine topped with goats' cheese on toasted brioche, or deep-fried plaice fillets. New since last year is a speedy two-course fixed-price lunch, changed twice weekly, offering perhaps crab and mullet quenelles, followed by chicken vol-au-vent, and a tart of roast pineapple with honey and almonds. Service is quick and cheerful, and wines are fairly priced. Note the half-dozen French country wines around £10.

CHEFS: Marco Smeeth and Hugh Cocker   PROPRIETORS: Tony and Wendy Perkins   OPEN: Tue to Sat L 12 to 1.45, Sun L 11.45 to 2.30, Tue to Sat D 6.30 to 9.45   CLOSED: 1 week Christmas, 1 Jan, Easter Tue   MEALS: alc (main courses £8 to £10.50). Set L Tue to Sat £9.75 (2 courses), Set L Sun (price not available at time of going to press). BYO £6   SERVICE: not inc   CARDS: Amex, Delta, Diners, MasterCard, Switch, Visa   DETAILS: 73 seats. 24 seats outside. Private parties: 12 main room, 30 private room. Car park. Vegetarian meals. No children under 7 at D. No smoking in 1 dining-room. Wheelchair access (1 step; not WC). No music. Air-conditioned

---

PLYMOUTH Devon   map 1

Chez Nous 🍷

13 Frankfort Gate, Plymouth PL1 1QA   COOKING 6
TEL/FAX: (01752) 266793   COST £42–£51

The surrounding area may be post-Blitz brutalist, but Jacques and Suzanne Marchal's small French restaurant is a magnet for those in the know. The royal-blue frontage and white louvred windows give the place a slightly anonymous look, and inside is tiny: this really is one of those small-scale operations where the emphasis is on what you eat, rather than on decorative fripperies.

'Cuisine spontanée' is the name of the game. Menus are written in non-metaphorical French and what turns up on the plate is also hearteningly direct and to the point, but cooked with undeniable talent. Scallops with garlic butter, chicken livers sauté in port, or crab and orange salad may start you off, to be followed by Barbican bouillabaisse (using seafood from nearby Barbican Quay), grilled cod with pistou, or beef fillet with mushrooms. At one level, this may look like straightforward bistro food, and yet there is a depth to the seasoning and saucing, and a proficiency with timing, that lift it out of the rough-and-ready class. At the end, choose from a fine showing of great French cheeses, or praline glacé with chocolate sauce and orange ice-cream, or perhaps treacle pudding with Devon clotted cream. Suzanne Marchal runs front-of-house with self-effacing calm. Although compiled with the help of Englishman David Sommerfelt of Christopher Piper Wines, the *carte des vins* is as Gallic as the rest of the establishment, with just a few wines from 'other countries' given houseroom. Clarets stretching back to the 1950s and burgundies to the early 1970s are its forte. House wines are £10.50. CELLARMAN'S CHOICE: Rully 1991, Raymond Dureuil-Janthial, £17.25; Bordeaux Supérieur, Ch. St-Jacques 1993, £16.

CHEF: Jacques Marchal   PROPRIETORS: Suzanne and Jacques Marchal   OPEN: Tue to Fri L 12.30 to 2, Tue to Sat D 7 to 10.30   CLOSED: 3 weeks Feb, 3 weeks Sep, bank hols   MEALS: Set L and D £30.50   SERVICE: not inc   CARDS: Amex, Diners, MasterCard, Switch, Visa   DETAILS: 28 seats. Private parties: 28 main room. Children welcome. Wheelchair access (not WC). Music. Air-conditioned

---

PONTELAND Northumberland   map 10

Café 21 £

35 The Broadway, Darras Hall, Ponteland NE20 9PW   COOKING 4
TEL: (01661) 820357   COST £20–£43

This unassuming, easy-going outpost of the Laybourne empire (headquarters is 21 Queen Street; see entry, Newcastle upon Tyne) is at the end of a row of suburban shops. It operates bistro-style with paper cloths and a blackboard menu, offering an appealing selection of dishes from soups (split pea, or smooth potato and bacon with Gruyère cheese croûtons) to cod with couscous, and sirloin steak with chips. Some ideas – terrine of ham knuckle, for example – come straight from Newcastle, some are as traditionally British as fish-cakes with creamy parsley sauce, while others have drifted up from the Mediterranean: grilled mackerel with pesto, maybe. There is usually a slow-cooked dish on offer too: shoulder of lamb 'full of flavour', or ham shank with pulses and salsa verde. Sound skills and modest ambition keep everything on track, including desserts of light ricotta cheesecake with raspberry coulis, or custard tart with nutmeg ice-cream. Service is friendly, and the short wine list is fairly priced.

All entries, including Round-ups, are fully indexed at the back of the Guide.

CHEF: Andrew Waugh PROPRIETORS: Terence and Susan Laybourne OPEN: Sat L 12 to 2, Tue to Sat D 5.30 (6 Sat) to 10.30 CLOSED: Christmas, bank hols MEALS: alc (main courses £8 to £13). Set L and D before 7pm £10.50 (2 courses) to £12.50 SERVICE: not inc CARDS: Amex, Delta, Diners, MasterCard, Switch, Visa DETAILS: 62 seats. Private parties: 70 main room. Vegetarian meals. Children's helpings. No-smoking area. Wheelchair access (1 step; also WC). Music

POOLE Dorset map 2

▲ *Mansion House* 🍷

Thames Street, Poole BH15 1JN COOKING 3
TEL: (01202) 685666 FAX: (01202) 665709 COST £27–£44

Built in the eighteenth century as a mayoral residence, the Mansion House is a sardine's throw from the quayside, in a quiet cobbled mews. Its dining-room is in the basement, extending through two connected rooms panelled in cherrywood, and is imbued with a full-dress feel that takes in linen napery and candles, and a baby grand piano. The kitchen, under the executive direction of Gerry Godden, has held fast to a gently rich style of cooking that brings both Gorgonzola ravioli with pesto and twice-cooked cheese soufflé on to the menu. Chinese duck salad with spring onions might be one way of sidestepping dairy fat, and there is an option of an intermediate soup course such as chunky mushroom with croûtons.

Main course choice is dauntingly wide, extending from loin of venison with truffled celeriac and raspberries, through crab-stuffed chicken breast sauced with ginger, lemon grass and coriander, to simpler salmon fillet in a nicely balanced white wine reduction sauce. Ices and sorbets seem to be reliable dessert bets, or wait for the trolley of admirable British and Irish cheeses to come round. Waiting staff have been described as charming, if still at the learning stage. The lengthy wine list is divided into two parts. The first sets an upper price limit of £30 (although many cost less than £15) and features a worldly collection, grouped by style. The second part contains French and New World classics with no price ceiling. House wines start at £12 a bottle, £2.45 a glass. CELLARMAN'S CHOICE: Cloudy Bay Sauvignon Blanc 1997, Marlborough, New Zealand, £29.95; Errázuriz, Don Maximiano Cabernet Sauvignon 1993, Aconcagua Valley, Chile, £17.95.

CHEFS: Gerry Godden and Darren Rocket PROPRIETOR: Robert Leonard OPEN: Sun to Fri L 12 to 2, Mon to Sat D 7 to 9.30 CLOSED: L bank hol Mons MEALS: Set L £14.50, Set D £19.50 (2 courses) to £24. Meal prices reduced by 15% for residents SERVICE: not inc CARDS: Amex, Delta, Diners, MasterCard, Switch, Visa DETAILS: 85 seats. Private parties: 100 main room, 14 to 100 private rooms. Car park. Vegetarian meals. Children's helpings. No children under 5 exc at Sun L. Occasional music. Air-conditioned ACCOMMODATION: 28 rooms, all with bath/shower. TV. Phone. B&B £57.50 to £125. Children welcome. Baby facilities. Dogs welcome by arrangement. Afternoon teas (*The Which? Hotel Guide*) (£5)

▲ *means accommodation is available.*

All entries in the Guide *are re-researched and rewritten every year, not least because restaurant standards fluctuate. Don't rely on an out-of-date* Guide.

PORTHLEVEN Cornwall

map 1

▲ Critchards ⅝※

The Harbourside, Porthleven TR13 9JA	COOKING 2
TEL: (01326) 562407 FAX: (01326) 564444	COST £26–£49

Since 1990, the Critchards have run this one-time millhouse as a likeable harbourside restaurant specialising in seafood, much of it from the Newlyn boats. Raw materials may be local, but Jo Critchard takes a world view of fish cookery, pulling in ideas and ingredients from far and wide, and spelling them out on her menu, right down to the last grain of fragrant Thai rice. Reporters regularly endorse Russian-style ceviche of salmon and also 'perfectly cooked' sea bass with a light mint, vermouth and yoghurt sauce, but there is much more besides. Crab and avocado wrapped in a buckwheat and tomato crêpe and baked in a thermidor sauce was deemed 'deliciously interesting and unusual' while monkfish given New Orleans treatment with green peppers, a slug of Southern Comfort and caramelised oranges has been 'sublime'. Those not fancying fish could order steak or duck, while vegetarians have their own daily menu. 'Divine' Italian chocolate nut slice is one of many noteworthy desserts. Service is fine enough, but it's worth noting that Steve Critchard has an 'idiosyncratic system of only taking orders every 15 minutes', so there may be a wait. Forty wines cover affordable territory from Cornwall's Lizard Peninsula to Chile and California. House French is £10.95.

CHEF: Jo Critchard   PROPRIETORS: Steve and Jo Critchard   OPEN: Mon to Sat D only 6.30 to 9.30   MEALS: alc (main courses £11 to £28). Set D £16.95   SERVICE: not inc, card slips closed   CARDS: MasterCard, Switch, Visa   DETAILS: 44 seats. Private parties: 30 main room. Vegetarian meals. Children's helpings. No children under 6. No smoking in dining-room. Music   ACCOMMODATION: 2 rooms, both with bath/shower. TV. B&B £46 to £55. No children under 6   £5

PORTLOE Cornwall

map 1

▲ Tregain ⅝※ £

Portloe TR2 5QU	COOKING 2
TEL: (01872) 501252	COST £20–£39

The location is a classic Cornish fishing village in a rocky inlet on the high-cliffed coastal path: in other words, completely alluring but jam-packed with tourists in summer. The premises are tiny, but Clare Holdsworth somehow manages to combine 'tea room, shop and licensed restaurant' with the duties of the local post office. It is hardly surprising that service can be stretched at peak times, although most visitors are more than happy with the kitchen's output. Crab soup continues to win votes as a starter, while treacle puddings (note the plural) with clotted cream hold their own as the best-selling dessert. In between, the evening menu gives top billing to fish: a medley of bass, monkfish, halibut, sole, scallops and giant prawns with cream and herbs is one possible option. Otherwise, there are carnivorous alternatives in the shape of naturally reared fillet steak, or chicken breast with crème fraîche, spinach and air-dried ham, for example. Call in during the day, and you will find pasties, pizzas, ploughman's, sandwiches and all kinds of sweets on offer. House wine is £8.50.

CHEF/PROPRIETOR: Clare Holdsworth   OPEN: all week L 10 to 5.30, Mon to Sat D 7 to 8.30 CLOSED: Nov to Mar   MEALS: alc (main courses £4 to £14)   SERVICE: not inc, card slips closed CARDS: Delta, MasterCard, Switch, Visa   DETAILS: 22 seats. 12 seats outside. Private parties: 22 main room. Vegetarian meals. Children's helpings. No smoking in dining-room. Occasional music   ACCOMMODATION: 2 rooms. B&B £20 to £40. Children welcome. High teas for children. Baby facilities. Dogs welcome but not to be left alone in rooms. Afternoon teas

---

PORTREATH Cornwall   map 1

Tabb's £   NEW ENTRY

Tregea Terrace, Portreath TR16 4LD   COOKING 2
TEL/FAX: (01209) 842488   COST £17–£39

The setting is an old forge, a low stone building cunningly hidden away beneath a viaduct near the turn-off to the little harbour. Nigel and Melanie Tabb decamped here from London a few years ago (he used to work at Langan's Brasserie; see entry, London), hung some work by local artists on the walls, and set about refining what they call 'Gulf Stream cuisine' – which is one way of describing north Cornish crossover cooking. The handwritten menus embrace pigeon and mushroom fricassee with cardamom rice (a substantial starter, that), robust fish soup with a dash of chilli oil and Parmesan, and market-fresh fish such as gurnard in mustard and vermouth sauce. Seasonings are delicate but intelligently considered: a Chinese note giving aromatic lift to steamed monkfish, rosemary and garlic adding pungency to a provençale stew with rabbit. Finish with challengingly dense, black chocolate fudge cake or 'lusciously creamy' home-made ice-creams, such as ginger or tutti-frutti. The wine list confines itself to one or two from each region at mostly friendly prices. House French is £8.95.

CHEF: Nigel Tabb   PROPRIETORS: Melanie and Nigel Tabb   OPEN: Sun L 12.15 to 1.45, Wed to Mon D 7 to 9   CLOSED: 2 weeks Nov and Jan   MEALS: alc (main courses £9.50 to £14.50). Set L Sun £10.50, Set D £11.50 (2 courses) to £14.50   SERVICE: not inc, card slips closed   CARDS: Delta, MasterCard, Visa   DETAILS: 30 seats. Private parties: 30 main room. Vegetarian meals. Children's helpings. No pipes/cigars in dining room. Music   £5

POULTON-LE-FYLDE Lancashire   map 8

▲ *River House*

Skippool Creek, Thornton-le-Fylde,
Poulton-le-Fylde FY5 5LF
TEL: (01253) 883497   FAX: (01253) 892083
from roundabout junction of A585 and B5412 follow   COOKING 1
signs to Skippool Creek   COST £34–£57

'We have not changed and have no intention of doing so!' insists Bill Scott, whose family have been custodians of the River House for more than three decades. Its 'secret location', by the tidal estuary with mud channels, rickety wooden walkways and various moored boats, doubtless helps to explain the enduring appeal of this 'very traditionally British' house. Bill's cooking is rooted firmly in the world of chateaubriand with béarnaise, pork schnitzel, and roast pheasant with game sauce, although there are occasional quantum leaps into salmon teriyaki or chicken in chilli and red pepper sauce. Begin with soufflé suissesse or sauté chicken livers with brandy and marjoram sauce, and finish with Apfelstrudel, chocolate mousse laced with Grand Marnier, or Ticky Tacky Pudding (the original sticky toffee pud, first served here in 1958). A note on the wine list indicates that supplies may be erratic, but the choice is wide and it is easy to drink affordably. House wine is £12.50.

CHEF: Bill Scott   PROPRIETORS: Bill and Linda Scott   OPEN: Mon to Sat 12 to 2, 7.30 to 9.30 (booking essential)   CLOSED: 25 and 26 Dec, 1 Jan   MEALS: alc (main courses £16 to £20). Set L and D £25   SERVICE: not inc   CARDS: Delta, MasterCard, Switch, Visa   DETAILS: 40 seats. Private parties: 40 main room, 14 private room. Car park. Children's helpings. No children under 7. Music   ACCOMMODATION: 4 rooms, all with bath/shower. TV. Phone. B&B £65 to £80. Children welcome (*The Which? Hotel Guide*)   (£5)

POWERSTOCK Dorset   map 2

Three Horseshoes ✸✶ £ | NEW ENTRY |

Powerstock DT6 3TF
TEL: (01308) 485328   COOKING 1
off A3066 at Gore Cross, 4m NE of Bridport   COST £25–£40

After some 12 years at the helm of this Dorset grey-stone pub, the Fergusons departed and handed over control and ownership to Mark and Sue Johnson. Reach the Three Horseshoes down winding lanes deep in Thomas Hardy's 'Wessex': the views are described as 'stunning'. Powerstock is only six miles from the sea, and daily blackboard menus are dominated by what the local day boats can provide. Simplicity is the key. Cornish scallops are grilled and served bathed in melted butter, hake is baked and 'smothered' in a colourful provençale sauce, while monkfish might come with salsa. Away from the sea, there is meat and game aplenty: pigeon breasts might be wrapped in bacon and served with a potent green peppercorn sauce, while sirloin steak could be given a dose of garlic. Desserts range from decent ice-creams and sorbets to bread-and-butter pudding glazed with honey. Staff are keen, reliable and well informed. Real ales are kept in good order and there are some workmanlike wines to be supped. House Australian is £8.20.

CHEFS: Mark Johnson and Ashley Stones   PROPRIETORS: Mark and Sue Johnson   OPEN: all week 12 to 2 (3 Sat and Sun), 7 to 9.30 (10 Sat)   CLOSED: 24 Dec D, 25 Dec L   MEALS: alc (main courses £10 to £14). Bar menu available   SERVICE: not inc, card slips closed   CARDS: Delta, MasterCard, Switch, Visa   DETAILS: 60 seats. 30 seats outside. Private parties: 50 main room, 20 private room. Car park. Vegetarian meals. Children welcome in restaurant. Children's helpings. No smoking in dining-room. Wheelchair access (also WC). No music

---

The 2000 Guide *will be published before Christmas 1999. Reports on meals are most welcome at any time of the year, but are particularly valuable in the spring (no later than June). Send them to* The Good Food Guide, *FREEPOST, 2 Marylebone Road, London NW1 1YN. Or email your report to guidereports@which.co.uk.*

PRESTBURY Cheshire   map 8

▲ *White House*

New Road, Prestbury SK10 4DG
TEL: (01625) 829376 FAX: (01625) 828627   COOKING 2
on A538, 4m N of Macclesfield   COST £23–£62

The setting is rural Cheshire at its prettiest, the White House a stylishly
decorated venue with a bright dining-room and conservatory extension at the
back. The style heads for the last word in trend-conscious internationalism:
griddled scallops with pak choi on a melon and ginger salsa, 'superb and
well-cooked' sea bass with a tomato and fennel compote, or shank of local lamb
glazed in hoisin and served with sweet potato mash, for example. Chocolate
galaxy comes not in a foil wrapper from the corner shop, but is an assiette of
delights that takes in parfait, pudding and ice-cream. Smartly attired staff bring
it all forth with commendable warmth and promptitude. French house wine is
£12.50, and ten wines are available by the glass at £2.25–£3.95.

CHEFS: Ryland Wakeham and Mark Cunniffe PROPRIETORS: Ryland and Judith Wakeham
OPEN: Tue to Sun L 12 to 2, Mon to Sat D 7 to 10 CLOSED: 25 Dec MEALS: alc (main courses
£10.50 to £17). Set L £12.95, Set D Mon to Fri £14.95 (2 courses) to £17.95. Bar menu Tue to Sat
L SERVICE: not inc, card slips closed CARDS: Amex, Delta, Diners, MasterCard, Switch, Visa
DETAILS: 80 seats. 12 seats outside. Private parties: 120 main room, 6 to 40 private rooms. Car
park. Vegetarian meals. Children's helpings. Wheelchair access (1 step; not WC). Music
ACCOMMODATION: 11 rooms, all with bath/shower. TV. Phone. Room only £70 to £120. No
children under 12. No dogs (*The Which? Hotel Guide*)

PRESTON Lancashire   map 8

Heathcote's Brasserie

23 Winckley Square, Preston PR1 3JJ
TEL: (01772) 252732 FAX: (01772) 203433   COOKING 4
EMAIL: heathcotes.co.uk   COST £20–£48

The Preston arm of Paul Heathcote's manifold operations occupies a stolid
Victorian town house, but behind the frosted glass, a streamlined modern room
has high-gloss floors, white Philippe Starck chairs, and background jazz to
emphasise the laid-back feel. Jamie Holland, who took over the role of head chef
in 1998, produces sound brasserie dishes using impeccably sourced materials,
some of them local. The effort to refine or extend recognisably northern dishes – a
Heathcote trade mark – stops short of pretension. 'Moist and fresh-tasting' cod
hotpot comes with buttered cabbage and a meat stock sauce; deep-fried spiced
sole comes with chips and hummus; while rabbit is stuffed with black pudding
and pork sausage, and sauced with walnuts and red wine.

Bread-and-butter pudding may arrive with anything from orange custard to
raspberry coulis, and for urban modernists there's poached pear with liquorice
and thyme sorbet. Breads and coffee are suitably classy, and service was
'superior' for one reporter, 'too speedy' for another. Downstairs, a seafood and
rotisserie bar does cheaper snacks. Everything on the wine list is available by the
125ml glass, allowing you to mix and match at will, France taking its place

unassumingly among the Mexicans and Tasmanians. Prices start at £11 a bottle, £2 a glass, for house wines from the Loire.

CHEF: Jamie Holland   PROPRIETOR: Paul Heathcote   OPEN: all week 12 (12.30 Sun) to 2.30, 7 (6 Sat and Sun) to 10.30 (9.30 Sun)   CLOSED: 25 Dec, 1 Jan   MEALS: alc (main courses £9 to £16). Set L Mon to Sat (Menu Rapide) £8.95 (2 courses) to £10.95. Set L Sun £13.50. Seafood and rotisserie menu Mon to Fri and Sat L. BYO (Mon only) £1   SERVICE: 10% (optional), card slips closed   CARDS: Amex, Delta, MasterCard, Switch, Visa   DETAILS: 90 seats. Private parties: 90 main room, 60 private room. Vegetarian meals. Children's helpings. No cigars/pipes in dining-room. Wheelchair access (2 steps; not WC). Music. Air-conditioned   £5

PULBOROUGH   West Sussex   map 3

Stane Street Hollow ❦ ✱✖

Codmore Hill, Pulborough RH20 1BG
TEL: (01798) 872819   COOKING 2
on A29, 1½m NE of Pulborough   COST £26–£48

René and Ann Kaiser moved into this beguiling cottage of Bargate stone in 1975. More than two decades later they still work hard, offering seasonal French cooking in a 'folksy-pretty' setting of low, beamed ceilings, candles and fresh flowers. Ann Kaiser works valiantly out front, while her husband holds sway in the kitchen. Menus – written in French with English translations – change from month to month, and the cooking seems to follow its own well-tried path unswayed by most current trends. In March you might begin with spicy parsnip soup or a warm salad of duck, bacon and lentils, before moving on to, say, sauté lambs' sweetbreads on creamed spinach and young nettles with Madeira sauce. Alternatives might include marinated chicken breast with lemon and cream sauce, or linzen knödels: lentil dumplings topped with Raclette cheese, no doubt a nostalgic tribute to René's native Switzerland. Desserts take in everything from flashy profiteroles to tiramisù. The carefully constructed, eclectic wine list manages to keep prices below £20 except when it moves on to the finer French bins. Swiss wines in all three colours keep the home flag flying. French 'open' table wines are £12 a litre. CELLARMAN'S CHOICE: Pinot d'Alsace 1995, Dom. Zind-Humbrecht, £15.50; Mercurey 1995, Ch. Phillipe le Hardi, £18.

CHEF: René Kaiser   PROPRIETORS: René and Ann Kaiser   OPEN: Wed to Fri and Sun L 12.30 to 1.15, Wed to Sat D 7.30 to 9.30   CLOSED: 24 Dec to 6 Jan   MEALS: alc (main courses £11 to £14). Set L Wed to Fri £12.50 (2 courses) to £15.50, Set L Sun £15.50 (2 courses) to £18.50   SERVICE: not inc, card slips closed   CARDS: Delta, MasterCard, Switch, Visa   DETAILS: 34 seats. Private parties: 20 main room, 14 and 20 private rooms. Car park. Vegetarian meals. Children's helpings. No smoking in dining-room. Wheelchair access (3 steps; not WC). No music

---

The text of entries is based on unsolicited reports sent in by readers, backed up by inspections conducted anonymously. The factual details under the text are from questionnaires the Guide sends to all restaurants that feature in the book.

All entries, including Round-ups, are fully indexed at the back of the Guide.

Village Restaurant ▮ ⌇✳

16–18 Market Place, Ramsbottom BL0 9HT
TEL: (01706) 825070   FAX: (01706) 822005
EMAIL: rammy.vics@which.net   COOKING 5
off A56/M66, 4m N of Bury   COST £15–£35

Ros Hunter and Chris Johnson have been running their highly idiosyncratic
north-Manchester restaurant for 14 years now. There have been tweaks and
reassessments along the way, changes of tone and format, but the backbone of
the operation – an unswerving commitment to quality organic produce cooked
sensitively, and served at fixed times only – remains firm. They have their loyal
regulars, and also first-timers who come away feeling it is like dining at the
house of friends who are capable and enthusiastic cooks and also knowledgeable about wines.

You may not expect to sit on church pews when eating with friends, but
nothing is quite ordinary here. Dinner is a four-course affair with a choice only at
the end. A typical menu in late May kicked off with Cheshire asparagus, went on
to a soup of Jerusalem artichokes, and then roast strip-loin of Pennine beef with
seasonal vegetables. Pudding options were ricotta cheesecake, sticky toffee, or
fresh fruits with tayberry ice-cream, or cheese. A willingness to try out new ideas
produced a mozzarella salad with fiery chilli dressing one October night, and a
Japanese seafood salad in spring. Supplementary helpings of both meat and veg
are liberally offered at no extra cost. Cumbrian ham, free-range corn-fed chicken
without antibiotics, good thick yoghurt to offset the sweetness of toffee pudding,
and an excellent creme brulée are among the citations in readers' letters. Ros
Hunter cooks entirely without salt, which provides its own kind of fascination.

A monthly-changing eclectic list of two dozen wines is presented in the
restaurant, but you are also invited to browse around the basement shop where
several hundred wines are stocked. A corkage charge of £5 for ordinary wines, or
£9 for fine wines (those costing £15 or more) will be added to the retail price. A
similar 'corkage' system is applied to beers and ciders if you can't find something
to tickle your fancy among the 80-plus wines listed upstairs. House French is £9
a bottle, £2 a glass.

CHEF: Ros Hunter   PROPRIETORS: Ros Hunter and Chris Johnson   OPEN: Wed to Fri L 12.45 (1
sitting), Sat L 12 and 2 (2 sittings), Sun L 1 and 3 (2 sittings), Wed to Sat D 8 (1 sitting)   MEALS:
Set L £6.50 (2 courses) to £9.50, Set D £19.50 to £26.50, Set D Sat £24.50   SERVICE: not inc,
card slips closed   CARDS: Amex, Delta, Diners, MasterCard, Switch, Visa   DETAILS: 40 seats.
Private parties: 30 main room, 10 and 30 private rooms. Vegetarian meals. Children welcome.
No smoking in dining-room. Music   £5

New main entries and restaurant closures are listed near the front of the book.

See inside the front cover for an explanation of the symbols used at the tops of entries.

The Good Food Guide *is a registered trade mark of Which? Ltd.*

RAMSGILL   North Yorkshire   map 8

▲ *Yorke Arms* ❀ £   **NEW ENTRY**

Ramsgill, nr Pateley Bridge HG3 5RL   COOKING 6
TEL/FAX: (01423) 755243   COST £25–£54

Gerald and Frances Atkins make a welcome return to the *Guide* after their last
main-entry appearance at Shaw's in London a couple of years ago. They have
chosen a tiny village – largely renovated in the mid-nineteenth century –
surrounded by moorland, near How Stean Gorge and the twitcher's paradise that
is Gouthwaite Reservoir. Fronting the green and covered in Virginia creeper, the
house is 'well maintained, but without pretension'. Thick walls, flagstoned
floors and bare wooden tables set the scene for some 'really accomplished
cooking' that is more cosmopolitan than in many a country inn, taking in
Thai-spiced fish-cakes, a salad of black pudding with poached egg, and
sweet-and-sour braised duck with oriental vegetables.

While the food has already taken root in Nidderdale lamb pie, and Yorkshire
ham and eggs with sauté potatoes, there are no concessions when it comes to
cooking. 'At last, somebody in Yorkshire knows what to do with tuna,' ventured
one visitor, obviously pleased to find it quickly seared and pink inside, served
with a herb-flecked sauce, a pile of rocket leaves and a few thin slivers of pear.
The combination of first-rate ingredients, accurate timing and typical Yorkshire
generosity was evident in a simply conceived September dish of 'three or four'
pink-roast grouse breasts, served with a few bilberries, a slice of brioche, and a
well-reduced game sauce. Daily specials add to the variety, residents get their
own set-price menu, and desserts have included a wedge of light custard tart
with raspberry sorbet. 'Open, honest' service is welcome for its lack of stuffiness,
and some 60 wines take their commitment to good value seriously, starting with
house French at £9.95.

CHEF: Frances Atkins   PROPRIETORS: Gerald and Frances Atkins   OPEN: all week L 12 to 2, Mon
to Sat D 7 to 9 (residents only Sun D)   MEALS: alc (main courses £6.50 to £14). Set D (residents
only) £25   SERVICE: not inc   CARDS: Amex, Delta, MasterCard, Switch, Visa   DETAILS: 80
seats. 60 seats outside. Private parties: 40 main room. Car park. Vegetarian meals. Children
welcome. No smoking in dining-room. Music   ACCOMMODATION: 14 rooms, all with
bath/shower. TV. Phone. B&B £50 to £130. Children welcome. Afternoon teas

---

REDMILE   Leicestershire   map 5

▲ *Peacock Inn* ❀   **NEW ENTRY**

Church Corner, Redmile NG13 0GA
TEL: (01949) 842554   FAX: (01949) 843746   COOKING 3
off A52, 7m W of Grantham   COST £28–£47

Redmile isn't too far from both the M1 and the A1, but far enough to be a picture
of bucolic tranquillity. The Peacock fits it like a glove, a traditional English
country inn, comfortably furnished in modern style with two restaurants, one a
large airy conservatory leading out to a patio-type garden, with tables for eating
outside in fine weather. There isn't much sense of pub tradition about the menus,
however, unless calf's liver on mash with onion gravy comes into that category.

For the rest, the full-dress Mediterranean/Asian mode comes into play, and Ross Barrett performs with considerable panache. Thai-spiced mussels steamed in coconut milk and coriander is a generous bowl of plump shellfish with unrestrained authentic seasonings, or there might be coarse-textured rabbit and pork terrine with sharp apple chutney.

The range of choice may appear dauntingly broad, and yet nothing fell short of the mark at inspection. Duck breast marinated in Chinese spices appeared with a 'loud and fruity' chunky citrus jam containing whole kumquats. Salmon escalope sauced with pink peppercorns and whisky indicates the scope and ambition with fish, as does seared turbot with saffron noodles, baby lobster tails and asparagus in white wine sauce. Milk chocolate mille-feuille filled with vanilla mousse or copybook toffee pudding with butterscotch sauce are among dessert possibilities. French waiting staff are highly commended. The compact wine list sources from Western Europe and the southern hemisphere, with prices kept well in check. House wines start from £8.50

CHEF: Ross Barrett   PROPRIETORS: Colin and Celia Crawford   OPEN: Mon to Sat 12 to 2, 7 to 9.30, Sun 12 to 9.30   MEALS: alc (main courses £9 to £15). Bar menu L   SERVICE: not inc   CARDS: Delta, MasterCard, Switch, Visa   DETAILS: 165 seats. 50 seats outside. Private parties: 70 main room, 35 private room. Car park. Vegetarian meals. Children's helpings. No smoking in 1 dining-room. Wheelchair access (also WC). Music   ACCOMMODATION: 8 rooms, all with bath/shower. TV. Phone. B&B £75 to £90. Children welcome. Baby facilities. No dogs (*The Which? Hotel Guide*)

REIGATE Surrey   map 3

Dining Room ⁵✳

59A High Street, Reigate RH2 9AE   COOKING 6
TEL: (01737) 226650   COST £23–£60

Abstract paintings of food decorate the cream-coloured walls of this first floor L-shaped room. The bright, inventive style brings together British comfort food, a few Mediterranean splashes, and some spicy Far Eastern flavours, though not always in the same dish. A sense of individual identity remains, whatever the context: in a tartlet of roasted Mediterranean vegetables with goats' cheese, for example, in tandoori swordfish brochettes, or in seared calf's liver with sticky cheese and bacon mash. Other versions of mash have included a sprout and bacon partnership served with guinea-fowl ('innovative and quite exciting'), while first-course salads on the fixed-price menu have combined black pudding, bacon and poached egg, and warm chorizo with smoked haddock.

Marinating, honey-roasting, and pesto-crusting are among the main-course treatments, while fillet of beef has been rolled in morel dust (one of this year's more fashionable sprinkles) and served with truffled scrambled eggs. Crisply seared, moist scallops come highly recommended, and some of the sharpest flavours seem to be reserved for fish, taking in spiced red mullet soup, crab-cakes with a hot and sweet sauce, and Thai-style casserole of lobster with lemon grass and coconut. The last two flavourings also appear at dessert stage, in a sorbet to accompany a passion-fruit mousse; otherwise there might be a twice-baked chocolate soufflé with a fondant centre and white chocolate sauce.

451

Service has divided reporters: 'some of the nicest waiters I have come across' according to one, 'aloof and arrogant' for another. Problems can be compounded by language difficulties. The restaurant's claim not to set a time limit on tables is challenged by one reporter, and other niggles relate to vegetarian choice, charges for vegetables as a separate item, and for extra coffee, both of which can bump up the bill. A short wine list stretches from house French at £9.50 to Acacia Pinot Noir at just over £20, with an even shorter list of fine bottles for bigger spenders.

CHEFS: Anthony Tobin and Nathan Darling   PROPRIETOR: Paul Montalto   OPEN: Mon to Fri L 12 to 2, Mon to Sat D 7 to 10.30   CLOSED: 1 week Christmas, 1 week Easter, 2 weeks summer   MEALS: alc (main courses £15 to £22). Set L £10 (2 courses) to £13.50, Set D Mon to Thur £14.95, Set D Fri and Sat £16.95   SERVICE: not inc   CARDS: Amex, MasterCard, Switch, Visa   DETAILS: 50 seats. Private parties: 40 main room. Vegetarian meals. Children's helpings. No smoking in 1 dining-room. Music. Air-conditioned   (£5)

RICHMOND Surrey   map 3

Burnt Chair ▼

5 Duke Street, Richmond TW9 1HP	COOKING 3
TEL: (0181) 940 9488 FAX: (0181) 940 7879	COST £31–£50

'After an electrifying *Dream of Gerontius* at Tiffins School, we adjourned here for more earthly sustenance,' noted one correspondent; others come from nearby Richmond Theatre to sample modern international cooking in a setting of unmatching chairs and colourful glass bottles. Organically reared 'wild' Devon beef remains a highlight on the monthly *carte*: it might be grilled and served with horseradish potato cake and a mustard reduction or be teamed up with 'pomme boudin noir', for example. Piscophiles have praised Thai fish soup, while vegetarians have been pleased with grilled tikka vegetables served with a tower of baby poppadoms 'cemented' with rice. Elsewhere, there has been a chorus of approval for exotic sounding duck breast with a stuffed fig and watermelon pickle, as well as lamb cutlets 'cut Barnsley-chop style', boned and stuffed with a lamb forcemeat. To finish, the assiette of sherbets is an intriguing palate cleanser; otherwise the choice of desserts might extend to chocolate brownie with candied orange ice-cream, or coconut parfait with tropical fruits scented with lemon grass. Owner Weenson Oo ensures that 'the feel-good factor' is much in evidence and is keen to treat his guests as future friends.

Refreshingly, menus are tailored to suit the wine list, the main focus of which is Burgundy and North America. Mr Oo's enthusiasm for these regions comes over loud and clear: the selections are highly astute and the accompanying tasting notes very knowledgeable. House vin de pays is £9.75. CELLARMAN'S CHOICE: Stonegate Winery Sauvignon Blanc 1996, Napa Valley, California, £25; Qupé Syrah 1995, Santa Barbara, California, £20.

CHEF/PROPRIETOR: Weenson Oo   OPEN: Mon to Sat D only 6 to 11   CLOSED: 1 week Christmas, bank hols, 10 days Aug   MEALS: alc (main courses £10 to £14). Set D 6 to 7.30 (7 Sat) £15 (2 courses). Cover £1   SERVICE: not inc   CARDS: Delta, MasterCard, Switch, Visa   DETAILS: 36 seats. Private parties: 36 main room. Vegetarian meals. Children's helpings. Smoking restricted till 10.30pm. Wheelchair access (not WC). Music   (£5)

Chez Lindsay £

11 Hill Rise, Richmond TW10 6UA	COOKING 2
TEL: (0181) 948 7473	COST £16–£54

Springtime colours and windows overlooking the Thames make this a pleasant Breton outpost for Richmond Brits seeking seafood, galettes and crêpes (pancakes, savoury and sweet). The galettes are available all day, with fillings to rival pizza toppings in number, including every conceivable combination of ham, cheese, tomato, egg, onion, mushroom, andouille and mustard sauce. At lunch-time and in the evening the menu expands, with aquaria of molluscs and crustacea served as assiettes, or even larger plateaux de fruits de mer. 'Mousse-like' salmon terrine with a minty tomato coulis, moules á la St Malo, and melted Camembert with scallops, langoustines and sliced potatoes, are all praised by reporters, along with a few meat and poultry dishes. For dessert, there are crêpes with apples and caramel sauce, or banana and chocolate sauce, for example. Drink Breton or Normandie cider, or wine from a short all-French list, which includes (according to the list) the deep-southern French provinces of Espagne and Australie!

CHEFS: Lindsay Wotton and Moise Diabate   PROPRIETOR: Lindsay Wotton   OPEN: Mon to Sat 11 to 3, 6 to 11, Sun 12 to 10   CLOSED: 25 Dec   MEALS: alc (main courses £4.50 to £17.50). Set L Mon to Sat £4.99 (2 courses), Set L and D Sun to Fri £9.99. Snack menu (salads, galettes, crêpes) available 11 to 12, 2.30 to 6 Mon to Sat and all day Sun   SERVICE: not inc   CARDS: Delta, MasterCard, Switch, Visa   DETAILS: 48 seats. Private parties: 50 main room, 36 private room. Children's helpings on request. No cigars/pipes while others eat. Wheelchair access (not WC). Music   £5

RIDGEWAY Derbyshire	map 9

Old Vicarage ♚ ⁂

Ridgeway Moor, Ridgeway S12 3XW	
TEL: (0114) 247 5814 FAX: (0114) 247 7079	
EMAIL: eat@theoldvicarage.co.uk	COOKING 6
off A616, on B6054 nearly opposite village church	COST £43–£67

Described as 'a comforting country house without pretension', this attractive old building works on a 'small, quiet' scale. It can feel a bit formal, lounge space is at a premium on busy nights, and there is so much vegetation in the candlelit conservatory it can feel 'like eating in the rain forest' but, as soon as canapés and an appetiser arrive, attention is firmly focused on the food. The menu is short, varied and full of interest, combining some classic European ideas with a few oriental and sometimes innovative flavours, especially when it comes to seafood: baked fillet of cod with a gremolata crust and anise-flavoured rhubarb sauce, or skewered, chargrilled scallops 'nicely browned, very fresh, very firm, well flavoured', served on coconut and basil rice with mango relish.

Materials are first-rate, and the kitchen has produced some 'faultless' dishes, among them 'brilliant, slow roast, tender' duck leg, and crisp-skinned breast, served on a bed of juniper-flavoured leeks with 'no sauce', or wild boar, tasting 'like pork should taste but never does', with a sage and thyme crust, served with two types of cabbage: crisp green and caramelised red. What struck an inspector, however, and half the reporters this year, was that, despite all the effort, precision and careful construction, dishes lacked the excitement of a real punch of flavour. But there are still highlights, not least a plate of 'oozing' cheeses, 'light as a feather' lemon soufflé, and a trio of strawberry desserts: soufflé, sorbet and tart.

'Friendly and attentive' Tessa Bramley oversees ordering and billing, but service from her uniformed team has not always been as organised or informed as reporters expect. Wines number just under 100 (plus 20 halves) and have been chosen to complement the style of cuisine. Some fine clarets, burgundies and old Alsace wines lend a touch of class to proceedings, and while prices are not low – house wines start at £16 – they do reflect the overall quality. CELLARMAN'S CHOICE: Franciscan Oakville Estate Chardonnay 1994, Napa Valley, California, £36; Amarone della Valpolicella 1994, Masi, £34.

CHEFS: Tessa Bramley, Nathan Smith and Andrew Gilbert   PROPRIETOR: The Old Vicarage (Ridgeway) Ltd   OPEN: Tue to Fri and Sun L 12.30 to 2.30, Tue to Sat D 7 to 10 (10.30 Sat) CLOSED: 26 and 31 Dec, 1 Jan   MEALS: Set D Tue to Fri £29 to £40, Set D Sat £40   SERVICE: not inc, card slips closed   CARDS: Amex, Delta, Diners, MasterCard, Switch, Visa   DETAILS: 50 seats. 20 seats outside. Private parties: 48 main room, 28 private room. Car park. Vegetarian meals. Children's helpings. No smoking in dining-room. Wheelchair access (3 steps; not WC). No music   £5

RIPLEY   North Yorkshire   map 9

▲ Boar's Head ♥ ✸

Ripley HG3 3HY
TEL: (01423) 771888   FAX: (01423) 771509   COOKING 4
EMAIL: boarshead@ripleycastle.co.uk   COST £26–£59

The village consists of one short street, plus a church, car park and castle, and might as well be called Ingilby, after the castle's owners, so omnipresent is the family and its works. They have shaped Ripley over the centuries, favouring cobbles and small shops, keeping the tackier tourist elements at bay, and making a go of the Boar's Head. Bar meals are served in the courtyard on sunny days, while the restaurant's preoccupation is with generally comforting dishes: from pot au feu or terrine of wild boar (the estate is a handy source of game), to warm tartlet of Finnan haddock with poached egg.

Novel touches have included an orange sauce with risotto, and a tomato sauce flecked with couscous to accompany seared tuna, and although timing (of fish, for example) is more approximate than it should be, the kitchen is well enough organised to serve a side dish of ten vegetables, and 14 different items (some tropical) in an 'assiette of seasonal fruits'. Roasted peach or poached pear ('all elements successful and attractively presented') might be among the alternatives. Wine service has on occasion left something to be desired, but the wines themselves tend to make up for this. Some 200 realistically priced bins offer a good range of winemaking styles from around the world, beginning with a seasonal selection of house wines at £9.95 and above. CELLARMAN'S CHOICE: Palliser Estate Sauvignon Blanc 1997, Martinborough, New Zealand, £17; Côtes du Lubéron, Ch. Val Joanis Rouge 1994, £11.

CHEF: Steven Chesnutt   PROPRIETORs: Sir Thomas and Lady Emma Ingilby   OPEN: all week 12 to 1.45, 7 to 9.30   MEALS: Set L Mon to Sat £13.50 (2 courses) to £17.50, Set L Sun £14.95, Set D £27.50 to £36. Bar menu available all week L and D   SERVICE: not inc, card slips closed   CARDS: Amex, Diners, MasterCard, Switch, Visa   DETAILS: 40 seats. 60 seats outside. Private parties: 30 main room. Car park. Vegetarian meals. Children's helpings. No children under 10. No smoking in 1 dining-room. No cigars/pipes in dining room. Wheelchair access (also WC). Music   ACCOMMODATION: 25 rooms, all with bath/shower. TV. Phone. B&B £90 to £125. Rooms for disabled. No children under 10. Baby facilities. No dogs in public rooms. Afternoon teas. Garden. Fishing (*The Which? Hotel Guide*)

RIPLEY Surrey   map 3

Michels'

13 High Street, Ripley GU23 6AQ
TEL: (01483) 224777   FAX: (01483) 222940   COOKING 6
off A3, 4m SW of Cobham   COST £31–£70

This imposing Georgian building is decorated with modern paintings, some 'weird' lamps, and what one visitor described as 'auntie' furniture: old but not quite antique. Erik Michel is 'a natural chef' who gives his first-class ingredients a contemporary European spin: in an Italianate 'terrine' of roast red pepper and aubergine with soft white goats' cheese in a green pasta envelope, or a chunk of home-smoked sea bass, 'immaculately' roasted, with braised fennel and a light cream sauce.

The food combines a few earthy touches such as black pudding or pig's trotter with more luxurious items, perhaps a starter of whole small lobster, served with baby artichokes and 'brilliantly emerald' skinned broad beans in a balsamic dressing. But this is not pretentious cooking, just accomplished, as in a 'masterpiece' of pink pigeon breast with wild mushrooms in a pastry 'pan', napped with garlic sauce; or in 'rosy roundels' of roast English lamb served with mash that was 'wickedly full of forbiddens', including Brie, olive oil and butter, 'and I think there was some potato there too'. If the *carte* tends to be expensive, dinner offers two four-course alternatives, neither with any choice, one of them including wines by the glass.

Cheeses have not always been in tip-top condition, and desserts are not usually the highlight. They tend to be fruity: passion-fruit tart with a confit of strawberries, or orange and grapefruit roasted with honey, served with mandarin sorbet and lemon syllabub. 'Well-trained' service has been known to start off cool but then warm up later. A few New World wines join the aristocratic French assembly, and nine house wines under £15 help to lighten the burden, starting at £9.50.

CHEF: Erik Michel   PROPRIETORS: Erik and Karen Michel   OPEN: Tue to Fri and Sun L 12.30 to 1.30, Tue to Sat D 7.30 to 9 (7 to 9.30 Sat)   CLOSED: early Jan   MEALS: alc (main courses £20 to £22). Set L £21, Set D Tue to Fri £23 to £30 (inc wine)   SERVICE: not inc   CARDS: Amex, Delta, Diners, MasterCard, Switch, Visa   DETAILS: 50 seats. Private parties: 12 main room, 12 private room. Car park. No smoking while others eat. Children welcome Sun L only. Wheelchair access (2 steps; not WC). No music

ROADE Northamptonshire

map 5

▲ *Roade House* ✸

16 High Street, Roade NN7 2NW
TEL: (01604) 863372   FAX: (01604) 862421   COOKING 5
off A508, 4m S of Northampton   COST £22–£41

After extensive refurbishment, with six bedrooms and more in the pipeline, the Roade House has a new identity. A welcoming entrance, a spacious bar with a real fire, and seven-days-a-week opening are part of its re-branding as a hotel, but alterations have not changed the 'pleasant, friendly feel' of the place. Sue Kewley is 'her usual alert knowledgeable self', welcoming and taking orders in the bar, supported by efficient help from mostly young girls in the dining-room. Lunch is a good-value set-price deal, dinner à la carte only, with service included as before.

The food has a comforting appeal, in pâté of duck foie gras, blinis with smoked salmon, or poached egg on brioche toast with mushrooms, and good materials have included smoked haddock in a moulded tower with waxy potatoes, fillet of John Dory with mussels in an 'intensely flavoured' cream sauce, and belly pork braised with ginger and soy as a first course. Acidity points up a number of items – raspberry vinegar with marinated salmon fillets, balsamic vinegar with a 'good thick piece' of pink calf's liver in a dark sauce with diced beetroot – but some dishes might benefit from a sharper focus, and vegetables still appear on side plates, correctly cooked but seeming, at least to one reporter, more anachronistic with every year that passes. Cheeses have included a collation of Dunsyre, Coverdale, Stilton and Sharpham, and among desserts the 'rich yet not cloying' chocolate mousse cake stands out. A fairly priced predominantly European list starts with a quartet of house wines at £10.

CHEFS: Christopher Kewley and Steven Barnes   PROPRIETORS: Christopher and Susan Kewley   OPEN: Tue to Fri and Sun L 12.30 to 2, Mon to Sat D 7 to 9.30   MEALS: alc (main courses £12.50 to £17). Set L £12.50 (2 courses) to £15, Set Sun L £16.50. BYO £7   SERVICE: net prices, card slips closed   CARDS: Amex, MasterCard, Switch, Visa   DETAILS: 50 seats. 8 seats outside. Private parties: 50 main room. Car park. Children's helpings. No smoking in dining-room. Wheelchair access (1 step; also WC). No music. Air-conditioned ACCOMMODATION: 6 rooms with bath/shower. TV. Phone. B&B £50 to £86. Rooms for disabled. Children welcome. High teas for children with prior notice. Baby facilities.

ROCHDALE Greater Manchester

map 8

After Eight ✸

NEW ENTRY

2 Edenfield Road, Rochdale OL11 5AA   COOKING 4
TEL: (01706) 646432   COST £26–£40

The origin of the name may seem something of a mystery, since not only may early-birds eat at seven, but nor will you get a chocolate mint in a paper envelope with your coffee. It's worth stressing that latter point since the Taylors pride themselves on making as much as possible of what they serve in-house, a practice that extends to petits fours as well as puff pastry and ice-creams. The building that it's all made in is a substantial stone house, with wrought-iron gate and a small garden close to the town centre. Buttoned-leather armchairs and bottle-bottom window panes lend the place an air of old-world comfort.

Geoff Taylor's aim is to offer the best of north-west produce at value-for-money prices. Fish from Fleetwood, suckling pig from Garstang, champion black puddings and wild elderberries picked nearby to go with venison are among the guiding lights of the kitchen. Technique is highly assured, bringing a lighter touch to classical ways, so that a scallop complete with its coral encased in puff pastry and sauced with hollandaise is a triumph of judgement, while poached turbot fillet with warm niçoise salad allows all its flavours to shine through, including that of the 'very fresh' fish. Noisettes of spring lamb, 'moist, pink and full of young flavour', come 'beautifully complemented' by purée asparagus to make a fine seasonal dish. The kitchen is especially proud of the copious side-plates of vegetables, which come with a small herb soufflé on a pastry base. Baking skills are much in evidence among puddings, too – perhaps in the form of a raspberry sablé that uses crushed hazelnut biscuits and comes with a powerful strawberry coulis – or there may be tiramisù torte or lime cheesecake. Vegetarians have their own menu to choose from. Although this is essentially a two-handed operation, reports attest that 'everything runs like clockwork'. Concise selections from most of the world's major wine regions come at prices that will gladden the heart. House French is £8.90.

CHEF: G.P. Taylor PROPRIETORS: G.P. and A. Taylor OPEN: Tue to Sat D only 7 to 9.30 CLOSED: 25 and 26 Dec, 1 Jan MEALS: alc (main courses £11 to £15) SERVICE: not inc CARDS: Amex, Delta, MasterCard, Switch, Visa DETAILS: 45 seats. Private parties: 30 main room, 15 and 30 private rooms. Vegetarian meals. Children's helpings. No smoking in dining-room. Music (£5)

ROMALDKIRK Co Durham   map 10

▲ *Rose & Crown* ⁵⚒

Romaldkirk DL12 9EB
TEL: (01833) 650213 FAX: (01833) 650828
EMAIL: rcrown@globalnet.co.uk   COOKING 1
on B6277, 6m NW of Barnard Castle   COST £32–£38

Visitors appreciate the warm welcome and traditional Englishness of this old village inn. It is 'one of the most hospitable bars imaginable', with an enormous stone fireplace, comfortable sofas and old mahogany-topped cast-iron pub tables. Four-course dinners 'with ample choice at each stage' might open with a gratin of 'sweet, plump, lightly cooked' scallops with vegetable tagliatelle, followed by 'well-made' fennel, tomato and orange soup, then pan-fried calf's liver with green peppercorns, onion marmalade and parsley noodles. At inspection an 'attractively presented' sauté pheasant breast came with rillettes of leg with 'velvety, creamy texture' and a sauce of oloroso sherry. Finish with crème caramel and spiced apricot compote, hot apple tart with calvados ice-cream, or a selection of British cheeses. Sunday lunch is a traditional affair, including roast leg of Yorkshire ham and rib of British beef. Service is friendly, attentive and helpful, and more than

120 wines include a wide-ranging New World section at reasonable prices. House Chilean is £9.50.

CHEFS: Christopher Davy and Dawn Stephenson PROPRIETORS: Christopher and Alison Davy OPEN: Sun L 12 to 1.30, Mon to Sat D 7.30 to 9 CLOSED: 24 to 26 Dec MEALS: Set L £12.95, Set D £24 SERVICE: not inc, card slips closed CARDS: MasterCard, Switch, Visa DETAILS: 24 seats. Private parties: 30 main room. Car park. Children's helpings. No children under 6 at D. No smoking in dining-room. No music ACCOMMODATION: 12 rooms, all with bath/shower. TV. Phone. B&B £60 to £90. Rooms for disabled. Children welcome. High teas for children. Dogs welcome in bedrooms only. Afternoon teas (*The Which? Hotel Guide*) £5

ROMSEY Hampshire map 2

Old Manor House 🍾

21 Palmerston Street, Romsey SO51 8GF COOKING 6
TEL: (01794) 517353 COST £33–£51

The wizened house of red brick and timber is a decidedly civilised place for a restaurant. Take drinks in a small lounge with a big fireplace before proceeding to one of the two dining-rooms, where fine china and handsome glassware reinforce the elevated tone. After nearly two decades, the Bregolis have the art of restauration off to a T, she leading a thoroughly hospitable front-of-house, he one of the more idiosyncratic and dedicated chefs in Southern England.

Game is properly hung, pork butchery approached with positively Victorian self-sufficiency, and wild mushrooms are gathered in the New Forest. The menu doesn't change much from one year to the next, but when so few places offer such items as coppa (cured pork neck), simply dressed in extra virgin and black pepper, one wouldn't really want it to. In order to allow these components to show at their best, cooking techniques are kept simple, the mushrooms going into a dish of tagliatelle, the wild boar ham air-dried and given piquancy with pickled cherries. At main course, the kitchen offers authentic bollito misto, incorporating beef shin, silverside and pork cotechino with salsa verde for the full meaty experience. Fish dishes are equally straightforward, and may include roasted tuna or a whole sea bass grilled with fresh herbs. For dessert, crème brûlée is a favourite, but usually endowed with some novel flavouring such as fennel, with perhaps bitter chocolate mousse and passion-fruit coulis among other options. This is substantial cooking, and it pays to take a healthy appetite, and if you have a healthy bank balance you might wish to treat yourself to one of the many prize vintage first-growth clarets or venerable burgundies on offer. But first take a look at the Bregolis' impressive collection of Italian bins, which includes four Biondi Santi Brunello di Montalcinos. Plenty of bottles under £20 are also offered, starting with a red and white from Chile at £11.50 each.

CHEF/PROPRIETOR: Mauro Bregoli OPEN: Tue to Sun L 12 to 2, Tue to Sat D 7 to 9.30 MEALS: alc (main courses £12.50 to £17.50) SERVICE: not inc, card slips closed CARDS: Amex, MasterCard, Switch, Visa DETAILS: 16 seats. Private parties: 18 main room. Car park. Children welcome. No cigars/pipes in dining-room. No music

---

Dining-rooms where music, either live or recorded, is never played are signalled by No music *in the details at the end of an entry.*

Pheasants ▌🍷⚹

52 Edde Cross Street, Ross-on-Wye HR9 7BZ	COOKING 3
TEL: (01989) 565751	COST £45–£57

Three-course meals are the form in this creeper-clad seventeenth-century inn. They begin with provençale black olives, then an introductory bowl of soup – black-bean with chilli salsa perhaps – and typically offer four or five choices at each stage. 'I cook to no particular style, just my own,' writes Eileen Brunnarius, although it is 'loosely based on country cooking from around the world'. That might take in Thai fish-cakes, a leek, ricotta and olive tart, and pot roast partridge with quince. She makes use of local organic suppliers, picks up pike from the Wye, and asparagus from just up the road. She now has her own orchard and garden for growing herbs and unusual vegetables. Bread-and-butter pudding is a fixture and continues to win approval, or there may be grilled figs with mascarpone and honey, or an old English apple dish of Friar's omelette.

Adrian Wells, helpful to a fault, 'presides theatrically over proceedings', but his particular forte is wine. He is always keen to chat about his highly idiosyncratic yet excitingly different list and eager to advise on wine selection. The list is grouped by style and varietals and intelligently annotated, and each dish on the menu is accompanied by a suggestion. Forty wines by the glass cost between £2.70 and £6. CELLARMAN'S CHOICE: Sandihurst Gewurztraminer 1996, Canterbury, New Zealand, £18.20; Tedeschi Capitel San Rocco Ripasso 1991, Veneto, £18.60.

CHEF/PROPRIETOR: Eileen Brunnarius   OPEN: Tue to Sat D only 7 to 9.30   CLOSED: 25 Dec to 2 Jan, 1 to 6 June   MEALS: Set D £27   SERVICE: not inc   CARDS: Amex, Delta, Diners, MasterCard, Switch, Visa   DETAILS: 22 seats. Private parties: 24 main room. Vegetarian meals. Children's helpings. No smoking in dining-room. Wheelchair access (not WC). Music £5

George & Dragon 🍷⚹

High Street, Rowde SN10 2PN	COOKING 6
TEL: (01380) 723053 FAX: (01380) 724738	COST £18–£53

A pub by the road in the middle of Rowde defies its landlocked location by specialising in market-fresh seafood. The fish is hauled in from Cornwall, while oysters and langoustines make the journey from Loch Fyne. The place is very small with a tendency to cheery clamour, and décor is plain (the lavatories are outside). That said, no one feels rushed, and the cooking, led by Tim Withers, is too good to pass up for want of a bit of cosseting.

Crab and asparagus salad is a 'sophisticated and original' starter with a dressing of Courchamps sauce (the dark meat of the crab whizzed up with Pernod, tarragon and lemon juice), and sauces generally are a strong point. One of crème fraîche with fish stock, cucumber, pieces of bacon and a dash of mustard was used to support stir-fried chunks of monkfish, while another stock-based version, enriched with crab shell, scallop coral and diced tomato, has done the same for fillet of halibut. Despite the obvious willingness to experiment, the kitchen is not above doing classics such as skate wing with capers and black butter, the fish timed to be 'meltingly soft'. Crisp, properly dressed salad leaves with a scattering of pine-nuts seem to make a more apposite side-dish than the rather perfunctory vegetables. Simple desserts include tropical fruits with mascarpone ice-cream, clementines in brandy, and a 'brilliantly decadent' version of crème brûlée that tasted as if it may have been made with clotted cream. The broadly based wine list furnishes plenty of choice, and – surprisingly for a fish-orientated menu – contains as many red wines as white. House wines from south-west France are £9.

CHEFS: Tim Withers, Hannah Seal and Kate Phillips PROPRIETORS: Tim and Helen Withers OPEN: Tue to Sat 12 to 2, 7 to 10 CLOSED: 25 Dec, 1 Jan MEALS: alc (main courses £8.50 to £21). Set L £8.50 (2 courses) to £10. BYO £5 SERVICE: not inc, card slips closed CARDS: Delta, MasterCard, Switch, Visa DETAILS: 35 seats. 24 seats outside. Private parties: 12 main room. Car park. Vegetarian meals. Children's helpings. No smoking in dining-room. No music

---

RYE East Sussex   map 3

Landgate Bistro £

5–6 Landgate, Rye TN31 7LH	COOKING 4
TEL: (01797) 222829	COST £20–£38

On a street named after the nearby imposing fourteenth-century stone entrance to Rye, the bistro consists of a bar and a brick-walled dining-room with cloth-covered sewing-machine tables, its credentials confirmed by candles and casual service. The place 'chugs along nicely' according to a regular visitor, with a generous *carte* supplemented by a mid-week three-course set-price option, made even better value by the inclusion of service. Ideas are appealing, from spicy chickpea fritters, or a white sausage of chicken and pork served with fried apples, to hot crab terrine, and wild rabbit with garlic and rosemary. Saucing is varied – a sharp lemony buttery herb-flecked one with salmon and smoked haddock fish-cakes, and a dark sauce speckled with mustard seeds for lambs' kidneys – and enthusiastic endorsements have covered leek tart, and 'perfectly cooked' whole baby sea bass. Vegetables on the *carte* (carrot and parsnip purée for example) are charged separately. Desserts might run to chocolate truffle loaf, or slices of quince in a sweet syrup, served with vanilla cream. Up to eight wines are available by the glass, on a savvy and affordable list that starts at £8.90.

CHEF: Toni Ferguson-Lees PROPRIETORS: Nick Parkin and Toni Ferguson-Lees OPEN: Tue to Sat D 7 to 9.30 (10 Sat) CLOSED: 1 week autumn, Christmas/New Year, 2 weeks summer MEALS: alc (main courses £9 to £12.50). Set D Tue to Thur £15.90 SERVICE: net prices, card slips closed CARDS: Amex, Delta, Diners, MasterCard, Switch, Visa DETAILS: 30 seats. Vegetarian meals. Children's helpings. No cigars/pipes in dining-room. Music £5

Net prices *in the details at the end of an entry indicates that the prices given on a menu and on a bill are inclusive of VAT and service charge, and that this practice is clearly stated on menu and bill.*

The Guide*'s longest-serving restaurants are listed near the front of the book.*

ST IVES Cornwall   map 1

Pig'n'Fish ✦

Norway Lane, St Ives TR26 1LZ   COOKING 4
TEL: (01736) 794204   COST £31–£44

The stone-built shed is up a side street, 'only a pilchard lob from the seafront'.
Climb the wooden stairs to a long, narrow, low-ceilinged dining-room, bigger
than you might imagine from outside, and 'surprisingly light and airy'. It is
seafood nearly all the way, from the ever-present fish soup – rich, smooth, deeply
coloured – via mussel salad with new potatoes, to roast cod with cannellini
beans. Reporters agree that freshness and quality of fish, mostly from the
Newlyn boats, 'cannot be faulted'. The selection varies by the day, although the
same species tend to swim round again and again.

Timing is spot on, and Paul Sellars has 'a gentle, subtle hand' when it comes to
composing and saucing dishes. One of the best items to come out of the kitchen
has been a bowl of quickly fried squid rings and tentacles, in a pool of
potato-thickened sauce flavoured with fennel seeds and the zip of chilli oil.
Turbot, meanwhile, might be sliced into a ceviche and given a sharp salsa
dressing, or lightly roasted and served with leeks in a sorrel and chive butter
sauce. Simple but good accompanying vegetables are sourced from a local
community project, and visitors who go in the asparagus or samphire season can
expect a bonus.

Finish with citrus tart, zabaglione ice-cream, or a 'wonderfully light' chocolate
soufflé cake 'like a good moist brownie', served with a blob of clotted cream.
Simple meals are now served all day, and a delicatessen has been opened next
door. Around three dozen wines, mostly whites, take in a good number of grape
varieties; quality is high and prices are fair. House Vin de Pays d'Oc is £10.

CHEF: Paul Sellars   PROPRIETORS: Debby and Paul Sellars   OPEN: Tue to Sat 12.30 to 1.30, 7 to
9; reduced opening Nov to Feb (phone for details)   MEALS: alc (main courses £12.50 to £16.50).
Set D £21.50 Light menu Mon to Sat 10 to 5   SERVICE: not inc   CARDS: MasterCard, Visa
DETAILS: 25 seats. 28 seats outside. Children's helpings. No children under 2. No smoking in
dining-room. Music

ST KEYNE Cornwall   map 1

▲ *Well House*

St Keyne PL14 4RN
TEL: (01579) 342001   FAX: (01579) 343891
on B3254, 3m S of Liskeard; at end of village near   COOKING 6
church follow sign to St Keyne Well   COST £37–£53

The grey-stone building, down a country lane, is a 'small and intimate' place.
Built at the turn of the century, in three acres of gardens, it makes the most of a
quiet rural location without feeling like the back of beyond. Prints abound, and
the dining-room's lemon-yellow walls add to the sense of brightness. Nick
Wainford 'has the knack of making you feel, on first acquaintance, that you've
known him for ever'. Attentive, courteous and relaxed, his tone is picked up by
'very professional' staff.

Cameron Brown's menus – the same at lunch and dinner – take a contemporary approach to some classical European ideas, combining risotto of wild mushrooms with grilled goats'-cheese tartlet in one main course, or encasing rump of lamb in a rosemary and truffle crust and serving it with couscous. Flavourful raw materials are presented sparely, as in a UFO-shaped disc of pasta filled with crab and ginger, sitting in a small puddle of langoustine sauce: a dish praised for its 'immaculate' textures and balance of flavours.

Fish is particularly enticing – tuna with spring onion brandade and lemon oil, or fillets of red snapper and rock grouper on deep-fried polenta – and timing is accurate in last-minute renderings such as calf's liver, whose 'impeccably judged' stock-based sauce at inspection contained a 'brilliant' combination of grain mustard and green peppercorns. Good-quality West Country cheeses precede desserts such as passion-fruit soufflé, berry soup, dark chocolate marquise, or 'fabulous' lemon tart. The cellar's traditional French backbone is fleshed out with reliable bottles from elsewhere, and prices are kept under control. House wine is £8.95.

CHEF: Cameron Brown   PROPRIETORS: Nick Wainford and Ione Nurdin   OPEN: all week 12.30 to 1.45, 7 to 9   MEALS: Set L and D £21.95 (2 courses) to £30.45   SERVICE: not inc, card slips closed   CARDS: Amex, Delta, Diners, MasterCard, Switch, Visa   DETAILS: 36 seats. 18 seats outside. Private parties: 30 main room. Car park. Vegetarian meals. No children under 8 at D. No cigars/pipes in dining-room. Wheelchair access (1 step; also WC). No music ACCOMMODATION: 9 rooms, all with bath/shower. TV. Phone. B&B £70 to £155. Rooms for disabled. Children welcome. High teas for children. Baby facilities. Swimming-pool (The Which? Hotel Guide)

ST MARGARET'S AT CLIFFE Kent   map 3

▲ Wallett's Court ⁜✻

West Cliffe, St Margaret's at Cliffe CT15 6EW
TEL: (01304) 852424   FAX: (01304) 853430
EMAIL: wallettscourt@compuserve.com
on B2058, off A258 Dover to Deal road, 3m NE of   COOKING 3
Dover   COST £38–£55

'The closest restaurant to the Continent in England' is the Oakleys' assessment, and their restoration of the seventeenth-century house, outbuildings and garden – on the site of a manor mentioned in the Domesday Book – now runs to a health spa. Perhaps prodded by the state of the nation's agriculture, the kitchen's attention has turned increasingly towards organic produce – including locally ground flour, and deer and boar from Wadhurst Park – all in the service of a defiantly country style of cooking: no fast-moving cosmopolitan cuisine here. Instead, local codling might be served with a mustard sauce, Romney Marsh lamb appears in a navarin, and rabbit has gone into the pot along with cider and Bramley apples. 'The food is good,' reckoned a reporter, 'without quite reaching the heights the menu might lead you to expect.' Desserts have included lemon and almond tart, and armagnac ice-cream with prunes. Generally affordable and predominantly French wines, with a decent spread of half-bottles, are headed by Aligoté and Pinot Noir house wines at £14 (£3.50 a glass).

CHEF: Christopher Oakley PROPRIETORS: the Oakley family OPEN: all week D only 7 to 9, 'late arrivals' menu 9 to 10.30. L by arrangement for groups of 12 or more CLOSED: 24 to 28 Dec MEALS: alc D (main courses £16 to £18.50). Set D £24.95. BYO £7 SERVICE: not inc CARDS: Amex, Delta, Diners, MasterCard, Switch, Visa DETAILS: 60 seats. Private parties: 40 main room, 40 private room. Car park. Vegetarian meals. Children's helpings. No children under 8 after 8pm. No smoking in dining-room. Wheelchair access (3 steps; not WC). Music ACCOMMODATION: 16 rooms, all with bath/shower. TV. Phone. B&B £55 to £120. Rooms for disabled. Children welcome. High teas for children. Dogs welcome by arrangement. Afternoon teas. Swimming-pool (The Which? Hotel Guide) £5

ST MARTIN'S Isles of Scilly   map 1

▲ St Martin's Hotel ᙏ✳

Lower Town, St Martin's TR25 0QW   COOKING 5
TEL: (01720) 422092 FAX: (01720) 422298   COST £37–£56

This is a good place to 'recharge stressed batteries', and those who make the journey (by air from Exeter seems the most popular) are accommodated in comfort 'with good service and excellent food'. Boats land on the quay, just in front of the grey stone cottages that constitute the island's only hotel, luggage is carried, champagne is on ice, and 'most of the staff seemed to know us by name', according to one new arrival. Dinner, now à la carte only, is a serious affair served in the 'sophisticated' first-floor dining-room with its modern paintings and sea views.

Luxury ingredients don't dominate, but might appear as, for example, lobster raviolis in a Dubarry soup, or a warm pigeon and foie gras tart. The cooking is technically ambitious, but Patrick Pierre Tweedie is well up to it, producing a frogs' leg fricassee, or chicken and morel sausage to start. Ideas tend to have a classical foundation, and fish shares the billing equally with meat. A summer menu, for example, turned up main courses of roast sea bream with fennel, and grey mullet on a broad-bean fricassee, alongside roast veal with creamed mustard sauce, and Barbary duckling with pesto stuffing. Presentation is a strong point, not least among desserts, which might feature 'American-style' pancakes with redcurrants and maple syrup ice-cream, a hot raspberry soufflé, or a dark chocolate 'délice' with passion-fruit sauce. The place is well run by 'young, efficient, happy staff'. As the questionnaire was not returned to us, some of the information below may not be correct. House wine is £14.

CHEF: Patrick Pierre Tweedie PROPRIETOR: Peter Sykes OPEN: all week D only 7 to 10 CLOSED: Nov to March MEALS: alc (main courses £12.50 to £18) SERVICE: not inc, card slips closed CARDS: Amex, Delta, Diners, MasterCard, Switch, Visa DETAILS: 60 seats. 50 seats outside. Private parties: 90 main room. Children welcome. No children under 12. No smoking in dining-room. Music ACCOMMODATION: 30 rooms, all with bath/shower. TV. Phone. D,B&B £100 to £260. Children welcome. High teas for children. Baby facilities. Dogs welcome in ground-floor rooms only. Afternoon teas. Swimming-pool (The Which? Hotel Guide)

ᙏ✳ indicates that smoking is either banned altogether or that a dining-room is maintained for non-smokers. The symbol does not apply to restaurants that simply have no-smoking areas.

ST MAWES Cornwall	map 1

▲ *Tresanton Hotel*   <u>NEW ENTRY</u>

27 Lower Castle Road, St Mawes TR2 5DR   COOKING 5
TEL: (01326) 270055   FAX: (01326) 270053   COST £26–£47

Olga Polizzi, Lord Forte's daughter, re-opened Tresanton in June. A cluster of cottages overlooking the Fal estuary and St Mawes harbour, it seems to have a touch of the Riviera about it. Having started life as a yacht club in the '40s, the hotel has been extensively renovated with stylish simplicity, and benefits from the added allure of Marco Pierre White-trained chef Richard Turner.

Start with drinks on the terrace in summer, to admire the wonderful views. Fixed-price menus, free of supplements, fit well with the straightforward design, and the choice is kept to a modest four items at each stage for dinner, two at lunch. A couple who couldn't wait to try it out came away from a July dinner feeling suitably impressed: with crab soup seasoned with cayenne and saffron, and tuna carpaccio in a lively balsamic marinade. Seafood is expected to be a strong suit – lobster is roasted with chillies and olives, while sole is grilled and dressed classically with lemon butter – but meat dishes are well-handled too. Suckling pig is a rolled cut, properly crisped and served with lightly baked apple and fennel, while a breast of corn-fed chicken has a herb mixture spread beneath the skin to deepen the flavour. Unfussy desserts might include strawberries set in champagne jelly with Cornish clotted cream or chocolate orange cake, or there is a selection of West Country cheeses. Service at this early stage seemed to be suffering only minor teething troubles. The wine list casts its net wide to bring in some creditable producers from all over the place, but with the cheapest Sancerre at £35, prices are not very forgiving. House Italians are £11.

CHEF: Richard Turner   PROPRIETOR: Olga Polizzi   OPEN: all week 12.30 to 2.30, 7 to 10.30 (supper menu at Sun D)   MEALS: Set L £18, Set D £30   SERVICE: not inc, card slips closed   CARDS: Amex, MasterCard, Switch, Visa   DETAILS: 50 seats. 50 seats outside. Private parties: 50 main room, 50 private room. Car park. Vegetarian meals. Children's helpings. No pipes in dining-room. No music   ACCOMMODATION: 26 rooms, all with bath/shower. TV. Phone. B&B £153 to £220. Children welcome. High teas for children. Afternoon teas

---

ST MICHAEL'S ON WYRE Lancashire	map 8

Mallards

Garstang Road, St Michael's on Wyre PR3 0TE   COOKING 1
TEL: (01995) 679661   COST £18–£35

'A good reliable restaurant that satisfies at a reasonable price,' sums up one visitor, pointing to qualities that should never be under-estimated. As far as value is concerned Sunday lunch is hard to beat. John Steel's cooking stays mostly simple – egg and prawn mayonnaise, cheese soufflé, fillet steak with a red pepper and mushroom sauce – and among the local materials might be an earthy-tasting black pudding 'with not too much fat and plenty of specks of white barley', served with a well-made cream and cheese sauce. Cream is a favourite saucing ingredient, perhaps flavoured with mild grainy mustard to partner a 'thick, moist and tasty' slice of roast local gammon. Vegetables with 'saucy blandishments' come on a side plate, and approved desserts have included smooth raspberry sorbet and hot apple crumble. A short but wide-ranging wine list starts with house French at £8.95.

CHEF: John Steel   PROPRIETORS: John and Ann Steel   OPEN: Sun L 12 to 2.30, Mon to Sat D 7 to 9 (9.30 Sat)   CLOSED: 1 week Oct, 1 week Jan, 1 week July   MEALS: Set L £11.50, Set D £16.50 (2 courses) to £19.95   SERVICE: not inc, card slips closed   CARDS: Delta, MasterCard, Switch, Visa   DETAILS: 28 seats. Private parties: 34 main room. Car park. Children's helpings. No smoking while others eat. Wheelchair access (also WC). Music   (£5)

SALE Greater Manchester   map 8

Hanni's £

4 Brooklands Road, Sale M33 3SQ   COOKING 2
TEL: (0161) 973 6606   COST £22–£37

Here is the other sort of Mediterranean. Hanni al-Taraboulsy's converted shop premises in a genteel suburb of south Manchester are the setting for cooking that describes a grand sweep from Greece through Lebanon across North Africa, taking in Tunisia, Algeria and Morocco. Red lighting and a maroon colour scheme set the tone, service is informative and 'there appears to be a faithful regular clientele,' according to a reporter. A wide range of meze includes kibbeh (crisp-fried minced lamb and spicy cracked wheat), properly garlicky hummus, falafel and dolmades. All come with sharply dressed saladings. Tunisian couscous may be served with two large fillets of halibut in a tomato sauce with pickled turnip and other roots, accompanied by a sauceboat of chilli dressing. Kleftiko is the real thing: 'succulent and tender' lamb cooked on the bone with tomatoes and okra. Meals end saltily with fried halloumi and olives, or sweetly with a salad of dried fruits. An enterprising wine list appropriately finds room for bottles from Lebanon, Greece and Turkey, among other offerings. Prices start at £9.50.

CHEF: Mr Hoonanian   PROPRIETOR: Hanni Al-Taraboulsy   OPEN: Mon to Sat D only 6 to 10.30 (11 Fri and Sat)   CLOSED: 25 and 26 Dec, Good Fri, Easter Mon, last 2 weeks Aug   MEALS: alc (main courses £8.50 to £13.50)   SERVICE: not inc   CARDS: Amex, Delta, MasterCard, Switch, Visa   DETAILS: 50 seats. Private parties: 50 main room. Vegetarian meals. Children's helpings. Wheelchair access (not WC). Music. Air-conditioned   (£5)

SANDGATE Kent   map 3

▲ Sandgate Hotel, La Terrasse ♈ 🍴

Wellington Terrace, The Esplanade,
Sandgate CT20 3DY   COOKING 7
TEL: (01303) 220444   FAX: (01303) 220496   COST £34–£70

Sandgate may not be a jewel in Kent's crown, but La Terrasse is a diamond in the south coast's tiara. In essence it is a Victorian seaside hotel done up with French flair and élan: only yards from the water, four storeys high, with France visible from the windows and an air of confidence about it that is more cosmopolitan than seaside, as are some of the prices. The lounge is comfortable, the

465

dining-room bright yellow, fresh and inviting. First courses consist almost entirely of shellfish and foie gras, local fish is a strong suit, and luxury oozes from the menu: ballottine of foie gras (from Samuel Gicqueau's native Loire) and Sauternes jelly with a lamb's lettuce and truffle (from Perigord) salad, for example. The 'modern classical French' style might embrace a salad of Rye Bay scallops and Jerusalem artichokes, or fillet of turbot with potato 'scales', served with braised cabbage and langoustine jus.

Despite its richness, a sense of clarity and purpose guides the cooking, producing 'nicely salted and perfectly cooked' slices of warm foie gras served with turnip and port-infused figs, and a texturally appealing dish of just-cooked turbot on the bone with chanterelles and celery: 'materials, timing and conception were first-rate'. A seasonal vein runs through the kitchen too, turning up venison tournedos in winter, pré-salé lamb in spring, and a gratin of fraises des bois in summer. Among desserts that have delighted are a triangular cooked chocolate mousse, the outside slightly firm, the inside warm and runny (served with a cream and almond sauce and verbena ice-cream), and a poached William pear encased in a layer of filo-style pastry, served with small blobs of Szechuan pepper ice-cream.

French gems sparkle throughout the wine list (only five bins hail from elsewhere), and the range extends from first-growth clarets through mature burgundies to leading Loires, '*naturellement*'. The professional wine service is helpfully backed up by detailed tasting notes. House wines are £13.50 a bottle, £3.50 a glass. CELLARMAN'S CHOICE: Saumur Vieilles Vignes 1994, Dom. Langlois-Château, £18.50; Bourgueil 'Cuvée Grand Mont' 1993, Pierre Jacques Druet, £27.

CHEF: Samuel Gicqueau PROPRIETORS: Zara and Samuel Gicqueau OPEN: Tue to Sun L 12.15 to 1.30, Tue to Sat D 7.15 to 9.30 CLOSED: mid-Jan to mid-Feb, first week Oct MEALS: alc (main courses £16 to £22.50). Set L and D £20.50 to £29.50 SERVICE: not inc CARDS: Amex, Delta, Diners, MasterCard, Switch, Visa DETAILS: 24 seats. Private parties: 28 main room. Car park (space for 4 cars only). Children's helpings. No smoking in dining-room. Music ACCOMMODATION: 15 rooms, all with bath/shower. TV. Phone. B&B £39 to £69. Children welcome. Baby facilities. Afternoon teas (*The Which? Hotel Guide*)

SANDIWAY Cheshire   map 7

▲ *Nunsmere Hall*

Tarporley Road, Sandiway CW8 2ES
TEL: (01606) 889100 FAX: (01606) 889055   COOKING 6
off A49, 4m SW of Northwich   COST £31–£64

The Hall's idyllic lakeside setting is perhaps why Sir Aubrey Brocklebank – chairman of a family shipping line that later merged with Cunard – chose this site to build his imposing residence at the turn of the century. It still exudes a sense of solid prosperity, the well-proportioned rooms, pastel colours and expansive tables contributing to a relaxed and genial mood. As Simon Radley departed for the Chester Grosvenor (see entry), sous-chef Duncan Mitchell slipped effortlessy into his shoes, producing a balanced output along the same lines as before: modern, with a penchant for the Mediterranean and a seasonal feel, plus a separate vegetarian menu that might offer a mille-feuille of baby leeks, asparagus and broad beans in a chervil butter sauce. The cooking is fresh, lively and clearly flavoured. First courses are notably generous: for example, a huge slab of ham knuckle and foie gras terrine, served with crunchy warm brioche and a grape salad, or an expertly dissected roast quail with a hint of honey, that was 'a sort of mini main course', served with masses of wild mushrooms. Dishes are also technically strong and 'well crafted', as in a 'fabulously flavoured' Barbary duck breast, served with an exquisitely made pithivier of hot, melting puff pastry filled with shredded leg meat that oozed 'lovely juices'; of all the possible duck and fruit combinations this one, with blackberries in the sauce, was judged to work 'particularly well'.

Desserts look 'very entertaining', and might run to a caramel trio, or a 'large box' of iced parfait with chunks of glacé fruit, topped with baked fruit, 'looking like it had been gift-wrapped'. Quite a lot of the professional but unobtrusive service is young and 'sweetly French'. The extensive wine list is not confined exclusively to French classics, but prices are stiff, with not much below £20 except for six house wines starting at £15.50.

CHEF: Duncan Mitchell   PROPRIETORS: Malcolm and Julie McHardy   OPEN: Sun to Fri L 12 to 1.45, Mon to Sun D 7 to 9.30 (9 Sun)   MEALS: alc (main courses £19.50 to £23.50). Set L £17.50 (2 courses) to £19.50, Set D £30   SERVICE: net prices, card slips closed   CARDS: Amex, Delta, Diners, MasterCard, Switch, Visa   DETAILS: 70 seats. 150 seats outside. Private parties: 70 main room, 22 to 45 private rooms. Car park. Vegetarian meals. No children under 10 at D. No smoking in dining-room. Wheelchair access (also WC). Music   ACCOMMODATION: 36 rooms, all with bath/shower. TV. Phone. B&B £90 to £325. Rooms for disabled. Children welcome. Baby facilities. No dogs. Afternoon teas (*The Which? Hotel Guide*)

SAWBRIDGEWORTH Hertfordshire   map 3

Shoes ⅝✳

52 Bell Street, Sawbridgeworth CM21 9AN	COOKING **2**
TEL: (01279) 722554 FAX: (01279) 832494	COST £23–£53

Home Counties denizens reckon that a drive out to Shoes is preferable to the London trek, and this converted coaching-inn-cum-shoe-shop pleases with its professional approach to things, and its affordable Anglo-French cooking. Reporters regularly endorse the timbale of crab and asparagus as a starter, although alternatives appear in the shape of calf's liver and truffle parfait, or ravioli of caramelised lambs' sweetbreads and chanterelles. Among main courses, chicken with watercress mousse and salsa has been approved, while the kitchen is also prepared to tackle elaborate-sounding dishes-of-many-parts: pan-fried suprême of salmon with aubergine caviare, brandade of cod and 'petit ratatouille' dressing, for example. As for desserts, there might be 'excellent' blueberry bavarois coupled with raspberries in batter, or apricot clafoutis with ice-cream. Service comes in for plenty of praise, and there is live jazz on Friday nights. A well-chosen wine list of sensible proportions includes a few real goodies such as Turckheim's 1996 Gewurztraminer. House wines start at £10.75.

See inside the front cover for an explanation of the symbols used at the tops of entries.

CHEF: Mark Green   PROPRIETORS: Lyndon Wootton, and Peter and Doreen Gowan   OPEN: Tue to Fri L 12 to 1.30, Mon to Sat D 7 to 9.30   CLOSED: 2 weeks Christmas, 2 weeks Aug, bank hol Mons   MEALS: alc (main courses £11.50 to £16). Set L £10 (2 courses) to £13.25, Set D Mon to Thu £19, Set D Fri £21.50   SERVICE: not inc   CARDS: Amex, Delta, MasterCard, Switch, Visa   DETAILS: 60 seats. Private parties: 40 main room, 20 private room. Vegetarian meals. Children's helpings. No smoking in 1 dining-room. Wheelchair access (1 step; also WC). Occasional music. Air-conditioned

---

SAWLEY Lancashire   map 8

▲ *Spread Eagle* ✳✸ £   NEW ENTRY

Sawley BB7 4NH
TEL: (01200) 441202   FAX: (01200) 441973   COOKING 4
off A59, 4m NE of Clitheroe   COST £14-£32

Steven Doherty of the Punch Bowl (see entry, Crosthwaite) is edging closer to Heathcote territory with his new outpost in the Trough of Bowland on the banks of the Ribble. The place was last in the *Guide* in 1970, when steaks and joints were the order of the day, and dinner cost 25 shillings a head. Now the menu takes in baked goats' cheese and aubergine with pesto, grilled tuna, and chicken with a balsamic tomato basil butter. Choose what to eat in the comfortable lounge bar, before moving into a split-level dining-room with small tables and large picture windows.

Both the aim (to serve 'honest food at sensible prices') and the style are close to the Crosthwaite original, and Doherty makes use of Goosnargh duck, farmhouse Lancashire cheeses, Cumbrian bacon and air-dried ham, local black puddings, and fish from Fleetwood: salmon, cod and prawn hash, or baked cod fillet. Simple grilled ribeye steak has worked well, as has sticky date and ginger sponge with 'an excellent butterscotch sauce'. An early evening 'beat the clock' system calculates the bill according to the time of ordering: at 6pm it costs £6; at half past seven, £7.30. It doesn't apply at lunch-time, otherwise everybody would turn up at one o'clock. Service is smartly dressed and friendly, and the short wine list takes affordability seriously, starting with house wine at £8.95.

CHEF: Steven Doherty   PROPRIETORS: Alan Bell, Lionel Yates, Steven and Marjorie Doherty   OPEN: all week 12 to 2, 6 to 9   CLOSED: 25 Dec   MEALS: alc (main courses £7 to £10). Set L Mon to Fri £5.95 (2 courses) to £11.25. Set L Sun £9.25 (2 courses) to £11.25. BYO £10   SERVICE: not inc, card slips closed   CARDS: Amex, Delta, MasterCard, Switch, Visa   DETAILS: 80 seats. Private parties: 16 main room, 80 to150 private room. Car park. Vegetarian meals. Children's helpings. No smoking in dining-room. Wheelchair access (2 steps; not WC). Occasional music   ACCOMMODATION: 10 rooms, all with bath/shower. TV. Phone. B&B £35 to £50. Rooms for disabled. Children welcome. No dogs. Afternoon teas

---

'"We have reserved a table for one o'clock. The name is Smith," we said. "Do you have a reservation?" was the scarcely intelligible response. "Yes. The name is Smith." "And what is your name?" This did not augur well.' (On eating in Manchester)

Occasional music in the details at the end of an entry means live or recorded music is played in the dining-room only rarely or for special events. No music means it is never played.

Plough Inn ⁵⅜

Headwell Lane, Saxton LS24 9PB
TEL: (01937) 557242   FAX: (01937) 557655   COOKING 3
off A162, between Tadcaster and Sherburn in Elmet   COST £21–£39

This 'hidden gem' (a status to which local signposting contributes) is still very much a village pub, where drinkers can outnumber diners. Indeed, there are no clues from outside as to the quality and broad appeal of Simon Treanor's food. Dishes are chalked on a board over the fireplace, and served by friendly staff at polished wooden tables with good glasses and paper napkins. The repertoire covers a lot of ground, from gravadlax to kedgeree, from seared tuna salad with balsamic vinaigrette to Chinese-style breast of duck with pak choi. Roast fillet of brill, and pork with apples and apricots, were evidence enough for one reporter of prime ingredients handled well, though gratin dauphinois might benefit from a return visit to the drawing-board. Desserts have included poached Conference pears with cinnamon cream, and rich chocolate tart. Around 60 interesting wines are as varied as the food, and all but a handful come in under £20. House French is £8.95.

CHEF: Simon Treanor   PROPRIETORS: Simon and Nicola Treanor   OPEN: Tue to Sun L 12 to 2, Tue to Sat D 6.30 to 9.30   CLOSED: first two weeks Jan.   MEALS: alc Tue to Sat (main courses £10.50 to £13). Set L Sun £13.95, Set D £29.50 (not always available)   SERVICE: not inc, card slips closed   CARDS: Delta, MasterCard, Switch, Visa   DETAILS: 65 seats. 16 seats outside. Private parties: 65 main room. Car park. Vegetarian meals. Children's helpings. No smoking in dining-room. Wheelchair access (also WC). Music

Lanterna £

33 Queen Street, Scarborough YO11 1HQ   COOKING 3
TEL/FAX: (01723) 363616   COST £21–£45

The warm atmosphere and charming service in this simple family-run restaurant are consistently approved by reporters who are equally enthusiastic about the cooking, and in particular the Alessios' almost obsessive concern with the quality and freshness of ingredients. The emphasis is on local fish in season, selected from Scarborough harbour, and the owners will tell you about dishes of the day, such as grilled black bream, baked sea bass, or goujons of Scarborough wolf-fish. There is much more than just fish though, with four conventional pasta dishes, and another four of pasta all'uovo 'handmade on the premises', including salmon ravioli in a cream sauce. Meat eaters can choose from beef, veal and chicken each prepared in four ways and, in season, wild hare in Barbera wine. Potatoes and two vegetables are always included, and, again, there are seasonal highlights such as locally picked wild mushrooms or asparagus, alongside deep fried aubergines or zucchini. Desserts offer few surprises, although home-made cassata, saffron ice-cream and passion-fruit or lemon sorbet sound promising. The short, mainly Italian wine list includes a useful selection of half-bottles; house wine is £9.95.

CHEF: Giorgio Alessio   PROPRIETORS: Giorgio and Rachel Alessio   OPEN: Mon to Sat 12 to 1.30,
6 to 11 (booking essential for lunch)   CLOSED: 25, 26 and 31 Dec   MEALS: alc (main courses
£9.50 to £17). BYO £5   SERVICE: not inc, card slips closed   CARDS: Delta, MasterCard, Switch,
Visa   DETAILS: 28 seats. Private parties: 30 main room. Vegetarian meals. Children welcome.
Wheelchair access (not WC). Music. Air-conditioned

SEAFORD   East Sussex   map 3

Quincy's ▼ ⅝✳

42 High Street, Seaford BN25 1PL   ·   COOKING 3
TEL: (01323) 895490   COST £34–£42

Low lighting, fresh flowers and laden bookshelves add to the charm of this
comfortable bow-fronted dining-room in the old part of town. 'Unfussy cooking
of excellent ingredients' is the style, and Ian Dowding's culinary intelligence is
striking: potted duck with spiced plums and duck crackling makes an
interesting starter, and main courses extend to loin of lamb stuffed with dried
cherries and Parma ham, or loin of venison with lentils, ceps and tarragon.
Interest is maintained at dessert stage by lemon and muscovado granita with
brandied fruits or vattalapam (spiced coconut custard with mango, garnished
with edible gold leaf). Service is 'first-class'. Some brain power has clearly been
applied to assembling the mostly French wine list (which includes a Quincy,
naturellement). The pricing policy is thoughtful, too, with plenty of choice under
£15, and the choice of half-bottles is generous. A quartet of French house wines
begins at £9.75. CELLARMAN'S CHOICE: Breaky Bottom Müller-Thurgau 1992,
England, £12.75; Côtes du Rhône 1994, E. Guigal, £13.25.

CHEF: Ian Dowding   PROPRIETORS: Ian and Dawn Dowding   OPEN: Sun L 12 to 2, Tue to Sat D
7.15 to 10   MEALS: Set L and D £20 (2 courses) to £24. BYO £5   SERVICE: not inc   CARDS:
Amex, MasterCard, Visa   DETAILS: 28 seats. Private parties: 20 main room. Vegetarian meals.
Children's helpings. No smoking in 1 dining-room. Music

SEATON BURN   Tyne & Wear   map 10

▲ Horton Grange ⅝✳

Seaton Burn, Northumberland NE13 6BU
TEL: (01661) 860686   FAX: (01661) 860308
EMAIL: andrew@horton-grange.co.uk
from A1 take A19 exit; at roundabout take first exit;
after 1m turn left, signposted to Brenkley and   COOKING 6
Dinnington; hotel 2m on right   COST £44–£52

The Shiltons' country hotel is a foursquare stone-built house reached by (very)
minor roads, so mark the directions carefully. In 1997 they spent a substantial
sum creating a new conservatory-style dining-room with verandah overlooking
a tranquil water garden. Shades of vernal green in the upholstery create a
soothing ambience, as does the tinkling of an indoor fountain.
    Steven Martin, who has been cooking here for a decade, has kept Horton
Grange on a steady trajectory by tempering artfulness with restraint, combining
care in presentation with a sense of generosity, all within the compass of a

fixed-price dinner menu of four courses, plus coffee and excellent incidentals. Bread rolls baked in-house are the size of tangerines, crisply crusty and yeasty within. A first-course terrine of salmon, white crabmeat and turbot wrapped in spinach successfully combines a variety of textures, its flavour boosted by 'enjoyable little bursts of heat' provided by green peppercorns. Soup or sorbet comes next, the former perhaps a delicate consommé of chicken with cheese straws, the latter of something sharp like Bramley apple. The choice is sweeping, but dishes are none the less rendered with real skill: grilled fillet of sea bass sits on gently spiced couscous with a ribbon of orientally spiced sauce, for example. Smoked bacon and potato gratin, 'lubricated with cream, cheese and mustard', makes a suitably opulent accompaniment to herb-crumbed rack of lamb. At inspection, banana tarte Tatin may have been short on technical shine but a prune and armagnac parfait that combined silky smoothness with 'jammy' prune and 'bouncy' sponge was spot on.

Only the wine list lets the whole operation down with a clunk. No vintages are given, and it does seem perverse to claim that the Sancerre is from 'a small producer who indelibly stamps his own character on the wine' without telling us his name. The cooking deserves better. House Spanish is £10.90.

CHEF: Steven Martin   PROPRIETORS: Andrew and Susan Shilton   OPEN: Mon to Sat D only 7 to 8.45   CLOSED: Christmas and New Year   MEALS: Set D £34   SERVICE: not inc, card slips closed   CARDS: Amex, MasterCard, Switch, Visa   DETAILS: 50 seats. Private parties: 65 main room. Car park. No children under 14. No smoking in dining-room. Wheelchair access (also WC). Occasional music   ACCOMMODATION: 9 rooms, all with bath/shower. TV. Phone. B&B £59 to £90. Rooms for disabled. No children under 14 (*The Which? Hotel Guide*)   £5

SHAFTESBURY Dorset   map 2

La Fleur de Lys ♟

25 Salisbury Street, Shaftesbury SP7 8EL   COOKING 4
TEL: (01747) 853717   COST £32–£53

Be on your toes, or you might miss this wood-panelled restaurant altogether. The entrance is along a passageway beside what looks like a private house, and the dining-room is in a converted loft over stables at the back. Driving the enterprise is a kitchen going about its work with diligence, and there are plenty of indications of dedicated, time-consuming technique in dishes such as steamed fillets of sea bass served with a mousseline of scallops and tarragon cream sauce, and roast charred saddle of venison wrapped in bacon with baked garlic in Madeira. But not all is elaboration: witness grilled Dover sole with lemon butter sauce. One couple who tried out the set Sunday lunch menu were more than pleased with an asparagus, courgette and coriander tart with herb sauce, which preceded poached salmon on a bed of 'wonderful' sauté fennel, and roast sirloin of beef with Yorkshire puddings ('note the plural'). Desserts on this occasion included 'exquisite' coffee beignets with dark and white chocolate sauce, or there might be apple and calvados parfait with caramel and calvados sauce, or a brandy-snap basket filled with prune and Muscat liqueur ice-cream.

The wine list is solid in its Old World selections, with added weight lent by a page of fine clarets, and there are rich pickings to be had in the New World section, which is ordered by grape variety. Prices are generally fair; French house wines from the Rothschilds are £11.50. CELLARMAN'S CHOICE: Paul Cluver Gewurztraminer 1995, Stellenbosch, South Africa, £13.95; Jim Barry McCrae Wood Shiraz 1994, Clare Valley, S. Australia, £22.

CHEFS: D. Shepherd and M. Preston   PROPRIETORS: D. Shepherd, M. Griffin and M. Preston
OPEN: Tue to Sun L 12 to 2.30 (3 Sun), Mon to Sat D 7 to 10   CLOSED: 2 weeks Jan   MEALS: alc
Tue to Sat L, all week D (main courses £12.50 to £18.50). Set L Sun £16.45 (2 courses) to £19.45,
Set D Mon to Thur £19.50 (2 courses) to £23.50, Set D Fri and Sat £23.50. BYO £6   SERVICE: not
inc   CARDS: Amex, Delta, Diners, MasterCard, Switch, Visa   DETAILS: 40 seats. Private parties:
40 main room. Vegetarian meals. Children's helpings. No smoking before 10 at D. Music

---

SHEFFIELD South Yorkshire   map 9

Rafters

220 Oakbrook Road, Nether Green, Sheffield S11 7ED   COOKING 2
TEL/FAX: (0114) 230 4819   COST £29–£37

The Bosworth brothers tell us that they have recently refurbished their restaurant in a terrace of shops in one of the city's 'prestigious' residential areas. Feature lights from Milan overhang the dining-room, which now boasts a terracotta and lemon colour scheme. What really attracts, however, is the quality and price of the food. 'Best value in Sheffield,' concluded one local correspondent who chose game terrine studded with foie gras, then braised lamb shank, and finished off with home-made ice-cream. Others have been well satisfied with gnocchi with pesto sauce, and chargrilled tuna (which might be served with stir-fried vegetables and an olive and pickled ginger salsa). The ever-present signature dessert of apple bread-and-butter pudding with sticky toffee sauce also continues to generate plaudits. A BYO policy applies from Monday to Thursday, although the workmanlike wine list delivers exactly what is required. House French is £8.90.

CHEFS/PROPRIETORS: Wayne and Jamie Bosworth   OPEN: Mon and Wed to Sat D only 7 to 10
CLOSED: 26 Dec, 1 Jan, some bank hols   MEALS: Set D £19.95. BYO (exc Fri and Sat) £2
SERVICE: not inc, card slips closed   CARDS: Amex   DETAILS: 40 seats. Private parties: 44 main
room. Vegetarian meals. Children's helpings. No children under 4. Music

---

Smith's of Sheffield ¾✖

34 Sandygate Road, Sheffield S10 5RY   COOKING 5
TEL: (0114) 266 6096   COST £29–£42

With an eye to the potential of food as theatre, Richard Smith has opened a new upstairs dining-room, where he puts on a bravura performance every Saturday night, cooking a no-choice six-course menu in the open kitchen. Meanwhile, the relaxed, brasserie-style restaurant downstairs continues to offer a snappy modern menu of bistro classics with a '90s twist. Richard Smith describes his cooking as 'representing a melting pot of influences from all over the world', but it's good to see that he hasn't forgotten his Northern roots: in among the Mediterranean ingredients and Asian spicing might be black pudding and brown sauce onions with calf's liver, 'Yorkshire breakfast salad', or Yorkshire rhubarb with crème brûlée.

The cooking may be eclectic but the approach is disciplined, and flavour remains the priority. A starter of marinated tomatoes with garlic prawns, pesto and provençale vegetables for one reporter was visually pleasing and oozing with fresh flavours, while subtle yet full-flavoured chicken foie gras sausage with creamed leeks was accompanied by soft, succulent caramelised apples and an intense sage jus. Portions are described as 'massively plentiful' and puddings may even come in threes: triple chocolate hedonism with a vanilla milkshake sauce, trio of crème brûlée (almond, chocolate and vanilla), and lemon three ways: soft meringue, 'subtle, creamy and sharp' syllabub, and sorbet with vanilla sauce. An interesting and varied wine list offers plenty of moderately priced bottles. House wines are £8.50.

CHEF: Richard Smith   PROPRIETORS: Richard and Victoria Smith, and John and Sallie Tetchner   OPEN: Tue to Sat D only 6.30 to 9.30   MEALS: alc (main courses £11 to £15). Set D Sat £35, BYO (Tue to Thurs only) £2.50   SERVICE: not inc, card slips closed   CARDS: Amex, MasterCard, Switch, Visa   DETAILS: 44 seats. Private parties: 50 main room, 20 private room. Vegetarian meals. Children's helpings. No smoking in dining-room. Wheelchair access (1 step; not WC). Music

---

SHELF West Yorkshire   map 8

Bentley's 🍴 £

| 12 Wade House Road, Shelf HX3 7PB | COOKING 3 |
| TEL: (01274) 690992   FAX: (01274) 690011 | COST £15–£35 |

The food in this 'handsome little basement dining-room' improves year by year according to one observer, and although the stone-flagged cellar floor doesn't make for the warmest feet, the place is full of 'real people', which brings its own warmth. The set-price lunch is a steal, and doesn't stint on choice – typically eight first and main courses – although around half the dishes attract a price supplement. A penny-pincher might stick to a salad of bacon chunks, crunchy croûtons, toasted pine kernels and dressed leaves with a tang of balsamic vinegar, followed by salmon with a puddle of buttery sauce, while a splasher-out could indulge in scallops in a leek and bacon sauce, and venison steak.

The *carte* has no secrets, sometimes confiding enough detail for you to make the dish at home, but the apparent complexity should not deter: trout fillet with dill, lemon, sliced almonds and currants, for example, has worked remarkably well, and ideas have also included black pudding and bacon tartlet with poached egg, and simple Whitby crab with mayonnaise. Timing sometimes requires a little more precision, but at its best has produced duck breast with ('miraculously these days') crisp skin and a just-pink centre. Try sherry trifle with white chocolate custard to finish, or 'jazzed up pancakes' with butterscotch sauce and ice-cream. Some 70 wide-ranging wines keep the balance of prices commendably below £15, starting at £8.95 for house vin de pays.

The Guide*'s longest-serving restaurants are listed near the front of the book.*

CHEFS: Paul Bentley and Anthony Bickers   PROPRIETORS: Paul and Pam Bentley   OPEN: Tue to Fri and Sun L 12 to 2, Tue to Sat D 6.30 to 9 (9.30 Fri and Sat)   CLOSED: 25 Dec to 30 Dec   MEALS: alc (main courses £10 to £12). Set L Tue to Fri £6.75 (2 courses) to £7.95, Set L Sun £9.95. BYO £3   SERVICE: not inc, card slips closed   CARDS: Delta, MasterCard, Switch, Visa   DETAILS: 44 seats. Private parties: 24 main room, 20 and 24 private rooms. Vegetarian meals. Children's helpings. No smoking in dining-room. Music   £5

SHEPTON MALLET Somerset   map 2

Blostin's £

29 Waterloo Road, Shepton Mallet BA4 5HH   COOKING 3
TEL/FAX: (01749) 343648   COST £25–£36

The Reeds' simple, unshowy country restaurant occupies a knock-through cottage conversion where the long, thin dining room is half divided by the remains of one of the demolished party-walls. A tiny bar with an open fire in winter creates the right sort of intimate welcome, and service from friendly local staff under Lynne Reed's tutelage is seamlessly efficient. The cooking doesn't aim to impress with complication, but just wants to do classic things well. A generous piece of foie gras on toasted brioche bears chestnut-brown stripes from the grill, and comes with salad leaves, or there may be salmon mousse wrapped in smoked salmon and sauced with watercress purée.

Main-course roasts are sure-fire bets, whether of 'plump, crisp-skinned' guinea-fowl with wild mushrooms in a cream sauce, or herb-crusted rack of spring lamb with a 'nice old-fashioned gravy'. A separate vegetarian menu shows considerate thought, and dinners might end with iced ginger meringue and cappuccino cream, sharply flavoured sorbets in a brandy-snap basket, or lemon tart. A varietally arranged wine list offers a modest range of decent drinking at commendable prices. Prices start at £8.95.

CHEF: Nick Reed   PROPRIETORS: Nick and Lynne Reed   OPEN: Tue to Sat D 7 to 9.30 (10 Sat)   CLOSED: 2 weeks Jan, 2 weeks Jun   MEALS: alc (main courses £11 to £13). Set D £13.95 (2 courses) to £15.95. BYO £5   SERVICE: not inc, card slips closed   CARDS: Delta, MasterCard, Switch, Visa   DETAILS: 50 seats. Private parties: 32 main room, 18 private room. Vegetarian meals. Children's helpings. No-smoking area. Wheelchair access (1 step; not WC). Occasional music   £5

▲ Bowlish House ▮

Wells Road, Shepton Mallet BA4 5JD
TEL/FAX: (01749) 342022
on A371 to Wells, ¼m from town centre opposite   COOKING 4
Horseshoe Inn   COST £32–£39

A stone-flagged entrance hall, with a table covered in guide books, greets visitors to this attractive eighteenth-century house on the edge of town. A couple who stayed and dined three nights running found enough choice on the menu to keep them happy, adding that it was all good value for money. Linda Morley typically builds a menu with five options per course, among which might be Denhay air-dried ham with salad leaves and Parmesan shavings, or an unusually flavoured soup such as lentil and apricot with cardamom. 'Featherlight' first-course soufflés are highly rated – perhaps red pepper and lovage – while main courses deftly juggle game (loin of venison with rösti potato) and fish (sea bass with a basil-butter sauce) alongside roast saddle of lamb or sirloin steak. 'Robust, elegantly sauced and presented,' summed up a reporter of the style. Vegetables are served plain.

Cheeses, perhaps including unpasteurised Cheddar or Devon blue, offer a realistic alternative to desserts of lemon semi-freddo with strawberries, or 'exceedingly rich' chocolate brownie with dark chocolate sauce and vanilla ice-cream. 'Attentive personal' service from Bob Morley, 'an excellent host', is a plus, and he also oversees the wine list which merits an A-plus for combining quality with interest and variety, offering maturity and youthful vigour, and all at very fair prices. Spain, Italy, California and the Lebanon all compete with France for attention. An eclectic group of house wines are £9.95 a bottle (£1.95 a glass), and there is a generous choice of half-bottles. CELLARMAN'S CHOICE: Saint-Aubin *premier cru* 'Les Frionnes', 1995, Sylvain Langoureau, £25; Côtes du Roussillon, Ch. de Canterrane 1982, £17.50.

CHEF: Linda Morley   PROPRIETORS: Bob and Linda Morley   OPEN: L first Sun of month 1.30 (1 sitting), all week D 7 to 9.30   CLOSED: 1 week autumn, 1 week spring   MEALS: Set Sun L £14.50, Set D £22.50. BYO £5   SERVICE: not inc, card slips closed   CARDS: Amex, MasterCard, Visa DETAILS: 24 seats. Private parties: 40 main room. Car park. Vegetarian meals. Children's helpings. No smoking while others eat. No music   ACCOMMODATION: 3 rooms, all with bath/shower. TV. B&B £48 to £58. Children welcome. High teas for children by arrangement. Baby facilities. Dogs welcome in bedrooms only (*The Which? Hotel Guide*) £5

▲ Charlton House, Mulberry Restaurant

Charlton Road, Shepton Mallet BA4 4PR
TEL: (01749) 342008   FAX: (01749) 346362   COOKING 5
EMAIL: reservations@charltonhouse.   COST £28–£66

This 'swish' Georgian country house is 'a shrine to the Mulberry Company products' (owner Roger Saul is chairman of the company), which helps to explain the rugs, heavy drapes, 'ye olde' ornaments and generally lavish furnishings. The brand extends to cutlery and crockery in the spacious dining-room. Things have changed a bit since last year, catching one or two readers on the hop. Trevor Brooks has gone to Kinnaird (see entry, Dunkeld) and Adam Fellows took over in February 1998. Set-price menus now offer no choice, pre-meal pastry nibbles have been replaced by olives, and vegetables are now incorporated into each dish, but the food retains its ability to soothe and comfort.

Luxuries play their part in this. Ballottine of salmon comes with a cauliflower and truffle purée, soup might be lettuce and oyster, and fillet of 'naturally reared' beef has been served with a slice of pan-fried duck liver. Locally sourced materials make a contribution, and the cooking has obliged by producing 'moist, pink' chicken liver parfait with a 'deep, satisfying flavour', and braised guinea-fowl in a 'full-bodied sauce' with Puy lentils. Desserts appear to be less successful, and service has left a lot to be desired. A short wine list is almost as strong on sparklers as on reds and whites, and is fairly priced, starting at £12.

CHEF: Adam Fellows   PROPRIETORS: Mr and Mrs R.J. Saul   OPEN: all week 12.30 to 2, 7.30 to 9.30   MEALS: alc (main courses L £9.50 to £16, D £17.50 to £21.50). Set L £12.50 (2 courses) to £16.50, Set D £27.50 to £31   SERVICE: not inc   CARDS: Amex, Diners, MasterCard, Switch, Visa   DETAILS: 50 seats. 24 seats outside. Private parties: 80 main room. Car park. Children's helpings. No smoking in dining-room. Wheelchair access (also WC). Music   ACCOMMODATION: 17 rooms, all with bath/shower. TV. Phone. B&B £85 to £285. Children welcome. Baby facilities. Afternoon teas. Dogs welcome in 1 room only. Swimming-pool. Fishing (*The Which? Hotel Guide*)

SHERE Surrey   map 3

Kinghams ✿✱

Gomshall Lane, Shere GU5 9HB
TEL: (01483) 202168   COOKING 3
just off A25 Dorking to Guildford road   COST £24–£45

'We strolled around the village on a mellow autumn day and returned to an excellent meal, served with a smile.' So wrote a pair from Essex who arrived at this comforting beamed cottage restaurant on the stroke of midday – only to be told that the kitchen needed 'another ten minutes or so to cook the potatoes'. That reassuring sense of freshness and sound ingredients also colours other reports: fish arrives daily from the market, duck in various guises (perhaps on a bed of Puy lentils) has been 'cooked to perfection', and visitors have also remarked on the quality of roast vegetables with olive oil and balsamic dressing, seared tuna ('pink inside') with avocado salsa, and monkfish in a cream-based sauce. Accompanying salads are imaginative, vegetables are 'competently presented', while desserts are praiseworthy offerings along the lines of richly satisfying chocolate tart. The mood of the place is thoroughly relaxing, and it's worth strolling out into the garden for coffee on fine evenings. Around 40 suitably varied wines are backed up by a clutch of half-bottles. Chilean house wine is £10.50.

CHEF/PROPRIETOR: Paul Baker   OPEN: Tue to Sun L 12 to 2.30, Tue to Sat D 7 to 9.30   CLOSED: 25 to 31 Dec   MEALS: alc (main courses £10 to £15). Set L £10.95 (2 courses), Set D Tue to Thur £12.50 (2 courses)   SERVICE: not inc   CARDS: Amex, Delta, MasterCard, Switch, Visa   DETAILS: 46 seats. 20 seats outside. Private parties: 28 main room, 20 and 28 private rooms. Car park. Vegetarian meals. Children's helpings. No smoking in dining-room. Wheelchair access (not WC). Music   £5

SHINFIELD Berkshire   map 2

L'Ortolan

The Old Vicarage, Church Lane, Shinfield RG2 9BY
TEL: (0118) 988 3783   FAX: (0118) 988 5391   COOKING 8
off A33, S of M4 junction 11   COST £38–£129

This modest, unimposing red-brick vicarage has a country feel to it, although distressed peach walls, maroon fabrics and silk-flower displays might convey something of the 'conference hotel aesthetic'. Fast, professional service is delivered by a team of young French staff who are fine provided they don't encounter anything unusual: front-of-house might benefit from an authoritative presence. That apart, 'exciting and highly innovative' food is presented in a number of formats; the beauty is that, although the most expensive starters on the *carte* can cost £30 and more, cheaper set-price meals are no less attractive.

One such lunch began with a dish of sweet-sour marinated salmon artfully contrasted with salty caviare and surrounded by a chive cream sauce. This was followed by a thick slab of roast cod on waxy potatoes which came with a 'dynamic' mustard cream sauce, a second sauce provided by the runny yolk of a poached egg. John Burton-Race has a light touch and enjoys layering dishes with contrasts of textures and carefully worked nuances of flavour. Complexity is his trademark, nothing is simple: for example, a dish of sole that is poached, then 'masked' with juices, then enriched with sabayon, then gratinated. One visitor likened him to a conductor who 'manages to direct the orchestra with a flourish, and keep to the beat'.

Results may not always transcend ingredients 'but the kitchen affords plenty of glimpses of its immense talent: 'five impressive mouthfuls' of lightly steamed truffle-topped langoustines on half-moon potato slices – 'looking like jewellery' – served with young leaves dressed with a 'perfumed and luscious' olive oil that 'stole the show'. Cameo parts also took the limelight in an inspector's breast of squab pigeon, bound together with a mousse, wrapped in Savoy cabbage leaves, steamed, and dramatically sliced to reveal red breast, pink mousse and green leaves. By its side was a 'brilliant' and eclipsing raviolo containing five tiny girolles in a clean-tasting Madeira sauce. Whatever else, you can at least see where the money goes when you reckon up the effort involved.

The same goes for desserts, still impressive although their impact may be less powerful: caramelised puff pastry circles sandwiching poached pear and vanilla ice-cream, or a variation on the raspberry theme incorporating a light mousse, punchy sorbet, miniature soufflé, and puff pastry leaves encasing plump fresh raspberries. The hefty tome that is the wine list continues to be dominated by a strong selection from classical France; indeed the number of fine clarets has greatly increased, numbering nine Ch. Haut-Brions (running back to 1964) and five Ch. Latours (from 1988 to 1971) among their ranks. Prices can be very high, although the house selection starts at £16 for a Vin de Pays de Vaucluse Chardonnay.

CHEF: John Burton-Race   PROPRIETOR: Burton-Race Restaurants plc   OPEN: Tue to Sun L 12 to 2.30, Tue to Sat D 7 to 10   MEALS: alc (main courses £26 to £36). Set L £22 to £39.50, Set D £42 (not Sat) to £75 (minimum 2).   SERVICE: not inc, card slips closed   CARDS: Amex, Delta, Diners, MasterCard, Switch, Visa   DETAILS: 60 seats. 20 seats outside. Private parties: 40 main room, 30 private room. Car park. Vegetarian meals. Children's helpings. Wheelchair access (2 steps; also WC). No music   £5

The Guide *office can quickly spot when a restaurateur is encouraging customers to write recommending inclusion. Such reports do not further a restaurant's cause. Please tell us if a restaurateur invites you to write to the* Guide.

The Guide *is totally independent, accepts no free hospitality, and survives on the number of copies sold each year.*

SHIPHAM Somerset   map 2

▲ *Daneswood House* ✲ | NEW ENTRY |

Cuck Hill, Shipham, nr Winscombe BS25 1RD
TEL: (01934) 843145 FAX: (01934) 843824   COOKING 2
EMAIL: daneswoodhousehotel@compuserve.com   COST £25–£50

The tall pebbledash and white building, at the top of a hairpin-bend drive, was
built at the turn of the century as a health hydro. It felt 'very boarding-house' to
one visitor, with its conservatory addition, dark green and gold wallpaper, brace
of dining-rooms, busy fabrics, and tiny oil paintings in ornate gold frames. Two-
and three-course menus, supplemented by vegetarian options, have produced
twice-baked herb and cheese soufflé, filo pastry tartlet of goats' cheese with
bacon rashers, and roast loin of wild boar. The style is not too ambitious, despite
a few luxury items, and the food seems to have 'home made' written all over it,
or 'home-smoked' in the case of chicken used in a roulade. Vegetables are
incorporated into main courses: no fewer than seven different types with one
reporter's grilled beef sirloin. Cheeses are British, and desserts have included
strawberry meringue, armagnac parfait, and bread-and-butter pudding. A
classically inclined wine list starts with a dozen-strong house selection under
£15.

CHEFS: Julian Prosser and Heather Matthews PROPRIETORS: David and Elise Hodges OPEN:
Sun to Fri L 12.15 to 1.45, all week D 7 to 9.30 (8 Sun) CLOSED: 26 Dec to 3 Jan. MEALS: Set L
Mon to Fri £15.95 to £29.95, Set L Sun £13.95 (2 courses) to £17.05, Set D £23.95 to £29.95
SERVICE: not inc, card slips closed CARDS: Amex, Delta, Diners, MasterCard, Switch, Visa
DETAILS: 50 seats. Private parties: 70 main room, 10 to 34 private rooms. Car park. Vegetarian
menu. Children's helpings. No smoking in dining-room. Wheelchair access (2 steps; also WC).
Occasional music ACCOMMODATION: 12 rooms, all with bath/shower. TV. Phone. B&B £65 to
£125. Children welcome. High teas for children. Baby facilities. No dogs. Afternoon teas (*The
Which? Hotel Guide*) £5

SHOTLEY Suffolk   map 6

Old Boot House ♥ £ ✲

Main Road, Shotley IP9 1EY
TEL: (01473) 787755   COOKING 3
10m SE of Ipswich on B1456   COST £21–£41

'Because of our location we may close if we have no bookings,' advises Ian
Chamberlain, so visitors are advised to telephone before embarking on a journey
to this remote Suffolk backwater. The place stands on a peninsula between the
Orwell and Stour surrounded by wheat, barley and beet fields. Ian's cooking is
defined not only by the locality, it also responds to the seasons. Ideas evolve as
the months go by. In the dark days of the year you might find baked hare fillets
wrapped in puff pastry with Suffolk black bacon and elderberry sauce, or spiced
lamb invigorated with cinnamon, cloves and allspice. Come summer, there
might be east coast crab sausage with pickled samphire to start, and grilled
peaches with honeysuckle syrup, or even a raspberry tart (tinged with rose
petals from bushes growing in front of the restaurant) to round things off.
Inspiration comes from far and wide, be it spätzli noodles with mushroom sauce,

or cleverly presented devilled kidneys in a pastry 'pot' ('I thought it was crockery until I saw it fall apart when I tackled [it],' observed one reporter).

Pam Chamberlain's forthright front-of-house style is not to everyone's taste, but her staff are always polite and helpful. Wine service is matter of fact, and the selection from both the Old and New Worlds (supplied by Adnams) offers a great range of styles and flavours at very competitive prices, beginning with house vins de pays at £8.50. CELLARMAN'S CHOICE: Vin de Pays des Côtes de Pérignan, Viognier 1996, £13.90; Crozes-Hermitage 1996, Dom. Pochon, £13.60.

CHEF: Ian Chamberlain PROPRIETORS: Ian and Pamela Chamberlain OPEN: Tue to Sun L 12 to 1.30, Tue to Sat D 7 to 9 (later by arrangement) MEALS: alc (main courses L £7 to £10, D £9 to £15.50). Set L Sun £11.50 (2 courses) to £14.75 SERVICE: not inc, card slips closed CARDS: MasterCard, Switch, Visa DETAILS: 45 seats. 12 seats outside. Private parties: 45 main room. Car park. Children's helpings. No smoking in dining-room. No music

---

SHREWSBURY Shropshire   map 5

Sol ⁵⭐ | NEW ENTRY |

82 Wyle Cop, Shrewsbury SY1 1UT   COOKING 5
TEL: (01743) 340560 FAX: (01743) 340552   COST £20–£47

Things are looking up for Shrewsbury, and not before time judging by the enthusiasm with which Sol has been greeted. After leaving the Old Vicarage Hotel (see entry, Worfield), John Williams took over a tapas bar in this steep town-centre street just as the last edition of the *Guide* appeared. He has left the décor more or less as it was, complete with high-tech lighting and 'brash' Mexican colour scheme with its aquamarine ceiling and sunny yellow walls. Against this background the 'grand-hotel food' might appear 'incongruous', but nobody minds that. The place is 'youthful, full of zest and a true pleasure', the dishes both sophisticated and technically accomplished.

A broadly Anglo-French approach produces escabèche of Cornish mackerel with fennel slaw, Ludlow venison with red cabbage wuntun and foie gras, and grilled fillet of salmon with polenta and lobster sauce. The food looks good, and main courses come complete (without the 'usual run-of-the-mill assorted vegetables'), although the style may hark back to earlier days with its garnishing gestures of a cone-shaped carrot mousse with roast rump of lamb, or decorative balls of courgette and carrot served with tortellini of smoked haddock. Ice-creams figure prominently among desserts; otherwise try a tall wedge of lightly glazed lemon tart with a 'luscious' filling.

Quantities are not large, although appetites are assuaged by copious nibbles, appetisers, 'impeccably professional' bread, and a two-tiered basket of petits fours, and value is considered good. Despite an element of 'pomp and circumstance' in the service, Mrs Williams oversees an efficient operation, dispensing wines from a short list that stays commendably under £20 for the most part, starting with four house wines at £8.95.

Use the lists towards the front of the book to find suitable restaurants for special occasions.

CHEF: John Williams   PROPRIETORS: J. and D. Williams, C. Cadwallader and S. Cousins   OPEN: Tue to Sat 12 to 2.30, 7 to 9.30   MEALS: alc L (main courses £6.50 to £7). Set D £25 to £29.50   SERVICE: not inc, card slips closed   CARDS: Amex, Delta, Diners, MasterCard, Switch, Visa   DETAILS: 50 seats. Private parties: 20 main room, 25 private room. Vegetarian meals. Children's helpings. No smoking in dining-room. Music £5

SHURDINGTON Gloucestershire   map 2

▲ *The Greenway* ♟ ⅝✳

Shurdington GL51 5UG

TEL: (01242) 862352   FAX: (01242) 862780   COOKING 3

on A46, 2½m S of Cheltenham   COST £32–£55

Set well back from the thrum of the A46, at the end of a long driveway, this creeper-clad Elizabethan manor house offers the kind of time-warp experience the Cotswolds specialise in. Soft furnishings and fresh flowers in the drawing-room, and conservatory dining with a view of lush gardens and the hills beyond, cast a comforting spell. Peter Fairclough does nothing to disrupt the tone, but plies the country-house line with quiet aplomb. Boned quail stuffed with wild mushrooms on buttered spinach with sherry vinegar jus makes an elegant and forthrightly flavoured starter, and the labour-intensiveness in a main course of monkfish tail with baby leeks, ravioli of scallop mousse and cream sauce infused with thyme seemed worth the trouble to one reporter. Timing, not always accurate, has nevertheless produced a correctly pink canon of lamb served with sarladaise potatoes, wild asparagus and rosemary sauce.

Puddings display fine technique in praline parfait with white chocolate mousse, or pistachio tart with some ingenious dried strawberry 'wafers'. Coffee comes with good petits fours, while service is highly formal and moves at a stately pace. A traditional list takes in most wine-producing countries but shows a marked preference for France, particularly Bordeaux and Burgundy. Excellent vintage ports, including a 1945 Warre, are a high point; house wines start at a lowly £13.50. CELLARMAN'S CHOICE: Cloudy Bay Sauvignon Blanc 1997, Marlborough, New Zealand, £33.50; Aloxe-Corton 'Les Chaillots' 1993, Dom. Latour, £43.

CHEF: Peter Fairclough   PROPRIETORS: David and Valerie White   OPEN: Sun to Fri L 12.30 to 2, all week D 7.30 to 9.30 (8.30 Sun)   CLOSED: first week Jan   MEALS: alc (main courses £9.75; not available Sun L). Set L Sun £14.50 (2 courses) to £18.50. Set D £32   SERVICE: not inc, card slips closed   CARDS: Amex, Diners, MasterCard, Switch, Visa   DETAILS: 50 seats. 16 seats outside. Private parties: 24 main room, 12 to 24 private rooms. Car park. Vegetarian meals. Children's helpings. No children under 7. No smoking in dining-room. Wheelchair access (also WC). Music   ACCOMMODATION: 19 rooms, all with bath/shower. TV. Phone. B&B £90 to £225. Rooms for disabled. No children under 7. No dogs. Afternoon teas (*The Which? Hotel Guide*)

Restaurateurs justifiably resent no-shows. If you quote a credit card number when booking, you may be liable for the restaurant's lost profit margin if you don't turn up. Always phone to cancel.

SNAPE Suffolk   map 6

▲ *Crown Inn* £

Main Street, Snape IP17 1SL   COOKING 2
TEL: (01728) 688324   COST £21–£41

This 500-year-old pub near the Maltings concert hall may be geared to 'the gentrified Aldeburgh set', but can't be accused of standing on ceremony. Show yourself to a seat, unpack your own cutlery, be prepared to chase the wine list, and pick your food off a blackboard. Local supplies include beef from a grass-fed herd, organic vegetables, and, of course, fish: grilled lemon sole, baked sea bass, or pan-fried skate wing. The menu, meanwhile, runs around the world, from a beef, Guinness and mushroom pie, via bresaola with Parmesan shavings and olive oil, to mussels with lemon grass, coriander and ginger. Some combinations may sound a bit risqué – salad of prawns with mango, lime and a salsa, for example – but soft herring roes on tapénade toast with capers was 'a nicely done pub dish', and puddings are in the familiar vein of chocolate fudge cake, spotted dick with custard, and crème brûlée. Around 70 wines from the Adnams list characteristically offer plenty of interest, much of it below £15. Prices start at £9.50 and there are more than a dozen by the glass.

CHEF: Diane Maylott PROPRIETORS: Paul and Diane Maylott OPEN: all week 12 to 2, 7 to 9 (pre-and post-concert meals by arrangement) CLOSED: 25 Dec, D 26 Dec MEALS: alc (main courses £7 to £14.50) SERVICE: not inc, card slips closed CARDS: Delta, MasterCard, Switch, Visa DETAILS: 50 seats. 24 seats outside. Private parties: 28 main room. Car park. Vegetarian meals. No children under 14. Wheelchair access (1 step; also WC). No music ACCOMMODATION: 3 rooms, all with bath/shower. B&B £35 to £50. No children under 14 £5

SOUTHALL Greater London   map 3

Brilliant £

72–76 Western Road, Southall UB2 5DZ   COOKING 3
TEL: (0181) 574 1928   FAX: (0181) 574 0276   COST £18–£36

'This place deserves its name,' insists one devotee, who maintains that it continues to deliver 'the best Indian food I have eaten in a restaurant'. Expansion into the fish and chip shop next door has allowed the place to absorb greater numbers of enthusiastic customers, but there has been 'no deterioration in standards'. Improvements out front have been mirrored in the kitchen, which now boasts a tandoor oven: this might be used for 'much-improved' breads or succulent king prawns, subtly marinated and cooked with consummate lightness and dexterity. Daily specials such as vegetable keema augment the 'rock-like' menu, although old favourites continue to draw most praise: chilli chicken 'cooked tenderly through', methi chicken with a 'vibrantly spicy' fenugreek sauce, and aloo gobi ('respecting the original texture of the potato and cauliflower') have been endorsed. Rice is suffused with flavour, and sweets range from gulab jamun to ice-cream with mangoes. Drink lassi or Indian bottled beer. House wine is £7.50. Members of the Anand family also run Madhu's Brilliant at 29 South Road, Southall; Tel: (0181) 574 1897.

CHEF: D.K. Anand PROPRIETORS: K.K. and D.K. Anand OPEN: Tue to Fri L 12.15 to 2.30, Tue to Sun D 6.15 to 11.15 (12 Fri and Sat) MEALS: alc (main courses £6 to £8). Set L £12.50, Set D £15 SERVICE: 10%, card slips closed CARDS: Amex, Delta, Diners, MasterCard, Switch, Visa DETAILS: 120 seats. Private parties: 120 main room, 80 private room. Vegetarian meals. Children's helpings. Wheelchair access (also WC). Music. Air-conditioned

Lahore Karahi & Tandoori £

162–164 The Broadway, Southall UB1 1LW
TEL: (0181) 574 8602 FAX: (0181) 574 1630   COOKING 1
EMAIL: gifto@virgin.net   COST £7–£26

Far from a 'curry' house – even the word is rare in the long menu – this a large Pakistani eating-house. The menu proclaims it as a subsidiary of a cash-and-carry, and its aim is to serve the local community without fuss or frills in décor or service. Strengths include tandoori and barbecue meat and fish accompanied by a variety of naan, roti and paratha breads. The long menu also offers Bombay chaats and puris as well as biryanis, butter chicken, and the unusual haleem (a mixture of crushed lentils and lamb). For those who crave something English, there's always 'tikka chicken masala'. The restaurant is unlicensed, though customers are welcome to bring their own wine (no corkage charge); or better yet, drink fruit juice or lassi by the glass or jug.

CHEF: Mohammad Muslim PROPRIETORS: Abdul Rahman and Arshad Mohammad OPEN: all week 12 to 11.30 (midnight Fri and Sat) MEALS: alc (main courses £1.60 to £9). Unlicensed: BYO (no corkage) SERVICE: not inc CARDS: Amex, Delta, Diners, MasterCard, Switch, Visa DETAILS: 190 seats. Private parties: 325 main room, 100 private rooms. Vegetarian meals. Children welcome. Music

---

SOUTH MOLTON Devon   map 1

▲ Whitechapel Manor ⅝✳

South Molton EX36 3EG   COOKING 5
TEL: (01769) 573377 FAX: (01769) 573797   COST £43–£60

Fronted by a well-kept terraced garden, this Grade I listed Elizabethan manor is the repository of a spectacular Jacobean carved oak screen, and William and Mary plasterwork and panelling. More than one reporter has remarked that the owners are not at all like typical hoteliers, which may be why the place is considered 'grand' and 'homely' at the same time. Materials are well sourced, taking in fish from the north Devon coast as well as pheasant, venison and partridge in season. The food's Anglo-French axis – Devon fillet steak with mash and grain mustard cream, or duck breast with lentils – is often given a Mediterranean tilt, especially when it comes to seafood: seared wild salmon with black olive purée, or red mullet with ratatouille and basil oil.

Output, according to one visitor, is typical of the 'professional school of modern British cookery', which is to say thoroughly accomplished, if 'fairly predictable'. There are minor changes from day to day, as sauces are rotated, and risottos varied: a saffron and herb version with seared Cornish scallops one night, a risotto nero with turbot the next. A hot lemon tart with passion-fruit sorbet lifted the spirits of one luncher, while another enjoyed iced coffee parfait with thinly sliced dark chocolate. Australia and New Zealand make a positive contribution to the wine list, though France remains dominant; bargain-hunters need to know their retail prices to get the best deal. House Chardonnay is £11.50, red Minervois £10.50.

CHEF: Matthew Corner   PROPRIETORS: Margaret Aris and Charles Brown   OPEN: all week D only 7 to 8.45 (booking essential) and L by arrangement for parties of 6 or more   MEALS: Set D £34   SERVICE: not inc, card slips closed   CARDS: Delta, Diners, MasterCard, Switch, Visa DETAILS: 30 seats. Private parties: 36 main room. Car park. Children's helpings. No smoking in dining-room. No music   ACCOMMODATION: 11 rooms, all with bath/shower. TV. Phone. B&B £70 to £170. Children welcome. Baby facilities. No dogs. Afternoon teas (*The Which? Hotel Guide*)

SOUTHWATER West Sussex   map 3

Cole's ✸✱

Worthing Road, Southwater RH13 7BS	COOKING 4
TEL: (01403) 730456	COST £23–£49

What was once a barn in a 'rather straggling' Sussex village has been transformed over the years into a restaurant complete with high ceilings and a grand inglenook fireplace. Elizabeth Cole and family have stamped their mark on the place, and the cooking continues to find favour with a loyal contingent of customers. Good ingredients are used judiciously in ways that are both comfortingly familiar and inviting. Nothing is forced or pretentious. Fish might show up in the guise of seared scallop and pancetta salad with orange and saffron dressing, or grilled fillets of sea bass with salsa verde garnished with straw potatoes. Those with different preferences could consider Caesar salad, fillet of Scotch beef on a grain mustard and brandy sauce, or wild mushroom risotto. The dessert menu is a safe run through fruit brûlée, sticky toffee pudding, and apple fritters with vanilla ice-cream. Service aims for smartness and professionalism rather than warmth. France is the main contender on the list of around 40 fairly priced wines, but there is also some tempting stuff from down under. House wines are £10.95.

CHEF: Elizabeth Cole   PROPRIETORS: the Cole family   OPEN: Tue to Fri and Sun L 12 to 2, Tue to Sat D 7 to 9   MEALS: alc Tue to Fri L and Tue to Sat D (main courses £12 to £19). Set L £12.95 (2 courses) to £15   SERVICE: not inc   CARDS: Amex, Delta, Diners, MasterCard, Switch, Visa DETAILS: 36 seats. Private parties: 36 main room, 10 private room. Car park. Vegetarian meals. Children's helpings. No smoking in dining-room. Wheelchair access (2 steps; also WC). Music (£5)

SOUTHWOLD Suffolk   map 6

▲ The Crown ▮ 🛏 ✸✱

90 High Street, Southwold IP18 6DP	COOKING 4
TEL: (01502) 722275 FAX: (01502) 727263	COST £22–£35

Wholesale staff changes in early 1998 have left a new regime out front, overseen by Anna Bostedt, and in the kitchen. But this old coaching-inn, the flagship of celebrated brewer and wine merchant Adnams, has barely wobbled since the changeover: both ingredients and cooking have remained 'well up to expectations'. The bar offers an easy-going *carte* of leek and mushroom soup, grilled calf's liver, and baked apple with fudge sauce, while the rather more formal dining-room goes in for fixed-price meals of two or three courses with an attractive deal on suggested wines by the glass.

Seafood still accounts for a fair slice of the kitchen's output, in the form of grilled monkfish with a saffron and mussel risotto, or salmon on puff pastry with sliced and 'beautifully dressed' new potatoes in a 'praiseworthy' cream sauce. Craig Dunn maintains interest without resorting to exotica, serving smoked chicken boudin with a herb mayonnaise, and breast of Aylesbury duck, cooked 'saignant' as requested, with minted couscous and a honey-flavoured sauce. Finish perhaps with strawberry crème brûlée (strawberries are not restricted to summer) or a sponge flan filled with a white chocolate 'cheesecake' mixture. The wine list sails around the world, finding plenty of good-value, quality bottles in every port (though the Italians and Australians look particularly appealing). House wines change every a month, and a fleet of drinkable bins cruises in under £10. CELLARMAN'S CHOICE: Mâcon Chardonnay 1996, Talmard, £12.80; Mitchell 'Growers Grenache' 1997, Clare Valley, S. Australia, £13.95.

CHEF: Craig Dunn   PROPRIETOR: Adnams Hotels plc   OPEN: all week 12.15 to 2.30, 7 to 9.30 CLOSED: 1 week early Jan   MEALS: Set L £14 (2 courses) to £17, Set D £19 (2 courses) to £23. BYO £6. Bar food available   SERVICE: not inc, card slips closed   CARDS: Amex, Delta, Diners, MasterCard, Switch, Visa   DETAILS: 22 seats. 12 seats outside. Private parties: 22 main room, 22 private room. Car park. Vegetarian meals. Children's holpings. No smoking in dining-room. No music. Air-conditioned   ACCOMMODATION: 12 rooms, all with bath/shower. TV. Phone. B&B £45 to £68. Children welcome. High teas for children (must be pre-booked). No dogs (*The Which? Hotel Guide*)

STADDLEBRIDGE   North Yorkshire   map 9

▲ *McCoy's Bistro*

The Cleveland Tontine, Staddlebridge DL6 3JB
TEL: (01609) 882671   FAX: (01609) 882660   COOKING 5
6m NE of Northallerton, at junction of A19 and A172   COST £31–£53

The stone-built inn stands on a small island between a slip road and the busy A19, gentle farmland to the west, wooded hills rising on the other side to the North Yorkshire moors. Double-glazing helps to keep it peaceful, and in any case McCoy's has always been 'an inward-looking place' somewhat cut off from the outside world. Those who cherish memories of the gloriously eccentric dining-room will either have to hang on to them, or book a private party, since this remarkably atmospheric room with its 1940s Muzak is now closed to casual visitors. But the basement bistro continues to serve up the same lively yet serious food in the same friendly atmopshere.

Begin, perhaps, with a pair of briefly grilled scallops on sweet potato salad, unusually accompanied by a spicy wuntun of chopped scallop with chillies, dressed with a ginger and coriander vinaigrette; or with a salad of black pudding with lyonnaise sausage and poached egg. Despite an accumulation of ingredients in many dishes, Marcus Bennett's sense of culinary reason prevails, producing for example squab pigeon on a purée of white beans, together with a cabbage-leaf parcel of minced pigeon, all in a glossy port-enriched reduction. Finish, perhaps with light strawberry mille-feuille, or that old-school favourite baked Alaska. The wine list is a short but impressive international jumble chosen for flavour, starting with house red and white at £10.95.

CHEF: Marcus Bennett   PROPRIETORS: the McCoy brothers   OPEN: all week 12 to 2, 7 to 9.30   CLOSED: 25 and 26 Dec, 1 Jan   MEALS: alc (main courses £13 to £17)   SERVICE: not inc   CARDS: Amex, MasterCard, Switch, Visa   DETAILS: 70 seats. Private parties: 50 main room. Car park. Vegetarian meals. Children's helpings. Music. Air-conditioned   ACCOMMODATION: 6 rooms, all with bath/shower. TV. Phone. B&B £75 to £90. Children welcome. High teas for children

---

STAITHES North Yorkshire   map 9

▲ Endeavour 🍴 £

1 High Street, Staithes TS13 5BH   COOKING 2
TEL: (01947) 840825   COST £24–£49

Captain James Cook once resided in this charm-laden fishing village, and Lisa Chapman's little restaurant close by the quay is named in honour of his ship. Fish from local boats always shows up prominently on her daily blackboard menu: ideas might be as simple as dressed crab salad or lobster with garlic butter, or as in tune as home-cured 'gravlax' of sea bass with blinis and lime vinaigrette, or pan-fried cod roe with Indian aubergine salad. Meat eaters and vegetarians are also well served: the former might go for duck breast with damson and red wine sauce, or noisettes of local lamb with black pudding and cider cream sauce, while the latter could choose mushroom pancake gâteau with wild mushroom sauce, or black-bean chilli with avocado salsa and crème fraîche. Best seller among the desserts is, apparently, crème brûlée, although the kitchen also turns its hand to pecan pie with home-made toffee ice-cream, and bayleaf bavarois with redcurrants. 'May we compliment the young ladies who run Endeavour,' pleaded one reporter after being affectionately looked after one bitterly cold Easter holiday. Forty wines provide reliable drinking at prices few would dispute. House wine is £8.45.

CHEF/PROPRIETOR: Lisa Chapman   OPEN: Mon to Sat L 12 to 2 (bookings only), all week D 6.45 to 9   CLOSED: 25 and 26 Dec, Sun and Mon autumn to early spring   MEALS: alc (main courses £8.50 to £19). BYO £5   SERVICE: not inc   CARDS: none   DETAILS: 45 seats. Private parties: 30 main room, 12 to 30 private rooms. Vegetarian meals. Children welcome. No smoking in dining-room. Occasional music   ACCOMMODATION: 3 rooms, 2 with bath/shower. TV. B&B £42 to £50. Children welcome. No dogs   (£5)

To find a restaurant in a particular area use the maps at the back of the book.

All details are as accurate as possible at the time of going to press, but chefs and owners often change, and it is wise to check by telephone before making a special journey. Many readers have been disappointed when set-price bargain meals are no longer available. Ask when booking.

STANTON Suffolk   map 6

Leaping Hare Vineyard Restaurant 🌶✕ 🍽 £

Wyken Vineyards, Stanton IP31 2DW
TEL: (01359) 250287   FAX: (01359) 252372   COOKING 3
signposted off A143 Bury St Edmunds to Diss road   COST £24–£39

East Anglia meets America's West Coast in this vineyard complex, run by Carla
Carlisle, who once cooked at Chez Panisse in California. A garden opens to the
public from Thursday to Saturday, and a shop stocks everything from Wyken
wines and jams to colourful New England patchwork quilts. The restaurant
occupies one end of a beautiful old barn, its wooden beams supporting a lofty
roof, with high windows adding to the airy ambience. Wooden tub chairs are
more comfortable than they look, and tables have colourful check cloths.

Brendan Daly's cooking is sophisticated but uncomplicated, with portions
designed to satisfy even the famished. Crisp, fresh home-grown leaves and
vegetables contribute to the success of seared scallop salad with sesame oil
dressing, or roast sea bass with samphire and warm tomato vinaigrette.
Carnivores have enjoyed local game, including partridge, smoked pheasant
breast, and Suffolk lamb 'finely flavoured outside, even better inside'.
Commended desserts have included poached pears with lemon syllabub, sticky
toffee and chocolate pudding with Jersey cream, and a light rhubarb sponge
pudding. The menu credits all its suppliers , including Neal's Yard for cheese
and Rocombe Farms for ice-cream. American hospitality and efficiency defines
the service, which is a model of teamwork. The short 'Guest Wine List' is
carefully chosen to supplement Wyken's own; most wines are available by the
glass, or try 'wine-like, delicious and addictive' Wyken cider.

CHEF: Brendan Daly   PROPRIETORS: Kenneth and Carla Carlisle   OPEN: Thur to Sun L 12 to
2.15, Fri and Sat D 7 to 9 (booking essential L and D). Café menu available   CLOSED: 24 Dec to 6
Feb   MEALS: alc (main courses £8.50 to £13)   SERVICE: not inc, card slips closed   CARDS:
Delta, MasterCard, Switch, Visa   DETAILS: 50 seats. 8 seats outside. Private parties: 50 main
room. Car park. Vegetarian meals. Children's helpings. No smoking in dining-room. Wheelchair
access (also WC). Music   £5

STOCKCROSS Berkshire   map 2

▲ Vineyard at Stockcross 🍾   NEW ENTRY

Stockcross RG20 8JU
TEL: (01635) 528770   FAX: (01635) 528398   COOKING 6
just off A4, 2m W of Newbury   COST £46–£97

The vineyard referred to – also owned by Sir Peter Michael – is several thousand
miles away in Napa Valley, which might explain something of the Californian
approach here. Ideally placed to attract an international clientele out of
Heathrow, it has had pots of money thrown at it, and is as much about 'the art of
fine dining' as anything. The first sight to catch the eye may well be six flames set
dramatically on a circular lake by the entrance, where a doorman stands ready to
park the car. Lounging and dining-areas form a 'semi-open plan' arrangement,
with artwork that looks more like a private than off-the-peg collection. Wine

stores are floor-to-ceiling, seats all have arms, and vineleaf and lily motifs are everywhere.

The overall effect is 'airy, light and relaxed', and one visitor summed it up as 'Savoy meets country club', reminding us that David Sharland used to cook at the Savoy Grill. His style is modern, with a French bias, and might be equally at home in San Francisco as in Newbury. A few luxuries appear – not surprisingly, given that all main courses on the *carte* are over £20 – fish and meat generally come as fillets, breasts or saddles, and there are lots of purées: this is easy-to-eat food. The menu lists key ingredients without always describing how they are put together, allowing for an element of surprise, but has turned out a fairly consistent array of dishes from crab risotto with 'a nice texture' to pink pigeon breast with couscous and girolles, from filo parcels of lobster to 'huge' wedges of pink duck breast with potato purée.

Cheeses – mostly French – have been 'all ripe and good' but, given a temperature controlled chocolate room (something of a rarity outside Switzerland) as part of the new kitchen, it makes sense to try the assiette of chocolate. Those who opt instead for crème brûlée with a fig and port purée at the bottom, or a 'little soup' of cherries with soft meringue 'snow eggs', will be able to catch up on chocolate with 'fabulous' petits fours. Wines are presented in two separate books: California and International. The Californian list is unique, being a collection from Sir Peter's and other small, family-owned vineyards, with many rarely seen in the UK. The international set is an equally impressive range of classic wines, particularly good in Bordeaux, Burgundy and Italy, but at prices designed to deflect you back to California. However, around 50 bins priced under £20 can be found. House wines are the Sir Peter Michael range, starting at £25. CELLARMAN'S CHOICE: Ojai Sauvignon Blanc/Semillon 1996, Santa Barbara, California, £27.50; Catfish Vineyard Zinfandel 1995, Mendocino, California, £26.50.

CHEF: David Sharland   PROPRIETOR: Sir Peter Michael   OPEN: Tue to Sun L 12 to 2, Tue to Sat D 7 to 10   MEALS: alc (main courses £21.50 to £28). Set L £33, Set D £70 (inc wine)   SERVICE: not inc   CARDS: Amex, Delta, Diners, MasterCard, Switch, Visa   DETAILS: 40 seats. Private parties: 8 main room, 25 private room. Car park. Vegetarian meals. No children under 12. Jacket and tie. Wheelchair access (also WC). Music. Air-conditioned   ACCOMMODATION: 15 rooms, all with bath/shower. TV. Phone. Room only £150 to £500. No children under 12. No dogs. Afternoon teas (£5)

STOKE HOLY CROSS   Norfolk   map 6

Wildebeest Arms ⅝✶

Norwich Road, Stoke Holy Cross NR14 8QJ
TEL: (01508) 492497   FAX: (01603) 766403
from Norwich take A140 Ipswich road; directly after
roundabout take the left turn signposted Stoke Holy   COOKING 2
Cross   COST £23–£43

While the eponymous creature has yet to turn up on the menu at this whitewashed country inn, its habitat is invoked in the wall decorations of tribal masks and assegais. Those who start with Cajun-spiced chicken with pineapple and lime salsa, or mushroom and spinach lasagne with pine-nuts and mascarpone, may feel they have lost their bearings completely. Do not worry. Eden Derrick's cooking mixes and matches in the modern way, using local ingredients to vibrant effect: in cod wrapped in Parma ham with mussels, spring onion mash and tomato velouté, or rump of lamb with a thyme-scented ragoût of sweet potatoes, Puy lentils and shallots. Chips to accompany come with their skins on. It is all 'carefully cooked with verve and flair'. Cheeses, or a savoury of Welsh rarebit with onion chutney, provide a viable alternative to desserts of two-tone chocolate mousse with bitter orange sauce, or perhaps banana, bourbon and honeycomb parfait with vanilla sauce. Sunday lunch, chalked up on a board, treads a more traditional route, usually offering a choice of two roasts. French wines and New World reds are the strong suits on the list. House selections start at £8.95.

CHEFS: Eden Derrick PROPRIETOR: Henry Watt OPEN: all week 12 to 2 (12.30 to 2.30 Sun), 7 to 9.30 CLOSED: 25 and 26 Dec MEALS: alc (main courses L £7.50 to £13, D £9 to £15). Set L £15 SERVICE: not inc, card slips closed CARDS: Amex, Delta, Diners, MasterCard, Switch, Visa DETAILS: 60 seats. Private parties: 60 main room. Car park. Vegetarian meals. Children's helpings. No smoking in 1 dining-room. Wheelchair access (1 step; not WC). Music

---

STOKESLEY North Yorkshire   map 10

▲ Chapters

27 High Street, Stokesley TS9 5AD   COOKING 4
TEL: (01642) 711888 FAX: (01642) 713387   COST £20 £46

Times are busy for Alan and Catherine Thompson. The bistro at the front of their three-storey hotel by the banks of the Leven has been given a complete re-fit and their main dining-room was receiving similar treatment as the *Guide* went to press. Also, Dave Connolly has been drafted in to help with an eclectic style of cooking in which the orient seems to be waxing more strongly than ever. King prawn tempura are served with spiced coriander aïoli and curried Malibu sauce, grilled sea bass comes with Japanese mushroom purée, 'marmade' of onions, coriander and sauce nero, while seared tuna gets the full '90s treatment with wasabi, shallot and soy dressing and a garnish of crispy aubergines. Here and there less exotic ideas surface, as in twice-baked leek and Gruyère soufflé, or pan-fried calf's liver with bubble and squeak, crispy onions and sauce aigre-doux. A substantial contingent of desserts might include semolina crisp with pineapple sorbet and a strawberry and lime coulis, or baked pear in mulled wine with white chocolate ice-cream. Around 40 wines reflect the owners' commitment to value as well as quality. House French from Duboeuf is £8.90.

CHEFS: Richard West and Dave Connolly PROPRIETOR: Alan Thompson OPEN: Mon to Sat L 12 to 2, all week D 6.30 to 9.30 CLOSED: 25 Dec, 1 Jan MEALS: alc (main courses L £5.50 to £10.50, D £12.50 to £17). BYO £3.50 SERVICE: not inc CARDS: Amex, Delta, Diners, MasterCard, Switch, Visa DETAILS: 120 seats. 25 seats outside. Private parties: 70 main room. Children's helpings. No no cigars/pipes in dining-room. Music ACCOMMODATION: 13 rooms, all with bath/shower. TV. Phone. B&B £40 to £65. Children welcome. Baby facilities (*The Which? Hotel Guide*) (£5)

Use the lists towards the front of the book to find suitable restaurants for special occasions.

▲ *Ston Easton Park* ▼ ✳

Ston Easton BA3 4DF
TEL: (01761) 241631 FAX: (01761) 241377
EMAIL: stoneaston@cityscape.co.uk   COOKING 6
on A37, 12m S of Bristol   COST £26–£71

Putting it in a nutshell, one visitor observed that this imposing Palladian
mansion built of Bath stone offers 'classy, elegant food in stunning surroundings
with particularly fine service'. It appeals partly because of the flexibility it offers:
a proper à la carte lunch as well as dinner, but also a set-price option at each. A
three-course lunch for £16 is good going, given that it might include smoked
duck salad, pan-fried collops of monkfish, and chocolate and praline roulade
with Kahlua sauce, 'with no service charge included or gratuity expected'. On
top of that, dishes from either menu can be mixed, adding to the feeling of an
accommodating operation that genuinely tries to please.

Mark Harrington might not take many risks with his cooking – Dover sole is
plainly grilled and served with asparagus, pork comes with poached apricots
and calvados juice – but he does use prime ingredients, and coaxes contentment
with a tartlet of smoked salmon and quail's egg, or a smooth and 'satisfyingly
mushroomy' bisque with a swirl of crème fraîche and crisp croûtons. A similar
feeling pervades a 'wobbly and light' twice-baked cheese soufflé in a rich,
buttery fondue sauce with chives; and by adding a couple of slices of foie gras to
pink roast pigeon served on a base of lentils, he turns an earthy dish into a luxury
one. But boldness is also apparent, in the 'robust' flavours of skate meunière
with capers, chopped anchovies and lemon; even the sun-dried tomatoes here
have a convincingly strong tomato flavour.

Pastry work is impressive, well-kept unpasteurised British and Irish cheeses
arrive on a trolley, and the usual country-house gestures range from appetising
appetisers to petits fours with the good espresso coffee. The wine list lives up to
its surroundings, offering page after page of fine French bottles at some fairly
imposing prices. A dozen wines under £20 open proceedings, and matters are
brought to a close by 30-odd bins from some the New World's most prestigious
producers. CELLARMAN'S CHOICE: Wairau River Sauvignon Blanc 1996, Marlborough, New Zealand, £16.50; Côtes du Castillon, Ch. Pitray 1990, £19.

CHEF: Mark Harrington PROPRIETORS: Peter and Christine Smedley OPEN: all week 12.30 to 2,
7 to 9.30 (10 Fri and Sat) MEALS: alc (main courses L £15 to £16, D £20 to £26.50). Set L £11 (2
courses) to £16, Set D £39.50 SERVICE: none, card slips closed CARDS: Amex, Delta, Diners,
MasterCard, Switch, Visa DETAILS: 45 seats. 18 seats outside. Private parties: 50 main room,
50 private room. Car park. Vegetarian meals. Children's helpings. No children under 7. Jacket
and tie. No smoking in dining-room. Wheelchair access (2 steps; not WC). No music
ACCOMMODATION: 20 rooms, all with bath/shower. TV. Phone. Room only £145 to £405. Children
welcome. High teas for children by arrangement. Baby facilities. Dogs welcome in basement
only. Afternoon teas (*The Which? Hotel Guide*)

▲ *denotes an outstanding wine cellar;* ▼ *denotes a good wine list, worth travelling for.*

The Guide *always appreciates hearing about changes of chef or owner.*

▲ *Manleys* ♥

Manleys Hill, Storrington RH20 4BT	COOKING 5
TEL: (01903) 742331 FAX: (01903) 740649	COST £33–£67

Chintz curtains and old beams decorate the brace of 'pretty' dining-rooms that constitute this long-established South Downs restaurant. They also herald a traditional approach: the menu announces everything in French and then translates it into English, which seems an odd thing for an Austrian to do in West Sussex, but there we are. In its defence the food is largely Anglo-French, from duck confit to pork with prunes, from scallops in puff pastry with a langoustine sauce to roasted veal kidneys in a grain-mustard sauce. It may not be the last word in originality, but the kitchen is obviously comfortable working within this framework, applying sound skills to good ingredients.

Wild duck, pheasant and venison are local, while fish might have landed anywhere from Devon to Newhaven to Scotland, producing pan-fried Dover sole with a chive beurre blanc, or roasted sea bass with fennel and Pernod. Fresh fruit gratin, or butterscotch meringue, may be among desserts, but Salzburger Nockerln for two sounds the thing to have. Wines come entirely from France and Germany, save for half a dozen from Austria (of course), Australia and New Zealand. Quality is high throughout, and this is reflected in the prices. French house wines are £14.80. CELLARMAN'S CHOICE: Pinot Blanc Kabinett, Ried Kuchelviertel 1990, Stift Klosterneuberg, Austria, £18.50; Côte Rôtie 'Les Jumelles' 1984, Jaboulet Aîné, £33.50.

CHEF/PROPRIETOR: Karl Löderer   OPEN: Tue to Sun L 12.15 to 2, Wed to Sat D 7.15 to 9   CLOSED: bank hol Mons   MEALS: Set L Tue to Sat £15 (2 courses) to £19.60, Set L Sun £23.50, Set L and D £32.50 (2 courses) to £33.50. BYO £8   SERVICE: not inc   CARDS: Amex, Delta, MasterCard, Switch, Visa   DETAILS: 48 seats. Private parties: 30 main room, 22 private room. Car park. Vegetarian meals. Children's helpings. No cigars/pipes in dining-room. Wheelchair access (also WC). No music. Air-conditioned   ACCOMMODATION: 1 room, with bath/shower. TV. Phone. B&B £55 to £95. No children. No dogs   (£5)

Old Forge ♥

6 Church Street, Storrington RH20 4LA	
TEL: (01903) 743402 FAX: (01903) 742540	COOKING 3
EMAIL: clive@oldforge.co.uk	COST £24–£37

Expect a friendly welcome from Cathy Roberts at this fifteenth-century oak-beamed restaurant, where the food keeps broadly up to date without making an issue of it. Simplicity helps the kitchen keep on top of things, from asparagus vinaigrette with crumbled Roquefort to a terrine of smoked ham and salt pork with basil. Despite an occasionally bold dish such as soy-marinated beef satay with chickpea relish, flavours tend not to be exotic, relying rather on pesto to infuse a leek and Parmesan risotto, or grain mustard to set off a piece of baked cod. What matters, as one reporter noted, is that 'everything is cooked with great care', and that goes for 'lovely and fluffy' game and mushroom suet pudding, as well as vegetables and roast potatoes. English farmhouse cheeses are properly explained and 'mercifully not fridge cold', and desserts – rhubarb crumble, or more ambitious prune and armagnac tart with cardamom ice-cream and chocolate sauce – come with a suggested list of wine by the glass. A short, savvy wine list avoids the obvious in favour of interest and variety at extremely friendly prices. House wines are £11, but for an extra £7.50 you can have Cloudy Bay Sauvignon. CELLARMAN'S CHOICE: Mâcon-Clessé, Dom. de la Bongran 1995, Jean-Claude Thévenet, £28; Noceto Sangiovese 1995, Shenandoah Valley, California, £17.

CHEFS: Clive Roberts and Jonas Tester PROPRIETORS: Cathy and Clive Roberts OPEN: Wed to Fri and Sun L 12.15 to 1.15, Wed to Sat D 7.15 to 9 CLOSED: Christmas and New Year, 2 weeks spring, 2 weeks autumn MEALS: Set L Wed to Fri £21.50 (2 courses) to £27.50, Set L Sun £15 (2 courses) to £18, Set D £17.50 (2 courses) to £27.50. BYO £5 SERVICE: not inc, card slips closed CARDS: Amex, Delta, Diners, MasterCard, Switch, Visa DETAILS: 34 seats. Private parties: 14 main room. Vegetarian meals. Children's helpings. No smoking while others eat. Occasional music £5

STRETE Devon   map 1

Laughing Monk

Blackawton Road, Strete TQ6 0RN
TEL: (01803) 770639   COOKING 2
5m S of Dartmouth, just off A379   COST £19–£33

'It must be very welcoming when there's a winter storm outside,' concluded one reporter after a visit to this comfortably converted old schoolhouse just off the Dartmouth to Kingsbridge coast road. The Rothwells have been in residence for more than a decade and have earned a reputation for rock-solid reliability. Blackboard menus follow the seasons, and the kitchen is now putting an increasing emphasis on fish, with specialities such as Dover sole with lime and spinach hollandaise, or tempura of local seafood served with roasted pepper and onion chutney, not to mention steamed sea bass stuffed with fennel (a dish which dazzled one recipient). Away from the sea, you might also find medallions of pork and apple in a mustard sauce, or crispy roast duck with a plum and ginger glaze. The approach of the sweet trolley seems to delight all who see it: lemon cream meringue produced 'tremors of sugary delight' in one lady customer. Around 50 reasonably priced wines suit the food admirably. House wines from France and Chile are £9.25.

CHEF: David Rothwell PROPRIETORS: David and Trudy Rothwell OPEN: Sun L 12 to 1.30, Tue to Sat D 7 to 9.30 MEALS: alc D (main courses £10.50 to £15.50). Set L £12.50 SERVICE: not inc, card slips closed CARDS: Diners, MasterCard, Switch, Visa DETAILS: 50 seats. Private parties: 60 main room. Car park. Vegetarian meals. Children's helpings. Occasional music

---

Report forms are at the back of the book; write a letter if you prefer; or email us at guidereports@which.co.uk.

CELLARMAN'S CHOICE: Wines recommended by the restaurateur, normally more expensive than house wine.

STUCKTON Hampshire   map 2

▲ *Three Lions* ❢ ⅙✳

Stuckton Road, Stuckton SP6 2HF
TEL: (01425) 652489 FAX: (01425) 656144
½m SE of Fordingbridge, off A338 but not signposted
from it: take the turn just S of Fordingbridge and   COOKING 7
follow a sign down a narrow country lane.   COST £32–£51

A sense of dedication prevails at this family-run restaurant in the tiny hamlet of
Stuckton. Although napkins are as starched as nuns' wimples, it steers well clear
of opulence and design, with pot plants, polished pine tables, an open-plan
layout and blackboard menu. It may be only 'a pub with knobs on', but what
knobs! 'I want to go back as soon as possible' is a typical sentiment from
reporters on the receiving end of a friendly welcome and 'caring, professional'
service from Jayne Womersley, who finds time to chat to regulars and
newcomers alike. The pattern is a *carte* of around seven or eight first and main
courses, with nearly as many desserts, and menu descriptions hide a great deal of
skill. 'They certainly seek out quality ingredients,' reckoned one visitor. Fish
from Poole might include grilled sardines, sea bass served with a warm
vinaigrette of shallots, tomato and basil, or a layer of fresh crab covered with a
crimped square of pasta, with a Madeira-like sauce.

Game is a feature – vine-roasted partridge, quail with ceps – and wild
mushrooms from the New Forest are liable to sprout almost anywhere: at
breakfast, in a first-course hotpot of lambs' kidneys served in a copper pan with
Puy lentils, or in main courses of loin of lamb, and beef fillet, where chanterelle,
oyster, St George and hedgehog fungi combined to produce a 'soft but
meaty-textured' accompaniment at one meal. Meat, like everything else, is
cooked with 'exemplary timing', and comes with separately served vegetables
including 'cheesy, garlicky, creamy dauphinoise potatoes'.

To finish there may be poached fanned pears with verbena ice-cream, or
properly made treacle tart, but it is difficult to better the hot chocolate pudding,
which is crispy outside and 'rich, soft and melting inside', and well worth the
15-minute wait. The Three Lions has a wine list to roar about, with a pride of
established names from the Old World and some bright young cubs from the
New. The house selection stays usefully under £20 (champagne excepted).
CELLARMAN'S CHOICE: Montagny *premier cru* 1992, Dom. Denizot, £23.50;
Taltarni Merlot 1991, Victoria, Australia, £21.50.

CHEF: Jayne Womersley PROPRIETORS: Mike and Jayne Womersley OPEN: Tue to Sun L
12.15 to 2, Tue to Sat D 7.15 to 9.45 (10 Sat) CLOSED: mid-Jan to mid-Feb MEALS: alc (main
courses £11.50 to £16). Set L Tue to Fri £13.50 (2 courses) SERVICE: not inc CARDS: Delta,
MasterCard, Switch, Visa DETAILS: 60 seats. Private parties: 60 main room. Car park.
Vegetarian meals. Children's helpings. No smoking in dining-room. Wheelchair access (not
WC). No music ACCOMMODATION: 3 rooms, all with bath/shower. TV. B&B £59.50 to £75.
Rooms for disabled. No children. No dogs

The Guide *relies on feedback from its readers. Especially welcome are reports on new
restaurants appearing in the book for the first time. All letters to the* Guide *are
acknowledged.*

STUDLAND Dorset   map 2

Shell Bay | NEW ENTRY |

Ferry Road, Studland BH19 3BA   COOKING 1
TEL: (01929) 450363   FAX: (01929) 450570   COST £24–£47

Big windows make the most of 'one of the best views ever', looking inland across
Poole Harbour to Brownsea Island. The décor is 'generally fishy in theme' and
furniture is very basic, but reporters appreciate the relaxed ambience, friendly
service and the 'no fuss' approach to seafood cooking. Typical of the short,
daily-changing *carte* might be a simple starter of 'perfect' seared scallops,
followed by skate with 'smashing' chips, courgettes and tomato sauce, or grilled
mackerel with ginger and black-bean dressing. Finish with watermelon and
bitter chocolate salad, or warm pear and almond tart with clotted cream. A short
list of decent wines at modest prices starts with house wines at £9.50.

CHEF: Charles Mumford   PROPRIETOR: Shell Bay Holdings Ltd   OPEN: all week 12.30 to 2.30,
7.30 to 9.30   CLOSED: Jan, L Thu to Sun and D Thu to Sat from end Oct to Easter   MEALS: alc
(main courses L £8 to £12, D £11 to £18)   SERVICE: not inc, card slips closed   CARDS:
MasterCard, Switch, Visa   DETAILS: 60 seats. 40 seats outside. Private parties: 60 main room.
Children's helpings. Music   £5

STURMINSTER NEWTON Dorset   map 2

▲ *Plumber Manor*

Sturminster Newton DT10 2AF
TEL: (01258) 472507   FAX: (01258) 473370
A357 to Sturminster Newton, take first left to   COOKING 4
Hazelbury Bryan, on left-hand side after 2m   COST £25–£50

The lovely old manor house, in peaceful rural surroundings and spacious
grounds, is run by owners whose family has lived here for centuries. It is thus a
very personal operation, with 'attentive and friendly' service from Richard
Prideaux-Brune. Brother Brian's food appeals for its simple Anglo-French
country style: asparagus in melted butter, grilled goats' cheese with red peppers,
or stuffed loin of pork with apricots and sage jus. Even the more exotic touches,
of chicken breast in a light curry sauce for example, are in the same vein.

Judging by the wide range of dishes recommended by reporters, output is
consistent across the board, from gravad lax, or sauté of wild mushrooms, via
plaice stuffed with smoked haddock, to 'duck with spices'. Fresh and 'homely'
vegetables accompany main courses, and although desserts come on a trolley
they are none the worse for that: crème brûlée perhaps, or chocolate and
Cointreau mousse. The host knows his wines, which are mostly French, and
good value across the board. House Vin de Pays d'Oc is £10.

---

*'The Continental waiter would describe every element of each dish he served in the most
painstaking detail but in incomprehensible English. Therefore a terrine of suckling pig,
chorizo and flageolets sounded like a street fight: "A tear-in with a socking pig, a corrh or
soand flayed gullet."'* (On eating in Oxfordshire)

CHEF: Brian Prideaux-Brune   PROPRIETOR: Richard Prideaux-Brune   OPEN: Sun L 12.30 to 1.30, all week D 7.30 to 9.30   CLOSED: Feb   MEALS: Set L £17.50, Set D £17.50 (2 courses) to £29. BYO £7.50, champagne £10   SERVICE: not inc, card slips closed   CARDS: Amex, Diners, MasterCard, Switch, Visa   DETAILS: 60 seats. Private parties: 50 main room, 14 to 45 private rooms. Car park. Vegetarian meals. Children welcome by arrangement. Wheelchair access (also WC). No music   ACCOMMODATION: 16 rooms, all with bath/shower. TV. Phone. B&B £75 to £140. Rooms for disabled. Children welcome. Baby facilities. Dogs welcome in some bedrooms only (£5)

SUDBURY Suffolk   map 6

Brasserie Four Seven ✸ £ | NEW ENTRY |

47 Gainsborough Street, Sudbury CO10 6ET   COOKING 1
TEL/FAX: (01787) 374298   COST £20–£36

Fraser and Fiona Green acquired what was Mabey's Brasserie in the summer of 1997, and it remains a welcoming place. Part of the dining-room is divided into compartments by shoulder-high wooden partitions, tables are polished pine, cooking is done behind a counter, and daily specials and puds are chalked on a board. Fraser Green used to cook here, which may account for the continuity in style: a sensible range of dishes taking in salads, giant fried prawns, creamy steamed mussels, and tempura of cod and haddock on egg noodles with a chilli and sesame dressing. Main courses – perhaps a 'large, succulent and tasty' chicken breast with first-rate dauphinoise potatoes – come with a dish of (very) mixed vegetables. As an alternative to crème brûlée, or marmalade sponge with hot chocolate sauce, there is usually a savoury: huge half-baguettes generously smothered with a well-browned spicy Welsh rarebit mixture. Outside France, wines on the 30-strong list lean towards the New World. House red and white are £7.95 a bottle, £1.75 a glass.

CHEFS: Fraser Green and Mark Bull   PROPRIETORS: Fiona and Fraser Green   OPEN: Tue to Sat 12 to 2, 7 to 10   MEALS: alc (main courses £6 to £12)   SERVICE: not inc, card slips closed CARDS: Amex, Diners, Switch, Visa   DETAILS: 56 seats. Private parties: 25 main room, 25 and 36 private rooms. Vegetarian meals. Children's helpings. No smoking in 1 dining-room. No music. Air-conditioned (£5)

Red Onion Bistro £

57 Ballingdon Street, Sudbury CO10 6DA   COOKING 2
TEL: (01787) 376777   FAX: (01787) 883156   COST £13–£31

Painted such a bright red that one might easily mistake it for the local fire station, the Onion takes on the air of a converted village hall inside, with a communal refectory table down the centre, and a 'jolly and relaxed' atmosphere. Reasonable prices are a big draw – look at the set lunch – and daily blackboard specials supplement the printed menus. 'We aim to be a simple local restaurant,' writes Gerry Ford, and reporters agree that the food is more homespun than adventurous, offering leek and mushroom gougère, crab-cakes, cod and chips with tartare sauce, and perhaps grilled rabbit loin with a tarragon mustard sauce. Puddings are also chalked on a board: maybe chocolate buttercrunch pie, or banana cheesecake with fudge sauce. Service is 'friendly, interested, attentive', and there is a short list of wines for those who don't want to choose their own from the cellar; prices start comfortably below £10.

CHEF: Darren Boyles   PROPRIETORS: Gerry and Jane Ford   OPEN: Mon to Sat 12 to 2, 6.30 to 9.30   CLOSED: Christmas to New Year, bank hols   MEALS: alc (main courses £6 to £10.50). Set L £5.95 (2 courses) to £7.75, Set D Mon to Thur £7.75 (2 courses) to £9.75   SERVICE: not inc, card slips closed   CARDS: Delta, MasterCard, Switch, Visa   DETAILS: 60 seats. 30 seats outside. Private parties: 25 main room. Car park. Vegetarian meals. Children's helpings. No cigars/pipes in dining-room. Wheelchair access (1 step; not WC). No music   £5

SUNDERLAND Tyne & Wear   map 10

Brasserie 21   NEW ENTRY

Low Street, Wylam Wharf, Sunderland SR1 2AD   COOKING 4
TEL: (0191) 567 6594   FAX: (0191) 510 3994   COST £23–£46

This is the latest addition to Terence Laybourne's cluster of budget-priced alternatives to his flagship Newcastle restaurant, 21 Queen Street (see entry). Adrian Watson has moved over from Bistro 21 in Durham (see entry) and is dishing up similar food: French bistro cooking geared to Northern sensibilities, with the inimitable Laybourne blend of robustness and refinement. The setting is a converted nineteenth-century warehouse on the southern bank of the river, a previously run-down area that is definitely 'on the up'. Old oak beams, pine flooring, silver-painted girders and a twisting metal staircase create a pleasantly light and spartan atmosphere. A concise, good-value blackboard menu at lunch-time might offer roast tomato soup followed by fish-cakes, or spinach and Parmesan tart, while dinner is à la carte, with more choice: spicy fried prawns with aubergine pickle, roast rabbit with provençale vegetables, or 'tender thin slices of succulent' grilled calf's liver and bacon on a bed of mash with an excellent jus. An inspector felt that some of the dishes might benefit from an extra element: a saffron risotto, for example, was buttery and cooked to the correct consistency but might have been helped by a contrasting flavour. Desserts are a highlight, lemon meringue pie and apricot and almond tart both winning praise for their 'flaky but light' pastry. The short but sensible wine list starts off with house Duboeuf at £9.50.

CHEF: Adrian Watson   PROPRIETORS: Terence and Susan Laybourne   OPEN: Mon to Sat 12 to 2, 6 to 10.30   CLOSED: 25 Dec, bank hols   MEALS: alc D (main courses £9.50 to £15). Set L £12 (2 courses) to £14.50   SERVICE: not inc   CARDS: Amex, Delta, Diners, MasterCard, Switch, Visa   DETAILS: 75 seats. 20 seats outside. Private parties: 50 main room. Car park. Vegetarian meals. Children's helpings. Wheelchair access (also WC). Music

---

Dining-rooms where music, either live or recorded, is never played are signalled by No music *in the details at the end of an entry.*

New main entries and restaurant closures are listed near the front of the book.

The Guide*'s top-rated restaurants are listed near the front of the book.*

SUTTON GAULT Cambridgeshire   map 6

▲ *Anchor Inn* ✣ | NEW ENTRY |

Sutton Gault CB6 2BD
TEL: (01353) 778537 FAX: (01353) 776180
off B1381 Sutton to Earith road, just S of Sutton, 6m W   COOKING 2
of Ely   COST £27–£44

Built around 1650, on the bank of the Hundred Foot Drain (as locals refer to the
New Bedford River), the white-painted Anchor 'feels like an old pub that is
seeing better days'. Still with sloping floors and scrubbed pine tables, it has been
given an injection of new blood since last year: Keeley Moyle out front and Geoff
in the kitchen have both worked at good London addresses. This has brought a
degree of confidence to the operation, which shows itself in simple but careful
'home cooking' of creamy mushroom soup, salmon fillet with lemon and parsley
butter, and accurately timed breast of guinea-fowl 'as tasty as guinea-fowl gets'.
Fish comes from Grimsby, and rare-breed meats might include three boneless
chops of Portland lamb in a dark gravy with celeriac mash. 'Take the puddings
without ice-cream or clotted cream,' advised one who enjoyed a 'fine version' of
freshly made crème brûlée served with a shortbread biscuit. Some 60 wines from
Lay & Wheeler combine quality with value (prices start around £11), and there is
usually a local real ale on draught.

CHEFS: Geoffrey Moyle, Richard Bradley and Jonathan Dunckley   PROPRIETORS: Robin and
Heather Moore   OPEN: all week 12 to 2, 7 to 9 (6.30 to 9.30 Sat)   MEALS: alc (main courses £9 to
£15). Set L Mon to Fri (2 courses) £7.50, Set L Sun £15.50   SERVICE: not inc   CARDS: Amex,
Delta, MasterCard, Switch, Visa   DETAILS: 70 seats. 40 seats outside. Private parties: 40 main
room. Car park. Vegetarian meals. Children's helpings. No children under 5 after 8pm. No
smoking in 3 dining-rooms. Wheelchair access (also WC). No music   ACCOMMODATION: 2
rooms, both with bath/shower. TV. Phone. B&B £50 to £82.50. Children welcome. No dogs
(£5)

SWAFFHAM Norfolk   map 6

▲ *Strattons* ♟ ✣

4 Ash Close, Swaffham PE37 7NH   COOKING 4
TEL: (01760) 723845 FAX: (01760) 720458   COST £40–£48

Just off the market square in Swaffham is the Scotts' elegant Palladian villa.
Although the façade may look imposing, the ambience within – especially in the
semi-subterranean dining-room – is refreshingly informal, testimony to the
proprietors' unstuffy approach. The kitchen benefits both from a great rapport
with local suppliers, and Vanessa Scott's missionary belief in what one reader
sums up as 'absolutely genuine cooking, using superb ingredients'. A tart of
Cromer crab and tomato in basil-scented custard might begin a meal, or there
may be pea soup with cheese straws or a memorable mushroom and Cashel Blue
soufflé. Vegetarian dishes are particularly highly commended, and may take in
choux buns filled with celery and cashew-nuts in a carrot and tarragon cream
sauce. Grilled sea bass with fennel, or duck breast sauced with redcurrants and
balsamic are among the alternatives.

Ices and sorbets are a feature, either at the outset (as blood orange with garden mint) or to finish, where apple and cinnamon ice may go into a meringue cake. In addition to puddings, there is an expertly chosen selection of British and Irish cheeses from Neal's Yard. The illustrated, handwritten and helpfully annotated wine list offers a broad range of styles and flavours from around the world at extremely modest prices. An impressive 45 wines are offered by the large glass from around £2. CELLARMAN'S CHOICE: Vin de Pays des Coteaux de l'Ardéche, Chardonnay Grand Ardéche 1995, Louis Latour, £15.86; Tinto do Anfora 1992, Alentejo, £10.98.

CHEFS: Vanessa Scott. Margaret Cooper and Hannah Scott   PROPRIETORS: Les and Vanessa Scott   OPEN: all week D only 7 to 8.30 (Sun residents only)   CLOSED: Christmas, 2 weeks summer   MEALS: Set D £25   SERVICE: not inc, card slips closed   CARDS: MasterCard, Switch, Visa   DETAILS: 22 seats. 8 seats outside. Private parties: 20 main room. Car park. Vegetarian meals. Children's helpings. No smoking in dining-room. Occasional music   ACCOMMODATION: 7 rooms, all with bath/shower. TV. Phone. B&B £65 to £135. Children welcome. Baby facilities. Afternoon teas

---

SWANAGE Dorset   map 2

Galley

9 High Street, Swanage BH19 2LN   COOKING 2
TEL: (01929) 427299   COST £27–£38

Nick Storer now has two more fishermen netting for him than he did last year, and his scallop-diver has gone full time, we learn, so devotees of the fresh, simple seafood dishes that his restaurant specialises in will be well supplied. Oysters and mussels come all the way from Loch Fyne, but most of the rest is locally caught. Once in the kitchen, it is given traditional treatments: herring fillets are cured in sherry and dill, and lobster is sauté in garlic butter. Sea bass is baked in a mound of sea salt and dressed with parsley pesto, and salmon may be poached with mushrooms and sorrel in white wine and cream. Meat-eaters are not neglected, and game pie full of rabbit and pigeon is expected to become a seasonal stalwart. Accompanying portions of vegetables tend to be large, but value is the kitchen's watchword. Crème caramel is a familiar way to finish, or try steamed fruit pudding with Muscat sauce. Wines are divided stylistically on the list, with plenty of New Worlders muscling in among the French. House wines from Chile, South Africa and Australia start at £8.50.

CHEF: Nick Storer   PROPRIETORS: N.D. and M.G. Storer   OPEN: all week D only 6.45 to 9.30 (10 Sat)   CLOSED: 3 weeks Nov, 1 Jan to 14 Feb   MEALS: Set D £18.50. BYO £5   SERVICE: not inc, card slips closed   CARDS: Amex, Diners, MasterCard, Visa   DETAILS: 34 seats. Private parties: 30 main room. Vegetarian meals. Children welcome. Wheelchair access (2 steps; not WC). Music. Air-conditioned

---

'My wife plucked up courage to tell the French waiter that the spinach was much too salty. "Oh, maybe the chef is in love," he replied. "I shall tell him in future: 'Hey, don't be in love when you are making the spinach, ha, ha, ha."' This was a timely reminder that, historically, the French are to dry humour what the British are to gastronomy.' (On eating in Oxfordshire)

TADCASTER North Yorkshire   map 9

▲ *Hazlewood Castle, Restaurant 1086* ✸ │ NEW ENTRY │

Paradise Lane, Hazlewood, Tadcaster LS24 9NJ
TEL: (01937) 535354   FAX: (01937) 530630   COOKING 4
off A64, 3½m SW of Tadcaster   COST £26–£67

In October 1997, this medieval castle opened as a luxurious hotel, with a
spacious Great Hall, various sitting-rooms, and sumptuously decorated
dining-room. The cooking is done by brothers John and Matthew
Benson-Smith, the latter perhaps familiar to *Guide* readers from his stint at the
Hole in the Wall in Bath (see entry). Various fixed-price options are available,
from a basic two-course lunch to a seven-course tasting menu at £45, but they are
given names such as 'Elementary' or 'Extravaganaza', whose 'pretentious and
silly' descriptions don't square with the serious intent of the kitchen. In their
favour, they suggest a different wine with each dish, on offer at £4 a glass.

'Mixed results' seems to sum up the run of early meals here. Impressive
seafood has included seared scallops on a sparse cream and mustard sauce, and
sea bass with a tangy sauce of red wine and orange, that was rated 'excellent' for
fish, sauce and presentation. 'Sweet and tender' fillet of lamb has been well
treated: as a starter, layered with sweetbreads and tomato in a charlotte,
surrounded by pesto; and as a main course, partnered with a 'moussaka-like'
preparation of minced lamb and sliced potato. Finish with the good selection of
well-kept unpasteurised cheeses, or a dessert such as deep-fried banana ravioli,
or fig and liquorice parfait. Appetisers (and some dishes) are on the small side,
though what is small in Yorkshire is often normal elsewhere. Freshly baked
breads are 'first-class', and service at its best has been 'attentive' and 'unobtrusive'. House wine is £11.50.

CHEFS: John and Matthew Benson-Smith   PROPRIETOR: Hazlewood Castle   OPEN: Tue to Fri
and Sun L 12.30 to 2, Tue to Sat D 6 to 9.45   MEALS: Set L £17.50 (rapid menu) to £45, Set D £15
to £45   SERVICE: not inc, card slips closed   CARDS: Amex, Delta, Diners, MasterCard, Switch,
Visa   DETAILS: 80 seats. Private parties: 80 main room, 30 to 120 private rooms. Car park.
Vegetarian meals. Children's helpings. No smoking in dining-room. Wheelchair access (also
WC). Music   ACCOMMODATION: 21 rooms, all with bath/shower. TV. Phone. B&B £95 to £165.
Children welcome. High teas for children. No dogs. Afternoon teas (£5)

Singers ✸ £

16 Westgate, Tadcaster LS24 9AB   COOKING 3
TEL: (01937) 835121   COST £24–£34

Patron-impresario Philip Taylor and his band of young waitresses are
commended by reporters for treating everyone as regulars in this popular place –
so popular that they operate a two-sittings policy, but softened by an early-
evening three-course menu. The longer main menu, also reasonably priced, but
with a few small supplements, has an emphasis on meat seemingly designed for
healthy Yorkshire appetites. Expect straightforward dishes such as 'thin, light
and tasty' glazed pancake of spinach and chicken with a hint of garlic; asparagus
and spinach soup; and roast rack of lamb with 'creamy and garlicky gratin

potatoes'. At inspection sea bass and salmon were crisp-skinned and pleasantly sauced, and roast potatoes and mint stood out in a generous bowl of mixed vegetables. Irish coffee cheesecake, and dark chocolate and orange iced terrine make satisfying conclusions. Twenty-five wines are ranged under £20, beginning at £8.50 for house Duboeuf.

CHEFS: David Lockwood and Richard Thompson PROPRIETORS: Philip Taylor and Guy Vicari OPEN: Tue to Sat D only 6 to 9.30 CLOSED: 25 and 26 Dec, 1 week Feb, 1 week Aug MEALS: Set D Tue to Fri before 7pm £10.95, Set D Tue to Thu £12.95 (2 courses) to £15.95, Set D Fri and Sat £15.95. BYO £5 SERVICE: not inc, card slips closed CARDS: Delta, MasterCard, Switch, Visa DETAILS: 38 seats. Private parties: 38 main room. Children welcome. No smoking in dining-room. Wheelchair access (not WC). Music (£5)

TADWORTH Surrey   map 3

Gemini ✸✷

28 Station Approach, Tadworth KT20 5AH   COOKING 3
TEL: (01737) 812179   COST £24–£45

The name is reflected in the twin figures doing handstands on the front of the menu. Otherwise, this is an unobtrusively decorated small neighbourhood restaurant with chintzy curtains at the leaded windowpanes, and mugs on hooks hanging around the original fireplace. Robert Foster's cooking is ambitious and inventive, with a particular fondness for oriental techniques, and comes as a fixed-price deal with one or two dishes carrying a surcharge. Smoked salmon and dill terrine topped with crabmeat and a langoustine is a sound, proficient starter, as is an artfully constructed main course of pork loin rolled around a herb mousse and served with a tartlet of caramelised apples and onions. Sauces can err on the heavy side, as can pastry, although a croustillant of figs with clove ice-cream offered 'melt-in-the-mouth delicate' puff and fine flavour combinations. Service can be pressed when the going gets busy. The short wine list stays mainly in France, with single-bottle showings from other countries. House wines start at £9.50.

CHEF/PROPRIETOR: Robert Foster OPEN: Tue to Fri and Sun L 12 to 2, Tue to Sat D 7 to 9.30 CLOSED: 2 weeks Christmas, 2 weeks summer MEALS: Set L £9.50 (1 course) to £15.50, Set D Tue to Thur £20 (2 courses) to £24.50, Set D Fri and Sat £24.50. BYO £4 SERVICE: not inc; 10% on parties of 8 or more CARDS: Amex, Delta, MasterCard, Switch, Visa DETAILS: 44 seats. Private parties: 42 main room. Vegetarian meals. Children welcome L only. No smoking in dining-room. Wheelchair access (1 step; not WC). Occasional music

---

TAPLOW Berkshire   map 3

▲ Cliveden, Waldo's ♥ 🍷 ✸✷

Taplow SL6 0JF
TEL: (01628) 668561 and (0800)
454063 FAX: (01628) 661837 and (0800) 454061   COOKING 8
off A4, 2m N of Taplow on Cliveden Rd   COST £63–£103

As the *Guide* went to press, Cliveden and its sister hotels (including Royal Crescent in Bath, see entry) were subject to well-publicised takeover bids, though we are assured that little will change. The house, if we may use such a modest term, has acres of ground and centuries of history under its belt, as well as a bit of a scandal from Profumo and Keeler in the 1960s to add allure. Given the size and splendour, it does seem a bit odd to serve food of the calibre that Gary Jones cooks, in a small, dimly lit, though sprucely furnished, basement.

The *carte* is sensibly limited to five choices per course, and although luxuries are *de rigueur*, this is not flamboyant food and there are no flashy flavour combinations. Gary Jones has cooked alongside Raymond Blanc and Michel Roux, and has obviously mastered the finer points of French haute cuisine, as well as developing a sharp sense of culinary judgement and a deft hand with presentation. An inspector was 'completely taken aback by the talent displayed in the cooking', not least in a single piece of film-like ravioli encasing a beautifully executed risotto, in the centre of which was a poached egg, the whole thing surrounded by mounds of mixed herb purée and slivers of pancetta.

Sauces are of 'stunning depth and complexity', notably in a 'dazzling' reduction of langoustines that surrounded a starter of pasta and langoustine meat with girolles and asparagus, and in a 'remarkably pure' reduction of fish stock and red wine that accompanied accurately timed turbot, served on a bed of spinach enclosing creamy mash. In another dish, the 'perfect creamy texture' of celeriac purée provided counterpoint for lightly pink Trelough duck breast heaped in the centre of the plate, served with roasted apple slices. Fine flavours and textures also characterise desserts: of hot caramel soufflé accompanied by a praline ice-cream, or jellied orange muscat terrine topped by a bittersweet chocolate sorbet. Cheese arrives on a marble board, which is common enough, but the waiter knows them intimately, and after choosing – from Penwood ewes' milk, St Marcellin, Lancashire blue, or Epoisse, all in prime condition – they are whisked away, arranged in order of strength, and returned together with a cheese soufflé made from Stinking Bishop.

The sommelier, praised for her excellent and knowledgeable service, oversees a cellar in which wines from France hold sway, although California and Australia make a significant contribution. Mark-ups can be high (there is not much under £20), but the lack of service charge does mitigate matters somewhat. CELLARMAN'S CHOICE: Juris Chardonnay 1996, Stiegelmar, Austria, £27; Coteaux du Tricastain 1993, Dom. du Vieux Micocoulier, £20. A second restaurant, the Terrace, has a better view, but its food is not in the same class; given that prices are not unrelated to the splendour of the place, the fixed-price lunch may be the most cost-effective option.

CHEF: Gary Jones   PROPRIETOR: Cliveden plc   OPEN: Tue to Sat D only 7 to 10.30   CLOSED: 24 Dec to 24 Jan   MEALS: Set D £52 to £75   SERVICE: net prices, card slips closed   CARDS: Amex, Diners, MasterCard, Switch, Visa   DETAILS: 28 seats. Private parties: 12 to 54 private rooms. Car park. Vegetarian meals. Children welcome. Jacket and tie at D. No smoking in dining-room. Wheelchair access (also WC). Music. Air-conditioned   ACCOMMODATION: 38 rooms, all with bath/shower. TV. Phone. Room only £235 to £750. Rooms for disabled. Children welcome. High teas for children. Baby facilities. Swimming-pool. Fishing

Card slips closed *in the details at the end of an entry indicates that the total on the slips of credit cards is closed when handed over for signature.*

TAUNTON Somerset map 2

Brazz £

SOMERSET 1999 BRASSERIE

NEW ENTRY

Castle Bow, Taunton TA1 1NF COOKING 3
TEL/FAX: (01823) 252000 COST £21–£45

Well tried in cities, the café-bar-brasserie idea is no less appealing in a county town the size of Taunton, where the Castle Hotel (see entry, below) opened this prime example in June 1998 amid much brazzamatazz and brazzle-dazzle. To get through the glass door, grasp a seven-foot-high stainless-steel handle fashioned from the initial B. Inside is 'spare, minimal and light', with much blond wood, chrome, and Susanna Bailey paintings. A low-ceilinged café with brushed-steel bar gives way, beyond the balcony rail, to a larger space with tropical aquarium and, ahead of the millennium, its own domed ceiling or 'dark blue cupola'.

The menu is so New it was put together on the back of focus groups, which may explain the prawn cocktail, grilled ribeye steak with chips and béarnaise, and sticky toffee pudding. But it also accounts for a seafood bias that takes in a 'soupy' smoked haddock risotto with chive oil and peas, and grilled mackerel; and for salads, vegetable and pasta options. Meat dishes include marinated chump of lamb with braised aubergines in an 'excellent sweet gravy'. Those in search of simple comfort might prefer smoked salmon, beefburger, fish-cakes with spinach and a well-made butter sauce, and rich-tasting chocolate tart with good pastry. Plentiful staff were still finding their feet when our inspector dined. A couple of dozen wines, mostly under £20, are well suited to the operation, though focus groups seem to have had a hand in the tasting notes. Prices start at £8.95.

CHEFS: Phil Vickery and Andy Knight PROPRIETORS: the Chapman family OPEN: all week 12 to 3, 6 to 10.30 (11 Fri and Sat) MEALS: alc (main courses £6 to £15) SERVICE: not inc, card slips closed CARDS: Amex, Delta, Diners, MasterCard, Switch, Visa DETAILS: 110 seats. 20 seats outside. Private parties: 150 main room. Vegetarian meals. Children's helpings. Wheelchair access (also WC). Music. Air-conditioned (£5)

▲ *Castle Hotel*

Castle Green, Taunton TA1 1NF
TEL: (01823) 272671 FAX: (01823) 336066 COOKING 7
EMAIL: reception@the-castle-hotel.com COST £30–£64

The past year has been eventful at the Castle. Peter Chapman, largely responsible for its post-war lease of life, died at the end of 1997, aged 82, while the present generation launched a new venture (see entry above). Just as the high street brand names that crowd the centre of town are at odds with the Castle's ancient air, so its own interior doesn't quite chime with either its seventeenth-century origins or the '90s; but it has to cope with large numbers, pressing various rooms into service for pre-meal drinks, filling them with chairs, squishy sofas and tables. The pink and green dining-room – 'comfortable but not exciting' – offers various fixed-price options. What distinguishes the more expensive dishes is not so much luxury ingredients as more demanding cooking and greater interest: mussel stew with coconut milk, for example, versus steamed lobster and crab sausage with roast artichoke and saffron couscous.

Cooking relies on simple ingredients well put together: gravlax with shrimp paste and roast pepper dressing perhaps, or Caesar salad made with crisp cos lettuce and good marinated anchovy fillets, with copious amounts of dressing and Parmesan. Although variations in quality of output have raised a few eyebrows – at one meal 'it felt like there were two different people cooking' – materials are generally first-rate, including Sunday's roast sirloin of beef, 'marbled with fat, oozingly rare and juicy'. Techniques are sufficiently varied to produce a good balance and offer a range of textures: from steamed sea bass with lovage mash, to sole deep-fried in tempura-style batter ('light as a whisker, studded with sesame seeds'), served with saffron mayonnaise 'the colour of gorse in May'.

The British vein that runs through the repertoire is seen at its most traditional among deserts such as baked egg custard with nutmeg ice-cream, steamed hazelnut sponge, or lemon-curd mousse. Good bread is multiple choice from a large basket. Service has been variable, though the wine waiter is knowledgeable and helpful. The wine list helpfully includes a short list of suggested bins priced up to £15, between £16 and £25, or over £25, then runs through a commendable number of half-bottles before moving on to the full list. Another nice touch is the listing of the shipper by each wine, in case customers want to lay in a supply for home drinking. France gets the most thorough treatment, backed-up by intelligent selections from the New World. House red and white is £11.50. CELLARMAN'S CHOICE: Sancerre 'Les Roches' 1996, Vacheron, £23; Niebaum-Coppola Rubicon 1986, Napa, California, £34.80.

CHEF: Phil Vickery   PROPRIETORS: the Chapman family   OPEN: all week 12.30 to 2.30, 7.30 to 9   MEALS: Set L £34 to £38.50, Set L Sun £14.90 (2 courses) to £18.90, Set D £23 to £39.50 SERVICE: not inc, card slips closed   CARDS: Amex, Diners, MasterCard, Switch, Visa   DETAILS: 65 seats. Private parties: 110 main room, 16 to 110 private rooms. Car park. Children's helpings. No smoking in dining-room. Wheelchair access (also WC). Occasional music ACCOMMODATION: 44 rooms, all with bath/shower. TV. Phone. B&B £85 to £210. Rooms for disabled. Children welcome. Baby facilities. Dogs welcome in bedrooms only. Afternoon teas

---

TAVISTOCK Devon	map 1

▲ *Horn of Plenty* ✦✖

Gulworthy, Tavistock PL19 8JD
TEL/FAX: (01822) 832528
3m W from Tavistock on A390, turn right at   COOKING 6
Gulworthy Cross   COST £27–£56

The Duke of Bedford built himself this foursquare Georgian mansion in the foothills of Dartmoor a couple of hundred years ago. It was later reborn as a restaurant-with-rooms (seven of them in the converted coach house), its slight severity eased by a mass of creepers, and colourfully in summer by camellias, azaleas and rhododendrons. The dining-room has been built out to one side to provide panoramic views of the gardens, echoing the floral theme in its wallpaper.

Peter Gorton cooks in a broad-based, contemporary way, wrapping monkfish in prosciutto and serving it with ratatouille, whipping up a tomato risotto to go with loin of lamb, and spicing lemon sole before deep-frying it in tempura batter for a starter. The cornucopia of the restaurant's name appears to refer more to the piling up of culinary technicalities in a dish than to the actual ingredients, so be prepared for lobster brandade galette, or celeriac ravioli filled with rabbit confit ragoût. One reporter enthused over a fillet of brill topped with crab mousse and accompanied by nicely tender asparagus, while another enjoyed duck with orange sauce, sweet potato mash and stir-fried pak choi. The 'Horn of Plenty vegetarian trio' is not a group of fastidious regulars, but a surprise main course for non-carnivores. Ices and sorbets are recommended desserts, and generally come with something like a lime and Grand Marnier syrup, or there may be glazed lemon tart with raspberry sauce. Service is by 'a team of long-serving and efficient waitresses, admirably marshalled by Elaine Gatehouse'. Mature clarets and burgundies lead a classic list that allows room at the end for a decent showing of southern hemisphere wines. House selections, which include a Cornish white, start at £11.25.

CHEF: Peter Gorton   PROPRIETORS: Ian and Elaine Gatehouse   OPEN: Tue to Sun L12 to 2, all week D 7 to 9.30   CLOSED: 25 and 26 Dec   MEALS: Set L £15.50 (2 courses) to £18.50, Set D £32.50   SERVICE: not inc   CARDS: Amex, Delta, MasterCard, Switch, Visa   DETAILS: 50 seats. 20 seats outside. Private parties: 50 main room, 12 private room. Car park. Vegetarian meals. No children under 13 exc at Sun L. No smoking in dining-room. Wheelchair access (also WC). No music   ACCOMMODATION: 7 rooms, all with bath/shower. TV. Phone. B&B £70 to £110. Rooms for disabled. No children under 13. Dogs welcome in bedrooms only (charge for second dog) (*The Which? Hotel Guide*)

TEFFONT EVIAS Wiltshire   map 2

▲ *Howard's House* ﹗✴

Teffont Evias SP3 5RJ
TEL: (01722) 716392   FAX: (01722) 716820
off B3089, W of Dinton and 9½m W of Salisbury,   COOKING 3
signposted Chicksgrove   COST £26–£40

A seventeenth-century dower house, with Victorian additions, set in the peaceful Nadder Valley offers a retreat for city escapees, or trippers wearied by the tourist stampede at Stonehenge. Although it has been decorated with evident refinement, the owners have refused to spoil the show by insisting on formal dress or banning children, with the result that everybody feels open-heartedly welcomed. Paul Firmin cooks to a fixed-price formula of three courses plus coffee, and the culinary style is the only thing likely to jolt you out of any old-English reverie. Start with pigeon breast and foie gras encased in puff pastry and dressed with cassis and balsamic, or maybe grilled sea bass served with crab mousseline, shellfish bisque and chilli noodles. The shock of the new runs through main courses such as seared salmon with lemon couscous and tempura-battered squid, or English veal en crépinette with sun-dried tomatoes and basil on a cep sabayon. Sunday lunch on a hot spring day delighted one pair right up to desserts of white and dark chocolate parfait on chocolate sauce, and calvados-laced bread-and-butter pudding, rounded off with coffee taken in the garden. Bordeaux and Burgundy make up the backbone of the extensive wine list, and prices throughout are pretty stiff. House selections start at £9.95 for a pair of vins de pays from south-west France.

CHEF: Paul Firmin   PROPRIETORS: Paul Firmin and Jonathan Ford   OPEN: Sun L 12.30 to 2, all week D 7.30 to 9.30 (Mon to Fri L by arrangement for parties of 4 or more)   CLOSED: 25 to 28 Dec   MEALS: Set L £18.50, Set D £22 (2 courses) to £25. BYO £6 to £8 (sparkling)   SERVICE: not inc, card slips closed   CARDS: Amex, Delta, Diners, MasterCard, Switch, Visa   DETAILS: 30 seats. 10 seats outside. Private parties: 40 main room. Car park. Children's helpings. No smoking in dining-room. Wheelchair access (not WC). Occasional music   ACCOMMODATION: 9 rooms, all with bath/shower. TV. Phone. B&B £75 to £135. Children welcome. Afternoon teas (*The Which? Hotel Guide*)   £5

THAME Oxfordshire   map 2

▲ *The Old Trout* ⅚✶ £   NEW ENTRY

29–30 Lower High Street, Thame OX9 2AA   COOKING 2
TEL: (01844) 212146   FAX: (01844) 212614   COST £21–£47

The Old Trout occupies two ancient thatched cottages with exposed beams and flagstone floors, the sage green walls of its many small rooms sympathetically decorated with black and white prints and portraits. On offer is a blend of modern and traditional ideas, which engage attention with their simple but lively approach. Reports praise the *entente cordiale* of fresh crab niçoise: chunks of crab in the shell, a decorative claw on top, and minute new potatoes scattered among the salad ingredients. Otherwise, there might be fish-cake on sauce gribiche, salmon steak on a lime and shrimp sauce, or rack of 'Old Spot' with spicy fruits. Pleasant, smiling service led by Ruth Jones may be stretched on busy weekend evenings. Wines on the attractively priced list offer a range of styles from both hemispheres, with plenty of good drinking under £20. Eight house wines are changed every four weeks, and are £11.95 a bottle.

CHEFS: Mark Jones and Simon Hallas   PROPRIETORS: Mr and Mrs Mark Jones   OPEN: Mon to Sat 12 to 2.30, 6.30 to 10   CLOSED: 25 Dec to 2 Jan, 17 Aug to1 Sep.   MEALS: alc (main courses L £5.50 to £10, D £9.50 to £15). Set L £10.25 (2 courses) to £13.50   SERVICE: not inc, card slips closed   CARDS: Delta, MasterCard, Switch, Visa   DETAILS: 70 seats. 40 seats outside. Private parties: 26 main room. Car park. Vegetarian meals. Children welcome. No smoking in 1 dining-room. Music   ACCOMMODATION: 8 rooms, all with bath/shower. TV. Phone. B&B £55 to £75. Children welcome. No dogs. Afternoon teas. (*The Which? Hotel Guide*)

THORNBURY South Gloucestershire   map 2

▲ *Thornbury Castle* ▼ ⅚✶

Castle Street, Thornbury BS35 1HH
TEL: (01454) 281182   FAX: (01454) 416188
EMAIL: 100070.2761@compuserve.com   COOKING 4
off B4061, at N end of town   COST £28–£67

This is 'a cracking good hotel' with elegance, style and warmth; indeed, there is nothing else quite like it. In the early days (of the sixteenth century, when it was built), Thornbury saw a succession of royals pass through its ivy-covered portals, among them Henry VIII, Anne Boleyn and Mary Tudor; nowadays a token suit of armour in the nineteenth-century Gothic interior has to serve as a reminder of its venerable state. Steven Black's raw materials are good, presentation is attractive, and many of his dishes, especially seafood ones, have Mediterranean leanings: roast salmon with a bouillabaisse sauce, or grilled sea bass on fennel and tomato compote with liguini and basil purée. Lunch offers a choice of three items per course, dinner six, perhaps ending with banana mousseline, or hot butterscotch pudding. Among the gripes this year, steaks (which carry a supplement on an already hefty set price) have been cooked longer than requested, and long waits for service haven't helped matters, but the wine list is a great soother. An advance sighting rewards fans of old and rare wines, as many have been 'down in the dungeons' for years (clarets date back to the First World War) and require a few hours to reach the correct serving temperature. Less ancient (and less expensive) bins include nine 'everyday wines' – three from the castle's own vineyards – starting at £12. CELLARMAN'S CHOICE: Gavi di Gavi 1996, Villa Lanata, £15, Errazuriz Cabernet Sauvignon 1993, Aconcagua, Chile, £19.

CHEF: Steven Black   PROPRIETOR: The Baron of Portlethen   OPEN: all week 12 to 2, 7 to 10   CLOSED: 3 days early Jan   MEALS: Set L £16.50 (2 courses) to £19.50, Set D £39.50. BYO £10   SERVICE: net prices, card slips closed   CARDS: Amex, Delta, Diners, MasterCard, Switch, Visa   DETAILS: 60 seats. Private parties: 30 main room, 14 and 20 private rooms. Car park. Vegetarian meals. No children under 12. Jacket and tie. No smoking in dining-room. Wheelchair access (not WC). Music   ACCOMMODATION: 20 rooms, all with bath/shower. TV. Phone. B&B £85 to £335. Rooms for disabled. No children under 12. No dogs. Afternoon teas (*The Which? Hotel Guide*)
(£5)

THORNTON CLEVELEYS Lancashire   map 8

Didier's Bistro £

Trunnah Road, Thornton Cleveleys FY5 4HF
TEL: (01253) 860619   FAX: (01253) 865350   COOKING 2
off A585, 3m N of Blackpool   COST £14–£34

Styling itself, since last year, a French bistro – there is no booking, and it's open all week – Didier's 'achieves what it sets out to achieve' by serving unfussy food in an informal conservatory setting. In fact, dishes on the laminated menu go beyond France: to the land of Caesar salad, where kiln-roasted salmon comes with ciabatta bread, and wild boar sausages are served with garlic mash, on over the rainbow to pan-fried ostrich fillet with gratin dauphinois, and four flavours of Häagen-Dazs ice-cream. It works because ingredients are sound, cooking is kept simple – a charcoal grill is applied to quail (as a starter), noisettes of lamb, and fillet and sirloin steaks – and service is 'crisp and efficient'. The short wine list stays mostly under £20, and there are drinkable bottles for less than half that, including house Chardonnay and Tempranillo at £6.95.

CHEF: Didier Guerin   PROPRIETORS: Louise and Didier Guerin   OPEN: all week 12 to 2, 6 to 10 (9.30 Sun)   MEALS: alc (main courses £7.50 to £11.50). Set L £6.50 (2 courses) to £8.50. BYO £6   SERVICE: not inc   CARDS: Amex, Delta, MasterCard, Switch, Visa   DETAILS: 104 seats. 40 seats outside. Private parties: 60 main room, 20 to 60 private rooms. Car park. Vegetarian meals. Children welcome. Music

TORQUAY Devon   map 1

Table

| 135 Babbacombe Road, Torquay TQ1 3SR | COOKING 4 |
| TEL/FAX: (01803) 324292 | COST £35–£42 |

Julie Tuckett does everything herself in this 'clean and cared-for' restaurant. One correspondent who found himself there on a quiet evening reported that 'the short menu evolved as we discussed it': soups were added, other courses offered, main dishes varied. Not all are fortunate enough to be offered this customised service, but dinner (the main meal) typically puts up three or four varied items each for first and main courses: starter salads of grilled Sussex goats' cheese or Torbay scallops, filo pastry parcels of crab, or fish soup.

Despite the proximity to the coast, 'red meats are my mainstay', writes Julie Tuckett. Barbary duck might be served on cabbage with a peppercorn sauce, and game from Exmoor might include venison fillet with juniper and Madeira. Chilled chocolate terrine with hot plums seems a favourite among puddings. The wine list has seen a few departures, but continues to offer an appealing range of food-friendly bins that stay mostly under £20. A dozen house wines start at £11 a bottle and are also available by the glass in three sizes.

CHEF/PROPRIETOR: Julie T. Tuckett   OPEN: Tue to Fri L 12.15 to 1.45, all week D 7.30 to 9.30   CLOSED: first 2 weeks Feb, last 2 weeks Mar   MEALS: Set L £8.50 (1 course) to £26.50, Set D £26.50   SERVICE: not inc, card slips closed   CARDS: Amex, MasterCard, Visa   DETAILS: 20 seats. Private parties: 20 main room. No children under 10. No smoking while others eat. Wheelchair access (not WC). No music   £5

TREVENEN Cornwall   map 1

Crahan ⁵✱   NEW ENTRY

Trevenen, Helston TR13 0ND	
TEL: (01326) 573090	COOKING 5
on A394, 2½m NE of Helston	COST £21–£33

A large sign stretches across the corner of the drive of this old farmhouse on the Helston to Falmouth road, announcing a proud Cornish newcomer. The Popes opened in 1997, after gutting the ground floor to provide a large open area with a huge chimney breast and fireplace (now only decorative), and filling in the apertures with a display of sculpted glass irises: blue is the colour dominating fabrics, furniture and pictures. Jacky Pope runs front-of-house in a 'friendly and efficient way', while David Pope's 'unblushing' culinary CV, printed on the menu, chronicles his experience with Brian Turner, Shaun Hill and Rick Stein, among others. Menus are sensibly arranged – set-price dinner offers no choice, lunch two or three options per course, the *carte* four or five – and meals are 'astonishing value'.

The food is not fussy, but appeals for its directness and 'harmonious' combinations: a green-leaf summer salad with asparagus, soft-boiled quail's eggs and slivers of Parmesan, or a 'light, fluffy' twice-baked Stilton soufflé, crisp outside, with a glossy hollandaise-type sauce. Spices are used well – a hint of curry in the fruity sauce that comes with a whole small guinea-fowl 'roasted to perfection', or a bolder 'pungent' first course of mackerel stuffed with ginger and coriander, served with a 'fiery' tomato salsa – but this is a chef who knows when to leave well alone: for example, a simply poached sea bass that needed no adorning beyond its moistening wine sauce. Plentiful accompanying vegetables include a 'prettily coloured medley', and well-browned, melting dauphinoise potatoes.

Desserts 'clearly show David Pope's origins as a pastry chef', according to one visitor for whom the rich chocolate torte made with chocolate pastry and served with raspberry coulis was 'the ultimate pudding'. Otherwise, there may be nougat parfait with a passion-fruit sorbet, or plump rum-soaked raisins in a caramel ice-cream, served with a puddle of butterscotch sauce. A straight-forward wine list keeps prices low, starting with house French at £7.50.

CHEF: David Pope   PROPRIETORS: David and Jacky Pope   OPEN: Fri and Sat L 12 to 2, Tue to Sat D 7 to 9   CLOSED: 25 Dec, 1 Jan   MEALS: Set L £11 (2 courses) to £15, Set D £18 (2 courses) to £21.50   SERVICE: not inc, card slips closed   CARDS: Delta, MasterCard, Switch, Visa   DETAILS: 36 seats. Private parties: 30 main room. Car park. Vegetarian meals. Children's helpings. No smoking in dining-room. Occasional music   £5

TUNBRIDGE WELLS Kent   map 3

▲ *Hotel du Vin & Bistro*   NEW ENTRY

Crescent Road, Tunbridge Wells TN1 2LY
TEL: (01892) 526455   FAX: (01892) 512044   COOKING 6
EMAIL: reception@tunbridgewells.hotelduvin.co.uk   COST £18–£50

Robin Hutson and Gerard Basset's first Hotel du Vin & Bistro, opened in 1994, brought a breath of fresh air to Winchester. This one does exactly the same for Tunbridge Wells. Restoration has brought charisma to the mellow eighteenth-century sandstone building in a less-than-inspiring civic quarter. Once through the imposing porch, lighting is subdued, walls are soft grey, and floors everywhere are 'simply wooden planks'. There may be an occasional suit or posh frock, but this is basically 'an up-market French bistro' in which to enjoy the essentials of eating without the distraction of British mannerisms.

Winchester's generous and broadly Mediterranean formula has been applied in the kitchen, producing a long list of recommended dishes from crab-cakes via sweet onion tart to 'well-seasoned, warm and satisfying' cream of mussel and saffron soup. A rich and creamy mushroom risotto ('an excellent test of a kitchen') impressed one visitor with its hint of 'earthy' truffle oil and large crisp curl of golden Parmesan. Variety extends to calf's liver, roast cod with curried basmati rice, richly sauced venison stew, and slices of chicken breast interleaved with mozzarella and 'sweet yet slightly tart' plums. 'Ultra-fresh' and plainly presented vegetables are ordered and charged for separately.

To finish, chocolate mousse comes with marinated cherries, and whole baked apple with lemon grass-flavoured custard. Service from 'masses of staff' – mostly French – is relaxed, affable, polite and efficient. Like its sister establishment, the hotel operates two wine lists: the daily selection of wines offered by the bottle or glass from £9.95/£2.50, and the 'Screwpull Cellar' list, which is a similarly cosmopolitan collection, taking in Switzerland and Uruguay, for example, as well as the usual classics. Again, value for money is the cornerstone of the operation.

CHEF: Chris Start   PROPRIETOR: Alternative Hotel Company   OPEN: all week 12 to 1.45, 7 to 9.30   MEALS: alc (main courses £8 to £14). Set L Sun £20   SERVICE: not inc, card slips closed   CARDS: Amex, Delta, Diners, MasterCard, Switch, Visa   DETAILS: 70 seats. Private parties: 70 main room, 12 to 70 private rooms. Car park. Vegetarian meals. Children's helpings. Wheelchair access (1 step; also WC). No music   ACCOMMODATION: 25 rooms, all with bath/shower. TV. Phone. Room only £75 to £119. Rooms for disabled. Children welcome. Baby facilities (*The Which? Hotel Guide*)

Thackeray's House ▼ ⁵⭑

85 London Road, Tunbridge Wells TN1 1EA COOKING 6
TEL/FAX: (01892) 511921 COST £29–£74

The Victorian novelist's house sits well amid the stolid environs of Royal Tunbridge Wells. Painted green and white, and floodlit after dusk, it is a striking sight. The upstairs lounge, a reporter tells us, retains a 'homely' and slightly threadbare air – 'don't change it,' she pleads – while the 'rather dark but elegant' dining-room is done up attractively in full Victorian fig.

Bruce Wass cooks a prix fixe menu at lunch, and à la carte in the evenings. Earthy flavours and bold combinations are the norm: pigeon breast and bacon salad with poached egg, ceviche of smoked haddock with crab and avocado, and 'just sufficiently cooked' pesto-crusted cod. The Italian accent has been gently incorporated, bringing grilled polenta into play with a herb-roasted chicken breast, and supporting red mullet with angel hair pasta and asparagus. Ingredients fashioned variously into 'cake' or 'loaf' form are a favoured method of presentation, including at dessert stage: 'delicate' chocolate and armagnac loaf with griotte cherries, for example. 'Quiet and supremely smooth' service copes well.

The main wine list includes mature vintages from the French regions, an expanded Italian section and a classy collection from the New World, plus over 60 half-bottles. Bruce Wass's personal choice of 40 wines still offers plenty of options for those in a hurry, and starts at £12.85 a bottle. Fans of whisky should note the ten cask-strength malts. CELLARMAN'S CHOICE: Mudhouse Sauvignon Blanc 1997, Marlborough, New Zealand, £22; Coteaux du Languedoc, Pic St-Loup 1995, Mas de Mortiès, £21.50.

CHEFS: Bruce Wass and Robert Mercer   PROPRIETOR: Bruce Wass   OPEN: Tue to Sun L 12.30 to 2 (3 Sun), Tue to Sat D 7 to 10   CLOSED: 5 days Christmas   MEALS: alc D (main courses £16.50 to £22.50). Set L Tue to Sat £13.50 (2 courses) to £19.50, Set L Sun £24.50   SERVICE: not inc   CARDS: Delta, MasterCard, Switch, Visa   DETAILS: 50 seats. 30 seats outside. Private parties: 55 main room, 12 to 55 private rooms. Children's helpings. No smoking in 1 dining-room. Wheelchair access (1 step; not WC). No music   £5

Prices quoted in the Guide are based on information supplied by restaurateurs. The prices quoted at the top of each entry represent a range, from the lowest meal price to the highest; the latter is inflated by 20 per cent to take account of likely price rises during the year of the Guide.

map 3

McClements

2 Whitton Road, Twickenham TW1 1BJ	COOKING 6
TEL: (0181) 744 9598 FAX: (01784) 240 593	COST £35–£48

Anyone who thinks that all Twickenham can offer is rugby should pay a visit to McClements. It's a cramped but cheery bistro close to the station serving perfectly executed French cooking that would not be out of place in a much grander establishment. 'Long may he stay at the stoves,' wrote an inspector of John McClements after enjoying 'a quite exceptional meal'.

Consistently fine ingredients, well-judged sauces and careful composition are backed up by attractive presentation. Stuffed pig's trotter might be served with a whole, 'very tender' lamb's tongue, a small heap of sweetbreads and an excellent jus to make a 'first class' dish. Leeks and scallops 'seared quickly to a perfect texture' make a delicate topping for a tarte Tatin, its caramelised sauce in no way overpowering the seafood. 'This was a dish I shall be going back for,' declared one reporter. Choice of puddings is limited but the 'exemplary' soufflé with calvados sauce has won plaudits.

The six-course menu including a glass of wine with each course is an idea that more restaurants might emulate. This *tour de force* typically starts with roast lobster ravioli and a glass of champagne, followed by tart of quail and ceps with a *grand cru* Gewurztraminer, then smoked salmon, blini, caviar and vodka. A choice of main courses comes next (for those still clear-headed enough to make a choice), then cheese with vintage port and dessert with orange muscat. More modest appetites may prefer the three-course option. House wine is £11. A new sister restaurant, Chez Clements, is at 108 Heath Road, Twickenham (tel: (0181) 891 0008.

CHEF/PROPRIETOR: John McClements   OPEN: Mon to Fri L 12 to 2, Mon to Sat D 7 to 11
CLOSED: 2 weeks Aug   MEALS: alc (main courses £14 to £15). Set L £18, Set D £23 to £40 (with wine) SERVICE: 10%   CARDS: Amex, MasterCard, Switch, Visa   DETAILS: 40 seats. Private parties: 200 seats private room. Children's helpings. No-smoking area. Wheelchair access (also WC). Music. Air-conditioned

---

UCKFIELD   East Sussex   map 3

▲ Horsted Place Hotel, Pugin Restaurant ⁵✗

Little Horsted, Uckfield TN22 5TS	
TEL: (01825) 750581 FAX: (01825) 750459	
EMAIL: hotel@horstedplace.co.uk	COOKING 5
on A26, 2m S of Uckfield	COST £29–£63

This Pugin house, enjoying expansive views over the rolling South Downs, is approached through mature woodland, the front elevation an imposing vision of untrammelled period grandeur. Window-seating in the lounge allows you to savour the vista, while the dining-room, upholstered in deep crimson, offers views of the changing evening sky. Short set-price menus have only two choices per course at lunch, three at dinner, but they are supplemented by a *carte*.

Allan Garth's kitchen participates enthusiastically in the modern movement, sourcing ideas from Europe, North Africa and Asia, without forcing them all together in one dish. Begin perhaps in Thai mode with cod-cake spiked with lime leaves and chilli, or go French for thyme-crusted rabbit confit with onion marmalade. Other options might include roast salmon on sweetcorn blinis with horseradish and crème fraîche, or there might be lightly smoked local ostrich (from the wild Sussex herds, no doubt), given a celeriac and shallot purée and Barolo sauce. Vegetarians have their own menu, which may take them from fennel and ricotta ravioli in tomato and basil consommé, to date and almond tagine with coriander dumplings. At the end comes chestnut vacherin sauced with armagnac and prunes, or pear tarte Tatin with cinnamon anglaise. Service from smartly attired staff is *comme il faut*. Wines are largely French, with just a couple of reds and whites from each of the other regions included, at mark-ups that emphasise the poshness of the surroundings. House wines from the Languedoc are £12.50.

CHEF: Allan Garth   PROPRIETOR: Granfel Hotels   OPEN: all week 12.30 to 2, 7.30 to 9.30
MEALS: alc (main courses £18 to £19.50). Set L Mon to Sat £17.95, Set L Sun £18.95, Set D £32.
Snack menu 11 to 9   SERVICE: not inc, card slips closed   CARDS: Amex, Delta, Diners,
MasterCard, Switch, Visa   DETAILS: 40 seats. 40 seats outside. Private parties: 24 main room,
16 to 24 private rooms. Car park. Vegetarian meals. Children's helpings. No children under 7. No
smoking in dining-room. Wheelchair access (not WC). Music   ACCOMMODATION: 20 rooms, all
with bath/shower. TV. Phone. B&B £80 to £285. Rooms for disabled. Children welcome. No
dogs. Afternoon teas. Swimming-pool (*The Which? Hotel Guide*)

ULLSWATER Cumbria   map 10

▲ *Sharrow Bay* 🍷 ⅝✳

Ullswater CA10 2LZ
TEL: (01768) 486301   FAX: (01768) 486349
2m from Pooley Bridge on E side of lake, signposted   COOKING 7
Howtown and Martindale   COST £42–£64

Nineteen-ninety-eight was Sharrow Bay's fiftieth season, an event whose celebration was sadly overshadowed by the death of Francis Coulson at the beginning of the year. Anybody writing a history of British cooking in the twentieth century will be unable to do so without paying tribute to his remarkable partnership with Brian Sack, the duo to whom the post-war invention of the country-house hotel is credited. They began when rationing was in force, endured long decades when British cooking was universally ignored or laughed at, and survived into an era when it is held in its highest esteem ever. Their part in this was to pioneer good food long before it was fashionable, and to set and maintain standards that inspired others, all with a modesty that seems quite unjustified. They stimulated loyalty in staff – Johnnie Martin and Colin Akrigg have been here since 1966 – and customers alike.

Reporters come for the whole Sharrow Bay experience, which begins with a view down Ullswater to the fells beyond: the location is 'second to none'. Chairs and settees crowd the lounge, and the feel is of 'comfort verging on luxury', overseen by staff 'with a tradition of real courtesy and care'. With traditional British food in vogue, Sharrow Bay's style can seem quite modern, taking in anything from a tomato, onion and mozarella tart to a dish of duck foie gras, braised pig's trotter and ham shank served with pease pudding. Lunch is four courses, dinner five, with a sorbet somewhere in the middle. Apart from the second set (fish) course – perhaps fillet of halibut with salmon mousseline and a soufflé suissesse – choice is more than generous, as are portions.

Soups terrines and pasta figure among starters, maybe a thin raviolo enclosing a 'light and bouncy' mixture of lobster and scallop, while main courses take in fowl, game and offal (a 'decently thick' slice of calf's liver with salty bacon and a cassis sauce) alongside fillet steak served with a small steak and kidney pudding. Vegetables are arranged on the plate, and might easily include three different kinds of potato. Adding to the already strongly native appeal is an impressive array of desserts, from 'eighteenth-century rum and chocolate pye', via 'memorable' lemon posset pudding, to a warm and 'expertly made' pastry tart of black figs with crème fraîche sauce. The all-embracing wine list is commendably high on quality while mark-ups are surprisingly low for a country house, including plenty of good bins under £20. House French is £13.95 and 33 wines are offered by the glass. CELLARMAN'S CHOICE: Fransola Gran Viña Sol 1996, Miguel Torres, Spain, £19.65; Glen Carlou Estate, Grande Classique 1994, Paarl, South Africa, £23.50.

CHEFS: Johnnie Martin and Colin Akrigg PROPRIETOR: Brian Sack OPEN: all week 12.30 to 1, 7.30 to 8 CLOSED: Dec, Jan and early Feb MEALS: Set L £36.25, Set D £47.25 SERVICE: net prices, card slips closed CARDS: Delta, MasterCard, Switch, Visa DETAILS: 65 seats. Private parties: 10 main room. Car park. No children under 13. No smoking in dining-room. No music. Air-conditioned ACCOMMODATION: 26 rooms, 24 with bath/shower. TV. Phone. D,B&B £120 to £380. No children. Afternoon teas. Fishing (*The Which? Hotel Guide*)

ULVERSTON Cumbria   map 8

▲ *Bay Horse Hotel* ♈ ⁙✳

Canal Foot, Ulverston LA12 9EL
TEL: (01229) 583972 FAX: (01229) 580502
EMAIL: reservations@bayhorse.furness.co.uk
off A590; just before centre of Ulverston, follow   COOKING **5**
signs to Canal Foot   COST £26–£46

When horse-drawn coaches traversed the sands of Morecambe Bay to Lancaster in the eighteenth century, this was one of the watering-holes they would pause at. Once a brewery, inn and fishermen's cottages, it is all now amalgamated as a restaurant and hotel, without losing the cheery, pubby feel that makes for a sense of warm hospitality. Robert Lyons is a John Tovey protegé, and once cooked at Miller Howe (see entry, Windermere). The Lakeland influence still runs strongly through his menus, and may best be identified by the profusion of ingredients in many dishes, and some quite interesting juxtapositions. Smoked chicken, spinach and mango come together in a salad dressed with hazelnut oil, while strips of beef fillet are stir-fried with chilli peppers, spring onions and soy, glazed with raspberry vinegar and honey and served on basmati rice. An extensive vegetarian menu embraces Emmental, leek and asparagus tartlet with caramelised apple and apricot, or perhaps a starter dish of devilled mushrooms on a peanut-butter croûton. Finish, maybe, with rich chocolate and orange liqueur slice, raspberry and Frangelico (hazelnut liqueur) mousse, or brown-sugar meringue with mango and papaya. Home-made truffles are served with coffee. Hand-pumped northern ales and the friendly approach add to the Bay Horse's pedigree, as does the wine list, which features well-bred producers from around the globe with nary a mongrel among them. An already strong New World presence has been bolstered by a number of attractive bins from the Americas. Prices are fair, ranging between £12.95 and £32.75, with seven by the glass.

CHEFS: Robert Lyons and Esther Jarvis   PROPRIETORS: John Tovey and Robert Lyons   OPEN: Tue to Sat L 12 to 1.30, all week D 7.30 for 8 (1 sitting)   MEALS: alc (main courses £15.50 to £17). Set L £16.75. BYO £5   SERVICE: 10% (optional), card slips closed   CARDS: Delta, MasterCard, Switch, Visa   DETAILS: 50 seats. Private parties: 50 main room. Car park. No children under 12. No smoking in dining-room. Wheelchair access (also WC). Music   ACCOMMODATION: 7 rooms, all with bath/shower. TV. Phone. D,B&B £85 to £160. No children under 12. Dogs in bedrooms only. Afternoon teas (*The Which? Hotel Guide*)

UPPER SLAUGHTER   Gloucestershire   map 5

▲ *Lords of the Manor* ⁵✳

Upper Slaughter, nr Bourton-on-the-Water GL54 2JD
TEL: (01451) 820243   FAX: (01451) 820696   COOKING 6
turn W off A429, 3m S of Stow-on-the-Wold   COST £34–£85

Although bang in the centre of this much-visited hamlet, the Cotswold stone manor-house is quite secluded, with eight acres running down to the River Eye, and a kitchen plot that grows herbs and fruit to flavour jams, oils and vinegars. It is an elegant, restful, friendly place, its pale yellow dining-room considered 'charming, glamorous and inviting'. John Campbell's food is classy and up to date, and although the style may not be strikingly original – ham hock and foie gras terrine owes a debt to Terence Laybourne, 'Jaffa cake' is very Gary Rhodes – this is a country-house hotel after all, and for one visitor it served 'consistently high-quality' meals over the course of a three-day break.

Campbell aims for workable ideas such as leek and potato soup with Welsh rarebit, and squab pigeon with celeriac purée and boudin blanc. He cooks up risottos – of artichoke, or black pudding – and is fond of the scent of truffle oil, which works its way into a parfait of foie gras with a Szechuan pepper jelly, and into baked cod or turbot with mashed peas. The cooking is 'technically very accomplished', raw materials are 'superb', timing is 'perfection itself', and sauces are 'beyond criticism'. One sign of a good chef is being able to make even ordinary-sounding dishes exciting, which happened in the case of one reporter's 'brilliantly executed' corn-fed chicken served with leeks and mushroom ravioli.

Some desserts such as warm chocolate fondant, or pear Tatin, need ordering in advance; otherwise there might be toffee and banana tart, apricot bread and butter pudding, or 'outstanding' cheese tart with lemon sorbet. 'Intelligent and human' staff are observant and attentive. Note that service charge is added to dinner only. The wine list was being totally re-vamped as we went to press, but a house Sauvignon from Touraine and a Syrah/Mourvèdre from the Pays d'Oc are £14.95.

CHEF: John Campbell PROPRIETOR: Empire Ventures Ltd OPEN: all week 12 to 2 (2.30 Sun), 7 to 9.30 MEALS: alc (main courses £19 to £25.50). Set L Mon to Sat £16.95 (2 courses) to £19.95, Set L Sun £21, Set D £32.50. Light L menu Mon to Sat SERVICE: not inc L, 12.5% D; card slips closed D CARDS: Amex, Delta, Diners, MasterCard, Switch, Visa DETAILS: 60 seats. 16 seats outside. Private parties: 60 main room, 24 to 30 private rooms. Car park. Vegetarian meals. Children's helpings. No smoking in dining-room. Wheelchair access (also men's WC). No music ACCOMMODATION: 27 rooms, all with bath/shower. TV. Phone. B&B £95 to £295. Rooms for disabled. Children welcome. High teas for children. Baby facilities. No dogs. Afternoon teas. Fishing

---

VIRGINSTOW Devon   map 1

▲ *Percy's at Coombeshead* 🕯✕

Virginstow EX21 5EA
TEL: (01409) 211236 FAX: (01409) 211275
EMAIL: percyscoombeshead@compuserve.com
follow signs to Percy's at Coombeshead from Gridley
corner on A388, or from B3218 at Metherell Cross   COOKING **5**
junction   COST £29–£43

The Bricknell-Webbs have taken the plunge and finally bid London goodbye. Since the last edition of the *Guide*, they have sold their restaurant in North Harrow and now concentrate on this Devon farmstead, where their own organic fruit and vegetables are the pride and glory of the kitchen. A makeover for the stables has produced eight guest rooms, while the dining goes on in two adjoining rooms.

A fixed-price menu with two or three supplements keeps things simple, though the same may not immediately be said of the cooking. Cornish smoked haddock is much favoured, served on tomato and fish stock velouté one night, and then – to great delight on another – on leeks with a poached egg and cream sauce. Seared king scallops, 'slightly smoky outside, melting within', were dressed with honey vinaigrette at a spring dinner, while turbot from the Cornish catch has been robustly treated by roasting it with smoked piquillo peppers, and saucing it with smoked garlic butter. Meat dishes take in Aberdeen Angus, perhaps served with 'spaghetti' of celeriac and a peppercorn sauce, as well as bacon-wrapped chicken breast stuffed with a mousse of ceps, leeks and tarragon. No holds are barred at dessert stage, either, where banana and hazelnut meringue is accompanied by mango and butterscotch sauce and rosemary ice-cream, and 'outstanding' crème brûlée may be beguilingly scented with lavender. Waits between courses can on occasion be lengthy. The wine list makes a decent fist of sourcing some good, positive flavours from around the world, the house selections starting at £8.95 for Loire Sauvignon and £9.95 for Cape Pinotage.

CHEF: Tina Bricknell-Webb PROPRIETORS: Tony and Tina Bricknell-Webb OPEN: all week 12 to 2, 6.30 to 9 MEALS: Set L and D £22 SERVICE: 10% (optional), card slips closed CARDS: Amex, Delta, MasterCard, Switch, Visa DETAILS: 44 seats. Private parties: 30 main room, 18 to 30 private rooms. Car park. No children under 12. No smoking in dining-room. Wheelchair access (1 step; not WC). Music ACCOMMODATION: 8 rooms, all with bath/shower. TV. B&B £49.50 to £79.50. Rooms for disabled. Children welcome. High teas for children. Baby facilities (*The Which? Hotel Guide*) (£5)

▲ *Manor House*

Northlands, Newbold Road, Walkington HU17 8RT
TEL: (01482) 881645 FAX: (01482) 866501   COOKING 2
off B1230 towards Beverley from Walkington   COST £26–£57

Décor in the conservatory dining-room is a 'remarkable collection of disparate elements which works better than you might expect', according to one visitor, who could not resist drawing a parallel with the food. Derek Baugh has the sort of 'wild energy' that throws all sorts of components into individual dishes, though this may leave some of them without a clear identity: for example, eight queen scallops served with eight different sauces, surely a record if nothing else. But his 'seat-of-the-pants' style of cooking has produced some notable successes, among them 'creamy textured and deeply flavoured' lobster bisque, and 'fresh and precisely judged' sea bass with a vivid yellow hollandaise.

Good saucing has included a rich and shiny stock reduction for a dish of lambs' tongues and kidneys, and a similarly dark and glossy one for oxtail. Baking skills are evident in breads and in desserts such as caramelised lemon tart. There are two menus, the cheaper with three choices at each stage, the dearer with eight: 'we couldn't decide whether the short menu was a bargain or the long menu overpriced'. Service is 'willing but unpolished', and classic French wines constitute the backbone of a 150-strong list, starting with house red and white at £11.95.

CHEF: Derek Baugh PROPRIETORS: Derek and Lee Baugh OPEN: Mon to Sat D only 7 to 9.15
CLOSED: 25and 26 Dec, bank hols Mon MEALS: Set D £18.50 to £30 SERVICE: not inc, card
slips closed CARDS: MasterCard, Switch, Visa DETAILS: 55 seats. Private parties: 30 main
room. Car park. No children under 12. No cigars/pipes in dining-room. Music
ACCOMMODATION: 7 rooms, all with bath/shower. TV. Phone. Room only £65 to £100. Children
welcome. Small dogs welcome (£5)

▲ *Priory Hotel* 🍷 ⁵⊁

Church Green, Wareham BH20 4ND   COOKING 5
TEL: (01929) 551666 FAX: (01929) 554519   COST £26–£72

Head for the village church: the five-centuries-old hotel occupies an 'idyllic' setting in four acres of well-cared-for grounds between that and the banks of the River Frome. Summer dinners may start with aperitifs on the terrace, before moving down to the 'light and airy' cellar dining-room for Stephen Astley's modern British country-house cooking.

The choice at dinner is either à la carte or a four-course set-price menu with soup – perhaps 'well-constructed and very filling' mushroom and tarragon – after the starter. Dishes are artfully composed but not too elaborate. A terrine of marinated herrings wrapped in smoked salmon with a sauce of cucumber and yoghurt shows 'superb balance', while roast guinea-fowl with creamed leeks, roasted shallots and a thyme jus was for one reporter 'probably one of the best dishes I have eaten this year'. Beef Wellington for two, carved at table and served with truffled Madeira sauce, gets star billing on the *carte*. A light touch with desserts brings commendations for blackcurrant mousse, and mango and lemon syllabub. Service is genuinely welcoming, and enhances the sense of occasion provided by the surroundings. The extensive wine list features a long line of grand clarets stretching back to 1955, some attractive Rhônes and Alsatians, and some fine bins from the New World. Numerous bottles under £20 and a wine waiter who knows his business add to the appeal. House wines from Dom. Laroche are £12.50.

CHEF: Stephen Astley   PROPRIETORS: Stuart and John Turner   OPEN: all week 12.30 to 2, 7.30 to 10   MEALS: alc (main courses £19.50 to £23, not available Sun L). Set L Mon to Sat £13.95 (2 courses) to £15.95, Set L Sun £19.95, Set D Sun to Fri £26.50, Set D Sat £31.50. Light L available   SERVICE: not inc, card slips closed   CARDS: Amex, Delta, Diners, MasterCard, Switch, Visa   DETAILS: 45 seats. 40 seats outside. Private parties: 45 main room, 25 and 45 private rooms. Car park. Vegetarian meals. No children under 8. No smoking in dining-room. Music   ACCOMMODATION: 19 rooms, all with bath/shower. TV. Phone. B&B £80 to £225. No children under 8. High teas for children over 8. No dogs. Afternoon teas. Fishing

---

WARMINSTER Wiltshire   map 2

▲ *Bishopstrow House* ⁵⨯

Warminster BA12 9HH
TEL: **(01985) 212312**   FAX: **(01985) 216769**
EMAIL: bishopstrow_house_hotel@msn.com   COOKING **2**
on B3414, SW of Warminster   COST £28–£64

Signs at the gate announce a spa, hair stylist, beauty treatment and restaurant 'in that order', and they are 'strong on swimming-pools', too, with one inside, one out. The country-house approach stops short of offering an appetiser before dinner, but does take a typically no-holds-barred line in toasted goats' cheese, Quantock duck confit with chilli, lentil and coriander dressing, and roast lamb with Mediterranean vegetables and olive gravy. Dishes tend to contain a lot of ingredients, but materials are generally good and meals 'well cooked and presented'. Finish, perhaps, with raspberry crème brûlée, or poached tamarillo turned into a 'tropical island scene' with the help of a biscuit palm tree and pineapple sorbet. Bottled water costs £3.70 a litre, and a 15 per cent 'voluntary' service charge hikes up the total. French wines dominate the list, but Argentina supplies house red and white at £13.50.

CHEF: Chris Suter   PROPRIETORS: Howard Malin, Simon Lowe and Andrew Leeman   OPEN: all week 12.30 to 2, 7.30 to 9 (9.30 Fri and Sat)   MEALS: alc L (main courses £4.50 to £10). Set D £29.50 to £34.50. Bar L available Sun to Thur   SERVICE: 15% (optional), card slips closed   CARDS: Amex, Delta, Diners, MasterCard, Switch, Visa   DETAILS: 85 seats. 50 seats outside. Private parties: 70 main room, 22 private room. Car park. Vegetarian meals. Children welcome. No smoking in dining-room. Music   ACCOMMODATION: 31 rooms, all with bath/shower. TV. Phone. Room only £90 to £295. Rooms for disabled. Children welcome. High teas for children. Baby facilities. Afternoon teas. Swimming-pool. Fishing (*The Which? Hotel Guide*)

'The young waitress was of the naïve school: "I were going to ask if everything was all right, but the way you're tucking in, I won't bother".' (On eating in Lancashire)

WATERHOUSES Staffordshire   map 5

▲ *Old Beams*   ▮ ⁵⤡

Leek Road, Waterhouses ST10 3HW
TEL: (01538) 308254   FAX: (01538) 308157   COOKING 6
on A523, 7m SE of Leek   COST £32–£63

The Wallises put a lot of effort into making their restaurant (with rooms in an annexe across the busy road) look attractive. The beamed part of the dining-room is considered 'cosier' than the plant-strewn conservatory, where the door to the loo is hidden in a huge Italianate mural, the reasoning presumably being that anyone desperate enough will find it. The food's classical European foundation is evident in calves' sweetbreads with morels and Madeira sauce, or an open tart of tomatoes with pesto dressing and Parmesan shavings, although Nigel Wallis is not averse to incorporating spicy couscous and a korma sauce into a roast cod starter. If dinner prices seem high, consider some of the luxuries they deal in: truffle-scented risotto with wild mushroom ravioli and a cep sauce, or foie gras terrine and duck confit with a Sauternes jelly.

Some combinations have raised eyebrows – fillet of lamb topped with crab ravioli, on a bed of red cabbage with wild mushrooms, was considered rather 'Masterchef' – but that sort of thing appears to be the exception rather than the rule. The thrust is firmly towards more sensible ideas along the lines of boned skate wing filled with lobster mousse, or wood pigeon with Puy lentils, a philosophy that also applies to desserts: rich chocolate tart with clotted cream, or one of the signature soufflés, either sweet (Grand Marnier) or savoury (goats' cheese). Good black olives arrive with drinks at the start, and 'coffee and petits fours are worthy of mention'. Ann Wallis is a busy, friendly hostess, and standards only seem to wobble when the proprietors take a break. Like the cuisine, classic European regions form the basis of the wine list, with the expected mature burgundies and vintage clarets joined by such luminaries as Zind-Humbrecht from Alsace and Italy's Angelo Gaja. Selections from the New World are small but sound, and half-bottles abound. A trio of French house wines starts at £13.90. CELLARMAN'S CHOICE: Pouilly-Fumé 'Clos des Chaudoux' 1995, Serge Dagueneau, £23.50; Ribera del Duero 1995, Pago de Carraovejas, £18.90.

CHEF: Nigel Wallis   PROPRIETORS: Nigel and Ann Wallis   OPEN: Wed to Fri and Sun L 12 to 1.45, Tue to Sat D 7 to 9.30   CLOSED: 3 weeks Jan, 1 week Aug   MEALS: Set L £15.95 (2 courses) to £21, alc D (main courses £16.50 to £18.50)   SERVICE: not inc, card slips closed   CARDS: Amex, Delta, Diners, MasterCard, Switch, Visa   DETAILS: 40 seats. Private parties: 40 main room. Car park. No children under 4. No smoking in dining-room. No music   ACCOMMODATION: 5 rooms, all with bath/shower. TV. Phone. B&B £65 to £120. Rooms for disabled. Children welcome. Baby facilities. Guide dogs only (*The Which? Hotel Guide*)   £5

Report forms are at the back of the book; write a letter if you prefer; or email us at guidereports@which.co.uk.

Several sharp operators have tried to extort money from restaurateurs on the promise of an entry in a guidebook that has never appeared. The Good Food Guide *makes no charge for inclusion.*

WATERMILLOCK Cumbria   map 10

▲ *Rampsbeck Hotel* ▼ ⚹

Watermillock, Ullswater CA11 0LP
TEL: (017684) 86442   FAX: (017684) 86688   COOKING 5
on A592 Penrith to Windermere road   COST £34–£59

Just off the road, down towards the water's edge, Rampsbeck is a quiet
eighteenth-century house that reminded one visitor of 'an old spa hotel'.
Afternoon tea can be taken by the fire, lunchtime snacks in the bar and main
meals in the large dining-room overlooking Ullswater, where the choice is
between two set-price four-course meals (plus a vegetarian version). The more
expensive menu offers a greater concentration of the kitchen's efforts, more
luxury and more choice: perhaps hot smoked salmon with new potato salad and
caviare to begin, then a middle course of sorbet or soup, followed by sea bass
with langoustine risotto, or pink breast of grouse with cabbage, game chips and
blackberries.

Supplies are well sourced – air-dried ham and Cumberland sausage from
Woodall's at Waberthwaite, shellfish from Loch Fyne – and the cooking is
considered 'professional and workmanlike': for example a starter of sea bass and
scallops, on a base of rösti potato and spinach, in red wine sauce. Warm chocolate
tart or poached pear might be among desserts, and Amaretto soufflé comes well
risen in its copper pan, with a Florentine biscuit adding a second nutty flavour. If
you like a touch of nuttiness in your wine, then concise and accurate tasting
notes on the list will lead you to a Mâcon-Igé with a 'hint of almonds'. Wines are
helpfully grouped by style, and prices are friendly too, starting at £11.25 for the
house selection. CELLARMAN'S CHOICE: Bodegas Con Class Sauvignon Blanc
1996, Rueda, £15; Parducci Petite Sirah 1995, Mendocino, California, £16.

CHEF: Andrew McGeorge   PROPRIETORS: Mr and Mrs T.I. Gibb and Mrs M.J. MacDowall
OPEN: all week 12 to 1, 7 to 8.30 (booking essential L)   CLOSED: Jan to mid-Feb   MEALS: Set L
£25, Set D £26 to £39. Light L available   SERVICE: not inc, card slips closed   CARDS: Delta,
MasterCard, Switch, Visa   DETAILS: 40 seats. Private parties: 12 main room, 16 private room.
Car park. Vegetarian meals. Children's helpings. No smoking in dining-room. No music
ACCOMMODATION: 21 rooms, all with bath/shower. TV. Phone. B&B £55 to £180. Children
welcome. High teas for children. Dogs welcome by arrangement. Afternoon teas (*The Which?
Hotel Guide*)

WATH-IN-NIDDERDALE North Yorkshire   map 8

▲ *Sportsman's Arms* ⚹

Wath-in-Nidderdale HG3 5PP
TEL: (01423) 711306   FAX: (01423) 712524
take B6156 or B6265 to Pateley Bridge, follow signs to   COOKING 4
village; 2m NW of Pateley Bridge   COST £25–£47

After 20 years at this seventeenth-century inn, the Carters are celebrating with
extensive refurbishment as we go to press, redecorating lounges and bedrooms,
and converting a stable-block. The food remains as before: straightforward,
appealing dishes chalked on a board in the bar, or a choice between à la carte or a
set-price menu with half a bottle of wine in the dining-room. Fish is a feature,

from Scottish salmon, via Nidderdale trout, to a daily delivery from the east coast: Scarborough woof, haddock, or plaice fillets served up with just butter, parsley and lemon. Lamb from the butcher in Pateley Bridge, just down the road, might be roasted along with some garlic cloves; soups are freshly made and flavourful, reflecting the 'simple honesty' of the style; and some of the cheeses are from the Dales. Summer pudding is a popular way to finish, or there may be raspberry crème brûlée or sticky toffee. Wines are strongest in France and prices are agreeably restrained, starting at £10.50 within the house French selection. Several wines by the glass at around £2 are changed daily.

CHEF: Ray Carter   PROPRIETORS: Jane and Ray Carter   OPEN: Sun L 12 to 2 (2.30 Sun), Tue to Sat D 6.30 to 9.30   CLOSED: 25 Dec   MEALS: alc (main courses £13.50 to £16). Set L Sun £15.50, Set D £21 (inc wine)   SERVICE: not inc, card slips closed   CARDS: MasterCard, Switch, Visa   DETAILS: 60 seats. 30 seats outside. Private parties: 55 main room, 10 private room. Car park. Vegetarian meals. Children's helpings. No smoking in dining-room. Wheelchair access (not WC). No music   ACCOMMODATION: 13 rooms, 11 with bath/shower. TV. B&B £25 to £80. Rooms for disabled. Children welcome. No dogs. Afternoon teas. Fishing (The Which? Hotel Guide)

WELLS Somerset   map 2

Ritcher's

5 Sadler Street, Wells BA5 2RR	COOKING 2
TEL/FAX: (01749) 679085	COST £15–£30

A short hop from Wells's market-place, Ritcher's can be found at the end of a passageway between shops. Sit in the courtyard outside the ground-floor bistro, or ascend the spiral staircase to the slightly more formal restaurant above. Bistro French is the style, taking in duck liver pâté with blackcurrant marmalade and brioche, steamed halibut on pasta with a mushroom cream sauce, or Stilton-glazed beef fillet on smoked bacon rösti sauced with red wine and shallots. More novel ideas, such as 'heavenly' courgette, tomato and basil strudel with béarnaise, are brought off with equal panache, and chocolate tart with caramel sauce or mango parfait with fresh fruits are sweet alternatives to fine English cheeses. Friendly, obliging service helps it all go with a swing. A good range of halves bolsters the French-led and considerably priced wine list. House burgundy is £8.95.

CHEFS/PROPRIETORS: Nicholas Hart and Kate Ritcher   OPEN: all week 12 to 2, 7 (5.30 Fri and Sat May to Sept) to 9.30 (10 Fri and Sat)   CLOSED: 26 Dec, 1 Jan   MEALS: Set L £5.50 (1 course) to £7.50, Set D Fri and Sat before 7pm May to Sept £9.95 (2 courses), Set D £13.95 (2 courses) to £16.95   SERVICE: not inc, card slips closed   CARDS: MasterCard, Switch, Visa   DETAILS: 40 seats. 12 seats outside. Private parties: 22 main room, 22 private room. Vegetarian meals. Children welcome. No children under 7 upstairs at D. No cigars/pipes in dining-room. Wheelchair access (not WC). Occasional music   (£5)

To find a restaurant in a particular area use the maps at the back of the book.

If you have access to the Internet, you can find The Good Food Guide *online at the* Which? *Online web site (http://www.which.net).*

Sakonis 🍴✕ £

119–121 Ealing Road, Wembley HA0 4BP
TEL: (0181) 903 9601   FAX: (0181) 903 7260   COOKING 2
EMAIL: enquiries@sakonis.co.uk   COST £11–£27

This real live wire of a place can pack in more than 300 customers sitting at Formica tables and enjoying genuine Indian vegetarian food at rock-bottom prices. The menu kicks off with an assortment of 'Bites' (snacks and appetisers), taking in everything from samosas, mogo chips (cassava), and dahi vadai to toasted sandwiches (including an anglicised version with cheese, onion, tomato and chilli). More substantial offerings are listed as 'Eats': here you might choose from potato bhajias, Mysore masala dosai, or even a vegetable burger with chips. The kitchen's appetite for crossover dishes extends even further into what the menu calls 'Vegetarian Chinese Cuisine (prepared Indian style)'. Spinach and bean sprouts with dried chillies, sea-spice aubergine, assorted noodles, and even American 'chopped' (*sic*) suey are the sort of things to expect. The chefs also make a fine job of exotic kulfis, milkshakes and shrikand. Take-aways and a delivery service are a boon to locals. There is a branch a couple of doors away at 129 Ealing Road (with the same phone number) and a further outlet at 114–116 Station Road, Edgware (tel: (0181) 951 0058). Sakonis is unlicensed.

CHEFS: R. And N. Bhimsiyani   PROPRIETOR: Everfresh Ltd   OPEN: all week 11 to 11 (11.30 Fri and Sat)   MEALS: alc (main courses £2.50 to £5)   SERVICE: 10%, card slips closed   CARDS: Delta, MasterCard, Switch, Visa   DETAILS: 330 seats. Private parties: 80 private room. Vegetarian meals. Children welcome. No smoking in dining-room. Wheelchair access (also WC). Music. Air-conditioned   (£5)

Riverside Restaurant £

West Bay DT6 4EZ
TEL: (01308) 422011   COOKING 2
off A35, 1m S of Bridport   COST £20–£52

The Watsons' seafood restaurant sits in an enclosed harbour in a tiny seaside resort, and is reached by a narrow wooden walkway. It is hugely popular and a hive of 'convivially noisy' activity. Printed menus are verbally amended at the table according to what hasn't been caught that day. What is offered is straightforwardly simple – and occasionally dazzling – fish cookery. The polish shows in a starter of scallops seared to 'a brown, nutty roastedness' on couscous with basil pesto: a 'quite gorgeous' combination revealing real culinary intelligence. To follow, cod comes in Guinness batter with mushy peas and chips, salmon with hollandaise, and baked sea bass is stuffed with fennel, garlic, ginger and spring onions. Childhay Manor ice-creams seem the best bets for afters; pastrywork in a prune and armagnac tart at inspection was very poor. Service is pacey but pleasingly casual at the same time. The predominantly white wines are a broad selection at reasonable mark-ups, with a good few available by the glass. House French is £11.95 a litre.

CHEFS: Michael Mills and Nick Larcombe PROPRIETORS: Arthur and Janet Watson OPEN: Tue to Sun L 12 to 2.30, Tue to Sat D 6.30 to 9 CLOSED: 1 Dec to 1 Mar MEALS: alc (main courses £6 to £17.50) SERVICE: not inc, card slips closed CARDS: Delta, MasterCard, Switch, Visa DETAILS: 70 seats. 20 seats outside. Private parties: 100 main room, 20 private room. Vegetarian meals. Children's helpings. No cigars/pipes in dining-room before 10.30pm. Wheelchair access (not WC). Occasional music

---

WEST TANFIELD North Yorkshire map 9

Bruce Arms |NEW ENTRY|

West Tanfield HG4 5JJ COOKING 4
TEL: (01677) 470325 FAX: (01677) 470796 COST £20–£37

Ivy covers the 'solid, handsome' stone walls of this restaurant-pub. An original fireplace, pewter tankards, guns on the wall and seating on cushioned church pews all contribute to the comfortable rustic atmosphere. The blackboard lists mainly traditional dishes presented in modern style with well-dressed salad garnishes. Smoked chicken and avocado with raspberry dressing pleased an inspector, while the richness of smooth chicken liver paté was offset by sharp Cumberland sauce. Bananas might appear in a starter (with bacon and curried mayonnaise), or in a main course of chicken breast and smoked ham in a mild curry sauce.

More firmly traditional offerings include avocado with prawns, and fillet steak au poivre. 'Tender and flavoursome' braised lamb shank with a tarragon and mustard sauce made an inspector wish there had been a little more of it; but sauces accompanying roast cod, and salmon with caramelised red cabbage were generously served. The high point of one meal was classic crème brûlée, although milk chocolate mousse ran it a close second. Vegetarian main dishes might include aubergine and tomato lasagne, wild mushroom gâteau and cashew-nut curry. Service has been described as 'warm, obliging, smiling and professional'. Some 50 modestly priced wines include a dozen by the glass and start with house French at £7.95. Of the few over £20, Château Pape Clément 1990 or 1993 should be a snip at £25.

CHEF: Geoff Smith PROPRIETORS: Geoff Smith and Amanda Donkin OPEN: Tue to Sun L 12 to 2 (2.30 Sun), Tue to Sat D 7 to 9.30 MEALS: alc (main courses £7 to £14) SERVICE: not inc CARDS: Delta, MasterCard, Switch, Visa DETAILS: 42 seats. 16 seats outside. Private parties: 30 private room. Car park. Vegetarian meals. Children welcome. Music (£5)

WETHERSFIELD Essex map 6

Dicken's 🍷

The Green, Wethersfield CM7 4BS COOKING 5
TEL/FAX: (01371) 850723 COST £30–£47

A relaxed regime obtains at this old house, parts of which date from the seventeenth century, where reporters come for food that is 'well prepared and competently served in pleasant surroundings'. John Dicken combines traditional ideas of beef and horseradish, or pork and apple, with a few more upbeat flavours, often with Mediterranean leanings: saffron risotto with roasted peppers, or skate with caper and sun-dried tomato pesto. Soups are a strength, including the ever-popular fish version with rouille, and steamed game or lamb puddings are judiciously spiced to meet the demands of the 'mid-Essex palate'. Sauces are delicate, and not over-reduced, but they can also pack a punch, judging by a dish of mussels with noodles and a 'sumptuous' coconut Thai sauce.

Take a tip from a regular and finish with lemon tart or sticky toffee pudding. On the question of value, bread (though good) is charged extra, while the two-course lunch for under a tenner is considered a steal. As for service, a proprietorial presence out front would be a boon. Rich pickings are to be had from a lengthy wine list that keeps interest high and sources reliable. Helpfully arranged by style and concisely annotated, it opens with John's personal selection of 19 bins to aid those who can't decide what the dickens to choose. Prices open at £10.25. CELLARMAN'S CHOICE: Madfish Bay Unwooded Chardonnay 1997, Margaret River, W. Australia, £17; Carneros Creek, Fleur de Carneros Pinot Noir 1995, Carneros, California, £20.25.

CHEF/PROPRIETOR: John Dicken   OPEN: Wed to Sun L 12.30 to 2, Wed to Sat D 7.30 to 9.30   CLOSED: bank hols   MEALS: alc (main courses L £6.50 to £15, D £11 to £15.50). Set L £10 (2 courses), Set D £19.50   SERVICE: not inc   CARDS: Delta, MasterCard, Switch, Visa   DETAILS: 60 seats. 12 seats outside. Private parties: 36 main room, 10 to 18 private rooms. Car park. Vegetarian meals. Children's helpings. Wheelchair access (1 step; also women's WC). Occasional music   £5

WHITBY North Yorkshire   map 9

Magpie Café ❉ £

14 Pier Road, Whitby YO21 3PU
TEL: (01947) 602058 and 821723   COOKING 2
FAX: (01947) 601801   COST £14–£44

'If you have to queue, queue; if you have to share a table, share,' noted a couple who remembered the Magpie with great affection. The location – a 200-year-old merchant's house overlooking the harbour – suggests fish, and that's exactly what you can expect. All kinds of spanking-fresh Whitby fish with chips are the stars of the show, although the menus offer a dauntingly large choice of everything, from suggestions for weightwatchers to special set meals served all day. In between, there might be griddled scallops with lemon oil, cod baked with sun-dried tomatoes, crab salad, and vegetarian shepherd's pie. Rounding off proceedings is a line-up of two dozen calorie-laden desserts ranging from steamed treacle sponge to profiteroles topped with cappuccino sauce. Service is as nice as can be, and 'the whole operation so well organised it cannot be praised too highly'. An affordable list of wines from Bibendum matches the food admirably. House wine is £6.95.

CHEF: Ian Robson   PROPRIETORS: Sheila and Ian McKenzie, Ian Robson and Alison McKenzie-Robson   OPEN: all week 11.30 to 9 (6.30 Sun Nov to mid-Mar)   CLOSED: 22 to 24 Dec, Jan   MEALS: alc (main courses £4.50 to £17). Set L and D £9.25 to £14.95   SERVICE: not inc, card slips closed   CARDS: Delta, MasterCard, Switch, Visa   DETAILS: 100 seats. Private parties: 50 main room. Vegetarian meals. Children's helpings. No smoking in dining-room. Occasional music. Air-conditioned   £5

WHITSTABLE Kent

map 3

▲ *Whitstable Oyster Fishery Co*

Royal Native Oyster Stores, The Horsebridge,
Whitstable CT5 1BU
TEL: (01227) 276856 FAX: (01227) 770666

COOKING 1
COST £25–£62

This bare-boarded Victorian oyster store, facing a shingle beach and the distant Isle of Sheppey, has a cavernous dining-room decorated with 'nautical clichés' as well as a blackboard menu and displays of seafood. 'Luxurious it is not,' claimed one reporter, but the aim is simplicity and no frills: oysters (natives in season) with shallot vinegar, langoustines in tarragon butter, or lightly battered squid rings served with a big blob of mayonnaise. Supplies come variously from Scottish farms, the West Country, local fishermen and Billingsgate, and typically end up being simply grilled: halibut or sea bass 'fresh as a daisy' served with chips, whole lemon sole, or perhaps skate wing with black butter sauce. Some items – smoked eel at £7.50 – can seem a little expensive, and not all reporters have been happy with the output. Service is casual, which might translate as either 'slow' or 'friendly and helpful', depending on circumstance. Drink Shepherd Neame bottled beer, or one of the ten white wines. House Chardonnay is £9.95.

CHEF: Chris Williams PROPRIETOR: Whitstable Oyster Fishery Co OPEN: all week 12 to 2 (2.30 Sat, 3 Sun), 7 to 9 (6.30 to 9.30 Sat) CLOSED: Sun D and Mon Oct to June MEALS: alc (main courses £8.50 to £22). Set L and D £25 SERVICE: not inc; 10% (optional) for parties of 6 or more CARDS: Amex, Delta, MasterCard, Visa DETAILS: 150 seats. 50 seats outside. Private parties: 40 main room. Children's helpings. No pipes in dining-room. Wheelchair access (1 step; not WC). Music ACCOMMODATION: 7 rooms, all with bath/shower. TV. Room only £55 to £85. Children welcome. No dogs (*The Which? Hotel Guide*)

WILLITON Somerset

map 2

▲ *White House* ▮ ⁵✻

11 Long Street, Williton TA4 4QW
TEL: (01984) 632306

COOKING 6
COST £45–£53

Palms, mimosas, clematis and fuchsias are part of the living décor in evidence at this plain white symmetrical building, which counts carved antique dining-tables among the furniture, and a Georgian square piano manufactured by the composer Clementi. Rough dark stone walls help to make it feel 'small and intimate', and a 'relaxed, unpretentious' atmosphere prevails. Unless they are really busy, owners Dick and Kay Smith share the well-paced, friendly and attentive service between them. The food's foundation is rock solid. Supplies are 'immaculate, top quality and of unsurpassed freshness' according to an inspector, and include local free-range meat, poultry, game, eggs and seasonal vegetables: try asparagus in early summer. Fish and shellfish are from Brixham, taking in steamed halibut with dill, roast monkfish with pesto, and a 'clean-tasting, warmly flavoured' starter of 'superbly' seared scallops with tomatoes and basil in the vinaigrette.

The cooking itself is fairly simple, that is to say it concentrates on perfect timing rather than elaborate technique. 'Rarely have I had a meal so bursting with flavour throughout,' confessed one whose roast grouse came in two waves: breasts first, then legs, both sliced, sitting on a potato and celeriac rosti, with little more than pan juices in the sauce. 'Immense care' extends to the smallest detail, from good olives and an appetiser soup, to bread that made an expert baker 'green with envy', to mashed potatoes that Dick Smith had been 'working on for months'. 'Classic flavour contrasts' are the norm: for example, a wedge of layered, open-textured chocolate sponge cake and 'intense' mousse, with a 'wicked blob' of cream and a few peeled orange segments. The three-course menu can be extended (for a small supplement) with soup or cheese, although 'it is hard to imagine many people wanting both courses'. However, it is easy to see how wine lovers would want to choose more than one bottle, for the White House list is a European treasure trove in which Germany and the Rhône shine out. A few New World gems sparkle, and around 20 dessert wines add a golden lustre. House wines start at £10.50. CELLARMAN'S CHOICE: Seresin Sauvignon Blanc 1997, Marlborough, New Zealand, £16.50; Ribera del Duero Tinto Crianza 1995, Teófilo Reyes, £27.

CHEFS/PROPRIETORS: Dick and Kay Smith   OPEN: all week D only 7.30 to 8.30   CLOSED: early Nov to mid-May   MEALS: Set D £31   SERVICE: not inc   CARDS: none   DETAILS: 22 seats. Private parties: 10 main room. Car park. Children's helpings. No smoking in dining-room. Wheelchair access (not WC). No music   ACCOMMODATION: 12 rooms 10 with bath/shower. TV. Phone. B&B £34 to £94. Rooms for disabled. Children welcome. Dogs by arrangement

---

WILMINGTON   East Sussex   map 3

▲ *Crossways* ⁵✳

Lewes Road, Wilmington BN26 5SG
TEL: (01323) 482455   FAX: (01323) 487811
EMAIL: crossways@fastnet co.uk   COOKING 4
on A27, 2m W of Polegate   COST £36–£42

A white-fronted Georgian house with green shutters and pillared porch, Crossways is set on the fringe of the South Downs, not far from the imposing chalk figure known as the Long Man of Wilmington. Mature shrubs and a big garden pond full of lilies lend an appealingly pastoral air to the approach, and the restful atmosphere is maintained in a dining-room done in salmon-pink with floral swags at the windows.

The format is a fixed-price dinner of four courses plus coffee, with a supplement only for beef fillet. What would once have been seen as modern British cooking is the furrow the kitchen ploughs, and starters may include such oddities as hot mushroom éclair or savoury cheese peach. A gratinated cheesy seafood pancake turns out to be an accomplished wafer-thin batter encasing fresh, clear flavours of salmon and prawns. The second course is soup of the day, perhaps a simple 'mild and lightly creamy' white onion potion with croûtons, followed by Gressingham duck breast with elderflower sauce, or a dish of monkfish collops coated with crunchy sesame and onion seeds, the flavours buttressed by a strong lobster sauce. Great craft is shown too in the unctuously textured dessert jelly of peaches and strawberries in Muscat wine that came on a minted cream sauce, 'its delicious vibrancy making a clean finish to the meal'. The proprietors run front-of-house with assured polish, the show extending to 'quick and amusing' explanations of the menu. The characterful wine list leads off with English and New World bottles, before delving into the classic French regions. Prices throughout are easy on the pocket, and house wines – a Chilean red and an English white – are £10.25.

CHEFS: David Stott and Juliet Anderson   PROPRIETORS: David Stott and Clive James   OPEN: Tue to Sat D only 7.30 to 8.45   CLOSED: from 24 Dec for 4 weeks   MEALS: Set D £26.95 SERVICE: not inc, card slips closed   CARDS: Amex, Delta, MasterCard, Switch, Visa   DETAILS: 24 seats. Private parties: 6 main room. Car park. No children under 12. No smoking in dining-room. Occasional music   ACCOMMODATION: 7 rooms, all with bath/shower. TV. Phone. B&B £46 to £74. No children under 12. No dogs

---

WILMSLOW Cheshire

map 8

Bank Square

NEW ENTRY

4 Bank Square, Wilmslow SK9 1AN
TEL: (01625) 539754

COOKING 4
COST £18–£51

Modern brasserie eating came to Wilmslow when this two-tiered restaurant and bar opened on the square of the same name in late 1996. Downstairs is a bustling music-filled bar, while the serious business takes place on the first floor, where a multi-levelled, alcoved room offers a pleasing sense of intimacy as well as some strikingly up-to-date food. Michael Dodds's menus might kick off with a salad of grilled asparagus and peppers with roast cherry tomatoes, Gruyère crisps and balsamic vinaigrette, and proceed to roast salmon on fennel with white bean and lentil ragoût.

An inspection meal began well with a slice of scallop-studded crab pâté with chive cream sauce, and a bowl of 'satisfyingly sweet and smooth' pea soup with chopped mint and a swirl of crème fraîche. Rump of lamb was appealingly charred on the outside and properly pink within; a triumph of timing and seasoning, it came with a gâteau of aubergine and potato. Puddings have embraced iced white chocolate nougatine with crêpes suzette, and hot pineapple soufflé with piña colada ice-cream. Staff are skilful and pleasant. The wine list is divided between France and the rest of the world, the latter offering slightly better value, although mark-ups throughout are fairly firm. The starting price is £11.95.

CHEF: Michael Dodds   PROPRIETORS: Janet and David Rivett   OPEN: Mon to Sat 12 to 2.30, 6.30 to 11   MEALS: alc (main courses £12.50 to £17). Set L £9.95 (2 courses), Set D Mon to Fri 6.30 to 7.30 £9.95 (2 courses) to £12.50. Set D Mon to Fri after 7.30 and Sat 6.30 to 7.30 £12.50 (2 courses) to £15. Bar food and light menus available to 6.30   SERVICE: not inc   CARDS: Amex, Delta, Diners, MasterCard, Switch, Visa   DETAILS: 52 seats. Private parties: 65 main room, 40 private room. Vegetarian meals. Children's helpings. Music. Air-conditioned   (£5)

(£5) *indicates that the restaurant has elected to participate in the* Good Food Guide *voucher scheme. For full details see page 6.*

WINCHCOMBE Gloucestershire   map 5

▲ *Wesley House* ▾ ✱

High Street, Winchcombe GL54 5LJ	COOKING 5
TEL: (01242) 602366 FAX: (01242) 602405	COST £27–£50

This endearingly uneven, half-timbered house on the Cotswold edge, taking its name from a possible connection with John Wesley, is a comfortable restaurant-with-rooms. Summer diners savour the chance to sit on the terrace and drink in the view, and Sudeley Castle can be seen from the dining-room. The cooking here has gradually evolved from a lush country-house style to incorporate some of the earthier flavours of modern times. Smoked duckling is presented in the form of carpaccio, dressed with truffle oil and served with raspberry relish, while a strudel of broccoli and Stilton comes with macadamia nuts and noodles. Slow-roasted belly-pork with black beans and ginger on garlic mash is the sort of main course that's wowing them in the West End of London now, but reporters appreciate the more classical modes too: fillet of sea bass with spinach mousseline, and noisettes of 'delicately pink' lamb, with a ragoût of beans and pine-nuts, for example. Pastry-work in desserts has been praised, as has nougat glacé with fruits in crème anglaise, and British and Irish cheeses are impeccably kept. Discreet but helpful service ensures that things run smoothly.

South Africa is the 'preferred country' of Wesley House, and wines have been sourced from some of her finest producers: Hamilton Russell, Kanonkop, Rust en Vrede and Thelema Mountain, to name just a few. For those less enamoured of the fruits of the Cape, some stylish bins from around the world are also provided. A dozen house wines start at £11.50. CELLARMAN'S CHOICE: Brampton Sauvignon Blanc 1997, Stellenbosch, South Africa, £18; Lievland Estate Merlot/Cabernet 1993, Stellenbosch, South Africa, £25.

CHEFS: Jonathan Lewis and James Lovatt PROPRIETORS: Matthew Brown and Jonathan Lewis OPEN: all week L 12 to 2, Mon to Sat D 7 to 9.30 CLOSED: 14 Jan to 10 Feb MEALS: alc L (main courses £10.50 to £15.50). Set L £12.25 (2 courses) to £16.50, Set D £23.50 (2 courses) to £28.50 SERVICE: not inc, card slips closed CARDS: Amex, Delta, MasterCard, Switch, Visa DETAILS: 55 seats. 16 seats outside. Private parties: 25 main room. Vegetarian meals. Children's helpings. No smoking in 1 dining-room. Music ACCOMMODATION: 6 rooms, all with bath/shower. TV. Phone. B&B single room £48, D,B&B double room £59 per person. Children welcome. Baby facilities. No dogs. Afternoon teas (*The Which? Hotel Guide*) £5

WINCHESTER Hampshire   map 2

▲ *Hotel du Vin & Bistro*

14 Southgate Street, Winchester SO23 9EF	COOKING 6
TEL: (01962) 841414 FAX: (01962) 842458	COST £28–£49

'Dining at Hotel du Vin must be a bit like receiving the OBE,' surmised one visitor, concluding that 'what you remember is the whole day'. The ensemble includes beautifully crafted surroundings of bare wood, small secluded walled gardens for al fresco eating, oenological paraphernalia by the bucket load, attentive service – get past the strong French accents and it is 'very professional, very observant, well informed' – and a lively atmosphere: anywhere that gets packed by 8pm on a Monday night has got to be doing things right. Tables may be small and close together, but this is a bistro that punches above its weight.

It is the sort of place that gives 'simple cooking' a good name, with lots of salady starters and much roasting and pan-frying. Despite a change of chef – Andy Clark arrived with experience at Le Manoir aux Quat' Saisons in Great Milton and Canteen and Quo Vadis in London (see entries) – the Mediterranean retains a strong pull but doesn't tie the kitchen down. Tempura of cod with pommes frites and aïoli (fish and chips, in other words) is indicative of the style, as are pea and Parma ham risotto, and seared scallops wrapped in bacon with pickled ginger and baby spinach. Bright ideas win support for 'the direct simplicity of their flavour combinations', and the kitchen brigade for 'the impeccability of their timing'. Then there's the excellence of raw materials to consider, including a rarity, 'pork to change all one's ideas about pork: juicy, tender, tasty, a delight', served with choucroute, chorizo, and sizzlingly good mange-tout that made the centrepiece of an inspector's 'exhilarating meal'.

The classical French undercurrent breaks surface at dessert stage, producing tarts of apple Tatin, and pear bourdaloue with a frothy eggy custard and 'excellent flavour and texture combinations'. Wines are taken seriously, hardly surprising as they are overseen by award-winning sommelier Gerard Basset and Vincent Gasnier. Diners are presented with two lists: a short one which changes daily to offer around a dozen wines by the bottle (from £9.95 to £25) or glass (from around £2.80) to partner the day's food, and a much longer 'cellar list'. The latter is a global collection which features many grand names but doesn't stint at providing plenty of bins under £20 as well.

CHEF: Andy Clark   PROPRIETORS: Robin Hutson and Gerard Basset   OPEN: all week 12 to 1.45, 7 to 9.30   CLOSED: 29 and 30 Dec   MEALS: alc (main courses £9 to £15)   SERVICE: not inc, card slips closed   CARDS: Amex, Delta, Diners, MasterCard, Switch, Visa   DETAILS: 60 seats. 35 seats outside. Private parties: 48 main room, 12 to 48 private rooms. Car park. Vegetarian meals. Children welcome. No cigars/pipes in dining-room. Wheelchair access (2 steps; not WC). No music   ACCOMMODATION: 23 rooms, all with bath/shower. TV. Phone. Room only £79 to £165. Rooms for disabled. Children welcome. Guide dogs only (*The Which? Hotel Guide*)

Hunters ¾✳ £

5 Jewry Street, Winchester SO23 8RZ	COOKING 2
TEL: (01962) 860006	COST £21–£38

After a brief sojourn away, Hunters returns to the listings amid bright cheerful yellows, whites and greens, with tiled floors, and candles on close-set tables. It feels lively and friendly, and the food comes as generous helpings on large plates. Choose between a *carte* or a set menu at dinner, and expect anything from a Thai herb salad with chilli dressing, via chicken leg with mango and ginger salsa, to pink roast rack of Scottish lamb with couscous and a redcurrant and apricot chutney. Fish – marlin with salsa verde and smoked paprika perhaps – appears as a special of the day. Endorsements have included fillet of Aberdeen Angus beef – 'cooked as ordered, wonderful flavour' – in a rich red wine sauce, and a dessert consisting of two wheels of rich chocolate truffe balanced on filo triangles; or there may be plum tartlet with peach ice-cream, or blueberry and brioche pudding with clotted cream. Service is helpful and informal rather than speedy. A serviceable round-the-world wine list stays mostly under £20, starting with House Reynier at £9.50.

CHEFS: Simon Cox and Jon Perrett   PROPRIETOR: David Birmingham   OPEN: Mon to Sat 12 to 2, 6.30 to 10   CLOSED: 24 Dec to 3 Jan, bank hols   MEALS: alc (main courses L £5.50 to £10, D £10 to £16). Set D £9.95 (2 courses) to £12.95   SERVICE: not inc   CARDS: Amex, Delta, Diners, MasterCard, Switch, Visa   DETAILS: 60 seats. Private parties: 12 main room, 30 private room. Vegetarian meals. Children's helpings. No smoking in 1 dining-room. Wheelchair access (not WC). Music (£5)

Old Chesil Rectory ⅝✳

1 Chesil Street, Winchester SO23 8HU	NEW CHEF
TEL: (01962) 851555 FAX: (01962) 869704	COST £32–£52

Although the Ruthven-Stuarts retain ownership of this comfortable 500-year old beamed rectory with its twin-peaked roof, as the *Guide* went to press they were about to move to the Old House Hotel in Wickham, which they purchased in summer 1998, and have therefore turned over the stoves to co-chef Philip Storey. If he continues in similar vein as before, he might produce such dishes as herb-crusted cod with sauce vierge, grilled peppered ribeye, or chocolate mousse with mango sorbet. Appreciable effort has clearly gone into sourcing good-value wines throughout, and there is an appendix of fine clarets and burgundies for the bigger spenders. A group of imaginative house wines opens with Argentinian Malbec at £12.95. Reports please.

CHEF: Philip Storey   PROPRIETORS: Nicholas and Christina Ruthven-Stuart   OPEN: Tue to Sat 12 to 2, 7 to 9.30   CLOSED: 2 weeks Christmas, 2 weeks summer   MEALS: Set L £15 (2 courses) to £20, Set D £27 (2 courses) to £30. BYO £8.50   SERVICE: not inc, card slips closed; 12.5% for parties of 6 or more   CARDS: Delta, Diners, MasterCard, Switch, Visa   DETAILS: 60 seats. Private parties: 40 main room, 10 and 14 private rooms. Children welcome. No smoking in 1 dining-room. Wheelchair access (3 steps; not WC). Occasional music

▲ Wykeham Arms ♥ ⅝✳ £

75 Kingsgate Street, Winchester SO23 9PE	COOKING 2
TEL: (01962) 853834 FAX: (01962) 854411	COST £19–£38

This seventeenth-century pub, neatly sandwiched between college and cathedral, holds fast to its heritage, although the main focus of attention is now food. Lunch – according to landlord Graeme Jameson – is a 'bustly affair', with everything from sandwiches and salads to steaks. Evening meals, by candle light, revolve around a daily-changing repertoire that mixes tradition with current trends and looks to France, Italy and the New World for much of its substance. Well-sourced meat includes Downland lamb with celeriac dauphinoise and a port and rosemary jus, as well as pan-fried calf's liver with rösti, caramelised shallots and garlic-scented pan juices. Seafood has also been commended, in the shape of spicy fish-cakes with sweet tomato chutney, and chunky salmon and cod terrine with salad leaves. Cheeses are kept in good order; otherwise finish with chocolate and brandy-soaked prune marquise, or ginger and banana upside-down cake. Service is brisk and efficient. Graeme Jameson continues to champion Burgundy and in particular the wines of Louis Jadot on his enthusiastically annotated list, while winemakers Randall Grahm (California) and Andre van Rensburg (South Africa) make welcome débuts in the spring and summer selection (the list changes with the seasons). Value for money is still a priority, beginning with house French at £10.95. CELLARMAN'S CHOICE: Pouilly-Fumé 'Villa Paulus' 1996, Dom. Masson-Blondelet, £17.95; Côtes du Rhône 1993, Dom. de St-Georges, £14.50.

CHEFS: Vanessa Booth and Belinda Watson   PROPRIETORS: George Gale & Co Ltd   OPEN: Mon to Sat 12 to 2.30, 6.30 to 9   MEALS: alc (main courses L £4.50 to £7, D £10 to £13)   SERVICE: not inc, card slips closed   CARDS: Amex, Delta, Diners, MasterCard, Switch, Visa   DETAILS: 75 seats. 30 seats outside. Private parties: 8 main room. Car park. Vegetarian meals. No children under 14. No smoking in dining-room. No music   ACCOMMODATION: 13 rooms, all with bath/shower. TV. Phone. Room only £45 to £117.50. No children under 14. Afternoon teas (The Which? Hotel Guide)

WINDERMERE Cumbria   map 8

▲ *Gilpin Lodge* ▼ ⁵⁄✕

Crook Road, Windermere LA23 3NE
TEL: (015394) 88818   FAX: (015394) 88058
EMAIL: hotel@gilpin-lodge.demon.co.uk   COOKING 5
on B5284, 2m SE of Windermere   COST £23–£54

The house occupies 20 acres of garden, woodland and moor: 'what a joy and a find,' enthused one visitor. Sofas and real fires contribute to the comfort level, and tables are laid with white cloths, flowers and candles. Four-course dinners are the main event, but lunch is flexibly priced by the dish, offering a good variety of starter-sized options including cep risotto, salmon- and crab-cakes, and perhaps pineapple and bacon rarebit. For those who stay, breakfast is a major event, and there is afternoon tea as well. Cooking is largely Anglo-French, along the lines of a gratin of oysters and artichoke hearts with watercress sabayon, or brill stuffed with anchovies in a warm niçoise salad with aïoli, and the kitchen makes use of Fylde fish, Waberthwaite hams, bacon and sausages, local pheasant and venison, and any cheese with a local ring to it.

Although some dishes may sound involved, results are generally clear and well judged: for example, a fricassee of wild mushrooms with a 'perfectly poached' egg on top – 'simple but effectively done' – or a soufflé of sole and smoked haddock on a thin pastry base with 'a star component' of a warm vinaigrette using good tomatoes, green peppercorns and 'something spicy' to give it depth. The only dish that disappointed an inspector was a rather 'careless' rendition of roast duckling, but a 'terrific' caramelised banana tarte Tatin raised the batting average. Proper organisation ensures that everything runs smoothly, and service is 'very civilised, notably good'. Wines are intelligently drawn from both hemispheres, with some elegant bins offered at fair prices. Five house wines start at £11.50 a bottle, and eight wines by the glass are priced from £2.85. CELLARMAN'S CHOICE: Traminer Aromatico 1996, Franz Haas, Alto Adige, £21.50; Muratie Estate Pinot Noir 1996, Stellenbosch, South Africa.

CHEF: Christopher Davies   PROPRIETORS: John and Christine Cunliffe   OPEN: all week 12 to 2.30, 7 to 8.45   MEALS: alc L Mon to Sat (main courses £7 to £12). Set L Sun £16.50, Set D £29.50   SERVICE: not inc   CARDS: Amex, Delta, Diners, MasterCard, Switch, Visa   DETAILS: 65 seats. 20 seats outside. Private parties: 28 main room, 14 and 28 private rooms. Car park. Vegetarian meals. No children under 7. No smoking in dining-room. Wheelchair access (1 step; not WC). Music   ACCOMMODATION: 14 rooms, all with bath/shower. TV. Phone. D,B&B £75 to £220. Rooms for disabled. No children under 7. No dogs. Afternoon teas   (£5)

▲ *Holbeck Ghyll* ⅝✳ | NEW ENTRY |

Holbeck Lane, Windermere LA23 1LU
TEL: (01539) 432375   FAX: (01539) 434743
EMAIL: accommodation@holbeck-ghyll.co.uk
off A591, take Holbeck Lane 3m N of Windermere   COOKING 5
signposted Troutbeck, hotel ½m on left   COST £27–£55

The house, run by the Nicholsons for a decade, overlooks Lake Windermere, away from traffic and noise. It has well-appointed lounges, real fires, and a couple of dining-rooms: one with oak panels, bare tables, and curtains in which a giraffe plays a starring role, and another in which it doesn't. Jake Watkins's impact has been to lay out a contemporary European spread that covers everything from tagliolini with Loch Fyne scallops, via home-cured air-dried pigeon with foie gras and cep oil, to braised ox-cheek with parsnip purée. Although the food has luxurious leanings – towards scrambled eggs with Perigord truffle for example – it owes its clear, convincing style to a carefully sourced range of materials, much of it local: goose, snipe, wigeon, teal, partridge, rabbit, sea trout, brown trout, wild mushrooms, beef ('grass fed and hung for 35 days on the bone') and suckling pig, perhaps served on a fondant potato with cubes of winter root vegetables.

The cooking has its sunnier side too, in a quickly seared red mullet fillet on 'mushy' risotto with a slick of intense red wine sauce, and the uncomplicated style is able to carry off familiar combinations with assurance, as in a hot chocolate fondant, cake-like on top, runny inside, with orange sorbet. Anybody who has spent the day walking will be pleased to hear of the waves of pre-meal nibbles, from pigeon breast on tapénade crostini to a salt cod beignet with hollandaise. The proprietors help with service, which made one visitor feel 'well looked after'. The geographical reach of the wine list is not quite matched by its accuracy (Mondavi's Woodbridge is not from Napa Valley), but choices are extremely good, if sometimes a little ungenerously priced, with house wines starting at £13.75.

CHEF: Jake Watkins   PROPRIETORS: David and Patricia Nicholson   OPEN: all week 12 to 2, 7 to 9   MEALS: Set L £14.50 (2 courses) to £17.95, Set D £29.50 to £34.50   SERVICE: not inc, card slips closed   CARDS: Amex, Diners, MasterCard, Switch, Visa   DETAILS: 50 seats. 25 seats outside. Private parties: 38 main room, 8 to 18 private rooms. Car park. Vegetarian meals. Children's helpings. No children under 8. No smoking in dining-room. Wheelchair access (2 steps; not WC). No music   ACCOMMODATION: 20 rooms, all with bath/shower. TV. Phone. D,B&B £79 to £230. Rooms for disabled. Children welcome. High teas for children. Baby facilities. Dogs welcome in bedrooms only. Afternoon teas (*The Which? Hotel Guide*)   (£5)

Jerichos ⚡✕

NEW ENTRY

Birch Street, Windermere LA23 1EG
TEL/FAX: (015394) 42522

COOKING 5
COST £30–£45

After 11 years at Miller Howe (see entry below), Chris Blaydes and his wife
opened their own place in February 1998 in a narrow double-yellow-lined street
just off the main shopping drag. They have transformed a former chippy into a
classy open-plan dining-area with plum-coloured fabrics and a view of the
kitchen. It 'looks inviting'. The format is a choice of five dishes per course, and
the food's 'ornate' style recalled a television cooking programme for one visitor,
'as though customers had brought a variety of unlikely ingredients and
challenged them to do what they can'. His evidence included a salty-crusted fillet
of smoked haddock laced with garlic, on a bed of cabbage and French beans,
surrounded by pieces of black pudding and a sage-flavoured tomato sauce.

There is much to admire in the balanced output – a bowl of 'excellent' leek,
fennel and watercress soup, a wild mushroom and king prawn risotto, or fat
asparagus tips seasoned with garlic and sea salt, served with rocket and
butter-beans – and a vegetarian main course is built in: perhaps roasted
provençale vegetables with couscous, beans and mushrooms. A couple of dishes
change weekly, depending on circumstance, but have so far included chargrilled
steak with chips and red wine sauce, and desserts of 'smooth, creamy' lemon
brûlée, iced chocolate parfait, and a light orange and ginger sponge. The sharply
chosen 40-strong wine list is fairly priced, starting with eight house wines at
£10.75, all available by the glass.

CHEFS: Chris Blaydes and Chris Dickson   PROPRIETORS: Chris and Jo Blaydes   OPEN: Tue to
Sun D only 6.45 to 10   MEALS: alc (main courses £11 to £15)   SERVICE: not inc   CARDS: Delta,
MasterCard, Switch, Visa   DETAILS: 38 seats. Private parties: 22 main room. Vegetarian meals.
No children under 12. No smoking in dining-room. Music £5

▲ Miller Howe ⚡ ✕

Rayrigg Road, Windermere LA23 1EY
TEL: (015394) 42536   FAX: (015394) 45664
EMAIL: lakeview@millerhowe.com
on A592, between Windermere and Bowness

COOKING 6
COST £25–£52

'Anyone going to Miller Howe not knowing it had changed hands would be
hard pushed to detect any changes,' ventured one reporter. After nearly 30 years
John Tovey has relinquished control over a business he spent a large part of his
lifetime building up, though he remains a 'consultant', and most of the key staff
are all 'personalities' from the old regime. Chris Blaydes has left to open his own
restaurant, Jericho's (see entry above), but Susan Elliott remains. Some changes
are 'mostly cosmetic': the flowery menu is now plainer, the service charge has
gone, lunch offers a choice of main course, and vegetables accompanying the
evening main course have at last dropped to a sensible three (from a high of
seven not so long ago). But the main change is that the dinner menu now has a
suggested no-choice option, plus an additional three starters and main courses
on a separate menu, to mix and match at no additional charge. The new owners –

Charles Garside is a former newspaper editor – say they are intent on 'evolution, not revolution'.

Over the course of 11 years, Susan Elliott has absorbed enough of the Tovey style to continue with hardly a ripple, turning out smooth smoked chicken and avocado terrine that 'could have been mistaken for foie gras', and two large slices of marinated tuna looking 'like pieces of rare steak', served with a chilli, soy and ginger dressing. A degree of innovation and some bold flavours continue to characterise the food: at one meal loin of pork on a savoury cake of black pudding and mustard, served with cabbage 'jazzed up with sesame'; the three accompanying vegetables were beetroot with orange juice, peppered green beans, and roast potatoes 'given a lift' with curry. Desserts might be coffee parfait, summer pudding, tiramisù, or a plate of pre-selected but well-kept cheese. Dinner starts with flavoured bread, while coffee (with chocolate truffles) now comes in an individual pot, 'which is an improvement'. A few good Old World wines are provided to keep traditionalists happy, but the list's heart lies firmly with the sunshine flavours and modern producers of the New World. Ebullient tasting notes make for an entertaining read, while the combination of reasonable prices and no added service charge lifts the spirits even higher. South African house red is £15.50.

CHEF: Sue Elliott PROPRIETOR: Charles Garside OPEN: all week 12.30 to 2, 8 (1 sitting) CLOSED: 2 Jan to 11 Feb MEALS: Set L £15, Set D £32 SERVICE: not inc, card slips closed CARDS: Amex, Diners, MasterCard, Visa DETAILS: 72 seats. 24 seats outside. Private parties: 40 main room, 32 private rooms. Car park. Vegetarian meals. No children under 8. No smoking in dining-room. Wheelchair access (1 step; not WC). Music. Air-conditioned ACCOMMODATION: 12 rooms, all with bath/shower. TV. Phone. No children under 8. Dogs welcome in bedrooms only (£3 per day). Afternoon teas (*The Which? Hotel Guide*) £5

Roger's ⁑✖ £

4 High Street, Windermere LA23 1AF   COOKING 4
TEL: (015394) 44954   COST £23–£50

This tiny, elegant, deep-green dining-room on the edge of Windermere near the tourist office is a 'warm and comfortable' spot with 'no views, just food'. The cooking mixes traditional mussels marinière, or osso buco, with more contemporary tiger prawns in a sauce of coconut, chilli and lemon grass. Sometimes the two worlds meet, as in calf's liver with bacon and mango. Good ingredients and fresh sauces are a hallmark, producing pink roast rack of Lakeland lamb 'trimmed but juicy' in a sauce with 'strong hints of both garlic and rosemary'. Fish is well handled too: a starter of crisply grilled tail-ends of sea bream with chilli coriander salsa, and main-course baked sea bass fillet – 'excellent fish, well cooked, firm textured, good flavour' – with asparagus and sorrel butter sauce. To finish, a 'posh' version of bread-and-butter pudding vies for attention with damson crème brûlée, and steamed chocolate pudding. Mrs Pergl-Wilson chats to regular customers, somebody else serves, and wines are varied and sympathetically priced, starting with house Duboeuf at £9.90.

The Guide *always appreciates hearing about changes of chef or owner.*

CHEF: Roger Pergl-Wilson PROPRIETORS: Roger and Alena Pergl-Wilson OPEN: Mon to Sat D only 7 to 9.30 MEALS: alc (main courses £6 to £14.50). Set D £16.50 SERVICE: not inc, card slips closed CARDS: Amex, Delta, Diners, MasterCard, Switch, Visa DETAILS: 45 seats. Private parties: 28 main room, 28 private room. Vegetarian meals. Children's helpings. No smoking in 1 dining-room. Music (£5)

WINKLEIGH Devon   map 1

Pophams ⅝✶ £

Castle Street, Winkleigh EX19 8HU   COOKING 5
TEL: (01837) 83767   COST £21–£39

This thoroughly idiosyncratic and enthusiastically supported lunchtime-only restaurant is unlicensed, but the post office next door can oblige if you've forgotten to get a bottle. Once a shop, the tiny space is now divided into a terracotta-tiled kitchen and dining-area by a cold counter. Stills of classic Hollywood film stars look down from walls, there are no printed menus (just a blackboard) and the welcome 'strikes the right balance between warmth and over-effusiveness'.

The range changes daily, with everything cooked to order. One April meal began with an appetisingly colourful salad of beetroot, orange, feta, honey-roasted pecans and asparagus in a citrus dressing, and proceeded flawlessly to roasted salmon fillet glazed with maple syrup, soy, lemon and garlic, served with creamy mash, wilted spinach and a vivid red pepper sauce. Prime meats are sympathetically treated, as in best end of lamb swaddled in puff pastry and sauced with paprika cream, or beef fillet – 'a princely two-inch-high cut' – in green peppercorn and brandy sauce. Technique is assured: reporters who watched an apple tart being assembled before their eyes saw Granny Smiths sliced on to a pastry case of crème patissière then covered with a glaze and served with a scoop of fine cinnamon ice-cream, with a pleasing result. Home-made bread underlines the dedication.

CHEF: Melvyn Popham PROPRIETORS: Melvyn Popham and Dennis Hawkes OPEN: Wed to Sat L only 11.30 to 4 CLOSED: Feb MEALS: alc (main courses £11 to £15.50). Unlicensed but BYO (no corkage) SERVICE: not inc CARDS: Delta, MasterCard, Visa DETAILS: 10 seats. Private parties: 10 main room. Vegetarian meals. No children under 14. No smoking in dining-room. Wheelchair access (not WC). Music. Air-conditioned

---

WINSFORD Somerset   map 1

▲ Savery's at Karslake House ⅝✶

Halse Lane, Winsford TE24 7JE   COOKING 5
TEL/FAX: (01643) 851242   COST £36–£47

This fifteenth-century malthouse in a small Exmoor village is best thought of as a restaurant-with-rooms, one of them a rectangular dining-room decorated with painted wooden ducks dating from the restaurant's days at Frampton-on-Severn. 'Revolutionary the food isn't,' claimed one visitor, nor is it particularly ambitious, but 'everything is quite perfect in its own way'. Eastern spicing makes itself felt now and again, but seems to be more the sign of an inquisitive cook than a fashion statement. A combination of freshness – fish supplies are clearly no problem – and care gives the food its impact, as in a dish of lightly battered, crisp prawns and courgettes with a mango salsa on well-dressed leaves: a 'clean, fresh, spare sort of dish', judged our inspector, just the kind of thing to give straightforward cooking a good name.

'Dead simple, dead right,' was another pronouncement, this time on a well-hung rack of lamb with light-textured mashed potato and a skilfully made mint and caper sauce. Main courses come with fresh, plainly prepared vegetables, including 'old-fashioned, classic' gratin dauphinoise. 'Carefully, honestly and freshly made' was an assessment of a warm wedge of almond and apple tart served with creamy Amaretto ice-cream, but is also a fair summing up of the whole style. Patricia Carpenter, we understand, is a keen gardener (there is a fully functioning greenhouse at the back) as well as being 'very good at making people relax and feel at home'. The understated sense of humour, modesty and lack of pretension are further helped by 'jolly ungrasping' prices, which also apply to the short and predominantly French wine list. It opens with four house wines at around £11.

CHEFS: John Savery and Nicky Plumb   PROPRIETORS: Patricia Carpenter and John Savery
OPEN: Mon to Sat D only 7 to 9.30 (9 in winter exc Sat)   CLOSED: Feb   MEALS: Set D £24.95
SERVICE: not inc, card slips closed   CARDS: Delta, MasterCard, Switch, Visa   DETAILS: 30
seats. Private parties: 36 main room. Car park. No children under 15. No smoking in
dining-room. No music   ACCOMMODATION: 7 rooms, all with bath/shower. TV. B&B £25 to £40.
Rooms for disabled. No children under 15. Dogs welcome (£2.50 supplement) (The Which?
Hotel Guide)

WINTERINGHAM North Lincolnshire   map 9

▲ *Winteringham Fields* ♈ ⁵✳

Winteringham DN15 9PF
TEL: (01724) 733096 FAX: (01724) 733898   COOKING 9
EMAIL: euroannie@aol.com   COST £31–£83

The Schwabs have achieved 'something of a miracle' in a remote, rather flat and unlovely part of North Lincolnshire. At first glance, thanks to various brick additions and extensions, it doesn't seem like a seventeenth-century farmhouse, but its 'old age comes alive' inside with low doorways, sloping floors, beams and much Victoriana. Take pre-dinner summer drinks on the terrace, or start in the conservatory, or in a warm winter parlour-like sitting-room, with a coffee-cupful of soup and a nibble on something fishy, and proceed to the small but comfortable dining-room with its large, well-set tables and high-backed upholstered chairs.

Germain Schwab's cooking runs on a mix of simple invention and great care with detail, delivering any amount of impressive flavours along the way. It is 'characterful' food, sometimes with a dash of orientalism or a hint of the Maghreb: perhaps a filo pastry tart of rabbit with duck liver, dredged with icing sugar 'in the manner of pastilla'. But most of all it is in contemporary European style: fine slices of lobster accompanied by a dariole of jellied gazpacho, or a long pink cylinder of Lincolnshire lamb, accompanied by a courgette flower filled with kidney mousse and then deep-fried. Menus may use rather elastic descriptions, but these are generally forgiven when the dish turns out to be, say, a 'wonderful' pot au feu of fresh, sweet scallops topped with foie gras in a full-flavoured vegetable-strewn broth.

Precision timing, and 'total command' of 'subtle but complex' saucing, spicing and flavour-balancing, work to produce, for example, a 'masterful' dish of halved scallops, arranged on a bed of couscous and squid ink, surrounded by red pepper coulis and yellow beurre blanc; not just 'visually stunning' but 'full of great sea flavours'. If Schwab's ideas are more an extension of conventional wisdom than wildly original, then that at least anchors the whole thing in the world of common sense. They combine familiarity with invention, as in desserts such as a 'brilliant' red pepper variation on the pineapple-and-pepper theme, the fruit served with 'an amazing aromatic' coconut custard in a tuile biscuit. Alternatively, there is always the 'superb' chariot of 'immaculate' cheeses. 'Outstandingly well-judged' service combining friendliness and correctness is 'as professional as you can get', a tribute to the warmth and skill with which Annie Schwab runs front-of-house. Prices are high but 'entirely justified'. The lengthy, Eurocentric wine list features bottles from Austria and Germain's native Switzerland as well as the expected French classics. Prices can make you blink, but five house wines are all £13.50. CELLARMAN'S CHOICE: Cape Mentelle Semillon/Sauvignon Blanc 1995, Margaret River, W. Australia, £27; Weinert Cabernet Sauvignon 1983, Mendoza, Argentina, £19.

CHEF: Germain Schwab PROPRIETORS: Annie and Germain Schwab OPEN: Tue to Fri L 12 to 1.30, Mon to Sat D 7.15 to 9.30 CLOSED: 2 weeks Christmas, first week Aug, bank hols MEALS: alc (main courses £25 to £26). Set L £15.50 (2 courses) to £18.50, Set D £29 to £46 SERVICE: not inc, card slips closed CARDS: Amex, Delta, MasterCard, Switch, Visa DETAILS: 46 seats. Private parties: 10 main room, 10 private room. Car park. Vegetarian meals. Children welcome. No smoking in dining-room. Wheelchair access (not WC). No music ACCOMMODATION: 7 rooms, all with bath/shower. TV. Phone. Room only £60 to £105. Rooms for disabled. No children under 8. No dogs (The Which? Hotel Guide)

WITHERSLACK Cumbria   map 8

▲ Old Vicarage ♥ ✳

Church Road, Witherslack LA11 6RS
TEL: (015395) 52381 FAX: (015395) 52373
EMAIL: hotel@old-vic.demon.co.uk   COOKING 2
off A590, take first left in village to church   COST £26–£47

'Serene' aptly describes this lovely Georgian house set in fruitfully productive grounds adjacent to the village church. Herbs and wild plants find their way into the kitchen along with impeccably sourced local supplies, including fish from Fleetwood, venison from the nearby estate and organically reared lamb from Mansergh Hall. Added to this are Morecambe Bay shrimps, black-leg chickens, Richard Woodall's dry-cured bacon, and more besides. Raw materials are undoubtedly excellent, and there is much to enjoy on the daily four-course dinner menu, although an inspector felt that handling and timing were not up to the standard of previous years. Even so, glorious home-baked breads (including a fine molasses version) have been singled out for praise, along with a robust dish of penne-type Capunti pasta with Italian sausage, fennel and Barolo; and roast leg of Tunstall pork coupled with honey-roasted ham and apple sauce. Home-made ice-creams are as luscious as can be, and everyone extols the virtues of the 'outstanding' British cheeseboard. The compact wine list neatly blends old favourites with enterprising newcomers, while a page of Italian house specialities adds a touch of the unusual. A good range of half-bottles adds to its appeal. CELLARMAN'S CHOICE: Vernaccia di San Gimignano 1996, Fattoria, Cusona, £14.50; C.J. Pask Cabernet/Merlot 1994, Hawkes Bay, New Zealand, £23.50.

CHEFS: Stanley Reeve and James Brown   PROPRIETORS: Jill and Roger Brown, and Irene and Stanley Reeve   OPEN: Sun L 12.30 to 1, all week D 7 to 8.30   MEALS: Set L £15.50, Set D £27.50   SERVICE: not inc, card slips closed   CARDS: Amex, Delta, MasterCard, Switch, Visa DETAILS: 40 seats. Private parties: 20 main room, 12 private room. Car park. Vegetarian meals. Children's helpings. No smoking in dining-room. Wheelchair access (2 steps; not WC). Music ACCOMMODATION: 14 rooms, all with bath/shower. TV. Phone. D,B&B £80 to £200. Rooms for disabled. Children welcome. Baby facilities. Dogs welcome in bedrooms only and not left unattended. Afternoon teas (The Which? Hotel Guide)

WOODBRIDGE Suffolk   map 6

Captain's Table ✠ £ | NEW ENTRY |

3 Quay Street, Woodbridge IP12 1BX   COOKING 4
TEL: (01394) 383145   FAX: (01394) 388508   COST £21–£34

The owners used to run the Normandie restaurant in Birtle – a stalwart of Guides past – and in summer 1998, finally hove into this new berth in a pale yellow sixteenth-century house in the centre of Woodbridge. Having retained the existing name, they emphasise the point by clothing staff in T-shirts that say 'Captain's Mate'. Three inter-connecting dining-rooms with low-beamed ceilings form the backdrop for Pascal Pommier's conscientious European style of cookery.

Fresh seafood shows up well in the shape of a generous serving of dressed white crab bound with mayonnaise and fringed with cucumber and tomato in a good strong vinaigrette. Fashionable ingredients are given uncomplicated treatments, as in an assemblage of roasted red peppers, tomatoes and onions served with olives and basil, or a pressed terrine of mackerel and potatoes with tartare sauce, while a speculative foray into Far Eastern modes has produced a successful pork teriyaki with spiced lentils. Vegetarian options have included mushroom ravioli with garlic and parsley cream sauce. Simple desserts such as home-made ice-creams and authoritative crème brûlée precede fine espresso that comes with memorable nut fudge. Service is willing, and prices seem very reasonable for the surroundings. Restraint in marking up is also evident among the wines, which are an imaginative modern jumble that span the geographical range from local Shawsgate to Moa Ridge Sauvignon from New Zealand, starting at £8.95.

The Guide *relies on feedback from its readers. Especially welcome are reports on new restaurants appearing in the book for the first time. All letters to the* Guide *are acknowledged.*

CHEF: Pascal Pommier   PROPRIETORS: Jo Moussa and Jo Moussa   OPEN: Tue to Sun L12 to 2 (3 Sun), Tue to Sat D 6.30 to 9.30 (10 Fri and Sat)   CLOSED: 2 weeks Jan   MEALS: alc (main courses £7 to £10.50). Set L Sun £15   SERVICE: not inc, card slips closed   CARDS: Delta, MasterCard, Switch, Visa   DETAILS: 50 seats. 12 seats outside. Private parties: 32 main room, 15 to 32 private rooms. Car park. Vegetarian meals. Children welcome. No smoking in 1 dining-room. Wheelchair access (not WC). No music

---

WOODSTOCK   Oxfordshire   map 2

▲ *Feathers Hotel* ⅙✳ ⌂

Market Street, Woodstock OX20 1SX
TEL: (01993) 812291   FAX: (01993) 813158   COOKING 7
EMAIL: enquiries@feathers.co.uk   COST £33–£70

The Feathers is a brick exception to the stone-built rule in this village at the gates of Blenheim. Dating from the seventeenth century, it boasts a series of small flag-floored terracotta-painted rooms for drinking and snacking, and a candlelit dining-room decorated in slate blue and canary yellow; talking of which, if you hear a strange noise it is probably the caged bird near the front door. The food has undergone a change since last year. Mark Treasure arrived as the last edition of the *Guide* went to press, and although the cooking seemed to go through a rocky patch over the winter, a summer inspection found it back on track, fulfilling the promise that Treasure showed when he was at Michael's Nook (see entry, Grasmere).

The kitchen works to demanding technical standards, servicing an evening *carte* (and related tasting menu) that wraps its luxuries in appealing guise: chilled gazpacho with seared warm scallops, or deep-fried lemon sole beignets with lobster sauce. The style is contemporary Anglo-French, and 'rather haute', but above all enticing. Ravioli of tarragon-flavoured chicken and ceps comes in a dark brown stock-based sauce, while duck breast might be poached, set on cabbage and beetroot, topped with creamed horseradish, and surrounded by a lake of truffle-oiled consommé with 'good deep flavour'. While judgement and balance may not always be perfect, they can reach impressive heights, as in a 'brilliant' creamy-textured risotto with white worm-like strands of baby calamari and a concentrated fresh fishy flavour.

Desserts, meanwhile, have produced a 'gem' of a chocolate sorbet to accompany pistachio crème brûlée, and 'wonderfully tasty' peach fritters in a crisp almondy batter. Dishes don't always correspond precisely with their menu description, and there are lots of garnishing flourishes, but even they don't blur the main focus. Staff are young and willing, though not as highly polished as the kitchen brigade. Mark-ups on the wine list are considered 'greedy', and although house Duboeuf is £11.75, Seaview Brut at £20.75 costs over three times the retail price. It is also worth remembering that a 'voluntary' gratuity of 15 per cent is added to all accounts.

⌂ *indicates that there has been a change of chef since last year's* Guide, *and the Editor has judged that the change is of sufficient interest to merit the reader's attention.*

CHEF: Mark Treasure   PROPRIETORS: Andrew Leeman, Simon Lowe and Howard Malin   OPEN: all week 12.30 to 2.15, 7.30 to 9.15 (9.45 Fri and Sat)   CLOSED: 25 Dec D to non-residents   MEALS: alc (main courses £17 to £22). Set L Mon to Sat £17.50 (2 courses) to £21, Set L Sun £20.50, Set D £44. Bar menu all week L, Mon to Fri D. BYO £8   SERVICE: 15% (optional), card slips closed   CARDS: Amex, Delta, Diners, MasterCard, Switch, Visa   DETAILS: 60 seats. 60 seats outside. Private parties: 60 main room. Vegetarian meals. Children's helpings. No smoking in dining-room. Music. Air-conditioned   ACCOMMODATION: 21 rooms, all with bath/shower. TV. Phone. B&B £88 to £260. Children welcome. Dogs welcome with own bedding and food (£5 per night). Afternoon teas (*The Which? Hotel Guide*) £5

WORCESTER Worcestershire   map 5

Brown's

24 Quay Street, Worcester WR1 2JJ   COOKING 4
TEL: (01905) 26263   FAX: (01905) 25768   COST £24–£48

'A multitude of swans' gliding by on the Severn predisposed one summer luncher to have a jolly good time at Brown's. It was built as a grain mill over 200 years ago, but a clean-lined and modern conversion made a smart restaurant of it in 1980. Simple cooking using quality raw materials is what the kitchen excels at, and so brochettes of langoustines and bacon, and chargrilled Scotch beef fillet come in for praise, though more complex roast duck with griottine cherries, in which the leg is prepared as a confit, has rated highly. A nod to fashion has brought crab-cakes with red onion salsa on to the lunch menu, and added chive and chilli dumplings in roast tomato and sweet pepper sauce to dinner offerings. Chewy meringue encases chocolate and chestnut pavlova, or there may be old-fangled rhubarb and ginger crumble, served not with custard, however, but with mascarpone. The wine list is stolidly classic in its Francophilia and vigorous mark-up policy, but the annotations make it approachable. Beaujolais is particularly well served for choice. House Australian is £11.50.

CHEF: W.R. Tansley   PROPRIETORS: W.R. and P.M. Tansley   OPEN: Tue to Fri and Sun L 12.30 to 1.45, Tue to Sat D 7.30 to 9.45   CLOSED: 24 to 31 Dec, bank hol Mons   MEALS: Set L £18.50, Set D £34.50   SERVICE: net prices, card slips closed   CARDS: Amex, Delta, MasterCard, Switch, Visa   DETAILS: 100 seats. Private parties: 80 main room. Vegetarian meals. No children under 8. No-smoking area. Wheelchair access (also WC). No music

---

WORFIELD Shropshire   map 5

▲ Old Vicarage Hotel 🍷 🍴

Worfield WV15 5JZ
TEL: (01746) 716497   FAX: (01746) 716552
EMAIL: v-old-vicarage@demon.co.uk   COOKING 4
2m N of A545, 3m E of Bridgnorth   COST £30–£61

Despite its age (Edwardian), the red-brick vicarage looks remarkably new from outside, and the modern conservatory with wooden seagulls dangling from the ceiling strikes a note of individuality in an otherwise 'English bourgeois' setting. Richard Arnold and Blaine Reed take advantage of good raw materials: Bollington wild boar, Ludlow venison, locally shot pheasant and partridge, and 'fantastic' seared Loch Fyne scallops (a starter, just two of them) sitting on a mound of something very like risotto sprinkled with chopped chives. What arrives does not always seem to tally with its description, but at inspection the kitchen's skills came together well in a main course of rabbit, combining chargrilled loin with roast leg that had been wrapped in bacon and stuffed with minced pork and dried apricot; 'good taste and texture contrasts' combined with a mustardy tarragon sauce to make it 'a thoroughly enjoyable dish'. Vegetables (the same for all, served separately) might be improved. Desserts have included banana and fudge-ice cream with glazed bananas, and spiced carrot cake with toffee cream and caramel sauce.

The appetiser is complimentary, but extras can stack up with supplements for some dishes, £7.50 for an additional course, and a charge for coffee and petits fours. Certainly the 'hand-made' British cheeses are worth a punt and, of all the incidentals, in-house bread stands out as 'extremely professional'. Service is efficient if 'rather stiff', and wines are taken seriously, with a detailed study of France and astute selections when the list ventures beyond her borders. Half-bottles are uncommonly generous, and French and Chilean house wines are £14. CELLARMAN'S CHOICE: Green Point Chardonnay 1996, Yarra Valley, S. Australia, £19; Ch. Musar 1990, Gaston Hochar, Lebanon, £19.50.

CHEFS: Richard Arnold and Blaine Reed   PROPRIETORS: Peter and Christine Iles   OPEN: Sun L 12 to 2, all week D 7 to 9   MEALS: Set Sun L £17.50, Set D £25 to £35 (Gourmet Menu)   SERVICE: not inc   CARDS: Amex, Diners, MasterCard, Visa   DETAILS: 40 seats. 10 seats outside. Private parties: 40 main room, 10 to 40 private rooms. Car park. Vegetarian meals. Children's helpings. No smoking in 1 dining-room. Wheelchair access (also WC). Music   ACCOMMODATION: 14 rooms, all with bath/shower. TV. Phone. B&B £70 to £160. Rooms for disabled. Children welcome. Baby facilities. Dogs by arrangement (*The Which? Hotel Guide*) £5

WORLESTON Cheshire   map 5

▲ *Rookery Hall* 🍴 ✶

Worleston CW5 6DQ
TEL: (01270) 610016   FAX: (01270) 626027   COOKING 4
on B5074, 2½m N of Nantwich   COST £29–£61

The whole place is built on a generous scale inside and out, with a stable block devoted to conferences, and a dining-room with ornate plaster ceilings and exuberantly carved shiny mahogany panelling. Craig Grant took over the kitchen in July 1997, and pursues a suitably elaborate style of cooking, picking up on contemporary flourishes such as a 'cappuccino' of mange-tout to serve with hot smoked salmon, or fashioning a 'cushion' of horseradish polenta to serve with beef. In this context 'feuilleté' doesn't refer to pastry, but perhaps to layers of crab interleaved with tomato 'wafers'. Dishes are spiked with oils and essences, and flavour combinations can be as ambitious as duck and plum ravioli served on girolle mushrooms with a smoked garlic cream.

The food is praised for being 'straightforward, with no unnecessary garnishes', and looks good, although ideas and achievements vary quite a bit. This is perhaps illustrated by an inspector's main course of 'superb' Welsh lamb that tried to combine homely bubble and squeak with Mediterranean vegetables, a strong mustard crust and an improvable dark sauce. Some desserts are prepared to order (soufflés, or warm apple tart), and British and Irish cheeses are among 'the finest', served by knowledgeable staff who are plentiful, keen, and always at the ready. Of the incidentals, 'exceptional' petit fours stand out. A good proportion of wines by the glass is a strength of the list, although wines under £20 a bottle are in the minority. Prices start at £16.

CHEF: Craig Grant   PROPRIETOR: Arcadian Hotels Ltd   OPEN: all week 12 to 2, 7 to 9.45
MEALS: alc L (main courses £13.50 to £14.50). Set L £18.50, Set D £38   SERVICE: not inc
CARDS: Amex, Delta, Diners, MasterCard, Switch, Visa   DETAILS: 40 seats. Private parties: 66
main room, 12 to 90 private rooms. Car park. Vegetarian meals. Children's helpings. No
smoking in dining-room. Wheelchair access (also WC). No music   ACCOMMODATION: 45 rooms,
all with bath/shower. TV. Phone. B&B £120 to £265. Rooms for disabled. Children welcome.
Dogs welcome in annexe only. Afternoon teas. Fishing   (£5)

WRIGHTINGTON Lancashire map 8

High Moor

Highmoor Lane, Wrightington WN6 9QA
TEL: (01257) 252364   FAX: (01257) 255120
off A5209, between M6 junction 27 and Parbold; take
Robin Hood Lane at crossroads W of Wrightington   COOKING 3
Hospital, then next left   COST £19–£49

The long, squat, white-painted building with black-framed windows has a quasi-rustic feel, with flagstone floor, beams and large tables in the bar, and a spacious, carpeted dining-room with padded banquettes. It is professionally run, and smartly dressed waitresses are clued up about the food and drink they are serving. Choose a simple soup-and-sandwich deal at lunch for £4, a set-price lunch or 'early doors' meal, or opt for the wide-ranging *carte* with hearty fare of more 'industrial' weight. Old-fashioned dishes such as corned beef and pickle, prawn cocktail, and knickerbocker glory confirm that this plain cooking has little truck with modern fads.

It prefers deep-fried fish and chips with mushy peas, or saddle of lamb with earthy vegetables, and its virtues are apparent in a dish of chicken livers that reminded one visitor of 'the goodness of home country-cooking'. Finish with creamy rice-pudding served with a marmalade-like compote of apricot and brandy, or bread-and-butter pudding with 'plenty of sultanas' and a dollop of ice-cream. France is the biggest player on the wine list, but the New World contributes some good examples. Each bottle is given a short paean of praise, and a generous selection of house wines starts at £9.75, all available by the glass from around £2.

CHEF: Darren Wynn   PROPRIETORS: James Simes and John Nelson   OPEN: all week 12 to 2,
5.30 to 10 (8.30 Sun)   CLOSED: 26 Dec, 1 Jan   MEALS: alc (main courses L £3.50 to £13.50, D
£5.50 to £17.50). Set L and D (before 7pm) £10 (2 courses) to £12   SERVICE: not inc, card slips
closed   CARDS: Amex, Delta, Diners, MasterCard, Switch, Visa   DETAILS: 100 seats. 12 seats
outside. Private parties: 120 main room. Car park. Vegetarian meals. Children's helpings.
Wheelchair access (not WC). Music. Air-conditioned

The Good Food Guide *is a registered trade mark of Which? Ltd.*

ENGLAND

WYE Kent   map 3

▲ *Wife of Bath*

4 Upper Bridge Street, Wye TN25 5AW
TEL: (01233) 812540   FAX: (01233) 813630   COOKING 3
just off A28, Ashford to Canterbury road   COST £24–£41

The connection with Chaucer is made in the oak-beamed bedrooms, named after
such pilgrims as Franklin, Knight and Miller (who, on reflection, sound more
like a firm of estate agents), although there is no hard evidence to suggest that
any of them actually stayed here. Nevertheless, this is a handy stop for anybody
en route to or from the Channel Tunnel. Fish is from Hythe (peppered skate wing
perhaps, or a terrine of sole and mussels), salad leaves are from Appledore, and
local fruits add a seasonal note, although the thrust of the cooking is towards
France and the Mediterranean, as in a tartlet of grilled tomatoes with peppers
and goats' cheese, or cod wrapped in Parma ham with aïoli. The menu changes
every two weeks, but John Morgan's assessment is that enthusiastic regulars
tend to put a brake on novelty: 'well-trusted dishes seem to be always
appreciated.' Good olives and bread add to the appeal, as do the wines, most of
which are under £20, with a good showing from the southern hemisphere.
House vin de pays is £12.25.

CHEF: Robert Hymers PROPRIETOR: John Morgan OPEN: Tue to Sat 12 to 2.30, 7 to 10.30
CLOSED: 25 Dec to 7 Jan MEALS: alc L (main courses £10 to £14.50). Set L £10 (2 courses) to
£13.75, Set D £23.50. BYO £5 SERVICE: not inc CARDS: Amex, Delta, Diners, MasterCard,
Switch, Visa DETAILS: 50 seats. Private parties. 55 main room. Car park. Vegetarian meals.
Children's helpings. No pipes in dining-room. Wheelchair access (1 step; not WC). No music
ACCOMMODATION: 6 rooms, all with bath/shower. TV. Phone. B&B £40 to £80. Rooms for
disabled. Children welcome (*The Which? Hotel Guide*) (£5)

YARM Stockton-on-Tees   map 10

D.P. Chadwick's ✸

104 High Street, Yarm TS15 9AU   COOKING 4
TEL: (01642) 788558   COST £24–£49

'A crowd pleaser that is easy to like because it takes its role seriously,' wrote one
reporter of this busy brasserie. Warm red and mustard coloured walls covered
with assorted paintings, and marble-topped tables all with fresh roses,
contribute to the veritable brasserie ambience. So do friendly, expert staff who
look 'Continental' in black and white, with black aprons. The sensibly short
menu offers a fashionably eclectic choice of starters, including bang bang
chicken salad, tandoori king prawns with Bombay salad, as well as Italian-
inspired dishes. There are three sorts of pasta, as well as old favourites with a
modern twist: calf's liver and bacon with bubble and squeak and sauce
aigre-doux, home-made fish-cakes with sauce Malibu, plus more homely dishes
such as grilled salmon, or pork and leek sausages with herb mash. Strongly
approved at inspection were 'heady and sweet' mushroom and asparagus salad
with a vinaigrette made from aged balsamic and 'really truffly' truffle oil,
followed by grilled sesame tuna with 'quite sweet and super spicy' mango salsa,

then 'hot and very nutty' walnut and pecan pie. Wines are modestly priced (only two over £20) and ten are available by the glass.

CHEF/PROPRIETOR: David Brownless   OPEN: Tue to Sat 12 to 2.30, 6 to 9.30   MEALS: alc (main courses £7 to £15)   SERVICE: not inc, card slips closed   CARDS: Delta, MasterCard, Switch, Visa   DETAILS: 70 seats. Vegetarian meals. Children's helpings. No smoking in 1 dining-room. Music

---

YARMOUTH   Isle of Wight   map 2

▲ *George Hotel* ♟

Quay Street, Yarmouth PO41 0PE   COOKING 7
TEL: (01983) 760331   FAX: (01983) 760425   COST £28–£51

Easy to find next to the ferry, the refurbished hotel (where Charles II once slept) continues to impress. It does a good job across the spectrum: locals use the log-fired bar, and the bright, summery yellow brasserie, with views across the water, offers wild mushroom tart with poached egg, and corned beef hash with pancetta. More serious business is done in the smart burgundy and grey dining-room – 'in winter, when the curtains are drawn, it feels like sitting in a dark red box' – where the deal is a set price for three courses. Before the arrival of Kevin Mangeolles, visitors had to make allowances when eating on the Isle of Wight, but no longer. He is at home with contemporary ingredients from couscous to cep powder, takes a European line, and draws on a high degree of imagination and skill, turning out ravioli of ox tongue with foie gras and garlic beignets, and galantine of rabbit with wild mushrooms and chorizo.

One visitor had barely recovered from the 'small sensation' of light and fluffy scrambled egg with truffle – 'utterly simple and truly gorgeous' – that appeared as an appetiser, before being hit by a 'triumph' of 'warm, soft, wobbly' Jerusalem artichoke mousse surrounded by slices of globe artichoke and thin asparagus spears: more truffle helped the combination along. The appeal of this food is that it does not allow the main component to be sidelined; the soloist is not upstaged by the chorus, but supported by it. Technique is thus not an end in itself, but sharpens the focus of the main idea; for example, roast pheasant breast is served with a 'dark, bloody and finely-textured' sausage of liver and leg-meat ('like a pheasant black pudding'), bringing a note of vitality to the dish; cabbage, lentils and foie gras helped as well.

For dessert, expect similarly workmanlike dishes of rhubarb and almond tart with a rhubarb and cardamom mousse and cranberry sorbet, or chocolate fondant with pain d'épices ice-cream and coffee sauce. Wines are enterprisingly grouped by price, opening with eleven bottles (including a white from the Isle of Wight's Adgestone vineyard) all at £11.50, then ten at £14.50, eleven at £17.50 and nine at £21.50, before moving on to more serious, mostly French, bins with no upper limit. CELLARMAN'S CHOICE: Firestone Chardonnay 1996, Santa Ynez, California, £17.50; Zevenwacht Estate Cabernet/Merlot 1996, Stellenbosch, South Africa £14.50.

See inside the front cover for an explanation of the symbols used at the tops of entries.

CHEF: Kevin Mangeolles PROPRIETORS: Jeremy and Amy Willcock, and John Illsley OPEN: restaurant Sun L 12.30 to 3, Tue to Sat D 7 to 10; brasserie all week 12 to 3, 7 to 10 MEALS: restaurant Set L £24.50, Set D £36.75; brasserie alc (main courses £6.95 to £14.50). BYO £6 SERVICE: none, card slips closed CARDS: Amex, Delta, MasterCard, Switch, Visa DETAILS: 40 seats (restaurant), 45 seats (brasserie), 60 seats outside. Private parties: 60 main room (restaurant), 12 main room (brasserie), 20 private room. Vegetarian meals (brasserie). Children's helpings. No children under 10 in restaurant. Wheelchair access to brasserie (not WC). No music. Air-conditioned (restaurant). No cigars/pipes in brasserie ACCOMMODATION: 16 rooms, all with bath/shower. TV. Phone. B&B £80 to £175. Children welcome. Baby listening. Dogs by arrangement. Afternoon teas (*The Which? Hotel Guide*) (£5)

YATTENDON Berkshire

map 2

▲ *Royal Oak* ⁵⚹

The Square, Yattendon RG18 0UG
TEL: (01635) 201325 FAX: (01635) 201926
off B4009, 5m W of Pangbourne

| NEW CHEF |
COST £27–£52

'We are just completing a three-year project to restore and revitalise the Royal Oak,' writes Corinne Macrae, and most effort seems to have been expended on accommodation: this is a brick-built, creeper-covered, French-style, family-run restaurant-with-rooms on the village's tiny green. The kitchen has not been neglected, but we learnt of Robin ZaZou's arrival only as we went to press. If the format remains, it will revolve around a *carte* in the brasserie, and three-course fixed-price meals in the restaurant, possibly taking in luxuries of salmon jelly with marinated salmon and caviare, striking a Mediterranean note in roast rack of lamb and couscous, and going in for rich and creamy desserts such as hot chocolate fondant with clotted cream. House French wine – also available by the glass – costs £9.95 a bottle.

CHEF: Robin ZaZou PROPRIETOR: Regal Hotel Group OPEN: restaurant all week L 12 to 2, Mon to Sat D 7 to 9.30 (10 Sat); brasserie all week L and D MEALS: restaurant Set L and D £32.50; brasserie alc (main courses £8 to £12.50) Set D £32 SERVICE: not inc CARDS: Amex, Delta, Diners, MasterCard, Switch, Visa DETAILS: 70 seats. 34 seats outside. Private parties: 32 main room, 10 private room. Car park. Children's helpings. No smoking in restaurant. No music in restaurant ACCOMMODATION: 5 rooms, all with bath/shower. TV. Phone. Room only £95 to £125. Children welcome. Baby facilities. Afternoon teas (*The Which? Hotel Guide*) (£5)

YORK North Yorkshire

map 9

Melton's ♟ ⁵⚹

7 Scarcroft Road, York YO23 1ND
TEL: (01904) 634341 FAX: (01904) 635115

COOKING 4
COST £21–£41

The small converted terraced house, with pastel walls and a colourful mural, is known for its modest surroundings – 'you would not come here for a comfortable evening' – and reasonable prices that include coffee, mineral water and service. Monthly-changing menus include a *carte* and a fixed-price version with a choice of three first and three main courses. Tuesdays see extra vegetarian dishes, Thursdays extra fish. Michael Hjort's practice of 'cooking what he likes' might not chime with every visitor, but it has produced fish soup with rouille, roast monkfish with home-cured cod and aïoli, and ox-tongue with charcutière sauce and parsnip purée.

The food can be 'a bit fussy', and flavours would gain by being more powerfully expressed – these days people want excitement on the plate – but the Hjorts are sensitive to special dietary needs and go out of their way to welcome families with children. Desserts might include a rhubarb version of baked Alaska, and the boozy trifle comes 'with jam rather than fruit'. Service is from local young women, and informality reigns: wine, for example, is brought already opened and, once approved, will be left for you to replenish your glass. Mark-ups are limited to a maximum of £10, meaning that the more expensive wines offer best value, but there is plenty to tempt at all price levels on the wide-ranging list. CELLARMAN'S CHOICE: St-Véran 'Les Chailloux' 1996, Dom. des Deux Roches, £15.20; Maranges *premier cru* 'Clos des Loyères Vieilles Vignes' 1995, Vincent Girardin, £21.50.

CHEFS: Michael Hjort and I.J. Drew   PROPRIETORS: Michael and Lucy Hjort   OPEN: Tue to Sun L 12 to 2, Mon to Sat D 5.30 to 10   CLOSED: 3 weeks Christmas, 1 week in summer   MEALS: alc (main courses £10.50 to £15). Set L £15, Set D £15 (to 6.15) to £19.50   SERVICE: net prices, card slips closed   CARDS: Delta, MasterCard, Switch, Visa   DETAILS: 40 seats. Private parties: 30 main room, 16 private room. Vegetarian meals. Children's helpings. No smoking in 1 dining-room. Wheelchair access (1 step; not WC). Music £5

▲ *Middlethorpe Hall* ▼ ⅝✳

Bishopthorpe Road, York YO23 2GB   COOKING 5
TEL: (01904) 641241   FAX: (01904) 620176   COST £23–£56

'Like a big block of chocolate ice-cream' was how Middlethorpe looked to one couple after they glided over a motorway bridge and saw it loom up on the right. Built at the close of the seventeenth century, it is certainly a stately pile, and the classical grandiosity of the interiors – a marble figurine in an illuminated cupola is the focal point of one of the three dining-rooms – is lightened by the friendly ministrations of highly proficient staff. Miniature fish-cakes of cod, potato and coriander are typical pre-dinner nibbles, and indicate the level of attention that goes into the food.

Andrew Wood is in his fifth year here, and standards remain as steady as ever. The style is modern British, with sound combinations of ingredients gilded with occasional oriental inflections. That brings on chargrilled monkfish with shiitake mushrooms, as well as lamb kofta with turmeric rice and red onions in yoghurt. A goats'-cheese salad is elevated into the premier division by a basil oil dressing, and praise has come in for roast pork and oyster mushrooms on a bed of mash with a wine and green peppercorn sauce. Hot soufflés are a grand way to finish: a 'perfectly timed' raspberry version lacked nothing in intensity. Alternatives might include a poached pear in a praline basket with ginger sabayon, and there is an option to take cheeses afterwards as an extra course. Coffee is served with plentiful, and hugely professional, petits fours. Fine champagnes, clarets and burgundies form an imposing introduction to a wine list which is brightened by the presence of some exciting bins from the New World. Prices are as stately as the setting, although wines under £20 can be found. Six French house wines start at £13. CELLARMAN'S CHOICE: Vin de Pays d'Oc, Viognier 1996, Dom. St-Hilaire, £19; Cousiño Macul Merlot Limited Release 1995, Maipo Valley, Chile, £20.

CHEF: Andrew Wood   PROPRIETOR: Historic House Hotels Ltd   OPEN: all week 12.30 (12 on race days) to 1.45, 7.30 to 9.45   CLOSED: 25 Dec (exc for residents)   MEALS: Set L Mon to Sat £12.50 (2 courses) to £14.50, Set L Sun £18.50, Set D £27.95 (2 courses) to £36.95. BYO £5, sparkling £7.50   SERVICE: net prices, card slips closed   CARDS: Amex, MasterCard, Switch, Visa   DETAILS: 60 seats. Private parties: 45 main room, 45 private rooms. Car park. Vegetarian meals. No children under 8. Jacket and tie at D. No smoking in dining-room. Wheelchair access (8 steps; not WC). Occasional music   ACCOMMODATION: 30 rooms, all with bath/shower. TV. Phone. Room only £99 to £230. Rooms for disabled. No children under 8. No dogs. Afternoon teas (*The Which? Hotel Guide*)   £5

Scotland

Faraday's

2–4 Kirk Brae, Cults, Aberdeen AB15 9SQ
TEL/FAX: (01224) 869666   COOKING 1
on A93, 3m from city centre   COST £21–£44

This narrow, Edwardian-style dining-room on the outskirts of Aberdeen was
once an electricity sub-station (hence Faraday's), although these days 'mains'
has a different meaning. Bar lunches look good value and come either cold with
pitta bread – roasted Mediterranean vegetables on couscous, for example – or
warm with vegetables: pan-fried ox liver with onions perhaps. Elsewhere the
food might combine a rustic theme (rough game terrine) with seafood dishes of
scampi tails in thermidor sauce, or tasty smoked salmon with prawn
mayonnaise. Staff recite desserts of caramelised apple tart, or a 'cake' of banana,
pear and rum served with vanilla ice and warm toffee sauce. Courtesy of a bowl
of soup, three-course weekday meals are extended to four on Friday and
Saturday. Credit card transactions attract a 2.5 per cent surcharge. An average
spend on wine might be around £20 a bottle, but four house wines weigh in at
£12.50.

CHEFS: Dorothy Skene, Paul Christie and Roger Ross   PROPRIETOR: John Inches   OPEN: Tue to
Sat 12 to 2, 6 (7 Fri and Sat) to 9.30   CLOSED: 26 Dec to 6 Jan   MEALS: alc (main courses £5.50
to £16). Set D £26.95. BYO £6.50   SERVICE: 10%, card slips closed   CARDS: Amex, Delta,
MasterCard, Switch, Visa (2.5% surcharge on credit cards)   DETAILS: 40 seats. Private parties:
40 main room. Car park. Vegetarian meals. Children's helpings. No smoking before 2pm L and
10pm D. Wheelchair access (also WC). Music. Air-conditioned   £5

Q Brasserie

9 Alford Place, Aberdeen AB10 1YD   COOKING 4
TEL: (01224) 595001   FAX: (01224) 582245   COST £24–£52

The old theological seminary above the College Bar is reached through a side
entrance, up a circular staircase. The rostrum end of the 'stark church lecture hall'
is a bar, the soaring ceiling is of dark 'ecclesiastical wood', the floor of bare
boards, and modern paintings decorate the walls. 'It could be the dining-hall of a
minor public school', were it not for the food, which starts with good olives and
tiny kebabs with drinks, and proceeds through a varied menu (even more lavish
in choice at dinner) of mostly Euro-style dishes: pressed terrine of chicken and

545

pencil leeks, Greek salad with feta and lemon, or roast saddle of rabbit with cep ravioli.

'The chef really knows his stuff, and has the confidence to be original,' wrote one who began with a potage of scallops and mussels in a rich fish stock with wuntuns and a 'sesame twist'. Another dined on 'fine fresh halibut' and 'rich, chunky, aromatic lamb' served with a plum chutney. Dauphinoise potatoes, 'garlicky and rich', are charged extra. Desserts 'in the first rank' have included a light Grand Marnier soufflé, and hot banana tart with almond brittle ice-cream. 'Staff could not explain the significance of the Q', but are chatty and helpful, and the wine list is short and to the point, starting with house French at £10.95. We are unable to confirm the details below as the restaurant has not returned our questionnaire.

CHEF: David MacCallum PROPRIETORS: J. and S. Clarkson OPEN: Mon to Fri L 12 to 1.45, Mon to Sat D 7 to 9.45 (10.45 Fri and Sat) MEALS: alc (main courses L £8.50 to £11.50, D £12 to £15) SERVICE: not inc CARDS: Amex, Delta, Diners, MasterCard, Switch, Visa DETAILS: 120 seats. Private parties: 120 main room, 16 private room. Vegetarian meals. Children's helpings. Music

Silver Darling 🍴✳

Pocra Quay, North Pier, Aberdeen AB11 5DQ	COOKING 4
TEL: (01224) 576229 FAX: (01224) 791275	COST £28–£60

Renovation has brought a change of tone to this harbourside restaurant. The original ground-floor dining-room is now reserved for private parties, and a new storey has been added, with a fresh white and yellow colour scheme; all-round windows give panoramic views over the harbour entrance, the city and out to sea. Lines are clear and uncluttered, the whole place is appropriately ship-shape, and the food is still 'French and proud of it'. Didier Dejean deals mainly in seafood, most of it locally landed, some of it simply chargrilled: a generous plate of monkfish, salmon and langoustine, for instance, or 'gloriously fresh' sea bass 'timed to the second'.

Such simplicity is a strength, but doesn't militate against more adventurous crab gratin soufflé with a lemon-grass and ginger sauce. Crusts and toppings are a favoured device – ground pecans for red snapper, brioche crumbs for steamed halibut fillet – and the à la carte format allows a few luxuries, such as oysters in a champagne and cream sauce, or lobster salad with mango and basil dressing. A meat dish, perhaps roast fillet of lamb, is offered for variety, and vegetables, though little more than 'a gesture', are included in the price. A French spirit pervades desserts of pancake with Grand Marnier parfait and bitter orange sauce, or caramelised apples with a calvados sorbet; and around 30, mostly white, wines follow suit, starting with house wine at £9.50.

CHEF: Didier Dejean PROPRIETORS: Didier Dejean and Catherine Wood OPEN: Mon to Fri L 12 to 2, Mon to Sat D 7 to 10 CLOSED: 2 weeks Christmas and New Year MEALS: alc (main courses £11.50 to £22) SERVICE: not inc, card slips closed CARDS: Amex, Delta, Diners, MasterCard, Switch, Visa DETAILS: 60 seats. Private parties: 15 main room. Children welcome. No smoking in 1 dining-room. Wheelchair access (1 step; also WC). Music

All entries, including Round-ups, are fully indexed at the back of the Guide.

ABERFELDY Perthshire & Kinross   map 11

▲ *Farleyer House* ⁵⨳

Aberfeldy PH15 2JE
TEL: (01887) 820332   FAX: (01887) 829430
EMAIL: andycole@compuserve.com
on B846, Aberfeldy to Kinloch Rannoch road, 1½m W | NEW CHEF |
of Weem   COST £23–£45

Perched on a hill, with fine views across the valley to mountains beyond,
Farleyer keeps two dining-rooms going: the more formal Menzies Room and a
more modest and casual 'bistro' with plain wooden tables and chairs. As the
Guide went to press, Richard Lyth left to open a new restaurant at No 7, The
Square, Aberfeldy, and his deputy Kieran Grant took over, presumably still with
good supplies of organic beef and Skye seafood at his fingertips. Reports are
welcome on both please. The wine list is generous with choice: start at the end
for bottles under £20, or try one of 11 house recommendations from £10.50
upwards.

CHEF: Kieran Grant   PROPRIETOR: Janice Reid   OPEN: all week 12 to 2.30, 6 to 10   MEALS: alc
(main courses £8 to £15). Set L and D £29. BYO £10   SERVICE: not inc   CARDS: Amex, Delta,
Diners, MasterCard, Switch, Visa   DETAILS: 110 seats. 20 seats outside. Private parties: 60
main room, 30 and 40 private rooms. Car park. Vegetarian meals. Children's helpings. No
smoking in 1 dining-room. Wheelchair access (also WC). Music   ACCOMMODATION: 19 rooms,
all with bath/shower. TV. Phone. D,B&B £110 to £210. Rooms for disabled. Children welcome.
Baby facilities. Dogs welcome in kennels. Afternoon teas. Fishing (£5)

ABERFOYLE Stirling   map 11

Braeval ❢ ◗

Aberfoyle FK8 3UY
TEL: (01877) 382711   FAX: (01877) 382400   COOKING 5
on A81, 1m SE of Aberfoyle   COST £30–£52

A stream still flows through the garden of the old stone mill, whose fireplace,
paved floor and beamed ceilings are softened by drapes, candles, and above all
by Fiona Nairn. Her smiling, relaxed but watchful presence is pivotal; she is
calm yet epitomises efficiency, and runs the operation 'brilliantly', leaving
visitors to feel 'quiet and relaxed'. Things seem to have stabilised after Nick
Nairn's departure to Glasgow (see entry, Nairns), and the direct flavours of Neil
Forbes's modern 'uncomplicated food' have strong appeal. The format is as
before: no choice on the three-course weekday lunch menus, and only a choice of
dessert on the four-course dinner and Sunday lunch menus.

Flavours impress right from the beginning – an appetiser of marinated salmon
on toast perhaps – and might reach their zenith in a langoustine bisque made
from 'superb shellfish stock', which induced 'ecstasy' in one visitor. Local
materials and European ideas combine to produce crisp-skinned breast of
maize-fed chicken with sauté wild mushrooms in a reduced stock sauce, served
simply with spinach and potato, and 'well-cooked' tuna with peppery rocket
and thin, soft chilli noodles, a dish kept moist by an abundance of 'subtle oils'.

Cheeses are a 'thin sliced selection of mature local delicacies', and while a May diner wondered where the blueberries, strawberries, raspberries and blackberries in his dessert might have come from, he had no complaints about the caramelised puff pastry and 'cinnamon cappuccino' with which they appeared. Wines are drawn almost entirely from the major regions and boast some prominent châteaux and famous producers. The French section is trimmer this season, while New Zealand is showing more weight. Prices are reasonable, starting with a baker's dozen of house wines between £15 and £20. CELLARMAN'S CHOICE: Marsannay 1996, Guyard, £19.95; Isabel Estate Pinot Noir 1996, Marlborough, New Zealand, £23.50.

CHEF: Neil Forbes   PROPRIETOR: Fiona Nairn   OPEN: Thur to Sun L 12.30 to 1.30, Wed to Sat D 7.30 to 9.30   CLOSED: 25 Dec, 1 and 2 Jan, 1 week Feb, 1 week June, 1 week Oct   MEALS: Set L Thur to Sat £19.50, Set L Sun £23.50, Set D £31.50   SERVICE: not inc   CARDS: MasterCard, Switch, Visa   DETAILS: 36 seats. Private parties: 30 main room. Car park. No children under 10. No cigars/pipes in dining-room. No smoking before coffee is served. Wheelchair access (1 step; also WC). No music

---

ABOYNE Aberdeenshire   map 11

White Cottage £✳

Dess, Aboyne AB34 5BP
TEL/FAX: (013398) 86265   COOKING 4
On A93, 2½m E of Aboyne   COST £23–£46

The façade is attractive, the garden 'unloved', and the only white bit is a Victorian porch, set against granite walls. Views across farmland from the conservatory may not be the most dramatic in Deeside, and general upkeep may not top the list of priorities, but seating is comfortable, the welcome is friendly, and the Mills oversee an operation that treats supplies and cooking with equal seriousness. Lunch-time offers a fairly hefty menu, although its à la carte format allows lighter meals of just starters and puddings, while set-price dinners helpfully offer the choice of either two or three courses.

A mildly inventive streak runs through the repertoire, producing a fragrant chicken and rice soup flavoured with coconut, lemon and sherry, a risotto that combines both rice and barley with mushrooms and chicken livers, and baked spinach roulade with fennel and beans in gazpacho sauce. Outright novelty is not the aim, rather ideas recur in different contexts: so the gazpacho sauce will on another occasion accompany crab-cakes with rösti potatoes, and the chicken livers will turn up with boiled potatoes for lunch. Cheeses might include Perthshire goats' or Irish Cooleeney, and puddings offer a balanced choice of perhaps fruit pavlova, baked lemon tart, or a melting chocolate mousse pancake. About half the 50 wines are French, the rest work their way around the world, and there is something to suit most pockets, starting at £12.

'At a table of six, three waiters are required for the dome-removing ceremony, clasping a dome in each hand. They lift the silver lids over their heads in perfect balletic unison, rocking back slightly on their heels, like a troupe of limp-wristed Morris dancers at the school fête.' (On eating in Oxfordshire)

CHEF: Laurie Mill PROPRIETORS: Laurie and Josephine Mill OPEN: Tue to Sat 11.30 to 2.45, 6 to 9.15 CLOSED: 1 week October, 5 days Christmas, 4 days New Year, one week Easter, one week July MEALS: alc L and D 6 to 7pm (main courses £7.50 to £14.50). Set D (from 7pm) £24 (2 courses) to £28.50 SERVICE: not inc CARDS: MasterCard, Switch, Visa DETAILS: 36 seats. 12 seats outside. Private parties: 45 main room, 24 private room. Car park. Vegetarian meals. Children's helpings. No smoking in 1 dining-room. Wheelchair access (also WC). Occasional music (£5)

ACHILTIBUIE Highland   map 11

▲ *Summer Isles Hotel* 🍷 ✳

Achiltibuie IV26 2YG
TEL: (01854) 622282 FAX: (01854) 622251
take A835 to Drumrunie, 10m N of Ullapool, then
single-track road for 15m; hotel 1m past Achiltibuie   COOKING 5
on left   COST £42–£51

Any visit to Summer Isles is bound to be memorable: not least for the remote location, peaceful setting, and 'spectacularly moody' views. A long, single-track road leads to a strung-out village where this rambling and serene Edwardian house looks out over the bay: a 'Highland gem', one visitor called it. Cream, white, gold and teal blue are keynote colours in the dining-room, and dinner is set for eight o'clock: five courses, one of them cheese, and no choice before dessert.

The emphasis, according to Gerry Irvine, moves increasingly towards fresh and simply prepared seafood, prodded by both supply (shellfish at least is bountiful, even if white fish stocks are threatened) and demand. Seared Tanera Bay scallops, grilled Lochinver halibut, and a plate of local langoustines and spiny lobsters are typical of the output, with praise registered for Achiltibuie smoked salmon with blini, and crab ravioli. Seafood is balanced on the well-constructed menus by roast grouse or saddle of rabbit, with perhaps a starter of leek and asparagus tart.

Isle of Mull Cheddar has figured among the generous array of cheeses, and desserts might include banana fritters, blueberry and apple roulade, or hazelnut, nectarine and raspberry torte. Service is discreet, attentive and 'always friendly', and knowledgeable advice on choosing wines is readily offered. The impressive list leans heavily towards classic France, but when it does tilt over to the New World it is perfectly sound. Prices are very fair, with a good selection of bins under £15 and house wines starting at £12.50; half-bottles are plentiful and Mark Irvine's inspired choice of wines by the glass to match the day's starters helps to reduce the knotty business of selecting even further. CELLARMAN'S CHOICE: Pelorus 1993, Cloudy Bay, Marlborough, New Zealand, £25; St-Joseph 'Les Grisières' 1994, André Perret, £23.

Prices quoted in the Guide *are based on information supplied by restaurateurs. The prices quoted at the top of each entry represent a range, from the lowest meal price to the highest; the latter is inflated by 20 per cent to take account of likely price rises during the year of the* Guide.

CHEF: Chris Firth-Bernard   PROPRIETORS: Mark and Gerry Irvine   OPEN: all week light L 12.30 to 2, D 8pm (1 sitting)   CLOSED: mid-Oct to Easter   MEALS: Set D £35. Light L available. BYO £5   SERVICE: net prices, card slips closed   CARDS: MasterCard, Switch, Visa   DETAILS: 28 seats. Private parties: 8 main room. Car park. Vegetarian meals. Children's helpings. No children under 6. No smoking in dining-room. No music   ACCOMMODATION: 12 rooms, all with bath/shower. Phone. B&B £50 to £106. No children under 6. Dogs welcome in bedrooms only, not left unaccompanied. Fishing (*The Which? Hotel Guide*)

ALEXANDRIA   Dumbarton & Clydebank   map 11

▲ *Cameron House, Georgian Room* ♥ ⅝✳

Loch Lomond, Alexandria G83 8QZ
TEL: (01389) 755565   FAX: (01389) 759522   COOKING 6
off A82, ½m N of Balloch roundabout, 1m S of Arden   COST £35–£95

The turreted old house with lawns sweeping down to Loch Lomond has been more or less sympathetically enlarged with extra bedrooms, conference facilities, a sports complex and time-share cottages. It is 'grand hotel' rather than 'country house', and 1930s at that, with chandeliers, red plush, and tinkling piano, but the tone is lightened by fresh flowers and a view across the loch. It delights in a degree of showiness. Staff, dressed in cherry-coloured jackets and black aprons, slice bread, deftly remove the butter label with a pair of tongs, lift earthenware domes and so forth, but it is all done without irritating pomp, and for all that service has been considered 'exceptional in its quiet efficiency and lack of fuss'.

Menus are clearly written, with attractive choices, and include a *carte*, set-price 'market' menus at both lunch and dinner, and a 'celebratory surprise' option of six courses. Peter Fleming looks at his materials through modern European spectacles, and keeps the focus sharp by staying simple. An inspection meal began with grilled goats' cheese on a croûton, 'unadorned and splendid', and with wild mushrooms in thin ravioli, followed by an 'outstanding, light' warm mousseline of lobster. A degree of comfort characterises the style, and a switch from lightness to richness according to context is welcome: thus a main course of two generous medallions of well-hung beef fillet in a claret jus on a 'gooey' truffled risotto were followed by a hot cherry soufflé with vanilla ice-cream.

Wine service is first-class, but you'll need a head for high prices to scale the peaks of the vintage claret, burgundy and Rhône ranges, although they do climb down below £20 in a few places on the lengthy list. There are no house wines; individual suggestions are made instead. Eighteen wines cost between £4 and £16.50 a glass, and there is an impressively extensive list of old malts. CELLARMAN'S CHOICE: Savennières 'Clos de Varennes' 1996, Ch. de Fesles, £24; Beaucanon Estate Cabernet Sauvignon 1994, Napa Valley, California, £23.50.

'*Home-made milk-chocolate ice-cream was very odd. It seemed, as time went by, to acquire the character of the bar of chocolate as which it no doubt started out. If I could have made it last another ten minutes I think it would have started to wrap itself in silver paper.*' (On eating in London)

CHEF: Peter Fleming   PROPRIETOR: De Vere Hotels   OPEN: Mon to Fri L 12 to 1.45, all week D 7 to 9.45   CLOSED: 26 Dec   MEALS: alc (main courses £22.50 to £31.50). Set L £17.50 (2 courses) to £21.50, Set D £38.50 to £45   SERVICE: not inc   CARDS: Amex, Delta, Diners, MasterCard, Switch, Visa   DETAILS: 220 seats. Private parties: 200 main room, 12 to 40 private rooms. Car park. Vegetarian meals. No children. Jacket and tie. No smoking in dining-room. Music. Air-conditioned   ACCOMMODATION: 96 rooms, all with bath/shower. TV. Phone. B&B £140 to £395. Rooms for disabled. Children welcome. High teas for children. Baby facilities. No dogs. Afternoon teas. Swimming-pool

---

ALYTH   Perthshire & Kinross   map 11

▲ *Drumnacree House* 🍴✳

St Ninians Road, Alyth PH11 8AP
TEL/FAX: (01828) 632194
EMAIL: allan.cull@virgin.net
turn off A926 Blairgowrie to Kirriemuir road to Alyth;
take first left after Clydesdale Bank; hotel entrance is   COOKING 4
300 metres on right   COST £27–£43

'We like very small hotels which serve excellent food,' wrote one couple, 'and this lived up to our expectations.' The Culls, who opened here a decade ago, offer 'no frills, just good value' in comfortable suroundings with polished but unhurried service. Dinner is now à la carte only. Allan Cull's speciality is spicy Cajun food, which might appear as a thick prawn and okra gumbo to start, and then blackened salmon, chicken or steak, accompanied by dirty rice. Otherwise he tends to cook a mix of Scottish favourites such as a warm mousse of Abroath smokies, or vension fillet with chanterelle mushrooms, alongside more exotic spiced chicken with couscous and wild apricots. Multi-leaved home-grown salads, some with nasturtium flowers, are attractively served in glass bowls, and herbs and vegetables come from the garden too. Scottish cheeses are served with warm oatcakes, and puddings cover the familiar territory of syrup sponge, chocolate mousse, or armagnac parfait with prunes. Some 40 wines, mostly French, start with a house trio at £12.

CHEF: Allan Cull   PROPRIETORS: Allan and Eleanor Cull   OPEN: Tue to Sat D only 7 to 9 CLOSED: Dec to Mar   MEALS: alc (main courses £11 to £14.50). BYO £5   SERVICE: not inc CARDS: Amex, MasterCard, Visa   DETAILS: 50 seats. Private parties: 50 main room, 12 and 30 private rooms. Car park. Children's helpings. No smoking in dining-room. Wheelchair access (also women's WC). Music   ACCOMMODATION: 6 rooms, all with bath/shower. TV. B&B £47.50 to £88. Children welcome. High teas for children. Well-behaved dogs welcome   £5

The 2000 Guide will be published before Christmas 1999. Reports on meals are most welcome at any time of the year, but are particularly valuable in the spring (no later than June). Send them to The Good Food Guide, FREEPOST, 2 Marylebone Road, London NW1 1YN. *Or email your report to* guidereports@which.co.uk.

£5 *indicates that the restaurant has elected to participate in the* Good Food Guide *voucher scheme. For full details see page 6.*

ANSTRUTHER Fife

map 11

Cellar

24 East Green, Anstruther KY10 3AA
TEL: (01333) 310378   FAX: (01333) 312544

COOKING 6
COST £25–£46

'This is a restaurant on good form, doing what it does best,' commented an inspector of Peter Jukes's seafood restaurant close to the harbour, adding that it is a prime example of what can be achieved with first-rate ingredients simply treated. The key to its success? 'Don't mess around with fabulous seafood,' according to Mr Jukes, whose respect for his raw materials extends to a strict adherence to the seasons, even for fish such as haddock and cod that are commonly thought of as year-rounders.

The Cellar's log fire, heavy curtains and thick stone walls create a comfortable setting in winter, though can be a touch gloomy on a sunny lunch time. Local seafood starters are treated in an appropriately northern style: a creamy Finnan haddock filling for an omelette, perhaps, or oak-smoked and hot-kiln-smoked salmon in a trio with gravad lax. Main courses may embrace the Mediterranean – basil oil and pesto with cod, tuna in a niçoise dressing – but very often the fish (monk, scallops, halibut) are just roasted, seared or grilled, to great effect. This combination of skill and simplicity extends to a daily meat dish: chicken breast with Dijon mustard sauce, for example, winning praise for its good, strong flavours.

Puddings are not always handled so deftly – a prune and armagnac parfait with good prunes and plenty of brandy deserved a better sauce – but there is comfort to be had in the home-made whisky truffles served with coffee, or the quintet of luscious dessert wines at the back of the list. While red wines are far from neglected in this classy collection, great attention has naturally been paid to providing a fine range of whites, notably from Alsace and Burgundy. Prices are fair across the board, starting at £12.50 for New World house wines. CEL-LARMAN'S CHOICE: Riesling d'Alsace 1993, Trimbach, £21.50; Côte de Nuits Villages 1992, Jayer-Gilles £23.50.

CHEF: Peter Jukes   PROPRIETORS: Peter and Susan Jukes   OPEN: Wed to Sun (Sat winter) L 12.30 to 1.30, all week (Tue to Sat and some Mons winter) D 7 to 9.30   CLOSED: 4 days Christmas   MEALS: alc L (main courses £7.50 to £12.0). Set D £25 (2 courses) to £28.50 SERVICE: not inc, card slips closed   CARDS: Amex, Delta, Diners, MasterCard, Switch, Visa DETAILS: 32 seats. Private parties: 36 main room. Children's helpings. No children under 8. No smoking in dining-room. Music

ARCHIESTOWN Moray

map 11

▲ *Archiestown Hotel* £

Archiestown AB38 7QL
TEL: (01340) 810218   FAX: (01340) 810239

COOKING 2
COST £22–£49

'Within sampling distance' of some fine distilleries, this hotel at the crossroads of a tiny village (pop. 165) typically caters for visitors who fish, golf, walk the

Speyside Way or totter the Whisky Trail. They go out for the day, returning with a healthy appetite for plain, wholesome food culled from the Scottish larder: oysters, smoked salmon, lobster mayonnaise or pheasant terrine to begin, then hare and pigeon casserole, devilled kidneys or Dover sole to follow. Judith Bulger might ring the changes with lamb cassoulet or chicken couscous, but the golden rule is 'nothing fancy'. Freshness, simple cooking and reasonable prices are the draw. Finish with a nursery pudding of spotted dick or apple flan, and drink from a short list of mostly French wines, starting with house vin de pays at £11.

CHEF: Judith Bulger   PROPRIETORS: Judith and Michael Bulger   OPEN: all week 12.30 to 1.45, 6.30 to 8.30   CLOSED: 1 Oct to 9 Feb   MEALS: alc (main courses £6.50 to £17.50).   SERVICE: not inc, card slips closed   CARDS: MasterCard, Visa   DETAILS: 40 seats. 12 seats outside. Private parties: 24 main room, 20 private room. Car park. No children after 8pm. Children's helpings. No music   ACCOMMODATION: 9 rooms, 7 with bath/shower. TV. Phone. B&B £35 to £85. Children welcome. High teas for children. Dogs welcome. Afternoon teas (£5)

ARISAIG Highland   map 11

▲ *Arisaig House* 🍴✳ ☕

Beasdale, by Arisaig PH39 4NR
TEL: (01687) 450622   FAX: (01687) 450626
EMAIL: arisaighse@aol.com   COOKING 5
on A830, 3m E of Arisaig   COST £27–£59

The mid-Victorian grey-stone manor is set in parkland among century-old beeches and vivid rhododendrons, but despite a formal air it is 'neither stuffy nor foreboding'. New chef Duncan Gibson arrived in March 1998, and an early inspection suggests unruffled continuity from the standard set by his predecessor. The classical country-house style means fixed-price dinner menus of four courses plus coffee, with a choice of soup or sorbet before the main. Local ingredients are enthusiastically used, but in ways that may surprise. Crispy wuntun of Mallaig prawns with pesto might just qualify as modern Scots cuisine, for want of any more precise definition, and salmon may be wrapped around an escalope of foie gras and given a sauce diable. Starters range from 'delicate and subtle' nage of west coast mussels with lemon and chive essence to 'strong, gamey' terrine of venison with a sweet redcurrant sauce, and may be followed by carrot and coriander soup 'of high quality'.

Monkfish on mash with sauce antiboise demonstrated a light touch at inspection, while more robust palates may be satisfied by guinea-fowl breast served with smoked bacon and sauerkraut. Puddings include coffee and chocolate gâteau with Drambuie cream, and crème brûlée with rhubarb, or there is a selection of Scottish and French cheeses. Lunch is simpler fare such as tagliatelle with Parma ham and grilled goats' cheese, or grilled sirloin with 'Café de Paris' butter. It is all served by 'kind and helpful' staff. Wines are predominantly French, with mature clarets in abundance, at prices that reflect the surroundings. House wines start at £14.50.

The Guide *always appreciates hearing about changes of chef or owner.*

CHEF: Duncan Gibson   PROPRIETORS: John, Ruth and Andrew Smither, and Alison Wilkinson   OPEN: all week 12.30 to 2, 7.30 to 8.30   CLOSED: Nov to Easter   MEALS: alc L (main courses £7.50 to £12.50). Set D £37.50   SERVICE: not inc, card slips closed   CARDS: MasterCard, Switch, Visa   DETAILS: 36 seats. Private parties: 10 main room. Car park. Vegetarian meals. No children under 10. No smoking in dining-room. No music   ACCOMMODATION: 14 rooms, all with bath/shower. TV. Phone. B&B £80 to £252. No children under 10. No dogs. Afternoon teas (*The Which? Hotel Guide*)

AUCHMITHIE Angus   map 11

But 'n' Ben ❦✹ £

Auchmithie DD11 5SQ
TEL: (01241) 877223   COOKING 1
on coast, 3m NE of Arbroath, off A92   COST £14–£37

Screens and partitions break up the space inside these two whitewashed cottages perched high on a clifftop, and a welcoming coal fire burns in the grate. But 'n' Ben opens most of the day and provides just what visitors are after: anything from half a dozen oysters, via home-made soup, to an Angus steak mince pie. It reflects its locality well, hoovering up materials from suppliers round and about, and offers salads of crab, lobster or prawn when available. If there is a centrepiece, it involves Arbroath smokies: served either simply hot and buttered, or (the house speciality) a fish-filled springy pancake dripping with buttery, eggy sauce. Baking seems to be a permanent activity, producing an array of inexpensive tarts, pies and cakes for dessert: 'portions are big'. Twenty basic wines start at £8 and, apart from champagne, stop at £20.

CHEFS: Margaret and Angus Horn   PROPRIETORS: Margaret, Ian and Angus Horn   OPEN: Wed to Mon 12 to 2.30, 4 to 5.30, 7 to 9.30   CLOSED: 26 Dec, 1 and 2 Jan   MEALS: alc (main courses L £5.50 to £10.50, D £7 to £13.50)   SERVICE: not inc, card slips closed   CARDS: Delta, MasterCard, Switch, Visa   DETAILS: 40 seats. Private parties: 40 main room. Car park. Vegetarian meals. Children's helpings. No smoking in dining-room. Wheelchair access (not WC). No music   (£5)

AUCHTERARDER Perthshire & Kinross   map 11

▲ Auchterarder House ♥ ❦✹

Auchterarder PH3 1DZ   COOKING 4
TEL: (01764) 663646   FAX: (01764) 662939   COST £26–£62

This 'big Victorian pile set smack in the middle of Scotland' operates on a large scale and, even though the décor may be in need of some TLC, feels reassuringly substantial. Kiernan Darnell makes use of quite a few native materials, from Shetland salmon to Perthshire lamb and red deer, but a lively and intelligent approach to the food means langoustine tempura comes with candied ginger and chilli sambal, while a terrine of potato, goats' cheese and chorizo is wrapped in Ayrshire bacon and given a sweet mustard dressing.

Lunch is a short, printed *carte*, not wholly representative of the variety offered at dinner; nevertheless it has produced some simple but good dishes. Reporters have endorsed open lasagne of scallops and langoustine with sun-dried tomatoes and vermouth butter sauce, and breast of chicken with peppers and salsa verde. Finish with hot raspberry soufflé with cinnamon essence and lime sorbet, or a plate of Scottish cheeses. 'Shambolic' service has let the side down badly on a couple of occasions, making a mockery of the kitchen's efforts, though at its best it has been 'courteous and efficient'. Wine service has also come in for some criticism, but the list continues to offer venerable bottles from the classic regions of France, a reasonable choice for fans of Germany, and some select bins from the New World. House Rioja, white and red, is £14.50. CELLARMAN'S CHOICE: Chablis premier cru 'Côte de Lêchet' 1994, Daniel Defaix, £38.50; Vosne-Romanée 1995, J Faiveley, £45.

CHEF: Kieran Darnell   PROPRIETOR: Wren Hotel Group   OPEN: all week 12.30 to 2.30, 7 to 9.45 MEALS: Set L Sun £16.50, Set D £32.50   SERVICE: not inc, card slips closed   CARDS: Amex, Delta, Diners, MasterCard, Switch, Visa   DETAILS: 70 seats. Private parties: 70 main room, 24 private rooms. Car park. Vegetarian meals. Children's helpings. No children under 10. Jacket and tie. No smoking in dining-room. Wheelchair access (also WC). Occasional music ACCOMMODATION: 15 rooms, all with bath/shower. TV. Phone. B&D £120 to £250. Rooms for disabled. No children under 10. Dogs by prior arrangement. Afternoon teas (£5)

AULDEARN Highland   map 11

▲ *Boath House* ⁵✸   NEW ENTRY

Auldearn IV12 5LE
TEL: (01667) 454896   FAX: (01667) 455469   COOKING 5
on A96, 2m E of Nairn   COST £29–£56

Rescued from neglect and refurbished over the past five years, this elegant, early nineteenth-century Regency-style house of pink granite, with an imposing pillared entrance, stands in 20 acres just outside Nairn. Rooms are spacious, windows tall, and much of the art is for sale. A log fire burns in the lounge, and the oval-shaped dining-room, candlelit for dinner, overlooks a man-made loch. The food is distinguished by freshness, accurate timing and 'complementary textures and flavours', or so an inspector felt after eating a dinner of fillet of turbot on a 'disc of perfect risotto' made with rich fish and shellfish stock, with half a dozen shelled Skye langoustines in a puddle of lightly truffled cream sauce to one side.

Charles Lockley's contemporary approach is labour-intensive, producing, for example, a sausage of halibut studded with chunks of 'sweet, juicy' scallop on a mound of leaves, with drizzles of basil and shellfish oil. Home-made pasta, meanwhile, has taken the form of tortellini filled with a 'pleasantly sharp' goats' cheese in a light, frothy, asparagus-flavoured bouillon. Success is helped by vegetables and herbs from the kitchen garden, and by home-made breads, and top-notch appetisers and petits fours.

Cheese consists of 'three generous wedges' from the list on offer, served with hefty triangles of crumbly oatcake, while desserts have included creamy, custardy, raspberry-flavoured crème brûlée with a thin, crisp topping, and more 'spectacular and substantial' sweets such as a 'richly flavoured' caramel banana torte with banana ice-cream and caramel sauce. A full house tests the organisation, but service is 'friendly and unobtrusive'. A wide-ranging wine list does well with the middle ground, and although it makes few concessions on price there is still acceptable drinking around £20. Six house wines start at £9.75.

CHEF: Charles Lockley   PROPRIETORS: Don and Wendy Matheson   OPEN: Wed to Sun D only 7 to 9 (L by arrangement)   MEALS: alc (main courses £12 to £20)   SERVICE: not inc   CARDS: Amex, Delta, Diners, MasterCard, Switch, Visa   DETAILS: 35 seats. Private parties: 40 main room, 8 and 27 private rooms. Car park. Vegetarian meals. Children's helpings. No smoking in dining-room. Wheelchair access (also WC). Music   ACCOMMODATION: 7 rooms, all with bath/shower. TV. Phone. B&B £45 to £120. Rooms for disabled. Children welcome. Baby facilities. Well-behaved dogs welcome by arrangement. Fishing   (£5)

AYR South Ayrshire map 11

Fouter's Bistro

2A Academy Street, Ayr KA7 1HS   COOKING 2
TEL: (01292) 261391   FAX: (01292) 619323   COST £20–£48

Trees and baskets of fruit are stencilled on to the white walls of this basement bistro, where the chargrill is applied generously: to sardines as a starter, tuna as a main course, and to ribeye, sirloin and fillet steaks, offered with a garlic or cream sauce for a small supplement. Simplicity is the key, producing anything from an old-fashioned prawn cocktail, to baked cod, to duck confit. A strong Scottish theme underscores the operation, yielding Ayrshire pigeon salad, Carrick wild venison with a burgundy and chocolate sauce, and Cloutie dumpling. A quartet of Swiss wines adds interest to a rather conservative list that starts with house French at £12.50.

CHEF: Laurie Black   PROPRIETORS: Laurie and Fran Black   OPEN: Tue to Sat 12 to 1.50, 6.30 to 10   CLOSED: 25 to 27 Dec, 1 to 3 Jan   MEALS: alc (main courses L £5 to £9, D £9 to £15.50). Set D £12.50 (2 courses) to £25   SERVICE: not inc   CARDS: Amex, Diners, MasterCard, Switch, Visa   DETAILS: 38 seats. Private parties: 30 main room, 14 private room. Children's helpings. No pipes in dining-room. Music. Air-conditioned   (£5)

BALLATER Aberdeenshire map 11

▲ *Darroch Learg* ♈ ⁵✳

Braemar Road, Ballater AB35 5UX   COOKING 6
TEL: (01339) 755443   FAX: (01339) 755252   COST £23–£41

An hour's drive west of Aberdeen, this 'Victorian pile' stands on a wooded hillside overlooking the golf course and River Dee. It is a comfortable but informal country-house hotel whose guests generally come to walk, fish, play golf, and visit castles and distillieres; or to eat. The dining-room opens out into a light, airy conservatory, candlelit at dinner, with well-spread tables, and David Mutter's contemporary strand of cooking does justice to many native ingredients on his daily- and monthly-changing menus. Salmon, for example, is home-smoked, and has been expertly partnered with 'perfectly cooked' seared scallops, with an intense but balancing vinaigrette. Accurate timing has also been applied to fillet of beef with 'real flavour', topped with a sticky confit of oxtail, served with a rich sauce of red wine and meat juices.

More exotic flavours are put to good use too, in starters of roast monkfish with avocado salsa and a saffron crab velouté, or salad of partridge breast with mango coulis that served its 'light and appetite-promoting' purpose. The kitchen's versatility allows it to deal with the sunny side of things – halibut and scallops with ratatouille and antiboise sauce – alongside slightly earthier ones such as breast of Gressingham duck with home-made boudin and truffle cream. To finish, iced aniseed soufflé has been served with chocolate and a summer berry compote, and one visitor raved about his lemon tart with light pastry, 'intensely sharp' lemon cream, and 'crisp, caramelised' topping. Families are welcomed and get a good deal.

The 34-page globe-trotting wine list makes almost as good reading as drinking, with intelligent notes describing the style of a wine, introducing the producer, suggesting food matches and highlighting alternative whites for members of the Anything But Chardonnay club. House wines start at £13.30 and 12 wines are available by the glass from £3. CELLARMAN'S CHOICE: Chablis 'Les Vaillons' 1992, Bernard Defaix, £25.40; Pelago 1994, Umani Ronchi, £22.

CHEF: David Mutter   PROPRIETORS: Nigel and Fiona Franks   OPEN: all week 12.30 to 2, 7 to 8.30 (9 Fri and Sat)   CLOSED: Christmas, 10 to 31 Jan   MEALS: alc L (main courses £5.50 to £16). Set L Sun £16.50, Set D £27.50   SERVICE: net prices, card slips closed   CARDS: Amex, Delta, Diners, MasterCard, Switch, Visa   DETAILS: 48 seats. Private parties: 48 main room. Car park. Vegetarian meals. Children's helpings. No smoking in dining-room. Wheelchair access (2 steps; not WC). No music   ACCOMMODATION: 18 rooms, all with bath/shower. TV. Phone. D,B&B £64 to £82. Rooms for disabled. Children welcome. High teas for children. Dogs welcome in bedrooms only. Afternoon teas (The Which? Hotel Guide)   £5

▲ Green Inn ♀

9 Victoria Road, Ballater AB35 5QQ
TEL/FAX: (01339) 755701   COOKING 6
EMAIL: royal_deeside@compuserve.com   COST £22–£42

A terraced granite house facing Ballater's village green 'gives the impression that it has always been cared for', according to one correspondent, and that is certainly true of the time during which the Purveses have owned it. Although not very large, the dining-room is arranged with a respectable amount of space between tables, and the furnishings are comfortable without being lavish.

Jeff Purves is scrupulous about the origins of his raw materials, taking environmental concerns very seriously, and according flavour paramount importance in his cooking. Off-beat accompaniments are used in counterpoint to the central elements in dishes: foie gras and chicken liver parfait, for example, comes with haricot beans and sultanas, and a mushroom tart is garnished with apricot chutney. More daring combinations, such as smoked haddock and Parma ham, may occasionally miss the mark, but on the whole reporters are full of praise. A 'sumptuous' starter of terrine of sea bass and John Dory with saffron oil may be followed by beef fillet with garlic purée on a parsley cream sauce. Steamed black treacle pudding with custard makes a very British way to finish; more unusual choices might include 'subtle' iced basil soufflé with sharply flavoured pear purée. Carol Purves serves with attentive professionalism.

Wine selections from each region are small but perfectly formed, and prices are fair. Austria's Willi Opitz makes a welcome appearance this year, contributing to both the main list and dessert section; indeed, fans of luscious stickies are well looked after. House wines are £10.45. CELLARMAN'S CHOICE: Gewurztraminer d'Alsace *grand cru* Speigel 1991, Dom. Eugene Meyer, £20.25; Regnié, Dom. des Buyats 1996, £12.25.

CHEF: Jeffrey Purves PROPRIETORS: Jeffrey and Carol Purves OPEN: Sun L 12.30 to 1.45, all week D 7 to 9 (closed Sun Oct to Mar) CLOSED: 21 to 27 Dec, 2 weeks Oct MEALS: Set L £10.25 (2 courses) to £13.50, Set D £21 (2 courses) to £25 SERVICE: not inc CARDS: MasterCard, Switch, Visa DETAILS: 32 seats. Private parties: 32 main room. Car park. Vegetarian meals. Children's helpings. No smoking while others eat. Wheelchair access (not WC). Music. Air-conditioned ACCOMMODATION: 3 rooms, all with bath/shower. TV. D,B&B £64 to £108. Children welcome. High teas for children. Baby facilities. Dogs welcome £5

BALQUHIDDER Stirling   map 11

▲ *Monachyle Mhor* £✕

Balquhidder FK19 8PQ   COOKING 2
TEL: (01877) 384622 FAX: (01877) 384305   COST £24–£45

This is a working farm on a 2,000-acre estate, complete with grouse moor, deerstalking, and salmon and trout fishing. There are scenic walks, a couple of lochs to gaze at, plenty of wildlife, and self-catering cottages, although Tom Lewis's cooking is enough to knock the last one on the head for most visitors. He swears by local materials and takes a gentle Franco-Scottish approach, particularly with seafood, serving seared Mallaig scallops with samphire and a lemon and dill hollandaise, for instance, or baked Tay salmon with a tarragon and lemon butter. Roasted pearl barley and Balquhidder ceps give the 'poacher's game bag' (rabbit and pigeon perhaps) a regional tag, but Tom Lewis is happy to straddle culinary boundaries, serving guinea-fowl with clapshot and a mild curry sauce, or lambs' sweetbreads with garam masala and courgette noodles. Fair prices and reliable producers characterise the wine list, which offers three or four house wines below £10.

CHEF: Tom Lewis PROPRIETORS: Robert and Jean Lewis, and Tom Lewis OPEN: all week 12 to 2, 7 to 9 CLOSED: last 2 weeks Jan MEALS: alc L (main courses £8 to £13.50). Set L £17.50 to £19.50, Set D £21 to £25 SERVICE: not inc, card slips closed CARDS: MasterCard, Switch, Visa DETAILS: 34 seats. 20 seats outside. Private parties: 34 main room. Car park. Vegetarian meals. No children under 12. No smoking in dining-room. Wheelchair access (also WC). No music. Air-conditioned ACCOMMODATION: 10 rooms, all with bath/shower. Phone. B&B £48 to £84. No children under 12. Afternoon teas. Fishing (*The Which? Hotel Guide*)

The Guide *is totally independent, accepts no free hospitality, and survives on the number of copies sold each year.*

Restaurateurs justifiably resent no-shows. If you quote a credit card number when booking, you may be liable for the restaurant's lost profit margin if you don't turn up. Always phone to cancel.

▲ *Kinloch House* ♥ ⅗✻

by Blairgowrie PH10 6SG
TEL: (01250) 884237   FAX: (01250) 884333
EMAIL: kinlochhouse@compuserve.com   COOKING 4
on A923, 3m W of Blairgowrie towards Dunkeld   COST £22–£61

Log fires and oak panelling are part of the abiding 'Scottish bourgeois' impression left by this stone-built 1840s house, and a high standard of housekeeping, combined with a degree of formality, suggest that Victorian values have never really deserted it. Kinloch is rightly proud of its materials: Aberdeen Angus beef, free-range eggs, wild fish, shellfish and game, and vegetables from its own renovated walled garden. Everything that can be made in-house, they reckon, is: sausages, bread, jams and marmalade, pickles and chutneys, terrines and pasta.

Dinner is the main business, and there are several add-ons to the basic menu, which typically takes in salmon marinated in brown sugar, honey and whisky, Angus sirloin steak, and Kyle of Lochalsh scallops. For anybody who feels this is not already Scottish enough, a separate 'Scottish menu' offers perhaps black pudding, Arbroath smokies or roast leg of lamb. Fillet steak, lobster and a few other items attract a price supplement, and vegetarians get their own menu, which might offer spinach and cheese soufflé, or a stir-fried noodle dish. To finish, a savoury is usually available as an alternative to lemon mousse or a more elaborate pancake filled with Drambuie soufflé and served with raspberry cranachan and hot chocolate sauce. A good spread of claret vintages reaching back to 1961 catches the eye in a wine list that is strongest in France, but the New World range also has some attention-seeking bins. Half-bottles are generous in number and 11 house wines start at £12.20.

CHEF: Bill McNicoll   PROPRIETORS: David and Sarah Shentall   OPEN: Sun L 12.30 to 2, all week D 7 to 9.15   CLOSED: Christmas   MEALS: Set L Sun £15.95, Set D £29.90. Bar L available Mon to Sat   SERVICE: net prices, card slips closed   CARDS: Amex, Delta, Diners, MasterCard, Switch, Visa   DETAILS: 50 seats. Private parties: 14 main room, 20 private room. Car park. Vegetarian meals. Children's helpings. No children under 7 at D. Jacket and tie. No smoking in dining-room. Wheelchair access (not WC). No music   ACCOMMODATION: 21 rooms, all with bath/shower. TV. Phone. D,B&B £89 to £189. Rooms for disabled. Children welcome. High teas for children. Baby facilities. Dogs welcome in bedrooms only. Afternoon teas. Swimming-pool. Fishing (*The Which? Hotel Guide*)

▲ *Harbour Inn* £

The Square, Bowmore PA43 7JR   COOKING 2
TEL: (01496) 810330   FAX: (01496) 810990   COST £16–£53

Visitors who come to Islay for the whisky will find every distillery on the island represented here, at what is essentially a pub with a nautically themed bar, and a 'suburban semi' dining-room with big windows at the back. Scott Chance's local supplies run to game birds, venison, rabbit, hare, and shellfish by the bucket load, including Gruinart oysters and Lagavulin scallops. Some old-fashioned dishes (gammon steak with pineapple) lurk among the stir-fried monkfish, ragoût of Jura venison, and pork fillet in cider sauce, but that hardly matters when the kitchen can turn out a 'pink and juicy' sirloin steak with green peppercorn sauce, accompanied by impressive vegetables. Puddings range from apple and calvados syllabub to steamed chocolate sponge, service is 'matter of fact', and wines are sympathetically priced, starting with house French at £8.90.

CHEF: Scott Chance   PROPRIETORS: Scott and Wendy Chance   OPEN: Mon to Sat L 12 to 2.30, all week D 6 to 9   CLOSED: 25 Dec, 1 Jan   MEALS: alc (main courses L £5 to £12, D £6 to £21). Bar meals. BYO £3   SERVICE: not inc   CARDS: Amex, Delta, MasterCard, Visa   DETAILS: 44 seats. Private parties: 40 main room. Vegetarian meals. Children's helpings. Wheelchair access (also men's WC). No music   ACCOMMODATION: 4 rooms, all with bath/shower. TV. Phone. B&B £32.50 to £55. Children welcome. Baby facilities. Dogs welcome. Afternoon teas   (£5)

CAIRNDOW Argyll & Bute   map 11

Loch Fyne Oyster Bar ⅙✱ £

Clachan Farm, Cairndow PA26 8BH
TEL: (01499) 600264   FAX: (01499) 600234   COOKING 3
on A83, at head of Loch Fyne   COST £21–£46

Despite its large size, this 'seafood brasserie' has a friendly feel to it. Staff radiate a 'sense of community' and look as if they care about what they do, which makes an impression on visitors. 'I would go out of my way to visit again,' professed one, which is just as well because most people have to. The low, whitewashed barn is at the head of a sea loch which is the source of much that appears on the table. The aim is to serve fish and shellfish, not least their own oysters, 'all through the day to all comers at reasonable prices', and is carried out with a commendable eye on the sustainability of resources.

The emphasis may be on simple and uncluttered cooking, but that doesn't prevent Morag Keith from serving six oysters baked with spinach and Mornay sauce, or six roasted queen scallops with bacon. But it does mean that those who wish to can opt for unadorned cold oysters of undisputed freshness, plainly served smoked salmon from the smokehouse at the back, or the increasingly well-travelled hot-smoked salmon (bradan rost) served either hot or cold with horseradish. One who sampled such a selection declared, 'I have never had better'. Of the two dozen wines, a quarter are available by the glass, including house white (£2.28, or £8.95 the bottle).

CHEF: Morag Keith   PROPRIETORS: John Noble and Andrew Lane   OPEN: all week 9 to 9 (9 to 6 Nov to end Mar)   CLOSED: 25 Dec and 1 Jan   MEALS: alc (main courses £5 to £8.50)   SERVICE: not inc, card slips closed   CARDS: Delta, Diners, MasterCard, Switch, Visa   DETAILS: 80 seats. Private parties: 45 main room, 45 private room. Car park. Vegetarian meals. Children's helpings. No smoking in 1 dining-room. Wheelchair access (also WC). Music   (£5)

£ *means that it is possible to have a three-course meal, including coffee, half a bottle of house wine and service for £25 or less per person, at any time the restaurant is open, i.e. at dinner as well as lunch. It may be possible to spend considerably more than this, but by choosing carefully you should find £25 or less achievable.*

CANONBIE Dumfries & Galloway	map 11

▲ *Riverside Inn* ▼ ⁵⭒ £

Canonbie DG14 0UX	
TEL: (013873) 71295 and 71512	COOKING 1
off A7, just over the border	COST £18–£32

'More classy than the usual village pub', this well-kept seventeenth-century inn, in a peaceful village just north of the border, has an air of 'bourgeois comfort'. It is run with care, and food is served in both the convivial bar and in the conventionally decorated dining-room, whose menu overlaps with the former's blackboard listings. Seen as pub food, it is impressive. Fine raw materials are simply treated to produce 'honest and straightforward' dishes that don't make too many demands on the kitchen: pea soup, a halved nectarine stuffed with cream cheese and covered with curry sauce, or 'wholesome' pigeon terrine. Main courses of duck confit, or pink chargrilled ribeye of beef, are served with roast potatoes and fresh crisp salads. Finish perhaps with coeur à la crème or a 'rough and ready' rhubarb crumble. North Yorkshire merchants Playford Ros now supply a favourably priced worldly bunch of wines from some good producers: Cline in California, Dampt in Chablis, for example. House wines are £9.50. CELLARMAN'S CHOICE: Cape Mentelle Semillon/Sauvignon 1996, Margaret River, W. Australia, £14.45; Brouilly, Ch. de Prieuré 1996, Piron, £14.65.

CHEFS/PROPRIETORS: Robert and Susan Phillips   OPEN: Sun L 12 to 2, Wed to Sat D 7.30 to 8.30   CLOSED: 25 and 26 Dec, 1 and 2 Jan, Feb   MEALS: Set L Sun £11.95, Set D £19.50. BYO £5. Bar food available   SERVICE: not inc   CARDS: Delta, MasterCard, Switch, Visa   DETAILS: 36 seats. 16 seats outside. Private parties: 30 main room. Car park. Vegetarian meals. Children's helpings. No smoking in dining-room. No music   ACCOMMODATION: 7 rooms, all with bath/shower. TV. B&B £55 to £90. No children under 5. Dogs by arrangement

CLYDEBANK Dumbarton & Clydebank	map 11

▲ *Beardmore Hotel, Citrus* ⁵⭒ | **NEW ENTRY** |

Beardmore Street, Clydebank G81 4SA	COOKING 5
TEL: (0141) 951 6000 FAX: (0141) 951 6018	COST £26–£39

Despite its 'international hotel ambience', this revamp at the Beardmore (the restaurant used to be called 'Symphony') now feels as if it belongs to Glasgow. Vast windows in the huge lounge overlook the Clyde, bold modern artwork decorates the walls, glass screens separate tables, and a lime-green and orange colour scheme (no prizes for guessing where that comes from) give it a fresh tone. It is relaxed and characterful, with low-key but highly efficient service, and Mark Knowles's 'precise cooking' has a bright edge to it without recourse to exotic flavours: mushroom pithiviers with celeriac cream and parsley oil, for example, and seared tuna with couscous and ratatouille.

If fixed-price meals are comparatively short on choice, vegetarian options are more than merely token offerings, and the *carte* is generous. Dishes are more than just good-looking: a terrine of leeks, morels and brioche, arranged in an eye-catching zig-zag pattern, impressed for its delicacy and purity of flavour, while a cavernous bowl of rich, creamy, velvety Jerusalem artichoke soup came with the comfort of two softly poached quails' eggs. Of two main courses at inspection, the winner was a bumper portion of tender calf's liver piled into a pyramid over mashed potato, with lightly smokey pancetta, and a mound of onion in red wine.

Cheeses are in British vein – Lanark blue, or Quicke's cheddar – and desserts have included fig tart with ginger clotted cream, and a parfait of 'scrunchy fresh hazelnuts', cut into pyramidal slices and served with a light coffee-flavoured sauce, dredged with 'a cloudburst of cocoa powder and icing sugar'. Coffee could be improved, but 'no hidden extras' translates into good value for money, helped by a short but varied list of wines with eight available by the glass. House vin de pays is £12.50.

CHEF: Mark Knowles   PROPRIETOR: Beardmore Hotel Ltd   OPEN: Mon to Fri L 12 to 2, all week D 7 to 9.30   MEALS: Set L £12.50 (2 courses) to £15.50, Set D £20.50. Bar menu available   SERVICE: not inc, card slips closed   CARDS: Amex, Delta, Diners, MasterCard, Switch, Visa   DETAILS: 56 seats. 80 seats outside. Private parties: 130 main room, 2 to 130 private rooms. Car park. Vegetarian meals. Children's helpings. No smoking in dining-room. Wheelchair access (also WC). Music. Air-conditioned   ACCOMMODATION: 168 rooms, all with bath/shower. TV. Phone. B&B £103 to £126. Rooms for disabled. Children welcome. Baby facilities. Guide dogs only. Afternoon teas. Swimming-pool   (£5)

COLBOST Highland   map 11

Three Chimneys ▼ ⚟

Colbost, by Dunvegan, Isle of Skye IV55 8ZT
TEL: (01470) 511258   FAX: (01470) 511358   COOKING 4
on B884, 4m W of Dunvegan   COST £19–£64

An unassuming pair of crofters' cottages are the frame for Eddie and Shirley Spear's restaurant, which is next to the Colbost Folk Museum and five or so miles from Dunvegan Castle. The sense of days gone by is reinforced by the plough and churn that stand outside, and also by the exposed rough-hewn stone walls within, where a blackened kettle dangles over the open fire. Home-baking is a forte of Shirley's kitchen, not just of breads such as lemon and fennel or basil and Parmesan rolls, but for the likes of smoked haddock soufflé too. Presentation is kept plain, so that a dollop of thick grouse pâté is served on a wedge of potato-cake and garnished with leaves dressed in lemon oil. Seafood specialities, of which the Spears are justly proud, take in robustly textured partan bree, grilled lobster seasoned with vanilla, and a brochette of fine scallops and monkfish with multicoloured peppers, moist couscous and a creamy saffron sauce. Meats may include grilled loin of Highland lamb with roasted sweet-tasting root vegetables and a 'light, well-balanced' sauce of redcurrants and port. Spiced rhubarb crumble full of oats and hazelnuts is well counterpointed by cinnamon ice-cream, or there may be cranachan parfait with crushed raspberries or top-drawer Scottish cheeses. Eddie Spear genially presides front-of-house. Light savouries and teas are served in the afternoon and, as the *Guide* went to press, plans were afoot to introduce accommodation in spring 1999.

The food-friendly wine list offers a fine range of whites to complement the seafood and a good spread of claret and Riojas for a traditional match with the lamb. Plenty of bottles fall under the £20 price-point, with house wines starting at £11.25. Eight wines are offered by the glass from £2.25 to £5.25 for champagne. CELLARMAN'S CHOICE: Dry River Estate Sauvignon Blanc 1996, Martinborough, New Zealand, £22.95; Savigny-lès-Beaune 'Les Lavières' 1992, Lucien Camus-Bruchon £24.25.

CHEF: Shirley Spear   PROPRIETORS: Eddie and Shirley Spear   OPEN: Mon to Sat 12.30 to 2.30, 2.30 to 4.30, 7 to 9 (plus Sun D Easter and Whitsun)   CLOSED: Nov to Mar   MEALS: alc (main courses L £5.50 to £25, D £15.50 to £27.50). Set D £24.50   SERVICE: not inc   CARDS: Delta, MasterCard, Switch, Visa   DETAILS: 30 seats. 6 seats outside. Private parties: 16 main room, 16 private room. Car park. Vegetarian meals. Children welcome. No children under 8 at D. No smoking in dining-room. Wheelchair access (1 step; not WC). Music   £5

CUPAR Fife   map 11

Ostlers Close ▮

25 Bonnygate, Cupar KY15 4BU   COOKING 6
TEL: (01334) 655574   FAX: (01334) 654036   COST £24–£51

'The interesting thing,' write the Grahams, still on their long voyage of discovery, 'is that it hasn't become mundane after 17 years.' Supporters of their restaurant, in an old stone-built knock-through, might echo the sentiment, and people come from miles around to avail themselves of the experience. Many establishments in the *Guide* lay claim to the use of local supply-lines, but the Grahams have elevated this principle to a pitch of rare discrimination. Organic vegetables come from growers who cultivate to their strict specifications, free-range poultry is bred especially for them, and James Graham is an enthusiastic forager after wild mushrooms, resourcefully gathering some wild cicely instead if the fungi prove elusive.

All of this translates into the kind of cooking our reporters praise fulsomely. A small fillet of cod, 'its skin blackened to within a whisker of disaster, but the pearly-white flakes of flesh succulent', sitting on herb-flecked mash surrounded by tarragon-scented shellfish sauce, offers a superb combination of flavours. Otherwise, roasted monkfish might be adorned with a necklace of scallop slices, and sauced with a light champagne cream, and still a popular fixture on the menu is duck breast and confit leg served with Puy lentils in a rich stock reduction. The range and care exhibited in vegetable accompaniments is impressive. Desserts may be slightly less successful, but are not without interest: a Drambuie ice-cream is given granular texture with plenty of toasted oatmeal and garnished with orange. If a pudding feels like too much, then wait for coffee and petits fours, which are numerous and carefully made.

'Intelligently chatty' service is another asset, as is the globe-trotting wine list, which offers a good variety of grapes and styles at some friendly prices. Chilean house wines are £9.50 for Chardonnay, £10.50 for Cabernet Sauvignon. CELLARMAN'S CHOICE: Sancerre, Chavignol les Comtesse 1996, £15.95; Neil Ellis Pinotage 1995, Stellenbosch, South Africa, £13.50.

CHEF: James Graham PROPRIETORS: James and Amanda Graham OPEN: Tue to Sat 12.15 to 2, 7 to 9.30 CLOSED: 25 and 26 Dec, 1 Jan MEALS: alc (main courses L £9 to £13, D £15 to £18). BYO £5 SERVICE: not inc, card slips closed CARDS: Amex, Delta, MasterCard, Switch, Visa DETAILS: 28 seats. Private parties: 28 main room. Children's helpings. No children under 6 at D. No smoking while others eat. No music (£5)

DALRY North Ayrshire

map 11

Braidwoods ✦✱

Drumastle Mill Cottage, Dalry KA24 4LN
TEL: (01294) 833544 FAX: (01294) 833553
1m off A737 on Dalry to Saltcoats road

COOKING 5
COST £26–£49

Very much off the beaten track – in the middle of a field, in fact – Braidwoods is a converted mill cottage. The small, well-tended gardens make for an agreeably picturesque setting and, inside, the restaurant has a 'relaxed and intimate feel'. It charms because Keith Braidwood's cooking seems to transcend these domestic confines.

Local supplies are extensively employed: turbot and scallops from the Ayrshire catch, served with lentils and coriander sauce, or red deer fillet sauced with wild mushrooms and Madeira. Menu prices are fixed according to the number of courses, starting perhaps with pasta – smoked salmon and mascarpone ravioli with a tomato and basil vinaigrette – before an intermediate soup option such as chowder of Arbroath smokie with leeks and sweetcorn. Reporters have been as impressed by the 'consummate timing' in a main course of guinea-fowl breast on mushroom risotto with thyme, as by 'marvellously tender' Aberdeen beef fillet with caramelised shallots and well-reduced tarragon and mustard sauce. Pecan parfait with tayberry and raspberry coulis, 'old-fashioned' bread-and-butter pudding, and lushly textured crème brûlée with rhubarb are typically rich dessert options. The wine list is strong in France, but also contains some high-flying New World names, and offers good value for money. Prices start at £11.95.

CHEFS/PROPRIETORS: Keith and Nicola Braidwood OPEN: Wed to Sun L 12 to 1.45, Tue to Sat D 7 to 9 CLOSED: first week Oct, 25 Dec, first three weeks Jan, last week Sept MEALS: Set L £14 (2 courses) to £16, Set D £26 to £29. BYO £5 SERVICE: not inc, card slips closed CARDS: Amex, Delta, MasterCard, Switch, Visa DETAILS: 24 seats. Private parties: 16 main room. Car park. No children under 12 at D. No smoking in dining-room. No music

---

DERVAIG Argyll & Bute

map 11

▲ Druimard Country House ✦✱

Dervaig, Isle of Mull PA75 6QW
TEL/FAX: (01688) 400345

COOKING 4
COST £30–£46

This unpretentious and comfortable house, next door to Mull Little Theatre, is set high above a small loch. Allow time 'to gawp at the sea loch, the sunset, the wild geese, church tower' and whatever else catches the eye. Inside, floral patterns, bird prints and 'Victorian knick-knacks' predominate. Dinner is four courses (but coffee is included) and starts early when the theatre is playing.

There are two set menus: one with no choice before dessert; and one with choice, confusingly called an à la carte. Not that it matters much because 'guests are free to choose from either or both'.

A Franco-Scottish theme runs through the short repertoire, producing chicken liver parfait with cranberries and oatcakes, and seared scallops with aubergine crisps. Native materials include Aberdeen Angus flamed in whisky (for a small supplement), and locally landed fish such as halibut, perhaps served with a bouillabaisse sauce. Mull lobster (subject to availability) also carries a supplement, requires 24 to 48 hours' notice, and might be served with a simple herb butter sauce.

Wendy Hubbard goes to town on presentation, strewing chervil flowers and diamonds of red and yellow pepper around a plate of mushrooms in filo, for example, and turns out a 'seductive' range of desserts, from chocolate truffle terrine, via fresh fruit fool, to sticky gingerbread pudding. Some three dozen wines hold few surprises, other than their reasonable pricing, starting with house Côtes de Duras at £8.95.

CHEF: Wendy Hubbard PROPRIETORS: Haydn and Wendy Hubbard OPEN: Mon to Sat D only 7 to 8.30 (Sun D residents only) CLOSED: Nov to Mar MEALS: Set D £22.50 SERVICE: not inc CARDS: MasterCard, Visa DETAILS: 28 seats. Private parties: 20 main room. Car park. Vegetarian meals. Children's helpings. No smoking in dining-room. Music ACCOMMODATION: 6 rooms, all with bath/shower. TV. Phone. D,B&B £69.50 to £139. Children welcome (*The Which? Hotel Guide*)

DORNOCH Highland　　　　　　　　　　　　　　　　　　　　map 11

▲ *Quail Restaurant* ✸　　　　　　　　　　| NEW ENTRY |

Castle Street, Dornoch IV25 3SN　　　　　　　　　　　　　　COOKING 4
TEL: (01862) 811811　　　　　　　　　　　　　　　　　　　COST £30–£36

Michael and Kerensa Carr proved themselves adept at running a popular small restaurant when they had Courtney's in Newcastle, a stalwart of previous editions of the *Guide*. This one is even smaller, two compact dining-rooms in a three-storey town house of Sutherland stone. Nearby is a championship golf course, some truly dramatic coastline and a ruined castle, so you won't be short of things to do beforehand. Dinner only is the drill, the menu a fixed-price format for three courses, with a choice of three items at each stage.

Before the main business comes a 'chef's surprise': perhaps an op art coffee cup containing pungent smoked duck soup, 'an excellent, unexpected treat' for one reporter. Simplicity is clearly considered a virtue: starters might include pork rillettes with thyme and garlic, asparagus with truffle oil and Parmesan, or 'palate-awakening' king prawns with 'vibrant' Thai flavourings. Main courses are served with gutsy accompaniments: chargrilled salmon has sundried tomatoes, black olives and pesto, while roast loin of spring lamb and vegetables comes with a rich thyme gravy. A ten-minute wait has proved more than worthwhile for 'moist yet flakily crisp' apple and blackberry strudel with 'creamy, smooth' honey ice-cream. Kerensa Carr runs front-of-house with eager politeness. The wine list is full of bright ideas and plenty of half-bottles, although reds are heavily weighted to Bordeaux. House Vin de Pays d'Oc is £9.50.

CHEF: Michael Carr   PROPRIETORS: Michael and Kerensa Carr   OPEN: Tue to Sat D only 7.30 to 9.30 (restricted opening in winter)   MEALS: Set D £22.50   SERVICE: not inc   CARDS: Amex, Delta, MasterCard, Switch, Visa   DETAILS: 20 seats. Private parties: 8 main room, 10 private room. Car park. Vegetarian meals. Children welcome. No smoking in dining-room. Music   ACCOMMODATION: 3 rooms, all with bath/shower. TV. B&B from £25 per person. No children under 10   (£5)

DRYBRIDGE Moray   map 11

Old Monastery £✳

Drybridge AB56 5JB
TEL/FAX: (01542) 832660
2½m S of Buckie, just over 2m S of junction of A98 and   COOKING 3
A942   COST £25–£54

This former holiday retreat for Benedictine monks still has an ecclesiastical feel to it, picked up by windows, chair backs, and heavy tapestry in the inner sanctum of the high-vaulted dining-room. Douglas Gray takes a commendably simple approach, using good stock for French onion soup, making game terrine, and roasting vegetables to fill a filo pastry tartlet. He doesn't aim to break any moulds, but uses native produce in familiar ways – Aberdeen Angus sirloin steak topped with Stilton, or Scottish salmon with lemon butter sauce – and finishes with rich chocolate tart, or raspberry ripple cheesecake. The wine list's careful choices (including 20 half-bottles) are matched by fair prices, starting below £12.

CHEF: Douglas Gray   PROPRIETORS: Maureen and Douglas Gray   OPEN: Tue to Sat 12 to 1.30 (1 Sat), 7 to 9 (Sat 9.30)   CLOSED: 25 and 26 Dec, 31 Dec, 1 Jan   MEALS: alc (main courses £7.50 to £20)   SERVICE: not inc, card slips closed   CARDS: Amex, MasterCard, Switch, Visa   DETAILS: 45 seats. Private parties: 45 main room. Car park. Children's helpings. No children under 8. No smoking in dining-room. No music

---

DUMFRIES Dumfries & Galloway   map 11

Wisharts

NEW ENTRY

Robert Burns Centre, Mill Road,
Dumfries DG2 7BE   COOKING 6
TEL: (01387) 259679   COST £20–£41

In the centre of town, the broad River Nith tumbles over a weir that once upon a time directed its waters to a brick-built mill. That mill is now the Robert Burns Centre (he lived, wrote and died in Dumfries), containing a museum, a film theatre and Wisharts, owned and run by two brothers. Chef Mark, the younger, appeared in last year's *Guide* at Marco Pierre White's Les Saveurs (see entry, London), so is no stranger to classy cooking. Their theatre of operations is an L-shaped room with red and green walls, paintings for sale, ornate candle-holders, and a view of the kitchen. The overall impression is 'that a limited budget has been sensibly deployed to redecorate the former café tastefully, but not lavishly'.

Efforts are concentrated on just three dishes per course, another shrewd move, and the food is thoughtful, skilful, and plated up simply but attractively. A debt to contemporary French classics is evident too. Everyone who works for Marco learns to turn out a test-piece foie gras parfait, this one served with a mild pear and raisin chutney. In another first course, sliced scallops are laid on a fine carrot and leek julienne in a shell, covered with flaky pastry and baked; the top is pierced at table and beurre blanc poured in. Simple or complex, it doesn't seem to matter, the food all works, as in a postcard-sized fillet of cod on a bed of Savoy cabbage, with dark earthy-flavoured Puy lentils scattered about, and fruity olive oil mash.

It may look easy, but high-quality ingredients and judicious flavour combinations have produced an 'exemplary' dish of alternating layers of stewed rhubarb and vanilla-flecked custard in a large wine glass, set off by a hint of ginger, and a topping of orange juice frozen into granita-like crystals: a dish 'for grown-ups'. Service is enthusiastic and well informed, and a handful of the 30 fairly priced wines escape from France to go on a brief world tour. House vin de table is £8.75.

CHEF: Mark Wishart   PROPRIETORS: Mark and Ian Wishart   OPEN: Tue to Sun 12.30 to 2.30, 7 to 10   CLOSED: 25 and 26 Dec, 1 Jan   MEALS: alc (main courses L £6 to £8, D £11.50 to £14.50) SERVICE: not inc, card slips closed   CARDS: Delta, Diners, MasterCard, Switch, Visa   DETAILS: 42 seats. 20 seats outside. Private parties: 42 main room. Car park. Children's helpings. No smoking before main course. No music

---

DUNKELD Perthshire & Kinross   map 11

▲ *Kinnaird*

Kinnaird Estate, Dunkeld PH8 0LB
TEL: (01796) 482440   FAX: (01796) 482289
from A9 2m N of Dunkeld, take B898, signposted   COOKING 5
Kinnaird, for 4½m   COST £37–£70

Kinnaird is very grand indeed, with a 9,000-acre estate around it, and large well-proportioned rooms, including a dining-room with Louis XIV aspirations. Trevor Brooks may be familiar to *Guide* readers from his days at the Table in Babbacombe near Torquay (see entry), and although the scale of things here is much bigger, his menu remains a manageable size: enough to provide variety, but no more than four or five items per course. He has easy access to Highland material, enabling him to produce galantine of wild salmon, ravioli of Loch Linnhe prawns in a concentrated asparagus soup, and rack of Perthshire lamb. 'Simple dishes, well-crafted and with good sauces,' is one summary of the result.

'Our meat is normally served underdone,' says the menu, although sadly it wasn't when our inspector visited. Fish was much better, including scallops that were 'sweet and succulent with a wonderful soft centre', combined with dill-fringed smoked salmon and assorted dressed leaves. Main courses – sea bass with a confit of cherry tomatoes in good olive oil, for example – are followed by 'an intimidatingly large' plate of British cheeses, and a dessert such as lemon tart with braised plum, a hot soufflé, or roast peppered pineapple. Ladies can wear what they like, but gentlemen are required to wear jacket and tie. The pace of meals, however, is more relaxed.

Wines (and prices) are as grand as their surroundings: those wishing to spend under £20 should look to French country wines or to Chile. Otherwise, you will see clarets dating back to 1961, mature burgundies and some classy Rhônes matched by some stellar productions from the New World. An abundance of half-bottles includes some luscious dessert wines. CELLARMAN'S CHOICE: Rongopai Chardonnay 1995, Waikato, New Zealand, £26; Bonny Doon Clos de Gilroy Grenache 1996, Santa Cruz, California, £24.

CHEF: Trevor Brooks   PROPRIETOR: Constance Ward   OPEN: all week 12 to 1.45, 7.15 to 9.30 CLOSED: Mon to Wed in Jan and Feb   MEALS: Set L £22.50 (2 courses) to £26, Set D £45. SERVICE: not inc, card slips closed   CARDS: Amex, Delta, MasterCard, Switch, Visa   DETAILS: 35 seats. Private parties: 35 main room, 20 private room. Car park. Vegetarian meals. No children under 12. Jacket and tie. No smoking in dining-room. Wheelchair access (also WC). No music   ACCOMMODATION: 9 rooms, all with bath/shower. TV. Phone. B&B £210 to £315. Rooms for disabled. No children under 12. Dogs welcome in kennels by arrangement. Afternoon teas. Fishing

---

DUNVEGAN Highland   map 11

▲ *Harlosh House* ⚡✳

Dunvegan, Isle of Skye IV55 8ZG
TEL/FAX: (01470) 521367
EMAIL: harlosh.house@virgin.net   COOKING 4
off A863, 3m S of Dunvegan   COST £36–£43

The remote, eighteenth-century croft-like tackman's house faces Loch Bracadale, with the Cuillin Hills beyond: a telescope in the lounge can be trained on otters, eagles and seals. It is more of a restaurant-with-rooms than a hotel, and Peter Elford now manages the place single-handedly; since he spends much of his time in the kitchen it is left to 'willing and friendly locals' to look after front of house. The emphasis is on fish and shellfish, and the pattern is four courses, the second a soup, with no choice before dessert.

'Mr Elford barely cooks his fish, so it tastes fresh and moist and full of flavour,' enthused a visitor who enjoyed roast monkfish with coriander sauce. An Eastern note has also cropped up in crab and coriander kedgeree in a coconut and tomato sauce, and grilled scallops served with spring onions, pickled ginger and thin white noodles. Soups are typically vegetable-based: pea, lettuce and mint maybe, or a 'smooth, intensely flavoured' watercress soup that proved 'an excellent example of its genre'. Finish, perhaps, with hazelnut and praline parfait, or date pudding with caramel sauce and crème anglaise. Breads, soups, desserts and chocolates are made in-house. Wines are understandably skewed towards whites, with a good variety of flavour options, and prices are fair, starting with house South African at £10.20.

CHEF/PROPRIETOR: Peter Elford   OPEN: all week D only 7 to 8.30   CLOSED: end Oct to Easter MEALS: Set D £25. BYO £6   SERVICE: not inc, card slips closed   CARDS: MasterCard, Switch, Visa   DETAILS: 16 seats. Private parties: 4 main room. Car park. Children's helpings. No children under 7. No smoking in dining-room. Music   ACCOMMODATION: 6 rooms, all with bath/shower. D,B&B £92.50 to £145. Children welcome. High teas for children. Baby facilities. No dogs. Afternoon teas (*The Which? Hotel Guide*) (£5)

Atrium ▼

10 Cambridge Street, Edinburgh EH1 2ED	NEW CHEF
TEL: (0131) 228 8882 FAX: (0131) 228 8808	COST £24–£39

On the ground floor of the Traverse Theatre complex, Atrium attracts a smart crowd. 'There's a sense of importance about the place, as though everyone is rather impressed with themselves for being there.' Perhaps that also applies to Alan Mathieson and David Ward, who arrived just as the *Guide* went to press, after having worked in some highly regarded kitchens. The food up to now has been as modern as food gets, with fish and vegetable dishes to the fore, a bit of game from time to time, and ingredients from here there and everywhere, all put together with the help of chilli oil, coriander, Chinese spices and the like. The unhurried pace of service is helped by friendly staff. On the floor above, the cosmopolitan Blue Bar Café (under the same ownership) serves a limited menu of uncomplicated and less-expensive dishes. A dozen sherries offered by the glass provide an appealing curtain-raiser to a wide-ranging collection of wines that is every bit as cosmopolitan as the Atrium's theatre-going clientele. The Old World tends to hold centre-stage, but New World selections make a fair bid for their share of the limelight. House French is £10.50. CELLARMAN'S CHOICE: Mitchelton Blackwood Park Riesling 1995, Victoria, Australia, £17.50; Neil Ellis Jonkershoek Valley Pinotage 1996, Stellenbosch, South Africa, £17.50.

CHEFS: Alan Mathieson and David Ward PROPRIETORS: Andrew and Lisa Radford OPEN: Mon to Sat 12 to 2.30, 6 to 10.30 (11 during Festival) CLOSED: 1 week Christmas and New Year MEALS: alc (main courses L £7.50 to £9.50, D £12.50 to £18.50). Light L available SERVICE: not inc CARDS: Amex, Delta, Diners, MasterCard, Switch, Visa DETAILS: 70 seats. Private parties: 100 main room. Vegetarian meals. Children's helpings. Wheelchair access (also WC). No music. Air-conditioned

▲ *Balmoral, Number One*

	NEW ENTRY
Princes Street, Edinburgh EH2 2EQ	COOKING 6
TEL: (0131) 557 6727 FAX: (0131) 557 8740	COST £34–£86

Bought by Sir Rocco Forte in summer 1997, Balmoral has taken a turn for the better, thanks to the arrival of Jeff Bland, who has cooked in some impressive kitchens, most recently at Cameron House Hotel in Alexandria (see entry). Described variously as 'fifties chic' and 'Eastern-inspired', the interior houses a bar 'awash with cocktails', and a dining-room with tables pressed against banquette seats. The food may seem 'hugely expensive', but then it uses hugely

If a restaurant is new to the Guide *this year (did not appear as a main entry in the last edition),* NEW ENTRY *appears opposite its name.*

NEW CHEF *is shown instead of a cooking mark where a change of chef occurred too late for a new assessment of the cooking.*

expensive materials, and does them justice. Menus combine variety and interest in several formats: a set-price 'Market' version with a couple of items per course; a more generously endowed *carte*; and a similar 'Classic' menu, which keeps its promise with duck foie gras on toasted brioche, grilled Dover sole with parsley sauce, and butterscotch tart.

Presentation – a strong card – adds interest to dishes that are as carefully constructed as they are simple: 'rich, creamy, densely flavoured' foie gras terrine with truffle jus, served on discs of crispy sauté potatoes and pancetta, or a dish of caramelised scallops, set on a leek timbale whose flavour matched the shellfish 'brilliantly', spiked with sauce vierge and topped with caviare. An indication of the modern spin put on classical ideas comes with osso buco, the meat layered on potatoes and morels, topped with veal sweetbreads, and sauced with a stock and Madeira reduction. 'Beautifully caramelised' pear tart, and rich, well-flavoured banana soufflé have both been served with improvable ice-creams, and in our inspector's view some of the saucing and pastrywork might also benefit from more attention, but his meal still left a strongly favourable impression. Staff are friendly 'without being obsequious'. Sommelier David Harvey has put together a serious wine list at some very serious prices: those on a tight budget will find little relief under £20. However, there's no doubting the quality, and wine lovers will find much to excite them from both hemispheres. Ten house wines include a Chilean Gewurztraminer for £17.50 and a Spanish Garnacha for £20. Another restaurant on the premises, Hadrian's, aims for a brasserie style.

CHEF: Jeff Bland PROPRIETOR: Rocco Forte Hotels OPEN: Mon to Fri L 12 to 2, all week D 7 to 10 (10.30 Fri and Sat) CLOSED: 1 week Jan MEALS: alc (main courses £19.50 to £29). Set L £14.95 (2 courses) to £17.95, Set D £32 SERVICE: not inc; 12.5% for parties of 6 or more CARDS: Amex, Delta, Diners, MasterCard, Switch, Visa DETAILS: 60 seats. Private parties: 80 main room, 40 private room. Car park. Vegetarian meals. Children's helpings. Wheelchair access (also WC). Music. Air-conditioned ACCOMMODATION: 184 rooms, all with bath/shower. TV. Phone. Room only £150 to £260. Rooms for disabled. Children welcome. High teas for children. Baby facilities. Afternoon teas. Swimming-pool

Café St-Honoré ✶✱

| 34 N.W. Thistle Street Lane, Edinburgh EH2 1EA | COOKING 2 |
| TEL: (0131) 226 2211 | COST £23–£47 |

Lunch-time is all business in this city-centre back-street French restaurant, and candles come out at night. Menus vary by the day, with a choice of half a dozen first or main courses. Starters can be as straightforward as pork and caper broth, or warm salad of langoustine and chorizo, while others take on more ample dimensions: casserole of quail with red cabbage and lentils, or asparagus risotto with basil and goats' cheese. Variety is achieved by ringing the changes on familiar ideas, which might produce breast of Barbary duck with beetroot and black pudding, and fish gets some interesting treatment, as in gurnard with samphire and black beans, or escalope of salmon with wild asparagus and couscous. Finish with kumquat mousse with saffron ice-cream, or hot pear crumble with cinnamon ice-cream. A sharp eye has picked out some good bottles on the short wine list, and seven house wines start at £9.50 (£3.20 a glass).

CHEF: Christopher Colverson PROPRIETORS: Christopher Colverson and Jerry Mallet OPEN: Mon to Fri L 12 to 2.15, Mon to Sat D 7 to 10.00 (open all week during Festival) CLOSED: 4 days Christmas, 2 weeks Easter, 1 week Oct/Nov MEALS: alc (main courses £7.50 to £17) SERVICE: not inc CARDS: Amex, Delta, Diners, MasterCard, Switch, Visa DETAILS: 40 seats. Private parties: 30 main room, 18 private room. Children's helpings. No smoking in dining-room. Wheelchair access (also WC). Music

Fishers Bistro £

1 Shore, Leith, Edinburgh EH6 6QW	COOKING 2
TEL: (0131) 554 5666	COST £21–£43

This converted pub, on a corner overlooking the Water of Leith and the harbour, serves its entire menu all day long. Informal, unpretentious, with bare wooden tables and paper napkins, it concentrates on seafood to the exclusion of almost everything else. Apart from lamb-stuffed nan bread with harissa, perhaps, and a few vegetable starters such as courgette, leek and fennel soup, or baked mushrooms, it revels in crab- and cod-cakes, whole grilled lemon or Dover sole, and generous quantities of scallops and crevettes combined with vegetables in a rich creamy sauce. A bright 'Pacific Rim' streak is evident in baby turbot with chilli jam, king prawns on a spicy salad with coconut satay, and grilled snapper with a mango, mint and lime relish. Puddings are not the highlight, but service is prompt, efficient and enthusiastic, and the modern collection of fair-value wines starts below £10.

CHEFS: Mary Walker and Brendan Sugars PROPRIETORS: Graeme Lumsden and Jake Millar OPEN: all week 12 to 10.30 CLOSED: 25 and 26 Dec, 1 Jan MEALS: alc (main courses £9 to £17) SERVICE: not inc; 10% for parties of 8 or more CARDS: Amex, Diners, MasterCard, Switch, Visa DETAILS: 45 seats. 20 seats outside. Private parties: 36 main room. Children's helpings. Wheelchair access (3 steps; not WC). No music

▲ Haldanes ⁵⁺✖

39A Albany Street, Edinburgh EH1 3QY	COOKING 4
TEL: (0131) 556 8407	COST £30–£52

Although in the basement of the Albany Townhouse Hotel, Haldanes overlooks a walled garden, and takes advantage of a patio for al fresco eating in fine weather. The house is Georgian, with an open fire in the sitting-room, and crisp linen and smart table settings in the light, attractive dining-room. George Kelso's larder is well stocked with native ingredients, and he typically spices them up with something from further south: a warm salad of Highland venison with lentils and balsamic dressing, for example, or saddle of Scottish lamb with a pesto crust. He takes a light approach to fish dishes in particular, serving trout mousse on a few crisp leaves dressed in a tangy vinaigrette, or baked West Coast monkfish with herb couscous and a lemon butter sauce, but finishes on a more indulgent note with terrine of dark chocolate, bread-and-butter pudding, or sticky toffee pudding with butterscotch sauce. Service is 'attentive', although 'the waitress seemed rather surprised that I should want to taste the wine.' Nearly 60 bins balance New World against Old, affordability is a priority, and house wines start at £10.50.

CHEF: George Kelso PROPRIETORS: George and Michelle Kelso OPEN: Mon to Fri L 12 to 2, all week D 6.30 to 9.30 (10.30 Fri and Sat) CLOSED: 25 and 26 Dec MEALS: alc (main courses £13.50 to £19). Set L £10 (2 courses) to £12.50. SERVICE: not inc CARDS: Amex, Delta, MasterCard, Switch, Visa DETAILS: 40 seats. 8 seats outside. Private parties: 40 main room, 20 private room. Vegetarian meals. Children's helpings. No smoking in dining-room. Music £5

Kalpna 🌱✸ £

2–3 St Patrick Square, Edinburgh EH8 9EZ	COOKING 2
TEL: (0131) 667 9890	COST £15–£24

In a modest setting of pink walls, 'most charming' ethnic hangings and functional furniture, a regular crowd of theatregoers, students and others continue to relish an exceedingly affordable selection of South Indian and Gujarati vegetarian dishes. The secret, according to one who knows, is in the way spices are mixed 'very cleverly' to give each dish its distinctive impact. Starters such as crisp samosa sabji (vegetable pastries), and pakoras (potato fritters as well as the more traditional kind) continue to please, while more substantial specialities are also well reported. Khumb masala (mushrooms in coconut sauce) is a firm favourite; also good are bhindi masala with 'chilli glowing nicely in the background' and aloo bangara, a potato dish with 'complex ethnic, but unfamiliar flavours'. Rice is well cooked and chapatis have been described as 'hot, fresh and tender'. Mango kulfi is a premier-league version, and there is also 'serro' (a vegan semolina-based sweet with raisins) to finish. Lunch is always a bargain price buffet. Drink Cobra beer or dip into the intelligently chosen wine list. House wine is £7.95.

CHEFS: Ajay Bhartdwaj and Kaushlandra Pandey PROPRIETORS: Ajay Bhartdwaj, Mrs Barton and Mr Jogee OPEN: Mon to Fri L 12 to 2, Mon to Sat D 5.30 to 11 CLOSED: 25 and 26 Dec, 1 Jan MEALS: alc (main courses £4.50 to £7.50). Set Buffet L £4.50, Set D £8.30 to £10.50 SERVICE: 10%, card slips closed CARDS: MasterCard, Visa DETAILS: 65 seats. Private parties: 70 main room, 35 to 40 private rooms. Vegetarian meals. Children welcome. No smoking in dining-room. Wheelchair access (2 steps; not WC). Music

Kelly's 🌱✸

	NEW ENTRY
46 West Richmond Street, Edinburgh EH8 9DZ	COOKING 3
TEL/FAX: (0131) 668 3847	COST £33–£40

Kelly's, handy for the Queen's Hall and Festival Theatre, has been taken over. Anne and Stephen Frost (who may be familiar to some readers from stints at Cromlix House, Kinbuck, and Stonor Arms, Stonor) returned to Scotland to run this small city-centre restaurant as the last edition of the *Guide* went to press. Now decorated in cool, creamy shades with a 'restrained, sophisticated' feel, it is comfortable, congenial and good value. Menus combine traditional and modern ideas without being too ambitious, producing rabbit with mustard, for example, and a terrine of wood pigeon and duckling served with beetroot and orange relish.

Dishes are attractively varied, winning support with a 'convincingly savoury' risotto of sun-dried tomatoes, and the 'strong, sweet' flavour of mutton, combined in a casserole with Toulouse sausage, haricot beans and a 'shiny dark gravy, oozing with chef-made richness'. Among impressive soups have been a 'soothing' cream of fennel, while desserts have produced wild cherry clafoutis, and a huge wedge of 'very professional' strawberry pavlova, the meringue 'crisp outside, marshmallowy within'. Some of the special deals are worth watching: two courses for £8 at Saturday lunch-time, plus weekday lunch and early-evening offers of, for example, a starter, pudding and coffee for £9.50. The wine list is to be given a 're-vamp', but for the moment the fruity Australian house wine is £10.

CHEF: Stephen Frost   PROPRIETORS: Stephen and Anne Frost   OPEN: Wed to Sat 12 to 2, 7 to 9.30 (pre-/post-theatre meals by arrangement)   CLOSED: 24 to 26 Dec, 1 and 2 Jan   MEALS: Set L Wed to Fri £12 (2 courses) to £15, Set L Sat £8 (2 courses) to £10, Set D £25   SERVICE: not inc   CARDS: Delta, MasterCard, Switch, Visa   DETAILS: 30 seats. Private parties: 34 main room. Vegetarian meals. Children's helpings. No children under 4. No smoking in dining-room. Wheelchair access (not WC). Music   £5

Martins ♥ ⅝

| 70 Rose Street North Lane, Edinburgh EH2 3DX | COOKING 3 |
| TEL: (0131) 225 3106 | COST £28–£55 |

The two-storey house looks as if it has been squeezed into its appointed spot between Rose Street and George Street, but inside all is simple layout, light and relaxing. After 15 years Martin and Gay Irons know their customers well enough, offering a straightforward set-price two-course lunch of, say, artichoke soup and pan-fried pigeon breast, as well as a short *carte*. Materials are 'organically grown or reared where possible', with some wild foods thrown in – berries, nettles, mushrooms among them – and the European strand of risotto or goats'-cheese ravioli is occasionally livened up with more exotic flavours: spiced couscous with roast salmon, or ginger, coriander and lime for king prawns. Desserts might include banana crème brûlée or rich chocolate torte, but one visitor noted that 'the cheeseboard is clearly Martin's pride and joy', and he keeps the flag flying for unpasteurised British and Irish cheeses. The Ironses can be just as proud of their wine list, which offers an eclectic range of bins at some reasonable prices. Selections from the Loire and California continue to impress, while Rolly-Gassman in Alsace remains a firm favourite.Four appealing house wines are priced from £10.95 to £11.80. CELLARMAN'S CHOICE: Bonny Doon, Ca'del Solo Il Pescatore 1993, Santa Cruz, California, £18.75; Gran Recosind Crianza 1989, Cellers Santamaría, Ampurdán-Costa Brava, £14.95.

CHEFS: Forbes Stott and Anthony Singh   PROPRIETORS: Martin and Gay Irons   OPEN: Tue to Fri L 12 to 2, Tue to Sat D 7 to 10 (open Mon L and D in Aug)   CLOSED: 24 Dec to 20 Jan, 1 week May/June, 1 week Sept/Oct   MEALS: alc (main courses £17 to £21). Set L £14.50 (2 courses)   SERVICE: not inc; 10% for parties of 6 or more   CARDS: Amex, Delta, Diners, MasterCard, Switch, Visa   DETAILS: 48 seats. Private parties: 8 and 12 private rooms. No children under 8. No smoking in dining-room. No music

£5 *indicates that the restaurant has elected to participate in the* Good Food Guide *voucher scheme. For full details see page 6.*

Shore ¦✳ £

3–4 The Shore, Leith, Edinburgh EH6 6QW
TEL/FAX: (0131) 553 5080   COOKING 2
off A199 on Firth of Forth, 2m E of city centre   COST £17–£36

The Shore contributes 'honest seafaring simplicity' to the new-look Leith, in the words of one reporter, referring to super-fresh fish and seafood dishes cooked with a minimum of elaboration. Choose between the cheerily noisy bar or a dining-area with white linen and flowers as a backdrop, and then enjoy the likes of poached Dublin Bay prawns adorned with wedges of garlic and unsalted butter. Melted butter is all the accompaniment that first-course seafood needs when, as here, it is 'sweet and juicy, and sings of the sea'. A little garnish is allowed on main courses, either asparagus and a couple of thick chunks of smoked salmon for a grilled lemon sole, or green leeks and wild mushrooms for lightly baked cod. Timing is accurate throughout. Those hankering for meat might go for loin of lamb wrapped in pancetta sauced with blackberries and port. Dead simple puddings – chocolate mousse, fruit ice-creams or lemon tart with an 'expert tangy, buttery filling' – are exactly what is expected. The wine list leans towards whites, offering plenty of youthful Chardonnay and Sauvignon at attractive prices. House wines are £9 for white, £9.60 for red.

CHEFS: Innes Gibson and Alison Bryant   PROPRIETOR: Stuart Linsley   OPEN: all week 12 to 2.30 (12.30 to 3 Sun), 6.30 to 10   CLOSED: 25 and 26 Dec, 1 and 2 Jan   MEALS: alc (main courses £8.50 to £16). Set L Mon to Sat £6.95 (2 courses), Set L Sun £10.50 (2 courses) to £13   SERVICE: not inc   CARDS: Amex, MasterCard, Visa   DETAILS: 36 seats. 12 seats outside. Private parties: 36 main room. Vegetarian meals. Children's helpings on request. No smoking in dining-room. Wheelchair access (1 step; not WC). Music

Skippers

1A Dock Place, Leith, Edinburgh EH6 6UY   COOKING 3
TEL: (0131) 554 1018   FAX: (0131) 553 5988   COST £21–£34

Allan and Jennifer Corbett have been serving top-quality fresh fish to the citizens of Leith and beyond since 1984. The secret of their success lies not only in the quality and handling of ingredients, but in the relaxed, confident mood of this converted pub in Dock Place. A comforting livery of dark wood, red paint and gleaming brass calls up echoes of the bistro's former incarnation, although there's a lighter undercurrent to proceedings in general. The kitchen majors in dishes such as moules marinière, pan-fried skate with capers, and whole lemon sole with herb butter, but also tips its hat to fashion with sauté scallops and coriander mash, or crispy fillet of salmon with tomato and basil vinaigrette. Those of a carnivorous persuasion are also catered for with baked lamb chops with onion confit, or sirloin steak with green peppercorn sauce. Puddings are mostly fruity or calorie-laden favourites such as rhubarb crumble, and plum and cinnamon torte. The wine list has some interesting New World offerings, and prices are far from greedy. George Duboeuf house wines are £9.

CHEFS: Kerr Marrian, Neil Wright and Jennifer Corbett   PROPRIETORS: Allan and Jennifer Corbett   OPEN: Mon to Sat 12.30 to 2, 7 to 10   CLOSED: 25 and 26 Dec, 1 and 2 Jan, 1 week Mar, 2 weeks Sept   MEALS: alc (main courses £7 to £14). Set D £17.50 (2 courses) to £21 SERVICE: not inc   CARDS: Amex, Delta, MasterCard, Switch, Visa   DETAILS: 58 seats. 12 seats outside. Private parties: 24 main room, 24 private room. Children welcome. No pipes in dining-room. Wheelchair access (also WC). Music. Air-conditioned   (£5)

Stockbridge Restaurant £ | NEW ENTRY

33A St Stephen Street, Edinburgh EH3 5AH
TEL: (0131) 225 9397

COOKING 3
COST £23–£36

Simply decorated with wooden tables and paper cloths, this unassuming restaurant opened its doors in December 1997. Tiled walls, mirrors, and beer posters give it the air of a 'basic French bistro', although the team that runs it comes with impressive London credentials: Keith McQuaid was manager of Bibendum (see entry, London), Rachel McQuaid worked for Gary Rhodes, and Paul Malinen has cooked with Alastair Little (see entries, London). Despite all that, the aims are modest, and the '90s European food is essentially simple, adding greatly to the appeal: caldo verde, risi e bisi, or plaice with tapénade crust.

Individual dishes change every few days, so the whole menu rolls over in about three weeks, producing a 'simple but perfectly cooked' wild mushroom risotto, zampone sausage with buttery Puy lentils and garlicky salsa verde, and moist, crisp-skinned poussin with lemon butter. Touchstones from other cultures bring variety in the form of smoked haddock fish-cakes, braised lamb shank with clapshot, and a 'rich' coconut tart. Cheese, which might include Isle of Mull Cheddar, comes with cream crackers. A very short and mostly French wine list keeps all but a couple of prices below £20. House Sicilian, red or white, is £8.95.

CHEF: Paul Malinen   PROPRIETORS: Keith, Moira and Rachel McQuaid, and Charles Hunter OPEN: Wed to Sat L 12.30 to 2.15, Tue to Sat D 6.30 to 10.15   CLOSED: 24 to 26 Dec   MEALS: alc (main courses £9 to £12)   SERVICE: not inc   CARDS: Delta, MasterCard, Switch, Visa   DETAILS: 24 seats. Private parties: 24 main room. Children welcome. Occasional music

Valvona & Crolla Caffè Bar ▮ ⁵⅌ £

19 Elm Row, Edinburgh EH7 4AA
TEL: (0131) 556 6066   FAX: (0131) 556 1668
EMAIL: sales@valvonacrolla.co.uk

COOKING 3
COST £20–£34

The spelling of 'caffè' is no mistake, for its spiritual home is Bologna. This simple wooden hut, dubbed 'a temple' by one reporter, is behind the shop, which opened over 60 years ago. Here you can buy complete dishes to take away, and most of their ingredients, as well as the remainder of the 600 listed wines which you didn't drink with your meal. The caffè is open for breakfast and lunch, plus dinner during the Festival. The danger lurking in its *prima colazione*, considering such temptations as the paesano breakfast of grilled sausage, smoked pancetta, egg, tomato and polenta, is that of spoiling your appetite for lunch. Coffee has been described simply as 'the best.' Main dishes in the *piatti del giorno*, which really do change daily, encompass a variety of pasta, vegetables, pizza and fish, plus one meat option. Antipasti always include home-made breads with virgin olive oil and balsamic vinegar. Occasionally, in deference to good Scottish sense, not one but two soups are offered; for instance, cream of mushroom and the renowned, but often traduced, eggy chicken soup, stracciatella. A noisy crowd enjoys the lunches despite a pace of service which is partly explained and excused by the menu note that hot dishes are cooked to order.

Lovers of great *vino* should do themselves a favour and make a pilgrimage here to wonder at the glorious array of Italy's finest. No major financial sacrifice is necessary either, as all the wines on the shop's list can be had for a corkage charge of only £3. If you find yourself unable to make a choice (or are simply pushed for time), then look to the regularly changing selection of ten wines starting at around £6 a bottle, £2 a glass.

CHEFS/PROPRIETORS: the Contini family OPEN: Mon to Sat 8am to 3pm (also D during Festival 6 to 10) CLOSED: 25 and 26 Dec, 1 and 2 Jan MEALS: alc (main courses £6 to £12). SERVICE: not inc, card slips closed CARDS: Amex, Delta, MasterCard, Switch, Visa DETAILS: 80 seats. 8 seats outside. Private parties: 60 main room, 80 private room. Vegetarian meals. Children's helpings. No smoking in dining-room. Music. Air-conditioned

---

Vintners Rooms ♀ ⅛✷

The Vaults, 87 Giles Street, Leith,
Edinburgh EH6 6BZ   COOKING 4
TEL: (0131) 554 6767   FAX: (0131) 467 7130   COST £24–£51

Hidden behind a high stone wall, these seventeenth-century wine cellars have the feel of a secret location that only the truly dedicated know about. Rococo vine motifs cover the high, vaulted ceiling, a gilded chandelier hangs down, and fresh flowers decorate pristine white tablecloths. The welcome is warm, service is courteous and efficient, and expectations are high for a menu that knows its way around the '90s repertoire: grilled goat's cheese on olive bread with oven-dried tomato, mango dressing for a Bayonne ham salad, or minted couscous with rack of lamb.

Vegetarians get a fair deal, and seafood is a strong suit, producing chargrilled scallops with rhubarb butter, and a fine puff pastry tartlet with chunks of crab and a delicate cheese sauce. Given the dockside location, the fish selection might be more enterprising, but saucing is the thing: sorrel with salmon, or a 'superb' sweet pepper and anise sauce with monkfish. Although more sensitive preparation of ingredients would have been appreciated at inspection, roast Aberdeen Angus with mushrooms, port and polenta was 'just as beef should be'. To finish, prune and armagnac ice-cream comes with a plum sauce, or there may be chocolate fudge cake, billed as 'chocolate silk'.

While the wine list's array of New World names might bewilder any ghostly merchants checking out their old haunt, the host of French classics remains familiar and reassuring. Modern-day visitors will be heartened by the reasonably down-to-earth prices with plenty of choice under £20. CELLARMAN'S CHOICE: Pouilly-Fuissé 1995, Dom. la Soufrandise, François Mélin, £27; De Loach Saitone Ranch Zinfandel 1996, Russian River, California, £30.50.

CHEFS: Tim Cumming and James Baxter   PROPRIETORS: A.T. and S.C. Cumming   OPEN: Mon to Sat 12 to 2, 7 to 10.30 (open later during festival)   CLOSED: 2 weeks Christmas and New Year   MEALS: alc (main courses £15 to £18). Set L £11 (2 courses) to £14.50   SERVICE: not inc   CARDS: Amex, Diners, MasterCard, Visa   DETAILS: 65 seats. Private parties: 36 main room. Car park. Vegetarian meals. Children's helpings. No smoking in dining-room. Wheelchair access (2 steps; not WC). No music

Winter Glen

3A1 Dundas Street, Edinburgh EH3 6QG   COOKING 4
TEL: (0131) 477 7060   FAX: (0131) 624 7087   COST £23–£44

'Our aim is to offer Scottish food without the stodgy image many perceive,' declare the proprietors. Their surnames jointly supply the name for a venue that might sound as though it is perched on a snowbound hillside, but is actually in Edinburgh's New Town. The interior is a pleasing mix of 'rough stone and smooth furniture', according to a reporter. Ideas revolve around the tried-and-true, so expect monkfish and smoked bacon brochette to start, then venison sitting on a rösti with toasted barley and a port glaze sauce. More adventurous dishes might include chicken breast marinated in chilli and lime, presented on a spiced purée of butter-beans and sauced with a coriander jus. Blueberry ice-cream with kiwi sauce or bananas baked in filo pastry make inspiring desserts. Presentation is thought delightful. Wines scour the New World before ascending in price through burgundies and clarets, and the choices are good and solid. House burgundy is £11.25.

CHEF: Graham Winter   PROPRIETORS: Graham Winter and Blair Glen   OPEN: Mon to Sat 12 to 2, 6 to 10 (10.30 Fri and Sat)   MEALS: Set L £10.95 (2 courses) to £12.95, Set D Mon to Fri £22.50 (2 courses) to £24.95, Set D Sat £27.50   SERVICE: not inc   CARDS: Amex, Delta, MasterCard, Switch, Visa   DETAILS: 60 seats. Private parties: 60 main room, 12 private room. Children's helpings. No smoking before 2pm L, 9pm D. Music. Air-conditioned

ERISKA Argyll & Bute   map 11

▲ Isle of Eriska ♥ ⚒

Ledaig, Eriska PA37 1SD
TEL: (01631) 720371   FAX: (01631) 720531   COOKING 7
off A828, 12m N of Oban   COST £46–£55

This may be a baronial pile on a private island, but it is also a 'surprisingly congenial' place. Built in 1884 from grey granite and red sandstone, it has been run by the Buchanan-Smiths for a quarter of a century and, for visitors who aim to do more than just observe badgers, roe deer and other wildlife, sporting attractions now include a golf course, swimming-pool, sauna and steam-room gym. The 'homely atmosphere' generated by aromatic wood-burning fires is appreciated, as is the 'impeccable attention' paid to housekeeping. A rather formal dining-room, with chintz curtains, bare mahogany tables, candles and gleaming crystal and sliver, makes a fitting setting for Robert MacPherson's six-course dinners.

'This is not fancy food, but really tasty fare,' claimed an inspector. Raw materials make use of local produce, including vegetables, herbs, saladings and soft fruits from the garden, and while the kitchen is undoubtedly ambitious, it has the skill to back this up. It has produced a starter of boned oxtail stuffed with a herb and vegetable mix – so soft it was 'like marshmallow' – in a light bouillon: 'a very accomplished dish'. It takes novel flavour blends in its stride, dressing plump langoustines with lemon and sweet shredded beetroot, and is very much at home with fish, evident from crisply seared sea bass on a 'great mixture' of vegetables, including garlic, aubergine, tomato and cucumber, with plenty of chervil.

'Expert presentation' extends to desserts of iced nougat parfait with a strawberry coulis and chocolate border, or an unusual dish of thickly sliced banana impaled on vanilla skewers, with a chocolate and honey sauce and a camomile sorbet. After this comes a savoury such as Kentish rarebit, Bedford toast, or Whitley goose 'We waited to be offered this course,' wrote one couple, 'but it never materialised, and wasn't mentioned. It was hardly necessary.' Cheeses might include Cashel Blue, sharp-sour Lochaber goat, or creamy, soft Bishop Kennedy. The wine list leans heavily towards classical France, with Trimbach flying the flag for Alsace, but fair-priced New World offerings from the likes of Cloudy Bay, Cape Mentelle and Opus One help to redress the balance. There is good choice under £15, even under £10, and half-bottles are plentiful. House French starts at £8.80.

CHEF: Robert MacPherson   PROPRIETORS: the Buchanan-Smith family   OPEN: all week D only 8 to 9   MEALS: Set D £37.50   SERVICE: none, card slips closed   CARDS: Amex, MasterCard, Switch, Visa   DETAILS: 40 seats. Private parties: 20 main room. Car park. Children welcome. Jacket and tie. No smoking in dining-room. Wheelchair access (not WC). No music ACCOMMODATION: 17 rooms, all with bath/shower. TV. Phone. B&B £110 to £230. Rooms for disabled. Children welcome. Baby facilities. Dogs by arrangement. Swimming-pool. Fishing (The Which? Hotel Guide)

FORT WILLIAM Highland   map 11

Crannog £✳ £

Town Pier, Fort William PH33 7NG	COOKING 1
TEL: (01397) 705589 FAX: (01397) 700134	COST £23–£45

'Superb views over the loch' make this a good place to stop: 'after days on the road on the west coast it can seem like an oasis.' What the food may lack in metropolitan finesse it makes up for in fishy simplicity: fresh oysters, smoked salmon, steamed mussels, or grilled fish of the day such as cod, haddock, hake or sole. The highlight is a plate of langoustines 'fresh from the loch' served either as a starter or main course, and either cold with a selection of dips or 'swimming in hot butter'. Some 20 wines include a handful, starting at £9.95, available by the glass and half-litre.

CHEF: Annie Mackinnon   PROPRIETOR: Finlay Finlayson   OPEN: all week 12 to 2.30, 6 to 9.30 (9 in winter)   MEALS: alc (main courses £8.50 to £15)   SERVICE: not inc   CARDS: Delta, MasterCard, Switch, Visa   DETAILS: 70 seats. Private parties: 70 main room. Vegetarian meals. Children's helpings. No smoking in 1 dining-room. Wheelchair access (also WC). Music

▲ *Inverlochy Castle* 🍶 ✸

Torlundy, Fort William PH33 6SN
TEL: **(01397) 702177** FAX: **(01397) 702953** COOKING **6**
3m N of Fort William on A82 COST £34–£76

This giant, luxurious hotel is set in spacious grounds amid rolling hills just north of Fort William. A pianist plays excerpts from musicals in the grandest of the lounges, while guests sink into comfortable chairs, nibble on venison sausages or smoked salmon, and read through the menu and enormous wine list. Balanced set-price menus of three courses at lunch, up to five at dinner, exude as much opulence as the furnishings: roast quail salad with white pudding, tartare of smoked haddock with Welsh rarebit and poached egg, or 'creamy and tasty' foie gras on a crunchy green bean salad with a sharp-sweet dressing to cut the richness. An à la carte was under development as the *Guide* went to press, which may do away with such oddities as a £3 supplement (on a £45 menu) for lobster salad.

Apparently simple ideas can be particularly effective, as in a 'brilliant' combination of crab and horseradish, the white meat sandwiched between buckwheat blinis, sitting on cubes of potato in a horseradish cream, the ensemble surrounded by three sauces, piles of avocado, and very hot chilli. Materials are first-rate, though sauces have varied from a disappointing chive beurre blanc with an outstanding and 'perfectly cooked' piece of turbot, to a well-judged meat stock that accompanied a saddle of spring lamb, its 'crisp fat' and 'succulent meat packed with flavour'.

After a pre-dessert such as pistachio parfait might come warm chocolate tart, the high cocoa solid filling oozing out and mixing with an orange sauce, or a rich combination of light puff pastry filled with perfectly executed vanilla-flavoured egg custard, layered with roasted banana. Petits fours are as good as the starter nibbles, and better than the coffee. Friendly but 'zealous' service appears anxious to top up glasses after every sip. Cost-conscious drinkers may feel a bit faint when they see the wine prices, but may well rally when they observe the sheer quality: classed-growth clarets dating back to 1961, many venerable burgundies (of both colours) and some classy New World bins. Wines under £20 can be found, although it might be wise to check that you haven't merely spotted one of the many half-bottles scattered throughout the list. House claret and white burgundy from Justerini & Brooks are £15.50 each.

CHEF: Simon Haigh PROPRIETOR: Inverlochy Castle Ltd OPEN: all week 12.30 to 1.45, 7 to 9.30 CLOSED: 5 Jan to 12 Feb MEALS: Set L £23 to £30, Set D £35 to £50. Light L available. BYO £10 SERVICE: net prices, card slips closed CARDS: Delta, MasterCard, Switch, Visa DETAILS: 40 seats. Private parties: 30 main room. Car park. Children's helpings. No children under 5. Jacket and tie. No smoking in dining-room. No music ACCOMMODATION: 17 rooms, all with bath/shower. TV. Phone. B&B £180 to £440. Children welcome. High teas for children. Baby facilities. Dogs welcome in bedrooms only. Afternoon teas. Fishing (*The Which? Hotel Guide*)

'Why is it that so many restaurants that would be mortified if accused of serving canned peas or canned peaches consider canned music acceptable?' (On eating out in general)

---

map 11

Café Gandolfi £

64 Albion Street, Glasgow G1 1NY
TEL: (0141) 552 6813

COOKING 2
COST £16–£33

Visitors to the 1999 City of Architecture and Design may be interested to know that the café opened in 1979 on the site of the derelict Old Cheese Market. Designer Tim Stead put in dark wood panelling, stained-glass windows and his solidly crafted furniture; reporters find it unstuffy in every sense and enjoy the lively ambience. Seumas MacInnes describes the cooking as 'Modern Scottish', a term broad enough to take in a large bowl of country-style broccoli soup, Indonesian stuffed peppers with salad, and Scandinavian apple and almond pudding. Alternatively, opt for more-local Cullen skink, Stornoway black puddings with mushrooms and pancakes, or potted Drumloch Cheddar with ale. It is all summed up as 'honest, rough-and-ready food using good materials'. Most wines on the basic, well-chosen list are offered by the small or large glass as well as bottles and halves; house wine is £9.95. Unusual bottled beers include organic ale, a self-fulfilling Golden Promise at £3.

CHEF: Maggie Clarence   PROPRIETOR: Seumas MacInnes   OPEN: all week 9am (12 Sun) to 11.30pm   CLOSED: 25 and 26 Dec, 1 and 2 Jan   MEALS: alc (main courses £5.50 to £11)   SERVICE: not inc; 10% (optional) for parties of 6 or more   CARDS: Delta, MasterCard, Switch, Visa   DETAILS: 65 seats. Private parties: 25 main room. Vegetarian meals. Children's helpings. No children after 8.30. No-smoking area. Music

Lux

NEW ENTRY

1051 Great Western Road, Glasgow G12 0XP
TEL: (0141) 576 7576   FAX: (0141) 576 0162

COOKING 3
COST £28–£46

The former railway station, some distance from the centre of Glasgow on the endless Great Western Road, was designed by Sir J.J. Burnet in homage to Frank Lloyd Wright's Prairie House. It went up in 1896, closed in 1942, suffered from vandalism and fire, and has twice been threatened with demolition. The present owners rescued it and opened up two restaurants in the spring of 1998. Stazione Mediterranean, once the booking office, has become a brasserie, while the spacious first-floor Lux has a bar with lots of windows letting in natural light, bright clean walls hung with modern prints, and a generously varied dinner menu (shorter at Sunday lunch-times) that combines round-the-world enthusiasm with more traditional ideas. Stephen Johnson used to cook at the Buttery, Glasgow.

In the old-fashioned camp, steak is served with a creamy pepper sauce, and sole with orange butter sauce, but alongside may be Thai fish salad with green salsa dressing; variation-on-a-theme cooking has produced pork with spiced apricots and coconut crème fraîche, and duck ravioli in a pool of zingy orange-flavoured stock. Fish impressed at inspection – salmon and potato in filo in a light, fragrant, creamy saffron sauce, and well-seasoned monkfish 'with good pesto on fine noodles' – and vegetables taste freshly cooked. Try crème brûlée to finish, or a plate of fresh and poached fruit served with a simple fruit syrup. Meals begin with bread and a bowl of 'wonderfully fruity' olive oil, and end with improvable coffee. Wines are arranged by style, with some interest under £20, and helpfully annotated. House red is £16, white £15.

CHEF: Stephen Johnson PROPRIETORS: David Maguire and Ronnie Sommerville OPEN: Sun L 12 to 2.30, all week D 6 to 11 CLOSED: 25 Dec, 1 Jan MEALS: Set L Sun £17.50, Set D £25 SERVICE: not inc, card slips closed; 10% on parties of 6 or more CARDS: Delta, MasterCard, Switch, Visa DETAILS: 70 seats. Private parties: 75 main room. Car park. Vegetarian meals. Children's helpings. No-smoking area. Music. Air-conditioned

Mitchells/Mitchells West End

157 North Street, Charing Cross, Glasgow G3 7DA
TEL: (0141) 204 4312 FAX: (0141) 204 1818
EMAIL: angus635@aol.com
31–35 Ashton Lane, West End, Glasgow G12 8SJ   COOKING 1
TEL: (0141) 339 2220   COST £19–£38

Both branches of Mitchells aim for a convivial approach, attracting a casual crowd with simple food and some bright flavours: home-made beefburger, chillied beef in a tortilla shell, Jamaican jerk chicken, and a pasta dish or two. Fish might be made into soup, or served as haddock on potato skins, and meatless items run to caramelised marsala and red onion tartlet, and potato and coriander cake with an apple and mustard-seed relish. Finish with steamed lemon pudding, or deep-fried choux pastry with a red fruit compote and vanilla ice-cream. Drink from a short wine list for less than £20, unless the occasion calls for champagne. House red and white are £10.95 each, £2 a glass.

CHEFS: Angus Boyd and Scott Baxter PROPRIETOR: Angus Boyd OPEN: Mitchells Mon to Fri L 12 to 2.30, Mon to Sat D 5 to 10.30; Mitchells West End Mon to Sat D only 5 to 10.30 CLOSED: 25 Dec, 1 Jan, L bank hols MEALS: Mitchells alc (main courses £5 to £12). Set D £8.95 (2 courses) to £10.95; Mitchells West End alc (main courses £7.50 to £12) SERVICE: not inc CARDS: Amex, Delta, Diners, MasterCard, Switch, Visa DETAILS: 50 seats (Mitchells), 34 seats (Mitchells West End). Private parties: 60 main room, 50 private room (Mitchells). Vegetarian meals. Children's helpings. No children under 12. Wheelchair access (also WC). Music £5

▲ Nairns   NEW ENTRY

13 Woodside Crescent, Glasgow G3 7UP   COOKING 6
TEL: (0141) 353 0707 FAX: (0141) 331 1684   COST £38–£48

Nick Nairn, not the first chef to turn himself via the medium of television into a 'celebrity', has come up trumps in his new venture, delighting the city with 'imaginative, carefully cooked food at a reasonable price'. A Victorian town house, in what is now 'officeland', has been converted into a restful, stylish modern restaurant with a small ground floor and larger basement dining-room. Grey pictures on steel grey walls induced a sense of 'Anouska Hempel meets Clydeside shipbuilders' in one reporter, but the place is both comfortable and welcoming. Nick Nairn's name is on everything, 'and if you're sad enough you can buy the menu with his signature on it for £1'. One or two items carry a supplement, but that doesn't detract from the overall impression of good value.

The food entices with a mix of classical ideas – terrine of chicken and leek with sauce gribiche, or lamb shank with fragrant, buttery tarragon mash – and a more inventive edge: duck samosa with chilli dressing, sweet potato soup with smoked paprika aïoli, or cod fillet with curried peas. Sauces and seasonings have varied in their impact, but combinations of ingredients have impressed reporters: a rich dish of pork fillet, for example, with pig's cheek and black pudding on a bed of Jerusalem artichokes in an 'old-fashioned, meaty gravy'.

Dan Hall's accurate timing has made the most of good materials, including a 'sensational' dish of chicken livers with black pudding and lentils 'in an intense stocky thyme jus', and among impressive vegetable dishes has been a 'hugely memorable' shiitake ragoût with crisply cooked courgette and salsify, all in a rich coriander pesto. Desserts typically come in two parts: steamed pear pudding with stem ginger ice-cream, mango Tatin with plum syrup, and 'outstanding' cherry clafoutis with vanilla ice-cream. Bread is served from a gigantic bowl, and service can be speedy. Around half of the 30 wines stay below £20, including four house wines.

CHEF: Dan Hall   PROPRIETORS: Nick and Christopher Nairn   OPEN: Tue to Sun 12 to 2, 6 to 10 CLOSED: 25 and 26 Dec, 1 and 2 Jan   MEALS: Set L £13.50 (2 courses) to £17, Set D £23.50 SERVICE: not inc; 10% for parties of 8 or more   CARDS: Amex, Delta, MasterCard, Switch, Visa DETAILS: 75 seats. Private parties: 40 main room. Vegetarian meals. Children welcome. No smoking before coffee is served. Wheelchair access (also WC). Music   ACCOMMODATION: 4 rooms, all with bath/shower. TV. Phone. Room only £90 to £125. Children welcome. No dogs

---

▲ One Devonshire Gardens ⛶✕

1 Devonshire Gardens, Glasgow G12 0UX	COOKING 5
TEL: (0141) 339 2001 FAX: (0141) 337 1663	COST £42–£70

The hotel, on the Great Western Road two or three miles out of the city centre, occupies three adjoining town houses in one of those handsome Victorian stone terraces of which Glasgow appears to have an unlimited supply. Three things might strike the visitor: an impression of space – high-ceilinged and generously proportioned rooms – a sense of opulent design, and a 'womb-like quality' engendered by wood panelling, dark wallpaper and subdued lighting.

Andrew Fairlie sets his sights on a brand of elegant, modern classical cooking which, although it doesn't aim to break through any barriers, would put many hotels of this kind to shame. He smokes lobster, giving it a herb and lime butter, and serves grilled halibut fillet with creamed goats'-cheese polenta. Sourcing, timing, balance and seasoning all impress. Importantly, 'everything tastes as it should', including an inspector's fricasee of prime, crisp-skinned sea bass, langoustine and scallop served in a tangy lemon grass broth with tiny sculpted vegetables, and a 'deeply satisfying autumn dish' of pink roast pheasant breast arranged on a bed of braised Savoy cabbage, with ceps, roasted shallots, whole garlic cloves and a dark thyme-flavoured jus.

British cheeses arrive already plated and in good condition, providing serious competition for desserts: passion-fruit gratin with mango coulis and bitter chocolate sorbet, perhaps, or a small tuile basket filled with cold, creamy rice pudding, sharing the plate with a granita of mulled wine and balsamic vinegar, plus a warm mound of blueberries, raspberries and strawberries. Service has been described as 'formal' and 'pleasant' but 'unsynchronised'. Wines are high in quality and price, with most of the usual under-£20 escape routes (including Chile and Argentina, for heaven's sake) sealed off. House wine is £19.

CHEF: Andrew Fairlie   PROPRIETOR: Ken McCulloch   OPEN: Sun to Fri L 12.15 to 2, all week D 7.15 to 9.45   MEALS: Set L £19 (2 courses) to £25, Set D £40. BYO £12.50   SERVICE: not inc CARDS: Amex, Delta, Diners, MasterCard, Visa   DETAILS: 50 seats. 16 seats outside. Private parties: 52 main room, 12 to 32 private rooms. Car park. Vegetarian meals. Children's helpings. No smoking in dining-room. Music   ACCOMMODATION: 27 rooms, all with bath/shower. TV. Phone. Room only £140 to £225. Rooms for disabled. Children welcome. Baby facilities. Afternoon teas (*The Which? Hotel Guide*)

La Parmigiana £

447 Great Western Road, Glasgow G12 8HH	COOKING 1
TEL: (0141) 334 0686	COST £15–£47

Regulars flock to this long, narrow, sandy-coloured, high-ceillinged room for defiantly untrendy Italian food: a standard run of dishes from Parma ham with melon via soup, and half a dozen pasta variations (spaghetti with seafood is highly rated), to chicken and veal two ways each. Cream and alcohol in the sauces, and a pepperpot flourish, indicate Parmigiana's traditional leanings, but the food's freshness appeals. The advice is to 'pounce on any daily specials involving fish or venison', among which might be 'fat, juicy, springy, sweet and impeccably timed' chargrilled scallops, or plump collops of gamey venison fillet with juniper berries and gin. For dessert, try the 'expertly whisked' zabaglione or the 'luscious' liqueur-drenched dolce al mascarpone. More careful service would be appreciated. Interesting Italian wines are fairly priced, starting at £12.50.

CHEF: Sandro Giovanazzi   PROPRIETORS: Angelo and Sandro Giovanazzi   OPEN: Mon to Sat 12 to 2.30, 6 to 11   CLOSED: Christmas, 1 Jan, bank hols   MEALS: alc (main courses £10.50 to £16). Set L Mon to Fri £8.50   SERVICE: not inc   CARDS: Amex, Diners, Delta, MasterCard, Switch, Visa   DETAILS: 50 seats. Private parties: 60 main room. Vegetarian meals. Children's helpings. No pipes in dining-room. Music. Air-conditioned

Puppet Theatre ✸ 🍴

11 Ruthven Lane, Glasgow G12 9BG	COOKING 3
TEL: (0141) 339 8444 FAX: (0141) 339 7666	COST £24–£47

'Dramatically different dining' is what the Puppet Theatre promises, as much in the extravagantly offbeat décor of the four dining-rooms – one, a narrow conservatory adorned with rattan blinds, dried hops and plaster busts – as in the kitchen's quirky culinary style. Chefs do seem to succeed one another at a rate of knots, but the style is somehow sustained. Vivid salads are strong suits among starters, perhaps combining soused mackerel, saffron potatoes and chermoula, or roasted beetroot, blood orange, red chicory and pine-nuts in orange oil. Inventive vegetarian dishes have included roast carrot risotto cakes with a sauté of wild mushrooms and asparagus, and oriental technique informs a raviolo of Thai-spiced salmon topped with pak choi in a lime, tomato and sesame broth. Dishes are certainly complex, but the components seem to pull together, most notably at dessert stage where passion-fruit parfait comes with poached pear and blackcurrant coulis, or banana Tatin is accompanied by honey ice-cream and a caramel sauce. Mature chesses, Costa coffee and the 'friendly and chatty' service add polish. French wines are bolstered by one or two each from other countries, and there is a generous spread of half-bottles. House wines start at £11.50.

CHEF: John Quigley   PROPRIETORS: Ron McCulloch and George Swanson   OPEN: Tue to Fri and Sun L 12 to 2.30, Tue to Sun D 7 to 10.30   CLOSED: 25 and 26 Dec, 1 and 2 Jan   MEALS: Set L Tue to Fri £12.95 (2 courses) to £14.50, Set L Sun £17.50, Set D £24.95 (2 courses) to £29.50 SERVICE: not inc; 10% for parties of 7 or more   CARDS: Amex, Delta, MasterCard, Switch, Visa DETAILS: 66 seats. Private parties: 28 main room, 10 to 28 private rooms. Car park. Vegetarian meals. Children welcome. No smoking in 1 dining-room. Music. Air-conditioned

Rogano

11 Exchange Place, Glasgow G1 3AN	COOKING 4
TEL: (0141) 248 4055 FAX: (0141) 248 2608	COST £27£60

Back in the main-entry section of the *Guide* after a change of chef just before we went to press last year, Rogano scores for its relaxed, friendly ambience, 1930s art deco interior with 'saucy mermaids', and generous way with fish. It attracts all ages, service is attentive and friendly in best Glasgow style, and the place 'hums with quiet enjoyment'. It also remains 'one of the few places in Glasgow where chilli and Thai spicing are mercifully absent', opting for more traditional fish soup, smoked salmon, fresh oysters, and poached or grilled fish such as halibut and sea bass. Fish is well sourced, if not always equally well sauced, judging by the cheese one for lobster thermidor (the pinnacle of the offerings if price is anything to go by) at one meal.

Impeccable timing, however, has shown to good effect in 'unctuous, just-seared' foie gras with a rich Sauternes jus, and in half a dozen 'fresh and sweet' scallops, still translucent, scattered with bits of tangy bacon and served with glistening leaves. Flavours may sometimes lack the courage of their convictions, as in a couple of desserts at inspection, for example, but the truffles that come with coffee pack a real dark chocolate punch. The sensible length wine list is not overpriced, and starts with House French at £9.85.

CHEF: William Simpson   PROPRIETOR: Allied Domecq Inns   OPEN: all week 12 to 2.30, 6.30 to 10.30   MEALS: alc (main courses £18 to £30). Set L £16.50   SERVICE: 10% (optional), card slips closed   CARDS: Amex, Delta, Diners, MasterCard, Switch, Visa   DETAILS: 70 seats. Private parties: 70 main room, 16 private room. Vegetarian meals. Children welcome. No smoking before 2 L and 10 D. Wheelchair access (not WC). Occasional music. Air-conditioned

78 St Vincent ⁵✳   NEW ENTRY

78 St Vincent Street, Glasgow G2 5UB	COOKING 2
TEL/FAX: (0141) 248 7878	COST £21–£42

Value for money is a big draw at this modern bistro, filling a gap 'plumb in the centre of Glasgow'. It occupies the old Phoenix Assurance building, restored with a marble staircase and wrought ironwork, and has an uncluttered but convivial feel. Pre-theatre meals cost less than a tenner, and the set-price dinner's vegetarian main course even has a 'negative supplement'. Despite a penchant for positive accompaniments (mango dressing, mustard mash, lavender jelly, curried cream), such flavours are not too intrusive; and despite an occasional 'huge portion' (timbale of brown crabmeat with honey-sweet pepper sauce), the tone is light and upbeat. Monkfish comes with coriander noodles, chicken with pesto yoghurt, and salmon appears in various guises: ceviche, terrine, fish-cakes, or smoked and layered with goats' cheese. Among meats, thick-cut slices of pink lamb appeal, plainly served with its juices. Potatoes seem to be the pick of the vegetables, and desserts might include marmalade crème brûlée, 'cocoa-rich' chocolate cake, or 'lightly scrunchy' nougat glacé. Informal service is 'cheerily Glasgow' with lots of chat. A second outlet was due to open in Bothwell Street as the *Guide* went to press. Forty-plus wines include eight by the glass (a large glass here is 250ml), starting with house red and white at £9.95 a bottle.

CHEF: Andrew Crawford   PROPRIETOR: Michael J. Conyers   OPEN: Mon to Sat L 12 to 3, all week D 6 to 10.30 (10.45 Fri and Sat)   CLOSED: 25 and 26 Dec, 1 and 2 Jan   MEALS: Set L £9.95 (2 courses) to £11.95, Set D 5 to 7, £8.95 (for 2 courses) to £19.95   SERVICE: not inc; 10% on parties of 7 or more   CARDS: Amex, Delta, Diners, MasterCard, Switch, Visa   DETAILS: 120 seats. Vegetarian meals. Children's helpings. No smoking in 1 dining-room. Wheelchair access (also WC). No music   (£5)

Splash ⚞ £

Royal Concert Hall, 2 Sauchiehall Street,
Glasgow G1 3NY   COOKING 1
TEL: (0141) 332 3163   FAX: (0141) 332 9238   COST £23–£33

At the start of Sauchiehall Street near the railway station, Splash is part of the Royal Concert Hall, its trading hours varying according to the concert programme. Cheerful Mediterranean yellows, oranges, reds and blues in the second-floor dining-room are matched by a bright menu that is now set-price only. It strikes a modern pose in langoustine soup with truffle sabayon, or salad of black pudding and seared pigeon breast to start, and keeps the risotto flag flying: choose between tomato, or wild mushroom with black olive croustade. Crushed potatoes are *de rigueur*, served with roast cod, while pepper-crusted chicken comes with roasted vegetables. Finish with strawberry and mascarpone cheesecake, or candied peach in filo. Twenty-one wines start with house French at £12.

CHEF: Michael Hughes   PROPRIETOR: Letheby & Christopher   OPEN: all week 12 to 2, 5 to 9.30   CLOSED: Sun when no concert, bank hols   MEALS: Set L and D £12.50 (2 courses) to £19   SERVICE: not inc, card slips closed   CARDS: Amex, Delta, MasterCard, Switch, Visa   DETAILS: 100 seats. Private parties: 100 main room, 100 to 400 private rooms. Children's helpings. No smoking in dining-room. Wheelchair access (also WC). Music. Air-conditioned   (£5)

⚞ *indicates that smoking is either banned altogether or that a dining-room is maintained for non-smokers. The symbol does not apply to restaurants that simply have no-smoking areas.*

Stravaigin

26 Gibson Street, Glasgow G12 8NX

COOKING 5

TEL: (0141) 334 2665 FAX: (0141) 334 4099

COST £28–£43

Glasgow readers will recognise this chef-proprietor, son of Ronnie Clydesdale, as a block off the old Chip (see entry below). His wooden-tabled basement café attracts a lively, youthful crowd, tempted in by low prices and a monthly changing 'globe-trotting' menu served until early evening. Service is as bright as the modern paintings on the walls, overseen by 'informed and humorous' Carol Wright, and the kitchen's strength is its use of high-quality Scottish materials: shellfish, white fish, beef, lamb, rabbit, venison and mushrooms among them. Its cosmopolitan menu thrives on 'innovatory flourishes' such as braised lamb shanks with herbed couscous and yam chips, or a robust dish of rabbit and firm-fleshed chicken with butter-beans in a 'good old-fashioned thickened gravy', served with a lime pesto.

Vegetable dishes are appealing – asparagus mousse in filo pastry with pine kernels and a rich and well-judged mushroom sauce, for example – and fish is well treated: as in baked hake 'superbly timed', served with a sharp and crunchy carrot chutney, or a Thai broth of squid, mussels, and chunks of cod and monkfish that impressed with 'a stunning blend' of flavours. Cheeses are from Iain Mellis, and showpiece desserts have included a light steamed sponge served with vanilla ice and Kahlua cream, and 'sticky, scrunchy' pineapple tart with grated coconut in a sweet ginger and lemon grass syrup. 'One of the best-value restaurants in Glasgow' was one summing-up, a status helped by a sharply chosen annotated list of wines, mostly under £20, 11 of them available by the glass for around £2.

CHEF/PROPRIETOR: Colin Clydesdale OPEN: Mon to Sat L 12 to 2.30, all week D 5 to 11 (12 Fri and Sat) CLOSED: 25 Dec, 1 and 2 Jan MEALS: alc (main courses £9.50 to £14). Set L and Mon to Thur D 5 to 7 £8.95 (2 courses). Bar menu available SERVICE: not inc CARDS: Amex, Delta, Diners, MasterCard, Switch, Visa DETAILS: 80 seats. Private parties: 80 main room. Vegetarian meals. Children's helpings. No smoking before 9pm. Music. Air-conditioned £5

Ubiquitous Chip 🍾

12 Ashton Lane, G12 8SJ

COOKING 4

TEL: (0141) 334 5007 FAX: (0141) 337 1302

COST £25–£49

Reporters come here for 'a good meal in a jolly place'. The heart of the Chip is an atmospheric barn-like dining-room full of tumbling green plants and lots of chunky pine furniture – 'slightly '70s' – where Ronnie Clydesdale's roots provide a strong 'Scottish traditional' foundation to the food. As well as clapshot, and haggis 'n' neeps, this includes a host of ingredients from Ayrshire bacon to Perthshire wood pigeon, and a very Scottish assembly of cheeses. The result is comfort food with an inventive streak: perhaps a simple starter of well-timed asparagus and poached egg, served on crunchy soda bread with hollandaise sauce.

There may be some 'rough corners' to the cooking, but those who are prepared for it seem to enjoy what they get. A sweet element pervades some savoury dishes, as when strips of marinated slow-cooked venison are accompanied by saffron mash and a 'sweet, bread-like substance which had raisins or sultanas in it'. 'Real home-made puds' deliver concentrated flavours, as in a syrup tart with crowdie cheese, or soft, creamy cinnamon ice-cream served with 'a big, flat, treacle and oatmeal biscuit'. Enthusiastic service typically gets off to a cracking start, and although dishes arrive quickly they have not always been piping hot. The wine list is full of gems both Old and New, and impresses with its combination of top producers, mature vintages and exciting off-beat flavours. Classical France has the strongest presence, although Germany also makes a fine showing. Magnums and half-bottles are numerous (if not ubiquitous), while wines by the glass in all three colours cost £2.75.

CHEFS: Ronald Clydesdale and Ian Brown   PROPRIETOR: Ronald Clydesdale   OPEN: all week 12 (12.30 Sun) to 2.30, 5.30 (6.30 Sun) to 11   CLOSED: 25 Dec, 1 and 2 Jan   MEALS: Set L £18.60 (2 courses) to £23.60, Set L Sun £16, Set D £26.60 (2 courses) to £31.60. Bar meals available   SERVICE: not inc   CARDS: Amex, Delta, Diners, MasterCard, Switch, Visa   DETAILS: 150 seats. Private parties: 80 main room, 25 private rooms. Vegetarian meals. Children's helpings. Wheelchair access (also WC). No music

Yes

22 West Nile Street, Glasgow G1 2PW	COOKING 4
TEL: (0141) 221 8044 FAX: (0141) 248 9159	COST £24–£49

'Very much a Glasgow restaurant', this spacious and 'quietly elegant' combination of bar, brasserie and dining-room is so well appointed – with 'Yes' handles on glass doors, bold colours, lots of blond wood, and good modern art on the walls – that it is 'better to look into than out of'. Scottish produce and ideas fuel the kitchen, which has come up with a gâteau of haggis, neeps and tatties, a soup of finnan haddock served with a mini Cheddar soufflé, and duck breast with clapshot and a whisky sauce.

The Mediterranean exerts a pull in the form of cod with pesto butter, and chicken served with pea and ham risotto, while the Pacific's input has produced Asian fish-cakes, and a casserole of West Coast seafood with a glaze of curry, coconut, mango and coriander. If only timing were more accurate. But reporters generally enjoy themselves, vegetarians get a four-course deal that incorporates wild foods, pulses and fruits, and puddings have included dark chocolate mousse with mango purée, and baked brioche custard with raspberry compote. The 50-strong wine list assembles a diverse range of grape varieties at generally affordable prices, starting with house vin de pays at £11.95.

CHEFS: Ferrier Richardson and Ian McMaster   PROPRIETOR: Ferrier Richardson   OPEN: Mon to Sat 12 to 2.30, 7 to 11   CLOSED: bank hols   MEALS: Set L £12.95 (2 courses) to £15.95, Set D £21.95 (2 courses) to £29.50   SERVICE: not inc, card slips closed   CARDS: Amex, Delta, Diners, MasterCard, Switch, Visa   DETAILS: 120 seats. Private parties: 100 main room, 20 private room. Vegetarian meals. Children's helpings. Music. Air-conditioned

Not inc *in the details at the end of an entry indicates that no service charge is made and any tipping is at the discretion of the customer.*

Use the lists towards the front of the book to find suitable restaurants for special occasions.

GULLANE East Lothian	map 11

▲ *Greywalls* ♟ ⅓✕ ⌂

Muirfield, Gullane EH31 2EG
TEL: (01620) 842144 FAX: (01620) 842241 COOKING 5
on A198, at W end of Gullane COST £25–£54

A Lutyens-designed house that has been in the Weaver family for the better part of the century, Greywalls is a charming old pile full of country-house creature comforts. Squashy sofas and wood panelling adorn the interior, and the dining-room – decorated in a cool shade of green – looks out over Muirfield golf course, so lunchers at least may get in a spot of spectating while enjoying roast Berwick cod with wild mushroom risotto, or perhaps just a chunky sandwich.

Novel but sensible combinations mark the new regime under Simon Burns, though the format is still fixed-price for four courses plus coffee, with an innovative soup such as curried parsnip with walnut paste, or beetroot consommé with orange oil, at second. An inspection dinner that opened with a slice of lightly cooked foie gras served with a 'sweet but sharp' melon chutney illustrates the scope. Main courses of poached fillet of veal with vanilla, or Barbary duck breast with blueberry sauce, offer much to divert the palate, while an 'outstanding' roast rump of lamb comes with piquant salsa verde and grain mustard mash, and roast sea bass is served with baby fennel and a langoustine jus.

Scottish cheeses from a good Edinburgh supplier are the alternative to puddings such as white peach fondant with lemon sorbet, or puréed strawberry 'soup' with vanilla ice-cream. Older vintages of classed growths take pride of place on a very attractive wine list which, while spotlighting classical France, also shines a light into other regions, new and old. There is plenty of choice at all price levels, starting at £12 with the house selection and rising to £1,000 for the Pétrus 1966. CELLARMAN'S CHOICE: Rully Rabourcé 1996, Leflaive, £25; Canon-Fronsac, Ch. Mazeris 1989, £24.

CHEF: Simon Burns PROPRIETOR: Giles Weaver OPEN: all week 12.30 to 2, 7.30 to 9.30
CLOSED: Nov to Mar MEALS: alc L (main courses £8.50 to £15). Set L £17, Set D £35 SERVICE:
not inc, card slips closed CARDS: Amex, Diners, MasterCard, Switch, Visa AILS: 50 seats.
Private parties: 10 main room, 20 private room. Car park. Children's helpings. Jacket and tie at
D. No smoking in dining-room. No music ACCOMMODATION: 23 rooms, all with bath/shower.
TV. Phone. B&B £95 to £190. Rooms for disabled. Children welcome. Dogs welcome in
bedrooms only. Afternoon teas (*The Which? Hotel Guide*) (£5)

La Potinière 🍾 ⅓✕

Main Street, Gullane EH31 2AA
TEL: (01620) 843214 COOKING 8
on A198, 4m SW of North Berwick COST £29–£48

GREAT
1999
VALUE

This might look like a village hall from outside, but inside all is 'quiet elegance', with a simple French provincial feel and a tiny dining-room with just seven tables. It is a place to come for 'consistent cooking of the highest class at almost absurdly low prices', which makes it 'one of the great culinary bargains of Britain'. Don't expect a puppyish welcome, or anxious enquiries about whether or not you are enjoying the food: service from David Brown is relaxed and friendly, but it is taken for granted that the food is up to scratch. Don't expect waves of appetisers before you begin: there aren't any. Don't expect a sommelier with a badge, hiding your wine several feet away and pouring from it now and again; wine and water are, quite rightly, left on the table for you to help yourself.

The pace of meals is naturally dictated by the kitchen, which tends to mean a fairly lengthy dinner, quite in keeping with the objectives. There is no choice, and portions are generous, but the four courses at lunch, five at dinner, are 'superbly balanced'. Menus are constructed by the day, often featuring old favourites, or variants on them, and fresh, usually seasonal, ingredients lay the foundation. A generous tureen of vegetable soup provides a 'satisfying start': lovage, or tomato and mint, or red pepper with a 'stunning intensity' of flavour and a rich texture that was 'as good as soup gets'. The second course is normally fish, perhaps scallops with mango and coriander oil, or 'memorable' stuffed mousseline of sole, flavoured with basil; one reporter, who recognised this as a tricky technical challenge, proclaimed it the equal of any.

Main courses typically combine breast of fowl or a game bird with either pulses or legumes: grouse with Puy lentils, or guinea-fowl with haricot beans. These come with the renowned 'perfect' dauphinoise potatoes, and offer up the 'good deep flavours' so characteristic of the cooking here. The 'cleansing salad' that follows is 'one of the best of its kind', and cheese is a single piece such as Brie de Meaux 'in perfect condition', served with apple. Far better that, is the conclusion, than half a dozen in mediocre condition. French is the culinary language throughout, but sometimes a dessert such as a 'small and extremely rich' caramel parfait will give way to a more novel idea: a warm 'cake' of almond and polenta, served with a rhubarb sorbet, delicately balancing sweetness and acidity.

Canny purchasing and a carefully maintained cellar has resulted in an impressive range of wines at some incredibly good prices, most notably from Bordeaux and Italy. South-west France has long been a particular enthusiasm, and attention is also being turned to South Africa and Spain for the quality and value these regions now offer. Half-bottles are generous in number, whereas wines by the glass are limited to house French (£3.35, or £12.75 a bottle) and whatever David Brown feels like opening. One reporter has suggested that an appropriate glass of wine for each course would be quite feasible with a set menu, and would relieve the customer of the burden of making a good match.

CHEF: Hilary Brown   PROPRIETORS: David and Hilary Brown   OPEN: Sun to Tue and Thur L 1pm (1 sitting), Fri and Sat D 8pm (1 sitting)   CLOSED: Oct, 25 Dec, 1 Jan, 1 week June   MEALS: Set L £20, Set D £30   SERVICE: not inc   CARDS: none   DETAILS: 28 seats. Private parties: 28 main room. Car park. Children welcome. No smoking in dining-room. Wheelchair access (1 step; not WC). No music

---

The Guide's *top-rated restaurants are listed near the front of the book.*

'The "rockery" is rather a dump of large boulders between the dining-room and the car park, which is of no importance except insofar as it relates to the pretensions of the place.' (On eating in Wales)

▲ *Culloden House* ⚞✶

Milton of Culloden, Inverness IV1 2NZ
TEL: (01463) 790461 FAX: (01463) 792181
EMAIL: 106237.663@compuserve.com
from Inverness take A96 to Nairn, turn right after 1m,   COOKING 2
then left at Culloden House Avenue   COST £28–£57

As one might expect of a residence with royal connections (the site was headquarters to Bonnie Prince Charlie before the Battle of Culloden in 1746), the ivy-covered house is built on an impressive scale. Sitting in a 40-acre estate, it is decked out with marble fireplaces, chandeliers, and pink and white plasterwork. Tureens, domes and decanters decorate the dining-room, where the option is a lunchtime *carte* or multi-course set-price dinner. Despite smoked salmon, timbale of haggis with neeps and tatties, and Atholl brose, the heritage card is not overplayed. Scottish lamb has been served with couscous and bordelaise sauce, halibut has taken on a cider and apple complexion, and beef has appeared with wild mushrooms. One of the three main courses at dinner is vegetarian, and desserts might include strawberry and coconut meringue, or sticky toffee pudding. There are some fancy prices on the heavyweight French-dominated wine list, but some decent drinking under £20 too. House red Bordeaux is £12.60, white burgundy £16.80.

CHEF: Michael Simpson PROPRIETOR: North American Country Inns OPEN: all week 12.30 to 2, 7 to 8.45 MEALS: alc L (main courses £9.50 to £16). Set L £12.50 (2 courses) to £17.50, Set D £35. BYO £8 SERVICE: not inc, card slips closed CARDS: Amex, Diners, MasterCard, Switch, Visa DETAILS: 60 seats. Private parties: 60 main room, 25 private rooms. Car park. Vegetarian meals. Children welcome by arrangement. Jacket and tie. No smoking in dining-room. Occasional music ACCOMMODATION: 28 rooms, all with bath/shower. TV. Phone. B&B £135 to £250. Children welcome by arrangement. High teas for children. Dogs welcome by arrangement. Afternoon teas (£5)

▲ *Dunain Park* ⚞✶

Inverness IV3 6JN
TEL: (01463) 230512 FAX: (01463) 224532
EMAIL: dunainparkhotel@btinternet.com   COOKING 2
on A82, 2m from Inverness   COST £37–£48

The Nicolls, who have run this Georgian country house just outside Inverness since 1985, have imbued it with a welcoming, homely, lived-in feel. Large bay windows overlook the valley, and it appears 'comfortable but unostentatious'. Ann Nicoll cooks Scottish meals with a French accent, along the lines of smoked haddock and whiting mousseline with a sabayon sauce, or layers of flaky pastry filled with wild mushrooms in a creamy white wine sauce.

Materials (including herbs, soft fruit and vegetables from the two-acre walled garden) are of high quality, and a steak menu offers fillet or sirloin – from Aberdeen Angus accredited herds – either plain or with a variety of sauces from garlic butter to whisky and oatmeal. Lamb is local too, and might appear as a pink loin wrapped in rösti potato on a rich sage-infused sauce. Vegetables are served plain, while puddings, typically creamy or chocolatey, are help-yourself from a buffet. Some good bottles are in evidence on the well-annotated wine list and, although most are over £20, prices reflect the quality. House French is £12.50.

CHEF: Ann Nicoll   PROPRIETORS: Ann and Edward Nicoll   OPEN: all week D only 7 to 9   MEALS: alc (main courses £16)   SERVICE: not inc, card slips closed   CARDS: Amex, Delta, MasterCard, Switch, Visa   DETAILS: 40 seats. Private parties: 20 main room. Car park. Vegetarian meals. Children's helpings. No smoking in dining-room. Wheelchair access (not WC). No music ACCOMMODATION: 12 rooms, all with bath/shower. TV. Phone. B&B £138 to £170. Rooms for disabled. Children welcome. High teas for children. Baby facilities. Dogs welcome by arrangement. Afternoon teas. Swimming-pool (*The Which? Hotel Guide*) £5

KILCHRENAN Argyll & Bute   map 11

▲ *Taychreggan* 🍴✕

Kilchrenan PA35 1HQ
TEL: (01866) 833211 and 833366
FAX: (01866) 833244
EMAIL: taychreggan@btinternet.com   COOKING 2
on B845, 7m S of Taynuilt   COST £24–£43

This 300-year-old inn beside Loch Awe, reached down a long, twisting single-track road, could not be more peaceful. Lunch is three courses, dinner a more leisurely five, eaten looking across the loch through floor-to-ceiling windows. The same style of food obtains at each, and typically makes use of Mull salmon, steamed Loch Etive mussels and roast loin of Argyll venison. Martin Wallace, who arrived in the kitchen just as the last edition of the *Guide* was going to press, seems happiest in traditional mode: a chicken-liver parfait with well-matched sweet chutney, for example, worked well at inspection. Finish, perhaps, with lemon meringue pie, or crisply caramelised, creamily smooth, coffee-flavoured crème brûlée. Wines from classic French regions are balanced by interesting bottles from elsewhere, and prices are fair. House wine is £9.95.

CHEF: Martin Wallace   PROPRIETOR: Annie Paul   OPEN: all week 12.30 to 2, 7.30 to 8.45 MEALS: Set L £17, Set D £28. Bar L available   SERVICE: not inc   CARDS: Amex, Delta, MasterCard, Switch, Visa   DETAILS: 45 seats. Private parties: 50 main room, 24 private room. Car park. Vegetarian meals. No children under 14. No smoking in dining-room. Wheelchair access (1 step; also WC). Music. Air-conditioned   ACCOMMODATION: 19 rooms, all with bath/shower. Phone. DB&B £80 to £220. No children under 14. Dogs welcome by arrangement. Fishing (*The Which? Hotel Guide*) £5

'Our excellent second-floor window seat ensured a good view of the local binmen clearing the remnants of the market, which was a first in terms of dining entertainment.' (On eating in London)

The Guide *relies on feedback from its readers. Especially welcome are reports on new restaurants appearing in the book for the first time. All letters to the* Guide *are acknowledged.*

map 11

▲ *Killiecrankie Hotel* ❧✶

Killiecrankie, by Pitlochry PH16 5LG
TEL: (01796) 473220   FAX: (01796) 472451   COOKING 3
off A9, 3m N of Pitlochry   COST £38–£45

Stuffed birds and animals set the tone in the hallway of this privately run hotel
on the side of a steep gorge, where ravens fly and where the imaginative might
conjure up echoes of a bloody battle dating from the Jacobite rebellion. Dinners
are served in two rooms, one pleasantly done out in shades of coral and
turquoise, the other a more modern conservatory-style addition. A new kitchen
brigade, headed by Mark Easton, continues to offer a daily, fixed-price menu of
three courses plus Scottish cheeses and coffee. Support for local and regional
ingredients is evident in cream of broccoli and Gowrie Cheddar soup, or
generous roast leg of Tombuie smoked lamb with red onion and mint compote
served with mash and a red wine sauce, which an inspector thought 'could not
be faulted'.

Desserts might range from a trio of fruit sorbets with meringue wafers to an
impressive version of tiramisù with coffee anglaise. Bar lunches have drawn
variable reports, although the owners tell us that they are pleased with their
range of French country breads. Colin Anderson is a 'notably gracious and
welcoming host'. The list of around 70 wines from Lay & Wheeler is fairly
divided between France and other producing nations. Prices of house wines
range from £10.50 to £14.85.

CHEF: Mark Easton   PROPRIETORS: Colin and Carole Anderson   OPEN: all week D only 7 to
8.30   CLOSED: Jan and Feb   MEALS: Set D £28. Bar L available   SERVICE: not inc, card slips
closed   CARDS: MasterCard, Switch, Visa   DETAILS: 34 seats. Private parties: 12 main room.
Car park. Vegetarian meals. Children's helpings. No children under 5. No smoking in
dining-room. No music   ACCOMMODATION: 10 rooms, all with bath/shower. TV. Phone. D,B&B
£60 to £160. Children welcome. High teas for children. Baby facilities. Well-behaved dogs
welcome (*The Which? Hotel Guide*) £5

---

 map 11

▲ *Ballathie House* ❧✶

Kinclaven, by Stanley PH1 4QN
TEL: (01250) 883268   FAX: (01250) 883396
EMAIL: email@ballathiehousehotel.com   COOKING 5
off B9099, take right fork 1m N of Stanley   COST £21–£50

This peaceful, turreted, Victorian house stands in a prime spot beside the Tay,
surrounded by 1,500 acres of woodland. It attracts all nationalities but has not
been unduly corporatised, and 'still retains some sense of a grand home', with
high ceilings, panelled wallpaper, ornate plasterwork, heavy draped curtains,
and damask tablecloths. Lunches (apart from Sunday) offer a choice between
sandwiches, and bar meals of smoked salmon or goujons of sole with tartare
sauce, while the Terrace menu might take in pickled herring, pan-fried pheasant
breast, and a vegetable and cheese flan.

The kitchen moves into another gear for set-price dinners that might start with, say, warm terrine of salmon mousseline served with horseradish and dill butter sauce, or salad of home-smoked wood pigeon with a sherry vinegar dressing. The second course is a soup (leek and smoked haddock perhaps) or sorbet, typically followed by a fish option such as steamed halibut fillet (served with creamed Savoy cabbage and smoked salmon), a meat along the lines of Chinese-spiced breast of Gressingham duck, or a vegetarian alternative of wild mushroom and artichoke charlotte.

To finish, there may be chilled citrus fruit tart, or sticky toffee pudding with fudge sauce and vanilla ice-cream. Skilled and obliging service from smartly dressed young staff is a plus, and the wine list's weight of French tradition is leavened by respectable and affordable wines from elsewhere. Around a dozen are available by the glass, with prices starting at £10.50 a bottle.

CHEF: Kevin MacGillivray   PROPRIETOR: Ballathie House Hotel Ltd   OPEN: all week 12 to 2, 7 to 9   MEALS: alc L Mon to Sat (main courses £5.50 to £7.50). Set L Sun £16.95, Set D £20.50 to £30. Bar L available Mon to Sat   SERVICE: not inc   CARDS: Amex, Delta, Diners, MasterCard, Switch, Visa   DETAILS: 80 seats. Private parties: 60 main room, 15 to 35 private rooms. Car park. Vegetarian meals. Children's helpings. No smoking in dining-room. Wheelchair access (also WC). No music   ACCOMMODATION: 38 rooms, all with bath/shower. TV. Phone. B&B £60 to £180. Rooms for disabled. Children welcome. Baby facilities. Dogs welcome in bedrooms only. Afternoon teas. Fishing

---

KINGUSSIE Highland   map 11

▲ *The Cross* 🍷 ✳

Tweed Mill Brae, Kingussie PH21 1TC   COOKING 6
TEL: (01540) 661166   FAX: (01540) 661080   COST £43–£51

This converted tweed mill off the main road, beside the burn that determined its location, is a haven of calm. Tony Hadley provides 'an easy, relaxed welcome', talks naturally and helpfully through the menu and wines, and the spacious dining-room and expansive tables are appreciated. Five-course dinners offer no choice of the first three, but are well-balanced, and advance notice of dietary or vegetarian requirements is dealt with sympathetically. Becca Henderson, new to the listings, has been at Ruth Hadley's elbow for four years now, taking an increasingly important role, but the gentle Scottish style continues as before.

Typical of the format might be a starter of game sausage (using pigeon and venison), or seafood boudin, made from a mix of scallops, prawns and turbot, and served with asparagus and mayonnaise. This is followed by soup, a 'well-flavoured' capsicum version for example, then perhaps a fish-cake or a tartlet: of Gigha goats' cheese and leeks, or mushrooms set in a savoury custard. Portion sizes take into account the number of courses, and dishes look good. Native materials may be treated simply – wild salmon 'caught this morning' with a sorrel sauce – or given a bit of a fillip: sliced duck breast with a sauce of sherry and soy that was 'light, clear, and not too Chinese-y'.

Meals finish with a choice of 'our usual selection of unusual cheeses', or one of two desserts: lemon cheesecake, or iced hazelnut meringue parfait. Tony Hadley is continuing the policy of reducing the number of French wines on his 400-plus list and increasing the range in all other areas, particularly South Africa. Prices are fair, with around 150 bins under £20, and some 70 half-bottles are available. There are no house wines as such, but six wines are chosen to match the evening's menu in both style and price (usually between £12.50 and £25), with a glass of something interesting offered at £3.

CHEFS: Ruth Hadley and Becca Henderson PROPRIETORS: Tony and Ruth Hadley OPEN: Wed to Mon D only 7 to 9 CLOSED: 1 to 26 Dec, 11 Jan to 25 Feb MEALS: Set D £35 SERVICE: not inc, card slips closed CARDS: Delta, MasterCard, Switch, Visa DETAILS: 28 seats. Private parties: 28 main room. Car park. No children under 12. No smoking in dining-room. Wheelchair access (also WC). No music ACCOMMODATION: 9 rooms, all with bath/shower. Phone. D,B&B £95 to £190. No children under 12 (*The Which? Hotel Guide*) £5

KINLOCHMOIDART Highland map 11

Kinacarra ⁵⋇ £

Kinlochmoidart PH38 4ND
TEL: (01967) 431238 COOKING 4
on A861, at head of Loch Moidart COST £14–£37

'The area around this restaurant must be one of the most beautiful and unspoilt in Scotland,' remarked a reporter. Angus and Frances MacLean's modest stone residence stands on the shores of Loch Moidart and continues to please all comers and all ages. Dinner is a *carte* that calls into play not only venison, but also Scottish sirloin steak, salmon, scallops and other regional produce. Typical starters are cream of mushroom and garlic soup, or smoked pheasant breast with melon slices, while main courses could range from breast of chicken marinated with lime and soy, via pork with apple, brandy and cream sauce, to a casserole of venison in wine with red peppers. A quartet of desserts might include a 'deliciously light' rhubarb and orange fool, steamed syrup sponge or home-made ice-creams. The light lunch menu is a more limited affair, with 'reasonable' prices to match: one couple were delighted with a meal that included salmon pâté, pasta with a vegetarian sauce and meringue with home-made coffee and praline ice-cream. The wine list from Lay & Wheeler bypasses Europe in favour of lively stuff from the New World. House Merlot from Chile is £10.50.

CHEF: Frances MacLean PROPRIETORS: Angus and Frances MacLean OPEN: Tue to Sun 12 to 2, 7 to 8.30 CLOSED: end Oct to Easter MEALS: alc (main courses L £4 to £7, D £9.50 to £13.50). Light L menu SERVICE: not inc CARDS: none DETAILS: 24 seats. 6 seats outside. Private parties: 24 main room. Car park. Vegetarian meals. Children's helpings. No smoking in dining-room. Wheelchair access (also WC). No music

---

LINLITHGOW West Lothian map 11

▲ Champany Inn ▮

Champany, Linlithgow EH49 7LU
TEL: (01506) 834532 FAX: (01506) 834302 COOKING 6
2m NE of Linlithgow at junction of A904 and A803 COST £34–£77

The Davidsons ply a unique trade in this low whitewashed old farm building, devoting themselves principally to cooking beef. Wander through a courtyard, past a cocktail bar, round a seawater pool of Loch Gruinart oysters and live lobsters, into a circular stone dining-room with wooden rafters and bare polished tables. Slabs of beef are laid out for approval beside the see-through kitchen and, depending on the season, there may be a basket of wild mushrooms or asparagus on display as well. The beef is Aberdeen Angus, hung for three weeks, butchered into strip loin, ribeye, porterhouse, chateaubriand and pope's eye. Either choose by eye, or take up their offer to 'cut a steak from the display to your requirements and charge according to weight'.

Accompaniments tend to be simple: black peppercorn sauce, for example, or a 'sticky, concentrated' sauce of stock and wild mushrooms. Anything that is not beef is likely to be lamb, poultry or seafood, among the latter may be flavourful salmon fillet with 'a nice sharp' lemon butter, or grilled lobster served with a sauce 'like hollandaise with chopped tomatoes and coriander'. Begin, perhaps, with Stilton soup, or slices of 'pungent and rich' home-smoked beef, with 'fantastic depth of flavour', dribbled with good olive oil; the smoked beef also finds its way into bread. Vegetables are charged extra, and prices can make this one of the *Guide*'s more expensive Scottish restaurants, but the Chop and Ale house – the 'indicated' venue for lunch – serves generous helpings of spicy king prawns, burgers, steaks, lamb chops and chips for rather less.

The weighty wine list with almost 1,000 bins is not for the faint-hearted (nor are the prices), but sommelier and maitre'd Mike Anthony will happily guide waverers, perhaps towards the exceptional range from South Africa. Otherwise, mature *grand cru* burgundies, vintage clarets and fine Rioja offer a wealth of choice to go with the beef. White wine lovers are equally well catered for, and house South African is £12.50. CELLARMAN'S CHOICE: Gewurztraminer d'Alsace Reserve 1996, Trimbach, £28.50; Thelema Mountain Vineyards Merlot 1994, Stellenbosch, South Africa, £35.

CHEF: Clive Davidson PROPRIETORS: Clive and Anne Davidson OPEN: Mon to Fri L 12.30 to 2, Mon to Sat D 7 to 10 MEALS: alc (main courses £14.50 to £27.50). Set L £15.75 (2 courses) SERVICE: 10%, card slips closed CARDS: Amex, Delta, Diners, MasterCard, Switch, Visa DETAILS: 50 seats. 20 seats outside. Private parties: 16 main room, 16 private room. Car park. Vegetarian meals. Children welcome. No children under 8. Wheelchair access (1 step; also WC). No music ACCOMMODATION: 16 rooms, all with bath/shower. TV. Phone. Rooms for disabled. Children welcome. No dogs

---

MILNGAVIE East Dunbartonshire   map 11

Gingerhill £

1 Hillhead Street, Milngavie G62 8AF
TEL: (0141) 956 6515   COOKING 2
off A81, 4m N of Glasgow   COST £7–£39

Modesty is a virtue in Carol Thomson's tiny upstairs bistro overlooking a suburban shopping precinct. It is a 'clean and tidy' little place with closely packed tables, plastic cloths and blue colour scheme. Customers come here for honestly prepared, hearty food – the kind of stuff that reminded one reporter of 'recipes for thrifty housewives in women's magazines'. Printed lunch and dinner menus are bolstered by a goodly number of blackboard specials and there is a bias towards fish and vegetarian dishes, although carnivores are not overlooked.

Organic produce (including beef) receives a good airing, and Scottish waters yield seasonal hauls of langoustines, diver-caught scallops, mussels and more besides. Soups – especially fish chowder – are well reported, and the kitchen also takes on board seared halibut with coriander, monkfish thermidor and vegetable crêpes with pine-nuts. To finish, hot chocolate fudge cake has been a winner, while bread-and-butter pudding is a pleasing version. Gingerhill is unlicensed, and there's no corkage if you BYO; bottled water comes free.

CHEFS: Heather Gorman and Carol Mercer   PROPRIETOR: Carol Thomson   OPEN: Mon to Sat 11.30 to 3, Thur to Sat 7pm (1 sitting)   MEALS: alc (main courses L £2 to £10.50, D £9 to £16.50). Unlicensed, BYO (no corkage)   SERVICE: not inc, card slips closed   CARDS: MasterCard, Visa   DETAILS: 24 seats. 14 seats outside. Private parties: 14 main room, 10 private rooms. Vegetarian meals. Children's helpings. No smoking while others eat. Music

---

MOFFAT   Dumfries & Galloway   map 11

▲ Well View ▾ ⅝✻

Ballplay Road, Moffat DG10 9JU   COOKING 3
TEL: (01683) 220184   FAX: (01683) 220088   COST £18–£39

A comfortable lounge and friendly atmosphere get things off to a good start in this double-fronted Victorian house, run by the Schuckardts for 15 years now. Even though there is little to ponder before dinner – no choice before dessert, and even then not much – the menu still comes with something appetising to nibble. John, a knowledgeable host, chats as he waits on table 'with exquisite patience' in the small dining-room. Meals are five courses plus a half-way citrus sorbet, and portions are well judged. A typical example might start with chicken terrine, before salmon and Kirkcudbright queenies in a cream and vegetable sauce, then fillet of Galloway beef in a red wine sauce; a long list of endorsements includes carrot and apricot soup, haggis and black-pudding rissoles, trout in oatmeal, and gammon with Cumberland sauce.

'Wonderfully kept' cheeses appear to be a hobby, and come with home-made chutney and 'interesting Scottish biscuits', while desserts might run to mango brûlée, or praline ice-cream with apple and ginger cake. Bread is brought to table warm 'and unwrapped like a new baby', and value for money is considered 'outstanding'. The simply annotated wine list manages to cover all bases while making some interesting hits to the outfield: Hungarian Blauer Spätburgunder, perhaps, or a trio of country wines from Scotland. House wines start at £10 a bottle, £2.20 a glass.

CHEF: Janet Schuckardt   PROPRIETORS: Janet and John Schuckardt   OPEN: Sun to Fri L 12.15 to 1.15 (booking essential), all week D 6.30 to 8.30   MEALS: Set L £13, Set D £27.50   SERVICE: none, card slips closed   CARDS: Amex, Delta, MasterCard, Switch, Visa   DETAILS: 24 seats. Private parties: 18 main room, 6 private room. Car park. No children under 6 at D. No smoking in dining-room. Wheelchair access (2 steps; not WC). No music   ACCOMMODATION: 6 rooms, all with bath/shower. TV. B&B £45 to £90. Children welcome. High teas for children. Baby facilities. Dogs welcome in bedrooms only and not left unattended. Afternoon teas (*The Which? Hotel Guide*)   £5

See inside the front cover for an explanation of the symbols used at the tops of entries.

▲ *The Dower House* ▼ ✻

Highfield, Muir of Ord IV6 7XN
TEL/FAX: (01463) 870090
EMAIL: thedowerhouse@compuserve.com   COOKING 3
on A862, 1m N of Muir of Ord   COST £38–£45

Three sets of antlers perched above the door greet visitors to this low stone building. Highfield House, to which it was attached, no longer exists, but the Dower House still has three acres of peaceful grounds to its name. Real fires, and stacks of books and local maps contribute to the welcoming friendly feel, and antique furniture adds a note of elegance. The Aitchisons, who have been here ten years, serve a simple-as-can-be three-course dinner with only one choice: either cheese or dessert.

Local supplies of seafood, beef, cheese, and game in season are the foundation, and are put to varied use in a repertoire that stretches from red wine risotto to hot-smoked chicken with oriental vegetables. The enterprising approach might also throw up grilled red gurnard with sweet pepper, and an Italian or Mediterranean streak is often detectable: in grilled polenta with Parma ham and a rosemary and anchovy dressing, for example. To finish, expect hot pineapple with rum sauce, perhaps, or lemon and rhubarb tart.

The wine list will suit both French traditionalists and New World adventurers, while over 50 half-bottles will aid those who like to pick and mix. Four French house wines are £13 each. CELLARMAN'S CHOICE: Mudhouse Sauvignon Blanc 1997, Marlborough, New Zealand, £17; Bonny Doon Carignan 1996, Santa Cruz, California, £17.

CHEF: Robyn Aitchison PROPRIETORS: Robyn and Mena Aitchison OPEN: all week D only 7.30 to 9.30 (L by arrangement) CLOSED: Christmas day MEALS: Set D £25. BYO £10 SERVICE: not inc, card slips closed CARDS: MasterCard, Visa DETAILS: 26 seats. 8 seats outside. Car park. Vegetarian meals. Children's helpings. No children under 6. No smoking in dining-room. Wheelchair access (also WC). No music ACCOMMODATION: 5 rooms, all with bath/shower. TV. Phone. B&B £45 to £120. Rooms for disabled. Children welcome. High teas for children. Baby facilities. Dogs welcome in bedrooms only. Garden (*The Which? Hotel Guide*)

▲ *Clifton House* ▮ ✻

Viewfield Street, Nairn IV12 4HW
TEL: (01667) 453119 FAX: (01667) 452836   COOKING 4
W of town roundabout on A96   COST £27–£43

This creeper-clad Victorian house is 'a must for lovers of a civilised, relaxing atmosphere'. It is also 'a feast of art' throughout, from paintings to the Pugin-designed drawing-room wallpaper: eat your heart out Lord Irvine. The menu changes every day 'depending on what we can make, buy, order, grow or kill', writes J. Gordon Macintyre, who also recognises that you don't get far in this business without good supplies. Lobsters and langoustines come from Skye, oysters and scallops from Loch Fyne, and white fish from Duncan Fraser 'with whom we have dealt since before the war': the house has been in the family since 1931. But Macintyre is always on the lookout for something new. This year's find is Mrs Jones in Inverurie, who supplies free-range chickens, an unusual breed of lamb, and a pig-boar cross that produces 'pork such as one used to have 30 years ago'.

Menus are written in 'very correct' French, as they have been for 45 years – 'I am too old to change now', confides Macintyre senior – and indeed some of the dishes have an old-fashioned ring to them, oeufs mayonnaise and crevettes Marie-Rose among them. But simple treatment keeps the whole thing on track, from turbot with beurre blanc to guinea-fowl provençale. A visiting academic marked his starter of smoked halibut and salmon 'alpha plus', and declared the cheese selection 'a meal in itself'. Full marks go to the huge collection of wines which are presented in a Latin-inscribed book and range from a drinkable bunch under £10 to the great and the good from classical France and beyond. Prices are keen enough to raise a smile, and 47 malts by the glass bring a cheery end to proceedings.

CHEFS: Charles Macintyre and J. Gordon Macintyre   PROPRIETOR: J. Gordon Macintyre   OPEN: all week 12.30 to 1, 7 to 9.30   CLOSED: Dec and Jan   MEALS: alc (main courses £11 to £15) SERVICE: none, card slips closed   CARDS: Amex, Diners, MasterCard, Visa   DETAILS: 40 seats. Private parties: 60 main room, 12 private room. Car park. Vegetarian meals. Children's helpings. No smoking in 1 dining-room. Music   ACCOMMODATION: 12 rooms, all with bath/shower. B&B £60 to £107. Children welcome. Afternoon teas (*The Which? Hotel Guide*)

NEWTON STEWART   Dumfries & Galloway   map 11

▲ *Kirroughtree Hotel* ⁵✳

Newton Stewart DG8 6AN
TEL: (01671) 402141   FAX: (01671) 402425
EMAIL: mcmhotel@mcmhotel.demon.co.uk   COOKING 2
off A712, just outside Newton Stewart   COST £21–£48

The white-painted eighteenth-century house and its croquet lawn stand in eight acres of landscaped gardens, a scale which is echoed inside. Burns used to recite poetry from the grand staircase, and the dining-rooms look as if they have been iced like giant wedding cakes. Ian Bennett's Franco-Scottish aspiratons are centred on dinner, which might start with chicken liver and foie gras parfait with onion chutney, or 'superlative' ravioli of wild mushrooms with deep-fried celeriac and a truffle sauce. Meaty fish such as halibut or turbot share main-course billing with Scottish beef and lamb, and roast rump of venison in a game sauce. Cheese (served with bannocks) has been highly rated, while desserts might run to hot caramel soufflé, or an apple dish combining parfait and fritters. The wine list makes an effort to supply plain drinking under £20, but is not averse to a few posh three-figure bottles either. House Vin de Pays d'Oc is £12.

All entries in the Guide *are re-researched and rewritten every year, not least because restaurant standards fluctuate. Don't rely on an out-of-date* Guide.

CHEF: Ian Bennett PROPRIETOR: McMillan Hotels Ltd OPEN: all week 12 to 1.30, 7 to 9
CLOSED: 3 Jan to mid-Feb MEALS: alc (main courses £10.50 to £14). Set L £13.50, Set D £30
SERVICE: not inc, card slips closed CARDS: Delta, MasterCard, Switch, Visa DETAILS: 50
seats. Private parties: 20 main room. Car park. Vegetarian meals. No children under 10. Jacket
and tie. No smoking in dining-room. Music ACCOMMODATION: 17 rooms, all with bath/shower.
TV. Phone. B&B £65 to £160. No children under 10. Dogs welcome in lower-ground-floor rooms
only. Afternoon teas

OBAN Argyll & Bute	map 11

▲ Heatherfield House, Poacher's Restaurant ⁵✳

Albert Road, Oban PA34 5EJ	COOKING 3
TEL/FAX: (01631) 562681	COST £22–£60

The Robertsons have tacked a canopied dining-area for al fresco summer eating
on to a terrace in the lower garden of their stone built Victorian house. Simpler
fare is on offer here than in the bare-boarded Poacher's Restaurant, but the
emphasis remains on home-smoked meats and home-cured fish. Game from
local shoots features in season. 'We should like to record our satisfaction in
particular with the seafood and smoked fish dishes,' wrote one couple. Those
may include salad of spiced potted crab, smoked salmon and cream-cheese
croissant, or seafood stew with tomato, pimento, leek and garlic. Rabbit
casseroled with cranberries, red wine and bacon has proved popular with
meat-eaters, and the dessert repertoire runs to fresh fruit pavlova or feuilleté of
pineapple with rum and a coffee caramel syrup. A good international wine list
takes in a serviceable selection of halves and wines by the glass. House French is
£9.95.

CHEF: Alasdair Robertson PROPRIETORS: Alasdair and Jane Robertson OPEN: all week 12.30
to 5.30, 7.30 to 9.30 (24-hour advance booking essential Nov to Mar) MEALS: alc (main courses
£10 to £25). Set L £9.95 (2 courses) to £15, Set D £16.50 (2 courses) to £22 SERVICE: not inc,
card slips closed CARDS: MasterCard, Visa DETAILS: 30 seats. 15 seats outside. Private
parties: 40 main room. Car park. Children's helpings. No smoking in dining-room. Music
ACCOMMODATION: 4 rooms, all with bath/shower. TV. D,B&B £43.50 to £87. Children welcome.
High teas for children. Baby facilities. Small well-behaved dogs welcome in bedrooms only
£5

▲ Knipoch Hotel ▮ ⁵✳

Knipoch, Oban PA34 4QT
TEL: (01852) 316251 FAX: (01852) 316249
EMAIL: 100745.1315@compuserve.com   COOKING 3
on A816, 6m S of Oban   COST £39–£60

Set back from the road a few miles south of Oban, Knipoch provides comfortable
leather armchairs and big sofas, log fires, an informal ambience, and a simple
dinner format. A typical three-course meal might start with either cauliflower
soup, or prawn and asparagus tossed in mayonnaise and served on toast,
followed by loin of pork stuffed with prunes and walnuts, served with a plum
sauce. Next comes either a Perthshire version of Brie, or an orange cake covered
in chocolate, on an orange and whisky sauce. To turn this into a five-course meal,

you simply eat the lot. There are specials too. In-house smoking is a favourite pastime (indeed, a mail-order business), so smoked salmon or Islay scallops make a natural alternative. Or there may be fillet of Aberdeen Angus with a sauce of mushrooms, wine and cream. The hotel has its own private spring, and provides this water free of charge

The gargantuan wine list opens with a selection of easy-drinking house varietals mostly costing £11.90, moves on to Colin Craig's recommended whites and reds, chosen for being 'good in their class' in the £10 to £20 range, and then proceeds to the list proper. While most people could probably find something to suit in the first three pages, it would be a shame to miss the delights of the main list, with its mature burgundies, vintage clarets and prized bins from Spain and Germany as well as the New World. Prices are fair too.

CHEFS: Colin and Kamma Craig   PROPRIETORS: the Craig family   OPEN: all week D only 7.30 to 9; L by arrangement   CLOSED: mid-Dec to mid-Feb   MEALS: Set D £29.50 to £39.50   SERVICE: not inc, card slips closed   CARDS: Amex, Delta, Diners, MasterCard, Switch, Visa   DETAILS: 36 seats. Private parties: 24 main room, 12 private room. Car park. Children's helpings. No smoking in dining-room. No music   ACCOMMODATION: 16 rooms, all with bath/shower. TV. Phone. B&B £35 to £154. Children welcome. High teas for children. Baby facilities. No dogs. Afternoon teas. Fishing

---

PEAT INN Fife	map 11

▲ Peat Inn 🍷 ✳

Peat Inn KY15 5LH
TEL: (01334) 840206   FAX: (01334) 840530   COOKING 5
at junction of B940 and B941, 6m SW of St Andrews   COST £26–£55

The Peat Inn is aptly named – a pleasant smoky odour hangs in the air – and if the interior appears to be a model of contemporary styling this may be partly because 'the 1970s are back in vogue'. The Wilsons believe strongly that a restaurant should reflect its surroundings, use local and regional produce, and thus respond to the seasons. This gives the food its identity, which here includes a distinctly red-blooded element in pan-fried venison liver and kidney, and a lighter component in the form of langoustine tails with wild mushrooms, or monkfish and lobster with artichoke hearts.

The *carte* offers around half a dozen choices at each stage, cost is not high, and the set four-course options are especially appreciated. Over the past year some reporters have enjoyed first-class meals, from 'simple but brilliant' fillet of halibut on a bed of roasted vegetables to 'wonderful' fillet of beef with potato cake and rich Madeira sauce; for one, this is 'still the standard-setter'. But the restaurant's performance has been variable: two inspectors dining independently on separate occasions found little to justify the reputation that the Wilsons have built up over a quarter of a century: problems with timing, seasoning and flavouring in general have taken the shine off things. Among desserts, chocolate tart shows Peat Inn at its best, the trio of caramels is well reported, and flavours and textures have 'worked really well' in baked apple with caramel sauce and crème anglaise. Service was 'friendly' for one visitor, though others have reported the opposite experience.

David Wilson lists some highly prestigious châteaux and producers but they are presented without pretension: he starts in France, moves on to similar wines from other countries, then back to the next French region. House wines, at £14, change throughout the year; there are plenty of bins around the £20 mark, though if you wish to spend £2,000 (for a 1945 Pétrus), you may, and half-bottles are plentiful. CELLARMAN'S CHOICE: Glenguin Unoaked Chardonnay 1996, Hunter Valley, Australia; £20; Haut-Médoc, Ch. Lamothe Bergeron 1988, £22.

CHEF: David Wilson and Angus Blacklaws   PROPRIETORS: David and Patricia Wilson   OPEN: Tue to Sat 1pm (1 sitting) 7 to 9.30   CLOSED: 25 Dec, 1 Jan   MEALS: alc (main courses £15.50 to £19.50). Set L £18.50, Set D £28 BYO £6   SERVICE: net prices, card slips closed   CARDS: Amex, Diners, MasterCard, Switch, Visa   DETAILS: 48 seats. Private parties: 24 main room, 12 private rooms. Car park. Vegetarian meals. Children's helpings. No smoking in dining-room. Wheelchair access (also WC). No music   ACCOMMODATION: 8 rooms, all with bath/shower. TV. Phone. B&B £75 to £135. Rooms for disabled. Children welcome (*The Which? Hotel Guide*)

PEEBLES Borders   map 11

▲ *Cringletie House* 🍽️ ✳️

Peebles EH45 8PL
TEL: (01721) 730233   FAX: (01721) 730244   COOKING 4
on A703, 2½m N of Peebles   COST £23–£46

Cringletie passed into corporate ownership in the autumn of 1997, but virtually nothing about the tone of the place has changed, and the new regime seems 'determined to keep high standards'. Arrive in the dark to experience the full majesty of the setting: a flood-lit turreted red sandstone pile with a hint of Hans Christian Andersen to it looms through trees above Eddleston Water. The lounge and dining-rooms have now swapped roles, but the ambience of restrained luxury is maintained, and is enhanced by 'friendly and attentive' staff.

Gregg Russell cooks in the country-house manner, so meals open with an appetiser, perhaps a sliver of quail meat in balsamic dressing. Presentation is a strong point. 'Perfectly cooked' fillet of sole is formed into a circular band and filled with a cheesy mousse; looking like a brooch, it is titled 'cameo' on the menu. 'Successful and enjoyable' at inspection was a salmon fillet on roughly mashed potato and cabbage with a gently aniseedy sauce. More robust appetites might prefer fillet of local beef with herb crumble sauced with port and shallots. Vegetables err on the firmer side of al dente. Desserts such as banana parfait with butterscotch sauce or lemon pudding with feathered vanilla and raspberry sauces are pleasing without raising the roof. Fine home-made fudge comes with 'notably good' coffee. Only France receives detailed attention on the wine list, the remainder being little more than a nod to the rest of the world. That said, the house wines are a catholic selection, and open at £9.95.

CELLARMAN'S CHOICE: *Wines recommended by the restaurateur, normally more expensive than house wine.*

The Guide *is totally independent, accepts no free hospitality, and survives on the number of copies sold each year.*

CHEF: Gregg Russell   PROPRIETOR: Wrens Group Ltd   OPEN: all week 12.30 to 2, 7 to 9
MEALS: Set L £14.95, Set D £29.50. Bar L available Mon to Sat. BYO £10   SERVICE: not inc
CARDS: Amex, Delta, MasterCard, Switch, Visa   DETAILS: 60 seats. Private parties: 60 main
room, 12 to 30 private rooms. Car park. Vegetarian meals. Children's helpings. Jacket and tie.
No smoking in dining-room. No music   ACCOMMODATION: 13 rooms, all with bath/shower. TV.
Phone. B&B £65 to £130. Children welcome. High teas for children. Baby facilities. Dogs
welcome in bedrooms only. Afternoon teas   £5

PERTH Perthshire & Kinross   map 11

Let's Eat ⅚✕

77 Kinnoull Street, Perth PH1 5EZ   COOKING 3
TEL: (01738) 643377   FAX: (01738) 621464   COST £21–£41

Once a theatre, now a low-ceilinged, coral-pink L-shaped room, this is a
comfortable if slightly 'cave-like' place offering a fairly long *carte* with extra
options chalked on blackboards. The menu could stand as a weathervane for the
late '90s, offering black pudding in a salad with bacon strips and a poached egg,
wild mushroom risotto with truffle oil and Parmesan, and spiced pink-roasted
tenderloin of lamb on minted couscous. Occasionally, there is a feeling that one
too many elements have been incorporated in a dish, but the urge to stimulate
tastebuds is paramount. Puddings can be substantial: witness a raspberry and
blackberry frangipane tart with a biscuit cup of intense raspberry ice-cream.
Otherwise, indulge yourself with banana and praline pavlova, or yardstick
crème brulée. Shona Drysdale leads front-of-house with relaxed civility. The
international wine list has its fair share of highlights, and prices are mostly
manageable. House South African is £9.75.

CHEFS: Tony Heath, Lewis Pringle and Thomas Burns   PROPRIETORS: Tony Heath and Shona
Drysdale   OPEN: Tue to Sat 12 to 2, 6.30 to 9.45   CLOSED: 25 Dec, 1 Jan, 2 weeks Jan and
July   MEALS: alc (main courses £7 to £14.50)   SERVICE: not inc, card slips closed   CARDS:
Amex, Delta, MasterCard, Switch, Visa   DETAILS: 70 seats. Private parties: 70 main room.
Vegetarian meals. Children's helpings. No smoking in dining-room. Wheelchair access (2 steps;
also WC). Music   £5

PORT APPIN Argyll & Bute   map 11

▲ Airds Hotel ▮ ⅚✕

Port Appin PA38 4DF
TEL: (01631) 730236   FAX: (01631) 730535   COOKING 7
2m off A828, on E shore of Loch Linnhe   COST £54–£64

The dining-room windows and a narrow conservatory make the most of the
'simply stunning' location: looking across Loch Linnhe to Lismore. This very
comfortable white-painted house attracts a cosmopolitan clientele and has a
slightly formal feel, perhaps engendered by the mechanics of ordering both
dinner and wine between 6 and 7pm, and by the single sitting, albeit with a
staggered start. If the rituals of service are 'a trifle fussy', they generally produce a
'purposive atmosphere', and staff themselves are perfectly relaxed. Local

materials might include lightly cooked Lismore oysters and smoked salmon with champagne jelly ('beautiful taste and texture'), or squat lobsters and crab ravioli with turbot, pointing to the classically European tenor of Graeme Allen's food. He serves breast of pigeon with foie gras, truffle and chanterelles, for example, and loin of lamb with aubergine and dauphinoise potatoes.

Meals typically begin with shellfish and offal – crabmeat sausage, or smooth chicken liver parfait – but have also included toasted goat's cheese on a crisp croûton with diced apple and caramelised onion, and a 'delightful' soup of pea and mint, 'the flavours in perfect balance, with lots of concentration'. After meaty main courses such as pink and 'perfectly timed' venison with two purées (celeriac and parsnip), and a reduced sauce of the cooking juices, come British cheeses 'in excellent condition', or one of half a dozen desserts: fine apple tart with vanilla ice-cream, iced chocolate and orange mousse, or date pudding with butterscotch sauce. Amuse-gueules and petits fours are first-rate, and wines are of the highest quality. Europe dominates the lengthy list with pages of fine bins from Burgundy, Alsace and Italy, but the smaller New World selections are spot-on. Prices are eminently reasonable, starting with an English table wine at £12, and there are nearly 40 half-bottles. The considerate placing of the list in bedrooms allows extensive browsing.

CHEF: Graeme Allen   PROPRIETORS: the Allen family   OPEN: all week D only 8 to 8.30   CLOSED: 20 to 27 Dec, 6 to 31 Jan   MEALS: Set D £40   SERVICE: not inc, card slips closed   CARDS: MasterCard, Switch, Visa   DETAILS: 30 seats. Private parties: 30 main room. Car park. Children's helpings. No smoking in dining-room. No music   ACCOMMODATION: 12 rooms, all with bath/shower. TV. Phone. B&B £160 to £200. Children welcome. High teas for children. Baby facilities. Dogs welcome by arrangement. Afternoon teas. Fishing (*The Which? Hotel Guide*)   £5

▲ *Pierhouse* £✳

Port Appin PA38 4DE
TEL: (01631) 730302   FAX: (01631) 730400
off A828, on E shore of Loch Linnhe,   COOKING 3
opposite Lismore ferry   COST £19–£49

Ferries leave from the other end of the jetty that gives this seafood restaurant its name, to cross the short stretch of water to Lismore. It is a fine view, and a reminder, if one were needed, that fresh supplies are never far away. One reporter expected the place to be grander than it is. Raffia mats, paper napkins and packet butter are the form, and although new owners took over in March 1998, Rita Thomson, who has straddled both regimes, continues in the kitchen much as before, serving Lismore oysters, scallops in lemon butter, fresh-out-of-the-water langoustines, and platters of salmon and shellfish. Other options include pasta, risotto, venison, sirloin steak, a couple of vegetarian dishes, and a blackboard of daily specials. 'We don't come here for puds,' reckoned one pair of regular visitors, happy to forgo crème brûlée, profiteroles, and sticky toffee pudding. Service might be more on the ball, while three dozen wines know their way around the major grape varieties, starting with four house whites below £12.

CHEF: Rita Thomson   PROPRIETORS: Mr D.M. and Mrs E.M. Hamblin   OPEN: all week 12.30 to 2.30, 6.30 to 9.30   CLOSED: 25 Dec   MEALS: alc (main courses L £6.50 to £20, D 11.50 to £20) SERVICE: not inc, card slips closed   CARDS: Delta, MasterCard, Switch, Visa   DETAILS: 70 seats. 20 seats outside. Private parties: 80 main room. Car park. Vegetarian meals. Children's helpings before 7. No smoking in dining-room. Wheelchair access (also WC). Music ACCOMMODATION: 11 rooms, all with bath/shower. TV. Phone. B&B £39.50 to £84. Children welcome. High teas for children. Baby facilities. Dogs welcome in bedrooms only. Afternoon teas

---

PORTPATRICK   Dumfries & Galloway   map 11

▲ *Knockinaam Lodge* ⁑✳

Portpatrick DG9 9AD

TEL: (01776) 810471   FAX: (01776) 810435   COOKING 4
off A77, 3m S of Portpatrick   COST £36–£60

A 'secret haven' at the end of a long, narrow road on the west coast of Scotland, Knockinaam is a peaceful retreat with a 'civilised atmosphere'. A lawn stretches down to a private sandy beach, Northern Ireland is visible across the water, and the house, built in 1869, is tastefully furnished without being ostentatious. The owners welcome guests and serve drinks, while staff are 'friendly, natural and attentive'. Dinner is a leisurely four courses, with only one choice – either cheese or dessert – but individual requirements are taken into account along the way. The pattern is a succession of small portions, and one couple who cleared all their plates felt 'simply satisfied' by the end.

Meals start with canapés, followed by an appetiser at table, and usually include both meat and fish. One typical example progressed from a light oriental chicken broth with coriander and ginger, via fresh flaky cod topped with pesto in a tomato sauce, to a 'visually enticing' tower of haggis, spinach and slices of roe deer covered with diced apple and prune. Our inspector felt that 'everything was cooked with exactness' and, although simple, the food impressed with its natural tastes. Desserts have included hot apricot and almond soufflé with ginger ice-cream, and a 'well-executed' chocolate sorbet with orange crème brûlée. Around 400 wines, half of them French, include some top claret properties and vintages, and the choice of half-bottles is generous. There are 15 house wines, although we cannot list prices, nor are we able to confirm details below, since the restaurant has refused to complete the *Guide*'s questionnaire.

CHEF: Tony Pierce   PROPRIETORS: Michael Bricker and Pauline Ashworth   OPEN: all week 12 to 2, 7 to 9.30   MEALS: Set L £27, Set D £38   SERVICE: not inc   CARDS: Amex, Delta, Diners, MasterCard, Switch, Visa   DETAILS: 32 seats. Private parties: 35 main room, 10 private room. Car park. Vegetarian meals. No children at D. No smoking in dining-room. Wheelchair access (also WC). Music   ACCOMMODATION: 10 rooms, all with bath/shower. TV. Phone. D,B&B £95 to £240. Children welcome. High teas for children. Baby facilities. Dogs welcome by arrangement. Afternoon teas. Fishing (*The Which? Hotel Guide*)

⁑✳ *indicates that smoking is either banned altogether or that a dining-room is maintained for non-smokers. The symbol does not apply to restaurants that simply have no-smoking areas.*

▲ *The Creel* ⁵⚹

Front Road, St Margaret's Hope KW17 2SL
TEL: (01856) 831311
off A961, 13m S of Kirkwall, on South   COOKING 7
Ronaldsay island   COST £37–£54

'We first visited this remarkable little restaurant three years ago, and have finally made it back, having fallen in love with both Orkney and The Creel.' The magnet seems to draw most visitors back sooner or later, for 'meals by a great Orcadian chef swimming against the tide of mediocrity in the islands'. Alan Craigie's food is an excellent ambassador for local produce, and the small family-run hotel, looking out over the water, offers 'wonderful value for money'. What struck a regular visitor was that the food has become even finer during 1998. Supplies of white fish and shellfish formerly destined for the Continent have been intercepted, improving the already good range, the repertoire has been expanded, and the cooking is done with greater care.

Seafood remains paramount: queen scallops in their shells in a thick puddle of garlic and herb butter, salmon fish-cakes 'the size and shape of golf balls', or a simple crab salad. Salt cod brandade is made in-house, raised to new heights by its accompaniments: an 'irresistible, thick, golden' herby mayonnaise, attractively dressed potatoes and salad leaves, and drops of a sweetish vinegar dotted with mustard seeds. 'World-class' soups may owe something to the 'outboard motor-sized blender' that Alan Craigie uses to extract 'every molecule of flavour' from his shellfish. Partan bree – a rich and intensely flavoured crab soup – can be dunked with beremeal bannocks, made from a rare and ancient form of wheat flour: grains dating back 4,000 years have been found at the Skara Brae settlement on the other side of Orkney.

Meat also features, perhaps Orkney beef marinated in a sweet beer pickle, smoked over oak chips, served with home-made rhubarb chutney, and called 'bresaola of the house'; or loin of North Ronaldsay lamb with a mustard and oatmeal crust, served with spicy lentils and a baby haggis. Although desserts have difficulty keeping up, they too have improved, and run the gamut from lemon pie or strawberry shortcake to clootie dumpling parfait, 'which sounds a bizarre idea but worked well'. Orkney farmhouse cheeses 'in excellent condition' are served with oatcakes or more bannocks. The wine list still lags a way behind, and 'could do with being taken in hand', but the 20 or so bottles are fairly priced, starting at £7.25.

CHEF: Alan Craigie PROPRIETORS: Joyce and Alan Craigie OPEN: Apr to Sept all week D only 7 to 9 (open Fri and Sat only Nov to Mar) CLOSED: 2 weeks Oct MEALS: alc (main courses £15.50 to £21). Set D £26.50 SERVICE: not inc, card slips closed CARDS: Visa DETAILS: 36 seats. Private parties: 36 main room. Car park. Children's helpings. No smoking in dining-room. Wheelchair access (2 steps; also WC). No music ACCOMMODATION: 3 rooms, all with bath/shower. TV. B&B £30 to £60. Children welcome. No dogs. Afternoon teas

The Guide *office can quickly spot when a restaurateur is encouraging customers to write recommending inclusion. Such reports do not further a restaurant's cause. Please tell us if a restaurateur invites you to write to the* Guide.

SPEAN BRIDGE Highland map 11

▲ *Old Pines* ⁵⫶✗

Spean Bridge PH34 4EG
TEL: (01397) 712324 FAX: (01397) 712433 COOKING 3
EMAIL: goodfood.at.oldpines@lineone.net COST £30–£36

This is a family affair – indeed Bill and Sukie Barber seem to have two of them: one consisting of children, the other of ducks and hens waddling round the yard. Taken together, these give a clue that the single-storey, Scandinavian-style house with magnificent views (Ben Nevis isn't far away) both exudes a very informal air and takes its supplies seriously. Just how informal becomes apparent at dinner when residents generally share tables. The fresh local ingredients at the heart of the operation mean that seasons – remarkably short in some cases – are properly observed.

Bread and pasta are home-made, salmon is home-smoked, trout is from a nearby loch, and Bill picks the ceps and chanterelles that go into a first-course pasta sauce or a second-course soup. Dinner is five set courses, organised around a centrepiece such as haunch of venison, John Dory, or roast leg of lamb (perhaps stuffed with kidney and fresh herbs), followed by caramelised rhubarb tart, or maybe brown sugar meringue with gooseberries and elderflower ice-cream. Scottish farmhouse cheeses bring up the rear, served with oatcakes. As we went to press a drinks licence was imminent, though customers are still welcome to bring their own wine with no corkage charge.

CHEF: Sukie Barber PROPRIETORS: Bill and Sukie Barber OPEN: all week D only 8pm (1 sitting, occasionally 7.30 in winter, May to Sept Sun D residents only) CLOSED: 2 weeks end Nov/early Dec MEALS: Set D £27.50. Light meals available all day. BYO (no corkage) SERVICE: not inc, card slips closed CARDS: MasterCard, Switch, Visa DETAILS: 30 seats. Private parties: 30 main room. Car park. Vegetarian meals. Children's helpings. No smoking in dining-room. Wheelchair access (also WC). Music ACCOMMODATION: 8 rooms, all with shower. D,B&B £55 to £120. Rooms for disabled. Children welcome. High teas for children. Baby facilities. Dogs welcome. Afternoon teas (*The Which? Hotel Guide*) £5

STEIN Highland map 11

▲ *Lochbay* ⁵⫶✗ £

1–2 Macleod Terrace, Stein, Isle of Skye IV55 8GA COOKING 1
TEL/FAX: (01470) 592235 COST £23–£47

Note that the name of the village is pronounced 'steen'; this will avoid confusion with any other Stein's seafood restaurant. The dining-room, with its crofter's cottage grate, and red quarry tiled floor is as cheerful and welcoming as Margaret Greenhalgh herself. Her knowledge, and repertoire, of seafood surpasses the ordinary. It includes pollan, the Finnish muikku, wolf fish, and the Icelandic steinbitur ('stone biter') named for the jaws which allow it to eat crabs, clams and other tough-carapaced prey. Particularly enjoyed by an inspector were squat lobster tails from Loch Bay (which is at the bottom of the garden), hearty, orangey-white fish soup, grilled skate, and seared wolf fish. The copious salads – some with pineapple, coleslaw, grape and sweetcorn – are perhaps less appropriate than the potatoes, either jacket or chips. Warm clootie dumpling with cream was 'a kind of Christmas pudding, rich and moist, with plenty of sultanas'. The wine list is short; ales, including grozot, elderberry, or gooseberry and wheat, may be more rewarding.

CHEF/PROPRIETOR: Margaret Greenhalgh   OPEN: Sun to Fri 12 to 2.30, 6 to 9   MEALS: alc (main courses £6 to £18). Snack L available   SERVICE: not inc   CARDS: MasterCard, Visa   DETAILS: 24 seats. 8 seats outside. Private parties: 6 main room. Car park. Children's helpings. No smoking in dining-room. Music   ACCOMMODATION: 2 rooms, both with bath/shower. TV. B&B £27 to £42. Children welcome. High teas for children. No dogs. Afternoon teas

---

STEWARTON   Argyll & Bute   map 11

▲ *Chapeltoun House* ♥ 🍮 ⚒

Irvine Road, Stewarton KA3 3ED
TEL: (01560) 482696   FAX: (01560) 485100
EMAIL: 106331.543@compuserve.com   COOKING 5
2m from Stewarton on B769 towards Irvine   COST £20–£44

The house was built for a Scottish industrialist and his English bride, hence thistle and rose motifs in the plaster mouldings and around the fireplace, and a scale that is somewhere between 'grand' and 'domestic'. Bay windows overlook sweeping lawns and mature trees, and luxurious old armchairs add to the feel of 'low key comfort'. New husband and wife management team David and Sarah Ostle arrived at the end of May 1998, and have sharpened up the cooking somewhat. Their well-sourced Scottish produce, from fish to beef to cheese, is treated with 'expert modern flair', although a classical background isn't hard to detect in terrine of foie gras and duck confit with lentils, or chicken boudin with wild mushrooms.

The menu's garnishing 'confits' of this and 'compotes' of that tend to be loose descriptions, but the cooking is more exact: sweet scallops 'seared in superb butter', with fondant garlic and a 'couple of artistic pop-art blobs' of gazpacho sauce, or equally well-timed venison fillet on an 'intensely gamey' red wine sauce. The kitchen garden, meanwhile, supplies materials for a 'sprightly tossed bouquet of chervil, frilly lettuce and dill' to accompany galantine of quail with a mousse-like wrapping. At inspection a light baked lemon tart was 'the best I have had for ages', with buttery pastry and a tangy, eggy, lemon-curdy filling. Portions are 'on the light, healthier side', petits fours are first-rate, and service is friendly and informal. Wines are strongest in France, with first-growth clarets from mature vintages offered at very favourable prices, though there is much of interest at less-exalted levels too. House recommendations from Australia and France are £11.95 and £11.50 respectively.

CHEF: David Ostle   PROPRIETOR: Anthony Dobson   OPEN: all week 12 to 2.30, 7 to 9 (9.30 Fri and Sat) MEALS: alc (main courses £6 to £8). Set L £13.95, Set D £20.80 (2 courses). BYO £7. Bar meals available   SERVICE: not inc, card slips closed   CARDS: Amex, MasterCard, Switch, Visa   DETAILS: 110 seats. Private parties: 60 main room, 25 and 60 private rooms. Car park. Vegetarian meals. Children's helpings. Jacket and tie. No smoking in dining-room. Wheelchair access (3 steps; not WC). Music ACCOMMODATION: 8 rooms, all with bath/shower. TV. Phone. B&B £79 to £145. Children welcome. High teas for children. Baby facilities. House-trained dogs welcome. Afternoon teas   (£5)

STONEHAVEN Aberdeenshire   map 11

Tolbooth

Old Pier, Stonehaven AB39 2JU
TEL/FAX: (01569) 762287   COOKING 3
16m S of Aberdeen   COST £24–£48

A first-floor dining-room, reached by a short flight of worn stone steps, occupies the length of the building and overlooks Stonehaven's small harbour. Fish is understandably the main business: cockles and hand-dived scallops from Orkney, mussels from the west coast, and langoustines from a local boat-owner. The cooking has a bright, spicy edge to it, evident in Thai fish-cakes with coconut curry sauce, in chargrilled tuna with chilli-spiked salsa and red pepper vinaigrette, and in a lentil sauce flavoured with cardamom and coriander served with monkfish. At the same time, a more European strand has produced scallops in a Sauternes butter sauce, and chargrilled smoked salmon fillet with blini, while the seasonal appearance of crab, sea trout, samphire, chanterelles, ceps and blackberries anchors the whole thing in the here and now. Meat is in the minority, but of high quality, perhaps Glenbervie Aberdeen Angus beef from just down the road, served with braised Savoy cabbage, red onion confit and red wine sauce. Youthful whites naturally dominate the wine list, and the southern hemisphere rates best for affordability. House French is £8.95.

CHEFS: Jean-François Meder and Andrew Ritchie   PROPRIETORS: Jean-François Meder and Chris McCarrey   OPEN: Sun L 12 to 2, Tue to Sun D 6.30 to 9.30   CLOSED: 25 and 26 Dec, first 2 weeks Jan   MEALS: alc Tue to Sat D (main courses £12 to £18.50).Set D Sun £18.95   SERVICE: not inc   CARDS: MasterCard, Visa   DETAILS: 44 seats. Private parties: 44 main room. Children's helpings. No children under 8. No cigars/pipes in dining-room. Music   £5

STRONTIAN Highland   map 11

▲ *Kilcamb Lodge* ❦ ✳

Strontian PH36 4HY
TEL: (01967) 402257   FAX: (01967) 402041   COOKING 3
on A861, by N shore of Loch Sunart   COST £38–£45

Way out on a westerly limb, this family-run hotel, whose 28 acres include half a mile of Loch Sunart's shoreline, is extremely well kept. Just as important, Peter Blakeway and his helpers are friendly and hospitable, making for a relaxed and convivial atmosphere. Four-course dinners (the second soup) are fairly priced, and generally adopt a European stance: confit of duck leg with mushroom risotto, or noisette of Highland lamb with tarragon mousse and polenta pancakes. Native materials range from pan-fried langoustine tails or Morar scallops to start, via roast fillet of Grampian pork with mushroom cake, to loin of Argyll venison with a game and chocolate sauce. A classic dimension to desserts produces glazed lemon tart with raspberry sauce, and apple and thyme tarte Tatin. Wines are a canny collection offering both value-for-money and a variety of styles and flavours. There are plenty of friendly faces from both hemispheres, with the odd surprise thrown in for good measure: we are all used to seeing Ch.

Musar from the Lebanon, but the Reserve du Couvent from Ksara will be unfamiliar to many. House wines start at £9.75.

CHEFS: Peter Blakeway and Neil Mellis   PROPRIETORS: the Blakeway family   OPEN: all week D only 7.30 (1 sitting)   CLOSED: Dec to Feb exc Hogmanay   MEALS: Set D £29.50   SERVICE: not inc, card slips closed   CARDS: Delta, MasterCard, Switch, Visa   DETAILS: 28 seats. Private parties: 30 main room. Car park. Vegetarian meals. Children's helpings. No children over 6. No smoking in dining-room. No music   ACCOMMODATION: 11 rooms, all with bath/shower. TV. D,B&B £70 to £180. Children welcome. High teas for children. Baby facilities. Dogs welcome by arrangement. Afternoon teas (*The Which? Hotel Guide*)

SWINTON Borders   map 11

▲ *Wheatsheaf Hotel* 🍴✳

Main Street, Swinton TD11 3JJ
TEL: (01890) 860257   FAX: (01890) 860688   COOKING 2
on A6112, Coldstream to Duns road   COST £20–£44

Shootin' and fishin' are among Alan Reid's pastimes, so if you find yourself eating woodcock or a piece of Tweed salmon here, the chances are he may have bagged or caught it himself. The Wheatsheaf is a rough-hewn old inn with a conservatory extension in the middle of a tranquil village. You eat as formally or as informally as you like, depending on whether you are in the market for fish and chips in the bar or venison fillet sauced with blackberry, juniper and port jelly in the grander but unstuffy dining-room. Reporters have praised chicken breast with red wine and mushrooms, and mustard-sauced grilled mackerel, while puddings range from rhubarb and ginger sponge to exotic-sounding coconut ice-cream with raspberry and Malibu coulis. Enthusiastic use of Highland produce in the cooking extends to Drambuie (in an iced parfait) and Glayva (in ice-cream). Don't miss the shortbread with coffee. The wine list is broadly based, reasonably priced and offers plenty of half-bottles. House wines are £9.50.

CHEFS: Alan Reid and John Keir   PROPRIETORS: Alan and Julie Reid   OPEN: Tue to Sun (and Mon D residents only) 12 to 2.15, 6 to 9.30   CLOSED: 25 Dec, 1 Jan,   MEALS: alc (main courses L £5 to £13, D £8 to £16)   SERVICE: not inc, card slips closed   CARDS: Delta, MasterCard, Switch, Visa   DETAILS: 50 seats. 24 seats outside. Private parties: 28 main room, 18 private room. Car park. Vegetarian meals. Children's helpings. No smoking in dining-room. Wheelchair access (2 steps; not WC). No music   ACCOMMODATION: 6 rooms, 4 with bath/shower. TV. B&B £34 to £95. Children welcome. High teas for children. Baby facilities. Dogs welcome by arrangement in bedrooms only (*The Which? Hotel Guide*)

TROON South Ayrshire   map 11

▲ *Highgrove House* 🛏 £

Old Loans Road, Troon KA10 7HL   COOKING 1
TEL: (01292) 312511   FAX: (01292) 318228   COST £18–£42

Built in the 1920s, Highgrove is less imposing than the Costleys' other restaurant, the flagship Lochgreen House (see entry below), and offers simple, affordable 'bistro-style' food with a Scottish accent. The wide-ranging repertoire pulls in some old favourites, from mussels cooked in white wine, or West Coast seafood chowder, to beef bourguignonne on champ potatoes, and plainly grilled peppered sirloin steak. Its broad appeal is bolstered by warm salads based on smoked haddock, or squid and langoustines, by an occasional vegetarian item such as stuffed pepper, and by a few distinctive borrowings: grilled goats' cheese with pickled ratatouille and Parma ham, or chicken on rice pilaff with Cajun spices and Thai curry sauce. Puddings might include bread-and-butter, vacherin, or tarte Tatin, and some 60 wines combine variety with reasonable prices, starting with three house wines at £9.95.

CHEF: William Costley PROPRIETORS: William and Catherine Costley OPEN: all week 12 to 2.30, 6 to 9.30 MEALS: alc (main courses L £6 to £8.50, D £9.50 to £14.50). Set L £12.95, Set D £16.95 to £22.50 SERVICE: not inc, card slips closed CARDS: Amex, Delta, MasterCard, Switch, Visa DETAILS: 80 seats. Private parties: 50 main room, 16 private room. Car park. Vegetarian meals. Children's helpings. Wheelchair access (not WC). Music ACCOMMODATION: 9 rooms, all with bath/shower. TV. Phone. B&B £69 to £99. Children welcome. Baby facilities. No dogs. Afternoon teas

▲ *Lochgreen House* ♦ ⁵⁄✕

Monktonhill Road, Southwood, Troon KA10 7EN   COOKING 4
TEL: (01292) 313343   FAX: (01292) 318661   COST £28–£49

Bill Costley cooks mostly at his other Troon restaurant (see entry above) but keeps a close eye on things here, where son Andrew oversees the day to day cooking. It is an attractive building set in large grounds 'which truly merit the description manicured', with oak panelling and a 'yesteryear' ambience. Lunchtime and evening menus are similar in scope, dinner offering an extra course (soup or sorbet) to make four, while ingredients, centred on Scottish produce, are 'demonstrably fresh and of high quality'. The food does not try to be innovative, but does include a few luxuries, in the form of goose liver parfait, or pan-fried Tay salmon served with crab and langoustine ravioli in a truffle-infused cream sauce, and is skilfully cooked.

Workmanship extends to filling a maize-fed chicken breast with a mousseline of smoked venison and wild mushrooms, and a degree of comfort is evident in the poached egg served with scallop risotto, and in desserts of bitter chocolate terrine with pistachio ice-cream, or roasted pears with apricot parfait and candied almonds. Attentive service from helpful local staff gives the place 'a homely and friendly touch', and wines are full of good breed and character, hailing mostly from France with some sound selections from around the world. Mark-ups can be on the high side, but there is plenty of choice below £20, beginning with half a dozen house wines priced between £14.50 and £17.95. CELLARMAN'S CHOICE: St-Aubin 'Le Charmois' 1993, Ch. de Chassagne-Montrachet, £30.10; Côte de Beaune Marcilly Reserve Bourgogne 1988, Double Blason, £28.10.

CHEFS: Andrew and William Costley PROPRIETORS: William and Catherine Costley OPEN: all week 12 to 2, 7 to 9 MEALS: Set L £17.95, Set D £29.95 SERVICE: not inc, card slips closed CARDS: Amex, Delta, MasterCard, Switch, Visa DETAILS: 85 seats. Private parties: 45 main room, 16 to 45 private rooms. Car park. Vegetarian meals. No smoking in dining-room. Wheelchair access (also WC). Music ACCOMMODATION: 15 rooms, all with bath/shower. TV. Phone. B&B £99 to £160. Rooms for disabled (*The Which? Hotel Guide*)

TURNBERRY South Ayrshire   map 11

▲ *Turnberry Hotel, Turnberry Restaurant*

Turnberry KA26 9LT   COOKING 6
TEL: (01655) 331000 FAX: (01655) 331706   COST £39–£135

This enormous white-painted 'golferama' hotel faces out to the tiny but dramatic
island of Ailsa Craig, the Mull of Kintyre and across the Irish Sea. It has acquired
new owners, but Stewart Cameron remains in executive charge of operations.
He has a lot to oversee: a Clubhouse and Bay Restaurant as well as the Turnberry
itself, which between them serve everything from big breakfasts to sandwiches
to afternoon teas, and Turnberry's twin-track dinners. The £48 set-price job
might sound a lot, but the cost covers four courses, and in any case the *carte* isn't
cheap: grilled Dover sole at £35, and roast lobster at £40, for example.

Big spenders can also enjoy seared foie gras, Loch Fyne oysters, and Beluga
caviar, but there is more to the cooking than mere luxury and prime cuts. It
doesn't attempt to break any moulds, serving roast Ayrshire lamb with garlicky
vegetables, or poached salmon with chervil hollandaise, but it does swim with
the tide, offering prawn and crab-cakes, or charred bresaola with aubergine
purée, oven-dried tomatoes and black olive dressing. Upbeat flavours characterise desserts such as summer berries with lime confit, or redcurrant and
blackberry mousseline with mango and ginger purée. House wine is £19.75.

CHEF: Stewart Cameron PROPRIETOR: Westin Hotels OPEN: Sun L 1 to 2.30, all week D 7.30 to
10 MEALS: alc D (main courses £26 to £44). Set L £25.95, Set D £45 SERVICE: not inc, card
slips closed CARDS: Amex, Delta, Diners, MasterCard, Switch, Visa DETAILS: 180 seats.
Private parties: 240 main room, 16 to 20 private rooms. Car park. Vegetarian meals. Children's
helpings. Jacket and tie at D. No pipes in dining-room. Wheelchair access (also WC). Music
ACCOMMODATION: 132 rooms, all with bath/shower. TV. Phone. D,B&B £215 to £590. Rooms for
disabled. Children welcome. Baby facilities. Dogs welcome in bedrooms only. Afternoon teas.
Swimming-pool (*The Which? Hotel Guide*)

UIG Western Isles   map 11

▲ *Baile-na-Cille* ⬥✳

Timsgarry, Uig, Isle of Lewis HS2 9JD
TEL: (01851) 672242 FAX: (01851) 672241
EMAIL: randjgollin@compuserve.com   COOKING 2
B8011 to Uig, then right down track on to shore   COST £28–£34

Britain's most remote hotel is beyond the back of beyond. A postcard entitled
'rush hour, high season' shows acres of white sand with not a soul in sight, and
people apparently come to this comfortable hotel to escape everything from
world tension to working out their tax returns. There is 'more decoration' this
year, a grand piano graces the sitting-room, and guests can still play tennis; the
hotel's grass court, which was washed away, has been replaced by a hard court
presented to the village. Joanna Gollin is now helped in the kitchen by Richard
Gollin and Margot Pratt. Four-course meals – one of them cheese – might start
with smoked salmon pâté or blue cheese quiche, followed by pork with
gingered leeks, or baked salmon with pesto sauce. A visiting vegetarian was

'most impressed' too. Finish with queen of puddings or chocolate roulade. Pick up a bottle of wine on the way into dinner – they cost either £8.50 or £12.50, a pricing structure unchanged since 1985 – and if you want a half-bottle, the Gollins simply drink the other half.

CHEFS: Joanna and Richard Gollin, and Margot Pratt   PROPRIETORS: Richard and Joanna Gollin   OPEN: all week, D only 7 (1 sitting)   CLOSED: 7 Oct to 7 Mar.   MEALS: Set D £24, BYO (no corkage); lunchtime snacks £2 to £10   SERVICE: net prices, card slips closed   CARDS: MasterCard, Visa   DETAILS: 30 seats. Private parties: 30 main room. Car park. Vegetarian meals. Children's helpings. No smoking in dining-room. No music   ACCOMMODATION: 14 rooms, 8 with bath/shower. B&B £24 to £48. Children welcome. Baby facilities. Afternoon teas. Fishing (*The Which? Hotel Guide*)

ULLAPOOL Highland	map 11

▲ *Altnaharrie Inn* ▮ ⊱✗

Ullapool IV26 2SS	COOKING 10
TEL: (01854) 633230	COST £77–£98

It may seem a little odd that one of Britain's best restaurants is the least accessible. It has no car park, no neighbours, no reception desk, no menu, not even mains electricity, making it the antithesis of the grand country house. There is no car park because there is no road. Leave your vehicle and the world behind in Ullapool (but hang on to your wellies), and escape across Loch Broom in the launch. 'One has to assess it as a place to eat and stay,' observed one reporter, 'since it's not practicable to do anything else.' Altnaharrie shuns all pretension, and is decorated with 'restrained good taste', the kind that mixes antique and modern, wood and stone, tactile and visual, the kind that grows on you. A motley crowd of guests gives the place 'a genuine house-party feel'.

An air of individuality and modesty extends to the dining-room with its bare wooden tables, where first courses typically impress with their combination of both delicacy and intensity of flavour: lobster in a light and frothy champagne sauce laced with chervil oil for example, or a mousseline of shellfish inlaid with crab, covered in a cloche of filo pastry, with a trio of sauces, one made from meat juices. The shellfish leitmotif might continue with a soup of lobster and truffles, before a change of gear to lamb split into three and variously stuffed with, topped with, or surrounded by ceps and morels, and given two sauces, one of lamb, one of creamed spinach.

'You need a good memory to dine in this place,' reckoned one visitor. The menu is recited by soft-spoken Fred Brown, not written down, which is all right to start with when there is no choice but, after a few glasses of wine, 15 cheeses ('of the highest quality') can be a bit taxing. Far from seeking the limelight, Gunn Eriksen is 'the invisible chef' who never leaves the kitchen to make a prima donna appearance, but her food is 'far greater than the sum of its parts'. Meals are treated as a totality rather than a succession of unrelated courses, at least until dessert stage when all three are delivered to each table: perhaps a brittle-shelled, soft-centred chocolate mousse with chocolate sauce and cassis; a circular puff pastry plum tart with peach liqueur and ice-cream; and rhubarb and almond crumble.

Service is 'perfect, and just happens in the most discreet and attentive way; guests are left to pour their own wine, for which a written order must be handed in by 6pm. Burgundy just has the edge over Bordeaux on a Francophile list which still manages to offer plenty of choice from other countries, with Austria making an entrance this year. Prices on the whole are fair, reflecting the quality of the wines on offer, although some might baulk at paying £8.70 for an albeit-large glass of champagne. Seventeen house wines begin with a Minervois at £10.90, and half-bottles are numerous.

CHEF: Gunn Eriksen PROPRIETORS: Fred Brown and Gunn Eriksen OPEN: all week D only 8pm (1 sitting) CLOSED: Nov to Easter MEALS: Set D £70 to £75 SERVICE: none, card slips closed CARDS: Delta, MasterCard, Switch, Visa DETAILS: 18 seats. Private parties: 18 main room. Car park. No children under 8. No smoking in dining-room. No music ACCOMMODATION: 8 rooms, all with bath/shower. D,B&B £165 to £420. No children under 8. Dogs by arrangement (*The Which? Hotel Guide*)

WALLS Shetland　　　　　　　　　　　　　　　　map 11

▲ *Burrastow House* ⁵✳

Walls ZE2 9PD
TEL: (01595) 809307 FAX: (01595) 809213
EMAIL: burr.hs.hotel@zetnet.co.uk
at Walls drive to top of hill, turn left, then follow road　　COOKING 3
for 2m to Burrastow　　　　　　　　　　　　　　　　COST £23–£46

The most northerly outpost of good food and wine in the country takes a 'friendly and natural' approach to things. One couple who arrived by taxi at 1pm and stayed until the bus went at 5.15 experienced 'faultless hospitality', while another was impressed by everything from accommodation to breakfast to packed lunches to dinner. It makes sense anywhere, but here particularly, to use local produce and cook it simply. There might be fillet of Shetland beef with a green and pink peppercorn sauce, plus a vegetarian option such as wild mushroom risotto, or even pickled red peppers with hummus as a starter one night, but it is 'fish and seafood that really shine'.

Star turns have included 'really terrific' mussels with wine and garlic, home-pickled herrings, kipper pâté, and flavourful lobster salad with cold hollandaise, which one reporter felt to be 'a clever way of getting round the raw egg problem with home-made mayonnaise'. Organic vegetables are plainly cooked, and salad leaves from the poly tunnel in the garden come 'with a lovely mustardy dressing'. 'If one has room for pudding', consider crêpes suzette, fresh fruit pavlova, or Atholl brose. There are some good bottled beers, and fairly priced wines include a number of organics, among them house French at £9.25

CHEF: Bo Simmons PROPRIETORS: Bo Simmons and Henry Anderton OPEN: L only by prior booking Tue to Sun 12 to 2.30, D Tue to Sat 7.30 to 9 CLOSED: 25 and 26 Dec, Jan and Feb, 1 week Oct MEALS: alc (main courses L £8.50 to £12.50, D £16 to £17.50) SERVICE: not inc, card slips closed CARDS: Amex, Delta, Diners, MasterCard, Switch, Visa DETAILS: 30 seats. Private parties: 12 main room, 25 private room. Car park. Vegetarian meals. Children's helpings. No smoking in dining-room. Wheelchair access (also WC). No music ACCOMMODATION: 5 rooms, all with bath/shower. B&B £50 to £100. Rooms for disabled. Children welcome. Baby facilities. Dogs by arrangement. Afternoon teas. Fishing (*The Which? Hotel Guide*) £5

Wales

▲ *Penhelig Arms Hotel* ▮ ✻

Aberdovey LL35 0LT
TEL: (01654) 767215   FAX: (01654) 767690
on A493 Tywyn to Machynlleth road, opposite   COOKING 2
Penhelig station   COST £18–£46

On the edge of Aberdovey, just across the road from where boats tie up in the estuary, this 'good local inn' dates back to the eighteenth century. Things have moved ahead since last year with a refurbished kitchen, and an enlarged bar separated from the dining-room by not very much. The 'pub-style' presentation accords neatly with unpretentious dishes of mushroom pancake, dressed local crab, and fillet of beef Stroganoff. Chargrilling is applied enthusiastically, and with varying degrees of success, to anything from lamb steaks to tuna, and reporters have enjoyed 'substantial' courgette and orange soup, first-rate lightly battered haddock, and simple desserts of fruit in a brandy-snap basket, and 'rich but not heavy' treacle tart with ice-cream. Polite, well-informed and friendly staff keep everything running smoothly. The pedigree and variety of wines on the generously priced list are guaranteed to gladden the heart, opening with a fine selection from the New World and finishing in the traditional reaches of France. A collection of 14 attractive bins from Italy is highlighted, and house wines start at £9.50. CELLARMAN'S CHOICE: Dan Morgan Chardonnay 1995, Monterey, California, £18.50; Agrelo Vineyard Cabernet Sauvignon 1994, Mendoza, Argentina, £14.90.

CHEF: Jane Howkins   PROPRIETORS: Robert and Sally Hughes   OPEN: all week 12 to 2, 7 to 9.30   CLOSED: 25 and 26 Dec   MEALS: alc (main courses £5.50 to £10). Set L Sun £12.50, Set D £19.50   SERVICE: not inc, card slips closed   CARDS: Amex, Delta, MasterCard, Switch, Visa   DETAILS: 34 seats. Private parties: 18 main room. Car park. Vegetarian meals. Children's helpings. No smoking in dining-room. No music   ACCOMMODATION: 10 rooms, all with bath/shower. TV. Phone. B&B £39 to £78. Children welcome. High teas for children. Baby facilities. Afternoon teas (*The Which? Hotel Guide*)   (£5)

The 2000 Guide *will be published before Christmas 1999. Reports on meals are most welcome at any time of the year, but are particularly valuable in the spring (no later than June). Send them to* The Good Food Guide, *FREEPOST, 2 Marylebone Road, London NW1 1YN. Or email your report to guidereports@which.co.uk.*

▲ *Porth Tocyn Hotel* 🕴✳

Abersoch LL53 7BU
TEL: (01758) 713303   FAX: (01758) 713538
on minor road 2m S of Abersoch through hamlets of   COOKING 4
Sarn Bach and Bwlchtocyn   COST £23–£46

Converted from a row of lead-miners' cottages in 1948, this is not a stuffed-shirt country house, but a characterful and user-friendly one, on a promontory overlooking Cardigan Bay, that seems to attract 'relaxed hedonists'. Lunch is a buffet, served al fresco in summer, that becomes a 'happy, laid-back extravaganza' on Sundays, delivering 'marvellous value'. Five-course dinners offer the option of a more slender two 'for those who cannot cope with so much food', and the menu changes daily, a boon for long-stay guests. Nick Fletcher-Brewer, a jovial host, takes care of the bar and beats the gong for dinner, helped by staff who are 'sophisticated finishing-school types'.

Louise Fletcher-Brewer's style is 'home cooking with flair', using good raw materials such as crisp-skinned corn-fed chicken breast, served with a grain mustard cream sauce and spinach tagliatelle. The food's appeal lies in its 'straightforward and unambitious' approach, as in a 'strong and uplifting' smoked garlic and tomato soup with basil cream that impressed an inspector with its depth of flavour. Seafood is naturally good, perhaps taking the form of a smooth salmon terrine wrapped in leek with an asparagus cream sauce, or poached lemon sole with stir-fried king prawns and vegetables flavoured with ginger and coriander. Desserts range from a rich whisky cream pie with chocolate chips in, served with blackberry coulis, to an upside-down turret of light, refreshing lemon jelly in a sea of passion-fruit sauce. A varied and dependable collection of wines starts with a page of house recommendations including a white vin de pays and red South African for £10.95.

CHEFS: Louise Fletcher-Brewer and David Carney   PROPRIETORS: the Fletcher-Brewer family
OPEN: all week 12.15 to 2, 7.15 to 9   CLOSED: mid-Nov to Easter   MEALS: Set L Sun £16.50, Set D £22 (2 courses) to £29. Bar L Mon to Sat. BYO (by arrangement)   SERVICE: not inc, card slips closed   CARDS: MasterCard, Switch, Visa   DETAILS: 50 seats. 30 seats outside. Private parties: 50 main room. Car park. Vegetarian meals. Children's helpings. No children under 7 at D. No smoking in dining-room. Wheelchair access (1 step; not WC). No music   ACCOMMODATION: 17 rooms, all with bath/shower. TV. Phone. B&B £46.50 to £112. Children welcome. High teas for children. Baby facilities. Dogs welcome exc in public rooms or by pool. Afternoon teas. Swimming-pool (*The Which? Hotel Guide*)

▲ *Riverside Hotel*

Abersoch LL53 7HW
TEL: (01758) 712419   FAX: (01758) 712671   COOKING 1
on A499, 6m SW of Pwllheli   COST £33–£39

John and Wendy Bakewell reached a milestone in 1998 when they chalked up 30 years here. Their style is 'pleasingly relaxed', and reporters appreciate the ample portions, unhurried service and good value on offer. Bar lunches of open sandwiches, or bacon and cheese croissant, are quite a contrast to the three-course dinners, but both are underpinned by local seafood, smoked fish, and meat from the Lleyn Peninsula. Caernarfon Bay crab tartlet, served with foaming hollandaise, struck a chord with one couple, roast leg of lamb has been served with a simple mint sauce, and meals finish with an assortment of Welsh farmhouse cheeses, or a dessert such as chocolate profiteroles with a crunchy nut centre. A vegetarian dish, though not listed, is usually available. Around 40 varied wines from Terry Platt are reasonably priced. House Californian is £12.95.

CHEFS/PROPRIETORS: John and Wendy Bakewell   OPEN: all week 12 to 2, 7.30 to 8.30 (8 early and late season)   CLOSED: Nov to Feb   MEALS: Set D £23.50. Bar L available   SERVICE: not inc, card slips closed   CARDS: Amex, MasterCard, Switch, Visa   DETAILS: 34 seats. Private parties: 34 main room. Car park. Children's helpings. Music   ACCOMMODATION: 12 rooms, all with bath/shower. TV. Phone. DB&B £38 to £88. Children welcome. Afternoon teas. No dogs. Swimming-pool

---

BASSALEG Newport   map 4

Junction 28 ▯ £

Station Approach, Bassaleg NP1 9LD
TEL: (01633) 891891
from M4 J28 take A468 towards Caerphilly, turn right   COOKING 2
at Tredegar Arms and take first left   COST £19–£52

Junction 28's generous opening hours and keenly priced 'Early Evening Flyer' menu proved 'a godsend' for one family travelling with three food-conscious children. As its name suggests, the restaurant occupies the site of the old Bassaleg railway station, and recent refurbishment has given the place what the owners describe as 'a bright and stylish relaxed atmosphere'. Whether you go for the Flyer or the regularly changing *carte*, you are likely to encounter plenty in the way of generous, robust flavours and neat but unaffected presentation. Starters might include anything from chicken tikka in a filo basket to warm salad of scallops, bacon and mange-tout, while main courses could range from lamb rump with creamed spinach and wild mushroom sauce, to escalope of salmon with spring onion fritters and hollandaise. Vegetables have been praised, while desserts aim to please with milk chocolate terrine, or steamed jam sponge. Service is prompt and casual throughout. Wines are arranged in ascending order of price on the carefully chosen list which therefore switchbacks around the globe, but stays right on track when it comes to offering value for money in a variety of styles and flavours. House vins de pays are £8.95. CELLARMAN'S CHOICE: Albariño 1995, Bodegas Martin Codax, Galicia, £13.50; Ribera del Duero 'Alion' 1993, Vega Sicilia £32.50.

CHEF: Jon West   PROPRIETORS: Richard Wallace and Jon West   OPEN: all week L 12 to 2 (4 Sun), Mon to Sat D 5.30 to 9.30   CLOSED: 26 Dec   MEALS: alc Mon to Sat (main courses £8 to £16). Set L Sun £9.95 (2 courses) to £11.95, Set D (5.30 to 7pm) £11.95. Light L available Mon to Sat. BYO £5   SERVICE: not inc, card slips closed   CARDS: Delta, MasterCard, Switch, Visa   DETAILS: 150 seats. Private parties: 50 main room, 50 private room. Car park. Vegetarian meals. Children welcome. Wheelchair access (also WC). Occasional music. Air-conditioned

---

To find a restaurant in a particular area use the maps at the back of the book.

▲ *Ye Olde Bulls Head* ♟ ⁵✳

Castle Street, Beaumaris LL58 8AP	COOKING 3
TEL: (01248) 810329 FAX: (01248) 811294	

As bulls' heads go, this is pretty ancient. But the fifteenth-century inn near the even older castle is about to experience one of its biggest changes in some time. Work starts on a new brasserie in the autumn of 1998, due for completion in spring 1999. It will open seven days a week, offering 'modern British' brasserie food, while bar snacks will become a thing of the past. Once the brasserie is up and running, the first-floor restaurant, reached by a roundabout staircase route, will close briefly for refurbishment, before re-opening with larger tables and higher prices, to give it a distinct identity from the brasserie. Until then, the restaurant continues on its course, offering plenty of variety on a *carte* that makes use of Hereford duck, Welsh Black beef, and roast loin of Caernarfon lamb served with aubergine crisps, garlic and thyme.

The kitchen is as happy in contemporary mode, with a starter of grilled goats' cheese, Carmarthen ham and salsa verde, as with a more traditional and earthy terrine of rabbit with pickled wild mushrooms, or roast Bresse pigeon with barley risotto. Desserts have included steamed orange sponge, and chocolate mousse of 'excellent intensity'. Wines are drawn from some impeccable sources, whether from Burgundy or the Rhône, California or New Zealand, and mark-ups are kept admirably in check. Five good house wines cost £13.75 a bottle, £3 a glass. CELLARMAN'S CHOICE: Mâcon-Viré, Dom. de Roally, 1993 Henri Goyard, £17.95; Amarone della Valpolicella 1991, Allegrini, £22.50.

CHEFS: Keith Rothwell and Soames Whittingham   PROPRIETOR: Rothwell and Robertson Ltd
OPEN: restaurant Mon to Sat D only 7.30 to 9.30, brasserie all week L and D (phone for details of times)   CLOSED: 25 and 26 Dec, 1 Jan   MEALS: (phone for details of prices)   SERVICE: not inc
CARDS: Amex, Delta, MasterCard, Switch, Visa   DETAILS: 60 seats (restaurant), 72 seats (brasserie). Private parties: 40 main room. Car park. Vegetarian meals. Children's helpings. No children under 7 at D. No smoking in dining-room. No music   ACCOMMODATION: 15 rooms, all with bath/shower. TV. Phone. B&B £49 to £81. Children welcome. Guide dogs only (*The Which? Hotel Guide*)

BROAD HAVEN   Pembrokeshire   map 4

▲ *Druidstone* £

Druidston Haven, nr Broad Haven SA62 3NE	
TEL: (01437) 781221 FAX: (01437) 781133	
from B4341 at Broad Haven turn right at sea; after 1½m	COOKING 3
turn left to Druidston Haven; hotel ¾m on left	COST £17–£32

Anyone who values individuality will warm to the Druidstone. Views are breathtaking, and to call the atmoshpere 'relaxed' hardly does justice to the laid-back approach: 'informality is the essence of our business,' writes Jane Bell, and she can write that again. The house, and indeed some of the guests, call to mind the 'Woodstock era'. After a quarter of a century in the *Guide*, responsibility is being handed over to the next generation, Angus, although no big changes are foreseen. The food is as varied as ever, taking in Basque fish soup, steak and kidney pie cooked in ale, and breast of duck with pickled ginger.

Non-meat dishes are part of the style, perhaps feta cheese and asparagus salad, shirred eggs, or a lentil version of moussaka. The Bells, committed to local and organic produce, are doing their best to overcome the difficulties of supply: at present it can be cheaper and easier to buy Pembrokeshire strawberries from Liverpoool market than from the grower 15 miles away. Other dessert ingredients include blueberries, in a cheesecake, and plum and apple, in a crumble. Thirty-plus wines are varied and sympathetically priced, starting with house French at £7.

CHEFS: Rod and Jane Bell, Donna Banner and Angus Bell PROPRIETORS: Rod and Jane Bell OPEN: Sun L 1 to 2, Mon to Sat D 7.30 to 9.30 CLOSED: Mon to Thur 9 Nov to 17 Dec and 4 Jan to 11 Feb MEALS: alc (main courses £6 to £12). Bar meals available. BYO £4 SERVICE: not inc, card slips closed CARDS: Amex, Delta, MasterCard, Switch, Visa DETAILS: 40 seats. 20 seats outside. Private parties: 40 main room, 10 private room. Car park Vegetarian meals. Children's helpings. Wheelchair access (also WC). Occasional music ACCOMMODATION: 9 rooms. B&D £29.50 to £70. Children welcome. High teas for children. Baby facilities. Dogs welcome. Afternoon teas (The Which? Hotel Guide)

CAPEL GARMON Conwy   map 7

▲ Tan-y-Foel ▼ ⁵✳

Capel Garmon, nr Betws-y-Coed LL26 0RE
TEL: (01690) 710507 FAX: (01690) 710681
take turning marked Capel Garmon and Nebo from
A470 about halfway between Betws-y-Coed and   ·   COOKING 4
Llanrwst   COST £36–£46

From outside, this is a stone-built sixteenth-century farmhouse overlooking the Conwy Valley. Inside, there is hardly a hint of the rustic, more a suggestion of flamboyance: a sitting-room with a clutter of ornaments and curtains 'like a Spanish rococo altar-piece', and a 'town house' dining-room with a conservatory extension. The dining-room may not blend with much else, but open fires strike a homely note, everything is impeccably kept, and Peter Pitman is a cordial host. There isn't much sign of a rustic element in the cooking either, which appears in fashionable modern mode with an emphasis on presentation: a piece of salmon on a curry-flavoured potato base, for example, surrounded by a salsa of lime, coriander and garlic.

Considering the limited choice – perhaps one main course, with two starters and puddings plus cheese – the food 'isn't exactly cheap' but it uses good raw materials, and meals include 'light and pleasant' canapés, and Belgian chocolates with coffee. Not all meals have gone swimmingly (one reporter failed to enjoy a dish of 'overcooked' skate flaked on to 'undercooked' potatoes), but an inspection showed up an impressive loin of lamb on a base of minted mushy peas, topped with a herb and cheese 'biscuit', and surrounded by pearl barley 'risotto'. One dessert is usually fresh fruit, the other may be apricot and almond tart, or steamed chocolate pudding. Wines range from Lebanon to New Zealand, and from Oregon to South Africa, picking up some interesting producers along the way. Prices start around £10 for the Mexican house wines. CELLARMAN'S

CHOICE: Montes Alpha Chardonnay 1996, Curico Valley, Chile, £19; Fixin, Dom. Pierre Gelin 1993, £24.

CHEF: Janet Pitman   PROPRIETORS: Peter and Janet Pitman   OPEN: all week D only 7.45 (1 sitting; booking essential)   CLOSED: mid-Dec and Christmas   MEALS: Set D £19.95 (2 courses) to £25   SERVICE: not inc, card slips closed   CARDS: Amex, Delta, Diners, MasterCard, Switch, Visa   DETAILS: 16 seats. Car park. No children under 7. No smoking in dining-room. No music   ACCOMMODATION: 7 rooms, all with bath/shower. TV. Phone. B&B £65 to £150. Children welcome. Afternoon teas. No dogs. Garden (*The Which? Hotel Guide*)

CARDIFF   Cardiff   map 4

Armless Dragon ⁝✳ £

97 Wyeverne Road, Cathays, Cardiff CF2 4BG   COOKING 2
TEL/FAX: (01222) 382357   COST £15–£38

Part of the gastronomic scene around Cardiff University for many years, David Richards's bistro is as popular as ever. The setting is a pair of converted terraced cottages embellished with greenery and decked out with modern artwork. A 'seemingly unchanging' menu of Dragon stalwarts such as laverballs with mushrooms, crab soup, various steaks, and a mixed vegetarian (or vegan) platter is bolstered by a blackboard of more invigorating specials which is brought to each table. A springtime sampling from the latter yielded a clean-flavoured salad of crispy preserved duck, followed by a lightly poached wing of skate with capers and 'aromatic butter', plus exemplary, 'absolutely fresh' vegetables. No fancy trimmings, no cheap shortcuts, just 'honest ingredients prepared in an honest way' was the verdict. Service is unhurried, pleasant and personal in a discreet kind of way. Around 40 wines – mainly from France – are augmented with a commendable number of half-bottles. House wine is £7.90.

CHEF/PROPRIETOR: David Richards   OPEN: Tue to Fri L 12 to 2.15, Tue to Sat D 7 to 10.15   CLOSED: Christmas   MEALS: alc (main courses £9 to £14). Set L £7.50 (2 courses) to £9.50. BYO £5   SERVICE: not inc   CARDS: Amex, Delta, Diners, MasterCard, Switch, Visa   DETAILS: 50 seats. Private parties: 50 main room. Vegetarian meals. Children's helpings. No smoking in dining-room. Wheelchair access (not WC). Music   (£5)

Le Cassoulet

5 Romilly Crescent, Canton, Cardiff CF1 9NP   COOKING 5
TEL/FAX: (01222) 221905   COST £25–£50

Le Cassoulet may be planted firmly in the Welsh capital but its heart belongs in south-west France. Small and snug, with a fine display of armagnac and posters of Toulouse-Lautrec (no mean cook himself), it offers a concise menu specialising in the rich, robust, carnivorous cooking of the region. Foie gras features strongly, both in a salade du sud-ouest, where the richness is cut with oranges, walnuts and wafer-thin celeriac crisps, and in a suprême de poulet fermier, the chicken breast served on spring onion mash and the leg, 'bursting with flavour', stuffed with spinach and foie gras. Duck breast comes with pommes sarladaises, and lamb with ratatouille, dauphinoise potatoes and rosemary jus. Cassoulet

Toulouse-style is a mainstay of the menu, served authentically in an earthenware dish.

The style may be rustic but it is serious cooking, assembled with a sure hand. Each ingredient is treated in an appropriate and considered way, with flavours, colours and textures all working well together. Desserts are composed with the same care and skill: strawberry tart with cardamom comes with a buttery, spiced red wine sauce that contrasts well with the fruit. Other choices might include warm prune and armagnac tart, or crème brûlée with roasted rhubarb. Or you could forgo dessert in favour of a 'splendid' platter of unpasteurised French cheeses. Although reporters have commented that it comes at a high price for Cardiff, they agree that 'Le Cassoulet is in a league of its own'. Service is formal but friendly. The almost entirely French wine list offers some fine vintages from notable châteaux and domaines. Seven wines come in under £15, including house vins de pays at £10.95.

CHEFS: Gibert Viader and Arnaud Tournier PROPRIETORS: Gilbert and Claire Viader OPEN: Tue to Sat 12 to 2, 7 to 10 (post-theatre D by arrangement) CLOSED: 2 weeks Christmas, Aug MEALS: alc (main courses £15 to £17.00). Set L £14.95 SERVICE: not inc CARDS: Amex, Delta, Diners, MasterCard, Switch, Visa DETAILS: 40 seats. Private parties: 40 main room. Vegetarian meals. Children's helpings. No cigars/pipes in dining-room. No music

Le Monde £

62 St Mary Street, Cardiff CF1 1FE
TEL/FAX: (01222) 387376
EMAIL: chefuk@globalnet.co.uk

COOKING 1
COST £24–£50

The three restaurants on this site belonging to Benigno Martinez share a common approach, although each is slightly different. The unifying formula is simple: all have sawdust on the floor; tables are not booked in advance (except for large parties); and there are no menus or wine lists, just a huge variety of blackboards listing food, wine and other drinks. Chilled cabinets display ingredients behind glass; point to what you want, and discuss how you want it cooked, or order something from the blackboard. Vegetarians get short shrift, and there are no puddings. Champers (tel. (01222) 373363), with a Spanish bodega theme, puts more of an emphasis on seafood, while La Brasserie (tel. (01222) 372164), with rustic French décor and wines, errs towards steak, with the added attraction of a two-course lunch for £5.95.

Le Monde, meanwhile, arguably the best of the three for food, can be called on for a mix of fish (sold by weight) and meat. As at the other two, the chargrill dominates cooking. Wander about to read what's on offer, join the jostling queue to place an order, hope for good chips and don't expect a wonderful salad. The food itself might include 'glistening, fresh, locally caught' sea bass cooked in rock salt, then split open and 'elegantly de-boned and filleted by the waitress'. Start perhaps with a pint of shrimps baked on a black cast iron platter, and finish with cheese and a glass of port. Wines generally offer good value for money, Marqués de Cáceres is Le Monde's house wine (£9.95 for white, £10.95 for red), and a hunt for bin ends displayed in the half-barrels can repay the effort.

CHEFS: David Legg and Chris Ruck PROPRIETOR: Benigno Martinez OPEN: Mon to Sat 12 to 2.30, 7 to 12 CLOSED: 25 and 26 Dec MEALS: alc (main courses £7 to £19) SERVICE: not inc CARDS: Amex, Diners, MasterCard, Visa DETAILS: 200 seats. Private parties: 30 main room, 100 private room. Children's helpings at manager's discretion. Music. Air-conditioned

---

CLYTHA Monmouthshire · map 2

▲ *Clytha Arms* ✸ £

Clytha NP7 9BW
TEL/FAX: (01873) 840206
off old Abergavenny to Raglan road, S of A40, 6m E of Abergavenny

COOKING 4
COST £24–£42

The exterior of this converted dower house on the fringes of Clytha Park reminded one visitor of 'a private grange', but it thrives contentedly as a country pub with a restaurant attached. 'Local support' keeps the bar going, doubtless owing to the fact that real ales are kept in tip-top condition. Andrew Canning and family have a vigorously keen attitude to pub food, toasting the Principality with the likes of leek and laverbread rissoles, 'first-class' ploughman's with Welsh cheeses, or faggots and peas. In the dining-room, menus change monthly and tradition is spiced with eclecticism. Reporters have singled out daube of wild boar, and roast monkfish with laverbread and crab sauce, as particularly good mains, although the choice takes in everything from seared tuna with polenta chips, to Caribbean fruit curry. Vegetables arrive in profusion, while desserts range from chocolate charlotte with white chocolate ice-cream to 'light as a feather' bread-and-butter pudding. The intention to produce good food in a vibrant, 'joyful' atmosphere is there, although the wheels of service may grind slowly at busy times. France holds pride of place on the wine list, although the New World is not to be outdone. House wine is £8.50.

CHEFS: Andrew and Sarah Canning PROPRIETORS: Andrew and Beverley Canning OPEN: Tue to Sun L 12.30 to 2.30 (3.30 Sun), Tue to Sat D 7.30 to 9.30 MEALS: alc (main courses £9.50 to £15). Set L Sun £13.95. Bar snacks available Mon L SERVICE: not inc, card slips closed CARDS: Delta, MasterCard, Switch, Visa DETAILS: 66 seats. Private parties: 50 main room, 18 private room. Car park. Vegetarian meals. Children's helpings. No smoking in dining-room. No music ACCOMMODATION: 3 rooms, all with bath/shower. TV. B&B £45 to £70. Children welcome. High teas for children. No dogs (£5)

COLWYN BAY Conwy · map 7

Café Niçoise

124 Abergele Road, Colwyn Bay LL29 7PS
TEL: (01492) 531555

COOKING 3
COST £23–£63

Attempts to create a Welsh café on France's Mediterranean coast would probably not meet with as much success as this family-run French-style bistro on the north Wales coast. The set-up includes a fixed-price 'menu touristique' at lunch-time and on weekday evenings, offering just the sort of sustenance that travellers appreciate: soup of the day, roast salmon with tapénade sauce, and meringues with black cherries and chantilly cream. Among local materials are Black beef,

CRICCIETH

maybe served with creamed cabbage and wild mushrooms, and Welsh lamb, perhaps teamed with provençale vegetables. The food is as informal as the surroundings, with an occasional game dish such as roast pheasant with smoked bacon, and an emphasis on workable combinations: mushrooms in garlic butter, rump steak with bordelaise sauce, or rum and raisin parfait. A good-value list groups wines by style, with half a dozen southern French house recommendations under £10.

CHEF: Carl Swift   PROPRIETORS: Carl and Lynne Swift   OPEN: Wed to Sat L 12 to 2, Mon to Sat D 7 to 10   CLOSED: 1 week Jan, 1 week June   MEALS: alc (main courses £7 to £14). Set L and D £11.95 (2 courses) to £13.95 (not available Sat D). BYO £3.75   SERVICE: not inc, card slips closed   CARDS: Amex, Delta, MasterCard, Switch, Visa   DETAILS: 32 seats. Private parties: 30 main room. Vegetarian meals. Children's helpings. No children under 7 at D. No-smoking area. Music

CREIGIAU Carditt   map 4

Caesar's Arms £

Cardiff Road, Creigiau CF4 8NN   COOKING 1
TEL: (01222) 890486   FAX: (01222) 892176   COST £21–£46

If you are eating in this greatly extended white stone country pub, you need to know the system. Check your booking at the food counter, find your table, then return to order; everything is on display in refrigerated cabinets and there is information in abundance chalked on boards overhead. Choose what you want and how it is to be cooked, then wait: but generally not for long because it is a simple formula which works. One reporter detected plenty of authentic flavours in mussels 'as you might find (them) in Spain' with a light tomato and pepper sauce, and in provençale fish soup with a good selection of seafood, strongly tinged with anise and pepper. Elsewhere there are variations on meat, poultry, fish and salads, ranging from fillet steak or honey-roast Barbary duck to hake, sea bass and crawfish tails, most of which can be had fried, grilled or poached, with or without sauces. Desserts might be sticky toffee pudding or raspberry Pavlova. Well-known names from France and Spain dominate the blackboard list of some 100 wines. House wine is £9.45.

CHEF: Earl Smikle   PROPRIETOR: Steadychance Ltd   OPEN: all week L 12 to 2.30 (3 Sun), Mon to Sat D 7 to 10.30   CLOSED: 25 Dec   MEALS: alc (main courses £5 to £17). Set L £5 (1 course)   SERVICE: not inc, card slips closed   CARDS: Amex, Delta, Diners, MasterCard, Switch, Visa   DETAILS: 180 seats. 40 seats outside. Private parties: 50 main room, 60 private room. Car park. Vegetarian meals. Children welcome. Wheelchair access (also WC). Music

CRICCIETH Gwynedd   map 7

Tir-a-Môr ♥ £   NEW ENTRY

1–3 Mona Terrace, Criccieth LL52 0HG   COOKING 3
TEL/FAX: (01766) 523084   COST £24–£43

This traditional town house on a corner site is 'exactly the sort of restaurant every small town should have'. Pristine but relaxing, it is set out brasserie-style with pine tables, a colonial fan, and large windows with green floral curtains.

Blackboards display daily specials and fish, which rely on local resources 'as far as possible' to produce fillet of sea bass with crab tartlet, Anglesey scallops with capers and sage, or rose beef from the Lleyn Peninsula served with dolcelatte crostini. Salad and pasta starters point to a Mediterranean theme, taken up by Moroccan tagine of mixed grilled fish, and squid stuffed with lemon risotto.

Martin Vowell is a wild-mushroom enthusiast, his seasonal haul perhaps served in a light, crisp pastry tart, or combined in a salad with smoked chicken. 'Good presentation and forthright flavours' are the style, evident in a hearty portion of seared tuna drenched with tapénade, or fillet of lamb cooked 'very pink as requested', served with both a mushroom risotto and vegetables, all 'delicious but far too much'. Puddings, somewhat unusually, continue in southern European vein with zuccotto, spumone Amaretto and baklava, and service comes with 'plenty of friendly banter'. A starter bowl of olives or a helping of flavoured Italian flat bread are charged extra, but prices are generally fair for both food and wine, the latter a compact but attractively varied collection from around the world, arranged broadly by style and helpfully annotated, starting around £10. CELLARMAN'S CHOICE: Friuli Chardonnay 1996, Aquileia, Italy, £9.95; Salice Salentino Riserva 1993, Italy, £11.95.

CHEF: Clare Vowell PROPRIETORS: Clare and Martin Vowell OPEN: Mon to Sat D only 6.30 to 9.30 CLOSED: Christmas and New Year, Mon to Thur Nov to Mar MEALS: alc (main courses £8 to £16) SERVICE: not inc, card slips closed CARDS: Delta, MasterCard, Switch, Visa DETAILS: 39 seats. Private parties: 25 main room. Vegetarian meals. Children's helpings. No children under 7. Wheelchair access (also WC). Music

---

CRICKHOWELL Powys   map 4

▲ *Bear Hotel*

Crickhowell NP8 1BW   COOKING 3
TEL/FAX: (01873) 810408   COST £29–£44

The Bear is a restored fifteenth-century coaching-inn, set in a market town on the River Usk, in the hills of the Brecon Beacons National Park. Inside is a 'rabbit warren of half-timbering' with antique furniture, open fires and lots of fresh flowers. The repertoire leaves hardly any cuisine untouched, as it makes contact with nori rolls, smoked haddock risotto, salmon pizza, and crab-cakes with ginger and lime butter. Pheasant and duck come from a local estate, lamb from a small farm, but there may also be wild boar, venison fillet, or ostrich. Although not all reporters have been equally happy, there have been endorsements for a number of dishes including twice-baked soufflé served with poached pear and salad leaves, and leg of lamb with a rosemary-scented *jus*. To finish, chilled Amaretto terrine is served with a warm toffee sauce, and bread-and-butter pudding comes with brown-bread ice-cream. Service is generally 'friendly' and 'attentive'. Wines are arranged according to style, and more exciting outside France than in; prices are fair, and around a dozen are available by the glass, including house French at £8.25 a bottle.

▌ *denotes an outstanding wine cellar;* ▼ *denotes a good wine list, worth travelling for.*

CHEF: Denvor Dodwell PROPRIETORS: Stephen and Judy Hindmarsh OPEN: all week L 12 to 2,
Mon to Sat D 7 to 9.30 MEALS: alc (main courses £12 to £17). BYO £12 SERVICE: not inc
CARDS: Amex, Delta, MasterCard, Switch, Visa DETAILS: 80 seats. 40 seats outside. Private
parties: 60 main room, 30 and 40 private rooms. Car park. Vegetarian meals. Children's
helpings. No children under 5. Wheelchair access (also WC). Music ACCOMMODATION: 35
rooms, all with bath/shower. TV. Phone. B&B £45 to £110. Rooms for disabled. Children
welcome (*The Which? Hotel Guide*)

Nantyffin Cider Mill Inn ¶ £

Brecon Road, Crickhowell NP8 1SG
TEL/FAX: (01873) 810775   COOKING 1
1½m W of Crickhowell at junction of A40 and A479   COST £20–£42

Looking across the River Usk to mountains beyond, this large stone barn, a
sixteenth-century drovers' inn, is built on two levels, with 'arrow slits' for
windows, massive wine racks, and a renovated cider press. The same food is
served in both bar and dining-room, and the menu – supplemented by a board of
daily specials – reads enticingly: spiced crab-cakes, smoked chicken risotto, grey
mullet with a pea and chorizo sauce, and loin of pork with a chilli dressing.
Intentions are good, local and seasonal produce (including game) features, and
flavourings range from Asian to Moroccan. Desserts of carrot cake with lemon
cream, and coconut parfait with apricot coulis and rum ice-cream, were the
highlights of one meal. At inspection, however, the kitchen simply 'failed to
deliver' much of what it promised, which may have something to do with the
acquisition of the Manor Hotel half a mile away, where Glyn Bridgeman is now
cooking. Nantyffin's wine list is an interesting one: it has gone totally American,
Sean Gerrard explains, because the wines offer good value, are exciting but
'easily understood', and still enable them to put together a balanced collection.
And don't neglect the traditional ciders. Chilean Sauvignon Blanc is £10.75,
Randall Grahm's Big House Red £13.50. CELLARMAN'S CHOICE: Wild Boy
Chardonnay 1996, Santa Maria, California, £20.95; Simi Vineyards 'Altaire'
1996, Sonoma, California, £15.95.

CHEFS: Sean Gerrard and Simon Kealy PROPRIETORS: Sean Gerrard and Glyn Bridgeman
OPEN: all week 12 to 2.30, 6.30 to 9.30 CLOSED: Mons Sept to May MEALS: alc (main courses
£5 to £14). Set L Sun £10.95 (2 courses) to £12.95, Set D Sun to Fri (6.30 to 7.45pm) £9.95 (2
courses) to £11.95. BYO £5 SERVICE: not inc, card slips closed CARDS: Amex, Delta,
MasterCard, Switch, Visa DETAILS: 100 seats. 40 seats outside. Private parties: 60 main room.
Car park. Vegetarian meals. Children's helpings. No cigars/pipes in dining-room. Wheelchair
access (also WC). Occasional music (£5)

DOLGELLAU Gwynedd   map 7

Dylanwad Da ¶ ✳ £

2 Ffôs-y-Felin, Dolgellau LL40 1BS   COOKING 2
TEL: (01341) 422870   COST £22–£29

'A lick of paint but not many changes,' reports Dylan Rowlands, who recently
celebrated a decade in residence at this eponymously titled, cheery bistro. He
continues in his own distinctive way, offering robust dishes with plenty of

flavours and a fondness for neat presentation. One reporter singled out a 'vibrant' warm salad of pigeon breast, bacon and grapes, as well as roast loin of top-notch lamb with spring-onion stuffing and a mint-tinged port gravy, but there is much more besides. Fillet of grey mullet is tossed in oatmeal and served with bilberry sauce, while Welsh sirloin steak receives a punchy sauce of peppers and chorizo sausage. The platter of generously sliced Welsh cheeses in perfect condition gets a round of applause, otherwise there are desserts such as treacle sponge or home-made lemon ice-cream topped with lemon marmalade sauce. A short but striking range of wines offers reliability and quaffability at some knockdown prices. Four house wines set the ball rolling at £9 a bottle, £1.80 a glass. CELLARMAN'S CHOICE: Agrelo Vineyard Chardonnay 1996, Mendoza, Argentina, £14.60; Antiguas Reservas Cabernet Sauvignon 1995, Cousiño Macul, Maipo, Chile, £12.20.

CHEF/PROPRIETOR: Dylan Rowlands   OPEN: Thur to Sat (Tue to Sun, July to Sept) D only 7 to 0 (all week Easter and Whitsun)   CLOSED: 6 weeks Feb and March   MEALS: alc (main courses £8.50 to £13). Set L and D £14 (only if pre-booked). BYO £5   SERVICE: not inc   CARDS: none
DETAILS: 30 seats. Private parties: 30 main room. Vegetarian meals. Children's helpings. No smoking in dining-room. Wheelchair access (1 step; not WC). Music   £5

EGLWYSFACH Powys   map 7

▲ *Ynyshir Hall* ❦ ✳

Eglwysfach SY20 8TA
TEL: (01654) 781209   FAX: (01654) 781366   COOKING 5
off A487, 6m SW of Machynlleth   COST £30–£54

One thing Ynyshir is not short of is colour. From its bright walls and vibrant fabrics to the deep blues and terracottas of Rob Reen's paintings, the effect is invigorating: 'the house is without doubt one of the most artistically decorated that we have ever stayed in,' and the Reens themselves are 'perfect hosts'. The menu now changes every two to three weeks instead of daily, but choice is greater than before: six items per course. The longer time scale gives Chris Colmer a 'chance to refine the dishes', which makes a lot of sense, especially since some of them seem to involve quite a bit of work: home-cured pastrami with coriander blinis, oak-smoked ham boudin with mushy peas, or veal bolognese with lobster ravioli. And that's just for starters.

These are intriguing and inventive ideas, worth spending time on, as are main courses of, for example, marinated seared cod with sweet-and-sour vegetables, and whole roast crisp-skinned lemon chicken, served with herb gnocchi. Desserts are no less attractive: wild strawberry tart with lemon-grass ice-cream, or plum tarte Tatin with thin crisp pastry and lots of fruit, served with an amaretto ice-cream. A stream of vintage clarets flowing back to a 1945 Margaux is a strong point of a fine French collection, but the 200-strong wine list also reaches out to Italy and the New World, and doesn't disappoint. Prices aren't the cheapest in Wales, but choice under £20 is reasonable, particularly southern France. CELLARMAN'S CHOICE: Joseph Hill Gewurztraminer 1996, Eden Valley, S. Australia, £21; Chassagne-Montrachet Rouge 1995, Déléger, £30.

CHEF: Chris Colmer PROPRIETORS: Joan and Rob Reen OPEN: all week 12.30 to 1.30, 7 to
8.30 CLOSED: 5 to 21 Jan MEALS: Set L £19.50, Set D £31 SERVICE: not inc, card slips
closed CARDS: Amex, Delta, Diners, MasterCard, Switch, Visa DETAILS: 35 seats. Private
parties: 28 main room, 18 private room. Car park. Vegetarian meals. No children under 9. No
smoking in dining-room. Music ACCOMMODATION: 8 rooms, all with bath/shower. TV. Phone.
B&B £95 to £170. No children under 9. Dogs welcome by arrangement. Afternoon teas (*The
Which? Hotel Guide*) (£5)

FISHGUARD Pembrokeshire   map 4

▲ *Three Main Street* ✣

3 Main Street, Fishguard SA65 9HG   COOKING 4
TEL: (01348) 874275   COST £31–£48

'We rent a cottage in Pembrokeshire twice a year, and the holiday is a success
because of the quality of the food we eat at Three Main Street,' runs one ringing
endorsement of this converted Georgian town house. It is a very personal
enterprise, involving talent in the kitchen, good supplies, and an unflappable
presence out front. Effort extends from morning coffee via light lunches – hot
Italian sandwich of roast peppers, aubergine and mozzarella, or home-baked
ham with spinach and Madeira sauce – to afternoon tea and dinner.

The menu is a manageable length, with many dishes reflecting the season and
locality: scallops from Cardigan Bay with a basil cream sauce, or sea bass from
Milford Haven, served with mashed potatoes and salsa verde. Marion Evans
uses organic vegetables and herbs from small producers, free-range eggs,
farmhouse cheeses, and her cook's tour takes her from Thai-spiced fish soup
with lemon grass, ginger and coconut, to warm tartlet of goats' cheese and
tomato. Puddings are enticing: pecan and chocolate tart with espresso ice-cream,
or fresh figs stuffed with mascarpone. The wide-ranging wine list picks up some
interesting bottles (if in doubt, try Italy) and passes them on at reasonable prices,
starting with house French at £10.25.

CHEF: Marion Evans PROPRIETORS: Inez Ford and Marion Evans OPEN: Tue to Sat 12 to 2, 7 to
9.30 CLOSED: Tues in winter, Feb MEALS: Set L and D £19.50 (2 courses) to £23.50 SERVICE:
not inc CARDS: none DETAILS: 35 seats. Private parties: 20 main room, 14 to 20 private rooms.
Vegetarian meals. Children's helpings. No smoking in dining-room. Wheelchair access (2 steps;
not WC). No music ACCOMMODATION: 3 rooms, all with bath/shower. TV. B&B £35 to £60.
Children welcome. No dogs (*The Which? Hotel Guide*)

GANLLWYD Gwynedd   map 7

▲ *Plas Dolmelynllyn* ♟ ✣ | NEW ENTRY |

Ganllwyd LL40 2HP
TEL: (01341) 440273 FAX: (01341) 440640   COOKING 2
on A470, 4m N of Dolgellau   COST £32–£39

Once frequented by Shelley and Grey, 'Dolly' dates in part from 1550,
stone-built on a small plateau in the Mawddach Valley. It has the air of a country
retreat, with spacious, high ceilings and a dining-room mahogany-panelled to
mantel level, with large pot plants to break up the space. Joanna Reddicliffe's

four-course menus are sensibly balanced, and her food combines flavours in a meaningful way: sometimes straightforwardly in a dish of duck with green peppercorns, or minted lamb baked in a sea-salt crust, and sometimes using variations on well-tested themes. Thus a filo parcel of goats' cheese is partnered with sweet, jammy red onions and a sharp blackcurrant and thyme sauce, while monkfish comes with a creamy mushroom sauce 'with a fine, deep, earthy savour'. Other successes have included a 'very tasty' puffed-up omelette of melting Teifi cheese, asparagus and smoked duck, and sticky toffee pudding with a 'hugely rich' toffee sauce, blobbed with crème fraîche.

Because this is a totally non-smoking hotel, wines can be enjoyed to the full. They are John Barkwith's hobby and he has put together a very attractive international list at some appealing prices; there are plenty of good bottles to be had under £15, even a few around £10. Halves are plentiful too. CELLARMAN'S CHOICE: Mâcon-Clessé, Dom. de la Bongran 1993, J. Thévenet, £27.50; Kemblefield Estate Cabernet Franc 1989, Hawkes Bay, New Zealand, £21.50.

CHEF: Joanna Reddicliffe   PROPRIETORS: Jonathan Barkwith and Joanna Reddicliffe   OPEN: all week D only 7 to 8.30   CLOSED: 1 Dec to 28 Feb   MEALS: Set D £24.50 (£22.50 for residents) SERVICE: not inc, card slips closed   CARDS: Amex, Diners, MasterCard, Visa   DETAILS: 20 seats. Private parties: 40 main room. Car park. Vegetarian meals. Children's helpings. No children under 8. No smoking in dining-room. Wheelchair access (1 step; not WC). No music ACCOMMODATION: 10 rooms, all with bath/shower. TV. Phone. B&B £45 to £115. Children welcome. High teas for children. Afternoon teas. Fishing (*The Which? Hotel Guide*)   £5

HARLECH Gwynedd

map 7

▲ Castle Cottage ♀ ⚒

Pen Llech, Harlech LL46 2YL

TEL/FAX: (01766) 780479

COOKING 2

COST £20–£35

Filling a gap between between the splendour of Harlech Castle and a fish and chip shop, Glyn Roberts's cottagey hotel-cum-restaurant continues to serve its neighbourhood well. The décor may be 'quaint' but the low beams, pictures and shelves of ornaments create their own atmosphere. Ingredients are drawn from sound local sources and the kitchen handles everything with a noticeable degree of competence. Fixed-price three-course dinner menus don't throw down many challenges, but ideas are lively and the cooking is sound. An excellent Welsh smoked salmon mousse and a salad of barbecued chicken, mango and bacon impressed at inspection, as did a Welsh Black steak cooked pink as requested and served with vegetables that included commendable potato cakes with sesame seeds. Home-made pistachio ice-cream delighted a youngster, while grown-ups have been equally pleased with rhubarb and ginger fool served with a shortbread biscuit. Bread rolls and coffee are both worthy of note. The wine list may be short but it does manage to net a good range of styles and varietals as it trawls the world's wine regions. Prices are keen, starting at £9.75, while a page of bin-ends increases both choice and the chances of picking up a bargain.

▲ *means accommodation is available.*

CHEF: Glyn Roberts   PROPRIETORS: Jacqueline and Glyn Roberts   OPEN: Sun L 12.30 to 2, all week L 7 to 9.30 (9 in winter)   CLOSED: 3 weeks Feb   MEALS: Set L £13, Set D £21.50. BYO £5 SERVICE: not inc, card slips closed   CARDS: Amex, Delta, MasterCard, Switch, Visa   DETAILS: 45 seats. Private parties: 45 main room. Vegetarian meals. Children's helpings. No smoking in dining-room. Music   ACCOMMODATION: 6 rooms, 4 with bath/shower. B&B £26 to £56. Children welcome. High teas for children. Baby facilities. Dogs welcome in bedrooms only (*The Which? Hotel Guide*)   (£5)

HAY-ON-WYE Powys

map 4

Nino's £

The Pavement, Hay-on-Wye HR3 5BU
TEL: (01497) 821932

COOKING 3
COST £19–£39

'What a sensible place this is,' noted a correspondent after lunching at this contemporary, café-style restaurant on a pavement corner opposite the clock tower. He went on to describe the window blinds, black furniture and halogen lighting as 'starkly but comfortably simple'. The kitchen turns out a menu of innovative, modern food, and chef Rod Lewis clearly has his finger on the Welsh culinary pulse. Influences are many, ingredients judiciously gleaned from local sources: Swansea fish shows up in the shape of pan-fried fillet of brill on crispy pasta with wild mushroom sauce, or chargrilled monkfish with Mediterranean vegetables. Meat is from a long-established family butcher: chump of Welsh lamb might be roasted and served with chargrilled fennel, polenta chips and garlic juices, and Herefordshire beef regularly puts in an appearance. Lunch is a short selection of lighter items taking in, say, avocado and tomato salad, 'absolutely perfect' Thai green chicken curry with jasmine rice, and cream caramel with rum-soaked sultanas. Below the restaurant is a low-beamed wine bar dealing in snacks and bargain-price dishes. Eight wines by the glass head the short, varied list. House wines start at £8.50.

CHEF: Rod Lewis   PROPRIETORS: Mr and Mrs C.A. Letts   OPEN: Wed to Sun and bank hol Mons 12 to 2, 7 to 9.30 (10 Sat)   CLOSED: 25 and 26 Dec, 1 and 2 Jan   MEALS: alc (main courses L £2 to £6, D £9 to £14). Set L £8 (2 courses), Set D £12. BYO £5   SERVICE: not inc, card slips closed   CARDS: Delta, MasterCard, Switch, Visa   DETAILS: 26 seats. 9 seats outside. Private parties: 26 main room. Vegetarian meals. Children's helpings. Music

---

LLANARMON DYFFRYN CEIRIOG Wrexham

map 7

▲ West Arms £

Llanarmon Dyffryn Ceiriog LL20 7LD
TEL: (01691) 600665   FAX: (01691) 600622
off A5 Llangollen to Oswestry road at Chirk, then
follow B4500 for 11m

COOKING 2
COST £20–£39

The area surrounding this tranquil village in the Berwyn mountains is 'one of Wales's best-kept secrets', according to the Evanses; the Principality's highest waterfall is nearby, and West Arms owns a couple of miles of private fishing on the River Ceiriog. The inn is four centuries old and looks it, with low-beamed ceilings and flagstone floors. It combines a small public bar for local drinkers and snackers with a restaurant that does a good line in locally bred fowl and game:

marinated duck breast with roast chestnuts and shallots, or Loton Park venison, served with wild mushrooms in a red wine sauce. The hills provide Welsh lamb, which might be wrapped in pastry and served with minted pesto, but even this far inland the kitchen manages to get hold of enough seafood to serve up scampi tails in basil cream, and turbot and sole fillets in saffron butter sauce. Dinner might finish with burnt lemon tart, or hot blackcurrant soufflé, and the wine list offers plenty of drinking under £20, starting with house French red and white at £8.95.

CHEFS: Grant Williams and David Smart   PROPRIETORS: R.J.W. and M.A. Evans   OPEN: all week 12 to 2.30, 7 to 9.30   MEALS: alc (main courses £8 to £15). Set L £14.50, Set D £17.50   SERVICE: not inc, card slips closed   CARDS: Delta, MasterCard, Switch, Visa   DETAILS: 120 seats. 100 seats outside. Private parties: 60 main room, 8 to 60 private rooms. Car park. Vegetarian meals. Children's helpings. No smoking in 1 dining-room. Wheelchair access (1 step; also WC). Music   ACCOMMODATION: 12 rooms, all with bath/shower. TV. Phone. B&B £40 to £80. Rooms for disabled. Children welcome. High teas for children. Baby facilities. Well-behaved dogs welcome. Afternoon teas. Fishing (The Which? Hotel Guide)   £5

LLANBERIS Gwynedd   map 7

Y Bistro ✷✶

43–45 High Street, Llanberis LL55 4EU
TEL/FAX: (01286) 871278
EMAIL: ybistro@nwi.co.uk
off A4086, at foot of Mount Snowdon

COOKING 2
COST £30–£36

For almost two decades Danny and Nerys Roberts have been providing sustenance for famished climbers and mountaineers, and their warmly welcoming bistro continues to do a roaring trade. 'Danny out front is unfailingly good-natured,' noted one correspondent, and 'Nerys is on a good patch,' helped by son-in-law Sion who is now playing a supporting role in the kitchen. The menu – written in Welsh with English translations – sings patriotically and the Robertses work in genuine sympathy with producers from the region. Penrhyn mussels steamed with leeks, fennel and orange is a typically flag-waving starter, while main courses might feature lamb, salmon and rump of Black beef, the last perhaps pan-fried and served with a sauce of mushrooms, garlic and port. Desserts stay mostly in the home country for mead ice-cream with bara brith or geographically apt 'Snowdon Pudding' (a steamed suet confection with oranges and sultanas). There are Welsh wines, too, with bottles from Aberaeron and the Llanerch Vineyard heading the short, international list. House wines are £8.95.

CHEFS: Nerys Roberts and Sion Llwyd   PROPRIETORS: Danny and Nerys Roberts   OPEN: Mon to Sat D only 7.30 to 9.45   CLOSED: occasional days in winter   MEALS: Set D £23. BYO £3.50 SERVICE: not inc, card slips closed   CARDS: Amex, Delta, MasterCard, Switch, Visa   DETAILS: 60 seats. Private parties: 44 main room, 10 and 22 private rooms. Vegetarian meals. Children's helpings. No smoking in dining-room. Wheelchair access (2 steps; not WC). Music   £5

'I can only describe the fish soup as thin porridge, heavily dependent on tomato purée with a few prawny afterthoughts. Dire. I almost forgot to mention the garnish, which consisted of a single strand of blond human hair.' (On eating in Kent)

LLANDDEINIOLEN Gwynedd   map 7

▲ Ty'n Rhos 🍴✗

Seion, Llanddeiniolen LL55 3AE
TEL: (01248) 670489   FAX: (01248) 670079
off B4366, 5m NE of Caernarfon on road signposted   COOKING 5
Seion   COST £22–£43

The whitewashed stone-built hotel, once a farmhouse, is growing, sprouting 'an even larger conservatory' at the back. It is well cared for, with a manicured garden, chintzy interior and relaxing feel. There is no choice on the cheaper set-price dinner menu, but the more expensive one offers six or seven items per course, many with a modern take on a classic idea: hake fish-cakes with lime and herbs, or game sausage with 'black pudding potatoes' and a Guinness sauce. Lynda Kettle writes that 'we are commited to supporting and encouraging local suppliers', whose produce is augmented by home-grown fruit, vegetables and herbs.

There seems to be a lot going on in some of the dishes: for example, a generous piece of brill topped with an almond crust, resting on a bed of spinach, surrounded by saffron sauce, with roast fennel niçoise, stir-fried vegetables and dauphinoise potatoes. At its best the kitchen has produced a 'simple but wonderful' starter of baked flat mushrooms with leeks and smoked bacon, topped with a garlic and herb crust, served with a lemon butter sauce, as well as a 'chewy and crumbly' iced hazelnut parfait, on a raspberry coulis with a poached pear. Service, which one visitor felt would have benefited from a hands-on proprietorial presence, has sometimes lacked organisation. The wine list may not always keep pace with what's left in the cellar, but is helpfully arranged, sympathetically priced, carefully chosen, and starts with ten house wines at £9.50, all available by the large glass for £2.50.

CHEFS: Carys Davies and Ian Cashen   PROPRIETORS: Lynda and Nigel Kettle   OPEN: Sun L 12 to 2, Mon to Sat D 7 to 9 (Sun D residents only)   CLOSED: 1 week Dec, 1 week Jan, 1 week Aug   MEALS: Set L £14.95, Set D £19.50 to £27.50. BYO £3   SERVICE: not inc, card slips closed   CARDS: Amex, Delta, MasterCard, Switch, Visa   DETAILS: 35 seats. 10 seats outside. Private parties: 30 main room, 20 private room. Car park. Vegetarian meals. Children's helpings. No children under 6. No smoking in dining-room. Wheelchair access (2 steps; not WC). No music   ACCOMMODATION: 14 rooms, all with bath/shower. TV. Phone. B&B £49 to £90. Rooms for disabled. No children under 6. Afternoon teas. No dogs. Fishing (*The Which? Hotel Guide*)
£5

LLANDEGLA Denbighshire   map 7

▲ Bodidris Hall 🍴✗

Llandegla LL11 3AL
TEL: (01978) 790434   FAX: (01978) 790335   COOKING 3
on A5104 9m SE of Ruthin   COST £24–£50

This stone-built, creeper-covered house, half a mile from the road along a track bordered with ancient trees, makes clear its Tudor heritage with beams, an inglenook fireplace, and a suit of armour. Kevin Steel's heritage is reflected in a country-house approach that serves a multi-course dinner decked out with an appetiser, mid-meal sorbet, and pre-dessert. In between all that may be salmon ravioli or game terrine to begin, followed by some ambitious main courses: seared tuna and scallops on a feta and asparagus salad with pesto dressing, or duck breast and confit leg served with lime marmalade and savoury cheese beignet. Fruit might feature in a number of dishes: in a first-course 'mosaic', or in a dessert of iced passion-fruit and pancake terrine served with caramelised banana and rum and raisin sauce. One reporter was surprised to be served by a knowledgeable waitress 'dressed like a gym teacher'. A dependable list of around 70 wines, updated every few months, starts with a ten-strong house selection in the region of £12 a bottle.

CHEF: Kevin Steel   PROPRIETOR: W.J. Farden   OPEN: all week 12 to 2, 7 to 9.15   MEALS: Set L £16, Set D £22 (available on request) to £30   SERVICE: not inc, card slips closed   CARDS: Amex, Delta, Diners, MasterCard, Switch, Visa   DETAILS: 36 seats. 24 seats outside. Private parties: 60 main room, 24 private room. Car park. Vegetarian meals. Children's helpings. No smoking in dining-room. Music   ACCOMMODATION: 0 rooms, all with bath/shower. TV. Phone. D,B&B £55 to £130. Children welcome. High teas for children. Afternoon teas. Fishing   (£5)

LLANDEILO Pembrokeshire   map 4

▲ *Cawdor Arms* ⚘✳

Rhosmaen Street, Llandeilo SA19 6EN   COOKING 2
TEL: (01558) 823500   FAX: (01558) 822399   COST £23–£36

Flagstones, polished oak, Chesterfield settees and antiques are the form at this Grade II-listed Georgian town house, where there is also occasional 'musical and dramatic entertainment' in the form of a pianist, or 'local thespians acting out anything from a Victorian murder mystery to Chaucer'. The inn acquired new owners just as the last edition of the *Guide* went to press, but Rod Peterson stayed on as head chef, turning out bright-sounding lunchtime dishes of chorizo risotto, or boudin of seafood mousseline for the 'sitting-room' menu, and leek and goats' cheese tartlet, or grilled mackerel fillets in the dining-room. There may be few surprises for cosmopolitan eaters, but raw materials are good and the food well crafted. Dinner might start with Cardigan Bay crab-cake, then grilled breast of St David's duckling with pork belly stir-fry, before steamed spotted dick, or pear and chocolate parfait. Sympathetic pricing appeals on the short French-dominated wine list, which starts at £9.90.

CHEFS: Rodney Peterson and Mohammedali Bashir   PROPRIETORS: John and Sylvia Silver OPEN: all week 12 to 2, 7.30 to 9   MEALS: Set L £11.50 (2 courses) to £13.50, Set D £17.50 (2 courses) to £20. Light L available   SERVICE: not inc, card slips closed   CARDS: Amex, Delta, MasterCard, Switch, Visa   DETAILS: 70 seats. Private parties: 100 main room, 40 private room. Car park. Children's helpings. No smoking in dining-room. Wheelchair access (2 steps; not WC). Occasional music   ACCOMMODATION: 16 rooms, all with bath/shower. TV. Phone. B&B £45 to £90. Children welcome. Well-behaved dogs welcome. Afternoon teas (*The Which? Hotel Guide*) (£5)

' "Goat, strong, medium, mild. What you like?" Thus the description of the enormous selection of cheeses by the hard-pressed waitress. At £15 per portion, one had hoped for a little more detail.' (On eating in Oxfordshire)

Walnut Tree Inn 🍷

Llandewi Skirrid NP7 8AW
TEL: (01873) 852797   COOKING **8**
on B4521, 3m NE of Abergavenny   COST £34–£67

'Everyone should, at least once in their lifetime, go to the Walnut Tree'. This whitewashed country pub on the edge of Abergavenny is a jewel of robust, imaginative cooking using the freshest ingredients. It is a hybrid in more ways than one, combining pub with restaurant, and Franco Taruschio's native Italy with his adopted Wales, expressed in a range of dishes from bresaola to Lady Llanover's salt duck. Hopeful unbooked diners queue before opening and soon fill the bar tables. They find themselves sitting 'buttock to buttock' with complete strangers, at tables too small for the largesse put before them. Barriers are broken by curiosity about the food on someone else's plate, and there is a 'deceptive air of chaos' as well as an engaging simplicity exemplified by the outside loo and messily written menu. All this reflects the Walnut Tree's resolute confidence in its own idiosyncratic approach.

Conventional wisdom dictates that we regard with suspicion anywhere, especially in a small village, that offers upwards of 50 dishes, but conventional wisdom doesn't apply here. 'Wonderful ingredients cooked with consummate skill and few frills' is the gist of Taruschio's appeal, from the well-known vincis grassi maceratese, a comforting dish of lasagne with wild mushrooms, truffle and Parmesan, to perfectly timed risotto, to 'fresh, firm, tasty, juicy, large pieces of white monkfish' roasted and served with meaty scallops, crevettes and a laverbread sauce with curls of sweet orange zest. Nobody pretends that every single dish is faultless, and some reporters come away disappointed, but there is often an extenuating circumstance. One visitor's brodetto of fish was marginally overcooked, but this was outweighed by the 'sumptuousness and generosity' of the vivid red soupy sauce of tomato, fish stock and garlic that evoked the home cooking of Naples. Likewise a thick slice of roast suckling pig flavoured with rosemary and garlic conjured up the 'porchetta rolls sold from stalls in Tuscan markets' for an inspector.

A 'cheeky' £1 cover charge pays for a basket of breads and a pre-meal slice of warm, tasty quiche, and there is an extra charge for vegetables: asparagus, Welsh bubble and squeak, or a rocket and chicory salad. Desserts might include a trio of chocolates, 'perfectly executed' strawberry crème brûlée, or a creamy citron tart – with a paper-thin caramelised crust and a long aftertaste of lemon zest – that would challenge the best. Service is from 'motherly' types in gathered skirts and flat sandals. The outstanding wine list, prepared with the assistance of Bill Baker and Reid Wines, opens with a roll-call of renowned Italian producers, then moves on to a classic collection of French bins, while fans of the New World are looked after with a small but astute selection. Prices are fair, starting with house Verdicchio and Rosso Piceno at £12.50 a litre.

CHEF: Franco Taruschio   PROPRIETORS: Franco and Ann Taruschio   OPEN: Tue to Sat 12.15 to 3.15, 7.15 to 10.15   MEALS: alc (main courses £8 to £18). Cover £1   SERVICE: not inc   CARDS: none   DETAILS: 106 seats. 30 seats outside. Private parties: 46 main room. Car park. Vegetarian meals. Children's helpings. Wheelchair access (also WC). No music. Air-conditioned

---

▲ *Tyddyn Llan* ⸙✳

Llandrillo LL21 0ST
TEL: (01490) 440264 FAX: (01490) 440414
EMAIL: tyddnllanhotel@compuserve.com COOKING 6
on B4401, 4½ miles S of Corwen COST £24–£58

This peaceful, stone-built Georgian country house is extremely well kept, but 'friendly' and 'unpompous', a combination rare enough in Wales for reporters to remark on. 'We felt totally relaxed as we walked through the door,' one couple subsequently summoned the energy to write. The Kindreds busy themselves with some refurbishment every January, this time smartening up a few bedrooms and posting French military prints in the bar. Jason Hornbuckle, meanwhile, continues his well-resourced and carefully crafted style of European cooking, turning out salt-cod brandade with gazpacho sauce, roast breast of Hereford duck with cabbage fondue, and monkfish tail with split pea purée.

This year a four-course 'gourmet' option joins the quarterly-changing dinner menu, offering more in the way of luxury: caramelised scallops and pasta to start perhaps, then a plate of lamb loin, breast, kidney and liver served with garlic-crushed potatoes, before grilled goats'-cheese salad and dessert. Other treats have been enjoyed by reporters – duck confit and foie gras terrine, peppered venison steak, and roast guinea-fowl with truffles and a vegetable salsa – but the food doesn't rely on indulgence for success, rather on good judgement. Choice after the main course, at least on the seasonal menu, includes a savoury Welsh rarebit, selection of cheese, or a dessert such as 'icky sticky soufflé', or caramelised pineapple with mascarpone mousse and Malibu ice-cream. 'There is no sense of rush' to the service, although greater generosity with the coffee would be appreciated. The well-balanced wine list has an eye for some interesting bottles (Duxoup's Charbono for one) and starts with a dozen house wines around £12–£16.

CHEF: Jason Hornbuckle PROPRIETORS: Peter and Bridget Kindred OPEN: all week 12.30 to 2, 7 to 9 MEALS: Set L £13 to £15.50, Set D £25 to £35. Bar L available SERVICE: not inc, card slips closed CARDS: Amex, Delta, Diners, MasterCard, Switch, Visa DETAILS: 50 seats. 15 seats outside. Private parties: 45 main room, 45 private room. Car park. Vegetarian meals. Children's helpings. No children under 8. No smoking in dining-room. Wheelchair access (also men's WC). Music ACCOMMODATION: 10 rooms, all with bath/shower. TV. Phone. B&B £64 to £130. Children welcome. High teas for children. Baby facilities. Dogs welcome in bedrooms only. Afternoon teas. Fishing (*The Which? Hotel Guide*) £5

▲ *Bodysgallen Hall* ♟ ⸙✳

Llandudno LL30 1RS
TEL: (01492) 584466 FAX: (01492) 582519 COOKING 2
off A470, 2m SE of Llandudno COST £24–£65

Made of local stone, the terraced hall is surrounded by secluded walled gardens – including one for kitchen use – with lots of yew and box trees. Nibbles come with an aperitif in the dark wood-panelled lounge, and meals in the pale yellow dining-room are at a set price with a few supplements: for smoked salmon, foie gras, or fillet of Welsh Black beef. Good raw materials showed at inspection, particularly a saddle of venison, roasted in a piece and well timed, then roughly sliced and placed on a cake of improveable mashed potato. Choice extends to grilled Dover sole, roast sea bass, and Welsh lamb with a compote of peas and broad beans, and dinner might begin with prune-filled saddle of rabbit, or a fillet of baby halibut covered in a mustardy Welsh rarebit (tasting much stronger than the fish) with a caper-dressed salad. 'Intensely flavoured' raspberry soufflé served with a Welsh honey ice-cream made a good finish to one meal, though coffee needs to go back to the drawing board. Service is plentiful but might be better organised. The wine list travels around the world, and prices reflect the country-house setting, but bins under £15 are scattered throughout and there is a generous number of half-bottles. Half a dozen French house wines set the ball rolling from £11.75. CELLARMAN'S CHOICE: Berry's Sauvignon Blanc 1996, Marlborough, New Zealand, £24.50; Castle Creek Cabernet Sauvignon 1996, Australia, £15.50.

CHEF: Mike Penny   PROPRIETOR: Historic House Hotels Ltd   OPEN: all week 12.30 to 1.45, 7.30 (7 in summer) to 9.30   MEALS: Set L £13.50 (2 courses) to £15.50, Set D £29.50. BYO £5 SERVICE: net prices, card slips closed   CARDS: Amex, Delta, MasterCard, Switch, Visa DETAILS: 60 seats. Private parties: 40 main room, 40 private room. Car park. Vegetarian meals. No children under 8. Jacket and tie. No smoking in dining-room. Wheelchair access (1 step; also WC). Occasional music. Air-conditioned   ACCOMMODATION: 35 rooms, all with bath/shower. TV. Phone. Room only £95 to £205. Rooms for disabled. No children under 8. Dogs welcome in cottage suites only. Afternoon teas. Swimming-pool (*The Which? Hotel Guide*) £5

▲ Martin's

11 Mostyn Avenue, Craig-y-Don,
Llandudno LL30 1YS   COOKING 3
TEL: (01492) 870070   FAX: (01492) 876661   COST £22–£50

Martin James offers a generous choice on his 'bill of fare' at this modest dining-room in a terrace of shops. It signals a busy kitchen, confirmed by the time he must spend making port wine crystals to partner melon cocktail, assembling warm layers of fish mousse to serve with seafood, and putting together a trio of pastas to go with steamed sea bass. There are some treats to look for – roast squab with a truffle and wine jus, or roast loin of Anglesey hare with pickled cabbage – as well as more homely leek and potato soup, and rack of Welsh lamb with onion marmalade. Cheeses are Welsh farmhouse, and desserts might include hot apple flan or passion-fruit soufflé. A set menu operates for pre-theatre bookings, and house vin de pays is £9.95.

CHEF: Martin James   PROPRIETORS: Martin James and Jan Williams   OPEN: all week 12.30 to 2.30, 6 to 9.30   MEALS: alc D (main courses £12 to £16). Set L £10.95 (2 courses) to £13.50, Set pre-theatre D Tue to Sat (5 to 7pm) £13.95 (2 courses) to £16.50 (reservations only). BYO £3 SERVICE: not inc, card slips closed   CARDS: Amex, MasterCard, Visa   DETAILS: 30 seats. 10 seats outside. Private parties: 30 main room. Children welcome. Vegetarian meals. No-smoking area. Wheelchair access (1 step; not WC). Music   ACCOMMODATION: 4 rooms, all with bath/shower. TV. B&B £45 to £55. Guide dogs only £5

Richard's

7 Church Walks, Llandudno LL30 2HD   COOKING 2
TEL: (01492) 877924 and 875315   COST £25–£41

Since 1990, Richard Hendey has been pleasing the crowds in his basement bistro not far from Llandudno pier. The fact that he seeks out his fresh fish 'personally and locally' counts for a great deal, and the results of his efforts show up well on the daily list of blackboard specials: here you can expect anything from Conwy mussels with pasta in a spinach and champagne cream sauce, to seared salmon steak with muscadet, spinach and watercress sauce. The theme of richness and 'indulgence' – portions are big – carries through to meat and game dishes such as chargrilled Welsh beef with red wine, whisky and Stilton cream sauce, or slow-roasted Shropshire duckling with plum sauce and orange segments. Desserts are also calorie-laden, as in toffee apple cheesecake with caramel sauce, and strawberry choux bun with strawberry praline sauce. A strong and well-annotated house selection is the highlight of the lively but affordable wine list. Prices start at £8.95.

CHEFS: Richard Hendey and Mark Roberts   PROPRIETOR: Richard Hendey   OPEN: all week D only 5.30 to 11   CLOSED: 25 and 26 Dec   MEALS: alc (main courses £11 to £14)   SERVICE: net prices, card slips closed   CARDS: Amex, Delta, MasterCard, Switch, Visa   DETAILS: 50 seats. Private parties: 20 main room. Vegetarian meals. Children's helpings. Music

▲ St Tudno Hotel 🍷 ⅛✳

Promenade, Llandudno LL30 2LP
TEL: (01492) 874411   FAX: (01492) 860407   COOKING 3
EMAIL: sttudnohotel@btinternet.com   COST £24–£47

One of the smaller hotels at the pier end of the promenade in this Victorian seaside town, St Tudno hardly looks any different from its neighbours. Inside, though, it is a cut above the rest. Restrained good taste in the lounges gives way to a sunny-bright 'make-believe conservatory' dining-room with hanging flower baskets and wicker garden chairs. David Harding's 'Gourmet' menu offers considerably more options and interest than the rather plain standard one, which might start with melon or a smoked chicken salad, then soup or sorbet, before grilled turbot, fillet of beef (for two only, with a supplement) or a vegetarian dish of the day.

Seafood is a speciality, impressing our inspector with a simply presented crab and avocado salad with a sharp brandy mayonnaise, a hotpot of seafood in a smooth, creamy champagne sauce, and salmon fillet served with a good lobster sauce. Welsh spring lamb and Black beef also feature, and accompanying buttered vegetables are 'simple and straightforward'. Puddings may not be particularly adventurous, but have included rhubarb sponge with custard, and a hot lemon pie topped with frothy meringue. Service, kept sharp by Janette Bland's watchful eye, is 'caring and professional'.

The well-organised wine list repays browsing at length as it features some classic bins from both hemispheres. Two pages of wines from Willi Opitz and Ch. Musar are a welcome new feature, and epicures should look out for the 'marriage of food and wine' evenings. House French is £9.50 or £11.50.

CELLARMAN'S CHOICE: Muskat Ottonel Trocken 1996, Opitz, Austria, £21; Hamilton Russell Pinot Noir 1995, Walker Bay, S. Africa, £26.50.

CHEF: David Harding   PROPRIETORS: Martin and Janette Bland   OPEN: Sun L 12.30 to 1.45, all week D 7 to 9.30 (9 Sun)   MEALS: alc L (main courses £7.50 to £14.50). Set L Sun £16.95, Set D £22 (2 courses) to £29.50. BYO £12.50   SERVICE: not inc, card slips closed   CARDS: Amex, Delta, Diners, MasterCard, Switch, Visa   DETAILS: 60 seats. Private parties: 75 main room. Car park. Vegetarian meals. Children's helpings. No very young children at D. No smoking in dining-room. Wheelchair access (not WC). Occasional music. Air-conditioned ACCOMMODATION: 20 rooms, all with bath/shower. TV. Phone. B&B £70 to £250. Children welcome. Baby facilities. Small dogs welcome, not left unattended. Afternoon teas. Swimming-pool (*The Which? Hotel Guide*)

LLANFIHANGEL NANT MELAN Powys   map 4

▲ Red Lion Inn 🍴 £

Llanfihangel nant Melan, nr New Radnor LD8 2TN
TEL/FAX: (01544) 350220
on A44 Rhayader to Kington road, 3m W of New   COOKING 4
Radnor   COST £18–£33

This modestly appointed roadside pub with conservatory extension impresses reporters for its 'warm welcome, friendly and informal atmosphere and unbelievably low prices' that the Johns family have made an integral part of its appeal. Décor may be pretty basic, extending to jigsaw-puzzles mounted on the walls, as if in tribute to the labour of whoever completed them, but Gareth Johns's accomplished cooking is what draws people in, and – in the evenings at least – may seem surprisingly sophisticated in the circumstances. A warm terrine of fresh and smoked salmon with appetising juicy texture has a mild herbed cream sauce, while toasted Pencarreg goats' cheese with relish is a fixture. Main courses at lunch may be as simple as pork and leek sausages with mash and onion gravy, but dinner options put on the style for Montgomery duck breast with whimberries – 'outstandingly good meat in an honest, well-balanced, fruity stock' – or medallions of tender Welsh Black beef in Madeira sauce. Vegetables are plentiful and attentively cooked. 'Simple but top-class' dark chocolate terrine delivers plenty of cocoa solids, or there may be banana sablé using excellent home-made shortbread. House wine is £4.95 per 500ml carafe.

CHEF: Gareth Johns   PROPRIETORS: Keith, Liz and Gareth Johns   OPEN: Sun L 12 to 2, Wed to Mon D 7 to 9 (9.30 Sat)   CLOSED: 1 week Nov   MEALS: alc (main courses £6 to £12)   SERVICE: none, card slips closed   CARDS: Amex, Delta, MasterCard, Switch, Visa   DETAILS: 54 seats. 16 seats outside. Private parties: 20 main room, 20 private rooms. Car park. Vegetarian meals. Children's helpings. No smoking in 1 dining-room. No music   ACCOMMODATION: 3 rooms, all with bath/shower. B&B £20 to £40. Children welcome

---

£ *means that it is possible to have a three-course meal, including coffee, half a bottle of house wine and service for £25 or less per person, at any time the restaurant is open, i.e. at dinner as well as lunch. It may be possible to spend considerably more than this, but by choosing carefully you should find £25 or less achievable.*

▲ *The Lake Country House* ♥ ⅝✳

Llangammarch Wells LD4 4BS
TEL: (01591) 620202   FAX: (10591) 620457   COOKING 4
off B483 at Garth, 6m W of Builth Wells   COST £25–£49

'Very rural,' summed up one visitor to this mock half-timbered Victorian-Edwardian house in 50 acres of grounds. What the place may lack in individuality it more than makes up for in sheer size; the lounge alone 'gives new meaning to the word spacious', while the dining-room's strong point is floral carpets and curtains. Jeremy Medley has cooked at some fine country houses, including Mallory Court (see entry, Bishops Tachbrook) and Buckland-Tout-Saints, and knows what goes down well. Here he comforts with pressed terrine of calf's liver, wild mushroom risotto with a poached egg, roast Welsh lamb, and local venison.

The food can be technically demanding, in first courses of venison pudding or a small quail pie, for example, or main courses such as saddle of rabbit, stuffed, rolled and sliced, on a bed of shredded cabbage. But the kitchen seems to thrive on this, producing at inspection a well-made hot banana soufflé with rum and raisin ice-cream that stole the show. Although dishes may not be cracking with excitement, fresh ingredients are the foundation, and menus are well planned. Service is plentiful, smart, well-paced, observant, and French: Mr and Mrs Mifsud 'clearly run a very tight ship'. Clarets are given serious consideration on the lengthy wine list, which divides them by growths, covers a good spread of vintages and provides helpful tasting notes. If you have your sights set on an appealing bin from the New World you will not be disappointed, but don't be surprised if the strong Spanish selection claims your attention instead. Two dozen house recommendations start at £9.75. CELLARMAN'S CHOICE: Forrest Estate Sauvignon Blanc 1996 Marlborough, New Zealand, £18.50; Vistalba Estate Syrah 1994, Mendoza, Argentina, £11.50.

CHEF: Jeremy Medley   PROPRIETORS: Mr and Mrs J.P. Mifsud   OPEN: all week 12.30 to 1.45, 7.30 to 9   MEALS: Set L £17.50, Set D £32.50   SERVICE: not inc   CARDS: Amex, Delta, Diners, MasterCard, Switch, Visa   DETAILS: 85 seas. Private parties: 85 main room. Car park. Vegetarian meals. Children's helpings. No children under 7 after 7.30pm. Jacket and tie. No smoking in dining-room. Wheelchair access (also WC). No music   ACCOMMODATION: 19 rooms, all with bath/shower. TV. Phone. B&B £80 to £235. Rooms for disabled. Children welcome. High teas for children. Baby facilities. Dogs welcome in bedrooms only. Afternoon teas. Fishing (*The Which? Hotel Guide*)

Welcome to Town ⅝✳ £   [NEW ENTRY]

Llanrhidian, Gower SA3 1EH
TEL: (01792) 390015   COOKING 1
on B4295, 10m W of Swansea   COST £24–£32

This long, low, whitewashed country inn opposite the church has been simply refurbished with modern beams and white walls, and is now '90 per cent restaurant and 10 per cent bar'. Robert Allen fronts the enterprise, and sets the friendly tone that ensures it lives up to its name, while his wife Sheila cooks with a light touch. A straightforward approach with fresh ingredients pays dividends, in crab and salmon fish-cakes, or a casserole of lamb and broad beans in a well-flavoured gravy served with earthy new Gower potatoes at one May meal. Food 'like the best that could be produced at home' might include a mini quiche filled with haddock and prawns, or with leeks and cream cheese, served with a crunchy salad. A star attraction is the 'Llanrhidian bun', a light brioche overflowing with laverbread, cockles, leeks and bacon. Finish with a sharp but creamy lemon tart with crumbly short pastry, or the 'softest and lightest' white chocolate and Grand Marnier brioche pudding that reminded an inspector of childhood bread-and-butter puddings. Like the menu, the short wine list changes every month, and offers equally good value. House wine is £9.

CHEF: Sheila Allen PROPRIETORS: Robert, Sheila and Timothy Allen OPEN: Tue to Sat 12.30 to 1.45, 7 to 8.45 CLOSED: Oct MEALS: alc (main courses £9 to £11) SERVICE: not inc, card slips closed CARDS: Amex, Delta, MasterCard, Switch, Visa DETAILS: 38 seats. Private parties: 8 main room. Car park. Vegetarian meals. No children under 14 at D exc by arrangement. No smoking in dining-room. Wheelchair access (1 step; not WC). Music (£5)

LLANSANFFRAID GLAN CONWY Conwy   map 7

▲ Old Rectory 🍷 ⁵⁺✳

Llanrwst Road, Llansanffraid Glan Conwy,
nr Conwy LL28 5LF
TEL: (01492) 580611 FAX: (01492) 584555
EMAIL: oldrect@aol.com   COOKING 6
on A470, ½m S of junction with A55   COST £39–£53

The 'gracious' Regency house, full of books and tasteful antiques, sits high above the Conwy estuary, overlooking the castle and Snowdonia. The Vaughans have been here for 15 years, and their approach is a dedicated one. Dinner is on their terms: one sitting at 8pm, with no choice of first or main course, apart from special requirements negotiated when booking. Local materials play a prominent part in proceedings, and the first course is usually fish: fillet of brill with spinach and brandade of cod, or a salmon platter that includes gravad lax, a mousse wrapped in spinach, pâté with salmon eggs, and a circle of salmon filled with brown shrimps.

Although the Black beef and Mountain lamb are Welsh, their treatment is more exotic, the former perhaps served with polenta and wild mushrooms, the latter with couscous and roasted vegetables. Alternatively, there might be roast breast of duck with goats' cheese mash and root vegetables. After that comes a choice of a couple of desserts or sorbet, and then a plate of four small Welsh cheeses. Michael Vaughan serves the food 'with courtesy and friendliness' at a leisurely pace: one couple, who felt that it helped 'to be in a state of supreme tranquility, and armed with plenty to talk about', arrived at 7.15 and reached coffee by 10.35. Another reporter found himself confronted by a harp recital in the drawing-room between ordering drinks and being called to table.

Fine wines from France form the centre-piece of a cleverly composed list, with intelligent selections from Germany, Italy, South Africa and the Americas providing agreeable side attractions. Half-bottles are plentiful. CELLARMAN'S

CHOICE: Pinot d'Alsace 'Les Princes Abbés' 1996, Schlumberger, £18.90; Crozes-Hermitage 'La Petite Ruche' 1996, Chapoutier, £17.90.

CHEF: Wendy Vaughan PROPRIETORS: Michael and Wendy Vaughan OPEN: all week D only 7.30 for 8 (1 sitting) CLOSED: limited opening Nov to Mar, closed 10 Dec to 1 Feb. MEALS: Set D £25 to £29.50 SERVICE: not inc, card slips closed CARDS: Amex, Delta, MasterCard, Switch, Visa DETAILS: 16 seats. Private parties: 12 main room. Car park. No children under 5. No smoking in dining-room. No music ACCOMMODATION: 6 rooms, all with bath/shower. TV. Phone. B&B £99 to £139. No children under 5. Dogs welcome in some rooms only (*The Which? Hotel Guide*)

LLANWDDYN Powys

map 7

▲ *Lake Vyrnwy Hotel* ✻

Lake Vyrnwy, Llanwddyn SY10 0LY
TEL: (01691) 870692   FAX: (01691) 870259
on B4393, at SE end of Lake Vyrnwy

COOKING 3
COST £24–£40

Vyrnwy reservoir was a typically grandiose Victorian project, built to provide water for Liverpudlians; at the time its dam was the largest in Europe. The hotel that once housed engineers and visiting dignitaries enjoys tranquility and a 'magical' vista, especially at sunset. Lunch changes daily, but the dinner menu, which offers a generous seven or eight items per course, stays in place for a couple of weeks, which one long-stay couple found rather restricting. Dinner might start with a crisply fried breaded fish-cake served with a spring onion, lime and chilli salsa, or a 'colourful and stylish' terrine of goats' cheese, roast red peppers and Jerusalem artichokes, served with beetroot and asparagus salad.

Andrew Wood's broadly European cooking has also taken in roast breast of guinea-fowl with crunchy buttered cabbage on a glossy red wine sauce, as well as a 'beautifully fresh' fillet of brill, served with chargrilled red peppers, aubergine and courgette swimming in a vermouth cream sauce. Desserts have ranged from lemon tart to a freshly baked hot apple crumble with rhubarb ice-cream and a tangy apricot syrup. 'Prompt, charming' service is from 'smiley local ladies done up in striped dresses and white frilly pinnies', and as a bonus it is 'so nice that children are treated as people'. A level-headed Eurocentric wine list takes in a brace of organic English wines, and isn't badly off for half-bottles. House vin de pays is £9.95.

CHEF: Andrew Wood PROPRIETOR: Market Glen Ltd OPEN: all week 12.30 to 1.45, 7.30 to 9.15 MEALS: Set L Mon to Sat £15.95, Set L Sun £16.95, Set D £25.50. BYO £6 SERVICE: not inc, card slips closed CARDS: Delta, Diners, MasterCard, Switch, Visa DETAILS: 80 seats. Private parties: 80 main room, 25 private rooms. Car park. Vegetarian meals. Children's helpings. Jacket and tie. No smoking in dining-room. Wheelchair access (not WC). No music ACCOMMODATION: 35 rooms, all with bath/shower. TV. Phone. DB&B £75 to £95. Children welcome. Baby facilities. Afternoon teas. Dogs welcome (heated kennels available). Fishing
£5

'The staff line up forlornly against one wall, as if wishing their dance card would suddenly become full'. (On eating in Cambridgeshire)

▲ Carlton House � ⁵✳

Dolycoed Road, Llanwrtyd Wells LD5 4RA	COOKING 6
TEL: (01591) 610248 FAX: (01591) 610242	COST £25–£53

This 'Edwardian slab of a building', set back from the street by a narrow walled garden, is a restaurant-with-rooms. The appeal is 'very good cooking, eaten in the best of atmospheres, at a decent price'. Since last year the format has changed: Carlton House is now also open for lunch, and an à la carte has taken over from the set-price menus. The dining-room has also changed, the homely yellow and blue room that struggled to seat above a dozen at once being replaced with a larger, brighter room at the front of the house with the added advantage of better views for diners.

Carefully sourced materials are the foundation, from Towy sewin (served with squid ink risotto) to Welsh Black beef that might appear as a first-course carpaccio with Pecorino and herbs, or as a pan-fried fillet with a wild mushroom sauce. A few exotic flavours surface from time to time – fillet of salmon in a pesto crust with couscous, or Welsh lamb with onion bhajias and spiced lentils – but most combinations work because they have a proven track record: pigeon breast with juniper-scented cabbage, or a croustade that plays off tart apple against the 'smooth roundness' of goats' cheese. If you don't fancy 'A Serious Attack by Chocolate', try the passion-fruit sorbet with a sweet coconut crème anglaise, or the cheeses, which are well-kept and generously served at the point of ripeness.

Service is from Alan Gilchrist 'with intermittent briefings from his wife', and a 'cracking breakfast' awaits those who stay over. The ever-expanding, helpfully annotated wine list continues to offer a variety of fresh styles and flavours from reliable producers. It might not cover the major regions fully but it does introduce some interesting minor ones, for example New York State. There are plenty of bottles under £15 with even a few under £10, including the Chilean house red and white at £9.95. CELLARMAN'S CHOICE: Pouilly-Fumé Buisson Ménard 1993, Didier Dagueneau, £28.75; Vin de Pays du Var Merlot 1995, Dom. de Triennes, £16.25.

CHEF: Mary Ann Gilchrist   PROPRIETORS: Alan and Mary Ann Gilchrist   OPEN: Tue to Sat L 12.30 to 1.45, Mon to Sat D 7 to 8.30   CLOSED: Christmas   MEALS: alc (main courses L £10 to £15, D £13 to £18.50)   SERVICE: not inc, card slips closed   CARDS: Delta, MasterCard, Switch, Visa   DETAILS: 14 seats. Private parties: 12 main room. Vegetarian meals. No children under 6. No smoking in dining-room. No music   ACCOMMODATION: 7 rooms, all with bath/shower. TV. B&B £30 to £70. Children welcome. Dogs welcome in bedrooms only (The Which? Hotel Guide)

▲ Griffin Inn ⁵✳ £

Llyswen LD3 0UR	COOKING 1
TEL: (01874) 754241 FAX: (01874) 754592	COST £21–£39

'[Our] food is grounded in true rural fare,' notes Richard Stockton, the senior partner at this 500-year-old whitewashed inn set in the Upper Wye Valley. Four generations of his family now run the Griffin and have fashioned it into a veritable haven for devotees of fish and game. In a setting of traditional timbers, stone floors and log fires, visitors can sample hearty, robust country cooking based around local supplies of everything from pigeons, rabbits and venison to Wye salmon and, occasionally, mutton. Eat in the bar or the dining-room from a menu that is dominated by stews, casseroles and the like: knuckle of Welsh lamb is braised and served on red cabbage with garlic and rosemary jus, Hereford beef is pot-roasted in claret, while duck might receive the cassoulet treatment. Elsewhere there's a charcoal grill for fish and vegetables, and the repertoire extends to 'succulent' baked cod in herb crust, and trout with smoked bacon and mushrooms. Welsh cheeses and familiar home-made desserts complete the picture. Drink real ale or dip into the global wine list. Seventeen house wines start at £8.55.

CHEFS: Richard Stockton and Andrew Addis-Fuller   PROPRIETORS: Richard and Di Stockton   OPEN: all week L 12 to 2, Mon to Sat D 7 to 9   CLOSED: 25 and 26 Dec   MEALS: alc (main courses L £6 to £8, D £10 to £16).   Bar L available Mon to Sat   SERVICE: not inc   CARDS: Amex, Delta, Diners, MasterCard, Switch, Visa   DETAILS: 40 seats. 16 seats outside. Private parties: 40 main room, 14 private room. Car park. Vegetarian meals. Children's helpings. No smoking in dining-room. Wheelchair access (not WC). No music   ACCOMMODATION: 7 rooms, all with bath/shower. TV. Phone. B&B £40 to £80. Children welcome. High teas for children. Baby facilities. Fishing (*The Which? Hotel Guide*)   £5

▲ *Llangoed Hall* £✕

Llyswen LD3 0YP
TEL: (01874) 754525   FAX: (01874) 754545
EMAIL: 101543.3211@compuserve.com
on A470, 2m NW of Llyswen

COOKING 6
COST £30–£61

To the extent that country-house hotels depend on their setting, ambience and service as much as food for effect, this place delivers. The Jacobean manor-house was restored by Sir Clough Williams-Ellis earlier in the century, then rescued by Sir Bernard Ashley, widower of Laura, in 1987. It doesn't immediately feel like a hotel – there is no reception desk, for example – which is part of its charm. Edwardian paintings hang from the walls, comfortable sofas cluster round coffee tables in the lounge, and the dining-room looks out over the valley, its tables laid with white cloths and Wedgwood china.

The menu's southern European thrust is evident in a terrine of Welsh lamb and Mediterranean vegetables, or sea bass with couscous and sun-dried tomatoes, and some of the preparation looks pretty demanding: a fillet of rabbit stuffed with wild mushrooms, wrapped in pastry on a cep risotto, with a tarragon sauce, or Black beef fillet on a foie gras potato cake with a tortellini of wild mushrooms, in a red wine sauce. Accurate timing gets the best out of materials, such as a briefly grilled fillet of Pembrokeshire cod, and vegetarians seem to do very well for themselves.

Flavour combinations are carefully considered, if generally traditional, as in a hot apple and cinnamon soufflé, or a coffee and chocolate roulade served with Bailey's ice-cream. Wines are impressive in scope and quality, and although many of them are for big spenders there are chinks of light for those with £20 or so: look to the cellarman's choice, house selection, and the New World. House Graves white and red are £18.50 and £19 respectively.

CHEF: Ben Davies   PROPRIETOR: Sir Bernard Ashley   OPEN: all week 12.15 to 2, 7.15 to 9.30
MEALS: alc (main courses £14 to £22). Set L Mon to Sat £15 (2 courses) to £18, Set L Sun £21.50,
Set D £35   SERVICE: not inc, card slips closed   CARDS: Amex, Delta, Diners, MasterCard,
Switch, Visa   DETAILS: 50 seats. 15 seats outside. Private parties: 50 main room, 15 to 50
private rooms. Car park. Vegetarian meals. No children under 8. Jacket and tie. No smoking in
dining-room. Wheelchair access (1 step; also WC). No music   ACCOMMODATION: 23 rooms, all
with bath/shower. TV. Phone. B&B £155 to £325. No children under 8. Dogs welcome in heated
kennels only. Afternoon teas. Fishing (*The Which? Hotel Guide*) (£5)

MATHRY Pembrokeshire   map 4

Ann FitzGerald's Farmhouse Kitchen ▼ £

Mabws Fawr, Mathry SA62 5JB
TEL: (01348) 831347   COOKING 3
off A487, 6m SW of Fishguard   COST £18–£44

The restored thirteenth-century farmhouse is out of the way, but easy to find
down a country lane. Go through the kitchen to reach a Victorian dining-room,
'cleanly decorated and comfortable', with a relaxed atmosphere and attentive
service from local girls. The country style of cooking runs to duck pâté with
onion chutney, rabbit with mustard, and a meaty fish such as brill or turbot
served with a sauce of mushrooms, cream and sherry. Materials include Welsh
Black beef which, although grass-fed and from a BSE-free accredited herd, is still
subject to the same restrictions as all other cattle. The FitzGeralds understandably lament the passing of oxtail, and stock made from bones – as a result
'our sauces have got lighter' – but the silver lining is that locally caught fish now
appears more often: grilled mackerel perhaps, or Fishguard Bay scallops in filo
pastry with Gower cockles and laverbread.

A few Eastern notes work their way into the repertoire, from curried crab
pancake roll to chicken with an Indonesian spice mix (salt and spices can
sometimes get the upper hand), but desserts are as familiar as apple tart, or bread
pudding with whisky custard. France remains to the fore on the attractive,
100-strong list, although an impressive dozen from Italy and some sound New
World selections vie for attention. Six house wines start at £9. CELLARMAN'S
CHOICE: Pinot Blanc Spätlese 1994, Opitz, Austria, £20; Cepparello 1986, Isole e
Olena, Tuscany, £31.

CHEFS/PROPRIETORS: Ann and Lionel FitzGerald   OPEN: all week 12 to 2, 6 to 9   MEALS: alc
(main courses L £6 to £13, D £10 to £14). Set L £10, Set D £17   SERVICE: not inc, card slips
closed   CARDS: MasterCard, Visa   DETAILS: 45 seats. 16 seats outside. Private parties: 45
main room. Car park. Vegetarian meals. Children's helpings. Wheelchair access (also WC).
Music (£5)

---

*The text of entries is based on unsolicited reports sent in by readers, backed up by
inspections conducted anonymously. The factual details under the text are from
questionnaires the* **Guide** *sends to all restaurants that feature in the book.*

▲ *Four Seasons*

Cwmtwrch Farm Hotel, Nantgaredig SA32 7NY
TEL: (01267) 290238   FAX: (01267) 290808   COOKING 3
on B4310, ½m N of Nantgaredig   COST £27–£33

This enticing set-up has grown out of a collection of traditional Welsh
agricultural buildings: the restaurant (and bedrooms) occupy one longhouse,
with a modern conservatory-style extension tacked on. In a pine-ceilinged
dining-room with chunky wooden furniture, rustic implements and displays of
local pottery, Charlotte Pasetti and Maryann Wright please visitors with a
four-course dinner menu that changes day by day. Here is a kitchen where
supplies of red pesto, balsamic vinegar and creme fraîche sit alongside
Carmarthen air-dried ham, Brechfa smoked salmon and Welsh Black beef. The
impression is of traditional – and often local – ingredients given a splash of
colour from the global palette: rack of salt-marsh lamb with aubergine caponata,
breast of chicken stuffed with leeks and wrapped in Parma ham, and salmon and
fennel cannelloni, for example. Welsh cheeses not only appear on the cheeseboard but also find their way into a number of dishes: Gwyn Bach in a salad
with avocado and tomato, Llanboidy paired with spinach in vegetarian
pancakes. A daily assortment of home-made desserts encompasses everything
from chocolate and whisky ice-cream to pear and almond tart. The owners
operate a small wine company from the restaurant, and their 50-strong list is
knowledgeably chosen and fairly priced. House wines are £9.50.

CHEFS/PROPRIETORS: Charlotte Pasetti and Maryann Wright   OPEN: Tue to Sat D only 7.30 to
9.30   CLOSED: 25 Dec   MEALS: Set D £20   SERVICE: not inc, card slips closed   CARDS: Delta,
MasterCard, Switch, Visa   DETAILS: 50 seats. Private parties: 60 main room. Car park.
Vegetarian meals. Children's helpings. No children under 5. Wheelchair access (not WC).
Occasional music   ACCOMMODATION: 5 rooms, all with bath/shower. TV. B&B £40 to £54.
Rooms for disabled. Children welcome. High teas for children. Baby facilities. Swimming-pool
(*The Which? Hotel Guide*) (£5)

▲ *Cnapan* 🍴

East Street, Newport SA42 0SY   COOKING 2
TEL: (01239) 820575   FAX: (01239) 820878   COST £15–£36

The homely feel of this rose-coloured restaurant-with-rooms in National Park
territory derives from its family ownership and the pleasant array of
knick-knacks inside. Food presentation is appealingly rough-and-ready, as
befits the surroundings. A reporter who stayed three nights roamed the culinary
range, enjoying along the way gratinated crab and laverbread with toasted garlic
ciabatta, skewered monkfish and salmon sauced with white wine, lemon and
prawns, and an enterprising dish of pork fillets with spiced lentils and banana in
a coconut curry sauce. Abundant Welsh cheeses make an alternative to puddings
such as apricot crumble and custard. The basic wine list is headed up by a trio of
house offerings at £8.75 a bottle or £1.70 the glass.

CHEFS: Eluned Lloyd and Judith Cooper   PROPRIETORS: Eluned and John Lloyd, and Michael and Judith Cooper   OPEN: Mon and Wed to Sat 12 to 2, 6.30 to 8.45 (Sun L bookings only) CLOSED: Christmas, Jan and Feb   MEALS: alc (main courses L £5, D £11.50 to £13.50) SERVICE: not inc, card slips closed   CARDS: Delta, MasterCard, Visa   DETAILS: 36 seats. 25 seats outside. Private parties: 30 main room. Car park. Vegetarian meals. Children's helpings. No smoking in dining-room. Wheelchair access (also WC). No music   ACCOMMODATION: 5 rooms, all with bath/shower. TV. B&B £44 to £88. Children welcome. High teas for children. Baby facilities. Guide dogs only (*The Which? Hotel Guide*)

PEMBROKE Pembrokeshire   map 4

Left Bank ﹩✳ £

---

63 Main Street, Pembroke SA71 4DA   COOKING 3
TEL: (01646) 622333   COST £24–£39

A one-time bank building on guess which bank of the River Cleddau has been transformed into a jazzy modern minimalist brasserie with bold modern artwork and a vibrant colour scheme. This is an enthusiastically run venue with a fashion-conscious French accent and a few Mediterranean whispers. Seasonal dinner menus are based resolutely on what west Wales can produce, and the kitchen works industriously to fill any gaps with breads, pastas and the like. The quality of raw materials impressed one couple who enjoyed perfectly timed free-range chicken with garlic sauce, and a great piece of excellent 'pig' with apple and juniper sauce. Chef Andrew Griffith and his team also get to work on roast pigeon with green peppercorns and braised cabbage, as well as smoked haddock ravioli with beurre blanc, and baked brill with shallots, bacon and lentils. Bread-and-butter pudding with vanilla custard has earned praise, while banana tart and ice-cream produced an emphatic 'Wow!' from one recipient. At lunch-time it is also possible to get snacks and light dishes ranging from club sandwiches to gravad lax salad. The manageable, varied wine list has some decent drinking at very reasonable prices. House wine is £6.95.

CHEFS: Andrew Griffith, Becky Bradshaw and Phil Tee   PROPRIETOR: Gareth Griffith   OPEN: Tue to Sat (and Mon in summer) 12 to 2, 7 to 10   CLOSED: 25 and 26 Dec, 1 Jan   MEALS: alc (main courses £10 to £15). Light L available   SERVICE: not inc, card slips closed   CARDS: Delta, MasterCard, Switch, Visa   DETAILS: 65 seats. Private parties: 30 main room, 30 private room. Vegetarian meals. Children's helpings. No smoking in dining-room. Wheelchair access (2 steps; not WC). Music. Air-conditioned £5

PENMAENPOOL Gwynedd   map 7

▲ *Penmaenuchaf Hall* ❢ ﹩✳

Penmaenpool LL40 1YB
TEL: (01341) 422129   FAX: (01341) 422787   NEW CHEF
off A493, 2m W of Dolgellau   COST £26–£55

Built for a Bolton cotton magnate back in 1860, this peaceful country house in Snowdonia National Park, just north of Cader Idris, sits in acres of gardens and has its own private fishing. Colour-co-ordinated fabrics and dark oak panelling give it a 'well-appointed' feel, and a 'charming welcome' sets the tone. As the

Guide went to press, Hugh Cocker left for Perkins (see entry, Plumtree) and Wayne Roberts arrived from Tre-Ysgawen Hall too late for us to make an assessment. If the past is anything to go by, local meats, fish from the Mawddach estuary, wild mushroooms, Celtic farmhouse cheeses, and the kitchen garden will all have a say in the end result.

The wine list offers plenty of variety in the grape department, running from Albariño to Zinfandel, and also in the regions, with Bulgaria and Wales both taking a bow. A string of fine clarets and burgundies brings a reassuring touch of class to proceedings, while a monthly-changing trio provides the opportunity to introduce innovative winemakers. CELLARMAN'S CHOICE: Schloss Castell Silvaner Trocken 1995, Franken, £17.50; Pomerol, Ch. Feytit-Clinet 1989, £32.80.

CHEF: Wayne Roberts PROPRIETORS: Mark Watson and Lorraine Fielding OPEN: all week 12 to 2, 7 to 9.30 (9 Sun) MEALS: alc Mon to Sat L, all week D (main courses L £6.50 to £9, D £15 to £18.50). Set L £12.06 (2 courses) to £14.95, Set D £25. BYO £7.50 SERVICE: not inc, card slips closed CARDS: Amex, Delta, Diners, MasterCard, Switch, Visa DETAILS: 36 seats. Private parties: 50 main room, 16 private room. Car park. Vegetarian meals. Children's helpings. No children under 6. No smoking in dining-room. Wheelchair access (also WC). Music ACCOMMODATION: 14 rooms, all with bath/shower. TV. Phone. B&B £70 to £155. Children welcome. No children under 6. Baby facilities. Dogs welcome by arrangement. Afternoon teas. Fishing (*The Which? Hotel Guide*) £5

PONTFAEN Pembrokeshire   map 4

▲ *Tregynon Farmhouse* ✸✳

Gwaun Valley, Pontfaen SA65 9TU
TEL: (01239) 820531 FAX: (01239) 820808
EMAIL: tregynon@uk-holidays.co.uk
at junction of B4313 and B4329, take B4313 towards   COOKING 2
Fishguard, then take first right, and first right again   COST £21–£34

Although in the Pembrokeshire Coast National Park, these renovated farm buildings, with thick stone walls and wooden beams, occupy a perfectly manicured landscape 'with not a blade of grass out of place'. Attention to detail is striking throughout, and one visitor on a gluten-free diet was accommodated 'from nibbles right through to desserts'. The recited menu is arranged in a 15-day rotating pattern, with optional supplements, for the benefit of long-stay residents. It relies on fresh, local, additive-free ingredients, and has turned out such crowd-pleasers as a thick and peppery tomato soup with bits of celery and 'more than a hint' of vodka and whisky, as well as a fried golden triangle of Brie-like Pencarreg, served with a cranberry and port sauce. 'Excellent home cooking with fine ingredients and substantial portions' was one summary, prompted in part by fresh, meaty monkfish tail in a chervil butter sauce, and home-smoked gammon that 'you could really get your teeth into'. Desserts, the least successful course at inspection, run from apple toasties, via tiramisù, to home-made ices that have 'many superlatives in the visitors' book'. Around 40 extensively annotated wines are carefully chosen and sensibly priced, starting with house Touraine at £10.95. Two local wines and a Welsh malt whisky also feature.

CHEFS: Peter and Jane Heard, and Sian Davies   PROPRIETORS: Peter and Jane Heard   OPEN:
all week D only 7.30 to 8.30   MEALS: Set D £19.95 (£18.95 for residents). BYO £5   SERVICE: not
inc   CARDS: Delta, MasterCard, Switch, Visa   DETAILS: 24 seats. Private parties: 16 main room,
10 private room. Car park. Vegetarian meals. No children under 8. No smoking in dining-room.
Music   ACCOMMODATION: 6 rooms, all with bath/shower. TV. Phone. Room only £60 to £76. No
children under 8. Afternoon teas. No dogs (*The Which? Hotel Guide*)

PORTHGAIN Pembrokeshire   map 4

Harbour Lights ⁵✳

Porthgain, nr St David's SA62 5BL
TEL/FAX: (01348) 831549
EMAIL: harblights@aol.com   COOKING 4
off A487 at Croesgoch, 4m W of Mathry   COST £31–£37

This stone-built cottage in a tiny seaside village, close to the harbour where local
boats drop off their catch, has a homely feel. It is a family-run business that
changes little but offers a warm welcome and friendly service. 'Everything
seems simple and straightforward', and the menu – four or five options per
course – is not too ambitious, enabling the kitchen to accomplish what it sets out
to do. Organic steak is always on the menu, but seafood is the main business, and
dinner might start with crab salad or local oak-smoked salmon, followed by
grilled Dover sole, wild salmon or sea bass. 'We pick our own laverbread,' writes
Annie Davies, who serves it with spinach and cockles, flavoured with organic
bacon and wild garlic. Llangloffan might be among the local cheeses, or there
may be chocolate pot to finish. Sixteen unusual wines, all except two under £20,
include an organic Bergerac. House French is £9.50.

CHEFS: Anne Marie Davies and Bernadette Barker   PROPRIETOR: Anne Marie Davies   OPEN:
Thu to Sun D only 6.30 to 9.30   MEALS: Set D £23   SERVICE: not inc   CARDS: Delta,
MasterCard, Switch, Visa   DETAILS: 40 seats. Private parties: 40 main room. Car park.
Vegetarian meals. No smoking in dining-room. Wheelchair access (1 step; not WC). Music

---

PORTMEIRION Gwynedd   map 7

▲ Hotel Portmeirion ▮ ⁵✳

Portmeirion LL48 6ET
TEL: (01766) 770000   FAX: (01766) 771331
EMAIL: hotel@portmeirion.wales.com   COOKING 3
off A487, signposted from Minffordd   COST £38–£46

Sir Clough Williams Ellis championed the idea that 'the development of a
naturally beautiful site need not necessarily lead to its defilement', and
expressed this over the course of a lifetime by building his 'ideal village' close to
the family estate, above Cardigan Bay. Some might consider the cluster of
Italianate buildings a giant folly, but few would argue that he proved his point.
Visitors stay in the suites and cottages, and eat in the curved 1930s dining-room
('it reminds me of an ocean liner') overlooking the estuary.

Country cooking – broccoli soup, pot-roast guinea-fowl, apple and almond
tart – is brought up to date with provençale-style dressings and herby sauces,

647

producing 'seriously good' roast loin of venison, and chicken liver parfait that is 'light and full of flavour'. Among Welsh ingredients to feature are goats' cheese in a first-course salad; beef, perhaps served with creamed celeriac and smoked bacon; and bara brith and butter pudding. Service has produced a mixed response, lacking the necessary graces for one, 'attentive, pleasant, helpful and chatty' for another. It would be hard to find fault with the wine list, however, which is high on quality and low on price. An astute collection of wines under £13.50 sets things rolling and then it's on to a tour of the major wine regions, as well as some of the minor ones, including Wales. If you'd like to add a touch of sparkle to your meal, the Champagne Portmeirion from Duval-Leroy would be well worth a try at £23.50 a bottle, £4.50 a glass.

CHEFS: Colin Pritchard and Billy Taylor   PROPRIETOR: Second Portmeirion Foundation   OPEN: Tue to Sun L 12.30 to 2, all week D 7 to 9.30   CLOSED: 10 to 23 Jan   MEALS: Set L Tue to Sat £10.50 (2 courses) to £13.50, Set L Sun £14, Set D £30   SERVICE: not inc, card slips closed   CARDS: Amex, Delta, Diners, MasterCard, Switch, Visa   DETAILS: 100 seats. 12 seats outside. Private parties: 100 main room, 12 and 30 private rooms. Car park. Vegetarian meals. No children under 7 at D. Children's helpings. No smoking in dining-room. No music ACCOMMODATION: 39 rooms, all with bath/shower. TV. Phone. Room only £80 to £150. Children welcome. High teas for children. Baby facilities. No dogs. Swimming-pool (*The Which? Hotel Guide*)

PWLLGLOYW Powys   map 4

Seland Newydd ⚡✖

Pwllgloyw LD3 9PY
TEL: (01874) 690282   COOKING 4
on B4520 Brecon to Builth Wells road   COST £25–£39

The name is Welsh for 'New Zealand', the native home of Freya Harvey, who bought this village pub (formerly the Camden Arms) in 1996. Since moving in, she and her partner have gone from strength to strength. The place still pays allegiance to its roots as a country hostelry, and bar meals please all comers, as do the real ales on handpump. But Seland Newydd also puts on a confident face as a restaurant with high aspirations, and it succeeds with colours flying. Raw materials are impressive, execution is persuasively good, presentation delights the eye.

The menu evolves regularly, although the formula – three à la carte courses plus a complimentary sorbet – remains intact. Home-cured gravad lax is bound in Greek yoghurt and served with a prawn, cucumber and dill dressing, while cream of leek and potato soup comes garnished with a softly poached egg. Technical complexity appears in the shape of leg of wild rabbit filled with a chorizo mousseline, wrapped in bacon and served with the seared loin and a cabbage parcel, or, in gutsier vein, roast rack of lamb with faggots, mash and wild mushroom sauce. To finish, expect desserts such as glazed lemon tart served with a honey wafer basket filled with iced lime parfait; otherwise opt for the selection of 'Welsh and Border cheeses'. The 'New Land' naturally looms large on the well-annotated wine list, although other countries fare well too. House French is £8.75.

CHEF: Maynard Harvey   PROPRIETORS: Maynard and Freya Harvey   OPEN: all week 12 to 2,
6.45 to 9 (9.30 Sat)   CLOSED: Tue and Wed L Oct to April, occasional days in winter   MEALS: alc
(main courses £11 to £14). Bar menu available   SERVICE: not inc, card slips closed   CARDS:
Delta, MasterCard, Switch, Visa   DETAILS: 35 seats. 40 seats outside. Private parties: 35 main
room, 12 private room. Car park. Vegetarian meals. Children's helpings. No pipes in dining
room. Wheelchair access (not WC). Music

PWLLHELI Gwynedd   map 7

▲ *Plas Bodegroes* 🍴 ✳

Nefyn Road, Pwllheli LL53 5TH
TEL: (01758) 612363   FAX: (01758) 701247   COOKING 6
on A497, 1m W of Pwllheli   COST £26–£53

Although officially a 'restaurant with-rooms', this verandahed Georgian manor
comes pretty close to being a fully fledged country house. In its own grounds,
full of ancient beechwoods, it strikes a 'restrainedly tasteful' and 'slightly
Scandinavian' note. Gunna Chown's 'elegant charm' pervades, service is
cheerful and professional, the pace leisurely, and arrivals are staggered for the
kitchen's benefit. Shaun Mitchell's approach is as contemporary as a filo parcel
of crab with coconut leeks and chilli salsa, but the focus is mainly on Italy and
the Mediterranean: a smooth, well-balanced, room-temperature gazpacho to
start, for example, or a pastry tartlet with goats' cheese and a layer of rich
caramelised onion.

Local produce provides a strong foundation: fish from Cardigan Bay, lobsters
from Anglesey, and meat and vegetables from farms round about. Rare rack of
lamb with a parsley 'paste', has been served with 'crunchy' garlic-flavoured
flageolet beans and a port sauce, and pan-fried loin of pork with a crisp and
deeply browned 'cake' of wild mushroom risotto in a light asparagus sauce.
'Solid technique' characterised an inspection meal, with saucing and puddings
stealing the show. One innovative dessert combined a 'profoundly tasty' jelly
made with sherry and Rioja, with orange segments in a caramel sauce, and
dollops of mascarpone, the whole dish seeming 'like a discord being resolved
into a chord'. Another of 'intense but complementary tastes' partnered first-rate
lemon tart with lemon milk sorbet in a honey wafer basket.

Meals begin with good olives and canapés, then an appetiser at table; bread is
'fresh and warm from the oven'; and fudge and chocolate truffles come with
coffee. As in previous years, the wine list opens with a food-friendly house
selection priced between £12 and £29, but you are still urged to look to Alsace for
finer fare. The number of wines from each region isn't high but quality is, prices
are sensible and half-bottles are generous in number. CELLARMAN'S CHOICE:
Gewurztraminer d'Alsace Vendange Tardive 1985, Willm, £32; Graves, Ch.
Beauregard-Ducasse 1994, £20.

---

*'There is also (because it's January) an all inclusive menu at £12.50 a head (not Saturday
evening) which seems like quite remarkable value for money. We choose from this list.
"Having the cheap menu, eh?" [the chef/proprietor] says. "That'll leave enough over for
an expensive bottle of wine."'* (On eating in Lincolnshire)

CHEF: Shaun Mitchell   PROPRIETORS: Chris and Gunna Chown   OPEN: Sun L 12 to 2, Tue to Sun D 7 to 9.30   CLOSED: Dec to Feb   MEALS: Set L Sun £16.50, Set D £31.50   SERVICE: not inc CARDS: Amex, Delta, MasterCard, Switch, Visa   DETAILS: 40 seats. Private parties: 40 main room, 16 private room. Car park. Children welcome. No smoking in dining-room. Wheelchair access (1 step; not WC). Occasional music   ACCOMMODATION: 11 rooms, all with bath/shower. TV. Phone. D,B&B £70 to £200. Children welcome. Baby facilities. Dogs welcome by arrangement   £5

REYNOLDSTON Swansea   map 4

▲ *Fairyhill* 🍷 ❋

Reynoldston SA3 1BS   COOKING 4
TEL: (01792) 390139   FAX: (01792) 391358   COST £29–£55

The Gower Peninsula was the first part of Britain to be designated an area of outstanding natural beauty, and Fairyhill is justly proud of its own 24-acre share of it. The grounds include a trout stream and lake, but if you decide to roam, you are asked to do so quietly and not disturb the moorhens. All the trimmings of a serious country-house operation are present, so the canapés served with aperitifs are followed at the table by an amuse-bouche, itself likely to be fairly complex: chorizo-stuffed chicken galantine with damson chutney, for example. Lengthy menus signal ambitious intent. Although one reporter thought the style pretentious, others have delivered enthusiastic praise for dishes such as warm seafood salad with crisped seaweed and samphire, and duck breast and confit leg with prune and chestnut charlotte and sage cream sauce.

A diverting dessert of apple and tarragon in layers of filo pastry is also approvingly mentioned by a couple of readers, or you may finish more conventionally with treacle tart and custard. Service makes an effort to make all feel at home: 'we were greeted like long-lost friends.' The comprehensive wine list includes classed-growth clarets back to 1955, Germany makes a welcome appearance, Henschke remains a highlight of a strong New World section, and Wales contributes 20 bins. Over 60 half-bottles aid those who like to change wines with each course, and lovers of dessert wine are particularly well served. House wines start at £12.50. CELLARMAN'S CHOICE: Savigny-lès-Beaune 1995, Bize, £29.50; Brouilly, Dom. Crête des Garanches, 1996, Bernard Dufaître, £19.50.

CHEFS: Paul Davies and Adrian Coulthard   PROPRIETORS: Andrew Hetherington, Paul Davies and Peter and Jane Camm   OPEN: all week 12.30 to 1.45, 7.30 to 9.15   CLOSED: 4 days Christmas, bank hols   MEALS: Set L £14.50 (2 courses) to £17.50, Set D £25 (2 courses) to £32 SERVICE: not inc, card slips closed   CARDS: Amex, Delta, MasterCard, Switch, Visa   DETAILS: 60 seats. 20 seats outside. Private parties: 40 main room, 20 and 40 private rooms. Car park. Vegetarian meals. Children's helpings. No children under 8 at D. No smoking in dining-room. Wheelchair access (also WC). Music   ACCOMMODATION: 8 rooms, all with bath/shower. TV. Phone. B&B £95 to £160. No children under 8. No dogs (*The Which? Hotel Guide*)   £5

All details are as accurate as possible at the time of going to press, but chefs and owners often change, and it is wise to check by telephone before making a special journey. Many readers have been disappointed when set-price bargain meals are no longer available. Ask when booking.

ROSEBUSH Pembrokeshire map 4

Tafarn Newydd ¦✳

Rosebush SA66 7RA
TEL: (01437) 532542 FAX: (01437) 532926
EMAIL: tafarn.newydd@u.s.a.net COOKING 2
on B4313, 8m SE of Fishguard COST £21–£42

The 'New Tavern' is an out-of-the-way Georgian farmhouse on the south side of the Preseli mountains. It was originally a drovers' inn, and the circus even stayed here in the days when it brewed its own beer. Diana Richards has remained true to the pub's roots, providing real ales and live folk music in the bar. She has also added three dining-areas, with abundant old beams, quarry tiles and a pleasing hotch-potch of wooden furniture. The mood is laid-back and casual: it's 'jeans and sweaters' rather than stuffed shirts. Blackboard menus suggest a broadminded approach to things culinary, as well as a crusading commitment to local produce. Fillet of Welsh Black beef may appear with a green peppercorn sauce, venison steak receives a rich, creamy sauce of wild garlic, and organic pork appears in several guises. The farmhouse tradition shows in mushroom and apple soup, and breast of 'well-fed' chicken with cider and apples, while there are exotic overtones to Korean pork patties with a punchy dip, Thai curry, and Basque vegetable risotto. Bread-and-butter pudding has just the right amount of old-fashioned richness and there are also some commendable Welsh cheeses (including a goats' made in the village). The short wine list provides plenty of easy, affordable drinking. House wine is £10.

CHEF: Diana Richards PROPRIETOR: Tafarn Newydd Ltd OPEN: all week 12 (12.30 Sun) to 2, 7 to 9 CLOSED: 25 Dec, second week Jan, Sun D mid-Nov to Apr MEALS: alc (main courses £10 to £15.50). Set L £7.25 (1 course) to £12.75 SERVICE: not inc, card slips closed CARDS: Delta, MasterCard, Switch, Visa DETAILS: 42 seats. 10 seats outside. Private parties: 25 main room. Car park. Vegetarian meals. No children in main restaurant. No smoking in dining-room. Wheelchair access (1 step; not WC). Occasional music

---

ST DAVID'S Pembrokeshire map 4

Morgan's Brasserie

20 Nun Street, St David's SA62 6NT COOKING 3
TEL/FAX: (01437) 720508 COST £23–£39

Ceri and Elaine Morgan's house-converted-to-restaurant maintains its smartish, relaxed approach, and continues to be a useful address in the diminutive city of St David's. A blackboard of fresh fish from the Pembrokeshire coast is the prime attraction and it's often given a Welsh flourish: Dover sole topped with Penclawdd cockles, or monkfish wrapped in smoked salmon with laverbread sauce, for example. Elsewhere, the shortish *carte* works its way confidently through fresh-tasting crab soup, fillet of Welsh Black beef ('very good meat', according to one recipient) served with Madeira demi-glace, roast loin of Welsh spring lamb with redcurrant jus, or pulse-laden Red Dragon Pie topped with organic Caerfai cheese. Desserts feature the likes of additive-free damson sorbet, strawberry crème brûlée and a sablé of fresh berries. Three dozen wines offer keenly priced drinking from most major producing countries, with France and Australia showing up particularly well. French house wines are £9 a bottle.

CHEF: Ceri Morgan   PROPRIETORS: Ceri and Elaine Morgan   OPEN: D only 6.30 to 9 as follows – Nov, Dec and Mar Fri and Sat, Jul to Aug Mon to Sat, Apr to Jun and Sept to Oct Tue to Sat   CLOSED: Jan and Feb   MEALS: alc (main courses £9 to £14)   SERVICE: not inc   CARDS: Amex, MasterCard, Visa   DETAILS: 34 seats. Private parties: 20 main room. Vegetarian meals. Children's helpings. No cigars/pipes in dining-room. Occasional music

---

ST GEORGE Conwy   map 7

Kinmel Arms ⅚✳ £ | NEW ENTRY |

St George LL22 9BP   COOKING 3
TEL: (01745) 832207   FAX: (01745) 832207   COST £20 £38

Just a short meander from the A55 sits this seventeenth-century coaching-inn with slate exterior and leaded windows. Very much a country pub, it serves cask-conditioned ales, but also boasts its own smokery and uses meats from the local estate, and tables are as smartly dressed as in somewhere much more formal. Gary Edwards, who has been at the stoves for five years now, is producing some confident and imaginative cooking. A late-summer meal delivered Conwy crab-cakes of 'good sweet fresh flavour and texture' with light chilli sauce (and some extraneous couscous), perfectly timed grilled fillet of sea bass with a lime-spiked beurre blanc, and succulent Debden duck – a juicy breast and crisped leg – on teriyaki noodles. The range of techniques, as well as impeccable raw materials, are likely to impress. Appealing desserts have included lemon tart garnished with a tuile basket of raspberry sorbet, and a chocolate-enriched version of crème brûlée. Service in both restaurant and bar is wholly charming and attentive. A Lilliputian jumble of wines is mostly well selected from a local merchant, and opens with a 'sommelier's selection' from £8.95.

CHEF: Gary Edwards   PROPRIETORS: Gary Edwards and Dermot McGee   OPEN: all week L 12 to 2, Tue to Sun D 7 to 9   CLOSED: 25 Dec   MEALS: alc (main courses £11 to £13). Set L and D £12.95. Bar meals available. BYO £5   SERVICE: net prices, card slips closed   CARDS: Delta, MasterCard, Switch, Visa   DETAILS: 52 seats. 20 seats outside. Private parties: 32 main room, 24 private room. Car park. Vegetarian meals. Children welcome. No smoking in dining-room. Wheelchair access (not WC). Music

---

SWANSEA Swansea   map 4

La Braseria £

28 Wind Street, Swansea SA1 1DZ   COOKING 1
TEL: (01792) 469683   FAX: (01792) 470816   COST £20–£39

The Spanish element may be only skin-deep, extending little further than wine boxes, sawdust and a sheet of tapas-style starters: calamares, gambas, sardines, chicken wings, spare ribs. But no matter, this is a determinedly straightforward operation with not an ounce of pretence. Main course meat and fish are displayed in cabinets, and simply chargrilled. That's it: no sauces, no garnishes, no towers of this or mille-feuilles of that; just lemon or Dover dole, turbot, lobster, hake, shark or swordfish, all priced by weight. A few fish – bass, snapper, bream – may be baked in rock salt from time to time, and there may also be honeyed duck or ostrich, but a feeling of 'no-nonsense value for money' prevails throughout. House wine is £1.60 a glass.

CHEFS: I. Wing and J. Robins   PROPRIETOR: Manuel Tercero   OPEN: Mon to Sat 12 to 2.30, 7 to 11.30   CLOSED: 25 and 26 Dec, 1 Jan   MEALS: alc (main courses £6 to £18). Set L £6.75 (2 courses)   SERVICE: not inc, card slips closed   CARDS: Amex, Delta, Diners, MasterCard, Switch, Visa   DETAILS: 185 seats. Private parties: 100 main room. Vegetarian meals. Children welcome. Wheelchair access (1 step; also WC). Music. Air-conditioned

Number One Wind Street

1 Wind Street, Swansea SA1 1DE   COOKING 3
TEL: (01792) 456996   COST £20–£36

A cheery, informal bistro, Number One Wind Street ('wind as in clock, not as in gusty') provides a convivial if slightly cramped setting for some classic French cooking and fine Welsh produce. Seafood is a strong point in the weekly-changing menu – perhaps simply grilled lemon sole with hollandaise sauce, or a more complex warm terrine of fresh sewin (sea trout), sole and hake with chive butter. 'Mouthwateringly fresh' poached local sea bass might be served with a laverbread sauce 'full of the flavour of the sea'. Meat dishes can fall short, however, although the accompanying vegetables have won praise. Desserts might include a couple of rich chocolate options, balanced by lighter choices such as fruit salad in Beaumes de Venise. Service is prompt and obliging, with Kate Taylor emerging from the kitchen from time to time for a chat, and wines are served without ceremony. The democratic list includes small selections from some very respectable producers around the globe. House wines in all three colours are £9.50.

CHEF: Kate Taylor   PROPRIETORS: Peter Gillen and Kate Taylor   OPEN: Tue to Sat 12 to 2.30, 7 to 9.30 (post-theatre D by arrangement)   CLOSED: 1 week Christmas, bank hols exc Good Fri   MEALS: alc L (main courses £7 to £14). Set D £17 (2 courses) to £21. BYO £5   SERVICE: not inc, card slips closed   CARDS: Amex, MasterCard, Visa   DETAILS: 50 seats. Private parties: 50 main room, 20 private room. Vegetarian meals. Children welcome. No pipes in dining-room. Wheelchair access (not WC). Music

---

TALSARNAU Gwynedd   map 7

▲ Maes-y-Neuadd ▼ £✳

Talsarnau LL47 6YA
TEL: (01766) 780200   FAX: (01766) 780211
EMAIL: jslatter@enterprise.co.uk   COOKING 4
off B4573, 1m S of Talsarnau   COST £20–£50

The old stone-built manor house, in the foothills above Cardigan Bay, manages to combine 'a feel of homeliness' with 'a touch of luxury'. It also has 'a thoughtful kitchen' with a measure of gentle invention and an ability to keep everything under control. The menu is structured around a manageable number of dishes, so choice at dinner is between two first courses, three mains (one of them vegetarian) and four last courses (one of them cheese). In between might come a soup, such as curried marrow, or heavily parsleyed artichoke, and, for those with the appetite, perhaps an intermediate course of seafood terrine with crab sauce.

Materials include salt marsh lamb, locally gathered mushrooms, and sea bass from Barmouth. Main courses have an eye for pheasant, venison and goose as much as chicken or beef, while unusual vegetables such as kale are given an opportunity to shine: underneath a glazed poached egg, for example, or deep-fried as an amuse-gueule ('like seaweed but tastier,' according to a reporter). The rural Welsh feel is also captured occasionally in a dessert of bara brith pudding with elderflower ice-cream. Service is well-timed, 'neither officious nor too chatty', and breakfasts are recommended. The attractively priced wine list takes a leisurely stroll through the classic French regions before venturing out into the big wide world where it finds much of quality and interest. House wines (three French, one Welsh) start at £9.75. CELLARMAN'S CHOICE: Au Bon Climat Chardonnay 1996, Santa Barbara, California, £28.45; Volnay 'Clos des Ducs' 1994, Dom. Marquis d'Angerville, £38.15.

CHEF: Peter Jackson   PROPRIETORS: Michael and June Slatter, and Malcolm and Olive Horsfall   OPEN: all week 12.15 to 1.45, 7 to 9   MEALS: Set L £9 (1 course) to £13.25, Set D £25 to £32. BYO £7.50   SERVICE: not inc, card slips closed   CARDS: Amex, Delta, Diners, MasterCard, Switch, Visa   DETAILS: 50 seats. Private parties: 50 main room, 12 private room. Car park. Vegetarian meals. Children's helpings. No children under 7 at D. No smoking in dining-room. Wheelchair access (also WC). Occasional music   ACCOMMODATION: 16 rooms, all with bath/shower. TV. Phone. D,B&B £76 to £223. Rooms for disabled. Children welcome. High teas for children. Baby facilities. No dogs in public rooms. Afternoon teas (*The Which? Hotel Guide*)
£5

TALYLLYN Gwynedd   map 7

▲ *Minffordd Hotel* ⅙✷

Talyllyn LL36 9AJ
TEL: (01654) 761665   FAX: (01654) 761517   COOKING 5
at junction of A487 and B4405, 8m SW of Dolgellau   COST £26–£31

In the wilds of west Wales, a little south of Cader Idris, Minffordd's locale is 'breathtaking'. The seventeenth-century hotel stands in four trim acres, and bases its appeal on the warmly unpretentious welcome extended by Mary McQuillan and Mark Warner, and on the latter's accurate and accomplished cooking. As guests gather at eight for dinner, non-residents are introduced to residents, and the atmosphere is of a private dinner party. Fixed-price menus offer four courses plus coffee, the last course always a plated selection of good British (predominantly Welsh) cheeses. Before that may have come coriandered salmon fish-cakes with avocado relish, Barbary duck breast with plum and ginger sauce, and a pudding such as baked strawberry ramekin. Ostentation is avoided and the locally sourced ingredients benefit from a simple approach. Game is particularly well treated, with fruity preparations of apples and cider applied to braised pheasant, or orange and port to venison. The proprietors make a point of joining guests in the lounge for a chinwag over coffee. Wines are unexciting, with standard French selections bolstered by scarcely more than one red and white each from other countries. Four house wines start at £8.45.

CHEF: Mark Warner PROPRIETORS: Mark Warner and Mary McQuillan OPEN: all week D only 7.30 for 8 (1 sitting) CLOSED: Dec to Feb MEALS: Set D £19.50 SERVICE: not inc, card slips closed CARDS: Delta, MasterCard, Visa DETAILS: 22 seats. Private parties: 6 main room. Car park. Children's helpings. No children under 5. No smoking in dining-room. No music ACCOMMODATION: 6 rooms, all with bath/shower. Phone. D,B&B £53 to £112. No children under 3. High teas for children. Guide dogs only (*The Which? Hotel Guide*)

TREFRIW Conwy   map 4

Chandler's ♥ ⅝✸

Trefriw LL27 0JH
TEL: (01492) 640991   COOKING 3
off B5106, NW of Llanrwst   COST £27–£40

The Rattenburys don't believe in flogging themselves to a standstill, which is why they open for two nights of the week, with lunches a summer speciality. For many small restaurants, this is the key to consistent success, and if longevity is any guide, then the 12 years they have now notched up must count for something. Their chosen formula is the best of Welsh produce simply but effectively cooked, with a range of trendy breads a retail sideline. A roving reporter told us that this was 'one of my summer's best experiences – marvellously fresh fish, perfectly sauced'. Cajun-blackened tuna steak rubs shoulders with Barbary duck breast sauced with orange and ginger among main courses, while imagination-stirring starters include a salad pairing of monkfish with Carmarthen ham in a red pepper dressing. Puddings bring on peach and almond crumble tart with raspberry ice-cream, or chocolate parfait cake with a custard made from Welsh whisky liqueur.

The short wine list has been put together with a keen eye for attractive offerings from reputable producers at some very friendly prices, and still finds room for lesser-known bins; not many establishments offer both a Welsh White and a Mexican Barbera. Chilean house wines are £9.50. CELLARMAN'S CHOICE: Jackson Estate Sauvignon Blanc 1997, Marlborough, New Zealand, £14.65; Wirra Wirra Church Block 1995, McLaren Vale, S. Australia, £16.10.

CHEFS/PROPRIETORS: Adam and Penny Rattenbury OPEN: Tue to Thu L (summer only) 12 to 2, Fri and Sat D 7 to 9.30 MEALS: alc D (main courses £9 to £14). Set L £8.50. BYO £5 SERVICE: not inc, card slips closed CARDS: MasterCard, Switch, Visa DETAILS: 24 seats. Private parties: 30 main room. Car park. Vegetarian meals. Children's helpings. No smoking in dining-room. Music (£5)

WELSH HOOK Pembrokeshire   map 4

▲ *Stone Hall*

Welsh Hook, Wolf's Castle SA62 5NS
TEL: (01348) 840212 FAX: (01348) 840815
1½m off A40, between Letterston and Wolf's Castle,   COOKING 1
W of Welsh Hook   COST £27–£40

A modest gravel drive flanked by rhododendrons takes one up to the door of this fifteenth-century stone-built manor-house, where the Watsons pay homage to

Gallic culture. Their chef is Gascon, menus are bilingual, and it isn't long before Enya cedes the background airwaves to Edith Piaf. Moules au pistou, duck rillettes, confit and cassoulet are what to expect. Sauces are used in a classical way to uplift the flavour of the main ingredient, the salty tang of Roquefort adding savour to beef fillet, for example. There seems as much duck on the menu as there would be in south-west France, perhaps magret served Agen-style with orange peel and armagnac-soaked prunes. Profiteroles au chocolat, ice-creams anointed with your choice of liqueur, or 'perfect' crisply caramelised crème Catalan emphasise the tone. South African and German wines bring up the rear on an otherwise French list, and mark-ups are reasonable throughout. House wines, a Sauvignon and a Gamay from Touraine, are £10.50.

CHEF: Jean-Yves Poujade   PROPRIETORS: Alan and Martine Watson   OPEN: all week D only 7 to 9.30   MEALS: alc (main courses £11.50 to £13.50). Set D £18. BYO £3.50   SERVICE: not inc   CARDS: Amex, Diners, MasterCard, Visa   DETAILS: 34 seats. Private parties: 45 main room, 20 private room. Car park. Vegetarian meals. Children's helpings. No cigars/pipes in dining-room. Wheelchair access (1 step; not WC). No music   ACCOMMODATION: 5 rooms, all with bath/shower. TV. B&B £46 to £70. Children welcome. High teas for children. Baby facilities. No dogs (£5)

WHITEBROOK Monmouthshire   map 2

▲ *The Crown at Whitebrook* ▼ ✴

Whitebrook NP5 4TX
TEL: (01600) 860254   FAX: (01600) 860607   COOKING 5
5m S of Monmouth, between A466 and B4293   COST £38–£46

The Bateses have now passed the decade milestone at their converted pub in the densely forested Wye Valley. Enter through a heavy door in the gable end, and be greeted by bare walls, beams and a stone fireplace, giving the place a real country-pub atmosphere. Welsh spindle-backed chairs furnish the dining-room. Sandra Bates cooks a largely but not exclusively Francophile menu, so starters may include 'saucisse chinois': pork, ginger and spring onion sausage served with stir-fried crispy vegetables in a dressing of five-spice and sesame oil. More obviously Gallic notes sound in a 'light but firm' chicken liver parfait accompanied by some whole sauté livers on a bed of mixed leaves tossed in raspberry vinaigrette. Labour-intensive fish courses, such as a darne of salmon with creamed leek tartlet and a shellfish sauce, compete with robust meat dishes along the lines of beef fillet on rösti topped with black pudding and sauced with port. Offal is accorded due prominence, either as braised ox tongue with celeriac purée and roasted shallots, or as lambs' kidneys partnering a roast rack. Desserts might include a citrus-based trio of lemon tart, crêpes suzette and pink grapefruit mousse, or 'excellent' pannacotta with poached rhubarb and spiced shortbread biscuits. A 'friendly but not effusive' welcome is appreciated.

Wines echo the food – you have to wait until bin no. 109 before crossing the French border – but the presence of Torres from Spain, Jane Hunter from New Zealand and Weinert from Argentina point to quality, whatever the region. House wines are £9.75 a bottle, £1.90 a glass. CELLARMAN'S CHOICE: Sancerre

1996, Dom. Cherrier et fils, £16.50; Weinert Cavas de Weinert 1992, Mendoza, Argentina, £19.95.

CHEF: Sandra Bates   PROPRIETORS: Rodger and Sandra Bates   OPEN: Tue to Sun L 12 to 1.30, Mon to Sat D 7 to 9 (Sun D residents only)   CLOSED: 2 weeks Jan, 2 weeks Aug   MEALS: Set L £15.95, Set D £27.95. BYO £5. Light L available   SERVICE: not inc   CARDS: Amex, Delta, Diners, MasterCard, Switch, Visa   DETAILS: 32 seats. 16 seats outside. Private parties: 24 main room, 12 private room. Car park. Vegetarian meals. Children's helpings. No smoking in dining-room. No music   ACCOMMODATION: 10 rooms, all with bath/shower. TV. Phone. D,B&B £66 to £130. Dogs welcome by arrangement in bedrooms only (*The Which? Hotel Guide*)

Channel Islands

GOREY Jersey	map 1

Village Bistro

NEW ENTRY

Gorey JE3 9EP

TEL: (01534) 853429

COOKING 6

COST £19–£42

Suns, moons and stars are the celestial decoration theme at this small, family-run restaurant in the heart of Gorey village, reached through a garden that has patio seating in fine weather. It has the feel of a particularly gracious café, with raffia roller blinds at the windows and dried chillies as table decorations. A weekly-changing fixed-price lunch menu supplements the longer *carte*, and while dishes appear firmly rooted in bistro idiom, sound culinary technique lends refinement to what appears on the plate.

Seared salmon comes as three thin cuts on a bed of leaves, the lemon dressing replete with saffron strands, the whole thing moistened with good olive oil and balsamic. Sauté scallops on carrots and basil are another well-reported first course, showing off the local seafood to its freshest advantage. Accompaniments to fish dishes span the ethnic range, embracing couscous and a spicy sauce for baby halibut, or chillied Thai noodles with brill. Meats are more mainstream, perhaps roast saddle of lamb on braised red cabbage with sultanas (served with redcurrant jelly and mint sauce), or good chicken breast with tagliatelle and a buttery sauce of wild mushrooms. Finish with admirably powerful ice-creams and sorbets, or armagnac crème brûlée with prunes and a syrup of Earl Grey. Relaxed and friendly service adds to the enjoyment. Wines are strongest in France but also feature some other European countries and around half a dozen from the New World. House French is £7.50.

CHEF: David Cameron   PROPRIETORS: Sandra Dalziel and David Cameron   OPEN: Tue to Sun 12 to 2 (3 Sun), 7 to 10 (9.30 Sun)   CLOSED: 21 Dec to 6 Jan   MEALS: alc (main courses £12 to £15). Set L Tue to Sat £12.50, Set L Sun £14.50   SERVICE: not inc   CARDS: MasterCard, Switch, Visa   DETAILS: 42 seats. 30 seats outside. Private parties: 42 main room. Children's helpings. No cigars/pipes in dining-room. Wheelchair access (1 step; not WC). Music

ST SAVIOUR Jersey   map 1

▲ *Longueville Manor* 🐜✳

St Saviour JE2 7WF
TEL: (01534) 25501   FAX: (01534) 31613   COOKING **6**
EMAIL: longman@itl.net   COST £25–£90

Malcolm Lewis, the present proprietorial incumbent, is of the third generation of
Lewises to run Longueville, which has been in his family since just after the war.
There is nothing fake about the sense of antiquity that overhangs the place, part
of which originates from the thirteenth century. Well-tended gardens and the
log-fired lounges are prize draws, and starched napery and immaculate
glassware establish a tone of quiet refinement in the oak-panelled
dining-rooms.

Andrew Baird has cooked here through the 1990s. Menus are long and
classical, and plumb in the country-house idiom. A ring of grilled scallops and
skinned tomatoes seasoned with basil demonstrates accurate cooking and a
certain amount of visual artistry. Much is made of the produce of the kitchen
garden (although asparagus served in mid-winter baffled one reporter), and
roast pheasant with game chips uses tender, well-matured meat, given point
with glazed pear and a scattering of cranberries. Casserole of beef comes with
Yorkshire pudding and horseradish hollandaise, or there might be seafood
panaché with griddled Mediterranean vegetables and aïoli. Desserts include
creamy rice-pudding ringed with banana slices, and passion-fruit soufflé, or
prune and apple sablé. Smartly attired staff ensure the place runs like
clockwork. Wines offer an encyclopedic choice, from old clarets to good
Chileans, but selections are less sound in the New World than in France. House
wines from France and Chile start at £9.

CHEF: Andrew Baird   PROPRIETORS: Malcolm Lewis and Sue Dufty   OPEN: all week 12.30 to 2,
7.30 to 9.30   MEALS: alc D (main courses £19 to £25). Set L £16 (2 courses) to £20, Set D £35 to
£75 (some inc wine). BYO from £7   SERVICE: net prices, card slips closed   CARDS: Amex, Delta,
Diners, MasterCard, Switch, Visa   DETAILS: 70 seats. 45 seats outside. Private parties: 70 main
room, 16 and 21 private rooms. Car park. Vegetarian meals. Children's helpings. No smoking in
1 dining-room. Wheelchair access (not WC). No music. Air-conditioned   ACCOMMODATION: 32
rooms, all with bath/shower. TV. Phone. B&B £142.50 to £320. Rooms for disabled. Children
welcome. High teas for children. Baby facilities. Dogs welcome in bedrooms only. Afternoon
teas. Swimming-pool

🐜✳ *indicates that smoking is either banned altogether or that a dining-room is maintained
for non-smokers. The symbol does not apply to restaurants that simply have no-smoking
areas.*

*All details are as accurate as possible at the time of going to press, but chefs and owners
often change, and it is wise to check by telephone before making a special journey. Many
readers have been disappointed when set-price bargain meals are no longer available.
Ask when booking.*

*The 2000 Guide will be published before Christmas 1999. Reports on meals are most
welcome at any time of the year, but are particularly valuable in the spring (no later than
June). Send them to* The Good Food Guide, FREEPOST, 2 Marylebone Road, London
NW1 1YN. *Or email your report to guidereports@which.co.uk.*

Northern Ireland

Ginger Tree

29 Ballyrobert Road, Ballyclare BT39 9RY   COOKING 4
TEL: (01232) 848176   FAX: (01232) 840777   COST £16–£54

A carefully planted and well-tended Japanese-style garden with pots and pebbles gives a clue to the focus of this Victorian farmhouse. If Japan is the Far East for the British, Ireland must be the Far West for the Japanese, but both worlds blend seamlessly: menus offer an easy way into a great cuisine, and glossaries and scattered notes offer clear explanations. Considering obvious problems of supply, the choice is wide. Of the fish so essential to the Japanese diet, one of the most prized is eel; here they grill Lough Neagh eel in various ways. Hors d'oeuvre include deep-fried bean curd, tempura prawns (Japan's definitive answer to fried fish), and ohitashi: blanched spinach with soy sauce and sesame seeds. Afterwards, try green tea ice-cream, or perhaps banana Osaka – bananas stuffed with soya bean paste and wrapped in pastry – and Japanese plum wine with, or even instead of, dessert.

CHEFS/PROPRIETORS: Elizabeth English and Shotaro Obana   OPEN: Mon to Fri L 12 to 2, Mon to Sat D 7 to 8.30 (9 Sat)   CLOSED: 24 to 26 Dec, 1 Jan, 12 and 13 July   MEALS: alc (main courses £9.50 to £15). Set L £8.10 to £10.75, Set D £14.95 (Mon to Fri only) to £28.50. BYO £5.50 SERVICE: not inc   CARDS: Amex, Diners, MasterCard, Visa   DETAILS: 70 seats. Private parties: 80 main room. Car park. Vegetarian meals. Children's helpings. No-smoking area. Wheelchair access (also WC). Music. Air-conditioned   (£5)

Shanks ▼

The Blackwood, 150 Crawfordsburn Road,
Bangor BT19 1GB   COOKING 6
TEL: (01247) 853313   FAX: (01247) 852493   COST £26–£62

Sir Terence Conran designed the interior of the Blackwood Golf Centre for the Marchioness of Dufferin and Ava, which may be why it seems 'as luxurious as a New York art gallery'. In 1997 the Millars bought the restaurant from the Blackwood company and are now masters of all they survey, while Robbie Millar is now into his fifth year in the kitchen. Menus are fixed-price at lunch and dinner, and the aim is to offer both value and innovation. Celeriac and black truffle soup with a Beaufort cheese croûton makes an intriguing first course, and celeriac crops up again in a salad with pear and walnuts to accompany a Roquefort tart with port-laced onion marmalade. The coast brings in lobsters, served at a supplement with garlic butter, or as spiced lobster aïoli; and there are organic meats, including game from the nearby Clandeboye estate: for example venison with coriandered lentils, roast cauliflower, sweet potato purée and a seasoning of Chinese five-spice.

Lighter lunch dishes include crumbed pork loin with mustard sauce and cabbage, and vegetarians have their own imaginative menus, featuring perhaps gratin of white beans and black truffle with spinach and morels. Fruits are used to optimum effect in desserts, as in sablé of pineapple, mango and coconut with passion-fruit sauce, or a trio of apple confections. Young, trendy staff suit the atmosphere to a T, and the cleverly constructed wine list offers wines of impeccable provenance from Worlds Old and New at very fair prices, with plenty of appealing bins under £15. House wines start at £10.95 a bottle, £2.50 a glass. CELLARMAN'S CHOICE: Cloudy Bay Sauvignon Blanc 1997, Marlborough, New Zealand, £22; Lytton Springs, Ridge Zinfandel 1995, Sonoma, California, £27.

CHEF: Robbie Millar   PROPRIETORS: Robbie and Shirley Millar   OPEN: Tue to Fri L 12.30 to 2.15, Tue to Sat D 7 to 10   CLOSED: 25 and 26 Dec, 1 Jan, Easter Tue   MEALS: Set L £12.95 (2 courses) to £28.50, Set D £28.50. BYO £5   SERVICE: not inc; 10% for parties of 6 or more   CARDS: Amex, MasterCard, Switch, Visa   DETAILS: 80 seats. 25 seats outside. Private parties: 28 main room, 28 private room. Car park. Vegetarian meals. Children's helpings. No-smoking area. Music

---

BELFAST   Co Antrim   map 16

La Belle Epoque £

61 Dublin Road, Belfast BT2 7HE   COOKING 3
TEL/FAX: (01232) 323244   COST £17–£36

In an area brimming with restaurants and bars of all descriptions, Belle Epoque is smart, relaxed, full of music and buzz. Green and cream wood panelling, and wall portraits that enable James Joyce to rub shoulders with Napoleon, provide a striking backdrop to essentially French cooking. Occasional forays beyond the Gallic repertoire into moussaka aux lentilles, or smoked chicken and whisky salami salad with ginger and honey dressing, indicate a broad-minded approach. Otherwise, the foundation is duck magret with apples and cider, grilled beef fillet béarnaise, or roasted salmon with a mix of tapénade, mustard, anchovies and garlic. Vegetarians might be offered deep-fried chickpea croquettes with red pepper coulis. The tricolour flies proudly over desserts, too, with the exception of tiramisù (which becomes 'Italian cheesecake' in translation), producing roasted pears with cinnamon ice-cream, or profiteroles filled with hazelnut and chocolate cream. Service is generally unobtrusive and helpful. Wines are by no means exclusively French or expensive, but the list doesn't trouble itself with the tiresome detail of vintages. House selections start at £7.50.

CHEF: Alain Rousse   PROPRIETORS: J. Delbart, G. Sanchez and Alain Rousse   OPEN: Mon to Fri L 12 to 5.30, Mon to Sat D 5.30 (6 Sat) to 11   CLOSED: 25 and 26 Dec, 1 Jan, 10 to 14 July   MEALS: alc (main courses £7 to £11.50). Set L £5.95 to £10.95 (both 2 courses), Set D Mon to Fri £15. BYO £3.50   SERVICE: not inc   CARDS: Amex, Delta, Diners, MasterCard, Switch, Visa   DETAILS: 84 seats. Private parties: 30 main room. Vegetarian meals. Children welcome. Wheelchair access (also WC). Music

Deane's

34–40 Howard Street, Belfast BT1 6PD	COOKING 7
TEL: (01232) 331134 FAX: (01232) 560000	COST £30–£71

'Deane's is currently *the* place to go in Belfast,' according to a reporter, who stressed the need to book weeks in advance for dinner in the main restaurant. It is not just a fashionable destination, although the stylish ochre and burnished-red dining-room, huge mirrors and towering flower arrangements give it an appealing air of *fin de siècle* decadence. Michael Deane's boldly original cuisine is the main draw. He mixes and matches ingredients with an alchemist's touch, yet knows when to leave well alone, and gives high priority to fish and game.

For such a baroque setting, the food is surprisingly simple, relying on quality ingredients and lively contrasts rather than fancy saucing or elaboration. Flavours are clean and distinctive, dishes refreshingly well balanced. Chicken and lobster sausage with scallion cream, for example, was 'an absolute hit', the individual flavours clearly defined, the weight perfectly judged for a starter. Spices are used with discretion but to great effect: a clear mushroom soup, for example, is brought to life with lemon grass, chilli and chicken wuntuns, and red curry oil. Simpler dishes achieve an impact too: 'light and spring-like' halibut fillet with chargrilled vegetables triumphed because of the dazzling freshness of ingredients.

Puddings continue the preference for Eastern flavourings: perhaps a papaya mousse with lychee sorbet and mango rice-pudding, or cinnamon-baked caramel with cardamom ice-cream. An assiette of toffee and apple desserts provides a fitting finale, with eight variations on the theme, including a sorbet that 'really captured the taste of fresh green apples' and a tiny caramel sponge 'with a lovely springy bite'. Downstairs in the brasserie Raymond McArdle also pulls in the punters with a more informal menu of fish-cakes, club sandwich, Thai chicken, or pasta with Asian greens. The wine list offers plenty of sassy New World choices, plus some European classics. House wines start at £12.95.

CHEFS: Michael Deane and Raymond McArdle   PROPRIETORS: Michael Deane and Brian and Lynda Smyth   OPEN: Thur and Fri L 12.15 to 2, Tue to Sat D 7 to 9.30   CLOSED: 25 and 26 Dec, 1 Jan, 1 week July   MEALS: Set L £16.50 (2 courses) to £19, Set D £27 (2 courses) to £45 SERVICE: not inc; 10% for parties of 6 or more   CARDS: Amex, Delta, MasterCard, Switch, Visa DETAILS: 40 seats. Private parties: 40 main room. Vegetarian meals. Children welcome. Music. Air-conditioned

Nick's Warehouse ▼ £

35–39 Hill Street, Belfast BT1 2LB	COOKING 5
TEL: (01232) 439690 FAX: (01232) 230514	COST £18–£41

Nick Price's wine bar-cum-restaurant is down a one-way thoroughfare (approach from the cathedral end), where in the evening cars may be parked on the pavement. The downstairs wine bar has now been expanded to cope with the lunchtime rush, and greater kitchen space has permitted a correspondingly expansive turn in the culinary doings. Lunch choices may offer tagliatelle carbonara with asparagus and basil, locally smoked haddock with Dijon mustard sauce and mushy peas, or sirloin steak with Cajun onion gravy.

In case you hadn't noticed, influences are drawn from 'food fashions of the moment', according to Nick, so expect Californian, Italian and grand-mère, including now-familiar combinations such as goats' cheese on fried polenta with sun-dried tomato salsa. A 'compost salad' [sic] mulches together crab, celeriac and wholegrain mustard mayo. Vegetarians may get to choose the most outlandish dishes of all, if spicy chickpea and peanut butter fritters with harissa and coriander sauce is anything to go by. Classic French and British puddings are alternatives to a house selection of Irish cheeses. Meticulously attentive service keeps things flowing, and a small but perfectly formed wine list manages to pack in some fun as well as respectable bins at prices low enough to make you grin. Eight house wines stay below £9 a bottle. CELLARMAN'S CHOICE: Sancerre, Les Celliers St-Romble 1996, André Dezat et fils, £15.95; Ribera del Duero 1995, Abadia Retuerta Rivola, £12.95.

CHEFS: Nick Price, Simon McCance and Alan Montgomery   PROPRIETORS: Nick and Kathy Price   OPEN: Mon to Fri L 12 to 0, Tue to Sat D 0 to 9.30   CLOSED: 25 and 26 Dec, Easter Mon and Tue, 12 and 13 July   MEALS: alc (main courses £5 to £14)   SERVICE: not inc, card slips closed; 10% for parties of 5 or more   CARDS: Amex, Delta, Diners, MasterCard, Switch, Visa   DETAILS: 180 seats. Private parties: 50 private room. Vegetarian meals. Children welcome. Wheelchair access (1 step; also WC). Occasional music. Air-conditioned   £5

Roscoff ▼

7 Lesley House, Shaftesbury Square, Belfast BT2 7DB	COOKING 7
TEL: (01232) 331532 FAX: (01232) 312093	COST £26–£47

Lucky Belfast residents are now spoiled for choice when it comes to eating well but, in its tenth year, Roscoff maintains its status as 'a marvellous, glamorous place serving some of the best food in the UK', according to one visitor. Despite TV stardom, Paul Rankin spends time where it counts – at the stoves – and it pays off. This is a restaurant where skill is rivalled by imagination, and where the exuberant, freewheeling approach to cooking is kept in check by a clear understanding of flavouring: the culinary equivalent of perfect pitch.

Huge glass vases of lilies and orchids, a mirrored bar and deep sofas create a feeling of light and space in the reception area, which is hung with modern paintings, all for sale at fabulous prices. The restaurant is a bright, white, ultra-modern room, uncluttered and elegant, making a fitting backdrop for an unfussy, pared-down style of cooking. The menu reflects the Rankins' nomadic lifestyle before they settled in Ireland, drawing on influences from California, Mexico, Asia and Europe. Thus, roast venison comes with hot and sour cabbage, scallops with spring rolls and coriander salsa, oysters on black risotto, and oriental rare beef salad with a spiced basil dressing. At the same time, warm potato pancake with wild mushrooms, or salmon with horseradish mash, remind diners that they are eating in Belfast rather than Berkeley, California. At an inspection meal, rabbit with pancetta and mustard sauce proved a hit, while roast monkfish with Mediterranean vegetables and a pool of 'subtle, intense' anchovy sauce was 'a great combination'.

Desserts have included an assiette of mango (tart, sorbet and pannacotta), and a chocolate sponge that was pure wizardry: thin, dark cake wrapped round a gooey chocolate centre, with a pool of chocolate sauce, a scoop of vanilla ice-cream and a scattering of tiny wild strawberries. Artistry continues with 'a gorgeous selection' of petits fours, while service, from courteous and efficient staff, is 'superb from start to finish'. The wine list is as well-travelled as the Rankins, picking up quality bins from Canada to Chile, and South Africa to New Zealand, as well as traditional European regions. An attractive collection of 15 house wines starts at £12, with eight available by the glass from £2.50. CELLARMAN'S CHOICE: Rochioli Chardonnay 1994, Russian River, Sonoma, California, £20.75; Ribera del Duero 1993, Alión, £24.15.

CHEF: Paul Rankin PROPRIETOR: Paul and Jeanne Rankin OPEN: Mon to Fri L 12.15 to 2.15, Mon to Sat D 6.30 to 10.15 CLOSED: 25 and 26 Dec, 1 Jan, 12 and 13 Jul MEALS: Set L £17.50, Set D £29.95 SERVICE: 10% (optional), card slips closed CARDS: Amex, Delta, Diners, MasterCard, Switch, Visa DETAILS: 65 seats. Private parties: 65 main room. Children's helpings. No-smoking area. Wheelchair access (also WC). Music. Air-conditioned

Strand £

| 12 Stranmillis Road, Belfast BT9 5AA | COOKING 1 |
| TEL: (01232) 682266 FAX: (01232) 663189 | COST £20–£42 |

The Strand appeals to a heterogeneous crowd beyond the students who form its most obvious constituency. Cool jazz and an arresting colour scheme set the tone, and menus change every six weeks lest the fine edge of pleasure be blunted. Red and green peppers stuffed with queen scallops and mango make an eye-catching first course, Dublin Bay prawns doused in white wine and garlic a more familiar one. Star billing is accorded to prime cuts of award-winning Northern Ireland beef, or there is honey-roast duck confit with a timbale of red lentil purée. A simpler menu of 'Lite Bites', more obviously aimed at students, takes in bangers and mash, or chicken curry with wild rice. House wines are £8.55.

CHEF: Sean McConnell PROPRIETORS: Stephen McCombe and Frank Cullen OPEN: Mon to Fri 12 to 11 (10 Mon, 11.30 Fri), Sat 10am to 11.30pm, Sun 10am to 10pm MEALS: alc (main courses £8 to £14). Set L £7.95 (2 courses), Set D Sun £12.95 SERVICE: not inc CARDS: Amex, Delta, Diners, MasterCard, Switch, Visa DETAILS: 60 seats. 12 seats outside. Private parties: 25 main room, 35 private room. Vegetarian meals. Children welcome. Music. Air-conditioned

---

LIMAVADY Co Londonderry   map 16

Lime Tree £   NEW ENTRY

| 60 Catherine Street, Limavady BT49 9DB | COOKING 2 |
| TEL: (015047) 64300 | COST £13–£40 |

The restaurant takes its names from Limavady's historical lime trees, donated to the town by an expat who became prime minister of New Zealand. Stanley and Maria Matthews have travelled, too, previously having run a pub in Kinsale in the Republic, but put down new roots here in 1996. A large old house on the high street, it is painted dark green and cream outside and muted orange and yellow within: 'all very soothing and relaxing'. The menu sticks largely to soundly cooked standards of the repertoire: a large disc of filo pastry topped with caramelised onions and a slab of melting goats' cheese for a starter, or chunky salmon fish-cakes with a creamy parsley sauce for a main course. Grander dishes include crab and prawn parcels dressed with chilli oil, and an enterprising treatment of hake roasted in a crust of smoked ham, breadcrumbs and herbs, and given a white wine sauce. Tip-top vanilla cheesecake with strawberry sauce scores for lightness, or finish with lemon meringue gâteau. Maria Matthews leads the operation well. A short international wine list is cannily chosen, with nearly everything offered well under £20. House wines are available by the glass at £1.80.

CHEF: Stanley Matthews PROPRIETORS: Stanley and Maria Matthews OPEN: Wed to Sun 12 to 2, 6 to 9.30 (bookings only Sat L), and Mon and Tue end July to end Aug and Dec CLOSED: 1 week Mar, 1 week July, 1 week Nov MEALS: alc (main courses L £5 to £7, D £8 to £14.50). Set L Wed to Fri £6.95, Set L Sun £10.95 SERVICE: not inc CARDS: Amex, Delta, MasterCard, Switch, Visa DETAILS: 30 seats. Private parties: 34 main room. Car park. Vegetarian meals. Children's helpings. Wheelchair access (also WC). Music

---

LONDONDERRY Co Londonderry map 16

▲ Beech Hill Country House, Ardmore Restaurant 🕏✖

32 Ardmore Road, Londonderry BT47 3QP
TEL: (01504) 349279 FAX: (01504) 345366
EMAIL: beechhill@btinternet.com
turn off A6 Londonderry to Belfast road at Faughan
Bridge and proceed to Ardmore chapel; hotel is | NEW CHEF |
opposite chapel   COST £23–£49

Beech Hill is a pastoral oasis just beyond the city outskirts, where a woodland walk through the grounds of the elegant eighteenth-century mansion will help to sharpen appetites. Or head straight for the genteel, pastel-painted dining-room and enjoy splendid views of the garden and waterfalls. The food has typically displayed a sumptuousness to match the setting, though it now falls to Cyril Strub to to decide whether to continue producing lemon sole with herb salsa, tarte Tatin of mushrooms with artichokes and onions, and white chocolate mousse gâteau with Bailey's sauce. New World wines head up the varied and fairly priced list, which starts at £10 for Spanish red and Chilean white.

CHEF: Cyril Strub PROPRIETOR: Seamus Donnelly OPEN: all week 12 to 2.30, 6 to 9.30 CLOSED: 24 and 25 Dec, L 26 Dec MEALS: alc D (main courses £14 to £17). Set L £15.95, Set D £23.95 SERVICE: not inc, card slips closed CARDS: Amex, MasterCard, Switch, Visa DETAILS: 45 seats. Private parties: 80 main room, 15 to 80 private rooms. Car park. Vegetarian meals. Children's helpings. No smoking in dining-room. Wheelchair access (also WC). Music ACCOMMODATION: 17 rooms, all with bath/shower. TV. Phone. B&B £52.50 to £85. Rooms for disabled. Children welcome. Baby facilities. No dogs. Afternoon teas

---

PORTRUSH Co Antrim map 16

Ramore ♟

The Harbour, Portrush BT56 8BN   COOKING 4
TEL: (01265) 824313 FAX: (01265) 823194   COST £27–£44

Downstairs is the wine bar, where you take pot luck to get a table: upstairs is the pleasantly appointed restaurant, which accepts bookings for two sittings a night. The atmosphere buzzes, and harbour views from the big picture windows are a bonus on fine days. Dinner revolves around a regularly changing *carte* bolstered by a generous helping of blackboard specials. George McAlpin's cooking shows plenty of invention across the board: a goats'-cheese samosa with beetroot and chilli jam, crème fraîche, beetroot leaf salad and walnut pesto is a typically vivid starter, while main courses could range from escalope of Irish salmon niçoise to pork fillet and black-bean sauce on garlic potatoes with mayonnaise and a Chinese salad.

To finish, you will find a handful of puddings along the lines of peppermint and chocolate soufflé with hot chocolate sauce, or an exotic coconut and fruit brûlée with mango, papaya and banana. The modish wine list features bins from top growers in both hemispheres at impressively low prices. House Sauvignon from New Zealand and Merlot from Chile are £8.95 and £9.25 respectively. CELLARMAN'S CHOICE: Cape Mentelle Sauvignon/Semillon 1997, Margaret River, W Australia, £14.95; Rochioli Pinot Noir 1995, Russian River, California, £22.25.

CHEF: George McAlpin   PROPRIETORS: George and Jane McAlpin   OPEN: Tue to Sat D only 6.30 to 10.30   CLOSED: 24 to 26 Dec, 1 Jan   MEALS: alc (main courses £11 to £13)   SERVICE: not inc   CARDS: Delta, MasterCard, Switch, Visa   DETAILS: 80 seats. Private parties: 80 main room. Car park. No children after 9pm. Wheelchair access (2 steps; not WC). Music. Air-conditioned

Republic of Ireland

We have not given marks for cooking for the Republic of Ireland entries because of a shortage of reports; please do give us feedback should you visit. To telephone the Republic from mainland Britain, dial 00 353 followed by the number listed, but dropping the initial 0. Prices are quoted in Irish punts.

ADARE   Co Limerick   map 16

▲ *Adare Manor* ⁑✳

Adare
TEL: (061) 396566   FAX: (061) 396124   COST £36–£70

The Manor manages to surprise even those who are used to the grandeur of country-house hotels. It is a veritable Versailles of south-west Ireland, all landscaped gardens and rolling golf course, so undeniably imposing that one reporter on a first visit here remarked that 'a beefburger and chips would have been OK'. Gerard Costello has set his sights a little higher than that, to deliver mango, avocado and crab tart with curry mayonnaise, red lentil and cracked wheat soup, and rack of lamb roasted in Guinness with buttered cabbage, oyster mushrooms and a rosemary and balsamic jus. Our reporter thought his stir-fried beef fillet with sherry sauce and wild rice 'a successful combination well brought off'. Finish with the likes of chocolate and mint parfait with crème anglaise, or plum and almond tart with fresh fruit coulis. The magisterial wine list carefully anatomises France before taking off into the New World, where – as so often – better value may be found. House Merlot and Chardonnay from France are £19.

CHEF: Gerard Costello PROPRIETORS: Mr and Mrs Kane OPEN: all week 12.30 to 2, 7 to 9.30
MEALS: alc D (main courses £17.50 to £22.50). Set L £21.50, Set D £34.50 SERVICE: 15%, card slips closed CARDS: Amex, Delta, Diners, MasterCard, Switch, Visa DETAILS: 280 seats. Private parties: 200 main room, 20 to 200 private rooms. Car park. Vegetarian meals. Children's helpings. Jacket and tie. No smoking in 1 dining-room. Wheelchair access (2 steps; also WC). Music ACCOMMODATION: 62 rooms, all with bath/shower. TV. Phone. Room only £120 to £215. Rooms for disabled. Children welcome. High teas for children. Baby facilities. No dogs. Afternoon teas. Swimming-pool. Fishing

---

AHAKISTA Co Cork
map 16

Shiro ✱

Ahakista
TEL: (027) 67030 FAX: (027) 67206   COST £53–£64

Golden pheasants sing outside this fascinating little place on the Sheep's Head Peninsula. Their sounds provide a tantalising and enticing backdrop for Kei and Werner Pilz's self-styled 'Japanese dinner house'. She paints, creates calligraphy, handcrafts sushi and cooks; he serves front-of-house. The evening's menu begins in authentic fashion with zensai appetisers and suinomo soup, before a choice of main courses that extends to tempura, sashimi, beef teriyaki and ton-katsu ('petite' pork cutlets with three dipping sauces, Japanese-style potato salad and vegetables). To finish there is usually home-made ice-cream. Drink tea, saké or something from the almost exclusively French wine list; prices start at £13.

CHEF: Kei Pilz PROPRIETORS: Kei and Werner Pilz OPEN: all week D only 7 to 9 CLOSED: 24 to 31 Dec MEALS: Set D £42. BYO £4 SERVICE: 10% CARDS: Amex, Diners, MasterCard, Visa
DETAILS: 18 seats. Private parties: 16 main room, 5 and 14 private rooms. Car park. Vegetarian meals. No children under 14. No smoking in dining-room. Music

---

BALLINA Co Mayo
map 16

▲ Mount Falcon Castle ✱

Foxford Road, Ballina
TEL: (096) 21172 FAX: (096) 71517
EMAIL: mfsalmon@iol.ie
on N57 between Foxford and Ballina   COST £34–£41

Mount Falcon runs to a successful formula, much as many places in the England's Lake District do. Dinner is at eight, taken at one long table, and is a five courses plus coffee. Fresh produce from the garden, salmon from the River Moy and Aberdeen Angus beef are among favoured ingredients, and the Aga cooking is soundly based on good domestic principles. One evening offered tomato vinaigrette to start, then chicken and vegetable soup, a choice of chilli con carne and rice, or roast leg of pork with apple sauce, Irish cheeses, and either fruit salad or apple and rice meringue. Wines are predominantly French and from some good growers. House red and white are £12.

CHEF: Denise Moyles   PROPRIETOR: Constance Aldridge   OPEN: all week D only 8pm (1 sitting)   CLOSED: 1 week Christmas, Feb, Mar   MEALS: Set D £25   SERVICE: not inc   CARDS: Amex, Diners, MasterCard, Visa   DETAILS: 22 seats. Private parties: 50 main room. Car park. Children's helpings. No smoking in dining-room. No music   ACCOMMODATION: 9 rooms, all with bath/shower. Phone. D,B&B £50 to £120. Children welcome. High teas for children. Baby facilities. No dogs in public rooms. Afternoon teas. Garden. Fishing

---

BALLYDEHOB   Co Cork   map 16

Annie's

Main Street, Ballydehob
TEL: (028) 37292   COST £31–£37

'The restaurant has a unique relationship with the pub across the road,' writes Anne Barry, meaning that it doubles as an aperitif area for the restaurant. Mind how you go when crossing Main Street: a vehicle of some sort comes by at least every hour. Annie's majors in simple homely food, with the emphasis on fresh fish and seafood. Mussels are stuffed with garlic butter and breadcrumbs, locally smoked salmon is fashioned into a roulade, and black sole is grilled on the bone. For meat people, pork is sauced with apples and Cointreau, and rack of lamb comes with tarragon and lemon sauce. The concise wine list shows off some pedigree growers, with prices starting at around £11.50.

CHEFS/PROPRIETORS: Dano and Anne Barry   OPEN: Tue to Sat D only 7 to 9.30   CLOSED: Oct to Nov, 4 days Christmas   MEALS: alc (main courses £14). Set D £22   SERVICE: not inc   CARDS: MasterCard, Visa   DETAILS: 24 seats. Private parties: 24 main room. Car park. Vegetarian meals. Children's helpings. Music

---

BALLYLICKEY   Co Cork   map 16

▲ Ballylickey Manor, Le Rendez-Vous

Ballylickey, Bantry Bay
TEL: (027) 50071   FAX: (027) 50124   COST £21–£57

The Graves family (Robert, the poet, was the present owner's uncle) have been running Ballylickey since just after the war. It is a 300-year-old shooting-lodge-turned-country-hotel, single-mindedly devoted to the creature comforts, where the cooking – now under Pascal Kirsch – has for long been in the grand French style. Smoked salmon is given a new twist with tapénade crêpes, and turbot is painstakingly coated with potato slices and sauced with a meat stock reduction. Lobster thermidor served with rice timbale is there, while duck magret is partnered with pearl barley and asparagus. Finish with 'la classique crème caramel' or orange and pink grapefruit gratin. The entirely French wine list is not exactly a bargain-hunter's paradise, and fails to list producers' names for many items. House Graves (but of course) is £11.

CHEF: Pascal Kirsch PROPRIETORS: Mr and Mrs Graves OPEN: Thur to Tue L 12.30 to 2, all week D 7 to 9 CLOSED: mid-Nov to Mar MEALS: alc (main courses L £7.50 to £11, D £10 to £16.50). Set L £12, Set D £28 SERVICE: 10%, card slips closed CARDS: Amex, Diners, MasterCard, Visa DETAILS: 30 seats. 15 seats outside. Car park. Vegetarian meals. Children's helpings. No children under 8 at D. Jacket and tie. No smoking in dining-room. Wheelchair access (not WC). Occasional music ACCOMMODATION: 11 rooms, all with bath/shower. TV. Phone. B&B £100 to £200. Children welcome. High teas for children. Baby facilities. No dogs. Swimming-pool. Fishing

---

BALLYVAUGHAN Co Clare   map 16

▲ *Gregans Castle* ♟ ⚕⚘

Ballyvaughan
TEL: (065) 7077005 FAX: (065) 7077111
EMAIL: gregans@iol.ie
on N67, 3½m S of Ballyvaughan   COST £45–£60

For those with a passion for natural history, the Burren – the name of the region hereabouts – is a botanical mecca: a hundred square miles of limestone scenery merging into Galway Bay and the Aran Islands beyond. At its heart is Gregans Castle, an ancestral residence since the seventeenth century and these days a family-run country-house hotel. The kitchen draws on supplies of Burren lamb, local fish and organic produce for fixed-price dinner menus with a modern accent. Confit of duck is served with crispy-fried celeriac and walnut dressing, pan-fried John Dory comes with saffron mash and a mild onion and pancetta dressing, while bacon and cabbage with parsley sauce strikes a more homespun note. Rounding things off are things like rhubarb parfait with raspberry coulis. Bar lunches and afternoon teas are served in the Corkscrew Room. Wines are a worldly collection chosen with an eye for respectable produces while keeping the other on variety and flavour. Eight house wines start at £14.50.

CHEF: Gary Masterson PROPRIETORS: the Haden family OPEN: all week D only 7 to 8.30 CLOSED: mid-Oct to late March MEALS: Set D £22.50 (2 courses) to £34. Bar L available SERVICE: not inc, card slips closed CARDS: Amex, MasterCard, Visa DETAILS: 50 seats. Private parties: 90 main room. Car park. Vegetarian meals. Children's helpings. No smoking in 1 dining-room. Wheelchair access (also WC). Music ACCOMMODATION: 22 rooms, all with bath/shower. Phone. B&B £84 to £280. Rooms for disabled. Children welcome. Baby facilities. Dogs welcome in stable only. Afternoon teas

---

BLACKLION Co Cavan   map 16

▲ *MacNean Bistro* ⚕⚘

Blacklion
TEL: (072) 53022 FAX: (072) 53404   COST £21–£51

The village of Blacklion is set among some of Ireland's most haunting landscape, where hill-walking, potholing and scrutinising Neolithic tombs are what folks get up to. Star billing goes to the Maguires' restaurant, which – set in a Victorian hotel building – neither looks nor feels like a bistro. Nor is Neven Maguire content just to trot out bistro standards. Offerings such as seared salmon with polenta cake and vanilla cream, or peppered rump of kangaroo with creamed lentils and roast garlic, are more his style, and reports suggest that the success rate is high. Crisply roasted duck with five-spice sauce shows a confident affinity with oriental technique, while desserts – whether chocolate tart, banana parfait, or crème brûlée – tend to be 'elaborately decorated with biscuit constructions, pools of sauces, little sorbets on the side and a variety of other dramatic effects'. A tied cookery school is to be the next departure. House wines start at around £10.

CHEF: Neven Maguire   PROPRIETORS: Vera and Joe Maguire   OPEN: Sun L 12.30 to 3.30, Tue to Sun D 6 to 8.45   CLOSED: 25 to 27 Dec   MEALS: alc D (main courses £12 to £15). Set L Sun £12, Set D £25 to £32. BYO £4   SERVICE: not inc   CARD: Visa   DETAILS: 40 seats. Private parties: 40 main room, 14 private room. Car park. Vegetarian meals. Children's helpings. No smoking in dining-room. Music   ACCOMMODATION: 10 rooms, all with bath/shower. TV. Phone. B&B £23 to £46. Children welcome. Baby facilities. No dogs. Afternoon teas

---

BRAY   Co Wicklow   map 16

Tree of Idleness

Seafront, Bray
TEL: (01) 2863498   FAX: (01) 2828183   COST £30–£52

A photographic exhibition of 'Old Cyprus' now adds to the atmosphere in Susan Courtellas's long-serving restaurant on Bray's seafront. Greek-Cypriot specialities form the bedrock of the menu, with roast suckling pig, saddle of lamb stuffed with feta cheese and olives, and rabbit stifado setting the tone. Elsewhere, the Mediterranean has its colourful say with lambs' kidneys and sweetbreads with mustard cream sauce, peppered monkfish in olive oil, or braised boned quail with grapes and caramelised honey sauce. 'Guests are encouraged to take as much as they desire' from the trolley of home-made ice-creams, exotic fruits, Greek yoghurt mousse, and chocolate puddings. The wine list is a heavyweight collection of more than 250 bins spanning everything from vintage clarets to the Crimean Massandra Collection. House Côtes du Rhône is £12.95.

CHEF: Ismail Basaran   PROPRIETOR: Susan Courtellas   OPEN: Tue to Sun D only 7.30 to 11 (10 Sun)   CLOSED: Christmas, last 2 weeks Aug   MEALS: alc (main courses £9.95 to £16.50). Set D Tue to Fri and Sun £20   SERVICE: 10%, card slips closed   CARDS: Amex, Diners, MasterCard, Visa   DETAILS: 50 seats. Private parties: 25 main room. Vegetarian meals. Children's helpings. Wheelchair access (not WC). Music

---

CASHEL   Co Tipperary   map 16

Chez Hans ▼

Moor Lane, Cashel
TEL: (062) 61177   COST £32–£51

Inhabiting a converted church at the foot of Cashel Rock, Chez Hans offers one of Ireland's more striking restaurant surroundings. Nothing changes much from year to year (this is the proprietor's thirtieth anniversary here), the menu remaining as rooted in classical principles as ever. Quenelles of turbot and brill with a wine and butter sauce, tian of avocado with shrimps, crab and smoked salmon, and, from a generous range of fish main courses, herb-crusted cod with mussels and mustard sauce are the kinds of dishes to expect. Meat-eaters may prefer rack of local lamb with rosemary jus, or roast duckling with garlic confit and a honey and thyme sauce. Reliable and forward-looking producers are the key to the wine list, which concentrates on France but also takes in the New World, Spain, Italy and Germany (a spätlese from Hans-Peter Matthiä's family vineyards). Eleven bottles under £12 form the opening attraction.

CHEF/PROPRIETOR: Hans-Peter Matthiä   OPEN: Tue to Sat D only 6.30 to 10   CLOSED: 24 to 26 Dec, first 3 weeks Jan, Good Fri,   MEALS: alc (main courses £15.50 to £21.50). BYO £3 SERVICE: not inc   CARDS: MasterCard, Visa   DETAILS: 75 seats. Private parties: 90 main room. Car park. Children's helpings. No-smoking area. Wheelchair access (also WC). Music. Air-conditioned £5

CASTLEBALDWIN Co Sligo   map 16

▲ Cromleach Lodge 🍴★

Castlebaldwin, via Boyle
TEL: (071) 65155   FAX: (071) 65455
EMAIL: cromleac@iol.ie   COST £36–£63

From the outside the Lodge 'seems to have grown sideways in stages' in the view of one couple, who thought it the 'best hotel we stayed at' during a grand tour of the Republic. Table occupancy is rotated for residents, so everyone gets to survey the magnificent hilltop views. Local organic produce lends class to Moira Tighe's cooking, the principal showcase for which is a six-course tasting menu. Quail breasts with creamed lentils, or blue cheese soufflé with pineapple and date chutney turn up among first courses on the regular menu, before an in-betweenie of soup or salad. Sorbet follows as standard, then it's turbot with redcurrants and walnuts, or Sligo beef with roast shallots, before subsiding into marbled two-tone chocolate mousse gâteau on Bailey's custard. House recommendations from £12.95 head up a classical French-led list with a decent showing of halves.

CHEF: Moira Tighe   PROPRIETORS: Christy and Moira Tighe   OPEN: all week D only 6.30 to 8.45   CLOSED: Nov to Jan   MEALS: alc (main courses £17). Set D £25 to £35 (tasting menu) SERVICE: not inc, card slips closed   CARDS: Amex, Diners, MasterCard, Visa   DETAILS: 50 seats. Private parties: 22 main room. Car park. Children's helpings. No children under 7 after 7pm. No smoking in dining-room. Wheelchair access (not WC). No music   ACCOMMODATION: 10 rooms, all with bath/shower. TV. Phone. B&B £60 to £140. Rooms for disabled. Children welcome. High teas for children. Baby facilities. Dogs welcome in kennels. Fishing

---

CORK Co Cork   map 16

▲ Arbutus Lodge 🍾

Middle Glanmire Road, Cork
TEL: (021) 501237   FAX: (021) 502893
EMAIL: arbutus@iol.ie   COST £23–£57

'A country house in a city' is how the Ryans invite us to think of the Lodge, one of Ireland's more renowned gastronomic addresses. Despite the grandeur of the surroundings, reporters are pleased to note that there is none of the stuffiness that can pervade such places. 'Franco-Irish' is the qualifier given to the cooking, which translates as foie gras terrine with toasted sour-dough bread, hot oysters glazed with Sauternes sabayon, and loin of lamb en crépinette stuffed with spinach and wild mushrooms. One couple appreciated the freshness and presentation in a starter combination of smoked salmon, pear and fennel, and agreed that Parma ham was a good thing to wrap monkfish in. Fine Irish cheeses are offered after the pudding trolley, which bears the expected gâteaux and tarts.

The impressive wine list is divided into three parts. The first is an extremely long line of the venerable and the up-to-the-minute from both hemispheres, the second helpfully lists bottles under £17 (of which there are 34), and the third repeats part one but with annotations. House wines start at £11.50. CELLARMAN'S CHOICE: Rockford Old Vine Riesling 1997, Barossa Valley, S. Australia, £18.50; Rockford Basket Press Shiraz 1994, Barossa Valley, S. Australia, £33.

CHEFS: Declan Ryan and Eric Theze   PROPRIETORS: Declan Ryan and family   OPEN: Mon to Sat 1 to 2, 7 to 9.30   CLOSED: 24 to 28 Dec   MEALS: alc (main courses £17 to £20). Set L £15.50, Set D £20.50 to £30. Bar L available   SERVICE: not inc   CARDS: Amex, Delta, Diners, MasterCard, Visa   DETAILS: 60 seats. Private parties: 12 main room, 25 to 100 private rooms. Car park. Vegetarian meals. Children's helpings. No cigars/pipes in dining-room. No music. Air-conditioned   ACCOMMODATION: 20 rooms, all with bath/shower. TV. Phone. B&B £52 to £125. Children welcome. High teas for children. Baby facilities. No dogs. Afternoon teas

Crawford Gallery Cafe £

Emmet Place, Cork
TEL: (021) 274415   COST £19–£32

Renovations to the entire Crawford Building are in the pipeline, says Chris O'Brien. In the meantime it's business as usual at his commendable daytime café. The setup is owned by Ballymaloe House (see entry, Shanagarry), and the menu always features their speciality breads and ice-creams. Weekly-changing menus bring together a goodly helping of open sandwiches, warm salads and fish alongside more substantial dishes such as minute steak with tomato and mango salsa, or grilled chicken breast with spiced lentils, carrot and ginger sauce. Afternoon teas are a restorative godsend for shoppers. House George Duboeuf is £10.

CHEF: Chris O'Brien   PROPRIETOR: Ballymaloe House   OPEN: Mon to Sat 10 to 5 (4.30 Sat) CLOSED: 25 Dec to 2 or 3 Jan, bank hols   MEALS: alc (main courses £7.50 to £8.50). Set L £12 SERVICE: not inc   CARDS: MasterCard, Visa   DETAILS: 80 seats. Private parties: 80 main room. Children's helpings. Wheelchair access (4 steps; also WC). Music   £5

DINGLE Co Kerry   map 16

Beginish ♥ ✻

Green Street, Dingle
TEL: (066) 51588   FAX: (066) 51591   COST £21–£47

A pair of English travellers commended the 'genteel but relaxed ambience and view of the beautiful garden from our table in the conservatory' at John and Pat Moore's Georgian terraced house. The menus offer wider choice than may be expected, but the kitchen copes well and is seemingly happy to cook fish according to the diner's specifications. Otherwise, there are Cromane mussels with pesto and garlic cream, tapénade-crusted salmon with leek fondue and citrus salsa, or beef fillet with Roquefort polenta, red onion marmalade and brandy cream sauce. Grand Marnier goes into crème brûlée, and there are always good Irish farmhouse cheeses. Service is 'efficient and unobtrusive'. The wine list is strongest in Bordeaux and Burgundy, but choice of producer is sound whatever the region: Trimbach in Alsace, Antinori in Tuscany, Cape Mentelle in Australia, Errázuriz in Chile. CELLARMAN'S CHOICE: Chablis 1996, Joseph Drouhin, £21; Savigny-lès-Beaune 1995, Louis Latour, £21.

CHEF: Pat Moore   PROPRIETORS: John and Pat Moore   OPEN: Tue to Sun 12.30 to 2.15, 6 to 10   CLOSED: Christmas   MEALS: alc (main courses L £5 to £16.50, D £11 to £16.50)   SERVICE: not inc, card slips closed   CARDS: Amex, Diners, MasterCard, Visa   DETAILS: 52 seats. Private parties: 20 main room. Vegetarian meals. Children's helpings. No smoking in 1 dining-room. Wheelchair access (not WC). Music. Air-conditioned

▲ Half Door ⁵✕

3 John Street, Dingle
TEL: (066) 51600 and 51883   FAX: (066) 51883   COST £19–£64

In this restaurant on the wind-buffeted Kerry peninsula, fish and shellfish remain the focus. A Gaelic greeting heads the menu, which itself is written in both French and English. It all translates into escalope of salmon with garlic beurre blanc, prawn and crab lasagne, or seafood chowder to start, with lobster thermidor, crisped monkfish in tomato and basil sauce, or cod on potatoes and chives to follow. For those hankering after red meat there's half a roast duckling in citrus and almond sauce. Strawberry shortbread with crème Chantilly, and crêpes flamed in Strega with lemon and lime are among the dessert offerings. The wine list reaches out to take in bottles from around the world, with house selections starting at £12.50.

CHEF: Denis O'Connor   PROPRIETORS: Denis and Teresa O'Connor   OPEN: Mon to Sat 12.30 to 2.30, 6 to 10   CLOSED: Jan and Feb   MEALS: alc (main courses L £4 to £28, D £12 to £28)   SERVICE: not inc   CARDS: Amex, MasterCard, Visa   DETAILS: 50 seats. Private parties: 20 main room, 20 private room. Vegetarian meals. Children's helpings. No children after 8pm. No smoking in 1 dining-room. Wheelchair access (not WC). Music. Air-conditioned   ACCOMMODATION: 8 rooms, all with bath/shower. TV. Phone. B&B £25 to £44. Children welcome

DONEGAL   Co Donegal   map 16

▲ Harvey's Point ⁵✕

Lough Eske, Donegal
TEL: (073) 22208   FAX: (073) 22352
EMAIL: harveyspoint@tinet.ie   COST £23–£53

'Time quite literally stands still' around these parts, says the brochure for Marc Gysling's Swiss-style hotel in rugged Donegal, though Harvey's Point itself is fast approaching its first decade of operations, offering cuisine that mixes and matches Swiss, French and Irish influences. Goose meat is fanned out on cold ratatouille vegetables and dressed with a coriander vinaigrette, while grilled sea bream appears on green tagliatelle with a basil butter sauce. Main courses tend towards the richer end of the spectrum, as in chicken breast stuffed with wild mushrooms and sauced with port, and desserts use Swiss chocolate for a pair of mousses, or fresh fruits with ice-cream and sorbet garnishes. Wines look like a cosmopolitan collection, but there are too many producers' names missing for an operation of this seriousness. Prices go upwards from around £12.

CHEF/PROPRIETOR: Marc Gysling   OPEN: all week 12.30 to 2, 6.30 to 9.30   CLOSED: Christmas and New Year, Mon to Fri Nov to Mar   MEALS: alc (main courses £8.50 to £18.50). Set L £10.45 to £13.75, Set D £27.50   SERVICE: 10%, card slips closed   CARDS: Amex, Diners, MasterCard, Visa   DETAILS: 80 seats. Private parties: 80 main room, 80 to 300 private rooms. Car park. Vegetarian meals. Jacket and tie. No smoking in 1 dining-room. Wheelchair access (also WC). Music. Air-conditioned   ACCOMMODATION: 20 rooms, all with bath/shower. TV. Phone. B&B £61 to £99. Afternoon teas

---

DOUGLAS   Co Cork   map 16

Lovetts ▼

Churchyard Lane, off Well Road, Douglas
TEL: (021) 294909 and 293604   FAX: (021) 294024   COST £24–£50

The Lovett family celebrated the start of its third decade of operations here by extensively refurbishing the place in 1998. A late-Georgian house with a polygonal extension, ten minutes out of Cork, it aims to offer 'serious cooking' in a variety of styles using fresh and free-range ingredients. The informal brasserie menu deals in simple dishes such as mussels with pesto, and chargrilled kidneys in mustard sauce, while more ambitious outings in the main dining-room have included lasagne of crab with shiitake mushrooms, and sirloin steak with caramelised onions and garlic butter. Wines in the brasserie comprise 20 bottles taken from the restaurant's lengthy, globe-trotting list, which combines grand names with appealing styles of winemaking. House wines from France and South Africa start at £12.50. CELLARMAN'S CHOICE: Santa Mónica Sauvignon Blanc 1996, Rapel, Chile, £14.85; Côtes du Rhône 1995, Coudoulet de Beaucastel, £20.75.

CHEFS: Marie Harding and Margaret Lovett   PROPRIETORS: Dermod and Margaret Lovett OPEN: Tue to Fri L 12.30 to 2, Tue to Sat D 7 to 9.30   CLOSED: 1 week Christmas, first week Aug MEALS: alc (main courses £13 to £18). Set L £15.50, Set D £24. Bar menu L; brasserie menu D SERVICE: not inc, card slips closed   CARDS: Amex, Diners, MasterCard, Visa   DETAILS: 50 seats. Private parties: 50 main room, 24 and 50 private rooms. Car park. Vegetarian meals. Children's helpings. Wheelchair access (not WC). Music

---

DUBLIN   Co Dublin   map 16

▲ Clarence, Tea Room

6–8 Wellington Quay, Dublin 2
TEL: (01) 6707766   FAX: (01) 6707833
EMAIL: clarence@indigo.ie   COST £27–£58

The Clarence is a lavishly restored hotel bankrolled by the Irish pop group U2. Mackintosh is the inspiration for the decorative style, although the split-level dining-room does not evoke unalloyed rapture. Michael Martin's cooking is a different matter altogether, his CV bristling with stints at London's most luxuriantly garlanded kitchens. The cooking splashes through the Mediterranean in approved modern manner, bringing a high degree of polish to dishes such as a salad of aubergine crisps, roast garlic, mesclun and red onion oil, or roast cured salmon with celeriac mash and braised peppers. Choice is wide, as befits the opulence of the environment, and the sense of value palpable. Meats are largely prime cuts, and desserts begin with soufflé Rothschild with peach flambé. An inspired international wine list contains some fine growers, but prices are not slow in leaving the £20 barrier. House South African is £15.

CHEF: Michael Martin PROPRIETOR: Brushfield Ltd. OPEN: Mon to Fri L 12.30 to 2.20, all week D 6.30 to 10.20 (10 Sun) MEALS: alc (main courses £13 to £18.50). Set L £13.50 (2 courses) to £17 SERVICE: not inc CARDS: Amex, Diners, MasterCard, Visa DETAILS: 90 seats. Private parties: 90 main room. Vegetarian meals. Children welcome. No-smoking area. Wheelchair access (also WC). Music ACCOMMODATION: 50 rooms, all with bath/shower. TV. Phone. Room only £175 to £190. Rooms for disabled. Children welcome. Baby facilities. No dogs. Afternoon teas

Commons

Newman House, 85–86 St Stephens Green, Dublin 2
TEL: (01) 4780530 FAX: (01) 4780551   COST £32–£78

Once the student refectory of University College, now a top-drawer restaurant boasting its own specially commissioned artworks in homage to James Joyce, Commons is part of the Georgian splendour of Newman House. The fine Swiss plasterwork and rococo style of the interiors should not be missed, nor should the chance of a terrace table in fine weather. Sebastien Masi's culinary style is firmly in modern brasserie mould, embracing a first-course salad of Clonakilty black pudding with caramelised apples dressed in balsamic, and a surf 'n' turf main course of rabbit loin with Dublin Bay prawns and Savoy cabbage. Escoffier classics such as tournedos Rossini and gâteau opéra rub shoulders with such unusual sounding dishes as ribbon of chestnut or spirit of Shanghai (both desserts). A predominantly French list offers considerably grander fare than student budgets could ever have coped with. House French is £18.

CHEF: Sebastien Masi PROPRIETOR: Michael Fitzgerald OPEN: Mon to Fri L 12.30 to 2.15, Mon to Sat D 7 to 10.15 CLOSED: 1 week Christmas, bank hols MEALS: alc (main courses £20 to £24). Set L £20, Set D £35 and £50 SERVICE: not inc CARDS: Amex, Diners, MasterCard, Visa DETAILS: 60 seats. 20 seats outside. Private parties: 70 main room, 20 and 60 private rooms. Children welcome. No-smoking area. Music. Air-conditioned

Le Coq Hardi 🍾 ⁵⋇

35 Pembroke Road, Dublin 4
TEL: (01) 6689070 and 6684130 FAX: (01) 6689887   COST £33–£88

A Dublin institution since the 1970s, Le Coq roosts in an imposing Victorian house on a corner site near Ballsbridge. It is unmistakably a full-dress restaurant, replete with sofas to get submerged in, well-kept period interiors and a kitchen unafraid to do gourmet classics from another era alongside more modern dishes. Lobster and prawn bisque enriched with cognac, fillets of turbot on buttered greens with tarragon cream sauce, or mallard with braised red cabbage and game chips are highlights of the menus. Generous portions are the norm, as was discovered by a reporter who enjoyed king scallops in bacon with garlic cream, saddle and leg of rabbit with colcannon, and 'wickedly rich' chocolate and brandy terrine: 'This is cooking at the very highest level – I was glad my wife was paying.' The lengthy wine list offers classed-growth clarets back to 1870, there's a river of classy Rhônes, and venerable burgundies include four Dom. de la Romanée-Contis. Fine wines from California provide the final feather in its cap. House wines are £16. CELLARMAN'S CHOICE: Sancerre 'La Poussie' 1996, de Ladoucette, £27; Canon-Fronsac, Ch. Mazeris 1990, £62.

CHEFS: John Howard and James O'Sullivan   PROPRIETORS: John and Catherine Howard
OPEN: Mon to Fri L 12.30 to 2.30, Mon to Sat D 7 to 11   MEALS: alc (main courses £18 to £27). Set
L £21, Set D £35   SERVICE: 12.5%, card slips closed   CARDS: Amex, Diners, MasterCard,
Visa   DETAILS: 80 seats. Private parties: 50 main room, 10 to 35 private rooms. Car park.
Vegetarian meals. Children welcome. Jacket and tie. No smoking in 1 dining-room. Occasional
music. Air-conditioned

L'Ecrivain ▮ ⁵✖   ⟦NEW ENTRY⟧

109a Lower Baggot Street, Dublin 2
TEL: (01) 6611919   FAX: (01) 6610617   COST £24–£55

Derry Clarke's restaurant, under an archway in a courtyard beside Lad Lane, has escaped our attention for too long. He has been here since 1989, producing highly refined modern cooking in a bright yellow room adorned with portraits of Irish writers (hence the name), from Joyce to Seamus Heaney, the star attraction being a life-sized bronze of Brendan Behan in his cups. Menus are full of bang-up-to-date touches: black pudding accompanied by port sauce and an orange and ginger sorbet, for example, and lightly spiced yellowfin tuna that comes on tomato and pepper crostini dressed with soy and sherry. A creamed root vegetable soup served in half a coconut might make an eye-catching way to start, and you might end with rhubarb compote with mascarpone or a selection of Irish farmhouse cheeses. Service is from friendly and knowledgeable staff. Wines on the well-written, international list are sourced from fine growers, notably from France, Italy and California. Prices can be high, particularly for some of the top-quality clarets, but plenty of good drinking can be had under £20, beginning with four Chilean house wines at £13 a bottle, £3 a glass.

CHEF: Derry Clarke   PROPRIETORS: Derry and Sallyanne Clarke   OPEN: Mon to Fri L 12.30 to 2,
Mon to Sat D 7 to 11   CLOSED: 25 Dec, bank hols   MEALS: alc D (main courses £19.50). Set L
£12.50 (2 courses) to £15.50, Set D £25 to £30   SERVICE: 10% on food only   CARDS: Amex,
Diners, MasterCard, Visa   DETAILS: 66 seats. 20 seats outside. Private parties: 58 main room,
10 private room. Vegetarian meals. Children's helpings. No smoking in 1 dining-room. Music.
Air-conditioned

Ernie's 🍳

Mulberry Gardens, Dublin 4
TEL: (01) 2693300   FAX: (01) 2693260
off Morehampton Road in Donnybrook village   COST £26–£66

The menu cover may whisk you away to a rustic cottage by a lough somewhere, but the Donnybrook part of Dublin is not without its own charm. Here, in a family-run restaurant overlooking a dramatically lit garden and plashing fountain, is one of the city's most attractive dining-rooms. John Sultan has taken over the kitchen since the last edition of the *Guide* and maintains the gentle mixture of traditional and modern modes that established Ernie's repute. Clonakilty black pudding arrives in a salad with pecans, and scallops go into a 'cassoulet' with blackeye beans in a lime and coriander butter. There may be steak and kidney pie at lunch-time, with baked custard to follow, but if the mood of experimentation has caught hold, chocolate mousse with Japanese meringue and morellos is on the menu too. A majestic run of clarets and a good slate of half-bottles add interest to the wine list. House selections start at £15.50 for Duboeuf Beaujolais-Villages.

CHEF: John Sultan   PROPRIETORS: the Evans family   OPEN: Tue to Fri L 12.30 to 2, Tue to Sat D 7.30 to 10.30   CLOSED: 23 Dec to 2 Jan   MEALS: alc (main courses £15.50 to £20). Set L £14.95, Set D £25   SERVICE: 12.5%   CARDS: Amex, Diners, MasterCard, Visa   DETAILS: 60 seats. Private parties: 70 main room. Vegetarian meals. Children's helpings. No-smoking area. No music. Air-conditioned

Les Frères Jacques ⅝✱

74 Dame Street, Dublin 2
TEL: (01) 6794555   FAX: (01) 6794725   COST £23–£63

Sited next to the Olympia Theatre, this French restaurant claims among its attractions, according to a local reader, 'the best pianist in Ireland'. In an infectiously buzzy atmosphere, Nicolas Boutin uses a daily supply of fresh fish and shellfish to conjure up seafood minestrone, dressed lobster salad with tarragon mayonnaise, and grilled tuna with sauce niçoise. Wicklow lamb is a menu stalwart, done at one session with minted rice and wine vinegar, at another with poached pear and a Roquefort sauce. Seasonality is a strong point right up to dessert stage, when summer's red fruits may be fashioned into a soup and served with pistachio ice-cream. The wine list is mainly French, but spares a corner for Spain, Australia and California too. House wines in three colours are £11.

CHEF: Nicolas Boutin   PROPRIETOR: Jean-Jacques Caillabet   OPEN: all week 12 to 2.30, 7 to 10.30 (11 Fri and Sat)   CLOSED: 24 Dec, 2 Jan, bank hols   MEALS: alc D (main courses £16.50 to £22). Set L £13.50, Set D £21   SERVICE: 12.5% (optional)   CARDS: Amex, Diners, MasterCard, Visa   DETAILS: 60 seats. Private parties: 15 to 40 main room, 15 to 40 private rooms. Vegetarian meals. Children's helpings. No smoking in 1 dining-room. Music (£5)

Kapriol

45 Lower Camden Street, Dublin 2
TEL: (01) 4751235   FAX: (01) 4753770   COST £34–£58

'A quaint and intimate atmosphere' is promised at Kapriol, an Italian restaurant of crimson frontage that offers an old-school trattoria menu of enduring popularity. 'Expect huge prawns!' is the owners' advice, and expect them dressed with lemon, butter and garlic or in a 'sea melody' with scallops, turbot and salmon in a cream and brandy sauce. Otherwise, classic cheese- and ham-coated veal scallopine and peppered steaks are the name of the game, and there's marinated pheasant in season. The pasta is all home-made. Wines are

Italian and French and somewhat pricey. House wines, a Frascati and a Sicilian red, are £13 a litre.

CHEFS: Ronan Flanagan and Maura Hughes PROPRIETOR: Ronan Flanagan OPEN: Tue to Sat D only 7 to 12 MEALS: alc (main courses £12 to £17.50) SERVICE: 12.5% CARDS: Amex, Diners, MasterCard, Visa DETAILS: 36 seats. Private parties: 36 main room. Vegetarian meals. Children's helpings. No children under 4. No-smoking area. Wheelchair access (not WC). Music

Patrick Guilbaud

21 Upper Merrion Street, Dublin 2
TEL: (01) 6764192 FAX: (01) 6610052   COST £29–£88

Patrick Guilbaud's restaurant at the new Merrion Hotel makes the most of its opulent setting in the heart of Georgian Dublin. The period garden is one of the undeniable charms of the place, as is Guillaume Lebrun's 'modern classic cuisine' that celebrates the pick of Ireland's provender. Green pea soup with wild mushroom tortellini is one way of having pasta to start; another may be lobster ravioli poached in coconut liquor and seasoned with curried olive oil. As may be seen, this is not quite the unmixed Mediterranean mode of recent times, and the menu is happy to make space for crubeens (trotters) served with bread pudding and a rosemary sauce. Otherwise, sole comes with truffled mash and an egg-yolk dressing, and meals end with palate-cleansing lemon ganache, or chocolate and hazelnut mousse. M.Guilbaud still won't let us see his wine list, although he informs us that house wines start at £17 a bottle, £3.50 per glass.

CHEF: Guillaume Lebrun PROPRIETOR: Patrick Guilbaud OPEN: Tue to Sat 12.30 to 2, 7.30 to 10.15 CLOSED: first week Jan MEALS: alc (main courses £24 to £35). Set L £20, Set D £65 SERVICE: net prices CARDS: Amex, Diners, MasterCard, Visa DETAILS: 80 seats. 20 seats outside. Private parties: 80 main room, 20 private room. Car park. Children welcome. Wheelchair access (also WC). No music. Air-conditioned

Peacock Alley   NEW ENTRY

Fitzwilliam Hotel, 119 St Stephen's Green, Dublin
TEL: (01) 6770708 FAX: (01) 6718854   COST £30–£81

Conrad Gallagher opened his restaurant in South William Street in the summer of 1996, and has just moved out to St Stephen's Green, where it forms part of the new Conran-designed Fitzwilliam Hotel. Establishing himself as one of the movers and shakers of contemporary Irish cooking, he has a cookery book to his name, as well as a hugely accomplished kitchen. 'New Irish' turns out to have been as absorptive of Mediterranean and pan-Asian techniques as its British counterpart, and so polenta tart with buffalo mozzarella, tomato fondue and gazpacho sauce, not to mention roast scallop with Indian herbs, grilled aubergine and coconut cream, are quite likely to crop up. A group who ate before the change of address endorsed many of the dishes, particularly a breast of guinea-fowl accompanied by three treatments of parsnip – roasted, in a risotto, and puréed with harissa. Crème brûlée with raspberries, warm peach sablé with spiced honey, and an enlivening range of sorbets are on offer among desserts. The wine list is long on Bordeaux and classical France, more perfunctory elsewhere, and prices reflect the pedigree. House selections start with Côtes du Roussillon red and white at £12.50.

CHEF/PROPRIETOR: Conrad Gallagher   OPEN: Mon to Sat 12.30 to 2.30, 6 to 12   CLOSED: 25 Dec, 1 Jan, some bank hols   MEALS: alc (main courses £18 to £22). Set L £18.95, Set D £21.50 (6 to 7.30) to £55   SERVICE: not inc; 12.5% for parties of 8 or more   CARDS: Amex, Diners, MasterCard, Visa   DETAILS: 75 seats. Private parties: 70 main room. Children's helpings. No-smoking area. Music. Air-conditioned

Roly's Bistro

7 Ballsbridge Terrace, Dublin 4
TEL: (01) 6682611   FAX: (01) 6608535   COST £19–£44

Colin O'Daly cooks up-to-the-minute fusion food at this flamboyant venue opposite the American embassy in smart Ballsbridge. It's difficult to see the appellation 'bistro' as anything other than tongue in cheek when you can seat 160, and there is certainly no slavish devotion to traditional French methods: witness pork and sweetbread terrine with pickled vegetables and fried almonds, deep-fried sole goujons with apricot salsa, and plum fool with nut meringue sandwich. The lunch menu represents outstanding value. A list of predominantly French wines is fairly priced and soundly chosen, with international house selections all £10.95.

CHEF: Colin O'Daly   PROPRIETORS: Roly Saul, John O'Sullivan, Angela O'Sullivan, and Colin O'Daly   OPEN: all week 12 to 2.45, 6 to 10 (10.30 Fri and Sat)   CLOSED: 25 to 27 Dec, Good Fri   MEALS: alc D (main courses £8.50 to £16). Set L £12.50. BYO £5   SERVICE: 10%, card slips closed   CARDS: Amex, Diners, MasterCard, Visa   DETAILS: 160 seats. Private parties: 12 main room. Vegetarian meals. Children's helpings. No-smoking area. Wheelchair access (1 step; also WC). Air-conditioned

Thornton's ♥ ⁂

1 Portobello Road, Dublin 8
TEL: (01) 4549067   FAX: (01) 4532947   COST £33–£73

The 'unlikely venue' for some very highly rated cooking is a converted terraced house some way out of town, on the canalside between Rathmines and Harold's Cross. Kevin Thornton is 'dedicated to providing the best seasonal food in elegant, chic surroundings' and wins praise for an imaginitive menu built on solid classical French foundations, the style illustrated by noisette of hare with ravioli and hazelnut sauce, and sea bass fillet with baby fennel, purple potatoes and a squid ink sauce. Small parcels of sole stuffed with crab mousse and served with new potatoes in a copper pan impressed one reporter for high standards in both presentation and flavour. Irish and French cheeses and a pre-dessert, perhaps a miniature crème brûlée, precede desserts such as nougat pyramid. Like the food, the wine list is based around classical France, with clarets dating back to 1961, luscious dessert wines including a 1945 Yquem and some fine burgundies, while choice New World offerings provide a youthful balance. House wines start at £13.50. CELLARMAN'S CHOICE: Beaune 'Clos des Mouches' premier cru 1996, Joseph Drouhin, £62; Cornas 1989, Etienne Clape, £31.

CHEF: Kevin Thornton   PROPRIETORS: Kevin and Muriel Thornton   OPEN: Tue to Fri 12.30 to 2,
Mon to Sat D 6.30 to 11   MEALS: alc (main courses £19.50 to £22). Set L £22, Set D £49 (for
whole table). BYO £6   SERVICE: 12.5%   CARDS: Amex, Diners, MasterCard, Visa   DETAILS: 40
seats. Private parties: 46 main room, 16 private room. Car park. Vegetarian meals. Children's
helpings. No smoking in 1 dining-room. Music. Air-conditioned

---

DURRUS   Co Cork   map 16

▲ *Blairs Cove*

Durrus, nr Bantry
TEL: (027) 61127   FAX: (027) 61487
1½m out of Durrus on Barleycove to Goleen road   COST £41–£48

The boxy shape of this restaurant-with-rooms will give the hint that it once
formed the outbuildings of a nearby manor-house. It is run in cheerfully
unpretentious fashion. There is no silver service, help yourself to starters from
the buffet table and puddings from the top of the grand piano. The former may
include gravad lax, crabmeat in cucumber boats, Greek salad, and sushi rolls,
while the latter take in chocolate terrine, strawberry and apple flan, and hazelnut
meringue roulade. Between times, you might have ordered roast monkfish with
marinated peppers, or rack of lamb with flageolet beans. The mainly French
wine list does its job in an unspectacular manner. House wines are £12.

CHEF: Sabine De Mey   PROPRIETORS: Philippe and Sabine De Mey   OPEN: Tue to Sat D only
7.30 to 9.30   CLOSED: Nov to Mar   MEALS: Set D £29   SERVICE: not inc, card slips closed
CARDS: Diners, MasterCard, Visa   DETAILS: 80 seats. Private parties: 40 main room. Car park.
Children's helpings. No cigars/pipes in dining-room. No-smoking area. Wheelchair access (not
WC). Occasional music   ACCOMMODATION: 3 suites (with kitchens), all with bath/shower. TV.
Phone. Room only £30 to £120. Children welcome

GOREY   Co Wexford   map 16

▲ *Marlfield House*

Courtown Road, Gorey
TEL: (055) 21124   FAX: (055) 21572
EMAIL: marlf@iol.ie   COST £47–£63

The Bowes celebrated 20 years at Marlfield in 1998, and the place, despite its
undoubted grandeur, still feels like the family-run business it is. Fourteen acres
of garden and woodland surround the house and, although there has been a
change of chef since the last edition of the *Guide*, the experimental style of the
fixed-price modern menus continues. Fashionable ingredients abound in a
starter of baked goats' cheese on a garlic croûton with Thai vegetables in a
beetroot and mango salsa, and duck foie gras on black pudding with Poire
Williams sorbet. An intermediate course is followed by, for example, monkfish
on potato and spring onion salad, or loin of lamb with vegetable ragoût and a
port sauce. Tarragon ice-cream is the accompaniment for warm pear tart. Service
is commended as excellent. Mature clarets kick off the wine list, which is also
good in Australia, and finds space for Greece and Lebanon too. House wines
are £16.

CHEF: Jo Ryan   PROPRIETORS: Mary and Ray Bowe   OPEN: Sun L 12.30 to 1.45, all week D 7 to
9 (8 Sun)   CLOSED: mid-Dec to end Jan   MEALS: Set L Sun £19.50 to £21.50, Set D £35 to £40.
Light L available   SERVICE: not inc, card slips closed   CARDS: Amex, Diners, MasterCard,
Visa   DETAILS: 65 seats. Private parties: 20 main room, 20 and 30 private rooms. Car park.
Vegetarian meals. Children's helpings. No children under 8 at D. Jacket and tie. No smoking in
dining-room. Wheelchair access (also WC). No music. Air-conditioned   ACCOMMODATION: 19
rooms, all with bath/shower. TV. Phone. B&B £80 to £490. Rooms for disabled. Children
welcome. High teas for children. Baby facilities. Dogs by arrangement

---

HOWTH   County Dublin   map 16

King Sitric ▮ ✳

East Pier, Howth
TEL: (01) 8325235 and 6729   FAX: (01) 8392442   COST £32–£62

Since 1971 the old harbourmaster's residence on East Pier has been home to the
MacManuses' well liked restaurant. The setting suggests fish, and that's exactly
what the kitchen delivers. During the summer a seafood bar provides light
lunches of Redbank oysters, plates of marinated salmon, Howth crab and the
like. The main business, however, is in the restaurant, where Aidan MacManus
shows off his affection for piscine gastronomy, old and new. Turbot may be
poached or grilled and served with hollandaise or béarnaise, black soles are
done in meunière or Colbert style and lobsters come in a variety of ways. But
there's also a liking for the orient in the shape of tempura prawns with noodles
and soy, or mixed sashimi, for example. Those inclined towards something from
the land might be persuaded by Dublin spiced beef with Bayonne ham and
elderberry sauce, while sweet-lovers can indulge in chocolate marquise or figs in
red wine. Wines are a regal collection of whites from the classic regions of France
backed up by some fish-friendly bins from around the world, while claret-lovers
are courted with a long line of vintages stretching back to the 1950s. House
wines start at £12.50. CELLARMAN'S CHOICE: Chablis premier cru, Montée de
Tonnerre 1995, Louis Michel, £27; Chassagne-Montrachet, Ch. de Chassagne-
Montrachet 1993, £23.

CHEF: Aidan MacManus   PROPRIETORS: Aidan and Joan MacManus   OPEN: Mon to Sat D only
6.30 to 10.30   CLOSED: 2 weeks Jan, bank hols   MEALS: alc (main courses £14.50 to £21). Set
D £28. BYO £5. Light L available Mon to Sat in summer   SERVICE: not inc   CARDS: Amex,
Diners, MasterCard, Visa   DETAILS: 75 seats. Private parties: 45 main room, 16 and 20 private
rooms. Vegetarian meals. Children's helpings. No smoking in 1 dining-room. Wheelchair access
(also women's WC). Music (£5)

KANTURK   Co Cork   map 16

▲ *Assolas Country House*

Kanturk
TEL: (029) 50015   FAX: (029) 50795
signposted from N72, NE of Kanturk, 8m W of Mallow   COST £43–£52

Loyalty to the seasons and local supplies dictates Hazel Bourke's cooking in this
early-seventeenth-century manor, the family home for more than six decades.
Dinner is a four-course affair, with soup or sorbet as a mid-meal interlude.

Duck livers with home-made pasta, lemon and garlic, or another starter of grilled mussels with pesto, suggest a broad-minded approach to things, but there's also a deep-rooted sense of home cooking in main dishes such as Aga-roasted free-range chicken breast served on braised onions with red-wine sauce, or loin of lamb with a caper and mint jus accompanied by Hazel's own mint jelly. A trolley of desserts or Irish cheeses precedes coffee 'served beside the fire'. The wine list focuses on long-standing names and families from France and other parts of Western Europe. Guigal's Côtes du Rhône heads the field at £14.50.

CHEF: Hazel Bourke   PROPRIETORS: the Bourke family   OPEN: all week D only 7 to 8.30 CLOSED: 1 Nov to 25 Mar   MEALS: Set D £32   SERVICE: none, card slips closed   CARDS: Amex, Diners, MasterCard, Visa   DETAILS: 28 seats. Private parties: 30 main room, 20 private room. Car park. Vegetarian meals. Children welcome. No music   ACCOMMODATION: 9 rooms, all with bath/shower. Phone. B&B £55 to £164. High teas for children. Baby facilities. Dogs by arrangement.Fishing

---

KENMARE Co Kerry   map 16

▲ *Park Hotel Kenmare* 🍷 ✳

Kenmare
TEL: (064) 41200   FAX: (064) 41402
EMAIL: phkenmare@iol.ie   COST £53–£87

Since arriving on the scene in 1989, chef Bruno Schmidt has stamped his mark firmly on the kitchen of this quirkily appointed Victorian stone mansion. His dinner menus show the kind of broad brushstrokes that typify so much eclectic hotel cooking in the 1990s. Roast quail filled with pistachio farce and accompanied by Sneem black pudding and a raspberry vinegar jus is a typically Euro-inspired starter, while main courses might veer off into pan-fried cod in Cajun spices on fresh noodles and baby fennel with a coconut and spring onion vinaigrette. Desserts, as one might expect, go the whole way with chilled Beaujolais soup, crystallised red fruit and cassis-scented parfait. The extensive wine list features some grand bottles from the Old World and some prestigious bins from the New, helpfully grouped by grape variety as well as region. Despite the preponderance of expensive clarets, there is plenty of good drinking to be had under £20, with French house wines leading the way at £16.95. CELLARMAN'S CHOICE: Waipara Springs Riesling 1996, Canterbury, New Zealand, £23; Carneros Creek 'Signature Reserve' 1993, Carneros, California, £58.

CHEF: Bruno Schmidt   PROPRIETOR: Francis Brennan   OPEN: all week D only 7 to 9   CLOSED: 1 Nov to 23 Dec 2 Jan to mid-Apr   MEALS: alc (main courses £18.50 to £24.50). Set D £39.50. Snacks available 11 to 6   SERVICE: not inc   CARDS: Amex, Diners, MasterCard, Visa   DETAILS: 120 seats. Private parties: 40 main room. Car park. Vegetarian meals. No children under 5. No smoking in 1 dining-room. Wheelchair access (not WC). Music   ACCOMMODATION: 50 rooms, all with bath/shower. TV. Phone. B&B £120 to £436. Rooms for disabled. Children welcome. High teas for children. Baby facilities. No dogs. Afternoon teas

---

All entries in the Guide *are re-researched and rewritten every year, not least because restaurant standards fluctuate. Don't rely on an out-of-date* Guide.

REPUBLIC OF IRELAND

▲ Sheen Falls Lodge, La Cascade ▮

Kenmare
TEL: (064) 41600 FAX: (064) 41386
EMAIL: sheenfalls@iol.ie
follow signs for Glengariff from Kenmare; hotel
signposted after about ½m   COST £54–£65

The iridescent peach of the exterior of this modern hotel and leisure complex provides a somewhat startling contrast with the surrounding tranquil green by Kenmare Bay. Nearby waterfalls give the restaurant its name, but what's happening on the plates may be even more attention-grabbing. The frequently changing menus essay such turns as rabbit loin on a plum tomato and tapénade tart (as a starter), local scallops on celeriac and horseradish purée and beetroot compote, beef fillet with truffled parsnips and roast garlic, and cardamom custard with spiced fruits. Service blends correctness and warmth in the Irish way. The wine list is a mighty tome, heavy on classed-growth clarets, with judicious selections from regional France, Germany, Italy and the New World providing added weight and interest. Some of the mark-ups are hefty, with just a handful of wines coming in under £20, but there is no question about quality. French house wines start at £18.50.

CHEF: Fergus Moore PROPRIETOR: Bent Hoyer OPEN: all week D only 7.15 to 9.30 CLOSED: 30 Nov to 23 Dec, 3 Jan to 5 Feb MEALS: Set D £37.50 SERVICE: not inc, card slips closed CARDS: Amex, Diners, MasterCard, Switch, Visa DETAILS: 120 seats. 20 seats outside. Private parties: 120 main room, 20, 30 and 60 private rooms. Car park. Vegetarian meals. Children's helpings. Wheelchair access (also WC). Music ACCOMMODATION: 61 rooms, all with bath/shower. TV. Phone. Room only £245. Rooms for disabled. High teas for children. Baby facilities. Afternoon teas. Swimming-pool. Dogs in stables only. Fishing

---

KILKENNY Co Kilkenny   map 16

▲ Lacken House

Dublin Road, Kilkenny
TEL: (056) 61085 FAX: (056) 62435
EMAIL: lackenhs@indigo.ie   COST £32–£52

Once Viscount Montmorency's dower house, and then for many years a nursing home, Lacken House has spent the past 15 years under the MacSweeneys' tutelage as a handsome restaurant and guesthouse. Eugene cooks a fixed-price dinner menu in the contemporary Irish idiom, offering perhaps pigeon terrine with juniper berry dressing to start, before main courses that range from baked sea trout with truffle oil butter and risotto to an Ozymandian-sounding 'tower of ostrich' on a rösti foundation with shiitake mushrooms and a Madeira glaze. At the end, it's marinated strawberries in a chocolate cup, pineapple in hot rum sauce with cinnamon cream, or Irish farmhouse cheeses. Star wines such as Opus One and Vega Sicilia add lustre to the French-led list, which opens – wait for it – with McGuinness's Côtes du Ventoux red and white at £13.

CHEF: Eugene McSweeney   PROPRIETORS: Eugene and Breda McSweeney   OPEN: Tue to Sat
D only 6.30 to 10.30   MEALS: alc (main courses £14 to £18). Set D £23   SERVICE: not inc, card
slips closed   CARDS: MasterCard, Visa   DETAILS: 30 seats. Private parties: 40 main room, 20
private room. Car park. Vegetarian meals. Children's helpings. No music. Air-conditioned
ACCOMMODATION: 8 rooms, all with bath/shower. TV. Phone. B&B £36 to £60. Children welcome.
High teas for children. No dogs

KINVARA Co Galway   map 16

▲ *Merriman* 🍳 ⭐ £

Kinvara
TEL: (091) 638222   FAX: (091) 637686   COST £17–£46

In a village on the southern edge of Galway Bay, the Merriman claims to have the
largest thatched roof in all Ireland. Mathias Salesses arrived to cook here late in
1997, and brings a new focus to the menus. The soup is no mere soup but 'velvet
crab bisque', further glamorised with mushroom ravioli and citrus Chantilly,
while smoked chicken mille-feuille is accompanied by crisp apple slices in a
honey and cider dressing. Enthusiastic support of local produce brings on rump
of lamb with celeriac purée, straw potatoes and thyme jus, while vegetarians
might like to go Moroccan with vegetable and chickpea ragoût with coriander
and raisined couscous. A Breton pudding with prune, walnut and armagnac
ice-cream is among the more unusual desserts. The Eurocentric wine list is
modest in scope and opens at £10.50.

CHEF: Mathias Salesses   PROPRIETOR: Lowstrand Properties   OPEN: Sun L 12.30 to 2, all week
D 7.15 to 9.30   CLOSED: 24 Dec to 17 Mar   MEALS: alc (main courses £7.50 to £16.50). Set L
Sun £10, Set D £19. Bar L available   SERVICE: not inc, card slips closed   CARDS: Amex, Diners,
MasterCard, Visa   DETAILS: 60 seats. Private parties: 60 main room, 30 private room. Car park.
Vegetarian meals. Children's helpings. No smoking in 1 dining-room. Wheelchair access (also
WC). Music   ACCOMMODATION: 32 rooms, all with bath/shower. TV. Phone. B&B £55 to £70.
Rooms for disabled. Children welcome. No dogs. Afternoon teas

---

LETTERFRACK Co Galway   map 16

▲ *Rosleague Manor* ⭐

Letterfrack
TEL: (095) 41101   FAX: (095) 41168
on N59 to Westport, 7m NW of Clifden   COST £26–£54

A 'splendid' setting and elegant furnishings set the tone in this part-Georgian
manor on the seaward fringes of Connemara. Nigel Rush offers guests light
lunches, but most of his efforts are reserved for evening meals in the reassuring
Anglo-French mould. One typically confident meal for two began with salmon,
trout and chive mousse, and a 'refined' chicken liver pâté with red fruit sauce
before pleasant-tasting soups (hot lovage and celery, cold carrot and orange).
Equally good were main courses of fried loin of veal and tip-top rabbit saddle
confit with mustard and pepper sauce. Seasonal vegetables and lightly crafted
desserts have also been enthusiastically received. Wines seem to play second
fiddle to the food, according to most reporters. House French is £11.50.

CHEFS: Nigel Rush and Rosaleen Curran PROPRIETORS: Patrick and Anne Foyle OPEN: all week 1 to 2.30, 8 to 9.30 CLOSED: Nov to Easter MEALS: alc (main courses L £7.50 to £12.50, D £14 to £16). Set D £28 to £30 SERVICE: not inc, card slips closed CARDS: Amex, MasterCard, Visa DETAILS: 60 seats. Private parties: 60 main room. Car park. Children's helpings. No smoking in dining-room. No music ACCOMMODATION: 20 rooms, all with bath/shower. Phone. B&B £40 to £140. Rooms for disabled. Children welcome. No dogs. Afternoon teas £5

MALLOW Co Cork map 16

▲ *Longueville House* ⁂

Mallow
TEL: (022) 47156 FAX: (022) 47459
on N72 Killarney road, 3m W of Mallow COST £42–£62

Home-produced supplies of lamb, pork, herbs and vegetables all find their way into the kitchen of this listed Georgian manor-house surrounded by a 500-acre working farm and estate. 'House-smoked' salmon from fish caught in the nearby Blackwater River also shows up as a starter on the menu in the Presidents' Restaurant. Chef William O'Callaghan offers a four-course, fixed-priced dinner with centrepieces of duck magret with pickled red cabbage in a tangerine and caraway sauce, or braised monkfish with potato and celeriac purée and a sauce tinged with chervil. Irish farmhouse cheeses are alternatives to desserts such as a pyramid of passion-fruit parfait with seasonal fruit salad. A dozen house wines (including a representative from Longueville itself) are the best bets on the wide-ranging list. Prices start at £14.

CHEF: William O'Callaghan PROPRIETORS: the O'Callaghan family OPEN: all week D only 6.30 to 9 (9.45 Fri and Sat) CLOSED: 21 Dec to 1 Feb MEALS: Set D £31 to £40; bar food available L SERVICE: not inc, card slips closed CARDS: Amex, Diners, MasterCard, Visa DETAILS: 72 seats. Private parties: 40 main room, 16 private room. Car park. Vegetarian meals. Children's helpings. No smoking in 1 dining-room. Wheelchair access (2 steps; also WC). Occasional music ACCOMMODATION: 23 rooms, all with bath/shower. TV. Phone. B&B £55 to £164. Children welcome. Baby facilities. No dogs. Afternoon teas. Fishing £5

MIDLETON Co Cork map 16

Farmgate ⁂ £

Coolbawn, Midleton
TEL/FAX: (021) 632771 COST £16–£42

The entrance to Máróg O'Brien's country restaurant does a good job of awakening the appetite. Stalls are laid out with fruit and vegetables to one side and tempting cakes to the other. As well as fine Irish dairy produce, she makes the most of local shellfish and free-range poultry in a style of cooking that aims to keep things simple and homely. The handwritten menus offer the likes of a warm salad of chicken marinated in soy and ginger with roasted red peppers, smoked Gubbeen wrapped in bacon with buttered leeks and Cumberland sauce, and a trade mark main course of sauté strips of beef fillet in a sauce of Jameson's whiskey. Tarts of one sort or another are the mainstays of the pudding list (lemon tart comes highly endorsed). Wine is not, alas, taken very seriously: vintages and many of the producers' names are not thought worth divulging. House wines change every fortnight or so and are normally around the £10 mark.

CHEFS: Máróg O'Brien and David Doran PROPRIETOR: Máróg O'Brien OPEN: Mon to Sat L 12 to 4, Thur to Sat D 6.30 to 9.45 MEALS: alc (main courses L £5 to £9, D £9 to £15) SERVICE: not inc CARDS: MasterCard, Visa DETAILS: 60 seats. 25 seats outside. Private parties: 60 main room, 20 private room. Vegetarian meals. Children's helpings. No smoking in 1 dining-room. Wheelchair access (1 step; also WC). Music

MOYCULLEN Co Galway map 16

Drimcong House 🍷

Moycullen
TEL: (091) 555115 and 555585 FAX: (091) 555836
EMAIL: drimcong@indigo.ie
on Galway to Clifden road, 1m W of Moycullen COST £32–£59

An expansion of the garden's organic range has been afoot this year at Drimcong, the Galvins' charming seventeenth-century manor in Ireland's wild west. The culinary style remains as inventive as ever, and à la carte dinner menus are supplemented by a fixed-price offering that takes in of turkey escalope in a thyme and broccoli cream sauce, as well as a pairing of pigeon and rabbit on spiced lentils. A full vegetarian menu of four courses plus coffee makes a change from the usual perfunctory showings, providing a broth of noodles, beans and 'sea vegetables' before chickpea cakes with goats' cheese and tomato salsa. Finish with hot lemon pudding and raspberry sauce, or a selection of Irish cheeses. The wine list is arranged by style, and flies around the world in 80 bins before coming to land in Portugal for some fine vintage ports. A strong French selection includes the organic Mas de Daumas Gassac. House wines start at £11.50. CELLARMAN'S CHOICE: Cloudy Bay Sauvignon Blanc 1997, Marlborough, New Zealand, £25; Tyrrell's Vat 9 Shiraz 1993, Hunter Valley, New South Wales, Australia, £25.

CHEF: Gerry Galvin PROPRIETORS: Gerry and Marie Galvin OPEN: Tue to Sat D only 6.30 to 10.30 CLOSED: Christmas to Mar MEALS: alc (main courses £17.50 to £19.50). Set D £17.50 (2 courses) to £26. BYO £5 SERVICE: not inc CARDS: Amex, Diners, MasterCard, Visa DETAILS: 50 seats. Private parties: 50 main room, 10 to 50 private rooms. Car park. Vegetarian meals. Children's helpings. No-smoking area. Wheelchair access (3 steps; also WC). Music

NEWPORT Co Mayo map 16

▲ *Newport House* 🍾 £✱

Newport
TEL: (098) 41222 FAX: (098) 41613
EMAIL: kjti@anu.ie COST £40–£50

The tranquil, creeper-covered, bay-fronted house may give no clue as to the pugnacity of its one-time owners, the O'Donel family, descendents of the fractious Earls of Tyrconnell who were despatched from Ulster to Mayo by Oliver Cromwell. It's all rather more relaxed now, as guests avail themselves of a spot of angling, and look forward to John Gavin's multi-course, fixed-price dinners. A hot terrine of salmon, sole and scallops in white wine, tomato and chive-butter sauce might set the ball rolling, followed by an optional half-dozen oysters, before a choice of soups. One reporter spoke highly of a main course of duck in orange and damson sauce. Irish farmhouse cheese precedes desserts, which might include rhubarb tartlets, nougat glacé with blackcurrant coulis, and poached pears with honey-and-walnut ice-cream. Classed-growth clarets from top vintages, mature Rhônes and venerable champagnes at commendably low prices head up a traditional wine list, which none the less offers room to some fine New World bins. French house wines begin at £12 a bottle, £2 a glass. CELLARMAN'S CHOICE; Côtes du Rhône 1996, Guigal, £15; Haut-Médoc, Ch. Lestage 1989, £25.

CHEF: John Gavin   PROPRIETORS: Kieran and Thelma Thompson   OPEN: all week D only 7 to 9.30   CLOSED: 6 Oct to 18 Mar   MEALS: Set D £30   SERVICE: not inc, card slips closed CARDS: Amex, Diners, MasterCard, Visa   DETAILS: 36 seats. Private parties: 12 main room. Car park. Children's helpings. No smoking in dining-room   Wheelchair access (also WC). No music   ACCOMMODATION: 18 rooms, all with bath/shower. Phone. Room only £70 to £146. Rooms for disabled. Children welcome. Baby facilities. High teas for children. Dogs welcome in some bedrooms only. Afternoon teas. Garden. Fishing   (£5)

OUGHTERARD   Co Galway   map 16

▲ *Currarevagh House* 🌟

Oughterard, Connemara
TEL: (091) 552312 and 552313   FAX: (091) 552731
4m NW of Oughterard on Hill of Doon Lakeshore road   COST £30–£36

The drill is a well-established one at the Hodgsons' Victorian family home set in wild and beautiful Connemara. Everybody eats at 8pm at a single sitting, June Hodgson's menu of the day being presented on a handwritten card. The format may be wholeheartedly domestic, but culinary ideas are by no means run-of-the-mill. One menu ran from grapefruit soufflé, through sauté plaice with caper cream, and duck confit with cassis sauce and pommes Anna, to a pudding called chocolate sandwich. More traditional ways bring on a main course of roast Irish beef with (expatriate) Yorkshire pudding, or there may be rack of lamb cooked in honey and Guinness. Meals always end with thoroughbred Irish cheeses. Wines from the classic French regions are the crown jewels of the list. House red and white Mercurey from Rodet are £9.80. Note that credit cards are not accepted.

CHEF: June Hodgson   PROPRIETORS: Harry and June Hodgson   OPEN: all week D only 8 (1 sitting)   CLOSED: 20 Oct to 1 Apr   MEALS: Set D £22   SERVICE: 10%   CARDS: none   DETAILS: 30 seats. Private parties: 10 main room. Car park. No smoking in dining-room. No music ACCOMMODATION: 15 rooms, all with bath/shower. B&B £50 to £105. Children by arrangement. Fishing

---

The Guide *relies on feedback from its readers. Especially welcome are reports on new restaurants appearing in the book for the first time. All letters to the* Guide *are acknowledged.*

SCHULL   Co Cork   map 16

▲ *Restaurant in Blue* 🕏✴

Gubbeen, Schull
TEL/FAX: (028) 28305   COST £33–£40

A conservatory extension has now been added to this Gershwinesque-sounding place, but the feeling of comforting domesticity is not lost. 'New friendships are readily forged in the squashy armchairs of the sitting-room,' writes a reporter, and there is no sense of hurry if you find yourself nattering on before dinner. Burvill Evans is a sensitive cook, filling a pimento with chilli-spiked crabmeat and dressing it with pesto, and bedding cabbage-wrapped lamb on rösti for textural counterpoint. Lavender jelly topped with peach ice-cream rounded off 'a delightful evening' for the reporter who chose these things. The wine list would appear to offer good value all round, but too many producers' names have been omitted. Prices start at £11 for Santa Carolina Chardonnay and Merlot from Chile.

CHEF: Burvill Evans   PROPRIETORS: Burvill Evans and Christine Crabtree   OPEN: Wed to Sun D only 6.30 to 9.30   CLOSED: winter, bank hol Mon   MEALS: Set D £24.50   SERVICE: not inc   CARDS: Amex, Diners, MasterCard, Visa   DETAILS: 50 seats. Private parties: 40 main room, 25 private room. Car park. Vegetarian meals. No children. No smoking in 1 dining-room. Wheelchair access (2 steps; not WC). Music   ACCOMMODATION: 2 rooms, both with bath/shower. B&B £35 to £75. No children. No dogs

---

SHANAGARRY   Co Cork   map 16

▲ *Ballymaloe House* 🕏✴

Shanagarry, nr Midleton
TEL: (021) 652531   FAX: (021) 652021
EMAIL: bmaloe@iol.ie
2m outside Cloyne on Ballycotton road   COST £26–£59

Cookery school, farmstead and welcoming country hotel, Ballymaloe seems to impress most with the relaxed assurance with which it operates. The daily-changing menus may not be cutting-edge, but there is a wealth of choice, and much of what is served is of a high order. Grilled cod with peperonata and chive butter, or courgette flowers stuffed with goats' cheese and basil are among the more up-to-date offerings, but roast goose with apple sauce and beetroot is the kind of dish people travel for. Stewed rhubarb with carrageen pudding makes a pleasingly novel way to finish. Breakfasts are praised to the skies. France, Australia and California form the backbone of a list that has been put together by a real enthusiast. House Duboeuf is £14.

CHEF: Rory O'Connell   PROPRIETORS: the Allen family   OPEN: all week 1 to 1.30, 7 to 9.30 (Sun to 7.30, residents only)   CLOSED: 24 to 26 Dec   MEALS: Set L Mon to Sat £16.50, Set L Sun £19.50, Set D £31.50   SERVICE: not inc   CARDS: Amex, Diners, MasterCard, Visa   DETAILS: 90 seats. Private parties: 30 main room, 10 to 24 private rooms. Car park. Vegetarian meals. Children welcome. No smoking in 1 dining-room. Wheelchair access (1 step; not WC). No music   ACCOMMODATION: 30 rooms, all with bath/shower. Phone. B&B £75 to £150. Rooms for disabled. Children welcome. High teas for children. Baby facilities. Swimming-pool

WATERFORD Co Waterford   map 16

Dwyers 💱✖

8 Mary Street, Waterford
TEL: (051) 877478 FAX: (051) 877480   COST £24–£43

A sense of comforting but smartly turned-out domesticity pervades the Dwyers'
town-centre restaurant, which is fast approaching its first decade. Martin Dwyer
cooks an early-evening set-price menu as well as the main *carte*, keeping things
simple rather than risking all on mind-blowing combinations. Lambs' kidneys
with horseradish and tarragon might be one way of starting, before considering
spring onion soup or elderflower sorbet as a second course. Chicken breast is
stir-fried with orange, honey and ginger, and mint mayonnaise is the accompaniment for chargrilled salmon. Fruity puddings encompass strawberries
marinated in Grand Marnier, or rhubarb syllabub with ginger biscuits. The wine
list is modestly proportioned, and French in orientation. Prices open at £11.75.

CHEFS: Martin Dwyer and Judith Hovenden PROPRIETORS: Martin and Sile Dwyer OPEN: Mon
to Sat D only 6 to 10 CLOSED: 1 week Christmas, bank hols MEALS: alc (main courses £10.50
to £15.50). Set D before 7.30 £15 SERVICE: not inc CARDS: Amex, Diners, MasterCard, Visa
DETAILS: 32 seats. Private parties: 24 main room, 8 private room. Vegetarian meals. Children's
helpings. No smoking in 1 dining-room. Wheelchair access (1 step; also WC). Music £5

WICKLOW Co Wicklow   map 16

▲ Old Rectory 💱✖

Wicklow
TEL: (0404) 67048 FAX: (0404) 69181
EMAIL: mail@oldrectory.ie   COST £37–£55

A thriving family concern, the Old Rectory is a Victorian country house where
the Saunders family take a lively and consuming interest in the business of
hospitality. The garden-fresh principle is accorded the highest prominence: the
house is filled with flowers and so, in the summer months at least, is the cooking.
A nine-course floral menu in celebration of the Wicklow Gardens Festival
suggests there is more to this genre than just nasturtiums, taking in as it does
lamb and lavender sausage, a sorbet of pineapple sage and dandelion wine,
pansy pancakes, and Cashel Blue garnished with sweet cicely. If it all sounds a
touch too Laura Ashley, revert to the main menu, where herb-crusted sea bream
comes with tomato, basil and lemon salsa, and venison is sauced with girolles
and Gewurztraminer. The idiosyncratic wine list is longer on bottle-aged Rioja
than claret, and is pretty good in Australia too. Prices open at £14.

CHEF: Linda Saunders PROPRIETORS: Paul and Linda Saunders OPEN: all week D only 8 (1
sitting) CLOSED: Jan and Feb MEALS: alc (main courses £17.50 to £22.50). Set D £30.50
SERVICE: none, card slips closed CARDS: Amex, MasterCard, Visa DETAILS: 20 seats. Private
parties: 24 main room. Car park. Vegetarian meals. Children's helpings. No smoking in
dining-room. Wheelchair access (3 steps; not WC). Music ACCOMMODATION: 8 rooms, all with
bath/shower. TV. Phone. B&B £75 to £100. Children welcome. High teas for children. Baby
facilities. No dogs

Round-ups

Looking for a suitable place to eat at can be a lottery, especially if you are travelling around the country with no set plans in mind. The Round-up section is intended to provide some interesting gastronomic possibilities, whether you find yourself in the West Country or the northern outposts of Scotland. Pubs are becoming increasingly valuable as sources of high-quality food, but the listings also include modest family-run enterprises in country towns, racy café/bars and ethnic restaurants in big cities, and a sprinkling of hotel dining-rooms in all parts of the land. Dip into this section and you are almost bound to find somewhere that suits your needs and your pocket. Entries are based on readers' recommendations supported by inspectors' reports. Sometimes restaurants appear in the Round-ups instead of the main-entry section because seasonal closures or weekly openings limit their usefulness, or because there are changes in the air, or because positive feedback has been thin on the ground. Reports on these places are especially welcome, as they help to broaden our coverage of good eating places in Britain. Round-up entries (outside London) are arranged alphabetically by location within England, Scotland, Wales and the Channel Islands.

England

● **ALDEBURGH** (Suffolk)
152 152 High Street, (01728) 454152. Small, informal high-street restaurant specialising in excellent fish 'straight from the beach' and cooked simply. Other recommended dishes have been caramelised onion and blue cheese tart followed by grilled salmon on noodles or crispy duck confit on a spiced parsnip pureé. Finish with rich mocha pop with brandy, or pear and ginger tarte Tatin.

● **ALTRINCHAM** (Greater Manchester)
Franc's 2 Goose Green, (0161) 941 3954. English owned, but Francophile by nature. Dishes are spelt out in French with useful tranlations and there are suggestions for recommended wines. Expect smoked chicken salad, chargrilled gigot of lamb, or fillets of snapper sauté in rosemary butter. A menu headed 'Les Snacks' satisfies famished shoppers with croque monsieur, baguettes and omelettes. There is a branch in Chester (see Round-up entry).

● **AMERSHAM** (Buckinghamshire)
Gilbey's 1 Market Square, (01494) 727242. Together with the Eton Wine Bar and Gilbey's in Ealing (see entry, London Round-ups) this trio of restaurants specialise in excellent wines at shop prices. Modern British cooking offers dishes such as roasted sweet pepper tart, or salmon and herb fish-cakes to start, followed by grilled Oxford sausages with parsley mash or pan-fried mullet with Parma ham. Finish with lemon tart or chocolate flan.

● **ARDINGTON** (Oxfordshire)
Boar's Head Church Street, (01235) 833254. New owners and a new chef moved into this Oxfordshire country pub in summer 1997 and – judging by reports – it seems to have taken a while for them to find their feet. Printed menus change monthly and the kitchen likes big flavours. Moules marinière is a generous bowlful, blackened duck breast comes on a bed of fine red cabbage, and the star of the dessert menu is burnt lemon cream. Carefully chosen wines.

● **BARHAM** (Kent)
Old Coach House Dover Road, (01227) 831218. 'Do not go to Barham, stay on the A2 until you see the sign for the hotel,' advises chef/proprietor Jean-Claude Rozard. He looks across the Channel for culinary inspiration, and his short dinner menus are old-school Gallic

to a T. Begin with soup, terrine or snails in garlic butter, move on to chicken in tarragon sauce and finish off with crème caramel or chocolate mousse. Also check the fish specials.

● **BARNARD CASTLE** (Co Durham)
Blagraves House 30–32 The Bank, (01833) 637668. A gem of a house, with 'bags of history', a stunning courtyard and a warmly furnished dining-room boasting an impressive moulded ceiling, mullioned windows and a stone fireplace. Best value is the fixed-price menu (served Tues to Fri) which features, say, chicken liver pâté with tomato chutney, braised brisket of beef in red wine sauce, and white chocolate mousse with berries. Affordable, 'worldly' wines.

Market Place Teashop 29 Market Place, (01833) 690110. 'Delightful establishment' in a converted gents' outfitters. Soups, vegetarian dishes and puddings have been given a hearty round of applause, and the kitchen is adept at everything from Welsh rarebit and salmon pie to rice-pudding and home-made scones. Pleasant staff.

● **BASLOW** (Derbyshire)
Cavendish Hotel Baslow, (01246) 582311. Gentrified country-house hotel with glorious views over Chatsworth Estate. Meals in the 'traditional English' restaurant run to salmon and seaweed terrine with red caviare and sour cream sauce, chargrilled calf's liver with citrus and Madeira sauce, and an assiette of chocolate desserts. Lighter dishes are served throughout the day in the conservatory-style Garden Room.

● **BATH** (Bath & N. E. Somerset)
Green Street Seafood Café Green Street, (01225) 448707. Small, casual restaurant on three floors above the Fish Market. Lunch from Tuesday to Saturday, but only open for dinner on Friday and Saturday. 'Spankingly fresh, high-quality' fish is the thing here. Apart from oysters, moules, fritto misto or fish soup, a particularly recommended dish has been roasted shellfish (mussels, crab, prawns, scallops and razorclams) with garlic, lemon and thyme, and French bread for

soaking up the liquor. Other specials might be seared tuna with North African salad, or roast cod with garlic mash. Open from Tue to Thur 11 to 3 and all day Fri and Sat.

Priory Hotel Weston Road, (01225) 331922. A Georgian Bath-stone house standing in two acres of grounds, yet only two miles from Bath. Set-price and à la carte menus (not cheap) might include poached quail's eggs in a pastry case with smoked chicken, medallions of venison and black pudding on an apple galette, and nougatine mousse to finish. Reasonably priced wine list. Swimming-pool and croquet lawn.

Rendez Vous Provençal 2 Margarets Buildings, (01225) 310064. Restaurant on two levels in a pedestrian street just off the Royal Crescent. Set-lunch menu (also available at dinner from Monday to Wednesday), otherwise a *carte* which changes every six to eight weeks. Expect gratin de fruits de mer, sauté d'agneau with aubergines and cream, rump steak with anchovy butter or salmon and plaice in saffron butter.

● **BERWICK-UPON-TWEED** (Northumberland)
Foxtons 26 Hide Hill, (01289) 303939. Café/bar and restaurant housed in a smart Georgian-fronted building. Light meals are served throughout the day, when sandwiches are supplemented by blackboard specials such as bruschetta with mozzarella or smoked haddock fish-cakes. Dinner heralds a few more up-market ideas such as air-dried beef with Parmesan or warm salad of scallops and salmon. Crème caramel with poached figs is a typical sweet. Fridays and Saturdays can get very noisy, warns owner David Foxton.

● **BEVERLEY** (East Riding of Yorkshire)
Cerutti 2 Beverley Station, (01482) 866700. Likeable East Riding address that has been owned by the Cerrutti family since 1989. Seafood shows up favourably in the shape of fish-cakes, crab thermidor, scallops with bacon and the like. Meat eaters and vegetarians could opt respectively for chicken with lemon and

herbs, and vegetable crêpes with cheese sauce. The original Cerrutti is a few miles away at 10 Nelson Street, Hull.

● **BIRKENHEAD** (Merseyside)
Banks Bistro   5 Rose Mount, (0151) 670 0446. Eclectic bistro food on the Wirral. Menus are peppered with ideas from the global larder and the kitchen flies the flag for free-range and organic produce. Here you might find black pudding with Bramley apple sauce, chicken teriyaki, Indonesian beef, and swordfish steak marinated in Cajun spices. Reporters greatly appreciate the friendly atmosphere and all-pervading helpfulness of the staff.

● **BIRMINGHAM** (West Midlands)
San Carlo   4 Temple Street, (0121) 633 0251. Real fun, 'just like being abroad', noted one fan. This lively, city-centre hot spot gets its charge from a happy-go-lucky crowd and waiters who are 'all colourful characters'. Pizzas and pasta (pappardelle with porcini, for example) receive regular plaudits, as do the fish specials. Fried squid and grilled halibut have been among recent successes.

● **BLACKMORE END** (Essex)
Bull   Blackmore End, (01371) 851037. Still very much a pub, although its prime function is now 'eating-house'. Current favourites from Christopher Bruce's blackboard menu include curried parsnip soup, chicken liver and red wine pâté, the vegetarian trio, and suprême of chicken in Dijon mustard sauce. Banana and toffee crumble is a good sweet. Service is 'second to none', and the wine list earns a universal 'thumbs up'.

● **BRADFORD** (West Yorkshire)
Bharat   502 Great Horton Road, (01274) 521200. A fixture of the Bradford Indian restaurant scene since 1987, and a shade more stylish than some ethnic neighbourhood places in the city. No surprises on the menu, but the kitchen serves up a classic repertoire ranging from tikkas and tandooris to dhansaks, biryanis and bhunas. Lunch and early-evening set menus are great value.

Mumtaz Paan House   390 Great Horton Road, (01274) 571 861. This bustling restaurant is a fair way from the city centre. A sign by the door says, 'You are entering an alcohol-free zone', but jugs of water are supplied and kept topped up. A limited menu gives the choice of dishes by the pound or half-pound: lamb, chicken or vegetable curries, or try bhel puris or garlic pakora with meat or fish. Efficient and speedy service.

Restaurant Nineteen   North Park Road, (01274) 492559. Sorely missed from the pages of the *Guide* last year, Stephen Smith and Robert Barbour's attractive property in a leafy suburb is open, although still on the market. Good-value three-course dinner offers quality dishes such as fillet of rabbit with tarragon rissoles and twice-baked cheese soufflé with smoked salmon for starters, followed by loin of English lamb with Mediterranean vegetables and wood pigeon stuffed with mushrooms and summer vegetables. Strawberry tartlets with a lemon curd ice-cream rounded off an 'excellent meal'. Well-chosen wines and 'charming' front-of-house complete the picture.

Symposium   7 Albion Street, (01274) 616587. Distinctively decorated wine bar/restaurant with black walls and a wacky mural painted across the ceiling. The atmosphere can be 'electric' and the food has plenty of up-to-the-minute touches. Chargrilled chicken breast with spinach and vine tomatoes, and roast sea bass on red onion confit with balsamic and pesto oil have been commended. Breads and ice-creams are made on the premises.

● **BRIGHOUSE** (West Yorkshire)
Brook's   6–8 Bradford Road, (01484) 715284. A collection of paintings and customers' doodles line the walls in Darrell Brook's eponymous bistro. His dinner menus also display a splash of colour. Expect anything from skewered marlin and shiitake mushrooms with pak choi and bean shoot salad to garlic-stuffed chicken breast with sweet potato crust and mango salsa. As a nostalgic starter, look for spam fritters with home-made tomato ketchup.

● **BRINKWORTH** (Wiltshire)
Three Crowns Brinkworth, (01666)
510366. Archetypal village pub. Snacks
from the blackboard might include jacket
potatoes, ploughman's or filled double-
decker rolls, while the conservatory
dining-room menu might offer quite
elaborate dishes of Somerset wild boar,
sauté strips of crocodile flamed with
whisky, or home-made seafood pie, all
served with a plentiful vegetable
selection. Extensive desserts might
include banoffi pie, sticky toffee and
bread-and-butter puddings, or melon and
Cointreau sorbet. Friendly staff.

● **BRISTOL** (Bristol)
Hullaballoos 16 Clifton Road, (0117)
973 2920. Formerly called Muset, but
recently brought into line with an ever-
expanding group of eating places run by
the same owners under the banner of
Hullaballoos. Nothing else has changed.
Expect high levels of atmosphere,
competitive prices, a BYO wine policy
(there is also a good list) and menus that
span everything from de-luxe
cheeseburgers to grilled salmon with
mussel and saffron sauce.
Red Snapper 1 Chandos Road, (0117)
973 7999. Lively modern venue in an
increasingly gentrified part of the city.
Menus are dominated by local and
seasonal supplies – including fish and
wild foods – and results draw enthusiastic
reports: warm salad of chicken livers and
bacon, and sea trout with samphire have
been well received. Snappy little wine list
with a bias towards the New World, plus
some heady bottled beers.

● **BURGH LE MARSH** (Lincolnshire)
Windmill 46 High Street, (01754)
810281. A change of owners since last
year at this small high street restaurant.
Set menus might include black pudding
and bacon salad, followed by salmon with
prawn sauce, finishing with meringue
with mango coulis. Good bread made on
the premises with their own 'Windmill'
flour. Excellent bin-end selection of
wines and a fine collection of vintage
ports.

● **BURLEY IN WHARFEDALE** (West
Yorkshire)
David Woolley's 78 Main Street, (01943)
864602. David Woolley is host and
showman, and his sense of theatre
defines the convivial mood in this local
restaurant. The setting is a stone cottage,
but the cooking is far from homespun:
here you might find anything from Far
Eastern contrivances to fashionable ideas
from the Med, and a nod or two to the
comforting tradition of English puddings.
A dish such as salmon teriyaki, with
cherry tomato, shrimp salsa and basil
linguine sums it up.

● **BURNHAM MARKET** (Norfolk)
Hoste Arms The Green, (01328) 738777.
Seventeenth-century former coaching-
inn, now a small hotel, overlooking the
village green. Reporters have approved
fresh Cromer crab and 'best ever' spicy
fish-cakes. Non-fish dishes might be roast
breast of pigeon, best end of English lamb
with dauphinoise potatoes, or chilli
chicken stir-fry. Finish with dark
chocolate mousse or iced orange parfait.
Friendly service.

● **BURPHAM** (West Sussex)
Burpham Country Hotel Burpham,
(01903) 882160. A pristine setting deep
in the South Downs is one reason for
visiting this tranquil hotel in a 200-year-
old hunting lodge. Formal meals are
served in the Rösti Room, where a fixed-
price dinner menu promises such things
as twice-baked cheese soufflé, and loin of
lamb with couscous and Madeira sauce
followed by a selection of home-made
desserts.

● **BURY ST EDMUNDS** (Suffolk)
Ravenwood Hall Rougham Green,
(01359) 270345. Secluded Tudor hall set
in seven acres of lawns and woodland.
Eat in the ornately timbered restaurant or
– for a special occasion – book the
converted Edwardian cricket pavilion.
Steamed meat pudding is a firm favourite,
but the kitchen deals industriously in
home-cured tuna with mustard dressing,
and oak-smoked fillet of beef with
chanterelles, plus fish and chips.

● **Buxton** (Derbyshire)
Columbine 7 Hall Bank, (01298) 78752.
A simple but attractive restaurant, with
new owners and chef. Tagliatelli with
shiitake mushrooms, lambs' liver in
mustard sauce, and rump steak with
cream and brandy sauce have all been
praised. A vegetarian menu, and two- or
three-course Festival Theatre menus are
also available. Varied and well-selected
wines. More reports, please.

● **Bythorn** (Cambridgeshire)
White Hart, Bennett's Restaurant,
Bythorn, (01832) 710226. The à la carte
menu for the restaurant in this whitewashed pub offers dishes such as Puy
lentil and salami salad, salmon tartare or
rabbit terrine, followed by pan-fried
saddle of venison, Barbary duck breast or
'catch of seafood'. Finish with chocolate
and rum parfait or pear gâteau.

● **Cambridge** (Cambridgeshire)
Sala Thong 35 Newnham Road, (01223)
323178. Long-running Thai restaurant
'unobtrusively located' by the mill pond.
Co-owner Supannee Taylor cooks a no-
frills 45-dish menu that runs from pork
toasts with sweet chilli sauce to honey-
roast duck with ginger pickle; reports
have praised the green chicken curry and
also pad thai (fried noodles with chicken
and prawns). Next door is an oriental
supermarket under the same ownership.

● **Campsea Ashe** (Suffolk)
Old Rectory Campsea Ashe, (01728)
746524. 'The nearest thing to eating in a
pre-war country house,' commented one
visitor. Stewart Bassett's creeper-clad
Georgian rectory has its own special
charm and his knowledgeable wine list is
guaranteed to hit the button. Fixed-price
dinners are served in the log-fired dining-
rooms or the summertime conservatory:
baked red mullet with a stew of mixed
peppers, roast marinated fillet of beef
with mustard and red wine sauce, then
raspberry shortcake might be the order of
the evening.

● **Canterbury** (Kent)
Café des Amis du Mexique 2 Westgate
Grove, (01227) 464390. Tex-Mex food

with a kick and a hefty helping of
authenticity is what is offered in this
informal venue. Classics such as nachos,
tostadas and enchiladas are backed up by
more unexpected offerings including
carnero à la Yucateca (citrus lamb stew
with coriander and achiote) or salsichas
(assorted sausages and Serrano ham with
chive mash and a chipotle-spiked sauce).

● **Cheam** (Surrey)
Bistro des Amis 22 Ewell Road, (0181)
643 8838. Friendly local venue that lives
up to its name, and offers good value
French cooking served by a team of
French staff. Favourites such as onion
soup and moules marinière put in regular
appearances, alongside carpaccio of
salmon, chicken breast with walnut
sauce, and orange crème brûlée.
Takeaway meals are a new attraction.

● **Cheltenham** (Gloucestershire)
Beaujolais 15 Rotunda Terrace, (01242)
525230. Smart venue in an up-market
Regency shopping street. The atmosphere
and décor are reminiscent of a town
house and the cooking has aspirations.
Well-reported lunches have featured
international dishes such as 'superb'
mussels with angel-hair pasta, venison
sausages with bubble and squeak and 'full
force' gravy, and pan-fried venison on
rösti with cranberry vinaigrette.

● **Chester** (Cheshire)
Franc's 14A Cuppin Street, (01244)
317952. French posters and a bicycle
hanging from the ceiling set the tone in
this lively, family-run bistro. Gallic
influences show in asparagus with
hollandaise, moules marinière and
profiteroles, but the kitchen also looks
further afield. Penne with mushrooms
and tarragon, and couscous with roasted
vegetables have been recommended of
late. Related to Franc's, Altrincham (see
Round-up entry).

● **Chettle** (Dorset)
Castleman Hotel Chettle, (01258)
830096. Former dower house in an estate
village, now functioning as a country
hotel and restaurant complete with
galleried hall and walled garden. Daily
dinner menus are built around local

supplies, and the repertoire might include guinea-fowl terrine with spiced damson ketchup, plaice fillets in white port and lime sauce, and 'excellent' walnut fudge tart. Sunday lunch has also been well received.

● CHICHESTER (West Sussex)
Comme Ça 67 Broyle Road, (01243) 788724. Converted old roadside pub with tables on a terrace and a lush garden. Recommended dishes have been crab salad with mango sauce, casserole of wild rabbit, and coffee ice-cream. Specials of the day might include courgette and hazelnut soup followed by a mini Selsey crab or pan-fried leg and breast of French partridge with a juniper berry sauce. Cheerful and prompt service.

● CHIPPING NORTON (Oxfordshire)
Morel's 2 Horsefair, (01608) 641075. Small restaurant at the entrance to the town with a good-value three-course dinner menu from Tuesday to Thursday, and a more expensive set dinner on Friday and Saturday. Menus might offer ballottine of guinea-fowl with foie gras terrine or 'omenière' of scottish salmon with avocado mousse, followed by pavé of veal with an olive tapénade or 'fish of the day'. Finish with pineapple parfait or home-made pear and almond tart.

● CHITTLEHAMHOLT (Devon)
Highbullen Chittlehamholt, (01769) 540561. Set in a 200-acre estate, this Victorian Gothic mansion stands on high ground with fine views. Set meals might include mushroom armenienne, loin of pork and iced apricot mousse. Outstanding, reasonably priced wine list. Attractions include an indoor swimming-pool and an 18-hole golf course.

● CLACTON ON SEA (Essex)
Wendle's 3 Rosemary Road, (01255) 426316. Amiable hosts Bernard and Diane Jinadasa have put their stamp on this popular local restaurant. Seafood from near and far shows up strongly in the shape of lobster salad, sea bass with lemon butter or red snapper with Creole sauce. Meaty alternatives might run to 'excellent' pheasant in red wine sauce, or Barbary duck breast cooked with wild

berries. A 'Royal Thai' menu is also served Tues to Fri evenings.

● CLANFIELD (Oxfordshire)
Clanfield Tavern Bampton Road, (01367) 810223. Built in 1610 and still a maze of beamed nooks and crannies. By contrast, the new conservatory zooms forward to the present day with its Italian tiles and bright fabrics. The food follows suit. Smoked salmon, steaks and pasta please the old guard, but the real action is on the specials board, where you might encounter breast of guinea-fowl stuffed with chicken and pistachio mousse on marsala sauce. Keenly priced wines.

● COGGESHALL (Essex)
Baumann's Brasserie 4–6 Stoneham Street, (01376) 561453. Paintings of all kinds adorn the walls of this well-supported Essex brasserie set in a historic timber-framed house. Light lunches are great value for Stilton soup and grilled Torbay sole with tomato, basil and champagne sauce. Otherwise, the full menu takes in braised belly pork with lentils and mushrooms, goose breast with blackcurrant juices, and butterscotch mousse.

● COLCHESTER (Essex)
North Hill Exchange Brasserie 19 North Hill, (01206) 769988. Cavernous brasserie in one of Colchester's best-known Georgian-fronted buildings. Fresh fish such as grilled sea bass with ginger, garlic and soy flesh out the printed menu, which runs from filo parcels of smoked chicken and Brie to rack of lamb with ratatouille, finishing with iced nougat terrine with apricot sauce. Good-value set lunches on weekdays.

● CONSTANTINE (Cornwall)
Trengilly Wartha Inn Nancenoy, (01326) 340332. Whitewashed pub in a lovely setting on a steep hillside, with a conservatory dining-room extension and bar. Reporters have commended crab-cakes with white wine sauce, salmon parcels with red peppers, meringues and good cheese platters. Other dishes from the set menu might be warm venison salad or crab strudel followed by roast saddle and leg of rabbit, finishing with

chocolate and prune terrine or apple and marzipan puff.

● **CORBRIDGE** (Northumberland)
Valley Old Station House, (01434) 633434/633923. Indian restaurant located in 'one of the world's oldest passenger railway stations' deep in the Tyne Valley. Customers can be ferried by train from Newcastle, courtesy of the management, and other deals are on offer. The menu ranges beyond tikkas and kormas into the realms of mangsho pesta ke shadi (spiced topside of beef with pistachio nuts). A second branch, Junction 397, is at the Old Station, Jesmond, Newcastle upon Tyne, tel (0191) 281 6397.

● **COWLAM** (East Riding of Yorkshire)
Old Rectory Cowlam, (01377) 267617. Converted Victorian rectory with glorious views across the Yorkshire Wolds towards the coast. Jeremy and Annabel Mooney offer a short dinner menu along the lines of cream of watercress soup or smoked trout, 'partridge in a pear tree' (breast of partridge with glazed pears) or grilled Dover sole, finishing with chocolate soufflé pudding or crespelle alla creme (rich cream-filled pancakes). If you are staying the night, breakfast comes highly recommended.

● **CUDDINGTON** (Buckinghamshire)
Annie Bailey's Ale & Eating House Upper Church Street, (01844) 291215. Once the Red Lion pub, now an 'ale and eating-house', named in honour of a landlady who ran the place in Victorian times. Jazzed-up blackboard menus advertise such things as seared tuna on rocket with coconut and lime dressing, breast of Lunesdale duck with confit of beetroot, and wild mushroom risotto with Parmesan biscuits.

● **DARLINGTON** (Co Durham)
Cottage Thai 94–96 Parkgate, (01325) 361717. Modest, family-run Thai restaurant with authentic decor and a 75-dish menu that majors in the staples of the cuisine. Satays, spring rolls and dim-sum precede soups, salads, noodles, curries and stir-fries; vegetarians are well

served and duck looms large among the list of specials. Drink Singha Thai beer.

● **DARTINGTON** (Devon)
Cott Inn Dartington, (01803) 863777. Venerable fourteenth-century thatched pub, once a favoured watering-hole for packhorse drivers, now a popular eating-house. Daily-changing evening menus promise a mixed bag of dishes from steak and kidney pie to Moroccan lamb curry, braised duck with blueberries and apple, and seared scallops with Parma ham, oyster mushrooms and truffle oil. Lunch is a hot and cold buffet.

● **DENSHAW** (Greater Manchester)
Rams Head Ripponden Road, (01457) 874802. On top of Saddleworth Moor, this old stone inn is more restaurant than pub, although anything from coffee and sandwiches to fixed-price and à la carte menus are available. Try daube de boeuf, fillet of sea bass on basil mash, or roast duck on puy lentils. Drink draught Tetley Bitter or Timothy Taylor Landlord, or choose from the large selection of wines by the glass.

● **DODDISCOMBSLEIGH** (Devon)
Nobody Inn Doddiscombsleigh, (01647) 252394. In a lovely remote location, the best pub we've ever stayed in'. Famous for its huge wine list, and praised for excellent food from ostrich liver pâté to Blue Vinney cheese soup, followed by loin of pork in a brandy chestnut and cream sauce or mixed seafood. Finish with baked American cheesecake or wonderful platters of cheese. First-class breakfasts, and friendly and efficient service add to the appeal.

● **EAST BUCKLAND** (Devon)
Lower Pitt East Buckland, (01598) 760243. In the centre of the hamlet near the church, this small restaurant in a peaceful house has charming service from owners Jerome and Suzanne Lyons. Among recommended dishes have been 'excellent' smoked trout and salmon roulade, 'locally reared' fillet steak with red wine and mushroom sauce, roast duckling with sage and apple purée, and king scallops with mushrooms and pancetta. Try apricot and almond tart

with crème fraîche to finish. Good-value wine list with plenty of half-bottles.

● **EAST STOKE** (Dorset)
Kemps East Stoke, (01929) 462563. Fine views of the Purbeck Hills are a bonus at Paul and Jill Warren's one-time Victorian rectory. Well-judged dinners feature such offerings as spinach and walnut terrine, salmon and crab fish-cakes and casseroled venison. Breads are home-baked and 'superb'-looking desserts might include crème brûlée and lemon mousse.

● **ELTON** (Cambridgeshire)
Loch Fyne Oyster Bar The Old Dairy, (01832) 280298. East of England sibling of the original oyster bar in Cairndow (see main entry, Scotland). In addition to Loch Fyne oysters, the flexible menu promises anything from shellfish bisque and marinated herring fillets to grilled salmon with cucumber sauce and a mighty lobster platter. Lively choice of wines and other beverages.

● **EVESHAM** (Worcestershire)
Evesham Hotel Coopers Lane, (01386) 765566. The dining- room of this Georgian hotel overlooks a superb Cedar of Lebanon in the garden. Supplies are chosen judiciously, influences are eclectic and menus are peppered with wacky comments. Chicken Seeberg is served on asparagus tips in a Cambozola cheese sauce, monkfish Raffael is garnished with deep-fried strips of ginger. Wines are a fascinating collection from everywhere except France and Germany, which have been excluded since 1977.

● **EXETER** (Devon)
La Chandelle 12 Lower North Street, (01392) 435953. Patriotically Gallic restaurant run by a dedicated husband-and-wife team where dinner menus offer generous helpings of classic dishes. Hot goats'-cheese salad, sauté guinea-fowl with armagnac in plum sauce, fillet of beef with green peppercorn sauce, and chocolate mousse have been recommended.

● **FAWLEY** (Buckinghamshire)
Walnut Tree Fawley, (01491) 638360. 'Incredibly peaceful' Chiltern country pub hidden away among the beechwoods. Choose between the bar menu or eat restaurant-style in the conservatory dining-room. Here you can expect such things as grilled goats' cheese en croute with raspberry vinaigrette, sauté calf's liver with wilted spinach and balsamic vinegar, and spiced apple torte. Well chosen wines.

● **FAWSLEY** (Northamptonshire)
Fawsley Hall Fawsley, (01327) 892000. Newly opened up-market baronial-style hotel in a large mainly Tudor mansion. The chef is Tim Johnson, who was in the 1997 *Guide* cooking at Simply Nico (see main entry, London). An early visitor recommended first-class salt cod and risotto of ceps, followed by lamb 'cooked to perfection' on a bed of ratatouille. Good selection of French wines. More reports, please.

● **FELSTED** (Essex)
Rumbles Cottage Braintree Road, (01371) 820996. Aptly named country restaurant in a white-painted 400-year-old cottage. Joy Hadley grows a lot of her own herbs and vegetables for a range of menus that try to offer something a bit different. Carrot and peanut butter soup, stuffed breast of chicken with Marsala, and Turkish Delight ice-cream are typical. The Guinea Pig menu introduces experimental new dishes to customers, with varying degrees of success.

● **FLETCHING** (East Sussex)
Griffin Inn Fletching, (01825) 722890. Sixteenth-century roadside inn popular with locals, tourists and walkers alike. The Pullan family offer a warm welcome and good service. Cosmopolitan dishes might include Fletching sausages, Thai prawn curry or fish pie. Desserts of prune and armagnac ice-cream, or savouries such as 'devils on horseback', have been recommended. Well-kept beers and a good selection of wines by the glass.

● **FLITWICK** (Bedfordshire)
Flitwick Manor Church Road, (01525) 712242. Plush Georgian country-house hotel. Limited choice set-price lunch menu might offer crostini of goats' cheese followed by roast rump of lamb. From the

more adventurous dinner menus try a gâteau of lambs' sweetbreads, followed by pan-fried suprême of chicken, finishing with almond soufflé or a trio of chocolate. Impressive, but highly priced wine list.

● **FORTON** (Lancashire)
El Nido Whinney Brow Lane, (01524) 791254. René and Tracey Mollinga's restaurant may be of old Lancashire stone, but the food is rooted in Spain. Tortillas, gazpacho and paella share the billing with duckling in Spanish liqueur sauce with strips of puff pastry. International brasserie dishes such as seared salmon, spinach lasagne, and chicken cooked in Thai spices are also on offer. Some quaffable Spanish wines head the list.

● **FUNTINGTON** (West Sussex)
Hallidays Watery Lane, (01243) 575331. Small restaurant converted from three cottages in the '60s. Chef Andrew Stephenson was in the 1996 *Guide* at the Angel in Midhurst (see Round-up entry, England). Much praised have been good bread, hot potato pancake with haddock ceviche, goats' cheese in filo with braised chicory, and main-course sea bass cooked niçoise style. Finish with lemon verbena, crème brûlée or chocolate cappuccino mousse. Good-value wine list. Closed Mon, Sat L and Sun D.

● **GEDNEY DYKE** (Lincolnshire)
Chequers Main Street, (01406) 362666. Friendly Fenland pub. Daily fresh seafood selection might include Cromer salad, or turbot fillet with watercress sauce. From the *carte* choose Bradan Orach (traditional strongly smoked salmon), or polenta cake with provençale sauce, followed by seared suprême of guinea-fowl or Cajun spiced chicken. Finish with iced orange soufflé or fresh fruit in a brandy-snap basket. Excellent choice of real ales, plus nine house wines, and wines of the month by the glass.

● **GILLAN** (Cornwall)
Tregildry Hotel Gillan, (01326) 231378. Delightful small hotel with a spectacular setting overlooking Gillan Creek, Helford River and Falmouth Bay. Dishes live up to their menu descriptions. Try a gâteau

of avocado and Atlantic prawns or a salad of tomato, mozzarella and basil, followed by poached fillets of fresh salmon or roast rack of local lamb with a herb crust. Puddings might be bread-and-butter or a brandy-snap basket with Cornish ice-cream and a selection of berries. Excellent breakfasts.

● **GOSFIELD** (Essex)
Green Man The Street, (01787) 472746. English 'country-style' food in the lively setting of a traditional Essex hostelry. Daily menus are chalked on blackboards: game soup with sherry, steak and kidney pudding, and blackberry pie with ice-cream are typical. Service is 'never less than first-class', confirmed one couple who have been eating here for more than a decade. Wines and other tipples are also taken seriously.

● **GRAMPOUND** (Cornwall)
Eastern Promise 1 Moor View, (01726) 883033. Popular place, packed to the gills, serving Peking and Szechuan cuisine to an appreciative crowd. Service by mostly non-Chinese staff who cope admirably, but food is firmly rooted in Asia. Seafood stands out with excellent fresh scallops with spring onion and garlic, plus sea bass and mussels. Of non-fish dishes, crispy duck has been particularly recommended.

● **GREAT YARMOUTH** (Norfolk)
Seafood Restaurant 85 North Quay, (01493) 856009. Loyally supported family-run restaurant in what was once the fish capital of East Anglia. Christopher and Miriam Kikis have lived and worked here since 1979 and their presence ensures consistency. Seafood dishes of the old school are their speciality: lobsters are kept live in tanks, and the menu ranges from skate with black butter to Dover sole with Dublin Bay prawn sauce. 'Painstaking', friendly service.

● **GUILDFORD** (Surrey)
The Gate 3 Milkhouse Gate, (01483) 576300. Small two-storey restaurant in an alleyway off the high street. Broadly Mediterranean cooking has received approval for excellent Caesar salad, seared tuna loin and scallops, oysters with

red onion salsa, and magret of duck 'cooked to perfection' with mustard mash and kale (both at an extra charge). Good service.

● **HARROGATE** (North Yorkshire)
La Bergerie 11–13 Mount Parade, (01423) 500089. Refugees from the nearby Conference Centre often seek sanctuary in this dyed-in-the-wool French restaurant on the ground floor of a corner terrace house. Cassoulet Toulousaine and gratin de coquilles St Jacques are listed as specialities; otherwise the menu offers warm salad of pigeon breast and avocado, monkfish in puff pastry with basil and anise butter sauce, and frangipane tart with pears.
Bettys 1 Parliament Street, (01423) 502746. The original of a mini-chain of North Country tea rooms, founded in 1919 by Swiss confectioner Frederick Belmont. Cakes, breads, scones and much more are produced in the bakery, and the menu extends to Yorkshire rarebits, Swiss rösti and warm chicken and bacon salad. Good choice of teas, not to mention Alsatian wines.
Garden Room Harlow Carr Botanical Gardens, Crag Lane, (01423) 505604. 'A great favourite' with visitors to Harlow Carr Botanical Gardens. Daytime snacks and light meals call into play open sandwiches, cakes, pastries and ice-creams. The dinner menu (served Thursday to Saturday) opens out into the realms of terrine of smoked salmon with anchovy and caper butter, grilled belly pork with mustard mash, black pudding and apple compote, and maple syrup and pecan crème brûlée.
Rick's Just for Starters 7 Bower Road, (01423) 502700. Build an entire meal from the selection of starters in Rick Hodgson's cleverly devised enterprise. Pick as much or as little as you like from a line-up that could include Caesar salad, grilled Cajun chicken strips with peppers and red onion marmalade, and spinach and oyster mushroom crêpes. Added to this are a handful of main courses, such as poached fillet of salmon with asparagus and hollandaise sauce.

● **HARVINGTON** (Worcestershire)
Mill at Harvington Anchor Lane, (01386) 870688. Severely flooded in spring 1998, this riverside hotel was hoping to re-open in the autumn, with first-rate country cooking based on seasonal ingredients. The lunch menu might offer cannelloni, pasta with pesto, or 'the bookmaker's sandwich (hot slices of beef fillet). Evening menus have included warm duck salad and mushroom croûte, followed by blanquette of veal and salmon in pastry. Finish with strawberry shortbread. Well-annotated wine list.

● **HEREFORD** (Herefordshire)
Café at All Saints High Street, (01432) 370415. 'Quite a remarkable place,' wrote one correspondent of this unusual venue, in a fully functioning church that provides its congregation with sustenance both spiritual and gastronomic. Equally popular with locals and the many tourists who come to Hereford, it offers afternoon coffee and cakes, and a menu of more substantial vegetarian dishes such as spicy Thai salad, cheese and chilli muffins, sandwiches (maybe of home-made olive bread filled with pesto, roast courgettes, mozzarella and tomato), and various quiches and casseroles. Only open from 8.30 to 5.30 Mon to Sat.

● **HOUGHTON CONQUEST** (Bedfordshire)
Knife & Cleaver The Grove, (01234) 740387. Sympathetically converted country pub that now calls itself a 'restaurant-with-rooms'. Meals are served in a pleasantly light conservatory dining-room, where regularly changing menus boast Parma ham and cep risotto, confit of duck with orange, bacon and tarragon, and gooseberry strudel, plus interesting fish specials. Well-considered wines.

● **ILKLEY** (West Yorkshire)
Bettys 34 The Grove, (01943) 608029. One of a Yorkshire chain of tea rooms offering patisserie, breads, scones and plenty of other choices, plus more solid dishes such as rarebits, salads, or Swiss rösti. Excellent choice of teas.

● **IVY HATCH** (Kent)
Plough High Cross Road, (01732) 810268. Kentish 'restaurant and bar' specialising in French-style food with a few English gestures. On the one hand there might be snails in garlic butter, rack of lamb with provençale herbs and pork cutlets dijonnaise; on the other, potted shrimps, lambs' liver and bacon, and steak with Stilton and port sauce. Ploughman's, quiches and other bar snacks are also served at lunch-time.

● **KING'S LYNN** (Norfolk)
Riverside Kings Lynn Arts Centre, 27 King Street, (01553) 773134. Five-hundred year-old listed building with some of the best river views you could wish for, plus tables on the terrace in fine weather. Lunch is a simple, honest affair, taking in lemon chicken salad, seafood pasta and the like. Dinners move up a gear for leek, coriander and goats'-cheese tart, baked sea bass with butter sauce, and roast duck with rhubarb and ginger sauce. Separate vegetarian menu.

● **KINTBURY** (Berkshire)
Dundas Arms 53 Station Road, (01488) 658263. Great views and an enviable waterside setting by the Kennet & Avon Canal are crowd-pulling assets at this long-serving Berkshire pub/restaurant. Another bonus is landlord David Dalzell-Piper's magisterial list of more than 200 fine wines from all corners of the globe. Bar and restaurant menus try to keep pace with home-cured gravlax, breast of duck with lemon-grass sauce, grilled rump steak and chocolate St Emilion.

● **LANGTOFT** (East Riding of Yorkshire)
The Old Mill Mill Lane, (01377) 267284. Two centuries ago, this was a farmhouse (with a corn mill attached), now it functions as a personally run hotel. Dinner menus promise such things as warm Roquefort cheesecake, medallions of beef with whisky and grain mustard sauce, and herb-crusted rack of local lamb; or choose 'something fishy', such as sauté monkfish and king prawns with tomato cream sauce and rice.

● **LEEDS** (West Yorkshire)
Bibis Minerva House, 16 Greek Street, (0113) 243 0905. Founded in 1974, this long-running trattoria does a particularly good line in blackboard specials. Lobster and asparagus risotto and seared duck breast with mirabelle plums are typically up-beat offerings, otherwise plunder the extensive main menu for pizzas, pasta and hearty dishes such as braised ham shank with hot pickled cabbage. Well-spread wine list.

La Grillade 31–33 East Parade, (0113) 2459707. High-ceilinged French brasserie with a balcony and tables outside for summer eating. Typical main courses might take in black pudding with apple, or canard a l'orange, while desserts have included mousse au chocolat, crème caramel, and the tart of the day. Good French wines. Express lunch menu for those in a hurry.

Olive Tree Oaklands, (0113) 256 9283. Likeable venue that evokes Greece in the setting of an English Victorian house on a city ring road. The long menu offers Greek-Cypriot dishes in abundance, with starters coming out on top: 'exquisitely cooked' kotopitakia pastries filled with chicken, and garlicky mashed aubergines have been recommended. Mains are mostly high in protein, desserts ooze honey syrup. Solicitous service and a 'very pleasant hands-on owner'.

● **LEICESTER** (Leicestershire)
Heath's Seafood Restaurant 169 Evington Road, (0116) 273 3343. Fishily decorated, small seafood restaurant. Downstairs for smokers, and a more spacious non-smoking room upstairs. Good-value set-lunch menus, more expensive evening *carte*. Try dressed Scarborough crab, oyster chowder with lardons and croûtons, or seafood casserole with a plentiful selection of fish. Puddings tend to be straightforward apple crumble or strawberry and raspberry bavarois.

● **LICHFIELD** (Staffordshire)
Chandlers Corn Exchange, (01543) 416688. Light, airy attractive restaurant

with a central atrium, doing brasserie-style cooking with Italian and English overtones. Good-value *plat du jour* plus a *carte* have produced recommendations for marinated duck breast salad, grilled sardines, seared salmon, and treacle tart. Reasonably priced wine list. Attentive and efficient service.

● LIVERPOOL (Merseyside)
Armadillo 31 Mathew Street, (0151) 236 4123. Convenient for tourists visiting 'Beatle-land.' Lunch and early-supper menus are good value for Kiwi mussels with chilli salsa, pan-fried chicken and sweetcorn fritters, and lemon tart. Dinners are fleshed out with a few more elaborate ideas such as roast monkfish with Parma ham and sauerkraut. Commendable home-baked bread.
Beluga Bar 24 Wood Street, (0151) 708 8896. City centre bar/restaurant with a friendly, relaxed atmosphere. Go for sandwiches and soup in the bar at lunch-time, or more substantial Cumberland sausage with herb mash and black pudding, or calamari and mussels in a tomato sauce. Dishes from the evening *carte* might take in spinach-wrapped salmon mousse or crab and noodle soup, followed by a tian of crumbed veal or roast duck breast with pancetta. Closed on Sunday.
Number Seven Café 7 Falkner Street, (0151) 709 9633. Contemporary style restaurant (once three shops) related to Ziba (see entry below), with adjacent deli selling cheese, olives etc., plus a contemporary art gallery at the rear. Choose from Thai fish soup or aubergine pâté followed by lamb meat balls or vegetable biriyani with tarka dahl. Chocolate mousse or sticky toffee are typical puddings.
Ziba 15–19 Berry Street, (0151) 708 8870. Sister restaurant to Number Seven Café (see entry above) in a converted car showroom with stark modern design. Start with poached egg with lobster and scallops or pan-fried foie gras, followed by 'particularly good' grilled fillet of turbot with roasted artichoke or Goosnargh duck with water chestnut rösti. Desserts

might include Gypsy tart or rum and raisin brûlée; ale is brewed in the owners' micro-brewery next door. More reports, please.

● LONGDON GREEN (Staffordshire)
Red Lion Inn Longdon Green, (01543) 490250. A welcoming pub on the edge of Cannock Chase forest. Blackboard menus yield avocado vinaigrette or rich home-made chicken liver paté, followed by whole grilled lemon sole, or half a roast Gressingham duck with Cointreau gravy. Finish with summer pudding or lemon tart.

● LONG MELFORD (Suffolk)
Chimneys Hall Street, (01787) 379806. Pleasing neighbourhood restaurant housed in a 400-year-old, timber-framed building complete with inglenook fireplaces and exposed beams. Menus run along the lines of terrine of red mullet with red pepper dressing, pot-roast guinea-fowl with grapes and Madeira, and glazed pineapple with honey and almond ice-cream. Sound wine list from Lay & Wheeler.

● LOWER ODDINGTON (Gloucestershire)
Fox Inn Lower Oddington, (01451) 870555. Sympathetically extended country pub in a 'lovely' Cotswold village with a pleasant interior and bags of genuine atmosphere. Recent successes from the regularly changing menu have included a 'quad' of Cotswold sausages, delicate salmon fish-cakes and 'perfect', chunky moussaka. Banana ice-cream with hot toffee sauce makes a fine finish. Better-than-average pub wines.

● LOW LAITHE (North Yorkshire)
Carters Knox Manor Summerbridge, (015423) 780607. Attractively converted eighteenth-century flax mill in the heart of the Yorkshire Dales. The kitchen works to a menu that offers ample choice across the board. Roast best-end of Nidderdale lamb with roast garlic and rosemary jus has impressed greatly, but the choice spans everything from seafood pancake to lemon tart. Relaxed atmosphere, friendly service. Related to the Sportsman's Arms,

Wath-in-Nidderdale (see main entry, England).

● **LUDLOW** (Shropshire)
Dinham Hall (01584) 876464. Historic 200-year-old mansion a stone's throw from Ludlow Castle. Daily fixed-price dinner menus (anything from two to five courses) run along the lines of apple and mushroom soup, foie gras terrrine, paupiette of salmon with basil beurre blanc, and vanilla and lavender crème brûlée.

● **LYMINGTON** (Hampshire)
Old Bank House 68 High Street, (01590) 671128. Reliable neighbourhood address noted for its 'casual' atmosphere and lively cooking. Chef/proprietor Miles Wickes offers his customers 'perfectly cooked' seared scallops with chilli sauce, salad of home-smoked duck breast with honey and mustard dressing, and chargrilled chicken breast with sweet pepper sauce. Service is 'willing and friendly'.

● **MANCHESTER** (Greater Manchester)
Brasserie St Pierre 57–63 Princess Street, (0161) 228 0231. Stylishly appointed city brasserie with a modern menu of mainly Anglo-French dishes: smoked haddock with poached egg, new potatoes and grain mustard, or calf's liver and bacon with bubble and squeak on the one hand; salad niçoise or Bourgogne-style beef fillet with parsnip purée on the other. Closed Sat L, Sun, Mon D.
Cafe Istanbul 79–81 Bridge Street, (0161) 833 9942. This basic but popular authentic Turkish café is fast approaching two decades of providing a wide selection of hot and cold meze, chargrilled meats and kebabs, and slow-cooked stews to appreciative Mancunians. Finish with home-made pastries, sweets and Turkish coffee. Reasonable prices, especially the bargain three-course lunch. Good service and a decent wine list complete the picture.
Market Restaurant 104 High Street, (0161) 834 3743. Small high street restaurant, where recommended dishes from the *carte* have included tiropitakia (deep-fried cheese and herb filled filo

pastry triangles), 'excellent' asparagus wrapped in prosciutto, roast cod fillet with a gratin of potatoes and celeriac, and date, almond and apricot macaroon cake. There are wonderful home-made chutneys and a prize-winning cinnamon meringue with white chocolate cream, dark chocolate sauce and cherries poached in wine. Good beers and wine; friendly, knowledgeable service. They also run regular 'pudding club' meals and sales of crockery, glass, olives and chutney.
Le Meridien Victoria & Albert Hotel Water Street, (0161) 832 1188. Riverside warehouse conversion. Modern cooking in the Sherlock Holmes restaurant covers the world. Clues to the style are found in sushi of crab and tuna, salad of Clonakilty black pudding with pancetta and quail's eggs, followed by turban of gingered monkfish, or veal and marjoram sausage with pommes mousseline. Finish with banana and caramel sablé or apple and calvados mousse. Café Maigret offers lighter meals. New chef, so more reports please.
Sanam 145–151 Wilmslow Rd, (0161) 224 1008/8824. Decorated in 'true over-the-top Indian style', this reliable curry house reminded one reporter of 'a real Indian restaurant you might find in Delhi'. Its authenticity is borne out by its popularity with local Asian families, who are also tempted in by its excellent value for money. Sweets are 'a real delight': sample the range of 20 different kinds of burfi, or traditional hot gulab jamun. Strictly no alcohol.
Yang Sing 3 Charlotte Street, (0161) 236 2200. Fire may have ravaged their Princess Street building, forcing Yang Sing into temporary premises, but they are back in business and plan to return to the original site in spring 1999. A daytime dim-sum fan enjoyed steamed baby octopus, fungus roll and stuffed chicken wings, while Peking duck and steamed Dover sole have met with approval at dinner. Finish with egg tarts or fruit platter. Keep your ears open for the move

back (they expect to keep the same telephone number).

● **MANNINGTREE** (Essex)
Stour Bay Café 39-43 High Street, (01206) 396687. The Brights took over the café in August 1997, and with chef Stas Anastasiades are producing a modern menu featuring lots of local fish. Starters have included crab and corn bisque and the chef's own Greek salad, while main courses run to sea bass with 'woked' vegetables, pickled ginger and soy sauce, or a trio of Gressingham duck. Fruits de mer contains lobster, oysters, crab, prawns, whelks and clams, and comes with the house spicy mayonnaise. 'Friendly and relaxed' atmosphere.

● **MELLOR** (Greater Manchester)
Devonshire Arms Longhurst Lane, (0161) 427 2563. Stone-built pub in a Manchester suburb. Still very much a local, but with much emphasis on food. A short menu has permanent fixtures such as gravadlax, and mussel chowder, while daily specials might include dim-sum with sweet-and-sour dip, pea and ham soup, followed by chicken masala or pan-fried breast of duck with cranberry sauce. Various crêpes are available from Grand Marnier to lemon, or try chocolate sponge.

● **MELMERBY** (Cumbria)
Village Bakery Melmerby, (01768) 881515. Daytime café/teahouse offering 'honest-to-goodness' home cooking. Filling soups, 'exciting' salads and dishes such as tuna baked with marinated vegetables get the thumbs up. Otherwise a cup of tea with scones, cakes or biscuits goes down well. Drink iced coffee in summer, or Dunkerton's cider, organic Golden Promise beer or home-made lemonade. A new chef was being appointed as we went to press, so more reports, please.

● **MERLEY** (Dorset)
Les Bouviers Oakley Hill, (01202) 889555. James Coward's comfortably designed restaurant – complete with a 'delightful conservatory' – is a godsend for the denizens of Bournemouth, Poole and beyond. Very pretty French cooking

is the order of the day, and lunch has drawn rave reviews for poached egg on brioche with smoked salmon, ballottine of chicken with shredded courgettes and a top-drawer lemon tart with clotted cream.

● **MIDHURST** (West Sussex)
Angel Hotel North Street, (01730) 812421. Redoubtable coaching inn that is very much the focus of Midhurst's social life. Formal meals based around fashionable ingredients are served in the spacious and airy Cowdray Room, while the Brasserie offers similar dishes in more casual surroundings; otherwise opt for a snack in the bar. There was a change of chef as we went to press, so more reports, please.

● **MILBORNE PORT** (Somerset)
Old Vicarage Sherborne Road, (01963) 251117. The owners, who used to run Noughts 'n' Crosses in Ealing, have taken to the country life. The vicarage may be nineteenth-century, but the food is Anglo-French by way of Asia, thanks partly to chef Anthony Ma's Hong Kong training. Watch out for pork and crabmeat in red pepper, ribeye beef with onion sauce, and an eighteenth-century trifle. Open for D only, Fri and Sat, plus bank hols.

● **MILTON ERNEST** (Bedfordshire)
Strawberry Tree 3 Radwell Road, (01234) 823633. Family-run country cottage restaurant in a small village, with an immaculate garden. Only open for lunch from Wednesday to Sunday and dinner from Thursday to Saturday. Special 'menu du jour' at lunch-time, and also a more expensive set menu (£28). Start with scallops and black pudding followed by Old Spot pork chop with morels and spinach, spring lamb cutlets, or ballottine of duck. Desserts might be chocolate fondant or poached pear with ginger ice-cream. More reports, please.

● **MORPETH** (Northumberland)
La Brasserie 59 Bridge Street, (01670) 516200. A customer-friendly Northumbrian double act. On the ground floor is Henri's Bar, an all-day free-house with a vast menu covering everything

from ciabatta sandwiches to tuna steak with chorizo and potato. Upstairs is the long-serving brasserie, where the same menu is bolstered by blackboard specials such as herb-crusted rack of lamb with leek and mushroom sauce.

● **NEWENT** (Gloucestershire)
Three Choirs Restaurant Newent, (01531) 890223. Large airy restaurant overlooking rolling vineyards. Recommended dishes have included chicken, ham and leek terrine with chutney, bacon salad with blue cheese dressing, and chargrilled chicken fillets. Interesting selection of breads and attentive, but not obtrusive service. Drink the estate's own wines.

● **NORTHALLERTON** (North Yorkshire)
Bettys 188 High Street, (01609) 775154. One of a mini-chain of tea rooms founded in 1919 by Frederick Belmont, a Swiss confectioner. Serving breads, cakes, scones and other baked items, alongside more substantial lunchtime salads, soups or Yorkshire rarebits. Excellent choice of teas and patisserie.

● **NORTH BOVEY** (Devon)
Blackaller Hotel North Bovey, (01647) 440322. 'All our produce comes from within the county,' write the owners of this idyllic Devon woollen mill on the banks of the Bovey. Organic Jacob's lamb, fish from the Teign and the Dart, home-produced honey and West Country cheeses all find their way onto the four-course dinner menus (Tue to Sat only). Start with salad of smoked chicken breast, finish with strawberry meringue roulade.

● **NORTON** (Shropshire)
Hundred House Hotel Bridgnorth Road, (01952) 730353. Roadside hotel with brasserie and restaurant menus. The former offers soup, pâtés and salads. Approved dishes from the restaurant's *carte* have been potato cake with onion rings and hollandaise, bruschetta, and 'nicely pink' rack of lamb with dauphinoise potatoes. Desserts could include crème brûlée or apple tart. Wonderful herb garden.

● **NORWICH** (Norfolk)
The Aquarium 22 Tombland, (01603) 629358. Laid-back, smart and airy restaurant offering modern British/Mediterranean-style food. The *carte* has dishes such as grilled goats'-cheese salad, and deep-fried corn cakes with chilli sauce, followed by mixed fish stew, hot and sour swordfish curry, and oriental duck. Desserts tend to be rich: chocolate and Amaretto torte, or vanilla cheesecake with fresh strawberries. There is also an excellent-value two-course lunch menu. Well-paced, friendly and informal service.
Brasted's 8–10 St Andrews Hill, (01603) 625949. A change of chef as we went to press for this small, city-centre restaurant. Well-tried ideas are based on good ingredients, as in spanking fresh lobster salad or loin of rabbit with baby onions and mushrooms. Finish with orange and Muscat jelly or bread-and-butter pudding with 'super smooth' vanilla ice-cream. More reports, please.

● **NOTTINGHAM** (Nottinghamshire)
Merchants Restaurant 29–31 High Pavement, (0115) 958 9898. In the Lace Market area next to St Mary's church, this restaurant opened in May with chef Clive Dixon, previously in the *Guide* at Lords of the Manor, Upper Slaughter and Hunstrete House, Hunstrete (see main entries, England). One, two or three dishes can be taken from the lunch menu. Early visitors choosing from the *carte* have enjoyed a terrine of salmon and brill, and ravioli of roast chicken with wild mushrooms, followed by cod with a basil crust and cutlets of new season's lamb. Reports, please.
Le Pub Français 9 Warser Gate, (0115) 955 6060. A new chef had just arrived at this cafe/bar/restaurant as we went to press, but the style remains much as before. The setting is the rejuvenated Lace Market, the atmosphere is buzzy, and the menu goes Gallic with grilled tuna and basil tartlet, herb-roasted rack of lamb with provençale vegetables, and fillet of pork with calvados and caramelised apples. Closed Sundays.

Saagar 473 Mansfield Road, (0115) 962 2014/969 2860. Long-running suburban Indian out of the city close to Mapperley Park. An extensive menu features mainly Punjabi dishes with a few regional detours and in-house specialities. Aubergine paneer, achar chicken (cooked in pickled mustard seed oil), South Indian kaalan lamb (with mango, yoghurt and coconut), and king prawn 'dil ruba' (with apricots, mint, cream and tomato) sound promising.

● ODIHAM (Hampshire)
Grapevine 121 High Street, (01256) 701122. Good-value deals are a feature of Matthew and Penny Fleet's popular bistro-restaurant. Two-course 'lunchtime quickies', tapas and an 'early-bird' menu (6 to 7.30pm) are just some of the options. Otherwise the kitchen works to a monthly menu that might range from chargrilled shark loin with cucumber and watercress salsa to sirloin steak au poivre, with puddings such as blackcurrant and cassis tart bringing up the rear.

● ORFORD (Suffolk)
Butley-Orford Oysterage Market Hill, (01394) 450277. A Suffolk institution comprising smokehouse, shop and functionally furnished café rolled into one. Best bets are the oysters from Butley Creek, no-frills crustaceans, excellent smoked salmon and other assemblages of cured fish. Over-run during the summer, a great favourite with the Aldeburgh Festival set, but less frantic in winter, when opening times are limited.

● OVER STRATTON (Somerset)
New Farm Over Stratton, (01460) 240584. The setting may be an old farm building that has been in the Bond family for five generations, but the cooking has vibrant, eclectic overtones. Monthly-changing menus could produce, say, Thai fish-cakes with sweet and sour vinaigrette; roast duck with chilli, fig and sun-dried tomato sauce; or polenta pancake with peperonata and smoked cheese. Regular theme nights.

● OXFORD (Oxfordshire)
Gee's 61A Banbury Road, (01865) 553540. An Oxford landmark, famed for its meticulously restored Victorian conservatory, which houses the dining-room. Menus are peppered with up-to-the-minute ingredients and the kitchen handles them competently. Chargrilled boned quails with braised red cabbage and parsnip galette, and grilled halibut with Swiss chard and red pesto show the style. Tarte Tatin is a typical sweet.

Restaurant Elizabeth 82 St Aldates, (01865) 242230. High-ceilinged, spacious first-floor dining-room in this long-serving restaurant. Offerings might include 'mouth-watering' prawns on a bed of rice with aïoli, then rack of lamb served 'pink and succulent', or medallions of monkfish wrapped in bacon. First-class crème brûlée or a creamy syllabub to finish. Friendly, informative, but unobtrusive service.

● PADSTOW (Cornwall)
Brock's Restaurant The Strand, (01841) 532565. Bright, airy restaurant near the harbour, decorated in yellow with oak beams and shuttered windows. Short *carte* at lunch-time, set dinner menu. Recommended dishes have included cep risotto, smoked trout, duck confit and fillets of John Dory. Finish with armagnac parfait or dark chocolate marquise. Excellent service. Mostly New World wines, with a recommended Chilean house wine under £10. More reports, please.

● POLPERRO (Cornwall)
Kitchen The Coombes, (01503) 272780. Diminutive cottage restaurant in a village that gets its full quota of seasonal tourists and holidaymakers. Ian and Vanessa Bateson provide sustenance for the visitors with cosmopolitan-sounding dishes such as duck, pork and chestnut terrine, crab Malabar, and paneer and chickpea korma. Open for dinner only Tue to Sat, Easter to October.

● POOL IN WHARFEDALE (West Yorkshire)
Monkman's Bistro Pool Bank, (0113) 284 1105. Chris Monkman's 'bistro with bedrooms' is a vibrant, buzzy place offering great value and sound, modern cooking for young and old alike. Set

lunches in particular have been praised, and reporters have mentioned filo parcels stuffed with goats' cheese and red peppers, chicken suprême on couscous, and Eton Mess. A smaller branch, Monkman's Cookhouse is at 52 The Grove, Ilkley, tel. (01943) 816496.

● **RICHMOND** (Surrey)
Petersham Hotel Nightingale Lane, (0181) 940 7471. Breathtaking views over one of the best-known stretches of the Thames are a big plus at this Victorian mansion on Richmond Hill. Seasonal fish and game show up well on the menus in Nightingales Restaurant, and the kitchen also delivers such things as gâteau of asparagus and avocado, baked loin of venison and 'sharp lemon tart'. Polite, prompt service.

● **SAFFRON WALDEN** (Essex)
Old Hoops 15 King Street, (01799) 522813. 'Popular local spot' with a good buzz and food that offers great value for money. Mussel and watercress soup is a signature dish, and there have been enthusiastic votes for fillet of lamb dijonnaise; calf's liver with green peppercorns, blackcurrants and cassis; and Grand Marnier choux buns. Caring, hands-on chef/proprietor and 'splendid, personalised, smiling service'.

● **SALISBURY** (Wiltshire)
Harpers 6–7 Ox Row, (01722) 333118. Rather sparse décor, but excellent food. Snacks also available, plus vegetarian dishes and a children's menu. Starters run to marinated king prawns wrapped in filo pastry, and pasta in a tomato sauce with fresh ginger and chilli. Red snapper with minted pea purée has been a recommended main course, or try ragoût of New Forest venison in a redcurrant sauce. Puddings might be home-made treacle tart or iced lemon cream. Good-value set-price menus also available. A new chef is assisting Adrian Harper in the kitchen, so more reports please.

● **SAMLESBURY** (Lancashire)
Campions Samlesbury, (01772) 877641. Only five minutes from junction 31 of the M6, in the shadow of the Whitbread brewery, this former pub offers a dailytwo-course menu, plus a *carte* and daily specials. Recommended dishes have included mussels with a tomato and chorizo sauce, 'well-flavoured' pork chops with black-pudding mash, and roast baby gammon joint with cranberries. Good frangipane tart and excellent sticky toffee pudding.

● **SCARBOROUGH** (North Yorkshire)
The Restaurant, Stephen Joseph Theatre Westborough, (01723) 368463. First-floor restaurant with 'modern chrome' décor and views of the street below. An 'all-day menu' features light, brasserie-style dishes along the lines of pork and chive sausage with mash, Spanish omelette, smoked salmon with scrambled eggs plus a few sandwiches and puddings. A more extensive evening *carte* puts in an appearance when the theatre season starts in April.

● **SEAVIEW** (Isle of Wight)
Seaview Hotel High Street, (01983) 612711. Small hotel in a one-way street near the sea decorated with marine photographs. Try the Seaview special – hot Island crab with cream and spices and a crusty cheese top – or choose from mushroom and liver pâté, smoked fish mash with pesto toast, and sea bass with a saffron sauce. Efficient service.

● **SHEFFIELD** (South Yorkshire)
Greenhead House 84 Burncross Road, (0114) 246 9004. Homely and welcoming atmosphere in this small restaurant only open for light lunches on Thur and Fri, and dinner from Wed to Sat. Expensive four-course evening menus offer Mediterranean vegetable salad, crab tartlets with grilled salmon roulade, and strawberry soufflé, while lunches run to crispy duck salad or navarin of lamb with couscous. Finish with chocolate and Bacardi cheesecake. Fairly priced wine list.

● **SHERBORNE** (Dorset)
Pheasants 24 Greenhill, (01935) 815252. Family-run restaurant-with-rooms occupying an old terraced building in the town centre. The interior might be described as 'English traditional bourgeois' and the cooking is based

around Anglo-French classics with a few personal touches. Those who approve of the place have enjoyed creamy mussel soup, marinated fillet of beef with girolles and red wine sauce, and chilled chocolate and rum soufflé.

● **SISSINGHURST** (Kent)
Rankins' Restaurant The Street, (01580) 713964. 'Delightful', enthused one couple who also commended the 'charming' service in Hugh and Lee Rankin's converted village shop. Fixed-price dinners (Wednesday to Saturday only) run along the lines of ceviche of cod and prawns; braised lamb fillets with cumin, apricots and mint, and coffee fudge pudding. Also open for Sunday lunch.

● **SPEEN** (Buckinghamshire)
Old Plow Inn Flowers Bottom Lane, (01494) 488300. Ask for directions, then follow the long and winding Chiltern country lanes to reach this Buckinghamshire watering-hole. Originally a pub, it is now a full-blown bistro/restaurant dealing in dishes with strong brasserie leanings. Provençale fish soup, chicken roasted with chestnuts and red wine sauce, and treacle tart with clotted cream have been singled out.

● **STEEPLE ASTON** (Oxfordshire)
Red Lion South Side, (01869) 340225. Lovely old pub in a rural village serving excellent value English food, with home-grown fresh vegetables particularly commended. Bar snacks at lunch-time feature salads, pâtés, cheeses and cold meats, with some hot dishes in the winter. More expensive set-price dinners are served in the dining-room (bookings only) from Tue to Sat. Start with Sefton of salmon, and go on to duck in peppercorn sauce or venison steak with a sour-cream sauce. Desserts range from charlotte mousse, to cold chocolate soufflé. There is a terrace for outdoor summer drinking. Very friendly service.

● **STOCKLAND** (Devon)
Kings Arms Inn Stockland, (01404) 881361. A very businesslike set-up providing food, drink and accommodation in an eighteenth-century

thatched country pub with additions. Lunchtime snacks are served in the Farmers' Bar, more formal meals in the Cotley Restaurant. Blackboard menus promise Mediterranean fish soup, rack of local lamb, pasta carbonara and crème brûlée. Real ales and some well-kept wines.

● **STOKE BRUERNE** (Northamptonshire)
Bruerne's Lock The Canalside, (01604) 863654. Sit outside for a drink at this canalside restaurant watching people struggle through the lock. Choose from the patio light-lunch menu (soup, pâtés or cheese), set lunch menu, or an evening *carte*. Main courses run to pork cutlets with rosemary and garlic cream, and roasted cod fillet in an anchovy and chive butter sauce. Puddings could be sticky toffee or cinnamon and apple crumble.

● **STRATFORD-UPON-AVON** (Warwickshire)
The Boathouse Swan's Nest Lane, (01789) 297733. Lovely setting on the Avon looking across to the town and theatre – only five minutes' walk away – stylishly decorated in Mediterranean colours. Starters of spicy sausage and pork terrine, or asparagus with crushed new potato and salmon niçoise, might be followed by Cajun dorade on a risotto galette or braised shoulder of spring lamb with baby vegetables. Finish perhaps with Thai rice-pudding with poached pineapple or bitter chocolate tart.

Desport's 13–14 Meer Street, (01789) 269304. Vibrant sixteenth-century beamed building. Julie and Paul Desport's menu divides into Earth (vegetarian), Land, Sea and Heaven (desserts, of course), and cooking is up to the minute. 'Fusion' is the driving force behind cumin-crusted turbot with fennel mash, Asian vinaigrette and spiced lentils; and confit of belly pork with five-spice, orange-braised chicory and peanut miso sauce. 'Green' risotto and crème brûlée sound a simpler note.

No 6 6 Union Street, (01789) 269106. Small bistro in a side street, just off the main shopping area, where blackboard menus major in fish. Start with pan-fried king prawns or sauté squid rings in a spicy salsa, followed by roasted medallions of monkfish or red snapper fillets. Non-fish eaters might prefer baked field mushrooms, or chargrilled spiced minced lamb, followed by pavé of Scotch beef or pan-fried breast of duck. A light lunch menu is also available. A short wine list starts with house French at £9.25. Pleasant smiling service. Closed Sun.

Russons 8 Church Street, (01789) 268822. Fresh seafood, pasta and vegetarian specials flesh out the repertoire in this diminutive venue close to the theatre. Main menus change every three weeks and dishes come from around the world, as in lamb and coriander meatballs in chilli sauce, Thai king prawns in filo pastry, and blackened Cajun chicken breast with mango and banana. One-dish lunches are good value.

● **STRETTON** (Rutland)
Ram Jam Inn Great North Road, (01780) 410776. The former managers are now the owners of this inn on the Great North Road named after a drink produced by a former publican. Open all day and serving an instant lunch between noon and 2pm of soup, farmhouse cheese and sweets of the day. Otherwise try salad niçoise or braised shoulder of lamb with mash and spinach. Desserts include homemade ice-creams and upside-down pear tart.

● **SUTTON COLDFIELD** (West Midlands)
La Truffe 65 Birmingham Road, (0121) 355 5836. A logo of a truffle-hunting pig tops the menu in this tastefully appointed 'restaurant français'. The kitchen deals in classical French cuisine in the shape of terrine of venison with redcurrant and orange jelly, escalope of salmon with beurre blanc, and chocolate and passion-fruit mousse.

● **TAVISTOCK** (Devon)
Neil's 27 King Street, (01822) 615550. Diminutive country restaurant set in a converted 400-year-old farmhouse. Chef/proprietor Janet Neil enthusiastically supports the local food network and her menus are built around a bedrock of

organic and free-range produce. Baked mushrooms filled with goats' cheese, Gressingham duck with leeks and spicy plum sauce, and apple and cider syllabub are typical. Keenly priced wines.

● **TIRRIL** (Cumbria)
Queens Head Tirril, (01768) 863219. Rambling Lakeland country pub/restaurant dating from 1719: old oak beams, thick walls and four open fireplaces set the tone. Good-value bar menus include ploughman's with a trio of local cheeses, sausages from a butcher in Kendal, pasta, and some homely puddings. Meals in the dining-room are a touch more ambitious.

● **TORQUAY** (Devon)
Mulberry Room 1 Scarborough Road, (01803) 213639. Lesley Cooper works wonders in this Victorian corner terrace house close to the seafront. Superior home cooking based around prime local ingredients is what she offers, and her modest blackboard menu is forever evolving. Typical examples might include roasted red pepper soup with sizzled herbs, slow-roast Devon farm duck with cherry brandy sauce, and banana and maple toffee trifle.

● **TRESCO** (Isles of Scilly)
Island Hotel (01720) 422883. 'Wonderful sea views' and some spectacular landscapes are great attractions at this hotel, which has been owned by the Dorrien Smith family since 1961. Local seafood and duck have been singled out for praise, although the kitchen also tackles roast best end of lamb with creamed spinach, roast garlic and rosemary sauce, and chargrilled chicken breast with braised pearl barley and lemon thyme. 'Adventurous' wine list with a good choice of half-bottles.

● **TRURO** (Cornwall)
Oliver's Castle Street, (01872) 273028. Reputable local restaurant in a basement below the Law Courts. Daily menus follow the market, and reporters have endorsed warm salad of scallops, a trio of locally caught fish, and fruit parfait. Other options might range from chargrilled medallions of pork with red wine jus to

ENGLAND

steamed chicken stuffed with asparagus. Closed Sun.

● **TUNBRIDGE WELLS** (Kent)
Sankey's 39 Mount Ephraim, (01892) 511422. Spacious town restaurant decorated with fishy paintings and prints. Start with excellent grilled oysters with spinach and cream, followed by skate with capers and black butter or monkfish wrapped in bacon with tomato sauce. Well-chosen, reasonably priced wine list.

● **WARWICK** (Warwickshire)
Findons 7 Old Square, (01926) 411755. 'The ideal way to end a day' after visiting historic Warwick. Findons is part of a Georgian house, and stands conveniently close to the centre of things. Those who have sampled the kitchen's output speak well of marinated chicken with feta cheese and salad, fillet of salmon with tarragon butter, and chocolate mousse laced with Baileys. Service is polite, the atmosphere 'classic English'.

Ricochet Inn 6 Castle Street, (01926) 491 232. Former pub now a small restaurant/wine bar in the middle of town. Recommendations have come in for warm salad of bacon and Brie, chicken liver salad, and rich and gooey chocolate fudge cake. Other options range from bacon and mushroom 'smokies' topped with Austrian cheese, roasted duck breast with red wine and thyme sauce, and strawberry and Amaretto cheesecake. Short wine list. Newspapers on poles to read. Closed Sun D.

● **WELLING** (Kent)
Tagore 3 Welling High Street, (0181) 304 0433. Last in the *Guide* in 1984 when he owned the Viceroy in Farnham, Nur Monie then spent ten years running a successful restaurant in Paris which achieved two Gault Millau toques. He has now returned to England to promote his Pahktoon (North-west Frontier) cuisine. Try marinated kebabs, varied curries, koh-e-avadh from Lucknow (lamb shanks off the bone in rich gravy) or mahi e ghazni (pomfret roasted in the tandoori). Impressive wine list.

● **WESTFIELD** (East Sussex)
Wild Mushroom Westfield Lane, (01424) 751137. Modest turn-of-the-century house in open country just north of Hastings, with a yellow painted L-shaped dining-room. Start off with crostini of goats' cheese with bacon, or squid and scallion risotto. Main-course pigeon breast with bubble and squeak and port sauce, or lemon sole with mussel and saffron sauce, might be followed by dark chocolate timbale. Only open for lunch on Sun, and Tue to Sat dinner.

● **WEYBOURNE** (Norfolk)
Gasche's The Street, (01263) 70220. Careful cooking of good local materials – Blakeney mussels and Cromer crabs among them – in this restaurant with a lovely atmosphere and very friendly service. Sunday lunch might offer crab-cakes with tomato salsa followed by roast sirloin of beef with Yorkshire pudding, finishing with chocolate mallow torte. On other days there might be chicken curry or poached salmon fillet with prawn and champagne sauce.

● **WEYMOUTH** (Dorset)
Perry's 4 Trinity Road, (01305) 785799. 'One of the satisfying things about going to Perry's is finding a decent fish restaurant overlooking a working harbour.' The setting counts for a lot, staff are ever helpful and the kitchen takes its cue from local supplies. Scallops with lemon and garlic, monkfish with chive and Chablis sauce, and sea bass with citrus and olive oil show off the quality of raw materials.

● **WHIMPLE** (Devon)
Woodhayes Whimple, (01404) 822237. Katherine and Michael Rendle were on the point of selling their delightful Georgian residence as we went to press; one hopes that new owners will keep things much the same as before. Expect an enchanting setting deep in apple-orchard country, and cooking that is based around trusted local supplies, plus a sound international wine list.

● **WILLINGTON** (Co Durham)
Stile 97 High Street, (01388) 746615. Wine tastings, a book review club and a

weekly French menu are just some of the novel attractions at Mike Boustred's out-of-town, bistro-style restaurant. Otherwise, there is a regularly changing menu featuring fish, seasonal game and other local produce: expect dishes such as crab and avocado salad, braised lamb shank with couscous and rosemary, and strawberry tart with rhubarb sauce.

● **WOBURN** (Bedfordshire)
Paris House Woburn Park, (01525) 290692. Built in 1878 for the Paris exhibition, dismantled and re-erected in Woburn Park, Paris House is a perfect location for a summer dinner. The menu du jour might offer lamb cutlets and raspberry crème brûlée, while the *carte* extends to creamed ragoût of mussels followed by venison in a port and redcurrant sauce. Finish with apple tarte Tatin or 'tulipe en fantaisie'.

● **WOOLTON HILL** (Hampshire)
Hollington House Woolton Hill, (01635) 255100. John and Penny Guy's peerless antipodean wine list is a major attraction for oenophiles. Others will doubtless be impressed by the grand décor of this golden-stone Edwardian country house set in 25 acres of mature grounds and gardens designed by Gertrude Jekyll. Sous-chef Matthew du Plessis took over the reins in the kitchen shortly before we went to press. Reports on his progress, please.

● **YORK** (North Yorkshire)
Bettys 6–8 St Helen's Square, (01904) 659142. The first-floor Belmont Room (named after Bettys' founder, who travelled on the maiden voyage of the Queen Mary) has recently been refurbished, retaining many original 1930s features based on one of the ship's state rooms. Open daily from 9am to 9pm for brunch, patisserie, afternoon teas and much more.

Grange Hotel Clifton, (01904) 644744. Classic Regency town house within striking distance of the city centre and the Minster. The intimate basement Brasserie offers good value in the shape of spinach and Parmesan tart, venison sausages with mash, and steamed marmalade sponge. Alternatively eat in the Seafood Bar or the elegant Ivy Restaurant, where menus move into the realms of peppered loin of lamb with polenta cake and ratatouille.

Scotland

● **ABERDEEN** (Aberdeen)
Courtyard 1 Alford Lane, (01224) 213795. Downstairs is Martha's Vineyard bistro dealing in salads, pasta, stir-fries and the like. Above is the main restaurant, where menus feature more substantial dishes, including a fine showing of fish. Around 30 youthful wines provide suitable back-up. There was a change of chef as we went to press, so reports, please.

● **ARDUAINE** (Argyll & Bute)
Loch Melfort Hotel Arduaine, (01852) 200233. Famed for its stunning views across Asknish Bay and for its location next to Arduaine Gardens (National Trust). Light lunches are served in the Chartroom Bar, formal five-course dinners in the main dining-room. Seafood shows up in the shape of sauté crawfish and squat lobsters with pistachios, or turbot with beurre blanc; steaks, lamb and game are also Scottish.

● **BALLATER** (Aberdeenshire)
Balgonie Country House Braemar Place, (013397) 55482. Scottish produce is the foundation at this impressive Edwardian country house close to the River Dee. Fish-cakes are made with a mix of turbot and sea trout, fillet of salmon comes garnished with ratatouille and a red pepper coulis, while Aberdeen Angus fillet steak is topped with foie gras and served with wild mushrooms. Sunday lunch has been enjoyed from start to finish.

● **BIGGAR** (South Lanarkshire)
Culter Mill Coulter Village, (01899) 220950. Atmospheric, centuries-old grain

mill, complete with an original water-wheel in the beer garden. Produce from the Glasgow markets shows up on the menus, which promise haggis risotto, casseroled wild rabbit with bacon, wine and wholegrain mustard, and poached salmon with lime hollandaise and asparagus. Closed Tue.

● **BROADFORD** (Highland)
Creelers Seafood Bistro Broadford, Isle of Skye, (01471) 822281. 'Simple log-cabin of a restaurant' with six café-style tables. Heather MacLeod works the kitchen, husband Les is out front. Their surprisingly long menu majors in seafood, and freshness counts for a great deal. Honest simplicity rules. Squat lobster bisque, 'succulent' grilled king scallops with fennel seeds, garlic and butter, and saddle of venison with red wine and juniper are typical. Open from 12 till 11; also offers take-away dishes.

● **CRINAN** (Argyll & Bute)
Crinan Hotel Crinan, (01546) 830261. Comfortable harbour-side hotel close to Loch Fyne. Light snacks such as quiches, filled rolls and pastries are available in the coffee-shop. On the Westward Restaurant's menus might be Loch Ettoe mussels or locally smoked wild Scottish salmon, followed by pan-fried Aberdeen Angus steak with a pepper sauce, or civet of Isle of Jura venison, finishing with strawberry cheesecake. Fish specials are landed every evening and served at 8pm in the more expensive Lock 16 Restaurant (May to September only, weather permitting): jumbo prawn Corryvreckan or lobster from the Sound of Jura, all served naturally. Reporters have noted a surfeit of cats.

● **EDINBURGH** (Edinburgh)
Ann Purna 45 St Patrick's Square, (0131) 662 1807. Ann Purna's traditional Gujerati cooking 'with style' draws the plaudits of even non-vegetarians. Breads, thalis and lentil dishes are reckoned to be 'superb', with top-quality ingredients and a judicious hand with spicing, and a pair of regulars say the food is now 'the best yet'. Baingan (aubergine curry), vegetable korma, and kumbai masala

(mushrooms in coconut milk) have been praised. Finish with pistachio and mango kulfi and drink Kingfisher beer or masala tea. More reports, please.

Fitz Henry 19 Shore Place, (0131) 555 6625. Relaxed atmosphere in this converted warehouse near the river. The menu changes frequently and recommended dishes have included scallops, pan-fried halibut, and roasted monkfish tail. Finish with Scottish berry mille-feuille. Good-value, eclectic wine list.

Howies 208 Bruntsfield Place, (0131) 221 1777. One of a trio of buzzy Edinburgh cosmopolitan venues serving a lively mix of dishes with an international flavour. Salmon and pistachio mousse gets a sweet mustard dressing, roast chicken suprême receives a sherry, ginger and soy glaze, and there might be tiramisù or raspberry cranachan to finish. Licensed, but you can BYO (corkage £1.30). Other branches are at 63 Dalry Road and 75 St Leonard's Street.

Siam Erawan 48 Howe Street, (0131) 226 3675. Miss Chinnapong's cheerful Thai restaurant sits in a basement on the corner of Howe Street and South-East Circus Place. Menus promise a wide choice of dishes from tom yum kai soup to kung tord tempura (deep-fried prawns, fish and vegetables in batter with chilli sauce). Set-lunch menus are particularly good value.

Silvio's 54 The Shore, (0131) 553 3557. Warmly welcoming Italian place overlooking the Water of Leith near the docks. New chef Bruno Confortini is following in the footsteps of his predecessor, although recent meals have been a shade variable. Mixed antipasti is 'a definite winner', while the repertoire extends to polenta with Gorgonzola, and pork chop with sage, rosemary and garlic. Vintage Barolos top the bill on the wine list.

● **FAIRLIE** (North Ayrshire)
Fins Fencefoot Farm, (01475) 568989. A converted one-storey farm building attached to a fish farm, with farm shop, cookshop and a mail-order business.

Approved dishes from the all-fish menu have been 'superb' scallops, cod and brill, Fairlie kippers and their own spring-reared trout, plus squat lobsters and a hot shellfish platter. Other choices could be smoked haddock with poached egg, spinach and sauté potatoes, or herb-crusted lemon sole. Friendly and professional service. Closed Sun D and all day Mon.

● **GATTONSIDE** (Borders)
Hoebridge Inn Gattonside, (01896) 9823082. Cheerful, brightly decorated restaurant just across the River Tweed from Melrose, with a very pleasant ambience. The menu makes a favourable impression with prawn ravioli in langoustine sauce, chicken liver parfait with quince jelly, guinea-fowl with red wine sauce, and saffron-and-basil-scented monkfish with mussels on a bed of black pasta. Well-turned-out staff 'could not be more helpful'. Booking is recommended.

● **GLASGOW** (Glasgow)
Killermont Polo Club 2022 Maryhill Road, (0141) 946 5412. Situated between Maryhill and Bearsden in a converted house and functioning as a polo club and a restaurant. Recommended dishes have been Garlic Nahu, vegetable pakoras, and a hot chocolate drink with spiced rum and marshmallows on top – a nice way to finish a meal. Other dishes might include tandoori chicken, Goan-style mussels or sirloin of beef with green peppercorns and brandy.

● **KILCHRENAN** (Argyll & Bute)
Ardanaiseig Hotel Kilchrenan, (01866) 833333. Up a single-track road, overlooking the shores of Loch Awe, is this isolated, crenellated country-house hotel. Luxury-based dinner menus run to ravioli of lobster with a nage of shellfish and herbs; poached breast of guinea-fowl with foie gras, braised cabbage and morel sauce; finishing up with prune and Armagnac soufflé or a pyramid of Amaretto praline.

● **MELROSE** (Borders)
Burts Hotel Market Square, (01896) 822285. Owned by the Henderson family since 1970, this listed eighteenth-century coaching-inn is very much a fixture of the Borders scene. The kitchen draws on Scotland's larder for menus that might include warm salad of pigeon with basil and garlic dressing, chargrilled lamb chops, and breast of maize-fed chicken on creamed leeks with honey and grape sauce. Excellent wine list. Light meals and cask ales in the bar.

● **MOFFAT** (Dumfries & Galloway)
Beechwood Country House Hotel Harthope Place, (01683) 220210. Twelve acres of beechwoods surround this aptly named Victorian country house overlooking the Annan valley and the town of Moffat. Dinner menus are based around local produce and dishes might include wild mushroom potato cakes, followed by breast of chicken stuffed with grapes and Mull of Kintyre cheese, with an Amaretto cream sauce. Finish with caramel rice-pudding with blueberry purée, or chocolate and blackcurrant mousse.

● **PERTH** (Perthshire & Kinross)
Kinfauns Castle nr Perth, (01738) 620777. Built for Lord Gray in 1820, this crenellated castle lies on the slopes of the Tay valley (Kinfauns is Gaelic for 'head of the slopes'). Comfortable, elegant interior. Start with excellent canapés, go on to terrine of pheasant with orange chutney followed by pot-roast chicken and finish with whisky parfait or butterscotch cheesecake. Good-value, well-balanced shortish wine list.

● **SCARISTA** (Western Isles)
Scarista House Scarista, (01859) 550238. Converted Georgian manse next to a secluded beach on the Isle of Harris – definitely somewhere to get away from it all. Open only for dinner, when menus might include scallops baked in their shells or Sound of Harris prawns to start, followed by fillet of beef with herbs and Madeira sauce, or skate in black butter. Finish with miniature strawberry soufflés or chocolate hazelnut meringue.

● **SHIELDAIG** (Highland)
Tigh an Eilean Shieldaig, (01520) 755251. Converted from a row of

terraced cottages, this small hotel in a pretty village, only yards from the beach, offers good food and service. Dinner menus might feature duck breast, jugged hare or 'well-sauced' sirloin steak. Rich pot of chocolate or home-made lemon flan to finish. Competitively priced wine list with some excellent *cru bourgeois* clarets.

● **SPEAN BRIDGE** (Highland)
Old Station Station Road, (01397) 712535. Arrive by train (or car) at this restaurant actually in the Victorian station building. Seasonal produce is used industriously for dinner menus that could include warm celery and Parmesan tart, Shetland salmon with a white wine, lemon and ginger sauce, and Amaretto and blackcurrant parfait. Open for dinner only April to October, Tue to Sun.

Wales

● **CARDIFF** (Cardiff)
De Courcey's Tyla Morris Ave, Pentyrch, (01222) 892232. Set in around three acres of landscaped grounds a short drive from the city centre and the M4, this set-up is tailor-made for the conference and function market. Dinners in the restaurant revolve around 'house' and 'gourmet' menus featuring, say, scallops with squid-ink risotto, breast of Trelough duck with Puy lentils, and pistachio crème brûlée. Sunday lunch is a simpler affair.

Le Gallois 6–8 Romilly Street, (01222) 341264. Family-run French restaurant on the site of the former Quayles, with Andrew Reagen, ex-Le Cassoulet (see entry, Wales), as the co-chef. Typical dishes might be grilled lobster, Thai-style pigeon with creamed cabbage, wild mushroom ravioli with thyme sauce, and seafood specials. Closed Mon. More reports, please.

Metropolis 60 Charles Street, (01222) 344300. Within easy reach of the city centre, this modern, bright restaurant offers well-cooked food at reasonable prices. Recommended dishes have been warm salad of quail and quail's eggs, 'brilliant' loin of lamb with good vegetables, and poached pear in red wine with vanilla cream. Enthusiastic staff.

Riverside Cantonese 44 Tudor Street, (01222) 372163. A dependable and long-serving Cantonese restaurant, and a useful venue for cooked-to-order dim-sum (served noon to 5pm). Otherwise dip

into the standard menu that trawls its way through old favourites such as sizzling king prawns with black-bean sauce, chicken with cashew-nuts, and sliced beef with ginger and spring onions. Open all day.

● **CARMARTHEN** (Carmarthenshire)
Quayside Brasserie The Quay, (01267) 223000. There are views over the River Towy from the balcony area outside this rustic, barn-like brasserie. William Noblett and his team work to a blackboard menu based almost entirely on local produce (plus an occasional exotic intruder such as kangaroo). Cockles au gratin, venison steak in port sauce, and fillet of red bream are the kinds of things to expect. Extensive wine cellar.

● **CRICKHOWELL** (Powys)
Gliffaes Country House Hotel (01874) 730371. Wonderfully relaxed country-house hotel in a 100-year-old grey-stone house high above the river of the same name. Reporters have enjoyed 'nicely roasted, accurately timed' boned quail with rocket salad and plum chutney followed by vanilla mousse with prunes steeped in rum. Excellent Sunday lunches might be cock-a-leekie soup, roast Welsh lamb with good vegetables and sticky toffee pudding.

● **GLANWYDDEN** (Conwy)
Queen's Head Glanwydden, (01492) 546570. Formerly a wheelwright's cottage, now a civilised country inn with a sound local reputation. Wide-ranging

menus are built around Welsh produce, and the choice extends to smoked goose breast, deep-fried Pencarreg cheese with cranberry preserve, and grilled lamb cutlets with raspberry and Amaretto sauce. Seafood is also a strong suit in the shape of Conwy mussels or poached salmon.

● **GRESFORD** (Wrexham)
Pant yr Ochain Old Wrexham Road, (01978) 853525. Idiosyncratically decorated old building in great countryside north of Wrexham. The cooking goes in for global brasserie ideas, ranging far and wide for deep-fried halloumi cheese with roasted Mediterranean vegetables, prawn and papaya salad, and curried lamb-burgers with mango relish. Ploughman's, pizzas and baguettes also available.

● **LAUGHARNE** (Carmarthenshire)
Cors Restaurant Laugharne, (01994) 427219. Converted Victorian rectory, now a tranquil retreat complete with a strikingly captivating garden. Owner Nick Priestland's talents as horticulturist, artist and chef are everywhere to be seen. His cooking revolves around quite sophisticated dishes with a Mediterranean slant: witness tomato, basil and mozzarella tartlet, rack of saltmarsh lamb with Parmesan crust and red onion confit, and lemon tart. More reports, please.

● **LLANABER** (Gwynedd)
Llwyndu Farmhouse Llwyndu, (01341) 280144. Down-to-earth hospitality from the Thompsons at this 400-year-old house standing above the sea just outside Barmouth. A short daily-changing menu might include starters of curried parsnip and apple soup or chicken livers with grapes, followed by game casserole (wild boar, mallard, venison, goose and guinea-fowl) or savoury seafood pancakes. Puddings might include pancakes with butterscotch bananas or chocolate fudge cake.

● **LLANFYLLIN** (Powys)
Seeds 5 Penybryn Cottages, High Street, (01691) 648604. Knick-knacks and children's toys adorn the Seagers' cosy flagstoned cottage deep in rural Powys. Their short fixed-price menu shows enterprise and dedication: warm fish mousse is served with cockle and mussel cream sauce, rib of beef is accompanied by locally picked wild mushrooms, and treacle tart is paired with home-made cherry brandy ice-cream. Meticulous, unobtrusive personal service. Surprisingly good wine list.

● **LLANGOLLEN** (Denbighshire)
Gales 18 Bridge Street, (01978) 860089. Family-friendly wine and food bar (with accommodation) a short stroll from the Llangollen Railway and Canal Wharf. Constantly changing blackboard menus always offer soup, quiches, jacket potatoes and the like, with daily specials and steaks in the evening. The extensive wine list is well worth exploring.

● **MOLD** (Flintshire)
Chez Colette 56 High Street, (01352) 759225. No-nonsense French bistro, personably run by Colette and Jacques Duvauchelle. They share duties in the kitchen and produce a repertoire of classic staples along the lines of mussels in garlic butter, beef bourguignon, ragoût of monkfish and pan-fried steak with brandy and cream sauce. Note the limited opening times: Fri and Sat L, Thurs to Sat D.

● **SOLVA** (Pembrokeshire)
Old Pharmacy 5 Main Street, (01437) 720005. Charming and gregarious restaurant housed in an old chemist's shop. Local fish (including Solva lobster) and Welsh lamb feature on the menu and vegetarians are given a fair crack of the whip. Garlic mushrooms, charcuterie with caper relish, and plaice provençale have been recommended, along with desserts such as fruit crème brûlée, or apple and almond pie. Decent crab sandwiches and BLTs too. Good for families.

● **SWANSEA** (Swansea)
L'Amuse 93 Newton Road, Mumbles, (01792) 366006. As we went to press, Kate Cole's bistro moved to new premises in Mumbles. Nothing else seems set to

change. Expect the eponymous 'amuse gueule' to start, before a repertoire of archetypal bistro dishes with a few delicate modern twists. Add to this friendly service and a clutch of good-value wines. Reports on the new set-up, please.

Annie's 56 St Helen's Road, (01792) 655603. Small restaurant with an intimate ambience offering good-value set-price dinner menus from Tuesday to Saturday only. Start with gazpacho or mussels in a curry sauce, followed by confit of Barbary duck, or pot-roast shank of Welsh lamb. Desserts might be apple mousse, or hot pear Tatin. Improving wine list.

Barrows 42 Newton Road, Mumbles, (01792) 361443. 'Bistro and bar' in a side street a stone's throw from Oystermouth Castle. The kitchen takes an eclectic view of things, serving Welsh lamb steak with cracked peppers and blueberry sauce, then looking further afield for baked fillet of monkfish with Thai spices and basmati rice. Similarly, desserts could range from bread-and-butter pudding to baked bananas with maple syrup and ice-cream. Closed Sun and Mon.

P.A.'s Wine Bar 95 Newton Road, (01792) 367723. Steve and Kate Maloney's neighbourhood wine bar sets its stall out with a shortish menu of sound bistro-style dishes with more than a nod to the Welsh larder. Deep-fried 'soufflés' are filled with cockles, laverbread and bacon; well-trimmed rack of lamb is served on gratin potatoes, while poached sewin comes with hollandaise sauce.

Channel Islands

● **GOREY** (Jersey)

Jersey Pottery Restaurant Gorey, (01534) 851119. Relaxing, airy conservatory restaurant attached to the pottery and overlooking well-tended gardens. Ambitious lunch menus always place a strong emphasis on the sea: lobster and crab salads are 'out of this world', and other dishes range from sea bass with braised fennel to chicken breast with oyster mushrooms and grain mustard sauce. Lemon tart is a bestseller among desserts.

● **ST PETER PORT** (Guernsey)

La Frégate Les Cotils, (01481) 724624. Converted eighteenth-century manor-house boasting panoramic views of the harbour and neighbouring islands. Classic French cooking is the kitchen's stock-in-trade and menus always feature a strong showing of seafood. Typical offerings might include home-smoked duck breast with cranberry and Cointreau sauce, lobster thermidor, roast rack of lamb, and fruit vacherin.

Le Nautique Quay Steps, (01481) 721714. A French menu is offered in this cellar restaurant right on the quay overlooking the marina. Expect classic dishes along the lines of salade niçoise, poached turbot with hollandaise, Guernsey lobsters every which way and fillet of beef with green peppercorn sauce. 'Attentive service.'

The Good Food Club 1998

Many thanks to all the following people who contributed to this year's
Guide . . .

Paul Abbey
Andrew Abbott
David Abbott
E. Abbott
Jean Aberdour
Dr A.H Abrahams
David Abrahams
A.D. Abrams
Sheila Adam
Dr Hazel Adams
Robert Adams
Stephen C.F. Adams
John and Leslie Aird
S.T. Akers
Hugh Aldersey-
   Williams
David Alexander
Minda Alexander
Mrs Gillian Allen
Mr and Mrs P.J.
   Allen
Janet Allom
Mrs S. Allott-Davey
Nigel Allsop
Sir Anthony Alment
B. Anderson
Gwen and Peter
   Andrews
Dr S.D. Andrews
J.N. Anker
Bryan Anson
Mrs Juliet Anstey
Mrs Cynthia Archer
P.F. Arden
Mrs Y. Aris
R. Arnheim
John Arnold
K. Ashken
Brian Atkinson
J.H. Atkinson
Martin Attewell
Mrs Cleone Augur
Mrs J.M. Austin
L. Avill
Mr and Mrs Michael
   Awty
Sarah Backhouse
Jane and Martin
   Bailey
Mrs Mary Bailey
Robert Bairamian
Mrs Jenny Baker

Mr and Mrs R.G.
   Baker
Tony Balazs
Graham Balfry
Richard Balkwill
Charlie Ballantyne
Mrs Debbie Balmer
Pat Barbrook
Micheael Bardsley
John Barford
Bryan Bargh
John Barker
Col Keith Barker
Mrs Glenice Barnard
Erica Barnett
J.M. Barney
R.A. Barnfield
Sam and Margaret
   Barr
Vicki Barrass
Tony Barrow
Jane Barry
Mr and Mrs J.
   Bartholomew
M.D. Bartlett
Mrs E.A. Barwood
A. Bassett
Mr and Mrs John
   Bateman
Mrs M.G. Bateson
T. Battle
Dr John Batty
Mrs S. Batty
Conrad Bayliss
Andrew Beale
Ms M. Beale
J.M. Beaugie
Lord Beaumont
F.R. Beckett
H. Beckingsale
J.P. Bee
Mr and Mrs M. Bega
Mr and Mrs I. Beggs
T. Bendhem
David Bennett
Mrs E. Bennett
Helen Bennett
J. Bennett
Mr and Mrs John
   Bennett
Patricia Benson
Ann Bentley

Diane Bentley
James Bentley
William Bentsen
Mr and Mrs H.I.
   Berkeley
Dr Peter Berkzeller
Mrs Gabriele
   Berneck
A.J. Berry
Mr and Mrs F. Berry
Daniel Besson
W.J. Best
Mrs V.A. Bingham
Mr and Mrs Chris
   Birch
E.R. Birch
Sir Roger Birch
Ray Birchley
Mrs S. Birn
R.G. Birt
Mrs Judith Bishop
Dr Nicholas Bishop
Anne Blackburn
C.T. Blackburn
Roger Blackburn
Natasha Blair
Diana Blake
Steven Blake
Edward Blincoe
Mr and Mrs S. Bliss
R.J. Bloomfield
Mr and Mrs Bodd
C.A. Bodega
Manuel Boger
Mrs Jo Boissevain
M.H. Boler
S.A. Bollans
J. Bolt
Christopher Bolton
Mrs Julia Bolwell
Rowland Bonham
Mr and Mrs E.W.
   Booth
Mr and Mrs W.H.
   Booth
John Bosomworth
Canon M.A
   Bourdeaux
Robin Bourne
Miss I.D. Bowden
A.J. Bowen
Rod Bowker

Miss E.R. Bowmer
Z.E Bowyer
Thomas Boyd
J. Boynton
Mr and Mrs Brackley
Lawrence
   Brackstone
R.J. Bradburn
Christopher
   Bradfield
Mrs Helen Bradley
Mr and Mrs J.
   Bradley
Kathleen Bradley
L. Bradley
Peter Bradshaw
M. Brady
John Bragge
Barry Brahams
Dr Robina Brand
A.S. Brasier
Wilma Brew
Mrs Jonica Bridge
Mr and Mrs John
   Brierley
T.G. Brierly
C.T. Briggs
Mrs J. Briggs
Maxine Brightman
John Brill
J.F. Broadhurst
Mr and Mrs Neil
   Brockbank
Roy Bromell
Patrick Bromley
Mr and Mrs Graham
   Brooker
Clinton Brookes
Dr David Brooks
Douglas Brooks
Jayne Brooks
Paula Brookwell
A. Brown
C.I. Brown
J.J. Brown
Judith Brown
Katherine Brown
Lawrence Brown
Charles Brune
Roger Brunger
Mr and Mrs S.G.
   Brunning

Miss D. Bryan
Mr and Mrs Max
 Bryan
Mr and Mrs Edgar
 Bryant
Ian Bryant
Mr and Mrs John
 Bryant
M. Bryden
P.M.A. Buckman
B.T. Bull
Susan Bunker
Mr and Mrs Stephen
 Bunn
John Burdett
Mrs Daphne
 Burgess
Morris Burgoyne
Geoffrey Burnaby
Mr and Mrs Burnett
Mr and Mrs Peter
 Burnstone
M.H. Burr
Richard Burridge
H.W. Burton
J. Burton
Richard Busby
J.T.H. Butcher
Geoff Butler
Mr and Mrs Paul
 Butler
Roy Butler
J.G. Butlin
Mr and Mrs F. Butt
A. Butterworth
Mr and Mrs P.G.
 Byrne
Peter Byworth
A.J. Cade
Prof Robert Cahn
Robert Caldicott
Mrs W. Caldwell
Dr Brian Campbell
Mrs J. Cantlay
Prof Linda Cardow
H. Carmichael
Mrs Patricia Carr
Dr John Carroll
N. Carter
P.E. Carter
W.D.A. Carter
J.A.H. Cartwright
Mrs Colette Carus
Michael Casey
Yvonne Cash
John Cass
Dr R.E. Catlow
Mr and Mrs B.F. Catt
Margaret Chalk
Dr C.R.
 Chandraserar
A.H. Chapman

Miles Chapman
Mr and Mrs Barry
 Charles
S. Charles
Sebastian Charles
Mrs A. Charlton
Vyvyan Chatterjie
Philip Chatwin
Mrs A. Cheek
R.J. Chenery
W.J. Chesneau
T. Chippendale
P.W. Christie
Mrs Grace Ciappara
Mrs B.E. Civval
J.C. Clair
Mr and Mrs J.
 Clapham
Lesley Clare
Mrs Patricia Clark
M. Clarke
Mrs Alison Clayton
Brian Cleary
John Cleese
Alan Clegg
Mrs Jennifer Clegg
E. Clifford White
J.D. Cloud
Dr B.M. Cockburn
W.F. Coghill
Pam Cohen
Dr Vivienne Cohen
Mr and Mrs Cole
James Cole
Mr and Mrs Roger
 Colebrook
Mr and Mrs J.D.
 Coles
Sally Coles
N.P. Coley
P.V. Collings
Mrs A. Collins
G. Collins
John Collins
Stephen Collinson
Hannah Colton
Mrs E.J. Colwell
R.T. Combe
M. Comninos
John Connell
Sean Connolly
Roger Connon
Mr and Mrs John
 Constable
Peter Cooper
Dr and Mrs J.C.W.
 Cope
David Coplowe
Laurence Coppel
Mr and Mrs E.
 Corcoran
Godfrey Cordery

Tom Cordiner
D.W. Costain
J. Courivald
Mike Court
Stephen Court
J.S. Coward
Janet Coward
Mrs Diane Cox
Michael Cox
Richard Coxon
Mrs E.P.M. Craghill
G. Craig
Mrs K. Craig
David Cramb
Lorna Cranston
P. Creech
Michael Crick
W.P. Crick
Tom Crompton
Helen Crookston
J.D. Crosland
John and Judy
 Cross
David Cubey
Fiona Cullen
A.A. Cunningham
Miss C. Cunningham
Miss K.E.
 Cunningham
Mrs M. Curd
I.J. Curruthers
Dr John Cuthbert
Dr K. Cwynarski
Dr S. da Prato
A.H. Dalton
G.W. Dalton
Mr and Mrs Dalzell
Mrs Samantha
 Dalziel
K. Dann
Mr and Mrs L. Darby
Richard Darlington
Mrs J. Davenport
Mr and Mrs D.W.M.
 Davidson
W.H. Davidson
Alun Davies
Andrew Davies
Mrs D. Davies
E.B. Davies
Gillian Davies
Andrew Davis
Mr and Mrs G. Davis
Mr and Mrs Davison
Mr and Mrs Geoff
 Daw
Dr and Mrs R.P.R.
 Dawber
Tom Dawson
Mrs P.A. de Laszlo
Mr and Mrs F.C. de
 Paula

Mr and Mrs J.I. de
 Villiers
R. Dean
N.C. Dee
M. Deeks
N. Dees
Mr G. Delmont
Mr and Mrs
 Jonathan Denby
C. Derby
Adele Dethick
Eric Deung
R.C.E. Devenish
I. Dewar
Ian Dewey
Mr and Mrs Paul
 Diggory
G.M. Dobbie
Martin Dobson
Mr and Mrs R.A.
 Docherty
M.L. Dodd
Jean Don
Dr and Mrs Donn
Mrs Irene Dorrington
Mrs Trixie Douglas
Sidney Downs
Colin Dowse
Danielle Drake
M. Draper
Miss Paula Draper
S.D. Draycott
Dr John Drury
Mr and Mrs F.K.A.
 Dubash
John Ducker
Mark Dudley
Rev J. Duncan
Mrs Heather Durham
Denis Durno
Clive Dutson
Jean Dyer
Paul Dyer
John Earthy
Mr and Mrs K.
 Eckett
Dr S. Eden
Adrian Edwards
Mrs Aileen Edwards
G.M. Edwards
Guy Edwards
Malcolm Edwards
Paul Edwards
Sarah and Paul
 Edwards
Mr and Mrs Philip
 Egerton
Max Eilenberg
John Elder
James Eldridge
G. Elflett
Richard Elias

Steven Elief
Mr and Mrs M.G. Elliott
John Elliott
L.C. Elliott
P.R. Ellis
Dr Elizabeth Eltoft
Michael and Anita Emmott
Tom Empson
Dr Edgar Ernstbrunner
Mr and Mrs John Ette
A.D.W. Evans
Mrs C.J. Evans
Peter Evans
Philip Evans
Sharon Evans
Margaret Ewart
John Fahy
B. Farrel
Ann Farrow
J.G. Faulkner
Gordon Fawthrop
Mark Fear
Elaine Fenn
D. Fenton
A.B.X. Fenwick
Miss Anna Fergusson
Allen Ferns
Silvana Ferrari
H. Fessler
Neville Filar
Jonathan Fingerhut
Paul Fishpool
Mrs R.M. Fitton
John Fitzmaurice
Mr and Mrs Alan Flaherty
Kim Fleming
Dr Ron Fletcher
Christine Fletcher-Walker
Mrs Alison Flood
P. Forbes
Dr John Ford
Geoffrey Forester
Mrs P.L. Forrest
Mr and Mrs Forster
T.R. Forsyth
David Fossett
Simon Foster
A.S. Foulds
R.J.N. Fowler
D.J. Fox
Paul Fox
Mrs P. Frankel
R. Frankenburg
Dr M.L. Franks
C. Fraser

John Frayne
M.R. Freeman
R. Freeman
Sean French
Mrs J. Frost
K. Frusher
Mrs Victoria Fuller
Dr A.M. Furness
B.A. Furse
Mrs Pam Gadsby
John Gagg
V.G. Gale
L.A. Gallimore
Mrs D. Garner
J.E.A. Garnett
Amanda Garrett
Martin Gates
Rev Andrew Gaundon
Dr Ian Cavin
Sqn Ldr M.S. Geddes
Mr and Mrs D.H. Geldard
Mr and Mrs Germain
Hunter Gholson
J. Gibbs
P. Gibbs
Tim Giles
David Gilham
John Gilks
Mr and Mrs Gill
D.A. Gilmour
John Glaze
Karen Glencross
Mrs P.M. Glover
Mrs Gillian Goddard
Alan Godwin
Mrs Rebecca Goldsmith
R.F. Gompertz
Tom Gondris
B.J. Gordon
Dr E. Gordon
Mrs V.K. Gordon
Robert Gower
M.B. Gowers
Mrs F.J. Gracie
Alan Graham
D. Graham
R.J. Graham
Jill Grain
Simon Grainger
Duncan Grant
Dr and Mrs Eric Grant
Gary Grant
M Grantham
Lady Gray
P.J. Green
Mr and Mrs Richard Greenhalgh

C. Greenhow
Dr Arthur Greenwood
W.N. Greenwood
Conal Gregory
Prof K.J. Gregory
Dr P.R. Gregory
A.K. Grice
R.F. Grieve
Edward Griffin
J.R. Griffin
Michael Griffin
Mr and Mrs Griffiths
Dorothy Griffiths
Mr and Mrs J.A Griffiths
P. Griffiths
Nigel Grimshaw
Lt K.R. Groves
N. Grunborg
John Guest
B.G. Gunary
Rosalind Gunning
Dr Bryan Hall
Patrick Hall
Prof Peter Hall
Mr and Mrs Michael Hallsworth
Mrs A. Hamer
S. Hamilton
Geoffrey Hammond
F.J.T. Hancock
Gordon Hands
Sir Jeremy Hanley
David Hansen
Mrs M. Hansford
Prof Colin Harbury
R.A. Harcourt
Belinda Harding
C.R. Harding
Cliff Hardy
George Hardy
Joan Hare
Jonathan Harfield
S. Hargadon
K. Hargreaves
Tim Harper
R.W. Harries
Elizabeth Harris
James Harris
Prof Malcolm Harris
Noel and Janet Harris
R.A. Harris
Raymond Harris
Frank Harris-Jones
Dr T.N. Harrison
Mr and Mrs Hart
Sir Graham Hart
Adeline Hartcup
J.D. Hartley
Mrs D. Hartog

Dr Harvey
Peter Harvey
Frank Hawkins
Ken Hay
Peter Hayden
Mr and Mrs M. Hayes
Mrs Gill Hayhurst
Louise Hazard
Henry Heaney
Dr and Mrs C.C. Heath
Canon Neil Heavisides
Mr and Mrs Helson
George Henderson
L. Henderson
Dr W.A Henderson
L. Henley
N.F. Honshaw
R.A. Hepher
P.R. Herbert
A. Heron
Drs G. and J. Heron
R.L. Herrick
Dr Andrew Herxheimer
Mrs V. Heseltine
Gad Heuman
Allan Hewitt
Mrs Kay Hickman
Mrs J. Higgins
Mrs Lynn Higgins
Rupert Higgins
M.J. Higgs
F.R. Hilborne
Caroline Hill
Mrs Jennifer Hill
Mr and Mrs J. Hill
Robert Hill
Wendy Hillary
Mr and Mrs D.W. Hills
Ruth Hills
E. Hinds
Mr and Mrs R. Hinds
Janet Hobley
C.N. Hobson
Mrs Nita Hodgett
Mrs U. Hofheinz
David Holbrook
Mr Holmes
Mr and Mrs David Holmes
Judith Holmes
Mr and Mrs R. Holmes
Mr and Mrs Honour
David Hooper
Mrs J. Hope
Derek Hopes
G. Hopkinson

Ralph Hopton
Mr and Mrs R.H. Horncastle
Mrs Bev Hornsby
Mrs P. Horrocks
Mr and Mrs Ray Horrocks
Mr and Mrs Geoff Horwood
Mr and Mrs Hoskin
Richard Houghton
David House
Beryl Howard-Allen
J. Howarth
D.P. Howell
M.R. Howes
Gwilym Hughes
John and Jennifer Hughes
Kit Hughes
M. Hughes
P.J. Hunt
Mrs Sheila Hunt
Dr Tim Hunt
D. Hunter
D.M. Hunter
D.R. Hunter
Graham Hurry
M. Hurwitt
T.J. Hypher
B.M. Igra
L.D. Incoll
Dr Wipada Ingkamast
Stuart Irving
Mrs E.A. Jackson
Mrs H.C. Jackson
James McG. Jackson
Dr P. Jacques
Mrs C.J. Jakins
Mrs R.G. James
J.R. Jameson
Mr and Mrs Robert Jameson
B.G.W. Jamieson
N. Jamieson
Frances Janusz
Stephen Jean
Gillian Jeens
Mrs Brenda Jeeves
Alan Jefferson
Miss Sarah Jeffery
Richard Jeffries
Mrs H. Jenkins
Jean Jenkins
Mr and Mrs G.J. Jennings
Paul Jerome
David Jervois
Stephen Jessel

Mr and Mrs Brian Jobson
Joyce Johnson
Patricia Johnson
F.P.M. Johnston
Dr Jacqueline Jolleys
Alan Jones
Anthony Jones
B. Jones
Douglas Jones
Ian Jones
Mel Jones
R. Jones
Dr W.J.G. Jones
Keith Jordan
Mr and Mrs Nathan Joseph
Mr and Mrs Alan Josey
Paul Joslin
Mr and Mrs M. Joyce
Mrs M. Judah
M.R. Judd
Mary Judge
Lesley Kant
Mrs Dianne Kaufman
Dr Leon Kaufman
J.Q. Kavanagh
Jeannine Kay
Sheila Keene
David Keers
Mrs Ann Kefalas
A. Kellett-Long
Miss S. Kelly
Mrs Vivien Kelvin
Roger Kenber
T.J. Kendall
Julia Kendrick
Mrs J. Kennedy
Mrs R. Kent
W.J. Kent
R.B. Kenyon
Mr and Mrs Kerrod
Rev Peter Kettle
Elizabeth Key
Mrs D. Kibble
David and Sally Kibble
Joanne Kicinski
Amanda Killip
G. Kingman
Dr B.W. Kington
K. Kinnear
Ruth Kitching
Bodo Klingelhofer
Mrs Sylvia Knapp
Mrs G. Knight
Robin Knight
C. Kone

Mr and Mrs Sebastian Kraemer
Mr and Mrs R. Krupinski
P.J. Kyte
Susan Laithwaite
A.J. Lamberty
Michael Lancaster
John Lane
N.A. Lane
P. Lane
Mrs J.H.S. Lang
Helen Lange
Mr and Mrs John Langford
Mr and Mrs W. Lapthorne
Mrs F. Latham
Laure Latham
Mr and Mrs K. Lavender
Mr and Mrs Lavous
Morag Law
Mr and Mrs R. Lawrence
Mr and Mrs David Le Fevre
David Lea
Mrs Ruth Leach-Bing
J.S. Ledbury
A.J.N. Lee
Geoffrey Lee
M.I. Leese
V.J. Legg
Frank Lempriene
P.L. Leonard
Richard Leonard
Mrs B.M. Lesley
Colin Leslie
D.J. Lethem
Michael Levene
Clive Lewis
Dr David Lewis
Mrs G.T. Lewis
L.H. Lewis
Leonard Lewis
Sandra Lewis
Mrs M. Lhandley
Mr and Mrs Leonard Licht
Peter Liechts
Harold Lievesley
R.W. Lindo
Jenny Linford
Dr and Mrs J.R. Ling
Mr and Mrs D.R. Linnell
Mrs J.D. Lister
Mrs Mary Lister

Mr and Mrs David Littaur
J.C.A. Little
Dr Neil Livesey
Dr David Lloyd
James Lloyd
Stephen Lloyd Phillips
David Lloyd-Jacob
Andrew Lobbenberg
Mrs Brigitta Lock
Janet Lock
Alan Locke
Mrs Janet Lockett
Mr and Mrs Lockley
Victoria Logue
Dr Debra Lomas
G.M. Lomas
Nigel Lomax
Mr Lommilia
Mrs A.J. Long
Michael Long
Mr and Mrs Oliver Long
Sheila M. Longbottom
M.G. Longhurst
R.C. Loombe
Prof P. Lord
Robert Lorrimer
Mrs R. Lovegrove
M.A. Loverock
Martin Lovett
Mr and Mrs P.A. Lowater
L. Lowenthal
Jeremy Lucas
Maurice Lucas
Paul Lucas
David Luck-Hille
Dr P.J. Lutman
Mr and Mrs Lyttelton
Mr and Mrs Miles MacEacharn
R.B. MacGeachy
A.J. Macintosh
Mrs S.A. Mackenzie
G.R. Mackie
Dr and Mrs M.D. Mackinnon
Mrs M. Mackley
Sharon Maclaren
Norman Maclean
Mrs A. Maclennan
John Macleod
Wendy MacMahon
Alison Maddock
Sean Magee
Dr B.A. Maguire
Peter Mahaffey
Richard Maher
W.J. Mallett

A. Mallinson
U. Malmgard
N.R. Manners
Paul Manners
Michael Manser
Mrs N.V. Marcelli
Jonathan Margolis
Prof Marshall
  Marinker
Laurence Marks
Dr C. Markus
Leonard Marlow
Patricia Marr
W.F. Marsden
P. Marsh
D.F. Marshall
Prof John Marshall
R.O. Marshall
Mr and Mrs Roger
  Marshall
Sophie Marshall
Mr and Mrs T.F.
  Marshall
Mrs Rosamond
  Marshall-Smith
Mrs P. Marston
M.D. Martin
Roger and Joan
  Martin
Janice Martynowicz
Clive Mason
K. Mason
Donald Massey
Andrew Matheson
Paul Mathieu
Dr Gerry Mattock
Mr and Mrs Roy
  Mauger
Melanie Mauthner
Gary Maxwell
Alan May
Mrs Elspeth May
Ian May
W.P. May
Andrew McDonald
D. McDonald
Kate McDowall
Charles McFeeters
Colin and Lilian
  McGhee
Dr Ian McGill
Siobhan McGovern
Mr and Mrs Maurice
  McKee
G.J. McKeown
Colin McKerrow
Ian McLaren
Peter McLeod
J.P McMahon
L.R. McMahon
R.H. McNeil
J.A.L. McNeilage

Mr and Mrs Archie
  McPherson
D.C. McQueen
Mr and Mrs Mark
  Medcalf
John Medley
Leo Meier
John Mellon
F. Mellor
Tim Menah
Mr and Mrs Malcolm
  Menzies
Marshall Meredith
Mr and Mrs J. Merritt
A. Metherell
Lord Mexborough
Michael Meyer
P.G. Middleton
Paul Milican
Mrs B.J. Miller
Mrs Catherine Miller
Don Mills
E. Mills
John Milne
Mrs S.B. Milne
D.C. Mitchell
Susan Mitchell
Mrs Julia Molitor
R. Molland
Dr J. Mollon
Dr Barry Monk
Prof Eric Moonman
Mr and Mrs Colin
  Moore
Colleen Moore
E.A. Moore
S.C. Moore
T.J. Moorey
Nick Morgan
R.C. Morgan
Mrs Sarah Morgan
Chris Morrell
Deborah Morris
Robin Morton-Smith
Brian Moss
Mrs Jean Moss
Mr and Mrs S.R.
  Moss
Mr and Mrs
  Christopher
  Mullins
Mr and Mrs William
  Mullins
David Mumford
Debbie Mumford
Laura Murphy
G.R. Murray
John Nabney
Lt Cdr and Mrs K.M.
  Napier
Colin Nash

Mr and Mrs B.
  Natton
Dr and Mrs A. Naylor
C.H. Naylor
J.I. Neill
Stephen Newell
Brian and Tessa
  Newman
David Newman
Martin Newman
Ming Ng
Mr and Mrs Bryan
  Nicholls
D.J.B. Nicholls
Mrs Kim Nicholls
Frank Nicol
Sarah Nissim
Dr John Nocton
Dr J.R. Norman
J.Q. Norris
Graham Norwood
Mr and Mrs B.D.
  O'Brien
Clive O'Connor
K.P. O'Mahoney
D. O'Melia
Sally O'Neill
W.B. O'Neill
Dr Michael
  O'Riordan
Dr P.A. O'Sullivan
Charles Oatwig-
  Thain
John Oddey
A. Offer
Anthony Ogden
Robin Ogle
H.N. Olden
Mrs E. Orme
Mr and Mrs Bill Orr
Dr C. Orsi
Mr and Mrs R.E.
  Osborne
Mr and Mrs G.
  Osbourne
Kathy Ott
William Pack
Mrs Meriel Packman
Mr and Mrs N. Page
Mrs Frani Pallas
Mrs S.M. Pannell
Margaret Parker
Tim Parkinson
Martin Parmiter
Dr Heather Parry
Pamela Parry
Simon Partridge
Miss Jane Paterson
Dr K. Patrick
G.C. Pattie
Iain Patton
David Pearson

Mrs Kay Pearson
Julie Peasgood
Tom Pendry
David Perry
Tim Perry
A.J. Peters
Claire Peters
Mr and Mrs Francis
  Peto
G.E. Pettifor
Michael Phelan
Stephen and Wendy
  Phillips
Barbary Phillips
Saskia Phillips
I. Pickering
J.M. Pickering
R. Pieraccini
Alison Pigram
Mary Pimm
Tim Pinder
Michael Pitel
Hugh Pitt
Gerard Platt
Prof Peter Plesch
Lucy Portch
Mr and Mrs D.V.
  Porter
R.T. Porter
Anne and Mel Potter
Dr J.M. Potter
R.E. Potter
Mr and Mrs Colin
  Potts
John Poulter
Joan Powell
J.E. Poynton
Mr and Mrs S.G.
  Pratt
M. Preston
Roger Price
Mrs S. Price
Dr A.E. Pruss
A. Pugh
Indra Pullen
Howard Pursey
Dr Mike Quigley
A.E.I. Rae
Dr and Mrs D.S.
  Rampton
Mrs D. Randall
Dr R.J. Rathbone
Chris Ray
Mrs Mary Rayner
Juliet Raynes
B.S. Read
Paul Reeve
A.J. Reeves
Mr and Mrs Andrew
  Reeves
C.W. Reid
Dr and Mrs W. Reith

Mrs Marilyn Relf
John Reuter
W.F. Rhodes
David Richards
Miss S.P. Richards
Dr T.M. Richards
C.J. Richardson
S.J. Richardson
Carol Riddick
Michael Riddle
R. Rigby
M. Riggs
N.R. Riley
Gordon Ringrose
J.T. Rissbrook
Dr B. Ritson
G.L. Rivers
Alan Roberts
Franklyn Roberts
Gareth Roberts
Glyn Roberts
Marc Roberts
Mrs R.N. Roberts
D.R. Robinson
Harry Robinson
Mr and Mrs John
  Robinson
Mrs Philippa
  Robinson
Mrs Sheila Robinson
Dr and Mrs W.
  Robinson
J. Rochelle
T. Rockley
F.S. Rodgers
Sir Frank Rogers
Dr John Rogers
Linda Rogers
R. Rokeby-Johnson
Mr and Mrs Jamie
  Rollo
Mrs Hope Roper
Mr and Mrs Jeffery
  Rose
Mrs Cicely Ross
Mrs Michael Ross
P.W.A. Ross
Sarah Ross
Mr and Mrs John
  Row
J.E. Rowe
Peter Rowe
Michael Rowland
Mr and Mrs D.
  Rowlands
Mrs Jill Rowley
I.J. Roxburgh
Mr and Mrs Ian
  Royle
J.M. Ruane
Peter Rudd
P. Rudge

N.S. Ruderman
A.J. Rugg
Bee Runciman
Elizabeth Russell
  Taylor
M. Rutherford
J.S. Rutter
Ilse Ryder
Miss N. Sacchetti
Lady Sachs
L. Saffron
Keith Salway
Mr and Mrs B.
  Sandham
Robert Sandys
Dr N. Sankaray
Louise Sargent
Christopher Saul
R. Savage
W.R. Savage
Canon Michael
  Saward
P. Sawbridge
A.N. Sawrey-
  Cookson
Paul Saxon
Derek Scantlebury
Mrs Frances Scarr
Mrs Judith Schofield
Mr and Mrs Scholey
Dr Joseph Schwartz
R. Schwarz
Esme Scott
Prof J.S. Scott
D.G. Scotter
G.D. Sedgley
J.R.E. Sedgwick
Mr and Mrs S.A.
  Seligman
Sancia Sell
Peter Sellar
P. Sellars
Philip Sellos
Mrs Alison Sennett
Dr and Mrs Servant
Jean Seul-Lawton
A.J. Shakespeare
Craig Sharp
Mr and Mrs A. Shaw
Peter Shaw
Avrill Sheldon
L.W. Sheldon
E. Shephard
C. Shepherd
Jeremy Sheppard
Dr Mary Sherry
Mrs N.A. Sherwood
Emma Shilman
Mrs E.J. Shirras
T. Shortt
John and Viv
  Siderfin

Daniel Silverstone
Mr and Mrs L.J
  Simmons
Richard Simon
J.L. Simpole-Clarke
Andrew Simpson
Mr and Mrs J.A.
  Simpson
Mrs Jane Simpson
Adam Singer
Ian Single
Peter Skinnard
Philip Skottowe
J.V. Sloane
Michael Slater
Mrs J. Small
Mrs S. Smalley
C.J. Smith
Charles and Jennie
  Smith
Frances Smith
Ivor Smith
J.B. Smith
J.H. Smith
Mrs Jane Smith
Mrs K.E. Smith
Mike Smith
Patricia Smith
Mrs J.C. Smye
Tara Smyth
Mr and Mrs S. Solley
David Soloman
Mrs M. Solomons
E.V. Somers
Mrs E. Sones
Mrs E.M. Southey
Mrs Elizabeth
  Spencer
Dr Seymour Spencer
Louise Spitz
L. Squire
Sheila Stacey
Nicholas Stanford
Mr and Mrs Stanley
Mr and Mrs Mike
  Staples
John Stead
Mrs F.A. Stear
Mrs G.M. Stein
Anthony Stern
Jonathon Stevens
Malcolm Stevens
Mr and Mrs P.
  Stevens
Robert Stevens
Dr Andrew
  Stevenson
John Stevenson
Mrs Carol Stewart
Capt and Mrs J.S.
  Stewart
James Stewart

Michael Stewart
Celia Stimson
Julian Stock
Mrs C.M.R.
  Stoneham
S.R. Stoneham
Dr D.W. Stooke
Mr and Mrs A.N.
  Storey
J.C. Stott
H.M. Stratford
Margaret Stratford
Douglas Stuart
Ian Stuart
Tessa Stuart
Mrs Elizabeth Sutter
J. Sutton
A.M. Sutton-Scott-
  Tucker
Mrs Erica Swift
Mrs Gillian Switalski
Mr and Mrs Sykes
Brenda Symes
J. Talbot
Dr J. Tanner
John Tarrant
Dennis Tate
Dr and Mrs P.H.
  Tattersall
Dr D.M. Taub
Mrs A.C. Taylor
A.M. Taylor
Chris Taylor
E.R. Taylor
George Taylor
J.D. Taylor
Jacqueline Taylor
Mrs Jean Taylor
L.G. Taylor
Roger Taylor
S. Taylor
Simon Taylor
Trevor Taylor
Mrs Wendy Taylor
John Teenan
Anne Telly
J. Temple
Mr and Mrs Stanley
  Templeton
Russell Thersby
Alan Thomas
Nicola Thomas
John Thompson
N.J. Thompson
Mr and Mrs Roger
  Thompson
John Thornburn
Doreen Thorne
Mr and Mrs G.N.
  Thornton
Harry Thuillier
E.A. Thwaite

Mr and Mrs L.J.
Tibbs
D. Ticehurst
Margaret Tillyard
G.G. Tiramani
Mike Tivnen
Julian Tobin
Mrs Jan Todd
Michael Tomlinson
W.P. Tonks
M. Toomer
M.E.W. Tooth
Dr C. Torrance
Michael Townson
Andrew Tozer
J. Tradlyn
John Trenchard
Judy Tringham
William Trodd
Gary True
Beryl and Dick
Tudhope
Sarah Tulwa
Mrs A.B. Tune
B.W.B. Turner
Patricia Turner
R.L. Turner
Stuart Turner
Mr and Mrs R.D.
Turvil
Mrs Curzon Tussaud
Gary Twynam
Penny Tyecke
Debbie Tyler
Elizabeth Tylor
Mrs Polly Vacher
Mrs Elizabeth
Valentine
Mr Van Bawer
Susan Vaughan
Barbara Vazana
Graham Venables
Bernend Versluis
Gerald Vinestock
Dr A. Voller
Michael Wace
Patience Waddilove
Mrs E. Wald
Mrs A.M. Walden

Mr and Mrs B.
Walden
Mr and Mrs B.
Walker
Dr David Walker
James Walker
Mr and Mrs M.F.
Walker
Mrs Margaret
Walker
Michael Walker
Mrs Val Walker-
Dendle
Andrew Wall
J.M. Waller
M.C Wallis
Mrs Chris Walmsley
Mr and Mrs Richard
Walmsley
B.E. Walton
G. Walton
Hilary Walton
Mrs J. Walton
Mr and Mrs D.L.
Ward
Mrs O.M. Ward
Stella Wardell
A.J. Wardrop
Tim Ware
R.A. Wartnaby
Jane Warwick
Toshio Watanabe
A. Waterfield
Martin Waterhouse
Mr and Mrs J.S.
Waters
G.W. Waterson
Jayne-Louise
Watkins
Mrs Elizabeth
Watson
Dr Grace Watson
Mr and Mrs J.
Watson
Katy Watt
P. Watters
E.K. Watts
Mrs J. Wayman
G.T. Webster

Mr and Mrs S.R.
Weeden
Pam Weiner
Mr and Mrs J. Weir
Ivan Welch
David Wells
Marion Wells
J.F.M. West
M.J. West
T.J.M. Weston
Mr and Mrs J.
Westwood
Julie Wheat
Mrs C. Wheeler
Mr and Mrs John
Wheeler
B. Whitaker
Dr G.T. Whitaker
Mrs J. Whitbread
F. White
Joy White
K.G. White
Roger White
Tanya White
Miss Sarah
Whitehead
Eric Whiteway
Mrs Sandra
Witham
K.A. Whitmee-
Haddock
Paul Whittaker
John Whittam
Paul Whittard
Neville Whittle
Mr and Mrs S.
Whittle
D.N. Whyte
W. Wick
D. Wiles
Mr and Mrs John
Wilhare
John Wilkin
David Wilkins
J.B. Wilkins
Gerald Wilkinson
P. Willer
Steve Willey
Donald Williams

I.G.K. Williams
K.G. Williams
Mrs M. Williams
Stephen Williamson
Mr and Mrs M.J.
Williets
Celia Wills
Drs. A. and C.
Wilson
Mr and Mrs E.
Wilson
Mrs Joy Wilson
Lesley Wilson
Prof P.N. Wilson
Peter Wilson
Ralph Wilson
Prof Richard Wise
Mr and Mrs Judy
Wiseman
Mr and Mrs David
Witcher
Charles Wittiver
Richard Witts
Martin Wolf
Mrs M. Wood
Stephen Wood
Barbara Wooldridge
Alan Worsdale
Mr and Mrs Peter
Worsfold
Nicholas Wraight
Dr Sally Wraight
Dr A.P. Wright
Alan Wright
Mr and Mrs G.L.
Wright
Sue Wright
Mr and Mrs P.
Wrightson
R.A. Wyld
Peter Yager
Mr and Mrs Yardley
Michael York-
Palmer
J.G. Young
Penny Young
Philip Young
Mrs Sybella Zisman

Index of entries

Names in bold are main entries. Names in italics are Round-ups.

To the Editor *The Good Food Guide*
FREEPOST, 2 Marylebone Road, London NW1 1YN

Or send your report by electronic mail to: *guidereports@which.co.uk*

From my personal experience the following establishment should/should not be included in the *Guide* (please print in BLOCK CAPITALS):

_____

_____

Telephone_____

I had lunch/dinner/stayed there on (date) _____ 19____

I would rate this establishment _____ out of ten.

please continue overleaf

My meal for _____ people cost £ _____ *attach bill where possible*

☐ Please tick if you would like more report forms

Reports received up to the end of **May 1999** will be used in the research of the 2000 edition.

I am not connected in any way with management or proprietors.
Name and address (BLOCK CAPITALS, please)

_____

_____

Signed _____